SAS Activity-Based Costing (ABC) S̶ ̶ ̶ ̶ion

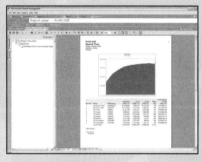

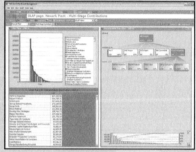

Activity-Based Costing (ABC) is a cost accounting method used by leading firms to accurately determine the costs of their product lines, service lines, distribution channels, and customers. SAS's Activity-Based Costing (ABC) Software is then used to identify the firm's most profitable products and customers, their inefficient operations, and their most effective and ineffective management methods.

The increasing breadth of diverse products and service lines, and the resulting expansion of indirect costs (overhead) to manage the resulting complexity and size of operations has created the need for ABC. In many ABC-using firms it has also required the use of effective software systems to maintain and process the information. Case material designed for Blocher/Chen/Cokins/Lin, *Cost Management: A Strategic Emphasis,* 3e uses the ABC software from SAS Institute Software of Cary, NC— software that is used worldwide for performance management functions/analysis.

The SAS ABC/M software (formerly called OROS) maintains and processes information about the activities within a company. OROS Quick, a simplified version of the fully functional software, includes all the steps of developing an activity-based costing system, including:

- Creating the necessary files of information about cost resources, activities, and cost objects
- Creating the cost driver assignments
- Data entry
- Calculating ABC costs
- Comparing ABC costs to traditional cost calculations

The OROS Quick software and a related tutorial are available for download at **www.mhhe.com/blocher3e**, the Online Learning Center (OLC) that accompanies Blocher/Chen/Cokins/Lin, *Cost Management: A Strategic Emphasis,* 3e. The software and tutorial are designed for those new to activity-based costing as well as the more experienced user.

The Blocher/Chen/Cokins/Lin *Cases & Readings Manual* and OLC include a short case that can be used with the tutorial and software to complete a short ABC application. The objective of the case and tutorial is to illustrate how a comprehensive ABC software system such as SAS can be used. While the case is greatly simplified, the software is capable of running large scale, complex applications. In this way, the case provides insight into actual applications of ABC that go well beyond the typical textbook examples. Additional cases will be added to the OLC as they become available.

Cost Management

A Strategic Emphasis

Cost Management

A Strategic Emphasis

Third Edition

Edward J. Blocher
University of North Carolina at Chapel Hill
Kenan-Flagler Business School

Kung H. Chen
University of Nebraska
School of Accountancy

Gary Cokins
Strategist, Performance Management Solutions
SAS/Worldwide Strategy

Thomas W. Lin
University of Southern California
Leventhal School of Accounting

McGraw-Hill Irwin

Boston   Burr Ridge, IL   Dubuque, IA   Madison, WI   New York   San Francisco   St. Louis
Bangkok   Bogotá   Caracas   Kuala Lumpur   Lisbon   London   Madrid   Mexico City
Milan   Montreal   New Delhi   Santiago   Seoul   Singapore   Sydney   Taipei   Toronto

 **McGraw-Hill
Irwin**

COST MANAGEMENT: A STRATEGIC EMPHASIS

Published by McGraw-Hill/Irwin, a business unit of The McGraw-Hill Companies, Inc., 1221 Avenue of the Americas, New York, NY, 10020. Copyright © 2005, 2002, 1999, by The McGraw-Hill Companies, Inc. All rights reserved. No part of this publication may be reproduced or distributed in any form or by any means, or stored in a database or retrieval system, without the prior written consent of The McGraw-Hill Companies, Inc., including, but not limited to, in any network or other electronic storage or transmission, or broadcast for distance learning.

Some ancillaries, including electronic and print components, may not be available to customers outside the United States.

This book is printed on acid-free paper.

4 5 6 7 8 9 0 DOW/DOW 0 9 8 7 6
ISBN-13: 978-0-07-281836-9
ISBN-10: 0-07-281836-0
Vice president and editor-in-chief: *Robin J. Zwettler*
Editorial director: *Brent Gordon*
Publisher: *Stewart Mattson*
Executive editor: *Tim Vertovec*
Developmental editor I: *Heather Sabo*
Marketing manager: *Richard Kolasa*
Senior producer, Media technology: *Ed Przyzycki*
Senior project manager: *Kari Geltemeyer*
Production supervisor: *Gina Hangos*
Designer: *Adam Rooke*
Senior supplement producer: *Carol Loreth*
Senior digital content specialist: *Brian Nacik*
Cover design: *Krista Lehmkuhl*
Typeface: *10.5/12 Times Roman*
Compositor: *GAC/Indianapolis*
Printer: *R. R. Donnelley*

Library of Congress Cataloging-in-Publication Data

Cost management : a strategic emphasis / Edward J. Blocher—[et al.].—3rd ed.
    p. cm.
   Previous ed. entered under E. Blocher.
   Includes index.
   ISBN 0-07-281836-0 (alk. paper)—ISBN 0-07-111210-3 (international : alk. paper)
    1. Cost accounting. 2. Managerial accounting. I. Blocher, Edward. Cost management.
HF5686.C8B559 2005
658.15'52—dc22

2003066613

We dedicate this edition . . .

To my wife Sandy, and our children Joseph and David

Ed Blocher

To my wife Mary, and our children Robert and Melissa

Kung Chen

To my wife Pam Tower, and my mentor Robert A. Bonsack, a true craftsman in the field of cost management

Gary Cokins

To my wife Angela, and our children Bill and Margaret

Tom Lin

Meet the Authors

Edward J. Blocher is Professor of Accounting at the Kenan-Flagler Business School at the University of North Carolina. He received his bachelor's degree in economics from Rice University, his MBA degree from Tulane University, and his PhD in accounting from the University of Texas at Austin. He has been a faculty member at the University of North Carolina since 1976. He has also been on the faculty of Northwestern University. Professor Blocher presents regularly on strategic cost management at the national meetings of both the American Accounting Association and the Institute of Management Accountants.

While he is involved in a number of accounting organizations, Professor Blocher has been most continuously active in the Institute of Management Accountants (IMA). He is a Certified Management Accountant (CMA), has taught review courses for the CMA exam, and has served on the Institute's national education committee. He also presents regularly at the annual national conference of the IMA. Professor Blocher is the author or coauthor of several articles appearing in various journals.

Putting research and teaching into practice is important to Professor Blocher, who has worked closely with other firms and organizations in developing products, publications, and teaching materials. He was the principal designer of an accounting analysis system developed by Financial Audit Systems, Inc. Also, he has worked with Blue Cross and Blue Shield of North Carolina, the American Institute of CPAs, KPMG Peat Marwick, Grant Thornton, and the Chancellor's Office at the University of North Carolina at Chapel Hill, among others.

Kung H. Chen is the Steinhardt Foundation Professor of Accounting and the Director of Graduate Programs in the School of Accountancy at the University of Nebraska-Lincoln. A graduate of National Taiwan University, he has his MBA degree from West Virginia University and a PhD from the University of Texas-Austin.

Professor Chen has published his research in various journals, including *The Accounting Review*, *Encyclopedia of Accounting*, *Internal Auditor*, *Journal of Business Finance and Accounting*, *Behavioral Research in Accounting*, *Journal of Accounting Literature*, *Advances in Accounting*, *Financial Management*, and *International Journal of Accounting*, and has presented research papers to audiences in several countries including the United States, New Zealand, Japan, Taiwan, Korea, and China.

Gary Cokins is a strategist in performance management solutions with SAS, the world's largest privately owned software vendor. He is an internationally recognized expert, speaker, and author in advanced cost management and performance improvement systems. Gary received a BS degree with honors in Industrial Engineering/Operations Research from Cornell University in 1971. He received his MBA from Northwestern University's Kellogg School of Management in 1974.

Gary serves on activity-based information committees including CAM-I, APICS, the Supply Chain Council, the Council for Logistics Management (CLM), the Institute of Management Accountants (IMA), the American Society for Quality (ASQ), the Purchasing Management Association of Canada (PMAC), the Institute of Industrial Engineers (IIE), Association for Management Information in Financial Services (AMI/fs), and the American Institute of CPA's (AICPA).

Thomas W. Lin is the Accounting Circle Professor of Accounting at the Leventhal School of Accounting at the University of Southern California. He received his BA in business administration from National Taiwan University, his MBA from National Chengchi University in Taiwan, his MS in accounting and information systems from UCLA, and a PhD in accounting from The Ohio State University. He has experience as a management accountant, a systems analyst and an assistant to the president of a multinational plastics firm, and as a computer auditor in an international accounting firm. Professor Lin has published 5 books and over 70 papers in various journals. He has presented seminars on new developments in cost management in North America and Asia.

Professor Lin has worked with many companies, including KPMG Peat Marwick, PricewaterhouseCoopers, Times Mirror, Carnation, Western Refuse and Hauling, City of Chino, Formosa Plastics, Intex Plastics, Zee Toys, FCBTaiwan California Bank, and General Bank. He is active in the American Accounting Association and the Institute of Management Accountants. A Certified Management Accountant (CMA), he was awarded a Certificate of Distinguished Performance by the Institute of Certified Management Accountants.

Blocher/Chen/Cokins/Lin:

A t first glance, the jumbled letters on the front cover of this text do not seem to serve a purpose. However, when one stands back from the cover and takes in the entire design at once, it's easy to see that the letters spell out *Cost Management, 3e*.

Just as the letters spelling out the book's title seem unclear at first, the same can be said of the course content by students first entering this course. Students fail to see the relevance of cost management concepts and procedures and how they will use this information in their future.

The strategic placement of the letters is clear when viewed as a whole—as the big picture. Similarly, *Cost Management: A Strategic Emphasis, 3e* by Blocher, Chen, Cokins, and Lin uses a **strategic emphasis** to make a connection for students between the concepts and procedures they learn in the class and how they will use them. In short, it makes cost information **relevant** for students.

Once viewed simply as technical experts in accounting methods and procedures, accountants are now participants on multifunctional management teams. *Cost Management: A Strategic Emphasis, 3e* helps students understand the critical role that cost management information plays in the overall success of an organization and teaches them the strategic and **decision-making skills** necessary to become tomorrow's cost accountant.

Strategic framework.
At the heart of the strategic emphasis of *Cost Management: A Strategic Emphasis, 3e* is its organization. The introductory chapters develop important strategic concepts used throughout the text—how firms compete and the nature of the key measures that managers must use to gain and maintain competitive advantage. Through the text Parts, *Cost Management: A Strategic Emphasis, 3e* emphasizes the role of cost management information in each of the four management functions. Each cost management method is clearly linked not only to the firm's overall strategy but also to each management function that uses the method:

> Part I: Strategic Management
> Part II: Planning and Decision Making
> Part III: Product Costing
> Parts IV and V: Operational Control and Management Control

Running theme: How does the topic we are discussing help the firm more effectively compete in its industry?
Cost Management: A Strategic Emphasis, 3e uses this strategic theme to integrate individual chapters into a coherent whole so that each of the text Parts contributes to overall understanding of the role of cost information and a firm's strategy for competitiveness. This organization helps students gain an understanding of cost accounting techniques and how they serve the company as a whole.

Bringing the Big Picture into **Focus** for Your Students

Problem Material.

The Blocher team has taken great care to develop problems and cases that effectively demonstrate the strategic issues presented in each chapter. Included are a variety of exercises and problems that deal with emerging **strategic**, **international**, **service**, and **ethics** issues. These problems are marked appropriately for easy identification:

 Strategy   International    Service   Ethics

Real-World Focus.

All firms strive to have a competitive edge—for some it may be low cost, for others it might be high quality or unique product features. To compete today, companies must develop a strategy to set themselves apart from competitors and ensure attractiveness to customers. *Cost Management: A Strategic Emphasis, 3e* teaches why, when, and how cost information is used to help accountants and managers develop a company's competitive strategy, focused on adding value for customers or shareholders. To augment this coverage, the Blocher team encourages students to explore real-world companies both in the text material, through the Chapter Openers and Real-World Focus and Cost Management in Action boxes, in the end-of-chapter material, and via the Cases and Readings Manual. Students are challenged to think about and use cost management information in a real-world setting.

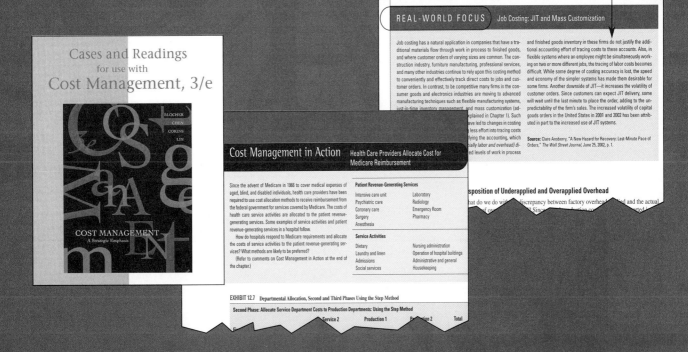

What's NEW about 3e?

Chapter 1: Cost Management and Strategy

- Coverage of strategy simplified by moving strategic positioning from Chapter 2 to Chapter 1
- Strategic positioning now presented as a fundamental concept of general knowledge

Chapter 2: Implementing Strategy

- Chapter 2 now deals entirely with the implementation of strategy, using accounting concepts and techniques, such as the balanced scorecard and the value chain
- Ethical and environmental concerns are enhanced through new material in Chapter 2 related to the Sarbanes-Oxley Act and additional material on sustainability

Chapter 3: Basic Cost Concepts

- General updating of material through new problems and exercises and new real-world focus boxes

Chapter 4: Job Order Costing

- The chapter on job costing was moved up in the text to provide a more orderly transition from the basic methods in Chapter 3 to ABC costing in Chapter 4. Also, it allows the instructor to cover job costing and overhead application prior to ABC costing, if desired
- The content of Chapter 4 was reduced somewhat to convey essential concepts of the chapter more simply and directly

Chapter 5: Activity Based Costing and Management

- Revised two-stage model depicting different drivers for different processes in cost assignment
- Section added with an extensive discussion on customer profitability analysis, including types of customers, customer cost categories, customer revenue analysis, and customer cost analysis
- General updating through new real world applications

Chapter 6: Cost Estimation

- General updating through new real world examples and problems
- Addition of the concept of mean absolute percentage error

Chapter 7: Cost-Volume-Profit Analysis

- General updating through new problems and examples
- ABC costing and sensitivity analysis incorporated

Chapter 8: Strategy and the Master Budget

- General updating through new problem and examples, with an emphasis on Excel applications

Chapter 9: Decision Making with Relevant Costs and a Strategic Emphasis

- General updating through new problems and examples, some incorporating Excel and ABC costing

Chapter 10: Cost Planning for the Product Life Cycle

- New section on pricing is added, including methods based on the cost life cycle and methods based on the sales life cycle
- Concept of Takt time is introduced

Chapter 11: Process Costing

- New section on the relationship of process costing to ABC costing
- New section on sustainability
- New section on the theory of constraints

Chapter 12: Cost Allocation

- General updating through new real world examples and problems

Chapter 13: The Flexible Budget and Standard Costing

- General updating through new real world examples and problems
- New emphasis on Excel applications

Chapter 14: Standard Costing: Factory Overhead

- General updating through new real world examples and problems
- New emphasis on Excel applications

Chapter 15: Productivity, Marketing Effectiveness, and Strategic Profitability Analysis

- Extensive discussion on strategic implications of marketing and productivity variances
- New section on operational profitability analysis examining effects on operating results attributable to growth, changes in price and cost, and variations in productivity over the years, including extensive discussion on strategic implications of these effects

Chapter 16: Total Quality Management

- General updating through new real world examples and problems
- New emphasis on Excel applications

Chapter 17: Management Control and Strategic Performance Measurement

- General updating through new real world examples and cases
- Greater emphasis on ethics

Chapter 18: Strategic Investment Units and Transfer Pricing

- General updating through new real world examples and cases

Chapter 19: Management Compensation and Business Valuation

- Revised chapter clarifies the difference between evaluating the performance of a business (for the purpose of evaluating top executives) from the valuation of a business (for the purpose of pricing the firm's shares, etc)
- New coverage of stock-based compensation incorporating recent developments

Chapter 20: Capital Budgeting

- General updating through new real world examples and problems
- Information added on uses of financial calculators to perform capital budgeting

Supplements

For Instructors . . .

Instructor's Resource CD-ROM (ISBN 0072835370): Contains all essential course supplements such as the Instructor's Resource Manual, Solutions Manual, Test Bank Word Files, Computerized Testbank by Brownstone, and PowerPoint® Presentations, and Excel Templates.

Online Learning Center (OLC): www.mhhe.com/blocher3e
The text website includes premium content for students for FREE with the purchase of a new book, including daily and weekly news feeds from the NY Times and PowerWeb. The Instructor Edition of the *Cost Management: A Strategic Emphasis, 3e* OLC is password-protected and another convenient place for instructors to access essential course supplements. Additional resources for professors include: Links to professional resources, Sample Syllabi, Text Updates, Solutions to the Student Excel Spreadsheets, and Solutions to Internet Exercises.

For Students . . .

Cases and Readings for use with *Cost Management: A Strategic Emphasis, 3e* (ISBN 0072835699): This manual contains a host of value-added resources. It includes an extensive set of longer cases pertaining to a variety of important topics. These case scenarios put students in situations that allow them to think strategically and to apply concepts they've learned in the course. Key readings have been chosen to give students more background into the evolution of strategic cost management topics. New cases have been added that incorporate the SAS software used by actual firms to calculate ABC cost information.

Study Guide (ISBN 0072835664): Prepared by Roger Doost (Clemson University), the study guide reviews the highlights of each chapter in *Cost Management: A Strategic Emphasis, 3e* and includes a variety of self-study questions for student review. Every chapter includes short-answer questions organized by learning objective, multiple-choice questions, and thorough exercises. Suggested answers to all questions and exercises are included.

Online Learning Center (OLC): www.mhhe.com/blocher3e The text website includes premium content for students for FREE with the purchase of a new book, including daily and weekly news feeds from the NY Times and PowerWeb. The Student Edition of the *Cost Management: A Strategic Emphasis, 3e* OLC also contains many tools designed to help students study including: Check Figures, Text Updates, Links to Professional Resources, eLearning Sessions, Chapter Overviews, Chapter Objectives, Multiple-Choice Quizzes, Flashcard Key Term Reviews, Internet Exercises, Excel Spreadsheet Exercises (watch for the Excel icon by selected end-of-chapter material), and PowerPoint® Presentations.

Acknowledgments

Our Sincerest Thanks . . .

In writing this book, we were fortunate to have received extensive feedback from a number of accounting educators. We want to thank our colleagues for their careful and complete review of our work. The comments that we received were invaluable in helping us to shape the manuscript. We believe that this collaborative development process helped us to create a text that will truly meet the needs of today's students and instructors. We are sincerely grateful to the following individuals for their participation in the process:

K. R. Balachandran,
New York University

Mohamed E. Bayou,
School of Mgmt.— U of MI—Dearborn

Wayne Bremser,
Villanova

Robert J. DePasquale,
Saint Vincent College

Robert W. Duron, Ph.D., CPA,
Chadron State College

Donald C. Gribbin,
Southern Illinois University

Linda Holmes,
University of Wisconsin—Whitewater

Dr. Norma C. Holter,
Townson University

Paul Juras,
Wake Forest University

Brian L. McGuire,
U of Southern Indiana

Cheryl E. Mitchem,
Virginia State University

Jennifer Gregorski Niece,
Assumption College

Margaret O'Reilly-Allen,
Rider University

Chei M. Paik,
George Washington University

Hugh Pforsich,
University of Idaho

Shirley Polejewski,
University of St. Thomas

Jenice Prather-Kinsey,
University of Missouri—Columbia

Dennis Shanholtzer,
Metropolitan State University

John L. Stancil,
Florida Southern College

Dr. Ronald A. Stunda,
Birmingham-Southern College

Finally, we are most appreciative of the outstanding assistance and support provided by the professionals of McGraw-Hill/Irwin: Stewart Mattson, our publisher, and Tim Vertovec, Executive Editor, for their guidance; our developmental editor, Heather Sabo, for her invaluable suggestions; Rich Kolasa, our marketing manager, for his significant promotional efforts; Kari Geltemeyer, our project manager, for her attention to detail; Adam Rooke, for the outstanding presentation of the text; Carol Loreth, our supplements coordinator, for her timeliness and accuracy in delivering the support material; and Edward Przyzycki, our media producer, for his technical expertise in delivering our online material. An added thanks to Beth Woods and Alice Sineath for their significant contributions to the accuracy of our text, as well as Roger Doost for his help with the Study Guide and Peggy Hussey for her work on the Interactive Excel Spreadsheets and Solutions found on our text's website.

Ed Blocher

Kung Chen

Gary Cokins

Tom Lin

Brief Contents

Contents

Chapter 4
Job Order Costing   92

Chapter 5
Activity-Based Costing and Management   130

PART TWO
PLANNING AND DECISION MAKING

Chapter 6
Cost Estimation   190

Chapter 7
Cost-Volume-Profit Analysis   238

Chapter 8
Strategy and the Master Budget   274

Cost Management

A Strategic Emphasis

CHAPTER ONE

Cost Management and Strategy: An Overview

After studying this chapter you should be able to . . .

1. Explain the use of cost management information in each of the four functions of management and in different types of organizations, with emphasis on the strategic management function
2. Explain how the contemporary business environment has influenced cost management
3. Explain the contemporary management techniques and how they have influenced cost management
4. Explain the different types of competitive strategies
5. Describe the professional environment of the management accountant, including professional organizations, professional certifications, and professional ethics
6. Understand the principles and rules of professional ethics and explain how to apply them

Talk about a success story! Wal-Mart has grown from its first discount store in 1962 to become the world's largest retailer. It has accomplished this through the day-to-day attention to its clear business mission: "We exist to provide value to the customer." It achieves this mission through a strategy that involves the extensive use of technology, and opportunity-oriented management style that values change and experimentation, a focus on friendly customer service, and aggressive efforts to grow the business globally.[1] This chapter shows how companies use these strategic initiatives and other important contemporary management techniques to make them more competitive and successful. For example, a section of the chapter on the global business environment shows how the worldwide liberalization of trade has helped firms like Wal-Mart succeed (to illustrate that success, Wal-Mart's sales outside the United States increased from 0 to 16.2 percent of total sales in a relatively short period, 1993 to 2002). Another section explains the increased importance of the customer; many business leaders now argue that business and other organizations have moved from a "product" orientation to a "consumer" orientation. As evidence of his focus on the customer, Sam Walton once led 100,000 Wal-Mart employees at a mid-1980s teleconference in the following:

> Now, I want you to raise your right hand. . . . I want you to repeat after me: From this day forward, I solemnly promise and declare that every time a customer comes within 10 feet of me, I will smile, look him in the eye, and greet him, so help me Sam.[2]

A key element in implementing Wal-Mart's Strategy was to set ambitious goals. Already a company with $44 billion in sales in 1992, it projected annual sales of more than $100 billion by 2000. In the 2002 fiscal year, Wal-Mart had net sales of $218 billion—almost a five-fold increase, a compound ten-year growth rate of about 18 percent!

---

[1] For more about the Wal-Mart success story, see the Wal-Mart website at www.wal-mart.com; James C. Collins and Jerry I. Porras, *Built to Last* (New York: Harper Business, 1994); Sam Walton and John Huey, *Sam Walton: Made in America* (New York: Doubleday, 1992); and "Wal-Mart vs. Inflation," *Business Week*, May 13, 2002, p. 32.

[2] Walton and Huey, *Sam Walton: Made in America*, p. 223.

This book is about how managers build a successful company as those at Wal-Mart have done. Everyone wants to be a winner, and so it is in business and accounting. We are interested in how the management accountant can play a key role in making a firm or organization successful. Now you might be asking, Don't we have to know what you mean by *success?* Absolutely! A firm must define clearly what it means by success in its mission statement. Then it must develop a roadmap to accomplish that mission, which we call *strategy.* In Wal-Mart's case, the mission was to achieve customer value, and the strategy involved the extensive use of technology, a management structure that welcomed change, and a constant focus on customer service. Recognize also that Wal-Mart, by succeeding in its mission and strategy, has built an enormous amount of wealth for its shareholders. Currently, the company's market value (number of shares outstanding times share price) is approximately $230 billion.

Because we are interested in how the management accountant can help a company be successful, we take a strategic approach throughout the book, beginning with an introduction to strategy in this chapter. The key idea is that success comes from developing and implementing an effective strategy aided by management accounting methods. These management accounting methods are covered in this text chapter by chapter; we discuss them because we know they have helped companies succeed. Before considering these management accounting methods, we introduce some basic concepts related to management accounting, the most basic of which is the concept of cost management information.

The most successful man in life is the man who has the best information.
Benjamin Disraeli, a nineteenth-century prime minister of England

---

LEARNING OBJECTIVE 1
Explain the use of cost management information in each of the four functions of management and in different types of organizations with emphasis on the strategic management function.

As Disraeli knew in the nineteenth century, having the best information is the key to success. In today's business environment, the development and use of information—especially cost management information—is a critical factor in the effective management of a firm or organization. As the business environment has changed, the role of cost management information has expanded to serve all management functions.

The Uses of Cost Management

Cost management information is the information the manager needs to effectively manage the firm or not-for-profit organization.

Cost management information is a broad concept. It is the information the manager needs to effectively manage the firm or not-for-profit organization and includes both *financial information* about costs and revenues as well as relevant *nonfinancial information* about productivity, quality, and other key success factors for the firm.[3]

Financial information alone can be misleading, because it tends to have a short-term focus, what we earned last month, for example. For competitive success, a firm needs to focus on longer-term factors, such as product and manufacturing advances, product quality, and customer loyalty. Emphasis on financial information alone could lead managers to stress cost reduction (a financial measure) while ignoring or even lowering quality standards (a nonfinancial measure). This decision could be a critical mistake, leading to the loss of customers and market share in the long term. Internationally known business consultants, such as W. Edwards Deming, Peter Drucker, and others, point out the importance of considering nonfinancial and long-term measures of operating performance if a firm is to compete successfully. A central theme of this book, then, is that cost management information includes the information—both financial and nonfinancial and both short-term and long-term—that managers need to lead their firms to competitive success.

---

[3] *Cost* is often defined as the use of a resource that has a financial consequence. In this text, we use the broader concept of cost management information that includes nonfinancial information as well as financial information.

If the management accountant were to focus on financial information only, how would he or she explain the success of a company like eBay? eBay has relatively few physical assets on the balance sheet, and the income statement looks mediocre, and yet its stock price shows it to be a better investment than some firms that have more assets and earnings. Investors are apparently betting on the long-term success of the firm, based on the popularity of its website and its customer loyalty. These strategic factors do not appear on the income statement or balance sheet. In fact, it is estimated that 30 percent–70 percent of stock prices are associated with factors that are not in the financial statements. Like these investors, the management accountant needs to focus on the measures that drive long-term success, and not just financial factors.

Source: "New Math for a New Economy," by Alan A. Webber, *Fast Company,* January–February 2000, pp. 214–224; "eBay: Bidding for Web Domination," by Amy Stone, *Business Week,* January 11, 2001; "Meg and the Machine," by Adam Lashinsky, *Fortune,* September 1, 2003, pp. 68–78.

Management accountants develop cost management information for which a firm's controller is responsible. The controller, who reports to the firm's chief financial officer (CFO), has a number of other duties, including financial reporting, maintaining financial systems, and other reporting functions (to industry organizations, governmental units, etc.), as illustrated in Exhibit 1.1. The CFO has the overall responsibility for the financial function; the treasurer manages investor and creditor relationships, and the chief information officer (CIO) manages the firm's use of information technology, including computer systems and communications.

In contrast to the cost management function, the financial reporting function involves preparing financial statements for *external users* such as investors and government regulators. These financial accounting reports require compliance with certain external requirements. Cost management information is developed for use *within* the firm to facilitate management and is not required to meet those requirements. The main focus of cost management information therefore must be *usefulness* and *timeliness;* the focus of financial reports must be *accuracy* and *compliance* with reporting requirements. However, strict adherence to accuracy can compromise the usefulness and timeliness of the information. The function of the financial systems department is to develop and maintain the financial reporting system and related systems such as

EXHIBIT 1.1

A Typical Organization Chart Showing the Functions of the Controller

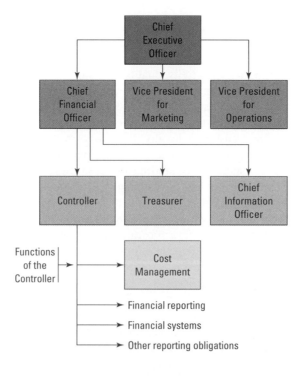

payroll, financial security systems, and tax preparation. The challenge for the controller is to reconcile these different and potentially conflicting roles.[4]

The Four Functions of Management

The management accountant develops cost management information for the CFO and other managers to use to manage the firm and make the firm more competitive and successful. Cost management information is provided for each of the four major management functions: (1) strategic management, (2) planning and decision making, (3) management and operational control, and (4) preparation of financial statements. (See Exhibit 1.2.) The most important function is **strategic management,** which is the development of a sustainable competitive position in which the firm's competitive advantage provides continued success. A strategy is a set of goals and specific action plans that, if achieved, provide the desired competitive advantage. Strategic management involves identifying and implementing these goals and action plans. Next, management is responsible for **planning and decision making,** which involves budgeting and profit planning, cash flow management, and other decisions related to the firm's operations, such as deciding when to lease or buy a facility, when to repair or replace a piece of equipment, when to change a marketing plan, and when to begin new product development.

The third area of responsibility, control, consists of two functions, operational control and management control. **Operational control** takes place when mid-level managers (e.g., plant managers, product managers, regional managers) monitor the activities of operating-level managers and employees (e.g., production supervisors and various department heads). In contrast, **management control** is the evaluation of mid-level managers by upper-level managers (the controller or the CFO).

In the fourth function, **preparation of financial statements,** management complies with the reporting requirements of relevant groups (such as the Financial Accounting Standards Board) and relevant federal government authorities (for example, the Internal Revenue Service and the Securities and Exchange Commission). The financial statement preparation role has recently received a renewed focus as accounting scandals have shown how crucial accurate financial information is for investors.[5] The financial statement information also serves the other three management functions, because this information is often an important part of planning and decision making, control, and strategic management.

Strategic Management and Strategic Cost Management

Effective strategic management is critical to the success of the firm or organization and is thus a pervasive theme of this book. The growing pressures of global competition,

Strategic management
is the development of a sustainable competitive position.

Planning and decision making
involves budgeting and profit planning, cash flow management, and other decisions related to operations.

Operational control
takes place when mid-level managers monitor the activities of operating-level managers and employees.

Management control
is the evaluation of mid-level managers by upper-level managers.

Preparation of financial statements
requires management to comply with the financial reporting requirements of regulatory agencies.

---

[4] A history of cost management is provided by Robert S. Kaplan, "The Evolution of Management Accounting," *The Accounting Review,* July 1984, pp. 390–418.

[5] The professional groups and the accountant's professional responsibility are identified and explained at the end of this chapter.

EXHIBIT 1.2
Cost Management Information Is Needed for Each of the Four Management Functions

1. **Strategic Management.** Cost management information is needed to make sound strategic decisions regarding choice of products, manufacturing methods, marketing techniques and channels, and other long-term issues.
2. **Planning and Decision Making.** Cost management information is needed to support recurring decisions regarding replacing equipment, managing cash flow, budgeting raw materials purchases, scheduling production, and pricing.
3. **Management and Operational Control.** Cost management information is needed to provide a fair and effective basis for identifying inefficient operations and to reward and motivate the most effective managers.
4. **Preparation of Financial Statements.** Cost management information is needed to provide accurate accounting for inventory and other assets, in compliance with reporting requirements, for the preparation of financial reports and for use in the three other management functions.

REAL-WORLD FOCUS   Why Strategy? Managers Tell Us Why

Our unique approach in this book is to demonstrate cost management from a strategic emphasis. Every cost management method we cover is linked to the firm's strategy, that is, how the method helps the firm to be successful. Why emphasize the strategic approach? Managers tell us why . . .

- A 1999 survey of 300 management accountants by the Institute of Management Accountants (the IMA is the main professional organization for those in cost management) showed that the accountants viewed themselves as broad finance professionals whose most important work activities, that is, "those that will be most critical to their company's success in three years," were the following:
  - Long-term strategic planning.
  - Financial and economic analysis.
  - Customer and product profitability.
  - Computer systems and operations.
  - Process improvement.

  These results show an important shift in the management accounting profession to strategic analysis, cost management information, and nonfinancial as well as financial information. This represents a move away from financial reporting only.

- The principal journal for the profession, *Management Accounting,* changed its name to *Strategic Finance* in April 1999. As noted in the IMA 1999 survey, managers now view accountants in the cost management function as finance professionals having an integral, strategic role in a firm's management. The work of accountants, no longer scorekeepers only, is better described as "strategic finance."

- The American Institute of Certified Public Accountants (AICPA), another key professional organization for accountants, has also recognized the change in the profession. The AICPA uses the term *new finance* to refer to the growing focus on strategy and "business partnership" for accountants who work within firms.

- Robert Half International, an executive recruitment firm, reported a 1999 survey of 1,400 CFOs of companies with more than 20 employees. CFOs expect that at least 40 percent of their work will be nonfinancial by the year 2004, indicating a greater need for business strategy and analysis but less need for financial reporting.

- The business press generally has set new and more strategic expectations for accountants. An example is the recent *Business Week* article, "Up From Bean Counter: The Role of the CFO Is Expanding to Strategist, Venture Capitalist, and Chief Negotiator." The title tells it all!

Sources: Gary Siegel, "Skills Needed for Entry-Level Management Accounting Positions," *Strategic Finance,* April 2000, pp.79–80; Ashish Garg, Debashis Gosh, James Hudick and Chuen Nowacki, "Roles and Practices in Management Accounting Today," *Strategic Finance,* July 2003, pp. 30–35. AICPA website (www.aicpa.org), "Center for Excellence in Financial Management"; Marcia Vickers, "Up From Bean Counter: The Role of the CFO Is Expanding to Strategist, Venture Capitalist, and Chief Negotiator," *Business Week,* August 28, 2000, pp. 119–120. Also the report of interviews and focus groups of dozens of accountants, businesspeople, and professors regarding the current and desired state of accounting education: W. Steve Albrecht and Robert J. Sack, "Accounting Education: Charting the Course through a Perilous Future," *Accounting Education Series Number 16* (American Accounting Association, 2000).

technological innovation, and changes in business processes have made cost management much more critical and dynamic than ever before. Managers must think *competitively;* doing so requires a strategy.

Strategic thinking involves anticipating changes; products and production processes are designed to accommodate expected changes in customer demands. Flexibility is important. The ability to make fast changes is critical as a result of the demand of the new management concepts of e-commerce, speed to market, and agile manufacturing. Product life cycles—the time from the introduction of a new product to its removal from the market—is expected to become shorter and shorter. Success in the recent past days or months is no longer a measure of ultimate success; the manager must be "driving" the firm by using the windshield, not the rear-view mirror.

The strategic emphasis also requires creative and integrative thinking, that is, the ability to identify and solve problems from a cross-functional view. The business functions are often identified as marketing, production, finance, and accounting/controllership. Instead of viewing a problem as a production problem, a marketing problem, or a finance and accounting problem, cross-functional teams view it from an integrative approach that combines skills from all functions simultaneously. The integrative approach is necessary in a dynamic and competitive environment. The firm's attention is focused on satisfying the customers' needs; all of the firm's resources, *from all functions,* are directed to that goal.

Because strategic issues are increasing in importance to management, cost management has moved from a traditional role of product costing and operational control to a

Strategic cost management is the development of cost management information to facilitate the principal management function, strategic management.

broader, strategic focus: strategic cost management. **Strategic cost management** is the development of cost management information to facilitate the principal management function, strategic management.

Types of Organizations

Cost management information is useful in all organizations: business firms, governmental units, and not-for-profit organizations. Business firms are usually categorized by industry, the main categories being merchandising, manufacturing, and service. Merchandising firms purchase goods for resale. Merchandisers that sell to other merchandisers are called *wholesalers;* those selling directly to consumers are called *retailers.* Examples of merchandising firms are the large retailers, such as Sears, Wal-Mart, and Amazon.com.

Manufacturing firms use raw materials, labor, and manufacturing facilities and equipment to produce products. They sell these products to merchandising firms or to other manufacturers as raw materials to make other products. Examples of manufacturers are General Motors, General Electric, and Cisco Systems.

Service firms provide a service to customers that offers convenience, freedom, safety, or comfort. Common services include transportation, health care, financial services (banking, insurance, accounting), personal services (physical training, hair styling), and legal services. In the United States, service industries are growing at a much faster rate than is manufacturing or merchandising, in part because of the increased demand for leisure and convenience and society's increased complexity.

Governmental and not-for-profit organizations provide services, much like the firms in service industries. However, these organizations provide the services for which no direct relationship exists between the amount paid and the services provided. Instead, both the nature of these services and the customers to receive them are determined by government or philanthropic organizations. The resources are provided by governmental units and/or charities. The services provided by these organizations are often called *public goods* to indicate that no typical market exists for them. Public goods have a number of unique characteristics, such as the impracticality of limiting consumption to a single customer (clean water and police and fire protection are provided for *all* residents).

Most firms and organizations use cost management information. For example, manufacturing firms use it to manage production costs. Similarly, retail firms such as Wal-Mart use cost management information to manage stocking, distribution, and customer service. Firms in the service industries, such as those providing financial services or other professional services, use cost management information to identify the most profitable services and to manage the costs of providing those services.

Cost management information is used in a wide variety of ways. Whatever the business, a firm must know the cost of new products or services, the cost of making improvements in existing products or services, and the cost of finding a new way to produce the products or provide the services. Cost management information is used to determine prices, to change product or service offerings to improve profitability, to update manufacturing facilities in a timely fashion, and to determine new marketing methods or distribution channels. For example, manufacturers such as General Motors study the cost implications of design options for each new product. The design study includes analysis of projected manufacturing costs as well as costs to be incurred after the product is completed, which include service and warranty costs. Service and warranty costs are often called *downstream costs* because they occur after manufacturing. By analyzing both manufacturing and downstream costs, General Motors is able to determine whether product enhancements might cause manufacturing and downstream costs to be out of line with expected increases in customer value and revenue for that feature.

Both large and small firms, in all types of industries use cost management information. A firm's degree of reliance on cost management depends on the nature of its competitive strategy. Many firms compete on the basis of being the low-cost provider of the industry's goods or services; for these firms, cost management is critical. Other firms, such as cosmetics, fashion, and pharmaceutical firms, compete on the basis of product leadership, in which the unusual or innovative features of the product make the firm successful. For these firms, the critical management concern is maintaining product leadership through product development and marketing. The role of cost management is to support the firm's strategy by providing the information managers need to succeed in their product development and marketing efforts, such as the expected cost of adding a new product feature, the defect rate of a new part, or the reliability of a new manufacturing process.

Not-for-profit and governmental organizations also must have a strategy to accomplish their mission and satisfy their constituents. Historically, governmental units and not-for-profit agencies have tended to focus on their responsibility to spend in approved ways rather than to spend in efficient and effective ways. Increasingly, however, these types of organizations are using cost management for efficient and effective use of their financial resources. Not-for-profit organizations especially need to predict the effect of an anticipated budget cut or increase on planned service levels. Cost management information usually serves as a starting point in assessing the effect of changing funding levels on activities and services. For example, the funding of Service Corps, a nonprofit provider of educational services, was cut by approximately 30 percent in a recent period. By studying its cost structure, the agency was able to project a cutback in service of approximately 50 percent based on the fact that a significant proportion of its costs (for facilities and administration) was not directly involved in providing the educational services and could not be reduced. Therefore, the cuts had to come from costs for classroom teachers. Thus, the analysis of the organization's cost structure explains why a 30 percent change in the budget had a greater effect on direct services.

The Contemporary Business Environment

LEARNING OBJECTIVE 2
Explain how the contemporary business environment has influenced cost management.

Many changes in the business environment in recent years have caused significant modifications in cost management practices. The primary changes are (1) increase in global competition, (2) advances in manufacturing technologies, (3) advances in information technologies, the Internet, and e-commerce (4) greater focus on the customer, (5) new forms of management organization, and (6) changes in the social, political, and cultural environment of business.

The Global Business Environment

A key development that drives the extensive changes in the contemporary business environment is the growth of international markets and trade. Businesses and not-for-profit organizations, as well as consumers and regulators, are all significantly affected by the rapid growth of economic interdependence and increased competition from other countries. The North American Free Trade Agreement (NAFTA), the World Trade Organization (WTO), the European Union (EU), and the growing number of alliances among large multinational firms clearly indicate that the opportunities for growth and profitability lie in global markets. Most consumers benefit as low-cost, high-quality goods are traded worldwide. Managers and business owners know the importance of pursuing sales and production activities in foreign countries, and investors benefit from the increased opportunities for investment in foreign firms.

The increasing competitiveness of the global business environment means that firms increasingly need cost management information to be competitive. Firms need financial and nonfinancial information about doing business and competing effectively in other countries.

Manufacturing Technologies

To remain competitive in the face of the increased global competition, firms around the world are adopting new manufacturing technologies. These include just-in-time inventory methods to reduce the cost and waste of maintaining large levels of raw

Going Global: The Growing Importance of Worldwide Markets

The following table indicates the percentage of sales coming from outside the home market for the listed companies.

	1993	2002
General Electric	16.5%	28.6%
Wal-Mart	0.0	16.2
McDonald's	46.9	63.7

Source: Company annual reports.

materials and unfinished product. Also, many firms are adopting the methods applied in Japanese manufacturing that have produced significant cost and quality improvements through the use of quality teams and statistical quality control. Other manufacturing changes include flexible manufacturing techniques developed to reduce setup times and allow fast turnaround of customer orders. A key competitive edge in what is called *speed-to-market* is the ability to deliver the product or service faster than the competition.

The New Economy: Use of Information Technology, the Internet, and E-Commerce

Perhaps the most fundamental of all business changes in recent years has been the increasing use of information technology, the Internet, and e-commerce. This *new economy* is reflected in the rapid growth of Internet-based firms (the dot-com's such as Amazon, eBay, and Etrade) and the increased use of the Internet for communications, sales, and business data processing. These technologies have fostered the growing strategic focus in cost management by reducing the time required for processing transactions and by expanding the individual manager's access to information within the firm, the industry, and the business environment around the world.

Focus on the Customer

A key change in the business environment is increased *consumer expectation* for product functionality and quality. The result has been a shorter product life cycle, as firms seek to add new features and new products as quickly as possible, thereby increasing the overall intensity of competition.

In past years, a business typically succeeded by focusing on only a relatively small number of products with limited features and by organizing production into long, low-cost, and high-volume production runs aided by assembly-line automation. The new business process focuses instead on customer satisfaction. Producing value for the customer changes the orientation of managers from low-cost production of large quantities to *quality, service, timeliness of delivery, and the ability to respond to the customer's desire for specific features.* Today many of the critical success factors (discussed later) are customer oriented. Cost management practices are also changing; cost management reports now include specific measures of customer preferences and customer satisfaction.

Management Organization

Management organization has changed in response to the changes in marketing and manufacturing. Because of the focus on customer satisfaction and value, the emphasis has shifted from financial and profit-based measures of performance to customer-related, nonfinancial performance measures such as quality, time to delivery, and service. Similarly, the hierarchical command-and-control type of organization is being

The communications industry is offering products that are dramatically changing the way people talk to one another. International Data Corp. estimates that one-third of the U.S. population and more than one-half of the populations of Europe and Japan use some form of wireless communication. Global giants such as Nokia, Motorola, and Ericsson provide the products, and other global giants such as Sprint, AT&T and Verizon (United States), Vodaphone (United Kingdom), Deutsche Tekekom (Germany), Telecom (France), and NTT Do-CoMo (Japan) provide the wireless services to what is expected to be 1 billion global customers within the next several years. The new wireless products and services are expected to push the growth of e-commerce and to provide entirely new services, such as wireless medical sensors that will alert doctors to medical emergencies. The cost management issues related to these products and services are emerging. How can the technologies be used to reduce the cost of providing such products and services? How can the wireless tools be used to provide a new competitive edge for established firms? Management accountants, as strategic partners, will be expected to have the expertise to assist managers in resolving these issues.

Source: "Wireless in Cyberspace," *Business Week,* special section May 29, 2000, pp. 136–64; and "Deutsche Telekom's Wireless Wager," *Business Week,* August 7, 2000, pp. 31–34.

replaced by a more flexible organizational form that encourages teamwork and coordination among business functions. In response to these changes, cost management practices are also changing to include reports that are useful to cross-functional teams of managers; the reports reflect the multifunctional roles of these teams and include a variety of operating and financial information: product quality, unit cost, customer satisfaction, and production bottlenecks, for example. The changes in manufacturing, marketing, and management in organizations are summarized in Exhibit 1.3.

EXHIBIT 1.3 **Comparison of Prior and Contemporary Business Environments**

	Prior Business Environment	Contemporary Business Environment
Manufacturing		
Basis of competition	Economies of scale, standardization	Quality, functionality, customer satisfaction
Manufacturing process	High volume, long production runs, significant levels of in-process and finished inventory	Low volume, short production runs, focus on reducing inventory levels and other non-value-added activities and costs
Manufacturing technology	Assembly line automation, isolated technology applications	Robotics, flexible manufacturing systems, integrated technology applications connected by networks
Required labor skills	Machine-paced, low-level skills	Individually and team-paced, high-level skills
Emphasis on quality	Acceptance of a normal or usual amount of waste	Goal of zero defects
Marketing		
Products	Relatively few variations, long product life cycles	Large number of variations, short product life cycles
Markets	Largely domestic	Global
Management Organization		
Type of information recorded and reported	Almost exclusively financial data	Financial and operating data, the firm's strategic success factors
Management organizational structure	Hierarchical, command and control	Network-based organization forms, teamwork focus—employee has more responsibility and control, coaching rather than command and control
Management focus	Emphasis on the short term, short-term performance measures and compensation, concern for sustaining the current stock price, short tenure and high mobility of top managers	Emphasis on the long term, focus on critical success factors, commitment to the long-term success of the firm, including shareholder value

Social, Political, and Cultural Considerations

In addition to changes in the business environment, significant changes have taken place in the social, political, and cultural environments that affect business. Although the nature and extent of these changes vary a great deal from country to country, they include a more ethnically and racially diverse workforce, a renewed sense of ethical responsibility among managers and employees, and an increased deregulation of business by the federal government.

The new business environment requires firms to be flexible and adaptable and to place greater responsibility in the hands of a more highly skilled workforce. Additionally, the changes tend to focus the firm on factors *outside* the production of its product or provision of its service to the ultimate consumer and the global society in which the consumer lives.

The Strategic Focus of Cost Management

The competitive firm incorporates the emerging and anticipated changes in the contemporary environment of business into its business planning and practices. The competitive firm is customer driven, uses advanced manufacturing technologies when appropriate, anticipates the effect of changes in regulatory requirements and customer tastes, and recognizes its complex social, political, and cultural environment. Guided by strategic thinking, the management accountant focuses on the factors that make the company successful rather than costs and other financial measures. We are reminded of the story of the Scottish farmer who had prize sheep to take to market. When asked why his sheep were always superior to those of his neighbors, the farmer responded, "While they're weighing their sheep, I'm fattening mine."[6] Similarly, cost management focuses not on the measurement per se but on the *identification of those measures that are critical* to the firm's success. Robert Kaplan's classification of the phases of the development of cost management systems describes this shift in focus:[7]

Stage 1. Cost management systems are basic transaction reporting systems.

Stage 2. As they develop into the second stage, cost management systems focus on external financial reporting. The objective is reliable financial reports; accordingly, the usefulness for cost management is limited.

Stage 3. Cost management systems track key operating data and develop more accurate and relevant cost information for decision making; cost management information is developed.

Stage 4. Strategically relevant cost management information is an integral part of the system.

The first two stages of cost system development focus on the management accountant's measurement and reporting role, and the third stage shifts to operational control. In the fourth stage, the ultimate goal, the management accountant is an integral part of management, not a reporter but a full business partner, with the skills of identifying, summarizing, and reporting the critical factors necessary for the firm's success. **Critical success factors (CSFs)** are measures of those aspects of the firm's performance essential to its competitive advantage and, therefore, to its success. Many of these critical success factors are financial, but many are nonfinancial. The CSFs for any given firm depend on the nature of the competition it faces.

Critical success factors (CSFs) are measures of those aspects of the firm's performance that are essential to its competitive advantage and, therefore, to its success.

---

[6] Sheep farmer story adapted from IEEE, *Spectrum,* January 1992, p. 25.

[7] Robert S. Kaplan, "The Four-Stage Model of Cost System Design," *Management Accounting,* February 1990, pp. 22–26.

Contemporary Management Techniques

LEARNING OBJECTIVE 3
Explain the contemporary management techniques and how they have influenced cost management.

Managers commonly use the following tools to implement the firm's broad strategy and to facilitate the achievement of success on critical success factors: benchmarking, total quality management, continuous improvement (*kaizen*), activity-based costing, reengineering, the theory of constraints, mass customization, just-in-time systems, computer-aided design and manufacturing, automation, target costing, life-cycle costing, the value chain, and the balanced scorecard.

Benchmarking

Benchmarking
is a process by which a firm identifies its critical success factors, studies the best practices of other firms (or other units within a firm) for achieving these critical success factors, and then implements improvements in the firm's processes to match or beat the performance of those competitors.

Benchmarking is a process by which a firm identifies its critical success factors, studies the best practices of other firms (or other units within a firm) for achieving these critical success factors, and then implements improvements in the firm's processes to match or beat the performance of those competitors. Benchmarking was first implemented by Xerox Corporation in the late 1970s.[8] Today many firms use benchmarking. Some firms are recognized as leaders, and therefore benchmarks, in selected areas (see Exhibit 1.4).

Benchmarking efforts are facilitated today by cooperative networks of noncompeting firms that exchange benchmarking information. For example, the International Benchmarking Clearinghouse (www.apqc.org) and the International Organization for Standardization (ISO) (www.iso.org) assist firms in strategic benchmarking.

Total Quality Management

Total quality management (TQM)
is a technique by which management develops policies and practices to ensure that the firm's products and services exceed customers' expectations.

Total quality management (TQM) is a technique by which management develops policies and practices to ensure that the firm's products and services exceed customers' expectations. This approach includes increased product functionality, reliability, durability, and serviceability. Cost management is used to analyze the cost consequences of different design choices for TQM and to measure and report the many aspects of quality including, for example, production breakdowns and production defects, wasted labor or raw materials, the number of service calls, and the nature of the complaints, warranty costs, and product recalls.

TQM efforts can build brand loyalty and help the company improve product quality and competitiveness quickly. For example, Hewlett-Packard has instituted a policy of taking back products returned by customers to retailers—something many computer manufacturers do only reluctantly. This policy builds retailer and customer loyalty, and it provides Hewlett-Packard an early warning of product problems.[9]

Continuous Improvement

Whether you think you can or whether you think you can't—you're right.

Henry Ford

---

[8] R. C. Camp, *Benchmarking: The Search for Industry Best Practices that Lead to Superior Performance* (Milwaukee, WI: American Society for Quality Control Press, 1989); and Alexandra Biesada, "Strategic Benchmarking," *Financial World*, September 29, 1992, pp. 30–58.

[9] "The Printer King Invades Home PCs," *Business Week*, August 21, 1995, pp. 74–75.

EXHIBIT 1.4
Leading Firms in Selected Benchmarks: Critical Success Factors

Sources: James C. Collins and Jerry I. Porras, *Built to Last* (New York: Harper Business, 1994); and "The Best Corporate Reputations in America," *The Wall Street Journal*, September 23, 1999, p. B-1.

Customer Service	Innovation and Product Development	Quality	Corporate Social Responsibility	Labor Relationships and Employee Training
L.L. Bean	3M	Toyota	Merck	Ford
FedEx	Apple Computer	Motorola	Johnson & Johnson	IBM
Nordstrom	Hewlett-Packard	IBM	General Electric	Johnson & Johnson
Home Depot	Sony		Ben & Jerry's	Lucent
Amazon.com	Nokia			Hewlett-Packard

One company, Dell Corporation, is a global manufacturer of PCs. In the last several years it has come to dominate the PC business, with market capitalization greater than Oracle, Sun, or Hewlett-Packard. In 2002 sales increased 9 percent and profits increased by 17 percent. Most important, this happened during a period of increasing price pressures and lower unit profits in the industry. Dell succeeded by reducing manufacturing time dramatically so that customers could expect their mail-order computers to arrive in a few days in comparison to the weeks that customers of other mail-order PC makers had to wait. As Michael Dell, chairman and CEO of Dell Computer, said, "Speed is everything in this business. We're setting the pace for the industry":

- Speed in order taking: Orders are confirmed to customers in 5 minutes.
- Speed in manufacturing: An order received by 9 A.M. Monday is shipped by 9 P.M. Tuesday.

- Speed in collection: Within 24 hours, phone and Web orders are collected in cash; in contrast, rival manufacturers that sell through dealers wait for a month or more to collect on sales.
- Speed in resupply: Circuit boards are restocked at the Austin, Texas, plant from suppliers in Mexico within 15 hours of an order.

Dell's speed reduces manufacturing costs and inventory holding costs as well as providing a key value for customers.

The second company, VF Corporation, a clothing manufacturer, helped its customers (such as Wal-Mart and J.C. Penney) forecast demand and proper stocking levels on its fastest moving items. It provides this service by linking the computers of the manufacturer and retailing customer. Using this technology, VF was able to re-stock its customers' shelves much faster, sometimes overnight.

Sources: "Dell, the Conqueror," *Business Week,* September 24, 2001, pp. 92–102; and "Just Get It to the Stores on Time," *Business Week,* March 6, 1995, pp. 66–67.

Continuous improvement
(the Japanese word is *kaizen*) is a management technique by which managers and workers commit to a program of continuous improvement in quality and other critical success factors.

Activity analysis
is used to develop a detailed description of the specific activities performed in the firm's operations.

Activity-based costing (ABC)
is used to improve the accuracy of cost analysis by improving the tracing of costs to products or to individual customers.

Activity-based management (ABM)
uses activity analysis to improve operational control and management control.

Reengineering
is a process for creating competitive advantage in which a firm reorganizes its operating and management functions, often with the result that jobs are modified, combined, or eliminated.

Henry Ford realized that the right attitude is important to success. That belief is what continuous improvement is all about. **Continuous improvement** (the Japanese word is *kaizen*) is a management technique by which managers and workers commit to a program of continuous improvement in quality and other critical success factors. Its origin is attributed to Japanese manufacturers who pursue quality tirelessly. Continuous improvement is very often associated with benchmarking and total quality management as firms seek to identify other firms as models to learn how to improve their critical success factors.

Activity-Based Costing and Management

Many firms have found that they can improve planning, product costing, operational control, and management control by using **activity analysis** to develop a detailed description of the specific activities performed in the firm's operations. The activity analysis provides the basis for activity-based costing and activity-based management. **Activity-based costing (ABC)** is used to improve the accuracy of cost analysis by improving the tracing of costs to products or to individual customers. **Activity-based management (ABM)** uses activity analysis to improve operational control and management control. ABC and ABM are key strategic tools for many firms, especially those with complex operations, or great diversity of products.

Reengineering

Reengineering is a process for creating competitive advantage in which a firm reorganizes its operating and management functions, often with the result that jobs are modified, combined, or eliminated. It has been defined as the "fundamental rethinking and radical redesign of business processes to achieve dramatic improvements in critical, contemporary measures of performance, such as cost, quality, service, and speed."[10] Under the pressure of global competition, many firms look to reengineering as a way to reduce the cost of management and operations and as a basis for careful reanalysis of the firm's strategic competitive advantage. Cost management supports the reengineering effort by providing the relevant information.

[10] The definition is provided by Michael Hammer and James Champy, *Re-Engineering the Corporation* (New York: Harper Press, 1993). Another useful reference is the book by Roy Harmon and Leroy D. Peterson, *Re-Inventing the Factory* (New York: Free Press, 1990).

The Theory of Constraints

The **theory of constraints (TOC)** is a strategic technique to help firms effectively improve a very important critical success factor: cycle time, the rate at which raw materials are converted to finished products.[11] TOC helps identify and eliminate bottlenecks—places where partially completed products tend to accumulate as they wait to be processed—in the production process.

In the competitive global marketplace common to most industries, the ability to be faster than competitors is often a critical success factor. Many managers argue that the focus on speed in the TOC approach is crucial. They consider speed in product development, product delivery, and manufacturing to be paramount as global competitors find ever higher customer expectations for rapid product development and prompt delivery. Many Internet firms, including sellers of computer products, clothing, and other consumer goods, are finding that promise of prompt delivery is sometimes the only way to make a sale since competition has forced all competing firms to provide excellent quality products and services.

> The **theory of constraints (TOC)** is a strategic technique to help firms effectively improve the rate at which raw materials are converted to finished products.

Mass Customization

Increasingly, many manufacturing and service firms find that customers expect products and services to be developed for each customer's unique needs. For example, a particular bicycle customer might expect the product to be designed to fit his or her height, weight, and usage requirements. Dell will assemble a computer based on the customer's exact specifications. Many firms have found that they can compete successfully with a strategy that targets customers' unique needs. In **mass customization**, marketing and production processes are designed to handle the increased variety that results from this type of business. This redesign involves a larger number of smaller production runs in manufacturing and specially designed marketing and service functions. The greater variety and complexity of production under mass customization increases a portion of production costs, although the costs of marketing and servicing the product might be reduced. Mass customization can be an effective way for a firm to compete in an industry in which the price and quality expectations of many consumers are met by existing manufacturers. It does this by distinguishing itself through providing a fast, customized service. The growth of mass customization is, in effect, another indication of the increased attention given to satisfying the customer.

> **Mass customization** is a management technique in which marketing and production processes are designed to handle the increased variety that results from delivering customized products and services to customers.

The Just-in-Time System

A **just-in-time (JIT) system** is a comprehensive production and inventory management system that purchases or produces materials and parts only as needed and just in time to be used at each stage of the production process. JIT can be applied to all aspects of business, including purchasing, production, and delivery. JIT focuses on eliminating waste, reducing inventories, and developing strong supplier relationships. The degree of coordination needed to implement effective JIT manufacturing systems highlights existing problems such as bottlenecks, inventory loss, and unreliable suppliers.

Kanban is used with JIT to greatly reduce lead times, decrease inventory, and improve productivity by linking all production operations in a smooth, uninterrupted flow.

Kanban is essentially a communication system; it can be a card, a label, a box or bin, a series of in trays, or a number of squares painted or taped on the factory floor or work surface. Its purpose is to inform the previous step in the process to make a part. The kanban card typically contains information identifying the part, its descriptive name, how many of each part should accompany the card, the delivery location, the reorder point, and the turnaround time.

> A **just-in-time (JIT) system** is a comprehensive production and inventory system that purchases or produces materials and parts only as needed and just in time to be used at each stage of the production process.

> **Kanban** is a set of control cards used to signal the need for materials and products to move from one operation to the next in an assembly line.

---

[11] Two of the best sources for descriptions of the theory of constraints are the following books: E. Goldratt and J. Cox, *The Goal* (New York: Free Press, 1986); and E. Goldratt, *The Theory of Constraints* (New York: North River Press, 1990).

Under a kanban system, the previous process or step cannot send parts or components to the subsequent step unless that downstream process or step requests them by means of a kanban card. Thus, no overproduction occurs, priority in production becomes obvious, and control of inventory becomes easier.

Computer-Aided Design and Manufacturing

Computer-aided design (CAD) is the use of computers in product development, analysis, and design modification to improve the quality and performance of the product. **Computer-aided manufacturing (CAM)** is the use of computers to plan, implement, and control production.

In the future, more companies will use CAD and CAM to respond to changing consumer tastes more quickly. These innovations allow companies to significantly reduce the time necessary to bring their products from the design process to the distribution stage.

Automation

Automation requires a relatively large investment in computers, computer programming, machines, and equipment. Many firms add automation gradually, one process at a time. To improve efficiency and effectiveness continuously, firms must integrate people and equipment into the smoothly operating teams that have become a vital part of manufacturing strategy. Flexible manufacturing systems (FMS) and computer-integrated manufacturing (CIM) are two integration approaches.

A **flexible manufacturing system (FMS)** is a computerized network of automated equipment that produces one or more groups of parts or variations of a product in a flexible manner. It uses robots and computer-controlled materials-handling systems to link several stand-alone, computer-controlled machines in switching from one production run to another.

Computer-integrated manufacturing (CIM) is a manufacturing system that totally integrates all office and factory functions within a company via a computer-based information network to allow hour-by-hour manufacturing management.

The major characteristics of modern manufacturing companies that are adopting FMS and CIM are production of high-quality products and services, low inventories, high degrees of automation, quick cycle time, increased flexibility, and advanced information technology. These innovations shift the focus from large production volumes necessary to absorb fixed overhead to a new emphasis on marketing efforts, engineering, and product design.

Target Costing

Target costing is a tool that has resulted directly from the intensely competitive markets in many industries. **Target costing** determines the desired cost for a product on the basis of a given competitive price, such that the product will earn a desired profit. Cost is thus determined by price. The firm using target costing must often adopt strict cost-reduction measures or redesign the product or manufacturing process to meet the market price and remain profitable.

$$\text{Target cost} = \text{Market-determined price} - \text{Desired profit}$$

Target costing forces the firm to become more competitive, and, like benchmarking, it is a common strategic form of analysis in intensely competitive industries where even small price differences attract consumers to the lower-priced product. The camera manufacturing industry is a good example of an industry where target costing is used. Camera manufacturers such as Minolta know the market price for each line of camera they manufacture, so they redesign the product (add/delete features, use less expensive parts and materials) and redesign the production process to get the manufacturing cost down to the predetermined target cost. The automobile industry also uses target costing.

Computer-aided design (CAD) is the use of computers in product development, analysis, and design modification to improve the quality and performance of the product.

Computer-aided manufacturing (CAM) is the use of computers to plan, implement, and control production.

A **flexible manufacturing system (FMS)** is a computerized network of automated equipment that produces one or more groups of parts or variations of a product in a flexible manner.

Computer-integrated manufacturing (CIM) is a manufacturing system that totally integrates all office and factory functions within a company via a computer-based information network to allow hour-by-hour manufacturing management.

Target costing determines the desired cost for a product on the basis of a given competitive price so that the product will earn a desired profit.

Life-Cycle Costing

Life-cycle costing
is a management technique used to
identify and monitor the costs of a
product throughout its life cycle.

Life-cycle costing is a management technique to identify and monitor the costs of a product throughout its life cycle. The life cycle consists of all steps from product design and purchase of raw materials to delivery and service of the finished product. The steps include (1) research and development; (2) product design, including prototyping, target costing, and testing; (3) manufacturing, inspecting, packaging, and warehousing; (4) marketing, promotion, and distribution; and (5) sales and service. Cost management has traditionally focused only on costs incurred at the third step, manufacturing. Thinking strategically, management accountants now manage the product's full life cycle of costs, including upstream and downstream costs as well as manufacturing costs. This expanded focus means that they pay careful attention, especially to product design, since design decisions lock in most subsequent life-cycle costs.

The Value Chain

The **value chain**
is an analysis tool firms use to
identify the specific steps required
to provide a product or service to
the customer.

The **value chain** is an analysis tool firms use to identify the specific steps required to provide a competitive product or service to the customer. In particular, an analysis of the firm's value chain helps management discover which steps or activities are not competitive, where costs can be reduced, or which activity should be outsourced. Also, management can use the analysis to find ways to increase value for the customer at one or more of the steps of the value chain. For example, companies such as Dell, General Electric, IBM, and Honeywell have found greater overall profits by moving downstream in the value chain to place a greater emphasis on high-value services and less emphasis on lower-margin manufactured products. A key idea of the value chain analysis is that the firm should carefully study each step in its operations, to determine how each activity contributes to the firm's profits and competitiveness.[12]

The Balanced Scorecard

Strategic information using critical success factors provides a road map for the firm to use to chart its competitive course and serves as a benchmark for competitive success. Financial measures such as profitability reflect only a partial, and frequently only a short-term, measure of the firm's progress. Without strategic information, the firm is likely to stray from its competitive course and to make strategically wrong product decisions, for example, choosing the wrong products or the wrong marketing and distribution methods.

To emphasize the importance of using strategic information, *both financial and nonfinancial,* accounting reports of a firm's performance are now often based on critical success factors in four different dimensions. One dimension is financial; the other three dimensions are nonfinancial:

1. Financial performance. Measures of profitability and market value, among others, as indicators of how well the firm satisfies its owners and shareholders.

2. Customer satisfaction. Measures of quality, service, and low cost, among others, as indicators of how well the firm satisfies its customers.

3. Internal business processes. Measures of the efficiency and effectiveness with which the firm produces the product or service.

4. Innovation and learning. Measures of the firm's ability to develop and utilize human resources to meet its strategic goals now and into the future.

The **balanced scorecard**
is an accounting report that
includes the firm's critical success
factors in four areas: (1) financial
performance, (2) customer
satisfaction, (3) internal business
processes, and (4) innovation and
learning.

An accounting report based on the four dimensions is called a **balanced scorecard.** The concept of balance captures the intent of broad coverage, financial and nonfinancial, of all factors that contribute to the firm's success in achieving its strategic goals.

---

[12] Richard Wise and Peter Baumgartner, "Go Downstream: The Profit Imperative in Manufacturing," *Harvard Business Review,* September–October 1999, pp. 133–141; Louis V. Gerstner, Jr., *Who Says Elephants Can't Dance* (New York: Harper Business, 2002).

Dell Computer was one of the biggest success stories of the last decade of the twentieth century. From 1995 to 2002, its stock price significantly outperformed that of its key rivals, Hewlett-Packard, IBM, Intel, and Cisco Systems. *Business Week* chose CEO Michael Dell as one of the Top Executives of the Year in 2003. Dell succeeded in all dimensions of company performance: profit growth, stock price gains, operating efficiency and speed, and customer service. These successes paid big dividends for the company, which more than doubled its sales in two years. Its stock price had almost a 100 percent average annual price increase throughout the 1990s—the best performing stock of the

decade! But trouble is ahead. Dell's sales increases fell nearly to the industry average.* Perhaps this is due to Dell's dependence on the PC market, which is showing signs of a slowdown. What should Dell do in this situation—stick with its strategy of dominance in the mail-order PC market or look to a new strategy of some kind? How might any of the contemporary management techniques just described in the text help?

* For current financial information about Dell, see http://finance.yahoo.com/.

Source: "The Top Executives," *Business Week*, January 13, 2003, p. 58.

The balanced scorecard provides a basis for a more complete analysis than is possible with financial data alone. The use of the balanced scorecard is thus a critical ingredient of the overall approach that firms take to become and remain competitive.

How a Firm Succeeds: The Competitive Strategy

If you do not know where you are going, you will probably get there.

(Anonymous)

A **strategy**
is a set of policies, procedures, and approaches to business that produce long-term success.

LEARNING OBJECTIVE 4
Explain the different types of competitive strategies.

A firm succeeds by implementing a **strategy,** that is, a set of policies, procedures, and approaches to business that produce long-term success. Finding a strategy begins with determining the purpose and long-range direction, and therefore the mission, of the company. Exhibit 1.5 lists excerpts from the mission statements of several companies. The mission is developed into specific performance objectives, which are then implemented by specific corporate strategies, that is, specific actions to achieve the objectives that will fulfill the mission. See the Sara Lee corporate strategy in Exhibit 1.6. Note that Sara Lee's broad mission statement is explained in terms of more specific objectives, which are in turn operationalized through specific corporate strategies.

Firms have responded to the changes in business in many ways, including reengineering operational processes, downsizing the workforce, outsourcing service functions, and developing smaller, more efficient, and more socially responsible organizational policies and structures. They have attempted to become more adaptable as the pace of change increases.

EXHIBIT 1.5
Mission Statements of Selected Companies

Ford Motor Company (ford.com)
Provide personal mobility for people around the world.

IBM (ibm.com)
To lead in the creation, development, and manufacture of the industry's most advanced information technologies, and to translate these into value for our customers.

United Parcel Service (ups.com)
To move at the speed of business.

Walt Disney (Disney.com)
To make people happy.

Merck (merck.com)
To preserve and improve human life.

Sara Lee (saralee.com)
To feed, clothe, and care for consumers and their families the world over.

EXHIBIT 1.6
Sara Lee Corporate Strategy

Source: Sara Lee Corporation (saralee.com).

We focus our efforts on building leadership brands in three global businesses: Food and Beverage, Intimates and Underwear, and Household Products. Seeking to be innovative in everything we do, we follow four principal strategies to create long-term shareholder value:

1. Drive profitable top-line growth by:
   • anticipating and meeting our consumers' needs.
   • partnering with our trade customers.
   • investing our cash flow behind internal opportunities and strategic acquisitions.
2. Achieve the lowest possible costs by leveraging our skills, scale, and technology, while striving for functional excellence in all business processes.
3. Be an employer of choice for highly talented people, retaining and attracting world-class individuals through a philosophy of empowerment and a system of providing rewards commensurate with performance.
4. Adhere to the highest standards of ethical business conduct, treating fairly, and with respect, all those we touch as a company.

EXHIBIT 1.7
Cost Management Focus in Prior and Contemporary Business Environments

	Prior Business Environment	Contemporary Business Environment
Cost management focus	Financial reporting and cost analysis; common emphasis on standardization and standard costs; the accountant as functional expert and financial scorekeeper	Cost management as a tool for the development and implementation of business strategy; the accountant as business partner

Firms also are beginning to use cost management to support their strategic goals. Cost management has shifted away from a focus on the stewardship role: product costing and financial reporting. The new focus is on a management-facilitating role: developing cost and other information to support the management of the firm and the achievement of its strategic goals. Before the changes in business processes, a focus on detailed methods for product costing and control at the departmental level was appropriate for the high-volume, standardized, infrequently changing manufacturing processes of that time. Now a firm's cost accounting system must be more dynamic to deal with the more rapidly changing environment and the increasing diversity of products and manufacturing processes. The cost management system must be able to assist management in this dynamic environment by facilitating strategic management. The contemporary business environment focuses on critical success factors, including both financial and nonfinancial factors (Exhibit 1.7).

Strategic Measures of Success

The strategic cost management system develops strategic information, including both financial and nonfinancial information. In the past, firms tended to focus primarily on financial performance measures, such as growth in sales and earnings, cash flow, and stock price. In contrast, firms in the contemporary business environment use strategic management to focus primarily on strategic measures of success, many of which are nonfinancial measures of operations, such as market share, product quality, customer satisfaction, and growth opportunities (see Exhibit 1.8). The financial measures show the impact of the firm's policies and procedures on the firm's *current financial position* and, therefore, its *current* return to the shareholders. In contrast, the nonfinancial factors show the firm's *current and potential competitive position* as measured from at least three additional perspectives from the balanced scorecard: (1) the customer, (2) internal business processes, and (3) innovation and learning. Additional perspectives include community and social impact, government relations, and ethical or professional management behavior. Strategic financial and nonfinancial measures of success are also commonly called *critical success factors* (CSFs).

EXHIBIT 1.8
Financial and Nonfinancial Measures of Success
Critical Success Factors

Financial Measures of Success	Nonfinancial Measures of Success
Sales growth	**Customer Measures**
Earnings growth	Market share and growth in market share
Dividend growth	Customer service
Bond and credit ratings	On-time delivery
Cash flow	Customer satisfaction
Increase in stock price	Brand recognition
	Positions in favorable markets
	Internal Business Processes
	High product quality
	Manufacturing innovation
	High manufacturing productivity
	Cycle time
	Yield and reduction in waste
	Learning and Innovation (Human Resources)
	Competence and integrity of managers
	Morale and firmwide culture
	Education and training
	Innovation and new products and manufacturing methods

EXHIBIT 1.9
Consequences of Lack of Strategic Information

- Decision making based on guesses and intuition only
- Lack of clarity about direction and goals
- Lack of a clear and favorable perception of the firm by customers and suppliers
- Incorrect investment decisions; choosing products, markets, or manufacturing processes inconsistent with strategic goals
- Inability to effectively benchmark competitors, resulting in lack of knowledge about more effective competitive strategies
- Failure to identify most profitable products, customers, and markets

Without strategic information, the firm is likely to stray from its competitive course, to make strategically wrong manufacturing and marketing decisions: to choose the wrong products or the wrong customers. Some of the consequences of a lack of strategic information are shown in Exhibit 1.9.

Developing a Competitive Strategy: Strategic Positioning

In developing a sustainable competitive position, each firm purposefully or as a result of market forces arrives at one of the two competitive strategies: cost leadership or differentiation.[13]

Cost Leadership

Cost leadership
is a competitive strategy in which a firm succeeds in producing products or services at the lowest cost in the industry.

Cost leadership is a strategy in which a firm outperforms competitors in producing products or services at the lowest cost. The cost leader makes sustainable profits at lower prices, thereby limiting the growth of competition in the industry through its success at price wars and undermining the profitability of competitors, which must meet the firm's low price. The cost leader normally has a relatively large market share and tends to avoid niche or segment markets by using the price advantage to attract a

---

[13] This section is adapted from Michael Porter, *Competitive Advantage* (New York: Free Press, 1985), chap. 1, except that we, for simplicity, omit a third strategy, focus. The Porter concept of competitive strategy is widely used. Another common view of competitive strategy is that of the Boston Consulting Group (B. D. Henderson, *Henderson on Corporate Strategy* [Cambridge, MA: Abt Books, 1979]). For a discussion of the Boston Consulting Group's view and that of others, see the chapter appendix.

large portion of the broad market. While most firms make strong efforts to reduce costs, the cost leader may focus almost exclusively on cost reduction, thereby ensuring a significant cost and price advantage in the market.

Cost advantages usually result from productivity in the manufacturing process, in distribution, or in overall administration. For example, technological innovation in the manufacturing process and labor savings from overseas production are common routes to competitive productivity. Firms known to be successful at cost leadership are typically very large manufacturers and retailers, such as Wal-Mart, Texas Instruments, and Dell.

A potential weakness of the cost leadership strategy is the tendency to cut costs in a way that undermines demand for the product or service, for example, by deleting key features. The cost leader remains competitive only so long as the consumer sees that the product or service is (at least nearly) equivalent to competing products that cost somewhat more.

Differentiation

Differentiation
is a competitive strategy in which a firm succeeds by developing and maintaining a unique value for the product as perceived by consumers.

The **differentiation** strategy is implemented by creating a perception among consumers that the product or service is unique in some important way, usually by being of higher quality. This perception allows the firm to charge higher prices and outperform the competition in profits without reducing costs significantly. Most industries, including automobile, consumer electronics, and industrial equipment, have differentiated firms. The appeal of differentiation is especially strong for product lines for which the perception of quality and image is important, as in cosmetics, jewelry, and automobiles. Tiffany, Bentley, Rolex, Maytag, and Mercedes-Benz are good examples of firms that stress differentiation.

A weakness of the differentiation strategy is the firm's tendency to undermine its strength by attempting to lower costs or by ignoring the necessity to have a continual and aggressive marketing plan to reinforce the differentiation. If the consumer begins to believe that the difference is not significant, lower-cost rival products will appear more attractive.

Other Strategic Issues

A firm succeeds, then, by adopting and effectively implementing one of the strategies explained earlier (and summarized in Exhibit 1.10). Recognize that although one strategy is generally dominant, a firm is most likely to employ both of the strategies at the same time. However, a firm following both strategies is likely to succeed only if it achieves one of them significantly. A firm that does not achieve at least one strategy is not likely to be successful. This situation is what Michael Porter calls "getting stuck in the middle." A firm that is stuck in the middle is not able to sustain a competitive advantage. For example, giant retailer Kmart has been stuck in the middle between trying to compete with Wal-Mart on cost and price, and with style-conscious Target on differentiation. Some have suggested that Kmart might find success by abandoning the

EXHIBIT 1.10
Distinctive Aspects of the Two Competitive Strategies

Source: A. A. Thompson and A. J. Strickland, *Strategic Management*, 10th ed. (New York: McGraw-Hill, 1998).

Aspect	Cost Leadership	Differentiation
Strategic target	Broad cross section of the market	Focused section of the market
Basis of competitive advantage	Lowest cost in the industry	Unique product or service
Product line	Limited selection	Wide variety, differentiating features
Production emphasis	Lowest possible cost with high quality and essential product features	Innovation in differentiating products
Marketing emphasis	Low price	Premium price and innovative, differentiating features

Which Is It: Cost Leadership or Differentiation?
Wal-Mart and Michelin

WAL-MART: WORKING CLASS OR BMW CROWD?
In the fiercely competitive retail business, Wal-Mart has established itself as a dominant force in discount retailing. Meanwhile upscale retailers, such as Nordstrom, focus on customer service and unique products. Can Wal-Mart attract both groups? Wal-Mart is now targeting well-off suburban areas and developing new stores with grocery sections that offer gourmet food and pricier products for these customers. This new strategy brings Wal-Mart in direct competition with more style-conscious stores, and at a distance from their base—the people who shop for necessities. One could argue that the new strategy simply reflects the fact that Wal-Mart cannot sustain its current rate of growth without moving to new markets. Wal-Mart believes that every shopper loves good prices, whether it be a basic item or something more pricey.

Source: Constance L. Hays, "Built on the Working Class, Wal-Mart Eyes BMW Crowd," *The Wall Street Journal*, February 24, 2002, p. C1.

MICHELIN: ARE AUTO TIRES A COMMODITY?
Michelin, the 114-year-old French manufacturer of tires, is the worldwide leader in tire sales; for example, in 2002 it had sales of more than $15 billion. But there are plenty of challenges. One is the growth of low-cost tire producers in Southeast Asia and elsewhere. Michelin knows that most tire buyers primarily are shopping for price, viewing tires as a commodity. This is true even though problems with Firestone and other tire makers in recent years have caused consumers to pay more attention to tire safety. To help differentiate his firm's product, Edouard Michelin (Michelin's CEO) is pushing development of technologically advanced tires that provide blowout protection and are more suited for high-performance use. So, is the auto tire a commodity? Edouard Michelin is betting he can continue to be successful with a differentiated product.

Note: What works for Michelin may not work for Goodyear Tire Company. Goodyear raised its prices and promoted a quality image following the recall of competitor Firestone's tires in 2000. The plan failed and Goodyear's sales and profits have fallen as a result.

Sources: "Michelin Rolls," *Business Week*, September 30, 2002, pp. 58–62; "How Goodyear Blew Its Chance to Capitalize on a Rival's Woes," by Timothy Aeppel, *The Wall Street Journal*, February 19, 2003, p. 1.

suburban locations where Target and Wal-Mart are strong and instead focusing on their many urban locations where they offer convenience to the urban shopper.[14]

The Professional Environment of Cost Management

Personally, I'm always ready to learn, although I do not always like being taught.
Winston Churchill

LEARNING OBJECTIVE 5
Describe the professional environment of the management accountant, including professional organizations, professional certifications, and professional ethics.

Winston Churchill, the former prime minister of the United Kingdom, understood the importance of continuous learning. His words apply equally well to the management accountant. Management accountants must continuously improve their technical and other skills and maintain a constant high level of professionalism, integrity, and objectivity about their work. Many professional organizations, such as the Institute of Management Accountants (IMA) and the American Institute of CPAs (AICPA), encourage their members to earn relevant professional certifications, participate in professional development programs, and continually reflect on the professional ethics they bring to their work.

Professional Organizations

The professional environment of the management accountant is influenced by two types of organizations: one that sets guidelines and regulations regarding management accounting practices and one that promotes the professionalism and competence of management accountants.

[14] Joann Muller, "Attention Kmart: Find a Niche," *Business Week*, February 4, 2002, p. 72.

REAL-WORLD FOCUS

Where to Look for Information on Professional Organizations

American Institute of CPAs (AICPA): http://www.aicpa.org/

Federal Trade Commission (FTC): http://www.ftc.gov/

Financial Executives Institute (FEI): http://www.fei.org

Institute of Internal Auditors (IIA): http://www.iia.org

Institute of Management Accountants (IMA): http://www.imanet.org

Internal Revenue Service (IRS): http://www.irs.gov

Securities and Exchange Commission (SEC): http://www.sec.gov/

Society of Management Accountants (SMAC, Canada): http://www.cma-Canada.org/

The Chartered Institute of Management Accountants (CIMA, UK): www.cima.org.uk

American Accounting Association Management Accounting Section (MAS): http://rutgers.edu/raw/aaa/aaamas

Consortium for Advanced Manufacturing (CAM-I): http://cam-i.org

Federal Government Accounting Standards: http://fasab.gov

The first group of organizations includes a number of federal agencies, such as the Internal Revenue Service, which sets product costing guidelines for tax purposes, and the Federal Trade Commission (FTC), which, to foster competitive practices and protect trade, restricts pricing practices and requires that prices in most circumstances be justified on the basis of cost. In addition, the Securities and Exchange Commission (SEC) provides guidance, rules, and regulations regarding financial reporting.

The role of the SEC was recently strengthened by the Sarbanes-Oxley Act of 2002 which created the Public Company Accounting Oversight Board (PCAOB) to establish rules for "auditing, quality control, ethics, independence, and other professional standards relating to the preparation of audit reports for issuers." Of particular importance to management accountants is that the SEC, in implementing the act, now requires each public company to disclose in its annual report whether it has a code of ethics covering its chief financial executives, including high-level management accountants such as the controller.

In the private sector, the Financial Accounting Standards Board (FASB), an independent organization, and the AICPA supply additional guidance regarding financial reporting practices. The AICPA also provides educational opportunities in the form of newsletters, magazines, professional development seminars, and technical meetings for management accountants.

Congress established the Cost Accounting Standards Board (CASB) in 1970 (Public Law 91–379), which operates under the Office of Federal Procurement Policy "to make, promulgate, amend and rescind cost accounting standards and interpretations thereof designed to achieve uniformity and consistency in the cost accounting standards governing measurement, assignment, and allocation of cost to contracts with the United States federal government." The CASB's objective is to achieve uniformity and consistency in the cost accounting standards used by government suppliers to reduce the incidence of fraud and abuse. Twenty standards cover a broad range of issues in cost accounting.

In addition, to enhance cost accounting standards and financial reporting by federal governmental entities, Congress established in 1990 the Federal Accounting Standards Advisory Board (FASAB; http://fasab.gov). The FASAB publishes reports and documents on cost accounting concepts and standards that are comparable to those used in business firms.

Another group of organizations supports the growth and professionalism of management accounting practice. The Institute of Management Accountants (IMA) is the principal organization devoted primarily to management accountants in the United States. The IMA provides journals, newsletters, research reports, management accounting practice reports, professional development seminars, and technical meetings that serve the broad purpose of providing continuing education opportunities for management accountants. In the United Kingdom, the Chartered Institute of Management Accountants (CIMA) performs a similar role, as does the Society of Management Accountants (SMA) in Canada, the Spanish Management Accounting Association, the French Accounting Association, and the Institutes of Chartered Accountants in Ireland, Australia, Scotland, and India. Similar organizations are present in most other countries around the world.

In areas related to the management accounting function, the Financial Executives Institute (FEI) provides services much like those provided by the IMA for financial managers, including controllers and treasurers.

Because one of the management control responsibilities of the management accountant is to develop effective systems to detect and prevent errors and fraud in the accounting records, the management accountant commonly has strong ties to the control-oriented organizations such as the Institute of Internal Auditors (IIA).

Even if you're on the right track, you'll get run over if you just sit there.

Will Rogers

Professional Certifications

The role of professional certification programs is to provide a distinct measure of experience, training, and performance capability for the management accountant. Certification is one way in which the management accountant shows professional achievement and stature. Three types of certification are relevant for management accountants. The first is the Certified Management Accountant (CMA) designation administered by the Institute of Management Accountants, which is achieved by passing a qualifying exam and satisfying certain background and experience requirements. The exam covers four areas of knowledge relevant to the practice of management accounting: (1) economics, finance, and management; (2) financial accounting and reporting; (3) management analysis and reporting; and (4) decision analysis and information systems. The material required for part (3) of the exam is covered throughout this book; portions of parts (1), (2), and (4) are also covered.

The second relevant certification is the Certified Financial Manager (CFM) program of the IMA. This program is intended for the broader responsibilities of the financial manager, such as those of the chief financial officer. The exam includes topics related to corporate financial management in addition to the topics covered on the CMA exam.

The third certification is the Certified Public Accountant (CPA) designation. Like the CMA and CFM, the CPA is earned by passing a qualifying exam, which the AICPA prepares and grades, and by satisfying certain background, education, and experience requirements. Unlike the CMA, which is an international designation, the CPA certificate is awarded and monitored in the United States by each state that has its own set of criteria. While the CPA designation is critical for those accountants who practice auditing, the CMA is widely viewed as the most relevant for those dealing with cost management issues.[15] Many countries have certificates that are similar to the CPA.

Professional Ethics

LEARNING OBJECTIVE 6
Understand the principles and rules of professional ethics and explain how to apply them.

Ethics is an important aspect of the management accountant's work and profession. Professional ethics can be summed up as the commitment of the management accountant to provide a useful service for management. This commitment means that the management accountant has the competence, integrity, confidentiality, and objectivity to serve management effectively.

---

[15] A fourth type of certification, the Certified Cost Analyst (CCA), is sponsored by the Institute of Cost Analysis. As with the others, its requirements include a qualifying exam and eight years of experience in cost analysis. The orientation of this exam and certification is accounting for federal contractors, especially defense contractors.

The IMA Code of Ethics

The ethical behavior of the management accountant is guided by the code of ethics of the Institute of Management Accountants (IMA). The IMA code of ethics specifies *minimum* standards of behavior that are intended to guide the management accountant and to inspire a very high overall level of professionalism. By complying with these standards, management accountants enhance their profession and facilitate the development of a trusting relationship in which managers and others can confidently rely on their work.

The IMA code of ethics contains four main sections: (1) competence, (2) confidentiality, (3) integrity, and (4) objectivity (Exhibit 1.11). The standard of competence requires the management accountant to develop and maintain the skills necessary for her or his area of practice and to continually reassess the adequacy of those skills as the firm grows and becomes more complex. The standard of confidentiality requires adherence to the firm's policies regarding communication of data to protect its trade secrets and other confidential information. Integrity refers to behaving in a professional manner (e.g., refraining from activities that would discredit the firm or profession, such as unfair hiring practices) and to avoiding conflicts of interest (e.g., not accepting a gift from a supplier or customer). Finally, objectivity refers to the need to maintain impartial judgment (e.g., not developing analyses to support a decision that the management accountant knows is not correct).

EXHIBIT 1.11
Institute of Management Accountants Code of Ethics

Source: Statement on Management Accounting No. 1C, "Standards of Ethical Conduct for Management Accountants." (Montvale, NJ: Institute of Management Accountants, June 1, 1983), pp. 1–2.

Competence
- Maintain an appropriate level of professional competence by ongoing development of knowledge and skills.
- Perform professional duties in accordance with relevant laws, regulations, and technical standards.
- Prepare complete and clear reports and recommendations after appropriate analyses of relevant and reliable information.

Confidentiality
- Refrain from disclosing confidential information acquired in the course of the work except when authorized, unless legally obligated to do so.
- Inform subordinates as appropriate regarding the confidentiality of information acquired in the course of the work and monitor one's activities to assure the maintenance of that confidentiality.
- Refrain from using or appearing to use confidential information acquired in the course of the work for unethical or illegal advantage either personally or through third parties.

Integrity
- Avoid actual or apparent conflicts of interest and advise all appropriate parties of any potential conflict.
- Refrain from engaging in any activity that would prejudice one's ability to carry out his or her duties ethically.
- Refuse any gift, favor, or hospitality that would influence or would appear to influence one's actions.
- Refrain from either actively or passively subverting the attainment of the organization's legitimate and ethical objectives.
- Recognize and communicate professional limitations or other constraints that would preclude responsible judgment or successful performance of an activity.
- Communicate unfavorable as well as favorable information and professional judgments or opinions.
- Refrain from engaging in or supporting any activity that would discredit the profession.

Objectivity
- Communicate information fairly and objectively.
- Disclose fully all relevant information that could reasonably be expected to influence an intended user's understanding of the reports, comments, and recommendations presented.

REAL-WORLD FOCUS | AICPA Guidance on Ethics for CPAs in Business

For management accountants who are also CPAs, the AICPA provides these helpful suggestions for handling ethics issues. These ideas should be helpful to non-CPAs as well. The AICPA also provides further ethics guidance in the form of a flowchart to aid management accountants in resolving ethics issues. This flowchart can be viewed and downloaded at http://www.aicpa.org/members/div/ethics/BAI/baimemb.htm.

• Do your best to resolve the issue within your own organization, whether that is your department in a larger organization or the company as a whole. Most issues are easily resolved.

• Be cognizant of your obligations to your employer's external accountants. You must be candid and must not knowingly misrepresent facts or fail to disclose material information to them.

• Maintain professional skepticism. If you get an explanation for the situation think about whether it makes sense. Continue to observe over time to see if the situation plays out as expected.

• Maintain documentation of the issue. Record your thoughts and decisions all along the way, as well as the parties with whom you discussed these issues to review later if necessary.

• Even if you are successful in a particular situation, you might find that other implications make it impossible to continue working at a company. In this situation you should seek employment elsewhere.

• Depending on the severity of the issue, you may want to consult with people that you respect from outside the company. Also, consider whether you need to consult with an attorney.

How to Apply the Code of Ethics

Handling situations in which an ethical issue arises can be very challenging and frustrating. To effectively resolve an ethical issue, it is crucial to understand the firm's business and strategy. Determining whether a particular action is ethical requires an understanding of the business context to understand the intent of the act—is it for a business purpose or is it intended to mislead or disguise fraud? An example is Sherron Watkins, an Enron Corporation employee, who is credited with bringing that firm's 2001 accounting fraud to light. She wrote a letter to the CEO about financial accounting practices at Enron that did not appear to fit the firm's business or strategy. Also, using the following step-by-step approach can be helpful:

First, the management accountant must consider the ethical principles or standards that might apply in the situation: competence, integrity, confidentiality, and objectivity. Also important is keeping in mind the broad objective of the code of ethics, which is to maintain management's confidence in the profession. The management accountant must consider how the resolution of the situation would affect a manager's trust and reliance on her or him and on other management accountants.

Second, the management accountant should discuss the situation with a superior. If the superior is part of the situation, the management accountant should seek out the person or persons *within the firm* who have the equivalent or higher level of responsibility, such as a manager in the firm's human resources department or a member of the audit committee. In keeping with the standard of confidentiality, the accountant does not communicate such problems outside the firm except as indicated in the fourth step. One exception is the use of a professional ethics hotline that assures confidentiality, such as ethics@imanet.org at the Institute of Management Accountants.

Third, if the ethical conflict cannot be resolved and the matter is significant, the management accountant might have to resign from the firm and communicate the reasons to the appropriate management level.

Fourth, the management accountant must, if resigning, consider his or her responsibility to communicate the matter outside the firm to regulatory authorities or to the firm's external auditor.

SUMMARY

The central theme of this book is that cost management information includes all the information that managers need to manage effectively to lead their firms to competitive success. Cost management information includes both financial and nonfinancial information critical to the firm's success. The specific role of cost management in the firm differs depending on the firm's competitive strategy, its type of industry and organization (manufacturing firm, service firm, merchandising firm, not-for-profit organization, or governmental organization), and the management function to which cost management is applied (the functions are strategic management, planning and decision making, management and operational control, and preparation of financial statements).

Changes in the business environment have altered the nature of competition and the types of techniques managers use to succeed in their businesses. These changes include (1) an increase in global competition, (2) advances in manufacturing technologies, (3) advances in information technologies, the Internet, and e-commerce, (4) a greater focus on the customer, (5) new forms of management organization, and (6) changes in the social, political, and cultural environment of business.

Of particular importance are the changes in business, especially the increase in global competition and the changes in management techniques, that have created the need for a new, strategic approach to management and to cost management. Cost management can assist the firm in using the new management techniques: benchmarking, total quality management, continuous improvement, activity-based costing and management, reengineering, the theory of constraints, mass customization, target costing, life-cycle costing, the value chain, and the balanced scorecard.

To apply new management methods effectively, it is crucial that the management accountant understand the firm's strategy. Strategy is the set of plans and policies that a firm employs to develop a sustainable competitive advantage. Using Michael Porter's framework, we see that a firm can compete effectively either as a cost leader or through differentiation.

A variety of professional organizations supports management accounting, including the Institute of Management Accountants (IMA), the American Institute of Certified Public Accountants (AICPA), and the Financial Executives Institute (FEI), among others. Several relevant certification programs recognize competence and experience in management accounting; they include the Certified Management Accountant (CMA) and the Certified Financial Manager (CFM) programs of the IMA and the Certified Public Accountant (CPA) program of the AICPA.

The management accountant is responsible to the firm and to the public for maintaining a high standard of performance, as set forth in the IMA code of professional ethics. The professional ethics standards of the management accountant include competence, integrity, objectivity, and confidentiality.

APPENDIX A

More about Strategy

Strategy is a complex topic for which there are many views. On a very basic level, some view strategy as the firm's broad purpose or direction (very much as we have used the concept of mission in the chapter); others see it as a way to determine a competitive position. Our approach, using Michael Porter's framework, is to use the latter view as a way to determine competitive positioning.[1]

The Boston Consulting Group (BCG) framework can be viewed as a mission-based approach, which argues that each firm or unit has one of the following three missions: to build, harvest, or hold. The *build mission* focuses the firm on revenue growth and market share; earnings and other goals are secondary. The *harvest mission* implies a short-term focus on increasing current earnings and cash flows. The *hold strategy* seeks to protect the firm's current competitive position.[2]

[1] The distinction between strategy as mission and strategy as competitive positioning is handled very well by Robert Simons, *Levers of Control* (Cambridge, MA: Harvard Business School Press, 1995), chap. 1; and John K. Shank and Vijay Govindarajan, *Strategic Cost Management* (New York: Free Press, 1993), chap. 5. See also Porter, *Competitive Advantage*.

[2] For more on the BCG approach, see "The Product Portfolio," *Perspectives* (Boston, MA: The Boston Group, Inc, 1970);

Again, our approach in this text is based on strategy as competitive positioning, for which Michael Porter's work is the key resource. Others have extended and clarified his concepts in important ways, as has Porter himself.[3] His 1996 extension of the original framework added a number of concepts. First, he advised managers not to confuse the concepts of operational effectiveness and strategy. Second, he added three new concepts of strategy; needs based, variety based, and access based. He explains and provides examples of each type.

Those who argue that, for many firms, cost leadership and differentiation are not separate strategies but must be achieved simultaneously take a somewhat different approach. Richard D'Aveni and Robert Gunther were among the first to advance this view of what they called *hypercompetition*. Similarly, Robin Cooper argued that, in an environment of lean competition, many firms compete simultaneously on cost, product features, and quality; he called this competition *confrontation*. These views have had an important influence on how managers think about strategy and choose strategies to employ. For example, Cooper shows how the confrontation strategy is consistent with the observed increased usage of target costing in certain industries.[4]

The most recent concept was advanced by Kathleen Eisenhardt and Donald Sull in what they call strategy by simple rules.[5] They argue that the increased complexity of business has caused firms to seek simple rules that arise from experience, rules such as, "Every question must be answered on the first call," or "R&D staff must rotate through customer service." To summarize, a comprehensive discussion of strategy goes beyond the goals of this text. The references here provide additional readings that present a deeper discussion of the different views of strategy.

B. D. Henderson, *Henderson on Corporate Strategy*. (Cambridge, MA: Abt Books, 1979); and Shank and Govindarajan, *Strategic Cost Management.*

[3] For Porters's follow-up on his framework, see Michael E. Porter, "What is Strategy?" *Harvard Business Review,* November–December 1996, p. 61; and Keith H. Hammonds, "Michael Porter's Big Ideas," *Fast Company*, March 2001. For extensions and clarifications of the framework, see Shank and Govindarajan, *Strategic Cost Management*; Robert Simons, *Performance Measurement and Control Systems for Implementing Strategy* (Upper Saddle River, NJ: Prentice Hall, 2000); Simons, *Levers of Control;* and Michael Treacy and Fred Wiersma, *The Discipline of Market Leaders* (Reading, MA: Addison-Wesley, 1995). A useful integration of the different concepts of strategy is presented by Kim Langfield-Smith, "Management Control Systems and Strategy: A Critical Review," *Accounting, Organizations and Society*, February 1997, pp. 207–232.

[4] Richard D'Aveni and Robert Gunther, *Hypercompetition: Managing the Dynamics of Strategic Maneuvering* (New York: Free Press, 1994); Robin Cooper, *When Lean Enterprises Collide: Competition through Confrontation* (Cambridge, MA: Harvard Business School Press, 1995); and Robin Cooper, "Costing Techniques to Support Corporate Strategy: Evidence from Japan," *Management Accounting Research*, 1996, pp. 219–46.

[5] Kathleen M. Eisenhardt and Donald N. Sull, "Strategy as Simple Rules," *Harvard Business Review*, January 2001, pp 107-116.

Key Terms

activity analysis, *13*
activity-based costing (ABC), *13*
activity-based management (ABM), *13*
balanced scorecard, *16*
benchmarking, *12*
computer-aided design (CAD), *15*
computer-aided manufacturing (CAM), *15*
computer-integrated manufacturing, (CIM) *15*
continuous improvement, *13*

cost leadership, *19*
cost management information, *3*
critical success factors (CSFs), *11*
differentiation, *20*
flexible manufacturing system (FMS), *15*
just-in-time (JIT) system, *14*
kanban, *14*
life-cycle costing, *16*
management control, *5*
mass customization, *14*
operational control, *5*

planning and decision making, *5*
preparation of financial statements, *5*
reengineering, *13*
strategic cost management, *7*
strategic management, *5*
strategy, *17*
target costing, *15*
theory of constraints (TOC), *14*
total quality management (TQM), *12*
value chain, *16*

Comments on Cost Management in Action

How Can Dell Retain Its Glitter?

Dell has achieved its dominant status in the PC market through aggressive cost cutting (its 10 percent ratio of operating expense to revenue is the lowest in the industry), advanced manufacturing techniques, and speed/quality of service. When growth in the PC industry slowed, Dell began to look elsewhere for growth and profit. Already second in the server market where margins are higher, with a 20 percent share, Dell has entered the market for printers, storage devices, and handhelds. Dell's business model is to offer low cost through direct sales and streamlined manufacturing operations. At 25 percent to 60 percent, the margins in storage devices and printers are much higher than those in the PC business and present great opportunities for the Dell approach. The relatively high margins of approximately 40 percent in the PC business in the late 1980s attracted Dell and made its model so effective there.

Sources: "The Dell Way," by Kathryn Jones, *Business 2.0*, February 2003, pp. 61–66; "Dell, the Conqueror," *Business Week*, September 24, 2001, pp. 92–102; "Whose Lunch Will Dell Eat Next," *Business Week*, August 12, 2002, pp. 66–67; http://www.dell.com.

Self-Study Problem
(For solution, please turn to the end of the chapter.)

An Ethical Problem

An ethical situation involving potential manipulation of accounting earnings occurred in Bausch & Lomb's (B&L) contact lens unit. Apparently, B&L used inappropriate accounting methods to inflate year-end sales. The story, as reported by *Business Week* (December 19, 1994, pp. 108–110), is as follows:

SEPTEMBER 1993: Independent contact lens distributors say B&L asks them to buy 4 to 6 months' worth of inventory. B&L says buildup supports a new marketing program, but distributors say uneven results leave them with 4 to 12 months' inventory in early December.

DECEMBER 13, 1993: B&L calls a meeting and tells distributors to take additional inventories ranging from one to two years' worth or face cutoff. B&L says the buildup is needed for programs aimed at getting high-volume accounts to buy from distributors rather than from the company.

DECEMBER 24, 1993: Insisting that lenses be ordered by December 24, B&L rushes out shipments. That tactic adds sales of $25 million, but distributors say B&L gave verbal assurances that the distributors would pay for lenses only when sold. B&L says small payments were set through June, when balances were due.

JUNE 15, 1994: With the new promotions lagging, less than 10 percent of the inventory is sold—or paid for. When the final payments fall due, most distributors refuse to pay. Meanwhile, B&L continues to sell directly to some high-volume accounts at prices below what the distributors paid.

OCTOBER 1994: With the majority of the inventory unsold, B&L takes most back. Distributors pay sharply discounted prices for the rest. B&L's third-quarter revenues drop 10 percent, to $449 million, and earnings plummet 86 percent, to $7.7 million, as a result of inventory reduction efforts and price cuts.

Required   What are the ethical issues in this case?

Questions

1–1 Give four examples of firms you believe would be significant users of cost management information and explain why.

1–2 Give three examples of firms you believe would *not* be significant users of cost management information and explain why.

1–3 What does the term *cost management* mean? Who in the typical firm or organization is responsible for cost management?

1–4 Name three professional cost management organizations and explain their roles and objectives.

1–5 What type of professional certification is most relevant for the management accountant and why?

1–6 List the four functions of management. Explain what type of cost management information is appropriate for each.

1–7 Which is the most important function of management? Explain why?

1–8 Identify the different types of business firms and other organizations that use cost management information, and explain how the information is used.

1–9 Name a firm or organization you know of that you are reasonably sure uses strategic cost management and explain why it does so. Does it use cost leadership or differentiation, and why?

1–10 As firms move to the Internet for sales and customer service, how do you expect their competitive strategies will change?

1–11 As firms move to the Internet for sales and customer service, how do you expect their need for cost management information will change?

1–12 What are some factors in the contemporary business environment that are causing changes in business firms and other organizations? How are the changes affecting the way those firms and organizations use cost management information?

1–13 Contrast past and present business environments with regard to the following aspects: basis of competition, manufacturing processes and manufacturing technology, required labor skills, emphasis on quality, number of products, number of markets, types of cost management information needed, management organizational structure, and management focus.

1–14 Name the 10 contemporary management techniques and describe each briefly.

Exercises

1–15 **Robert Half Survey, New Skills for the CFO** A number of firms in the Thomasville–High Point area of North Carolina are either directly or indirectly involved in furniture manufacturing. Paul Descoll, the CFO of one of these firms, Thomasville Furniture Industries, was asked to respond to the recent survey of 1,400 CFOs by Robert Half International, Inc. The survey projected large increases in hiring for new finance and accounting professionals in firms throughout the United States. The survey also reported that the CFOs expected in the coming years to see far greater emphasis placed on business strategy and less placed on financial report preparation as part of the finance function. They predicted that computer technologies would continue to affect the finance function by reducing the time and effort involved in processing transactions and by transferring the focus to the interpretation and use of the information available from the computer systems.

Required What do you think the implications of the Robert Half survey are for finance and accounting professionals? As the top financial manager of a large manufacturing company, what do you think CFO Descoll had to say about the role of finance and accounting professionals?

1–16 **Strategy, Real Estate Services** As a management accountant in a small real estate services firm, you have become aware of a strategic initiative in your firm to promote its services to a new class of customers. Currently, most of your firm's customers lease space in large office buildings where they might occupy three or more floors of the building. Your firm provides maintenance, security and cleaning services for the office space leased by these customers. The strategic initiative you have discovered is to seek out smaller firms that occupy as small a space as a few thousand square feet. You know that most of these smaller firms are now serviced in a haphazard manner, with part-time help for which turnover is very high; some of the smaller office buildings might not employ security of any kind. You expect that the demand for your company's services among firms of this smaller size will be good, but you are worried about the profitability of these new customers. In fact, although you cannot prove it with hard numbers, you are sure that this new strategy will cause big losses for your firm. You have not been consulted about this new strategy by the firm's owners because you are not viewed as part of the management decision-making team. You would like very much, however, to be more involved in the company's strategy development and decision making.

Required What should you do or say about this new strategic initiative?

1–17 **The Theory of Constraints, Manufacturing vs. Retail** Manufacturing firms such as General Motors and General Electric utilize the concept of the theory of constraints and emphasize speed of throughput in their manufacturing operations.

Required Discuss whether the concept of throughput in the theory of constraints is appropriate for retail and service industries. Take as a specific example the Wal-Mart chain of retail stores. How would or could you, apply this management technique to Wal-Mart?

Problems

1–18 **Contemporary Management Techniques** Tim Johnson is a news reporter and feature writer for *The Wall Street Review,* an important daily newspaper for financial managers. Tim's assignment is to develop a feature article on target costing, including interviews with chief financial officers and operating managers. Tim has a generous travel budget for research into company history, operations, and market analysis for the firms he selects for the article.

Required

1. Tim has asked you to recommend industries and firms that would be good candidates for the article. What would you advise? Explain your recommendations.
2. Assume that Tim's assignment is a feature article on life-cycle costing. Answer as you did for requirement 1.
3. Assume that Tim's assignment is a feature article on the theory of constraints. Answer as you did for requirement 1.

1–19 Professional Organizations and Certification   Ian Walsh has just been hired as a management accountant for a large manufacturing firm near his hometown of Canton, Ohio. The firm manufactures a wide variety of plastic products for the automobile industry, the packaging industry, and other customers. At least initially, Ian's principal assignments have been to develop product costs for new product lines. His cost accounting professor has suggested to Ian that he begin to consider professional organizations and professional certifications that will help him in his career.

Required   Which organizations and certifications would you suggest for Ian, and why?

1–20 Balanced Scorecard   Johnson Industrial Controls, Inc. (JIC), is a large manufacturer of specialized instruments used in automated manufacturing plants. JIC has grown steadily over the past several years on the strength of technological innovation in its key product lines. The firm now employs 3,500 production employees and 450 staff and management personnel in six large plants located across the United States. In the past few years, the growth of sales and profits has declined sharply, because of the entrance into the market of new competitors. As part of a recent strategic planning effort, JIC identified its key competitive strengths and weaknesses. JIC management believe that the critical strengths are in the quality of the product and that the weakness in recent years has been in customer service, particularly in meeting scheduled deliveries. The failure to meet promised delivery dates can be quite costly to JIC's customers, because it is likely to delay the construction or upgrading of the customers' plants and therefore delay the customers' production and sales.

JIC's management believes that the adoption of the balanced scorecard for internal reporting might help the firm become more competitive.

Required

1. Explain how the balanced scorecard might help a firm like JIC.
2. Develop a brief balanced scorecard for JIC. Give some examples of the items that might be included in each of these four parts of the scorecard: (a) customer satisfaction, (b) financial performance, (c) manufacturing and business processes, and (d) human resources.

1-21 Banking, Strategy, Skills   A large U.S.–based commercial bank with global operations recently initiated a new program for recruiting recent college graduates into the financial function of the bank. These new hires will initially be involved in a variety of financial functions, including transactions processing, control, risk management, business performance reporting, new business analysis, and financial analysis. Recognizing that they are competing with many other banks for the relatively small number of qualified graduates, the firm has assigned you to develop a skills statement to be used in college recruiting as well as an in-house training program for new hires. You have some old training manuals and recruiting guides to assist you, but your boss advises you not to use them but to start with a fresh page. The reason for developing new materials is that the bank recently reorganized based on new management methods.

Required

1. Briefly explain 8 to 10 critical success factors for this bank. Consider how a bank of this size remains competitive and successful.
2. Develop a one-page outline of the skill statement and training program that your boss requested. Be brief and specific about the proper job description of a new employee in the finance area of the bank.

1-22 **Consulting, Skills** A consulting firm offering a broad range of services will soon visit your college to recruit graduates. This firm has more than 20,000 professional staff in 275 offices of 11 different countries. Most of its clients are large corporations in a variety of different industries. Because of the opportunity for the experience and travel, you are very interested in getting a job with this firm. You have an interview in two weeks, and you're planning to do some research about the firm and the job to be as well prepared as you can be for the interview.

Required Write a brief, one-half page statement of what you think the job description for this employer is. What skills would you need to succeed as a consultant in this firm?

1-23 **Activity Analysis in a Bank** Mesa Financial is a small bank located in west Texas. As a small bank, Mesa has a rather limited range of services: mortgage loans, installment (mostly auto) loans, commercial loans, checking and savings accounts, and certificates of deposit. Mesa's management has learned that activity analysis could be used to study the efficiency of the bank's operations.

Required

1. Explain how activity analysis might help a bank like Mesa.
2. Give six to eight examples of activities you would expect to identify in Mesa's operations.

1-24 **Ethics, Product Quality** HighTech, Inc., manufactures computer chips and components. High-Tech has just introduced a new version of its memory chip, which is far faster than the previous version. Because of high product demand for the new chip, the testing process has been thorough but hurried. As the firm's chief of operations, you discover after the chip has been on the market for a few months and is selling very well that it has a minor fault that will cause hard-to-discover failures in certain, very unusual circumstances.

Required Now that you know of the chip's faults, what should you disclose and to whom should you disclose it?

1-25 **Strategy, General Motors** In the late 1990s, management at General Motors decided to improve the competitiveness of its products by stressing product quality, style, and innovation. The objective was to improve the image of GM vehicles and thus improve sales and brand loyalty. Managers decided to push this strategy in both the manufacturing and marketing divisions of the firm. One of the key moves to implement this strategy was to insist that GM dealers stop price-cutting and push brand value and image instead. GM exerted some control over dealers' pricing/selling strategy in part by reducing the money it set aside for dealers to use in local ads.

Required Is General Motors following a strategy of cost leadership or differentiation at this time? Comment on how effective you think the new strategy in dealer relations is likely to be.

1-26 **Strategy, Calvin Klein** For many, the name Calvin Klein (CK) is synonymous with high-fashion clothing and accessories, super models, and fashion shows. It has an image of quality and style. In reality, a significant amount of CK products are sold by discount retailers such as Costco. How can this be? The answer is that 60-year-old designer Calvin Klein licensed Warnaco Group and other manufacturers to produce his products. Under this arrangement, CK receives a royalty based on Warnaco's sales. As it turns out, Warnaco found that it could be more successful with the brand through a broad strategy involving a number of retailers, including discounters.

Required What type of strategy (cost leadership or differentiation) is Calvin Klein following at this time? Comment on how effective you think the relationship with Warnaco is likely to be.

1-27 **Strategy, Oracle Corp.** Oracle Corp., the maker of high-level business software, has had to change its strategy. Facing the weak economy of early 2003 and corporate buyers with less money to spend, Oracle changed its sales strategy from "push sales" to customer service. Rather than encouraging aggressive sales tactics in its sales force, Oracle is now pushing efforts to develop and retain customers, focusing instead on value for the customer. For example, now Oracle develops its sales presentations around the customer's specific technology and business needs, in contrast to its more general-purpose presentations of the past.

See: "Oracle Puts Priority on Customer Service," *The Wall Street Journal*, January 21, 2003.

Required

1. Identify the financial measures of success Oracle has probably used up until its recent change in sales strategy. Why have these measures worked so well in the past? Are they likely to work as well now and into the future?

2. Name three or four nonfinancial measures that Oracle managers might track given their focus on customer service.

1–28 **Strategy, Branding Beef** The steaks, roasts, and hamburger you buy at the supermarket are what many would call a commodity. Based on a certain degree of leanness, or a certain USDA grade, you can obtain the same products from supermarket to supermarket. As a commodity, beef is doing pretty well with annual supermarket sales of $60 billion relative to cereal sales of $7.5 billion or soda sales of $13.1 billion. However, the taste for beef is down, and supermarket demand for beef has fallen by 41 percent over the last 25 years. Some meatpackers attribute this to broad social and economic trends, including the fact that two-wage-earner families have less time to prepare meals, and cooking a roast can take hours. So some meatpackers have improved the convenience of their meat products by offering precooked roasts and specially prepared cuts of meat that can be cooked quickly at higher heat levels.

See: "A Roast Is a Roast? Not in the New Game of Marketing Meat," *The Wall Street Journal,* February 20, 2002, p. 1.

Required

1. Would you describe the strategy of the meatpacking industry as cost leadership or differentiation? Why?

2. Do you think the meatpacker's new products will improve sales of beef? Why or why not?

1–29 **Ethics, Product Quality** Green Acres, Inc., is a large U.S.-based multinational producer of canned fruits and vegetables. While Green Acres has a reputation of traditionally using only organic suppliers for its fruits and vegetables, it has recently experimented with produce from farmers known to have genetically modified crops. These genetically modified fruits and vegetables are often cheaper than their organic counterparts because farmers are able to achieve greater yields than with organic crops, and they have provided the firm with a way to cut its production costs. As Green Acres' chief of operations, the firm's marketing researchers have informed you that consumers continue to view Green Acres' products as organic despite the fact that Green Acres has never placed the word *organic* on its product labels. Moreover, the marketing researchers have discovered that Green Acres' sales and profits have dramatically increased due to this misperception in the wake of debates over the health and environmental consequences of genetically modified organisms.

Required Now that you know of your consumers' misperception about your product, should you disclose your use of genetically modified crops to the public?

Solution to Self-Study Problem

An Ethical Problem

As reported, B&L apparently made several direct efforts to improperly inflate earnings through forced sales to distributors. The ethical principles involved are integrity and objectivity, both of which have been violated in this case.

CHAPTER TWO

Implementing Strategy: The Balanced Scorecard and the Value Chain

After studying this chapter, you should be able to . . .

1. Explain how to implement a competitive strategy by using Strengths-Weaknesses-Opportunities-Threats (SWOT) Analysis
2. Explain how to implement a competitive strategy by focusing on the execution of goals.
3. Explain how to implement a competitive strategy using value chain analysis.
4. Explain how to implement a competitive strategy using the balanced scorecard.
5. Explain how to expand the balanced scorecard by integrating sustainability.

Amazon.com typifies successful competition in the new economy far more than any other firm. Some would say that Amazon invented the Internet retailing business model that all other dot-coms are struggling to copy. Amazon understands well the strategy (i.e., business model) of developing and maintaining customer loyalty, which is the key to success in retail e-business, and implements it effectively.[1] Walter Mossberg, technology commentator for *The Wall Street Journal,* puts it this way:

> While Amazon.com is price competitive, it didn't get to be the Web's largest retailer, with 23 million customers, by having the lowest prices on all items all the time. It doesn't guarantee to match or beat others' prices. Instead, Amazon has won the loyalty of millions by building an online store that is friendly, easy to use, and inspires a sense of confidence and community among its customers. People trust Amazon, partly because it knows their tastes and does what it promises. For me, and apparently many others, it wouldn't be worth roaming all over the Web to save a few bucks shopping elsewhere.[2]

LEARNING OBJECTIVE 1

Explain how to implement a competitive strategy by using Strengths-Weaknesses-Opportunities-Threats (SWOT) Analysis.

The amazing thing about Amazon is that it created such a successful strategy for e-commerce at a time when there was no model to use as a guide. As Mossberg suggests, Amazon's success appears to come from its ability to deliver excellent customer service with very low prices. It has differentiated itself through efficient and error-free operating systems that provide reliable, convenient service. Amazon's operations are so efficient that it is now performing the e-tail order-taking and order-filling services for other retailers such as Toys 'R' Us, Borders, Target, and Circuit City. Another growing service area is that of used merchandise. The great news for Amazon is that these new services provide fat margins, from 45 to 85 percent, far higher than e-tail

[1] See Frederick F. Reichheld and Phil Schefter, "E-Loyalty: Your Secret Weapon on the Web," *Harvard Business Review,* July–August 2000, pp. 105–113.

[2] Walter S. Mossberg, "Amazon.com Still Remains a Web Shopping Model," *The Wall Street Journal,* September 21, 2000, p. B-1.

sales.[3] How did Amazon implement this strategy? By careful planning and disciplined execution.

Firms choose to compete on either cost leadership or differentiation, as explained in Chapter 1. This chapter considers the various means for implementing that competitive strategy: (1) SWOT analysis, (2) focus on execution, (3) value chain analysis, and (4) the balanced scorecard.

The firm might also choose to *expand* its competitive strategy to the broader social and environmental setting in which the firm operates; these broader issues are called sustainability, which we examine at the close of the chapter.

Strengths-Weaknesses-Opportunities-Threats (SWOT) Analysis

SWOT analysis
is a systematic procedure for identifying a firm's critical success factors: its internal strengths and weaknesses and its external opportunities and threats.

Skills or competencies that the firm employs especially well are called **core competencies.**

One of the first steps in implementing strategy is to identify the critical success factors that the firm must focus on to be successful. **SWOT analysis** is a systematic procedure for identifying a firm's critical success factors: its *internal* strengths and weaknesses and its *external* opportunities and threats. Strengths are skills and resources that the firm has more abundantly than other firms. Skills or competencies that the firm employs especially well are called **core competencies.** The concept of core competencies is important because it points to areas of significant competitive advantage for the firm; core competencies can be used as the building blocks of the firm's overall strategy. In contrast, weaknesses represent a lack of important skills or competencies relative to the presence of those resources in competing firms.

Strengths and weaknesses are most easily identified by looking inside the firm at its specific resources:

- **Product lines.** Are the firm's products innovative? Are the product offerings too wide or too narrow? Are there important and distinctive technological advances?

- **Management.** What is the level of experience and competence?

- **Research and development.** Is the firm ahead of or behind competitors? What is the outlook for important new products and services?

- **Manufacturing.** How competitive, flexible, productive, and technologically advanced are the current manufacturing processes? What plans are there for improvements in facilities and processes?

- **Marketing.** How effective is the overall marketing approach, including promotion, selling, and advertising?

- **Strategy.** How clearly defined, communicated, and effectively implemented is corporate strategy?

Opportunities and threats are identified by looking outside the firm. Opportunities are important favorable situations in the firm's environment. Demographic trends, changes in regulatory matters, and technological changes in the industry might provide significant advantages or disadvantages for the firm. For example, the gradual aging of the U.S. population represents an advantage for firms that specialize in products and services for the elderly. In contrast, threats are major unfavorable situations in the firm's environment. These might include the entrance of new competitors or competing products, unfavorable changes in government regulations, and technological change that is unfavorable to the firm.

Opportunities and threats can be identified most easily by analyzing the industry and the firm's competitors:

- **Barriers to entry.** Do certain factors, such as capital requirements, economies of scale, product differentiation, and access to selected distribution channels, protect the firm from newcomers? Do other factors, including the cost of buyer switching,

---

[3] "How Amazon Cleared that Hurdle," *Business Week*, February 4, 2002, pp. 60–61; "How Hard Should Amazon Swing?" *Business Week*, January 14, 2002, p. 38.

REAL-WORLD FOCUS Retailing and the Internet: What's the Right Strategy?

In his recent book, Bill Gates provides some useful thoughts on how the Internet will affect retail business and other service providers. In his chapter "The Middleman Must Add Value," he says:

> The Internet is a great tool for helping customers find the best deal they can. It is reasonably easy for consumers to jump from one retail Web site to another to find the best prices on some goods. . . . The Web will provide more value in areas where matching buyers and sellers is more difficult, such as services, or where markets are small or dispersed. How does a consumer easily find a used product—car, computer, stereo—with certain capabilities and a certain price range? People trying to buy or sell hard-to-find items of any kind, such as antiques, parts for older equipment, or specialty items, will benefit. The GAP, for instance, is finding that the most frequent customers of its online clothing store are people looking for sizes that are not normally stocked in stores. . . . For service industries, the Internet requires you to be either a high-volume,

low-cost provider or a high-touch, customer-service provider. For the high-volume, low-cost model you use Internet technology to create a self-service approach. You make a lot of information available to customers and you drive a lot of traffic and transactions through your Internet site offering the best price. Because only a few companies in any market will be the high-volume players, most companies will have to find ways to use the Internet not just to reduce costs, but also to deliver new services.

Based on Bill Gates's comments, it seems that the Internet can help a company achieve either a cost leadership or a differentiation strategy and that the determination of this strategy depends on whether the firm can achieve very high volumes or satisfy unique and special customer requirements.

Source: Bill Gates, *Business @ The Speed of Thought* (New York: Warner Books, 1999), p. 9.

REAL-WORLD FOCUS Implementing Strategy for Research Triangle Park, North Carolina

Strategic positioning and implementation of strategy are common in business firms and increasingly common for municipalities and governmental entities such as Research Triangle Park (RTP) located between Raleigh and Durham, North Carolina. A group of RTP area leaders invited Michael Porter (author of *Competitive Advantage*, and of the strategy concepts of cost leadership and differentiation) to study the RTP and make recommendations regarding how to sustain its competitive success. The RTP, like other research parks and cities throughout the United States, competes vigorously for

research-oriented firms such as IBM and GlaxoSmithKline (GSK) that already have significant investments in the RTP area. The rewards are great to the local economy when the RTP succeeds. Porter presented his recommendations at a meeting of civic leaders in January 2002, calling for improved execution—better roads and schools, and better coordination and cooperation among local civic leaders.

Source: Charlene Hempel, "Piece by Piece; What Will Sustain the Triangle," *The News & Observer*, January 27, 2002, pp, A17–18.

---

government regulations and policies that favor the firm, and educational and licensing restrictions, restrict competition? To what degree is the firm protected from competition from new entrants to the industry?

- **Intensity of rivalry among competitors.** Intense rivalry can be the result of high entry barriers, specialized assets (and therefore limited flexibility for a firm in the industry), rapid product innovation, slow growth in total market demand, or significant overcapacity in the industry. How intense is the overall industry rivalry facing the firm?

- **Pressure from substitute products.** Will the presence of readily substitutable products increase the intensity level of the firm's competition?

- **Bargaining power of customers.** The greater the bargaining power of the firm's customers, the greater the level of competition facing the firm. Bargaining power of customers is likely higher if switching costs are relatively low and if the products are not differentiated.

- **Bargaining power of suppliers.** The greater the bargaining power of a firm's suppliers, the greater the overall level of competition facing the firm. The bargaining power of suppliers is higher when a few large firms dominate the group of suppliers and when these suppliers have other good outlets for their products.

REAL-WORLD FOCUS   Globalization, Strategy, and Exchange Rates: The Euro

Since January 1999, the euro has been used as the common currency of many European countries. For the first 20 months following its introduction, the euro steadily lost about 25 percent in its value relative to the U.S. dollar. Due to changing economic circumstances, the euro then began to rise in early 2002 to a value of $1.13 in July 2003. The constant change of the value of the euro relative to the dollar creates two types of strategic issues for U.S. and European firms.* One is the effect on import and export opportunities. For example, when the euro was falling this meant a higher cost for U.S. goods in euro countries, which caused problems for U.S. exporters, especially for smaller firms. For example, Hatteras Yacht Company

* The Economic and Monetary Union (EMU) of Europe has 15 member countries: Austria, Belgium, Denmark, Finland, France, Germany, Greece, Ireland, Italy, Luxembourg, the Netherlands, Portugal, Spain, Sweden, and the United Kingdom. As of August 2003, all of these countries except Denmark, Sweden, and the United Kingdom had adopted the euro. The EMU is the long-term project for the economic unification of Europe. A major milestone in this effort was the creation of the euro, the new single currency for Europe, on January 1, 1999, by fixing exchange rates for adopting countries. For more information, see http://europa.eu.int/euro/entry.html; see also, "Euro's Drop Is Hardest for the Smallest," *The Wall Street Journal,* October 2, 2000, International Section, p. 1; and Michael M. Phillips, "Ship Those Boxes; Check the Euro," *The Wall Street Journal,* February 7, 2003, p. C1; Liliana Hickman-Riggs and William A. Riggs, "Accounting for the Euro," *Management Accounting Quarterly,* Spring 2001, pp. 34–40; Michael R. Sesit, "How High Can the Euro Climb?" *The Wall Street Journal,* May 28, 2003, p. C1.

of New Bern, North Carolina, has lost some sales of its large boats to European customers. Other companies, such as Vermeer Manufacturing Company (of Pella, Iowa), maker of agricultural and industrial machines, have adopted dealer incentives to reduce the effect of the euro's change on its European customers. Larger firms, such as McDonald's, for many years protected overseas profits by hedging the exchange rates, that is, buying and selling overseas currencies at fixed prices to guarantee a given exchange rate in its business transactions. Of course, the issue is reversed when the dollar is falling relative to the euro, producing an advantage for the U.S. exporter. For example, the rise of the euro relative to the dollar in 2002 produced $16 million in foreign-exchange related profits for Amazon.com for the quarter ended December 31, 2002, enough to change what would have been a net loss into net income.

The second strategic issue is that the falling euro causes those holding U.S. dollars to favor purchases in these European countries. This means that U.S. firms have the opportunity to make strategically beneficial investments in European companies at a favorable net cost, considering the exchange rate. Of course, the reverse is again true when the dollar falls as it did in 2003. The message is that firms, small or large, with a significant global component to their business must plan strategically for dealing with the effects of changing exchange rates on their business.

REAL-WORLD FOCUS   CEO Strategies for Success

The Gallup Organization recently surveyed chief executive officers, presidents, and owners of firms with 100 or more employees, asking what was most important in their firms for competitive advantage and success. The results follow:

Critical Success Factor	Percentage Choosing This Factor as Most Important
Customer service	27%
Product (or service) quality	25
Operating efficiency	18
Communication and information technology	9
Flexibility and adaptability	9
Innovation	7
Speed to market	2
Don't know	3

These responses tell us not only what the heads of these firms view as critical success factors but also something about the firms' strategies. Some of these CSFs, such as customer service, speed to market, and innovation, are consistent with the differentiation strategy; operating efficiency is consistent, however, with the cost leadership strategy. The other CSFs could be associated with either type of strategy.

Source: *USA Today,* August 18, 1999, p. 1.

SWOT analysis guides the strategic analysis by focusing attention on the strengths, weaknesses, opportunities, and threats critical to the company's success. By carefully identifying the critical success factors in this way, executives and managers can discover differences in viewpoints. For example, what some managers might view as a strength others might view as a weakness. SWOT analysis therefore also serves as a means for obtaining greater understanding and perhaps consensus among managers regarding the factors that are crucial to the firm's success.

A final step in the SWOT analysis is to identify quantitative measures for the Critical Success Factors (CSFs). At this step the firm converts, for example, the CSF of customer service to a quantitative measure such as number of customer complaints, or a customer satisfaction score.

Developing measures for the CSFs involves a careful study of the firm's business processes. Product development, manufacturing, marketing, management, and financial functions are investigated to determine in which specific ways these functions contribute to the firm's success. The objective at this step is to determine the specific measures that will allow the firm to monitor its progress toward achieving its strategic goals. Exhibit 2.1 lists sample CSFs and ways in which they might be measured.

EXHIBIT 2.1
Measuring Critical Success Factors

Critical Success Factor	How to Measure the CSF
Financial Factors	
• Profitability	Earnings from operations, earnings trend
• Liquidity	Cash flow, trend in cash flow, interest coverage, asset turnover, inventory turnover, receivables turnover
• Sales	Level of sales in critical product groups, sales trend, percent of sales from new products, sales forecast accuracy
• Market value	Share price
Customer Factors	
• Customer satisfaction	Customer returns and complaints, customer survey
• Dealer and distributor	Coverage and strength of dealer and distributor channel relationships; e.g., number of dealers per state or region
• Marketing and selling	Trends in sales performance, training, market research activities; measured in hours or dollars
• Timeliness of delivery	On-time delivery performance, time from order to customer receipt
• Quality	Customer complaints, warranty expense
Internal Business Processes	
• Quality	Number of defects, number of returns, customer survey, amount of scrap, amount of rework, field service reports, warranty claims, vendor quality defects
• Productivity	Cycle time (from raw materials to finished product); labor efficiency; machine efficiency; amount of waste, rework, and scrap
• Flexibility	Setup time, cycle time
• Equipment readiness	Downtime, operator experience, machine capacity, maintenance activities
• Safety	Number of accidents, effects of accidents
Learning and Innovation	
• Product innovation	Number of design changes, number of new patents or copyrights, skills of research and development staff
• Timeliness of new product	Number of days over or under the announced ship date
• Skill development	Number of training hours, amount of skill performance improvement
• Employee morale	Employee turnover, number of complaints, employee survey
• Competence	Rate of turnover, training, experience, adaptability, financial and operating performance measures
Other Factors	
• Governmental relations	Number of violations, community service activities

Execution

> It is very hard to develop a unique strategy, and even harder, should you develop one, to keep it proprietary. Sometimes a company does have a unique cost advantage or a unique patented position. Brand position can also be a powerful competitive position—a special advantage that competitors strive to match. However, these advantages are rarely permanent barriers to others. . . . So, execution is really the critical part of a successful strategy. Getting it done, getting it done right, getting it done better than the next person is far more important than dreaming up new visions of the future.
>
> **Louis V. Gerstner, Jr.**

Louis V. Gerstner, Jr., *Who Says Elephants Can't Dance?* (New York: Harper Business, 2002), pp. 229–230.

LEARNING OBJECTIVE 2

Explain how to implement a competitive strategy by focusing on the execution of goals.

Lou Gerstner is credited with the remarkable success of IBM in the 1990s. He became CEO of IBM at a very troubled time for the company. He rejected the notion that he could save the company with some high vision, but instead he determined that the company needed to focus on execution. This meant determining the critical success factors and putting in place the processes to develop, achieve, and regularly inspect these processes. At IBM this meant a focus on the customer: beginning with a careful understanding of the customer's needs, then working on "faster cycle times, faster delivery times, and a higher quality of service." The service focus has served IBM well as its profits have grown to $8 billion in recent years compared to the $8 billion loss in 1993, the year Gerstner took over at IBM.

The nature of the types of CSFs that the manager executes depend, of course, on the type of strategy. For cost leadership firms, the CSFs are likely to relate to operational performance and quality, while differentiated firms are more likely to focus on the customer or innovation. Exhibit 2.2 summarizes the differences between the two types of competition, the nature of the required skills and resources, and the focus of efforts in execution. Also, while most topics we cover in the text are applicable to executing strategy for both cost leadership and differentiated firms, the topics in Part 4 (Operational Control) are particularly relevant for the cost leadership firm, while those in Part 2 (Planning and Decision Making) are most relevant for differentiated firms.

Looking more closely at differentiated firms, the key CSFs and execution issues are in marketing and product development—developing customer loyalty and brand recognition, emphasizing superior and unique products, and developing and using detailed and timely information about customer needs and behavior. This is where the marketing and product development functions within the firm provide leadership, and

EXHIBIT 2.2

Effects of Competitive Strategy on Required Skills and Execution

Source: Michael E. Porter, *Competitive Advantage* (New York: Free Press, 1985), p. 40.

Strategy	Required Skills and Resources	Execution
Cost leadership	• Substantial capital investment and access to capital • Process engineering skills • Intense supervision of labor • Products designed for ease of manufacturing	• Tight cost control • Frequent, detailed control reports • Structured organization and policies • Incentives based on meeting strict quantitative targets
Differentiation	• Strong marketing abilities • Product engineering • Corporate reputation for quality or technological leadership • Long tradition in the industry or unique skills drawn from other businesses	• Strong coordination among functions: research, product development, manufacturing, and marketing

the management accountants support these efforts by gathering, analyzing, and reporting the relevant information. Firms that excel in the execution of these functions include Coca-Cola, Microsoft, and IBM which have been the top three global brands for the last three years.[4]

Both cost leadership and differentiation firms also can improve on execution through benchmarking and total quality improvement. The Malcolm Baldrige National Quality Program (U.S. Department of Commerce; www.quality.nist.gov) sets forth improvement criteria and awards firms that excel on these criteria. The criteria include a wide variety of business functions, including leadership, strategic planning, marketing, information and analysis, human resources, process management, and business results. Another resource for benchmarking is the International Organization for Standardization, a network of national standards institutes from 145 counties (www.iso.org).

Value-Chain Analysis

LEARNING OBJECTIVE 3

Explain how to implement a competitive strategy using value-chain analysis.

Because execution is so important in implementing strategy, managers must know how the firm's strategy and its CSFs are implemented *in each and every phase of the firm's operations*. In other words, managers must implement their firm's strategy at the detail level of operations. This sequence of activities must include all the steps necessary to satisfy customers. Value chain analysis is a means to reach this detail level of analysis.

Value-chain analysis is a strategic analysis tool used to better understand the firm's competitive advantage, to identify where value to customers can be increased or costs reduced, and to better understand the firm's linkages with suppliers, customers, and other firms in the industry. The activities include all steps necessary to provide a competitive product or service to the customer. For a manufacturer, this starts with product development and new product testing, then to raw materials purchases and manufacturing, and finally sales and service. For a service firm, the activities begin with the concept of the service and its design, purpose, and demand and then moves to the set of activities that provide the service to create a satisfied customer. Although the value chains are sometimes more difficult to describe for a service firm or a not-for-profit organization because they might have no physical flow to visualize, the approach is applied in all types of firms. A firm might break its operations into dozens or hundreds of activities; in this chapter, it is sufficient to limit the analysis to no more than six to eight activities.

The term *value chain* is used because each activity is intended to add value to the product or service for the customer. Management can better understand the firm's competitive advantage and strategy by separating its operations according to activity. If the firm succeeds by cost leadership, for example, management should determine whether each individual activity in the value chain is consistent with that overall strategy. A careful consideration of each activity should also identify those activities in which the firm is most and least competitive.

The value-chain analysis focuses on the product's total value chain, from its design to its manufacture to its service after the sale. The underlying concept of the analysis is that each individual firm occupies a selected part or parts of this entire value chain.

The determination of which part or parts of the value chain to occupy is a strategic analysis based on the consideration of comparative advantage for the individual firm, that is, where the firm can best provide value to the ultimate consumer at the lowest possible cost. For example, some firms in the computer-manufacturing industry focus on the manufacture of chips (Texas Instruments) while others primarily manufacture processors (Intel), hard drives (Seagate and Western Digital), or monitors (Sony). Some manufacturers (Hewlett-Packard, Apple Computer) combine purchased and manufactured components to manufacture the complete computer; others (Dell,

---

[4] "The Top 100 Brands," *Business Week*, August 5, 2002, p. 95; "Brands," *Business Week*, August 4, 2003, p. 69; "The World's Most Valuable Brands," *Business 2.0,* November 28, 2000, p. 155. See also, Larry Bossidy and Ram Charan, *Execution: Translating Strategies into Results,* Crown Business (2002).

As the value chain in Exhibit 2.3 suggests, the profits in the PC industry are largely downstream, in services. This is often true of technology companies generally. For example, IBM says it has moved up the stack. The *stack* is the IBM term for the structure of products and services in the software industry. At the bottom of the stack are operating systems such as Windows or Linux, the foundation of all software systems. Moving up the stack, database and systems management, "middleware," and accounting or Internet application software provide crucial computing products for business firms. At the top of the stack is customer services; system integration, training, and maintenance software is more profitable to IBM than the others, and thus IBM's move "up the stack."

Similarly, price competition and saturation in equipment sales have caused technology firms, such as Ericsson, Lucent, Nortel, and Alcatel, to move their strategic focus toward the ultimate customer by providing network management and other services to consumers of their products.

Source: Louis Gerstner, *Who Says Elephants Can't Dance?* (New York: Harper Business, 2002), p. 155; "Ericsson Moves to Service as Equipment Sales Plunge," Bloomberg News Service, February 4, 2003.

EXHIBIT 2.3
Profits in the PC Industry

Source: Adapted from Orit Gadiesh and James Gilbert, "Profit Tools: A Fresh Look at Strategy," *Harvard Business Review*, May–June 1998, pp. 139–147.

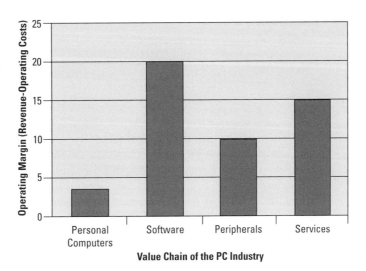

Gateway) depend primarily on purchased components. In the sport-shoe industry, Reebok manufactures its shoes and sells them to large retailers; Nike concentrates on design, sales, and promotion, contracting out all manufacturing. In effect, each firm establishes itself in one or more parts of the value chain on the basis of a strategic analysis of its competitive advantage.

Value-chain analysis has two steps:

Step 1: Identify the Value-Chain Activities

Value activities
are activities that firms in the industry must perform in the process of converting raw material to final product, including customer service.

The firm identifies the specific **value activities** that firms in the industry must perform in the processes of designing, manufacturing, and providing customer service. For example, see the value chain for the computer-manufacturing industry in Exhibit 2.4.

The development of a value chain depends on the type of industry. For example, the focus in a service industry is on operations and on advertising and promotion rather than on raw materials and manufacturing (an example of a service industry value chain is shown in self-study problem 1 at the end of the chapter). The activities also should be determined at a relatively detailed level of operations, that is, at the level of business unit or process just large enough to be managed as a separate business activity.

Step 2: Develop a Competitive Advantage by Reducing Cost or Adding Value

In this step, the firm determines the nature of its current and potential competitive advantage by studying the value activities and cost drivers identified earlier. In doing so, the firm must consider the following:

EXHIBIT 2.4
Value Chain for the Computer-Manufacturing Industry

Step in the Value Chain	Activities	Expected Output of Activities
Step 1: Design	Performing research and development	Completed product design
Step 2: Raw materials acquisition	Mining, developing, and refining	Silicon, plastic, various metals
Step 3: Materials assembled into components	Converting raw materials into components and parts used to manufacture the computer	Desired components and parts
Step 4: Intermediate assembly	Converting, assembling, finishing, testing, and grading	Boards, higher-level components
Step 5: Computer manufacturing	Final assembling, packaging, and shipping the final product	Completed computers
Step 6: Wholesaling, warehousing, and distribution	Moving products to retail locations and warehouses, as needed	Rail, truck, and air shipments
Step 7: Retail sales	Making retail sale	Cash receipts
Step 8: Customer service	Processing returns, inquiries, and repairs	Serviced and restocked computers

1. Identify competitive advantage (cost leadership or differentiation). The analysis of value activities can help management better understand the firm's strategic competitive advantage and its proper positioning in the overall industry value chain. For example, IBM, Ericsson, Boeing, General Electric, and other firms have increased emphasis on services for their customers, as many of these services are more profitable than the sale of their basic products.

2. Identify opportunities for added value. The analysis of value activities can help identify activities in which the firm can add significant value for the customer. For example, food-processing plants and packaging plants are now commonly located near their largest customers to provide faster and cheaper delivery. Similarly, large retailers such as Wal-Mart use computer-based technology to coordinate with suppliers to efficiently and quickly restock each of its stores. In banking, ATMs (automated teller machines) were introduced to provide improved customer service and to reduce processing costs. Banks have begun to develop on-line computer technologies to further enhance customer service and to provide an opportunity to reduce processing costs further.

3. Identify opportunities for reduced cost. A study of its value activities can help a firm determine those parts of the value chain for which it is *not* competitive. For example, firms in the information technology business, such as Flextronics International Ltd., Solectron Corp., and SCI Systems, Inc., have become large suppliers of parts and subassemblies for computer manufacturers and other information technology manufacturers such as Hewlett-Packard, Sony, and Cisco Systems Inc. The brand-name manufacturers have found that outsourcing some of the manufacturing to firms such as Flextronics reduces total cost and can improve speed, quality, and competitiveness.

4. Exploit linkages among activities in the value chain. The decision to provide an activity internally or to outsource it is sometimes influenced by the way that activity is affected by another activity in the value chain. For example, Iowa Beef Processors moved its processing plants to be near the feedlots in the southwest and midwest states, thereby saving transportation costs and reducing the loss in weight that the animals usually suffered during transportation. Firms such as Otis Elevator and Whirlpool Corporation have found that it is important to provide customer service internally since service representatives are sources of valuable information from customers; they can feed information regarding product weaknesses and desirable new features to product designers and manufacturing managers in a timely manner.

Value-Chain Analysis in Computer Manufacturing

The computer industry offers excellent opportunities to show value-chain analysis in action. The Computer Intelligence Company (CIC) manufactures computers for small businesses. CIC has an excellent reputation for service and reliability as well as a growing list of customers. The manufacturing process consists primarily of assembling components purchased from various electronics firms plus a small amount of metal-working and finishing. The manufacturing operations cost $250 per unit. The purchased parts cost CIC $500, of which $300 is for parts that CIC could manufacture in its existing facility for $190 in materials for each unit plus an investment in labor and equipment that would cost $55,000 per month. CIC is considering whether to make or continue to buy these parts.

CIC can contract out to another firm, JBM Enterprises, the marketing, distributing, and servicing of its units. This would save CIC $175,000 in monthly materials and labor costs. The cost of the contract would be $130 per machine sold for the average of 600 units sold per month. CIC uses value-chain analysis to study the effect of these options on its strategy and costs. The analysis is summarized in Exhibit 2.5.

EXHIBIT 2.5
Value-Chain Analysis for CIC Manufacturing Company

Value Activity	Option 1: Continue Current Operations	Option 2: Manufacture Components and Contract Out Marketing, Distributing, and Servicing Functions
Acquiring raw materials	CIC is not involved at this step in the value chain.	CIC is not involved at this step in the value chain.
Manufacturing computer chips and other parts	CIC is not involved at this step in the value chain; the cost of these parts is $200 to CIC.	CIC is not involved at this step in the value chain; the cost of these parts is $200 to CIC
Manufacturing components, some of which CIC can make	CIC purchases $300 of parts for each unit	CIC manufactures these parts for $190 per unit plus monthly costs of $55,000.
Assembling	CIC's costs are $250.	CIC's costs are $250.
Marketing, distributing, and servicing	CIC's costs are $175,000 per month.	CIC contracts out servicing to JBM Enterprises for $130 per unit sold

Summary of Costs that Differ between Options

1. Unit costs for purchased components: $300	1. Unit costs for manufacturing components ($190) plus cost of JBM contract ($130): $320
2. Monthly costs for marketing, distributing, and servicing: $175,000	2. Monthly costs for labor and equipment: $55,000
Total relevant costs for this option (assuming 600 units sold per month): $300 × 600 + $175,000 = $355,000 per month	Total relevant costs for this option (assuming 600 units sold per month): $320 × 600 + $55,000 = $247,000 per month

REAL-WORLD FOCUS   Value-Chain Analysis to Help Find Downstream Profits:
U-Haul, Boeing, and General Electric

Some firms are finding that their traditional core business is under continuing profit pressure and that the route to profitability is to expand downstream. A good example is U-Haul, which, under intense price competition from Ryder and Hertz-Penske in the truck rental business, adopted the strategy of charging low rental rates to build volume and to simultaneously expand downstream by advancing the sale of its accessories: boxes, insurance, packaging materials, and other moving supplies. U-Haul barely broke even on truck rentals but was profitable on the accessory and other downstream business. It effectively redefined the truck rental business by looking downstream for the profits.

Manufacturers such as Boeing and General Electric also use the value-chain concept to find profits downstream. For example, Boeing offers a number of products and services in addition to the aircraft it manufactures: financing, local parts supply, ground maintenance, logistics management, and pilot training. In the cyclical industry in which it operates, Boeing can find profits from them during the slack manufacturing times.

General Electric has connected its locomotive manufacturing business to its financing unit, GE Capital, to provide customer financing for not only locomotives but also boxcars and other rail assets. Other GE units profit by refurbishing and reselling boxcars and by developing advanced rail tracking systems. In effect, GE finds providing a broad range of services to the locomotive customer more profitable than manufacturing only.

Sources: Orit Gadiesh and James L. Gilbert, "Profit Pools: A Fresh Look at Strategy," *Harvard Business Review,* May–June 1998, pp. 139–47; and Richard Wise and Peter Baumgartner, "Go Downstream: The New Profit Imperative in Manufacturing," *Harvard Business Review,* September–October 1999, pp. 133–41.

The value-chain analysis in Exhibit 2.5 shows that CIC can save $108,000 per month ($355,000 − $247,000) by choosing option 2; thus, from a cost advantage, it prefers option 2. However, CIC also must consider its strategic competitive position. If its customers rely on CIC primarily for its service and reliability, then contracting out the marketing, distributing, and servicing functions is unwise; CIC should retain control over these critical success factors. Moreover, by moving to a strategy of making rather than buying the components, CIC is moving in the direction of competing on cost leadership with other computer manufacturers. It is unlikely that CIC can succeed at cost leadership because of its relatively small size and the presence of effective competitors already in this part of the value chain (Hewlett-Packard, Dell, and Gateway, to name a few). Thus, option 2 pulls CIC away from its proven competitive advantage of emphasis on customer service. From a strategic view, option 1 is preferred, even though the costs are higher.[5] The value-chain analysis provides a useful framework for studying CIC's options and determining where it can reduce costs and where it can compete most effectively on the value chain.

The Balanced Scorecard

LEARNING OBJECTIVE 4
Explain how to implement a competitive strategy using the balanced scorecard.

The balanced scorecard (BSC), a performance report based on a broad set of both financial and nonfinancial measures, is a crucial part of the firm's efforts to better understand and to implement its strategy. The BSC provides a comprehensive performance measurement tool that reflects all the measures critical for the success of the firm's strategy. Prior to the wide use of the BSC in the late 1980s, firms tended to focus only on financial measures of performance, and as a result, some of their critical nonfinancial measures were not sufficiently monitored and achieved. In effect, the BSC enables the firm to employ a strategy-centered performance measurement system, one that focuses managers' attention on critical success factors, and rewards them for achieving these critical factors.

---

[5] The options facing CIC can also be viewed as two separate outsourcing decisions, one for the manufacture of components and the other for marketing, distributing, and servicing. Both favor outsourcing. The manufacturing decision favors outsourcing for a savings of $11,000 ($300 × 600 − $190 × 600 − $55,000), and the marketing, distributing, and servicing decision favors outsourcing for a savings of $97,000 ($175,000 − $130 × 600).

Now a rapidly increasing number of firms, not-for-profit organizations, and governmental units use the BSC to assist them in implementing strategy.[6] The balanced scorecard consists of four perspectives, or groupings of critical success factors: (1) the *financial perspective* includes financial performance measures such as operating income and cash flow; (2) the *customer perspective* includes measures of customer satisfaction; (3) the *internal process perspective* includes measures of productivity and speed, among others; and (4*) learning and innovation* includes such measures as employee training hours and the number of new patents or new products (Exhibit 2.1). The BSC provides four key benefits:

- A *means for implementing strategy* by drawing managers' attention to strategically relevant critical success factors, and rewarding them for achievement of these factors.

- A framework firms can use to *achieve a desired organizational change in strategy*, by drawing attention to and rewarding achievement on factors that are part of a new strategy. The BSC makes the nature and direction of the desired change clear to all.

- A fair and objective basis for firms to use in determining each manager's compensation and advancement.

- A framework that coordinates efforts within the firm to achieve critical success factors. BSC enables managers to see how their activity contributes to the success of others.

There are also limitations. The BSC must be designed and used to:

- Provide accurate measures for each of the elements of the scorecard. Even though the reliability of much of the financial information is assured by the firm's accounting internal control systems and through the financial statement audit, some of the nonfinancial information is subject to the reliability of the sources and processes used.

- Assure that the information is handled confidentially where appropriate. For example, information about individual employees in the learning and innovation perspective should be confidential.

- Require timely, appropriate reporting of some elements of the scorecard. For example, many of the measures in the internal processes perspective require frequent—perhaps daily—updates while the financial measures may be required monthly or quarterly. The scorecard must be adapted to the different decision needs of the four perspectives.

The Balanced Scorecard Reflects Strategy

The BSC can be viewed as a two-way street. Since it is designed to help implement strategy (strategy → BSC), it also should reflect strategy (BSC → strategy). One should be able to infer a firm's strategy by a careful study of the firm's BSC. For example, consider the BSC of an electronics manufacturer shown in Exhibit 2.6. Does this firm follow a cost leadership strategy or a differentiation strategy, and why? The answer shows how this BSC reflects the strategy of the electronics firm. Notice that the firm does not use the standard four perspectives identified above; instead this firm uses five perspectives to implement its unique strategy. Note also the inclusion of an "employees and community" perspective that reflects this firm's strategic emphasis and desire to achieve in these areas.

Exhibit 2.6 shows that the electronics firm places the customer perspective at the top of the scorecard. Also, while price is mentioned, note that the emphasis is on customer satisfaction, through quality, innovation, and service. A strong theme through the entire scorecard is the importance of innovation and new products. This seems to fit

[6] Robert S. Kaplan and David P. Norton, *The Strategy-Focused Organization: How Balanced Scorecard Companies Thrive in the New Business Environment* (Boston: Harvard Business School Press, 2001), pp. 1–26.

EXHIBIT 2.6 **The Balanced Scorecard for an Electronics Firm**

Source: Chee W. Chow, Kamal M. Haddad, James W. Williamson, "Applying the Balanced Scorecard to Small Companies," *Management Accounting*, August 1997, pp. 21–27.

CSF	Measures
Customer Perspective	
Quality	Own quality relative to industry standards; number of defects; delivered product quality
Price	Own price relative to competitive market price; sales volume; customer willingness to pay
Delivery	Actual versus planned; number of ontime deliveries
Shipments	Sales growth; number of customers that make up 90 percent of shipments
New products	Number of new products; rate of technology improvements; percent of sales from products introduced in last two years
Support	Response time; customer satisfaction surveys
Internal Capabilities	
Efficiency of manufacturing	Cycle time; lead time; manufacturing overhead cost/quarter; rate of increase in use of automation
New product introduction	Rate of new product introduction/quarter
New product success	New products' quarterly sales; number of orders
Sales penetration	Actual sales versus plan; increases in number of $1 million customers each quarter
New businesses	Number of new businesses each year
Innovation	
Technology leadership	Product performance compared to competition; number of new products with patented technology in them
Cost leadership	Manufacturing overhead per quarter as a percent of sales; rate of decrease in cost of quality per quarter
Market leadership	Market share in all major markets; number of systems developed to meet customer requests and requirements
Research and development	Number of new products; number of patents
Financial Perspective	
Sales	Annual growth in sales and profits
Cost of sales	Extent it remains flat or decreases each year
Profitability	Return on total capital employed
Prosperity	Cash flows
Employees and Community Perspective	
Competitive benefits and salaries	Salaries compared to norm in local area
Opportunity	Individual contribution; personal satisfaction in job
Citizenship	Company contributions to community and the institutions that generate the environment

pretty well a firm that succeeds through differentiation based on quality and innovation, and the scorecard reflects that. Cost control is mentioned in the innovation perspective, but as supportive of the differentiation strategy, rather than in conflict with it.

The Strategy Map

A **strategy map**
is a cause-and-effect diagram of
the relationships among the BSC
perspectives.

While the electronics firm in Exhibit 2.6 placed the customer perspective at the top of the BSC to show its priority, it is also possible to create a strategy map by linking the perspectives in the order they contribute to the overall success of the firm. A **strategy map** is a cause-and-effect diagram of the relationships among the BSC perspectives. Managers use it to show how the achievement of CSFs in each perspective affect the achievement of goals in other perspectives, and finally the overall financial performance of the firm.[7]

[7] The strategy map is developed and illustrated by applications in a variety of firms and organizations by Robert S. Kaplan and David P. Norton, *The Strategy-Focused Organization* (Boston: Harvard Business School Press, 2001). See also "Transforming the Balanced Scorecard from Performance Measurement to Strategic Management," by the same authors, *Accounting Horizons*, March 2001, pp. 87–104.

For most firms, the ultimate goal is stated in financial performance, and for public firms in particular, in shareholder value. So, the financial perspective of the BSC is the target in the strategy map. The other BSC perspectives contribute to financial performance in a predictable, cause-and-effect way. For many firms, the learning and innovation perspective is the base upon which the firm's success is built. The reason is that learning and innovation—resulting in great products and great employees—drives performance in the internal processes perspective and also the customer perspective. Similarly, great performance in the internal processes perspective drives performance in the customer perspective; better operations mean more satisfied customers. Finally, satisfied customers lead directly to improved financial performance, as illustrated in Exhibit 2.7, a possible strategy map for Dell. The map shows that the foundation for Dell's success is learning and innovation, as measured by the number of innovations in manufacturing processes to speed up the manufacturing and delivery of their product. These efforts in learning and innovation are realized in improvements in operating performance, as measured by speed and quality. High performance in internal processes should lead to high customer satisfaction as measured by customer perceptions and customer retention. The bottom line is that customer satisfaction should lead to strong financial performance as measured by revenue growth, gross margin, and so on. The strategy map can enhance the usefulness of the BSC by showing the performance relationships among the perspectives, as a way to better understand and manage the performance drivers in the firm.

EXHIBIT 2.7
A Strategy Map for Dell Computer

Source: Adapted from Peter Brewer, "Putting Strategy into the Balanced Scorecard," *Strategic Finance*, January 2002, pp. 44–52.

Learning and Innovation
Measures (by product segment):
- Training dollars per employee
- Number of emerging technologies evaluated
- Number of new manufacturing processes developed
- Number of new manufacturing processes under development

↓

Internal Processes
Measures (by product segment):
- Product manufacturing time
- Raw materials inventory
- Order processing time
- Manufacturing defects

↓

Customer
Measures (by product segment):
- Customer perception of order-taking convenience and accuracy
- Customer perception of product quality
- Customer retention
- Customer satisfaction with speed of service

↓

Financial Performance
Measures (by product segment):
- Revenue growth
- Gross margin
- Operating cost ratio
- Selling expense to sales ratio

Expanding the Balanced Scorecard: Sustainability

Sustainable growth seeks to make more of the world's people our customers—and to do so by developing markets that promote and sustain economic prosperity, social equity, and environmental integrity.

Chad Holliday, CEO of DuPont[8]

Sustainability
means the balancing of short- and long-term goals in all three dimensions of the company's performance—economic, social, and environmental.

LEARNING OBJECTIVE 5
Explain how to expand the balanced scorecard by integrating sustainability.

In 2002, 45 percent of the 250 largest global companies prepared environmental and social responsibility reports, as compared to 35 percent in 2001. These companies are concerned about the **sustainability** of their business, that is, the balancing of short- and long-term goals in all three dimensions of the company's performance—economic, social, and environmental. Economic performance is measured in traditional ways, while social performance relates to health and safety of employees and other stakeholders. The environmental dimension refers to the impact of the firm's operations on the environment.

Those who measure the public's perceptions of large firms have recently begun to develop rankings for environmental and social responsibility. For example, the 2001 rankings showed Johnson & Johnson, Coca-Cola, and Wal-Mart as tops in a survey of 21,000 Americans. Moreover, firms like DuPont are lowering greenhouse emissions as required by the United Nation's Kyoto Protocol (www.unfccc.int), even though the United States had not signed the protocol as of January 2003. DuPont expects to benefit in the longer term by accumulating greenhouse gas emission credits that can be traded or sold to other firms around the world.[9]

Overall, we are seeing rapidly increasing interest within business and government to improve the sustainability of a firm's operations. This interest is driving firms such as Royal Dutch/Shell to develop environmental reports. These reports can be integrated with the firm's annual report, or issued as a separate report, as in the case of Royal Dutch/Shell. Separate, internal reports can be incorporated into the firm's BSC, in the fashion suggested by the BSC of the electronics firm in Exhibit 2.7, which has a perspective on employees and community. In effect, to expand a firm's strategy to include sustainability requires the extension of the BSC to include a new perspective, that of sustainability. The measures in this perspective can be similar to those employed by Shell and other firms that have adopted sustainability (see the Real-World Focus box on the next page).

Environmental performance indicators (EPIs) are the CSFs in a sustainability perspective; they are defined in three categories by the World Resources Institute (WRI) www.wri.org:[10]

- Operational indicators measure potential stresses to the environment; for example, fossil fuel use.
- Management indicators measure efforts to reduce environmental effects; for example, hours of environmental training.
- Environmental condition indicators measure environmental quality; for example, ambient air pollution concentrations.

---

[8] See Chad Holliday, "Sustainable Development the DuPont Way," *Harvard Business Review*, September 2001, pp. 129–134. Holliday is also chair of the World Business Council for Sustainable Development, a coalition of 150 global companies.

[9] For cited information see *Business Week*, September 2, 2002, p. 12 and the 2001 Harris Interactive Reputation Survey; also, see Jeffrey Ball, "New Market Shows Industry Moving on Global Warming," *The Wall Street Journal*, January 16, 2003, p. 1; and Stuart L. Hart, "Beyond Greening: Strategies for a Sustainable World," *Harvard Business Review*, January–February, 1997, pp. 66–76.

[10] "Measuring Up: Toward a Common Framework for Tracking Corporate Environmental Performance," by Daryl Ditz and Janet Ranganathan, the World Resources Institute, Washington, DC, 1997. The World Resources Institute is an independent center for policy research and technical assistance on global environmental and development issues.

Sustainable Development and the Balanced Scorecard at Royal Dutch/Shell

Royal Dutch/Shell Companies (Shell) uses a version of the balanced scorecard concept to define its business strategy and to report its performance in achieving this strategy. Shell is a global company operating in 135 countries with almost 100,000 employees, delivering a wide variety of products in the oil, chemical, and related industries. The firm's strategy is based on the principle of sustainable development, which in broad terms means that it is dedicated to developing natural capital, promoting economic prosperity, and developing social capital in all the countries in which it operates. Using the balanced scorecard, this broad principle is implemented by measuring and improving critical success factors grouped into four categories (the CSF list is partial):

- Economic measures.
  - Crude oil prices.
  - Operating profit.
  - Total debt ratio.
  - Net income.
- Environmental measures.
  - Greenhouse gas emissions.
  - Carbon dioxide emissions.
  - Emissions of nitrogen oxides.
  - Total number of spills of oil and chemical products.
- Social measures.
  - Number of countries using procedures to ensure equal employment opportunities.
  - Gender diversity, by management level.
  - Number of countries screening against the use of child labor.
  - Number of health and safety incidents.
- Shell employees and partners/business integrity and business principles.
  - Number of reported cases of bribery.
  - Number of countries with a screening process for compliance with Shell business principles.
  - Number of responses to the "Tell Shell" program.

These CSFs were reported in the Shell 2001 annual report; many were verified by independent auditors.

Source: The Royal Dutch/Shell Group of Companies Annual Report: People, Planet, and Profits 2001; and its website, www.shell.com.

Firms sometimes give the operational indicators the greatest attention, because they often deal with regulatory compliance issues. The operational indicators include four areas:

- Materials used in manufacturing and other operations
- Energy used, including different fuel types
- Waste, nontoxic waste of materials and energy
- Pollutants released to the air, water, or earth, including toxic waste and greenhouse gasses

The role of the sustainability perspective is to make these EPIs an integral part of management decision making, not only for regulatory compliance but also for product design, purchasing, strategic planning, and other management functions. As for the BSC, there are a number of implementation issues, including measurement problems and confidentiality issues. For example, the Global Reporting Initiative (GRI) www.globalreporting.org, an independent global institution in partnership with the United Nations and other groups, has a goal of developing generally accepted standards for sustainability reporting.

In summary this chapter has discussed three cost management resources for implementing strategy: SWOT analysis, value-chain analysis, and the balanced scorecard. We can see the broad perspective in which the three strategic resources are linked in a comprehensive strategic analysis. The first, SWOT analysis, helps to implement strategy by providing a system and structure in which to identify the firm's critical success factors. The second, value-chain analysis, builds on the CSFs developed in the first step by breaking them down into detailed activities. This provides the firm a way to better understand its strategy and, in particular, to identify activities that are (or are not) contributing to the firm's overall success. The final step, the balanced scorecard, provides a way to implement the detailed strategy developed through SWOT analysis and

EXHIBIT 2.8
Linking Strategic Resources for Strategy Implementation

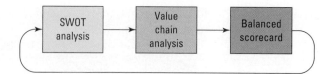

value-chain analysis by providing the processes for evaluating the firm's achievement of the CSFs needed for success. The balanced scorecard provides even more; as a reflection of the firm's strategy, it is a concrete and dynamic basis for continual reassessment of the firm's strategy. Thus, a feedback loop exists from the balanced scorecard to SWOT analysis as illustrated in Exhibit 2.8. Because of its key role in performance evaluation, we encounter the balanced scorecard again in Chapter 17.

Not-For-Profit Organizations

Competitive strategy is likely to be somewhat different in not-for-profit or governmental organizations than in for-profit organizations. These organizations must satisfy funding authorities, political leaders, and the general public as to their effectiveness and efficiency. The balanced scorecard can be used to monitor and evaluate the organization's performance on the key internal processes (e.g., efficiency measures such as pounds of trash removed), customer satisfaction measures (with the public and political leaders as the customers), key financial measures (e.g., credit rating, fund balance), and human resources measures.

Additionally, value-chain analysis can be used to determine at what points costs can be reduced or value added in the organization's value chain. In contrast to the acquisition of raw materials or the process of advertising and promotion, the first step in the value chain for a not-for-profit or governmental organization is likely to be to develop a statement of the organization's broad social mission, including the specific public needs served. The second step is to develop resources for the organization, including both personnel and facilities. The third and fourth steps are to operate the organization and deliver its service to the public, respectively.[11]

SUMMARY

The use of cost management facilitates a firm's strategic management. The management accountant has moved from a procedural, stewardship role to more of a strategic facilitation role, to a business partnership role in the firm. Michael Porter's work in strategic management explains the fundamentals of how firms compete. This grounding in the competitive environment of the firm determines the cost management role. That is, knowing how a firm competes and identifying its critical success factors are necessary to know how the firm's cost management system should be designed.

Three important management techniques for implementing strategy are SWOT analysis, the balanced scorecard, and value-chain analysis. SWOT analysis is a technique for identifying a firm's critical success factors based on an identification of its strengths, weaknesses, opportunities, and threats in the business environment. Value-chain analysis is a technique for assisting the management accountant in identifying opportunities for reducing cost and/or adding value to the firm's products and services. The balanced scorecard is a cost management report that summarizes the critical success factors for management, and thus provides a basis for monitoring and rewarding achievement of the CSFs. The balanced scorecard includes four or more perspectives

---

[11] Some good examples of applications of the value chain and the balanced scorecard in not-for-profit hospitals and governmental units such as the City of Charlotte, North Carolina, are described by Robert S. Kaplan and David P. Norton in *The Strategy-Focused Organization* (Boston: Harvard Business School Press, 2001); and Russ Kershaw and Susan Kershaw in "Developing a Balanced Scorecard to Implement Strategy at St. Elsewhere Hospital," *Management Accounting Quarterly*, Winter 2001, pp. 28–35.

(groups of CSFs): the financial, customer, internal processes, and learning and innovation. An additional perspective many firms have added is sustainability, that is, the ability of a firm to develop a strategy that balances its short-term and long-term social and environmental goals as well as its financial goals.

The implication of strategic analysis is that the management accountant must also adopt a strategic focus, that is, develop integrative skills for working with teams of operations, marketing, and other managers in the organization to lead the company to competitive success.

Key Terms

core competencies, *35*	sustainability, *48*	value activities, *41*
strategy map, *46*	SWOT analysis, *35*	

Comments on Cost Management in Action

Automakers and Parts Manufacturing: Spin Off the Parts?

The consensus of analysts and the business press is that Ford and General Motors were wise to spin off their parts manufacturing units, Visteon and Delphi, respectively. The reasons can be tied to a value-chain analysis of the automakers. The first reason is that the parts manufacturers are more cost efficient at operating the specialized design teams and manufacturing processes for these parts than the automakers. A second reason is that the spin off allows each automaker to look for the best technology at the best price by shopping around to other parts manufacturers. A third reason is that the spin off allows the automaker to reduce its total capital requirement and investment risk by divesting itself from the fixed costs associated with operating the parts units.

The new approach is consistent with another development in auto design, modular manufacturing, in which suppliers provide not just parts but entire sections of the car: the interior, the chassis, and so on. Automakers argue that handling the complexity of manufacturing today's auto is easier if the manufacturing is broken down into modules using the design and manufacturing skills of these suppliers.

The spin-off is a win-win strategy as well, since Delphi and Visteon are able to compete more effectively for business from other automakers and to independently develop their technologies and manufacturing expertise.

Sources: "Maybe What's Good for GM Is Good for Ford," *Business Week,* April 24, 2000, p. 60; "GM: Modular Plants Won't Be a Snap," *Business Week,* November 9, 1998, pp. 168–72; and "Souping Up the Supply Chain," *Business Week,* August 31, 1998, pp. 110–12

Self-Study Problems
(For solutions, please turn to the end of the chapter.)

1. Value-Chain Analysis

Jack Smith, a consultant for the Waynesboro Bulls AA baseball team, has been asked to complete a value-chain analysis of the franchise with a particular focus on a comparison with a nearby competing team, the Durham Buffaloes. Jack has been able to collect selected cost data as follows for each of the six steps in the value chain. Single-ticket prices range from $4.50 to $8.00, and average paying attendance is approximately 2,200 for Waynesboro and 5,000 for Durham.

Average Cost per Person at Scheduled Games

Waynesboro Bulls	Activities in the Value Chain	Durham Buffaloes
$0.45	Advertising and general promotion expenses	$0.50
0.28	Ticket sales: At local sporting goods stores and the ballpark	0.25
0.65	Ballpark operations	0.80
0.23	Management compensation	0.18
0.95	Players' salaries	1.05
0.20	Game-day operations: security, special entertainment, and game-day promotions	0.65
$2.76	Total Cost	$3.43

Required   Analyze the value chain to help Jack better understand the nature of the competition between the Bulls and the Buffaloes and to identify opportunities for adding value and/or reducing cost at each activity.

2. Competitive Strategy, Ethics

Frank Sills, the CEO and founder of Enviro-Wear, is facing the first big challenge to his young company. He began the company on the principle of environmental consciousness in the manufacture of sports and recreation wear. His idea was to develop clothing that would appeal to active people concerned about quality, waste in manufacturing and packaging, and the environmental impact of manufacturing the goods they purchased. Starting with a small shop in Zebulon, North Carolina, Frank was able to develop his small business through strategic alliances with mail-order merchandisers and through effective public relations about his environmentally concerned processes. A special advantage for the young firm was Frank's knowledge of accounting and his prior experience as a CPA in a national public accounting firm and as the controller of a small manufacturing firm. He is also a certified management accountant.

Enviro-Wear had reached $25,000,000 in sales in its sixth year when a disastrous set of events put the firm and its prospects in a tailspin. A news reporter overheard one of the key sales managers telling jokes about the poor quality of the firm's clothing, and the story spread quickly. At the same time, rumors (largely unfounded) spread that the firm was not really as environmentally conscious in its manufacturing and packaging as it claimed. The result was an immediate decline in sales; some retailers even returned goods.

Frank intends to fire the manager and publicly deny any association with the manager's comments and to defend the firm's environmental record.

Required

1. On the basis of Porter's analysis of strategic competitive advantage, what type of competitive strategy has Enviro-Wear followed? What type of strategy should it follow in the future?
2. What are the ethical issues involved in the case? How would you resolve them?

Questions

2–1   Identify and explain the two types of competitive strategy.

2–2   Identify three or four well-known firms that succeed through cost leadership.

2–3   Identify three or four well-known firms that succeed through product differentiation.

2–4   How are the three strategic resources—SWOT analysis, the value chain, and the balanced scorecard—linked in a comprehensive strategic analysis?

2–5   Explain the steps of implementing a competitive advantage for a firm using SWOT analysis.

2–6   What is a strategy map and how is it used?

2–7   What is SWOT analysis? For what is it used?

2–8   What is the role of the cost manager regarding nonfinancial performance measures such as delivery speed and customer satisfaction?

2–9   Explain the difference between short-term and long-term performance measures, and give two or three examples of each.

2–10 What is a critical success factor? What is its role in strategic management and in cost management?

2–11 Identify four or five potential critical success factors for a manufacturer of industrial chemicals. Explain why you consider those factors critical for the firm to be successful.

2–12 Identify four or five potential critical success factors for a large savings and loan institution.

2–13 Identify four or five potential critical success factors for a small chain of retail jewelry stores.

2–14 Identify four or five potential critical success factors for a large retail discount store that features a broad range of consumer merchandise.

2–15 Identify four or five potential critical success factors for a small auto-repair shop.

2–16 What is a balanced scorecard? What is its primary objective?

2–17 Contrast using the balanced scorecard with using only financial measures of success.

2–18 What is sustainability and what does it mean for a business?

2–19 Explain the uses of value-chain analysis.

Exercises

2–20 **Special Order, Strategy**   Joel Deaine, CEO of Deaine Enterprises, Inc. (DEI), is considering a special offer to manufacture a new line of women's clothing for a large department store chain. DEI has specialized in designer women's clothing sold in small, upscale retail clothing stores throughout the country. To protect the very elite brand image, DEI has not sold clothing to the large department stores. The current offer, however, might be too good to turn down. The department store is willing to commit to a large order, which would be very profitable to DEI, and the order would be renewed automatically for two more years, presumably to continue after that point.

Required   Analyze the choice Joel faces based on a competitive analysis.

2–21 **Strategy, Competitive Advantage**   In the mid-1990s, a large retailer of auto parts, Best Parts, Inc. (BPI), was looking for ways to invest an accumulation of excess cash. BPI's success was built on a carefully developed inventory control system that guaranteed the availability of a desired part on demand 99 percent of the time and within one business day for the remaining 1 percent. The speed and quality of service set BPI apart from other parts dealers, and the business continued to grow.

On the advice of close friends and consultants, BPI's owner and CEO decided to invest a significant portion of the excess cash in a small chain of gift and craft stores in shopping malls.

Required   Determine BPI's competitive advantage (cost leadership or differentiation) in the auto-parts business. Assess whether this competitive advantage will or will not facilitate success in the new venture.

Problems

2–22 **Strategy, Balanced Scorecard, Health Care**   Consumers, employers, and governments at all levels are very concerned about the rising costs of health care. As a result, health care systems nationwide are experiencing an ongoing demand to improve the efficiency of their operations. The health care industry faces significant challenges due to changing patient needs, reduced reimbursement, and the fierce competitive environment. The industry is experiencing consolidations through systemwide mergers and acquisitions as a way to reduce operating costs. Patients and payors are demanding a one-stop shopping approach. While improving operations is necessary, the quality of the health care delivered must not be jeopardized. The Medical University of Greenbelt is feeling the impact of the increasing penetration of its market by managed-care companies. As a result, management has been asked to develop a strategic plan to ensure that its funding sources will continue to meet the demands of its patients.

Because it is an academic medical center, the Medical University of Greenbelt's mission encompasses three components: clinical care, education, and research. Management must consider these competing objectives in the proposed plan:

Required

1. What should the Medical University of Greenbelt's strategy emphasize?
2. Do you think a balanced scorecard could help ensure the success of the Medical University of Greenbelt? What advantages does a balanced scorecard have over a traditional approach?
3. Determine four or five critical success factors for each of the four areas within the balanced scorecard. Remember that in addition to patients, its employees, employers, suppliers/distributors, other training entities, community, and payors are considered customers.
4. What types of challenges will management face in implementing a balanced scorecard? How can employee buy-in be increased?

2–23 **Strategic Positioning**   Fowler's Farm is a 1,000-acre dairy and tobacco farm located in southern Virginia. Jack Fowler, the owner, has been farming since 1982. He initially purchased 235 acres and has made the following purchases since then: 300 acres in 1985, 150 acres in 1988, dairy equipment and buildings worth $350,000 in 1988, and 315 acres in 1998. The cost of farmland has inflated over the years so that, although Jack has a total investment of $1,850,000, the land's current market value is $2,650,000. The current net book value of his buildings and equipment is $300,000, with an estimated replacement cost of $1,250,000. Current price pressures on farm commodities have affected Fowler's Farm as well as others across the country. Jack has watched as many of his neighbors either have quit farming or have been consolidated into larger, more profitable farms.

Fowler's Farm consists of three different operating segments: dairy farming, tobacco, and corn and other crops intended for livestock feed. The dairy farm consists of 198 milk-producing cows that are grazed on 250 acres of farmland. The crop farm consists of the remaining acreage that covers several types of terrain and has several types of soil. Some of the land is high and hilly, some of it is low and claylike, and the rest is humus-rich soil. Jack determines the fertilizer mix for the type of soil and type of crop to be planted by rules of thumb based on his experience.

The farm equipment used consists of automated milking equipment, six tractors, two tandem-axle grain bed trucks, and numerous discs, plows, wagons, and assorted tractor and hand tools. The farm has three equipment storage barns, an equipment maintenance shed, and a 90,000-bushel grain elevator/drier. The equipment and buildings have an estimated market value of $1,500,000.

Jack employs five full-time farmhands, a mechanic, and a bookkeeper and has contracted part-time accounting/tax assistance with a local CPA firm in Pittsboro. All employees are salaried; the farmhands and the bookkeeper make $25,000 a year, and the mechanic makes $32,000 annually. The CPA contract costs $15,000 a year.

In 2003, the farm produced 256,000 gallons of raw milk, 23,000 bushels of tobacco, and 75,300 bushels of corn. Jack sells the tobacco by contract and auction at the end of the harvest. The revenue in 2003 was $1,345,000, providing Jack a net income after taxes of $233,500.

Jack's daughter Kelly has just returned from college. She knows that the farm is a good business but believes that the use of proper operating procedures and cost management systems could increase profitability and improve efficiency, allowing her father to have more leisure time. She also knows that her father has always run the farm from his experience and rules of thumb and is wary of scientific concepts and management principles. For example, he has little understanding of the accounting procedures of the farm, has not participated in the process, and has adopted few, if any, methods to maintain control over inventories and equipment. He has trusted his employees to maintain the farm appropriately without using any accounting or operating procedures over inventories or equipment, preventive maintenance schedules, or scientific application of crop rotation or livestock management.

Required   Identify and describe briefly the competitive strategy for Fowler's Farm and explain your choice.

2–24 SWOT Analysis

Required   Develop a SWOT analysis for Fowler's Farm based on Problem 2–23. The analysis should include two to three items in each category: strengths, weaknesses, opportunities, and threats.

2–25 Value Chain Analysis

Required   Develop a value chain of six to nine activities for Fowler's Farm based on problem 2–23.

2–26 The Balanced Scorecard

Required   Develop a balanced scorecard with three or more groups of CSFs for Fowler's Farm based on problem 2–23. Explain your choice of groups and identify four to five CSFs in each group. Make sure that your CSFs are quantitative and can be measured.

2–27 Strategic Positioning   Tartan Corporation has been manufacturing high-quality home lighting systems for more than 80 years. The company's first products in the 1920s—the classic line—were high-quality floor lamps and table lamps made of the highest-quality materials with features that other manufacturers did not attempt: multiple switches, adjustable heights, and stained glass. In the 1950s and 1960s, the company introduced a number of new products that were in demand at the time, including track lighting and lava lamps, which became the company's Modern line. In keeping with its brand image, Tartan ensured that these new products also met the highest standards of quality in the industry. A new customer style emerged in the 1960s and 1970s, which resulted in another new line of products, contemporary. It was followed in more recent years by two new product lines, Margaret Stewart and Western.

Jess Jones, the company's chief financial officer, had become concerned about the performance of some of the product lines in recent years. Although total sales were growing at an acceptable rate, approximately 10 percent per year, the sales mix was changing significantly, as shown in the following product line sales report. Jess was particularly concerned about the Classic line because of its sharp drop in sales and its high costs. Because of the high level of craftsmanship required for the Classic line, it always had higher than average costs for labor and materials. Furthermore, attracting and retaining the highly skilled workers necessary for this product line were becoming more and more difficult. The workers in the Classic line in 2003 were likely to be older and very loyal employees who were paid well because of their skill and seniority. These workers displayed the highest level of workmanship in the company and, some would argue, in the entire industry. Few newer employees seemed eager to learn the skills required in this product line.

Moreover, manufacturing capacity was experiencing an increasing strain. The sharper than expected increase in sales for the Western styles had created a backlog of orders for them, and plant managers had been scrambling to find the plant capacity to meet the demand. Some plant supervisors suggested shutting down the Classic line to make capacity for the Western line. Some managers of the Margaret Stewart line argued the same thing. However, eliminating the Classic line would make obsolete about $233,000 worth of raw materials inventory that is used only in the manufacture of Classic line products.

Tom Richter, the firm's sales manager, acknowledged that sales of the Classic line were more and more difficult to find and that demand for the new styles was increasing. He also noted that the sales of these products reflected significant regional differences. The Western line was popular in the south and west, and the Contemporary, Modern, and Stewart styles were popular nationally. The Classic line tended to have strong support only in the northeast states. In some sales districts in these states, Classic sales represent a relatively high proportion of total sales.

Kelly Arnold, the firm's CEO, is aware of these concerns and has decided to set up a task force to consider the firm's options and strategy in regard to these problems.

Product Line Sales Report

	Classic	Contemporary	Margaret Stewart	Modern	Western
2000	20%	33%	5%	40%	2%
2001	16	35	11	34	4
2002	14	33	14	33	6
2003	9	31	18	31	11

Required Describe Tartan's competitive strategy. On the basis of this competitive strategy, what recommendation would you make to the task force?

2–28 SWOT Analysis

Required Develop a SWOT analysis for Tartan Corporation based on Problem 2–27. The analysis should include two to three items in each category: strengths, weaknesses, opportunities, and threats.

2–29 Value Chain Analysis

Required Develop a value chain of six to eight items for Tartan Corporation described in problem 2–27. Why would the value chain be useful to a firm like Tartan?

2–30 The Balanced Scorecard

Required Develop a balanced scorecard with three or more groups of CSFs for Tartan Corporation described in problem 2–27. Explain your choice of groups and identify four to five CSFs in each group. Make sure that your CSFs are quantitative and can be measured.

2–31 Strategic Analysis Jim Hargreave's lifelong hobby is racing small sailboats. Jim has been successful both at the sport and in the design of new equipment to be used on small sailboats to make them easier to sail and more effective in racing. Jim is now thinking about starting a mail-order business in his garage to sell products he favors as well as some he has designed himself. He plans to contract out most of the manufacturing for the parts and equipment to machine shops and other small manufacturers in his area.

Required Develop a strategic analysis for Jim's new business plan. What should be his competitive position; that is, how should he choose to compete in the existing market for sailboat supplies and equipment? How is he likely to use cost management information in building his business?

2–32 Strategic Analysis Consider the following companies, each of which is your consulting client:

1. Performance Bicycles, a mail-order company that supplies bicycles, parts, and bicycling equipment and clothing.

2. The Oxford Omni, a downtown hotel that primarily serves convention and business travelers.

3. The Orange County Public Health Clinic, which is supported by tax revenues of Orange County and public donations.

4. The Harley-Davidson motorcycle company.

5. The Merck pharmaceutical company.

6. St. Sebastian's College, a small, private liberal arts college.

Required   Determine each client's competitive strategy and related critical success factors.

2–33 **Strategic Analysis, the Camera Industry**   Olympus, Kodak, Canon, and other firms in the market for low-cost cameras have experienced significant changes in recent years. The rate of introduction of new products has increased significantly. Entirely new products, such as the digital camera, are coming down in cost, so they are likely to be a factor in the low-cost segment of the market in the coming years. Additionally, product life cycles have fallen from several years to several months. The new products in this market are introduced at the same price as the products they replace, but the new products have some significant advances in functionality, such as integrated flash, zoom lens, and "red-eye" reduction. Thus, there are price points at which the customer expects to purchase a camera of a given functionality. In effect, the camera manufacturers compete to supply distinctive and therefore competitive functionality at the same cost as that of the previous models.

The manufacturing process for Olympus, one of the key firms in the industry, is representative of the others. Olympus makes extensive use of suppliers for components of the camera. Working closely with the suppliers, not only in a supplier's manufacturing process but also in the supplier's design of the parts, ensures the quality of the parts. Each supplier is, in effect, part of a team that includes the other suppliers and Olympus's own design and manufacturing operations.

Required

1. How does this type of competition differ from the Porter framework of cost leadership and differentiation?

2. Develop a value chain for Olympus camera company. What are the opportunities for cost reduction and/or value enhancement for Olympus?

2–34 **Strategic Analysis, the Balanced Scorecard, and Value-Chain Analysis; the Packaging Industry**   Dana Packaging Company is a large producer of paper and coated-paper containers with sales worldwide. The market for Dana's products has become very competitive in recent years because of the entrance of two large European competitors. In response, Dana has decided to enter new markets where the competition is less severe. The new markets are principally the high end of the packaging business for products that require more technological sophistication and better materials. Food and consumer products companies use these more advanced products to enhance the appeal of their high-end products. In particular, more sturdy, more colorful, more attractive, and better-sealing packaging has some appeal in the gourmet food business, especially in coffees, baked goods, and some dairy products. As a consequence of the shift, Dana has had to reorient its factory to produce the smaller batches of product associated with this new line of business. This change has required additional training for plant personnel and some upgrading of factory equipment to reduce setup time.

Dana's manufacturing process begins with pulp paper, which it produces in its own mills around the world. Some of the pulp material is purchased from recycling operators when price and availability are favorable. The pulp paper is then converted into paperboard, which is produced at Dana's own plants or purchased at times from outside vendors. In most cases, the paperboard plants are located near the pulp mills. At this point in the manufacturing process, the paperboard might be coated with a plastic material, a special embossing, or some other feature. This process is done at separate plants owned by Dana. On occasion, but infrequently when Dana's plants are very busy, the coating and embossing process is outsourced to other manufacturers. The final step in the process is filling the containers with the food product or consumer product. This step is done exclusively at Dana-owned plants. Dana has tried to maintain a high reputation for the quality of the filling process, stressing safety, cleanliness, and low cost to its customers.

Required

1. Describe Dana Company's new strategic competitive position.
2. Develop a value chain for Dana. What are its opportunities for cost reduction and/or value enhancement?
3. Dana's management is considering the use of a balanced scorecard for the firm. For each of the four areas within the balanced scorecard, list two or three examples of measurable critical success factors that should be included.

2–35 Strategic Positioning: The Airline Industry

Required Since 9/11/01, the airline industry has struggled with increased security-related costs and a sharp decline in the number of passengers. Which airlines do you believe are most competitive right now, and why? Describe the nature of the competition in the airline industry right now and into the future.

2–36 Value-Chain Analysis

Required Develop a value chain for the airline industry. Identify areas in which any given airline might find a cost advantage by modifying the value chain in some way. Similarly, identify areas of the value chain in which the airline might be able to develop additional value for the airline customer. For example, consider ways the ticketing operation might be reconfigured for either cost or value-added advantage.

2–37 Value-Chain Analysis
Sheldon Radio manufactures yacht radios, navigational equipment, and depth-sounding and related equipment from a small plant near New Bern, North Carolina. One of Sheldon's most popular products, making up 40 percent of its revenues and 35 percent of its profits, is a marine radio, model VF4500, which is installed on many of the new large boats produced in the United States. Production and sales average 500 units per month. Sheldon has achieved its success in the market through excellent customer service and product reliability. The manufacturing process consists primarily of the assembly of components purchased from various electronics firms plus a small amount of metalworking and finishing. The manufacturing operations cost $110 per unit. The purchased parts cost Sheldon $250, of which $130 is for parts that Sheldon could manufacture in its existing facility for $80 in materials for each unit plus an investment in labor and equipment that would cost $35,000 per month.

Sheldon is considering outsourcing the marketing, distributing, and servicing for its units to another North Carolina firm, Brashear Enterprises. This would save Sheldon $125,000 in monthly materials and labor costs. The cost of the contract would be $105 per radio.

Required

1. Prepare a value-chain analysis for Sheldon to assist in deciding whether to purchase or manufacture the parts and whether to contract out the marketing, distributing, and servicing of the units.
2. Should Sheldon (a) continue to purchase the parts or manufacture them and (b) continue to provide the marketing, distributing, and servicing or outsource these activities to Brashear? Explain your answer.

2–38 Strategy, Ethics
The tire business is becoming increasingly competitive as new manufacturers from Southeast Asia and elsewhere enter the global marketplace. At the same time, customer expectations for performance, tread life, and safety continue to increase. An increasing variety of vehicles, from the small and innovative gas/electric vehicles to the large SUVs, place more demands on tire designers and on tire manufacturing flexibility. Established brands such as Goodyear and Firestone must look to new ways to compete and maintain profitability.

Required

1. Is the competitive strategy of a global tire maker cost leadership or differentiation? Explain your answer.
2. What are the ethical issues, if any, for tire manufacturers?

2–39 Strategy, Value Chain In the late 1990s, the bike maker Cannondale Corp. faced a variety of key strategic issues. One was the firm's continued dependence on Shimano Inc. of Japan to supply many parts for its bikes, particularly the derailleur, brakes, and crankset. A particularly troublesome aspect of this situation was that Shimano's high-quality and highly innovative parts were relatively expensive. Cannondale wished to reduce its dependency on these outsourced parts. A second issue was the increasing competition from Trek Bicycle Corp and Specialized Bicycle Components Inc. for bicycles in the upper-end range of the market where Cannondale competed. Cannondale had built a successful business on the basis of high quality and innovative products. Its customers were bicyclists who expected the highest quality and most advanced features. Industry analysts predicted consolidation in the industry for manufacturers that use Shimano parts but cannot differentiate their products effectively; these bicycle makers will likely be forced to compete on price.

Required

1. Consider the use of Shimano parts as one aspect of the value chain for Cannondale. Describe Cannondale's current strategy. How should this strategy change, if at all, to compete effectively with Trek and Specialized?

2. Should Cannondale continue to outsource Shimano parts? Why or why not?

2–40 Value Chain; Harly-Davidson Harley-Davidson Inc. (HD) is one of the most recognized brands worldwide. The motorcycle manufacturer has one of the most loyal owner groups of any company. Unfortunately, the firm's success has come at a price. New customers are sometimes frustrated at long waiting lists for a new bike, and other potential new customers say they are turned off at the enthusiasm of some of the current owners. HD has a *Wild Bunch* reputation that drives some customers away. Other potential customers are simply intimidated at the idea of riding a 400+ pound Harley-Davidson. To deal with these concerns, and to try to encourage new owners, HD developed the Rider's Edge program in which anyone who could pass the Motorcycle Safety Foundation's written test and driving test would be eligible for instructions on how to ride a Harley. The instructions are provided by local dealers (at this point 35 of HD's 600+ dealers participate in the program).

Required Where does this program fit in the Harley-Davidson value chain? From a value chain perspective, how does the Rider's Edge program at Harley-Davidson support the firm's strategy?

2–41 The Balanced Scorecard; Strategy Map; Banking Carlos Aguilar, a CMA and consultant in Los Angeles, has been asked to help develop a balanced scorecard for a local medium-sized commercial bank. Carlos is familiar with the area around the bank and he knows that the bank has succeeded in part because of good community ties and customer service. The bank managers also realize that employee morale is an important factor in the success of the bank.

Required Carlos has asked you to help him in the initial phases of this project. Specifically, he has asked you to identify the balanced scorecard perspectives you would use for this bank, and a short list of four to five critical success factors that you would include in each perspective. Also, he is interested in knowing how the concept of a strategy map might be applicable for this client. Prepare a brief report for Carlos.

Solutions to Self-Study Problems

1. Value-Chain Analysis

The cost figures Jack has assembled suggest that the two teams' operations are generally quite similar, as expected in AA baseball. However, an important difference is the amount the Durham team spends on game-day operations, more than three times that of the Waynesboro Bulls. That difference has, in part, built a loyal set of fans in Durham where gate receipts average more than twice that of Waynesboro ($28,500 versus $12,350). The Buffaloes appear to have found an effective way to compete by drawing attendance to special game-day events and promotions.

To begin to compete more effectively and profitably, Waynesboro might consider additional value-added services, such as game-day activities similar to those offered in Durham. Waynesboro's costs per person are somewhat lower than Durham's, but its cost savings are probably not enough to offset the loss in revenues.

On the cost side, the comparison with Durham shows little immediate promise for cost reduction; Waynesboro spends on the average less than Durham in every category except management compensation. Perhaps this also indicates that instead of reducing costs, Waynesboro should spend *more* on fan development. The next step in Jack's analysis might be to survey Waynesboro fans to determine the level of satisfaction and to identify desired services that are not currently provided.

2. Competitive Strategy, Ethics

1. Enviro-Wear's strategy to this point is best described as a differentiation strategy, with which Frank has been able to succeed by differentiating his products as environmentally sound. This approach has appealed to a sufficient number of sportswear customers, and Enviro-Wear has grown accordingly. However, given the unfortunate jokes made by the sales manager and the rumors, the differentiation strategy is unlikely to continue to work; the offense of the jokes and the disclosure of some discrepancies in the manufacturing methods will likely undermine the appeal of environmentally sound manufacturing. Frank must work quickly to maintain differentiation, perhaps through a quick response that effectively shows the firm's commitment to quality and environmental issues. If that fails, he should quickly decide what change in strategy is necessary for the firm to survive and continue to succeed. He should consider a new strategy, perhaps based on cost leadership. The cost leadership strategy would bring the company into competition with different types of firms, and Frank must determine whether Enviro-Wear could successfully compete in that type of market.

2. This case has a number of ethical issues that are especially important to Frank as a CPA and a CMA with previous experience in public accounting practice. He should try to identify and understand the different options and the ethical aspects of the consequences of each option. For example, should Frank deny all charges against the company? Should he undertake an investigation to determine what his other sales managers think (do they have the same view as the offensive sales manager)? Do the firm's manufacturing processes really live up to the claimed quality and environmental standards? The relevant ethical issue requires communicating unfavorable as well as favorable information and disclosing fully all relevant information that could reasonably be expected to influence a consumer's understanding of the situation. To disguise or mislead consumers and others would conflict with the professional standards with which Frank is very familiar.

   Also at issue is whether it is appropriate to fire the offensive sales manager. Most would probably agree that the firing is appropriate since the sales manager has publicly put himself at odds with the firm's strategic goals. However, others might want to consider the consequences of the firing and its fairness to the employee.

CHAPTER THREE

Basic Cost Concepts

After studying this chapter, you should be able to . . .

1. Explain the cost driver concepts at the activity, volume, structural, and executional levels
2. Explain the cost concepts used in product and service costing
3. Demonstrate how costs flow through the accounts
4. Prepare an income statement for both a manufacturing firm and a merchandising firm
5. Explain the cost concepts related to the use of cost information in planning and decision making
6. Explain the cost concepts related to the use of cost information for management and operational control

Maker of such well-known brands as Tide detergent and Crest toothpaste, Procter & Gamble (P&G) is recognized as one of the leading consumer products companies in the world. It has achieved success through product excellence and continuous improvement.[1] One key area of continuous improvement is the firm's emphasis on cost reduction through product and process simplification. To accomplish this, P&G uses a concept that we study in this chapter: the influence of product and process complexity on overall costs. In the early 1990s, P&G had as many as 50 different varieties of some of its brands, including different size containers, flavors, and so on. In addition to variety, the number of trade promotions, discounts, rebates, and coupons that affected P&G's net price were complex. The high complexity in products and pricing increased manufacturing costs, inventory holding costs, selling and distribution costs, customer service costs, administrative and accounting costs, and other operating costs. Over a period of five years, P&G reduced its product variety by one-half, and its profits surged. P&G's message for consumer products companies is to compete with the best but watch out for product and process complexity!

The importance of product simplification to P&G is also reflected by its recent strategic decision not to complete a merger with the drug makers American Home Products Corp. and Warner-Lambert Co. At first glance, the marriage of these three powerful firms might seem to offer a good way to achieve market dominance and economies of scale. On second thought, however, would P&G's capabilities in developing and marketing consumer brands such as Tide detergent be a competitive advantage in developing and marketing drugs? The technologies and expertise from product development to product marketing and distribution are quite different. Moreover, P&G has established an enviable reputation as a consumer-goods company, but it does not have a reputation as a health-focused company (as, for example, does Johnson & Johnson). The firm is not likely to maintain a dual image. In fact, a successful strategy normally requires a single focused image in the marketplace, and the merger would dilute and confuse P&G's already excellent reputation as a consumer-products company. Again, simplicity and clarity of strategy are winners.

This chapter explains the importance of the key cost concepts used throughout the text. Of the four groups of key concepts, the first group consists of the basic concepts and relationships among cost objects and cost drivers (e.g., complexity as a cost driver and P&G's products as the cost objects). Each of the remaining three groups includes

[1] For further information on P&G's strategy and continuous improvement efforts, see "Too Many Choices," Emily Nelson, *The Wall Street Journal,* April 20, 2001, p. B1; and "Make it Simple," *Business Week,* September 9, 1996, pp. 96–104. For additional background on P&G's merger decision, see "P&G's Cold Feet May Have Averted a Misstep," *Business Week,* February 7, 2000, p. 42; and "Procter and Gamble: Just Say No to Drugs," *Business Week,* October 9, 2000, p. 128.

concepts related to the three management functions: product and service costing, planning and decision making, and management and operational control. The concepts related to strategic management are covered in Chapters 1 and 2.[2]

Cost Drivers, Cost Pools, and Cost Objects

A cost driver
is any factor that causes a change in the cost of an activity.

LEARNING OBJECTIVE 1
Explain the cost driver concepts at the activity, volume, structural, and executional levels.

A cost
is incurred when a resource is used for some purpose.

Cost pools
are the meaningful groups into which costs are often collected.

A cost object
is any product, service, customer, activity, or organizational unit to which costs are assigned for some management purpose.

Cost assignment
is the process of assigning costs to cost pools or from cost pools to cost objects.

A direct cost
can be conveniently and economically traced directly to a cost pool or a cost object.

An indirect cost
has *no* convenient or economical trace from the cost to the cost pool or from the cost pool to the cost object.

A critical first step in achieving a competitive advantage is to identify the key cost drivers in the firm or organization. A **cost driver** is any factor that has the effect of changing the level of total cost. For a firm that competes on the basis of cost leadership, management of the key cost drivers is essential. For example, to achieve its low-cost leadership in manufacturing P&G carefully watches the design and manufacturing factors that drive the costs of its products. It makes design improvements when necessary, and the manufacturing plants are designed and automated for the highest efficiency in using materials, labor, and equipment. For firms that are not cost leaders, the management of cost drivers may not be so critical, but attention to the key cost drivers contributes directly to the firm's success. For example, because an important cost driver for retailers is loss and damage to merchandise, most of them establish careful procedures for handling, displaying, and storing it.

A firm incurs a **cost** when it uses a resource for some purpose. For example, a company producing kitchen appliances has costs of materials (such as sheet metal and bolts for the enclosure), costs of manufacturing labor, and other costs. Often costs are collected into meaningful groups called **cost pools**. Individual costs can be grouped in many different ways, and therefore a cost pool can be defined in many different ways, including by type of cost (labor costs in one pool, material costs in another), by source (department 1, department 2, and so on), or by responsibility (manager 1, manager 2, and so on). For example, an assembly department or a product engineering department might be treated as a cost pool.

A **cost object** is any product, service, customer, activity, or organizational unit to which costs are assigned for some management purpose. Products, services, and customers are generally cost objects; manufacturing departments are considered either cost pools or cost objects, depending on whether management's main focus is on the costs for the products or for the manufacturing departments. The concept of cost objects is a broad concept. It also includes groups of products, services, departments, and customers; suppliers; telephone service providers; and so on. Any item to which costs can be traced and that has a key role in management strategy can be considered a cost object.

Cost Assignment and Cost Allocation: Direct and Indirect Costs

Cost assignment is the process of assigning costs to cost pools or from cost pools to cost objects. A **direct cost** can be conveniently and economically traced directly to a cost pool or a cost object. For example, the cost of materials required for a particular product is a direct cost because it can be traced directly to the product.

The materials cost is accumulated in cost pools (manufacturing departments) and then is traced to each product manufactured, which is the cost object. Similarly, an airline's cost of preparing a passenger's meal is a direct cost that can be traced to each passenger (the cost object). For a direct cost, the cost driver is the number of units of that object, for example, the number of cartons of Tide produced by P&G, or the number of passengers on Flight 617 for Delta Airlines. Total direct cost increases directly in proportion to the number of cartons or passengers.

In contrast, there is no convenient or economical way to trace an **indirect cost** from the cost to the cost pool or from the cost pool to the cost object. The cost of supervising manufacturing employees and the cost of handling materials are good examples of

[2] Useful information on cost terms is also available in the IMA's *Statement on Management Accounting No. 2*, "Management Accounting Terminology" (Montvale, NJ: Institute of Management Accountants, June 1, 1983).

costs that generally cannot be traced to individual products and therefore are indirect costs for the products. Similarly, the cost of fueling an aircraft is an indirect cost when the cost object is the individual airline customer since the aircraft's use of fuel cannot be traced directly to that customer. In contrast, if the cost object for the airline is the flight, the cost of fuel is a direct cost that can be traced directly to the aircraft's use of fuel for that flight.

Since indirect costs cannot be traced to the cost pool or cost object, the assignment for indirect costs is made by using cost drivers. For example, if the cost driver for materials handling cost is the number of parts, the total cost of materials handling can be assigned to each product on the basis of its total number of parts relative to the total number of parts in all other products. The result is that costs are assigned to the cost pool or cost object that caused the cost in a manner that is fairly representative of the way the cost is incurred. For example, a product with a large number of parts should bear a larger portion of the cost of materials handling than a product with fewer parts. Similarly, a department with a large number of employees should bear a large portion of the cost of supervision provided for all departments.

Cost allocation
is the assignment of indirect costs to cost pools and cost objects.

Allocation bases
are the cost drivers used to allocate costs.

The assignment of indirect costs to cost pools and cost objects is called **cost allocation,** a form of cost assignment in which direct tracing is not possible, so cost drivers are used instead. The cost drivers used to allocate costs are often called **allocation bases.** The relationships between costs, cost pools, cost objects, and cost drivers in appliance manufacturing are illustrated in Exhibit 3.1 and Exhibit 3.2. This simplified example includes two cost objects (dishwasher, washing machine), two cost pools (assembly department, packing department), and five cost elements (electric motor, materials handling, supervision, packing material, and final product inspection). The electric motor is traced to the assembly department and from there directly to the two products. Similarly, the packing material is traced directly to the packing department and from there directly to the two products. In contrast, since the cost of final inspection has no cost pool, it is traced directly to each of the two products. The two indirect costs, supervision and materials handling, are allocated to the two cost pools (assembly and packing departments) and are then allocated from the cost pools to the products (the allocation bases are shown in Exhibit 3.2).

Direct and Indirect Materials Costs

Direct materials cost
includes the cost of the materials in the product and a reasonable allowance for scrap and defective units.

Direct materials cost includes the cost of materials in the product or other cost object (less purchase discounts but including freight and related charges) and usually a reasonable allowance for scrap and defective units (e.g., if a part is stamped from strip

EXHIBIT 3.1

Relationships between Costs, Cost Pools, Cost Objects, and Cost Drivers in Appliance Manufacturing

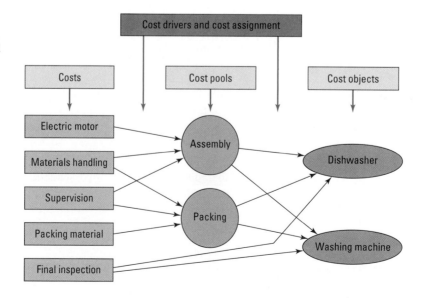

REAL-WORLD FOCUS   Replacing Indirect Costs with Direct Costs in the Textile Industry: Pluma, Inc.

Pluma, Inc., of Eden, North Carolina, manufactures textile products including fleece and jersey active wear. The firm recently announced cost-cutting measures including the elimination of 90 to 100 jobs involving indirect manufacturing activities such as machine repair and maintenance, human resources, and materials handling. The measures were taken to make Pluma more cost competitive. Those whose positions were eliminated were offered direct labor positions, that is, jobs in activities directly involved in manufacturing the firm's products.

This case illustrates that a high level of indirect costs can be a sign of poor cost management. The indirect costs are necessary for the manufacturing process but do not add value directly to the product. A firm such as Pluma does well to continually review the nature and extent of its indirect costs to determine whether some of the indirect activities causing them can be deleted and to focus on the direct activities that provide benefit to the customer.

Source: "Pluma to Cut Indirect Jobs to Reduce Annual Labor Costs," *Greensboro News and Record,* October 14, 1998.

EXHIBIT 3.2
Selected Examples of Costs, Cost Pools, Cost Objects, and Cost Drivers in Appliance Manufacturing

Cost	Cost Driver	Cost Pool	Cost Driver	Cost Object
Direct Costs				
Electric motor	Direct trace	Assembly department	Direct trace	Dishwasher and washing machine
Packing material	Direct trace	Packing department	Direct trace	Dishwasher and washing machine
Final inspection	Direct trace	Not applicable	Not applicable	Dishwasher and washing machine
Indirect Costs				
Supervision	Allocation base: Number of employees in the department	Assembly and packing departments	Allocation base: Direct labor-hours for each product	Dishwasher and washing machine
Materials handling	Allocation base: Number of parts in the product	Assembly and packing departments	Allocation base: Number of parts in the product	Dishwasher and washing machine

steel, the material lost in the stamping is ordinarily included as part of the product's direct materials).[3]

On the other hand, the cost of materials used in manufacturing that are not part of the finished product are **indirect materials cost.** Examples include supplies used by manufacturing employees, such as rags and small tools, or materials required by the machines, such as lubricant.[4]

Direct and Indirect Labor Costs

Direct labor cost includes the labor used to manufacture the product or to provide the service plus some portion of nonproductive time that is normal and unavoidable, such as coffee breaks and personal time. Other types of nonproductive labor that are

Indirect materials cost
refers to the cost of materials used in manufacturing that are not physically part of the finished product.

Direct labor cost
includes the labor used to manufacture the product or to provide the service.

---

[3] For additional information about the nature of direct materials cost, see *Statement on Management Accounting No. 4E,* "Practices and Techniques: Definition and Measurement of Direct Material Cost" (Montvale, NJ: Institute of Management Accountants, June 3, 1986).

[4] For convenience and simplicity, direct materials that are a very small part of materials cost, such as glue and nails, are sometimes not traced to each product but are included instead in indirect materials.

discretionary and planned, such as downtime, training, and setup time, usually are included not as direct labor but as indirect labor.[5]

Indirect labor costs provide a support role for manufacturing. Examples of indirect labor costs include supervision, quality control, inspection, purchasing and receiving, materials handling, janitorial labor, downtime, training, and cleanup. Note that an element of labor can sometimes be both direct and indirect, depending on the cost object; for example, labor for the maintenance and repair of equipment might be direct to the manufacturing department where the equipment is located but indirect to the products manufactured in that department.

Although these examples of direct and indirect costs are from a manufacturing setting, the concepts also apply to service companies. For example, in a restaurant where the cost object is each meal served, the food and food preparation costs are direct costs, but the costs of purchasing, handling, and storing food items are indirect costs. Similarly, in professional services firms such as law firms or accounting firms, the professional labor and materials costs for providing client service are direct costs, but the costs of research materials, nonprofessional support staff, and training professional staff are indirect costs.

Other Indirect Costs

In addition to labor and materials, other types of indirect costs are necessary to manufacture the product or provide the service. They include the costs of facilities, the equipment used to manufacture the product or provide the service, and any other support equipment, such as that used for materials handling.

All indirect costs—for indirect materials, indirect labor, and other indirect items—are commonly combined into a cost pool called **overhead**. In a manufacturing firm, it is called **factory overhead**.

The three types of costs—direct materials, direct labor, and overhead—are sometimes combined for simplicity and convenience. Direct materials and direct labor are sometimes considered together and called **prime costs**. Similarly, direct labor and overhead are often combined into a single amount called **conversion cost**. The labor component of total manufacturing costs for many firms that have highly automated operations is relatively low, and these firms often choose to place their strategic focus on materials and facilities/overhead costs by combining labor costs with overhead.

Types of Cost Drivers

Most firms, especially those following the cost leadership strategy, use cost management to maintain or improve their competitive position. Cost management requires a good understanding of how the total cost of a cost object changes as the cost drivers change. The four types of cost drivers are activity based, volume based, structural, and executional. Activity-based cost drivers are developed at a detailed level of operations and are associated with a given manufacturing activity (or activity in providing a service), such as machine setup, product inspection, materials handling, or packaging. In contrast, volume-based cost drivers are developed at an aggregate level, such as an output level for the number of units produced or the number of direct labor-hours used in manufacturing. Structural and executional cost drivers involve strategic and operational decisions that affect the relationship between these cost drivers and total cost. An example of cost drivers at Pennsylvania Blue Shield is shown in Exhibit 3.3.

Activity-Based Cost Drivers

Activity-based cost drivers are identified by using activity analysis, a detailed description of the specific activities performed in the firm's operations. The description

Indirect labor cost includes supervision, quality control, inspection, purchasing and receiving, and other manufacturing support costs.

All indirect costs are commonly combined into a single cost pool called **overhead** or, in a manufacturing firm, **factory overhead**.

Prime costs refer to direct materials and direct labor that are sometimes considered together.

Conversion cost refers to direct labor and overhead combined into a single amount.

[5] For additional information about the nature of direct labor cost, see *Statement on Management Accounting No. 4C*, "Practices and Techniques: Definition and Measurement of Direct Labor Cost," (Montvale, N.J.: Institute of Management Accountants, June 13, 1985).

EXHIBIT 3.3
Costs, Cost Pools, Cost Objects, and Cost Drivers at Pennsylvania Blue Shield

Source: Angela Norkiewicz, "Nine Steps to Implementing ABC," *Management Accounting,* April 1994, pp. 28–33.

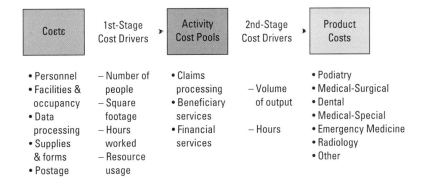

includes each step in manufacturing the product or in providing the service. For each activity, a cost driver is developed to explain how the costs incurred for that activity change. For example, the activities and cost drivers for a bank are illustrated in Exhibit 3.4. The total cost to the bank is affected by the cost driver for each activity.

The detailed description of the firm's activities helps the firm achieve its strategic objectives by enabling it to develop more accurate costs for its products and/or services. The activity analysis also helps improve operational and management control in the firm since performance at the detailed level can be monitored and evaluated, for example, by (1) identifying which activities are contributing value to the customer and which are not and (2) focusing attention on those activities that are most costly or that differ from expectations. These two benefits are achieved by activity-based costing and activity-based management, which are explained in Chapter 5.

Volume-Based Cost Drivers

Many types of costs are volume based, such as direct materials and direct labor. Total cost for a volume-based cost has a nonlinear relationship with the volume-based cost driver, which is the number of units of output for the product or service. As illustrated in Exhibit 3.5, at low values for the cost driver, costs increase at a decreasing rate, due in part to factors such as more efficient use of resources and higher productivity through learning. The pattern of increasing costs at a decreasing rate is often referred to as *increasing marginal productivity,* which means that the inputs are used more productively or more efficiently as manufacturing output increases.

EXHIBIT 3.4
Bank Activities and Cost Drivers

Activity	Cost Driver
Provide ATM service	Number of ATM transactions
Provide cashier service	Number of banking customers using cashier
Open and close customer accounts	Number of accounts opened or closed
Advise customers on banking services	Number of customers advised
Issue traveler's checks	Number of requests for checks
Update customer account balances	Number of accounts updated
Investigate unusual transactions	Number of transactions investigated
Periodically test controls over cash	Number of tests; based on company policy
Prepare applications for new loans	Number of loan applications prepared
Process loan applications	Number of loan applications processed
Prepare approved loans and disburse funds	Number of loans approved
Mail customer statements	Number of accounts
Process interbank transfers of funds	Number of transfers
Respond to customer inquiries	Number of inquiries

EXHIBIT 3.5
Total Cost and the Effect of Capacity Limits

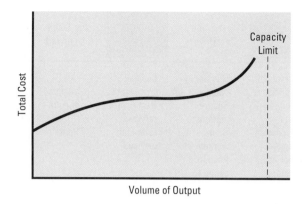

At higher levels of the cost driver, costs begin to increase at an increasing rate, due in part to inefficiency associated with operating nearer the limit of capacity; the less efficient resources are now being used, overtime may be required, and so on. This cost behavior in the higher levels of the cost driver is said to satisfy the *law of diminishing marginal productivity.*

The nonlinear cost relationships depicted in Exhibit 3.5 present some difficulties in estimating costs and in calculating total costs since linear, algebraic relationships cannot be used. Fortunately, we are often interested in only a relatively small range of activity for the cost driver. For example, we might know in a certain instance that the *volume-based* cost driver will fall somewhere between 3,500 and 3,600 units of product output. We observe that within this range, the total cost curve is approximately linear. The range of the cost driver in which the actual value of the cost driver is expected to fall and for which the relationship is assumed to be approximately linear is called the **relevant range**.

This simplification process is illustrated in Exhibit 3.6 and Exhibit 3.7. Exhibit 3.6 shows the curved actual total cost line and the relevant range of 3,500 to 3,600 units; Exhibit 3.7 shows the linear approximation of actual total cost; within the relevant range, the behavior of total cost approximates that shown in Exhibit 3.6. Note that the cost line above 3,600 and below 3,500 in Exhibit 3.7 is in color to indicate that this portion of the line is not used to approximate total cost because it is outside the relevant range.

The **relevant range** is the range of the cost driver in which the actual value of the cost driver is expected to fall and for which the relationship is assumed to be approximately linear.

Variable cost is the change in total cost associated with each change in the quantity of the cost driver.

Fixed and Variable Costs

Total cost is made up of variable costs and fixed costs. **Variable cost** is the change in total cost associated with each change in the quantity (volume) of output. Common

EXHIBIT 3.6   **Total Cost and the Relevant Range**

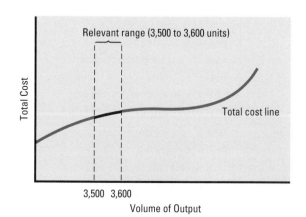

EXHIBIT 3.7   **Linear Approximation for Actual Cost Behavior, within the Relevant Range**

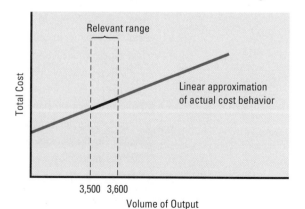

Fixed cost
is the portion of the total cost that does not change with a change in the quantity of the cost driver within the relevant range.

examples of variable costs are costs of direct materials and direct labor. In contrast, **fixed cost** is that portion of the total cost that does not change with output within the relevant range. *Total* fixed costs and *unit* variable costs are expected to remain approximately constant within the relevant range. Fixed cost is illustrated as the horizontal dashed line at $3,000 in Exhibit 3.8. Variable cost is $1 per unit, total cost is the upward-sloping line, and total variable cost is the difference between total cost and fixed cost. Total cost of $6,500 at 3,500 units is made up of fixed cost ($3,000) plus total variable cost (3,500 × $1 = $3,500); similarly, total cost at 3,600 units is $6,600 ($3,000 fixed cost plus 3,600 × $1 = $3,600 variable cost).

Fixed costs include many indirect costs, especially facility costs (depreciation or rent, insurance, taxes on the plant building, and so on), production supervisors' salaries, and other manufacturing support costs that do not change with the number of units produced. However, some indirect costs are variable since they change with the number of units produced. An example is lubricant for machines. The term **mixed cost** is used to refer to total cost that includes costs for both variable and fixed components as illustrated.

Mixed cost
is the term used to refer to total cost when total cost includes both variable and fixed cost components.

The determination of whether a cost is variable depends on the nature of the cost object. In manufacturing firms, the cost object is typically the product. In service firms, however, the cost object is often difficult to define because the service can have a number of qualitative as well as quantitative dimensions. Let's develop cost objects for one type of service firm, a hospital, which could use a number of measures of output including the number of patients served, the number successfully treated, and so on. However, a common approach in hospitals is to use the number of patient-days since this measure most closely matches the way the hospital incurs costs.

It has sometimes been said that all costs are variable in the long run; that is, with enough time, any cost can be changed. While it is true that many fixed costs do change over time (for example, the cost of rent might increase from year to year), that does not mean these costs are variable. A variable cost is a cost for which *total costs change with changes in the volume of output*. Fixed costs are defined for a period of time rather than in relationship to volume of output, and it is assumed that fixed costs will not change during this period of time which is usually taken to be a year.

Step Costs

A cost is said to be a **step cost** when it varies with the cost driver but in steps.

A cost is said to be a **step cost** when it varies with the cost driver but does so in steps (Exhibit 3.9). Step costs are characteristic of certain clerical tasks, such as order filling and claims processing. For example, if a warehouse clerk can fill 100 orders in a day, 10 clerks will be needed to process approximately 1,000 orders; as demand exceeds 1,000 orders, an eleventh clerk must be added. The steps correspond to specific levels of the cost driver for which an additional clerk is required; in effect, each step

EXHIBIT 3.8 **Total Cost, Total Variable Cost, and Fixed Cost**

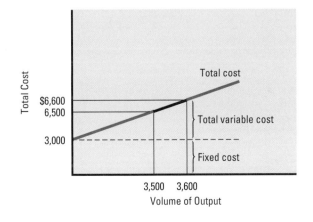

EXHIBIT 3.9 **A Step Cost**

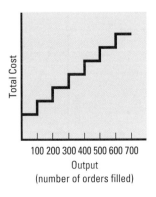

corresponds to one additional clerk. The steps will be relatively narrow if clerks are added for relatively small increases in the cost driver; the steps will be wider for large increases.

Unit Cost and Marginal Cost

Unit cost (or **average cost**) is the total manufacturing costs (materials, labor, and overhead) divided by units of output. It is a useful concept in setting prices and in evaluating product profitability, but it can be subject to some misleading interpretations. To properly interpret unit cost, we must distinguish *unit variable* costs, which do not change as output changes, from *unit fixed costs*, which do change as output changes. See Exhibit 3.10. For example, a driver's cost per mile is likely lower for a person who keeps a car for 200,000 miles than it is for a person who keeps a car for only 40,000 miles because the fixed costs are spread over more miles. These relationships are illustrated graphically in Exhibit 3.11. The management accountant is careful in using the terms *average cost* and *unit cost* because of the potential for misleading interpretations.

The term **marginal cost** is used to describe the additional cost incurred as the cost driver increases by one unit. Under the assumption of linear cost within the relevant range, the concept of marginal cost is equivalent to the concept of unit variable cost.

Structural and Executional Cost Drivers

Structural and executional cost drivers are used to facilitate strategic and operational decision making.[6] **Structural cost drivers** are strategic in nature because they involve plans and decisions that have long-term effects. Issues such as the following should be considered:

1. Scale. How much should be invested? How large should the firm become? Larger firms have lower overall costs as a result of economies of scale. For example, a retail firm such as Wal-Mart or The Gap must determine how many new stores to open in a given year to achieve its strategic objectives and compete effectively as a retailer.

2. Experience. How much prior experience does the firm have in its current and planned products and services? The more experience, the lower the development, manufacturing, and distribution costs are likely to be. For example, a manufacturer such as

[6] See John K. Shank and Vijay Govindarajan, *Strategic Cost Analysis* (New York: Free Press, 1993), pp. 20–22.

Unit cost (or **average cost**) is the total manufacturing cost (materials, labor, and overhead) divided by units of output.

Marginal cost is the additional cost incurred as the cost driver increases by one unit.

Structural cost drivers are strategic in nature and involve plans and decisions that have a long-term effect with regard to issues such as scale, experience, technology, and complexity.

EXHIBIT 3.10
Illustration of Total Fixed Cost and Variable Cost per Unit

	Fixed Cost		Variable Cost	
Units of output	10,000	20,000	10,000	20,000
Per unit	$ 10	$ 5	$ 8	$ 8
Total	100,000	100,000	80,000	160,000

EXHIBIT 3.11
Average Variable Cost and Average Fixed Cost

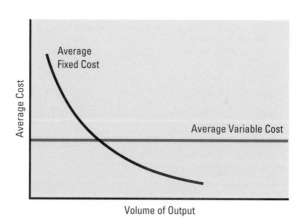

REAL-WORLD FOCUS   Survey of Practice: Cost Classification in U.S. Firms

A survey of 350 U.S. manufacturing firms provides the following results regarding how these firms treat selected indirect cost categories (the data show the percentage of the firms treating each type of indirect cost as a variable, step, or fixed cost).

Activity	Variable	Step Cost	Fixed	Other
Setup labor	49%	20%	12%	19%
Material handling labor	40	29	15	16
Quality control labor	28	30	25	17
Repairs and maintenance	23	36	24	17
Tooling	24	27	25	24
Energy	21	36	23	20
Supervision	3	22	58	17
Engineering	5	18	61	16
Data processing	2	12	69	17
Building occupancy	1	5	77	17
Taxes and insurance	1	9	74	16
Depreciation—machinery and equipment	1	6	78	15
Work-in-process inventory carrying cost	19	25	24	32

Source: Il-Woon Kim and Ja Song, "Accounting Practices in Three Countries," *Management Accounting,* August 1990, p. 28.

REAL-WORLD FOCUS   Is It Fixed or Variable: Auto Insurance, Lincoln Electric, and TV Celebrities

CAR INSURERS SET MILEAGE-BASED RATES

Patrick Butler is on a quest. On discovering that women drove fewer miles than men but paid the same insurance rates, he began to champion a movement to have insurers adopt mileage-based rates. A representative of one insurer that has pilot-tested the program says, "This is absolutely the future of auto insurance." In effect, Patrick is converting what has been a fixed cost into a variable cost for auto insurance.

CROSS-TRAINING AT LINCOLN ELECTRIC COMPANY

To retain skilled employees instead of letting them go when demand falls, Lincoln Electric trains employees for other tasks in the company. The Cleveland-based manufacturer of welding and cutting parts has integrated the approach in all its operations, so that it can guarantee employment for all employees who have been with the company for three or more years. This policy has worked for 60 years! The effect of the policy on cost is that labor expense, while fixed in total expenditure, is in reality a variable expense. Labor is flexible and can be moved from job to job or plant to plant as demand dictates; that is, labor cost at the plant level fluctuates with demand at each plant, while total labor cost at the firm stays fixed.

Other companies such as Nestle and Apex Precision Technology accomplish the same goal of keeping their employees as demand fluctuates by using part-time arrangements with the employees. Thus, instead of incurring a fixed cost for labor, the company's total labor costs are flexible and vary with demand, as part-time labor is added when needed.

TV CELEBRITY PAY BASED ON COST-PER-VIEWER?

TV celebrities such as David Letterman, Conan O'Brien, and Paula Zahn negotiate for multimillion dollar salaries based on their viewer drawing ability. These salaries are of course fixed in amount. While Letterman is the clear leader with $16 million per year, to O'Brien's $8 million, and Zahn's $2 million, they all have approximately the same amount of pay per viewer. The cost per viewer is $3.68, $3.14, and $3.70 for Letterman, O'Brien, and Zahn, respectively. Are these salaries fixed or variable? It would appear that the number of viewers is a key driver in the salary negotiations each year for these celebrities. From this perspective, these salaries might be viewed as variable costs. If the networks' advertising revenues are also based on number of viewers, then treating celebrities this way makes sense. It also might be used to explain why certain celebrities have higher or lower per-viewer rates, due presumably to different revenue rates for the shows; advertisers might be willing to pay more for a certain type of viewer.

Source: Russell Gold and Christopher Oster, "New Push to Let Car Insurers Set Mile-Based Rate," *The Wall Street Journal,* February 20, 2002, p. B1; Clare Ansberry, "In the Workplace, Jobs Morph to Suit Rapid Pace of Change," *The Wall Street Journal,* March 22, 2002, p. 1; Lisa De Moraes, "Conan the Cost: NBC's Thrifty Numbers Game," *The Washington Post,* February 8, 2002, p. C7.

Cost Management in Action   Product Complexity in Consumer Goods Manufacturing

In the mid-1990s, a large consumer goods manufacturer moved its customer base from department and specialty stores to mass merchandising. This strategic change required it to reconsider the complexity of its product lines (numbers of different products, patterns, and colors). The firm approached a large consulting firm to help it identify the nature of the complexity and some desired solutions.

The consulting firm observed the following:

1. As many as 10 different vendors provided certain purchased items.

2. Of the firm's customers after the strategic shift, 98 percent were responsible for only 7 percent of sales volume.

3. The wide variety of pricing discounts and promotional programs added complexity to the accounts receivable collection process because of increased disputes over customers' balances.

4. Seventy-five percent of the firm's volume involved products with five color combinations.

5. Customers' demands for fast delivery of new orders had caused a shift in manufacturing to smaller batch sizes and more frequent equipment setups. Thus, total setup-related costs increased.

As a consultant to the consumer goods manufacturer, what changes would you make in its operations and cost management practices?

(Refer to comments on Cost Management in Action at the end of the chapter.)

Hewlett-Packard uses existing manufacturing methods as much as possible for new products to reduce the time and cost necessary for workers to become proficient at manufacturing the new product. Additionally, health care management firms such as Columbia/HCA use their knowledge of experience-related cost drivers to reduce the time and cost necessary to improve the profitability of newly acquired hospitals.

3. Technology. What process technologies are used in designing, manufacturing, and distributing the product or service? New technologies can reduce these costs significantly. For example, manufacturers such as Procter & Gamble use computer technology to monitor the quantities of its products that its customers (typically, large retailers) have on hand so that it can promptly restock these products as needed. Technological innovation at Intel has lowered the cost of computing dramatically by improving the capability of microprocessors used in personal computers. While the capability of the microprocessors has increased exponentially, their manufacturing costs per unit have not changed significantly. This example of Moore's law describes the costs of digital technology falling (by one-half) every 18 to 24 months.

4. Complexity. What is the firm's level of complexity? How many different products does the firm have? As noted in the opening discussion of Procter & Gamble, firms with many products have higher costs of scheduling and managing the production process, as well as the upstream costs of product development and the downstream costs of distribution and service. These firms often use activity-based costing to better identify the costs and therefore the profitability of their different products, suppliers, and customers.

Strategic analyses using structural cost drivers help the firm improve its competitive position. These analyses include value-chain analysis and activity-based management. Value-chain analysis can help the firm assess the long-term consequences of its current or planned commitment to a structural cost driver. For example, the growth in size and capability of parts manufacturers for automakers should cause the automakers to reassess whether they should outsource the manufacture of certain parts.

Executional cost drivers
are factors the firm can manage in the short term to reduce costs, such as workforce involvement, design of the production process, and supplier relationships.

Executional cost drivers are factors the firm can manage in short-term, operational decision making to reduce costs. They include the following:

1. Workforce involvement. Are the employees dedicated to continual improvement and quality? This workforce commitment will lower costs. Firms with strong employee relationships, such as Federal Express, can reduce operating costs significantly.

2. Design of the production process. Can the layout of equipment and processes and the scheduling of production be improved? Speeding up the flow of product

through the firm can reduce costs. Innovators in manufacturing technology, such as Motorola and Allen-Bradley, can reduce manufacturing costs significantly.

3. Supplier relationships. Can the cost, quality, or delivery of materials and purchased parts be improved to reduce overall costs? Wal-Mart and Toyota, among other firms, maintain a low-cost advantage partially by agreements with their suppliers that they will provide products or parts that meet the companies' explicit requirements as to their quality, timeliness of delivery, and other features.

Plant managers study executional cost drivers to find ways to reduce costs. Such studies are done as a part of operational control, which is covered in Part Four.

Cost Concepts for Product and Service Costing

LEARNING OBJECTIVE 2
Explain the cost concepts used in product and service costing.

Accurate information about the cost of products and services is important in each management function: strategic management, planning and decision making, management and operational control, and financial statement preparation. The cost accounting systems to provide this information are explained in this section.

Cost Accounting for Products and Services

Cost accounting systems for the firms that manufacture products and for the merchandising firms that resell those products differ significantly. Merchandising firms include both retailers, which sell the final product to the consumer, and wholesalers, which distribute the product to retailers. Service firms often have little or no inventory, so their costing systems are relatively simple.

Product Costs and Period Costs

Product inventory for both manufacturing and merchandising firms is treated as an asset on their balance sheets. So long as the inventory has market value, it is considered an asset until the inventory is sold; then the cost of the inventory is transferred to the income statement as **cost of goods sold,** an expense. This is the life cycle of product cost, from design and manufacture (or purchase and stocking, in the merchandising firm) to sales and service, that is, from asset on the balance sheet to expense on the income statement.

Cost of goods sold
is the cost of the product transferred to the income statement when inventory is sold.

Product costs
for a manufacturing firm include *only* the costs necessary to complete the product: direct materials, direct labor, and factory overhead.

Product costs for a manufacturing firm include *only* the costs necessary to complete the product:

1. Direct materials. The materials used to manufacture the product, which become a physical part of it.

2. Direct labor. The labor used to manufacture the product.

3. Factory overhead. The indirect costs for materials, labor, and facilities used to support the manufacturing process.

Product costs for a merchandising firm include the cost to purchase the product plus the transportation costs paid by the retailer or wholesaler to get the product to the location from which it will be sold or distributed.

Period costs
are all nonproduct expenditures for managing the firm and selling the product.

LEARNING OBJECTIVE 3
Demonstrate how costs flow through the accounts.

All other expenditures for managing the firm and selling the product are expensed in the period in which they are incurred; for that reason, they are called **period costs.** These costs are expensed because there is no expectation that they will produce future value; in contrast, the sale of inventory will produce future earnings. Period costs primarily include the general, selling, and administrative costs that are necessary for the management of the company but are *not* involved directly or indirectly in the manufacturing process (or in the purchase of the products for resale). Advertising costs, data processing costs, and executive and staff salaries are good examples of period costs. See Exhibit 3.12. In a manufacturing or a merchandising firm, period costs are also sometimes referred to as *operating expenses* or *selling and administrative expenses.* In a service firm, these costs are often referred to as *operating expenses.*

EXHIBIT 3.12 Furniture Manufacturing Costs: Variable/Fixed, Direct/Indirect, and Product/Period Costs

The manufacture of dining table sets is used to provide examples of costs for each cost concept: variable/fixed, direct/indirect, and product/period. The furniture manufacturer for these dining table sets has organized its manufacturing by product line: dining table sets, upholstered chairs, sofas, bedroom furniture, end tables, and outdoor furniture. Each product line has its own manufacturing team although much of the equipment in the plant is shared among product lines (e.g., multiple product lines use the table saws). The company owns its retail sales outlets, each of which offers all of the firm's products. The cost object in this illustration is the *product line* for dining table sets (*not* each dining set produced).

Variable/Fixed, Direct/Indirect, and Product/Period Costs for the Product Line, Dining Table Sets

	Product Cost		Period (Nonproduct) Cost
	Direct	**Indirect**	
Variable	Wood and fabric	Power for table saws	Sales commissions for sales
Fixed	Salary of manufacturing supervisor for dining table sets	Depreciation on table saws	Insurance and depreciation on company-owned sales outlets

Notes: This illustration is based on the *cost object*, the product line for dining table *sets*. The examples would not change if we had chosen instead to have the cost object be *each set* manufactured except that the manufacturing supervisor's salary would no longer be a direct fixed product cost. It would become an *indirect* fixed product cost because the salary can be traced to the product line but not to each table set manufactured.

Manufacturing, Merchandising, and Service Costing

The cost flows in manufacturing, retail, and service firms are illustrated in Exhibits 3.13, 3.14, 3.15a, and 3.15b. The left-hand side of Exhibit 3.13 presents a graphic representation of the flows of costs for a manufacturing firm. The first step of the manufacturing process is to purchase materials. The second step involves adding the three cost elements—materials used, labor, and overhead—to work in process. In the third step, as production is completed, the production costs that have been accumulating in the Works in Process account are transferred to the Finished Goods Inventory account and from there to the Cost of Goods Sold account when the products are sold.

In the merchandising firm, shown on the right-hand side of Exhibit 3.13, the process is somewhat simpler. It purchases merchandise and places it in the Product Inventory account. When sold, it is transferred to the Cost of Goods Sold account. The merchandising and manufacturing firms in Exhibit 3.13 are shown side by side to emphasize the difference: The merchandising firm purchases inventory but the manufacturing firm manufactures inventory using materials, labor, and overhead.

Manufacturing firms use three inventory accounts: (1) **Materials Inventory,** where the cost of the supply of materials used in the manufacturing process is kept; (2) **Work-in-Process Inventory,** which contains all costs put into manufacture of products that are started but not complete at the financial statement date; and (3) **Finished Goods Inventory,** which holds the cost of goods that are ready for sale. Each account has its own beginning and ending balances.

Materials Inventory
keeps the cost of the supply of materials used in the manufacturing process or to provide the service.

Work-in-Process Inventory
contains all costs put into the manufacture of products that are started but not complete at the financial statement date.

Finished Goods Inventory
holds the cost of goods that are ready for sale.

An inventory formula relates the inventory accounts, as follows:

Beginning inventory + Cost added = Cost transferred out + Ending Inventory

The terms *cost added* and *cost transferred out* have different meanings, depending on which inventory account is being considered:

Inventory Account	Cost Added	Cost Transferred Out
Materials Inventory	Purchases of materials	Cost of materials used in production
Work-in-Process Inventory	1. Cost of materials used	Cost of goods manufactured, for
	2. Labor cost	products completed this period
	3. Overhead cost	
Finished Goods Inventory	Costs of goods manufactured	Cost of goods sold

EXHIBIT 3.13
**Cost Flows in Manufacturing
and Merchandising Firms**

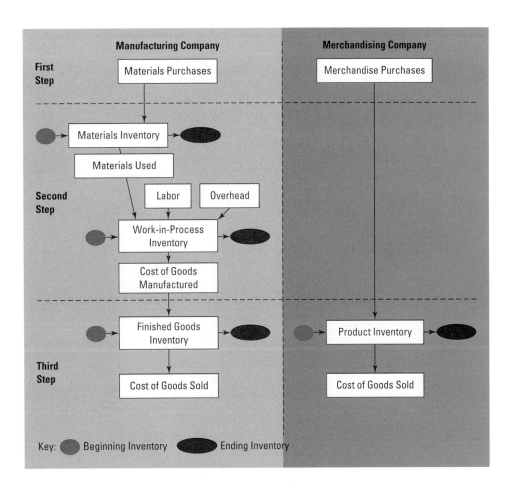

The inventory formula is a useful concept to show how materials, labor, and over-head costs flow into Work-in-Process Inventory, then into Finished Goods Inventory, and finally into Cost of Goods Sold. Exhibit 3.14 illustrates the effects of the cost flows on the accounts involved when the manufacturing firm converts materials into finished products and then sells them and when the merchandising firm sells merchandise inventory.

LEARNING OBJECTIVE 4
Prepare an income statement for both a manufacturing firm and a merchandising firm.

The illustration in Exhibit 3.14 shows the accounts for a manufacturing company that begins the period with $10 in Materials Inventory, $10 in Work-in-Process Inventory, $20 in Finished Goods Inventory. During the period, it purchases $70 of materials, uses $75 of materials and $80 of direct labor, and spends $100 for factory overhead. Also during the period, $215 of goods are completed and transferred from the Work-in-Process Inventory account to the Finished Goods Inventory account, and $210 of goods are sold. These events leave ending inventories of $5 in the materials account, $50 in the work-in-process account, and $25 in the finished goods account. The merchandising company purchased merchandise of $250 and made sales of $230, and its Merchandise Inventory account increases from $40 to $60.

Exhibit 3.15a shows how the accounting relationships are finally represented in the income statements for the two types of firms. Note that the manufacturing firm requires a two-part calculation for cost of goods sold: the first part combines the cost flows affecting the Work-in-Process Inventory account to determine the amount of **Cost of Goods Manufactured,** that is, the cost of the goods finished and transferred out of work in process during this period. The second part combines the cost flows for the Finished Goods Inventory account to determine the amount of the cost of the goods sold and net income, assuming $50 of selling expense for the manufacturing firm and $40 of operating expense for the merchandising firm.

Cost of Goods Manufactured
is the cost of goods finished and transferred out of the Work-in-Process Inventory account this period.

EXHIBIT 3.14
Account Relationships for Manufacturing and Merchandising Companies

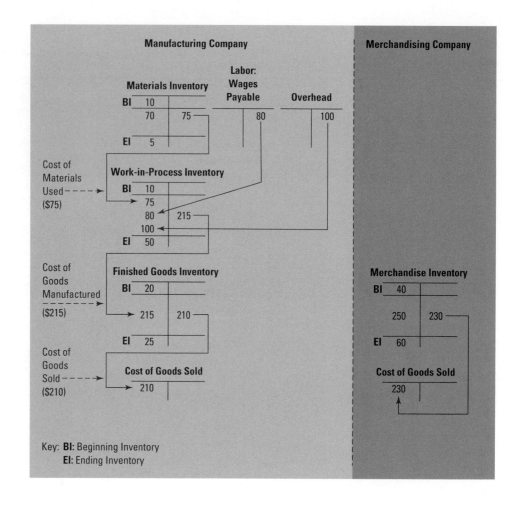

Exhibit 3.15b shows the relatively simple income statement for a service firm with $300 in sales, $60 in materials costs, $40 in labor costs, and $100 in other operating expenses for an operating income of $100.

Cost Concepts for Planning and Decision Making

LEARNING OBJECTIVE 5
Explain the cost concepts related to the use of cost information in planning and decision making.

To facilitate management decision making and planning, the management accountant provides relevant, timely, and accurate information at a reasonable cost. Relevance is the most critical of the decision-making concepts; timeliness, accuracy, and cost are unimportant if the information is irrelevant.

Relevant Cost

The concept of relevant cost arises when the decision maker must choose between two or more options. To determine which option is best, the decision maker must determine which option offers the highest benefit, usually in dollars. Thus, the decision maker needs information on relevant costs. A **relevant cost** has two properties: (1) it *differs for each decision option* and (2) it will be *incurred in the future*. If a cost is the same for each option, including it in the decision only wastes time and increases the possibility for simple errors. Costs that have already been incurred or committed are irrelevant because there is no longer any discretion about them.

A **relevant cost** has two properties: (1) *it differs for each decision option* and (2) it will be *incurred in the future.*

Differential Cost

A **differential cost** is a cost that differs for each decision option and is therefore relevant for the decision maker's choice. A differential cost arises either as the direct cost of selecting an option (the purchase cost of a new machine is the direct effect of replacing

A **differential cost** is a cost that differs for each decision option and is therefore relevant.

EXHIBIT 3.15a   **Statements for Manufacturing and Merchandising Firms**

Manufacturing, Inc. Statement of Cost of Goods Manufactured For the Year Ended December 31, 2004			(No need for a Cost of Goods Manufactured Statement for Merchandising Inc.)
Direct Materials			
Beginning Inventory	$ 10		
Purchases	70		
Direct Materials Available	$ 80		
Ending Direct Materials Inventory	5		
Direct Materials Used		$ 75	
Direct Labor		80	
Factory Overhead		100	
Total Manufacturing Cost		$255	
Add: Beginning Work-in-Process Inventory		10	
Total Manufacturing Cost to Account for		265	
Less: Ending Work-in-Process Inventory		50	
Cost of Goods Manufactured		$215	

Manufacturing, Inc. Income Statement For the Year Ended December 31, 2004				Merchandising, Inc. Income Statement For the Year Ended December 31, 2004		
Sales		$300		Sales		$300
Cost of Goods Sold				Cost of Goods Sold		
Beginning Finished Goods Inventory	$ 20			Beginning Finished Goods Inventory	$ 40	
Cost of Goods Manufactured	215			Purchases	250	
Cost of Goods available for sale	235			Cost of Goods available for sale	$290	
Ending Finished Goods Inventory	25	210		Ending Finished Goods Inventory	60	230
Gross Margin		90		Gross Margin		$ 70
Selling and Administrative expenses		50		Operating expenses		40
Net Income		$ 40		Net Income		$ 30

EXHIBIT 3.15b
Income Statement for a Service Firm

Service, Inc. Income Statement For the Year Ended December 31, 2004		
Revenues		$300
Operating Expenses		
Materials	$ 60	
Labor	40	
Other Operating Expenses	100	200
Operating Income		$100

an old machine) or as the indirect cost associated with the choice (replacing a machine creates a difference in certain costs, such as those for maintenance or electric power).

Opportunity Cost

Opportunity cost
is the benefit lost when choosing one option precludes receiving the benefits from an alternative option.

Opportunity cost is the benefit lost when choosing one option precludes receiving the benefits from an alternative option. For example, if a sales manager chooses to forgo an order from a new customer to ensure that a current customer's order is filled on time, the potential profit from the lost order is the manager's *opportunity cost* for this decision. Ensuring the loyalty of an existing customer has a difficult-to-quantify but significant long-term value, but the short-term loss of the new order, while quantifiable, is not so important.

Sunk costs
are costs that have been incurred
or committed in the past and are
therefore irrelevant.

Sunk Cost

Sunk costs are costs that have been incurred or committed in the past and are therefore irrelevant for decision making because the decision maker no longer has discretion over them. For example, if a company purchased a new machine without warranty that failed the next day, the purchase price is *irrelevant* for the present decision to replace or to repair the machine. Only future costs are relevant, and the purchase price of the recently acquired machine has no effect on future costs.

An important additional issue related to sunk costs must be considered. There is apparently an inherent bias for decision makers to include sunk costs as relevant to the analysis. Studies by psychologists Kahneman and Tversky found that decision makers are more willing to invest money to "recover" sunk costs than to invest the money to earn the same net return. Similarly, a study by Whyte found that decision makers tend to escalate commitments to sunk costs. The practical implication of these findings is that the management accountants must be particularly careful to develop information for decision makers that separates sunk costs from differential future costs.[7]

Attributes of Cost Information for Decision Making

Accuracy

The experienced decision maker does not use accounting information without considering the potential for inaccuracy. Inaccurate data can mislead, resulting in potentially costly mistakes. A primary way to ensure accurate data for decision making is to design and monitor an effective system of internal accounting controls. The system of **internal accounting controls** is a set of policies and procedures that restrict and guide activities in the processing of financial data with the objective to prevent or detect errors and fraudulent acts.

The system of **internal accounting controls**
is a set of policies and procedures
that restrict and guide activities in
the processing of financial data
with the objective to prevent or
detect errors and fraudulent acts.

Timeliness

Cost management information must be available to the decision maker in a timely manner to facilitate effective decision making. The cost of delay can be significant in many decisions, such as in filling rush orders that may be lost if the necessary information is not timely. The cost of identifying quality defects *early* in a manufacturing process can be far less than the cost of materials and labor wasted until the defect is detected later in the process.

Cost and Value of Cost Information

Thinking of cost management information as having a certain cost and value emphasizes that the management accountant is an information specialist, very much like other financial professionals, such as tax advisers, financial planners, and consultants. The management accountant provides an information service that has both a preparation cost and a value to the user. The preparation costs for cost management information should be controlled as should any other service provided within the firm. These preparation costs are likely influenced by the desired accuracy, timeliness, and level of aggregation; when increased accuracy, timeliness, and detail are desired, the preparation costs are higher.

Cost Concepts for Management and Operational Control

LEARNING OBJECTIVE 6
Explain the cost concepts related to the use of cost information for management and operational control.

A crucial role for cost management information is to provide a basis for motivating and rewarding managers' and employees' efforts and effectiveness. Key cost concepts applicable for this management function include controllability and risk preferences.

[7] Daniel Kahneman and Amos Tversky, "Prospect Theory: An Analysis of Decisions under Risk," *Econometrica,* March 1979, pp. 263–91; and Glen Whyte, "Escalating Commitment to a Course of Action: A Reinterpretation," *Academy of Management Review,* 1986, pp. 311–21.

REAL-WORLD FOCUS   Teaching Risk Taking at Trilogy Software, Inc.

Trilogy Software, Inc., an Austin, Texas, developer of software that helps companies manage product pricing, sales plans, and commissions, is in a stiff head-on competition with rivals Siebel Systems, Inc., and SAP AG. Joe Liemandt, CEO of Trilogy, understands the importance of managers in his company taking risks if Trilogy is to be successful. To prepare managers for risk taking and innovation, he put all new hires through an intense training program that divided them into groups to compete to develop new products and services. Everyone was rewarded with a trip to Las Vegas following the training period. In Las Vegas, to motivate and reward risk taking, Liemandt provided $2,000 cash to each recruit willing to bet that money

at the casinos in Las Vegas. Winners kept their winnings, but losers had to pay back the money to Trilogy in monthly deductions of $400 from their paychecks. Thirty-six of 300 recruits chose to take the bet. Whether winner or loser, all 36 came out ahead. One of the thirty-six, a loser, said, "We are known [at Trilogy] as risk takers, an important attribute in the high-tech world." These 36 are known as the "L2K Club" for "lost $2,000" although one of the 36 actually won $72,000. One employee says, "Joe knows every L2K pretty well."

Source: "How Trilogy Software Trains Its Raw Recruits to Be Risk Takers," *The Wall Street Journal*, September 21, 1998, p. 1.

Controllability

A cost is said to be **controllable** if the manager or employee has discretion in choosing to incur it or can significantly influence its amount within a given, usually short, period of time.

A cost is said to be **controllable** if the manager or employee has discretion in choosing to incur it or can significantly influence its amount within a given, usually short, period of time. For example, the shop supervisor ordinarily *cannot* control rent expense and insurance on the plant facility nor would the division manager ordinarily have discretion over the amount of corporate-level administrative costs. In contrast, employees typically have control over the labor and materials used in their work area. Costs such as advertising and maintenance ordinarily are within the scope of the product or division manager's control.

There are two views of the importance of controllability in the context of employee and manager motivation. One view holds that the manager or employee should be responsible only for the costs that he or she controls. This view is consistent with the argument that to hold managers responsible for changes in costs beyond their control is unfair and unmotivating. The second view is that many "uncontrollable" costs, such as corporate-level administrative costs, are in fact controllable by all managers *taken as a whole;* thus, to include these costs on the managers' costs reports sends a clear message that the firm benefits when managers manage these costs properly.

The Effect of Risk Preferences on Motivation and Decision Making

Risk preferences
describe the way individuals differentially view decision options because they place a weight on *certain* outcomes that differs from the weight they place on *uncertain* outcomes.

A manager's risk preferences are important in management and operational control because they can have unexpected and undesirable effects on his or her behavior. Assume that a manager must make a decision for which each option has a different outcome and some outcomes are more certain to happen than others. **Risk preferences** describe the way individuals differentially view decision options because they place a weight on *certain* outcomes that differs from the weight they place on *uncertain* outcomes. The risk associated with uncertain outcomes can be undesirable to the decision maker regardless of the value of the outcome itself. It is necessary to separate the value of the outcome from the positive or negative weight associated with the risk due to uncertainty. For example, people commonly dislike risk and thus prefer a certain $50 over a 50–50 chance at $100. People who prefer risk, on the other hand, would choose to have the chance to win the $100.

Many managers are risk averse; that is, they seek to avoid options with high risk and would choose an option with lower expected value if it had less risk. Other managers are risk prone; they seek risky projects that promise some chance of a high benefit, although the projects may have a significant risk of low benefit. These differences in risk preferences can significantly affect motivation under different supervision and reward techniques. For example, the risk-averse manager is most likely to be highly motivated by supervision that rewards the reduced risk; the opposite is likely true for the risk-prone manager.

Moreover, risk preferences can interfere with proper decision making. For example, a risk-averse manager might choose not to take a risky action that top management would take (for example, to install a costly new machine that would probably reduce operating costs) because of the personal consequences that a potentially unfavorable outcome would have for the manager. For proper motivation and decision making, management and operational control systems should be designed to reduce the negative effects of risk preferences.

Summary

There are several important concepts for the management accountant, which Chapter 3 presents in four groups: (1) cost objects, cost drivers, and cost pools, (2) product and service costing for the preparation of financial statements, (3) planning and decision making, and (4) operational and management control. Group 1 includes concepts that are important in all management functions, while groups 2, 3, and 4 are three of the four management functions. Concepts for the fourth management function, strategic management, are covered in Chapters 1 and 2.

The first group of concepts includes the four types of cost drivers: activity based, volume based, structural, and executional. Activity-based cost drivers are at the detail level of operations: equipment setup, materials handling, and clerical or other tasks. In contrast, volume-based cost drivers are at the aggregate level: usually the number of units produced. Structural cost drivers involve plans and decisions having long-term effects; executional cost drivers have short-term decision frames. The most important volume-based concepts are variable costs, which change according to a change in the level of output, and fixed costs, which do not. Direct costs are defined as costs that can be traced directly to a cost object in contrast to indirect costs, which cannot.

The important concepts in product costing are product costs, which are the costs of direct materials, direct labor, and indirect manufacturing (called *overhead*) required for the product and production process. Nonproduct costs (also called *period costs*) are the selling, administrative, and other costs not involved in manufacturing. The inventory formula is used to determine the cost of materials used in production, the cost of goods manufactured, and the cost of goods sold for a given period.

The most important concept in planning and decision making is relevant cost—a cost that differs for each option and will occur in the future. When considering options, the management accountant considers relevant costs. All past costs (also called *sunk costs*) are irrelevant because they will not change regardless of the option chosen.

The two key concepts in management and operational control are controllability and risk preferences. Distinguishing controllable costs from other costs is important because evaluation, even in part, on the basis of costs a manager cannot control can be negatively motivating. It is also important for the management accountant to recognize in the development of cost management systems that managers tend to be relatively risk averse, which can cause them to make decisions that are not consistent with top management's objectives.

Key Terms

allocation bases, *62*
average cost, *68*
controllable cost, *77*
conversion cost, *64*
cost, *61*
cost allocation, *62*
cost assignment, *61*
cost driver, *61*

cost object, *61*
cost of goods manufactured, *73*
cost of goods sold, *71*
cost pools, *61*
differential cost, *74*
direct cost, *61*
direct labor cost, *63*

direct materials cost, *62*
executional cost drivers, *70*
factory overhead, *64*
finished goods inventory, *72*
fixed cost, *67*
indirect cost, *61*
indirect labor cost, *64*

Comments on Cost Management in Action

Product Complexity in Consumer Goods Manufacturing

The consultant's observations indicate that the manufacturer was incurring large costs in operations, distribution, and administration due to the high level of complexity in its products. Maintaining relationships with 10 vendors for a single item contributed to high purchasing and stocking costs. Similarly, most of the firm's volume was made up of products with five color combinations, causing manufacturing, warehousing, shipping, and selling costs to be high relative to products with fewer color combinations. The high product variety also required smaller batch production and more frequent setups, which increased manufacturing costs. The variety of different customers, prices, and promotional programs increased manufacturing, shipping, and customer service costs as well as accounting costs related to customer invoices and account balances.

The solution? The firm reduced complexity by reducing the number of customers; the value of each customer was reviewed, and some with low value were not continued. The firm also developed a review process for proposed products or new variations on existing products to ensure their likely profitability. Furthermore, the firm reduced the complexity of equipment setups so that it could meet customers' demands for smaller batch sizes without increasing overall costs. As a result of the reduced complexity, overall profit margins improved. The manufacturer had found a way to deal with the cost consequences of its strategic initiative.

The firm also adopted new cost management practices that included nonfinancial measures such as setup time and frequency, percent of orders shipped on time, percent of orders made on a just-in-time basis, and the number of vendors for the top 20 commodity raw materials items. In addition, the firm began to calculate and regularly review customer profitability by type of market and customer size.

Source: Frank A. J. Gonsalves and Robert G. Eiler, "Managing Complexity through Performance Measurement," *Management Accounting,* August 1996, pp. 34–39. For another example, see "How IBM Turned Around Its Ailing PC Division," by Raju Narisetti, *The Wall Street Journal,* March 12, 1998, p. B1.

Self-Study Problem

(For solution, please turn to the end of the chapter.)

The following data pertain to Spartan Products Company:

Sales revenue	$1,000,000
Direct materials inventory, Jan. 1, 2004	20,000
Direct labor—Wages	350,000
Depreciation expense—Plant and equipment	80,000
Indirect labor—Wages	5,000
Heat, light, and power—Plant	12,000
Supervisor's salary—Plant	40,000
Finished goods inventory, Jan. 1, 2004	35,000
Work-in-Process inventory, Dec. 31, 2004	25,000
Supplies—Administrative office	6,000
Property taxes—Plant	13,000
Finished goods inventory, Dec. 31, 2004	40,000
Direct materials inventory, Dec. 31, 2004	30,000
Sales representatives' salaries	190,000
Work-in-Process inventory, Jan. 1, 2004	35,000
Direct materials purchases	100,000
Supplies—Plant	4,000
Depreciation—Administrative office	30,000

Required Prepare a statement of cost of goods manufactured and an income statement for Spartan Products Company for the year ended December 31, 2004, similar to the one in Exhibit 3.15a.

Questions

3–1   For what particular management function is relevant cost information needed?

3–2   Distinguish between direct and indirect costs and give several examples of each.

3–3   Are all direct costs variable? Explain.

3–4   Are all fixed costs indirect? Explain.

3–5   Define *cost driver*.

3–6   What is the difference between variable and fixed costs?

3–7   Explain step costs and give an example.

3–8   Define *relevant range* and explain its use.

3–9   What is a conversion cost? What are prime costs?

3–10 Why might the term *average cost* be misleading?

3–11 How do total variable costs, total fixed costs, average variable costs, and average fixed costs react to changes in the cost driver?

3–12 What does the term *marginal cost* mean?

3–13 Distinguish between product costs and period costs.

3–14 Explain the difference between cost of goods sold and cost of goods manufactured.

3–15 What are the three types of inventory in a manufacturing firm?

3–16 Cost management information should be relevant, timely, and accurate. Which of these attributes is most important? Why?

3–17 What is a relevant cost?

3–18 Define *differential cost, opportunity cost,* and *sunk cost.*

3–19 Should managers be responsible for the costs they cannot control directly? Why or why not?

3–20 What problem can arise if the firm and its employees have different risk preferences? What can be done about this problem?

Exercises

3–21 **Classification of Costs**   The following costs were taken from the accounting records of the Barnwell Manufacturing Company:

1. State income taxes
2. Insurance on the manufacturing facilities
3. Supplies used in manufacturing
4. Wages for employees in the assembly department
5. Wages for employees who deliver the product
6. Interest on notes payable
7. Materials used in the production process
8. Rent for the sales outlet in Sacramento
9. Electricity for manufacturing equipment
10. Depreciation expense on delivery trucks
11. Wages for the sales staff
12. Factory supervisors' salaries
13. Company president's salary
14. Advertising expense

Required   Classify each item as either a product cost or a period cost. Classify all product costs as direct or indirect, assuming that the cost object is each unit of product manufactured.

3–22 **Classification of Costs**   Following is a list of costs from Oakland Company, a furniture manufacturer:

1. Wood used in chairs
2. Salaries of inspectors
3. Lubricant used in machinery
4. Factory rent
5. Wages of assembly workers
6. Workers' compensation insurance
7. Sandpaper

8. Fabric used for upholstery
9. Property taxes
10. Depreciation on machinery

Required   Classify each cost as direct or indirect assuming that the cost object is each item manufactured. Also indicate whether each cost is a variable or fixed cost.

3–23 **Classification of Costs**   The following is a list of costs from the accounting records of Sunshine Pool Management, Inc. Each of Sunshine's 77 customers owns a pool. Sunshine maintains each customer's pool by providing supplies, cleaning, and repairs.

1. Lifesaving supplies
2. Salaries of Sunshine's managers
3. Pool chemicals
4. Sunshine's office rental expense
5. Wages of lifeguards
6. Workers' compensation insurance
7. Training for lifeguards
8. pH testing supplies
9. Office expense, including bookkeeping and clerical
10. Depreciation on cleaning and testing equipment

Required   Classify each item as direct or indirect assuming that the cost objects are each of 77 pools.

3–24 **Activity Levels and Cost Drivers**   Tartan Manufacturing Company produces four lines of high-quality lighting fixtures in a single manufacturing plant. Products are built to specific customer specifications. All products are made-to-order. Management of the plant lists the following as the key activities at the plant:

a. Product design
b. Production scheduling
c. Cost of purchasing department
d. Receipt and inspection of materials
e. Machine set-ups
f. Product inspection, done for each product
g. Plant security
h. Customer credit check
i. Machine operation
j. Machine maintenance

Required   Identify a cost object and a cost driver for each activity.

3–25 **Average and Total Costs**   The Business Students Association wants to have a Christmas dance for its members. The cost of renting a nightclub is $250, and the cost of refreshments will be $1 per person.

Required

1. What is the total cost if 100 people attend? What is the average cost?
2. What is the total cost if 200 people attend? What is the average cost?
3. Explain why average total cost differs with changes in total attendance.

3–26 **Classification of Costs**   Fran McPhair Dance Studios is a chain of 45 wholly owned dance studios that offer private lessons in ballroom dancing. The studios are located in various cities throughout the southern and southeastern states. McPhair offers a set of 12 private lessons; students may pay for the lessons one at a time, but each student is required to enroll for at least a 12-lesson plan. The 20-, 40-, and 100-lesson plans offer savings. Each dance instructor is paid a small salary plus a commission based on the number of dance lessons provided.

Required

1. McPhair's owner is interested in a strategic analysis of the business. The owner wants to understand why overall profitability has declined slightly in the most recent year while other studios in the area seem to be doing well. What is the proper cost object to begin this analysis? Explain your choice.
2. For each of the cost elements determine the cost classification from the following list for the cost object you chose in requirement 1. (In some cases, two or more classifications apply.)

Cost Elements

1. Each dancing instructor's salary.
2. Manager's salary.
3. Music tapes used in instruction.
4. Utilities for the studio.
5. Part-time studio receptionist.
6. Planning and development materials sent from the home office.
7. Free lessons given by each studio as a promotion.
8. Regional TV and radio advertisements placed several times a year.

Cost Classifications

a. Direct
b. Indirect
c. Variable
d. Fixed
e. Controllable by studio manager
f. Uncontrollable by studio manager

3–27 **Activities and Cost Drivers in a Hospital**   Greenbelt Hospital has the following activities in its value chain of providing service to each inpatient admission:

1. Schedule patient.
2. Verify insurance.
3. Admit patient.
4. Prepare patient's room.
5. Review doctor's report.
6. Feed patient.
7. Order tests.
8. Move to/from laboratory.
9. Administer lab tests.
10. Order pharmaceuticals.
11. Complete patient report.
12. Check patient's vital signs.
13. Prepare patient for operation.
14. Move to/from operating room.
15. Operate.
16. Collect charges.
17. Discharge patient.
18. Bill insurance.

Required   Assume that the cost object is the individual patient. Determine the appropriate cost driver(s) for each activity.

3–28 **Fixed, Variable, and Mixed Costs**   Adams Manufacturing's five manufacturing departments had the following operating and cost information for the two most recent months of activity:

	May 2004	June 2004
Units produced	10,000	20,000
Costs in each department		
Department A	$10,000	$10,000
Department B	25,000	50,000
Department C	35,000	45,000
Department D	18,000	64,000
Department E	22,000	44,000

Required   Identify whether the cost in each department is fixed, variable, or mixed.

3–29 **Relevant, Differential, and Opportunity Costs**   Jackson Farm Tools, Inc., has two options for repairing its office space, which received extensive wind damage in a recent storm.

	Option 1	Option 2
Cost 1	$ 8,000	$ 8,000
Cost 2	6,420	2,500
Cost 3	16,000	0
Cost 4	20,400	40,800
Total cost	$50,820	$51,300

Required   Identify the relevant, differential, and opportunity costs in this situation.

3–30 **Military Contracts and Direct vs. Indirect Costs**   In contracts with the U.S. government, direct costs are reimbursable. Indirect costs can be a problem however, when a contract is terminated because the approved cost assignment procedures are no longer appropriate.

The determination of whether a cost is direct or indirect can be critical in some situations. To understand the problem, consider this typical case. A contractor enters into a multiyear, fixed-price development contract with the military. The job requires a significant investment in inspection equipment that the contractor uses only for the military contract. Equipment cost is not treated as a direct cost, however, because governmental cost standards require depreciation costs of all similar assets to be treated consistently, either as direct or indirect costs. Thus, the inspection equipment must be treated as an indirect cost. Because the equipment is an indirect cost, its cost cannot be fully recovered until the project is completed. If the contract is terminated early, only a portion of the cost of the inspection equipment can be recovered.

Required   How do you think this issue should be resolved?

3–31 **Basic Cost Terms**   Following are descriptions of costs for a small-town cafe (column A) and cost types (column B). The cost object is each meal served.

A—Costs

1. Cost of part-time workers (seasonal fluctuations in breakfast and lunch trade)
2. Rent of the cafe building
3. Cost of full-time workers
4. Cost of utilities (telephone, gas, electric, and trash)
5. Cost of a leased gas-powered grill
6. Cost of cooking ingredients

B—Cost Types

a. Variable cost
b. Step cost
c. Fixed cost

Required   Match each cost in column A to a cost type in column B.

3–32 **Interpreting Average Cost**   Concern for gas emissions and depletion of nonrenewable resources has caused environmentalists and others to push for higher fuel-efficiency standards for new cars. The current corporate automotive fuel efficiency (CAFE) standards require automakers to produce an overall fuel efficiency of 26.2 miles per gallon for all autos produced.

Currently the U.S. government supports the development of hybrid autos that combine gas and electric power as the solution to the problem. Others propose simply raising the CAFE standards for auto manufacturers. To study the issue, the American Council for an Energy-Efficient Economy (ACEEE) conducted research to determine the cost for raising fuel efficiency for the different proposals. Their findings are as follows:

Option to reduce emissions and provide better fuel economy	Fuel Efficiency (mpg)	Cost for each gallon of gas saved
Current mileage standards	26.2	—
Moderate increase in CAFE	40.8	$0.57
Significant increase in CAFE	45.8	$0.60
Partial hybrid (15% of power from electricity)	52.6	$1.38
Full hybrid (40% of power from electricity)	59.3	$1.80

The increase in fuel economy required by higher CAFE standards would require automakers to use conventional technology to improve engines and transmissions. The hybrid vehicles require newer technology and electric motors.

Required   Give a brief critical review of the ACEEE's research results. What questions would you have for the researchers who presented these results?

3–33 **Interpreting Average Cost**   Recently the American Institute of CPAs (AICPA) and the Hackett Group, a consulting firm, partnered to study the trends in the nature and amount spent on the accounting function in corporations. A key finding was that the world's best accounting departments were able to function effectively at relatively low cost; these department's total costs were only about 1 percent of their firm's total revenues. In contrast, less efficient accounting departments required on the average 1.4 percent of total revenue, 40 percent higher. The world-class accounting departments were also faster in preparing regular financial reports (less than two days for the best departments, compared to five to eight days for the others). The study also found that larger firms spent less on accounting:

Manufacturing Firms	Finance Cost as a Percent of Total Revenue
Firms with less than $1 billion in revenues	1.6%
$1 billion to $5 billion	1.4%
More than $5 billion	1%
Service Firms	
Less than $1 billion in revenues	2.1%
More than $1 billion	1.6%

Required   Give a brief critical review of these research results. What questions would you have for the researchers who presented these results?

3–34 **Differential Costs**   A nonprofit health organization is studying two methods to increase the number of children in the area who receive measles immunization. The first method involves hiring an educator at $25,000 annual salary. In addition, the educator's expenses, including materials, would be $40,000.

The second method being considered is to strictly enforce an existing law requiring all schoolchildren to be immunized as they enroll for kindergarten. For this program, a staff would be hired to review all necessary paperwork, to send home notices if a child is not in compliance, and to do whatever follow-up work is necessary. Two clerical workers at a total cost of $35,000, including benefits, would be needed to accomplish the task. Cost of supplies and other materials to support the new staff in their jobs would be $15,000.

Required   The health organization must choose between the methods.

1. What are the relevant costs in the decision?
2. What other information might be important?

3–35 Cost of Goods Manufactured   The following information pertains to the Chambers Company:

Prime costs	$160,000
Conversion costs	185,000
Direct materials used	65,000
Beginning work in process	75,000
Ending work in process	62,000

Required   Determine the cost of goods manufactured.

Problems

3–36 Product Costs and Period Costs   Galletas Americanas is a cookie company in Guadalajara, Mexico, that produces and sells high-quality American-style cookies. The owner wants to identify the various costs incurred each year to be able to plan and control the business costs. Galletas Americanas's costs are the following (in thousands of pesos):

Utilities for the bakery	1,600
Paper used in packaging product	70
Salaries and wages in the bakery	15,000
Cookie ingredients	27,000
Bakery labor and fringe benefits	1,000
Administrative costs	800
Bakery equipment maintenance	600
Depreciation of bakery plant and equipment	1,500
Uniforms	300
Insurance for the bakery	600
Rent for administrative offices	13,200
Advertising	1,500
Boxes, bags, and cups used in the bakery	700
Manager's salary	10,000
Overtime premiums	2,000
Idle time	400

Required

1. What is the total amount of product and period costs?
2. Assume that Galletas is planning to expand its business into the United States and Canada, initially targeting the United States. This expansion will not require additional baking facilities, but labor and materials costs will increase, and advertising costs and packaging costs will increase substantially. Also, U.S. authorities will require certain documentation and inspections that will be an added cost for Galletas.
   a. Which of the additional costs are product costs?
   b. Which costs are relevant for the decision whether to expand into the United States?

3–37 Executional Cost Drivers, Internet Retailer   Assume that you are a consultant for a start-up Internet retailer, Bikes.com, which provides a variety of bicycle parts and accessories in a convenient and effective customer service approach. The firm operates from an office building and nearby warehouse located in Danville, Virginia. Currently, the firm has 10 permanent administrative staff, 6 customer service representatives who respond to customer inquiries, and 12 employees who pick, pack, and ship customer orders. All orders are placed over the firm's website. An 800 telephone number is available for customer service. The firm's sales increased at about 20 percent per year in the last two years, a decline from the 50 percent rate in its first three years of operation. Management is concerned that the decline will delay the firm's first expected profit, which had been projected to occur in the next two years. The firm is privately held and has been financed with a combination of bank loans, personal investments of top managers, and venture capital funding.

Required   What specific executional cost drivers are important in this business? How should the firm use them to improve its sales rate?

3–38 **Structural Cost Drivers**

Case A. Food Fare is a small chain of restaurants that has developed a loyal customer base by providing fast-food items with more choices (e.g., how the hamburger should be cooked; self-serve toppings) and a more comfortable atmosphere. The menu has a small number of popular items, including several different hamburgers, grilled chicken sandwiches, and salads. Recently, to broaden its appeal, Food Fare added barbecue, seafood, and steak to its menu.

Case B. Gilman Heating and Air Conditioning, Inc., provides a broad range of services to commercial and residential customers, including installation and repair of several different brands of heating and air conditioning systems. Gilman has a fleet of 28 trucks, each operated by one or more service technicians, depending on the size of a job. A recurrent problem for Gilman has been coordinating the service teams during the day to determine the status of a job and the need for parts not kept in the service vehicle as well as to identify which team to send on emergency calls. Gilman's service area is spread over an urban/rural area of approximately 20 square miles. The company has developed cost and price sheets so that the service technicians accurately and consistently price the service work they perform.

Required For each case, identify the important structural cost drivers for the company and the related strategic issues that it should address to be competitive.

3–39 **Cost of Goods Manufactured and Sold** Allure Company produces women's clothing. During 2004, the company incurred the following costs:

Factory rent	$265,000
Direct labor	325,000
Utilities—Factory	88,000
Purchases of direct materials	465,000
Indirect materials	70,000
Indirect labor	35,000

Inventories for the year were as follows:

	January 1	December 31
Direct materials	$ 90,000	$50,000
Work in process	40,000	85,000
Finished goods	115,000	95,000

Required

1. Prepare a statement of cost of goods manufactured.
2. Calculate cost of goods sold.

3–40 **Cost of Goods Manufactured** The following data pertain to Duvernoy Company for the year ended December 31, 2004:

	December 31, 2003	December 31, 2004
Purchases of direct materials		$60,000
Direct labor		45,000
Indirect labor		25,000
Factory insurance		12,000
Depreciation—Factory		80,000
Repairs and maintenance—Factory		15,000
Marketing expenses		66,000
General and administrative expenses		55,000
Direct materials inventory	$20,000	35,000
Work-in-process inventory	33,000	35,000
Finished goods inventory	23,000	20,000

Sales in 2004 were $500,000.

Required   Prepare a schedule of cost of goods manufactured and an income statement for Duvernoy Company similar to those in Exhibit 3.15a.

3–41 Cost of Goods Manufactured, Income Statement   Consider the following information for Household Furnishings, Inc. for the year ended December 31, 2004

Depreciation expense—Administrative office	$ 33,000
Depreciation expense—Plant and equipment	88,000
Direct labor—Wages	487,000
Direct materials inventory, Dec. 31, 2004	25,000
Direct materials inventory, Jan. 1, 2004	18,000
Direct materials purchases	155,000
Finished goods inventory, Dec. 31, 2004	38,000
Finished goods inventory, Jan. 1, 2004	15,000
Heat, light, & power—Plant	44,000
Indirect labor	25,000
Property taxes—Plant	34,000
Sales representatives' salaries	145,000
Sales revenue	1,500,000
Factory Supervisor's salary	66,000
Supplies—Administrative office	16,000
Supplies—Plant	29,000
Work-in-Process inventory, Dec. 31, 2004	9,000
Work-in-Process inventory, Jan. 1, 2004	23,000

Required   Prepare a statement of cost of goods manufactured and an income statement for Household Furnishings for the year ended December 31, 2004, similar to the one in Exhibit 3.15a.

3–42 Cost of Goods Manufactured, Calculating Unknowns   The following information was taken from the accounting records of Blazek Manufacturing Company. Unfortunately, some of the data were destroyed by a computer malfunction.

	Case A	Case B
Sales	$100,000	$?
Finished goods inventory, Jan. 1, 2004	15,000	8,000
Finished goods inventory, Dec. 31, 2004	16,000	?
Cost of goods sold	?	43,000
Gross margin	25,000	3,000
Selling and administrative expenses	?	1,000
Operating income	10,000	2,000
Work in process, Jan. 1, 2004	?	14,000
Direct material used	18,000	8,000
Direct labor	15,000	9,000
Factory overhead	20,000	?
Total manufacturing costs	?	35,000
Work in process, Dec. 31, 2004	7,000	?
Cost of goods manufactured	?	45,000

Required   Calculate the unknowns indicated by question marks.

3–43 Cost of Goods Manufactured, Income Statement   Norton Industries, a manufacturer of cable for the heavy construction industry, closes its books and prepares financial statements at the end of each month. The statement of cost of goods sold for April 2004 follows:

Norton Industries
Statement of Cost of Goods Sold
For the Month Ended April 30, 2004
($000 omitted)

Inventory of finished goods, March 31	$ 50
Cost of goods manufactured	790
Cost of goods available for sale	$840
Less inventory of finished goods, April 30	247
Cost of goods sold	$593

Additional Information

- Of the utilities, 80 percent relates to manufacturing the cable; the remaining 20 percent relates to the sales and administrative functions.
- All rent is for the office building.
- Property taxes are assessed on the manufacturing plant.
- Of the insurance, 60 percent is related to manufacturing the cable; the remaining 40 percent is related to the sales and administrative functions.
- Depreciation expense includes the following:

Manufacturing plant	$20,000
Manufacturing equipment	30,000
Office equipment	4,000
	$54,000

- The company manufactured 7,825 tons of cable during May 2004.
- The inventory balances at May 31, 2004, follow:
- Direct materials inventory $ 23,000
- Work-in-process inventory   220,000
- Finished goods inventory   175,000

Norton Industries
Preclosing Account Balances
May 31, 2004
($000 omitted)

Cash and marketable securities	$ 54
Accounts and notes receivable	210
Direct materials inventory (4/30/04)	28
Work-in-process inventory (4/30/04)	150
Finished goods inventory (4/30/04)	247
Property, plant, and equipment (net)	1,140
Accounts, notes, and taxes payable	70
Bonds payable	600
Paid-in capital	100
Retained earnings	930
Sales	1,488
Sales discounts	20
Other revenue	2
Purchases of direct materials	510
Direct labor	260
Indirect factory labor	90
Office salaries	122
Sales salaries	42
Utilities	135
Rent	9
Property tax	60
Insurance	20
Depreciation	54
Interest expense	6
Freight-in for materials purchases	15

Required Based on Exhibit 3.15, prepare the following:

1. Statement of cost of goods manufactured for Norton Industries for May 2004.
2. Income statement for Norton Industries for May 2004.

(CMA Adapted)

3–44 Risk-Aversion and Decision Making John Smith is the production manager of Elmo's Glue Company. Because of limited capacity, the company can produce only one of two possible products. Product A is a space-age bonding formula that has a 15 percent probability of making a $1,000,000 profit and an 85% chance of generating a $200,000 profit. Product B is a re-formulated household glue that has a 100 percent chance of making a $310,000 profit. John has the responsibility to choose between the two products. Assume that he is more risk averse than Elmo's top management. He receives a bonus of 20 percent of the profit from his department.

Required

1. Which product will John choose? Why?
2. Is this the product Elmo's top management would choose? Why or why not?
3. How can Elmo's change its reward system so that John makes decisions that are consistent with top management's wishes?

3–45 Risk Aversion, Strategy John Holt is the production supervisor for ITEXX, a manufacturer of plastic parts, with customers in the automobile and consumer products industries. On a Tuesday morning, one of ITEXX's sales managers asked John to reschedule his manufacturing jobs for the rest of the week to accommodate the manager's special order from a new customer. The customer required fast turnaround, which meant not only delaying the current production schedule but also running all three production shifts for the remainder of the week. This would make it impossible to complete the regularly scheduled maintenance on the equipment that John had planned for mid-week. The sales manager was determined to get the new customer, which could mean an important increase in overall sales and output at the plant. However, John worried not only about the delay of the current jobs but also about the chance that the maintenance delay would cause one of the machines to fail, which would back up the orders in the plant for at least a week, meaning a substantial delay for the new order as well as those currently scheduled.

Required How do you think John should resolve this problem? What is a good policy for handling such issues in the future?

Solution to Self-Study Problem

SPARTAN PRODUCTS COMPANY
Statement of Cost of Goods Manufactured
For the Year Ended December 31, 2004

Direct materials		
Direct materials inventory, Jan. 1, 2004	$ 20,000	
Purchases of direct materials	100,000	
Total direct materials available	$120,000	
Direct materials inventory, Dec. 31, 2004	30,000	
Direct materials used		$ 90,000
Direct labor		350,000
Factory overhead		
Heat, light, and power—Plant	12,000	
Supplies—Plant	4,000	
Property taxes—Plant	13,000	
Depreciation expense—Plant and equipment	80,000	
Indirect labor	5,000	
Supervisor's salary—Plant	40,000	
Total factory overhead		154,000
Total manufacturing costs		$594,000
Add: Beginning work-in-process inventory, Jan. 1, 2004		35,000
Total manufacturing costs to account for		$629,000
Less: Ending work-in-process, Dec. 31, 2004		25,000
Cost of goods manufactured		$604,000

SPARTAN PRODUCTS COMPANY
Income Statement
For the Year Ended December 31, 2004

Sales revenue		$1,000,000
Cost of goods sold		
Finished goods inventory, Jan. 1, 2004	$ 35,000	
Cost of goods manufactured	604,000	
Total goods available for sale	$639,000	
Finished goods inventory, Dec. 31, 2004	40,000	
Cost of goods sold		599,000
Gross margin		$ 401,000
Selling and administrative expenses		
Sales representatives' salaries	190,000	
Supplies—Administrative office	6,000	
Depreciation expense—Administrative office	30,000	
Total selling and administrative expenses		226,000
Net income		$ 175,000

CHAPTER FOUR

Job Order Costing

After studying this chapter, you should be able to . . .

1. Explain the types of costing systems
2. Explain the strategic role of product costing
3. Explain the flow of costs in a job costing system
4. Explain the application of factory overhead costs in a job costing system
5. Calculate underapplied and overapplied overhead and show how to dispose of it at the end of the period
6. Apply job costing in service industries
7. Explain an operation costing system

Determining the accurate cost of a product or service plays a critical role in the success of firms in most industries. For example, Smith Fabrication, Inc. of Kent, Washington (www.smithfabinc.com), uses a product costing system to estimate costs and to charge customers for the sheet metal products it provides to other manufacturers in the aviation, computer, telecom, and medical products industries. The product costing method it uses provides a competitive edge by providing accurate cost information in a form that customers can easily understand. Similarly, Kurz Industries (www.gkurzind.com) offers competitive pricing of its machining services through the use of fair market value product costing. What these and many companies have found is that a simple yet accurate method for determining product cost is crucial to their competitive success. Another example is home construction and remodeling, where product costing plays a key role in cost estimating and pricing the work (www.housingzone.com).

Smith Fabrication, Kurz Industries, and most home builders use a type of product costing called job costing which is explained in this chapter. Job costing is one of a variety of cost determining systems that companies can use. The job costing system is particularly appropriate for companies that produce made-to-order products such as machining, metal working, and home building. The manufacturing or service is based on a specific customer order. This is in contrast to firms that manufacture products in large quantities for sale by wholesalers or retailers. These firms do not deal directly with the ultimate customers. A soda bottler, food processing company, or toiletries manufacturer would be good examples. This latter type of firm has more of a process orientation to manufacturing than the customer-order orientation of firms like Smith or Kurz. In terms of Chapter 3 concepts, the job costing applications are used where it is easy to trace the cost of materials and labor to each customer's order. In the process-oriented firms, costs are usually traced to manufacturing departments and then allocated to individual products.

Product Costing Systems

Product costing
is the process of accumulating, classifying, and assigning direct materials, direct labor, and factory overhead costs to products or services.

Product costing is the process of accumulating, classifying, and assigning direct materials, direct labor, and factory overhead costs to products or services. Product costing provides useful cost information for both manufacturing and nonmanufacturing firms.

Several different product costing systems are available; these include the (1) cost accumulation method—job or process costing systems, (2) cost measurement method—actual, normal, or standard costing systems, and (3) overhead assignment method—traditional or activity-based costing systems.

The choice of a particular system depends on the nature of the industry and the product or service, the firm's strategy and management information needs, and the costs and benefits of acquiring, designing, modifying, and operating a particular system.

Cost Accumulation: Job or Process Costing

In a job costing system, the jobs or batches of products or services are the cost objects. This means that for the purposes of determining product cost, all manufacturing costs incurred are assigned to jobs. In a process costing system, on the other hand, production processes or departments are the cost objects. In the manufacture of appliances, for example, the metal fabrication department might be one cost center and the assembly department another.

A job costing system is appropriate in any environment in which costs can be readily identified with specific products, batches, contracts, or customers. The process costing system, on the other hand, is usually used by firms having homogeneous products. These firms engage in continuous mass production of one or a few products. Job costing systems are often used by medium to small firms that produce individual orders for customers. In contrast, process costing is likely to be used in large firms that produce one or a few homogenous products. This chapter describes job costing systems. Chapter 11 explains process costing systems.

Cost Measurement: Actual, Normal, or Standard Costing

Costs in either a job or process costing system can be measured in their actual, normal, or standard amount. An *actual costing system* uses actual costs incurred for all product costs including direct materials, direct labor, and factory overhead. Actual costing systems are rarely used because they can produce unit product costs that fluctuate significantly, causing potential errors in pricing, adding/dropping product lines, and for performance evaluations. Also most actual factory overhead costs are known only at or after the end of the period rather than at the completion of the batch of products. Thus, actual costing systems cannot provide accurate unit product cost information on a timely basis.

A *normal costing system* uses actual costs for direct materials and direct labor and normal costs for factory overhead. Normal costing involves estimating a portion of overhead to be assigned to each product as it is produced. A normal costing system provides a timely estimate of the cost of producing each batch of product.

A *standard costing system* uses standard costs and quantities for all three types of manufacturing costs: direct materials, direct labor, and factory overhead. Standard costs are target costs the firm should attain. Standard costing systems provide a basis for cost control, performance evaluation, and process improvement. This chapter explains actual costing and normal costing systems, and Chapters 13 and 14 present standard costing systems. See Exhibit 4.1.

Overhead Assignment under Normal Costing: Traditional or Activity-Based

Traditional product costing systems allocate overhead to products or jobs using a volume-based cost driver, such as units produced. This approach relies heavily on the assumption that each product uses the same amounts of overhead, since each product

	Types of Cost Used For		
Costing System	**Direct Materials**	**Direct Labor**	**Factory Overhead**
Actual costing	Actual cost	Actual cost	Actual cost
Normal costing	Actual cost	Actual cost	Applied overhead cost (using predetermined rate(s))
Standard costing	Standard cost	Standard cost	Standard cost

is charged the same amount. Many accountants argue that instead of an equal amount, the overhead in each product should be proportional to the direct labor hours needed to manufacture that unit, because more labor time also means increased overhead costs for equipment, supervision, and other facilities costs. Generally, neither of these assumptions turns out to be sufficiently accurate in many companies, so these firms use an activity-based approach.

Activity-based costing (ABC) systems allocate factory overhead costs to products using cause-and-effect criteria with multiple cost drivers. ABC systems use both volume-based and nonvolume-based cost drivers to more accurately allocate factory overhead costs to products based on resource consumption during various activities. Chapter 5 explains ABC systems.

The Strategic Role of Product Costing

To compete successfully, firms need accurate product cost information, irrespective of their competitive strategies. And this is even more likely to be true for cost leadership firms that rely on a high level of manufacturing efficiency and quality to succeed. Effective management of manufacturing costs requires timely and accurate cost information. Getting this timely and accurate information requires that the firm choose a cost system that is a good match for its competitive strategy. For example, a cost leadership firm that produces a commodity product is also likely to be in a process industry, such as food or chemical processing, or assembly line manufacturing. Thus, process costing systems are likely to be a good fit. Because accurate costs are important, such firms are likely to use activity-based costing, which is more accurate than the traditional method for overhead assignment. And finally, this type of firm is likely to choose a standard costing system to provide the cost targets and regular reports on meeting these targets. In sum, the commodity/cost leadership type of firm might very well use a cost system that combines elements of process costing (Chapter 11), activity-based costing (Chapter 5), and standard costing (Chapters 13 and 14).

In contrast, firms with a wide variety of distinct products usually use a *job costing system,* which is applied to low-volume goods and services. Firms with homogeneous products over a significant time period use the *process costing system,* which is applied to high-volume goods when individual units cannot be specifically identified and assigned a cost. In practice, many firms appropriately use job costing for some products or departments and process costing for other products or departments. Automobile manufacturing firms are an example; their products not only have many common features but also have unique features. Automakers cannot use either a pure job costing or a pure process costing system.

Many firms' manufacturing environments are changing rapidly. To provide meaningful information, a product costing system must keep up with the constantly changing manufacturing environment. Many firms change their product costing system from a single volume-based cost driver system to a multiple cost driver ABC system because of changes in their manufacturing environments.

An important strategic issue and a potential ethical issue for product costing involves the decisions the firm makes about the basis for allocating overhead costs. For example, if a firm manufactures products for two types of markets, one of which is price competitive and the other is not (e.g., cost-plus government contracts), the manner of overhead allocation involves both strategic and ethical issues. When manufacturing cost-plus products, managers can be tempted to overcost them by choosing an allocation basis that achieves the desired result.

LEARNING OBJECTIVE 2

Explain the strategic role of product costing.

Job costing

is a product costing system that accumulates costs and assigns them to a specific job.

Job Costing: The Cost Flows

Job costing is a product costing system that accumulates costs and assigns them to specific jobs. The production departments of these firms perform tasks that often vary from product to product. Because each product or service can require different

FMI Forms Manufacturers Uses Job Costing

FMI Forms Manufacturers is a machine-intensive printing company that produces business forms. The resources demanded by a specific job depend on the type and amount of paper used and the composition and construction of the business form. All jobs are constrained by the time on a press and a collator capable of producing forms at the required size.

FMI uses a separate factory overhead rate for each machine. Costs of machine operator, support personnel, and supplies are identified directly with presses and collators. Other factory overhead costs, including insurance, supervision, and office salaries, are allocated to machines based on their processing capacity (cost driver is the number of feet of business form per minute), weighted by the maximum paper width and complexity (cost driver is number of colors and/or stations) that they are capable of handling.

When FMI receives a request for a bid on a particular job, it uses a computer software program to determine direct materials costs based on the type and quantity of paper. Then it identifies the least expensive press and collator that are capable of handling the job specifications. Then FMI estimates the total press and collator processing costs by using specific cost driver rates per machine time multiplied by the estimated processing time. The bid price is calculated by adding a standard markup to the total press, collator, and direct materials costs. A higher markup is used for rush jobs and those requiring special features.

Based on information in Jacci L. Rodgers, S. Mark Comstock, and Karl Pritz, "Customize Your Costing System," *Management Accounting,* May 1993, pp. 31–32.

REAL-WORLD FOCUS Job Costing at Topnotch Auto Repair Shop

Topnotch Auto Repair Shop in Rowland Heights, California, is a business well-suited to job costing. The firm typically performs a wide variety of tasks from changing tires to repairing engines. Although shop personnel are likely asked to do some tasks several times a day, rarely are they asked to do the same task throughout the day. For example, two customers asking for engine tune-ups have differ-

ent models of cars that vary in their complexity and in the cost of repair. One customer might ask them to rotate the tires on the car. Therefore, it makes more sense for Topnotch to track the costs of repairing each car rather than the total monthly costs of the individual tasks.

LEARNING OBJECTIVE 3
Explain the flow of costs in a job costing system.

operations, the best way to determine the cost of a product or service is to accumulate costs for a job or batch. Therefore, in job costing, the product or service costs are obtained by gathering and assigning costs to a specific job or individual customer order for one or more products. The unit cost of each product or service is calculated by dividing total job costs by number of units produced in that batch or order.

Industries that use job costing include printing shops, shipbuilders, custom furniture-manufacturing plants, contractors, film-producing companies, accounting firms, law firms, advertising agencies, consulting firms, medical clinics, custom-made machine tool or equipment companies, construction companies, and research, engineering, and development services among others. Each job in these businesses is likely to be different. Examples of companies using job costing systems include Kinko's (www.kinkos.com); Paramount Pictures (www.paramount.com); Jiffy Lube International (www.jiffylube.com); Accenture (www.accenture.com), Kaiser Permanente (www.kaiserpermanente.org), and Hyatt Corporation (www.hyatt.com).

Job Cost Sheet

A **job cost sheet** records and summarizes the costs of direct materials, direct labor, and factory overhead for a particular job.

The basic supporting document in a job costing system is the **job cost sheet.** It records and summarizes the costs of direct materials, direct labor, and factory overhead for a particular job.

The job cost sheet in Exhibit 4.2 is started when the production or processing of a job begins. A job cost sheet has spaces for all three cost elements (materials, labor, overhead) and other detailed data management requires. The job cost sheet follows the product as it goes through the production process; all costs are recorded on the sheet as

Sally Industries, Inc., is a small manufacturer of animatronic figures known as entertainment robots such as E.T., the Extraterrestrial. Because entertainment robots are custom orders, Sally Industries uses a job costing system to help managers make project planning, cost control, performance measurement, and pricing decisions. Each job cost sheet is separated into direct materials, direct labor,

and factory overhead. Since Sally Industries is still a small business, it has a relatively simple job costing system that is maintained largely on spreadsheets.

Based on information in Thomas Barton and Frederick M. Cole, "Accounting for Magic," *Management Accounting,* January 1991, pp. 27–31.

EXHIBIT 4.2   Job Cost Sheet

Intellimechanics, Inc.
Job Cost Sheet

Product   Robot   Job No.   351

Date begun   June 6, 2004   Quantity   20

Date completed   July 15, 2004   Unit cost $3,761

	Direct Materials				Direct Labor					Factory Overhead			
Dept.	Date	Requisition Number	Units	Cost	Date	Hours	Rate	Ticket	Amount	Labor-Hours	Application Rate	Amount	Total Cost
A	6/6	A–4024	20	$1,500	6/6 to 6/25	100	$10	A–1101 through A–1150	$1,000	100	$5.00	$ 500	$3,000
B	6/26	B–3105	15	400	6/26 to 6/30	60	15	B–308 through B–320	900	60	6.70	402	1,702
C	7/2	C–5051	10	300	7/1 to 7/15	140	12	C–515 through C–500	1,680	140	6.00	840	2,820
Total				$2,200					$3,580			$1,742	$7,522

materials and labor are added. On completion of production, the overhead is added up based usually on a certain dollar amount per labor hour, as shown for IntelliMechanics Inc. in Exhibit 4.2. The total of all costs recorded on the job cost sheet is the total cost of the job. The average cost per unit is determined by dividing the number of units in the job by its total cost.

All costs shown in the job cost sheet are recorded in the Work-in-Process Inventory account. The subsidiary accounts to the Work-in-Process Inventory account (such as direct materials, direct labor, and various factory overhead accounts) consist of job cost sheets that include the manufacturing costs incurred during or prior to the current period. The total on all job cost sheets equals the total amount on the debit side of the Work-in-Process Inventory account. This total is reported on the statement of cost of goods manufactured (for review, see Exhibit 3.14 and 3.15).

Because a separate job cost sheet is prepared for each job, cost sheets for jobs started but not finished support the subsidiary ledger that shows the ending Work-in-Process Inventory. When a job is complete, the appropriate cost sheet is placed in a group of cost sheets representing the cost of goods manufactured.

Direct Materials Costs

When materials are purchased for $2,200, for example, the accountant (1) checks the supporting documents of purchase orders, receiving reports, and invoices and

(2) records the purchase amounts in the Receipts column of the subsidiary ledger, the material ledger. These support the following journal entry:

(1)	Materials Inventory	2,200	
	Accounts Payable		2,200

A general ledger control account sums the similar detailed account balances in the related subsidiary ledger. The Materials Inventory amount is the sum of all direct and indirect materials in the subsidiary ledger.

A **materials requisition form** is a source document that the production department supervisor uses to request materials for production.

A product costing system uses materials requisition forms to document and control all materials issued. A **materials requisition form** is a source document that the production department supervisor uses to request materials for production. The production department prepares materials requisition forms to request materials from the warehouse; copies are sent to the accounting department. The warehouse releases the materials based on the requisition. The materials requisition indicates the job charged with the materials used. In an online computer environment, the information is entered electronically. A detailed listing of all the materials needed for a given job is often developed in a *bill of materials.* For example, a bill of materials used by Thomasville Furniture Industries, Inc., (www.thomasville.com) in the manufacture of an end table is shown in Exhibit 4.3. Thomasville Furniture Industries (TFI) is a large manufacturer of high-quality furniture, with dedicated galleries in more than 600 stores worldwide and another 125 company-owned stores. TFI is located in Thomasville, North Carolina.

EXHIBIT 4.3

Bill of Materials for End Table Model 14531-210 for Thomasville Furniture Industries, Inc.

Thomasville Furniture Industries, Inc.
Bill of Materials

CHANGES FOR 14521-211

PLANT "T"

STYLE 14531-210 ARTICLE GEORGIAN END TABLE DATE 1-19-04 SHEET 1 OF 2

LINE		NO. PCS.	DESCRIPTION	FINISH SIZE L	FINISH SIZE W	FINISH SIZE T	FINISH SIZE BS	MULTI	ROUGH SIZE L	ROUGH SIZE W	ROUGH SIZE T	FOOTAGE	SKETCH
1	14531-210 ONLY	1	TOP	26	20	13/16		1	27	21	9/16		
2		1/2	TOP CORE					1	17	47 1/2	3/4		
3		1	TOP CORE SIDE BANDS	47 1/2	2	3/4		1	47 1/2	2	4/4		
4		2	TOP CORE FRT. & BK. BANDS	21	2	3/4		1	21	2	4/4		
5													
6		2	SIDE PANELS	22 3/8	4 15/16	3/4	21 3/8	4	23 7/8	21 3/4	5/8		4/4 POP CORE
7		2	SIDE APRON RAIL	22 3/8	1 7/8	1 7/16	21 3/8	1	23 3/8	2 1/8	8/4		
8		1	BACK PANEL	16 3/8	4 15/16	3/4	15 3/8	4	17 7/8	21 3/4	5/8		4/4 POP CORE
9		1	BACK APRON RAIL	16 3/8	1 7/8	1 7/16	15 3/8	1	17 3/8	2 1/8	8/4		
10		2	FRONT POST	22 3/4	2 1/2	2 1/2		1	23 3/4	2 3/4	3 pcs 5/4		
11		2	BACK POST	22 3/4	2 1/2	2 1/2		1	23 3/4	2 3/4	3 pcs 5/4		
12													
13	14531-210 ONLY	1	DRAWER FRONT	14 7/8	3 7/8	3/4		3	16 7/16	16 5/16	5/8		4/4 POP CORE
14		2	DWR. SIDES	20	3	7/16		1	21	3 1/4	5/8		
15		1	DWR. BACK	14 11/16	2 7/8	7/16							
16		1	DWR. BOTTOM	14 1/4	19 13/16	3/16		1	15 3/4	20 7/8	R.C.		
17		1	DWR. GUIDE—FEMALE	20 1/2	13/32	9/16	19 13/16	1	21 1/2	2 1/4	4/4		
18		1	DWR. GUIDE—MALE	22 1/2	1	1/2		1	23 1/2	1 1/4	4/4		
19		1	DWR. HOWE PULL										
20													

EXHIBIT 4.4
Materials Requisition Form

MATERIALS REQUISITION FORM

No. A–4024

Job Number _____ 351 _____   Date _____ June 6, 2004 _____

Department _____ A _____   Received by _____ Tom Chan _____

Authorized by _____ Juanita Peres _____   Issued by _____ Ted Mercer _____

Item Number	Description	Quantity	Unit Cost	Total Cost
MJI 428	Drawer Pull	10	$1.50	$15

Based on the information in materials requisition forms, costs of direct materials issued to production are recorded on the job cost sheet. This document is the source document for determining materials costs for individual jobs. Notice that the materials requisition form in Exhibit 4.4 specifically identifies the job that will use the materials.

For example, Thomasville Furniture Industries' Department A incurred $450 of costs for direct materials for Job 351 ($15 for drawer pulls and $435 for other materials).

(2)	Work-in-Process Inventory	450	
	Materials Inventory		450

Indirect materials are treated as part of the total factory overhead cost. Typical indirect materials are factory supplies and lubricants. They are recorded in the overhead cost sheet subsidiary ledger and the factory overhead general ledger account. The journal entry to record the issue of an indirect materials cost of $50 to support departments is

(3)	Factory Overhead	50	
	Materials Inventory		50

Exhibit 4.5 describes cost flows for direct materials and indirect materials of transactions (1), (2), and (3) through related general ledger T-accounts, subsidiary ledgers, and various source documents.

Direct Labor Costs

A time ticket
shows the time an employee worked on each job, the pay rate, and the total cost chargeable to each job.

Direct labor costs are recorded on the job cost sheet by means of a time ticket prepared daily for each employee. A **time ticket** shows the amount of time an employee worked on each job, the pay rate, and the total cost chargeable to each job. Analysis of the time tickets provides information for assigning direct labor costs to individual jobs. Note the typical time ticket form in Exhibit 4.6. The cost of the $1,000 direct labor incurred in TFI's Department A for Job 351 is recorded by the following journal entry:

(4)	Work-in-Process Inventory	1,000	
	Accrued Payroll		1,000

EXHIBIT 4.5 **Materials Cost Flows**

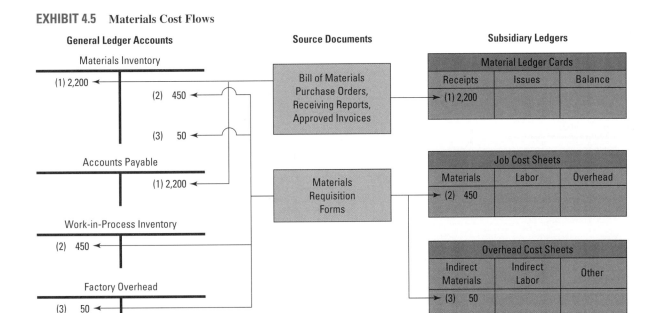

EXHIBIT 4.6
Time Ticket

TIME TICKET

Employee Number _____ 015 _____   Date _____ June 6, 2004 _____

Employee Name _____ Dale Johnson _____   Job Number _____ #351 _____

Operation _____ Assembly _____   Approved by _____ Juanita Perez _____

Time Started	Time Completed	Hours Worked	Rate	Cost
8:00 a.m.	11:00 a.m.	3.00	$10.00	$30.00

Total Cost $30.00

In addition to time tickets, clock or time cards are widely used for cost assignment and payroll. The times reported on an employee's time tickets are compared with the related clock cards as an internal check on the accuracy of the payroll computation.

Indirect labor costs are treated as part of the total factory overhead cost. Indirect labor usually includes items such as salaries or wages for supervisors, inspectors, rework labor, and warehouse clerks. They are recorded in the Indirect Labor column of the overhead cost sheet subsidiary ledger. The following is a journal entry to record the $100 indirect labor cost incurred:

(5)	Factory Overhead	100	
	Accrued Payroll		100

Exhibit 4.7 shows direct labor and indirect labor cost flows through related general ledger T-accounts, subsidiary ledgers, and various source documents.

EXHIBIT 4.7 **Labor Cost Flows**

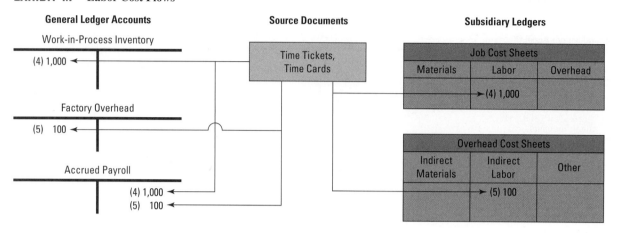

Factory Overhead Costs

Overhead application
is a process of assigning overhead costs to the appropriate jobs.

Overhead application is a process of allocating overhead costs to the appropriate jobs. Allocation is necessary because overhead costs are not traceable to individual jobs. The two approaches in allocating overhead costs to various jobs are actual costing and normal costing.

Actual Costing System

An **actual costing system**
uses actual costs incurred for direct materials and direct labor and applies actual factory overhead to various jobs.

Actual factory overhead
costs are costs incurred in an accounting period for indirect materials, indirect labor, and other indirect factory costs, including factory rent, insurance, property tax, depreciation, repairs and maintenance, power, light, heat, and employer payroll taxes for factory personnel.

An **actual costing system** uses actual costs incurred for direct materials and direct labor and applies actual factory overhead to various jobs.

Actual factory overhead costs are incurred each month for indirect materials, indirect labor, and other indirect factory costs, including factory rent, insurance, property tax, depreciation, repairs and maintenance, power, light, heat, and employer payroll taxes for factory personnel. Different firms use terms such as *manufacturing overhead, overhead,* or *burden* in referring to factory overhead.

Indirect materials of $50 and indirect labor of $100 were discussed in transactions (3) and (5), respectively. Other factory overhead costs such as depreciation, utilities, and insurance are accumulated in an overhead cost sheet subsidiary ledger under the Other column. The documents to support these costs include vouchers, invoices, and memos. This journal entry records the actual overhead costs of factory utilities, depreciation, and insurance for Department A.

(6)	Factory Overhead	350	
	Accounts Payable		80
	Accumulated Depreciation—Plant		150
	Factory Insurance		120

Assume Job 351 is the only job in Department A for the current month. The journal entry to record the overhead application ($50 + $100 + $350 = $500) to Job 351 for TFI's Department A is

| (7) | Work-in-Process Inventory | 500 | |
| | Factory Overhead Applied | | 500 |

EXHIBIT 4.8 **Factory Overhead Cost Flows: Actual Costing**

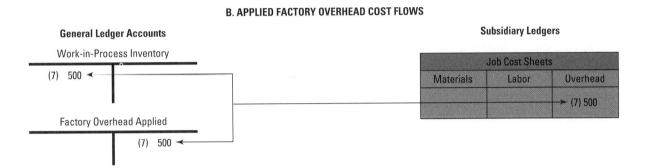

A. ACTUAL FACTORY OVERHEAD COST FLOWS

B. APPLIED FACTORY OVERHEAD COST FLOWS

Exhibit 4.8 illustrates actual factory overhead and applied factory overhead cost flows through related general ledger T-accounts, subsidiary ledgers, and source documents.

When Job 351 is complete, the finished products are transferred from the production department to finished goods. The management accountant finds the total cost incurred for Department A and transfers the total $1,950 cost (Direct materials $450 + Direct labor $1,000 + Factory overhead $500) to the Finished Goods Inventory account from the Work-in-Process Inventory account with this journal entry:

| (8) | Finished Goods Inventory | $1,950 | |
| | Work-in-Process Inventory | | $1,950 |

Normal Costing System

Normal costing system
uses actual costs for direct materials and direct labor and applies factory overhead to various jobs using a predetermined rate basis.

Actual factory overhead costs are not always readily available to most manufacturers at the end of a production process or period, nor can they be easily traced to individual products. In practice, many firms adopt a **normal costing system** that uses actual costs for direct materials and direct labor and applies factory overhead to various jobs using a single rate used throughout the year.

The motive for normalizing factory overhead costs is to avoid the fluctuations in cost per unit under actual costing resulting from changes in the month to month volume of units produced and overhead costs. Using a predetermined *annual* factory overhead rate normalizes overhead cost fluctuations, hence, the term *normal costing*.

The fluctuations in unit cost under actual costing are illustrated in Exhibit 4.9. Another reason for firms to favor normal costing is that this procedure allows management to keep product costs current. If, for example, the management of TFI wants to know the cost of tables manufactured on completion of a job, the controller can immediately provide the actual materials and labor costs incurred because this information is readily available. The controller, however, usually could not compute the actual

EXHIBIT 4.9
Monthly Per-Unit Fixed Factory Overhead Cost Fluctuations under Actual Costing

Steece Machine Tools, Inc., has a monthly total fixed factory overhead of $60,000 and variable manufacturing costs per unit of $10 for its only product. The firm produced 50,000 units in January but only 10,000 units in February because it had a large inventory of unsold goods at the end of January. The unit costs would be as follows if actual costing were used to determine the manufacturing cost per unit:

Month	Production Units	Variable Cost per Unit	Fixed Cost per Unit	Total Unit Cost
January	50,000	$10	$60,000/50,000 = $1.20	$11.20
February	10,000	10	60,000/10,000 = 6.00	16.00

This fluctuation in unit cost certainly does not represent the actual costs to produce the identical products and therefore is not desirable. Predetermined overhead rates, used for a year or longer, are easy to apply and reduce volatility and monthly fluctuations in job costs caused by changes in the production volume and/or overhead costs throughout the year.

per-unit overhead cost of the tables until the end of the accounting period or until some later time when all bills of factory overhead items arrived from the vendors. The costs for overhead elements such as electricity and repair and maintenance, for example, are most likely not available until the end of the period or later. Management certainly would not be satisfied with having to wait until the end of the period to review the manufacturing costs if it wants to bill customers promptly. Use of a predetermined factory overhead rate enables the controller to determine the cost of the product in a timely manner.

The Application of Factory Overhead

To apply overhead cost to each job, normal costing requires a per product rate (ratio of total overhead to the output of product), which is often called a predetermined rate since it is calculated at the beginning of the accounting period.

The predetermined factory overhead rate
is an estimated factory overhead rate used to apply factory overhead cost to a specific job.

The **predetermined factory overhead rate** is an estimated factory overhead rate used to apply factory overhead cost to a job. The amount of overhead assigned to a job using a predetermined factory overhead rate is called **factory overhead applied rate.**

To obtain the predetermined overhead rate, follow these four steps:

Factory overhead applied rate
is the amount of overhead assigned to a specific job using a predetermined factory overhead rate.

1. Estimate total factory overhead costs for an appropriate operating period, usually a year.
2. Select the most appropriate cost drivers for charging the factory overhead costs, usually direct labor hours or machine hours.
3. Estimate the total amount or activity level of the chosen cost drivers for the operating period, again, usually direct labor hours or machine hours.
4. Divide the estimated factory overhead costs by the estimated activity level of the chosen cost drivers to obtain the predetermined overhead rate.

Cost Drivers for Factory Overhead Application

LEARNING OBJECTIVE 4

Explain the application of factory overhead costs in a job costing system.

The base for applying a predetermined overhead rate can be either a volume- or activity-based cost driver. The important consideration is that it be closely related to the behavior of the total overhead costs. The best cost driver choice is the activity or output measure that best represents what drives or causes overhead.

Direct labor-hours, direct labor costs, and machine-hours are among the most frequently used volume-based cost drivers for applying factory overhead. The proper bases or cost drivers for a labor-intensive firm are probably direct labor-hours, direct labor costs, or some labor-related activity measure. In contrast, if factory overhead costs are predominantly related to the equipment operation, the proper cost driver is probably machine-hours or a related measure.

Applying Factory Overhead Costs

The predetermined overhead rate usually is calculated at or before the beginning of the year as follows:

$$\text{Predetermined overhead rate} = \frac{\text{Estimated factory overhead amount for the year}}{\text{Estimated level of cost driver for the year}}$$

For example, suppose TFI has a total estimated factory overhead cost of $200,000 for the coming year. TFI's total overhead costs vary with the total number of machine-hours worked. Thus, management decided to use machine-hours as the cost driver for overhead application. TFI has the following budgeted and actual data.

Estimated annual overhead for all departments	$200,000
Expected annual machine-hours for all departments	16,000
Actual machine-hours for department A for Job 351	26
Actual units for Job 351	10

Thus, the predetermined overhead rate is

$$\frac{\text{Estimated overhead}}{\text{Estimated number of machine-hours}} = \frac{\$200,000}{16,000} = \$12.50 \text{ per machine hour}$$

The overhead cost applied to Job 351 for Department A is $325, and the overhead cost per unit is $32.50:

$$\text{Overhead applied to Job 351 is } \$12.50 \times 26 = \$325$$

$$\text{Overhead cost per unit is } \frac{\$325}{10} = \$32.50$$

There is a difference of $175 ($17.50 per unit) between the $325 overhead applied for Department A under normal costing versus $500 overhead applied under actual costing (page 100). The $17.50 difference is due to the fluctuations in volume and overhead costs month by month. Normal costing assures that the unit cost of Department A overhead in each end table will be $32.50 throughout the year.

Firms lacking a Factory Overhead Applied account credit the Factory Overhead account. We use the separate Factory Overhead Applied account to clearly distinguish between actual and applied factory overhead costs.

Using a predetermined overhead rate to apply overhead cost to products can cause total overhead applied to the units produced to exceed the actual overhead incurred in periods when production is higher than expected. Alternatively, applied overhead might exceed incurred overhead if the amount incurred is less than estimated. **Overapplied overhead** is the amount of factory overhead applied that exceeds the actual factory overhead cost incurred.

On the other hand, it is possible that applied overhead will be less than the incurred amount of overhead, due either to the fact that the actual amount of incurred overhead was greater than expected and/or the actual production level was smaller than expected. **Underapplied overhead** is the amount by which actual factory overhead exceeds factory overhead applied. If the predetermined overhead rate has been determined carefully, the overapplied or underapplied difference should be small.

Overapplied overhead
is the amount of factory overhead applied that exceeds actual factory overhead cost.

Underapplied overhead
is the amount by which actual factory overhead exceeds factory overhead applied.

REAL-WORLD FOCUS Job Costing: JIT and Mass Customization

Job costing has a natural application in companies that have a traditional materials flow through work in process to finished goods, and where customer orders of varying sizes are common. The construction industry, furniture manufacturing, professional services, and many other industries continue to rely upon this costing method to conveniently and effectively track direct costs to jobs and customer orders. In contrast, to be competitive many firms in the consumer goods and electronics industries are moving to advanced manufacturing techniques such as flexible manufacturing systems, just-in-time inventory management, and mass customization (advanced manufacturing methods are explained in Chapter 1). Such changes in manufacturing processes have led to changes in costing methods for these firms that are putting less effort into tracing costs to jobs. Instead these firms are simplifying the accounting, which *will charge some of these costs (especially labor and overhead) directly to cost of goods sold.* The reduced levels of work in process

and finished goods inventory in these firms do not justify the additional accounting effort of tracing costs to these accounts. Also, in flexible systems where an employee might be simultaneously working on two or more different jobs, the tracing of labor costs becomes difficult. While some degree of costing accuracy is lost, the speed and economy of the simpler systems has made them desirable for some firms. Another downside of JIT—it increases the volatility of customer orders. Since customers can expect JIT delivery, some will wait until the last minute to place the order, adding to the unpredictability of the firm's sales. The increased volatility of capital goods orders in the United States in 2001 and 2002 has been attributed in part to the increased use of JIT systems.

Source: Clare Ansberry, "A New Hazard for Recovery: Last-Minute Pace of Orders," *The Wall Street Journal,* June 25, 2002, p. 1.

Disposition of Underapplied and Overapplied Overhead

What do we do with the discrepancy between factory overhead applied and the actual amount of overhead incurred? Since actual production costs should be reported in the period they were incurred, total product costs at the end of the accounting period should be based on actual rather than applied overhead.

Underapplied or overapplied overhead can be disposed of in two ways:

1. Adjust the Cost of Goods Sold account.
2. Adjust the production costs of the period; that is, prorate the discrepancy among the amounts of the current period's applied overhead remaining in the ending balances of the Work-in-Process Inventory, the Finished Goods Inventory, and the Cost of Goods Sold accounts.

When the amount of underapplied or overapplied overhead is not significant, it generally is adjusted to Cost of Goods Sold. On the other hand, if the amount is significant, it is often prorated.

Adjustment to Cost of Goods Sold

Adjusting Cost of Goods Sold is the more expedient of the two methods for disposing of overhead discrepancies. The difference between the actual factory overhead incurred and the amount applied to production is disposed of by adding to or subtracting from the Cost of Goods Sold account for the period, whichever is appropriate.

Suppose that TFI applied $200,000 of overhead but found at the end of the year that the actual total amount of overhead incurred was $205,000. The $5,000 discrepancy represents underapplied overhead. The appropriate adjusting entry to the Cost of Goods Sold account is

LEARNING OBJECTIVE 5
Calculate underapplied and overapplied overhead and show how to dispose of it at the end of the period.

Cost of Goods Sold	5,000	
Factory Overhead Applied	200,000	
Factory Overhead		205,000
To record the disposition of underapplied overhead.		

This entry closes the Factory Overhead and Factory Overhead Applied accounts and increases the cost of the goods sold for the period by $5,000.

To dispose of the $5,000 difference only in the Cost of Goods Sold account ignores the fact that some portion of current production costs also can be in ending Work-in-Process Inventory or ending Finished Goods Inventory; so when the overhead difference is significant, a management accountant usually chooses to use proration.

Proration among Inventories and Cost of Goods Sold

Proration is the process of allocating underapplied or overapplied overhead to Work-in-Process Inventory, Finished Goods Inventory, and Cost of Goods Sold accounts.

Because factory overhead is one of the manufacturing cost elements that entered into the Work-in-Process Inventory account, underapplied or overapplied overhead affects the value of the work in process, which, in turn, affects the amount transferred out of the Work-in-Process Inventory account and charged to the Finished Goods Inventory account. Eventually, the amount in the Cost of Goods Sold account for the period is also affected because it is determined by the amount in the Finished Goods Inventory account.

If all units placed into production are completed and sold at the end of a period, adjusting for any discrepancy between actual overhead and applied overhead can be accomplished with entries to the Cost of Goods Sold account as just explained. If, on the other hand, all units processed are not completed and/or all units completed are not sold at the end of the period, the adjustment made for underapplied or overapplied overhead should affect the Work-in-Process Inventory account and the Finished Goods Inventory account, in addition to the Cost of Goods Sold account. For these ending inventories to reflect the actual cost incurred, the amount of overapplied or underapplied overhead must be prorated among the three accounts.

The proration of the difference is based on the current period's applied overhead in the ending inventories of the Work-in-Process Inventory, Finished Goods Inventory, and Cost of Goods Sold accounts at the end of the period. To determine the ratios for the proration, we compute the sum of the applied overhead in the ending inventories of the Work-in-Process Inventory, Finished Goods Inventory, and Cost of Goods Sold accounts at the end of the period. The ratio of each of the components to this sum is the amount of the underapplied or overapplied overhead that should be prorated to the cost of the component.

To illustrate the proration of an overhead variance, assume that TFI's accounts had the following applied overhead balances for the end of period:

Ending Work-in-process inventory	$ 20,000
Ending Finished goods inventory	30,000
Cost of goods sold	150,000
Total factory overhead applied	$200,000
Factory overhead incurred (actual)	$205,000

Suppose that TFI uses the Factory Overhead account to record the actual overhead incurred and the Factory Overhead Applied account to record the application of overhead to the job. The proration of the $5,000 underapplied factory overhead among the Work-in-Process Inventory, Finished Goods Inventory, and Cost of Goods Sold accounts is computed as follows:

Amount	Applied Overhead	Underapplied Percentage of Total	Overhead Prorated
Work-in-process inventory	$ 20,000	10%	$ 500
Finished goods inventory	30,000	15	750
Cost of goods sold	150,000	75	3,750
Total	$200,000	100%	$5,000

In the late 1980s and early 1990s, the U.S. defense industry was in a slump; the end of the Cold War caused significant reductions in the national defense budget. ITT's Federal Service Corporation (ITTFSC), a long-time air force contractor, faced higher overhead costs, a long delay in billings because of a host of outdated technologies, and a government customer that no longer could afford outside consultants and other interim solutions. ITTFSC's managers needed more timely and reliable information to evaluate strategic options for changing the way to manage the business and promote service excellence. Managers wanted more accurate and timely job costing information to ensure a competitive advantage and optimize the company's service and support. What changes did ITTFSC make in the firm's cost management practices? (Refer to Comments on Cost Management in Action at the end of the chapter.)

REAL-WORLD FOCUS · Job Costing and Sustainability

Many firms in the metal processing industry use job costing because their business is driven by customer orders which tend to vary somewhat, making it easy to trace materials and labor to each job. One firm, a steel-plating facility, discovered in 1996 that it could reduce overall costs by integrating the costs of environmental compliance with the costing system, by carefully integrating and managing (a) the marketing plans, (b) the manufacturing plans, (c) the capacity of the firm's waste treatment facility, and (d) alternate means to eliminate or reduce environmentally sensitive waste. In contrast to many firms in the industry that relied only on environmental engineers to redesign the plant and treatment facility to achieve environmental compliance, this firm decided to take a business approach that integrated the marketing plans, the manufactur-

ing plans, and the required waste treatment efforts. The firm was able to install a new nickel steel product line and appropriate waste treatment methods that suitably matched the firm's product demand for $600,000 less than the estimates of the environmental engineers. The answer was to tailor the needed waste treatment to the nature and extent of expected product demand, and to seek a variety of ways to achieve environmental compliance, including new ways to prevent waste, different ways to dispose of waste, and new ways to treat waste in the manufacturing plant. The solution was a win-win economically and environmentally.

Source: Jasbinder Singh, "Making Business Sense of Environmental Compliance," *Sloan Management Review*, Spring 2000, pp. 91–100.

The appropriate adjusting entry is

Factory Overhead Applied	200,000	
Work-in-Process Inventory	500	
Finished Goods Inventory	750	
Cost of Goods Sold	3,750	
Factory Overhead		205,000

Some firms prefer to use the balances of Work-in-Process Inventory, Finished Goods Inventory, and Cost of Goods Sold accounts rather than the applied overhead in the accounts to calculate the percentages.

When a substantial difference between the actual factory overhead incurred and the factory overhead applied occurs, the total manufacturing cost as recorded on the debit side of the Work-in-Process Inventory account is understated (underapplication) or overstated (overapplication). Left unadjusted, the inventory and Cost of Goods Sold accounts would be substantially distorted.

No matter which method is used, underapplied or overapplied overhead is usually adjusted only at the end of a year. Nothing needs to be done during the year because the predetermined factory overhead rate is based on annual figures. A variance is expected between the actual overhead incurred and the amount applied in a particular month or quarter because of seasonal fluctuations in the firm's operating cycle. Furthermore, an underapplied factory overhead in one month is likely to be offset by an overapplied amount in another month (and vice versa).

Job Costing in Service Industries

Job costing is used extensively in service industries such as advertising agencies, construction companies, hospitals, and repair shops, as well as consulting, architecture, accounting, and law firms. Instead of using the term *job,* accounting and consulting firms use the term *client* or *project;* hospitals and law firms use the term *case,* and advertising agencies and construction companies use the term *contract* or *project.* Many firms use the term *project costing* to indicate the use of job costing in service industries.

LEARNING OBJECTIVE 6

Apply job costing in service industries.

Job costing in service industries uses recording procedures and accounts similar to those illustrated earlier in this chapter except for direct materials involved (there could be none or an insignificant amount). The primary focus is on direct labor. The overhead costs are usually applied to jobs based on direct labor-hours or dollars.

Suppose that Freed and Swenson, a Los Angeles law firm, has the following budget of estimated costs for 2004:

Compensation of professional staff	$ 500,000
Other costs	500,000
Total budgeted costs for 2004	$1,000,000

Other costs include indirect materials and supplies, photocopying, computer-related expenses, insurance, office rent, utilities, training costs, accounting fees, indirect labor costs for office support personnel, and other office expenses.

Freed and Swenson charges overhead costs to clients or jobs at a predetermined percentage of the professional salaries charged to the client. The law firm's recent data show that chargeable hours average 80 percent of available hours for all categories of professional personnel. The nonchargeable hours are regarded as additional overhead. This nonchargeable time might involve training, idle time, inefficiency in resource allocation, and similar factors.

Using these data, the firm's budgeted (that is, estimated) direct labor costs and budgeted overhead costs are:

1. Budgeted direct labor costs:

   $500,000 \times 80\% = \$400,000$

2. Budgeted overhead costs:

Other costs	$500,000
Salary costs for nonchargeable hours:	
$500,000 - \$400,000 =$	100,000
	$600,000

The predetermined overhead rate is

$$\frac{\text{Budgeted overhead costs}}{\text{Budgeted direct labor costs}} = \frac{\$600,000}{\$400,000} = 150\%$$

Exhibit 4.10 presents relevant data and job costs for the law firm's recent client, George Christatos.

REAL-WORLD FOCUS Job Costing at an Advertising Agency

The job costing system used by a New York City advertising agency provided information that assisted management in identifying highly profitable and extremely unprofitable accounts. The advertising agency used its job costing system to discover that a certain account was being served by personnel at a supervisory level while less expensive staff-level personnel would have been adequate. The firm then decided to assign staff personnel to the account, resulting in considerable savings. The job costing system also aided in budgeting costs and revenues for various accounts so that account managers could more effectively manage them. Overall, the system helped the firm improve its planning, control, and performance evaluation processes.

Based on information in William B. Mills, "Drawing Up a Budgeting System for an Ad Agency," *Management Accounting*, December 1983, pp. 47–49.

EXHIBIT 4.10
Job Costing for Freed and Swenson Law Firm

Client: George Christatos

Employee Charges	Hours	Salary Rates	Billing Rates (300 percent)
Partners	10	$80	$240
Managers	20	50	150
Associates	100	20	60
	130		

Total Revenues and Costs for This Client's Job
Service revenues   ($240 × 10) + ($150 × 20) + ($60 × 100) = $11,400
Cost of services

Direct labor ($80 × 10) + ($50 × 20) + ($20 × 100) = $3,800
Overhead $3,800 × 150%   = 5,700
Total costs of services   9,500
Operating income for this client $1,900

Operation Costing

Operation costing
is a hybrid costing system that uses job costing to assign direct materials costs and process costing to assign conversion costs to products or services.

LEARNING OBJECTIVE 7
Explain an operation costing system.

Operation costing is a hybrid costing system that uses job costing to assign direct materials costs to jobs, and a departmental approach to assign conversion costs to products or services.

Manufacturing operations whose conversion activities are very similar across several product lines, but whose direct materials used in the various products differ significantly use operation costing. After direct labor and factory overhead conversion costs have been accumulated by operations or departments, these costs are then assigned to products. On the other hand, direct materials costs are accumulated by jobs or batches, and job costing assigns these costs to products or services.

Industries suitable for applying operation costing include clothing, food processing, textiles, shoes, furniture, metalworking, jewelry, and electronic equipment. For example, chair manufacturing has two standard operations: cutting and assembling. Different jobs, however, require different wood and fabric materials. Therefore, an operation costing system can be well-suited for this situation.

Suppose that Irvine Glass Company manufactures two types of glass for sheets, clear glass and colored glass. Department 1 produces clear glass sheets, some of which are sold as finished goods. Others are transferred to Department 2, which adds metallic oxides to clear glass sheets to form colored glass sheets, which are then sold as finished goods. The company uses operation costing.

Irvine Glass Company finished two jobs: Job A produced 10,000 sheets of clear glass and job B produced 5,000 sheets of colored glass. Manufacturing operations and costs applied to these products follow.

Direct materials		
Job A (10,000 clear glass sheets)		$400,000
Job B (5,000 colored glass sheets)		
Materials for clear glass sheets in Department 1	$200,000	
Materials added to clear glass sheets in Department 2	100,000	300,000
Total direct materials		$700,000
Conversion costs		
Department 1		$180,000
Department 2		50,000
Total conversion costs		$230,000
Total costs		$930,000

Notice in this table that operation costing identifies direct materials by job but that it identifies conversion costs with the two production departments.

The unit product cost for each type of glass sheet is computed as follows:

	Clear Glass	Colored Glass
Direct materials		
Job A ($400,000/10,000)	$40	
Job B ($300,000/5,000)		$60
Conversion: Department 1 ($180,000/15,000)	12	12
Conversion: Department 2 ($50,000/5,000)		10
Total product cost per unit	$52	$82

Notice in this table that each glass sheet receives the same conversion costs in Department 1 since this operation is identical for the two products. Total product costs are calculated as follows:

Clear glass sheets ($52 × 10,000)	$520,000
Colored glass sheets ($82 × 5,000)	410,000
Total	$930,000

The following journal entries record Irvine Glass Company's flow of costs. Department 1 makes the first entry by recording the requisition of direct materials when Job A entered production:

Work-in-Process Inventory: Department 1	400,000	
Materials Inventory		400,000

Department 1 makes the following entry to record the requisition of direct materials when Job B enters production:

Work-in-Process Inventory: Department 1	200,000	
Materials Inventory		200,000

Conversion costs are applied in Department 1 with the following journal entry:

Work-in-Process Inventory: Department 1	180,000	
Conversion Costs Applied		180,000

The following entry records the transfer of completed clear glass sheets to finished goods:

Finished Goods Inventory	520,000	
Work-in-Process Inventory: Department 1		520,000

Direct materials $400,000 + Conversion ($12 \times 10,000$) = $520,000

The following entry records the transfer of partially completed colored glass sheets to Department 2:

Work-in-Process Inventory: Department 2	260,000	
Work-in-Process Inventory: Department 1		260,000

Direct materials $200,000 + Conversion ($12 \times 5,000$) = $260,000

The following entry records the requisition of the materials by Department 2 when job B enters production:

Work-in-Process Inventory: Department 2	100,000	
Materials Inventory		100,000

Conversion costs are applied in Department 2 with the following journal entry.

Work-in-Process Inventory: Department 2	50,000	
Conversion Costs Applied		50,000

Finally, the completed colored glass sheets are transferred to finished goods.

Finished Goods Inventory	410,000	
Work-in-Process Inventory: Department 2		410,000

Department 2 work-in-process $260,000 + Materials for colored glass $100,000 + Conversion ($10 \times 5,000$) = $410,000

Summary

Product costing is the process of accumulating, classifying, and assigning direct materials, direct labor, and factory overhead costs to products or services. Product costing provides useful cost information for both manufacturing and nonmanufacturing firms for (1) product and service cost determination and inventory valuation, (2) management planning, cost control, and performance evaluation, and (3) managerial decisions.

Several different product costing systems are available and can be classified as the (1) cost accumulation method—job or processing costing systems, (2) cost measurement method—actual, normal, or standard costing systems, (3) overhead assignment method—traditional or activity-based costing systems. The choice of a particular system depends on the nature of the industry and the product or service; the firm's strategy and its management information needs; and the costs and benefits to acquire, design, modify, and operate a particular system.

Job costing uses several general ledger accounts to control the product cost flows. Direct materials costs are debited to the Materials Inventory account at purchase time and debited to the Work-in-Process Inventory account when production requests materials. Direct labor costs are debited to the Work-in-Process Inventory account when they are incurred. Actual factory overhead costs are debited to the Factory Overhead account when they are incurred. Factory overhead applied using the predetermined factory overhead rate in normal costing is debited to the Work-in-Process Inventory account and credited to the Factory Overhead Applied account. When a job is complete, the cost of goods manufactured is transferred from the Work-in-Process Inventory account to the Finished Goods Inventory account.

The predetermined factory overhead rate is an estimated factory overhead rate used to apply factory overhead cost to a specific job. The application of a predetermined overhead rate has four steps: (1) estimate factory overhead costs for an appropriate operating period, usually a year, (2) select the most appropriate cost drivers for charging the factory overhead costs, (3) estimate the total amount or activity level of the chosen cost drivers for the operating period, and (4) divide the budgeted factory overhead costs by the estimated activity level of the chosen cost drivers to obtain the predetermined factory overhead rates.

The difference between the actual factory overhead cost and the amount of the factory overhead applied is the overhead variance; it is either underapplied or overapplied. It can be disposed of in two ways: (1) adjust the Cost of Goods Sold account or (2) prorate the discrepancy among the Work-in-Process Inventory, the Finished Goods Inventory, and the Cost of Goods Sold accounts.

Job costing is used extensively in service industries such as advertising agencies, construction companies, hospitals, repair shops and consulting, architecture, accounting, and law firms.

Operation costing is used when most of the plant's products have a similar conversion cycle, but materials costs may differ significantly. In this case, materials costs are traced to jobs, while conversion costs are traced to departments and then to jobs.

Appendix A

Spoilage, Rework, and Scrap in Job Costing

In today's manufacturing environment, firms adopt various quality improvement programs to reduce spoilage, rework units, and scrap. **Spoilage** refers to unacceptable units that are discarded or sold for disposal value. **Rework** units are units produced that must be reworked into good units that can be sold in regular channels. **Scrap** is the material left over from the manufacture of the product; it has little or no value.

SPOILAGE

The two types of spoilage are normal and abnormal. **Normal spoilage** occurs under normal operating conditions; it is uncontrollable in the short term and is considered a normal part of production and product cost. That is, the cost of spoiled unit costs is absorbed by the cost of good units produced. **Abnormal spoilage** is in excess over the amount of normal spoilage expected under normal operating conditions; it is charged as a loss to operations in the period detected.

Normal spoilage can be classified as that incurred (1) for a *particular job* and (2) *in common* with all jobs because it relates to the production process in general.

Spoilage cost for a particular job can be reduced by the estimated disposal value or selling price of the spoiled goods. Commonly, spoilage cost is transferred from the particular job cost into the Factory Overhead account. Abnormal spoilage is charged to the Loss from Abnormal Spoilage account.

Spoilage
refers to an unaccepted unit that is discarded or sold for disposal value.

Rework
is a produced unit that must be reworked into a good unit that can be sold in regular channels.

Scrap
is the material left over from the manufacture of the product; it has little or no value.

Normal spoilage
is waste that occurs under normal operating conditions.

Abnormal spoilage
is waste that should not arise under normal operating conditions.

Suppose during June, Wang Company's job A21 had normal spoilage with the estimated disposal value of $500 attributable to it, and job B32 had normal spoilage with the estimated cost of $700 due to the general production process failure plus abnormal spoilage of $100. The proper journal entries follow:

Materials Inventory (disposal value or selling price of the spoilage goods)	500	
Work-in-Process Inventory: Job A21		500
Factory Overhead (normal spoilage cost)	700	
Loss from Abnormal Spoilage	100	
Work-in-Process Inventory: Job B32		800

REWORK

Like spoilage, there are three types of rework: (1) rework on normal defective units for a particular job, (2) rework on normal defective units common with all jobs, and (3) rework on abnormal defective units not falling within the normal range. The cost of rework units is charged to one of three accounts depending on its nature. Normal rework for a particular job is charged to that specific job's Work-in-Process Inventory account. Normal rework common to all jobs is charged to the Factory Overhead account and abnormal rework is charged to the Loss from Abnormal Rework account.

SCRAP

Scrap can be classified according to (1) a specific job and (2) common to all jobs. To account for the first type of scrap, reduce the selling price of the scrap from the Work-in-Process Inventory account. For the second type, reduce the selling price of the scrap from the Factory Overhead account.

Suppose that Arnold Machine Shop incurred and sold the scrap from a specific job for $100 cash and sold the scrap common to all jobs for $200 cash in July. The proper journal entries follow:

Cash	100	
Work-in-Process Inventory		100
Cash	200	
Factory Overhead		200

Key Terms

abnormal spoilage, *111*	normal costing system, *101*	proration, *105*
actual costing system, *100*	normal spoilage, *111*	rework, *111*
actual factory overhead, *100*	operation costing, *108*	scrap, *111*
factory overhead applied	overapplied overhead, *103*	spoilage, *111*
rate, *102*	overhead application, *100*	time ticket, *98*
job cost sheet, *95*	predetermined factory	underapplied overhead, *103*
job costing, *94*	overhead rate, *102*	
materials requisition form, *97*	product costing, *92*	

Comments on Cost Management in Action

ITTFSC Battled Overhead Costs, Billing Delays, and Military Cutbacks

In the early 1990s, ITT's Federal Service Corporation (ITTFSC) assembled a strike team to reengineer its financial and accounting services. The team decided to replace the firm's 20-year-old mainframe accounting system because of its inflexibility and sluggish performance. The team wanted a system that could easily handle hundreds of concurrent users and process thousands of journal entries in hours rather than in days or weeks. ITT instigated an extensive review of proposals from 40 accounting system vendors and narrowed the list to four for an in-depth review and on-site demonstrations. Based on cost-effective superior functionality, the company decided to install Maxwell Business Systems' Job Cost Accounting/Management Information System (JAMIS).

JAMIS offered a flexible system for modifying ITT's job number structure. ITT cut the waiting period for the internal users dramatically because various department users collect the data themselves and generate reports in a matter of minutes rather than days. Billing, once a labor- and paper-intensive task, became automatic. The system's interactive approach kept ITT's payroll and billing information current and accurate. The new job costing system resulted in a 50 percent reduction in data processing and financial staffing requirements. Billings in the millions of dollars to the federal government could be submitted in days rather than weeks. Now ITT can support the special needs of its government contract and promote service excellence.

Source: "ITT Boosts Financial Productivity, Customer Service," *Management Accounting,* September 1996, pp. 32–33.

Self-Study Problem
(For solution, please turn
to the end of the chapter.)

Journal Entries and Accounting for Overhead

Watkins Machinery Company uses a normal job costing system. The company has this partial trial balance information on March 1, 2004, the last month of its fiscal year:

Materials Inventory (X, $3,000; Y, $2,000; Indirect materials, $5,000)	$10,000
Work-in-Process Inventory—Job 101	6,000
Finished Goods Inventory—Job 100	10,000

These transactions relate to the month of March:

a. Purchased direct materials and indirect materials with the following summary of receiving reports:

Material X	$10,000
Material Y	10,000
Indirect materials	5,000
Total	$25,000

b. Issued direct materials and indirect materials with this summary of requisition forms:

	Job 101	Job 102	Total
Material X	$5,000	$3,000	$ 8,000
Material Y	4,000	3,000	7,000
Subtotal	$9,000	$6,000	$15,000
Indirect materials			8,000
Total			$23,000

c. Factory labor incurred is summarized by these time tickets:

Job 101	$12,000
Job 102	8,000
Indirect labor	5,000
Total	$25,000

d. Factory utilities, factory depreciation, and factory insurance incurred is summarized by these factory vouchers, invoices, and cost memos:

Utilities	$ 500
Depreciation	15,000
Insurance	2,500
Total	$18,000

e. Factory overhead costs were applied to jobs at the predetermined rate of $15 per machine-hour. Job 101 incurred 1,200 machine-hours; job 102 used 800 machine-hours.

f. Job 101 was completed; job 102 was still in process at the end of March.

g. Job 100 and job 101 were shipped to customers during March. Both jobs had gross margins of 20 percent based on manufacturing cost.

The company closed the overapplied or underapplied overhead to the Cost of Goods Sold account at the end of March.

Required

1. Prepare journal entries to record the transactions and events. Letter your entries from a to g.
2. Compute the ending balance of the Work-in-Process Inventory account.
3. Compute the overhead variance and indicate whether it is overapplied or underapplied.
4. Close the overhead variance to the Cost of Goods Sold account.

Questions

4–1   What is the purpose of a product costing system?

4–2   Give three ways that management uses product costs.

4–3   Distinguish between job costing and process costing.

4–4   Explain when companies are likely to use a job costing system or a process costing system. Provide several examples.

4–5   Which product costing system is extensively used in the service industry for hospitals, law firms, or accounting firms? Explain why.

4–6   What document is prepared to accumulate costs for each separate job in a job costing system? What type of costs are recorded in the document?

4–7   Explain how predetermined factory overhead rates are computed and why they are used to apply factory overhead to units of products instead of actual overhead costs.

4–8   What is the role of material requisition forms in a job costing system? Time tickets? Bills of materials?

4–9   What does the statement that accounting for overhead involves an important cost-benefit issue mean? Why is that issue important?

4–10 Describe the flow of costs through a job costing system.

4–11 What do *underapplied overhead* and *overapplied overhead* mean? How are these amounts disposed of at the end of a period?

4–12 Why are some manufacturing firms switching from direct labor-hours to machine-hours as the cost driver for factory overhead application?

4–13 Explain why overhead might be overapplied in a given period.

4–14 Distinguish between an actual costing system and a normal costing system. What are the components of the actual manufacturing costs and the components of the normal manufacturing costs?

4–15 Factory overhead includes a variety of costs that vary greatly with respect to the production process. What is the best way to choose an appropriate cost driver when applying factory overhead?

4–16 What is the difference between normal cost of goods sold and adjusted cost of goods sold?

Exercises

4–17 **Basic Job Costing**   Assume the following for Round Top, Inc., for 2004. Round Top applies overhead on the basis of units produced.

Budgeted overhead	$350,000
Actual overhead	$360,000
Actual labor hours	22,000
Actual number of units sold	650,000
Overapplied overhead	$ 30,000
Budgeted production	700,000

Required   How many units were produced in 2004?

4–18 **Basic Job Costing**   Davis Inc. is a job-order manufacturing company that uses a predetermined overhead rate based on direct labor-hours to apply overhead to individual jobs. For 2004, estimated direct labor-hours are 95,000, and estimated factory overhead is $579,500. The following information is for September 2004. Job A was completed during September, and Job B was started but not finished.

September 1, 2004, inventories	
Materials inventory	$ 7,500
Work-in-process inventory (All Job A)	31,200
Finished goods inventory	67,000
Material purchases	104,000
Direct materials requisitioned	
Job A	45,000
Job B	33,500
Direct labor-hours	
Job A	4,200
Job B	3,500
Labor costs incurred	
Direct labor ($5.50/hour)	42,350
Indirect labor	13,500
Supervisory salaries	6,000
Rental costs	
Factory	7,000
Administrative offices	1,800
Total equipment depreciation costs	
Factory	7,500
Administrative offices	1,600
Indirect materials used	12,000

Required

1. What is the total cost of Job A?
2. What is the total factory overhead applied during September?
3. What is the overapplied or underapplied overhead for September?

4–19 **Journal Entries**   Carlson Company uses a job costing system with normal costing and applies factory overhead on the basis of machine-hours. At the beginning of the year, management estimated that the company would incur $1,008,000 of factory overhead costs and use 72,000 machine-hours.

Carlson Company recorded the following events during the month of May:

a. Purchased 180,000 pounds of materials on account; the cost was $2.50 per pound.
b. Issued 120,000 pounds of materials to production of which 15,000 pounds were used as indirect materials.
c. Incurred direct labor costs of $240,000 and $40,000 of indirect labor costs.
d. Recorded depreciation on equipment for the month, $15,700.
e. Recorded insurance costs for the manufacturing property, $3,500.
f. Paid $8,500 cash for utilities and other miscellaneous items for the manufacturing plant.
g. Completed Job H11 costing $7,500 and Job G28 costing $77,000 during the month and transferred them to the Finished Goods Inventory account.
h. Shipped Job G28 to the customer during the month. The job was invoiced at 35 percent above cost.
i. Used 7,700 machine-hours during May.

Required

1. Compute Carlson Company's predetermined overhead rate for the year.
2. Prepare journal entries to record the events that occurred during May.
3. Compute the amount of overapplied or underapplied overhead and prepare a journal entry to close overapplied or underapplied overhead into cost of goods sold on May 31.

4–20 Accounting for Overhead Yamashita Company is a furniture manufacturing firm in a suburb of Tokyo, Japan. It uses a job costing system. It applies factory overhead costs in yen on the basis of direct labor-hours. At the beginning of 2004, management estimated that the company would incur ¥284,000 of factory overhead costs for the year and work 71,000 direct labor-hours.

During the year, the company actually worked 75,000 direct labor-hours and incurred these factory overhead costs:

a. Paid ¥75,400 cash for utilities, power, and other miscellaneous items for the manufacturing plants.

b. Recognized ¥58,000 depreciation on manufacturing property, plant, and equipment for the year.

c. Paid ¥25,000 cash for the insurance premium on manufacturing property and plant.

d. Incurred advertising costs, ¥10,000.

e. Incurred indirect labor costs, ¥54,600.

f. Incurred indirect material costs, ¥53,000.

g. Paid the ¥55,000 salary of the factory superintendent.

h. Accrued sales and administrative salaries, ¥85,000.

Required

1. Compute the firm's 2004 predetermined overhead rate.

2. Compute the amount of factory overhead that should be applied to the Work-in-Process Inventory account for the year.

3. Compute the amount of overapplied or underapplied overhead to be closed into the Cost of Goods Sold account at the end of the year.

4. Check the most recent issue of *The Wall Street Journal* to find the exchange rate between the U.S. dollar and the Japanese yen.

4–21 Underapplied or Overapplied Overhead Tyson Company uses a job costing system that applies factory overhead on the basis of direct labor-hours. No job was in process on February 1. During the month of February, the company worked on these three jobs:

	Job Number		
	A23	**C76**	**G15**
Direct labor ($8/hour)	$24,000	?	$8,800
Direct materials	42,000	61,000	?
Overhead applied	?	24,750	6,050

During the month, the company completed and transferred Job A23 to the finished goods inventory at the cost of $82,500. Jobs C76 and G15 were not completed and remain in work in process at the cost of $148,650 at the end of the month. Actual factory overhead costs during the month totaled $48,600.

Required

1. Compute the amount of underapplied or overapplied overhead for February.

2. What is the predetermined factory overhead rate?

3. Compute the cost of direct materials issued to production during the month.

4. Prepare a journal entry showing the transfer of the completed job to Finished Goods Inventory.

4–22 Application and Proration of Factory Overhead Tomek Company uses a job costing system that applies factory overhead on the basis of direct labor-hours. The company's factory overhead budget for 2004 included the following estimates:

Budgeted total factory overhead	$568,000
Budgeted total direct labor-hours	71,000

At the end of the year, the company's ledger shows these results:

Actual factory overhead	$582,250
Actual direct labor-hours	71,500

The following amounts of the year's applied factory overhead remained in the various manufacturing accounts:

	Applied Factory Overhead Remaining
Work-in-process inventory	$139,000
Finished goods inventory	216,840
Cost of goods sold	200,160

Required

1. Compute the firm's predetermined factory overhead rate for 2004.
2. Calculate the amount of overapplied or underapplied overhead.
3. Prepare a journal entry to prorate overapplied or underapplied overhead to Work-in-Process Inventory, Finished Goods Inventory, and Cost of Goods Sold accounts.

4–23 **Overhead Rate, Pricing**   Buckey Associates is an advertising agency in Columbus, Ohio. The company's controller estimated that it would incur $325,000 in overhead costs for 2004. Because the overhead costs of each project change in direct proportion to the amount of direct professional hours incurred, the controller decided that overhead should be applied on the basis of professional hours. The controller estimated 25,000 professional hours for the year. During October, Buckey incurred the following costs to make a 20-second TV commercial for Central Ohio Bank:

Direct materials	$32,000
Direct professional hours ($23/hour)	1,200

Actual overhead costs to make the commercial totaled $14,700. The industry customarily bills customers at 150 percent of total cost.

Required

1. Compute the predetermined overhead rate.
2. What is the total amount of the bill that Buckey will send Central Ohio Bank?

4–24 **Operation Costing**   Pomona Company manufactures two sizes of T-shirts, medium and large. Both sizes go through cutting, assembling, and finishing departments. The company uses operation costing.

Pomona's conversion costs applied to products for April were $45,000 for the cutting department, $22,500 for the assembling department, and $15,000 for the finishing department. April had no beginning or ending work-in-process inventory.

The quantities and direct materials costs for April follow:

Job Number	Size	Quantity	Direct Materials
401	Medium	5,000	$20,000
402	Large	10,000	50,000

Each T-shirt, regardless of size, required the same cutting, assembling, and finishing operations.

Required

1. Compute both unit cost and total cost for each shirt size produced in April.
2. Prepare journal entries to record direct materials and conversion costs incurred in the three departments and finished goods costs for both shirt sizes.

4–25 Spoilage and Scrap Liu Textile Company's job X12 had normal spoilage with the estimated disposal selling price of $300 in May attributable to this particular job. Its job Y34 had a normal spoilage with the estimated cost of $400 from the general production process failure and abnormal spoilage of $200. The company also incurred scrap due to a specific job and sold it for $80. It also sold the scrap common to all jobs for $120 cash in May.

Required

1. Make the necessary journal entries to record normal and abnormal spoilage costs.
2. Make the necessary journal entries to record both types of scrap sold.

Problems

4–26 Application and Disposition of Factory Overhead Work in process inventory for Department 203 at the beginning of period:

Job	Materials	Labor	Overhead	Total
1376	$17,500	$22,000	$33,000	$72,500

Department 203 Costs for 2004:

	Incurred by Jobs			
Jobs	Materials	Labor	Other	Total
1376	$ 1,000	$ 7,000	—	$ 8,000
1377	26,000	53,000	—	79,000
1378	12,000	9,000	—	21,000
1379	4,000	1,000	—	5,000

	Materials	Labor	Other	Total
Indirect materials and supplies	$15,000	—	—	$ 15,000
Indirect labor	—	$ 53,000	—	53,000
Employee benefits	—	—	$23,000	23,000
Depreciation	—	—	12,000	12,000
Supervision	—	20,000	—	20,000
Total	$58,000	$143,000	$35,000	$236,000

Department 203 Overhead rate for 2004:

Budgeted overhead	
Variable	
Indirect materials	$ 16,000
Indirect labor	56,000
Employee benefits	24,000
Fixed	
Supervision	20,000
Depreciation	12,000
Total	$128,000
Budgeted direct labor dollars	$ 80,000
Rate per direct labor dollar ($128,000/$80,000)	160%

Required

1. What was the actual factory overhead for Department 203 for 2004?
2. What was Department 203's underapplied overhead for 2004?
3. Job 1376 was the only job completed and sold in 2004. What amount was included in the cost of the goods sold for this job?
4. What was the amount of Work-in-Process Inventory at the end of 2004?

5. Assume that factory overhead was underapplied in the amount of $14,000 for department 203. If underapplied overhead were distributed between the cost of the goods sold and inventory, how much of the underapplied overhead was charged to the year-end Work-in-Process Inventory?

(CMA Adapted)

4–27 Choice of Costing System

Required

1. The following is a list of websites for a number of companies. Briefly describe each company and indicate whether it is more likely to use job costing or process costing. Explain why in each case.

   a. New Century Software Inc. at www.newcenturysoftware.com.

   b. Kinko's at www.kinkos.com.

   c. Riverside Cement (TXi) at www.txi.com.

   d. Paramount Pictures at www.paramount.com.

   e. Evian at www.evian.com.

   f. Ircon International Limited at www.irconinternational.com.

2. Briefly describe two additional companies (and give their websites), one that would use a job costing system and the other that would use a process costing system. Explain why for each company.

4–28 Choice of Costing System

Required

1. The following is a list of websites for a number of non–U.S. companies. Briefly describe each company and indicate whether it is more likely to use job costing or process costing. Explain why in each case.

   a. Formosa Plastics Corporation at www.fpc.com.tw.

   b. Zurich Financial Services Group at www.zurich.com.

   c. Toyota Motor at www.global.toyota.com.

   d. Nestle S.A. at www.nestle.com.

   e. Nokia at www.nokia.com.

   f. SAP at www.sap.com

2. Briefly describe two additional non–U.S. companies (and give their websites), one that would use a job costing system and the other that would use a process costing system. Explain why for each company.

4–29 Job Costing   The following information applies to the Hartsook Company for March 2004:

a. Purchased direct materials and indirect materials with the following summary of receiving reports:

Material A	$16,000
Material B	12,000
Indirect materials	3,000
Total	$31,000

b. Issued direct materials and indirect materials with this summary of requisition forms:

	Job X	Job Y	Total
Material A	$6,000	$15,000	$21,000
Material B	2,000	7,000	9,000
Subtotal	$8,000	$22,000	$30,000
Indirect materials			42,000
Total			$72,000

c. Factory labor incurred is summarized by these time tickets:

Job X	$16,000
Job Y	12,000
Indirect labor	28,000
Total	$56,000

d. Factory utilities, factory depreciation, and factory insurance incurred is summarized by these factory vouchers, invoices, and cost memos:

Utilities	$ 2,000
Depreciation	18,000
Insurance	1,500
Total	$21,500

e. Factory overhead costs were applied to jobs at the predetermined rate of $46 per machine-hour. Job X incurred 1,200 machine-hours; Job Y used 800 machine-hours.

f. Job X was completed; Job Y was still in process at the end of March.

g. Job X was shipped to customers during March. Job X had a gross margin of 20 percent based on manufacturing cost.

The company closed the overapplied or underapplied overhead to the Cost of Goods Sold account at the end of March.

Required

1. Calculate the amount of overapplied or underapplied overhead and state whether the cost of goods sold account will be increased or decreased by the adjustment.

2. Calculate the total manufacturing cost for Job X and Job Y for March 2004.

4–30 **Schedule of Cost of Goods Manufactured**   Benaline Company uses a job costing system for its production costs. It uses a predetermined factory overhead rate based on direct labor costs to apply factory overhead to jobs. During the month of July, the firm processed three jobs: A12, C46, and M24. A small fire in the administration office during the early hours of August 1 left only these fragments of the company's factory ledger:

Inventories, July 1	
Materials inventory (all direct)	$ 42,500
Work-in-process inventory (job A12)	54,000
Finished goods inventory	75,000
Inventories, July 31	
Materials inventory (all direct)	?
Work-in-process inventory (job C46 and job M23)	?
Finished goods inventory	96,080
Cost of goods sold, July	102,000
Direct materials purchased, July	25,000
Direct materials issued to production	63,340
Job A12	21,340
Job C46	26,000
Job M23	16,000
Factory labor-hours used ($5.50/hour)	
Job A12	2,800
Job C46	3,800
Job M23	1,700
Indirect labor	900
Other factory overhead costs incurred	
Rent	29,500
Utilities	8,600
Repairs and maintenance	4,600
Depreciation	27,100
Other	6,600

Job A12 is the only job completed during the month; cost of goods manufactured totaled $123,080.

Required

1. Compute the predetermined factory overhead rate.
2. Compute the amount of factory overhead applied during July.
3. Compute the actual factory overhead cost incurred during July.
4. What was the ending balance of the Work-in-Process Inventory account?
5. Compute the amount of overapplied overhead or underapplied overhead.
6. Prepare a schedule of cost of goods manufactured.

4–31 **Journal Entries and Accounting for Overhead**   Humming Company manufactures highly sophisticated musical instruments for professional musicians. The company uses a normal costing system that applies factory overhead on the basis of direct labor-hours. For 2004, the company estimated that it would incur $120,000 in factory overhead costs and 8,000 direct labor-hours. The April 1, 2004, balances in inventory accounts follow:

Materials inventory	$27,000
Work in process inventory (S10)	10,500
Finished goods inventory (J21)	54,000

Job S10 is the only job in process on April 1, 2004. The following transactions were recorded for the month of April.

a. Purchased materials on account, $90,000.

b. Issued $91,000 of materials to production, $4,000 of which was for indirect materials. Cost of direct materials issued:

Job S10	$23,000
Job C20	42,000
Job M54	22,000

c. Incurred and paid payroll cost of $20,460:

Direct labor cost ($13/hour; total 920 hours)	
Job S10	$ 6,110
Job C20	4,030
Job M54	1,820
Indirect labor	2,500
Selling and administrative salaries	6,000

d. Recognized depreciation for the month:

Manufacturing assets	$ 2,200
Selling and administrative assets	1,700

e. Paid advertising expenses $ 6,000

f. Incurred factory utilities costs $ 1,300

g. Incurred other factory overhead costs $ 1,600

h. Applied factory overhead to production on the basis of direct labor-hours.

i. Completed Job S10 during the month and transferred it to the finished goods warehouse.

j. Sold Job J21 on account for $59,000.

k. Received $25,000 of collections on account from customers during the month.

Required

1. Calculate the company's predetermined overhead rate.
2. Prepare journal entries for the April transactions.

3. What was the balance of the Materials Inventory account on April 30, 2004?

4. What was the balance of the Work-in-Process Inventory account on April 30?

5. What was the amount of underapplied or overapplied overhead?

4–32 **Journal Entries, Schedule of Cost of Goods Manufactured** Apex Corporation manufactures eighteenth-century, classical-style furniture. It uses a job costing system that applies factory overhead on the basis of direct labor-hours. Budgeted factory overhead for 2004 was $1,235,475, and management budgeted 86,700 direct labor-hours. These transactions were recorded during August:

a. Purchased 5,000 square feet of oak on account at $25 per square foot.

b. Purchased 50 gallons of glue on account at $36 per gallon (indirect material).

c. Requisitioned 3,500 square feet of oak and 30.5 gallons of glue for production.

d. Incurred and paid payroll costs of $187,900. Of this amount, $46,000 were indirect labor costs; direct labor personnel earned $22 per hour on average.

e. Paid factory utility bill, $15,230 in cash.

f. August's insurance cost for the manufacturing property and equipment was $3,500. The premium had been paid in March.

g. Incurred $8,200 depreciation on manufacturing equipment for August.

h. Recorded $2,400 depreciation on an administrative asset.

i. Paid advertising expenses in cash, $5,500.

j. Incurred and paid other factory overhead costs, $13,500.

k. Incurred miscellaneous selling and administrative expenses, $13,250.

l. Applied factory overhead to production on the basis of direct labor-hours.

m. Completed goods costing $146,000 manufactured during the month.

n. Made sales on account in August, $132,000. The cost of goods sold was $112,000.

Required

1. Compute the firm's predetermined factory overhead rate for 2004.

2. Prepare journal entries to record the August events.

3. Calculate the amount of overapplied or underapplied overhead to be closed to the Cost of Goods Sold account on August 31, 2004.

4. Prepare a schedule of cost of goods manufactured and sold.

5. Prepare the income statement for August.

4–33 **Cost Drivers; Application and Proration of Factory Overhead** Northcoast Manufacturing Company, a small manufacturer of parts used in appliances, has just completed its first year of operations. The company's controller, Vic Trainor, has been reviewing the actual results for the year and is concerned about the application of factory overhead. He is using the following information to assess operations:

• Northcoast's equipment consists of several machines with a combined cost of $2,200,000 and no residual value. Each machine has a product output of five units per hour and a useful life of 20,000 hours.

• Selected actual data of Northcoast's operations for the year just ended follow:

Products manufactured	650,000 units
Machine utilization	130,000 hours
Direct labor usage	35,000 hours
Labor rate	$15 per hour
Total factory overhead	$1,130,000
Cost of goods sold	$1,720,960
Finished goods inventory (at year-end)	$430,240
Work-in-process inventory (at year-end)	$0

• Total factory overhead is applied using direct labor cost and a predetermined plantwide rate.

- The budgeted activity for the year included 20 employees, each working 1,800 productive hours, to produce 540,000 units of product. Each employee can simultaneously operate two to four machines, which are highly automated. Normal activity is for each employee to operate three machines. Machine operators are paid $15 per hour.
- Budgeted factory overhead costs for the past year for various levels of activity are shown in the following table:

Northcoast Manufacturing Company
Budgeted Annual Costs for Total Factory Overhead

Units of product	360,000	540,000	720,000
Labor-hours	30,000	36,000	42,000
Machine-hours	72,000	108,000	144,000
Total factory overhead costs			
Plant supervision	$ 70,000	$ 70,000	$ 70,000
Plant rent	40,000	40,000	40,000
Equipment depreciation	288,000	432,000	576,000
Maintenance	42,000	51,000	60,000
Utilities	144,600	216,600	288,600
Indirect materials	90,000	135,000	180,000
Other costs	11,200	16,600	22,000
Total	$685,800	$961,200	$1,236,600

Required

1. Based on Northcoast's actual operations for the past year
    a. Determine the dollar amount of total over/underapplied factory overhead and explain why this amount is material.
    b. Prepare the appropriate journal entry to close out Northcoast's total Factory Overhead account.
2. Vic Trainor believes that the company should use machine-hours to apply total factory overhead. Using the data given,
    a. Determine the dollar amount of total over/underapplied factory overhead if machine-hours had been used as the application base.
    b. Explain why machine-hours would be a more appropriate application base.

(CMA Adapted)

4–34 **Costing in System Selection, Underapplied or Overapplied Overhead**   Whittier Clinic is a large, profitable medical complex staffed by doctors who provide a variety of services. It has a net income of $200,000. When a patient goes to an appointment, the doctor fills out a computerized form that lists the services provided the patient during the visit. The clinic mails the patient the completed form with prices noted as the bill.

Required

1. Should Whittier Clinic use a job costing system, or should it try another system? Why?
2. Whittier Clinic's applied overhead was $108,475. The clinic found out, however, that actual overhead was $113,775. Is this overhead underapplied or overapplied? By what amount?
3. What would your answer be if the clinic's applied overhead were $127,850, and actual overhead were $122,950?
4. Should there be a difference between overhead applied and the actual overhead?
5. Using your numerical answer for requirement 2, show with journal entries how you would deal with the underapplied or overapplied overhead amount. Explain why you did it this way and when this procedure should be done.

4–35 **Job Costing; Service Industry**   The Jackson and Bird CPA firm has the following budget for 2004:

Direct labor (for professional hours charged to clients)	$180,000
Overhead	
Indirect materials	$ 25,000
Indirect labor	125,000
Depreciation—Building	25,000
Depreciation—Furniture	2,500
Utilities	28,000
Insurance	2,400
Property taxes	2,600
Other expenses	14,500
Total	$225,000

The firm uses direct labor cost as the cost driver to apply overhead to clients.
During January, the firm worked for many clients; data for two of them follow:

Barry account	
Direct materials	$ 200
Direct labor	1,500
Miles account	
Direct materials	$2,690
Direct labor	6,300

Required

1. Compute Jackson and Bird's budgeted overhead rate. Explain how this is used.
2. Compute the amount of overhead to be charged to the Barry and Miles accounts using the predetermined overhead rate calculated in requirement 1.
3. Compute a separate job cost for the Barry and the Miles accounts.

4–36   **Job Cost Sheets; Departmental Rates**   Decker Screw Manufacturing Company produces special screws made to customer specifications. During June, the following data pertained to these costs:

Summary of Direct Materials Requisitions				
Department Number	Job Number	Requisition Number	Quantity	Cost per Unit
1	2906	B9766	4,550	$ 1.34
2	2907	B9767	110	22.18
1	2908	B9768	1,000	9.00
1	2906	B9769	4,430	1.35
2	2908	B9770	23	48.00

Summary of Direct Labor Time Tickets				
Department Number	Job Number	Ticket Number	Hours	Cost per Unit
1	2906	1056-1168	1,102	$6.50
2	2907	2121-2130	136	8.88
1	2908	1169-1189	151	6.50
2	2908	2131-1239	32	8.88
1	2906	1190-1239	810	6.50

Summary of Factory Overhead Application Rates	
Department Number	Basis of Application Rates
1	$3 per direct labor-hour
2	150% of direct labor cost

Decker had no beginning work-in-process inventory for June. Of the jobs begun in June, Job 2906 was completed and sold on account for $30,000, Job 2907 was completed but not sold, and Job 2908 was still in process.

Required

1. Calculate the direct materials, direct labor, factory overhead, and total costs for each job started in June.

2. Perform the same calculations as in requirement (1), but assume that the direct labor-rate per hour increased by 10 percent in Department 1 and 25 percent in Department 2.

4–37 **Assigning Overhead to Jobs; Ethics**   Aero Systems is a manufacturer of airplane parts and engines for a variety of military and commercial aircraft. It has two production departments. Department A is machine intensive; Department B is labor intensive. Aero Systems has adopted a traditional plantwide rate using the direct labor-hour-based overhead allocation system. The company recently conducted a pilot study using a departmental overhead rate costing system. This system used two overhead allocation bases: machine-hours for Department A and direct labor-hours for Department B. The study showed that the system, which will be more accurate and timely, will assign lower costs to the government jobs and higher costs to the company's nongovernmental jobs. Apparently, the current (less accurate) direct labor-based costing system has overcosted government jobs and undercosted private business jobs. On hearing of this, top management has decided to scrap the plans for adopting the new departmental overhead rate costing system because government jobs constitute 40 percent of Aero Systems' business and the new system will reduce the price and thus the profit for this part of its business.

Required   As the management accountant participating in this pilot study project, what is your responsibility when you hear of top management's decision to cancel the plans to implement the new departmental overhead rate costing system? Can you ignore your professional ethics code in this case? What would you do?

4–38 **Operation Costing**   Brian Canning Co., which sells canned corn, uses an operation costing system. Cans of corn are classified as either sweet or regular, depending on the type of corn used. Both types of corn go through the separating and cleaning operations, but only regular corn goes through the creaming operation. During January, two batches of corn were canned from start to finish. Batch X consisted of 800 pounds of sweet corn and batch Y consisted of 700 pounds of regular corn. The company had no beginning or ending work-in-process inventory. The following cost information is for the month January:

Raw sweet corn	$5,200
Raw regular corn	2,450*
Separating department costs	1,500
Cleaning department costs	900
Creaming department costs	210

*Included $300 for cream

Required

1. Compute the unit cost for sweet corn and regular corn.

2. Record appropriate journal entries.

3. Post journal entries to T-accounts.

4–39 **Spoilage, Rework, and Scrap**   Richport Company manufactures products that often require specification changes or modifications to meet customer needs. Consequently, Richport employs a job costing system for its operations.

Although the specification changes and modifications are commonplace, Richport has been able to establish a normal spoilage rate of 0.025 of normal input. The company recognizes normal spoilage during the budgeting process and classifies it as a component of factory overhead. Thus, the predetermined overhead rate used to apply factory overhead costs to jobs includes an allowance for net spoilage cost for normal spoilage. If spoilage on a job exceeds the normal rate, it is considered abnormal and then must be analyzed and the cause of the spoilage must be submitted to management.

Randa Duncan, one of Richport's inspection managers, has been reviewing the output of Job N1192-122 that was recently completed. A total of 122,000 units had been started for the job, and 5,000 units were rejected at final inspection, meaning that the job yielded 117,000 good units.

Randa noted that 900 of the first units produced were rejected due to a very unusual design defect that was corrected immediately; no more units were rejected for this reason. Rejected units were disposed of at an additional cost of $1,200 to Richport.

Randa was unable to identify a pattern for the remaining 4,100 rejected units. They can be sold at a salvage value of $7 per unit.

The total costs accumulated for all 122,000 units of Job N1192-122 follow. Although the job is completed, all of these costs are still in the Work-in-Process Inventory account (i.e., the cost of the completed job has not been transferred to Finished Goods Inventory account).

Direct materials	$2,196,000
Direct labor	1,830,000
Applied factory overhead	2,928,000
Total cost of job	$6,954,000

Required

1. Explain the distinction between normal and abnormal spoilage.
2. Distinguish between spoiled units, rework units, and scrap.
3. Review the results and costs for Job N1192-122.
   a. Prepare an analysis separating the spoiled units into normal and abnormal spoilage by first determining the normal input required to yield 117,000 good units.
   b. Prepare the appropriate journal entries to properly account for Job N1192-122 including spoilage, salvage value, disposal, and/or transfer of costs to the Finished Goods Inventory account.

(CMA Adapted)

4–40 **Job Cost Sheets**   Boston Screw Manufacturing Company produces special screws made to customer specifications. During June, the following data pertained to these costs:

	Summary of Direct Materials Requisitions		
Department Number	**Job Number**	**Quantity**	**Cost per Unit**
1	88X	6,650	$8.31
1	88Y	2,130	2.52
1	88Z	1,818	9.16
1	88Y	921	4.18
1	88Z	63	3.23

	Summary of Direct Labor Time Tickets	
Department Number	**Job Number**	**Hours**
1	88X	554
2	88Y	321
2	88Z	618
1	88Y	25
1	88Z	613

The labor rate in Department 1 is $10.50 and in Department 2 is $9.50. The overhead rate in Department 1 is based on direct labor hours, at $4.50 per hour; in Department 2 the rate is 125 percent of direct labor cost.

Decker had no beginning work-in-process inventory for May. Of the jobs begun in May, Job 88X was completed and sold on account for $86,000, Job 88Y was completed but not sold, and Job 88Z was still in process.

Required

1. Calculate the direct materials, direct labor, factory overhead, and total costs for each job started in May.

2. Perform the same calculations as in requirement (1), but assume that labor rates in both departments have increased by 20 percent.

4–41 **Quarterly and Annual Overhead Application (Excel Icon)**   The Mansfield Machine Shop is a family-owned business with 25 employees. The founding brothers, Steve and George, started the business with a single milling machine, a grinder, and a lathe in 1974. The brothers now own a business with 27 machines, and operating revenues of more than $5 million per year. The brothers have noticed that they are losing business to new competitors and they have heard from some of their customers that their competitors have better prices. So they have asked you to study their operations and summary financial reports for the prior year and to make recommendations.

The information available to you includes:

1. The business is very seasonal, as it reflects the seasonality of the businesses of its major customers in the manufacturing and construction industries. The first and third quarters of the year have relatively low demand, while their busiest periods are the second and fourth quarters. George and Steve measure the volume of their business in machine-hours, since they charge by the machine-hour and the materials costs are negligible. The machine-hours demand for last year was 5,000 hours in the first quarter, 12,500 in the second quarter, 7,500 in the third quarter, and 11,250 in the fourth quarter.

2. Mansfield has 27 machines in the plant, and while some are newer and more technologically advanced than others, the differences are not great. Because of this, the brothers charge the same price for machining on each of the machines. George and Steve realize that their business is very seasonal and that their machines and operators will be busier at times, but to keep the machines in good shape and operators rested, they try to limit the work to approximately 150 hours per month per machine.

3. Because of the seasonality of the business, George and Steve have always recalculated the overhead rate for each quarter. The overhead rate is determined at the end of each quarter based on actual total overhead costs for the quarter (which are $450,000 per quarter) and the actual machine-hours for that quarter. This machine-hours-based rate is then used in the following quarter, and is revised accordingly at the end of each quarter.

4. Mansfield's variable costs are $45 per machine-hour. The firm charges a 50 percent markup over full cost, the sum of variable costs and overhead charges per unit.

5. In addition to $450,000 fixed operating costs per quarter, Mansfield has $25,000 administrative fixed costs per quarter.

Required

1. Calculate the overhead rates and machine-hour pricing rates using the quarterly overhead system now used by the firm.

2. Recalculate the overhead rates and machine-hour pricing rates using an annual overhead rate.

3. Calculate total contribution and operating income for the year and for each quarter under both the quarterly and annual rates.

4. Interpret your findings in parts 1 through 3. How does the choice of a quarterly overhead rate affect pricing for Mansfield? Which overhead rate, quarterly or annual, do you think Mansfield should use and why?

Solution to Self–Study Problem

Journal Entries and Accounting for Overhead

1. Journal entries:

(a)	Materials Inventory	25,000	
	Accounts Payable		25,000
	To record the purchase of direct materials and indirect materials.		
(b)	Work-in-Process Inventory	15,000	
	Factory Overhead	8,000	
	Materials Inventory		23,000
	To record direct and indirect materials issued.		
(c)	Work-in-Process Inventory	20,000	
	Factory Overhead	5,000	
	Accrued Payroll		25,000
	To record factory labor incurred.		
(d)	Factory Overhead	18,000	
	Accounts Payable		500
	Accumulated Depreciation—Factory		15,000
	Prepaid Insurance		2,500
	To record actual overhead costs incurred, including factory utilities, depreciation, and insurance.		
(e)	Work-in-Process Inventory	30,000	
	Factory Overhead Applied		30,000
	To record the application of factory overhead to jobs.		

Summary of factory overhead applied

Job 1 ($15 × 1,200)	$18,000
Job 2 ($15 × 800)	12,000
Total	$30,000

(f)	Finished Goods Inventory	45,000	
	Work-in-Process Inventory		45,000
	To record the job finished.		

Total manufacturing cost for job 101

Beginning inventory	$6,000
Direct materials added	9,000
Direct labor incurred	12,000
Factory overhead applied	18,000
Total	$45,000

(g)	Accounts Receivable	66,000	
	Sales		66,000
	To record the total sales revenue of two jobs.		
	Cost of Goods Sold	55,000	
	Finished Goods Inventory		55,000
	To record the total cost of goods sold.		

Summary of the total cost in shipping orders

Job 100	$10,000
Job 101	45,000
Total	$55,000

Sales = $55,000 × 120% = $66,000

2. Ending balance of the Work-in-Process Inventory account for Job 102:

Direct materials	$ 6,000
Direct labor	8,000
Factory overhead applied	12,000
Total ending balance	$26,000

3. Factory overhead variance:

Actual factory overhead

Indirect materials	$ 8,000	
Indirect labor	5,000	
Utilities	500	
Depreciation	15,000	
Insurance	2,500	$31,000
Applied factory overhead		30,000
Underapplied factory overhead		$ 1,000

4. To record the disposition of underapplied factory overhead by closing both Factory Overhead and Factory Overhead Applied accounts to the Cost of Goods Sold account.

Factory Overhead Applied	30,000	
Cost of Goods Sold	1,000	
Factory Overhead		31,000

CHAPTER FIVE

Activity-Based Costing and Management

After studying this chapter, you should be able to ...

1. Explain why volume-based costing systems tend to undercost or overcost products or services
2. Describe an activity-based costing system and its benefits and limitations
3. Compute and contrast product costs using volume-based and activity-based costing systems
4. Describe an activity-based management system and distinguish between high-value-added and low-value-added activities
5. Describe how activity-based costing systems are used in the manufacturing industry
6. Describe how activity-based costing systems are used in marketing and administrative activities
7. Demonstrate how activity-based costing systems are used in service and not-for-profit organizations
8. Analyze factors affecting revenues and selling and administrative costs and determine customer profitability
9. Describe customer cost categories and identify the costs to serve a customer
10. Conduct customer profitability analysis and determine customer value
11. Relate activity-based costing to strategic cost management
12. Identify key factors for a successful ABC/M implementation

The word *allocation* effectively means misallocation.

An ABC/M practitioner

Chapters 3 and 4 describe costing systems that use simple overhead rates to assign indirect costs to products or services. These simple systems are adequate in providing costing information as long as (1) indirect resources are not a significant cost in manufacturing products or providing services or (2) all products or services use more or less equal or proportional amounts of indirect resources. When a firm increases the variety of its products or services and these products or services consume different amounts of indirect resources, a simple overhead costing system is likely to generate inaccurate product or service cost information and lead to improper pricing or management decisions. Many managers did not grasp the true profitability of their products or the best mix of products because they did not really know what resources or activities went into producing their products. When indirect costs are a major operating cost, the cost distortion become even more serious. Today many firms, including Dow Chemical, an international Fortune 100 company, use activity-based costing and management (ABC/M) to help implement their new strategy for achieving their goals.[1]

In 1993 Dow Chemical began to shift its strategy from diversification to specialization in its core business of chemicals and plastics to enhance its competitiveness in highly competitive markets. Dow identified its corporate goal as supplying the optimal combination of cost and quality and providing the highest value to its customers.

---

[1] For more about the Dow Chemical success story, see its website at www.dow.com. Also see James W. Damitio, Gary W. Hayes, and Philip L. Kintzele, "Integrating ABC and ABM at Dow Chemical," *Management Accounting Quarterly,* Winter 2000, pp. 22–26.

EXHIBIT 5.1
Volume-Based versus ABC
Responsibility Reports:
Nelson Insurance Company
Claims Processing Department
For the Month Ended March
31, 2005

Volume-Based (Based on General Ledger)		ABC Data Based	
Salaries & wages	$625,000	Input claims	$ 45,000
Equipment depreciation	140,000	Verify and analyze claims	154,000
Supplies	36,000	File claims	24,000
Travel	90,000	Determine eligibility	166,000
Utilities	24,000	Make copies	125,000
Office rental	22,000	Respond to inquiries	240,000
Total	$937,000	Write correspondence	63,000
		Attend training	120,000
		Total	$937,000

ABC/M provided Dow Chemical managers with information that enabled them to truly understand the costs of manufacturing and selling products and to guide their decisions regarding pricing, product mix, product design, process restructuring, and improving customer profitability. Dow also integrated ABC into its budget process and tracked activities as well as costs with its enterprise resource planning system.

Firms around the world have been facing changes in business environment, technology, and manufacturing and operating practices. Managers realized the inadequacy of volume-based costing systems in providing accurate and relevant cost information for operational controls and for decision making. Exhibit 5.1 illustrates the inadequacy of a volume-based monthly responsibility report for the Claims Processing Department of an insurance company. The left side shows a typical volume-based monthly report that managers of responsibility centers receive. If you ask managers who receive this report questions such as "How much insight you get from the report on the content of work of your employees?" "How much of the expenses do you have control?" "What expenses and how much of the expenses will change if the number of claims decreased by 10 percent?" chances are they cannot give you answer based on the report they received. In contrast, the right side of Exhibit shows a monthly responsibility report generated based on an ABC data base. Managers who receive such a report would have a better insight into activities that consume resources.

Worse, many managers also discovered that volume-based costing systems often generated distorted cost data and led too many managers to erroneous decisions at the expense of profitability or even survival of their operations. ABC helps firms to eliminate or reduce cost distortions and provides accurate product costs. It offers a clear view of how a firm's diverse products, services, and activities contribute to the firm's bottom line.

For years, ABC/M was considered an expensive project that only large organizations with extensive resources could undertake. With vast advancement of information technology and proliferation of computers for gathering data and computing in the last decade, the cost of data collection, measurement, and reporting has fallen rapidly. Today, not only are such activity measurement and cost determination systems affordable, but much of the information already exists in some form within the organization. Information technology has dramatically improved the deployment of ABC/M data for viewing, planning, and decision making.

This chapter shows how managers in manufacturing, marketing, merchandising, service, and not-for-profit firms use ABC/M to gain a better understanding of cost structures, promote efficiency, become more competitive and effective in attaining goals and objectives. ABC/M also helps firms increase values received by customers, raise profits, and facilitate the determination and management of strategy.

Limitations of Volume-Based Costing Systems

Chapter 3 explains that manufacturing cost elements include direct materials, direct labor, and factory overhead. Volume-based costing systems were developed when direct

LEARNING OBJECTIVE 1
Explain why volume-based costing systems tend to undercost and overcost products or services.

costs, including direct labor costs, accounted for the bulk of product costs incurred inside a firm or factory. *Factory overheads* serve as a catch-all account for all production costs that cannot be directly identified with, or economically traced to, products or services. Factory overheads include such costs as repair and maintenance, depreciation, utilities, insurance, property taxes, and supervisory salaries.

In the past, labor activities were a major manufacturing activity. The other major manufacturing cost item, direct materials costs, consists of payments to vendors rather than costs incurred inside the factory. With labor costs being a primary manufacturing cost and labor activities being the major activity in the manufacture of a product, volume-based costing systems focus on measuring and controlling direct labor costs. Factory overheads are a small fraction of the labor cost and are deemed as resources expended to support labor activities. Tying to direct labor costs, a traditional overhead costing system becomes a volume-based costing system. As volumes (units) change, direct labor costs, as do overhead costs, vary in proportion to changes in units of production.

Volume-based costing systems have served well since the inception of cost accounting. A volume-based costing system is sufficient when technology is stable, when the range of products is limited, and when direct labor and materials costs dominate product costs. However, recent changes in manufacturing and business environments such as advances in manufacturing technology, changes in the competitive environment, expansions in product diversity, and astronomical increases in factory overhead amounts and categories have made volume-based costing systems fall short as a reliable and accurate product costing system. More and more factory overheads, such as setup cost, materials-handling cost, and product design and research and development costs, are unrelated to the number of units produced. By relying on volume-related measures to determine product costs, volume-based costing systems do a poor job in reflecting supporting costs for manufacturing and distribution of products or services.

Furthermore, automation in manufacturing decreases labor costs and increases factory overhead. As a result, the percentage of direct labor in total manufacturing costs has been decreasing consistently, with corresponding increases in the fraction of fixed overhead costs. By using a decreasing base-activity such as direct labor hours or direct labor costs to assign ever-increasing factory overhead costs to cost objects, a volume-based costing system generates distorted product or service costs because products or services do not consume support resources in proportion to their volumes.

Volume-Based Overhead Rate

The factory overhead rate in a volume-based costing system is either a single overhead rate for the entire operation (plantwide rate) or a set of overhead rates with various rates for different departments or divisions (departmental rates). These overhead rates use an output-volume-based activity or activities to assign (or to spread) factory overhead costs to products or services. An output-volume-based costing system spreads costs evenly so that each cost object (product or service) receives the same amount.

Plantwide Overhead Rate

A plantwide overhead rate uses one rate for the entire operation (factory or office) to assign the cost of indirect resources to products or services. The chosen base for assigning overhead is usually the total direct labor hour or direct labor cost of the factory or operation.

A plantwide overhead rate is determined by dividing the total budgeted overhead cost by the total budgeted direct labor hours or cost. For example, Dole Company has two divisions: Machining and Finishing. Machining is highly automated while Finishing is labor intensive. The company has budgeted the following operations for the year:

	Machining	Finishing	Total
Budgeted factory overhead cost	$400,000	$200,000	$600,000
Budgeted direct labor hours	10,000	50,000	60,000
Budgeted machine hours	20,000	4,000	24,000

Dole uses a single plantwide overhead rate based on direct labor hours to assign overhead. The firm budgeted $600,000 total factory overhead and 60,000 total direct labor hours for the year, the firm's plantwide predetermined overhead rate for the year is $10 per direct labor hour computed as:

$$\frac{\text{Budgeted Overhead}}{\text{Budgeted Direct Labor Hours}} = \frac{\$600,000}{60,000} = \$10 \text{ per direct labor hour}$$

Dole spent the following hours in July to manufacture 2,000 units of each of its two products, Widget and Gidget:

	Machining	Finishing	Total
Widget			
Number of direct labor hours	500	4,000	4,500
Number of machine hours	900	300	1,200
Gidget			
Number of direct labor hours	500	1,000	1,500
Number of machine hours	1,000	300	1,300

Using the predetermined plantwide overhead rate of $10 per direct labor hour, the firm calculates the factory overhead costs for these two products as follows:

	Total Direct Labor Hours	Overhead Rate Per Direct Labor Hour	Total Overhead	Total Units Manufactured	Overhead Cost per Unit
Widget	4,500	$10	$45,000	2,000	$22.50
Gidget	1,500	10	15,000	2,000	7.50
Total			$60,000		

A plantwide overhead rate assumes that all products or services benefit from or consume overhead costs in proportion to the quantity of the chosen activity (driver) for applying overhead. In the previous example, each direct labor hour spent on Widget uses the same amount of overhead as each direct labor hour spent on Gidget.

Departmental Overhead Rate

A departmental overhead rate method uses a separate volume-based driver to determine the overhead rate for each of the manufacturing departments. The departments may use different drivers or the same driver with an individual overhead rate for each department. If, for example, Dole Company decides to adopt departmental overhead rates and management has decided to use a machine-hour-based rate for the Machining Department and a direct-labor-hour-based rate for the Finishing Department, the firm's overhead rate would be:

Overhead Rate for Machining Department

$$\frac{\text{Budgeted Departmental Overhead}}{\text{Budgeted Machine Hours}} = \frac{\$400,000}{20,000} = \$20 \text{ per machine hour}$$

Overhead Rate for Finishing Department

$$\frac{\text{Budgeted Departmental Overhead}}{\text{Budgeted Direct Labor Hours}} = \frac{\$200,000}{50,000} = \$4 \text{ per direct labor hour}$$

Using departmental overhead rates, the factory overhead cost assigned to the two products is

	Widget	Gidget
Machining (driver: machine-hours)		
$20 × 900	$18,000	
$20 × 1,000		$20,000
Finishing (driver: labor-hours)		
$4 × 4,000	16,000	
$4 × 1,000		4,000
Total overhead applied	$34,000	$24,000
Number of units manufactured in July	2,000	2,000
Overhead cost per unit	$ 17.00	$ 12.00

The following table summarizes the amounts of applied overhead in July with different overhead application rates.

	Plantwide Rate Based on Direct Labor Hours		Departmental Rate	
	Total Overhead	Overhead per Unit	Total Overhead	Overhead per Unit
Widget	$45,000	$22.50	$34,000	$17.00
Gidget	15,000	7.50	24,000	12.00
Total	$60,000		$58,000	

Widget's overhead per unit with the plantwide overhead rate is $22.50, which is $5.50 higher than the overhead determined with departmental rates ($17.00). In contrast, Gidget's overhead per unit with the plantwide overhead rate is $7.50, which is $4.50 lower than the overhead calculated with departmental overhead rates ($12.00). The amounts of overheads applied to Gidget using the departmental rates are higher than those applied using the plantwide rate based on direct labor hours, both in total and in per unit, because, using only direct labor hours as the driver to determine applied overheads, the single plantwide overhead cost rate does not consider the sizable machine hours the Machining Department spent on Gidget.

Product costs based on departmental rates are likely to be more accurate than costs based on plantwide rates because departmental rates can reflect differences in amounts and types of resources consumed during the manufacturing of products in different departments. Departmental rates, however, do not consider the varying overhead costs of different activities within a department when not all factory overhead costs are volume based. Overhead costs such as machine setup cost, product design cost, purchase ordering cost, and materials handling cost are most likely not to vary in proportion to a volume-based driver such as direct labor-hours or machine-hours.

Volume, Size, and Complexity

A volume-based costing system may provide reasonably accurate costs when a firm's operation possesses the following characteristics:

- Few and very similar products and service lines.
- Relatively low overhead expenses.
- Homogeneous conversion processes for all products or services.
- Similar distribution channels, customer demands, and customers.

A volume-based overhead costing system, whether plantwide or departmental, often leads to inaccurate product costs, especially for firms with complex manufacturing operations—firms with varieties of products or heterogeneous production processes. As firms increase in variety of product, volume, size, or complexity, resources used and costs spent on supporting activities, such as handling and processing activities, increase. Distortions of volume-based overhead cost systems increase as product diversity increases because the cost system (1) is designed to cost products in the aggregate, not to relate to unique manufacturing characteristics in different operations; (2) uses a common plantwide or departmental cost driver and ignores differences in activities for different products or production runs within the plant or department; (3) employs a common activity volume for all operations such as direct labor-hours or dollars as the base to distribute overhead costs to all products while the selected activity is a small portion of the overall production activities; and (4) deemphasizes long-term product analysis.

Users of traditional volume-based cost data who are aware of likely distortions in cost data from a volume-based costing system, often attempt to make intuitive, and likely, imprecise adjustments to the volume-based cost information without understanding their complete effect and, thereby, distort the cost information further. Inaccurate cost information can lead to undesirable strategic results, such as wrong product-line decisions, unrealistic pricing, and ineffective resource allocations.[2]

Activity-Based Costing

To refine a costing system we need to understand relationships among resources, activities, and products or services. Resources are spent on activities and products or services are a result of activities. Many of the resources used in an operation can be traced to individual products or services and identified as direct materials or direct labor costs. Most overhead costs relate only indirectly to final products or services. Nevertheless, overhead costs are resources spent on a firm's activities to manufacture products, provide services, or facilitate manufacturing. A good costing system needs to identify costs with activities that consume resources and assign resource costs to cost objects such as products, services, or intermediate cost pools based on activities performed for the cost objects.

Activities, Resources, Cost Drivers, Resource Consumption Cost Drivers, and Activity Consumption Cost Drivers

Before discussing activity-based costing, we need to define several important terms: *activity, resource, cost driver, resource consumption cost driver,* and *activity consumption cost driver.*

An activity is an action or an aggregation of actions performed within an organization.

An **activity** is a specific deed, action, or work performed. An activity can be a single action or an aggregation of several actions. For example, moving inventory from workstation A to workstation B is an activity that may require only one action. Production set-up is an activity that may include several actions. Activities include actions, movements, or work sequences.[3]

A resource is an economic element needed or consumed in performing activities.

A **resource** is an economic element needed or consumed in performing activities. Salaries and materials, for example, are resources needed or used in performing manufacturing activities.

As defined in Chapter 3, a *cost driver is* a factor that causes or relates to a change in the cost of an activity. Because cost drivers cause or relate to cost changes, measured or quantified amounts of cost drivers are excellent bases for assigning resource costs to activities and the cost of one or more activities to other activities or cost objects.[4]

---

[2] Cooper demonstrates how traditional costing systems overcost large-size, high-volume products and undercost small-size, low-volume products when product diversity exists within the same operation. Robin Cooper, "The Rise of Activity-Based Costing—Part One: What Is an Activity-Based Cost System?" *Journal of Cost Management,* Summer 1988, pp. 45–54.

[3] Norm Raffish and Peter B. B. Turney, "Glossary of Activity-Based Management," *Journal of Cost Management,* Fall 1991, pp. 53–63. Other definitions from this glossary also are used in this chapter.

[4] Statement No. 4T, "Implementing Activity-Based Costing" (Institute of Management Accountants, 1993), p. 34, states that "Cost drivers reflect the consumption of costs by activities and the consumption of activities, products, or services."

REAL-WORLD FOCUS — Cost Drivers at Cal Electronic Circuits, Inc.

Cal Electronic Circuits, Inc., has 10 cost drivers to assign to overhead costs to printed circuit boards (PCB):

1. Number of setups.
2. Number of holes drilled in PCB.
3. Number of layers in PCB.
4. Number of drill sizes required.
5. Number of images per panel in PCB.
6. PCB length and width.
7. Number of parts per panel.
8. Number of engineering hours.
9. Lot size.
10. Volume of chemical waste.

Source: John Lee. "Activity Based Costing at Cal Electronic Circuits," *Management Accounting,* October 1990, pp. 36–38.

A resource consumption cost driver
is an activity or characteristic that consumes resources.

A cost driver is either a *resource consumption cost driver* or an *activity consumption cost driver.* A **resource consumption cost driver** is a measure of the amount of resources consumed by an activity. It is the cost driver for assigning a resource cost consumed by or related to an activity to a particular activity or cost pool. Examples of resource consumption cost drivers are the number of items in a purchase or sales order, changes in product design, size of factory buildings, and machine hours.

An activity consumption cost driver
measures how much of an activity a cost object uses.

An **activity consumption cost driver** measures the amount of an activity performed for a cost object. It is used to assign activity cost pool costs to cost objects. Examples of activity consumption cost drivers are the number of machine hours in the manufacturing of product X, the number of batches used to manufacture Product Y.

What Is Activity-Based Costing?

Activity-based costing (ABC)
is a costing approach that assigns resource costs to a cost object based on activities performed for the cost object.

Activity-based costing (ABC) is a costing approach that assigns resource costs to cost objects such as products, services, or customers based on activities performed for the cost objects. The premise of this costing approach is that a firm's products or services are the results of activities and activities use resources which incur costs. Costs of resources are assigned to activities based on the activities that use or consume resources (resource consumption drivers), and costs of activities are assigned to cost objects based on activities performed for the cost objects (activity consumption drivers). ABC recognizes the causal or direct relationships between resource costs, cost drivers, activities, and cost objects in assigning costs to activities and then to cost objects.

LEARNING OBJECTIVE 2
Describe an activity-based costing system and its benefits and limitations.

ABC assigns factory overhead costs to cost objects such as products or services by identifying the resources and activities as well as their costs and amounts needed to produce output. Using resource consumption cost drivers, a firm determines the resource costs consumed by activities or activity centers (activity cost pools) and calculates the cost of a unit of activity. The firm then assigns the cost of an activity or activity center to products or services by multiplying the cost of each activity by the amount of the activity consumed by each of the cost objects.

Two-Stage Cost Assignment Procedure

A two-stage cost assignment
assigns factory overhead costs to activity centers or cost pools and then to cost objects.

A **two-stage cost assignment** procedure assigns resource costs such as factory overhead costs to activity cost centers or cost pools and then to cost objects to determine the amount of resource costs for each of the cost objects. Volume-based costing systems assign factory overhead costs first to plant or departmental cost pools (cost centers) and second to products or services (see Exhibit 5.2). A volume-based two-stage cost assignment procedure, however, is likely to distort product or service costs. This is true especially in the second stage where the volume-based costing system uses a cost driver such as direct labor-hours, or output unit as the plantwide rate or departmental rates

EXHIBIT 5.2   The Volume-Based Two-Stage Procedure

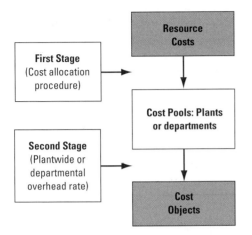

EXHIBIT 5.3   The Activity-Based Two-Stage Procedure

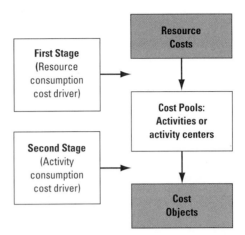

to assign factory overhead costs. Because all products or services do not always consume factory overhead resources in a cost pool in proportion to the volume-based measure or measures the firm uses to assign factory overhead costs, a volume-based system often leads to inaccurate measures for the costs of support activities in its operations. This distortion becomes more serious especially when a substantial portion of factory overhead costs is not output-volume related and the firm manufactures a diverse mix of products with differences in volumes, sizes, or complexities.

Activity-based costing systems differ from volume-based costing systems by tracing uses of resources to activities and linking activity costs to products, services, or customers (see Exhibit 5.3). The first-stage assigns factory overhead costs to activities or activity cost centers (activity cost pools) by using appropriate resource consumption cost drivers. The second-stage assigns the costs of activities or activity cost pools to cost objects using appropriate activity consumption cost drivers that measure the demands cost objects place on the activity or pool of activities. By using activities in both the first and second stage cost assignments, activity-based costing systems provide more accurate measures of product or service costs for the cost of activities that are not proportional to the volume of outputs produced.

In summary, activity-based costing systems differ from volume-based costing systems in two ways: First, the ABC system defines cost pools as activities or activity centers rather than production plant or department cost centers. Second, the cost drivers that the ABC system uses to assign activity costs to cost objects are drivers based on an activity or activities performed for the cost object. The traditional volume-based approach uses an arbitrarily selected cost allocation procedure to allocate costs to cost pools and a volume-based cost driver that often bears little or no relationship to the consumption of resource cost by the cost object or objects to assign costs to products or services (See Chapter 12 for the arbitrary cost allocation procedures).

The two-stage allocation procedure in an activity-based costing system identifies clearly the costs of activities of a firm. The assignment of activity costs to cost objects uses a measure or measures that represent the demands the cost objects make on activities of the firm. As a result, activity-based costing systems report more accurate product or service costs than traditional volume-based costing systems do.

When Is an Activity-Based Costing System Needed?

An activity-based costing system can provide better costing information and help management manage efficiently and gain a better understanding of the firm's competitive advantages, strengths, and weaknesses. Often, managers recognize needs for a better

REAL-WORLD FOCUS | Traditional Costing System Distorted Product Costs at Xi'an Electronics in China

Xi'an Electronics produces special electronics with more than 250 products that have in excess of 600 specifications. Researchers collected data for 25 of the company's products during the last half of 1997 and grouped them into two product categories, high volume and low volume. They found that the unit conversion cost (direct labor and overhead) was 29.58 percent higher under traditional costing (using direct labor hours as the cost driver) than ABC (using 30 cost drivers) for high-volume products and was 45.95 percent lower

under traditional costing than ABC for low-volume products. Their findings show that traditional costing overestimates the costs of high-volume products and underestimates the costs of low-volume products.

Source: Pingxin Wang, Qinglu Jin, and Dagang Ke, "Activity-Based Costing and Its Application in Chinese Enterprises," *China Accounting and Finance Review,* March 2000, pp. 138–55.

costing system such as activity-based costing when they experiencing increased lost sales due to erroneous pricing that resulted from inaccurate costing data. Many managers also observed that the costing data from a volume-based system often were out of sync with operations, especially when the manufacturing processes were complex or the operation involved multitude of products in number of products, volume, or size. They noticed that products easy to make had high costs while products challenging to manufacture had low costs, that units manufactured in large quantities had relatively high unit costs while units manufactured in small batches had relatively low unit costs.[5]

In recent years an increasing number of firms are using ABC systems and find that benefits of adopting this system exceed the costs of its implementation. An activity-based costing system has the most impact, according to Kaplan and Cooper, on firms that have areas with large, increasing expenses or have numerous products, services, customers, processes, or a combination of these.[6] Example are plants that produce standard and custom products, high-volume and low-volume products, or mature and new products. Firms that accept small and large orders, offer standard and customized deliveries, or satisfy all customers including those who demand frequent changes and services either before or after the delivery, and customers who hardly ever request special services can benefit substantially from activity-based costing systems.

According to a survey conducted by the Cost Management Group of the Institute of Management Accountants, 54 percent of responding companies that have tried ABC are using it to make decisions outside the accounting function. Of these companies, 89 percent say that ABC is worth the implementation costs. Who tries ABC? The survey indicated that the higher the potential for cost distortions, the more motivated an organization is to adopt ABC. It also reported that adopting firms had a higher percentage of overhead costs to total production costs. Based on questions relating to competition, cost-reduction efforts, and the basis for pricing decisions, adopting ABC firms ranked the decision usefulness of their cost information higher than non-ABC firms.[7]

Another survey by ABC Technologies, Inc., reported that the top four objectives of adopting ABC were product/service costing (58 percent), process analysis (51 percent), performance management (49 percent), and profitability assessment (39 percent).[8]

[5] Robin Cooper, "The Rise of Activity-Based Costing—Part Two: When Do I Need an Activity-Based Cost System?" *The Journal of Cost Management,* Fall 1988, pp. 41–48.

[6] Robert S. Kaplan and Robin Cooper, *Cost and Effects: Using Integrated Cost Systems to Drive Profitability and Performance* (Boston: Harvard Business School Press, 1997), pp. 100–101.

[7] Kip R. Krumwiede, "ABC: Why It's Tried and How It Succeeds," *Strategic Finance,* April 1998, pp. 32–38.

[8] Mohan Nair, "Activity-Based Costing: Who's Using It and Why?" *Management Accounting Quarterly,* Spring 2000, pp. 29–33.

Steps in Designing an Activity-Based Costing System

Designing an activity-based costing system entails three steps: (1) identifying resource costs and activities, (2) assigning resource costs to activities, and (3) assigning activity costs to cost objects.

Step 1: Identify Resource Costs and Activities

A firm engages in activities to manufacture products or provide services. Activities consume resources and resources cost money. The first step in designing an ABC system is to conduct an activity analysis to identify resource costs and activities of the firm. Most firms record resource costs in general ledger or its subsidiary accounts. Examples of these accounts include materials, supplies, purchasing, materials handling, warehousing, office expenses, furniture and fixtures, buildings, equipment, utilities, salaries and benefits, engineering, and accounting. These accounts can provide many resource costs. However, special efforts most likely will be needed to determine appropriate resource costs for activity-based costing because firms follow the generally accepted accounting principles in setting up their general ledgers and recording of accounts. Several different resource costs may be recorded in a single account or the costs for an activity may be recorded in several accounts. For example, a firm may use a single Factory Supplies account for all supplies in its operations that include several manufacturing operations. Costs to complete a purchasing order may spread out over several accounts including accounts for warehousing, purchasing, and receiving.

Through activity analyses a firm identifies the work it performs to carry out its operations. Activity analyses include gathering data from existing documents and records, as well as collecting additional data using questionnaires, observations, or interviews of key personnel. Questions that ABC project team members typically ask employees or managers in gathering activity data include:

- What work or activities do you do?
- How much time do you spend performing these activities?
- What resources are required to perform these activities?
- What value does the activity have for the product, service, customer, or organization?

With the help of industrial engineers, the team also collects activity data by observing the work performed and making a list of all the activities involved.

Cost Hierarchies

To identify resource costs for various activities, a firm needs to classify all activities according to the way in which the activities consume resources. Robin Cooper suggests four levels for classifying manufacturing activities:[9]

A **unit-level activity** is performed for each unit of the cost object.

1. A **unit-level activity** is performed on each individual unit of products or services of the firm. Examples of unit-level activities include using direct materials, using direct labor-hours, inserting a component, and inspecting every unit. A unit-level activity is volume-based. The required activity varies in proportion with the quantity of the cost object. The resource consumption driver and the activity consumption driver are most likely to be the same for unit level activities.

A **batch-level activity** is performed for each batch or group of products or services.

2. A **batch-level activity** is performed for each batch or group of units of products or services. A firm incurs a batch-level activity for each batch or group of units of products or services scheduled to be processed together, rather than for each individual unit of the cost object. A batch has more than one unit of a product or service or more than one product or service. Examples of batch-level activities are setting

[9] Robin Cooper, "Cost Classification in Unit-Based and Activity-Based Manufacturing Cost Systems," *Journal of Cost Management,* Fall 1990, pp. 5–14.

EXHIBIT 5.4
Activities and Activity Levels at Siemens Electric Motor Works

Adapted from Robin Cooper, "Cost Classification in Unit-Based and Activity-Based Manufacturing Cost Systems," *Journal of Cost Management,* Fall 1990, pp 5–14.

Activity	Activity Level
Direct materials	Unit
Direct labor-hours	Unit
Machine-hours	Unit
Number of production orders	Batch
Number of special components	Batch

A **product-sustaining activity** supports the production of a specific product or service.

A **facility-sustaining activity** supports the operation in general.

up machines, placing purchase orders, scheduling production, conducting inspections by batch, handling materials, and expediting production.

3. A **product-sustaining activity** supports the production of a specific product or service. Examples of product-sustaining activities include designing products, administering parts required for products, and engaging in engineering changes to modify products.

4. A **facility-sustaining activity** supports the operation in general. These activities are not caused by products or customer service needs and cannot be traced to individual units, batches, or products. Examples of facility sustaining activities include providing security and safety, performing maintenance of general purpose machines, managing the plant, incurring factory property taxes and insurance and closing of the books each month. Some firms refer to these activities as business or infrastructure sustaining activities.

Exhibit 5.4 illustrates activity level classifications at Siemens Electric Motor Works.

Step 2: Assign Resource Costs to Activities

Activity-based costing uses resource consumption cost drivers to assign resource costs to activities. Because activities drive the cost of resources used in operations, a firm should choose resource consumption cost drivers based on cause-and-effect relationships. Typical resource consumption cost drivers include the number of (1) labor hours for laborintensive activities; (2) employees for payroll-related activities; (3) setups for batch-related activities; (4) moves for materials-handling activities; (5) machine-hours for machine repair and maintenance; and (6) square feet for general maintenance and cleaning activities.

Although a firm's general ledger is a good starting point to find information about the cost of resources, most general ledger systems report the costs of different resources, such as indirect labor, electricity, equipment, and supplies, but do not report the cost of activities performed. New accounting systems are needed to obtain and track resource costs for activities.

The cost of the resources can be assigned to activities by direct tracing or estimation. Direct tracing requires measuring the actual usage of resources by activities. For example, power used to operate a machine can be traced directly to that machine's operation by reading the meter attached to the machine.

When direct measurement is not available, department managers and supervisors need to estimate the amount or percentage of time (or effort) employees spend on each identified activity.

Multiple resource consumption cost drivers often are needed to assign different resource costs to activity or activity center cost pools. Exhibit 5.5 illustrates resources and resources consumption drivers for factory overhead costs at AT&T's New River Valley plant.

Step 3: Assign Activity Costs to Cost Objects

The final step is to assign costs of activities or activity cost pools to outputs based on the appropriate activity consumption cost drivers. Outputs are the cost objects for which firms or organizations perform activities. Typical outputs for a cost system are products and services; however, outputs also can include customers, projects, or business units. For example, the outputs of an insurance company may be individual insurance policies

REAL-WORLD FOCUS — Sample Resource Consumption Cost Drivers at Hughes Aircraft

For years, Hughes Aircraft allocated service department costs to operating departments using the number of employees as the primary resource consumption cost driver because of its simplicity.

In 1991 the company adopted activity-based costing to improve its costing system. Hughes Aircraft uses the following service departments and resource consumption cost drivers:

Service Department (Resources)	Allocation Bases (Resource Consumption Cost Drivers)
Human resources	Number of employees
	Number of new hires
	Training hours
Security	Square footage
Data processing	Lines printed
	CPU minutes
	Storage units

Source: Jack Haedicke and David Fail, "Hughes Aircraft Sets the Standard for ABC," Management Accounting, February 1991, pp. 29–33.

EXHIBIT 5.5

Resource and Resource Consumption Cost Drivers at AT&T's New River Valley Plant

Source: Based on F. B. Green, Felix Amenkhienan, and George Johnson, "Performance Measures and JIT," *Management Accounting*, February 1991, p. 53.

Resource	Resource Consumption Cost Driver
Personnel	Number of workers
Storeroom	Number of items picked for an order
Engineers	Time worked
Materials management	Time worked
Accounting	Time worked
Research and development	Number of new codes developed
Quality	Time worked
Utilities	Square-footage

sold to customers, claims processed, types of policies offered, insurance agents, or divisions or subunits of the company.

Firms use activity consumption cost drivers to assign activity costs to cost objects. Activity cost drivers should explain why the cost of a cost object goes up or down. Typical activity consumption cost drivers are purchase orders, receiving reports, inspection reports or hours, parts stored, payments, direct labor-hours, machine-hours, and setups and manufacturing cycle time. Careful analyses should be conducted in determining proper activity consumption cost drivers. For example, at the Hewlett-Packard (HP)'s Surface Mount Center in Boise, the ABC system has been fully operational since the early 1990s. This facility manufactures about 50 electronic circuit boards for internal HP customers. The center's accounting, production, and engineering staffs jointly conducted an intense analysis of the production process and cost behavior patterns to select cost drivers. This combination of accounting and engineering analysis helped management choose cost drivers.[10]

Benefits and Limitations of an Activity-Based Costing System

Since the early 1980s an increasing number of firms have adopted the activity-based costing system. These firms adapt ABC because of the benefits it offers.

---

[10] C. Mike Merz and A. Hardy, "ABC Puts Accountants on Design Team at HP," *Management Accounting*, September 1993, pp. 22–27.

Benefits

Initially, many firms adopt activity-based costing to reduce distortions in product costs often found in their volume-based costing systems. In a volume-based costing system, the creation of many arbitrary cost allocation procedures often generates product or service costs bearing little or no relationship to activities and resources consumed in operations. ABC clearly shows the effect of differences in activities and changes in products or services on costs. Among the major benefits of activity-based costing that many firms have experienced are:

1. **Better profitability measures.** ABC provides more accurate and informative product costs, leading to more accurate product profitability measurements and to better-informed strategic decisions about pricing, product lines, and market segments.

2. **Better decision and control.** ABC provides more accurate measurements of activity-driving costs, helping managers to improve product and process value by making better product design decisions, better cost controlling, and fostering value-enhancement projects.

3. **Better information for controlling capacity cost.** ABC helps managers identify and control the cost of unused capacity.

Limitations

Although activity-based costing provides better product or service costs than volume-based systems, managers should be aware of its limitations:

1. **Allocations.** Not all costs have appropriate or unambiguous activity or resource consumption cost drivers. Some costs require allocations to departments and products based on arbitrary volume measures because finding the activity that causes the cost is impractical. Examples are facility-sustaining costs such as the costs of the information system, factory manager's salary, factory insurance, and property taxes for the factory.

2. **Omission of costs.** Product or service costs identified by an ABC system are likely to not include all costs associated with the product or service. Product or service costs typically do not include costs for such activities as marketing, advertising, research and development, and product engineering even though some of these costs can be traced to individual products or services. Product costs do not include these costs because generally accepted accounting principles (GAAP) for financial reporting require them to be treated as period costs.

3. **Expense and time.** An ABC system is not cost free and is time-consuming to develop and implement. For firms or organizations that have been using a traditional volume-based costing system, installing a new ABC system is likely to be very expensive. Furthermore, like most innovative management or accounting systems, ABC usually requires a year or longer for successful development and implementation.

A Comparison of Volume-Based and Activity-Based Costing Systems

Activity-based costing systems trace costs to products through activities. Factory overhead costs are assigned to homogeneous cost pools or activity centers rather than to departments. Costs in activity centers are then assigned to products or services. The process has three steps. First, costs traced to the same or similar resource drivers are assigned to the same cost pool or activity center. Second, an overhead rate is calculated for each activity center based on a selected activity consumption cost driver. Third, the overhead costs are assigned to each product by multiplying the specific overhead rate by the amount of the activity consumption cost driver required to complete the product. The major differences between a traditional volume-based and an activity-based costing system lie in the second and third steps. Exhibit 5.6 summarizes these major differences.

EXHIBIT 5.6
Differences between Traditional and Activity-Based Costing Systems

Volume-Based Costing System	Activity-Based Costing System
Uses volume-based cost drivers	Uses activity-based cost drivers (including both volume-based and nonvolume-based)
Allocates overhead costs first to departments and second to products or services	Assigns overhead costs first to activity cost centers and second to before products or services
Focuses on managing costs of functional departments or responsibility centers	Focuses on managing processes and activities and cross-functional problem solving

Illustration of System Comparison

LEARNING OBJECTIVE 3
Compute and contrast product costs using traditional and activity-based systems.

The following example contrasts Steps 2 and 3 of the volume-based costing system using direct labor-hours as the cost driver with an activity-based costing system that uses both volume-based and non-volume-based cost drivers.

Haymarket BioTech, Inc. (HBT) produces and sells two secure communication systems, AW (Anywhere) and SZ (SecureZone). AW uses satellite technology and allows parties whose DNA is implanted in the device to communicate anywhere on the earth. SZ uses similar technology except it allows communication between two parties who are within 10 miles of each other. HBT has the following operating data for the two products:

	AW	SZ
Production volume	5,000	20,000
Selling price	$400.00	$200.00
Unit direct materials and labor	$200.00	$ 80.00
Direct labor-hours	25,000	75,000
Direct labor-hours per unit	5	3.75

Volume-Based Costing System   The volume-based costing system that the firm uses assigns factory overhead (OH) based on direct labor-hours (DLH). The firm has a total budgeted overhead of $2,000,000. Since the firm budgeted 100,000 direct labor hours for the year, the overhead rate per direct labor hour is $20 per direct labor hour.

Total overhead		$2,000,000
Total DLH	25,000 + 75,000 =	100,000
Overhead rate per DLH		$ 20.00

Since the firm spent 25,000 direct labor hours to manufacture 5,000 units of AW, the factory overhead assigned to AW is $500,000 in total and $100 per unit:

Total OH assigned to AW	$20 × 25,000 =	$500,000
Number of units of AW		5,000
Factory overhead per unit of AW		$ 100.00

The factory overhead for SZ is $1,500,000 in total and $75 per unit since the firm spent 75,000 direct labor hours to manufacture 20,000 units of SZ:

Total OH assigned to SZ	$20 × 75,000 =	$1,500,000
Number of units of SZ		20,000
Factory overhead per unit of SZ		$ 75.00

In Exhibit 5.7 we show a product profitability analysis under the firm's volume-based costing system.

EXHIBIT 5.7
Product Profitability Analysis under the Volume-Based Costing System

	AW		SZ	
Unit selling price		$400		$200
Unit product cost:				
Direct materials and labor	$200		$ 80	
Factory overhead	100		75	
Cost per unit		300		155
Product margin		$100		$ 45

Activity-Based Costing Analysis   In an attempt to use an activity-based costing, HBT has identified the following activities, budgeted costs, and activity consumption cost drivers:

Activity	Budgeted Cost	Activity Consumption Cost Driver
Engineering	$ 125,000	Engineering hours
Setups	300,000	Number of setups
Machine running	1,500,000	Machine-hours
Packing	75,000	Number of packing orders
Total	$2,000,000	

HBT also has gathered the following operating data pertaining to each of its products:

	AW	SZ	Total
Engineering hours	5,000	7,500	12,500
Number of setups	200	100	300
Machine-hours	50,000	100,000	150,000
Number of packing orders	5,000	10,000	15,000

Using the gathered data, the cost driver rate for each activity consumption cost driver is calculated as follows:

(1) Activity Consumption Cost Driver	(2) Cost	(3) Activity Consumption	(4) = (2)/(3) Activity Rate
Engineering hours	$ 125,000	12,500	$ 10
Number of setups	300,000	300	1,000
Machine-hours	1,500,000	150,000	10
Number of packing orders	75,000	15,000	5

Factory overhead costs are assigned to both products by these calculations:

AW (5,000 units)

(1) Activity Consumption Cost Driver	(2) Activity Rate	(3) Activities	(4) = (2) × (3) Total Overhead	(5) Overhead Per Unit
Engineering hours	$ 10	5,000	$ 50,000	$ 10
Number of setups	1,000	200	200,000	40
Machine-hours	10	50,000	500,000	100
Number of packing orders	5	5,000	25,000	5
Overhead cost per unit			$775,000	$155

SZ (20,000 units)

(1) Activity Consumption Cost Driver	(2) Activity Rate	(3) Activities	(4) = (2) × (3) Total Overhead	(5) Overhead Per Unit
Engineering hours	$ 10	7,500	$ 75,000	$ 3.75
Number of setups	1,000	100	100,000	5.00
Machine-hours	10	100,000	1,000,000	50.00
Number of packing orders	5	10,000	50,000	2.50
Overhead Cost Per Unit			$1,225,000	$61.25

Exhibit 5.8 presents a product profitability analysis under the activity-based costing system and Exhibit 5.9 compares product costs and profit margins under the two costing systems.

Remember that one major limitation of a volume-based costing system is that it tends to undercost complex low-volume products and overcost high-volume products. The activity-based costing system presents a more accurate measurement of product costs by tracing overhead consumption. The preceding comparison shows that the volume-based product costing system significantly undercosts AW (a low-volume product) and overcosts SZ (a high-volume product), when considering the actual overhead consumptions of the two products. Distorted or inaccurate product costing can lead to inappropriate inventory valuations, incorrect product-line decisions, unrealistic pricing, ineffective resource allocations, misplaced strategic focus, misidentified critical success factors, and lost competitive advantage.

EXHIBIT 5.8
Product Profitability Analysis under the ABC Costing System

	AW		SZ	
Unit selling price		$400		$200.00
Unit product cost				
Direct materials and labor		$200		$80.00
Factory overhead:				
Engineering	$ 10		$ 3.75	
Setups	40		5.00	
Machine running	100		50.00	
Packing	5	155	2.50	61.25
Cost per unit		355		141.25
Product margin		$ 45		$ 58.75

EXHIBIT 5.9
Comparison of Alternative Costing Approaches

	(1) Volume-Based	(2) ABC	(1) − (2) Difference
AW			
Total overhead	$ 500,000	$ 775,000	$(275,000)
Unit overhead cost	100	155	(55)
Unit margin	100	45	55
SZ			
Total overhead	$1,500,000	$1,225,000	$ 275,000
Unit overhead cost	75	61.25	13.75
Unit margin	45	58.75	(13.75)

In the last decade of the twentieth century, Whirlpool Corporation, an internationally known manufacturer of home appliances, faced increasing competition, overhead, and product diversity. The traditional costing system in use at the time made managers feel ill-equipped and uncomfortable in using costing data to make decisions. They needed reliable information to evaluate strategic options and promote manufacturing excellence. They wanted more accurate unit product costs for the following objectives:

1. Identification of profitable products
2. Analysis of competitiveness
3. Cost reduction
4. Analysis of investments
5. Budget development
6. Analysis for make-or-buy-decisions

As the consultant to Whirlpool's top management, what suggestions would you make to improve the firm's costing system? What are the requisite steps they can use to implement your suggestions?

(Refer to Comments on Cost Management in Action at the end of the chapter.)

Activity-Based Management

LEARNING OBJECTIVE 4
Describe an activity-based management system and distinguish between value-added and non-value-added activities.

Benefits of activity-based costing systems are not limited to improving product costings. After having an activity-based costing system in place, management often discovers that information from a well-designed ABC system helps to increase both the value customers received and the profits to the firm, especially for firms that embrace activity-based management.[11]

What Is Activity-Based Management?

Activity-Based Management (ABM) manages activities to improve the value of products or services to customers and increase the firm's profit. ABM draws on ABC as its major source of information and focuses on the efficiency and effectiveness of key business processes and activities. Using ABM, management can pinpoint avenues for improving operations, reducing costs, or increasing values to customers. By identifying resources spent on customers, products, and activities, ABM improves management's focus on the firm's critical success factors and enhances its competitive advantage. After Stockham Valve and Fittings implemented activity-based management, it redesigned parts to minimize manufacturing costs, and modified equipment to reduce costs. The firm increased prices of products priced below ABC cost, and dropped unprofitable products, and earned higher profits.[12]

Cooper and Kaplan classify ABM applications into two categories: operational ABM and strategic ABM.[13] Operational ABM enhances operation efficiency and asset utilization, and lowers costs; its focuses are on doing things right and performing activities more efficiently. Operational ABM applications use management techniques such as activity management, business process reengineering, total quality management, and performance measurement.

Strategic ABM attempts to alter the demand for activities and increase profitability at the current or improved activity efficiency. Strategic ABM focuses on choosing appropriate activities for the operation. By using strategic ABM firms improve profitability by reducing unprofitable activities, eliminating nonessential activities, and selecting the most profitable customers. Strategic ABM applications use management techniques such as process design, product-line and customer mix, supplier relationships, customer relationships (pricing, order size, delivery, packaging, etc.), market segmentation, and distribution channels.

---

[11] Peter B. B. Turney, "Activity-Based Management," *Management Accounting,* January 1992, pp. 20–25.

[12] Peter B. B. Turney, "Activity-Based Management," *Management Accounting,* January 1992, pp. 20–25.

[13] Robert S. Kaplan and Robin Cooper, *Cost and Effects: Using Integrated Cost Systems to Drive Profitability and Performance* (Boston: Harvard Business School Press. 1998), p. 4.

EXHIBIT 5.10
The Role of ABC/M Tools

Critical Questions	ABC/M Tools
What do we do?	Activity analysis, cause-and-effect diagram, Pareto analysis
How much does it cost?	Activity-based costing
How well do we do it?	Performance measurement
How can we do it better?	Benchmarking, using just-in-time processes, performing process redesign, eliminating low-value-added activities

Cost driver analysis
examines, quantifies, and explains the effects of the cost driver on the cost of an activity.

A cause-and-effect diagram
maps out causes that affect an activity, process, stated problem, or outcome.

A Pareto analysis
is a histogram of cost drivers that contribute to the total cost.

Performance measurement
identifies the work performed and the results achieved by an activity, process, or organizational unit.

Activity-based management uses cost driver analysis, activity analysis, and performance measurement to improve operations. A **cost driver analysis** examines, quantifies, and explains the effects of the cost driver on the cost of an activity. Its purpose is to search for the root causes of activity costs. Tools used in cost driver analysis include benchmarking, cause-and-effect diagrams, and Pareto analysis.

As discussed in Chapter 1, *benchmarking* is the search for the best practices anywhere to identify ways to improve the operation for a task, activity, or process.

A **cause-and-effect diagram** maps out causes that affect an activity, process, stated problem, or desired outcome. Because of the shape of the diagram, it is also called a *fishbone* diagram or *Ishikawa* diagram after its inventor.[14]

A **Pareto analysis** is a histogram of cost drivers that contribute to the total cost. Most Pareto analyses show that 20 percent of the cost drivers are responsible for 80 percent of the total cost incurred. These tools are discussed in more detail in Chapter 16.

Performance measurement identifies the work performed and the results achieved by an activity, process, or organizational unit. Performance measures include both financial and nonfinancial. Examples of financial performance measures are the cost per unit of output, return on sales, and cost of every department's high-value-added and low-value-added activities.

Nonfinancial performance measures evaluate operating characteristics of manufacturing processes and measures of or feedbacks from customers or personnel. Examples of nonfinancial performance measures are the number of customer complaints, customer satisfaction, number of defective parts or outputs, number of output units, cycle time, on-time delivery rate, number of employee suggestions, and scores on employee morale. Exhibit 5.10 illustrates questions that tools from ABC/ABM can help to answer.

Activity Analysis

To be competitive a firm must assess each of its activities based on its need by the product or customer, its efficiency, and its value content. A firm performs an activity because it is:

- Required to meet the specification of the product or service or satisfy customer demand;
- Required to sustain the organization; or
- Deemed beneficial to the firm.

A firm may or may not perform an activity at the highest level of efficiency. A discretionary activity may be conducted per operating procedure or custom of the organization or the activity may not be required to meet the specification, to satisfy customer demand, to sustain the organization, or to carry out an operating procedure of the organization. Examples of activities required to sustain the organization are providing plant security and compliance with government regulations. Although these activities have no direct effect on the product or service or customer satisfaction, they cannot be eliminated. Examples of discretionary activities deemed beneficial to the firm include a holiday party and free coffee. Exhibit 5.11 depicts activity analysis.

[14] Ishikawa proposed the diagram in 1943. The popularity of his concepts, including the fishbone diagram, prompted the republication of his work. See Karou Ishikawa, *Guides to Quality Control*, 2nd ed. (Tokyo: Asian Productivity Organization, 1986).

EXHIBIT 5.11 **Activity Analysis**

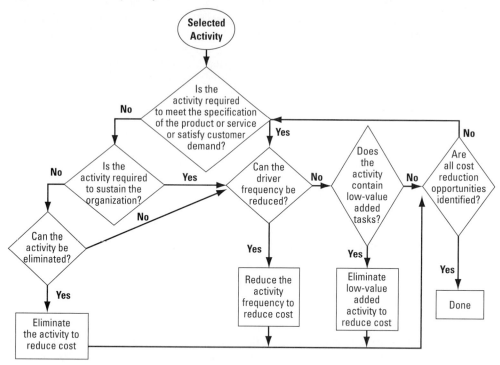

Source: Adapted from a presentation by Gary Cokins, SAS Institute.

High-Value-Added and Low-Value-Added Activities

Eliminating activities that add little or no value to customers reduces resource consumption and allows the firm to focus on activities that increase customer satisfaction. Knowing the values of activities allow employees to see how work really serves customers and which activities may have little value to the ultimate customers and should be eliminated or reduced.

A **high-value-added activity** increases significantly the value of the product or service to the customers. Removal of a high-value-added activity decreases perceptively the value of the product or service to the customer. Inserting a flange into a part, pouring molten metal into a mold, and preparing a field for planting are examples of high-value-added activities. Installing software to protect a computer from spam is a high-value-added activity to customers annoyed by bombardments of unwanted e-mail. Designing, processing (manufacturing), and delivering products and services are high-value-added activities.

Exhibit 5.12 illustrates high-value-added and low-value-added activities of a television news broadcasting firm. For a television news broadcasting company a high-value-added activity is one that, if eliminated, would affect the accuracy and effectiveness of the newscast and decrease total viewers as well as ratings for that time slot. An activity that shortens delivery from three to two days is a high-value-added activity. Activities that verify story sources to ensure the story's accuracy are high-value-added activities. Activities to plan newscasts so that viewers can follow transitions from one story to the next are high-value-added activities.

High-value-added activities are those:

- Necessary or required to meet customer requirements or expectations;
- That enhance purchased materials or components of a product;
- That, if more of them are accomplished, the customer would pay more for the product or service;
- That are critical steps and cannot be eliminated in a business process;
- That are performed to resolve or eliminate quality problems;

A **high-value-added activity**
increases the value of the product
or service to the customers.

REAL-WORLD FOCUS How Daton Technologies Identifies High-Value-Added and Low-Value-Added Activities

Daton Technologies asks five questions in identifying activities as high-value-added or low-value-added:

1. Is the activity of value to an external customer?
2. Is the activity required to meet corporate rules?
3. Is the activity required for sound business practices?
4. Is the activity of value to an internal customer?
5. Is the activity a waste?

The company classifies positive answers to the first two questions under high-value-added activities and to the last three questions under low-value-added activities, and tries to eliminate any activity in question 5. For questions 3 and 4, the company tries to improve the activity or reduce its frequency. Otherwise, try to eliminate that activity. Examples of high-value-added activities in Daton Technologies are making extrusion runs, shipping, designing parts, and making tools. Examples of low-value-added activities are setup, inspection, regrind, and process returns.

Source: Neal R. Pemberton, Logan Arumugam, and Nabil Hassan, "ABM at Daton Technologies: From Obstacles to Opportunities," *Management Accounting,* March 1996, pp. 20–27.

EXHIBIT 5.12
Television News Broadcasting Firm's High-Value-Added and Low-Value-Added Activities

A *high-value-added activity* is one that, if eliminated, would affect the accuracy and effectiveness of the newscast and decrease total viewers as well as ratings for that time slot.

1. Activities that augment accuracy
    *   Verification of story sources and acquired information.
2. Activities that augment effectiveness
    *   Efficient electronic journalism to ensure effective taped segments.
    *   Newscast story order planned so that viewers can follow from one story to the next.
    *   Field crew time used to access the best footage possible.
    *   Meaningful news story writing.
    *   Contents of the newscast planned so that viewers get the best possible package of stories.

A *low-value-added activity* is one that, if eliminated, would not affect the accuracy and effectiveness of the newscast. The activity contributes nothing to the quest for viewer retention and improved ratings.

1. Activities that generate excess
    *   Developing stories not used in a newscast.
    *   Assigning more than one person to develop each facet of the same news story.
2. Activities that augment delay (downtime)
    *   Newscast not completed on time because of one or more inefficient processes.
    *   Too many employees on a particular shift or project.

*   That are performed upon request of a satisfied customer; and
*   That you would do more of, if time permitted.

A **low-value-added activity** consumes time, resources, or space, but adds little or does not contribute to satisfying customer needs.

A **low-value-added activity** consumes time, resources, or space, but adds little in satisfying customer needs. If eliminated, customer value or satisfaction decreases inperceptibly or remains unchanged. Moving parts between processes, waiting time, repairing, and rework are examples of low-value-added activities. A low-value-added activity for a television news broadcasting company is one that, if eliminated, would have little or no effect on the accuracy and effectiveness of the newscast; the activity contributes little or nothing to the quest for viewer retention and improved ratings. Activities such as developing stories not used in a newscast and finishing segments of a story after broadcasting the story are examples of low-value-added activities for a television broadcasting company. In fact, many would consider these activities as non-value-added. Inventory, transportation, overprocessing, waiting, and correction are examples of low-value-added activities.

EXHIBIT 5.13
A Classification of High-Value-Added and Low-Value-Added Activities.

Activity	High-Value-Added	Low-Value-Added
Designing product	X	
Setting up		X
Waiting		X
Moving		X
Processing	X	
Reworking		X
Repairing		X
Storing		X
Inspecting		X
Delivering product	X	

Low-value-added activities do not generate sufficient benefits to the firm to justify the actions and non-value-added activities are waste. Reductions or eliminations of low-value-added activities reduce cost and increase profit. In the early 1990s, General Motors Corporation persuaded its parts suppliers to reduce or eliminate many low-value-added activities including overproducing, overstocking, moving, waiting, reworking, idling equipment, idling space, and making a product with features not required by customers. As a result, GM was able to reduce substantially the prices it paid its suppliers.[15] Exhibit 5.13 illustrates a classification of high-value-added and low-value-added activities.

Low-value-added activities are those that:

* Can be eliminated without affecting the form, fit, or function of the product or service;
* Begin with prefix "re" (such as rework or returned goods);
* Result in waste and add little or no value to the product or service;
* Are performed due to inefficiencies or errors in the process stream;
* Are duplicated in another department or add unnecessary steps to the business process;
* Are performed to monitor quality problems;
* Are performed due to a request of an unhappy or dissatisfied customer;
* Produce an unnecessary or unwanted output; and
* If given the option, you would prefer to do less of.

Firms need to realize that low-value-added activities decrease competitiveness and profitability. Efforts to eliminate or reduce low-value-added activities are never ending tasks.

Manufacturing Industry Applications

LEARNING OBJECTIVE 5
Describe how activity-based costing systems are used in manufacturing industry.

Activity-based costing started in the manufacturing industry. Many manufacturing companies, such as Hewlett-Packard and Advanced Micro Devices, have successfully implemented activity-based costing and management systems.

ABC at Hewlett-Packard

The Roseville Network Division (RND) of Hewlett-Packard (HP) was one of the first divisions to use activity-based costing. At RND the combined impact of increasing the variety of products manufactured and decreasing product lives made the design of products and their production processes critical factors for the division's success. The

---

[15] Joe Cyr, "Waste Removal Now," *CMA Magazine*, June 1993, p. 23.

EXHIBIT 5.14
Cost Drivers at Hewlett-Packard's Roseville Network Division

Source: Robin Cooper and Peter B. B. Turney, "Internally Forced Activity-Based Cost Systems," in *Measures for Manufacturing Excellence*, ed. R. S. Kaplan (Boston: Harvard Business School Press, 1990), p. 17.

Cost Driver	Activity Level	Cost Driver	Activity Level
Number of axial insertions	Unit	Number of radical insertions	Unit
Number of DIP insertions	Unit	Number of manual insertions	Unit
Number of test hours	Unit	Number of solder joints	Unit
Number of boards	Product	Number of parts	Product
Number of slots	Product		

costing system RND had been using, however, did not provide information that managers could use to compare the production costs of different designs.

RND redesigned its costing system and focused on the costs of the different activities at each production process. The new system started with only two cost drivers, direct labor-hours and number of insertions. Eventually the division identified nine cost drivers, as shown in Exhibit 5.14.

The activity-based costing system greatly influenced the design of new products. For example, after the ABC system discovered that manual insertions were three times as expensive as automatic insertions, engineers redesigned products to allow for more automatic insertion.

ABC at Advanced Micro Devices

Advanced Micro Devices (AMD), a major semiconductor manufacturer, completed an activity-based costing project at its test and assembly facility in Penang, Malaysia. The ABC project uncovered significant product cost distortions (high-volume, simple products were overcosted by 20 to 30 percent, and low-volume, complex products were undercosted by 600 to 700 percent). ABC provided AMD management with a more accurate basis for setting transfer prices between divisions.

Key non-volume-based cost drivers include (1) line items (for production scheduling and setup activities), (2) quality problems (for process-sustaining activities), and (3) decreases in volume (to below a certain point for yield and quality improvement activities).

The high total of expenses driven by these non-volume-based costs underscored the inaccuracies in the old system that allocated all expenses to products using labor- and machine-hours.

The success of the project was described by the director of finance, who stated, "ABC provided AMD with a cost system solution that enables and supports AMD's strategy of managing profitable growth."[16]

Marketing and Administrative Applications

LEARNING OBJECTIVE 6
Describe how activity-based costing systems are used in marketing and administrative activities.

Activity-based costing also can be used for marketing activities such as sales calls, advertising, selling, order filling, shipping, warehousing, return and restocking, and credit and collection processing. For administrative activities ABC is used for accounting, data processing, personnel, quality assurance, printing and duplicating, security, maintenance, and administrative services.

The procedures to apply ABC to marketing and administrative activities are similar to the steps described earlier for manufacturing applications. The firms track marketing costs to activity cost pools before tracing costs to product lines and territories. Exhibit 5.15 presents examples of cost drivers for marketing activities.

The deregulation of telecommunication industry made it critical for firms in the industry to carefully manage all activities and reduce operating costs to remain

[16] Robin Cooper, Robert Kaplan, Lawrence Maisel, Eileen Morrissey, and Ronald Oehm, *Implementing Activity-Based Cost Management: Moving from Analysis to Action-Implementing Experiences at Eight Companies* (Montvale, NJ: Institute of Management Accountants, 1992), p. 56.

REAL-WORLD FOCUS Robotics Distributor Identified Activities and Cost Drivers for Sales and Administration

Robotics Distributor is a U.S. distributor of robots for welding, materials handling, dispensing, cutting, and other industrial operations. Unhappy with its traditional costing system for sales and adminis-

tration activities, management launched a study to implement an ABC system by identifying the following major activities and cost drivers for its sales and administration costs:

Activities	Cost Drivers
Application engineering	Number of proposals
Engineering design	Number of bookings
Documentation	Number of bookings
Sales administration	Number of customers
Marketing	Number of customers
Sales	Number of customers
Customer support administration	Spare parts
Integrator support	Number of integrator customers
Transplant support	Revenue dollars
Finance	Revenue dollars

The implementation of ABC increased Robotics' monthly operating income from sales of its standard robotic product line by almost $150,000 and validated management's concerns about the previous allocation method. This information also facilitated strategic decision making on which product to emphasize.

Source: David Bukovinsky, Hans Sprohge, and John Talbott, "Activity-Based Costing for Sales and Administrative Costs: A Case Study," *The CPA Journal*, April 2000, pp. 70–72.

EXHIBIT 5.15
Cost Drivers for Marketing Activities

Source: Ronald J. Lewis, "Activity-Based Costing for Marketing," *Management Accounting*, November 1991, pp. 33–36.

Marketing Activity Cost Pool	Cost Driver
Advertising	Sales units or dollars Number of sales calls
Selling	Sales dollars Number of orders obtained
Order filling, shipping, warehousing	Weight of shipped product Number, weight, or size of units ordered Units of shipped product
General office (e.g., credit and collection)	Number of customer orders Number of invoice lines

competitive. AT&T found out it could no longer simply allocate costs to functional divisions as had been done since its inception more than a hundred years ago. To remain competitive, AT&T implemented an activity-based costing system to help managers gain a better understanding of the activities driving their business.

AT&T managers selected the business billing center as an ABC pilot project. Its activities included monitoring billing records; editing checks; validating data; correcting errors; and printing, sorting, and dispatching invoices to business customers. A cross-functional team prepared a flowchart of the business operations that identified the relationships between resources and activities, between activities and processes, and between process outputs and services provided to each customer.

The cost of services provided to different customers was determined by identifying activity and cost driver consumption characteristics. The firm selected several cost drivers, including the number of customers tested, number of change requests, number of service orders, number of printer hours, and number of pages printed.

AT&T managers found the ABC model developed in the pilot study useful in helping the firm manage costs and improve its internal operating processes, supplier relationships, and customer satisfaction.[17]

Service and Not-For-Profit Applications of ABC

LEARNING OBJECTIVE 7
Demonstrate how activity-based costing systems are used in service and not-for-profit organizations.

Many service and not-for-profit organizations have developed and implemented ABC systems, including Alexandria Hospital; Union Pacific Railroad; Amtrak Auto-Ferry Service; Data Services, Inc.;[18] Fireman's Fund;[19] American Express;[20] U.S. Postal Service;[21] and DSL Client Services.[22]

Service and not-for-profit organizations have many operating characteristics that make them different from manufacturing companies. Among them are changeable outputs, less predictability on service request activity, and ambiguous relationships between overhead or indirect costs and products or service outputs. Consequently, service and not-for-profit organizations often do not have ABC systems similar to those of manufacturing firms. Nevertheless, these organizations can benefit from ABC costing.

An Illustrative Comparison of Volume-Based and ABC Systems for a Service Firm

The accounting firm of Achuck, Buniel & Hinckley performed two audits this week. Both audits required 100 professional labor-hours. The average wage for its audit staff members is $50 per hour, including fringe benefits. An audit engagement often requires researching, on-site observations, documenting, e-mailing, and long-distance calls.

Costing Using a Volume-Based Costing System

The direct labor-based costing system that the firm is using assigns costs to cost objects based on the number of professional labor-hours. The firm's overhead rate is 160 percent of the cost of professional labor hours. For the accounting firm the cost object is defined as an audit.

Because both audits require 100 professional labor hours, the volume-based costing system reports that the total cost for both audits is $13,000.

	(1) Professional Hours	(2) Hourly Rate	(3) = (1) × (2) Total Professional Labor Cost	(4) Overhead Rate	(5) = (3) × (4) Applied Overhead	(6) = (3) + (5) Total Cost
Audit 1	100	$50	$5,000	160%	$8,000	$13,000
Audit 2	100	50	5,000	160	8,000	13,000

[17] Terence Hobdy, Jeff Thomson, and Paul Sharman, "Activity-Based Management at AT&T," *Management Accounting,* April 1994, pp. 35–39.

[18] William Rotch, "Activity-Based Costing in Service Industries," *Journal of Cost Management,* Summer 1990, pp. 5–14.

[19] Michael Crane and John Meyer, "Focusing on True Costs in a Service Organization," *Management Accounting,* February 1993, pp. 41–45.

[20] David A. Carlson and S. Mark Young, "Activity-Based Total Quality Management at American Express," *Journal of Cost Management,* Spring 1993, pp. 48–58.

[21] Terrell L. Carter, Ali M. Sedaghat, and Thomas D. Williams, "How ABC Changed the Post Office," *Strategic Finance,* February 1998, pp. 28–32.

[22] Barbara Gauharou, "Activity-Based Costing at DSL Client Services," *Management Accounting Quarterly,* Summer 2000, pp. 5–11.

REAL-WORLD FOCUS   Distorted Medicare Reimbursement with Inappropriate Cost Drivers

Hospitals must complete a Medicare cost report each year to be eligible for government reimbursement for services rendered to Medicare patients. Government uses this cost information to set amounts for various Medicare reimbursement parameters. Hospitals often use the same cost information as the basis for determining the charges for privately insured patients. For inpatient care costs, Medicare requires that all operating costs pertaining to patient care be allocated to patients based only on the number of days a patient spends in the hospital (patient-days). Thus, Medicare cost reporting does not explicitly consider the possibility of multiple cost drivers.

Huang and Kirby noted at least two cost drivers for patient care costs: (1) the number of patient-days and (2) the number of patients admitted. Patient-day costs include costs of meals, laundry, and basic nursing care. Admission costs include costs for taking patients' history upon admission, preparing patients for surgery, intensive care immediately following surgery, preparing rooms for new patients, and handling medical coding and billing. The first cost driver,

the number of patient-days, is a unit-level cost driver while the second cost driver is likely a batch-level cost driver.

Using publicly available data, Huang and Kirby compared the results of current Medicare reimbursement procedures that use a single volume-based, unit-level cost driver (patient-days), with the results that would be obtained if Medicare reimbursements were based on two cost drivers: a unit-level cost driver (patient-days) and a batch-level cost driver (number of admissions). Their study results suggest that Medicare is potentially overcharged by between $66 million and $1.98 billion per year for hospital patient care! The main reason is that Medicare patients tend to be older and have a much longer average length of hospitalization than private insurance patients do. Because Medicare reimbursements consider only patient-days, Medicare is charged for a disproportionately large share of admitted patients.

Source: Yuchang Huang and Alison L. Kirby, "Distorted Medicare Reimbursements: The Effect of Cost Accounting Choices," *Journal of Management Accounting Research,* Fall 1994, pp.128–43.

Activity-Based Costing System

Unsatisfied with its current billing based on a volume-based costing system, the accounting firm embarks on a cost study and has estimated the following costs of activities:

Activities	Cost Drivers	Indirect Cost Application Rate
Direct labor	Number of hours	$ 50 per hour
Copying/faxing	Number of copies/faxes	0.50 per page
Long-distance calls	Number of calls made	10 per call
Research/information services	Number of research/information items	400 per item
Data processing	Number of minutes	100 per minute

Audit 1 is more resource intensive; it required the following photocopies, long-distance calls, information service calls, and data processing to complete the audit.

Activity	Amount	Rate	Applied OH
Copying/faxing	5,000 copies	$0.50	$ 2,500
Long-distance calls	100 calls	10	1,000
Research/information	80 items	400	32,000
Data processing	70 minutes	100	7,000
Total			$42,500

In contrast, Audit 2 is less resource intensive. The breakdown of activities for Audit 2 follows:

Activity	Amount	Rate	Applied OH
Copying/faxing	2,000 copies	$0.50	$ 1,000
Long-distance calls	30 calls	10	300
Research/information	10 items	400	4,000
Data processing	30 minutes	100	3,000
Total			$ 8,300

Activity-based costing can be applied to measure and manage e-retailing business. Notice that four of the following e-retailing activities (2, 5, 7, and 9) are unique to e-business.

Source: Thomas L. Zeller, "Measuring and Managing E-Retailing with Activity-Based Costing," *Journal of Cost Management,* January/February 2000, pp. 17–30.

E-Retailing Activities

1. Service routine customers
2. Electronic customer order processing
3. Service customer issues
4. Merchandise inventory selection and management
5. Imaging and annotation
6. Purchasing and receiving
7. Virtual storefront optimization
8. Customer acquisition and retention
9. Customer acquisition and retention/revenue share
10. Information systems support
11. Business/administration support
12. Business/production support
13. Facility/administration maintenance
14. Facility/production maintenance

Cost Drivers

1. E-mail and phone inquiries
2. Time (hardware and software depreciation)
3. E-mail and phone inquiries
4. Number of new products
5. Number of changes to inventory database
6. Number of orders
7. Time (hours dedicated to Web page development)
8. Number of targeted customers
9. Number of affiliate links (i.e., affiliate) marketing
10. Number of desktop machines
11. Number of predominant drivers
12. Number of product categories
13. Square footage in the administrative area
14. Square footage in the production area

The ABC costing brings to light that the firm is actually losing money on Audit 1 while it might have substantially overcharged on Audit 2.

Customer Profitability Analysis

LEARNING OBJECTIVE 8
Analyze factors affecting revenues and selling and administrative costs and determine customer profitability.

ABC/ABM product costing can be extended to customer profitability analysis to identify the best customers. If two customers purchased from your company the exact same amount and mix of products and services at the exact same prices during the exact same time period, would both customers be equally profitable? Most likely not. Some customers place standard orders with no fuss, whereas others demand nonstandard everything, such as special delivery requirements. Some customers just buy your product or service line, and you hardly ever hear from them. Others you always hear from—to change their delivery requirements, inquire about and expedite their order, or return or exchange their goods.[23] Exhibit 5.16 depicts types of customers.

Customer profitability analysis focuses on selling, general, and administrative costs. It analyzes activities, identifies proper cost drivers, and determines realized profits from customers. Customer profitability analysis allows managers to:

- Identify most profitable customers—the champions;
- Manage each customer's "costs-to-serve" to a lower level;
- Establish a surcharge for or re-pricing expensive "costs-to-serve" activities;
- Reduce services;
- Introduce new products and services;
- Raise prices for demanders;
- Abandon products, services, or customers;

[23] Similar questions can be asked about the inbound costs from suppliers. Not all suppliers are equally easy to work with and deliver similar quality of services. Some suppliers can be so much more difficult to work with that the cost ultimately drags down the organization's profit.

EXHIBIT 5.16
Profitability Matrix

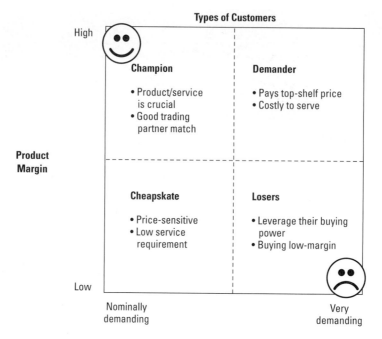

Source: Adapted from a presentation by Gary Cokins, SAS Institute.

- Improve the process;
- Offer the customer profit-positive service level options;
- Shift the customer's purchase mix toward richer, higher-margin products and service lines;
- Discount to gain more volume with low "costs-to-serve" customers.
- Select customer mix — What types of customer should we market to? What types should we not market to? or
- Choose kinds of after-sale services to provide.

A good understanding of the profitability of a firm's current and potential customers can help firms to achieve goals, raise earnings to a higher level, and strengthen strategic positions. Management accountants, as strategic management partners, can enhance both short- and long-term successes of the organization by providing good customer profitability analyses.

Customer profitability analysis
traces and reports customer revenues and customer costs.

Customer profitability analysis traces and reports customer revenues and customer costs. During the recent economic slowdown, many corporate managers found themselves knee-deep in expensive programs to improve customer relationships, such as overnight delivery and 360-degree customer service. However, many managers could not tell if these expensive projects were actually doing anything to increase business and improve profits.[24] Customer profitability analysis can help to separate profitable customers from money-losers, provide valuable insights into factors that contribute to the differences, point out ways to raise profits without raising prices, and improve the firm's profitability or the organization's effectiveness in attaining its goals. Many corporations have found these benefits of customer profitability analysis:

- Providing better services to highly profitable customers.
- Securing highly profitable customers from competitors.
- Setting prices based on the cost to serve; charging higher prices for expensive services and granting discounts, if necessary, to gain customers requiring lower costs.
- Negotiating with customers to reach mutually beneficial levels of services.

[24] David M. Katz, "Activity-Based Costing (ABC)," *CFO*, December 2002 (CFO.com).

- Transforming unprofitable customers through targeted negotiations on price, quantity, product mix, order processing, delivery terms, and payment arrangements.
- Identifying and conceding permanent loss customers to competitors.[25]

Customer profitability analysis includes the assessment of customer revenue, customer cost, and customer value.

Customer Revenue Analysis

Customer revenue analysis considers all activities that affect the net amount received from the customer.

A **customer revenue analysis** considers all activities that affect the net amount received from the customer. It traces prices, discounts, including sales and cash discounts, to customers and identifies financing costs associated with customer revenues. Not all sales dollars contribute equally to a firm's net revenue. Net revenues from customers can differ because of price discounting, sales terms, sales returns and allowances, and the length of time that customer accounts remain outstanding. Exhibit 5.17 illustrates revenue-related activities for three major customers of Winsome Office Supply.

At times, salespersons grant sales discounts and special sales terms to secure sales. To win the business from GereCo. and Advance Tek, the salespersons offered a 5 percent price discount. Both GereCo. and HomeServ paid their accounts within the specified payment terms. In fact, GereCo. paid its accounts within 10 days to take advantage of the cash discount. Advance Tek's accounts were usually overdue, and the firm did not take advantage of the cash discount. On average, Advance Tek's accounts remained outstanding for three months. Winsome estimates its cost of capital to be approximately 1 percent per month.

The three customers generate approximately the same amount of total sales. However, an analysis of the net revenues from these customers yields a different picture of profitability because of differences in sales discounts and sales terms granted to these customers, the amount and frequency of sales returns and allowances, and the pattern of payments by these customers. Exhibit 5.18 illustrates the analysis.

The net invoice price billed to a customer is the net amount after subtracting sales discounts granted to the customer from the total sales prices. For sales to GereCo, the

[25] Robert S. Kaplan and Robin Cooper, *Cost & Effect* (Boston: Harvard Business School, Press, 1998), p. 181.

EXHIBIT 5.17
Selected Sales Activity of Winsome Office Supply

	GereCo.	HomeServ Inc.	Advance Tek
Total sales	$500,000	$480,000	$540,000
Sales discounts	5%	0%	5%
Sales terms			
Payment	2/10, n/30	net 30	2/10, n/30
Delivery	FOB destination	FOB destination	FOB shipping point
Sales returns and allowances	1.0%	0.5%	6.0%

EXHIBIT 5.18
Customer Revenue Analysis, Winsome Office Supply

	GereCo.	HomeServ Inc.	Advance Tek
Total sales	$500,000	$480,000	$540,000
Less: Sales discounts	(25,000)	—	(27,000)
Net invoice amount	$475,000	$480,000	$513,000
Less: Sales returns and allowances	4,750	2,400	30,780
Net sales	$470,250	$477,600	$482,220
Less: Cash discounts	9,405	—	—
Finance charge*	(3,072)	—	9,644
Net proceeds	$463,917	$477,600	$472,576

*Finance charges:
GereCo.: Net proceeds on the 10th day: $470,250 − 9,405   = $460,845
              Interest earned for 20 days: $460,845 × 1% × 20/30 =   3,072
   Advance Tek: $482,220 × 1% × 2 months   =   9,644

list price is $500,000. The salesperson agreed to a 5 percent sales discount. The net invoice amount, therefore, is $475,000 [$500,000 − ($500,000 × 0.05)]. GereCo. returned and was granted a sales return and allowance of 1 percent of the goods it received or $4,750 (0.01 × 475,000). The net sales to GereCo. totaled $470,250 ($475,000 − $4,750), which is the amount it owed Winsome and is the basis for calculating cash discounts if GereCo. pays within 10 days. At the 2 percent cash discount agreed to, the cash discount is $9,405 ($470,250 × 2%).

Adjustments for finance charges allow comparisons of net proceeds from firms with different payment patterns. GereCo pays within 10 days. The funds Winsome receives on the 10th day are, therefore, available to Winsome 20 days earlier than the funds it receives from HomeServ, which pays its accounts in 30 days. Winsome can earn interest on the cash payment received on the 10th day or save the finance charge that the firm might have to incur if the funds were not available until the 30th day. At 1 percent cost of funds per month, the funds that GereCo remits, $460,845 ($470,250 − $9,405), on the 10th day, Winsome can save the finance charge on the funds needed in operations that it would have to raise elsewhere. The savings from having the funds available 20 days earlier is $3,072 [($460,845 × 0.01 × (20 days/30 days)].

The customer revenue analysis shows that the amount of net proceeds to Winsome from sales to HomeServ is the highest among the three customers, despite the fact that the total sales to HomeServe are only $480,000, the lowest of the three. This analysis suggests that HomeServ is the best customer in terms of net proceeds from sales.

Customer Cost Analysis

LEARNING OBJECTIVE 9
Describe customer cost categories and identify costs to serve a customer.

Not all customers require similar activities either before or after the sales. Examples of customer-specific activities include:

- Order processing costs;
- Billing, collection, and payment processing costs;
- Accounts receivable and carrying costs;
- Customer service costs;
- Return or allowance processing costs;
- Restocking costs; and
- Selling and marketing costs.

Customer cost analysis
identifies activities and cost drivers to service customers.

Customer cost analysis identifies activities and cost drivers to service customers before and after sales, not including product costs. Traditionally these costs are hidden in the customer support, marketing, and sales function. ABC/M can help managers to grasp activities and their costs to serve customers.

Different activities often have different cost drivers. Based on the activities and cost drivers involved in services performed to acquire and complete a transaction, customer costs can be classified into the following categories:

- *Customer unit-level cost*—resources consumed for each unit sold to a customer. Examples include sales commissions based on the number of units sold or sales dollars, shipping cost when the freight term is FOB destination and the freight charge is based on the number of units shipped, and cost of restocking each of the returned units.
- *Customer batch-level cost*—resources consumed for each sales transaction. Examples include order-processing costs, invoicing costs, and recording of sales returns or allowances every time a return or allowance is granted.
- *Customer-sustaining cost*—resources consumed to service a customer regardless of the number of units or batches sold. Examples are salespersons' travel costs to visit customers, monthly statement processing costs, and collection costs for late payments.
- *Distribution-channel cost*—resources consumed in each distribution channel the firm uses to service customers. Examples are operating costs of regional

warehouses that serve major customers and centralized distribution centers that serve small retail outlets.

- *Sales-sustaining cost*—resources consumed to sustain sales and service activities that cannot be traced to an individual unit, batch, customer, or distribution channel. Examples are general corporate expenditures for sales activities, and salary, fringe benefits, and bonus of the general sales manager.

Exhibit 5.19 reports customer-related activities, cost drivers and their rates, and the cost category of each of the activities of Winsome Office Supply. These activities are based on the results of a careful study of the firm's selling, administrative, and general expenditures, as well as customer transactions for the last three years. Exhibit 5.20 reports the detailed customer-related activities that Winsome experienced for the sales to the firm's three major customers reported in Exhibit 5.17.

Both customer activity costs, cost categories, and their cost drivers illustrated in Exhibit 5.19 and the detailed customer-related activities reported in Exhibit 5.20 provide the basis for analyzing customer costs. Exhibit 5.21 reports customer cost analyses for Winsome's three customers.

As illustrated in Exhibit 5.20, costs to service customers often differ because they do not require the same amount of services and attention. These three customers purchased approximately equal amounts from Winsome. The costs to serve these customers, however, ranged from $1,555 to $10,795. To evaluate customer profitability, we must review customer revenue analysis and customer cost analysis as illustrated next.

EXHIBIT 5.19
Customer-Related Activity, Cost Driver, Cost Rate, and Cost Category

Activity	Cost Driver and Rate	Cost Category
Order taking	$30 per order	Customer batch-level
Order processing	$20 per order, and	Customer batch-level
	$1 per item	Customer unit-level
Delivery	$100 per trip, and	Customer batch-level
	$1 per mile	Customer batch-level
Expedited order taking, processing, and delivery (additional costs)	$800 per order	Customer batch-level
Customer visit	$200 per visit	Customer sustaining
Monthly billing:		
First statement	$5 per statement	Customer sustaining
Subsequent reminder	$25 per notice	Customer sustaining
Sales returns	$100 per occurrence	Customer batch-level
Restocking	$5 per item returned	Customer unit-level
Sales office		
Salaries and fringe benefits	$100,000 per month	Sales sustaining
Office expenses	$50,000 per month	Sales sustaining

EXHIBIT 5.20
Customer-Related Activity for Selected Customers Winsome Office Supply

	GereCo.	HomeServ Inc.	Advance Tek
Number of orders	2	20	80
Average number of items per order	400	38	8
Delivery miles	10	15	20
Number of expedited orders	0	0	5
Number of visits by salesperson	1	2	5
Sales returns			
Number of requests	2	1	10
Average units per return	3	4	2

EXHIBIT 5.21   **Customer Cost Analysis, Winsome Office Supply**

	GereCo.	HomeServ Inc.	Advance Tek
Customer unit-level cost			
Order processing	400 × 2 × $1 = $800	38 × 20 × $1 = $760	8 × 80 × $1 = $640
Restocking	2 × 3 × $5= 30	1 × 4 × $5 = 20	10 × 2 × $5 = 100
Customer batch-level cost			
Order taking	2 × $30 = 60	20 × $30 = 600	80 × $30 = 2,400
Order processing	2 × $20 = 40	20 × $20 = 400	80 × $20 = 1,600
Delivery			
Trips	2 × $100 = 200	20 × $100 = 2,000	
Miles	10 × 2 × $1 = 20	15 × 20 × $1 = 300	
Expedited orders	—	—	$800 × 5 = 4,000
Sales returns	2 × $100 = 200	1 × $100 = 100	10 × $100 = 1,000
Customer-sustaining costs			
Sales visits	1 × $200 = 200	2 × $200 = 400	5 × $200 = 1,000
Monthly billings	1 × $5 = 5	1 × $5 = 5	1 × $5 = 5
Subsequent reminders	—	—	2 × $25 = 50
Sales-sustaining costs	0	0	0
Total	$1,555	$4,585	$10,795

Customer Profitability Analysis

A customer profitability analysis combines customer revenue and customer cost analyses to assess customer profitability and helps identify actions to improve customer profitability. Exhibit 5.22 illustrates customer profitability analyses for Winsome.

The customer profitability analysis verifies that HomeServ is the most profitable among Winsome's three major customers, even though HomeServ made the lowest

EXHIBIT 5.22
Customer Profitability Analysis, Winsome Office Supply

	GereCo.	HomeServ Inc.	Advance Tek
Total sales	$500,000	$480,000	$540,000
Less: Sales discounts	25,000	—	27,000
Net invoice amount	$475,000	$480,000	$513,000
Less: Sales returns and allowances	4,750	2,400	30,780
Net sales	$470,250	$477,600	$482,220
Less: Cash discounts	9,405	—	—
Finance charges	(3,072)	0	9,644
Net proceeds	$463,917	$477,600	$472,576
Customer costs			
Order processing	$ 800	$ 760	$ 640
Restocking	30	20	100
Order taking	60	600	2,400
Order processing	40	400	1,600
Delivery			
Trips	200	2,000	—
Miles	20	300	—
Expedited orders	—	—	4,000
Sales returns	200	100	1,000
Sales visits	200	400	1,000
Monthly billings	5	5	5
Subsequent reminders	0	0	50
Total customer costs	$ 1,555	$ 4,585	$ 10,795
Net customer profit	$462,362	$473,015	$461,781

An important part of customer profitability is the cost to acquire a new customer. Bain and Company, a consulting firm, estimated that the cost of obtaining a new customer in the consumer electronics industry needs more than four years of business from each new customer to break even, but more than half of the new customers will defect before the four-year breakeven point. The numbers are similar for the apparel industry. Many firms are now trying to acquire new customers through the Web. What would be the effect of the Web acquisition on profitability?

purchases from Winsome. The analysis also shows that although Advance Tek made the highest total purchases of the three, it yields the lowest net customer profit.

The reasons that GereCo. is not as profitable as HomeServ relate to sales activities. Winsome granted GereCo. much more favorable sales terms than the terms granted to HomeServ. GereCo. also had a high amount of sales returns and allowances; it returned twice as often as HomeServ did.

Price discounts and sales returns are contributing factors for the low profitability of Advance Tek. Although Advance Tek had the highest total sales, it generated the lowest profit of the three customers. Winsome should be concerned about Advance Tek's high returns and its frequency of expediting orders. The high returns could be a result of the customer's dissatisfaction with Winsome's products. Winsome needs to look into the reason for the high returns before losing the customer to competition. Late payments also add cost to serve Advance Tek; they might indicate Advance Tek's dissatisfaction with Winsome's sales and services or tightness of Advance Tek's financial condition.

Customer Value Assessment

Customer profitability analysis provides valuable information to the assessment of customer values. In addition, firms must weigh other relevant factors before determining the action appropriate for each customer. The following are among these relevant factors:

- Growth potential of the customer, the customer's industry, and its cross-selling potential.
- Possible reactions of the customer to changes in sales terms or services.
- Importance of having the firm as a customer for future sales references, especially when the customer could play a pivotal role in bringing in additional business.

Activity-Based Costing and Strategic Cost Management

LEARNING OBJECTIVE 11
Relate activity-based costing to strategic cost management.

Activity-based costing facilitates strategic cost management. ABC not only shows how activities consume resources and how products or customers trigger activities but also assigns costs to products or customers according to the resources they consume. ABC describes a firm as a series of activities whose performance is designed to satisfy customers' needs. It provides information for managers to manage activities to improve competitiveness, and achieve strategic goals.

Strategic choices determine activities. Successful firms use their resources on activities that lead to the greatest strategic benefit. Through measurement of costs of activities and identification of activities in manufacturing products or providing services ABC/M helps managers to understand the relationship between the firm's strategy and the activities and resources needed to implement the strategy.

Porter identifies business strategies to be either cost leadership or differentiation as mentioned in Chapter 2. For firms following a cost leadership strategy to gain competitive advantages, ABC/M is critical because it identifies key activities, cost drivers, and ways to improve processes to reduce cost. ABC/M also helps managers of firms with a differentiation strategy to identify value-enhancement opportunities; develops a customer strategy; supports a technological leadership strategy; and establishes a pricing strategy by identifying and analyzing key activities, processes, cost drivers, and improvement methods. In general, ABC/M provides answers to these strategic cost management questions, facilitates identification of the best strategy, and helps the firm to attain its strategic goals:

- How do a firm's cost structures and profits compare to those of its competition?
- How does switching from volume-based costing to an ABC costing system impact pricing, product design, process design, manufacturing technology, and product-line decisions?
- What are the cost effects on different products when a firm adopts a new strategy; for example, a change from mass production of standardized products to the production of small lots of customized products?
- What behavior changes occur for the product designers when a firm selects a cost driver to encourage the use of common components instead of many specialized components?
- Could the production process of a particular product be changed to reduce its unit cost?
- Has a firm adopted the most profitable distribution system for its product?
- How would changes in activities and components affect the suppliers and customers in the value chain?
- How will changes in a firm's processes impact the bottom line?
- What are the potential cost savings if a firm uses ABM to identify and eliminate low-value-added activities to achieve its low-cost strategy?
- How can ABC/M help a firm make changes to achieve its competitive strategy of high performance and short lead time in delivery of its products?

Implementation Issues

LEARNING OBJECTIVE 12
Identify key factors for a successful ABC/M implementation.

A successful ABC/M implementation requires close cooperation among management accountants, engineers, and manufacturing and operating managers. They need to act as a team in identifying activities, cost drivers, and requisite information, both financial and nonfinancial.

Most likely the information necessary to implement an ABC/M cost system is not readily available because most companies do not collect it in their traditional volume-based accounting systems. To obtain the information necessary for new cost management and measurement systems, employees directly involved in operating activities must be interviewed to find out daily activities of the operation. Activities of each operating and support department should be carefully studied and analyzed. This process facilitates the identification of cost pools of homogeneous cost drivers responsible for each cost category. It is not unusual for a department to have multiple activity cost pools, each with a different cost driver. For example, a quality control department could have three activity cost pools: inspection of incoming materials (cost driver: purchase orders), inspection of work in process (cost driver: setups), and inspection of finished goods (cost driver: cost of goods sold).

Understanding the production process and identifying cost drivers require persistent efforts. Efforts to redesign cost systems usually are rewarded when organizations have high product diversity, various cost drivers, multiple distribution channels, and heterogeneous batch sizes.

Following are processes found in many successful implementations of ABC/M:

Implementing Strategy	Justification
Involve management and employees in creating an ABC system	Allows them to become familiar with ABC/M. They could then be more willing to implement the system because they feel included and share in ownership of the new system.
Maintain a parallel system	Allows individuals to adapt gradually to the ABC/M system. Abruptly changing cost systems can confuse and frustrate management and employees.
Use ABC/M on a job that will succeed	Shows how and why the process works. Successfully completing one job enables individuals to see the benefits of ABC/M more clearly.
Keep the initial ABC/M design simple	Avoids overwhelming users and holds costs down; also reduces implementation time.
Create desired incentives	Reassures employees that they will be properly evaluated in accordance with their performance.
Educate management	Uses seminars to educate management about ABC/M to enable them to understand the concept and appreciate the benefits. Management becomes aware of the activities that drive the business.

Shields and McEwen conducted a survey of 143 companies.[26] Seventy-five percent of the firms reported a significant financial benefit from implementing ABC. Based on the survey results, Shields and McEwen identified seven factors for a successful ABC implementation: (1) top management support; (2) linkage to competitive strategy, stressing quality and JIT/speed; (3) linkage to performance evaluation and compensation; (4) training; (5) nonaccounting ownership (the belief by nonaccountants that the ABC system is of practical use to people throughout the company, not just to the accounting department); (6) adequate resources; and (7) consensus and clarity of the ABC objectives. They also found that a main reason for unsuccessful implementations was that many companies overemphasized the architectural and software design of ABC systems and failed to pay adequate attention to other issues.

[26] Michael D. Shields and Michael A. McEwen, "Implementing Activity-Based Costing Systems Successfully," *Journal of Cost Management,* Winter 1996, pp. 15–22.

Summary

Many companies have replaced their volume-based costing systems with activity-based accounting systems to gain better product costing and pricing. ABC facilitates activity-based management that improves competitiveness, reduces costs, increases productivity, and augments flexibility in meeting customer needs.

Volume-based costing systems use a volume-based overhead rate, either a single rate for the entire plant or departmental rates. These volume-based overhead rates typically use measures such as direct labor-hours, machine-hours, or direct labor costs for all products or services, even if the firm has diverse products, manufacturing processes, and volumes. For firms with more than one product or process, these overhead rates often generate inaccurate and significantly distorted product costs.

Activity-based costing (ABC) assigns costs to products or services based on consumptions of resources and activities. ABC systems recognize the fact that products or services are results of activities and that activities consume resources and incur costs; it recognizes the causal relationships of cost drivers to activities. ABC systems use a two-stage procedure to assign costs to products or services. The first-stage allocation is a resource cost assignment process by which factory overhead costs are assigned to activity cost pools or groups of activities called *activity centers* using appropriate resource consumption cost drivers. The second-stage allocation is an activity cost assignment process by which the costs of activities are assigned to products or services using appropriate activity consumption cost drivers.

Activity-based costing helps to reduce cost distortions often found in volume-based costing systems and provides more accurate product costs. It also yields a clear view of how a firm's diverse products, services, and activities contribute to the firm's bottom line. Even though developing and implementing an ABC system is expensive and time consuming, many firms found the benefit exceeds the cost of installing an ABC system.

Activity-based management (ABM) improves efficiency and effectiveness of an organization. Uses of ABM increase not only the value received by customers but also the firm's profits.

Manufacturing, marketing, and administrative organizations as well as service and not-for-profit groups have successfully applied ABC and ABM. Activity-based costing is closely tied to strategic cost management. Managers can have more meaningful information to determine the potential impacts on pricing, product design, process design, manufacturing technology, and product line decisions by switching from a volume-based costing system to an activity-based costing system.

Numerous factors play important roles in implementing ABC/ABM. To be successful, management accountants need to cooperate with engineers and manufacturing and operating managers to form a design team. Activities and cost drivers need to be identified; both financial and nonfinancial performance indicators are required.

Customer profitability analysis traces factors affecting revenues and customer costs to customers to allow management to determine customer profitability and to provide more attentive service to high-profit customers, acquire new high-profit customers, and improve the profitability of current customers. Customer profitability analysis includes customer revenue analysis, customer cost analysis, customer profitability analysis, and customer value assessment.

Key Terms

activity *135*
activity-based costing, *136*
activity consumption cost driver, *136*
batch-level activity, *139*
cause-and-effect diagram, *147*
cost driver analysis, *147*
customer cost analysis, *158*
customer profitability analysis, *156*

customer revenue analysis, *157*
facility-sustaining activity, *140*
high-value-added activity, *148*
low-value-added activity, *149*
Pareto analysis, *147*
performance measurement, *147*

product-sustaining activity, *140*
resource, *135*
resource consumption cost driver, *136*
two-stage cost allocation, *136*
unit-level activity, *139*

Comments on Cost Management in Action, Part 1

Competition Pressure, High Overhead Costs, and Product Diversity at Whirlpool

In the 1990 production year, Whirlpool's Evansville, Indiana, plant began as an ABC pilot project for all product lines. The plant's implementation team consisted of two full-time Whirlpool employees with accounting backgrounds and experience in production and operations. KPMG Peat Marwick provided an ABC consultant who acted as an adviser. The implementation of the ABC pilot program took approximately 16 weeks of full-time work. Whirlpool used the following steps to implement the ABC pilot project:

1. Develop an activities dictionary.
2. Identify respondents for an activity survey.
3. Conduct activity-work survey sessions.
4. Validate responses with follow-up interviews.
5. Enter people-related time and dollars into Whirlpool's structured productivity analysis system, SPANS (including both financial and nonfinancial cost drivers), and generate activity reports.

6. Download SPANS into the ABC system.

7. Enter expenses (i.e., general ledger data) into the ABC system.

8. Define activity centers.

9. Define and assign resource consumption cost drivers.

10. Define and assign activity consumption cost drivers.

11. Develop activity consumption cost driver quantities.

12. Generate product-costing reports.

13. Validate results.

Using ABC information, Whirlpool found that volume and complexity affected product costing at the plant. Managers have found that the ABC cost information is more accurate and useful in planning cost-reduction strategies and making decisions about outsourcing than volume-based systems. It now uses ABC cost data to analyze make-or-buy decisions. Whirlpool also uses the ABC data to manage costs by setting priorities for developing and improving cost-reduction plans. For example, it used the ABC system to demonstrate and quantify the cost savings to be gained from using bar codes to record the receipt of inventory.

In addition to realizing these benefits, Whirlpool found that maintaining its ABC system is not expensive; it now requires only about 120 hours per year to maintain.

Source: Cynthia B. Greeson and Mehmet C. Kocakulah, "Implementing an ABC Pilot at Whirlpool," *Journal of Cost Management,* March/April 1997, pp. 16–21.

Comments on Cost Management in Action, Part 2

Customer Profitability: Retention is the Key

The overall cost to acquire a new customer has a strong effect on customer profitability. These costs can be as high as $50 or more per customer. When customer retention is low, as it is in some industries, these costs lower overall customer profitability. For example, customer retention in the apparel industry is far higher than in the consumer electronics industry. A number of firms use the Web to acquire new customers, and some do it more effectively than others. For example, America Online, Amazon.com, and Dell Computer have sophisticated programs for identifying potential new customers and for improving the retention of existing customers. Interestingly, studies have shown that Web customers tend to be more loyal; their retention rates are somewhat higher than for traditional customers. Studies show that Web customers are most interested in convenience, not the lowest price, as is commonly thought. When they find a convenient Web source that meets their needs, they tend to consolidate their purchases there. E-loyalty is the road to success for these companies.

Source: Frederick F. Reichheld and Pohil Schefter, "E-Loyalty; Your Secret Weapon on the Web," *Harvard Business Review,* July–August 2000, pp. 105–113.

Self-Study Problem

(For solution, please turn to the end of the chapter.)

Volume-Based Costing versus ABC

Carter Company manufactures two products, Deluxe and Regular, and uses a traditional two-stage cost allocation system. The first stage assigns all factory overhead costs to two production departments A and B, based on machine-hours. The second stage uses direct labor-hours to allocate overhead to individual products.

For 2006, the firms budgeted $1,000,000 total factory overhead cost for these operations.

	Production Department A	Production Department B
Machine-hour	4,000	16,000
Direct labor-hour	20,000	10,000

The following information relates to the firm's operations for the month of January, 2006:

	Deluxe	Regular
Units produced and sold	200	800
Unit cost of direct materials	$100	$ 50
Hourly direct labor wage rate	$ 25	$ 20
Direct labor-hours in Department A per unit	2	2
Direct labor-hours in Department B per unit	1	1

Carter Company is considering implementing an activity-based costing system. Its management accountant has collected the following information for activity cost analysis:

Activity	Budgeted Overhead	Cost Driver	Budgeted Quantity	Driver Consumption	
				Deluxe	Regular
Material movement	$ 7,000	Number of production runs	350	150	200
Machine setups	400,000	Number of setups	500	20	40
Inspections	588,000	Number of units	19,600	200	800
Shipment	5,000	Number of shipments	250	50	100
	$100,000				

Required

1. Calculate the unit cost for each of the two products under the existing volume-based costing system.
2. Calculate the overhead per unit of the cost driver under the proposed ABC system.
3. Calculate the unit cost for each of the two products if the proposed ABC system is adopted.

Questions

5–1 Explain why a costing system that uses either a plantwide or a departmental overhead rate is likely to produce distorted product costs.

5–2 "Undercosting a product increases the profit from the product and benefits the firm." Do you agree? Why?

5–3 Firms sell products with high costs at high prices. High selling prices increase revenues and profits. Why then should managers worry about product overcosting?

5–4 What is activity-based costing, and how can it improve an organization's costing system?

5–5 Describe general levels of cost hierarchy in activity-based costing systems.

5–6 What is the second-stage procedure in tracing costs to products when using an activity-based costing system?

5–7 What type of company needs an activity-based costing system?

5–8 What are unit-level activities? Give two examples of unit-level activities.

5–9 What are batch-level activities? Give two examples of batch-level activities.

5–10 What are product-sustaining activities? Give two examples of product-sustaining activities.

5–11 What are facility-sustaining activities? Give two examples of facility-sustaining activities.

5–12 Why do product-costing systems using a single, volume-based cost driver tend to overcost high-volume products? Will there be any undesirable strategic effects from such product cost distortion?

5–13 What is activity-based management?

5–14 Give three examples of high-value-added activities in an organization that you choose.

5–15 Give three examples of low-value-added activities in an organization that you choose.

5–16 How can activity-based costing and management be used in service organizations?

5–17 Identify opportunities afforded by customer profitability analysis.

5–18 List important factors in conducting customer revenue analysis.

5–19 Explain customer cost categories.

Exercises

5–20 **Activity Levels and Cost Drivers** Al's Speedy Gourmet, a small hamburger shop, has identified the following resources used in its operations:

a. Bread	f. Advertising for Triple-Burger special
b. Hourly help	g. Salary for the store managers
c. Store rent	h. Utilities
d. Ground beef	i. $1-off-coupon for the second order
e. Catsup	j. Bags

Required

1. Classify its costs as unit-level, batch-level, product-sustaining, or facility-sustaining costs.
2. Suggest a proper driver for each of the above items.

5–21 Activity Levels and Cost Drivers Shroeder Machine Shop has the following activities:

a. Machine operation   f. Machine maintenance
b. Machine setup   g. Product improvement
c. Production scheduling h. Parts administration
d. Materials receiving   i. Final inspection
e. Research and development j. Materials handling

Required

1. Classify each of the activities as a unit-level, batch-level, product-sustaining, or facility-sustaining activity.
2. Identify a proper cost driver for each activity in requirement 1.

5–22 Activity Levels and Cost Drivers Richardson Industries manufactures industrial tools after creating a mold for each newly designed tool. Richardson personally inspects every unit during the trial run of a new mold and 10 percent of the units manufactured in the first three batches. Some of the activities of the firm follow:

a. Designing molds   f. Requesting and moving materials
b. Creating molds   g. Machining
c. Inspecting products   h. Insuring equipment
d. Modifying molds   i. Paying suppliers
e. Setting up production   j. Heating the factory

Required

1. Classify each of the activities as a unit-level, batch-level, product-sustaining, or facility-sustaining activity.
2. Identify a proper cost driver for each activity in requirement 1.

5–23 Activity Levels and Cost Drivers, Service Company Platte Valley Laboratories offers complete laboratory service for agriculture and the environment. A subdivision of its Agriculture Testing Department conducts soil tests (ST) and pesticide residues tests (PRT). The current costing system aggregates all $2,100,000 operating costs of the subdivision into a single overhead cost pool and charges a rate of $70 per test-hour. ST uses 10,000 test-hours, and PRT uses 20,000 test-hours. In an effort to establish a better costing structure, the controller has identified the following costs:

a. Salaries and wages of lab technicians $1,200,000. These costs can be traced to ST, $540,000, and PRT, $660,000.

b. Equipment-related costs such as depreciation, maintenance, insurance and taxes, and energy, $300,000. The cost driver is the number of test-hours.

c. Setup costs, $240,000, to be assigned on the basis of the number of setup hours. ST has 8,500 setup hours, and PRT has 11,500 setup hours.

d. Costs of test designs, $360,000. These costs are to be assigned to ST and PRT on the basis of the time required to design the tests. ST requires 5,800 hours, and PRT requires 4,200 hours.

Required

1. Classify each activity cost a through d as output unit-level, batch-level, product (or service) sustaining, or facility sustaining cost.
2. Calculate the cost per test-hour for ST and PRT using an improved costing structure. Explain briefly the reasons for these costs to be different from the $70 per test-hour under the current costing system.
3. Set up a spreadsheet and verify your answer for 2 above.
4. Use the spreadsheet you set up for requirement 3 to answer this question. What will be the cost per test hour for ST and PRT if $360,000 of the salaries and wages should have been included in the setup cost and $540,000 of the salaries and wages should have been included in the costs of test designs? Should the firm determine cost per testing on the basis of test-hour? (Of the remaining $300,000 salaries and wages for lab technicians, $135,000 for 2,500 hours can be traced to ST and $165,000 for 5,000 hours can be traced to PRT.)

(CMA Adapted)

5–24 Volume-Based Costing Versus ABC   Many companies recognize that their cost systems are inadequate for today's powerful global competition. Managers in companies selling multiple products are making important product decisions based on distorted cost information. This happens because most volume-based cost systems focused on inventory valuation. To elevate the level of management information, current literature suggests that companies should have as many as three cost systems for (1) inventory valuation, (2) operational control, and (3) activity-based costing.

Required

1. Discuss why the volume-based cost system developed to value inventory distorts product cost information.
2. Identify the purpose and characteristics of each of the following cost systems:
   a. Inventory valuation
   b. Operational control
   c. Activity-based costing
3. Describe the benefits that management can expect from activity-based costing.
4. List the steps that a company using a volume-based cost system would take to implement activity-based costing.

(CMA Adapted)

5–25 Activity-Based Costing   Hakara Company has identified the following overhead cost pools and cost drivers:

Cost Pools	Activity Costs	Cost Driver	Driver Consumption
Machine setup	$360,000	Setup hours	3,000
Materials handling	100,000	Pounds of materials	25,000
Electric power	40,000	Kilowatt-hours	40,000

The following cost information pertains to the production of its products A and B:

	A	B
Number of units produced	4,000	20,000
Direct materials cost ($)	$40,000	$50,000
Direct labor cost ($)	$24,000	$40,000
Number of setup hours	200	240
Pounds of materials used	1,000	3,000
Kilowatt-hours	2,000	4,000

Required   Use the activity-based costing approach to calculate the unit cost for each product.

5–26 Volume-Based Versus ABC Overhead Rate   GWS Hospital uses a hospitalwide overhead rate based on nurse-hours. The intensive care unit (ICU), which has 30 beds, applies overhead using patient-days. Its budgeted cost and operating data for the year follow:

Budget information

Hospital total overhead	$69,120,000
Hospital total nurse-hours	1,152,000

Budget Cost Driver Information for ICU for the Month of June

Cost Pool	Budget Cost	Cost Driver	Budget Cost Driver Activity
Beds	$810,000	Number of bed-days	900
Equipment	422,500	Number of patient-days	845
Nursing care	457,500	Number of nurse-hours	6,000

In June, GWS's intensive care unit had the following operating data:

5,900 nurse-hours
870 patient-days

Required

1. Calculate the ICU's overhead costs for the month of June using
   a. The hospitalwide rate
   b. The ICU departmentwide rate
   c. The cost drivers for the ICU department
2. Explain the differences and determine which overhead assignment method is more appropriate.

5–27 Product Selection Strategy Johans Computer Company has two product lines, Desktop and Tablet. The firm's costing system shows that each Desktop costs $550 to manufacture. Johans sells 9,000 Desktops at $660 per unit. A national low-price store has introduced a similar desktop computer with a market price of $380. Tablet computer is a new model that a handful of companies, including Johans, introduced recently. Each Tablet computer costs Johans $750 to produce and sells for $2,750. Johans sells approximately 150 Tablet computers. The marketing vice president suggests shifting the sales mix in favor of Tablet computer. Unfortunately, Tablet computer is more complicated to make and few are produced.

Required Should Johans focus its sales on the Desktop or Tablet computer? Explain your answer.

5–28 High-Value-Added and Low-Value-Added Activities The Radiology Department of the Lindex General Hospital has the following activities:

a. Admitting patients
b. Retrieving patients from the waiting area
c. Assessing need for lab work
d. Sending patients to the lab
e. Bringing patient to the MRI machine
f. Taking images
g. Checking images to determine the need for more images
h. Taking more images to get right pictures
i. Preparing report to the primary physician

Required Classify each item as a high-value-added, or a low-value-added activity.

5–29 High-Value-Added and Low-Value-Added Activities The Lindex General Hospital has determined the activities of a nurse including the following:

a. Report for duty and review patient charts
b. Visit each patient and take her/his temperature
c. Update patients' records
d. Coordinate lab and radiology works
e. Wait for the attending physician to arrive
f. Accompany attending physician
g. Explain treatments to patients
h. Call kitchen to have the wrong meal tray replaced
i. Perform CPR

Required Classify each item as a high-value-added or a low-value-added activity.

5–30 High-Value-Added and Low-Value-Added Activities Mazon.com sells merchandise through orders placed on its Web site. Some of the firm's activities are

a. Print order forms
b. Review orders to ensure the accuracy of prices and the totals
c. Secure approval of charges on credit cards
d. Deliver order forms to supervisor to secure her/his approval
e. Make a copy of each order to send to the warehouse
f. Pick and pack items ordered
g. E-mail customer for items not in stock
h. E-mail customer on the shipment of the order with a thank-you note

Required Classify each item as a high-value-added or low-value-added activity.

5–31 **Plantwide or Departmental Overhead Rate** MacPorter & Associates (MPA) specializes in business intelligence systems. The firm charges clients for both professional time and support activities. MPA has three levels of professionals:

Professional Rank	Billing Rate per Hour
Partner	$800
Senior consultant	400
Consultant	200

The firm does not track and itemize support activities and charges 40 percent of the professional time billed for support activities.

MPA completed works for two of its major clients last month. The hours of professional time spent on each client are as follows:

	Hours Spent	
Professional Rank	B&J Cream	Mini Mart (MM)
Partner	50	10
Senior consultant	30	30
Consultant	20	60

Required

1. What amounts did MPA bill B&J Cream and MM?
2. What amounts would MPA bill these two clients if MPA charges $60 per professional hour for support activities (instead of 40 percent of the professional times billed)?
3. Which is the more appropriate way for MPA to bill for support activities, 40 percent of the total professional time billed or $60 per professional hour?

5–32 **Plantwide Overhead Rate** Flexmetal Manufacturing Company specializes in manufacturing components for industrial equipment based on specifications supplied by the equipment manufacturers. It has three main manufacturing departments: engineering (E), precision tooling (PT), and molding and fabrication (MF).

For many years, Flexmetal determined overhead costs based on direct labor hours. Upon the suggestion of several major customers, the firm switched to machine hours in recent years. Summary budget data of 2006 for total overhead and cost driver information are:

	Budget Data	
Department	Machine Hours	Total Overhead
Engineering	10,000	$3,600,000
Precision tooling	30,000	1,800,000
Molding and fabrication	120,000	2,400,000

Details pertaining to budgeted cost driver usages and the budgeted number of units to manufacture for the firm's three major customers are:

Customer	Machine Hour	Number of Unit
Dellway Computer	4,000	500,000
Leland Motors	8,000	40,000
PH Company	148,000	200,000

Required

1. Compute the plantwide manufacturing overhead rate for the budget year.
2. Compute the total manufacturing overhead for each of the three major customers.
3. Compute the manufacturing overhead per unit for each of the three major customers.

5–33 **Department Overhead Rate (Continuation of Exercise 5–32)** Even though the managers believe that the use of machine-hours as the basis for overhead application is an improvement, several customers still complain about the high and unfair overheads they have to pay. Upon analyzing manufacturing data, the CIO suggests different cost drivers be used for different manufacturing operations to determine overhead costs. Summary budget data of 2006 for total overheads and cost driver information follow:

		Budget Data			
		Activity Level			
Department	Cost Driver	Engineering	Direct Labor	Machine	Overhead
Engineering	Engineering-hours	30,000	600	10,000	$3,600,000
Precision tooling	Direct labor-hours	2,400	96,000	30,000	1,800,000
Molding and fabrication	Machine-hours	3,600	23,400	120,000	2,400,000

Details pertaining to cost driver usage for the firm's three major customers are:

Customer	Engineering-Hours	Direct Labor-Hours	Machine-Hours	Number of Units
Dellway Computer	24,000	2,000	3,000	500,000
Leland Motors	2,400	84,000	6,000	40,000
PH Company	3,600	10,000	111,000	200,000

Required

1. Compute the department manufacturing overhead rate for the budget year.
2. Compute the total manufacturing overhead for each of the three major customers.
3. Compute the manufacturing overhead per unit for each of the three major customers.
4. Compare your answer in requirements 2 and 3 to that in requirements 2 and 3 of Exercise 5–32. Comment on the differences.

5–34 **ABC and Job-Costing** Hood Company designs and manufactures machines that facilitate DNA sequencing. Depending on the intended purpose of each machine and its functions, each machine is likely to be unique. The job-order costing system in its Norfolk plant has five activity cost pools, in addition to direct materials and direct labor. Job TPY–2306 requires 1,000 printed-circuit boards. The cost per board that passes the final inspection is $240. On average, only 50 percent of the completed units pass the final inspection. The prime costs per completed board are direct materials $25 and direct labor $5. Information pertaining to manufacturing overheads for printed-circuit boards follows:

Activity Cost Pool	Cost Driver	Overhead Rate per Units of Cost Driver	Unit of Cost Driver per Board	Factory Overhead per Board
Axial insertion	Number of axial insertions	$0.15	30	$A?
Hardware insertion	Number of hardware insertions	1.85	B?	37.00
Hand load	Boothroyd time	C?	5	35.50
Masking	Number of points masked	0.08	100	D?
Final test	Test time	F?	10	E?

Required Fill in the unknowns identified as A through F.

5–35 **Cost of Meal**   The following excerpt appeared in a syndicated advice column (March 20, 2003).

Dear Annie:

I attend out-of-town meetings and often am invited to join clients and associates for dinner. There is no way for me to politely refuse. The problem is, I can only afford so much for my meal. However, when the server comes to take our orders, one of the Big Shots invariably says to put the meal on one check. The others proceed to order expensive meals and wine, and we split the bill equally. I end up paying for a dinner that I can't afford, yet to ask for a separate check would be embarrassing.

How can I handle this situation?

Bottom of the Totem Pole in Wisconsin

Required   If you were Annie, how would you respond to this reader?

5–36 **Product-Line Profitability, ABC**   Supermart Food Stores (SFS) has experienced net operating losses in its frozen food products line in the last few periods. Management believes that the store can improve its profitability if SFS discontinues frozen foods. The operating results from the most recent period are:

	Frozen Food	Baked Goods	Fresh Produce
Sales	$120,000	$90,000	$158,125
Cost of goods sold	105,000	67,000	110,000

SFS estimates that store support expenses are approximately 20 percent of revenues.

The controller says that not every sales dollar requires or uses the same amount of store support activities. A preliminary analysis reveals store support activities for these three product lines are:

	Frozen Food	Baked Goods	Fresh Produce
Order processing (number of purchase orders)	10	55	90
Receiving (number of deliveries)	10	70	120
Shelf-stocking (number of hours per delivery)	2	0.5	4
Customer support (items sold)	30,000	40,000	86,000

The controller estimates activity-cost rates for each activity as follows:

Order processing	$ 80 per purchase order
Receiving	$110 per delivery
Shelf-stocking	$ 15 per hour
Customer support	$0.20 per item

Required

1. Prepare a product-line profitability report for SFS under the current costing system.
2. Prepare a product-line profitability report for SFS using the new information the controller provides.
3. What new insights does the ABC system in requirement 2 provide to SFS managers?

5–37 **Customer Revenue Analysis**   JD Company designs and manufactures athletic shoes. The following data pertain to two of its major customers: Transworld Shoes (TS) and Centermin Sports (CS).

	TS	CS
Total sales	$800,000	$880,000
Sales discount	12%	15%
Sales terms	1/15, n/45	Net 30
Sales returns	0.5%	0.75%

Both firms pay their accounts according to the terms agreed to. In fact, TS pays its accounts within the discount period. The controller estimates that the cost of working capital is approximately 1.5 percent per month.

Required Compare the net proceeds to JD Company 30 days after the sale.

5–38 Customer Cost Analysis Doreen Company has gathered the following data pertaining to activities it performed for two of its major customers.

	Jerry Inc.	Donald Co.
Number of orders	5	30
Units per order	1,000	200
Sales returns:		
Number of returns	2	5
Total units returned	40	175
Number of sales calls	12	4

Doreen sells its products at $200 per unit, net 30. The firm's gross margin ratio is 25 percent. Both Jerry and Donald pay their accounts promptly and no accounts receivable is over 30-days. After a careful analysis using a business intelligence software on the operating data for the past 30 months the firm has determined the following activity costs:

Activity	Cost Driver and Rate
Sales calls	$1,000 per visit
Order processing	$ 300 per order
Deliveries	$ 500 per order
Sales returns	$ 100 per return and $5 per unit returned
Sales salary	$100,000 per month

Required

1. Classify activity costs into cost categories and compute the total cost for Doreen Company to service Jerry Inc. and Donald Co.
2. Compare the profitability of these two customers (ignore cost of funds).

5–39 Customer Profitability Garner Industries manufactures precision tools. The firm uses an activity-based costing system. CEO Deb Garner is very proud of the accuracy of the system in determining product costs. She noticed that since the installment of the ABC system 10 years earlier the firm had become much more competitive in all aspects of the business and earned an increasing amount of profits every year.

In the last two years the firm sold 1 million units to 4,100 customers each year. The manufacturing cost is $600 per unit. In addition, Garner has determined that the order-filling cost is $100.50 per unit. The $784.56 selling price per unit includes 12 percent markup to cover administrative costs and profits.

The order-filling cost per unit is determined based on the firm's costs for order-filling activities. Order filling capacity can be added in blocks of 60 orders. Each block costs $60,000. In addition, the firm incurs $1,500 order-filling costs per order.

Garner serves two types of customers designated as PC (Preferred Customer) and SC (Small Customer). Each of the 100 PCs buys, on average, 5,000 units in two orders. The firm also sells 500,000 units to 4,000 SCs. On average each SC buys 125 units in 10 orders. Ed Cheap, a buyer for one PC, complains about the high price he is paying. Cheap claims that he has been offered a price of $700 per unit and threatens to take his business elsewhere. Garner does not give in because the $700 price Cheap demands is below her cost. Besides, she has recently raised the price to SC to $800 per unit and experienced no decline in orders.

Required

1. Demonstrate how Garner arrives at $100.50 order-filling cost per unit.
2. What would be the amount of loss (profit) per unit if Garner sells to Cheap at $700 per unit?
3. What is the amount of loss (profit) per unit at the $800 selling price per unit for units sold to SC?

Problems

5–40 **Cost Pools and Cost Drivers**   Based on a recent study of its manufacturing operations Johnston Manufacturing Corporation has identified six resource consumption cost drivers. These cost drivers and their budgeted activity levels for the coming year are:

Cost Driver	Activity Level
Number of purchase orders	6
Number of production runs (2,500 per production run)	40
Machine hours	100,000
Factory space (square feet)	24,000
Units of production	100,000
Engineering hours	20,000

The firm has budgeted the following costs for the year:

Engineering design	$600,000
Depreciation—building	50,000
Depreciation—machine	40,000
Electrical power (for factory building)	6,000
Electrical power (for machining)	30,000
Insurance	20,000
Property taxes	15,000
Machine maintenance—labor	11,000
Machine maintenance—materials	9,000
Natural gas (for heating)	8,000
Inspection of finished goods	7,000
Setup wages	20,000
Receiving	10,000
Inspection of direct materials on receiving	3,000
Purchasing	20,000
Custodial labor	51,000

With the exception of the factory space cost pool, which uses machine hours as the activity consumption cost driver, other cost pools have identical resource and activity consumption cost drivers.

Required

1. Identify the most appropriate activity cost pool for each of the cost items and cost driver for each activity cost pool you identified.
2. Johnston has received a request to quote the price for 4,000 units of a new product. The production will require 100 engineering-hours and 4,250 machine-hours. What is the manufacturing overhead per unit the firm should use in determining the price?

5–41 **Volume-Based Costing Versus ABC**   Nelson Company manufactures control boxes for irrigation devices. It has identified these overhead (OH) cost drivers:

OH Cost Pool	Cost Driver	Budgeted OH Cost	Budgeted Level of Cost Driver
Quality control	Number of inspections	$ 50,000	100
Machine operation	Machine-hours	100,000	40,000
Purchasing	Purchase orders	3,250	25
Other OH cost	Direct labor-hours	30,000	5,000

Nelson has an order for 500 control boxes; production requirements for this order are:

Number of inspections	5
Machine-hours	1,400
Number of purchase orders	1
Number of direct labor-hours	400

Required

1. How much overhead would be included in this order if Nelson uses a plantwide overhead rate based on direct labor-hours? What is the overhead cost per control box?
2. If Nelson uses an activity-based costing method, what is the total overhead cost assigned to the order? What is the overhead cost per control box?
3. Would you recommend the use of ABC or the direct labor-based method to this company? Why?

5–42 **Activity-Based Costing, Value Chain Activities**   Hoover Company uses activity-based costing and provides this information:

Manufacturing Activity	Cost Driver	Overhead Rate
Materials handling	Number of parts	$ 0.45
Machinery	Number of machine-hours	51.00
Assembly	Number of parts	2.85
Inspection	Number of finished units	30.00

Hoover has just completed 80 units of a component for a customer. Each unit required 105 parts and 3 machine-hours. The prime cost is $1,200 per finished unit. All other manufacturing costs are classified as manufacturing overheads.

Required

1. Compute the total manufacturing costs and the unit costs of the 80 units just completed.
2. In addition to the manufacturing costs, the firm has determined that the total cost of upstream activities including research and development and product design is $180 per unit. The total cost of downstream activities, such as distribution, marketing, and customer service is $250 per unit. Compute the full product cost per unit, including upstream, manufacturing, and downstream activities. What are strategic implications of this new cost result?
3. Explain to Hoover Company the usefulness of calculating the total value-chain cost and of knowing costs of different value-creating activities.

5–43 **Volume-Based Costing Versus ABC**   The California Cooking Oil Company (CCO) has been using machine-hours as the basis to determine overhead costs for all products. An ABC project team points out that the firm manufactures several products, each of which use significantly different factory supporting resources. As a start, the team suggests the following overhead cost pools, cost drivers, and estimated cost driver levels for manufacturing overheads:

Overhead Cost Pool	Cost Driver	Estimated Cost Driver Level	Budgeted Overhead
Machine setups	Number of setups	100	$100,000
Materials handling	Number of barrels	8,000	80,000
Quality control	Number of inspections	1,000	200,000
Other overhead cost	Machine-hours	10,000	100,000

CCO has recently completed production of 500 barrels each of P5 and G23. P5 is a corn-based oil distributed primarily through supermarkets. G23 is made from olive oil, flaxseed oil, and other exotic ingredients and sold to up-scale restaurants as gourmet foods. The productions require the following operations:

Overhead Cost Pool	Number of Cost Drivers	
	P5	**G23**
Machine setups	1 setup	50 setups
Materials handling	500 barrels	500 barrels
Quality inspections	2 times	20 times
Machine-hours	1,000 hours	1,000 hours

Required

1. Determine the overhead costs per barrel of P5 and G23 using the current single cost driver system based on machine-hours.
2. Determine the overhead costs per barrel of P5 and G23 using the multiple cost driver system suggested by the ABC project team.

5–44   **Volume-Based Costing Versus ABC**   West Chemical Company produces three products. The operating results of 2007 are:

Product	Sales Quantity	Target Price	Actual Price	Difference
A	1,000	$279.00	$280.00	$1.00
B	5,000	$294.00	$250.00	<$44.00>
C	500	$199.50	$300.00	$100.50

The firm sets the target price of each product at 150 percent of the product's total manufacturing cost. Recognizing that the firm was able to sell Product C at a much higher price than the target price of the product and lost money on Product B, Tom Watson, CEO, wants to promote Product C much more aggressively and phase out Product B. He believes that the information suggests that Product C has the greatest potential among the firm's three products since the actual selling price of Product C was almost 50 percent higher than the target price while the firm was forced to sell Product B at a price below the target price.

Both the budgeted and actual factory overheads for 2007 are $493,000. The actual units sold for each product also are the same as the budgeted units. The firm uses direct labor dollars to estimate manufacturing overhead costs. The direct materials and direct labor costs per unit for each product are:

	Product A	**Product B**	**Product C**
Direct materials	$50.00	$114.40	$65.00
Direct labor	20.00	12.00	10.00
Total prime cost	$70.00	$126.40	$75.00

The controller noticed that not all products consumed factory overheads similarly. Upon further investigations, she identified the following usages of factory overheads during 2007:

	Product A	**Product B**	**Product C**	**Total Overhead**
Number of setups	2	5	3	$ 8,000
Weight of direct materials (pounds)	400	250	350	100,000
Waste and hazardous disposals	25	45	30	250,000
Quality inspections	30	35	35	75,000
Utilities (machine-hours)	2,000	7,000	1,000	60,000
Total				$493,000

Required

1. Determine the amount of overhead cost per unit and the total overhead for each of the products.
2. Is Product B the least profitable and Product C the most profitable under both the current and the ABC costing systems?

3. What is the new target price for each product based on 150 percent of the new costs under the ABC system? Compare this price with the actual selling price.

4. Comment on the result. As a manager of West Chemical, describe what actions you would take based on the information provided by the activity-based unit costs.

5-45 **Volume-Based Versus Activity-Based Costing**   Addison, Inc., manufactures and sells three models of MP3-CD digital radios:

Elite, annual sales 5,000 units
Standard, annual sales 20,000 units
Junior, annual sales 50,000 units

Addison uses estimated factory overhead based on direct-labor dollars. The direct-labor wage rate is $20 per hour. The cost of each product follows:

	Elite	Standard	Junior
Direct materials	$22.50	$15.00	$ 7.50
Direct labor	15.00	12.00	8.00
Factory overhead	60.00	48.00	32.00
Total	$97.50	$75.00	$47.50

Addison's retail price for radios is usually marked up at 200 percent of its full cost.

	Elite	Standard	Junior
Product cost	$ 97.50	$ 75.00	$ 47.50
Target price	195.00	150.00	95.00
Actual price	180.00	150.00	110.00

Addison has noticed that it sells Junior box radios at a price higher than the target price with no effect on sales, while it has to lower the prices on Elite model to sell the radio. The newly installed enterprise software provides the following data on overhead costs:

		Activity Level		
	Total Overhead	Elite	Standard	Junior
Engineering (Engineering-hours)	$ 840,000	900	375	225
Quality control (Inspection-hours)	951,000	5,000	10,000	15,000
Machinery (Machine-hours)	544,000	640	2,100	2,700
Materials handling (DM cost)	525,000	?	?	?
Total	$2,860,000			

The controller has determined that material handling overheads vary with the direct materials costs.

Required

1. Using the current product costing system, what is Addison's most profitable product? The least profitable product?

2. Using a multiple cost drivers product costing system, what is Addison's most profitable product? The least profitable product?

3. Compare and explain differences in product. What are the implications for Addison's pricing strategy?

5-46 **Ethics, Cost System Selection**   Aero Dynamics manufactures airplane parts and engines for a variety of military and civilian aircrafts. The company is the sole provider of rocket engines for the U.S. military that it sells for full cost plus a 5 percent markup.

Aero Dynamics's current cost system is a direct labor-hour-based overhead allocation system. Recently, the company conducted a pilot study on the feasibility of using an activity-based costing system. The study shows that the new ABC system, while more accurate and timely, will result in the assignment of lower costs to the rocket engines and higher costs to the company's other products. Apparently, the current direct labor-based costing system overcosts the rocket engines and undercosts the other products. On hearing of this, top management has decided to scrap the plans to adopt the ABC system because its rocket engine business with the military is significant and the reduced cost would lower the price and, thus, the profit for this part of Aero Dynamics's business.

Required   As the management accountant participating in this ABC pilot study project, what is your responsibility when you learn that top management has decided to cancel the plans for the ABC system? Can you ignore your professional ethics code in this case? What would you do?

5–47   **Volume-Based Costing Versus ABC**   Gorden Company produces a variety of electronic equipment. One of its plants produces two laser printers, Speedy and Deluxe. At the beginning of 2006, the following data were prepared for this plant:

	Deluxe	Speedy
Quantity	50,000	400,000
Selling price	$475.00	$300.00
Unit prime cost	$180.00	$110.00
Unit overhead cost	$ 20.00	$153.60

The unit overhead cost is calculated using the predetermined overhead application rate based on direct labor-hours.

Upon examining the data, the marketing manager was particularly impressed with the per-unit profitability of the Deluxe printer and suggested that more emphasis be placed on producing and selling this product. The plant supervisor objected to this strategy, arguing that the Deluxe model required a very delicate manufacturing process. The supervisor believed that the cost of the Deluxe printer was likely to be much higher than reported.

The controller suggests a multiple-cost-driver costing system for overheads and provided the following data pertaining to the budgeted period:

Overhead Activity	Cost Driver	Activity Consumption		
		Pool Rate*	Deluxe	Speedy
Setups	Number of setups	$2,800	200	100
Machine costs	Machine-hours	100	100,000	400,000
Engineering	Engineering-hours	40	45,000	120,000
Packing	Packing orders	20	50,000	200,000

*Cost per unit of cost driver

Required

1. Using the projected data based on the firm's current costing system, calculate gross profit per unit and gross profit percentage for each product.
2. Using the suggested multiple cost drivers overhead rates, calculate the overhead cost per unit for each product and determine gross profit per unit and gross profit percentage for each product.
3. Based on your results, evaluate the suggestion of the marketing manager to emphasize the Speedy model.
4. How does ABC add to Gorden's competitive advantage?

5–48   **Volume-Based Costing Versus ABC**   Hairless Company manufactures a variety of electric shavers for men and women. The company's plant is partially automated. The company uses an activity-based cost system based on the following budget data:

Overhead Cost Pool	Overhead Cost	Cost Driver	Level for Cost Driver
Machine depreciation/maintenance	$135,000	Machine-hours	27,000 Machine-hours
Factory depreciation/utilities/insurance	$120,000	Machine-hours	30,000 Machine-hours
Product design	$504,000	Hours in design	42,000 Design hours
Material purchasing/storage	$147,000	Raw materials cost	$980,000

Two current product orders have these requirements:

	15,000 Men's Shavers	20,000 Women's Shavers
Direct labor-hours	24	12
Raw materials cost	$30,000	$26,000
Hours in design	15	37.5
Machine-hours	50	40

Required

1. What total overhead should be assigned to each product order?
2. What is the overhead cost per shaver?
3. Compute the predetermined overhead rate if the firm uses a plantwide overhead rate based on direct labor-hours. The direct labor budget for the year is 3,020 hours.
4. Compute the total overhead cost assigned to each production order using the plantwide overhead rate.
5. What is the overhead cost per shaver using the plantwide overhead rate?

5–49 **Volume-Based Costing Versus ABC**   The current manufacturing costing system of Auer Corporation has two direct cost categories (direct materials and direct labor). Indirect manufacturing costs are applied to products using a single indirect cost pool based on direct labor-hours at $120 per direct labor-hour.

Auer Corporation is in the process of changing to an activity-based costing system. The plant has five activity areas, each with its own supervisor and budget responsibility. Pertinent data follow:

Activity	Cost Driver	Overhead Rate
Materials handling	Number of parts	$ 0.70
Lathe work	Number of turns	0.35
Milling	Number of machine-hours	15.00
Grinding	Number of parts	0.60
Shipping	Number of orders shipped	2,180.00

The operating data for two jobs just completed are

	Job 101	Job 102
Direct materials cost	$45,300	$ 5,700
Direct labor cost	$16,800	$ 1,400
Number of direct labor-hours	420	35
Number of parts	1,500	600
Number of turns	80,000	15,000
Number of machine-hours	750	70
Number of shipments	1	1
Number of units	450	20

Required

1. Compute the per-unit manufacturing cost of each job under the existing single cost pool manufacturing costing system based on direct labor-hours.

2. Compute the per-unit manufacturing cost of each job under the ABC approach.

3. Compare the per-unit cost figures for job orders 101 and 102 computed in requirements 1 and 2.

4. Why do they differ?

5. How does ABC add to Auer's competitive advantage?

5–50 **Volume-Based Costing Versus ABC**   Moden Lighting Inc. (MLC) manufactures and sells lighting fixtures. The company has two main product lines, ceiling fixtures and luxury pendants. Its products are sold through industry and wholesale suppliers. During a recent executive meeting, Bob Brighten, the vice president of marketing, made three observations: First, the price of the Ceiling Fixture (CF), a high-volume product for the firm, is often higher than that of competitors' products. Second, MLC has been struggling to maintain its market share of CF. Third, the firm has sold approximately the same number of units of Luxury Pendant (LP), a high margin product, despite a 7.5 percent increase in price. Noting that the profit margin per unit of LP is higher than that of CF, Brighten has suggested that MLC should push for producing and selling of LP. Regina Jones, the plant manager, objected to this strategy because the manufacturing processes of LP were much more complicated than those for CF. The total manufacturing costs would increase substantially if MLC shifted its product line to emphasize LP.

Aaron Higgins, the vice president of finance, observes that MLC uses a direct labor cost-based system to determine the amount of manufacturing overhead for all of its products. For each direct labor dollar the firm attaches $2.00 overhead cost. Selected operating data for the year 2007 follow:

| Product | Units Sold | Cost per Unit | | Selling Price per Unit |
		Direct Materials	Direct Labor	
LP	4,000	$20	$8	$70
CF	40,000	10	5	40

Aaron also has collected the following data on activity cost pools and their cost drivers:

Cost Pools/Activities	Cost Drivers
Machine operation	Machine-hours
Support labor overhead	Direct labor costs
Machine setup	Setup hours
Assembly	Number of parts
Inspection	Inspection hours

Estimated Overhead Costs and Activity Consumption Information for Cost Pools and Activities

| Activity Cost Pool | Overhead | Activity Consumption Levels | | |
		Total Activity	LP	CF
Machine operation	$160,000	10,000	1,500	8,500
Support labor	81,200	232,000	32,000	200,000
Machine setup	68,000	2,500	1,000	1,500
Assembly	88,550	402,500	192,500	210,000
Inspection	66,250	4,000	1,600	2,400
Total	$464,000			

Aaron explained why these cost drivers were appropriate:

• The overhead costs for machine operation had nothing to do with the direct labor-hours. These costs were more likely to vary with the number of machine-hours.

- The support labor included allowances for benefits, break periods and costs related to the supervising and engineering staff. This overhead was indirect to the products but was related to the direct labor costs.
- The setup overhead was generated by changing the job to be run and should be related to the setup hours rather than the direct labor-hours.
- The assembly overheads related to costs incurred to assemble parts. The more parts needed, the higher the overhead costs. Therefore, the correct cost driver should be the number of parts.
- The inspection overhead arose from checking the finished goods. The higher the number of finished units, the higher the inspection overhead costs. The appropriate cost driver should be the number of hours spent on the inspection.

Required

1. Using the current costing system, which uses direct labor costs as the basis to determine overhead costs, calculate the unit manufacturing costs of the two products.
2. Using the activity-based costing system, calculate the unit manufacturing costs of the two products.
3. Under ABC, is the Luxury Pendant as profitable as the vice president of marketing thinks it is under the existing costing system?
4. Evaluate the marketing vice president's suggestion to shift the sales mix in favor of the Luxury Pendant units.
5. Give at least two reasons for the differences between the results for the two different costing systems.

5–51 **Volume-Based Costing Versus ABC**   ADA Pharmaceutical Company produces three drugs: Diomycin, Homycin, and Addolin belonging to the analgesic (pain-killer) family of medication. Since its inception four years ago, ADA has used a direct labor-hour-based system to assign manufacturing overhead costs to products.

Eme Akpaffiong, the president of ADA Enterprises, has just read about activity-based costing in a trade journal. With some curiosity and interest, she asked her financial controller, Takedo Simon, to examine differences in product costs between the firm's current costing and activity-based costing systems.

ADA has the following budget information for the year:

	Diomycin	Homycin	Addolin
Cost of direct materials	$ 205,000	$265,000	$258,000
Cost of direct labor	250,000	234,000	263,000
Number of direct labor-hours	7,200	6,800	2,000
Number of capsules	1,000,000	500,000	300,000

ADA has identified the following activities as cost drivers and has allocated them to total overhead cost of $200,000 as follows:

Activity	Cost Driver	Budgeted Overhead Cost	Budgeted Cost Driver Volume
Machine setup	Setup hours	$ 16,000	1,600
Plant management	Workers	36,000	1,200
Supervision of direct labor	Direct labor-hours	46,000	1,150
Quality inspection	Inspection-hours	50,400	1,050
Expediting orders	Customers served	51,600	645
Total overhead		$200,000	

Takedo selected the cost drivers with the following justifications:

SETUP HOURS: The cost driver of setup hours is used because the same product takes about the same amount of setup time regardless of size of batch. For different products, however, the setup time varies.

NUMBER OF WORKERS: Plant management includes plant maintenance and corresponding managerial duties that make production possible. This activity depends on the number of workers. The more workers involved, the higher the cost.

SUPERVISION OF DIRECT LABOR: Supervisors spend their time supervising production. The amount of time they spend on each product is proportional to the direct labor-hours worked.

QUALITY INSPECTION: Inspection involves testing a number of units in a batch. The time varies for different products but is the same for all similar products.

NUMBER OF CUSTOMERS SERVED: The need to expedite production increases as the number of customers served by the company increases. Thus, the number of customers served by ADA is a good measure of expediting production orders.

Takedo gathered the following information about the cost driver volume for each product:

	Diomycin	Homycin	Addolin
Machine setups	200	600	800
Plant management	200	400	600
Supervision of direct labor	200	300	650
Quality inspection	150	200	700
Expediting production orders	45	100	500

Required

1. Use the firm's current costing system to calculate the unit cost of each product.
2. Use the activity-based cost system to calculate the unit cost of each product.
3. The two cost systems provide different results; give several reasons for this. Why might these differences be strategically important to ADA Enterprises? How does ABC add to ADA's competitive advantage?
4. How may firms in the pharmaceutical industry use ABC?

5–52 **Volume-Based Costing Versus ABC**   Alaire Corporation manufactures several different printed-circuit boards; two of the boards account for the majority of the company's sales. The first product, a television (TV) circuit board, has been a standard in the industry for several years. The market for this board is competitive and price sensitive. Alaire plans to sell 65,000 of the TV boards in 2007 at $150 per unit. The second product, a personal computer (PC) circuit board, is a recent addition to Alaire's product line. Because it incorporates the latest technology, it can be sold at a premium price. The 2007 plans include the sale of 40,000 PC boards at $300 per unit.

Alaire's management group is meeting to discuss strategies for 2007. The current topic of conversation is how to spend the sales and promotion dollars for 2007. The sales manager believes that the market share for the TV board could be expanded by concentrating Alaire's promotional efforts in this area. In response to this suggestion, the production manager said, "Why don't you go after a bigger market for the PC board? The cost sheets that I get show the contribution from the PC board is about double the contribution from the TV board. I know we get a premium price for the PC board; selling it should help overall profitability."

Alaire's current volume-based costing system shows these data for TV and PC boards:

	TV Board	PC Board
Direct materials	$80	$140
Direct labor	1.5 hours	4 hours
Machine time	.5 hour	1.5 hours

The current costing system uses three types of factory overhead: variable factory, materials handling, and machine time. Variable factory overhead is applied on the basis of direct labor-hours. For 2007, Alaire budgeted at $1,120,000 variable factory overhead and 280,000 direct labor-hours. The hourly rates for machine time and direct labor are $10 and $14, respectively. Alaire applies a materials-handling charge at 10 percent of direct materials cost, which is not included in variable factory overhead. Total 2007 expenditures for direct materials are budgeted at $10,800,000.

The company conducted an activity analysis and collected the following information for 10 activities:

Budgeted Overhead Costs	Cost Driver	Annual Activity for Cost Driver
Materials-related overhead		
Procurement	$ 400,000	Number of parts	4,000,000
Production scheduling	220,000	Number of boards	110,000
Packaging and shipping	440,000	Number of boards	110,000
	$1,060,000		
Variable overhead		
Machine setup	$ 446,000	Number of setups	278,750
Hazardous waste disposal	48,000	Pounds of waste	16,000
Quality control	560,000	Number of inspections	160,000
General supplies	66,000	Number of boards	110,000
	$1,120,000		
Manufacturing overhead		
Machine insertion	$1,200,000	Number of insertions	3,000,000
Manual insertion	4,000,000	Number of insertions	1,000,000
Wave soldering	132,000	Number of boards	110,000
	$5,332,000		

Required per Unit	TV Board	PC Board
Parts	25	55
Machine insertions	24	35
Manual insertions	1	20
Machine setups	2	3
Hazardous waste	0.02lb.	0.35lb.
Inspections	1	2

Ed Welch, Alaire's controller, believes that before the management group proceeds with the discussion about allocating sales and promotional dollars to individual products, it might be worthwhile to look at these products on the basis of the activities involved in their production. As Ed explained to the group, "Activity-based costing integrates the cost of all activities, known as cost drivers, into individual product costs rather than including these costs in overhead pools." He prepared the preceding information to help the management group understand this concept.

"Using this information," Ed explained, "we can calculate an activity-based cost for each TV board and each PC board and then compare it to the standard cost we have been using. The only cost that remains the same for both cost methods is the cost of direct materials. The cost drivers will replace the direct labor, machine time, and overhead costs in the old standard cost figures."

Required

1. Identify general advantages associated with activity-based costing.
2. On the basis of Alaire's current costing system and its cost data (direct materials, direct labor, materials-handling charge, variable overhead, and machine time overhead) given in the problem, calculate the total contribution margin expected in 2007 for Alaire Corporation's TV board and PC board.
3. On the basis of activity-based costs, calculate the total contribution margin expected in 2007 for Alaire Corporation's TV board and PC board.
4. Explain how the comparison of the results of the two costing methods might affect the sales, pricing, and promotion decisions made by Alaire Corporation's management group.

(CMA Adapted)

5–53 **Volume-Based Costing Versus ABC**   Coffee Bean, Inc. (CBI) processes and distributes a variety of coffee. CBI buys coffee beans from around the world and roasts, blends, and packages them for resale. Currently the firm offers 15 coffees to gourmet shops in one-pound bags. The major cost is direct materials; however, a substantial amount of factory overhead is incurred in the predominantly automated roasting and packing process. The company uses relatively little direct labor.

Some of the coffees are very popular and sell in large volumes; a few of the newer brands have very low volumes. CBI prices its coffee at full product cost, including allocated overhead, plus a markup of 30 percent. If its prices for certain coffees are significantly higher than the market, CBI lowers its prices. The company competes primarily on the quality of its products, but customers are price conscious as well.

Data for the 2007 budget include factory overhead of $3,000,000, which has been allocated by its current costing system on the basis of each product's direct labor cost. The budgeted direct labor cost for 2007 totals $600,000. The firm budgeted $6,000,000 for purchases and use of direct materials (mostly coffee beans).

The budgeted direct costs for one-pound bags of two of the company's products are as follows:

	Mona Loa	Malaysian
Direct materials	$4.20	$3.20
Direct labor	0.30	0.30

CBI's controller, Mona Clin, believes that its current product costing system could be providing misleading cost information. She has developed this analysis of the 2007 budgeted factory overhead costs:

Activity	Cost Driver	Budgeted Activity	Budgeted Cost
Purchasing	Purchase orders	1,158	$ 579,000
Materials handling	Setups	1,800	720,000
Quality control	Batches	720	144,000
Roasting	Roasting-hours	96,100	961,000
Blending	Blending-hours	33,600	336,000
Packaging	Packaging-hours	26,000	260,000
Total factory overhead cost			$3,000,000

Data regarding the 2007 production of two of its lines, Mona Loa and Malaysian, follow. There is no beginning or ending direct materials inventory for either of these coffees.

	Mona Loa	Malaysian
Budgeted sales	100,000 pounds	2,000 pounds
Batch size	10,000 pounds	500 pounds
Setups	3 per batch	3 per batch
Purchase order size	25,000 pounds	500 pounds
Roasting time	1 hour per 100 pounds	1 hour per 100 pounds
Blending time	0.5 hour per 100 pounds	0.5 hour per 100 pounds
Packaging time	0.1 hour per 100 pounds	0.1 hour per 100 pounds

Required

1. Using Coffee Bean, Inc.'s current product costing system,
   a. Determine the company's predetermined overhead rate using direct labor cost as the single cost driver.
   b. Determine the full product costs and selling prices of one pound of Mona Loa coffee and one pound of Malaysian coffee.

2. Using an activity-based costing approach, develop a new product cost for one pound of Mona Loa coffee and one pound of Malaysian coffee. Allocate all overhead costs to the 100,000 pounds of Mona Loa and the 2,000 pounds of Malaysian. Compare the results with those in requirement 1.

3. What are the implications of the activity-based costing system with respect to CBI's pricing and product mix strategies? How does ABC add to CBI's competitive advantage?

(CMA Adapted)

5-54 **Customer Profitability Analysis**   Boston Depot sells office supplies to area corporations and organizations. Tom Delayne, founder and CEO, has been disappointed with the operating results and the profit margin for the last two years. Business forms are mostly a "commodity" business with low profit margins. To increase profit margins and gain competitive advantages, Delayne introduced "Desk-Top Delivery" service. The business seems to be as busy as ever. Yet, the operating income has been declining. To help identify the root cause of declining profits, he decided to analyze the profitability of two of the firm's major customers: Omega International (OI) and City of Albion (CA).

According to the customer profitability analysis that Boston Depot conducts regularly, Boston Depot has the same amount of total sales with both OI and CA. However, the firm earns a higher gross margin and gross margin ratio from CA than those from the sales to OI, as demonstrated here:

	Customer Profitability Analysis	
	Omega International	**City of Albion**
Sales	$ 80,000	$ 80,000
Product cost	(50,000)	(48,000)
Service fees (17.5% of sales)	(14,000)	(14,000)
Gross margin	$ 16,000	$ 18,000
Gross margin percent	20%	22.5%

Boston Depot adds a flat 17.5 percent to all sales for expenses incurred in such activities as handling customers' requests, pick-packing, order delivery, warehousing, and data entry. However, not all customers require the same level of services. Operation Manager, Jamie Steel, points out that CA has been a much heavier service user than OI. She shows the following data to support her belief:

Distribution Services Activities for OI and CA		
	OI	**CA**
Number of requisitions	300	700
Requisition line (all pick-packing)	900	2,100
Average number of cartons in warehouse	50	500
Number of miles per delivery	5	6

Controller Rod Jay has been investigating ways to determine the costs of performing various activities. He summarized his findings:

Activity	Total Estimated Annual Expense	Cost Driver	Estimated Annual Activity Level
Requisitions handling	$3,000,000	Requisitions	300,000
Warehouse	1,050,000	Number of cartons	70,000
Pick-packing	900,000	Pick-pack lines	600,000
Data entry	600,000	Pick-pack lines	600,000
Delivery charge	$10 per requisition (delivery) plus $0.30 per mile		

Steel points out that activities cost money. Two customers who request different service activities most likely are not costing the firm the same.

Required

1. Using activity-based costing, compute the charges per unit of service activities.
2. Using activity-based costing, compute the total distribution costs for each of the customers.
3. Is the City of Albion a more profitable customer?
4. Is Omega International a better customer for Boston Depot?

5–55 **Activity-Based Costing**   Miami Valley Architects Inc. provides a wide range of engineering and architectural consulting services through its three branch offices in Columbus, Cincinnati, and Dayton, Ohio. The company allocates resources and bonuses to the three branches based on the net income of the period. The results of the firm's performance for the year 2006 follows ($ in thousands):

	Columbus	Cincinnati	Dayton	Total
Sales	$1,500	$1,419	$1,067	$3,986
Less: Direct labor	382	317	317	1,016
Direct materials	281	421	185	887
Overhead	710	589	589	1,888
Net income	$ 127	$ 92	$ (24)	$ 195

Miami Valley accumulates overhead items in one overhead pool and allocates it to the branches based on direct labor dollars. For 2006, this predetermined overhead rate was $1.859 for every direct labor dollar incurred by an office. The overhead pool includes rent, depreciation, and taxes, regardless of which office incurred the expense. Some branch managers complain that the overhead allocation method forces them to absorb a portion of the overhead incurred by the other offices.

Management is concerned with the 2006 operating results. During a review of overhead expenses, management noticed that many overhead items were clearly not correlated to the movement in direct labor dollars as previously assumed. Management decided that applying overhead based on activity-based costing and direct tracing wherever possible should provide a more accurate picture of the profitability of each branch.

An analysis of the overhead revealed that the following dollars for rent, utilities, depreciation, and taxes could be traced directly to the office that incurred the overhead ($ in thousands):

	Columbus	Cincinnati	Dayton	Total
Direct overhead	$180	$270	$177	$627

Activity pools and their corresponding cost drivers were determined from the accounting records and staff surveys as follows:

General administration	$ 409,000
Project costing	48,000
Accounts payable/receiving	139,000
Accounts receivable	47,000
Payroll/Mail sort and delivery	30,000
Personnel recruiting	38,000
Employee insurance processing	14,000
Proposals	139,000
Sales meetings/Sales aids	202,000
Shipping	24,000
Ordering	48,000
Duplicating costs	46,000
Blueprinting	77,000
	$1,261,000

Cost Driver	Volume of Cost Drivers by Location		
	Columbus	Cincinnati	Dayton
Direct labor cost	$ 382,413	317,086	317,188
Timesheet entries	6,000	3,800	3,500
Vendor invoices	1,020	850	400
Client invoices	588	444	96
Employees	23	26	18
New hires	8	4	7
Insurance claims filed	230	260	180
Proposals	200	250	60
Contracted sales	1,824,439	1,399,617	571,208
Projects shipped	99	124	30
Purchase orders	135	110	80
Copies duplicated	162,500	146,250	65,000
Blueprints	39,000	31,200	16,000

Required (Round all answers to thousands)

1. What overhead costs should be assigned to each branch based on ABC concepts?
2. What is the contribution of each branch before subtracting the results obtained in requirement 1?
3. What is the profitability of each branch office using ABC?
4. Evaluate the concerns of management regarding the volume-based cost technique currently used.

(Adapted from Beth M. Chaffman, CPA, and John Talbott, CMA, IMA Management Accounting Campus Report)

5–56 **Customer Profitability Analysis** Spring Company collected the following data pertaining to its activities with selected customers.

	HS Inc.	Adventix	Baldwin
Total sales	$600,000	$750,000	$900,000
Sales discount	2%	3%	2%
Sales terms	2/10, n/30	1/15, n/60	2/10, n/eom
Shipping terms	FOB Shipping point	FOB Destination	FOB Destination
Sales returns	2%	1%	3%
Number of orders	10	5	50
Units per order	100	250	30
Expedited order	0	2	5
Sales visits	1	1	2
Number of sales returns	3	4	10

Spring Company mails monthly statements on or before the first day of each month. HS pays all of its account payables within the cash discount periods. Baldwin does not take advantage of cash discounts. However, it pays its accounts on the specified due dates. Adventix pays half of its accounts on the date that these accounts are due and pays the remainder at the end of the following month. Joan Lieberman, the controller of Spring Company, has estimated that the cost of working capital is approximately 2 percent per month.

Lieberman also gathered the following cost data:

Activity	Cost Driver and Rate
Order taking	$ 50 per order
Order processing	$ 75 per order
Delivery	$300 per delivery
Expedited orders	$500 per order
Restocking	$ 10 per unit plus $200 per return
Sales visits	$800 per visit

Required Prepare a customer profitability analysis for Spring Company.

5–57 Team Project Assignment, Activity Analysis

Required   This is a group assignment. Each group is to select a real-world organization and conduct an activity analysis of one of its processes such as sales and collection, purchase and payment, college admissions, student enrollment, warehousing, or bank deposits. Your written report should include the following:

1. Organization name, background information, persons contacted or interviewed.
2. Descriptions of activities and cost drivers in this process.
3. Process inputs, outputs, and performance measures.
4. Value- and non-value-added activities.
5. Unique features of the costing system of this organization.
6. Suggested improvements.

Solution to Self-Study Problem

Volume-Based Costing Versus ABC

1. Volume-based costing system

Stage 1 Allocation

Total overhead allocated to Department A

$$\$1,000,000 \times (4,000/20,000) = \$200,000$$

Total overhead allocated to Department B

$$\$1,000,000 \times (16,000/20,000) = \$800,000$$

Stage 2 Allocation

	Per Unit Cost	
	Deluxe	**Regular**
Overhead allocated to		
Department A		
($200,000/20,000) × 2 =	$ 20	
($200,000/20,000) × 2 =		$ 20
Department B		
($800,000/10,000) × 1 =	80	
($800,000/10,000) × 1 =		80
Total	$100	$100

Product cost per unit:

	Deluxe	Regular
Direct materials	$100	$ 50
Direct labor		
$25 × (2 + 1) =	75	
$20 × (2 + 1) =		60
Factory overhead	100	100
Unit cost	$275	$210

2. Budgeted overhead rates for cost drivers.

Cost Driver	Budgeted Overhead	Budgeted Cost Driver Quantity	Budgeted Overhead Rate
Number of production runs	$ 7,000	350	$ 20
Number of setups	400,000	500	800
Number of units	588,000	19,600	30
Number of shipments	5,000	250	20
	$100,000		

3. ABC system

	Deluxe	Regular
Overhead allocated to		
Material movement		
$20 × 150 =	$ 3,000	
$20 × 200 =		$ 4,000
Machine setups		
$800 × 25 =	16,000	
$800 × 50 =		32,000
Inspections		
$30 × 200 =	6,000	
$30 × 800 =		24,000
Shipment		
$20 × 50 =	1,000	
$20 × 100 =		2,000
Total	$30,000	$70,000
Unit overhead cost	$ 150	$ 87.50
Product cost per unit		
Direct materials	$ 100	$ 50
Direct labor	75	60
Factory overhead	150	87.50
Unit cost	$ 325	$197.50

Note that the volume-based costing system overcosts the high-volume regular product and under-costs the low-volume deluxe product.

CHAPTER SIX

Cost Estimation

After studying this chapter, you should be able to . . .

1. Understand the strategic role of cost estimation
2. Apply the six steps of cost estimation
3. Use each of the cost estimation methods: the high-low method, work measurement, and regression analysis
4. Explain the data requirements and implementation problems of the cost estimation methods
5. Use learning curves in cost estimation when learning is present
6. Use statistical measures to evaluate a regression analysis

LEARNING OBJECTIVE 1
Understand the strategic role of cost estimation.

Cost management information is critical in cost planning and decision making (planning for a new product or plant expansion and making other decisions). However, a basic requirement for cost effective planning is to use *accurate cost estimates* in the planning process. This chapter shows the methods to develop accurate estimates.

Cost estimation is particularly important for the construction industry. Large construction projects are often obtained on the basis of competitive bids. The contractors that bid on these projects must have accurate cost estimation methods to win their share of the bids and to be profitable. Cost estimation methods for contractors develop detailed analyses of the material and labor costs that are directly traceable to the project, as well as projections of the indirect costs, preferably using activity analysis as described in Chapter 5.

Cost estimation for construction contractors is such a critical aspect of these firms' success that a number of consultants and software developers have created tools and techniques to assist the contractors in cost estimation. The American Society of Professional Estimators (www.aspenational.com) and other professional organizations provide education and opportunities for professional development for cost managers involved in construction cost estimation. A number of consultants (e.g., Cost Concepts, Inc., www.costconcepts.com; and Davis Langdon Adamson Associates, www.davis langdon.com) and software providers such as Prosoft Inc., (www.prosoftinc.com) provide additional services.

One of the world's largest construction firms is Daewoo Construction Corp. of Korea, which has residential, commercial, and civil construction offices and construction projects in 30 countries throughout Asia, North America, and other parts of the world (http://www.dwconst.co.kr). Daewoo's corporate mission is to build "a creative company to lead global construction through technology and quality excellence." One critical part of the implementation of that corporate mission is the use of world-class cost estimation.

Strategic Role of Cost Estimation

The strategic cost literature suggests that management accountants should actively participate in early strategic decision making. Their contributions at early stages are likely to be in the form of predictions of (1) costs of alternative activities, processes, or organizational forms—both of the firm and its competitors, (2) financial and operational impacts of alternative strategic choices, and (3) costs (dollars and time) of alternative implementation strategies. If management accountants do not fill this role, others will.[1]

As Jalinski and Selto indicate, a critical starting point for strategic cost management is having accurate cost estimates. The strategic approach is forward looking, and thus cost estimation is an essential element of it. **Cost estimation** is the development of a well-defined relationship between a cost object and its cost drivers for the purpose of predicting the cost.

Cost estimation facilitates strategic management in two important ways. First, it helps predict future costs using previously identified activity-based, volume-based, structural, or executional cost drivers. Second, cost estimation helps identify the key cost drivers for a cost object and which of these cost drivers are most useful in predicting cost.

Cost estimation
is the development of a well-defined relationship between a cost object and its cost drivers for the purpose of predicting the cost.

Using Cost Estimation to Predict Future Costs

Strategic management requires accurate cost estimates for many applications, including these:

1. **To facilitate strategic positioning analysis.** Cost estimates are particularly important for firms competing on the basis of cost leadership. Cost estimates guide management in determining which contemporary management techniques, such as target costing or total quality management, the firm should employ to succeed in its chosen strategy.

2. **To facilitate value-chain analysis.** Cost estimates help the firm identify potential opportunities for cost reduction by reconfiguring the value chain. For example, cost estimates are useful in determining whether overall costs and value to the product can be improved by manufacturing one of its components in-house or by purchasing it from a supplier.

3. **To facilitate target costing and life-cycle costing.** Cost estimates are an integral part of target costing and life-cycle costing. Management uses cost estimates of different product designs as part of the process of selecting the particular design that provides the best trade-off of value to the customer versus manufacturing and other costs. Similarly, cost estimates are used to determine the minimum expected life-cycle cost for a product or service. Target costing and life-cycle costing are covered in Chapter 10.

Cost Estimation for Different Types of Cost Drivers

The cost estimation methods explained in this chapter can be used for any of the four types of cost drivers: activity based, volume based, structural, or executional. The relationships between costs and activity-based or volume-based cost drivers often are best fit by the linear cost estimation methods explained in this chapter because these relationships are at least approximately linear within the relevant range of the firm's operations.

Structural cost drivers involve plans and decisions that have a long-term and therefore strategic impact on the firm. Such decisions include manufacturing experience, scale of product, product or production technology, and product or production complexity. Technology and complexity issues often lead management to use activity-based costing and linear estimation methods. In contrast, experience and scale often require nonlinear methods. As a cost driver, experience represents the reduction in unit cost due to learning. The effect on total cost of experience is nonlinear: that is, costs decrease with increased manufacturing experience. The learning effect is explained in

---

[1] Dale W. Jalinski and Frank H. Selto, "Integration of Accounting and Strategy: A Longitudinal Field Study," working paper, University of Colorado at Boulder, July 1995.

Appendix A to the chapter. Similarly, the relationship between the structural cost driver, scale, and total cost is nonlinear. *Scale* is the term used to describe the manufacture of similar products that differ in size—for example, pipe valves of different capacity. A common effect of scale is that total manufacturing cost increases more rapidly than the increase in the size of the product. For example, the manufacture of a 22-inch industrial valve requires more than twice the cost of an 11-inch valve. The relationship between manufacturing cost and valve size can be predicted by a mathematical estimation model called the *power law* that is used in industrial engineering.[2]

Using Cost Estimation to Identify Cost Drivers

Often the most practical way to identify cost drivers is to rely on the judgment of product designers, engineers, and manufacturing personnel. Those who are most knowledgeable about the product and production processes have the most useful information on cost drivers. Cost estimation sometimes plays a discovery role and at other times a collaborative role to validate and confirm the judgments of the designers and engineers. For example, Hewlett-Packard uses cost estimation to confirm the usefulness of cost drivers selected by teams of engineers and production personnel.[3]

Six Steps of Cost Estimation

LEARNING OBJECTIVE 2
Apply the six steps of cost estimation.

The six steps of cost estimation are to (1) define the cost object for which the related costs are to be estimated, (2) determine the cost drivers, (3) collect consistent and accurate data on the cost object and the cost drivers, (4) graph the data, (5) select and employ an appropriate estimation method, and (6) evaluate the accuracy of the cost estimate.

Step 1: Define the Cost Object to Be Estimated

Although it might seem elementary, defining the particular cost to be estimated requires care. For example, if the goal is to estimate product costs to improve product pricing, the relevant cost objects are the products manufactured in the plant; product cost is relevant for pricing. In contrast, if the goal is to reward the managers most effective at reducing cost, the most appropriate cost objects are the individual manufacturing departments in the plant since costs are most directly controllable by department managers.

Step 2: Determine the Cost Drivers

Cost drivers are the causal factors used in the estimation of the cost. Some examples of estimated costs and their related cost drivers follow on the next page:

---

[2] Based on information in Phillip F. Ostwald and Timothy S. McLaren, *Cost Estimating for Engineering and Management* (Englewood Cliffs, N.J.: Prentice Hall, 2003).

[3] Based on information from Mike Merz and Arlene Hardy, "ABC Puts Accountants on Design Team at HP," *Management Accounting,* September 1993, pp. 22–27.

Cost to Be Estimated	Cost Driver
Fuel expense for auto	Miles driven
Heating expense for a building	Temperature to be maintained in the building
Maintenance cost in a manufacturing plant	Machine-hours, labor-hours
Product design cost	Number of design elements, design changes

Identifying cost drivers is the most important step in developing the cost estimate. A number of relevant drivers might exist, and some might not be immediately obvious. Fuel expense for a large delivery truck, for example, might be primarily a function of miles traveled, but it is also affected by the average weight delivered, the number of hours of operation, and the nature of the delivery area.

Step 3: Collect Consistent and Accurate Data

Once the cost drivers have been selected, the management accountant collects data on the cost object and cost drivers. The data must be consistent and accurate. *Consistent* means that each period of data is calculated on the same accounting basis and that all transactions are properly recorded in the period in which they occurred.

The accuracy of the data depends on the nature of the source. Sometimes data developed within the firm are very reliable, as a result of management policies and procedures to ensure accuracy. Accuracy also varies among external sources of data, including governmental sources, trade and industry publications, universities, and other sources. The choice of cost drivers requires trade-offs between the relevance of the drivers and the consistency and accuracy of the data.

Step 4: Graph the Data

The objective of graphing data is to identify unusual patterns. Any shift or nonlinearity in the data must be given special attention in developing the estimate. For example, a week's downtime to install new equipment causes unusual production data for that week; such data should be excluded when developing a cost estimate. Any unusual occurrences can be detected easily by studying a graph.

Step 5: Select and Employ the Estimation Method

The three estimation methods presented in the next section of the chapter differ in their ability to provide superior accuracy in cost estimation relative to the cost of the expertise and resources required. The management accountant chooses the method with the best precision/cost trade-off for the estimation objectives.

Step 6: Assess the Accuracy of the Cost Estimate

A critical final step in cost estimation is to consider the potential for error when the estimate is prepared. This involves considering the completeness and appropriateness of cost drivers selected in step 2, the consistency and accuracy of data selected in step 3, the study of the graphs in step 4, and the precision of the method selected in step 5.

A common approach for assessing the accuracy of an estimation method is to compare the estimates to the actual results over time. For example, when a firm predicts overhead costs each year, over a 10-year period there are 10 estimation errors to evaluate. These errors can be evaluated using the **mean absolute percentage error (MAPE)** that is calculated by taking the absolute value of each error, and then averaging these errors and converting the result to a percentage of the actual values of overhead.

The **mean absolute percentage error (MAPE)** is calculated by taking the absolute value of each error, and averaging these errors and converting the result to a percentage of the actual values of overhead.

Cost Estimation Methods

The three estimation methods are (1) the high-low method, (2) work measurement, and (3) regression analysis. The methods are listed from least to most accurate. However, the cost and effort in employing the methods are inverse to this sequence; the high-low

EXHIBIT 6.1
Trade-Offs among Estimation Methods

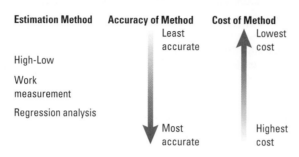

EXHIBIT 6.2
Graph of Maintenance Costs

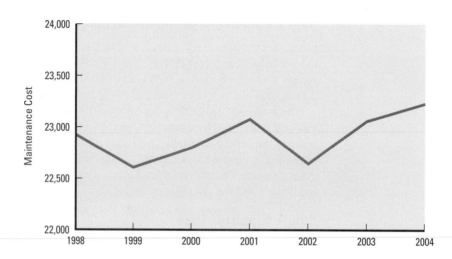

LEARNING OBJECTIVE 3
Use each of the cost estimation methods: the high-low method, work measurement, and regression analysis.

method is the easiest and least costly, and the regression analysis method is both the most accurate and most costly, requiring more time, data collection, and expertise (see Exhibit 6.1). In choosing the best estimation method, management accountants must consider the level of accuracy desired and any limitations on cost, time, and effort.[4]

Ben Garcia's Data on Maintenance Costs

To illustrate the three methods, we use the example of a management accountant named Ben Garcia who is developing cost estimates of maintenance costs for a large manufacturing company. Garcia has the following data on maintenance costs:

	1998	1999	2000	2001	2002	2003	2004
Maintenance cost ($)	22,843	22,510	22,706	23,030	22,413	22,935	23,175

As a first step, Garcia graphs the data (Exhibit 6.2) and observes that maintenance costs are increasing, although not steadily. Based only on the graphs, he also predicts that maintenance costs will be between $22,500 and $23,500 in the coming year, 2005. Since this prediction is rough and he wants to improve its accuracy, he turns to the cost estimation methods, beginning with the high-low method.

---

[4] A fourth estimation method, the *account classification method,* is used when the management accountant's information for cost estimation purposes is limited to the balances in the financial statement accounts. In this case, the accountant simply chooses for each cost account (rent, labor, materials, etc.) whether the costs in the account are fixed (e.g., rent expense) or variable (e.g., manufacturing direct labor). A difficulty with this method is that the costs in most accounts are mixed (e.g., the manufacturing labor account includes both direct and indirect labor, and thus both variable and fixed costs) and cannot be classified as simply fixed or variable. Because of the limited use of this method and the availability of much better methods, we do not consider it any further.

High-Low Method

The **high-low method** uses algebra to determine a *unique* estimation line between representative high and low points in the data. The high-low method accomplishes two important objectives for Garcia. First, it adds a degree of quantitative precision to the estimate, which is based on a unique cost line rather than a rough estimate based on a view of the graph. Second, it permits him to add information that might be useful in predicting maintenance costs. For example, he knows that total maintenance costs are likely to include both variable and fixed costs. The fixed cost portion is the planned (preventive) maintenance that is performed regardless of the plant's volume of activity. Also, a part of maintenance cost varies with the number of operating hours; more operating hours mean more wear on the machines and thus more maintenance costs. Garcia collects the additional information, operating hours, as follows:

	1998	1999	2000	2001	2002	2003	2004
Total operating hours	3,451	3,325	3,383	3,614	3,423	3,410	3,500
Maintenance costs ($)	22,843	22,510	22,706	23,030	22,413	22,935	23,175

To use the high-low method, Garcia enters the data into a graph, as shown in Exhibit 6.3, and then selects two points from the data, one representative of the lower points and the other representative of the higher points. Often these can be simply the lowest and highest points in the data. However, if either the highest or lowest point is a great distance from the other points around it, a biased estimation can result. Both points must be representative of the data around them.

The high-low estimate is represented as follows:

$$Y = a + b \times H$$

where: Y = the value of the estimated maintenance cost

H = the cost driver, the number of hours of operation for the plant

a = a fixed quantity that represents the value of Y when H = zero

b = the slope of the line. In the plant maintenance example, it is the unit variable cost for maintenance

EXHIBIT 6.3
Ben Garcia's Data on
Maintenance Cost and Hours

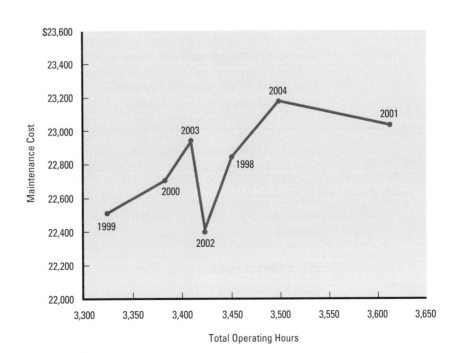

To obtain the high and low points, Garcia draws a freehand line through the data to help select the high and low points (try this yourself on Exhibit 6.3). He then chooses a high and a low point reasonably close to the freehand line. Suppose that he has chosen the points for 1999 and 2001. Then he calculates the value for b:

$$b = \text{Variable cost per hour}$$

$$= \frac{\text{Difference between } \textbf{costs} \text{ for high and low points}}{\text{Difference for the value of the } \textbf{cost driver} \text{ for the high and low points}}$$

$$b = \frac{\$23,030 - \$22,510}{3,614 - 3,325} = \$1.80 \text{ per hour}$$

Next, the value for a (the fixed quantity) can be calculated using either 1999 or 2001 data:

Using 2001 Data

$$a = Y - (b \times H) = \$23,030 - \$1.80 \times 3,614 = \$16,525$$

Using 1999 data gives the same value for a because fixed cost is the same at both levels of operating hours; only total variable costs for the two levels differ:

Using 1999 Data

$$a = Y - (b \times H) \times \$22,510 - \$1.80 \times 3,325 = \$16,525$$

So the estimation equation using the high-low method is:

$$Y = \$16,525 + \$1.80 \times H$$

This equation can be used to estimate maintenance cost for 2005. Suppose that 3,600 operating hours are expected in 2005. Then maintenance costs are estimated as follows:

$$\text{Maintenance cost in 2005} = \$16,525 + \$1.80 \times 3,600$$

$$= \$23,005$$

Management accountants find the high-low equation useful for estimating *total costs* but not the amount of fixed costs alone. The reason is that the estimate applies only to the *relevant range* of the cost driver used to develop the estimate, the range from 3,325 to 3,614 hours. The value of a, a measure that is relevant at zero hours only, is too far from the relevant range to be properly interpreted as a fixed cost. Its role is to serve only as the constant part of the estimation equation used to *predict total cost.*

The key advantage of the high-low method is to provide a precise mathematical cost equation. However, the high-low method is limited; it can represent only the best possible line for the two selected points, and the selection of the two points requires judgment. The next two methods, work measurement and regression, are more accurate because they use statistical estimation, which provides greater mathematical precision. By including estimation error directly in the analysis, they also provide useful measures of their estimation accuracy. The accuracy of the high-low method can be evaluated only subjectively; work measurement and regression have objective, quantitative measures of their estimation accuracy. Thus, the latter two methods provide a much superior basis for completing step 6 in cost estimation: assessing the accuracy of the cost estimate.

Work Measurement

Work measurement
is a statistical cost estimation method that makes a detailed study of some production or service activity to measure the time or input required per unit of output.

Work measurement is a statistical cost estimation method that makes a detailed study of some production or service activity to measure the time or input required per unit of output. For example, work measurement is applied to manufacturing operations to determine the labor and/or materials needed to manufacture the part or subassembly completed in that operation. In the nonmanufacturing context, the method is used to measure the time required to complete certain tasks, such as processing receipts or processing bills for payment.

Although a variety of work measurement methods are used in practice, the most common is **work sampling,** a statistical method that makes a series of measurements about the activity under study. These measurements are analyzed statistically to obtain estimates of the time and/or materials the activity requires.

As an example, suppose that Kupper Insurance Company provides insurance coverage for automobile drivers. The cost of processing claims has increased significantly in recent years, and the firm is studying that cost. A careful statistical analysis including data for several different employees and several types of claims, is completed over a three-week period. The mean processing time is found to be 18 minutes, and the range is such that 95 percent of the claims required between 14 and 22 minutes. On the basis of this study, Kupper is able to estimate processing costs more accurately and to evaluate the processing clerks more effectively and more fairly. For example, if a given claims-processing clerk requires 24 minutes on average per claim, that clerk likely needs training or supervision because this amount of time is outside the 95 percent likelihood range. Kupper considers the work measurement to be an ongoing activity and continues to sample the processing times throughout the year and to make adjustments to estimated times as needed.[5]

Regression Analysis

Regression analysis is a statistical method for obtaining the unique cost-estimating equation that best fits a set of data points. Regression analysis fits the data by *minimizing the sum of the squares* of the estimation errors. Each error is the distance measured from the regression line to one of the data points. Because regression analysis systematically minimizes the estimation errors in this way, it is called **least squares regression.**

A regression analysis has two types of variables. The **dependent variable** is the cost to be estimated.[6] The **independent variable** is the cost driver used to estimate the amount of the dependent variable. When one cost driver is used, the analysis is called a *simple regression analysis.* When two or more cost drivers are used, it is called *multiple regression.*

The regression equation has both an intercept and a slope term, much like the high-low method. In addition, the amount of the estimation error is considered explicitly in the regression estimate, which is

$$Y = a + bX + e$$

where: Y = the amount of the *dependent variable,* the cost to be estimated

a = a *fixed quantity,* also called the *intercept* or *constant term,* which represents the amount of Y when $X = 0$

X = the value for the *independent variable,* the cost driver for the cost to be estimated; there may be one or more cost drivers

b = the *unit variable cost,* also called the *coefficient* of the independent variable, that is, the increase in Y (cost) for each unit increase in X (cost driver)

e = the *estimation error,* which is the distance between the regression line and the data point

To illustrate the method, Exhibit 6.4A and the accompanying table show three months of data on supplies expense and production levels. (To simplify the presentation, only three data points are used; applications of regression usually involve 12 or

Work sampling
is a statistical method that makes a series of measurements about the activity under study.

Regression analysis
is a statistical method for obtaining the unique cost estimating equation that best fits a set of data points.

Least squares regression,
which minimizes the sum of the squares of the estimation errors, is widely viewed as one of the most effective methods for estimating costs.

The **dependent variable**
is the cost to be estimated.

The **independent variable**
is the cost driver used to estimate the value of the dependent variable.

[5] Sample applications of work measurement are provided on the website of the software firm, SimpleWorks (www.simpleworks.com/WS/whycare.htm).

[6] Although the dependent variable is a cost in most of the cases we consider, the dependent variable also could be a revenue or some other type of financial or operating data.

EXHIBIT 6.4A **Supplies Expense Data for Regression Application**

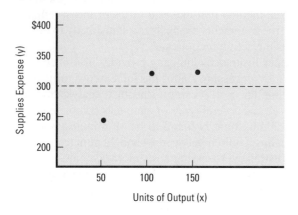

EXHIBIT 6.4B **The Regression Line for Supplies Expense with Units of Output as the Cost Driver (i.e., independent variable)**

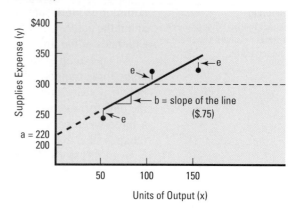

more data points.) The management accountant's task is to estimate supplies expense for month 4, in which the production level is expected to be 125 units.

Month	Supplies Expense (Y)	Production Level (X)
1	$250	50 units
2	310	100
3	325	150
4	?	125

The regression for the data is determined by a statistical procedure that finds the unique line through the three data points that minimizes the sum of the squared error distances. The regression line (see Exhibit 6.4B) is[7]

$$Y = \$220 + \$0.75\ X$$

And the estimated value for supplies expense in month 4 is

$$Y = \$220 + \$0.75 \times 125 = \$313.75$$

Regression analysis gives management accountants an objective, statistically precise method to estimate supplies expense. Its principal advantage is a unique estimate that produces the least estimation error for the data. On the other hand, since the errors are squared to find the best fitting line, the regression analysis can be influenced strongly by unusual data points called **outliers,** with the result that the estimation line is not representative of most of the data. Such a situation is illustrated in Exhibit 6.5. To prevent this type of distortion, management accountants often prepare a graph of the data prior to using regression and determine whether any outliers are present. Each outlier is reviewed to determine whether it is due to a data-recording error, normal operating condition, or a unique and unrecurring event. Guided by the objective of developing the regression that is most representative of the data, the accountant then decides whether to correct or remove the outlier.

Outliers
are unusual data points that strongly influence a regression analysis.

Choosing the Dependent Variable

Development of a regression analysis begins with the choice of the cost object, the dependent variable. The dependent variable might be at a very aggregate level, such as total maintenance costs for the entire firm, or at a detail level, such as maintenance costs for each plant or department. The choice of aggregation level depends on the

---

[7] The derivation of the intercept ($220) and coefficient ($0.75) for this regression line is done in Excel or other software. See also textbooks on basic probability and statistics such as that by Bruce Bowerman and Richard O'Connell, *Essentials of Business Statistics* (New York. McGraw-Hill, 2004). Appendix B to this chapter also has a technical reference on regression analysis.

EXHIBIT 6.5
The Effect of Outliers on Regression

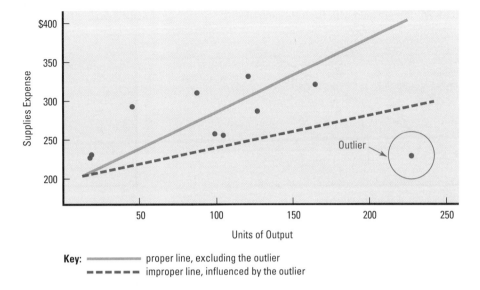

Key: ——————— proper line, excluding the outlier
      ─ ─ ─ ─ ─ improper line, influenced by the outlier

objectives for the cost estimation, data availability and reliability, and cost/benefit considerations. When a key objective is accuracy, a detailed level of analysis often is preferred.

Choosing the Independent Variables (Cost Drivers)

To identify the independent variables, management accountants consider all financial, operating, and other economic data that might be relevant for estimating the dependent variable. The goal is to choose variables that (1) are relevant; that is, they change when the dependent variable changes, and (2) do not duplicate other independent variables. As an example, Exhibit 6.6 presents some dependent and independent variables that might be appropriate for the study of costs in a chain of retail stores.

EXHIBIT 6.6   Independent Variables for Selected Dependent Variables
Types of Independent Variables: Financial, Operating, Economic, and Other

Selected Dependent Variables	Independent Variables			
	Financial Data	**Operating Data**	**Economic Indicators**	**Other**
• Sales	• Selling expense • Advertising expense	• Store size • Store type	• Price level index • Index of local economic conditions	• Dummy variable for change in credit policy
• Labor expense	• Wage rates • Sales • Units produced	• Hours worked • Dummy variable for change in labor mix • Number of employees	• Index of local wage rates	• Trend variable • Dummy variable for significant pay rate change
• Utilities expense	• Sales • Units produced	• Average daily temperature • Dummy variable for change in thermostat setting • Number of hours store is open		• Dummy variable for significant change in utility rate • Trend variable
• General expenses: office salaries and supplies, telephone, printing and duplicating, and repairs	• Sales • Total expense • Net fixed assets	• Store type • Store size • Number of employees	• Index of local price level	• Age of store • Dummy variable for change in office automation

EXHIBIT 6.7A Regression with High *R*-Squared

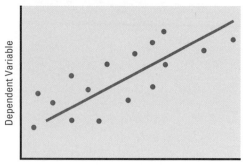

EXHIBIT 6.7B Regression with Low *R*-Squared

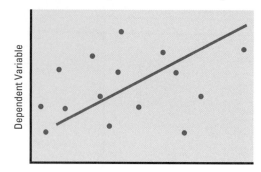

A **dummy variable**
is used to represent the presence or absence of a condition.

Most often the data in a regression analysis are numerical amounts in dollars or units. Another type of variable, called a **dummy variable,** represents the presence or absence of a condition. For example, dummy variables can be used to indicate seasonality. If the management accountant is estimating costs of production, and if production is always high in March, a dummy variable with a value of 1 for March and 0 for the other months could be used.

Evaluating a Regression Analysis

In addition to a cost estimate, regression analysis also provides quantitative measures of its precision and reliability. *Precision* refers to the accuracy of the estimates from the regression, and *reliability* indicates whether the regression reflects actual relationships among the variables, that is, is it likely to continue to predict accurately? These measures can aid management accountants in assessing the usefulness of the regression. Three key measures are explained here. These and other statistical measures are explained more fully in Appendix B in this chapter.

1. *R*-squared, also called the *coefficient of determination.*
2. The *t*-value.
3. The standard error of the estimate (*SE*).

R-squared and the *t*-value are used to measure the reliability of the regression, the standard error is a useful measure of the precision, or accuracy, of the regression.

R-squared
is a number between zero and 1 and often is described as a measure of the explanatory power of the regression, that is, the degree to which changes in the dependent variable can be predicted by changes in the independent variable(s).

R-squared is a number between zero and 1 and is often described as a measure of the explanatory power of the regression; that is, the degree to which changes in the dependent variable can be predicted by changes in the independent variables. A more reliable regression is one that has an *R*-squared close to 1. When viewed graphically, regressions with high *R*-squared show the data points lying near the regression line; in low *R*-squared regressions, the data points are scattered about, as demonstrated in Exhibit 6.7A (high *R*-squared) and 6.7B (low *R*-squared). Most regression analyses involving financial data have *R*-squared values above 0.5, and many have values in the 0.8 to 0.9 range.[8]

The **t-value**
is a measure of the reliability of each independent variable, that is, the degree to which an independent variable has a valid, stable, long-term relationship with the dependent variable.

The **t-value** is a measure of the statistical reliability of each independent variable. *Reliability* is the degree to which an independent variable has a valid, stable, long-term relationship with the dependent variable. A relatively small *t*-value (generally, the *t*-value should be more than 2) indicates little or no relationship between the independent and dependent variables. A variable with a low *t*-value should be removed from

[8] The square root of *R*-squared, or simply *R*, is called the *correlation coefficient* and is interpreted in the same manner as *R*-squared. The correlation coefficient is a number between −1 and +1; a value near zero is interpreted as a lack of relationship between the independent and dependent variables. When *R* is positive, the relationship is direct; that is, when one variable increases, so does the other. When *R* is negative, the relationship is inverse; that is, when one variable increases, the other decreases.

EXHIBIT 6.8A   Regression with Narrow (Good) Standard Error

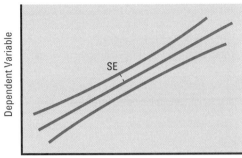

EXHIBIT 6.8B   Regression with Wide (Poor) Standard Error

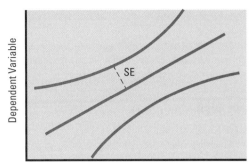

the regression to simplify the model and because it can lead to less accurate cost estimates.[9]

When two or more independent variables exist, the presence of a low *t*-value for one or more of these variables is a possible signal of what is called **multicollinearity,** which means that two or more independent variables are highly correlated with each other. As suggested by the name, independent variables are supposed to be independent of each other, not correlated. **Correlation** among variables means that a given variable tends to change predictably in the same (or opposite) direction for a given change in the other variable. For example, the number of machine-hours used in manufacturing is correlated with the number of labor-hours because both are affected by the same factor, the number of units produced. Moreover, because a common trend tends to affect many types of financial data, accounting and operating data are often highly correlated.

The effect of multicollinearity is that the regression is less reliable and the estimates less accurate. Thus, when a management accountant has reason to believe that two or more of the variables in the equation are correlated and the *t*-values are relatively low, additional regressions that remove one or more of these independent variables should be considered.

The **standard error of the estimate (SE)** is a measure of the accuracy of the regression's estimates. It is a range around the regression estimate in which we can be reasonably sure that the unknown actual value will fall. For example, if the regression estimate is $4,500 and the *SE* is $500, there is reasonable confidence that the unknown actual value lies in the range $4,500 +/− $500, that is, between $4,000 and $5,000.[10]

Because it is used to measure a confidence range, the *SE* must be interpreted by its relationship to the average size of the dependent variable. If the *SE* is small relative to the dependent variable, the precision of the regression can be assessed as relatively good. How small the *SE* value must be for a favorable precision evaluation is a matter of judgment, but a threshold of approximately 5 to 10 percent of the average of the dependent variable can be used. The confidence ranges for two regressions are illustrated in Exhibit 6.8A (good precision) and 6.8B (relatively poor precision).

Note that in Exhibits 6.8A and 6.8B the *SE* value increases as points on the regression line move farther in either direction from the mean of the independent variable. This is consistent with the concept of the relevant range. The estimate is most accurate near the mean of the independent variable and less accurate the farther it is from the mean.

Multicollinearity means that two or more independent variables are highly correlated with each other.

Correlation means that a given variable tends to change predictably in the same (or opposite) direction for a given change in the other, correlated variable.

The **standard error of the estimate (SE)** is a measure of the accuracy of the regression's estimates.

[9] As for the correlation coefficient (footnote 8), the *t*-value can be positive or negative, depending on the nature of the relationship between the dependent and independent variables.

[10] The standard error of the estimate provides a quantitative measure of the confidence one has with the accuracy of the estimate. See Appendix B for a more detailed explanation. An excellent discussion of the standard error and other regression measures, including a spreadsheet illustration, is provided in Adel M. Novin, "Applying Overhead: How to Find the Right Bases and Rates," *Management Accounting*, March 1992, pp. 40–43.

Applications of Regression Analysis

Regression analysis is used for cost estimation and a wide variety of financial management functions that the management accountant is likely to encounter. Five functions (and references for additional reading) are given here.

PREDICTING OVERHEAD COSTS

Regression is used to identify the best of several alternative overhead applications bases. (G. R. Cluskey Jr., Mitchell H. Raiborn, and Doan T. Modianos, "Multiple-Cost Flexible Budgets and PC-Based Regression Analysis," *Journal of Cost Management,* July–August 2000, pp. 35–47; and Adel M. Novin, "Applying Overhead: How to Find the Right Bases and Rates," *Management Accounting,* March 1992, pp. 40–43.)

REAL ESTATE APPRAISAL

Regression is used to estimate the value of commercial real estate properties using a variety of financial, operating, and general economic independent variables. (Stephen T. Crosson, Charles G. Dannis, and Thomas G. Thibodeau, "Regression Analysis: A Cost-Effective Approach for the Valuation of Commercial Property," *Real Estate Finance,* Winter 1996.)

CASH FLOW PROJECTIONS FOR RESTAURANTS

Luby's Inc. (www.lubys.com), a chain of Texas-based restaurants, uses regression analysis to predict cash flows at its different locations, as a part of overall financial planning at the corporate level. (See Luby's 2001 Annual Report, http://www.lubys.com/financials/2001ar.pdf.)

COST ESTIMATION AND COST MANAGEMENT IN PHARMACIES

Pharmacists use regression analysis to estimate and manage the costs of patient services in their pharmacies. Approximately 35 percent of patients receiving prescriptions require pharmacists to provide one or more of five patient services:

- **Patient consultation,** including discussing the patient's expectations and concerns
- **Patient monitoring,** or follow-up at planned intervals to ensure that new drug therapy problems do not arise
- **Patient education,** including recommendations and referrals

- **Patient assessment,** covering the patient's entire drug therapy, to identify current or potential drug interactions or other problems
- **Patient care plan** to establish specific therapy goals, including a written record of how patient problems are resolved

By applying regression analysis to pharmacy costs, pharmacists found that a key cost driver is the acuity, or degree of severity, of the patient's medical problems. Those with higher acuity require more pharmacy services. One analysis showed that at the lowest level of acuity, patient care assessment and planning costs were $1.30 per patient, while at the highest acuity level, the costs were $6.49 per patient. (David Tipton, "Pharmaceutical Care: Cost Estimation and Cost Management," *Drug Store News,* February 16, 1998.)

PUBLIC UTILITY RATE REGULATION

Connecticut's Department of Public Utility Control (CDPUC) has concluded that regression-based methods, if applied correctly, are accurate enough to forecast natural gas usage. Simple regressions are found to be very effective at forecasting average usage based on degree days. Degree days are defined by the U.S. National Weather Service as "a quantitative index demonstrated to reflect demand for energy to heat or cool houses and businesses. This index is derived from daily temperature observations at nearly 200 major weather stations in the contiguous United States." Other possible independent variables noted by the CDPUC include:

- Weather trends
- Days of the week (demand differs on weekends)
- Holidays
- Seasons
- Shoulder periods both in and out of the winter season

Most gas public utilities serving Connecticut report levels of accuracy of from 4 percent to 10 percent using regression. State of Connecticut: Department of Public Utility Control, "Application of the Yankee Gas Services Company for an Increase in Rates," March 17, 1999, http://www.nega.com/ctdpuc31799.doc

---

Using Regression to Estimate Maintenance Costs

We continue the case developed earlier, Ben Garcia's estimation of maintenance costs. Following the six steps outlined in the first section of the chapter, Garcia defined the cost object and the relevant cost driver as maintenance cost and operating hours, respectively. He also collected and graphed the data (Exhibit 6.3). The next step is to solve the regression using regression software such as the Excel spreadsheet program, with the following findings (Y represents maintenance cost and H represents operating hours):

$$Y = \$15,843 + \$2.02 \times H$$

Garcia expects approximately 3,600 operating hours in 2005, so the amount of maintenance cost for 2005 is estimated to be

$$Y = \$15,843 + \$2.02 \times 3,600 = \$23,115$$

Regression analysis is commonly used as one means to estimate the value of commercial real estate properties. It is used for two key types of properties: income-producing properties, such as apartment buildings and office buildings, and nonincome-producing properties, such as warehouses and manufacturing plants. Identify what you think are the two or three key independent variables for estimating the value for each type of property. (Refer to Comments on Cost Management in Action at the end of the chapter.)

The statistical measures are:

R-squared = .461

t-value = 2.07

Standard error of the estimate = $221.71

Ratio of SE to the mean of the dependent variable = 0.98%

Garcia notes that R-squared is less than 0.5, the t-value is greater than 2.0, and the SE is approximately 1 percent of the mean of the dependent variable. The SE and t-values are very good. However, since the R-squared is low, Garcia asks his accounting assistant, Jan, to review the regression.

Jan looks at the regression and the related graphs and comments immediately that in 2002 maintenance cost dropped significantly, and operating hours experienced a modest drop. Garcia observes that the drop in 2002 was probably due to the unusually poor economic conditions that year; thus, output was reduced and operating hours and maintenance fell accordingly. Recalling that dummy variables can be used to correct for isolated variations and seasonal or other patterns, Jan suggests that Garcia run the regression again with a dummy variable having a value of 1 in 2002 and a value of zero otherwise (the symbol D represents the dummy variable). The new regression result is as follows:

$$Y = \$16,467 + \$1.856 \times H - \$408.638 \times D$$

With the revised regression, the estimate of maintenance costs for 2005 is as follows (assuming no unusual unfavorable event in 2005, and thus $D = 0$):

$$Y = \$16,467 + \$1.856 \times 3,600 - \$408.638 \times 0$$
$$= \$23,149$$

The statistical measures are as follows:

R-squared = .772

t-values:

Hours: 2.60

Dummy variable: 22.33

Standard error of the estimate (SE) = $161.27

Ratio of SE to the mean of the dependent variable = 0.71%

Garcia observes that the inclusion of the dummy variable improves R-squared, the t-values, and the SE of the regression. For this reason, he relies on the estimate from the latter regression.

Using Spreadsheet Software for Regression Analysis

Suppose that WinDoor Inc. is developing a regression cost equation for the indirect costs in its plant. WinDoor manufactures windows and doors used in home construction; both products are made in standard and custom sizes. Occasionally, a very large

EXHIBIT 6.9
Indirect Costs, Labor- and
Machine-Hours for
WinDoor Inc.

Date	Total Indirect Costs	Direct Labor-Hours	Machine-Hours
June 2003	$274,500	26,940	2,009
July	320,000	35,690	3,057
August	323,200	32,580	3,523
September	219,900	24,580	1,856
October	232,100	19,950	2,168
November	342,300	34,330	3,056
December	427,800	43,180	3,848
January 2004	231,000	21,290	1,999
February	257,300	28,430	2,290
March	248,700	24,660	1,894
April	248,400	27,870	2,134
May	338,400	31,940	3,145

order substantially increases the direct and indirect costs in a given month. The indirect costs primarily consist of supplies, quality control and testing, overtime, and other indirect labor. Regression is to be used to budget indirect costs for the coming year, primarily for cash management purposes. The management accountant, Charlotte Williams, knows from prior years that both direct labor-hours and machine-hours in the plant are good independent variables for estimating indirect costs. She gathers the data in Exhibit 6.9 for the most recent 12 months.

Williams develops the regression for these data using a spreadsheet program, Excel. To use Excel, she selects the Regression option from the Tools/Data Analysis menu, then selects the X and Y ranges for the independent and dependent variables, and obtains the regression results in Exhibit 6.10 (where L represents labor-hours and M represents machine-hours):

$$Y = \$35,070 + \$5.090 \times L + \$40.471 \times M$$

The statistical measures follow:

R-squared $= .935$

t-values:

Labor-hours: 2.976

Machine-hours: 2.505

Standard error of the estimate $(SE) = \$17,480$

Ratio of SE to mean of the dependent variable $= 6.05\%$

The regression satisfies our statistical criteria: R-squared is relatively high, and the t-values and SE are good. Thus, WinDoor can use the regression for estimates with a reasonable degree of confidence.

Data Requirements and Implementation Problems

LEARNING OBJECTIVE 4
Explain the data requirements and implementation problems of the cost estimation methods.

To develop a cost estimate using regression or any other estimation method, management accountants must consider those aspects of data collection that can significantly affect precision and reliability. Three main issues are (1) data accuracy, (2) time period choice, and (3) nonlinearity.

Data Accuracy

All methods previously explained rely on the accuracy of the data used in the estimation. Whether it be financial data, operating data, or economic indicators (examples shown in Exhibit 6.6), management must carefully consider the source of the data and

EXHIBIT 6.10 **Excel Regression Results for WinDoor Data, Showing Regression Dialog Box**

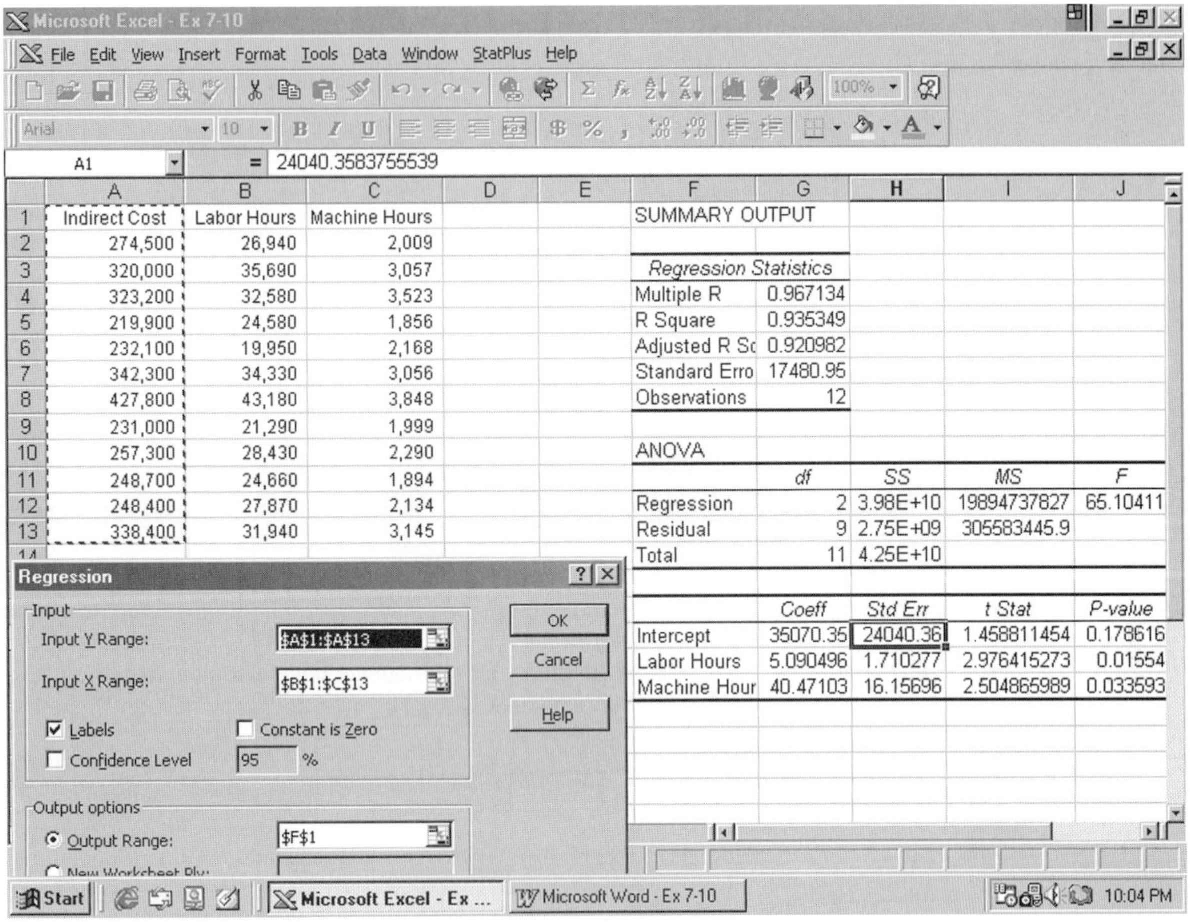

This exhibit shows both the regression results and the dialog box used to produce the regression results shown in the exhibit. Note that the independent variables (*X* Range) and dependent variable (*Y* Range) are entered into the dialog box. Labels are used in the top row of each column of data. The output is presented in the cells to the right and below the selected cell, F1. The dialog box is accessed by choosing **Data Analysis** under the Tools menu in Excel. If you do not find Data Analysis there, you must install it using **Add-Ins . . . ,** which is also under the Tools menu. After selecting **Add-Ins . . . ,** choose to install **Analysis ToolPak,** which contains data analysis and regression.

its reliability. If the source is inside the firm (usually financial and operating data), management can develop reporting requirements to ensure the accuracy of the data. For external economic data, management determines the reliability of data by considering the source. For example, trade and industry associations commonly provide industry and economic data for association members; by reputation, some providers are more reliable than others. Economic data are available from the U.S. government, local and state governments, and research firms and universities; some have better reputations for accuracy than do others. Management accountants must determine how much to rely on the data used in the estimation method.

Selecting the Time Period

1. **Mismatched time periods.** The data for each variable must be from the same time period. Mixing biweekly and monthly data is a problem, as is using data for sales based on the calendar month and for wages expense based on four consecutive weekly periods. Difficulties also arise when supplies are purchased in one period but used in the next.

2. **Length of time period.** The period can vary from daily to weekly or annually. If the period is too short, the chance of mismatch increases because of recording lags or errors. On the other hand, if the period is too long, important short-term relationships in the data might be averaged out, and the regression will not have much explanatory

EXHIBIT 6.11
Adjusting for Trend and Seasonality Using First Difference or a Price Index

| | | Price Index Adjustment | |
| | | Hypothetical Price Index for Supplies Expense | Supplies Expense Adjusted for Price Index |
Supplies Expense	First Difference		
$250	—	1.00	$250/1.00 = $250
310	$60	1.08	310/1.08 = 287
325	15	1.12	325/1.12 = 290

power. Moreover, a longer period reduces the number of data points needed to improve the precision and reliability of the regression. Management accountants must determine which time period best satisfies the competing objectives for a reliable and precise regression.

Nonlinearity Problems

Nonlinearity causes other problems to arise because of certain time-series patterns to the data. These patterns are trend, seasonality, outliers, and data shift.

　　1. **Trend and/or seasonality.** A common characteristic of accounting data is a significant trend that results from changing prices and/or seasonality that can affect the precision and reliability of the estimate. When trend or seasonality is present, a linear regression is not a good fit to the data, and the management accountant should use a method to deseasonalize or to detrend a variable. The most common methods to do this follow:

- Use of a price change index to adjust the values of each variable to some common time period.
- Use of a decomposition technique that extracts the seasonal, cyclical, and trend components of the data series.[11]
- Use of a trend variable. A **trend variable** takes on values of 1, 2, 3, . . . for each period in sequence.
- Replacement of the original values of each of the variables with the first differences. **First difference** for each variable is the difference between each value and the succeeding value in the time series.

A **trend variable** is a variable that takes on values of 1, 2, 3, . . . for each period in sequence.

First difference for each variable is the difference between each value and the succeeding value in the time series.

　　You can see the index approach and the first difference approach in Exhibit 6.11 using the supplies expense data from Exhibit 6.2.

　　Trend is present in virtually all financial time series data used in management accounting because of inflation and growth in the economy. Thus, it is a pervasive issue in the proper development of a regression analysis.

　　2. **Outliers.** As mentioned earlier, when an error in the data or an unusual or nonrecurring business condition affects operations for a given period, the result might be a data point that is far from the others, an outlier. Because outliers can significantly decrease the precision and reliability of the estimate, they should be corrected or adjusted (using, for example, a dummy variable) if it is clear that they are unusual or nonrecurring.

　　3. **Data Shift.** In contrast to the outlier, if the unusual business condition is long lasting, such as the introduction of new production technology or other permanent change, the average direction of the data has a distinct shift that should be included in the estimate. One way to handle this is to use a dummy variable to indicate the periods before and after the shift.

---

[11] An explanation of the decomposition of time series is beyond the scope of this introductory material. Decomposition is presented in basic texts on probability and statistics, such as S. Ross, *Introductory Statistics.*

Summary

Cost estimation is one of the most important activities the management accountant performs in supporting the firm's strategy. It has an important role in developing a strategic competitive position as well as in using value-chain analysis, target costing, and other planning and evaluation contexts within cost management.

To use cost estimation effectively, the management accountant develops and evaluates a cost-estimating model in six steps: (1) define the cost object, (2) determine the cost drivers, (3) collect consistent and accurate data, (4) graph the data, (5) select and apply a cost estimation method, and (6) evaluate the accuracy of the cost estimate.

This chapter presents three estimation methods. The high-low method develops a unique estimation equation using algebra and the representative low and high points in the data. Two statistical methods, work measurement and regression analysis, also are presented. Work measurement is a study of a work activity to measure the time or input required per unit of output. Regression analysis obtains a unique best-fitting line for the data. The chapter's focus is on the proper interpretation of the three key measures of the precision and reliability of the regression: *R*-squared, the *t*-value, and the standard error of the estimate.

In applying any cost estimation method management accountants consider the three main implementation problems: (1) inaccurate data, (2) mismatched data from different time periods and time periods that are too short or too long, and (3) nonlinearity in the data.

The most reliable and accurate method available to the management accountant is regression analysis, which can be solved using spreadsheet software such as Microsoft Excel. An advantage of regression analysis is that its results include quantitative and objective measures of the reliability and accuracy of the regression estimate.

Appendix A

Learning Curve Analysis

LEARNING OBJECTIVE 5
Use learning curves in cost estimation when learning is present.

One prominent example of nonlinear cost behavior is a cost influenced by learning. When an activity has a certain labor component and repetition of the same activity or operation makes the labor more proficient, the task is completed more quickly with the same or a higher level of quality. Learning can occur in a wide variety of ways, from the individual level as new employees gain experience, to the aggregate level in which a group of employees experiences improvement in productivity. We consider the latter instance in this appendix.

A **learning curve analysis** is a systematic method for estimating costs when learning is present.

Costs are affected by learning in a wide variety of contexts, especially in large-scale production settings, such as the manufacture of airplanes and ships. In each case, we can model the expected improvement in productivity and use this information in the estimation of future costs. A **learning curve analysis** is a systematic method for estimating costs when learning is present.

The **learning rate** is the percentage by which average time (or total time) falls from previous levels as output doubles.

One of the first well-documented applications of learning curves occurred in the World War II aircraft industry.[1] Studies showed that the total time to manufacture two airplanes declined by approximately 20 percent of the total time without learning. In other words, the average *per-unit* time to build the first two units was 80 percent of the time for the first unit. For example, if the time to build the first unit is 20 hours, the *average* time to build the first two units is 16 hours (20×0.8), or a total of 32 hours (16×2) for two units. Without learning, it would take 40 hours (20×2). The **learning rate** is the percentage by which average time (or total time) falls from previous levels

[1] Frank J. Andress, "The Learning Curve as a Production Tool," *Harvard Business Review,* January–February 1954; and Harold Asher, "Cost Quality Relationships in the Airframe Industry," Report R–291 (Santa Monica, CA: The RAND Corporation, July 1956).

EXHIBIT 6.12
Average Cost with Learning

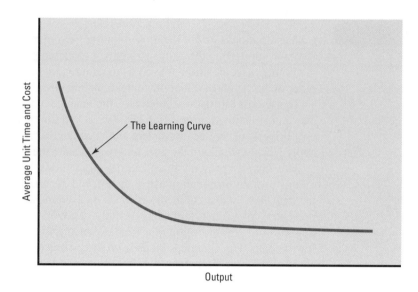

as output doubles. In this example, the rate is 80 percent. The unit cost behavior of the learning curve is illustrated in Exhibit 6.12.

Additional evidence of the practical importance of learning curves is the common reference to start-up costs in corporate annual reports and the financial press. A commonly accepted business principle is that new products and production processes have a period of low productivity followed by increasing productivity. Thereafter, the rate of improvement in productivity tends to decline over time until it reaches some equilibrium level where it remains relatively stable until another change in the product line or production process occurs.[2]

LEARNING CURVES IN SOFTWARE DEVELOPMENT

SofTech, Inc., is a vendor of software for financial analysts. SofTech's development staff recently changed its development language, T-Base, to a new language, Z-Base, which permits faster development and provides certain object-oriented programming benefits. Now SofTech is calculating the learning time needed for its programmers to come up to speed in the new language. These estimates are important because programming costs have increased 10 percent to $65 per hour in the past year and are expected to rise as quickly in the coming years. For purposes of this analysis, SofTech estimates the learning rate for Z-Base to be 80 percent and the initial time for coding 500 lines of good code in Z-Base to be 100 hours. The time and related cost required for developing the first 4,000-line application in Z-Base can be determined by using the learning curve; see Exhibit 6.13.

EXHIBIT 6.13
Softech, Inc.'s Learning Curve for Z-Base

Output (Multiples of 500 Lines)	Average Time (Coding for 500 Lines)	Total Time
500 lines	100 hours	100 hours
1,000 lines	$100 \times .8 = 80$ hours	$80 \times 2 = 160$ hours
2,000 lines	$80 \times .8 = 64$ hours	$64 \times 4 = 256$ hours
4,000 lines	$64 \times .8 = 51.2$ hours	$51.2 \times 8 = 409.6$ hours

[2] As in the World War II airplane production example, the common learning rate is approximately 80 percent. Two conventional models are used in learning curve analysis. One measures learning on the basis of average unit cost, the other on the basis of marginal cost. Both models are conceptually and mathematically similar, although the average cost model tends to lead to lower unit costs. The average cost model is the more common, and for clarity and simplicity, it is the only model we present here. For a full explanation and comparison of the two models, see J. Chen and R. Manes, "Distinguishing the Two Forms of the Constant Percentage Learning Curve Model," *Contemporary Accounting Research*, Spring 1985, pp. 242–52.

REAL-WORLD FOCUS Applications of Learning Curves

Learning curve analysis is commonly used to improve cost estimates in situations when learning is likely to occur. Three example applications follow.

AIRCRAFT GUIDANCE SYSTEMS

One of the earliest applications of the learning curve was in aircraft manufacturing. The British firm Above & Beyond, Ltd., continues this tradition by using the learning curve to estimate the reduction in costs for its development of guidance systems for space shuttles. The firm's engineers estimate the learning rate to be about 87 per-

cent. (G. J. Steven, "The Learning Curve: From Aircraft to Spacecraft?" *Management Accounting* (London), May 1999, pp. 64–65.)

PROJECT MANAGEMENT

When projects involve repetitive operations, the learning curve is applicable, as this study illustrates. (Jean-Pierre Amor and Charles J. Teplitz, "An Efficient Approximation for Project Composite Learning Curves," *Project Management Journal,* September 1998, pp. 28–42.)

Learning rates are obtained by reviewing and analyzing historical data. The methods vary from the simple high-low method to regression analysis based on fitting a nonlinear relationship to the historical data.[3]

Note also that a learning rate of *1 is equivalent to no learning.* A *learning rate of .5 is best interpreted as the maximum learning rate* because the total time for actual production equals the time for a single unit. Thus, the learning rate is always a number greater than .5 and less than 1. Actual case studies reveal that the learning rate most often falls near .8.

WHAT DECISIONS ARE INFLUENCED BY LEARNING?

Because the productivity of labor is a vital aspect of any production process, learning curve analysis can be an important way to improve the quality of a wide range of decisions. For example, when product prices are based in part on costs, learning curves could be used to determine a life-cycle plan for a new product for product pricing. Moreover, learning curves would be helpful in these areas:

1. **The make-or-buy decision (Chapter 9).** When the cost to make a part is affected by learning, the analysis can be used to more accurately reflect the total cost over time of the make option.

2. **Preparation of bids for production contracts; life-cycle costing (Chapter 10).** Learning curves play an important role in ensuring that the contract cost estimates are accurate over the life of the contract.

3. **Cost-volume-profit analysis (Chapter 7).** The determination of a breakeven point might be significantly influenced by the presence of learning.[4] Failing to consider learning causes overstatement of the actual number of units required for breakeven.

4. **Development of standard product costs (Chapters 13 and 14).** When learning occurs, standard costs change over time, and the appropriate labor costs must be adjusted on a timely basis.[5]

5. **Capital budgeting (Chapter 20).** Learning curves capture cost behavior more accurately over the life of the capital investment by including the expected improvements in labor productivity due to learning.

---

[3] For example, see methods described in Patrick B. McKenzie, "An Alternative Learning Curve Formula," *Issues in Accounting Education,* Fall 1987, pp. 383–88. Software can be used to facilitate the use of learning curves. Examples include an Excel add-in Foresee. See Charles D. Bailey, "Estimation of Production Costs and Labor Hours Using an Excel Add-in," *Management Accounting Quarterly,* Summer 2000, pp. 25–31; www.bus.ucf.edu/bailey.

[4] Edward V. McIntyre, "Cost-Volume-Profit Analysis Adjusted for Learning," *Management Science,* October 1977, pp. 149–60.

[5] Jackson F. Gillespie, "An Application of Learning Curves to Standard Costing," *Management Accounting,* September 1981, pp. 63–65.

6. **Budgeting production levels and labor needs (Chapter 8).** Another useful application of learning curves is the development of the annual or quarterly production plan and related labor requirement budget. When the activity or operation is affected by learning, the production and labor budgets should be adjusted accordingly.

7. **Management control (Chapters 17 and 18).** The use of learning curves is important in properly evaluating managers when costs are affected by learning. The evaluation should recognize the pattern of relatively higher costs at the early phase of the product life cycle.

LIMITATIONS OF LEARNING CURVE ANALYSIS

Although learning curve analysis can significantly enhance the ability to predict costs when learning occurs, three inherent limitations and problems are associated with the use of this method.

The first and key limitation of using learning curves is that the approach is most appropriate for labor-intensive contexts that involve repetitive tasks performed for long production runs for which repeated trials improve performance, or learning. When the production process is designed to maximize flexibility and very fast set-up times for manufacturing machinery using robotics and computer controls as many manufacturers now do, the manufacturing setting requires relatively little repetitive labor and consequently relatively little opportunity for learning.

A second limitation is that the learning rate is assumed to be constant (average labor time decreases at a fixed rate as output doubles). In actual applications, the decline in labor time might not be constant. For example, the learning rate could be 80 percent for the first 20,000 units, 90 percent for the next 35,000 units, and 95 percent thereafter. Such differences indicate the need to update projections based on the observed progression of learning.

Third, a carefully estimated learning curve might be unreliable because the observed change in productivity in the data used to fit the model was actually associated with factors other than learning. For example, the increase in productivity might have been due to a change in labor mix, a change in product mix, or some combination of other related factors. In such cases, the learning model is unreliable and produces inaccurate estimates of labor time and cost.

Appendix B

Regression Analysis

LEARNING OBJECTIVE 6
Use statistical measures to evaluate a regression analysis.

This appendix uses an example to explain the development of a regression estimate and the related statistical measures. Then we interpret the statistical measures to assess the precision and reliability of the regression.

THE REGRESSION ESTIMATE

To illustrate the manner in which a regression estimate is obtained, we use the data in Exhibit 6.4 (page 198). Recall that regression analysis finds the unique line through the data that minimizes the sum of the squares of the errors, where the error is measured as the difference between the values predicted by the regression and the actual values for the dependent variable. In this example, the dependent variable, supplies expense (Y), is estimated with a single independent variable, production level (X). The regression for the three data points is

$$Y = a + b \times X = \$220 + \$0.75 \times X$$

The intercept term, labeled a, and the coefficient of the independent variable, labeled b, are obtained from a set of calculations performed by spreadsheet and other programs and are described in basic textbooks on probability and statistics. The calculations themselves are beyond the scope of this text. Our focus is on the derivation and interpretation of the statistical measures that tell management accountants something about the reliability and precision of the regression.

STATISTICAL MEASURES

The statistical measures of the reliability and precision of the regression are derived from an analysis of the variance of the dependent variable. *Variance* is a measure of the degree to which the values of the dependent variable vary about its mean. The term *analysis of variance* is used because the regression analysis is based on a separation of the total variance of the dependent variable into error and explained components. The underlying concept is that in predicting individual values for the dependent variable, the regression is *explaining changes (i.e., variance) in the dependent variable* associated with changes in the independent variable. The variance in the dependent variable that is not explained is called the residual, or *error variance.* Thus, the regression's ability to correctly predict changes in the dependent variable is a key measure of its reliability and is measured by the proportion of explained to error variances. Based on the data in Exhibit 6.4, Exhibit 6.14 shows how the variance measures are obtained.

The first two columns of Exhibit 6.14 show the data for the independent (X) and dependent (Y) variables. Column (3) shows the mean of the dependent variable (YM), and column (4) the regression prediction (YE) for each of the points. The last three columns indicate the three variance measures. Column (5) shows the total variance, or variance of the dependent variable, measured as the difference between each data point and the mean of the dependent variable ($Y - YM$). Column (6) shows the variance explained by the regression ($YE - YM$), and column (7) shows the error variance, ($Y - YE$). The measures in these last three columns are squared and summed to arrive at the desired values for *total* variance, explained variance, and error variance, respectively. The sum of the error and explained variance terms equals total variance. These terms are illustrated in Exhibit 6.15 and the values calculated in Exhibit 6.16.

The three variance terms are the basic elements of the statistical analysis of the regression. This is best illustrated in the analysis of variance table in Exhibit 6.16. The **analysis of variance table** separates the total variance of the dependent variable into both error and explained components. The first two columns of the table show the type and amount of variance for each of the three variance terms. The third column shows the **degrees of freedom** for each component, which represents the number of independent choices that can be made for that component. Thus, the number of degrees of freedom for the explained variance component is always equal to the number of independent variables, and the total degrees of freedom is always equal to the number of data points less 1. The error degrees of freedom equal the total less the explained degrees of freedom.

The fourth column, **mean squared variance**, is the ratio of the amount of the variance of a component (in the second column) to the number of degrees of freedom (in the third column).

The **analysis of variance table** separates the total variance of the dependent variable into both error and explained variance components.

The **degrees of freedom** for each component of variance represent the number of independent choices that can be made for that component.

Mean squared variance is the ratio of the amount of variance of a component to the number of degrees of freedom for that component.

EXHIBIT 6.14 Variance Components for Regression Analysis: Total Variance, Regression Variance, and Error Variance

1	2	3	4	Variance Components		
				5	6	7
Dependent Variable Y	Independent Variable X	Mean of Y (YM)	Regression Prediction for Y (YE)	Total Variance of Y (T) = (Y − YM)	Regression Variance (R) = (YE − YM)	Error Variance (E) = (Y − YE)
250	50	295	257.5	(45)	(37.5)	(7.5)
310	100	295	295.0	15	0.0	15.0
325	150	295	332.5	30	37.5	(7.5)

EXHIBIT 6.15
Variance Components for Regression Analysis

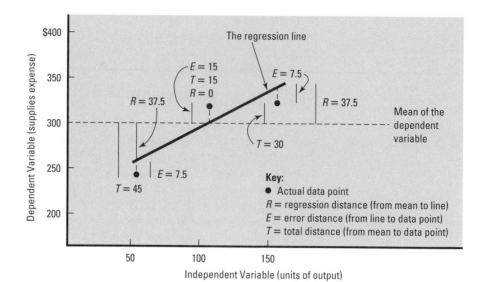

EXHIBIT 6.16
Analysis of Variance Table for Regression Analysis

Source of Variance	Variance of Each Component of the Regression (also called *sum of squares*)	Degrees of Freedom	Mean Squared Variance
Explained (regression)	$37.5^2 + 0^2 + 37.5^2 = 2,812.5$	1	2,812.5
Error	$7.5^2 + 15^2 + 7.5^2 = 337.5$	1	337.5
Total	$(45)^2 + (15)^2 + (30)^2 = 3,150.0$	2	1,575.0

EXHIBIT 6.17
Six Key Statistical Measures

Precision

1. Precision of the regression (measured by the standard error of the estimate)

Reliability

2. Goodness of fit (*R*-squared)
3. Statistical reliability (*F*-statistic)
4. Statistical reliability for each independent variable (*t*-value)
5. Reliability of precision (rank-order correlation)
6 Nonindependence of errors (Durbin-Watson statistic)

The analysis of variance table serves as a useful basis to discuss the key statistical measures of the regression. Of the six principal measures in Exhibit 6.17 (page 201), one measure refers to the precision of the regression and five measures refer to the reliability of the regression. *Precision* refers to the ability of the regression to provide accurate estimates—how close the regression's estimates are to the unknown true value. *Reliability* refers to the confidence the user can have that the regression is valid; that is, how likely the regression is to continue to provide accurate predictions over time and for different levels of the independent variables.

After explaining each of the statistical measures, we summarize the explanations in Exhibit 6.20 (on page 216).

Precision of the Regression

The standard error of the estimate (*SE*) is a useful measure of the accuracy of the regression's estimates. The standard error is interpreted as a range of values around the regression estimate such that we can be approximately 67 percent confident the actual value lies in this range (see Exhibits 6.8A and 6.8B). An inverse relationship, and therefore a trade-off, exists between the confidence level and the width of the interval.

The value of the *SE* for a given regression can be obtained directly from the analysis of variance table as follows:

$$SE = \sqrt{\text{Mean Square error}}$$

$$= \sqrt{337.5} = 18.37$$

The precision and accuracy of the regression improve as the variance for error is reduced and as the number of data points increases, as illustrated in the preceding formula for *SE*.

The standard error of the estimate can also be used to develop confidence intervals for the accuracy of the prediction, as illustrated in Exhibits 6.8A and B. A **confidence interval** is a range around the regression line within which the management accountant can be confident the actual value of the predicted cost will fall. A 67 percent confidence interval is determined by taking the regression line and identifying a range that is 1 standard error distance on either side of the regression line; a 95 percent confidence interval would be determined from 2 standard error distances. Confidence intervals are useful and precise tools for management accountants to describe the degree of precision obtained from the regression.

A **confidence interval** is a range around the regression line within which the management accountant can be confident the actual value of the predicted cost will fall.

Goodness of Fit (*R*-squared)

R-squared (also called the *coefficient of determination*) is a direct measure of the explanatory power of the regression. It measures the percent of variance in the dependent variable that can be explained by the independent variable. *R*-squared is calculated in Exhibit 6.16:

$$R^2 = \frac{\Sigma \text{ of squares (explained)}}{\Sigma \text{ of squares (total)}}$$

$$= \frac{2,812.5}{3,150} = .892$$

The explanatory power of the regression improves as the explained sum of squares increases relative to the total sum of squares. A value close to 1 reflects a good-fitting regression with strong explanatory power.

Statistical Reliability

The **F-statistic** is a useful measure of the statistical reliability of the regression. Statistical reliability asks whether the relationship between the variables in the regression actually exists or whether the correlation between the variables is an accident of the data at hand. If only a small number of data points are used, it is possible to have a relatively high *R*-squared (if the regression is a good fit to the data points), but this offers relatively little confidence that an actual stable relationship exists.

The larger the *F*, the lower the risk that the regression is statistically unreliable. The determination of an acceptable *F*-value depends on the number of data points, but the required *F*-value decreases as the number of data points increase. Most regression software programs show the *F*-value and the related risk score, which should be less than approximately 5 percent. The *F*-statistic can be obtained from the analysis of variance table as follows:

$$F = \frac{\text{Mean square (explained)}}{\text{Mean square (errors)}}$$

$$= \frac{2,812.5}{337.5} = 8.333$$

The *R*-squared value and the *F*-statistic usually tell the same story; that is, they are both favorable or unfavorable. However, if the regression used a very large number of data points (a few hundred or more), it is possible to have a good score for the

The **F-statistic** is a useful measure of the statistical reliability of the regression.

F-statistic but a poor fit based on the R-squared value. The number of data points in such a case is so large that the mean square error is very small (and therefore F is large) although the sum of squares for error is large, and therefore R-squared is poor. In this case, management accountants should interpret the regression as having statistical reliability (it is not by chance), but having perhaps little practical reliability (goodness of fit). That is, the management accountant can be relatively confident that it is a poor regression. The reverse is true for very small samples. The implication is that R-squared and the F-statistic must be interpreted carefully when the sample size is either very small or very large.

Statistical Reliability for Each of the Independent Variables (*t*-value)

The t-value is a measure of the reliability of each independent variable and as such, it has an interpretation very much like that of the F-statistic. The t-value equals the ratio of the coefficient of the independent variable to the standard error of the coefficient for that independent variable. The standard error of the coefficient is not the same as the standard error of the estimate, but it is interpreted in the same way. However, the SE cannot be obtained directly from the analysis of variance table. For the data in Exhibit 6.14, the value of the standard error for the coefficient is .2598.[6] The t-value is thus

$$t = .75/.2598 = 2.8868$$

A t-value larger than 2.0 indicates that the independent variable is reliable at a risk level of approximately 5 percent and is therefore a reliable independent variable to include in the regression. Regression software such as Excel shows the 95 percent confidence range for the coefficient of each of the independent variables. The range of the standard error of the estimate should be relatively small. A small range provides confidence in the accuracy of the coefficient's value.

Reliability of Precision (Nonconstant Variance)

Nonconstant variance is the condition when the variance of the errors is not constant over the range of the independent variable.

For certain sets of data, the standard error of the estimate varies over the range of the independent variable. The variance of the errors is not constant over the range of the independent variable. This is the case, for example, when the relationship between the independent and dependent variables becomes less stable over time. This type of behavior is illustrated in Exhibit 6.18.

If there is non-constant variance, the SE value provided by the regression is not uniformly accurate over the range of the independent variable. To detect nonconstant variance, we calculate the rank-order correlation between the position of the data and the size of the error. The **rank-order correlation** is a statistic that measures the degree to which two sets of numbers tend to have the same order, or rank. A relatively high rank-order correlation is evidence of nonconstant variance. For the data in Exhibit 6.14, the Spearman rank-correlation coefficient is .125, a relatively small correlation that indicates little evidence of nonconstant variance. The calculation of rank-order correlation

The **rank-order correlation** is a statistic that measures the degree to which two sets of numbers tend to have the same order or rank.

[6] The standard error of the coefficient is calculated as follows:

$$\text{Standard error} = SE/(\text{Std. deviation of the independent variable})$$

$$= \frac{18.37}{\sqrt{(50-100)^2 + (100-100)^2 + (150-100)^2}} = .2598$$

EXHIBIT 6.18
Nonconstant Variance

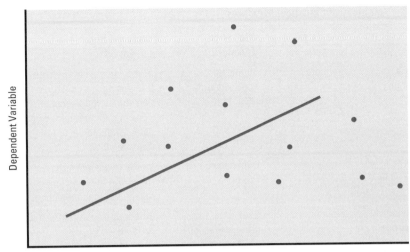

is beyond the scope of this introductory chapter but can be found in many statistics texts.

To fix the problem of nonconstant variance, management accountants should transform the dependent variable with the log or square root to see whether this improves the behavior of the errors. If it does not fix the condition, management accountants should be very cautious in interpreting the *SE* value.

Nonindependent Errors (Durbin-Watson Statistic)

A key assumption of regression is that the relationship between the independent and dependent variables is linear. If the data are nonlinear because of seasonality or a cyclical pattern, for example, the errors are systematically related to each other, that is, are not independent. This assumption is violated frequently because financial data are often affected by trend, seasonality, and cyclical influences. The relationship between the variables might also be inherently nonlinear, as when learning occurs or a multiplicative rather than an additive relationship exists (such as predicting payroll costs from hours worked and wage rates). Then the regression is unreliable and subject to greater than expected estimation errors. One type of nonlinearity (nonindependence of errors) is illustrated in Exhibit 6.19.

A common method that detects nonlinearity is the **Durbin-Watson (DW) statistic.** It is calculated from the amount and change of the errors over the range of the independent

The **Durbin-Watson statistic** is a measure of the extent of nonlinearity in the regression.

EXHIBIT 6.19
Nonindependence of Errors

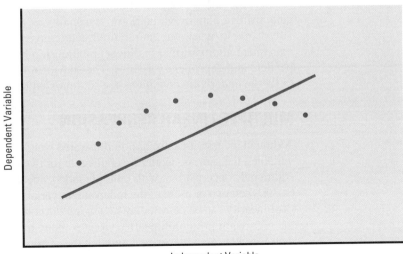

EXHIBIT 6.20 **Summary of Statistical Measures**

Measure Concerns	Statistical Measure	What Is an OK Value?*	What Is the Right Fix If Not OK?	Consequence If Not Fixed
Reliability— Goodness of fit	R-squared	Should be approximately .75 or better	• Add or delete independent variables • If DW is poor, could need transforms (lag, log, first differences, . . .) • Correct measurement errors in the data, for example, cutoff errors, or reporting lags	• Inaccurate estimates
Statistical reliability for the regression	F-statistic	Depends on sample size	• Increase sample size • Other changes as suggested for reliability—goodness of fit	• Inaccurate estimates
Statistical reliability for the independent variables	t-value	Should be greater than 2.0	• Delete or transform the independent variable	• Inaccurate estimates
Precision of the regression	Standard error of the estimates (SE)	Should be small relative to the dependent variable	• Same considerations as for reliability—goodness of fit above	• Inaccurate estimates
Reliability of precision (non constant variance)	Rank-order correlation	Should be small	• Square root or log transform the dependent variable • Add a dummy variable	• SE is unreliable
Reliability— Potential nonlinearity (nonindependence of errors)	Durbin-Watson statistic (DW)	Between 2.0 and 3.0	*For certain series:* • Deseasonalize • Detrend • Use dummy variable for shift *For nonlinear relationship* • Log transform • Some other nonlinear transform	• Inaccurate estimates • SE is unreliable

* The values shown here are useful for a wide range of regressions. The exact values for a specific regression depend on a number of factors including the sample size and the number of independent variables. A recent study of regression analysis applied to 20 different overhead cost accounts showed that most of the R-squared values fall between .83 and .93. The values for the standard error of the estimates averaged 12 percent of the mean of the dependent variable, with most falling between 5 percent and 20 percent. See G. R. Cluskey Jr., Mitchell H. Raiborn, and Doan T. Modianos, "Multiple-Cost Flexible Budgets and PC-Based Regression Analysis," *Journal of Cost Management*, July–August 2000, pp. 35–47.

variable. The DW value falls between zero and 4.0; with 20 or more data points, a value of DW between approximately 1.0 and 3.0 indicates little chance of a nonlinearity as described earlier; values less than 1.0 or greater than 3.0 should indicate the need to study the data and to choose appropriate fixes if necessary.

The problem of nonindependent errors usually can be fixed by deseasonalizing the data, using a dummy variable for seasonality, or using an index to remove the trend. Alternatively, what may be required is to convert a multiplicative relationship to an equivalent additive (that is, linear) relationship by taking the logarithm of the independent and dependent variables. The statistical measures, their indicators, and ways to fix the underlying conditions are summarized in Exhibit 6.20.

MULTIPLE LINEAR REGRESSION

Although the previous discussion illustrated simple linear regression (one independent variable), the same concerns are applicable for two or more independent variables. One additional concern arises with multiple independent variables: multicollinearity, which exists when two or more of the independent variables are significantly correlated. Multicollinearity can be detected by reviewing the correlation values given in the output of the regression. Multicollinearity violates the regression assumption that the independent variables are independent and that the relationships are linear and additive. When present, multicollinearity can show good values of R-squared, but it also can lead management accountants to overestimate the degree of reliability actually present in the regression. Thus, multicollinearity does not so much degrade the estimation performance of the regression as it distorts the confidence that management accountants should have in the regression.

Key Terms

analysis of variance table, *211*	high-low method, *195*	outlier, *198*
confidence interval, *213*	independent variable, *197*	rank-order correlation, *214*
correlation, *201*	learning curve analysis, *207*	regression analysis, *197*
cost estimation, *191*	learning rate, *207*	*R*-squared, *200*
degrees of freedom, *211*	least squares regression, *197*	standard error of the
dependent variable, *197*	mean absolute percentage	estimate, *201*
dummy variable, *200*	error (MAPE), *193*	trend variable, *206*
Durbin-Watson statistic, *215*	mean squared variance, *211*	*t*-value, *200*
first difference, *206*	multicollinearity, *201*	work measurement, *196*
F-statistic, *213*	nonconstant variance, *214*	work sampling, *197*

Comments on Cost Management in Action

Using Regression to Estimate the Value of Commercial Real Estate

Estimating Real Estate Values for Apartment Buildings and Office Buildings

As expected, real estate appraisers performing regression analysis to appraise the value of an apartment building or an office building use as the dominant independent variable the property's past, current, and expected future net operating income (NOI). That is, the chief determinant of the value of the property is its ability to produce cash flows and profits. Other variables regarding the property include its size (as measured by the number of units, number of square feet, number of two-bedroom and one-bedroom apartments, etc.), its age, and the relevant vacancy rate in the property and in the submarket area where it is located. Since the regression analysis is usually built from actual sales numbers over a period of time, these appraisers also use a trend variable to tie the sales price of the property to the year it was sold.

Estimating Real Estate Values for Warehouses and Manufacturing Plants

Similarly, real estate appraisers have developed regression analyses for warehouses and manufacturing plants using their size, age, and location. The NOI variable is usually not relevant. They also use a trend variable to distinguish sales of properties in different years. For example, an analysis of sales value (per square foot) of industrial properties in the Los Angeles area in the early 1990s showed a significant trend variable (−$2.83 per square foot per year); the coefficient on the trend variable was negative because prices were falling during that period. A significant size variable (−$2.43 per square foot, per 100,000 square feet of space) indicated that larger buildings had on average lower sales prices per square foot. Age was also a factor, the coefficient being −$0.41 per square foot per year of age. The location variable was also significant, showing that properties in certain counties in the Los Angeles area (Orange County, San Bernadino, etc.) were predicted to have as much as a $2.32 difference in value per square foot.

Sources: Stephen T. Crosson, Charles G. Dannis, and Thomas G. Thibodeau, "Regression Analysis: A Cost-Effective Approach for the Valuation of Commercial Property," *Real Estate Finance*, Winter 1996; Maxwell O. Ramsland Jr. and Daniel E. Markham, "Market-Supported Adjustments Using Multiple Regression Analysis," *The Appraisal Journal*, April 1998, pp. 181–91; and Stephen C. Kincheloe, "Linear Regression Analysis of Economic Variables in the Sales Comparison and Income Approaches," *The Appraisal Journal*, October 1993.

Self-Study Problems
(For solutions, please turn to the end of the chapter.)

1. Using the High-Low Method

Hector's Delivery Service uses four small vans and six pickup trucks to deliver small packages in the Charlotte, North Carolina, metropolitan area. Hector spends a considerable amount of money on the gas, oil, and regular maintenance of his vehicles, which is done at a variety of service stations and repair shops. To budget his vehicle expenses for the coming year, he gathers data on his expenses and number of deliveries for each month of the current year.

	Total Vehicle Expenses	Total Deliveries
January	$145,329	5,882
February	133,245	5,567
March	123,245	5,166
April	164,295	6,621
May	163,937	6,433
June	176,229	6,681
July	180,553	7,182
August	177,293	6,577
September	155,389	5,942
October	150,832	5,622
November	152,993	5,599
December	201,783	7,433

Required   Use the high-low estimation method to determine the relationship between the number of deliveries and the cost of maintaining the vehicles.

2. Using Regression Analysis

George Harder is the Imperial Foods Company's plant manager of one of the processing plants. George is concerned about the increase in plant overhead costs in recent months. He has collected data on overhead costs for the past 24 months and has decided to use regression to study the factors influencing these costs. He has also collected data on materials cost, direct labor-hours, and machine-hours as potential independent variables to use in predicting overhead.

George runs two regression analyses on these data, with the following results:

	Regression 1 (labor-hours only)	Regression 2 (labor-hours and machine-hours)
R-squared	.65	.58
Standard error	$12,554	$13,793
Standard error as a percent of the dependent variable	12%	14%
t-values		
Materials cost	2.0	−1.6
Labor-hours	4.5	3.8
Machine-hours		1.4

Required   Which of the two regressions is better and why?

3. Using Both High-Low and Regression

John Meeks Company is a medium-size manufacturing company with plants in three small mid-Atlantic towns. The company makes plastic parts for automobiles and trucks, primarily door panels, exterior trim, and related items. The parts have an average cost of $5 to $20. The company has a steady demand for its products from both domestic and foreign automakers and has experienced growth in sales averaging between 10 and 20 percent over the last 8 to 10 years.

Currently, management is reviewing the incidence of scrap and waste in the manufacturing process at one of its plants. Meeks defines scrap and waste as any defective unit that is rejected for lack of functionality or another aspect of quality. The plants have a number of different inspection points, and failure or rejection can occur at any inspection point. The number of defective units is listed in the following table; management estimates the cost of this waste in labor and materials is approximately $10 per unit.

An unfavorable trend appears to exist with regard to defects, and management has asked you to investigate and estimate the defective units in the coming months. A first step in your investigation is to identify the cost drivers of defective parts, to understand what causes them, and to provide a basis on which to estimate future defects. For this purpose, you have obtained these recent data on the units produced, the units shipped, and the cost of sales since these numbers are easily available and relatively reliable on a monthly basis:

	Units Produced (000s)	Cost of Sales (000s)	Units Shipped (000s)	Defective Units
Jan 2003	55	$ 689	50	856
Feb	58	737	53	1,335
Mar	69	886	64	1,610
Apr	61	768	56	1,405
May	65	828	60	1,511
Jun	69	878	64	1,600
Jul	75	962	70	1,570
Aug	81	1,052	76	1,910
Sep	70	1,104	80	2,011
Oct	79	1,224	89	2,230
Nov	82	1,261	92	2,300
Dec	70	1,020	74	1,849
Jan 2004	67	850	62	1,549
Feb	72	916	67	1,669
Mar	85	1,107	80	2,012
Apr	75	968	70	1,756
May	81	1,037	76	1,889
Jun	85	1,103	80	1,650
Jul	92	1,208	87	2,187
Aug	100	1,310	95	2,387
Sep	91	1,380	101	2,514
Oct	101	1,536	111	2,787
Nov	105	1,580	115	2,310
Dec	88	1,270	92	2,311

Required Use the high-low method and regression analysis to estimate the defective units in the coming months and to determine which method provides the best fit for this purpose.

Questions

6–1 Define *cost estimation* and explain its purpose in each of the management functions.

6–2 Explain the assumptions used in cost estimation.

6–3 List the three methods of cost estimation. Explain the advantages and disadvantages of each.

6–4 Explain the implementation problems in cost estimation.

6–5 What are the six steps in cost estimation? Which one is the most important? Why?

6–6 Contrast the use of regression analysis and the high-low method to estimate costs.

6–7 How is cost estimation used in activity-based costing?

6–8 Explain how to choose the dependent and independent variables in regression analysis.

6–9 What are nonlinear cost relationships? Give two examples.

6–10 List four advantages of regression analysis.

6–11 Explain what dummy variables are and how they are used in regression analysis.

6–12 How do we know when high correlation exists? Is high correlation the same as cause and effect?

6–13 What does the coefficient of determination (*R*-squared) measure?

6–14 Cost Classification: Match each cost to the appropriate cost behavior pattern shown in the graphs (a) through (l). Any graph can fit two or more patterns.

1. The cost of lumber used to manufacture wooden kitchen tables.

2. The cost of order fillers in a warehouse. When demand increases, the number is increased, and when demand falls off, the number is decreased.

3. The salary of the plant's quality control inspector, who inspects each batch of products.

4. The cost of water and sewer service to the manufacturing plant. The local municipality charges a fixed rate per gallon for usage up to 10,000 gallons, and a higher charge per gallon for usage above that point.

5. The cost of an Internet connection of $23 per month.

6. The cost of an Internet connection of $10 per month plus $2 per hour of usage above 10 hours.

7. The cost to make copies of a given document at a printing shop, which reduces the per-copy charge for customers who make more than 100 copies of the document.

8. The total cost of manufacturing a new camera over its entire life cycle.

9. To discourage excess usage and to level the demand, especially in peak load times, the local electric utility increases the per-kilowatt-hour charge for each additional 5,000 kilowatt-hours' usage.

10. A clothing store in the SunnyVale Mall pays a fixed rental charge of $1,000 per month plus 2 percent of gross sales receipts.

11. The cost of repair for a machine used in manufacturing.

12. A shoe store in the SunnyVale Mall pays 6 percent of gross sales receipts, up to a maximum of $3,000 per month as a rental charge.

Exercises

6–15 Cost Relationships   Comptech hired Erwin & Associates to design a new computer-aided manufacturing facility that has the capacity to produce 250 computers per day. The variable costs for each computer are $150 and the fixed costs total $62,250 per month.

Required   What is the average cost per unit if the facility normally expects to operate at 80 percent of capacity?

6–16 Cost Relationships   The following costs are for Optical View Inc., a contact lens manufacturer:

Output in Units	Fixed Costs	Variable Costs	Total Costs
250	$4,750	$7,500	$12,250
300	4,750	9,000	13,750
350	4,750	10,500	15,250
400	4,750	12,000	16,750

Required

    1. Graph total cost, total variable costs, and total fixed costs.

    2. Graph the per-unit total cost, per-unit variable cost, and per-unit fixed cost.

    3. Discuss the behavior of the fixed, variable, and total cost.

6–17 Cost Estimation, Average Cost   Maribeth's Cafe bakes croissants that it sells to local restaurants and grocery stores in the Raleigh, North Carolina, area. The average costs to bake the croissants are $0.55 for 500 and $0.50 for 600.

Required   If the total cost function for croissants is linear, what will be the average cost to bake 560?

6–18 Cost Estimation Using Graphs, Service   Lawson Advertising Agency is trying to persuade Kansas City Sailboards Company to spend more money on advertising. The agency's argument is that a positive linear relationship exists between advertising and sales in the sailboard industry. Sue Lawson presents these data taken from industry data for stores similar in size and market share to Kansas City Sailboards:

Advertising Expense	Annual Sales
$2,500	$ 95,000
3,000	110,000
3,500	124,000
4,000	138,000
4,500	143,000
5,000	147,000
5,500	150,000

Required

    1. Graph annual sales and advertising expense.

    2. Do the data prove Sue's point?

6–19 Cost Estimation: High-Low Method   Better Blind Manufacturing Inc. produces blinds and other window treatments for residential homes and offices. The owner is concerned about the maintenance costs for the production machinery, as maintenance costs for the previous fiscal year were higher than he expected. He has asked you to assist him in estimating his future maintenance costs so that he can better predict his firm's profitability. Together, you have determined that the best cost driver for maintenance costs is machine-hours. These data are from the previous fiscal year for maintenance expense and machine-hours:

Month	Expense	Hours	Month	Expense	Hours
1	$2,625	1,575	7	$2,865	1,785
2	2,670	1,590	8	2,830	1,720
3	2,720	1,605	9	2,780	1,695
4	2,750	1,620	10	2,760	1,625
5	2,855	1,775	11	2,590	1,550
6	2,930	1,800	12	2,570	1,525

Required   What is the cost equation for maintenance cost using the high-low method?

6–20 Cost Estimation, High-Low Method   Ethan Manufacturing Inc. produces floor mats for automobiles. The owner, Joseph Ethan, has asked you to assist him in estimating his maintenance costs. Together, you and Joseph determine that the single best cost driver for maintenance costs is machine-hours. These data are from the previous fiscal year for maintenance expense and machine-hours:

Month	Maintenance Expense	Machine-Hours
1	$2,600	1,690
2	2,760	1,770
3	2,910	1,850
4	3,020	1,870
5	3,100	1,900
6	3,070	1,880
7	3,010	1,860
8	2,850	1,840
9	2,620	1,700
10	2,220	1,100
11	2,230	1,300
12	2,450	1,590

Required   What is the cost equation for maintenance cost using the high-low method?

6-21   **Interpreting Regression Results**   Recent research into the cost of various medical procedures has shown the impact of certain complications encountered in surgery on the total cost of patient's stay in the hospital. The researchers used regression analysis and found the following results:

Total Cost for Patient = Constant, plus

   a × length of stay (measured in days), plus

   b × presence of one or more complications (= 1 if true, 0 if false), plus

   c × use of a laparoscope (= 1 if true, 0 if false)

Where:

- a, b, c are coefficients of the regression model, and
- The laparoscope is an instrument somewhat like a miniature telescope with a fiber optic system which brings light into the abdomen. It is about as big around as a fountain pen and twice as long.

The research, based on 57 patients, showed the following regression results:

r-squared: 53%
constant term: $3,719

Coefficients and t-values for independent variables:

	Length of Stay	Complication	Laparoscope
coefficient	$861	$1,986	$908
t-value	10.76	4.89	2.54

Required

1. What is the estimated cost for a patient who has complications and stays in the hospital two days, and whose surgery requires a laparoscope?
2. Which, if any, dummy variables are used in this regression?
3. Comment on the statistical measures for the model.

Problems

6–22   **Cost Estimation, High-Low Method**   Jay Bauer Company specializes in the purchase, renovation, and resale of older homes. Jay Bauer employs several carpenters and painters to do the work for him. It is essential for him to have accurate cost estimates so he can determine total renovation costs before he purchases a piece of property. If estimated renovation costs plus the purchase price of a house are higher than its estimated resale value, the house is not a worthwhile investment.

Jay has been using the home's interior square feet for his exterior paint cost estimations. Recently he decided to include the number of openings—the total number of doors and windows in a house—as a cost driver. Their cost is significant because they require time-consuming preparatory work and careful brushwork. The rest of the house usually is painted either by rollers or spray guns, which are relatively efficient ways to apply paint to a large area. Jay has kept careful records of these expenses on his last 12 jobs:

House	Square Feet	Openings	Cost
1	2,600	13	$3,300
2	3,010	15	3,750
3	2,800	12	3,100
4	2,850	12	3,150
5	4,050	19	4,700
6	2,700	13	3,250
7	2,375	11	2,800
8	2,450	11	2,800
9	2,600	10	2,875
10	3,700	16	4,100
11	2,650	13	3,200
12	3,550	16	3,950

Required

1. Using the high-low cost estimation technique, determine the cost of painting a 3,300-square-foot house with 14 openings. Also determine the cost for a 2,400-square-foot house with 8 openings.

2. Plot the cost data against square feet and against openings. Which variable is a better cost driver? Why?

6–23 Cost Estimation, Machine Replacement, Ethics   SpectroGlass Company manufactures glass for office buildings in Arizona and Southern California. As a result of age and wear, a critical machine in the production process has begun to produce quality defects. SpectroGlass is considering replacing the old machine with a new machine, either brand A or brand B. The manufacturer of each machine has provided SpectroGlass these data on the cost of operation of its machine at various levels of output:

Output (square yards)	Machine A Estimated Total Costs	Machine B Estimated Total Costs
4,000	$ 54,600	$ 70,000
7,000	78,800	100,000
9,000	90,300	115,000
14,000	114,900	137,000
16,000	132,400	146,000
24,000	210,000	192,000

Required

1. If SpectroGlass's output is expected to be 22,000 square yards, which machine should it purchase? At 15,000 square yards?

2. As a cost analyst at SpectroGlass, you have been assigned to complete requirement 1. A production supervisor comes to you to say that the nature of the defect is really very difficult to detect and that most customers will not notice it, so he questions replacing it. He suggests that you modify your calculations to justify keeping the present machine to keep things the way they are and save the company some money. What do you say?

3. Assume that brand A is manufactured in Germany and brand B is manufactured in Canada. As a U.S.–based firm, what considerations are important to SpectroGlass, in addition to those already mentioned in your answer to requirement 1?

6–24 **Cost Estimation, High-Low Method** Antelope Park Amoco (APA) in Antelope Park, Alaska, has noticed that utility bills are substantially higher the colder the average monthly temperature is. The only thing in the shop that uses natural gas is the furnace. Because of prevailing low temperatures, the furnace is used every month of the year (though less in the summer months and very little in August). Everything else in the shop runs on electricity, and electricity use is fairly constant throughout the year.

For a year, APA has been recording the average daily temperature and the cost of its monthly utility bills for natural gas and electricity.

	Average Temperature	Utility Cost
January	31°F	$760
February	41	629
March	43	543
April	44	410
May	46	275
June	50	233
July	53	220
August	60	210
September	50	305
October	40	530
November	30	750
December	20	870

Required Use the high-low method to estimate utility cost for the upcoming months of January and February. The forecast for January is a near record average temperature of 10°F; temperatures in February are expected to average 40°F.

6–25 to 6–29 **Regression Analysis** Problems 6–25 through 6–29 are based on Armer Company, which is accumulating data to use in preparing its annual profit plan for the coming year. The cost behavior pattern of the maintenance costs must be determined. The accounting staff has suggested the use of linear regression to derive an equation for maintenance hours and costs. Data regarding the maintenance hours and costs for the last year and the results of the regression analysis follow:

	Hours of Activity	Maintenance Costs
January	480	$ 4,200
February	320	3,000
March	400	3,600
April	300	2,820
May	500	4,350
June	310	2,960
July	320	3,030
August	520	4,470
September	490	4,260
October	470	4,050
November	350	3,300
December	340	3,160
Sum	4,800	$43,200
Average	400	3,600

Average cost per hour ($43,200/4,800) = $9.00

a (intercept)	684.65
b coefficient	7.2884
Standard error of the estimate	34.469
R-squared	.99724
t-value for b	60.105

Required (6–25) If Armer Company uses the high-low method of analysis, the equation for the relationship between hours of activity and maintenance cost follows:

    a. $y = 400 + 9.0x$

    b. $y = 570 + 7.5x$

    c. $y = 3,600 + 400x$

    d. $y = 570 + 9.0x$

    e. None of the above

(CMA Adapted)

Required (6–26) Based on the data derived from the regression analysis, 420 maintenance hours in a month mean that maintenance costs should be budgeted at

    a. $3,780

    b. $3,461

    c. $3,797

    d. $3,746

    e. None of the above

(CMA Adapted)

Required (6–27) The coefficient of determination for Armer's regression equation for the maintenance activities is

    a. 34.469/49.515

    b. .99724

    c. square root of .99724

    d. $(.99724)^2$

    e. None of the above

(CMA Adapted)

Required (6–28) The percent of the total variance that can be explained by the regression equation is

    a. 99.724%

    b. 69.613%

    c. 80.982%

    d. 99.862%

    e. None of the above

(CMA Adapted)

Required (6–29) At 400 hours of activity, Armer management can be approximately two-thirds confident that the maintenance costs will be in the range of

    a. $3,550.50 to $3,649.53

    b. $3,551.37 to $3,648.51

    c. $3,586.18 to $3,613.93

    d. $3,565.54 to $3,634.47

    e. None of the above

(CMA Adapted)

6–30 **Regression Analysis** Whittenberg Distributors, a major retailing and mail-order operation, has been in business for the past 10 years. During that time, its mail-order operations have grown from a sideline to represent more than 80 percent of the company's annual sales. Of course, the company has suffered growing pains. At times, overloaded or faulty computer programs resulted in lost sales, and scheduling temporary workers to augment the permanent staff during peak periods has always been a problem.

Peter Bloom, manager of mail-order operations, has developed procedures for handling most problems. However, he is still trying to improve the scheduling of temporary workers to take customer telephone orders. Under the current system, Peter keeps a permanent staff of 60 employees who handle the base telephone workload and supplements this staff with temporary workers as needed. The temporary workers are hired on a daily basis; he determines the number needed for the next day the afternoon before based on his estimate of the upcoming telephone volume.

Peter has decided to try regression analysis to improve the hiring of temporary workers. By summarizing the daily labor hours into weekly totals for the past year, he determined the number of workers used each week. In addition, he listed the number of orders processed each week. After entering the data into a spreadsheet, Peter ran two regressions. Regression 1 related the total number of workers (permanent staff plus temporary workers) to the number of orders received. Regression 2 related only temporary workers to the number of orders received. The output of these analyses follows:

$$\text{Regression model: } W = a + b \times T$$

where: W = workers; T = telephone orders

	Regression 1	Regression 2
a	21.938	−46.569
b	.0043	.0051
Standard error of the estimate	3.721	1.495
t-value	1.95	2.04
Coefficient of determination	.624	.755
Durbin Watson statistic	1.33	1.67

Required

1. Peter Bloom estimates that Whittenberg Distributors will receive 12,740 orders during the second week of December.

   a. Predict the number of temporary workers needed for this week using regression 1. Round your answer to the nearest whole number.

   b. Using regression 2, predict the number of temporary workers needed during this week. Round your answer to the nearest whole number.

2. Which of the two regression analyses appears to be better? Explain your answer.

3. Describe at least three ways that Peter Bloom could improve his analysis to make better predictions than either of these regression results provides.

(CMA Adapted)

6–31 **Regression Analysis** Pilot Shop is a catalog business providing a wide variety of aviation products to pilots throughout the world. Maynard Shephard, the recently hired assistant controller, has been asked to develop a cost function to forecast shipping costs. The previous assistant controller had forecast shipping department costs each year by plotting cost data against direct labor-hours for the most recent 12 months and visually fitting a straight line through the points. The results were not satisfactory.

After discussions with the shipping department personnel, Maynard decided that shipping costs could be more closely related to the number of orders filled. He based his conclusion on the fact that 10 months ago the shipping department added some automated equipment. Furthermore, he believes that using linear regression analysis will improve the forecasts of shipping costs. Cost data for the shipping department have been accumulated for the last 25 weeks. He ran two regression analyses of the data, one using direct labor-hours, and one using the number of cartons shipped. The information from the two linear regressions follows:

	Regression 1	Regression 2
Equation	$SC = 804.3 + 15.68DL$	$SC = 642.9 + 3.92NR$
R-squared	.365	.729
Standard error of the estimate	2.652	1.884
t-value	1.89	3.46

where: SC = total shipping department costs

DL = total direct labor-hours

NR = number of cartons shipped

Required

1. Identify which cost function (regression 1 or regression 2) that Pilot Shop should adapt for forecasting total shipping department costs and explain why.

2. If Pilot Shop projects that 600 orders will be filled the coming week, calculate the total shipping department costs using the regression you selected in requirement 1.

3. Explain two or three important limitations of the regression you selected in requirement 1, and identify one or two ways to address the limitations. Specifically include in your discussion the effect, if any, of the global nature of Pilot Shop's business.

(CMA Adapted)

6–32 **Regression Analysis**   United States Motors Inc. (USMI) manufactures automobiles and light trucks and distributes them for sale to consumers through franchised retail outlets. As part of the franchise agreement, dealerships must provide monthly financial statements following the USMI accounting procedures manual. USMI has developed the following financial profile of an average dealership that sells 1,500 new vehicles annually.

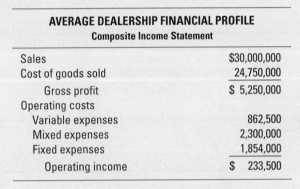

AVERAGE DEALERSHIP FINANCIAL PROFILE	
Composite Income Statement	
Sales	$30,000,000
Cost of goods sold	24,750,000
Gross profit	$ 5,250,000
Operating costs	
Variable expenses	862,500
Mixed expenses	2,300,000
Fixed expenses	1,854,000
Operating income	$ 233,500

USMI is considering a major expansion of its dealership network. The vice president of marketing has asked Jack Snyder, corporate controller, to develop some measure of the risk associated with the addition of these franchises. Jack estimates that 90 percent of the mixed expenses shown are variable for purposes of this analysis. He also suggested performing regression analyses on the various components of the mixed expenses to more definitively determine their variability.

Required

1. Calculate the composite dealership profit if 2,000 units are sold.

2. Assume that regression analyses were performed on the separate components of the mixed expenses and that a coefficient of determination value of .60 was determined as applicable to aggregate mixed expenses over the relevant range.

    a. Define the term *relevant range*.

    b. Explain the significance of an *R*-squared value of .60 to USMI's analysis.

    c. Describe the limitations that may exist in applying the composite-based relationships to specific new dealerships that have been proposed.

    d. Define the *standard error of the estimate*.

3. The regression equation that Jack Snyder developed to project annual sales of a dealership has an *R*-squared of 60 percent and a standard error of the estimate of $4,500,000. If the projected annual sales for a dealership total $28,500,000, determine the approximate 95 percent confidence range for Jack's prediction of sales.

4. What is the strategic role of regression analysis for USMI?

(CMA Adapted)

6–33 **Cost Estimation, High-Low Method, Regression Analysis**   DVD Express is a large manufacturer of affordable DVD players. Management recently became aware of rising costs resulting from returns of malfunctioning products. As a starting point for further analysis, Bridget Forrester, the controller, wants to test different forecasting methods and then use the best one to forecast quarterly expenses for 2004. The relevant data for the previous three years follows:

2001 Quarter	Return Expenses	2002 Quarter	Return Expenses	2003 Quarter	Return Expenses
1	$15,000	1	$16,200	1	$16,600
2	17,500	2	17,800	2	18,100
3	18,500	3	18,800	3	19,000
4	18,600	4	17,700	4	19,200

The result of a simple regression analysis using all 12 data points yielded an intercept of $16,559.09 and a coefficient for the independent variable of $183.22. ($R$-squared $= .27$, $t = 1.94$, $SE = 1128$).

Required

1. Calculate the quarterly forecast for 2004 using the high-low method and regression analyses. Recommend which method Bridget should use.
2. How does your analysis in requirement 1 change if DVD Express manufactures its products in multiple global production facilities to serve the global market?

6–34 **Cost Estimation, High-Low Method, Regression Analysis** Clothes for U is a large merchandiser of apparel for budget-minded families. Management recently became concerned about the amount of inventory carrying costs and transportation costs between warehouses and retail outlets. As a starting point in further analyses, Gregory Gonzales, the controller, wants to test different forecasting methods and then use the best one to forecast quarterly expenses for 2004. The relevant data for the previous three years follows:

Quarter	Warehouse and Transportation Expense ($000)
1/2001	$12,500
2	11,300
3	11,600
4	13,700
1/2002	12,900
2	12,100
3	11,700
4	14,000
1/2003	13,300
2	12,300
3	12,100
4	14,600

The results of a simple regression analysis using all 12 data points yielded an intercept of $11,854.55 and a coefficient for the independent variable of $126.22 ($R$-squared $= .19$, $t = 1.5$, $SE = 974$).

Required

1. Calculate the quarterly forecasts for 2004 using the high-low method and regression analysis. Recommend which method Gregory should use.
2. How does your analysis in requirement 1 change if Clothes for U is involved in global sourcing of products for its stores?

6–35 **Learning Curves** The Air Force Museum Foundation has commissioned the purchase of 16 Four F Sixes, pre–World War II aircraft. They will be built completely from scratch to the exact specifications used for the originals. As further authentication, the aircraft will be made using the technology and manufacturing processes available when the originals were built. Each of the 16 will be flown to Air Force and aviation museums throughout the country for exhibition. Aviation enthusiasts can also visit the production facility to see exactly how such aircraft were built in 1938.

Soren Industries wants to bid on the aircraft contract and asked for and received certain cost information about the Four F Sixes from the Air Force. The information includes some of the old cost data from the builders of the original aircraft. The available information is for the total accumulated time as the first, eighth, and thirty-second aircraft, respectively, were completed.

Output	Total Hours
1	250
8	1,458
32	4,724

Required

1. If Soren Industries expects that the time spent per unit will be the same as it was in 1938, how many hours will it take to build the 16 aircraft for the Air Force Museum Foundation?

2. What is the role of learning curves in Soren Industries' business for contracts such as this?

6–36 Learning Curves   Ben Matthews and David Everhart work for a landscaping company in Twin Cities, Oklahoma. Their principal job is to lay railroad ties to line the sidewalks around apartment complexes and to install flower boxes. The first time Ben and David undertook one of these projects, they spent 17 hours. Their goal by the end of the summer was to be able to finish an apartment complex in 8 hours, one working day. They performed eight of these jobs and had an 80 percent learning curve. Assume that all apartment complexes are approximately the same size.

Required   Did they reach their goal? If not, what would the learning rate have to have been for them to have accomplished their goal?

6–37 Learning Curves   Emotional Headdress (EH) is a Des Moines, Iowa, manufacturer of avant garde hats and headwear. On March 11, 2004, the company purchased a new machine to aid in producing various established product lines. Production efficiency on the new machine increases with the workforce experience. It has been shown that as cumulative output on the new machine increases, average labor time per unit decreases up to the production of at least 3,200 units. As EH's cumulative output doubles from a base of 100 units produced, the average labor time per unit declines by 15 percent. EH's production varies little from month to month and averages 800 hats per month.

Emotional Headdress has developed a new style of men's hat, the Morrisey, to be produced on the new machine. One hundred Morrisey hats can be produced in a total of 25 labor-hours. All other direct costs to produce each Morrisey hat are $16.25, excluding direct labor cost. EH's direct labor cost per hour is $15. Fixed costs are $8,000 per month, and EH has the capacity to produce 3,200 hats per month.

Required

1. Emotional Headdress wishes to set the selling price for a Morrisey hat at 125 percent of the hat production cost. At the production level of 100 units, what is the selling price?

2. The company has received an order for 1,600 Morrisey hats from Smiths, Inc. Smiths is offering $20 for each hat. Should the company accept Smiths' order and produce the 1,600 hats? Explain.

6–38 Learning Curves   Hauser Company, a family-owned business, engineers and manufactures a line of mopeds and dirt bikes under the trade-name Trailite. The company has been in business for almost 20 years and has maintained a profitable share of the recreational vehicle market due to its reputation for high-quality products. In addition, Hauser's engineering department has kept the company in the forefront by incorporating the latest technology in the Trailite bikes. Most subassembly work for the bikes is subcontracted to reliable vendors. However, the final assembly and inspection of all products is performed at Hauser's plant. Hauser recently developed a new braking system for the Trailite Model-500 dirt bike. Because of the company's current availability of production capacity, Jim Walsh, production manager, recommended that the first lot of the new braking system be manufactured in-house rather than by subcontractors. This 80-unit production run has now been completed. The cumulative average labor-hours per unit for the braking system was 60 hours. Hauser's experience with similar products indicates that a learning curve of 80 percent is applicable and that the learning factor can be expected to extend only through the fourth production run (80 per batch). Hauser's direct labor cost is $14.50 per direct labor-hour. Its management must decide whether to continue producing the braking system in its own plant or to subcontract this work. Joyce Lane, Hauser's purchasing agent, has received a proposal from MACQ, a company specializing in component assembly. MACQ has done work in the past for Hauser and has proved to be efficient and reliable. The terms of MACQ's proposal are negotiable, and before beginning discussions with them, Joyce has decided to conduct some relevant financial analysis.

Required

1. Hauser Company has an immediate requirement for a total of 1,000 units of the braking system. Determine Hauser's future direct labor costs to produce the required braking system units if it manufactures the units in-house.

2. A consultant has advised Joyce that the learning rate for this application might be closer to 75 percent. What is the effect on projected costs of using a 75 percent learning curve as opposed to an 80 percent learning curve?

3. What conditions in a manufacturing plant, if present, would offset the potential benefits of the learning curve? What is the strategic role of learning curve analysis for Hauser Company?

(CMA Adapted)

6–39 **Cost Estimation, Regression Analysis**   Plantcity is a large nursery and retail store specializing in house and garden plants and supplies. Jean Raouth, the assistant manager, is in the process of budgeting monthly supplies expense for 2004. She assumes that in some way supplies expense is related to sales, either in units or in dollars. She has collected these data for sales and supplies expenses for June 2001 through December 2003, and has estimated sales for 2004:

Date	Supplies Expense	Sales Units	Sales Dollars
Jun 2001	$2,745	354	$2,009
Jul	3,200	436	2,190
Aug	3,232	525	2,878
Sep	2,199	145	1,856
Oct	2,321	199	2,168
Nov	3,432	543	2,152
Dec	4,278	1,189	2,463
Jan 2002	2,310	212	1,999
Feb	2,573	284	2,190
Mar	2,487	246	1,894
Apr	2,484	278	2,134
May	3,384	498	3,210
Jun	2,945	424	2,850
Jul	2,758	312	2,265
Aug	3,394	485	2,435
Sep	2,254	188	1,893
Oct	2,763	276	2,232
Nov	3,245	489	3,004
Dec	4,576	1,045	3,309
Jan 2003	2,103	104	2,195
Feb	2,056	167	2,045
Mar	3,874	298	2,301
Apr	2,784	398	2,345
May	2,345	187	1,815
Jun	2,912	334	2,094
Jul	2,093	264	1,934
Aug	2,873	333	2,054
Sep	2,563	143	1,977
Oct	2,384	245	1,857
Nov	2,476	232	2,189
Dec	3,364	1,122	3,433

(continued)

Date	Supplies Expense	Sales Units	Sales Dollars
Jan 2004 (estimated)		180	$1,600
Feb		230	2,000
Mar		190	1,900
Apr		450	2,400
May		350	2,300
Jun		350	2,300
Jul		450	2,500
Aug		550	3,000
Sep		300	2,500
Oct		300	2,500
Nov		450	3,200
Dec		950	3,900

Required

1. Develop the regression that Jean should use based on these data and using the regression procedure in Excel or an equivalent regression software program. Evaluate the reliability and precision of the regression you have chosen.

2. What are the predicted monthly figures for supplies expense for 2004?

6–40 Regression Analysis: Cross-Sectional Analysis; Calculation of a Regression Equation   Jim Manzano is the general partner of an investment group that owns a number of commercial and industrial properties, including a chain of 15 convenience stores located in the greater metropolitan area of Cleveland, Ohio. Jim is concerned about the recent increase in inventory theft and waste (he calls it "spoilage") in his stores. Spoilage has increased by more than 20 percent in each of the past two years. In some stores, the main reason is theft; in others, it is damage and vandalism; and in still others, merchandise actually does spoil and must be thrown out. Jim has collected data on spoilage at each of his stores in the recent month and is looking for patterns of spoilage relative to store size (measured by square feet of floor space, number of employees, and total sales) and to the location of the store (location 1 is an area where few arrests for theft, disorderly conduct, or vandalism are made, and location 3 is for areas with high arrests). Jim is not sure, but he suspects, based on his experience managing convenience stores, that a relationship exists among these factors. A colleague told him that a type of regression called "cross-sectional" regression would suit his needs. The cross-sectional regression takes data from a single time period and determines predictions for the dependent variable at different cost objects (in this case, different stores). The objective of the cross-sectional regression is to compare the actual known value for the dependent variable to the predicted value as a basis for assessing the reasonableness of the actual value. This approach is often used in cases similar to Jim's in which the accuracy or reasonableness of the reported dependent variable is a concern. In effect, the cross-sectional regression develops a model that represents the overall patterns in all the data, and the unusual stores will be identified by the largest error terms in the regression. The following data are for the most recent month's operations:

Store Number	Inventory Spoilage	Square Footage	Number of Employees	Location	Sales
1	$ 1,512	2,400	8	1	$ 312,389
2	3,005	3,900	10	2	346,235
3	1,686	3,200	12	1	376,465
4	1,908	3,400	12	1	345,723
5	2,384	3,750	9	2	453,983
6	4,806	4,800	10	3	502,984
7	2,253	3,500	8	1	325,436
8	1,443	3,000	10	1	253,647
9	3,755	5,550	15	2	562,534
10	1,023	2,250	15	1	287,364
11	1,552	2,500	9	1	198,374

(continued)

Store Number	Inventory Spoilage	Square Footage	Number of Employees	Location	Sales
12	2,119	3,500	16	2	$ 333,984
13	5,506	7,500	15	3	673,345
14	3,034	5,700	16	2	588,947
15	772	2,200	8	1	225,364
Totals	$36,758	57,150	173		$5,786,774

Required

1. Using Excel or an equivalent software program, prepare a regression analysis that predicts inventory spoilage at each of the 15 stores. Use any of the four potential independent variables (or a combination) you think appropriate and explain your answer. Also evaluate the precision and reliability of the regression you select.

2. Using the regression equation you developed in requirement 1, determine which of the 15 stores might have inventory spoilage that is out of line relative to the entire chain of stores. Explain your choice.

6–41 **Regression Analysis; Multiplicative Terms** Since the early months of 2000, stock markets throughout the world have been subject to significant swings in value. It is now common for the stock indexes to fluctuate by 2 to 3 percent a day or more. The volatility in stock prices has unnerved investors and has been one of the causes, some say, of reduced stock investment. (See *Business Week,* March 10, 2003, for feature coverage of the issue.)

To investigate the broad effects of volatility in stock markets, researchers are planning to study the effect of the volatility of stocks on investing strategies and related financial measures such as interest rates. Furthermore, it is likely that the relationships will differ from country to country around the world. For example, suppose the researchers gather a sample of stocks from 30 countries and calculate the volatility of each of these stocks, and then come up with a weighted average volatility measure for each country (here volatility could be measured as the standard deviation of the stock price). Also, we look to the International Monetary Fund and similar organizations to determine an overall country credit rating for each of the 30 countries. Here credit rating is measured on a scale from zero to one, with a number closer to one meaning more creditworthy. Suppose the data we have gathered are in the following table. We identify each country as either a developed or an emerging economy because the difference might have a strong impact on the data.

Country	Emerging/ Developed	Volatility	Credit Rating
1	E	55.7	8.3
2	D	23.9	71.2
3	E	27.2	57.0
4	E	55.0	8.7
5	D	20.3	90.9
6	D	20.6	89.1
7	E	30.3	46.1
8	D	22.3	79.2
9	D	22.1	80.3
10	E	47.9	14.1
11	E	54.9	8.8
12	D	20.2	91.6
13	E	36.7	30.0
14	E	24.3	69.1
15	E	31.8	41.6
16	D	24.3	69.4
17	E	46.2	15.8
18	D	28.6	51.8
19	E	38.6	26.4
20	D	23.4	73.7

(continued)

Country	Emerging/Developed	Volatility	Credit Rating
21	E	60.5	6.0
22	D	22.2	79.9
23	D	21.4	84.6
24	D	23.3	74.1
25	E	45.1	17.0
26	E	46.3	15.7
27	D	20.8	87.8
28	D	20.3	90.7
29	E	36.9	29.5
30	E	36.2	31.0

Required

1. Calculate a regression equation using Excel or equivalent software to predict a country's stock volatility based on credit rating and country status (emerging or developed economy). Interpret your results briefly.

2. The results in part 1 assumed two independent variables were truly independent. Suppose on further reflection you believe that the two independent variables are correlated, and that developed countries are likely to have higher credit ratings than emerging countries. Calculate a new regression using, in addition to the current variable, the following new variable: the product of country status and credit rating. If the two variables are correlated this new variable should be an important factor in the regression, with a significant t value. What did you find?

6–42 Regression Analysis in Tax Court Cases   Since at least the late 1960s, the court systems in the United States and elsewhere have accepted regression analysis as evidence in court cases. In many instances, however, because of limitations or errors in developing the regression analysis, tax courts question or deny the regression evidence. A study was performed recently to determine the factors in the regression analysis that the court considered in determining whether regression evidence was admissible.

Required   What factors regarding the development of a regression analysis do you suspect the tax courts considered in determining the acceptability of a regression analysis as evidence?

Solutions to Self-Study Problems

1. Using the High-Low Method

Begin by graphing the data to determine whether there are any unusual (i.e., seasonal) patterns or outliers in Exhibit 6.21.

The graph shows no unusual patterns or outliers, so the high-low estimate can be determined directly from the low point (March) and the high point (December) as follows:

To determine the slope of the line (unit variable cost)

$$(\$201,783 - \$123,245)/(7,433 - 5,166) = \$34.644 \text{ per delivery}$$

To determine the intercept

$$\$201,783 - 7,433 \times \$34.644 = -\$55,726$$

$$\$123,245 - 5,166 \times \$34.644 = -\$55,726$$

The estimation equation is

$$\text{Vehicle costs} = -\$55,726 + \$34.644 \times \text{Number of deliveries/Month}$$

Note that the intercept is a negative number, which simply means that the relevant range of 5,166 to 7,433 deliveries is so far from the zero point (where the intercept is) that the intercept cannot be properly interpreted as a fixed cost. The estimation equation therefore is useful only within the relevant range of approximately 5,000 to 7,500 deliveries and should not be used to estimate costs outside that range.

EXHIBIT 6.21
Plot of Data for Hector's Delivery Service

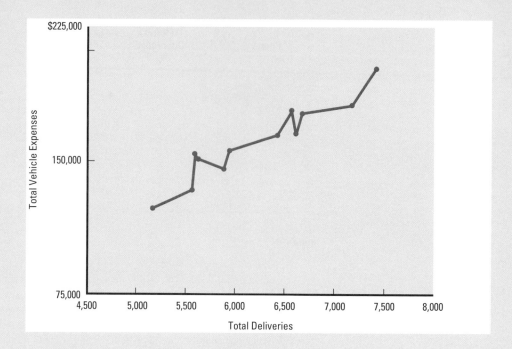

2. Using Regression Analysis

All relevant criteria favor the first regression based on higher *R*-squared and *t*-values and lower standard error. Moreover, the sign on the materials cost variable in regression 2 is negative, which is difficult to explain. This variable should have a direct relationship with overhead; thus, the sign of the variable should be positive. The reason for the improvement of regression 1 over regression 2 might be that machine-hours are highly correlated with either materials costs, labor-hours, or both, thus causing multicollinearity. By excluding machine-hours as an independent variable, George reduced or removed the multicollinearity, and the regression improved as a result. He should therefore use regression 1.

3. Using Both High-Low and Regression

Begin by graphing the data for the number of defective units, as shown in Exhibit 6.22. The objective is to identify any unusual patterns that must be considered in developing an estimate.

Exhibit 6.22 shows that the number of defective units varies considerably from month to month and that a steady increase has occurred over the past two years. Knowing that the production level also has been increasing (as measured either by cost of sales, units produced, or units shipped), we

EXHIBIT 6.22
Defective Units from January 2003 to December 2004

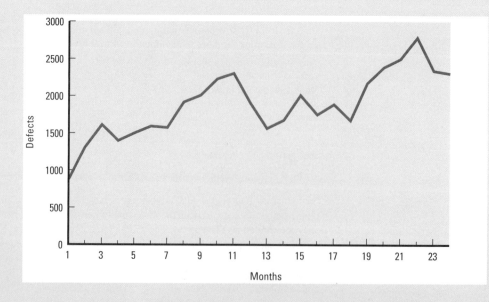

EXHIBIT 6.23

Defective Units vs. Production Level from January 2003 to December 2004

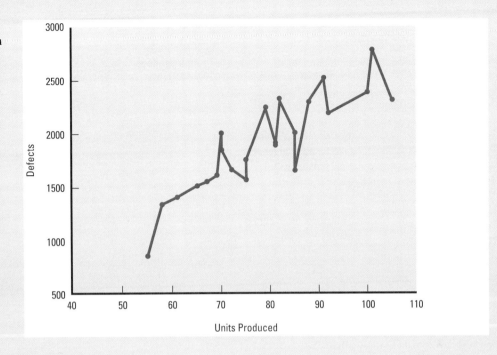

now want to determine whether the relationship between defects and production level (Exhibit 6.23) has changed.

We begin with units produced as the independent variable, since it should have the most direct relationship with defects; the other independent variables can be tried later. The second graph (Exhibit 6.23) makes clear that a relationship exists between units produced and the number of defects.

The next step is to quantify this relationship with the high-low method and regression analysis. We begin with the high-low analysis. For Exhibit 6.23, we identify February 2003 and December 2004 as representative low and high periods, respectively.

We calculate the high-low estimate as follows (these two points are not the absolute lowest and highest points, but they produce a line that is representative of the data):

$$\text{slope} = (2{,}311 - 1{,}335)/(88 - 58) = 32.533$$

And

$$\text{Intercept} = 2{,}311 - 32.533 \times 88 = 1{,}335 - 32.533 \times 58 = -552$$

Thus, the estimation equation is

$$\text{Number of defects} = -552 + 32.533 \times \text{Production level}$$

The high-low estimate is subject to the limitations of subjectivity in the choice of high and low points and because it uses only those two data points to develop the estimate. Regression is thus performed to provide a more precise estimate. Thus, the next step is to obtain a regression analysis from the previous data and to assess the precision and reliability of the regression estimate. The regression can be completed with a spreadsheet program or any of a number of available software systems. The results for three regression analyses are presented in Exhibit 6.24. The dependent variable in each case is the number of defective units.

Regression 1 has the following independent variables: cost of sales, units shipped, and units produced. R-squared and SE are OK, but we observe that all three t-values are less than 2.0, indicating unreliable independent variables. Because a priori we expect correlation among these variables and because of the low t-values, we suspect multicollinearity among these variables. To reduce the effect of multicollinearity, we try regression 2, which removes the variable units shipped since that variable is likely to be least associated with defective units and has among the lowest of the t-values. R-squared for regression 2 is essentially the same as for regression 1, although SE improves very slightly, and the t-value for cost of sales is now OK. The results of regression 3, with the cost of sales variable only, show that SE and the t-value improve again while R-squared is unchanged. Because it has the best SE and t-values, and a very good R-squared, the third regression is the best choice.

EXHIBIT 6.24   Regressions for the Number of Defects

Intercept	Coefficient of Independent Variable	*t*-value for Independent Variable	*R*-squared	Standard Error of the Estimate
Regression 1				
103.20			.883	161
	−38.974 (units shipped)	−.44		
	−2.849 (units produced)	−.38		
	4.702 (cost of sales)	.72		
Regression 2				
92.24			.881	158
	−2.230 (units produced)	−.309		
	1.837 (cost of sales)	4.54		
Regression 3				
43.95			.881	155
	1.720 (cost of sales)	12.77		

CHAPTER SEVEN

Cost-Volume-Profit Analysis

After studying this chapter, you should be able to . . .

1. Explain cost-volume-profit (CVP) analysis, the CVP model, and the strategic role of CVP analysis
2. Apply CVP analysis for breakeven planning
3. Apply CVP analysis for revenue and cost planning
4. Apply CVP analysis for activity-based costing
5. Employ sensitivity analysis to more effectively use CVP analysis when actual sales are uncertain
6. Adapt CVP analysis for multiple products
7. Apply CVP analysis in not-for-profit organizations
8. Identify the assumptions and limitations of CVP analysis and their effect on the proper interpretation of the results

For some companies, just about each product or service is new and different. This is true for SFX Entertainment, Inc. (www.sfx.com), the world's largest provider of live entertainment events. SFX produces live entertainment, mostly musical entertainment, in more than 70 locations. Each show offers a new opportunity for SFX to be profitable, but careful planning is necessary to achieve success. A key part of this planning for SFX is to use cost-volume-profit analysis, the topic of this chapter. SFX uses cost-volume-profit (CVP) analysis to project estimated profits for each live event, given the company's projections about attendance; that is, CVP analysis shows the relationship between volume of attendance and the event's related costs and profits.

LEARNING OBJECTIVE 1

Explain cost-volume-profit (CVP) analysis, the CVP model, and the strategic role of CVP analysis.

Some of SFX's events are planned on a fixed-fee basis; that is, the entertainer is paid a fixed amount for the performance that is not tied to attendance. Other events are planned so that the entertainer receives a payment based on attendance. The fixed-fee arrangement is somewhat riskier for SFX because it bears the risk of low attendance and therefore low profits or losses; of course, the upside is that SFX does well if attendance is high. In contrast, the entertainer paid on the basis of attendance shares some of the risk.

For fixed-fee events, SFX uses attendance projections and cost-volume-profit analysis to carefully project costs and profits and to plan levels of advertising and other expenses. This type of planning is critical for SFX's overall success and profitability.

Cost-Volume-Profit Analysis

Cost-volume-profit (CVP) analysis
is a method for analyzing how various operating decisions and marketing decisions will affect net income.

Cost-volume-profit (CVP) analysis is a method for analyzing how operating decisions and marketing decisions affect net income based on an understanding of the relationship between variable costs, fixed costs, unit selling price, and the output level. CVP analysis has many applications:

- Setting prices for products and services.
- Introducing a new product or service.
- Replacing a piece of equipment.

- Deciding whether to make or buy a given product or service.
- Performing strategic what-if analyses.

CVP analysis is based on an explicit model of the relationships between its three factors—costs, revenues, and profits—and how they change in a predictable way as the volume of activity changes. The CVP model is

$$\text{Profit} = \text{Revenues} - \text{Total costs}$$

or equivalently, since total costs include both fixed and variable cost elements:

$$\text{Revenues} = \text{Fixed costs} + \text{Variable costs} + \text{Profit}$$

Now, replacing revenues with the number of units sold times price, and replacing variable cost with unit variable cost times the number of units sold, the CVP model is

$$\text{Units sold} \times \text{Price} = \text{Fixed cost}$$
$$+ \text{Units sold} \times \text{Unit variable cost}$$
$$+ \text{Profit}$$

For easier use, the model is commonly shown in a symbolic form

where: Q = units sold

v = unit variable cost

f = total fixed cost

p = unit selling price

N = operating profit (profits *exclusive* of unusual or nonrecurring items and income taxes)

$$p \times Q = f + v \times Q + N$$

Contribution Margin and Contribution Income Statement

The **unit contribution margin** is the difference between unit sales price and unit variable cost and is a measure of the increase in profit for a unit increase in sales.

Effective use of the CVP model requires an understanding of three additional concepts: the contribution margin, the contribution margin ratio, and the contribution income statement. The contribution margin is both a unit and a total concept. The **unit contribution margin** is the difference between unit sales price and unit variable cost:

$$p - v = \text{Unit contribution margin}$$

The **total contribution margin** is the unit contribution margin multiplied by the number of units sold.

The unit contribution margin measures the increase in profit for a unit increase in sales. If sales are expected to increase by 100 units, profits should increase by 100 times the contribution margin. The **total contribution margin** is the unit contribution margin multiplied by the number of units sold.

For example, suppose that Household Furnishings, Inc. (HFI), a manufacturer of home furnishings, is interested in developing a new product, a wooden TV table, that would be priced at $75 and would have variable costs of $35 per unit. The investment would require new fixed costs of $5,000 per month. HFI expects sales of 2,400 units in the first year and 2,600 units in the second year. The data for HFI are summarized in Exhibit 7.1.

The unit contribution margin for each table would be $40 ($75 − $35). Using the unit contribution margin, we see that if HFI expects to sell 2,400 tables in 2003, it can

EXHIBIT 7.1

Data for Household Furnishings, Inc. (HFI): TV Table

	Per Unit	2003	2004
Fixed cost		$60,000	$60,000
Revenue	$75		
Variable cost	35		
Planned production		2,400 units	2,600 units
Planned sales		2,400 units	2,600 units

expect to increase total contribution margin in 2003 by $96,000 ($40 × 2,400) and operating profit by $36,000 ($96,000 − $60,000 fixed cost). In 2004 the profits increase as sales increase by 200 units, from 2,400 to 2,600 units. Since fixed costs are the same in both years, the increase in profits from 2003 to 2004 is equal to the change in total contribution margin from 2003 to 2004, that is, unit contribution of $40 times the increase in units sold, or $8,000 ($40 contribution per unit × 200 units).

The **contribution margin ratio** is the ratio of the unit contribution margin to unit sales price $(p - v)/p$.

A measure of the profit contributions per sales dollar is the **contribution margin ratio,** which is the ratio of the unit contribution margin to unit sales price $(p - v)/p$. The contribution margin ratio for HFI's proposed TV table is 53.33% = ($75 − $35)/$75. The ratio identifies the amount of increase (or decrease) in profits caused by a given increase (or decrease) in sales dollars. What is the effect on profits of an increase of the $15,000 in sales from 2003 to 2004? We can quickly calculate that profits will increase by $8,000 ($15,000 × 0.5333) from 2003 to 2004.

The **contribution income statement** focuses on variable costs and fixed costs, in contrast to the conventional income statement in Chapter 3, which focuses on product costs and nonproduct costs.

A useful way to show the information developed in CVP analysis is to use the contribution income statement. The **contribution income statement** begins with revenues and subtracts variable and fixed costs to obtain the total contribution margin and net income, respectively. In contrast, the conventional income statement that we prepared in Chapter 3 begins with revenues and subtracts product costs and nonproduct costs to obtain gross margin and net income, respectively. Exhibit 7.2 shows the contribution income statement for HFI for the years 2003 (2,400 units sold) and 2004 (2,600 units sold). Note that the sales increase of 200 units and $15,000 caused an $8,000 increase in profits as predicted by the contribution margin and contribution margin ratio. The key advantage of the contribution income statement is that it provides an easy and accurate prediction of the effect of a change in sales on profits. This is not possible with the conventional income statement, which does not separate variable and fixed costs.

EXHIBIT 7.2 **Contribution Income Statements for HFI's Proposed TV Table**

	2003		2004			
	Amount	Percent	Amount	Percent	Change	Notes
Sales	$180,000	100.00%	$195,000	100.00%	$15,000	
Variable costs	84,000	46.67	91,000	46.67	7,000	
Contribution margin	$ 96,000	53.33%	$104,000	53.33%	$ 8,000	53.33% is the contribution margin rate
Fixed costs	60,000		60,000		0	
Profit	$ 36,000		$ 44,000		$ 8,000	$8,000 = 0.5333 × $15,000

Strategic Role of CVP Analysis

CVP analysis can help a firm execute its strategy by providing an understanding of how changes in its volume of sales affect costs and profits. Many firms, especially cost leadership firms, compete by increasing volume (often through lower prices) to achieve lower overall operating costs, particularly lower unit fixed costs. CVP analysis provides a means to predict the effect of sales growth on profits. It also shows the risks in increasing volumes in this manner—more fixed costs and less flexibility if volumes fall.

Also, CVP analysis is important in using both life-cycle costing and target costing (Chapter 10). In life-cycle costing, CVP analysis is used in the early stages of the product's cost life cycle to determine whether the product is likely to achieve the desired profitability. Similarly, CVP analysis can assist in target costing at these early stages by showing the effect on profit of alternative product designs at expected sales levels.

In addition, CVP analysis can be used at later phases of the life cycle, during manufacturing planning, to determine the most cost-effective manufacturing process. Such manufacturing decisions include when to replace a machine, what type of machine to buy, when to automate a process, and when to outsource a manufacturing operation. CVP analysis is also used in the final stages of the cost life cycle to help determine the

REAL-WORLD FOCUS   The High Cost of Low Loyalty

Recent studies on the cost of obtaining and serving customers over the entire product life cycle have highlighted the very high cost to acquire customers in some industries. Some estimates show that increasing the customer retention rate by a modest 5 percent can improve profits by as much as 95 percent. One study showed that the cost to acquire a customer averaged between $50 and $80 in three industries: consumer electronics/appliances, groceries, and apparel. The years to breakeven for each customer varied from approximately one year in the apparel industry to more than four years in the consumer electronics/appliance industry. These firms are careful to use breakeven analysis to study all phases of the product life cycle for a new product or a marketing promotion.

In Internet-based retailing, breakeven analysis can be particularly important: It costs 20 to 40 percent more for e-tailers to acquire customers than for brick-and-mortar retailers. However, the cost of serving the customers, the downstream costs, are significantly lower for e-tailers than for other retailers. The bottom line—customer retention and customer loyalty are critical for e-tailers. This is the lesson learned by the most successful ones, including Dell, Amazon.com, and eBay and by other Internet-based businesses such as America Online. For example, Amazon.com has a strong reputation for good customer service, including its one-click ordering. eBay has taken special steps to ensure the reliability of its transactions and to prevent fraud. The competitive strategy for these firms is to differentiate themselves from others by providing superior customer service. Customers appreciate these efforts and respond with their loyalty.

Source: Frederick F. Reichheld and Phil Schefter, "E-Loyalty: Your Secret Weapon on the Web," *Harvard Business Review,* July–August 2000, pp. 105–13.

EXHIBIT 7.3
Strategic Questions Answered by CVP Analysis

1. What is the expected level of profit at a given sales volume?
2. What additional amount of sales is needed to achieve a desired level of profit?
3. What will be the effect on profit of a given increase in sales?
4. What is the required funding level for a governmental agency, given desired service levels?
5. Is the forecast for sales consistent with forecasted profits?
6. What additional profit would be obtained from a given percentage reduction in unit variable costs?
7. What increase in sales is needed to make up a given decrease in price to maintain the present profit level?
8. What sales level is needed to cover all costs in a sales region or product line?
9. What is the required amount of increase in sales to meet the additional fixed charges from a proposed plant expansion?
10. What additional sales are needed to improve profits by a desired amount?

best marketing and distribution systems. For example, CVP analysis can be used to determine whether paying salespeople on a salary basis or a commission basis is more cost effective. Similarly, it can help to assess the desirability of a discount program or a promotional plan. Some of the strategic questions answered by CVP analysis are outlined in Exhibit 7.3.

CVP analysis also has a role in strategic positioning. A firm that has chosen to compete on cost leadership needs CVP analysis primarily at the manufacturing stage of the cost life cycle. The role of CVP analysis here is to identify the most cost-effective manufacturing methods, including automation, outsourcing, and total quality management. In contrast, a firm following the differentiation strategy needs CVP analysis in the early phases of the cost life cycle to assess the profitability of new products and the desirability of new features for existing products.

CVP Analysis for Breakeven Planning

LEARNING OBJECTIVE 2
Apply CVP analysis for breakeven planning.

We first survey the plot, then draw the model;
And when we see the figure of the house,
Then we must rate the cost of the erection;
Which, if we find outweighs ability,
What do we then but draw anew the model.

William Shakespeare, Henry IV, Part II, Act 1

The starting point in many business plans is to determine the **breakeven point,** the point
at which revenues equal total costs and profit is zero. This point can be determined by
using CVP analysis. The CVP model is solved by inserting known values for v, p, and
f, setting N equal to zero, and then solving for Q. We can solve for Q in two ways: the
equation method and the contribution margin method. Each method can determine the
breakeven point in units sold or sales dollars.

Equation Method: For Breakeven in Units

The equation method uses the CVP model directly. For example, the equation for the
analysis of HFI's sale of TV tables is

$$P \times Q = f + v \times Q + N$$
$$\$75 \times Q = \$5,000 + \$35 \times Q$$

Solving for Q and assuming $N = 0$, we determine that the breakeven point is $Q = 125$
TV tables per month (1,500 units per year).

$$(\$75 - \$35) \times Q = \$5,000$$
$$Q = \$5,000/(\$75 - \$35)$$
$$Q = \$5,000/\$40 = 125 \text{ units per month}$$

The contribution to profit per TV table is measured directly by the unit contribution
margin, $p - v$, which is \$40 per table. So, since at sales of 125 units the profit is zero,
at 126 units the profit is \$40 (one unit past breakeven at \$40), at 127 units the profit
is $2 \times \$40 = \$80$, and so on. Using the unit contribution margin gives us a quick way
to determine the change in profit for a change in sales units. At the 128-unit level,
profit is

Sales: 128 units at \$75/unit	\$9,600
Less:	
Variable costs: 128 at \$35/unit	4,480
Contributing margin costs	\$5,120
Fixed costs	5,000
Total profit	\$ 120

Equation Method: For Breakeven in Dollars

Sometimes units sold, unit variable cost, and sales price are not known, or it is impractical to determine them. For example, suppose that a firm has many products and
is interested in finding the overall breakeven level for all products taken together. It is
not practical to find the breakeven in units for each product, but it is possible to find
the breakeven in sales dollars for all products. We use the equation method in a revised
form, where Y is the breakeven point in *sales dollars*:

$$Y = (v/p) \times Y + f + N$$

Using algebra, we can see that this model is equivalent to the model used earlier for
breakeven in units, except that Q is replaced by Y/p (i.e., sales in dollars $= Y = Q \times p$). Continuing with the HFI data in Exhibit 7.2, assume that we do not know that price
is \$75 and that unit variable cost is \$35; instead, we know only total variable cost
(\$84,000) and total sales (\$180,000). We can obtain the ratio, $v/p = 0.4667$
(\$84,000/\$180,000), and solve for breakeven in dollars:

$$Y = 0.4667 \times Y + \$5,000$$
$$Y = \$9,375 \text{ per month}$$

REAL-WORLD FOCUS Breakeven Analysis in Community Banking

In a competitive business such as community banking, management carefully plans to ensure the profitability of new products and services. New locations of a branch bank in a supermarket represent a key part of some community banks' growth strategy. To make this decision, banks must determine the amount of funds and fees that a specific supermarket location will generate and then determine the expected revenues and expenses from that funding level. This analysis requires estimates of the direct expenses of opening and maintaining the branch as well as the interest expense on funds developed at the branch and any increase in indirect expenses caused by opening the branch. The analysis often shows that the branch will not be profitable unless its fee income is relatively high. The following analysis shows how projections of deposits, interest revenue and expense, and direct and indirect expense can be used to project the amount of fee revenue needed for breakeven; in this example, the required fee revenue is $125,000 per year.

BREAKEVEN ANALYSIS: BRANCH BANK, SUPERMARKET LOCATION

Average Deposits, First Year of Operations (projected)

Gross funds	$7,500,000
Less: Nonearning funds	250,000
Net funds provided	$7,250,000

Projected Income Statement, First Year of Operation*

Interest revenue from new funds		$ 525,000
Fee revenue (required for breakeven)		**125,000**
Total revenue		$ 650,000
Expenses		
Interest expense	$345,000	
Direct expenses	200,000	
Indirect expenses	105,000	650,000
Net income		$ 0

*Projections for direct and indirect expense amounts and for interest revenue and expense are based on the expense and revenue experience of similar branch banks, given the projected funding level.

Source: Tom Flynn, "The Supermarket Branch Revisited," *Banking Journal*, October 1997 (www.banking.com/aba/community_1097.asp).

Contribution Margin Method

A convenient method for calculating the breakeven point is to use the equation in its equivalent algebraic form (derived by solving the model for Q):

$$Q = \text{Fixed costs/Unit contribution margin}$$

$$= \frac{f + N}{p - v}$$

The contribution margin method (so-called because the contribution margin is the denominator of the ratio) produces the same result as the equation method (for $N = 0$):

$$Q = (\$5,000)/(\$75 - \$35) = 125 \text{ units per month}$$

The contribution margin method can also be used to obtain breakeven in dollars, using the contribution margin ratio (replacing $p \times Q$ with Y and solving for Y)

$$Y = \frac{F + N}{(p - v)/p}$$

where:

$(p - v)/p =$ the contribution margin ratio

For the HFI example, the contribution margin ratio is 0.5333 and

$$Y = \$5,000/0.5333 = \$9,375 \text{ per month}$$

Some people find the equation method easier to use, and others prefer to use the contribution margin method. Use the method with which you are most comfortable. Both methods produce the same results.

The **CVP graph** illustrates how the levels of revenues and total costs change over different levels of output.

CVP Graph and the Profit-Volume Graph

Breakeven analysis is illustrated graphically in Exhibit 7.4. It shows the CVP graph at the top and the profit-volume graph beneath. The **CVP graph** illustrates how the

EXHIBIT 7.4
The CVP Graph (A) and the Profit-Volume Graph (B)

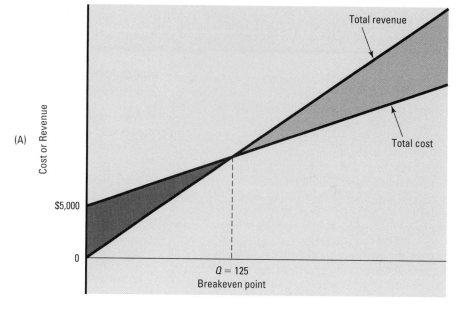

(A)

Cost or Revenue

Total revenue

Total cost

$5,000

0

$Q = 125$
Breakeven point

Output volume

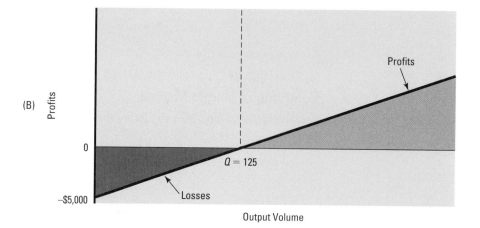

(B)

Profits

Profits

0

$Q = 125$

−$5,000

Losses

Output Volume

levels of revenues and total costs change over different levels of output. Note in the CVP graph that at output levels lower than 125 units, the revenue line falls below the cost line, resulting in losses. In contrast, all points above the 125-unit level show profits.

The **profit-volume graph** at the lower portion of the exhibit illustrates how the level of profits changes over different levels of output. At 125 units, profits are zero, and positive profits appear for output levels greater than 125. The slope of the profit-volume line is the unit contribution margin; therefore, the profit-volume graph can be used to read directly how total contribution margin, and therefore profits, change as the output level changes.

> The **profit-volume graph** illustrates how the level of profits changes over different levels of output.

Summary of Breakeven Methods

The Equation Methods

1. Breakeven in units (Q = sales in units)

$$p \times Q = v \times Q + f + N$$

2. Breakeven in dollars (Y = sales in dollars)

$$Y = (v/p) \times Y + f + N$$

The Contribution Margin Methods

3. Breakeven in units −

$$\frac{f + N}{p - v}$$

4. Breakeven in dollars =

$$\frac{f + N}{(p - v)/p}$$

CVP Analysis for Revenue and Cost Planning

LEARNING OBJECTIVE 3
Apply CVP analysis for revenue and cost planning.

CVP analysis can be used to determine the level of sales needed to achieve a desired level of profit. The two possible objectives are revenue planning and cost planning.

Revenue Planning

CVP analysis assists managers in revenue planning to determine the revenue required to achieve a desired profit level. For example, if HFI's management needs to know the sales volume necessary to achieve $48,000 in annual profits, we substitute $60,000 for fixed costs and $48,000 for desired profit; the solution in units is

$$Q = \frac{f + N}{p - v} = \frac{\$60,000 + \$48,000}{\$75 - \$35} = 2,700 \text{ units per year}$$

The solution in sales dollars is

$$p \times Q = \$75 \times 2,700 = \$202,500 \text{ per year}$$

Cost Planning

For cost planning decisions, the manager knows the value of Q and the desired profit but needs to find the value of the required variable cost or fixed cost. Four examples follow.

Trade-offs between Fixed and Variable Costs

To facilitate target costing, CVP analysis is used to determine the most cost-effective trade-off between different types of costs. To continue with the HFI example, assume sales of 2,700 units per year. Management is now considering the purchase of a new piece of production machinery that will reduce variable costs but also increase fixed costs by $2,250 per month. How much must unit variable costs fall to maintain the current level of profit, assuming that sales volume and all other factors remain the same?

$Q = 2,700$ units

$p = \$75$

$v =$ an unknown (previously $35)

$f = \$5,000 + \$2,250 = \$7,250$ per month ($87,000 per year)

$N = \$48,000$ per year

Now, instead of solving for Q (which is given as 2,700 units), we solve for v, as follows:

$$Q = \frac{f + N}{p - v}$$

$$p - v = \frac{f + N}{Q}$$

$$v = p - \frac{f + N}{Q}$$

$$v = \$75 - (\$87,000 + \$48,000)/2,700 = \$25$$

REGIONAL DENTAL PRACTICE

Katherine G. Collier, owner of a $1.3 million-grossing dental practice in Baltimore, uses breakeven analysis to evaluate the profitability of her business as the volume of patients increases. In a recent instance, the analysis convinced her that a planned expansion of her practice to an additional medical office was not likely to be profitable, and she canceled the expansion plans.

A PIZZA FRANCHISE

Christopher Lau saved his money from cooking, serving, and delivering pizzas with the dream of owning a franchise of the locally popular Blackjack Pizza Restaurant. Christopher used his knowledge as a business student to study the cost-volume relationships in the pizza business. He concluded that he needed to gross about $8,000 per week, or about 1,217 pies a week to break even given his planned investment in a Blackjack franchise.

ANALYSIS OF SOCIAL SECURITY RETIREMENT BENEFITS

By using data from the U.S. Social Security Administration (www.ssa.gov), a person thinking about retiring can develop a breakeven model to determine when to apply for benefits. The question is, if one delays applying for benefits until after age 62 (the earliest one can apply for benefits), how long will it take for the total of those larger (due to applying later) payments to add up to the total that would have been received by applying earlier? A convenient website provides the answer (www.social-security-table.com). For example, a person deciding whether to retire at the age of 65 or at 70 can use the analysis in the following graph. This analysis shows that retirees who survive beyond the breakeven age of 82 would receive greater lifetime benefits (not adjusted for the time value of money).

Total Cumulative Retirement Benefits at Different Ages

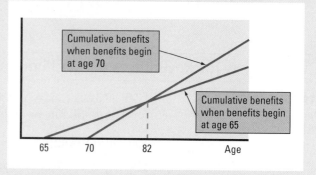

BREAKEVEN IN THE MUSIC BUSINESS

Although popular recording artists are very profitable to the music industry, developing unknown talent can be very costly and risky. One example is the artist, Carly Hennessy. MCA invested $2.2 million in Carly, an investment it has not yet recovered. Industry experts say that a major-label album must sell a breakeven 500,000 copies to recover the average investment. Unfortunately, of the 6,455 new albums released in 2001, only 100 sold more than 500,000 copies, and more than 6,000 sold fewer than 100,000. Because a relatively small number of artists keep the industry profitable, its challenge is finding new profitable artists.

Sources: "The Pizza Franchise Was His Dream; Then the 'Unfathomable,'" *Wall Street Journal*, June 23, 1999, p. 1; Jennifer Ordonez, "MCA Spent Millions on Carly Hennessy—Haven't Heard of Her?" *The Wall Street Journal*, February 20, 2002, p. 1.

In effect, for sales and profits to remain unchanged with the increase in fixed costs, unit variable costs must fall from $35 to $25.

Sales Commissions and Salaries

Another cost planning use of CVP analysis is to determine the most cost-effective means to manage downstream costs such as selling costs. To illustrate, HFI management is reviewing sales salaries and commissions and finds that $1,000 of the monthly $5,000 fixed costs is for sales salaries, that $7.50 of the $35.00 of unit variable cost is a 10 percent sales commission, and that $27.50 of variable cost is not commission based. Suppose that the salespeople are asking for a $450 increase in salary. Management responds that the salaries can be raised only if the commission rate is decreased. How much must management reduce the commission rate to keep profits the same, assuming that sales volume and all other factors remain unchanged?

With the proposed changes in variable and fixed costs to accommodate the new salary and commission plan, fixed costs increase by $450 per month and variable costs decrease as a result of the decrease in the commission rate, r:

$$v = \text{Commission rate} \times \text{Sales price}$$
$$+ \text{ Other noncommission-based unit variable costs}$$

$$v = r \times \$75 + \$27.50$$

And:

$$f = \text{Current monthly fixed costs} + \text{Increase in monthly salary}$$

$$f = \$5,000 + \$450 = \$5,450 \text{ per month, or } \$65,400 \text{ per year}$$

Now we use the CVP model to solve for v:

$$Q = \frac{f + N}{p - v}$$

$$v = p - \frac{f + N}{Q}$$

and substituting for v and f with $N = \$48,000$ and $Q = 2,700$ as before:

$$r \times \$75.00 + \$27.50 = \$75.00 - (\$65,400.00 + \$48,000.00)/2,700$$

$$r = 0.0733$$

In this situation, the manager must reduce the commission rate from 10 to 7.33 percent to keep profits the same and pay an additional monthly salary of $450 to the salespeople.

Including Income Taxes in CVP Analysis

The manager's decisions about costs and prices usually must include income taxes because taxes affect the amount of profit for a given level of sales. In the HFI example if we assume that the average tax rate is 20 percent, to achieve the desired annual *after-tax* profit of $48,000, HFI must generate before-tax profits of at least $60,000 [$48,000/(1 − .2)]. Thus, when taxes are considered, the CVP model is as follows, where the average tax rate is t:

$$Q = \frac{f + \dfrac{N}{(1-t)}}{(p - v)}$$

or

$$Q = \frac{\$60,000 + \$48,000/(1 - 0.2)}{\$75 - \$35} = 3,000 \text{ units per year}$$

This amount is an increase of 300 units over the 2,700 units required for the before-tax profit level.

CVP Analysis for Activity-Based Costing

LEARNING OBJECTIVE 4
Apply CVP analysis for activity-based costing.

The conventional approach to CVP analysis is to use a volume-based measure, that is, a measure based on units of product manufactured and sold. The preceding discussion has assumed a volume-based approach. An alternative approach is activity-based costing. Activity-based costing identifies cost drivers for detailed-level indirect cost activities, such as machine setup, materials handling, inspection, and engineering. In contrast, the volume-based approach combines the costs of these activities and treats them as fixed costs since they do not vary with output volume.

Activity-based costing provides a more accurate determination of costs because it separately identifies and traces indirect costs to products rather than combining them in a pool of fixed costs as the volume-based approach does. Returning to the HFI example, we show how CVP analysis can be adapted when activity-based costing is used.

The conventional, volume-based CVP analysis provides:

$$Q = (\$60,000 + 48,000)/(\$75 - \$35) = 2,700 \text{ units}$$

How does the activity-based CVP analysis work? Suppose that the cost accounting staff has been able to trace approximately $10,000 of last year's fixed costs to batch-level activities such as machine setup and inspection. This estimate was made when the firm was operating at 100 batches per year. These costs can be traced directly to each batch, although not to each unit of output. The staff has also learned that this year's production of 3,000 units is to be produced in batches of 30 units, so 100 batches will be produced again this year. We assume that batch-level costs increase in proportion to an increase in the number of batches produced during the year; that is, $100 per batch ($10,000/100). The activity-based CVP model is thus developed in the following way.

First, we define new terms for fixed cost: $f = f^{VB} + f^{AB}$, where:

> f^{VB} = the volume-based fixed costs, the portion of fixed costs that *do not* vary with the activity cost driver, $50,000 ($60,000 − $10,000)
>
> f^{AB} = the portion of fixed costs that do vary with the activity cost driver, $10,000; we assume that $10,000 is necessary for 3,000 units of output, requiring 100 production batches of 30 units each

Second, we define the following terms:

> v^{AB} = the cost per batch for the activity-based cost driver, $10,000/100 = $100 per batch
>
> b = the number of units in a batch, 30 units (3,000/100)
>
> v^{AB}/b = the cost per unit of product for batch-related costs when the batch is size b; v^{AB}/b = $3.33 ($100.00/30)

Third, the CVP model for activity-based costing is

$$Q = \frac{f^{VB} + N}{p - v - (v^{AB}/b)}$$

Fourth, substituting data from the HFI example,

$$Q = \frac{\$50,000 + \$48,000}{\$75 - \$35 - \$100/30} = 2{,}673 \text{ units}$$

$$= 89.1 \text{ batches } (2{,}673/30)$$

This method assumes that we hold batch size constant and vary the number of batches as the total volume changes. The number of batches must be a whole number, however. In this case, 90 batches are required for the 2,673 units; 89 batches of 30 units each (89 × 30 = 2,670 units) plus one additional batch. The analysis should be recalculated for exact breakeven using 90 batches as follows, where the cost of 90 batches is 90 × $100 per batch = $9,000:

$$Q = \frac{\$50,000 + \$9,000 + \$48,000}{\$75 - \$35} = 2{,}675 \text{ units}$$

The solution for the activity-based model is slightly lower than for the volume-based model (2,675 units versus 2,700 units) because the ABC method allows for lower total batch-level costs. Instead of a fixed batch-level cost of $10,000 under the volume-based approach, the ABC method allows the batch-level costs to decrease (or increase) as volume decreases (or increases).

To illustrate the effect of batch size on the solution, suppose that production is scheduled in smaller batches of 20 units and that batch costs continue to be $100 each. How many units must be sold now to earn $48,000? The answer is 2,800 units and 140 batches, as shown here. Note that the cost of batch-level activities has now increased substantially, from $10,000 for 100 batches to $14,000 for 140 batches.

$$Q = (\$50,000 + \$48,000)/(\$75 - \$35 - \$100/20)$$

$$= 2{,}800 \text{ units}$$

or

$$= 140 \text{ batches } (2{,}800/20) \text{ of } 20 \text{ units each}$$

We also could determine this from the following, using $14,000 for total batch level costs:

$$Q = \frac{\$50{,}000 + \$14{,}000 + \$48{,}000}{\$75 - \$35} = 2{,}800 \text{ units}$$

Notice that the number of units to achieve breakeven increases when the batch size is decreased. This is due directly to the increase in the total batch-level costs as batch size is decreased. CVP analysis based on activity-based costing can provide a more precise analysis of the relationships among volume, costs, and profits by considering batch-level costs.[1]

Sensitivity Analysis Of CVP Results

LEARNING OBJECTIVE 5
Employ sensitivity analysis to more effectively use CVP analysis when actual sales are uncertain.

CVP analysis becomes an important strategic tool when managers use it to determine the sensitivity of profits to possible changes in costs or sales volume. If costs, prices, or volumes can change significantly, the firm's strategy might also have to change. For example, if there is a risk that sales levels will fall below projected levels, management would be prudent to reduce planned investments in fixed costs (i.e., investments to increase production capacity). The additional capacity will not be needed if sales fall, but it would be difficult to reduce the fixed costs in the short term. **Sensitivity analysis** is the name for a variety of methods that examine how an amount changes if factors involved in predicting that amount change. Sensitivity analysis is particularly important when a great deal of uncertainty exists about the potential level of future sales volumes, prices, or costs. We present three of the most common methods for sensitivity analysis: (1) what-if analysis using the contribution margin and contribution margin ratio, (2) the margin of safety, and (3) operating leverage.[2]

Sensitivity analysis
is the name for a variety of methods used to examine how an amount will change if factors involved in predicting that amount change.

What-if Analysis of Sales: Contribution Margin and Contribution Margin Ratio

What-if analysis
is the calculation of an amount given different levels for a factor that influences that amount.

What-if analysis is the calculation of an amount given different levels for a factor that influences that amount. It is a common approach to sensitivity analysis when uncertainty is present. Many times it is based on the contribution margin and the contribution margin ratio. For example, the contribution margin ($40) and contribution margin ratio (0.5333) for HFI provide a direct measure of the sensitivity of HFI's profits to changes in volume. Each unit change in volume affects profits by $40; each dollar change in sales affects profits by $0.5333. Use of a spreadsheet such as Excel and tools such as data tables, scenarios, and goal-seek can facilitate the analysis.[3] An example of a data table for HFI is shown in Exhibit 7.5; units sold, fixed cost, and price are held constant, and we examine the effect of changes in unit variable cost on profits.

Margin of Safety

The margin of safety
is the amount of sales above the breakeven point.

The **margin of safety** is the amount of sales above the breakeven point:

$$\text{Margin of safety} = \text{Planned sales} - \text{Breakeven sales}$$

[1] See the discussion of CVP analysis for activity-based costing in Lawrence M. Metzger, "The Power to Compete: The New Math of Precision Management," *The National Public Accountant,* May 1993, pp. 14–32; and Robert C. Kee, "Implementing Cost-Volume-Profit Analysis Using an Activity-Based Costing System," *Advances in Management Accounting* 10 (2001), pp. 77–94.

[2] Other approaches to sensitivity analysis go beyond the coverage of this text and include analytical methods and spreadsheet simulation methods; see Jimmy E. Hilliard and Robert A. Leitch, "Breakeven Analysis of Alternatives under Uncertainty," *Management Accounting,* March 1977, pp. 53–57; and David R. Fordham and S. Brooks Marshall, "Tools for Dealing with Uncertainty," *Management Accounting,* September 1997, pp. 38–43.

[3] Data tables, scenarios, and goal-seek are functions of Microsoft Excel. Use of these tools in what-if analysis is explained in Stephanie M. Bryant, "Hey, What If...?" *Journal of Accountancy,* June 2000, pp. 35–45.

EXHIBIT 7.5
What-If Sensitivity Analysis for HFI, Inc. Using a Data Table

Units Sold	Unit Variable Cost	Fixed Cost	Price	Profit
1,500	$30	$60,000	$75	7,500
1,500	35	60,000	75	—
1,500	40	60,000	75	−7,500
1,500	45	60,000	75	−15,000

Returning to the HFI example, assume that the planned number of sales of TV tables is 3,000 units per year; since the breakeven quantity is 1,500 units, the margin of safety is

$$\text{Margin of safety in units} = 3,000 - 1,500 = 1,500 \text{ units}$$

or

$$\text{Margin of safety in sales dollars} = 1,500 \times \$75 = \$112,500$$

The margin of safety also can be used as a ratio, a percentage of sales:

$$\text{Margin of safety ratio} = \text{Margin of safety/Planned sales}$$
$$= 1,500/3,000 = .5$$

The **margin of safety ratio** is a useful measure for comparing the risk of two alternative products, or for assessing the risk in any given product.

The **margin of safety ratio** is a useful measure for comparing the risk of two alternative products or for assessing the risk in any given product. The product with a relatively low margin of safety ratio is the riskier of the two products and therefore usually requires more of management's attention.

Operating Leverage

Changes in the contemporary manufacturing environment include improved production techniques through automation, work-flow enhancements, and other techniques. As these changes take place, the nature of CVP analysis also changes. For example, in a fully automated production environment, labor costs are less important, and variable costs consist primarily of materials costs. In some cases, such as the manufacture of certain electrical parts and components, the materials cost is also relatively low so that fixed costs are very high relative to total cost. In this context, CVP analysis can play a crucial strategic role because profits are more sensitive to the number of units manufactured and sold. In other manufacturing operations, with low fixed costs and relatively high variable costs, profits are less sensitive to changes in sales, and CVP is relatively less important.

Consider two firms: One has relatively low fixed costs and relatively high unit variable costs (a labor-intensive firm), and the other has relatively high fixed costs and relatively low variable costs (a fully automated firm). Sample data for two such firms are shown in Exhibit 7.6.

These two situations are compared in Exhibit 7.7A (relatively high fixed costs) and Exhibit 7.7B (relatively low fixed costs). Note that the breakeven point is the same in each case, 50,000 units. However, if we examine the profit at 25,000 units above breakeven or the loss at 25,000 units below breakeven, a strong contrast emerges. For the firm with relatively high fixed costs (Exhibit 7.7A), the loss at 25,000 units is relatively large, $250,000, while the profit at 75,000 units is also relatively large,

EXHIBIT 7.6
Contrasting Data for Automated and Labor-Intensive Firms

	Automated: High Fixed Cost	Labor Intensive: Low Fixed Cost
Fixed cost/year	$500,000	$150,000
Variable cost/unit	2	9
Price	12	12
Contribution margin	10	3

EXHIBIT 7.7A
CVP Graph for a Firm with Relatively High Fixed Costs

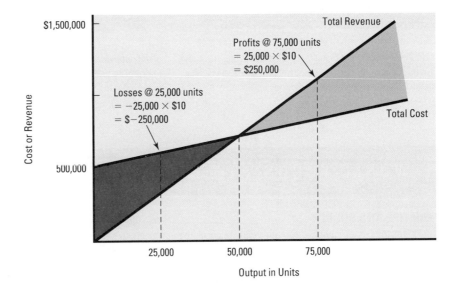

EXHIBIT 7.7B
CVP Graph of a Firm with Relatively Low Fixed Costs

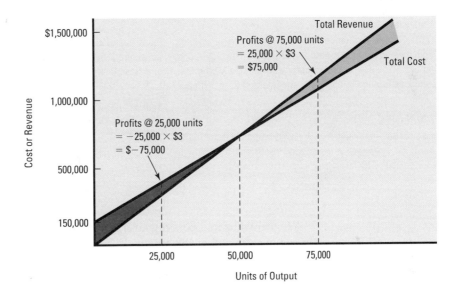

$250,000. In contrast, when fixed costs are low (Exhibit 7.7B), the loss at 25,000 units is only $75,000 and the profit at 75,000 units is only $75,000.

Clearly, a firm with high fixed costs is riskier because profits are very strongly affected by the level of activity. High profits are earned beyond breakeven, but high losses result from falling below breakeven. In this context, CVP analysis is particularly important in planning the use of new manufacturing technologies that have the potential to change the relationship between fixed and variable costs.

The potential effect of the risk that sales will fall short of planned levels, as influenced by the relative proportion of fixed to variable manufacturing costs, can be measured by **operating leverage,** which is the ratio of the contribution margin to profit. For the HFI data (Exhibit 7.2), the operating leverage for 2003 is as follows:

Operating leverage
is the ratio of the contribution margin to profit.

$$\text{Operating leverage} = \text{Contribution margin/Before Tax Profit}$$

$$= \$96,000/\$36,000 = 2.667$$

Operating leverage of 2.667 means that since HFI's sales increased 8.33 percent ($15,000/$180,000) from 2003 to 2004, profits should increase by 22.22 percent (2.667 × 8.33%). A quick calculation demonstrates that profit has increased by 22.22 percent ($8,000/$36,000).

At the end of 2001 only 23 percent of dot-com start-ups were profitable. For many of them, the struggle was to build revenues in a weak economy. Yet some were very successful. How did they accomplish it? What is the nature of the cost structure for dot-coms that is likely to influence their ability to deal with fluctuations in the economy and in overall customer demand?

REAL-WORLD FOCUS   Operating Leverage and Corporate Strategy

GOODYEAR TIRE AND RUBBER

Learning hard lessons from intensive foreign competition in the 1980s, many large U.S. manufacturers trimmed their manufacturing capacity. When demand surged in the 1990s, they did not expand their plants, but achieved the additional capacity by using overtime labor and machine utilization approaching 24 hours a day, every day. The additional variable costs of overtime labor, expensive overnight materials shipments, high employee turnover, and sky-rocketing machine repair and maintenance costs were judged to be a better strategy than the commitment to hard-to-lose fixed costs required to expand capacity. The automotive industry was especially affected, as was Goodyear Tire and Rubber, Inc., and Intermet Corp, a manufacturer of auto parts.

UNITED AIRLINES

While most airlines—including United—were profitable in the boom times of the 1990s, they have suffered huge losses with the falloff in air traffic since 2001. The large fixed cost structure in the industry has aggravated these losses for these carriers. While Southwest has prospered on a lean cost structure, American Airlines has made strong efforts to reduce its capital investments. Meanwhile, carriers such as United have large fixed costs associated with their fleets of aircraft and due to their inflexible labor costs which are largely based on air traffic volume. Between 1995 and 1999 things were not much better. The carriers filled 72.4 percent of their seats, just 2 percentage points more than their breakeven level of 70.4 seats. During these years, airline profits came from a relatively small number of passengers over breakeven—the airlines were highly leveraged and close to breakeven.

Source: "Just-in-Time Manufacturing Is Working Overtime," *Business Week,* November 6, 1999, p. 36; Robert Lowenstein, "Into Thin Air," *The New York Times Magazine,* February 17, 2002, pp. 40–45; Wendy Zellner, "The Airlines Unlikely Catalyst for Change," *Business Week,* March 17, 2003, p. 44; and "Bob Crandall, an American Gladiator," *Business Week,* April 27, 1998, p. 44.

A higher value for operating leverage indicates a higher risk in the sense that a given change in sales will have a relatively greater impact on profits. When sales volume is strong, a high level of leverage is desirable, but when sales begin to fall, a lower level of leverage is preferable. Each firm chooses the level of operating leverage that is consistent with its competitive strategy. For example, a firm with a dominant position in its market might choose a high level of leverage to exploit its advantage. In contrast, a weaker firm might choose the less risky low-leverage strategy.

CVP Analysis with Multiple Products

LEARNING OBJECTIVE 6
Adapt CVP analysis for multiple products.

One simplifying assumption made in the chapter to this point is to develop the CVP model for only a single product. How does the analysis change if we must deal with two or more products? What if the two or more products share the same fixed costs? Can we still calculate a breakeven value for each product? This section adapts the CVP model to answer questions such as these.

Our adaptation of the CVP model requires one key assumption: The sales of the product will *continue at the same sales mix.* That is, the sales of each product will remain at the same proportion of total sales.

Assuming a constant sales mix allows us to treat the two or more products as one combined product mix by computing a weighted-average contribution margin. The weighted-average contribution margin or contribution market rate is used to determine the total sales necessary to attain the desired operating result.

To illustrate, we use the example of Windbreakers, Inc., which sells light-weight sport/recreational jackets. Windbreakers has three products, Calm, Windy, and Gale.

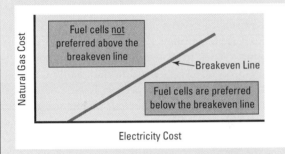
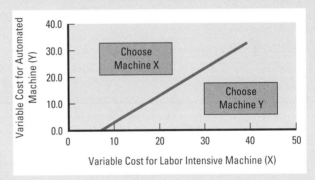
Relevant information for these products is in Exhibit 7.8. The total fixed costs for the period are expected to be $168,000.

From this information, we can calculate the weighted-average contribution margin ratio as follows, using the ratio of sales relative to total sales for each product.

$$0.5(0.2) + 0.4(0.25) + 0.1(0.1) = 0.21$$

The breakeven point for all three products can be calculated as follows:

$$Y = \$168,000/0.21 = \$800,000$$

EXHIBIT 7.8
Sales and Cost Data for Windbreakers, Inc.

	Calm	Windy	Gale	Total
Last period's sales	$750,000	$600,000	$150,000	$1,500,000
Percent of sales	50	40	10	100%
Price	$ 30	$ 32	$ 40	
Unit variable cost	24	24	36	
Contribution margin	$ 6	$ 8	$ 4	
Contribution margin ratio	0.20	0.25	0.10	

This means that for Windbreakers to breakeven, $800,000 of all three products must be sold in the same proportion as last year's sales mix. The sales for each product are as follows:

For Calm	0.5($800,000) = $400,000	(13,334 jackets at $30)
For Windy	0.4($800,000) = 320,000	(10,000 jackets at $32)
For Gale	0.1($800,000) = 80,000	(2,000 jackets at $40)
Total	$800,000	

The sale of jackets in the correct sales mix produces exactly the breakeven contribution margin of $168,000:

$$\$6(13,334) + \$8(10,000) + \$4(2,000) = \$168,000$$

For practicality, this approach is also best utilized with a small number of products. With a large number of products, the best approach is to approximate the overall contribution margin ratio (perhaps by product group or by knowledge of mark-up rates) and determine the overall breakeven in sales dollars.

CVP Analysis for Not-For-Profit Organizations

LEARNING OBJECTIVE 7
Apply CVP analysis in not-for-profit organizations.

Not-for-profit organizations and service firms can also use CVP analysis. To illustrate, consider a small mental health agency experiencing financial difficulty. Orange County Mental Health Center's financial support comes from the county, whose funding is falling because of a recession in the local economy. As a result, the county commissioners have set an across-the-board budget cut of about 5 percent for the new fiscal year. The center's funding was $735,000 last year and is projected to be approximately $700,000 next year. Its director figures that variable costs (including medications, handout publications, and some administrative costs) amount to approximately $10 per visit for the almost 300 patients who regularly see counselors at the center. All other costs are fixed, including salaries for the counselors, record-keeping costs, and facilities costs. How will the budget cuts affect the level of services the center provides?

To answer this question, we must determine precisely the center's activity with the associated fixed and variable costs. Although we could define activity in a variety of ways, we choose the number of patient visits as a logical measure of the center's activity. The director estimates 13,500 visits last year and that unit variable costs are constant at $10 per visit in the range of 10,000 to 14,000 visits per year; total variable costs were therefore $135,000 ($10 × 13,500) last year. We determine total fixed costs for last year:

$$\text{Funding} = \text{Total cost}$$
$$= \text{Total fixed costs} + \text{Total variable costs}$$
$$\$735,000 = \text{Total fixed costs} + \$135,000$$
$$\text{Total fixed costs} = \$600,000$$

Now the director can analyze the effect of the budget change on the center's service levels. At the $700,000 budget level expected for next year, the activity level is approximately 10,000 visits. Total cost of $700,000 less fixed cost of $600,000 leaves variable costs of $100,000; thus, $100,000/$10 = 10,000 visits. The director can now see that the approximate 5 percent cut in the budget is expected to result in an approximate 26 percent drop in patient contact [(13,500 − 10,000)/13,500].

Assumptions and Limitations of CVP Analysis

Linearity and the Relevant Range

The CVP model assumes that revenues and total costs are linear over the relevant range of activity. Although actual cost behavior is not linear, we use the concept of the relevant range introduced in Chapter 3 so that within a given limited range of output, total costs are expected to increase at an approximately linear rate. The caution for the manager is therefore to remember that the calculations performed within the context of a given CVP model should not be used outside the relevant range.

Step Costs

As illustrated in Exhibit 7.9, the cost behavior under examination may be so "lumpy" (step costs) that an approximation via a relevant range is unworkable. Although CVP analysis can be done, it becomes somewhat more cumbersome. Exhibit 7.9 illustrates a situation with a price of $18, a unit variable cost of $10, an initial fixed cost of $100,000, and an incremental fixed cost of another $100,000 when output exceeds 10,000 units. The expenditure of the additional fixed cost provides capacity for up to 30,000 units. A CVP analysis requires that the manager determine the breakeven point for each range (below and above the point at 10,000 units). For these data, we find no breakeven below the 10,000 unit level of output, but the breakeven point can be obtained for the upper range as follows:

$$Q = f/(p - v) = \$200,000/(\$18 - \$10) = 25,000 \text{ units}$$

Thus, losses will be incurred up to the 25,000-unit level, and the additional investment in capacity will be necessary to achieve this production and sales level. Of potential concern to the manager is the relatively narrow range of profitability, between 25,000 and 30,000 units. Therefore, additional analysis might be advisable to better determine the extent of demand for the product and the cost of extending capacity beyond 30,000 units.

Identifying Fixed and Variable Cost for CVP Analysis

Fixed Costs to Include

Suppose that management wants to calculate the breakeven point for a new product for Household Furnishings, Inc. The new product is a computer table designed for easy assembly and intended for the low-price end of the market. Is the cost of the president's salary a relevant fixed cost for this calculation? It is not because the president's salary does not change whether HFI introduces the computer table; it is a fixed cost for the corporation, but it is irrelevant for the analysis of the short-term profitability of the new product.

In a short-term analysis, relevant fixed costs are those expected to change with the introduction of the new product. These include costs of any new production facilities, salaries of new production personnel, and similar costs.

EXHIBIT 7.9
CVP Analysis with Step Cost Behavior

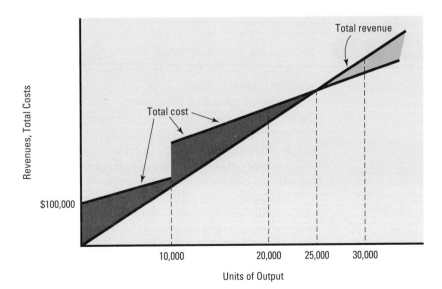

If a new product does not require any new fixed costs because existing facilities and personnel can handle the added production, what is the breakeven point? For a *short-term analysis,* the breakeven point is zero since the new product must cover no new fixed costs. That is, each product sold, beginning with the first, contributes to profit in the excess of price over variable cost. In contrast, for a *long-term analysis* of breakeven, all current and expected future fixed costs associated with the production, distribution, and sale of the product are relevant. Moreover, for a long-term analysis, the methods discussed in Chapter 20 could also be used, including the discounting of future cash flows. Failure to do so when considering breakeven over two or more years can lead to an unwarranted favorable bias to the analysis since discounting future cash flows reduces the value of these amounts, especially when relatively high discount rates are applicable.[4]

The Period in Which the Cost Was Incurred

The fixed costs in a CVP analysis can include the expected cash outflows for fixed costs in the period for which breakeven is expected; alternatively, they can include the fixed costs as determined by accrual accounting. The cash flow fixed costs include all cash outflows for insurance, taxes, and salaries but exclude the noncash items such as depreciation, amortization of patents, and other noncash expenses. The advantage of the cash flow approach is its focus on the company's cash needs.

An accrual accounting approach to determine the amount of fixed costs includes all costs normally expensed in the income statement, including depreciation, amortization, and accrued expenses. The advantage of this approach is that it ties the CVP analysis to the income statement. In choosing between these two approaches, a manager considers the relative benefits of information most relevant for cash flows or for accrual net profit.[5]

Unit Variable Costs

In measuring unit variable cost, the management accountant must be careful to include all relevant variable costs, not only production costs but also selling and distribution costs. Thus, expense for commissions is properly included as a unit variable cost. Any transportation or warehousing costs, if they change with level of output, are relevant.

---

[4] Mark Freeman and Kerrie Freeman make this point in "Considering the Time Value of Money in Breakeven Analysis," *Management Accounting* (London), January 1993, pp. 50–52.

[5] Some useful references for cash flow and accrual breakeven analysis are Bipin Ajikkya, Rowland Atiase, and Linda Bamber, "Absorption versus Direct Costing: Income Reconciliation and Cost-Volume-Profit Analysis," *Issues in Accounting Education,* Fall 1986, pp. 268–81; and David Solomons, "Breakeven Analysis under Absorption Costing," *The Accounting Review,* July 1968, pp. 447–52.

Summary

This chapter develops CVP analysis, a linear model of the relationships between costs, revenues, and output levels. The analysis is used for breakeven planning, revenue planning, and cost planning.

Breakeven planning determines the output level at which profits are zero. Breakeven analysis is used in planning and budgeting to assess the desirability of current and potential products and services. CVP analysis is also used in revenue planning to determine the sales needed to achieve a desired profit level by adding desired profit to the breakeven equation. In cost planning, CVP analysis is used to find the required reduction in costs to meet desired profits or to find the required change in fixed cost for a given change in variable cost (or vice versa).

Two additional concepts—activity-based costing and sensitivity analysis—enhance revenue and cost planning. Activity-based costing breaks fixed costs into batch- and unit-related costs, so CVP analyses can be performed at either (or both) the batch or unit level.

Sensitivity analysis is useful because profits of firms with relatively high fixed costs are more sensitive to changes in the level of sales. The sensitivity, or risk, of changes in sales levels is measured by the margin of safety and operating leverage.

With two or more products, the use of CVP analysis requires the assumption of a constant sales mix between them, and the weighted-average contribution margin is used to calculate the breakeven point.

Not-for-profit and service firms also use breakeven analysis. We presented the example of a municipal health agency's use of breakeven analysis to predict the effects of changing funding levels on its operations.

A number of limitations must be considered in using breakeven analysis. For example, we assume that total fixed costs and unit variable cost do not change.

Key Terms

breakeven point, *242*
contribution income
statement, *240*
contribution margin ratio, *240*
cost-volume-profit, (CVP)
analysis, *238*

CVP graph, *243*
margin of safety, *249*
margin of safety ratio, *250*
operating leverage, *251*
profit-volume graph, *244*
sensitivity analysis, *249*

total contribution
margin, *239*
unit contribution
margin, *239*
what-if analysis, *249*

Comments on Cost Management in Action

The Dot-com Start-Ups: Will They Make it?

An important characteristic of dot-com industry firms is making the large investments in infrastructure necessary to operate their businesses and satisfy their customers. The infrastructure for any given dot-com might include computer systems, warehouses, distribution systems, communication systems, and other technology. This means a relatively high degree of operating leverage for these companies. As a result, they are very sensitive to fluctuations in demand, and many depend on continued high growth levels for survival. When demand is strong, these firms have a big payoff in profits. For example, many of these firms have increased revenues substantially in 2002, so that by the end of that year 40 percent of the publicly held dot-coms were profitable—twice as many as in 2001.

Sources: "Building the Perfect E-tailer," *Business Week*, October 23, 2000, p. EB34; "The Web Is Finally Catching Profits," *Business Week*, February 17, 2003, p. 68; and David Marshall, Wayne McManus, and Daniel Viele, *Accounting: What the Numbers Mean* (New York: McGraw Hill, 2004), pp. 438–439.

Self-Study Problem
(For solution, please turn to the end of the chapter.)

The following data refer to a single product, the TECHWHIZ, made by the Markdata Computer Company:

Sales price = $5,595
Materials cost (including purchased components) = $899
Direct labor cost = $233
Facilities cost (for a highly automated plant mainly includes rent, insurance, taxes, and depreciation) = $2,352,000 per year

Required

1. What is the unit contribution margin?
2. What is the breakeven point in units and dollars?
3. What is the desired level of sales if the company plans to increase fixed costs by 5 percent (to improve product quality and appearance) and achieve a desired before-tax profit of $200,000?
4. If the company's income tax rate is 22 percent, what unit sales are necessary to achieve an after-tax profit of $150,000?

Questions

7–1   What is the underlying relationship in CVP analysis?
7–2   When might it be better to find the breakeven point in sales dollars rather than in units?
7–3   What is the contribution margin ratio and how is it used?
7–4   What are the basic assumptions of CVP analysis?

7–5 Why might the percentage budget cut for a not-for-profit agency not equal the resultant change in the activity level?

7–6 If a new product does not require any new fixed costs because the company utilizes the existing capacity of facilities and personnel, what is the breakeven point?

7–7 Is CVP analysis used in profit planning, cost planning, or revenue planning?

7–8 Why does the issue of taxes not affect the calculation of the breakeven point?

7–9 Why is CVP analysis important in planning the use of new manufacturing technologies?

7–10 What type of risk does sensitivity analysis address?

7–11 Explain the four methods for calculating the breakeven point.

7–12 What is the margin of safety, and for what is it used?

7–13 What is operating leverage, and for what is it used?

7–14 How are step costs treated in CVP analysis?

7–15 Desired before-tax net income equals the desired after-tax net income multiplied by _____?

7–16 How is CVP analysis used to calculate the breakeven point for multiple products?

7–17 Why do management accountants use sensitivity analysis?

Exercises

7–18 Make Or Buy, Two Machines   Calista Company manufactures electronic equipment. It currently purchases the special switches used in each of its products from an outside supplier. The supplier charges Calista $2 per switch. Calista's CEO is considering purchasing either machine X or machine Y so the company can manufacture its own switches. The projected data are

	Machine X	Machine Y
Annual fixed cost	$135,000	$204,000
Variable cost per switch	0.65	0.30

Required

1. For each machine, what is the minimum number of switches that Calista must make annually for total costs to equal outside purchase cost?
2. What is the most profitable alternative for producing 200,000 switches per year?
3. What volume level would produce the same total costs regardless of the machine purchased?

7–19 Operating Leverage   These sales and cost data (000s) are for two companies in the transportation industry:

	Company A		Company B	
	Amount	Percent of sales	Amount	Percent of sales
Sales	$100,000	100%	$100,000	100%
Variable costs	60,000	60	30,000	30
Contribution margin	$ 40,000	40%	$ 70,000	70%
Fixed costs	15,000		40,000	
Net income	$ 25,000		$ 30,000	

Required

1. Calculate the operating leverage for each company. If sales increase, which company benefits more? How do you know?
2. Assume that sales rise 10 percent in the next year. Calculate the percentage increase in profit for each company. Are the results what you expected?

7–20 CVP Analysis   Holden, Inc., a manufacturer of quality electric ice cream makers, has experienced a steady growth in sales over the past few years. Since her business has grown, Jo Holden, the president, believes she needs an aggressive advertising campaign next year to maintain the company's growth. To prepare for the growth, the accountant prepared the following data for the current year:

Variable costs per ice cream maker	
Direct labor	$ 11.75
Direct materials	15.25
Variable overhead	5.00
Total variable costs	$ 32.00
Fixed costs	
Manufacturing	$ 31,000
Selling	42,000
Administrative	356,000
Total fixed costs	$429,000
Selling price per unit	$ 65.00
Expected sales (units)	30,000

Required

1. If the costs and sales price remain the same, what is the projected profit for the coming year?
2. What is the breakeven point in units for the coming year?
3. Jo has set the sales target for 35,000 ice cream makers which she thinks she can achieve by an additional fixed selling expense of $200,000 for advertising. All other costs remain as in requirement 1. What will be the before-tax net income if the additional $200,000 is spent on advertising and sales rise to 35,000 units?
4. What will be the new breakeven point if the additional $200,000 is spent on advertising?
5. If the additional $200,000 is spent for advertising in the next year, what is the required sales level in units to equal the current year's income at 30,000 units?

7–21 **Multiple Product CVP Analysis**   Reader's Retreat is a small book store that rents space in a neighborhood shopping mall for $19,200 a year. Its utilities add another $7,800 yearly. The total staff salaries and benefits projected for next year equal $56,000. Reader's Retreat also spends $900 on advertising and $2,400 on professional services. Other overhead expenses total $11,500.

Jamie Davis, the company's owner, would like to make a $40,000 profit after taxes next year, when her tax rate will be 33 percent. The store sells hardbound books, paperback books, and magazines. The average cost of each category of items and Reader's markup on cost is $12.00 and 50 percent, hardbacks; $2.40 and 60 percent, paperbacks; and $1.90 and 60 percent, magazines.

In past years, 70 percent of the store's sales revenue came from hardback books, 20 percent from paperbacks, and the remaining 10 percent from magazines.

Required

1. What is the contribution margin of each sales item?
2. What are the store's projected fixed costs for next year?
3. What is the breakeven point for Reader's Retreat to achieve zero profit?
4. What sales level will the store need to reach the target after-tax profit?

7–22 **The Role of Income Taxes**   In 2004, Triad Company had fixed costs of $200,000 and variable costs of 80 percent of total sales revenue, earned $70,000 of net income after taxes, and had an income tax rate of 30 percent.

Required   Determine (1) before-tax operating income, (2) total contribution margin, (3) total sales, and (4) breakeven point in dollar sales.

7–23 **CVP Analysis with Taxes**   Jeffrey Company produces and sells socks. Variable costs are $3 per pair, and fixed costs for the year total $75,000. The selling price is $5 per pair.

Required   Calculate the following:

1. The breakeven point in units.
2. The breakeven point in sales dollars.
3. The units required to make a before-tax profit of $10,000.
4. The sales in dollars required to make a before-tax profit of $8,000.
5. The sales units and sales dollars required to make an after-tax profit of $12,000 given a tax rate of 40 percent.

7–24 Margin of Safety   Harold McWilliams owns and manages a general merchandise store in a rural area of Virginia. Harold sells appliances, clothing, auto parts, and farming equipment, among a wide variety of other types of merchandise. Because of normal seasonal and cyclical fluctuations in the local economy, he knows that his business will also have these fluctuations, and he is planning to use CVP analysis to help him understand how he can expect his profits to change with these fluctuations. Harold has the following information for his most recent year. Cost of goods sold represents the cost paid for the merchandise he sells, while operating costs represent rent, insurance, and salaries, that are entirely fixed.

Sales	$650,000
Cost of goods sold	422,500
Gross margin	227,500
Operating costs	105,000
Operating income	$122,500

Required

1. What is Harold's margin of safety in dollars? What is the margin of safety ratio?
2. What is Harold's margin of safety and operating profit if sales should fall to $500,000?

7–25 Budget Cuts   Student Health Services Pharmacy provides certain medications to students free of charge. Currently, 40 percent of the pharmacy's costs are fixed; the other 60 percent are variable. The pharmacy's budget was $200,000 last year, but the university recently cut this year's budget by 20 percent.

Required   What is the percentage decrease in the amount of services the pharmacy can provide this year?

7–26 Multiple Products CVP   Julia Company can produce two types of carpet cleaners, the Brighter and Smarter. The data on the two machines is as follows:

	Brighter	Smarter
Sales volume in units	200	300
Unit sales price	$750	$1,000
Unit variable cost	225	450

The number of machine-hours to produce Brighter is 1 and to produce Smarter is 2. Total fixed costs for the manufacture of both products are $132,000.

Required   Using a spreadsheet, determine the breakeven point for Julia Company, assuming that the sales mix remains constant in sales dollars.

Problems

7–27 CVP Analysis, Strategy   Frank's Western Wear is a western hat retailer in Dallas, Texas. Although Frank's carries numerous styles of western hats, each hat has approximately the same price and invoice (purchase) cost, as shown in the following table. Sales personnel receive large commissions to encourage them to be more aggressive in their sales efforts. Currently, the Dallas economy is really humming, and sales growth at Frank's has been great. The business is very competitive, however, and Frank has relied on his knowledgeable and courteous staff to attract and retain customers who otherwise might go to other western wear stores.

Because of the rapid growth in sales, Frank is also finding the management of certain aspects of the business, such as restocking of inventory and hiring and training new salespeople, more difficult.

Sales price	$ 30.00
Per unit variable expenses	
Invoice cost	15.50
Sales commissions	4.50
Total per unit variable costs	$ 20.00
Total annual fixed expenses	
Advertising	$ 20,000
Rent	25,000
Salaries	105,000
Total fixed expenses	$150,000

Required

1. Calculate the annual breakeven point in unit sales and dollar sales.
2. If Frank's sells 20,000 hats, what is its net income or loss?
3. If Frank's sells 25,000, what is its margin of safety and margin of safety ratio?
4. Frank is considering the elimination of sales commissions completely and increasing salaries by $82,000 annually. What would be the new breakeven point in units? What would be the net income or loss if 20,000 hats are sold with the new salary plan?
5. Identify and discuss the strategic issues in the decision to eliminate sales commissions (see requirement 4). How do these strategic concerns affect Frank's decision?

7–28 Contribution Income Statements Using Excel; Sensitivity Analysis; Goal Seek

Required

1. Using the data in Exhibit 7.1, create an Excel spreadsheet to provide a sensitivity analysis of the effect on operating profit of potential changes in demand for HFI, Inc. Use Exhibit 7.2 as a guide.
2. Use the Goal Seek tool within Excel to determine which sales price would allow HFI to earn $100,000 operating profit, assuming that all the other cost information is the same as in Exhibit 7.1.

7–29 Multiple Products   Most businesses sell several products at varying prices. The products often have different unit variable costs. Thus, the total profit and the breakeven point depend on the proportions in which the products are sold. Sales mix is the relative contribution of sales among various products sold by a firm. Assume that the sales of Hycel, Inc., are the following for a typical year:

Product	Units Sold	Sales Mix
A	8,000	80%
B	2,000	20
Total	10,000	100%

Assume the following unit selling prices and unit variable costs:

Product	Selling Price	Variable Cost per Unit	Unit Contribution Margin
A	$ 90	$70	$20
B	140	95	45

Fixed costs are $200,000 per year.

Required

1. Determine the breakeven point in units.
2. Determine the number of units required for a before-tax net profit of $40,000.

7–30 **Multiple Product CVP Analysis**   Neptune Company recently acquired the technology needed to produce small, standard, and super marine bilge pumps. Budgeted fixed costs for the manufacture of all three products total $425,000. The *budgeted* sales by product and in total for the coming year are as follows:

	Small		Standard		Super	
	Amount	Percent	Amount	Percent	Amount	Percent
Sales	$175,000	100%	$400,000	100%	$250,000	100%
Variable costs	120,750	69	100,000	25	125,000	50
Contribution	$ 54,250	31%	$300,000	75%	$125,000	50%

Actual sales for the year were not as planned; the following lists sales by product:

Small	$400,000
Standard	225,000
Super	200,000
	$825,000

Required

1. Prepare a contribution income statement for the year based on actual sales data.
2. Compute the breakeven sales dollars for the year based on both budgeted and actual sales, assuming that the sales mix remains constant in sales dollars.
3. The company president knows that total actual sales were $825,000 for the year, the same as budgeted. Because she had seen the budgeted income statement, she was expecting a nice profit from producing the bilge pumps. Explain to her what happened.

7–31 **CVP Analysis, Taxes**   Elmire Company produces and sells watches. It projects the following information for next year:

Sales price per unit	$ 60
Variable production cost per unit	30
Fixed production costs (total)	200,000
Variable selling costs per unit	5
Fixed selling costs (total)	150,000

Required

1. Determine the breakeven point in units and dollars.
2. How many units does the company need to sell to earn a pretax profit of $150,000?
3. What will Elmire's pretax profit be at 40,000 units?
4. Elmire is subject to a tax rate of 40 percent. If the CEO wants an after-tax profit of $150,000, how many units must it sell?
5. Elmire is considering an alternate strategy to reduce fixed production costs by $50,000. However, this would cause variable production costs to increase to $35 per unit. What is the number of units at which the company is indifferent as to the original production strategy and the new strategy?
6. Prepare a CVP graph based on the original data.

7–32 **CVP Analysis in a Professional Service Firm**   A local CPA firm has been asked to bid on a contract to perform audits for three counties in its home state. Should the firm be awarded the contract, it must hire one new staff member at a salary of $45,000 to handle the additional workload. (Existing staff are fully scheduled.) The managing partner is convinced that obtaining the contract will lead to additional new profit-oriented clients from the respective counties. Expected new work (excluding the three counties) is 800 hours at an average billing rate of $50.00. Other relevant information follows about the firm's annual revenues and costs:

Firm volume in hours (normal)	30,750
Fixed costs	$470,000
Variable costs	$ 5.00/hr

Should the firm win the contract, these audits will require 900 hours of expected work.

Required

1. If the managing partner's expectations are correct, what is the lowest bid the firm can submit and still expect to increase annual net income?
2. If the contract is obtained at a price of $20,000, what is the minimum number of hours of new business in addition to the county work that must be obtained for the firm to break even on total new business?

7–33 **CVP Analysis**   Greengrow Company, a manufacturer of riding lawn mowers, has a projected income for 2004 as follows:

Sales (12,000 units)		$36,000,000
Operating expenses		
Variable expenses	$22,500,000	
Fixed expenses	7,500,000	
Total expenses		30,000,000
Net income		$ 6,000,000

Required

1. Determine the breakeven point in units.
2. Using the contribution margin ratio, determine the breakeven in sales revenue.
3. Determine the required sales in dollars to earn an income of $7,250,000.
4. What is the breakeven point in units if the variable cost increases by 10 percent?

7–34 **CVP Analysis, Activity-Based Costing, Taxes**   Sports Plus, Inc., produces software for personal computers. The company's main product is Swing!, a golf training program. The total variable cost of the product is $10. Fixed manufacturing expenses are $60,000 per month, and the price of the product is $300. In the coming year, the company plans to spend $100,000 for advertising and $50,000 for research and development. Because this proprietorship is managed from a personal residence, it incurs no other fixed costs. The federal and state tax rate for the proprietor is 40 percent. The company expects 6,000 units of sales for the next year.

Required

1. Determine the breakeven point for the coming year in number of units.
2. Suppose that 20 percent of the manufacturing fixed costs are batch-level costs from testing and packaging. Because of the nature of the testing process, all production has the same batch size of 20 units. Calculate revised breakeven point.
3. Determine the number of units required for the coming year to cover a 100 percent increase in advertising expenses and a $12,000 after-tax profit per month.

7–35 **CVP Analysis**   The nonprofit Cardiac Diagnostic Screening Center (CDSC) is contemplating purchasing a blood gases analysis machine at a cost of $750,000. Useful life for this machine is 10 years. The screening center currently serves 5,000 patients per year, 30 percent of whom need blood gases analysis data as part of their diagnostic tests. The blood samples are presently sent to a private laboratory that charges $85 per sample. In-house variable expenses are estimated to be $40 per sample if CDSC purchases the analysis machine.

Required

1. Determine the indifference point between purchasing the machine or using the private laboratory.

2. Determine how many additional patients would be needed so that CDSC would be indifferent between purchasing the analysis machine and the $85 lab charge.

3. Determine the amount of the private laboratory charge so that CDSC would be indifferent as to purchasing the analysis machine or using the private laboratory, assuming the current service level of 5,000 patients per year.

7–36 **CVP Analysis; Sensitivity Analysis; Strategy**   GoGo Juice is a combination gas station and convenience store located at a busy intersection. Recently a national chain opened a similar store only a block away; consequently sales have decreased for GoGo. In an effort to reclaim lost sales, GoGo has implemented a promotional effort; for every $10 purchase at GoGo, the customer receives a $1 coupon for the purchase of gasoline. The average gasoline customer purchases 15 gallons of gasoline at $1.129 per gallon, for a total sale of $16.94. This promotional effort should encourage gasoline customers to purchase additional items so the sale totals $20. For spending $20, the customer is entitled to two coupons rather than one. The results of an average month, prior to this coupon promotion are shown in the following chart.

Not included on the chart is the monthly cost of printing the coupons that is estimated to be $500. Coupons are issued on the basis of total purchases regardless of whether the purchases are paid in cash or paid by redeeming coupons. Assume that coupons are distributed to customers for 80 percent of the total sales. Also assume that all coupons distributed are used to purchase gasoline.

	Sales	Cost of Sales
Gasoline	$100,000	$.84675 per gallon
Food and beverages	60,000	60%
Other products	40,000	50%

	Other Costs
Labor—station attendants	$ 9,000
Labor—supervision	2,500
Rent, power, supplies, interest, and misc.	46,500
Depreciation (pumps, computers, counters, fixtures, and building)	2,500

Required

1. If GoGo Juice implements the promotional coupon effort, calculate the profit (loss) before tax if the sales volume remains constant and the coupons are used to purchase gasoline. Assume the product mix; percentages of gasoline, food, and beverages; and other products, remain the same.

2. Calculate the breakeven sales for GoGo Juice if the promotional effort is implemented. Assume that the product mix remains constant.

3. Disregarding your responses to Requirements 1 and 2, assume the weighted contribution margin, after implementation of the coupon program, is 30 percent. Calculate the profit (loss) before tax for GoGo Juice, assuming sales increase 20 percent due to the new program. Assume that the sales mix remains constant.

4. GoGo Juice is considering using sensitivity analysis in combination with cost-volume-profit analysis. Discuss the use of sensitivity analysis with cost-volume-profit analysis. Include in your discussion at least three factors that make sensitivity analysis prevalent in decision making.

(CMA Adapted)

7–37 **CVP Analysis**   Headlines Publishing Company (HPC) specializes in international business news publications. Its principal product is *HPC-Monthly*, which is mailed to subscribers the first week of each month. A weekly version, called *HPC-Weekly*, is also available to subscribers over the Web at a higher cost. Sixty percent of HPC's subscribers are nondomestic customers. The company experienced a fast growth in subscribers in its first few years of operation, but sales have begun to slow in recent years as new competitors have entered the market. HPC has the following cost structure and sales revenue for its subscription operations on a yearly basis. All costs and all subscription fees are in U.S. dollars.

Fixed Cost

$306,000 per month

Variable Costs

Mailing	$0.60	per issue
Commission	3.00	per subscription
Administrative	1.50	per subscription

Sales Mix Information

HPC-Weekly	20	percent
HPC-Monthly	80	percent

Selling Price

HPC-Weekly	$ 47	per subscription
HPC-Monthly	$ 19	per subscription

Required   Use these data to determine the following:

1. Contribution margin for weekly and monthly subscriptions.
2. Contribution margin ratio for weekly and monthly subscriptions.
3. HPC's breakeven point in sales units and sales dollars.
4. HPC's breakeven point to reach a target before-tax profit of $75,000.
5. What are the critical success factors for HPC? For its domestic subscribers? For its international subscribers? How can CVP analysis be used to make HPC more competitive?

 7–38 **CVP Analysis, Commissions, Ethics**   Marston Corporation manufactures pharmaceutical products sold through a network of sales agents in the United States and Canada. The agents are currently paid an 18 percent commission on sales; that percentage was used when Marston prepared the following budgeted income statement for the fiscal year ending June 30, 2004.

MARSTON CORPORATION
Budgeted Income Statement
For the Year Ending June 30, 2004
($000 omitted)

Sales		$26,000
Cost of goods sold		
Variable	$11,700	
Fixed	2,870	14,570
Gross profit		$11,430
Selling and administrative costs		
Commissions	$ 4,680	
Fixed advertising cost	750	
Fixed administrative cost	1,850	7,280
Operating income		$ 4,150
Fixed interest cost		650
Income before income taxes		$ 3,500
Income taxes (40 percent)		1,400
Net income		$ 2,100

Since the completion of the income statement, Marston has learned that its sales agents are requiring a 5 percent increase in their commission rate (to 23 percent) for the upcoming year. As a result, Marston's president has decided to investigate the possibility of hiring its own sales staff in place of the network of sales agents and has asked Tom Markowitz, Marston's controller, to gather information on the costs associated with this change.

Tom estimates that Marston must hire eight salespeople to cover the current market area, at an average annual payroll cost for each employee of $80,000, including fringe benefits expense. Travel and entertainment expense is expected to total $600,000 for the year, and the annual cost of hiring a sales manager and sales secretary will be $150,000. In addition to their salaries, the eight salespeople will each earn commissions at the rate of 10 percent. The president believes that Marston also should increase its advertising budget by $500,000.

Required

1. Determine Marston Corporation's breakeven point in sales dollars for the fiscal year ending June 30, 2004, if the company hires its own sales force and increases its advertising costs.

2. If Marston continues to sell through its network of sales agents and pays the higher commission rate, determine the estimated volume in sales dollars for the fiscal year ending June 30, 2004, that would be required to generate the same net income as projected in the budgeted income statement.

3. Describe the general assumptions underlying breakeven analysis that limit its usefulness.

4. What is the indifference point in sales for the firm to either accept the agents' demand or adopt the proposed change? Which plan is better for the firm?

5. Assume that total sales for the year ending June 30, 2005, will remain approximately the same as for the year ending June 30, 2004. Would you, as the head of the sales agents' union, demand an increase in commission rate?

6. What are the ethical issues, if any, that Tom should consider before adopting the new program?

(CMA Adapted)

7–39   **CVP Analysis, Different Production Plans**   The PTO Division of Galva Manufacturing Company produces power take-off units for the farm equipment business. The PTO Division, headquartered in Peoria, has a newly renovated, automated plant in Peoria and an older, less-automated plant in Moline. Both plants produce the same power take-off units for farm tractors that are sold to most domestic and foreign tractor manufacturers.

The PTO Division expects to produce and sell 192,000 power take-off units during the coming year. The division production manager has the following data available regarding the unit costs, unit prices, and production capacities for the two plants.

- All fixed costs are based on a normal year of 240 work days. When the number of work days exceeds 240, variable manufacturing costs increase by $3 per unit in Peoria and $8 per unit in Moline. Capacity for each plant is 300 working days.

- Galva Manufacturing charges each of its plants a per-unit fee for administrative services such as payroll, general accounting, and purchasing because management considers these services to be a function of the work performed at the plants. For each plant at Peoria and Moline, the fee is $6.50 and represents the variable portion of general and administrative expense.

Wishing to maximize the higher unit profit at Moline, PTO's production manager has decided to manufacture 96,000 units at each plant. This production plan results in Moline's operating at capacity and Peoria's operating at its normal volume. Galva's corporate controller is not happy with this plan because she does not believe it represents optimal usage of PTO's plants.

	Peoria	Moline
Selling price	$150.00	$150.00
Variable manufacturing cost	72.00	88.00
Fixed manufacturing cost	30.00	15.00
Commission (5 percent)	7.50	7.50
General and administrative expense	25.50	21.00
Total unit cost	$135.00	$131.50
Unit profit	$ 15.00	$ 18.50
Production rate per day	400 units	320 units

Required

1. Determine the annual breakeven units for each PTO plant.

2. Determine the operating income that would result from the division production manager's plan to produce 96,000 units at each plant.

3. Determine the optimal production plan to produce the 192,000 units at PTO's plants in Peoria and Moline and the resulting operating income for the PTO Division. Be sure to support the plan with appropriate calculations.

(CMA Adapted)

7-40   CVP Analysis, Bid Pricing   Jason Fibers Inc. specializes in the manufacture of synthetic fibers that the company uses in many products such as blankets, coats, and uniforms for police and firefighters. Jason has been in business since 1975 and has been profitable each year since 1983.

Jason recently received a request to bid on the manufacture of 800,000 blankets scheduled for delivery to several military bases. The bid must be stated at full cost per unit plus a return on full cost of no more than 9 percent after income taxes. *Full cost* has been defined as all variable costs of manufacturing the product, a reasonable amount of fixed overhead, and a reasonable incremental administrative cost associated with the manufacture and sale of the product. The contractor has indicated that bids in excess of $27 per blanket are not likely to be considered.

To prepare the bid for the 800,000 blankets, Andrea Lightner, cost management analyst, has gathered the following information concerning the costs associated with the production of the blankets. The fixed overhead costs represent an allocation of the cost of currently used facilities. No new fixed costs are needed for the order.

Raw material per pound of fibers	$ 1.50
Direct labor per hour	$ 7.00
Direct machine costs per blanket*	$ 10.00
Variable overhead per direct-labor hour	$ 3.00
Fixed overhead per direct labor-hour	$ 8.00
Incremental administrative costs per 1,000 blankets	$2,500.00
Special fee per blanket‡	$ 0.50
Material usage	6 pounds per blanket
Production rate	4 blankets per direct labor hour
Effective tax rate	40 percent

* Direct machine costs consist of items, such as special lubricants, replacement needles used in stitching, and maintenance costs, that are not included in the normal overhead rates.

‡ Jason recently developed a new blanket fiber at a cost of $750,000. To recover this cost, it adds a $0.50 fee to the cost of each blanket using the new fiber. To date, the company has recovered $125,000. Andrea knows that this fee does not fit within the definition of full cost because it is not a cost to manufacture the product.

Required

1. What is the breakeven price per blanket using Jason's full cost system?

2. Calculate the minimum price per blanket that Jason Fibers could bid without reducing the company's net income.

3. Using the *full cost* criteria and the maximum allowable return specified, calculate the bid price per blanket for Jason Fibers.

4. Without prejudice to your answer to requirement 3, assume that the price per blanket that Jason calculated using the cost-plus criteria specified is higher than the maximum allowed bid of $27 per blanket. Discuss the strategic factors that the company should consider before deciding whether to submit a bid at the maximum acceptable price of $27 per blanket.

(CMA Adapted)

7-41   CVP Analysis, Probability Analysis   Don Masters and two colleagues are considering the opening of a law office in a large metropolitan area to make inexpensive legal services available to people who cannot otherwise afford these services. They intend to provide easy access for their clients by having the office open 360 days per year, 16 hours each day from 7:00 A.M. to 11:00 P.M. A lawyer, paralegal, legal secretary, and clerk-receptionist would staff the office for each of the two 8–hour shifts.

To determine the feasibility of the project, Don hired a marketing consultant to assist with market projections. The consultant's results show that if the firm spends $500,000 on advertising the first year, the number of new clients expected each day would have the following probability distribution:

Number of New Clients per Day	Probability
20	.10
30	.30
55	.40
85	.20

Don and his associates believe these numbers to be reasonable and are prepared to spend the $500,000 on advertising. Other pertinent information about the operation of the office follows.

The only charge to each new client would be $30 for an initial consultation. The firm will accept all cases that warrant further legal work on a contingency basis with the firm earning 30 percent of any favorable settlements or judgments. Don estimates that 20 percent of new client consultations will result in favorable settlements or judgments averaging $4,000 each. He does not expect repeat clients during the first year of operations.

The hourly wages for the staff are projected to be $95 for the lawyer, $35 for the paralegal, $15 for the legal secretary, and $10 for the clerk-receptionist. Fringe benefit expense will be 40 percent of the wages paid. A total of 400 hours of overtime is expected for the year; this will be divided equally between the legal secretary and the clerk-receptionist positions. Overtime will be paid at one and one-half times the regular wage, and the fringe benefit expense will apply to the full wage.

Don has located 6,000 square feet of suitable office space that rents for $28 per square foot annually. Associated expenses will be $22,000 for property insurance and $32,000 for utilities. The group must purchase malpractice insurance expected to cost $180,000 annually.

The initial investment in office equipment will be $60,000; this equipment has an estimated useful life of four years. The cost of office supplies has been estimated to be $4 per expected new client consultation.

Required

1. Determine how many new clients must visit the law office that Don and his colleagues are considering for the venture to break even its first year of operations.

2. Using the probability information provided by the marketing consultant, determine whether it is feasible for the law office to achieve breakeven operations.

3. Explain how Don and his associates could use sensitivity analysis to assist in this analysis.

(CMA Adapted)

7–42   **CVP Analysis, Strategy, Critical Success Factors**   Garner Strategy Institute (GSI) presents executive-level training seminars nationally. Eastern University (EU) has approached GSI to present 40 one-week seminars during 2004. This activity level represents the maximum number of seminars that GSI is capable of presenting annually. GSI staff would present the week-long seminars in various cities throughout the United States and Canada.

Terry Garner, GSI's president, is evaluating three financial options for the revenues from Eastern: accept a flat fee for each seminar, receive a percentage of Eastern's "profit before tax" from the seminars, and form a joint venture to share costs and profits.

Estimated costs for the 2004 seminar schedule follow.

	Garner Strategy Institute	Eastern University
Fixed costs		
Salaries and benefits	$200,000	N/A*
Facilities	48,000	N/A*
Travel and hotel	0	$210,000
Other	70,000	N/A*
Total fixed costs	$318,000	$210,000

(continued)

* Eastern's fixed costs are excluded because the amounts are not considered relevant for this decision (i.e., they will be incurred whether or not the seminars are presented). Eastern does not include these costs when calculating the "profit before the tax" for the seminars.

	Garner Strategy Institute	Eastern University
Variable costs		Per Participant
Supplies and materials	0	$47
Marketing	0	18
Other site costs	0	35

EU plans to charge $1,200 per participant for each one-week seminar. It will pay all variable promotion, site costs, and materials costs.

Required

1. Assume that the seminars are handled as a joint venture by GSI and EU to pool costs and revenues.
    a. Determine the total number of seminar participants needed to break even on the total costs for this joint venture. Show supporting computations.
    b. Assume that the joint venture has an effective income tax rate of 30 percent. How many seminar participants must the joint venture enroll to earn a net income of $169,400? Show supporting computations.
2. Assume that GSI and EU do not form a joint venture, but that GSI is an independent contractor for EU. EU offers two payment options to GSI: a flat fee of $9,500 for each seminar, or a fee of 40 percent of EU's "profit before tax" from the seminars. Compute the minimum number of participants needed for GSI to prefer the 40 percent fee option over the flat fee. Show supporting computations.
3. What are the strategic and implementation issues for GSI to consider in deciding whether to enter into the joint venture? For Eastern?

(CMA Adapted)

7–43 **CVP Analysis, Strategy, Uncertainty** Computer Graphics (CG) is a small manufacturer of electronic products for computers with graphics capabilities. The company has succeeded by being very innovative in product design. As a spin-off of a large electronics manufacturer (ElecTech), CG management has extensive experience in both marketing and manufacturing in the electronics industry. A long list of equity investors is betting that the firm will really take off because of the growth of specialized graphic software and the increased demand for computers with enhanced graphics capability. A number of market analysts say, however, that the market for the firm's products is somewhat risky, as it is for many high-tech start-ups because of the number of new competitors entering the market, and CG's unproven technology.

CG's main product is a circuit board (CB3668) used in computers with enhanced graphics capabilities. Prices vary depending on the terms of sale and the size of the purchase; the average price for the CB3668 is $100. If the firm is able to take off, it might be able to raise prices, but it might have to reduce the price because of increased competition. The firm expects to sell 150,000 units in the coming year, and sales are expected to increase in the following years. The future for CG looks very bright indeed, but it is new and has not developed a strong financial base. Cash flow management is a critical feature of the firm's financial management, and top management must watch cash flow numbers closely.

At present, CG is manufacturing the CB3668 in a plant leased from ElecTech using some equipment purchased from ElecTech. CG manufactures about 70 percent of the parts in this circuit board.

CG management is considering a significant reengineering project to significantly change the plant and manufacturing process. The project's objective is to increase the number of purchased parts (to about 55%) and to reduce the complexity of the manufacturing process. This would also permit CG to remove some leased equipment and to sell some of the most expensive equipment in the plant.

The per unit manufacturing costs for 150,000 units of CB3668 follow:

	Current Manufacturing Cost	Proposed Manufacturing Costs
Materials and purchased parts	$ 6.00	$15.00
Direct labor	12.50	13.75
Variable overhead	25.00	30.00
Fixed overhead	40.00	20.00

(continued)

	Current Manufacturing Cost	Proposed Manufacturing Costs
Manufacturing information for CB3668		
Number of setups	3,000	2,300
Batch size	50	50
Cost per setup	$300	$300
Machine hours	88,000	55,000

General, selling, and administrative costs are $10 per unit and $1,250,000 fixed; these costs are not expected to differ for either the current or the proposed manufacturing plan.

Required

1. Compute the contribution margin and breakeven in units for CB3668, both before and after the proposed reengineering project. Assume all setup costs are included in fixed overhead.
2. Determine the number of sales units at which CG would be indifferent as to the current manufacturing plan or the proposed plan.
3. Explain briefly (a) what CG's strategy is (b) what you think it should be and (c) why.
4. Should CG undertake the proposed reengineering plan? Using a spreadsheet, support your answer with sensitivity analysis and a discussion of short-term and long-term considerations.

7–44   CVP Analysis; ABC Costing   Using the information in Problem 7–43, complete the following:

Required

1. Compute the breakeven in units for both the current and proposed manufacturing plans, assuming that setup costs vary with the number of batches. Assume that setup costs are the only costs that vary with the number of batches.
2. Compare your solution above to that for Problem 7–43 and interpret the difference.

7–45   New Manufacturing Facility, Strategy   Julius Brooks, plant manager for ICL, Inc., a manufacturer of auto parts, has been successful in recent years because of the very high quality of his products and the speed of delivery. A growing market for ICL is automakers who want it to participate in the design of the car and to design certain parts. The ICL design team supervised by Julius has developed an excellent reputation among the automakers for quality designs, which have reduced warranty and service costs for the automakers. The result has been that a substantial part of the plant's revenues are now from design work, and sometimes ICL subcontracts the actual manufacturing to other manufacturers. Nevertheless, competitors continue to cut prices, and Julius is finding it more difficult to cut costs to meet the competition. Working with top management, he has helped design a new, automated factory in Georgia to take advantage of the tax breaks allowed by the State of Georgia and the local community.

Required   Discuss the strategic aspects of the plan for the new factory.

7–46   CVP Analysis   Babbott Bicycle Company (BBC) is a high-end manufacturer of bicycles. Its products are sold in specialty retail bike stores throughout the United States and Canada. This year's expected production is 10,000 units, but demand in the bicycle market has fluctuated in recent years so that BBC is also predicting that the actual production/sales figure could be anywhere between 7,000 and 15,000 bikes. To control quality, BBC currently makes most of the parts for its bikes, including the rear brake. BBC's accountant reports the following costs for making the 10,000 rear brake assemblies:

	Per-Unit Costs	Costs for 10,000 Units
Direct materials	$10.00	$100,000
Direct manufacturing labor	6.00	60,000
Variable manufacturing overhead (power and utilities)	3.00	30,000
Inspection, setup, materials handling	2.00	20,000
Machine lease	3.40	34,000
Allocated fixed plant administration, taxes, and insurance	6.00	60,000
Total costs		$304,000

An outside vendor has offered to supply up to 20,000 brake assemblies to BBC for $25 each. The following additional information is available:

- BBC's machine lease costs are for the equipment used to make the brakes. If BBC buys all brakes from the outside vendor, it will be able to cancel the lease and avoid this cost. All other fixed costs will not be affected.

Required Assume that if BBC purchases the brake assemblies from the outside supplier, the facility where it currently makes them will remain idle for at least the next year. At that point, BBC might consider leasing the space or using it for an alternative use. Should BBC accept the outside supplier's offer? Support your answer using CVP analysis. Include an assessment of the strategic issues facing BBC that might affect your answer.

7–47 **CVP Analysis; ABC Costing** Using the information in Problem 7–46 above, complete the following.

Required Assume that inspection, setup, and materials-handling costs vary directly with the number of batches in which the bikes are produced, and that BBC produces brakes in batches of 1,000 units. Compute the indifference quantity between making the brakes or purchasing the brakes. Compare your solution to that in Problem 7–46 and interpret the difference.

7–48 **CVP Analysis** Hemp, an agricultural product, is a natural fiber that has many industrial and commercial uses, including handbags, backpacks, hats, paper, rope, industrial fabrics, and clothing. In some areas of the world, particularly Australia, Canada, and the United States, hemp is viewed as a potentially significant new opportunity for agricultural production, and business and agricultural leaders are studying the strategic issues involved in making further investments in the crop. For example, an agricultural analysis by the Manitoba, Canada, Department of Agriculture has developed the following estimated costs for producing hemp. This analysis is based on an average farm in which 180 acres would be planted. Assume machinery operating costs, crop insurance, land taxes, licensing fees, sampling and analytical fees, and other costs are fixed relative to the production of hemp, while the other costs are variable per pound produced. Also, assume seed prices of $4.00 per pound, a 20 pound per acre seeding rate, and crop yield of 400 pounds per acre. The costs associated with investment in land and machinery are ignored in the analysis, on the assumption that these costs would remain the same whether or not the farmer grows hemp.

Estimated Operating Costs per Acre for the Production of Hemp

Seed	$80.00
Fertilizer	38.15
Chemicals	10.00
Fuel	11.00
Machinery operating costs	15.00
Crop insurance	6.00
Other costs	7.50
Land taxes	5.50
Licensing fee	15.00
Sampling and analytical fees	15.00
Drying costs	3.57
Cleaning costs	5.00
Interest on operating costs	7.44

Required Calculate the price per pound that a farmer on an average-sized farm would have to receive to break even on the production of hemp.

Solution to Self-Study Problem

Breakeven Analysis

1. Unit contribution margin = $5,595 − $899 − $233 = $4,463

2. Breakeven

   In units:

   $$Q = (f + N)/(p − v)$$

   $$Q = \$2,352,000/\$4,463 = 527 \text{ units}$$

   In dollars:

   $$p \times Q = \$5,595 \times 527 = \$2,948,565$$

   Or

   $$p \times Q = \frac{f + N}{(p − v)/p} = \frac{\$2,352,000}{0.797676} = \$2,948,565$$

3. New level of fixed costs = $2,352,000(1 + .05) = $2,469,600

   Breakeven:

   $$Q = (f + N)/(p − v)$$

   $$Q = (\$2,469,600 + \$200,000)/(\$4,463)$$

   $$= 599 \text{ units}$$

4. Incorporate a tax rate of 22 percent and desired profit of $150,000:

   $$Q = \{\$2,352,000 + [\$150,000)/(1 − 0.22)]\}/\$4,463$$

   $$= 570 \text{ units}$$

CHAPTER EIGHT

Strategy and the Master Budget

After studying this chapter, you should be able to . . .

1. Describe the role of a budget in planning, communicating, motivating, controlling, and evaluating performance

2. Discuss the importance of strategy and its role in budgeting and identify factors common to successful budgets

3. Outline the budgeting process

4. Prepare a master budget and explain the interrelationships among its supporting schedules

5. Identify unique budgeting characteristics of service and international firms and not-for-profit organizations

6. Apply zero-base, activity-based, and kaizen budgeting

7. Discuss the roles of ethics and behavioral concerns in budgeting

---

If you don't know where you're going, you'll end up somewhere else.

Yogi Berra

Johnson & Johnson, one of the largest manufacturers of health care products and providers of related services for the consumer, pharmaceutical, and professional markets in the world, started as a small manufacturer of health and well-being-related products in New Jersey in 1887.[1] Today, it has more than 99,000 employees and more than 190 operating companies in 51 countries and sells its products in more than 175 countries. Surveys conducted over the years by *Business Week, Forbes, Fortune,* and other business journals repeatedly have ranked Johnson & Johnson as one of the most innovative, well-managed, and admired firms in the world. Its employees and job applicants consider the firm to be among the best to work for.

How does Johnson & Johnson do it? It relies on a comprehensive formal planning, budgeting, and control system in formulating and implementing strategy, coordinating and monitoring operations, and reviewing and evaluating performance. Johnson & Johnson is organized on the principles of decentralized management with its Executive Committee as the principal management group responsible for the entire firm's operation. Executive Committee members also serve as worldwide chairpersons of group operating committees. These committees oversee and coordinate the activities of domestic and international companies related to each consumer, pharmaceutical, and professional segment of business. The operating management of each company reports directly, or through a line executive, to a group operating committee. Consistent with its policy of decentralization, operational managers are responsible for all aspects of their units including budget preparation, revision, and implementation. Every January, each operating company reviews and revises its 5- and 10-year plans from the previous year and its mission statement and prepares the budget for the coming year and a

---

[1] For more information about the company, see its website: jnj.com.

two-year plan. The budgeting process is not completed until the approval of the profit plan in December.[2]

Johnson & Johnson is not unique. Budgeting is a common tool companies use for planning and controlling what they must do to serve their customers and succeed in the marketplace. This chapter discusses the budgeting processes and techniques that many successful companies such as Johnson & Johnson use as part of their management processes. Harold S. Geneen believed that a well-managed firm implemented the planned strategy and operations to achieve the planned results. Growth and long-term profitability are results of good planning and implementation. Firms need to plan for success; seldom does a firm get more than the expected (budgeted). [3]

Business continually deals with the future and uncertainty. Planning is a process of charting the future course in this uncertain and dynamic world to attain desired goals. Good planning helps managers attain goals, recognize opportunities, and minimize the negative effects of unavoidable events. Successful organizations are the result of careful planning and diligent implementation. Conversely, failure to plan often results in compromising goals and can lead to financial disaster. The budget is one aspect of planning used by many organizations, for profit, not for profit, large or small, service, or manufacturing.

Role of a Budget

A **budget**
is an organization's operation plan for a specified period; it identifies the resources and commitments required to fulfill the organization's goals for the period.

Budgeting
is the process of preparing a budget.

LEARNING OBJECTIVE 1
Describe the role of a budget in planning, communicating, motivating, controlling, and evaluating performance.

A **budget** is an organization's operation plan for a specified period; it identifies the resources and commitments required to fulfill the organization's goals for the period identified. A budget includes both financial and nonfinancial aspects of the planned operations. The budget for a period is both a guideline for operation and a projection of the operating results for the budgeted period. The process of preparing a budget is called **budgeting**.

Budgets and the budgeting process are intertwined with all aspects of management. In addition to being a plan of operations, a budget plays an important role in allocating resources, coordinating operations, identifying constraints and limitations, and communicating expected actions and results, authorizing activities, motivating and guiding implementation, providing guidelines for control of operations, managing cash flows, and serving as criteria in performance evaluations.

In preparing a budget, a firm's management needs to be forward looking in assessing upcoming events and situations as they pertain to the firm's strategic goals. Budget preparations allow management time to work out any problems the company might face in the coming periods. This extra time enables the firm to minimize the adverse effects that anticipated problems could have on operations. Because all divisions are not likely to think alike and have the same plan for their operations, completion of a budget for all units of an organization also mandates coordinating operations among all budgeted units and synchronizing the operating activities of various departments. Use of budgets helps firms to run smoother operations and achieve better results.

The budget also can help managers identify current and potential bottlenecks in operations. Critical resources then can be mustered to ease any bottlenecks and prevent them from becoming obstacles to attaining budgetary goals.

---

[2] A description of the budgeting process at Johnson & Johnson can be found in Robert Simon, "Planning, Control, and Uncertainty: A Process View," in William J. Bruns, Jr., and Robert S. Kaplan, eds., *Accounting and Management: Field Study Perspectives* (Boston: Harvard University Press, 1987), pp. 339–62. A case study, Codman & Shurtleff, Inc. (Harvard Business School: 187–081), describes the budgeting process of a subsidiary of Johnson & Johnson.

[3] Harold S. Geneen, a trained accountant before becoming the legendary CEO of ITT from 1959 to 1977 relied on the numbers to manage ITT's operation and growth over the years. Under Geneen's management, ITT grew from a relatively unknown company to an international conglomerate in manufacturing, telecommunication, oil, services, and other businesses with more than 250 profit centers. For details, see Harold S. Geneen, *Managing* (New York: Avon Books, 1984), chapter 9, "The Numbers."

REAL-WORLD FOCUS   How Can Moviemakers Keep Their Heads (Budgets) above Water?

When a movie is released, a common sport is to speculate about the amount by which the project exceeded its budget. Why do moviemaking budgets often get out of hand? Doesn't the movie industry worry about budgets and profitability like other corporations and industries?

According to Bill Mechanic, chairman of Twentieth Century Fox, the industry learned a good deal regarding budget management from the making of "Titanic." "We learned some lessons making 'Titanic'... We have tightened up our budget controls, made sure we had more representatives on the set. Making movies for a budget is

about planning and execution, and we have learned a great deal about that." Mechanic noted that having more accounting systems in place to keep track of where and why money is spent help achieve effective cost control. As he put it, "You start to treat this like a real business . . . we all knew the budget [for 'Titanic'] was a bit soft. It would have helped some if we had known ahead of time what we were really in for."

Source: "Online Original: Q & A with Bill Mechanic of Twentieth Century Fox," *Business Week,* January 12, 1998.

A budget is a formal expression of plans for future actions. In many organizations, budgets are the only formal expression of future plans. A budget also serves as a communication device through which top management defines its plans and goals for the period so that other managers and employees have access to this information. The operation plan of a budget allows each division to know what it needs to do to satisfy the needs of other divisions. The manufacturing division knows, for example, that it needs to complete the production of a given product before a certain date if the marketing division budget schedules the delivery of that product to a customer on that date. Budgets prescribe what performance the organization expects of all divisions and all employees for the period.

A budget also is a motivating device. With the expected activities and operating results clearly delineated in the budget, employees know what is expected of them; this in turn motivates people to work to attain the budgeted goals. To enhance the role of budget as a motivating device, many organizations have employees participate in the budgeting process, thus helping employees identify the budget as their own.

During operations, budgets serve as frames of reference. They become guidelines for operations, criteria for monitoring and controlling activities, and authorizations for actions. An organization's success requires that all of its subunits carry out their operations as planned. Through a budget, all subunits know the operations they need to perform to attain the budgeted results. Knowing the expected actions and operating results facilitates coordination of activities. The authorization function of budgets is especially important for government and not-for-profit organizations because budgeted amounts often serve both as approval of activities and as a ceiling for expenditures.

At the end of an operating period, the budget of the period serves as a basis for assessing performance. The budget represents the specific results expected of the firm's divisions and employees for the period against which actual operating results can be measured.

Budgets and budgeting processes also perform many other functions. Covaleski and Dirsmith state that budgeting systems accomplish many purposes beyond achieving planning and control. Budgeting systems are at once forms and sources of power, and they serve as a political advocacy device used by both budgeters and budgetees in the internal resource allocation process.[4]

---

[4] Mark A. Covaleski and Mark W. Dirsmith, "Dialectic Tension, Double Reflexivity and the Everyday Accounting Researcher: On Using Qualitative Methods," *Accounting, Organizations and Society* 15, no. 6, pp. 543–574.

Strategy, the Long-Term Plan, and the Master Budget

LEARNING OBJECTIVE 2

Discuss the importance of strategy and its role in budgeting and identify factors common to successful budgets.

Importance of Strategy in Budgeting

A firm's strategy is the path it chooses for attaining its long-term goals and mission. It is the starting point in preparing its plans and budgets. American Express Company considers itself a personal financial services company. Corporate financial services, such as investment banking, do not fit into the firm's strategic course and therefore have been removed from its operations. B. F. Goodrich Company determined in the early 1980s that for competitive reasons, it would not stay in the automobile tire business and focused its strategy on other rubber products. Finally, Varity Corporation, a leading maker of diesel engines and automotive parts, decided not to be in the farm equipment business, even though its farm equipment manufacturing subsidiary, Massey-Ferguson, accounted for nearly 90 percent of its total revenue. Again, for competitive reasons, the firm made the strategic decision to leave the farm equipment business. Subsequent budgets of these firms reflect those strategic decisions.

The process of determining a firm's strategy begins by assessing external factors that affect operations and evaluating internal factors that can be its strengths and weaknesses. External factors typically include competition, technological, economic, political, regulatory, social, and environmental factors. A careful examination of such factors can help the organization identify opportunities, limitations, and threats. An organization's internal factors include operating characteristics such as financial strength, managerial expertise, functional structure, and organizational culture. Matching the organization's strengths with its identified opportunities and threats enables it to form its strategy. Exhibit 8.1 shows the development of a firm's product strategy.[5]

The importance of strategy in planning and budgeting cannot be overemphasized. Too often organizations view the budget for the coming period as a continuation of the budget for the current period with at best a scant attempt to link the budget to their strategy. A budget should start with a careful review and study of the organization's strategic plan. The objective is to build a budget to achieve the organization's strategic goals and objectives. Not relying on its strategic plan, an organization very likely would not be able to fully utilize its strengths and take full advantage of opportunities. Repeated missed opportunities and underperformances can cause an organization to stagnate. In the worst cases, an inappropriate strategy or lack of one leads to the eventual demise of organizations.

In the late 1960s and early 1970s, U.S. auto manufacturers decided not to develop compact and subcompact automobiles; thus, they did not plan and budget the necessary resources for developing and manufacturing such vehicles. This strategy later proved to be a costly mistake, and automakers suffered for almost 20 years because of this strategic decision. They did not begin to recover until the early 1990s.

Motorola suffered from a similar strategic mistake in the late 1990s. Motorola, which once dominated the wireless communication markets in the United States and most of the world, lost its dominating and very profitable position when it decided to continue pushing for analog technologies and invested only minimum amounts in digital technologies in the early 1990s. In early 2001 telecommunications companies such as Global Crossing, Lucent, and Level-3 followed budgets of yesteryears that emphasized expansions and, as a result, plunged their market values to less than 1 percent of the levels reached prior to 2000.

The success stories of many business firms are stories of good strategy. Wal-Mart Stores took advantage of its experience in operating stores in medium-size towns and expanded nationally into these markets, becoming the largest retailer in the world.

---

[5] Adapted from Robert N. Anthony and Vijay Govindarajan, *Management Control System,* 8th ed. (Burr Ridge, IL: Richard D. Irwin, 1995), p. 265.

EXHIBIT 8.1
Formulation of Strategy

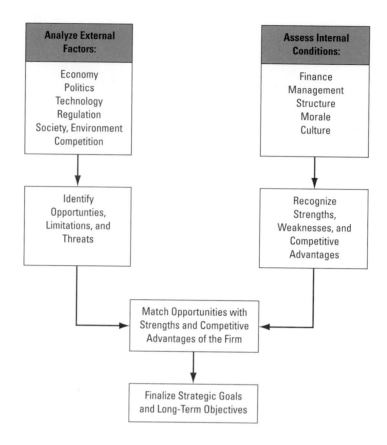

American Express, B. F. Goodrich, and Varity all have enjoyed appreciations in their stock returns greater than the S&P 500 since adopting their new strategies.

Formulation of Strategy

Formulation of strategy starts with analyzing external factors and assessing internal capabilities. Examining external factors surrounding an organization such as the economy, politics, regulations, society, environment, and competition helps the organization to identify opportunities, limitations, and threats. Opportunities available during a booming economy can be substantially different from those available in other times. Political situations and regulations often define the best course of action for firms and organizations.

Assessing internal conditions such as finance available to the organization; strength and capability of the management; and the structure, morale, and culture of the organization can help the firm recognize its strengths, weaknesses, and competitive advantages. In 1993 when he took over as CEO Louis Gerstner recognized that lumbering size and insular corporate culture had placed IBM on a watch list for extinction. The firm lost $16 billion in 1993 alone. Gerstner took hold of the company and demanded that managers work together to reestablish IBM's mission as a customer-focused provider of computing solutions. By the time he retired at the end of 2001, IBM was once again among the premier companies in the world.[6]

Having analyzed external factors surrounding the organization and assessed the internal situations it possesses, management can match opportunities with the strengths and competitive advantages of the organization and determine its strategies and long-term objectives.

Strategic Goals and Long-Term Objectives

An organization attains its strategic goals and long-term objectives through capital and master budgets. Strategy provides the framework within which a long-range plan is

---

[6] Louis V. Gerstner, Jr., *Who Says Elephants Can't Dance?* (New York: HarperCollins Publishers, 2002).

EXHIBIT 8.2   Translating Strategy with the Balanced Scorecard

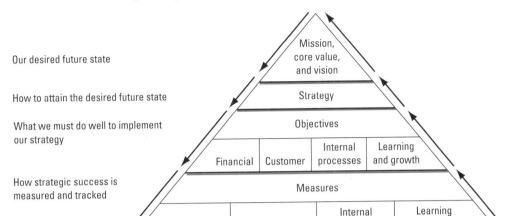

Long-range plan

identifies actions over a 5- to 10-year period to attain the firm's strategic goal.

Capital budgeting

is a process for evaluating proposed major projects and planning for resource requirements.

developed. The organization's **long-range plan** identifies required actions over a 5- to 10-year period to attain the firm's strategic goal. For instance, expecting higher demands for its products, a firm starts to plan for a new factory three years prior. B. F. Goodrich accomplished its strategic goal of leaving the automobile tire business by gradually phasing out its automobile tire manufacturing operations. Varity chose to liquidate Massey-Ferguson by downsizing and diversification over a period of several years. To divest its investment banking business, American Express Company decided in January 1994 to infuse more than $1 billion into its investment-banking arm, Lehman Brothers Inc. The capital infusion lifted the subsidiary's credit rating and American Express was able to sell Lehman Brothers Inc. in May 1994. These actions required long-range planning and coordination for the organizations to attain the goals set forth in their strategies.

Long-range planning often entails **capital budgeting**, which is a process for evaluating proposed major projects such as purchases of new equipment, construction of a new factory, and addition of new products and planning for resource requirements. Capital budgets are prepared to bring an organization's capabilities into line with the needs of its long-range plan and long-term sales forecast. An organization's capacity is a result of capital investments made in prior budgeting periods.

Short-Term Objectives and the Master Budget

Short-term objectives are goals for the coming period, which can be a month, a quarter, a year, or any length of time desired by the organization for planning purposes. A firm determines short-term objectives for the budget period based on strategic goals, long-term objectives and plans, operating results of past periods, and expected future operating and environmental factors including economic, industry, and marketing conditions. These objectives serve as the basis for preparing the master budget for a period.

Recognizing that the objective of an organization is multi-dimensional, more and more firms are employing the balanced scorecard to translate their strategy into objectives.[7] Exhibit 8.2 depicts translation of strategy into short-term objectives with the balanced scorecard.[8] The arrows suggest that the process is both a top-down and bottom-up process. Top-down arrows represent intended strategy—desired future states and plans that managers attempt to implement based on such things as mission, core value, vision, opportunities, and current capabilities. Bottom-up arrows are strategic learning that results from budgeting and day-to-day operations. Strategies that result

[7] Robert S. Kaplan and David P. Norton, *The Balanced Scorecard* (Boston: Harvard Business School Press, 1996). Robert S. Kaplan and David P. Norton, "Transforming the Balanced Scorecard from Performance Measurement to Strategic Management," *Accounting Horizon,* March 2001. Paul R. Niven, *Balanced Scorecard Step-by-Step* (New York: John Wiley & Sons, 2002).

[8] Adapted from Paul R. Niven, *Balanced Scorecard,* p. 107.

EXHIBIT 8.3 The Relationship Between Strategic Goals, Long-Term Objectives, Master Budgets, and Operations

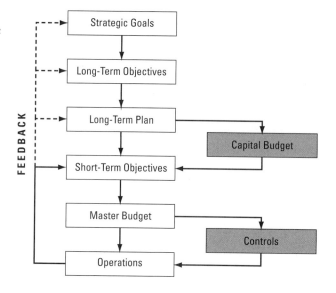

A **master budget**
is an organization's operating and financing plans for a specified period.

from the bottom-up process are emergent strategies—strategies that emerge in the organization as subunits and employees respond to opportunities and threats.[9]

A **master budget** translates the organization's short-term objectives into action steps. A master budget is an organization's operating and financing plans for a specified period that is usually short—a year, a quarter, or a month. A master budget expounds action plans to attain the organization's short-term objectives and financial plans for acquisitions and commitments of financial resources for the budgeted operations during the budget period. Exhibit 8.3 illustrates the relationship between strategic goals, long-term objectives and plans, short-term goals, budgets, operations, and controls.

A master budget plans activities for the coming period and commits resources for these activities. Such commitments must be made with a clear idea of where the organization is heading and be consistent with its strategic goals, long-range plans, and short-term objectives.

A master budget differs from a long-range plan in at least two respects. First, a master budget is a short-term operating plan that typically covers a period of no more than one year; a long-term plan extends over a longer period, such as three to five years.[10] Second, the focal point of a master budget is a responsibility center; a long-range plan is most likely structured along strategic business units, programs, activities, or product lines.

The operating results of recent years—including the expected results of the year that is about to end—impose limitations on the courses of action available to the organization in preparing a master budget. The expected future events simultaneously shape the set of actions from which a firm can choose to attain its goals. Both the operating results of recent years and the expected future events can affect a firm's strategic goals and long-range plans.

Operating budgets
are plans that identify resources needed in operating activities and the acquisition of these resources.

A master budget is also a comprehensive financial summarization of the organization's budgets and plans for operating activities of its subunits for the year. It comprises operating budgets and financial budgets. **Operating budgets** are plans that identify resources needed to carry out the budgeted activities such as sales and services, production, purchasing, marketing, and research and development and the acquisition of these resources. Operating budgets include production, purchase, personnel, and marketing budgets.

Financial budgets
identify sources and uses of funds for the budgeted operation, present budgeted operating result, and delineate financial position at the end of the budgeted period.

Financial budgets identify sources and uses of funds for the budgeted operation, present budgeted operating results, and delineate financial condition at the end of the

---

[9] Henry Mintzberg, "Patterns in Strategy Formation," *Management Science* 24 (1978), pp. 934–48; and Robert Simons, *Performance Measurement & Control System for Implementing Strategy* (Upper Saddle River, NJ: Prentice-Hall, 2000).

[10] It is not unusual for businesses with two distinct seasons to have two operating budgets within a year. For example, many sports teams have two operating budgets for a year.

budget period. Financial budgets include budgets for cash inflows and outflows, operating incomes, and financial position.

Both operating and financial budgets communicate to all subunits and employees the expected operating results and committed resources.

Common Factors of Successful Budgets

Successful budgets share many common factors. Most important among them is the acceptance and support of the budget by all managers and employees. A successful budget often becomes a personalized budget of the people who have the responsibility for carrying it out. They feel it is their budget, not a detached, impersonal institutional budget. They own the budget and are the ones who bring the budgeted goal to fruition.

A budget is more likely to be successful if employees perceive it as a planning and coordinating tool to help them to do their jobs, not as a pressure device to squeeze the last drop of their energy out of them. Nor is a budget likely to be an asset when it is viewed as a tool for management to place blame.

A successful budget is a motivating device that helps people work toward the goal of the organization and a better operating result; it is never used as an excuse for not doing things strategically important to the organization. The expression *not in the budget* never crops up at an organization with a successful budget.

A successful budget always has technically correct and reasonably accurate numbers. A technically incorrect budget is likely to be ignored. A budget with inaccurate numbers will fail to gain confidence and be rendered useless.

Budgeting Process

LEARNING OBJECTIVE 3
Outline the budgeting process.

The budgeting process can range from the informal simple processes small firms use that take only days or weeks to complete to elaborate, lengthy procedures large firms or governments employ that span over months from the start to the final approval. The process usually includes the formation of a budget committee; determination of the budget period; specification of budget guidelines; preparation of the initial budget proposal; budget negotiation, review, and approval; and budget revision.

Budget Committee

The budget committee oversees all budget matters and often is the highest authority in an organization for all matters related to the budget. The committee sets and approves the overall budget goals for all major business units, directs and coordinates budget preparation, resolves conflicts and differences that may arise during budget preparation, approves the final budget, monitors operations as the year unfolds, and reviews the operating results at the end of the period. The budget committee also approves major revisions of the budget during the period.

An effective budget committee has at least one member of the senior management serving as the head of the committee. A typical budget committee includes the chief executive officer or one or more vice presidents, heads of strategic business units, and the chief financial officer. The size of the committee depends on such factors as size of the organization, number of people involved in budget matters, extent of organizational units' participation in the budget processes, and management style of the chief executive officer.[11]

Budget Period

A budget usually is prepared for a set time, most commonly one year with subperiod budgets for each of the quarters or months. Although a budget period can be independent of its fiscal year, the budget year for most organizations coincides with their

---

[11] In some organizations, the chief executive officer makes all budget decisions and there is no committee.

A **continuous (rolling) budget** maintains a budget for a set number of months, quarters, or years at all times.

fiscal years. Synchronizing the budget period with the organization's fiscal period eases budget preparation and facilitates comparisons and reconciliation of actual operating results with the budgeted amounts.

An increasing number of companies prepare continuous budgets. A **continuous (rolling) budget** is a budget system that has in effect a budget for a set number of months, quarters, or years at all times. Thus, as a month or quarter ends, the original budget is updated based on the newly available information, and the budget for a new month or quarter is added. Advances in information technology and availability of easy-to-use budgeting and planning software facilitate the continuous updating of budgets and have greatly increased the number of firms that use continuous budgets. These companies no longer view their budgets as cast in stone at the start of a fiscal year but as living documents they can revise on an ongoing basis throughout the year.

Johnson & Johnson's continuous budget prepares two annual budgets each year, one for each of the next two years. Each year, the second-year budget is revised and updated based on the information that has become available since the last budget preparation period. This second-year budget then becomes the master budget for the coming period and a new second-year budget is prepared. A popular continuous budgeting system has in place 4 quarterly or 12 monthly budgets at all times. A survey showed that 15 percent of firms maintained 4 quarterly budgets; another 5 percent had 12 monthly budgets.[12]

In addition to having a constant budget period at all times, continuous budgets yield other benefits. With continuous budgets, managers are more likely to constantly scrutinize budgeted operations for the remainder of the budget period and examine operations beyond the immediate future. Budgeting and planning are no longer once-a-year events.[13] Firms using continuous budgets are more likely than firms with a traditional budgeting approach to have up-to-date budgets because the preparation of a budget for a new quarter or month often leads to revision of the existing budget.

In practice, firms seldom have budgets for only one year. The budgets for the years beyond the coming year, however, usually contain only the essential operating data. For example, Johnson & Johnson has only skeleton budgets for its 5- and 10-year budgets. Having a long-term budget in parallel with the master budget allows alignment of strategic goals and short-term operations.

Budget Guidelines

The budget committee is responsible for providing initial budget guidelines that set the tone for the budget and govern its preparation. The committee issues budget guidelines after careful considerations on the general outlook of the economy and the market, the organization's strategic goals, long-term plan, expected operating result of the current period, specific corporate decisions or policies such as mandates for downsizing, reengineering, pollution control, and special promotions, and short-term objectives. All responsibility centers (or budget units) follow the budget guidelines in preparing their budgets.

Initial Budget Proposal

Each responsibility center prepares its initial budget proposal based on the budget guidelines. In addition, budget units need to consider a number of internal factors in preparing their budget proposals including:

[12] William P. Cress and James B. Pettijohn, "A Survey of Budget-Related Planning and Control Policies and Procedures," *Journal of Accounting Education,* Fall 1985, pp. 61–78.

[13] However, John Fanning of World Class Finance, KPMG Consulting points out that to attain an effective use of a rolling budget approach, firms need to heed three caveats: First, the firm needs to ensure that the overall volume of information required is reasonable. The amount of details required needs to be substantially reduced so that the overall effort required is no more than that needed under the traditional approach despite the greater frequency of projections. Second, senior management needs to be actively involved and provide critical input to the process. Projections based on a superficial overview will not suffice and consequent budget revisions will most likely be perfunctory. The re-forecasts and re-budgets must be based on a thorough analysis of the changes in operating variables and the marketplace in which the firm operates. Third, care must be taken to ensure that adopting the re-forecasting and rolling budget does not reinforce the concentration on financial measures and result in the exclusion of other critical operating measures.
Source: John Fanning, "Budgeting in the 21st Century," *Management Accounting* (British), November 1999.

- Changes in availability of equipment or facilities.
- Adoption of new manufacturing processes.
- Changes in product design or product mix.
- Introduction of new products.
- Changes in expectations or operating processes of other budget units that the budget unit relies on for its input materials or other operating factors.
- Changes in other operating factors or in the expectations or operating processes in those other budget units that rely on the budget unit to supply them components.

Inevitably, external factors have effects on operations and a budget cannot be completed without careful examinations of important external factors such as:

- The industry's outlook for the near term,
- Competitors' actions,
- Threat to entry,
- Substitute products,
- Bargaining power of customers, and
- Bargaining power (availability and price) of input suppliers (raw materials, components, and labor).[14]

Negotiation, Review, and Approval

The superiors of budget units examine initial budget proposals. The examination includes determining adherence to the budget guidelines, verifying that the budget goals can be reasonably attained and are in line with the goals of the immediately higher organizational unit, and assuring that the budgeted operations are consistent with those of other budget units, including all units directly and indirectly affected. These reviews identify needed changes to the original budget and are made according to negotiations between the budget unit and its superior.

As budget units complete their budgets within the units, the budgets go through the successive levels of the organization until they reach the final level and the combined unit budgets become the organization's budget. Negotiations occur at all levels of the organization and are completed when the budget meets the approval of the budget committee. Negotiations are perhaps the core of the budgeting process and would likely take up the bulk of the budget preparation time.

The budget committee reviews the budget for consistency with the budget guidelines, attainment of the desired short-term goals, and fulfillment of the strategic plan. The budget committee gives final approval, and the chief executive officer then approves the entire budget and submits it to the board of directors.

Revision

No budget is ever cast in stone. As operations unveil, newly learned internal factors or external situations may make it necessary to revise the budget. Procedures for budget revision vary among organizations. Once a budget has been approved, some organizations allow for revision only under special circumstances; others, such as firms adopting continuous budget systems, build in quarterly or monthly revisions.

For organizations that allow budget revisions only under special circumstances, obtaining approval to modify a budget can be difficult. Not all events, however, unfold as predicted in a budget. Strictly implementing a budget as prescribed even when the actual events differ significantly from those expected certainly is not a desirable behavior. In such cases, managers should be encouraged not to rely on the budget as the absolute guideline in operations.

---

[14] Michael Porter considers the last five factors as five competing forces that firms need to scrutinize in determining strategy and planning for action. For details, see Cynthia A. Montgomery and Michael E. Porter, *Strategy* (Boston: Harvard Business Review Press, 1991).

Systematic, periodic revision of the approved budget or the use of a continuous budget can be an advantage in dynamic operations. An updated budget provides better operating guidelines. Regular budget revision, however, might encourage responsibility centers not to prepare their budgets with due diligence. Organizations with systematic budget revisions need to ensure that revisions are allowed only if circumstances have changed significantly and are beyond the control of the budget unit or the organization.

Master Budget

LEARNING OBJECTIVE 4
Prepare a master budget and explain the interrelationships among its supporting schedules.

A master budget is a comprehensive budget for a specific period. It consists of many interrelated operating and financial budgets. Some firms refer to the process of preparing a master budget as profit planning or targeting. Exhibit 8.4 delineates the relationships among components of a master budget.

Strategic Planning and Budgeting

The master budget is the document an organization relies on as it carries out its strategic plan to meet the organization's strategic goals. The master budget for a period is prepared based on the budget guidelines for the period, which were concocted to implement the strategy of the organization.

Sales Budget

A firm attains its desired goals through sales. Almost all activities of a firm emanate from efforts to attain sales goals and sales growth. For this reason, a sales budget often is regarded as the cornerstone of the entire budget.

Sales Forecast

The starting point in preparing a sales budget is sales forecasts. An inaccurate sales forecast can render the entire budget a futile exercise and often imposes costly expenses to the firm as well as its suppliers.[15]

Sales forecasting by its nature is subjective. To reduce subjectivity in forecasts, many firms, as a standard or routine procedure, generate more than one independent sales forecast before preparing the sales budget for the period. One firm has its market research staff at the headquarters, the manager of the business unit, and the sales department of the budget unit each prepare separate and independent sales forecasts. The resulting sales amount in the sales budget is one that all parties agree to be the most likely activity level for the period.

The following factors should be considered in sales forecasting:

- Current sales levels and sales trends of the past few years.
- General economic and industry conditions.
- Competitors' actions and operating plans.
- Pricing policies.

[15] At the end of its fiscal year on July 29, 2000, Cisco reported $1.2 billion in inventory. The firm reported in early February 2001 that it had inventories of $2.5 billion—an increase of more than 100 percent in six months, despite the fact that Cisco's sales grew 25 percent during that same period. The increase in inventory led Cisco's suppliers to suffer a similar fate. The inventory of Solectron, one of Cisco's major suppliers, went up from $1.8 billion in February 2000 to $4.5 billion at year-end. Flextronics, another supplier to Cisco, reported increases in inventories from $470 million at the end of 1999 to $1.73 billion at the end of 2000. Much of Solectron's and Flextronics' inventory was intended for Cisco. "Cisco's (sales) forecasts were wrong . . . and these guys are feeling its pain." At a cost of 1 percent per month, the increases in inventory added tremendous financial burdens to these firms and increased Cisco's costs. Fred Vogelstein, "Valley Talk Missed Earnings: The Contagion is Spreading and Oracle may be Next," *Fortune*, March 5, 2001, p. 42.

EXHIBIT 8.4
The Master Budget

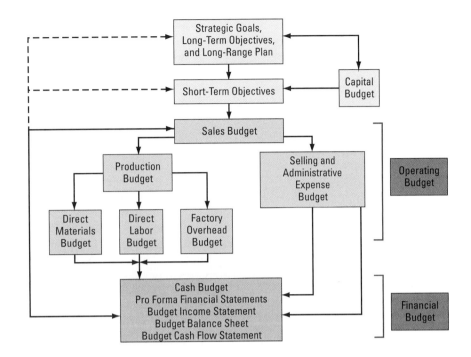

- Credit policies.
- Advertising and promotional activities.
- Unfilled back orders.

Many sales forecasting tools are available. Among them are trend analysis and econometric models. A trend analysis can range from a simple visual plotting of past data on a graph to a sophisticated time-series model. Trend analysis uses past data to map out the sales volume for the budget period. Since all the data needed for the analysis are from the firm's records, it has the advantage of not requiring special efforts to obtain data; this is also the least expensive way to obtain a forecasted sales level. History, however, seldom repeats itself. The forecasted sales level needs to be adjusted for events that may deviate from the perceived historical trend.

Econometric models such as regression or time-series analyses can incorporate past sales data and other factors that affect sales. In sales forecasts a firm may use an econometric model that includes national and regional economic indicators, unemployment rates, consumer-confidence indexes, and age-group distributions, in addition to factors the firm uses in trend analyses.[16] The advantages of using econometric models include objectivity, verifiability, explicit measures of reliability, and inclusion of more comprehensive relevant factors. The use of econometric models has become more common in recent years partly because of the wider availability of powerful, inexpensive computers, and user-friendly software. No model, however, can replace human judgment, no matter how complete or sophisticated it might be. A good forecast often is a combined result of experienced judgment and uses of excellent forecasting models.

---

[16] *Time* magazine attributes the use of an advanced data mining system to perform sales forecasting as one reason for Wal-Mart's success. "By analyzing years' worth of sales data—and then cranking in variables such as the weather and school schedules—the [advanced data mining] system could predict the optimal number of cases of Gatorade, in which flavors and sizes, a store in Laredo, Texas, should have on hand on Friday before Labor Day. Then, if the weather forecast suddenly called for temperatures 5° hotter than last year, the delivery truck would automatically show up with more." Bill Saporito, "Can Wal-Mart Get Any bigger?" *Time*, January 13, 2003, p. 43. Chapter 7 discusses quantitative techniques useful in sales forecasting in more detail.

EXHIBIT 8.5
Sales Budget

KERRY INDUSTRIAL COMPANY Sales Budget For the Quarter Ended June 30, 2007				
	April	**May**	**June**	**Quarter**
Sales in units	20,000	25,000	35,000	80,000
Selling price per unit	× 30	× 30	× 30	× 30
Total sales	$600,000	$750,000	$1,050,000	$2,400,000

Sales Budget

A **sales budget**
shows expected sales in units at
their expected selling prices.

A **sales budget** shows expected sales in units at their expected selling prices. A firm prepares the sales budget for a period based on the forecasted sales level, production capacity for the budget period, and long-term plan and short-term goal of the firm.[17]

A sales budget is the cornerstone of budget preparation because a firm can complete the plan for other activities only after it identifies the expected sales level. A manufacturing firm cannot complete its production schedule without knowing the number of units it must produce, and the number of units to be produced can be ascertained only after the firm knows the number of units budgeted to be sold for the period. Only after determining the number of units to be manufactured and the units of materials to be purchased can the number of employees needed for the operation and the required factory overheads be determined. The desired sales level also determines the expected selling and administrative expenses.

Exhibit 8.5 illustrates the sales budget for Kerry Industrial Company for the first quarter of the 2007 fiscal year. After examining its sales forecast for the coming year, operating results of the year to date, strategic goals, long-range plans for the firm and the product, and the budget guidelines, Kerry sets the sales levels shown and a selling price of $30 per unit.

Production Budget

A **production budget**
is a plan for acquiring the
resources needed to carry out the
manufacturing operations to
satisfy the expected sales and
maintain the desired ending
inventory.

A firm prepares a production budget after determining the number of units that it expects to sell. A **production budget** is a plan for acquiring the resources needed to carry out the manufacturing operations to satisfy the expected sales and maintain the desired ending inventory. The total number of units to be produced depends on the budgeted sales, the desired units of finished goods ending inventory, and the units of finished goods beginning inventory as described in the following:

$$\begin{array}{c}\text{Budgeted} \\ \text{production} \\ \text{(in units)}\end{array} = \begin{array}{c}\text{Budgeted} \\ \text{sales} \\ \text{(in units)}\end{array} + \begin{array}{c}\text{Desired ending} \\ \text{inventory} \\ \text{(in units)}\end{array} - \begin{array}{c}\text{Beginning} \\ \text{inventory} \\ \text{(in units)}\end{array}$$

Selecting the desired ending inventory for a period requires balancing opposing goals. Insufficient inventory loses sales. However, it is costly to maintain excessive inventory. An important determining factor for the optimal inventory level is the quickness with which a firm can adjust as the demand for its product fluctuates. With a real-time system throughout its operations, a firm with a just-in-time system needs no inventory.

Other factors that affect the production budget include company policies regarding stabilizing production versus flexible production schedules that minimize finished inventories, conditions of production equipment, availability of production resources such as materials and laborers, and the firm's production yields and quality.

[17] The Muncie, Indiana, plant of Borg-Warner Automotive drives its budget with cost targets by product line and department. The initial step in its budgeting process is to develop sales estimates for the coming year. Current costs then provide baselines. From there, the firm incorporates basic assumptions, such as inflation, planned product and process changes, and special program costs, to arrive at a base budget. Before completing the budgeting processes, operating managers work with accounting to fine-tune assumptions and incorporate other goals and objectives. George E Hanks, Michael A. Freid, and Jack Huber, "Shifting Gears at Borg-Warner Automotive," *Management Accounting*, February 1994, p. 28.

EXHIBIT 8.6
Production Budget

KERRY INDUSTRIAL COMPANY
Production Budget
For the Quarter Ended June 30, 2007

	April	May	June	Quarter
Budgeted sales in units	20,000	25,000	35,000	80,000
Add: Desired ending inventory of finished units	7,500	10,500	12,000	12,000
Total units needed	27,500	35,500	47,000	92,000
Less: Beginning inventory of finished units	5,000	7,500	10,500	5,000
Budgeted production in units	22,500	28,000	36,500	87,000

To illustrate, Kerry expects to have 5,000 units on hand at the beginning of the quarter, April 1. The firm's operation guideline requires the inventory on hand at the end of each month to be 30 percent of the following month's predicted sales. Kerry expects its total sales in May 2007 to be 25,000 units. The desired ending inventory on April 30, therefore, is 7,500 units as shown in step 1. Step 2 calculates that 22,500 units are to be manufactured in April.

Step 1. Determine the desired units of ending inventory (April 30):

Expected sales in May	25,000 units
$\times$ Desired percentage of the next month's sales to be on hand on April 30	$\times$ 30%
Desired ending inventory on April 30	7,500 units

Step 2. Calculate the budgeted production units during April:

Number of sales units budgeted for April	20,000 units
+ Desired ending inventory on April 30	+ 7,500 units
Total number of units needed in April	27,500 units
− Beginning inventory on hand on April 1	− 5,000 units
Number of production units budgeted for April	22,500 units

Exhibit 8.6 shows Kerry's production budget for the first quarter of 2007. This budget is based on the sales budget (Exhibit 8.5) and the expected sales of the next month.

Most of the quarterly amounts are simply the sums of the appropriate monthly figures. For example, in Exhibit 8.5 the budgeted sales for the quarter, 80,000 units, is the sum of the budgeted sales in April (20,000 units), May (25,000 units), and June (35,000 units). The desired ending finished inventory of the quarter, however, is the desired ending inventory of June, the end of the quarter, not the sum of the desired ending amount in each of the three months. The amount of beginning inventory for the quarter is the beginning inventory of the first month of the quarter. These two amounts refer to specific times in the quarter, not the amount for the entire period.

Before finalizing a production budget, the production manager reviews the feasibility of the budgeted production, in view of the available facilities and other activities scheduled for the same period. In the event that the budget production exceeds the maximum capacity available, management needs to either revise the budgeted sales level or find alternatives to satisfy the demand. If the available capacity exceeds the budgeted production level, the budget allows management ample time to find alternative uses of the idle capacity or to schedule other activities such as preventive maintenance and trial runs of new production processes. This ability to coordinate sales needs and production activities is another benefit of having a budget that allows firms to identify mismatches between capacity and output.

The sales budget for the quarter shows that Kerry expects increasing sales. When sales vary over periods, management can either change the production level as needed, as Kerry did, or choose to maintain a stable production level and schedule the production of 29,000 units per month.

Maintaining a constant production level enables the firm to keep a constant employment level. However, manufacturing excess units during slow periods builds up inventory that is costly to maintain. The new manufacturing environment and increasing adoptions of just-in-time in recent years have led many firms to adjust production activity to changes in sales volume.

Direct Materials Usage and Purchases Budget

A **direct materials usage budget** shows the direct materials required for production and their budgeted cost.

The information in the production budget becomes the basis for preparing several manufacturing-related budgets. One is the **direct materials usage budget** (Exhibit 8.7), which shows the amount of direct materials required for production and their budgeted cost. The last line of the production budget (Exhibit 8.6) shows the number of units of the product that Kerry Industrial Company plans to manufacture in April: 22,500 units. This amount becomes line 1 of Exhibit 8.7, Kerry's direct materials usage budget. The product specification requires 3 pounds of aluminum alloy for each unit of the product, which is entered into line 2 of Exhibit 8.7. Kerry needs a total of 67,500 pounds of aluminum (line 3) to produce the 22,500 units budgeted for the product. The remainder of the direct materials usage budget (Exhibit 8.7, part B) identifies the cost of direct materials for the budget period, which can be completed only after Kerry prepares the direct materials purchase budget for the month (Exhibit 8.8).

EXHIBIT 8.7
Direct Materials Usage Budget

		KERRY INDUSTRIAL COMPANY				
		Direct Materials Usage Budget				
		For the Quarter Ended June 30, 2007				
Line	Item	April	May	June	Quarter	Calculation
A.	*Production Requirement*					
1.	Budgeted production	22,500	28,000	36,500	87,000	
2.	Pounds of aluminum alloy for one unit of product	× ___3___	× ___3___	× ___3___	× ___3___	
3.	Total pounds of aluminum alloy needed in production	67,500	84,000	109,500	261,000	
B.	*Cost of Direct Materials*					
4.	Pounds of aluminum alloy from beginning inventory	7,000	8,400	10,950	7,000	
5.	Cost per pound	× $ 2.40	× $ 2.45	× $ 2.50	× $ 2.40	
6.	Total cost of aluminum alloy beginning inventory	$ 16,800	$ 20,580	$ 27,375	$ 16,800	(4) × (5)
7.	Total cost of aluminum alloy purchases	+ 168,805	+ 216,375	+ 284,310	+ 669,490	*
8.	Total cost of aluminum alloy available	$185,605	$236,955	$311,685	$686,290	(6) + (7)
9.	Desired ending inventory of aluminum alloy in units	8,400	10,950	10,800	10,800	*
10.	Cost per unit	× $ 2.45	× $ 2.50	× $ 2.60	× $ 2.60	*
11.	Aluminum alloy ending inventory	− $ 20,580	− $ 27,375	− $ 28,080	− $ 28,080	(9) × (10)
12.	Total cost of aluminum alloy used in production	$165,025	$209,580	$283,605	$658,210	(8) − (11)

* = Exhibit 8.8

A direct materials purchase budget shows the amount of direct materials to be purchased during the period (in both unit and cost) to meet the budgeted needs in operation. Kerry prepares its direct materials purchase budget to ensure having sufficient direct materials to meet both production needs and the required direct materials ending inventory and to ensure having sufficient funds for the purchases. A direct materials purchase budget starts with the amount of direct materials needed in production for the current period, which was determined in Line 3 of Exhibit 8.7. Kerry needs 67,500, 84,000, and 109,500 pounds of aluminum alloy to meet the production needs for April, May, and June, respectively.

The firm's operation guidelines require the ending direct materials inventory of each period to contain 10 percent of the next period's production needs (line 2). Line 3 of Exhibit 8.7 shows that the firm needs 84,000 pounds of aluminum alloy for the budgeted production in May. Thus, the firm needs to maintain 8,400 pounds of aluminum alloy on hand at the end of April (10% of 84,000), as shown in line 2 of Exhibit 8.8. The sum of lines 1 and 2 (Exhibit 8.8) is the total amount of direct materials needed for April, 75,900 pounds.

Kerry expects to have 7,000 pounds of aluminum alloy on hand at the beginning of April (March's ending inventory). Subtracting the quantity expected to be on hand on April 1 from the total amount needed for April, Kerry must purchase 68,900 pounds in April (line 5 of Exhibit 8.8) to meet the expected needs in April. These steps summarize the calculations in Exhibit 8.8:

Total amount of direct materials needed in production during the month		Line 1
+ Required ending direct materials inventory at the end of the month	+	Line 2
= Total direct materials needed for the month	=	Line 3
− Direct materials on hand at the beginning of the month	−	Line 4
= Direct materials to be purchased during the month	=	Line 5

Kerry's purchasing department estimates the cost of aluminum alloy to be $2.45 per pound in April. The total cost for the 68,900 pounds to be purchased is $168,805, as shown in line 7 of Exhibit 8.8.

At the beginning of April, Kerry has on hand 7,000 pounds of aluminum alloy. At a cost of $2.40 per pound, the total cost of the beginning inventory is $16,800 (Exhibit 8.7, line 6). Adding the purchase cost of $168,805 in April (calculated in line 7 of Exhibit 8.8), the total cost of the direct materials available in April is $185,605 (line 8 of Exhibit 8.7). Using the FIFO inventory valuation, Kerry's cost of ending inventory in April is priced at the most recent purchase price paid, which is $2.45 per pound, or

EXHIBIT 8.8
Direct Materials Purchase Budget

KERRY INDUSTRIAL COMPANY
Direct Materials Purchase Budget
For the Quarter Ended June 30, 2007

Line	Item	April	May	June	Quarter
1.	Total direct materials needed in production (from part A of Exhibit 8.7)	67,500	84,000	109,500	261,000
2.	Add: Desired direct materials ending inventory +	8,400 +	10,950 +	10,800 +	10,800
3.	Total direct materials needed	75,900	94,950	120,300	271,800
4.	Less: Direct materials beginning inventory	− 7,000	− 8,400 −	10,950 −	7,000
5.	Total direct materials purchases	68,900	86,550	109,350	264,800
6.	Purchase price per pound	× $ 2.45 ×	$ 2.50 ×	$ 2.60	
7.	Total cost of direct materials purchases	$168,805	$216,375	$284,310	$669,490

$20,580 (line 11). Subtracting the cost of ending inventory, $20,580, from the total cost of the direct materials available, $185,605, the total cost of the direct materials to be used in April is $165,025 (line 12).

Following the same procedure, the firm completes the purchase budgets for May and June. June's direct materials ending inventory of 10,800 pounds is based on the 36,000 units to be manufactured in July (3 pounds per unit × 36,000 = 108,000 pounds and 10% × 108,000 = 10,800 pounds).

Direct Labor Budget

To prepare the direct labor budget, Kerry would use its production budget. Each firm needs a requisite number of employees with the required skills to carry out the operation as budgeted. The direct labor budget enables the personnel department to plan for hiring and repositioning of employees. A good labor budget helps the firm to avoid emergency hiring, prevent labor shortages, and reduce or eliminate the need to lay off workers. Erratic labor employment diminishes employees' sense of loyalty, increases their insecurity, and leads to inefficiency and decreased productivity.

Many firms have stable employment policies or labor contracts that prevent them from hiring and laying off employees in direct proportion to their production needs. A direct labor budget enables the firm to identify circumstances when it can either reschedule production or plan temporary employee reassignments to perform other tasks. Manufacturing cells common to many firms that adopt new manufacturing technologies often use the direct labor budget to plan for maintenance, minor repairs, installation, testing, learning and growth, or other activities.

A company usually prepares a direct labor budget for each type of labor; for instance, Kerry has skilled and semiskilled factory workers. The production process uses 0.5 hour of semiskilled labor and 0.2 hour of skilled labor for each unit. The hourly wages are $8 and $12 for semiskilled and skilled laborers, respectively. Exhibit 8.9 illustrates the direct labor budget for the first quarter of 2007.

Factory Overhead Budget

A factory overhead budget often includes all production costs other than direct materials and direct labor. Unlike direct materials and direct labor, which vary in direct proportion with the number of units manufactured, manufacturing overhead costs include

EXHIBIT 8.9
Direct Labor Budget

KERRY INDUSTRIAL COMPANY Direct Labor Budget For the Quarter Ended June 30, 2007				
Line	April	May	June	Quarter
Semiskilled Labor				
1. Budgeted production	22,500	28,000	36,500	87,000
2. Semiskilled direct labor-hours per unit	× 0.5 ×	0.5 ×	0.5 ×	0.5
3. Total semiskilled direct labor-hours needed	11,250	14,000	18,250	43,500
4. Hourly wage rate of semiskilled labor	× $ 8 ×	$ 8 ×	$ 8 ×	$ 8
5. Total wages for semiskilled labor	$ 90,000	$112,000	$146,000	$348,000
Skilled Labor				
6. Budgeted production	22,500	28,000	36,500	87,000
7. Skilled direct labor-hours per unit	× 0.2	× 0.2	× 0.2	× 0.2
8. Total skilled direct labor-hours needed	4,500	5,600	7,300	17,400
9. Hourly wage for skilled labor	× $12 ×	$ 12 ×	$ 12 ×	$ 12
10. Total wages for skilled labor	$ 54,000	$ 67,200	$ 87,600	$208,800
Total Labor				
11. Total cost for direct manufacturing labor (5 + 10)	$144,000	$179,200	$233,600	$556,800
12. Total direct manufacturing labor-hours (3 + 8)	15,750	19,600	25,550	60,900

costs that vary in direct proportion with the units manufactured as well as costs that vary with either the kind of facilities the firm has or the way in which the firm carries out its operations. Examples include costs of facilities, which usually do not change with changes in usage, and materials retrieval costs, which are likely to vary with the number of batches in production.

In addition to the number of units to be produced during the budget period, budgeting for factory overhead costs requires knowing the way in which the production is to be carried out. Many firms separate the factory overhead items into variable and fixed overhead costs. Exhibit 8.10 shows Kerry's factory overhead costs budget for the first quarter of 2007.

Cost of Goods Manufactured and Sold Budget

The cost of goods manufactured production cost and the cost of goods sold budget reports the total budgeted cost of units sold for a period. Exhibits 8.6 through 8.10 provide the data needed to complete this budget for each of the months and the quarter. Exhibit 8.11 shows the cost of goods manufactured and sold budget for the first quarter of 2007 prepared by Kerry Industrial Company. The company's finished goods inventory on April 1 shows a unit cost of $18.

Upon completion of the cost of goods manufactured and sold budget for a period, two items in this budget appear in other budgets for the same period. The income statement budget uses the cost of goods sold to determine the gross margin of the period, and the balance sheet includes the finished goods ending inventory in total assets. These two financial statements are discussed later.

Merchandise Purchase Budget

A merchandising firm does not have a production budget. Instead, the manufacturing firm's production budget, as illustrated in Exhibit 8.6, is replaced by a merchandise purchase budget.

EXHIBIT 8.10
Factory Overhead Budget

KERRY INDUSTRIAL COMPANY
Factory Overhead Budget
For the Quarter Ended June 30, 2007

	Rate Per DLH*	April	May	June	Quarter
Total direct labor-hours		15,750	19,600	25,550	60,900
Variable factory overhead:					
Supplies	$0.12	$ 1,890	$ 2,352	$ 3,066	$ 7,308
Indirect labor	1.00	15,750	19,600	25,550	60,900
Fringe benefits	3.00	47,250	58,800	76,650	182,700
Power	0.20	3,150	3,920	5,110	12,180
Maintenance	0.08	1,260	1,568	2,044	4,872
Total variable factory overhead	$4.40	$ 69,300	$ 86,240	$112,420	$267,960
Fixed factory overhead:					
Depreciation		$ 30,000	$ 30,000	$ 40,000#	$100,000
Factory insurance		2,500	2,500	2,500	7,500
Property taxes		900	900	900	2,700
Supervision		8,900	8,900	8,900	26,700
Power		1,250	1,250	1,250	3,750
Maintenance		750	750	750	2,250
Total fixed factory overhead		$ 44,300	$ 44,300	$ 54,300	$142,900
Total factory overhead		$113,600	$130,540	$166,720	$410,860

*Direct labor-hour.
#Kerry purchased equipment in January for $200,000 to be delivered and installed in May (see item 8 on page 295).

EXHIBIT 8.11
Cost of Goods Manufactured
and Sold Budget

KERRY INDUSTRIAL COMPANY
Cost of Goods Manufactured and Sold Budget
For the Quarter Ended June 30, 2007

	April	May	June	Quarter
Direct materials (Line 12, Exhibit 8.7)	$165,025	$209,580	$283,605	$ 658,210
Direct labor (Line 11, Exhibit 8.9)	144,000	179,200	233,600	556,800
Total factory overhead (Exhibit 8.10)	113,600	130,540	166,720	410,860
Total cost of goods manufactured	$422,625	$519,320	$683,925	$1,625,870
Finished goods beginning inventory	90,000#	140,875	194,745	90,000
Total cost of goods available for sale	$512,625	$660,195	$878,670	$1,715,870
Finished goods ending inventory*	140,875	194,745	224,852	224,852
Cost of goods sold	$371,750	$465,450	$653,818	$1,491,018

#Finished goods beginning inventory, April 1, 5,000 units (Exhibit 8.6, p. 287) at $18 per unit.
*Computations for Cost Per Unit and Finished Goods Ending Inventory:

Budget usage:			
DM (8.7, Line 12)	$165,025	$209,580	$283,605
DL (8.9, Line 12)	144,000	179,200	233,600
OH (8.10, last line)	113,600	130,540	166,720
Total manufacturing cost	$422,625	$519,320	$683,925
Budget production unit (8.6, last line)	÷ 22,500 ÷	28,000 ÷	36,500
Cost per unit	$18.7833	$18.5471	$18.7377
Desired ending inventory (8.6, Line 2)	× 7,500 ×	10,500 ×	12,000
Finished goods ending inventory	$140,875	$194,745	$224,852

A **merchandise purchase budget** of a firm shows the amount of merchandise it needs to purchase during the period.

A firm's **merchandise purchase budget** shows the amount of merchandise it needs to purchase during the period. The basic format of a merchandise purchase budget is the same as the production budget. Instead of budgeted production as shown in Exhibit 8.6, however, the last items in a merchandise purchase budget are budgeted purchases.

Selling and General Administrative Expense Budget

A selling and general administrative expense budget delineates plans for all non-manufacturing expenses. As shown in Exhibit 8.12, Kerry Industrial Company's selling and general administrative expense budget for the first quarter of 2007, this budget includes all the planned expenditures for selling and general administrative expenses. This budget serves as a guideline for selling and administrative activities during the budget period.

Many selling and general administrative expenditures are discretionary. Firms are known to reduce or eliminate selling and administrative expenses to increase operating income for the period. For example, in an attempt to increase operating income and to show good control of operating expenses, the manager of a retailer proposes to cut customer service expenditures by $15 million from $20 million to $5 million. Although reduced customer services are likely to lead to decreases in sales, the budgeted total saving in expenditures exceeds the budgeted decrease in earnings for the year and the firm expects its budgeted operating income for the year to increase by $11 million as a result. Decreases in customer services, however, will likely have negative effects on the firm's reputation as well as its future sales. Firms must be wary of taking a short-term perspective when preparing a selling and administrative expense budget.

Cash Budget

A **cash budget** depicts effects of all budgeted activities on cash.

Having adequate cash on hand at all times is crucial for a business's survival and growth. A **cash budget** brings together the effects of all budgeted activities on cash receipts and disbursements. A cash budget depicts the firm's cash position during the budget period. By preparing a cash budget, management can take steps to ensure

EXHIBIT 8.12
Selling and General
Administrative Expense
Budget

	KERRY INDUSTRIAL COMPANY Selling and General Administrative Expense Budget For the Quarter Ended June 30, 2007			
	April	May	June	Quarter
Selling expenses				
Variable selling expense:				
Sales commissions	$ 30,000	$ 37,500	$ 52,500	$120,000
Delivery expenses	2,000	2,500	3,500	8,000
Bad debts expenses	9,000	11,250	15,750	36,000
Total variable selling expense	$ 41,000	$ 51,250	$ 71,750	$164,000
Fixed selling expense:				
Sales salary	$ 8,000	$ 8,000	$ 8,000	$ 24,000
Advertising	50,000	50,000	50,000	150,000
Delivery expenses	6,000	6,000	6,000	18,000
Depreciation	20,000	20,000	20,000	60,000
Total fixed selling expense	$ 84,000	$ 84,000	$ 84,000	$252,000
Total selling expense	$125,000	$135,250	$155,750	$416,000
General administrative expenses (all fixed)				
Administrative salaries	$ 25,000	$ 25,000	$ 25,000	$ 75,000
Accounting and data processing	12,000	12,000	12,000	36,000
Depreciation	7,000	7,000	7,000	21,000
Other administrative expenses	6,000	6,000	6,000	18,000
Total administrative expense	$ 50,000	$ 50,000	$ 50,000	$150,000
Total selling and administrative expense	$175,000	$185,250	$205,750	$566,000

having sufficient cash on hand to carry out the planned activities, allow sufficient time to arrange for additional financing that may be needed during the budget period and thus avoid high costs of emergency borrowing, and plan for investments of excess cash on hand to earn the highest possible return. For smaller firms and those with seasonal business, the cash budget is especially critical to ensuring smooth operations and avoiding crises. The importance of cash budgets cannot be overemphasized.

A cash budget includes all items that affect cash flows and pulls data from almost all parts of the master budget. Preparing a cash budget requires a careful review of all budgets to identify all revenues, expenses, and other transactions that affect cash. A cash budget generally includes three major sections: (1) cash available, (2) cash disbursements, and (3) financing.

The cash available section includes all sources of cash that will be available to the organization. Sources of cash include cash on hand at the beginning of the budget period and cash collections during the budget period. Cash collections are cash sales, collections of accounts and notes receivable, and cash received from nonroutine transactions. Factors that may have effects on cash from sales and cash collections of accounts receivable include sales level, sales pattern, credit policy, and collection experience. A firm also may engage in nonroutine transactions that generate cash during a budget period. Examples are disposal of plant, property, and equipment and sales of investments or nonoperating assets such as land purchased for the site of a factory that the firm no longer intends to build. All proceeds from such sales should be included in the cash available section.

The cash disbursements section describes expected payments during the budget period—payments for purchases of raw materials, supplies, and equipment, wages and salaries, operating expenses, interest expenses, and taxes.

The difference between cash available and cash disbursements is the *ending cash balance* before financing.

EXHIBIT 8.13
Cash Receipts Budget

KERRY INDUSTRIAL COMPANY Cash Receipts Budget For the Quarter Ended June 30, 2007					
Sales data:	March	April	May	June	Quarter
Cash and credit card sales (70% of total sales)	$315,000	$420,000	$525,000	$735,000	$1,680,000
Credit sales (30% of total sales)	135,000	180,000	225,000	315,000	720,000
Total sales	$450,000	$600,000	$750,000	$1,050,000	$2,400,000
Cash received from cash sales					
(60% of cash and credit card sales)		$252,000	$315,000	$441,000	$1,008,000
Cash received from credit card sales					
(40% of cash and credit card sales × 97%)		162,960	203,700	285,180	651,840
Collections of accounts receivable:					
From credit sales the month before this month					
Within cash discount period					
(Prior month credit sales × 80% × 60% × 98%)		63,504	84,672	105,840	254,016
After the cash discount					
(Prior month credit sales × 80% × 40%)		43,200	57,600	72,000	172,800
From sales two months before this month					
(75% of 20% of credit sales two months prior)		18,000	20,250	27,000	65,250
Total cash collections		$539,664	$681,222	$931,020	$2,151,906

A firm needs to arrange for additional funds if its cash balance is expected to fall below the desired minimum balance. On the other hand, a firm needs to determine the best avenues to invest excess cash if it expects to have significant cash receipts over cash disbursements. The firm needs to weigh return, liquidity, and risk in considering alternative investments. Both the additional funding and planned investments are included in the financing section.

Exhibit 8.13 and Exhibit 8.14 shows the cash receipts budget and cash budget, respectively, of the Kerry Industrial Company for the quarter ended June 30, 2007. In addition to reviewing Exhibits 8.5 through 8.12 to identify items that involve either cash inflow or cash outflow, management must gather additional information about the firm's operating characteristics and policies to complete the cash budget. The following are relevant operating characteristics and policies of Kerry Industrial Company that affect the availability of cash or the requirement to expend cash during the budget period:

1. The firm expects to have $75,000 cash on hand on April 1 and has a requirement of maintaining a minimum cash balance of $50,000.
2. The firm expects 70 percent of the total sales to be cash and credit card sales. The remainders are made to Kerry's customers on open accounts. The firm estimates that 40 percent of cash customers use credit cards for their purchases. The bank charges a 3 percent service fee to process credit card charges.
3. Kerry e-mails statements to its customers on the first of each month with terms of 2/10, n/eom.[18] Customers also can access their accounts any time on Kerry's website to find out the status of their accounts. Eighty percent of the credit customers pay within the month; of these, 60 percent pay within the discount period. Seventy-five percent of the remaining balances at the end of the month pay within the month. The remainders are bad debts. Most payments are made via electronic fund transfers.
4. Kerry purchases raw materials and supplies with a term of n/30. The firm pays 60 percent of its purchases in the month of the purchase and the remainder in the following month.
5. All expenses and wages are paid as incurred.

[18] Customers who pay within 10 days receive a 2 percent discount. The account is due on or before the end of the month.

EXHIBIT 8.14
Cash Budget

KERRY INDUSTRIAL COMPANY
Cash Budget
For the Quarter Ended June 30, 2007

	April	May	June	Quarter
Cash Available				
Cash balance, beginning	$ 75,000	$ 84,781	$ 91,916	$ 75,000
Cash collections (Exhibit 8.13)	539,664	681,222	931,020	2,151,906
Total cash available	$614,664	$766,003	$1,022,936	$2,226,906
Cash Disbursement				
Purchases of raw materials:				
Current month purchases[a]	$101,283	$129,825	$ 170,586	$ 401,694
Last month's purchases[b]	62,000	67,522	86,550	216,072
Total payment for purchases of raw materials	$163,283	$197,347	$ 257,136	$ 617,766
Direct labor wages (Exhibit 8.9, line 11)	$144,000	$179,200	$ 233,600	$ 556,800
Factory overheads (Exhibit 8.10, last line, less depreciation)	$ 83,600	$100,540	$ 126,720	$ 310,860
Operating expenses: (Exhibit 8.12)				
Sales commissions	$ 30,000	$ 37,500	$ 52,500	$ 120,000
Sales salary	8,000	8,000	8,000	24,000
Administrative salaries	25,000	25,000	25,000	75,000
Delivery expenses	8,000	8,500	9,500	26,000
Advertising	50,000	50,000	50,000	150,000
Accounting and data processing	12,000	12,000	12,000	36,000
Other selling and general administrative expenses	6,000	6,000	6,000	18,000
Total payment for operating expenses	$139,000	$147,000	$ 163,000	$ 449,000
Equipment purchase		$200,000		$ 200,000
Total cash disbursement	$529,883	$824,087	$ 780,456	$2,134,426
Cash balance before financing	$ 84,781	$(58,084)	$ 242,480	$ 92,480
Financing				
First National Bank		$150,000		$ 150,000
Payment to First National Bank:				
Principal			(150,000)	(150,000)
Interest			(1,500)	(1,500)
Total effect of financing		$150,000	$(151,500)	$ (1,500)
Ending cash balance	$ 84,781	$ 91,916	$ 90,980	$ 90,980

[a]For April for purchases in April: $168,805 × 0.6 = $101,283
For May for purchases in May: $216,375 × 0.6 = $129,825
For June for purchases in June: $284,310 × 0.6 = $170,586
[b]For April for purchases in March: $155,000 × 0.4 = $62,000
For May for purchases in April: $168,805 × 0.4 = $67,522
For June for purchases in May: $216,375 × 0.4 = $86,550

6. Total sales were $400,000 in February and $450,000 in March.
7. The firm purchased a total of $155,000 raw materials in March.
8. Equipment purchased in January for $200,000 will be delivered in May, terms COD.
9. The firm has a revolving 30-day account at 1 percent per month with the First National Bank for all temporary financing needs. The account must be drawn in increments of $50,000 with repayment occurring no sooner than 30 days.

Budget Income Statement

The budget income statement describes the expected operating results from the budgeted operations. An operation involves numerous activities carried out by divisions

EXHIBIT 8.15
Budget Income Statement

KERRY INDUSTRIAL COMPANY				
Budget Income Statement				
For the Quarter Ended June 30, 2007				
	April	May	June	Quarter
Sales (Exhibit 8.5)	$600,000	$750,000	$1,050,000	$2,400,000
Cost of goods sold (Exhibit 8.11)	371,750	465,450	653,818	1,491,018
Gross margin	$228,250	$284,550	$ 396,182	$ 908,982
Selling and general administrative expenses (Exhibit 8.12)	175,000	185,250	205,750	566,000
Net operating income	$ 53,250	$ 99,300	$ 190,432	$ 342,982
Less: Interest expense (Exhibit 8.14)			1,500	1,500
Income before taxes	$ 53,250	$ 99,300	$ 188,932	$ 341,482
Less: Income taxes (30%)	15,975	29,790	56,680	102,445
Net income	$ 37,275	$ 69,510	$ 132,252	$ 239,037

and subdivisions of a firm. A budget income statement allows management a glimpse of the likely operating result upon completion of the budgeted operation. In the event that the budgeted income for the period falls short of the goal, management can then investigate actions to improve the budgeted operating outcome before completing the budgeting process.

Once the budget income statement has been approved, it becomes the benchmark against which the performance of the period is evaluated. Exhibits 8.5, 8.11, and 8.12 provide information needed to prepare the budget income statement for the period in Exhibit 8.15.

Budget Balance Sheet

The last step in a budget preparation cycle usually is to prepare the budget balance sheet. The starting point in preparing a budget balance sheet is the expected financial positions at the end of the current operating period—the beginning balances of the budget period. Exhibit 8.16 presents the expected (budget) balance sheet as of March 31, 2007, the end of Kerry Industrial Company's current operating period. The balance in each of the accounts in this statement is the account's beginning balance of the budgeted balance sheet.

Starting with the beginning balance, the budget balance sheet incorporates the effects of operations during the budget period and shows the balances at the end of the budget period. Exhibit 8.17 shows the budget balance sheet at the end of the budget period. For example, the amount of cash in Exhibit 8.17, $90,980, is taken from the ending cash balance of the cash budget of the period (Exhibit 8.14). The ending balance of raw materials, $28,080, is from Exhibit 8.7. The gross amount for building and equipment, $964,000, is the sum of the beginning balance in the Building and Equipment account reported in Exhibit 8.16, $764,000, and the purchase of new equipment during the budget period, $200,000, as shown in the cash budget for May and, again, for the quarter (Exhibit 8.14). In addition, Kerry estimates that, on June 30, 2007, the balance of office supplies will be $38,906 and the sales tax to be remitted will be $7,812.

Budgeting in Service Companies International Firms, and Not-For-Profit Organizations

Service companies, international firms, and not-for-profit organizations have different operating characteristics, operating environments, and considerations than those of the manufacturing and merchandising firms. This section examines special concerns in

EXHIBIT 8.16
Budget Balance Sheet,
March 31, 2007

KERRY INDUSTRIAL COMPANY
Budget Balance Sheet
March 31, 2007

Assets

Current assets

Cash	$ 75,000	
Account receivables (net)	146,250	
Raw materials inventory	16,800	
Finished goods inventory	90,000	
Office supplies	10,250	
Total current assets		$338,300

Plant, property, and equipment

Land		$ 40,000	
Buildings and equipment	$764,000		
Less: Accumulated depreciation	168,000	596,000	
Total plant, property, and equipment			636,000
Total assets			$974,300

Liabilities and Stockholders' Equity

Current liabilities

Accounts payable	$ 62,000	
Sales tax payable	4,500	
Total liabilities		$ 66,500

Stockholders' equity

Common stock	$303,300	
Retained earnings	604,500	
Total stockholders' equity		907,800
Total liabilities and stockholders' equity		$974,300

LEARNING OBJECTIVE 5
Identify unique budgeting characteristics of service and international firms and not-for-profit organizations.

budgeting for service companies, international firms, and not-for-profit organizations as well as their budgeting approaches.

Budgeting in Service Industries

Similar to budgeting for manufacturing or merchandising firms, budgeting for service firms plans for the resources available from operations and the required resources in operations to fulfill budgeted goals. The difference is in the absence of production or merchandise purchase budgets and their ancillary budgets. A service organization achieves its budgeted goals and fulfills its mission through providing services. An important focal point in its budgeting is personnel planning. A service firm must ensure that it has personnel with the appropriate skills to perform the services required for the budgeted service revenue.

As an example, AccuTax, Inc., provides tax services to small firms and individuals. It expects to have these total revenues from preparing tax returns for the year ended August 31, 2007:

Tax returns for business firms		$1,000,000
Individual tax returns:		
Simple tax forms	$1,640,000	
Complex tax forms	1,200,000	2,840,000
Total revenues		$3,840,000

EXHIBIT 8.17
Budget Balance Sheet,
June 30, 2007

KERRY INDUSTRIAL COMPANY
Budget Balance Sheet
June 30, 2007

Assets

Current assets:

Cash (Exhibit 8.14)	$ 90,980	
Accounts receivable[a]	333,000	
Raw materials inventory (Exhibit 8.7, line 11)	28,080	
Finished goods inventory (Exhibit 8.11)	224,852	
Office supplies	38,906	
Total current assets		$ 715,818

Plant, property, and equipment:

Land (Exhibit 8.16)		$ 40,000	
Buildings and equipment	$964,000		
Less: Accumulated depreciation[b]	349,000	615,000	
Total plant, property, and equipment			655,000
Total assets			$1,370,818

Liabilities and Stockholders' Equity

Liabilities:

Accounts payable[c]	$113,724	
Sales tax payable	7,812	
Income tax payable (Exhibit 8.15)	102,445	
Total liabilities		$ 223,981

Stockholders' equity:

Common stock (Exhibit 8.16)	$303,300	
Retained earnings[d]	843,537	
Total stockholders' equity		1,146,837
Total liabilities and stockholders' equity		$1,370,818

---

[a]June Sales:

Total credit sales in June	$1,050,000 × 0.30 =	$315,000	
Allowance for bad debts	$315,000 × 0.05 =	15,750	
Total net accounts receivable from sales in June			$ 299,250

May Sales:

Total credit sales in May	$750,000 × 0.30 =	$225,000	
Allowance for bad debts	$225,000 × 0.05 =	11,250	
Total net accounts receivable as of May 31		$213,750	
Collections in June	$225,000 × 0.80 =	180,000	
Remaining accounts receivable from May sales			33,750
Accounts receivable, June 30, 2007			$ 333,000

[b]Accumulated depreciation, March 31, 2007 (Exhibit 8.16) $ 168,000

Depreciation expenses:

Factory (Exhibit 8.10)	$100,000	
Selling (Exhibit 8.12)	60,000	
General administrative (Exhibit 8.12)	21,000	
Total depreciation expense for the quarter ended June 30, 2007		181,000
Accumulated depreciation, June 30, 2007		$ 349,000

[c]Direct materials purchases in June, 2007 (Exhibit 8.8) $ 284,310

Payments (Exhibit 8.14)	170,586
Accounts payable, June 30, 2007	$ 113,724

[d]Retained earnings, March 31, 2007 (Exhibit 8.16) $ 604,500

Net income for the quarter ended June 30, 2007 (Exhibit 8.15)	239,037
Retained earnings, June 30, 2007	$ 843,537

The firm has 2 partners, 8 senior consultants, and 20 consultants. On average, a partner works 50 hours a week and is paid $250,000 a year. Both senior consultants and consultants are expected to work 40 hours a week and are paid, respectively, $90,000 and $60,000 a year. The annual compensation for supporting staff is $40,000 per full-time equivalent. The number of supporting staff varies with the size of the firm. In general, one staff is needed for every two partners, one for every four senior consultants, and one for every ten consultants. After allowing for vacation, sickness, and continuing education days, the weeks per year available to work with clients are 40 weeks for each partner, 45 weeks for each senior consultant, and 48 weeks for each consultant. All partners and senior consultants are full-time employees. The firm estimates the following required staff times for each hour spent to complete a tax return:

	Business Return	Complex Individual	Simple Individual
Partner	0.4 hour	0.1 hour	
Senior consultant	0.6 hour	0.4 hour	0.1 hour
Consultant		0.5 hour	0.9 hour

The general and administrative expenses are $150,000 per year plus 10 percent of the total payroll. The firm charges $250 per hour for business returns, $100 per hour for individual returns with complicated tax matters, and $50 per hour for simple individual tax returns. The budgeted revenues and the total hours for each of the returns for the coming year follow:

	Budgeted Revenue		Hourly Rate		Required Hours
Business returns	$1,000,000	÷	$250	=	4,000
Individual returns:					
Simple returns	$1,640,000	÷	$ 50	=	32,800
Complex returns	$1,200,000	÷	$100	=	12,000
Total					48,800

The following table shows the staff requirements for the budgeted revenue:

	Total Hours	Partner	Senior Consultant	Consultant
Business return	4,000	1,600	2,400	
Complex individual	12,000	1,200	4,800	6,000
Simple individual	32,800		3,280	29,520
Total hours	48,800	2,800	10,480	35,520
Hours per week		÷ 50	÷ 40	÷ 40
Number of weeks		56	262	888
Weeks per year		÷ 40	÷ 45	÷ 48
Number of employees needed		2	6	18.5

The budget shows that AccuTax has sufficient staff to support the expected activity. Assume AccuTax plans no change in personnel and maintains the same staff level, its budgeted operating income will be $808,000 as shown in Exhibit 8.18.

Budgeting in Not-for-Profit Organizations

The objectives of not-for-profit organizations such as governments, state universities or colleges, secondary and primary schools, charity organizations, museums, and foundations are different from those of for-profit organizations. Not-for-profit organizations have no single bottom-line, such as operating income that often serves as a verifiable goal in budgeting.

A not-for-profit organization's objective is to provide services efficiently and effectively as mandated in its charter, while not spending more than the allowed expenditure level. With no clear standard by which to measure performance in delivering services, and with a clear mandate not to exceed budgeted expenditures, the master

EXHIBIT 8.18
**Budgeted Operating Result
with no Change in Staffing**

ACCUTAX INC. Budget Income Statement For the year ended August 31, 2007			
Revenue			$3,840,000
Payroll expenses:			
Partners	2 × $ 250,000 =	$ 500,000	
Senior consultants	8 × $ 90,000 =	720,000	
Consultants	20 × $ 60,000 =	1,200,000	
Supporting staff	5 × $ 40,000 =	200,000	2,620,000
General and administrative expenses	$150,000 + 10% × $2,620,000 =		412,000
Operating income			$ 808,000

budget of a not-for-profit organization often becomes an authorization document for allowable expenditures and activities. In effect, the budget for a not-for-profit organization often becomes the source of both the power and limitations of the budgeted unit.

A not-for-profit organization begins its budget preparation by estimating the total revenues for the budget period. Because these organizations often do not have the option to increase revenues by increasing marketing activities, they must decide how best to allocate limited resources to competing activities and subunits. The budget must show that the organization can at least break even at the estimated amount of revenue.[19] Once approved, the budget shows the resources the organization plans to use in carrying out its activities. Revisions are seldom made during the budget period, and the organization's operations usually follow the budget.

Budgeting in International Settings

A multinational company (MNC) faces additional unique budgeting issues that arise because of cultural and language differences, dissimilar political and legal environments, fluctuating monetary exchange rates, and discrepancies in the inflation rates of different countries, among others. An acceptable operating procedure in one country may be against the law of another country. Also, fluctuating currency exchange rates and different inflation rates must be incorporated into the budget because changes in these rates affect the MNC's budgeted purchasing power, operating income, and cash flows.

Subsidiaries or subdivisions of a multinational firm often have their own budgets. They must follow the firm's budget procedure and coordinate their budgets with other divisions of the firm. A subsidiary of an international firm in Belgium, for example, must negotiate its budget with the European headquarters or the business unit to which the subsidiary belongs. The superior divisions then approve the budget in sequence until the final approval by the corporate budget committee.

Alternative Budgeting Approaches

LEARNING OBJECTIVE 6
Apply zero-base, activity-based, and kaizen budgeting.

Over the years many alternative approaches have been proposed to facilitate budget preparation and improve operations. When used properly these approaches—zero base, activity-based, and kaizen budgeting—improve budget effectiveness.

Zero-Base Budgeting

Zero-base budgeting
is a budgeting process that requires managers to prepare budgets from a zero base.

Zero-base budgeting is a budgeting process that requires managers to prepare budgets from a zero base. A typical budgeting process is an incremental process that starts with the current budget. The process assumes that most, if not all, current activities and functions will continue into the budget period. The primary focus in a typical budgeting process is on changes to the current operating budget.

[19] The budget for the federal government of the United States is an exception.

In contrast, a zero-base budgeting process allows no activities or functions to be included in the budget unless managers can justify their needs. Zero-base budgeting requires managers or budgeting teams to perform in-depth reviews and analyses of all budget items. Such a budgeting process encourages managers to be aware of activities or functions that have outlived their usefulness or have been a waste of resources. A tight, efficient budget often results from zero-base budgeting.

Zero-base budgeting has drawn considerable attention since the 1970s. A good budgeting process should follow the fundamental concept of zero-base budgeting; namely, regular, periodic review of all activities and functions. Do not approve a budget item simply because it has always been recommended and approved in the past. All expenditures should be examined with a fresh look and without any preconceived notion.

The amount of work and time needed to perform a true zero-base budgeting to all aspects of operations of an organization can be monumental, however. An organization may find it practically impossible to review and examine all of its activities from the zero-budget level every year. As an alternative, many organizations schedule zero-base budgeting periodically or perform zero-base budgeting for different divisions each year. For example, the highway department of a state government could adopt a rotating five-year zero-base budgeting. All divisions of the department would be subject to in-depth review of their activities every fifth year, not every year as a true zero-base budgeting requires, with the process applied to different divisions each year.

Organizations with considerable turnover at middle or senior levels are good candidates for using zero-base budgeting. Management turnover decreases resistance and reduces or eliminates the parochial knowledge on which previous budgets are based.

Activity-Based Budgeting

Activity-based budgeting (ABB)
is a budgeting process based on
activities and cost drivers
of operations.

Activity-based budgeting (ABB) is a budgeting process based on activities and cost drivers of operations. ABB starts with the budgeted output and segregates costs required for the budgeted output into homogeneous activity cost pools such as unit, batch, product-sustaining, and facility-sustaining activity cost pools based on similarity of their resource and activity consumption cost drivers.[20]

Activity-based budgeting can be a simple extension of a firm's activity-based costing system that has grouped its costs into activity cost pools. The firm needs to review the appropriateness of its activity cost pools and accuracy of its activity costs for the budget period, however, before employing them in budgeting. Either internal or external relevant operating factors may have changed and rendered the data from the current activity-based costing inaccurate or irrelevant, especially when a firm has experienced inexplicable variances. For example, the management may decide to increase the batch size so that fewer batches and fewer batch-related costs such as setup and materials requisition costs are needed for the budgeted output. Or they may acquire new equipment that decreases setup time per batch and supervisory time during both setup and production, and increase hourly wage rates to ensure labor stability, or raise skill levels of employees.

Exhibit 8.19 illustrates an activity-based budgeting for the factory overhead budget of the quarter ended June 30, 2007, for Kerry Industrial Company illustrated in Exhibit 8.10. In addition to data used in Exhibit 8.10, the ABB also used additional data given in Part A of Exhibit 8.19.

The result of an activity-based costing by Kerry Industrial Company suggests that the factory overhead cost varies with hours of semiskilled labor ($0.60 per hour), hours of skilled labor ($0.20 per hour), machine-hours ($3.20 per hour), number of batches ($1,700 per batch), and number of products ($5,000 each). In addition, there is a $50,000 facility cost per month. The firm has a standard batch size of 2,500 units and expects to operate 6,650, 8,220, and 10,510 machine-hours respectively in April, May, and June. Starting with five products in April, Kerry plans to introduce one additional product each month.

[20] Chapter 5 discusses activity-based costing in detail.

EXHIBIT 8.19
Factory Overhead Budget
Using Activity-Based
Budgeting

KERRY INDUSTRIAL COMPANY
Factory Overhead Budget (Activity-Based Budgeting)
For the Quarter Ended June 30, 2007

		April	May	June	Quarter
A: Data					
Units of output		22,500	28,000	36,500	87,000
Direct labor-hours					
Semiskilled		11,250	14,000	18,250	43,500
Skilled		4,500	5,600	7,300	17,400
Machine-hours		6,650	8,220	10,510	25,380
Number of batches (2,500/batch)		9	11.2	14.6	34.8
Number of products		5	6	7	
B: Activity-Based Budget					
Activity cost:	**Cost Rate**				
Semiskilled Hour	$0.60	$ 6,750	$ 8,400	$ 10,950	$ 26,100
Skilled hour	$0.20	900	1,120	1,460	3,480
Machine-hour	$3.20	21,280	26,304	33,632	81,216
Batch	$1,700	15,300	19,040	24,820	59,160
Product	$5,000	25,000	30,000	35,000	90,000
Facility/per month	$50,000	50,000	50,000	50,000	150,000
Total factory overhead		$119,230	$134,864	$155,862	$409,956

EXHIBIT 8.20
Traditional versus Activity-
Based Budgeting

	Volume-Based Budgeting	**Activity-Based Budgeting**
Budgeting unit	Expressed as the cost of functional areas or spending categories	Expressed as the cost of activities or cost drivers
Focus on	Input resources	High-value-added activities
Orientation	History	Continuous improvement
Roles of suppliers and customers	Does not formally consider suppliers and customers in budgeting	Coordinates with suppliers and considers the needs of customers
Control objective	Maximizes managers' performance	Synchronize activities
Budget base	Cost behavior patterns: variable and fixed costs	Utilized and unutilized capacity

Exhibit 8.20 contrasts traditional budgeting and ABB. Firms with volume-based costing systems usually prepare budgets for functional units such as cutting, assembling, and finishing and focus on cost elements, such as materials, labor, and manufacturing overhead, incurred in functional units using volume drivers as Kerry did for the budget shown in Exhibit 8.10. Aggregations of resource costs into functional units often obscure relationships between resource consumption and output and complicate decisions regarding resource utilizations and output levels. As a result, traditional cost systems emphasize allocations of past costs and expenses to products via a simplified volume-based measure, such as labor-hours, machine-hours, units of materials used, or output units. The obscure and complicated relationship between costs and outputs under volume-based costing systems makes it difficult to assess effects of changes on operating results and, as a result, the budget is merely an extension of past data using a much simplified and often arbitrary procedure.

An activity-based budgeting system prepares budgets based on the costs to perform the budgeted activities and links resource consumption to activities. An ABB system strives to define a clear relationship between resource consumption and output. Clear relationships among activities, cost, and output enable managers to examine effects on budgeted resource demands when changes are made to the products offered, product design, product mix, manufacturing processes, market share, customer mix, batch-size, and costs of input resources. ABB directs attention to costs for performing various activities. Budgeting systems under ABB can easily incorporate future-oriented cost data and make the budget relevant for the target period.

ABB facilitates continuous improvement. The process in preparing a budget under ABB highlights opportunities for cost reduction and elimination of wasteful activities. ABB facilitates identification of high-value-added activities and reduction or elimination of low-value-added activities. In contrast, history often is the underlying guidance in a traditional budget.

A volume-based budget confines its activities within the organization and seldom reaches beyond the firm's loading docks. The firm treats the activities of its suppliers or customers as given conditions to the budget. In contrast, a successful ABB requires coordinating closely with suppliers and meeting the needs of customers. As a control tool, a volume-based budget focuses on minimizing variances and maximizing responsibility units' performances. The primary objective for control in ABB is to coordinate and synchronize activities of the entire firm to better serve customers.

The changes made at Digital Semiconductor in its budgeting procedure illustrate the advantages of ABB. Digital Semiconductor, a strategic business unit of Digital Corporation, designed and manufactured Alpha microprocessors and other semiconductor products. In May 1998, the unit was experiencing rapid major technology changes, facing major investment decisions, and feeling increasing pressure to improve its performance. Digital Semiconductor adopted activity-based budgeting (ABB) to gain a better understanding of its cost structure and to establish reasonable product projections.

Digital Semiconductor's adoption of ABB evolved from the firm's activity-based costing and followed the firm's value chain, providing cost and accounting data by activity and beneficiary of those activities across functional areas of the firm. The successful installation of an ABC and, subsequently, an ABB system at Digital Semiconductor significantly improved the assignment of costs and clearly identified high-value-added and low-value-added activities. As a result, management gained a better understanding of activity cost drivers and cost projections. ABB influenced managers to focus on the amount of activities rather than the amount of budget spending. This, in turn, changed managers' behaviors. Product design, manufacturing, and finance managers were able to communicate better using the common language of ABB. Fabrication, assembly, and test operations were managed more effectively as the costs of department and division activities became clear.[21]

Kaizen (Continuous Improvement) Budgeting

Kaizen budgeting is a budgeting approach that explicitly demands continuous improvement in operation processes and incorporates the improvements in the budget. A firm using kaizen budgeting prepares budgets based on the desired future operating processes for the budget period. This is an improvement over the current operating processes, rather than the continuation of the current practices as is often the case in traditional budgeting. Chapter 1 noted that continuous improvement (kaizen) has become a common practice for firms operating in today's globally competitive environment.

Kaizen budgeting begins by analyzing practices to identify areas for improvement and determine expected changes needed to attain the desired improvements. Budgets are prepared based on improved practices or procedures. As a result, budgeted costs often are lower than those in the preceding period, and the firm expects to be able to manufacture products or render services at a lower cost. Kaizen budgeting may mandate, for example, a 10 percent decrease in a product's manufacturing cost for the budget period. The cost to manufacture a product that previously required labor costs of $500 has a budgeted manufacturing labor cost of $450 in a kaizen budget.[22]

Kaizen budgeting
is a budgeting approach that explicitly demands continuous improvement and incorporates the expected improvements in the budget.

[21] Richard J. Block and Lawrence P. Carr, "Activity-Based Budgeting at Digital Semiconductor," *Journal of Cost Management*, November/December 1999, pp. 11–20.

[22] Borrowing the concept of zero-base budgeting, Ewing Kauffman dealt with creeping expenses by insisting all budgets start at an expense level 10 percent lower than that of the current year. The departments had to justify adding the 10 percent before they could add any more expenses for the coming year. The practice worked well enough for Kauffman, who went on to own the Kansas City Royals and to found Ewing Marion Kauffman Foundation. Source: *Inc.*, December 1995, p. 13.

Kaizen budgeting is not limited to internal improvements. Many firms expect and demand continuous improvements of their suppliers and explicitly incorporate consequent effects on costs and delivery schedules of parts and components in budgeted production cost and manufacturing schedules. For example, Citizen Watch demands its suppliers to decrease their costs a minimum of 3 percent per year and includes this decrease in the budget. Suppliers keep any cost savings in excess of 3 percent.[23]

A kaizen budget decrease is not the same as the budget cuts we often see firms or governments make when facing a budget crunch because of diminishing profits, decreasing sales, or declining tax revenues. A budget cut often is a reluctant passive response to a mandate that is accomplished by reducing productive activities or services. In contrast, kaizen budgeting promotes active engagement in reforming or altering practices. A decrease in cost in a kaizen budget is a result of performing the same activity more efficiently and with higher quality; it is not a result of arbitrary elimination of activities or components.

Computer Software in Budgeting and Planning

Budget preparation is a laborious, time-consuming process requiring intensive coordination, number crunching, and reconciliation. This is one reason that a budget, once completed, tends to remain as unchanging as a statue. Neither a budget that is not changed once prepared nor the painstakingly slow processes most likely required to revise a budget can keep up with the needs of companies operating in today's rapidly changing business conditions.

Spreadsheet programs such as Microsoft Excel and similar programs can help ease the burden of number crunching and reduce detail work done manually in preparing or revising a budget. However, the usefulness of spreadsheets in budgeting and planning varies greatly with the abilities of the firm's programmers who develop the spreadsheet-based budgeting and planning module as well as the comfort of others using the program. Furthermore, spreadsheet modules often lack the ability to coordinate the budgets of various divisions and render a fragmented budgeting process.

Many integrated budgeting and planning programs now available integrate strategic planning, budgeting, management reporting, sensitivity analysis, and financial consolidations into one package. The online architecture of most of these programs makes it easy to involve more people in the budgeting and planning processes, provide instant feedback, and allow constant updates of budgets in response to changing circumstances.[24] The online budgeting-planning capability facilitates communication and enables firms to use both top-down and bottom-up budgeting approaches.

Executives and division managers can easily access the same application simultaneously while working on the same budget. The real-time capability eliminates the need to e-mail ideas, changes, and results back and forth. Top management can provide budget guidelines, goals, and objectives, and departmental managers and field personnel can enter their contributions and budget requests directly into the application.

A computer-based budgeting and planning system also can aid sensitivity analyses. Executives can pose what-if questions and the system analyzes the effects of changes and generates the results quickly.[25] For example, Amway Corp. uses its planning software to test changes in strategic assumptions and different budget scenarios, such as a new hiring plan, a new pricing schedule, a change in the cost of materials, a 10 percent decrease in sales because of a higher-than-expected unemployment in an area, a 5 percent cut in travel expenses across the board, or a supplemental incentive program for

[23] Robin Cooper, Citizen Watch Company, Ltd., Harvard Business School case 9–194033. © 1993 by the President and Fellows of Harvard College.

[24] For example, Comshare Inc.'s Comshare MPC; Hyperion Solution Corporation's Hyperion Planning; Cognos Inc.'s Cognos Finance 5.0; OutlookSoft Corp.'s Everest; and Adaytum Software Inc.'s e.Planning. Enterprise software by Oracle, Peoplesoft, SAP, and J. D. Edwards—among others—also offer extensive budgeting and planning capability.

[25] Rick Whiting, "Budget Planning: The Next Generation," *Information Week*, September 25, 2000, p. 163.

high performers. It can see what impact such changes have on the profits and losses and other aspects of the budget.

Recent rapid developments in computer-based online integrated budgeting and planning tools have greatly shortened budgeting processes. It is not unusual for firms to take almost an entire year to prepare budgets without using budgeting and planning software. In contrast, firms employing fully integrated software usually can complete the same processes in two months or less. Budgeting and planning software also allows integration of various operating and financial functions, frequent updates to reflect changing business conditions, in-depth analyses of likely scenarios, and active involvement of more personnel throughout the organization.

One example is the changes Fujitsu made in its budgeting process. Fujitsu Computer Products of America, the San Jose, California, manufacturer of mass data storage products such as disk drives and tapes, found in late 1990s that its traditional planning and budgeting processes spent a tremendous amount of time in administrative aspects of budgeting, distributing spreadsheets, and collecting information. The process took so long that by the time Fujitsu had completed critical assumptions, such as expected market growth, they no longer were valid.

At Fujitsu, department managers forecast product availability and customer expectations independent of each other and then kicked the estimates upstairs for review. The budgets would go through much churning, traveling up and down the corporate ladder until they were final. This circuitous routine took two months, an exceptionally long time in the fast-paced computer industry. Following the suggestion of KPMG, a Big Four accounting firm, Fujitsu replaced its Excel spreadsheet with software links to the firm's enterprise resource planning (ERP) software. The link to its ERP programs allowed the firm to provide information generated by its ERP to serve as a front-end planning database and an analytic tool. The process was arduous and expensive. The result, however, justified the effort. Fujitsu now uses a monthly rolling budget that enables its financial managers to measure real performance and allows for more careful analysis and planning.

The new system reaped dividends for Fujitsu in 1999, when it became apparent that its disk drive business was headed for a period of oversupply. Fujitsu entered the information into the new budgeting system, which advised the company to hold back on hiring and other capital investment plans during the period. Following these suggestions, the firm changed its budget. The system provided other benefits and more than paid for the cost of the system. Fujitsu's management now works as a team; by using enterprise planning software tools, it determines strategic and tactical assumptions before doing any detailed planning. The team discusses product launches, customer and competitive issues, pricing assumptions, and target market shares; documents that information; and then brings in competitive analyses before reaching overall planning objectives. When it is completed, the strategic plan goes to Fujitsu's product-line and sales managers, who create a forecast and tactics to support the corporate objectives. Their observations are compiled and reviewed to ensure that they conform to the original target. When the forecast and tactic fall short of the firm's objectives for the period, Fujitsu's financial managers make corrective changes before the budget is approved.

Moreover, unsupported assumptions are no longer repeated up and down the management ladder. Fujitsu's process now encompasses one up-and-down cycle. The new system eliminated multi-iterative budgets that waste time and replaced them with continuous plans owned by department managers. As a result, its planning and budgeting process takes about 10 to 15 days compared with six to eight weeks under the previous system. Because managers spend less time on budgeting, they devote more time to understanding Fujitsu's individual businesses. In contrast there wasn't enough time left over after the budgeting process in the past. Although Fujitsu is a very large corporation with more than $1 billion in annual sales, management has had no trouble understanding the consolidated results.[26]

---

[26] Russ Banham, "Better Budgets," *Journal of Accountancy*, February 2000, pp. 37–40.

Ethical, Behavioral, and Implementation Issues in Budgeting

A budget can be successful only if the person responsible for its implementation makes it happen. Successful implementations require proper ethical and other behavior. To encourage persons responsible for budget preparation and implementation to attain the organization's goals, management must take into consideration ethical and behavioral factors in budgeting.

Ethics in Budgeting

Ethical issues permeate all aspects of budgeting. Budgets often serve as an important criterion in evaluating budgeters' performances. Yet, budgeters provide input data on which the firm prepares budgets. Employees may breach the code of ethics if the firm fails to take preventive measures that discourage efforts to lower performance expectations in budgets.

A budget is also a result of negotiations. Too often people believe that it is better to promise too little and deliver more than to promise too much and deliver less. This might involve negotiating a goal of 12 percent growth in earnings and achieving 14 percent rather than negotiating a goal of 16 percent and delivering 15 percent. The 15 percent actual performance is certainly a better result for the firm, but when facing a choice between offering a budget with the likelihood of 12 percent growth and one with 16 percent growth, managers usually choose the 12 percent budget because it is easier to achieve and represents a lower risk to their careers. The advantages of having a budget are diminished when, as the retired CEO Jack Welch of General Electric stated, "(Budgets) are always getting the lowest out of people, because everyone is negotiating to get the lowest number." A successful budget needs to avoid making a budget an exercise in minimization.

Including budget slack, or padding the budget, is the practice of managers knowingly including a higher amount of expenditures in the budget than they actually believe is needed. They often justify such practices as insurance against uncertain future events. After all, no one knows exactly how the future will unfold. Budget slack, however, wastes resources and could lead employees to make half-hearted efforts to meet or exceed the budget.

Spending the budget is another serious ethical issue in budgeting. Managers might believe that their future budgets will be reduced if they do not use up all the budgeted amounts. As a result, managers might resort to wasteful spending to exhaust the remaining budgeted amount before the end of the period. This wastes precious resources on activities that yield little or no benefit to the firm or acquire unnecessary assets to use up remaining funds. Furthermore, managers waste time on unproductive efforts in trying to exhaust the budgeted expenditure.

Goal Congruence

Goal congruence is consistency between the goals of the firm, its subunits, and its employees. Ideally, a firm should strive for perfect goal congruence. Realistically, perfect goal congruence almost never exists because resources for satisfying short-term goals of individuals often conflict with those of the firm. For example, employees often desire to earn a high salary with minimum effort, whereas a firm seeks to offer employees low compensation while receiving maximum efforts from them.

Still, a firm's goals must be as consistent as possible with the goals of its employees. A budget devoid of considerations for goal congruence is likely not to achieve the most desirable results. A budget that aligns the firm's goals with those of its employees has a much better chance to realize successful operations and attain desirable results. One approach that encourages goal congruence is to actively involve all employees throughout the entire budgeting process. Employees are more likely to identify a budget as their own when they have participated actively during the budgeting process.

EXHIBIT 8.21
Budget Difficulty and Effort

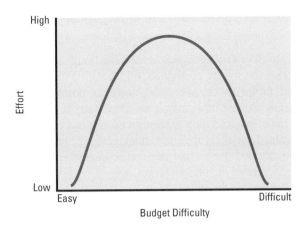

Difficulty Level of the Budget Target

An easy budget target may fail to encourage the employees to give their best efforts. A budget target that is very difficult to achieve can, however, discourage managers from even trying to attain it. Exhibit 8.21 depicts research findings on the relationship between the level of employees' efforts and level of difficulty of budget targets. Ideally, budget targets should be challenging yet attainable. But what is a challenging and attainable budget target?

To determine the difficulty level of a budget target, managers must consider the multiple functions a budget serves. A budget allows a manager to convert the organizational strategies and goals into budget goals for operating divisions. Budgeting, however, is a planning, coordinating, motivating, controlling, and evaluating tool. For planning and coordinating purposes, budget goals should be set at the level that most managers are likely to attain. Good planning identifies events likely to occur and allows managers to plan actions accordingly to attain the goals of their divisions as well as the goals of the organization. A budget with targets that managers cannot possibly attain is no plan at all and may undermine the coordination function of the budget.

For motivational purposes, the optimal budget target should be set at a level attainable by, say, fewer than half the managers. On the other hand, a budget that allows fewer than half the operations to occur as planned certainly is not a good plan, nor is it a very good guideline for coordinating activities.

Research by Merchant and Manzoni suggests that a highly achievable target, a target achievable by most managers 80 to 90 percent of the time, serves quite well in the vast majority of organizations, especially when accompanied by extra rewards for performances exceeding the target.[27] According to Merchant (1990), the advantages of using a highly achievable budget target include:

1. Increasing managers' commitment to achieving the budget target.
2. Maintaining managers' confidence in the budget.
3. Decreasing organizational control cost.
4. Reducing the risk that managers will engage in harmful earnings management practices or violate corporate ethical standards. Twenty-nine percent of workers responding to a survey felt pressure to violate the ethical standards of their firms because of overly aggressive business goals.[28]
5. Allowing effective and efficient managers greater operating flexibility.

[27] Kenneth A. Merchant, "How Challenging Should Profit Budget Targets Be?" *Management Accounting,* November 1990, pp. 46–48; Kenneth A. Merchant, *Rewarding Results: Motivating Profit Center Managers* (Cambridge, MA: Harvard Business School Press, 1989); and Kenneth A. Merchant and J. Manzoni, "The Achievability of Budget Targets in Profit Centers: A Field Study," *The Accounting Review,* July 1989, pp. 539–58.

[28] J. P. Miller, T. Burton, and R. Smith, "W. R. Grace is Roiled by Flap," *The Wall Street Journal,* March 10, 1995, p. A2.

6. Improving predictability of earnings or operating results.

7. Enhancing the usefulness of a budget as a planning and coordinating tool.

One risk of using highly achievable budgets is that some managers, especially those who are not highly motivated, might not be challenged enough to put forth their maximum performance. Merchant, however, points out that this problem might not be significant because most managers are already highly motivated. Most have risen through the ranks because they perform well and have strong competitive and self-satisfaction drives. More likely than not, managers will continue at the same pace even after they have attained the budget targets. To ensure that managers do not slack off once they have achieved the budget target, some firms provide bonuses for performance exceeding the budget target.

Authoritative or Participative Budgeting

Budgeting processes are either top down or bottom up. In a top-down budgeting process, top management prepares budgets for the entire organization, including those for lower-level operations. This process often is referred to as authoritative budgeting. A participative budgeting process, on the other hand, is a bottom-up approach that involves the people affected by the budget, including lower-level employees, in the budget preparation process.

Authoritative budgeting provides better decision-making control than does participative budgeting. Top management sets the overall goals for the budget period and prepares a budget for operations to attain the goals. An authoritative budget, however, often lacks the commitment of lower-level managers and employees responsible for implementing it. Furthermore, an authoritative budget does not communicate; it issues or dictates orders. People are likely to resent orders and are more willing to devote extra effort to attain goals they perceive as their own.

A participative budget is a good communication device. The process of preparing a budget often gives top management a better grasp of the problems their employees face and provides the employees a better understanding of the dilemmas that the top management deals with. A participative budget is more likely to gain the employees' commitment to fulfill the budgetary goals. Unless properly controlled, however, a participative budget can lead to easy budget targets or targets not in compliance with the organization's strategy or budget.

An effective budgeting process often combines both top-down and bottom-up budgeting approaches. Divisions prepare their initial budgets based on the budget guidelines issued by the firm's budget committee. Senior managers review and make suggestions to the proposed budget before sending it back to the divisions for revisions. The final budget usually is reached after several rounds of negotiations.

Top Management Involvement

To what extent and in what ways should top management be involved in budgeting? For a budget to be effective, top management must be involved and show strong interest in the budget results. Too much involvement, however, can make the budget an authoritative budget and alienate lower managers. The right approach is a good balance of top management involvement with active participation of lower-level managers throughout the entire budgeting preparation.

The budget review and approval process ensures top management that budget guidelines are being followed. Top management's active involvement in reviewing and approving the proposed budget is an effective way to discourage lower-level managers from playing budget games.[29] The active involvement of top management also

---

[29] Hofstede examines several budget games that people play. Among them are submitting budgets with easy targets and adding slack to a budget. For details, see G. H. Hofstede, *The Game of Budget Control* (New York: Barnes & Noble, 1968).

A recent survey of chief financial officers (CFOs) by Pricewaterhouse Coopers shows that 74 percent of these executives believe that the master budget has one of the highest priorities in the coming years. On a 5-point scale to rank importance, the executives scored the master budget as 4.1. Unfortunately, the executives also reported that the master budget was poorly implemented at their firms (an average score of 2.1 out of 5). Those writing up the study also noted that Jack Welch, former CEO of General Electric, has called the master budget the "bane of corporate America." What are some of the implementation problems these CFOs are concerned about, and how do you think they might address these problems?

motivates lower managers to believe in the budget, be candid in its preparation, and be dedicated to attaining its goals because they know that the boss cares about the budget.

Role of the Budget Department or Controller

The budget department, and in some organizations the controller, is actively engaged throughout the entire budget preparation process examining data accuracy and ensuring consistency and conformity with the organization's budget guidelines and goals. The budget department provides the technicians who put the budget together.

Unfortunately, many of the tasks that the budget department must perform can be perceived as negative if not carried out tactfully and gingerly. In putting together a budget, the budget department may detect budget slack, excessive inventory, inefficient operations, and other potential problems in the proposed operations. As the budget department directs attention to these problems, operational units may feel encroachment or interference of their authority. Nevertheless, a firm needs to eliminate budget slack, reduce excessive inventories, and improve operation efficiency if the firm is to have an efficient and effective budget.

Staff members in the budget department should be good communicators. They also must earn a reputation for being fair and impartial and for having personal integrity. A person who possesses such characteristics can offer much as an effective facilitator and coordinator of budgeting.

SUMMARY

An organization's budget is a quantitative plan that identifies the resources required and commitments to fulfill its goal for the budget period. Budgeting allows management to plan ahead, communicate the plan and goals for the budget period to all divisions and employees, and motivate employees. A budget also serves as a blueprint for operations, a guideline for controlling operations, and a basis for performance evaluation.

Strategy helps a firm to be more focused in its operations and to take advantage of its strengths and opportunities. A firm carries out its strategy through long-range plans and master budgets. Strategy provides a framework within which the organization develops its long-range plan. An annual master budget is an extension of the organization's long-range plan to fulfill organization goals and objectives. A successful budget is accepted and supported by the key management, becomes a personalized budget for the people responsible for implementing it, and is perceived by all personnel as a tool to help them to do a better job, not as a pressure device. A successful budget is also a motivating device and must be technically accurate.

Budgeting processes include formation of a budget committee; determination of the budget period; specification of budget guidelines; preparation of the initial budget proposal; budget negotiation, review, and approval; and budget revisions. A budget committee oversees all budget matters and usually consists of at least one key senior manager. The committee issues budget guidelines based on plans emanating from reviews of the firm's strategy, external and internal factors, goals and objectives of the budget period, and experience gained from implementing the current budget. Based on the budget guidelines, managers prepare initial budgets and discuss and negotiate their budget proposals with superiors. The budget committee or the chief executive officer gives final approval of the budget.

The master budget includes sales, production, direct materials, direct labor, factory overhead, selling, and administration expense budgets, and the budget cash statement, income statement, and balance sheet.

A service firm prepares a budget following set procedures just as a manufacturing or merchandising firm does. A major difference between budgets for service firms and those for manufacturing or merchandising firms is the absence of a production budget or merchandise purchase budget and its ancillary budgets for service firms. The budgeting procedures and all other budget items are the same for both service and manufacturing or merchandising firms. A service firm must carefully plan its activities for securing the required resources, frequently focusing on the labor force to render the planned services to fulfill the budgeted activities. A budget for a not-for-profit organization reflects its authorized activities.

A multinational company should carefully consider in its budget such issues as cultural and language differences, dissimilar political and legal environments, fluctuating monetary exchange rates, and discrepancies in inflation rates of different countries.

Zero-base budgeting differs from traditional budgeting in that it is not an incremental budget of the current budget. Zero-base budgeting requires managers to evaluate and justify all activities included in the budget. Activity-based budgeting focuses on the activities and cost drivers in preparing budgets. Kaizen budgeting integrates expected improvements into budgets.

Ethical issues in budgeting include preventing concealment of information, avoidance of having a higher budget goal, inclusion of budget slack, and spending the budget to avoid having it cut back. Behavioral issues in budgeting encompass the difficulty level of budget targets, the drawbacks and advantages of authoritative and participative budgeting processes, the extent of involvement of top management in budgeting, and the role of the budget department or controller in budgeting.

Key Terms

activity-based budgeting, *301*
budget, *275*
budgeting, *275*
capital budgeting, *279*
cash budget, *292*
continuous (rolling) budget, *282*

direct materials usage budget, *288*
financial budget, *280*
goal congruence, *306*
kaizen budgeting, *303*
long-range plan, *279*
master budget, *280*

merchandise purchase budget, *292*
operating budget, *280*
production budget, *286*
sales budget, *286*
zero-base budgeting, *300*

Comments on Cost Management in Action

What's Wrong with the Budget Process?

While most chief financial officers are convinced of the importance of the master budget, they are not satisfied with the budget process in their firms. Among the issues the CFOs identify for improvement are:

1. Many firms use a bottom-up budget process—department managers initiate the process and prepare detailed budgets for top management's review and approval. However, firms that use a top-down budgeting process find the top-down approach is preferable because it places a greater focus on the strategic plans developed by top management and because it is faster and more flexible to execute. Most importantly, it can be more difficult to integrate strategy into the budget when it has a bottom-up process. General Electric, in particular, insists that strategic thinking must be integrated throughout the budget process.

2. Many firms that use the annual budget process fail to update for changes during the year. As a result, these firms are not prepared for changes in market conditions and operating factors—changes that require fast response and perhaps a change in strategy. Johnson & Johnson, General Electric, Roche, and other firms use continuous budgets that require frequent updates of forecasts and reassessment of competitive factors throughout the year.

3. At some firms, a problem is that financial managers are not effective in communicating the importance and the benefits of the master budget to department heads. This means that the

budget is not fully and properly utilized. Firms such as Warner Lambert and General Electric work hard to make sure that financial managers working on the budget are effective at supporting the department heads, and that the budget process is understood and valued throughout the firm.

Source: Richard Harborne, "Power Planning: An Integrated Business Planning Process," *Strategic Finance,* October 1999, pp. 47–53.

Self-Study Problems
(For solutions, please turn to the end of the chapter)

1. Master Budget

Hansell Company's management wants to prepare budgets for one of its products, duraflex, for July 2007. The firm sells the product for $80 per unit and has the following expected sales units for these months in 2007:

April	May	June	July	August	September
5,000	5,400	5,500	6,000	7,000	8,000

The production process requires 4 pounds of dura-1000 and 2 pounds of flexplas. The firm's policy is to maintain a minimum of 100 units of duraflex on hand at all times with no fewer than 10 percent of units on hand at the end of a period to meet the expected sales for the following month. All materials inventories are to be maintained at 5 percent of the production needs for the next month, but not to exceed 1,000 pounds. The firm expects all inventories at the end of June to be within the guidelines. The purchase department expects the materials to cost $1.25 per pound and $5.00 per pound of dura-1000 and flexplas, respectively.

The production process requires direct labor at two skill levels. The rate for labor at the K102 level is $50 per hour and for the K175 level is $20 per hour. The K102 level can process one batch of duraflex per hour; each batch consists of 100 units. The manufacturing of duraflex also requires one-tenth of an hour of K175 workers' time for each unit manufactured.

Manufactured overheads are $1,200 per batch and $80 per direct labor-hour.

Required

On the basis of the preceding data and projections, prepare the following budgets for July 2007:

a. Sales budget (in dollars).

b. Production budget (in units).

c. Production budget for August (in units).

d. Direct materials purchase budget (in pounds).

e. Direct materials purchase budget (in dollars).

f. Direct manufacturing labor budget (in dollars).

2. Cash Budget and Income Statement

Hansell Company expects its trial balance on June 30 to be as follows:

HANSELL COMPANY
Budget Trial Balance
June 30, 2007

	Debit	Credit
Cash	$ 40,000	
Accounts receivable	80,000	
Allowance for bad debts		$ 3,500
Inventory	25,000	
Plants, property, and equipment	650,000	
Accumulated depreciation		320,000
Accounts payable		95,000
Wages and salaries payable		24,000
Note payable		200,000
Stockholders' equity		152,500
Total	$795,000	$795,000

Typically, cash sales represent 20 percent of sales and credit sales represent 80 percent. Sales terms are 2/10, n/30. Hansell bills customers on the first day of each month. Experience has shown that 60 percent of the billings will be collected within the discount period, 25 percent by the end of the month after sales, 10 percent by the end of the second month after the sale, and 5 percent will be uncollectible. The firm writes off uncollectible accounts after 12 months.

The purchase terms for materials are 2/15, n/60. The firm makes all payments within the discount period. Experience has shown that 80 percent of the purchases are paid in the month of the purchase and the remainder are paid in the month immediately following. In June 2007, the firm budgeted purchases of $25,000 for dura-1000 and $22,000 for flexplas.

Sixty percent of the factory overhead is variable. The firm has a monthly fixed factory overhead of $50,000, of which $20,000 is depreciation expense. The firm pays all manufacturing labor and factory overhead when incurred.

Total budgeted marketing, distribution, customer service, and administrative costs for 2007 are $2,400,000. Of this amount, $1,200,000 is considered fixed and includes depreciation expenses of $120,000. The remainder varies with sales. The budgeted total sales for 2007 are $4 million. All marketing and administrative costs are paid in the month incurred.

Management desires to maintain a minimum cash balance of $40,000. The firm has an agreement with a local bank to borrow its short-term needs in multiples of $1,000 up to $100,000 at an interest rate of 12 percent.

Required

1. Prepare the cash budget for July 2007.
2. Prepare the budget income statement for July 2007.

Questions

8–1   Describe at least three benefits, other than facilitating operational controls, that an organization can expect to realize from implementing a budget.   (CMA adapted)

8–2   Explain the difference between a strategic plan and a master budget.

8–3   Is a capital budget part of a master budget?

8–4   Differentiate master, operating, and financial budgets.

8–5   List at least three common characteristics of successful budgets.

8–6   What are the roles of a budget committee?

8–7   Is sales forecast and sales budget synonymous?

8–8   Why is the sales budget the cornerstone of a budget?

8–9   When sales volume is seasonal in nature, certain items in the budget must be coordinated. What are the three most significant items to coordinate in budgeting seasonal sales volume?
                                                                                    (CMA Adapted)

8–10 In addition to the sales budget, what additional information does a firm need to complete its materials purchase budget?

8–11 Which two factors determine the amount of factory overhead?   (CMA Adapted)

8–12 List the major components of a cash budget.

8–13 Explain similarities and differences between cash budgets and cash flow statements required for external financial reporting.

8–14 Contrast the budgeting considerations for service organizations and manufacturing companies.

8–15 What are the major differences in the preparation and uses of budgets for a business firm and a not-for-profit organization?

8–16 What is zero-base budgeting?

8–17 Is kaizen budgeting the Japanese term for activity-based budgeting?

8–18 Define slack in budgets. Why is it common to find slack in budgets?

8–19 What is a highly achievable budget? Why do firms prefer such a budget?

8–20 List the role of top management in participative budgeting.

Exercises

8–21 **Budgeting for Control**   Kallert Manufacturing currently uses the company's budget only as a planning tool. Management has decided that it would be beneficial also to use the budget for control purposes.

Required   What must the management accountant do so that the firm's budgeting and accounting systems implement this change successfully?

(CMA Adapted)

8-22 Purchase Budget and Payment   Janet DeVolris, purchasing manager of Corkin Manufacturing, a small Midwest manufacturer of specialty tools, was frustrated because her efforts to reduce the use of expensive overnight shipping appeared to be futile. Rush orders, last-minute changes, and other operating emergencies seemed to be the firm's way of life. Although she vowed to keep last minute actions to a minimum, overnight shipping shows no sign of abatement after six months.

At a recent convention, several suppliers mentioned that Corkin Manufacturing rarely takes advantage of the discount terms she worked so hard for them to grant. She was very surprised because sales terms of 2/10, n/30 or better yielded an annual return of at least 36 percent.

Tony Blair, the firm's CEO, recently praised Janet lavishly for her performance for the last six months and gave her a generous raise. Still, she feels frustrated and unfulfilled.

Required   What could Janet do to overcome her frustration?

8-23 Budget Slack and Zero-Base Budgeting   Bob Bingham is the controller of Atlantis Laboratories, a manufacturer and distributor of generic prescription pharmaceuticals. He is currently preparing the annual budget and reviewing the current business plan. The firm's business unit managers prepare and assemble the detailed operating budgets with technical assistance from the corporate accounting staff. The business unit managers then present the final budgets to the corporate executive committee for approval. The corporate accounting staff reviews the budgets for adherence to corporate accounting policies but not for reasonableness of the line items within the budgets.

Bob is aware that the upcoming year for Atlantis could be a difficult one because of a major patent expiration and the loss of a licensing agreement for another product line. He also knows that during the budgeting process, budget slack is created in varying degrees throughout the organization. Bob believes that this slack has a negative effect on the firm's overall business objectives and should be eliminated where possible.

Required

1. Define *budget slack*.
2. Explain the advantages and disadvantages of budget slack from the point of view of (a) the business unit manager who must achieve the budget and (b) corporate management.
3. Bob Bingham is considering implementing zero-base budgeting in Atlantis Laboratories.
   a. Define *zero-base budgeting*.
   b. Describe how *zero-base budgeting* could be advantageous to Atlantis Laboratories in controlling budgetary slack.
   c. Discuss the disadvantages Atlantis Laboratories might encounter in using zero-base budgeting.

(CMA Adapted)

8-24 Production Budget   Shocker Company has the following sales budget for the next year:

Quarter 1	10,000 units	Quarter 3	12,000 units
Quarter 2	8,000 units	Quarter 4	14,000 units

Company policy is to have a finished goods inventory at the end of each quarter equal to 20 percent of the next quarter's sales.

Required   What is the budgeted production for the second quarter of the next year? (CMA Adapted)

8-25 Production Budget   Merhendra Company's sales budget shows these projections for the year 2006:

Quarter	Units
First	60,000
Second	80,000
Third	45,000
Fourth	55,000
	240,000

Inventory on December 31, 2005, is expected to be 18,000 units. The firm desires the finished goods inventory at the end of each quarter to be 30 percent of the next quarter's sales.

Required   Determine the number of units that the firm needs to manufacture in each of the first two quarters of 2006.

8–26   **Production and Materials Purchase Budgets**   DeVaris Corporation's budget calls for the following sales for next year:

Quarter 1	45,000 units	Quarter 3	34,000 units
Quarter 2	38,000 units	Quarter 4	48,000 units

Each unit of the product requires 3 pounds of direct material. The company's policy is to begin each quarter with an inventory of the product equal to 10 percent of that quarter's sales requirements and an inventory of direct materials equal to 20 percent of that quarter's direct materials requirements for productions.

Required   Determine the production and materials purchase budgets for the second quarter.

8–27   **Production and Materials Purchase Budgets**   Willard Company is budgeting sales of 100,000 units of its model GS30 small generator for September. One unit of GS30 requires 2 pounds of aluminum and 3 pounds of alloy. Willard plans to have the following inventories for September:

	Beginning Inventory	Desired Ending Inventory
GS30	20,000 units	10,000 units
Aluminum	25,000 pounds	18,000 pounds
Alloy	22,000 pounds	24,000 pounds

Required   How many pounds of aluminum and alloy is Willard Company planning to purchase during September?

8-28   **Production and Materials Budgets—Processing Costing**   Uecker Company budgets on an annual basis. The planned beginning and ending inventory levels (in units) for the fiscal year of July 1, 2005, through June 30, 2006, for one of its products, XPL30, are as follows:

	July 1, 2005	June 30, 2006
Raw materials	40,000	50,000
Work in process	10,000	20,000
Finished goods	80,000	50,000

Two units of raw materials are needed to complete one unit of finished products. All materials are added at the beginning of production. The firm completes all work in process before starting a new batch and plans to sell 480,000 units during the 2005–2006 fiscal year?

Required

1. How many units of XPL30 must Uecker Company complete?
2. How many units of XPL30 must Uecker Company start into production during the 2005–2006 fiscal year?
3. How many units of raw materials must Uecker Company purchase during the 2005–2006 fiscal year?

8–29   **Production and Materials Budgets—Processing Costing**   Use the data for Uecker Company (8–28) and complete the requirements assuming that the firm adds all required materials right before the completion of the manufacturing process for XPL30.

8–30   **Cash Budget**   Carla Inc. has the following budget data for 2006:

Cash balance, beginning	$ 10,000
Collections from customers	150,000
Expenses:	
Direct materials purchases	25,000
Operating expenses	50,000
Payroll	75,000
Income taxes	6,000
Machinery purchases	30,000

Operating expenses include $20,000 depreciation for buildings and equipment. The firm requires a minimum cash balance of $20,000.

Required Compute the amount the firm needs to finance or excess cash available for Carla to invest.

8–31 **Cash Budget** Bill Joyce, CEO of Joyce and Associates, expects the firm to have $12,000 cash on hand at the end of 2006. He estimates the total revenues in 2007 to be $250,000, of which $175,000 will be collected during the year. Payroll and fringe benefits constitute the bulk of the firm's expenditures and will amount to $160,000 in 2007. Other operating expenses, including $5,000 for depreciation and $3,000 for property taxes, are $18,000. The property taxes expense is an increase of $500 from the current year. In addition, Bill Joyce plans to update the office equipment for $24,000 in 2007. He expects the payment in 2007 for the office equipment will be $6,000 to be paid for by reducing the minimum cash balance to $6,000. The county in which the firm is located requires payment of at least one-half of property taxes before the end of the year and the remainder before June 30 of the following year.

Required Can Bill meet the minimum cash balance?

8–32 **Estimate Cash Collections** Ishikawa Corporation has collected the following data relating to its accounts receivable in preparing the budget for the month of May:

Estimated credit sales for May	$200,000
Actual credit sales for April	150,000
Estimated collections in May:	
For credit sales in May	25%
For credit sales in April	70%
For credit sales prior to April	$ 16,000
Estimated write-offs in May for uncollectible accounts	8,000
Estimated provision for bad debts in May due to credit sales that month	7,000

Required What are the estimated cash receipts from accounts receivable collections in May?

(CPA Adapted)

8–33 **Accounts Receivable Collections** Esplanade Company's credit sales have the following historical pattern:

70 percent collected in the month of sale
15 percent collected in the first month after sale
10 percent collected in the second month after sale
 4 percent collected in the third month after sale
 1 percent uncollectible

These sales on open account (credit sales) have been budgeted for the last six months in 2006:

July	$60,000	October	90,000
August	70,000	November	100,000
September	80,000	December	85,000

Required

1. Determine the estimated total cash collections from accounts receivable during October 2006.
2. Compute the estimated total cash collections during the fourth quarter from credit sales of the fourth quarter.

(CMA Adapted)

8–34 **Accounts Receivable Collections**   Doreen Company is preparing its cash budget for the month of May. The following information is available concerning its accounts receivable:

Actual credit sales for March	$120,000
Actual credit sales for April	$150,000
Estimated credit sales for May	$200,000
Estimated collections in the month of sale	25%
Estimated collections in the first month after the month of sale	60%
Estimated collections in the second month after the month of sale	10%
Estimated provision for bad debts in the month of sale	5%

The firm writes off all uncollectible accounts at the end of the second month after the month of sale.

Required   Determine for Doreen Company for the month of May

1. The estimated cash receipts from accounts receivable collections.
2. The gross amount of accounts receivable at the end of the month.
3. The net amount of accounts receivable at the end of the month.

8–35 **Cash Discount**   Ben's Auto Parts e-mails monthly statements to area auto repair shops on the last day of each month with terms of 2/10, n/30. Selected sales data follow.

May (actual)	$50,000
June (actual)	60,000
July (budgeted)	75,000

Ben's experience is that 40 percent of the total sales are cash sales. Of the credit sales, 80 percent pay before the 10th of each month, 12 percent pay before the due day, and 5 percent pay in 60 days. The remainders are deemed uncollectible.

Required   Prepare a schedule of cash receipts for July.

8–36 **Cash Discount**   Yeopay Plumbing Supply accepts bank charge cards and offers established plumbers charge accounts with terms of 1/eom, n/45. Yeopay's experience is that 25 percent of its sales are for cash and bank credit cards. The remaining 75 percent are on credit. Of the cash sales, 40 percent pay cash and the remaining 60 percent pay with bank credit cards. Yeopay receives payments from the bank on credit card sales at the end of the day. However, Yeopay has to pay 3 percent for these services. An aging schedule for accounts receivable shows the following pattern on credit sales:

20 percent pay in the month of sale.
50 percent pay in the first month following the sale.
15 percent pay in the second month following the sale.
12 percent pay in the third month following the sale.
 3 percent are never collected.

All accounts not paid by the end of the second month following the sale are considered overdue and are subject to 2 percent monthly late charge. Yeopay has prepared the following sales forecasts:

June	$60,000
July	80,000
August	90,000
September	96,000
October	88,000

Required Prepare a schedule of cash receipts for September.

8–37 **Cash Discount with Spreadsheet Application** Use the data for Yeopay Plumbing Supply in Exercise 8–36.

Required

1. At the top of a new spreadsheet, create an "Original Data" section with three subheads: Sales Data, Sales Term, and Collection Pattern.
2. Enter all pertinent data from Exercise 8–36 for determination of cash receipts.
3. Create a new section to calculate cash receipts for September with rows for Cash Sales, Credit Card Sales, Collections of accounts receivable from sales of each of the months, and a Total Cash Inflow and columns for Total Sales, Percentage of Sales for cash and bank credit card sales, and credit sales, Payment Percentage for the proportions collection, Percentage Collected to allow for cash discounts or late charges, and Cash Receipts.
4. Program your spreadsheet to perform all necessary calculations for determinations of cash receipts for September. Do not type in any amounts. All the amounts you enter into this new section should derive from data from the Original Data section using a formula.
5. Verify the accuracy of your spreadsheet by calculating the total cash receipts in September. The total cash receipts for September should be $86,082.
6. Create a new section entitled October. Program your spreadsheet to perform all necessary calculations for determinations of cash receipts for October and verify the accuracy of your spreadsheet by showing that the total cash receipts for October is $88,141.

8–38 **Activity-Based Budgeting** OFC Company of Kansas City prints business forms and other specialty paper products, such as writing paper, envelopes, note cards, and greeting cards. Its Business Services division offers inventory management services and desktop delivery on request. The division uses an activity-based costing system. The budgeted usage of each activity cost driver and cost-driver rates for January 2006 for the Business Services division are:

Activity	Cost Driver	Budgeted Activity	Cost Driver Rate
Storage	Cartons in inventory	400,000	$0.4925/carton/month
Requisition handling	Requisitions	30,000	$12.50
Pick packing	Lines	800,000	$1.50
Data entry	Lines	800,000	$0.80
	Requisitions	30,000	$1.20
Desktop delivery	Per delivery	12,000	$30.00

The division made 11,700 deliveries to deliver 1,170,000 cartons to customers. The division expects the average delivery size in January 2006 to remain unchanged.

Required

1. What is the total budgeted cost for each activity and for the Business Services Division in January 2006?
2. What is the cost per delivered carton and the total budgeted cost for the Business Services Division if the firm uses a single cost rate based on the number of cartons delivered to estimate cost?
3. Dories Supply Chain Management Company offers to install an electronic order processing system that transmits customer requisitions via the Internet to the Business Services Division for immediate pick, packing, and delivery. No requisition handling and data entry will be needed once the system is fully functional. How much savings can the Business Services

Division expect from switching to the new system before considering the payment to Dories? Can you estimate the amount if the firm uses a single cost rate based on the number of cartons delivered to determine the budgeted cost for the division?

8–39 **Activity-Based Budgeting with Continuous Improvements**   OFC Company (Exercise 8–38) has decided to implement a continuous improvements program to improve operation efficiency. After a careful study, the management and employees agree that the firm will be able to reduce cost rates for batch-level activities by 2 percent and unit-level activities by 1 percent per month during the first year of its implementation starting February 2006. The firm has decided to delay the implementation of the program for customer sustaining and facility levels activities until 2007. The firm expects the amount of cost-driver usage in each of the next two months to be the same as those in January. (Use 4 decimal points for all cost rates.)

Required

1. Identify unit-level and batch-level activities.
2. What are the total budgeted costs for each activity and for the division in February and March?
3. Identify three factors that are likely to be critical for a successful kaizen program.

8–40 **Cash Budget**   Information pertaining to Noskey Corporation's sales revenue includes this:

	November 2005 (Actual)	December 2005 (Budget)	January 2006 (Budget)
Cash sales	$ 80,000	$100,000	$ 60,000
Credit sales	240,000	360,000	180,000
Total sales	$320,000	$460,000	$240,000

Management estimates 5 percent of credit sales to be uncollectible. Of collectible credit sales, 60 percent is collected in the month of sale and the remainder in the month following the sale. Purchases of inventory each month include 70 percent of the next month's projected total sales. Additional units are purchased in the month of sales to meet sales needs. All inventory purchases are on account; 25 percent are paid in the month of purchase, and the remainder is paid in the month following the purchase. The purchase costs are approximately 60 percent of the selling price.

Required   Determine for Noskey:

1. Budgeted cash collections in December 2005 from November 2005 credit sales.
2. Budgeted total cash receipts in January 2006.
3. Budgeted total cash payments in December 2005 for inventory purchases.

(CPA Adapted)

8–41 **Service Firm Budget**   Refer to AccuTax, Inc. in the chapter. One of the partners is planning to retire at the end of the year. May Higgins, the sole remaining partner, plans to add a manager at an annual salary of $90,000. She expects the manager to work, on average, 45 hours a week for 45 weeks per year. She plans to change the required staff time for each hour spent to complete a tax return to the following:

	Business Return	Complex Individual	Simple Individual
Partner	0.3 hour	0.05 hour	
Manager	0.2 hour	0.15 hour	
Senior consultant	0.5 hour	0.40 hour	0.2 hour
Consultant		0.40 hour	0.8 hour

The manager earns no overtime pay. The senior consultant receives time and half for overtime. The firm plans to keep all the senior consultants and adjust the number of consultants as needed including employing part-time consultants. The partner has also decided to have five supporting staff at $40,000 each. All other operating data remain unchanged. The manager will share 10 percent of any excess profit over $500,000 before bonus.

Required

1. What is the budgeted overtime premium for senior consultants?
2. How many full-time consultants should be budgeted?
3. Determine the manager's total compensation, assuming that the revenues from preparing tax returns remain unchanged.

8–42 **Service Firm Budget**   Refer to AccuTax, Inc., in the chapter and the additional data given in Exercise 8–41. May Higgins observed that the manager was overworked and, as a result, the quality was not as high as she wanted it to be. She is planning to add another manager and change the work assignments to the following:

	Business Return	Complex Individual	Simple Individual
Partner	0.2 hour	0.05 hour	
Manager	0.3 hour	0.20 hour	0.05 hour
Senior consultant	0.5 hour	0.55 hour	0.25 hour
Consultant		0.20 hour	0.70 hour

She expects the additional manager and the rearrangement of work assignments will improve quality and, as a result, increase the total revenue. May estimates the total revenue from business returns will increase 20 percent and each of the individual returns will increase 10 percent. She plans to add one supporting staff, two new senior consultants, and additional managers as needed when the workload exceeds the total hours available by 20 percent. In addition, she plans to increase managers' bonus to 15 percent. All managers are full time employees. All other operating data remain unchanged.

Required

1. What is the budgeted overtime premium for senior consultants?
2. How many full-time consultants should be budgeted?
3. Determine the manager's total compensation, assuming that the revenues from preparing tax returns remain unchanged.

Problems

8–43 **Small Business Budget**   Small businesses usually are the first to feel the effects of a recessionary economy and generally are the last to recover. Two major reasons for these difficulties are managerial inexperience and inadequate financing or financial management.

Small business managers frequently have problems in planning and controlling profits, including revenue generation and cost reduction activities. These important financial methods are especially critical during a recessionary period. The financial problems of small business are further compounded if the firm keeps poor accounting records and is inexperienced in the management of money.

Required

1. Profit planning is critical for the planning and controlling of profits of a small business. Identify key features that should be considered when developing a profit plan.
2. The management accountant can help ensure that good accounting records exist in an organization. Discuss the key features that form the basis for a good accounting system that will support management decisions.
3. Explain how the management accountant can assist an organization in adopting measures to ensure appropriate money management.

(CMA Adapted)

8–44 **Ethics in Budgeting**   Norton Company, a manufacturer of infant furniture and carriages, is in the initial stages of preparing the annual budget for 2006. Scott Ford recently joined Norton's accounting staff and is interested in learning as much as possible about the company's budgeting process. During a recent lunch with Marge Atkins, sales manager, and Pete Granger, production manager, Scott initiated the following conversation:

Scott: Since I'm new around here and am going to be involved with the preparation of the annual budget, I'd be interested to learn how the two of you estimate sales and production numbers.

Marge: We start out very methodically by looking at recent history, discussing what we know about current accounts, potential customers, and the general state of consumer spending. Then, we add that usual dose of intuition to come up with the best forecast we can.

Pete: I usually take the sales projections as the basis for my projections. Of course, we have to make an estimate of what this year's closing inventories will be, and that sometimes is difficult.

Scott: Why does that present a problem? There must have been an estimate of closing inventories in the budget for the current year.

Pete: Those numbers aren't always reliable since Marge makes some adjustments to the sales numbers before passing them on to me.

Scott: What kind of adjustments?

Marge: Well, we don't want to fall short of the sales projections so we generally give ourselves a little breathing room by lowering the initial sales projection anywhere from 5 to 10 percent.

Pete: So you can see why this year's budget is not a very reliable starting point. We always have to adjust the projected production rates as the year progresses and, of course, this changes the ending inventory estimates. By the way, we make similar adjustments to expenses by adding at least 10 percent to the estimates; I think everyone around here does the same thing.

Required

1. Marge Atkins and Pete Granger have described the use of budgetary slack.
   a. Explain why Marge and Pete behave in this manner, and describe the benefits they expect to realize from the use of budgetary slack.
   b. Explain how the use of budgetary slack can adversely affect Marge and Pete.
2. As a management accountant, Scott Ford believes that the behavior described by Marge and Pete may be unethical and that he may have an obligation not to support this behavior. By citing the specific standards of competence, confidentiality, integrity, and/or objectivity from the Standards of Ethical Conduct for Management Accountants, explain why the use of budgetary slack may be unethical.

(CMA Adapted)

8–45 **Master Budget** SecCo manufactures and sells security systems. The company started by installing photoelectric security systems in existing offices and has since expanded into the private home market. SecCo has developed its basic security system into three standard products, each of which can be upgraded to meet the specific needs of customers. SecCo's manufacturing operation is moderate in size; it outsources the bulk of component manufacturing to independent contractors. The security systems are approximately 85 percent complete when SecCo receives them from contractors and require only final assembly in its own plant. Each product passes through at least one of three assembly operations.

SecCo operates in a community that is flourishing. Evidence indicates that a great deal of new commercial construction will take place in the near future, and SecCo's management has decided to pursue this new market. To be competitive, SecCo must expand its operations.

In view of the expected increase in business, Sandra Becker, SecCo's controller, believes that the company should implement a master budget system. She has decided to make a formal presentation to SecCo's president explaining the benefits of a master budget system and outlining the budget schedules and reports that would be required.

Required

1. Explain what benefits can be derived from implementing a master budget system.
2. If Sandra Becker is going to develop a master budget system for SecCo,
   a. Identify, in order, the schedules and/or statements that must be prepared.
   b. Identify the subsequent schedules and/or statements to be derived from the schedules and statements identified in requirement 2a.

(CMA Adapted)

8–46 **Comprehensive Profit Plan** Spring Manufacturing Company makes two components identified as C12 and D57. Selected budgetary data for 2006 follow:

	Finished Components	
	C12	D57
Requirements for each finished component:		
RM 1	10 pounds	8 pounds
RM 2	0	4 pounds
RM 3	2 pounds	1 pound
Direct labor	2 hours	3 hours
Product information:		
Sales price	$150	$220
Sales unit	12,000	9,000
Estimated beginning inventory	400	150
Desired ending inventory	300	200

	Raw Materials Information		
	RM1	RM2	RM3
Cost per pound	$2.00	$2.50	$0.50
Estimated beginning inventory in pounds	3,000	1,500	1,000
Desired ending inventory in pounds	4,000	1,000	1,500

The firm expects the average hourly wage rate to be $25 per hour in 2006. Spring Manufacturing uses direct labor-hours to apply overheads. Each year the firm determines the overhead application rate for the year based on the budgeted operation for the year. The firm maintains negligible work-in-process inventory and expects the cost per unit for both beginning and ending finished products inventories to be identical.

	Factory Overhead Information
Indirect materials—variable	$ 10,000
Miscellaneous supplies and tools—variable	5,000
Indirect labor—variable	40,000
Supervision—fixed	120,000
Payroll taxes and fringe benefits—variable	250,000
Maintenance costs—fixed	20,000
Maintenance costs—variable	10,080
Depreciation—fixed	71,330
Heat, light, and power—fixed	43,420
Heat, light, and power—variable	11,000
Total	$580,830

	Selling and Administrative Expense Information
Advertising	$ 60,000
Sales salaries	200,000
Travel and entertainment	60,000
Depreciation—warehouse	5,000
Office salaries	60,000
Executive salaries	250,000
Supplies	4,000
Depreciation—office	6,000
Total	$645,000

The income tax rate of the firm is 40 percent.

Required   Prepare the following schedules or statements for 2006:

1. Sales budget
2. Production budget.

3. Raw materials purchase.
4. Direct labor budget.
5. Factory overhead budget.
6. Cost of goods sold and finished component ending inventory budgets.
7. Selling and general administrative expense budget.
8. Budgeted income statement.

8–47 Comprehensive Profit Plan Using Spreadsheet   (Use information in Problem 8–46 for Spring Manufacturing Company.) C12 is a mature product. The sales manager believes that the price of C12 can be raised to $160 per unit with no effect on sales quantity. D57 is a new product introduced last year. Management believes D57 has a great potential and is considering lowering the price to $180 to expand market size and gain market share. The lowering of D57's price is likely to double the total units sold.

Required

1. Set up a spreadsheet to complete requirements 1 through 8 in Problem 8–46. What effect do the changes have on the firm's after-tax operating income?
2. Would you recommend that the firm execute this strategy?

8–48 Comprehensive Profit Plan (Kaizen Budgeting)   (Use information in Problem 8–46 for Spring Manufacturing Company.) Spring Manufacturing Company has had a continuous improvement (kaizen) program for the last two years. According to the kaizen program, the firm is expected to manufacture C12 and D57 with the following specifications:

Cost Element	C12	D57
Raw materials 1	9 pounds	7 pounds
Raw materials 2	- 0 -	3.6 pounds
Raw materials 3	1.8 pounds	0.8 pounds
Direct labor	1.5 hours	2 hours

The firm specifies that the variable factory overheads are to decrease by 10 percent while the fixed factory overheads are to decrease by 5 percent, except for depreciation expenses. The firm does not expect the price of the materials to change. However, the hourly wage is likely to be $30 per hour.

Required

1. What is the budgeted after-tax operating income if the firm can attain the expected operation level as prescribed by its kaizen program?
2. What are the benefits of Spring Manufacturing Company adopting a continuous improvement program? What are the limitations?

8–49 Retailer Budget   D. Tomlinson Retail seeks your assistance in developing cash and other budget information for May, June, and July. The store expects to have the following balances at the end of April:

Cash	$ 5,500
Accounts receivable	437,000
Inventories	309,400
Accounts payable	133,055

The firm follows these guidelines in budget preparations:

- **Sales.** All sales are on credit with terms of 3/10, n/30. Tomlinson bills customers on the last day of each month. The firm books receivables at gross amounts and collects 60 percent of the billings within the discount period, 25 percent by the end of the month, and 9 percent by the end of the second month. The firm's experience suggests that 6 percent is likely to be uncollectible and is written off at the end of the third month.
- **Purchases and expenses.** All purchases and expenses are on account. The firm pays its accounts payable over a two-month period with 54 percent in the month incurred. Each

month's units of ending inventory equal 130 percent of the next month's units of sales. The cost of each unit of inventory is $20. Selling and general and administrative expenses, of which $2,000 is depreciation, equal 15 percent of the current month's sales.

Actual and projected sales follow:

Month	Dollars	Units	Month	Dollars	Units
March	$354,000	11,800	June	342,000	11,400
April	363,000	12,100	July	360,000	12,000
May	357,000	11,900	August	366,000	12,200

Required

1. Prepare schedules showing budgeted purchases for May and June.
2. Prepare a schedule showing budgeted cash disbursements during June.
3. Prepare a schedule showing budgeted cash collections during May.
4. Determine gross and net balances of accounts receivable on May 31.

(CMA Adapted)

8–50 **Sales Budget and Pro Forma Financial Statements**   Mark Dalid founded Molid Company three years ago. The company produces PDAs that are compatible with the most operating systems including Palm, MS Windows, and Linus with UBS connection and WiFi capability. Since the company's inception its business has expanded rapidly.

Bob Wells, the company's general accountant, prepared a budget for the fiscal year ending August 31, 2007, based on the prior year's sales and production activity. In view of the general business slowdown, Mark believes that the sales growth experienced during the prior year will not continue at the same pace. The pro forma statements of income and cost of goods sold prepared as part of the budget processes follow:

MOLID COMPANY
Pro Forma Statement of Income (in thousands)
For the budget year ended August 31, 2007

Net sales		$31,248
Cost of goods sold		20,765
Gross profit		$10,483
Operating expenses:		
Selling	$3,200	
General administrative	2,200	5,400
Income from operations before income taxes		$ 5,083

MOLID COMPANY
Pro Forma Statement of Cost of Goods Sold (in thousands)
For the budget year ended August 31, 2007

Direct materials:		
Materials inventory, 9/1/2006	$ 1,360	
Materials purchases	14,476	
Materials available for use	$15,836	
Materials inventory, 8/31/2007	1,628	
Cost of direct materials used		$14,208
Direct labor		1,134
Factory overhead:		
Indirect materials	$ 1,421	
General factory overhead	3,240	4,661
Cost of goods manufactured		$20,003
Finished goods inventory, 9/1/2006		1,169

(continued)

Cost of goods available for sale	$21,172
Finished goods inventory, 8/31/2007	407
Cost of goods sold	$20,765

On December 10, 2006, Mark and Bob met to discuss the first quarter operating results (September 1 through November 30, 2006). Bob believed that several changes should be made to the original budget assumptions that had been used to prepare the pro forma statements. He prepared the following notes summarizing the changes that had not become known until the first quarter results had been compiled. He submitted the following data to Mark:

a. The estimated production in units for the fiscal year should be revised upward from 162,000 units to 170,000 units with the balance of production being scheduled in equal segments over the last nine months of the fiscal year. Actual first quarter production was 35,000 units.

b. The planned ending inventory for finished goods of 3,300 units at the end of the fiscal year remains unchanged. The finished goods inventory of 9,300 units as of September 1, 2006, had dropped to 9,000 units by November 30, 2006. The finished goods inventory at the end of the fiscal year will be valued at the average manufacturing cost for the year.

c. The direct labor rate will increase 8 percent as of June 1, 2007, as a consequence of a new labor agreement signed during the first quarter. When the original pro forma statements were prepared, the expected effective date for this new labor agreement had been September 1, 2007.

d. Direct materials sufficient to produce 16,000 units were on hand at the beginning of the fiscal year. The plan to have sufficient direct materials inventory at the end of the fiscal year for 18,500 units of production remains unchanged. Direct materials inventory is valued on a first-in, first-out basis. Direct materials equivalent to 37,500 units of output were purchased for $3,300,000 during the first quarter of the fiscal year.

   Molid's suppliers have informed the company that direct materials prices will increase 5 percent on March 1, 2007. Direct materials needed for the rest of the fiscal year will be purchased evenly through the last nine months.

e. On the basis of historical data, indirect materials cost is projected at 10 percent of the cost of direct materials consumed.

f. One-half of general factory overhead and all of selling and general administrative expenses are considered fixed.

   After an extended discussion, Dalid asked for new pro forma statements for the fiscal year ending August 31, 2007.

Required

1. Based on the revised data that Bob presented, calculate Molid Company's sales for the year ending August 31, 2007 in (a) number of units sold, and (b) dollar volume of net sales.

2. Prepare the pro forma statement of cost of goods sold for the year ending August 31, 2007, that Mark Dalid had requested.

3. Bob suggests that the firm adopt a JIT strategy to better serve customers and to reduce obsolescence costs. He points out that the firm needs to incorporate new manufacturing technologies to maintain its competitive advantage. Mark is reluctant to make changes because he does not want to upset the proven successful business. He knows that any changes cost money, and he does not want to commit fresh capital just to change the business procedures. Bob argues that no additional capital will be needed to fund the changes. He points out that a JIT system maintains no finished goods inventory and no more materials than those needed to produce 100 units of the finished products.

   a. How much will the firm save by changing to a JIT system?

   b. Should the firm follow Bob's suggestion?

   c. What other factors should be considered in making the decision?

(CMA Adapted)

8–51 **Budget for Merchandising Firm**   Kelly Company is a retail sporting goods store that uses an accrual accounting system. Facts regarding its operations follow:

• Sales are budgeted at $220,000 for December and $200,000 for January, terms 1/EOM, n/60.

• Collections are expected to be 60 percent in the month of sale and 38 percent in the month following the sale. Two percent of sales are expected to be uncollectible and recorded at the end of the month of sales.

- Gross margin is 25 percent of sales.
- All accounts receivable are from credit sales. Uncollected balances are written off as bad debts at the end of the month following the sale.
- Kelly desires to have 80 percent of the merchandise for the following month's sales on hand at the end of each month. Payment for merchandise is made in the month following the purchase.
- Other expected monthly expenses to be paid in cash total $22,600.
- Annual depreciation is $216,000.

Kelly Company's statement of financial position at the close of business on November 30 follows:

KELLY COMPANY
Statement of Financial Position
November 30, 2007

Assets

Cash	$ 22,000
Accounts receivable (net of $4,000 allowance for doubtful accounts)	76,000
Inventory	132,000
Property, plant, and equipment (net of $680,000 accumulated depreciation)	870,000
Total assets	$1,100,000

Liabilities and Stockholders' Equity

Accounts payable	$ 162,000
Common stock	800,000
Retained earnings	138,000
Total liabilities and equity	$1,100,000

Required

1. What is the total of budgeted cash collections for December?
2. How much is the book value of accounts receivables at the end of December?
3. How much is the net income (loss) before income taxes for December?
4. What is the projected balance in accounts payable on December 31, 2007?
5. What is the projected balance in inventory on December 31?

(CMA Adapted)

8–52 **Budget for Service Firm**   Triple-F Health Club (Family, Fitness, and Fun) is a not-for-profit family-oriented health club. The club's board of directors is developing plans to acquire more equipment and expand club facilities. The board plans to purchase about $25,000 new equipment each year and wants to establish a fund to purchase the adjoining property in four or five years. The adjoining property has a market value of about $300,000.

The club manager, Jane Crowe, is concerned that the board has unrealistic goals in light of the club's recent financial performance. She has sought the help of a club member with an accounting background to assist her in preparing a report to the board supporting her concerns.

The member reviewed the club's records, including this cash basis income statement:

TRIPLE-F HEALTH CLUB
Income Statement (Cash Basis)
For Years Ended October 31 (in thousands)

	2007	2006
Cash revenues:		
Annual membership fees	$355.0	$300.0
Lesson and class fees	234.0	180.0
Miscellaneous	2.0	1.5
Total cash revenues	$591.0	$481.5

(continued)

Cash expenses:		
Manager's salary and benefits	$ 36.0	$ 36.0
Regular employees' wages and benefits	190.0	190.0
Lesson and class employees' wages and benefits	195.0	150.0
Towels and supplies	16.0	15.5
Utilities (heat and light)	22.0	15.0
Mortgage interest	35.1	37.8
Miscellaneous	2.0	1.5
Total cash expenditures	$496.1	$445.8
Increase in cash proceeds	$ 94.9	$ 35.7

- Other financial information as of October 31, 2007:

    Cash in checking account, $7,000.

    Petty cash, $300.

    Outstanding mortgage balance, $360,000.

    Accounts payable arising from invoices for supplies and utilities that are unpaid as of October 31, 2007, $2,500.

- No other unpaid bills existed on October 31, 2007.

- The club purchased $25,000 worth of exercise equipment during the current fiscal year. Cash of $10,000 was paid as of October 31, 2007.

- The club began operations in 2003 in rental quarters. In October 2003, it purchased its current property (land and building) for $600,000, paying $120,000 down and agreeing to pay $30,000 plus 9 percent interest annually on October 31 starting the following year until the balance is paid off.

- Membership rose 3 percent in 2007. The club has experienced approximately this same annual growth rate since it opened.

- Membership fees increased by 15 percent in 2007. The board has tentative plans to increase the fees by 10 percent in 2008.

- Lesson and class fees have not been increased for two years. The board policy is to encourage classes and lessons by keeping the fees low. The members have taken advantage of this policy, and the number of classes and lessons has increased significantly each year. The club expects the percentage growth experienced in 2007 to be repeated in 2008.

- Miscellaneous revenues are expected to grow at the same rate as in 2007.

- Operating expenses expected to increase:

    Hourly wage rates and the manager's salary: 15 percent.

    Towels and supplies, utilities, and miscellaneous expenses: 25 percent.

Required

1. Prepare a cash budget for 2008 for the Triple-F Health Club.

2. Identify any operating problems that this budget discloses for the Triple-F Health Club. Explain your answer.

3. Is Jane Crowe's concern that the board's goals are unrealistic justified? Explain your answer.

(CMA Adapted)

8–53 **Estimate Foreign Sales Revenue**   Multiplex Electronics Corporation manufactures custom-designed central processing computer chips for specialized applications. The firm expects to sell 9 million units during the coming year. Total foreign sales are approximately 80 percent of the units sold domestically. Since its inception of the firm five years ago, the foreign currency exchange rates have been stable. The firm receives $30 per unit and earns a contribution margin of $15 per unit for all units sold. However, financial crises began in September of this year in several countries in the region where the firm makes most of its foreign sales. Consequently, the firm's sales revenue in U.S. dollars has substantially decreased.

For the coming year, the firm expects the exchange rate to be about 60 percent of the level before the devaluation.

Required

1. Estimate the total sales and contribution margin for the coming year if the firm chooses not to alter its selling prices in foreign currencies.

2. Determine the unit-selling price for foreign sales for the coming year if the firm desires to receive $30 per unit.

3. Compute the unit-selling price for the coming year for all units (for both domestic and foreign markets) if the firm desires to earn the same total amount of contribution margin in U.S. dollars as before the financial crises.

8–54 **Strategy, Product Life Cycle, and Cash Flow**   Burke Company manufactures various electronic assemblies that it sells primarily to computer manufacturers. Burke has built its reputation on quality, timely delivery, and products that are consistently on the cutting edge of technology. Burke's business is fast paced: A typical product has a short life; the product is in development for about a year and in the growth stage, with spectacular growth sometimes, for about a year. Each product then experiences a rapid decline in sales as new products become available.

Burke has just hired a new vice president of finance, Devin Ward. Shortly after reporting for work at Burke, he had a conversation with Andrew Newhouse, Burke's president. A portion of the conversation follows.

Andrew: The thing that fascinates me about this business is that change is its central ingredient. We knew when we started out that a reliable stream of new products was one of our key variables, in fact, the only way to cope with the threat of product obsolescence. You see, our products go through only the first half of the traditional product life cycle—the development stage and then the growth stage. Our products never reach the traditional mature product stage or the declining product stage. Toward the end of the growth stage, products dies as new ones are introduced.

Devin: I suppose your other key variables are cost controls and efficient production scheduling?

Andrew: Getting the product to market on schedule, whether efficiently or not, is important. Some firms in this business announce a new product in March to be delivered in June, and they make the first shipment in October, or a year from March, or sometimes, never. Our reputation for delivering on schedule could account for our success as much as anything.

Devin: Where I previously worked, we also recognized the importance of on-time deliveries. Our absorption cost system set 93 percent on time as a standard.

Andrew: The key variable that is your responsibility is cash management. It took us a while to recognize that. At first, we thought that profit was the key and that cash would naturally follow. But now we know that cash is the key and the profits naturally follow. Still, we don't manage cash well. Improving our cash management is the main thing we expect from you.

Required

1. Discuss the cash-generating and cash usage characteristics of products in general in each of the four stages of the product life cycle—development, growth, maturity, and decline.

2. Describe the cash management problems confronting Burke Company.

3. Suggest techniques that Devin might implement to cope with Burke Company's cash management problems.

(CMA Adapted)

8–55 **Continuous Budget**   WestWood Corporation is a woodstove manufacturer in southern Oregon. WestWood manufactures three models: small stoves for heating a single room, medium-sized units for use in mobile homes and as a supplement to central heating systems, and large stoves with the capacity to provide central heating.

The manufacturing process consists of shearing and shaping steel, fabricating, welding, painting, and finishing. Molded doors are custom-built at an outside foundry in the state, brass plated at a plater, and fitted with custom etched glass during assembly at WestWood's plant. The finished stoves are delivered to dealers either directly or through regional warehouses located throughout the western United States. WestWood owns the three tractor trailers and one large truck used to ship stoves to dealers and warehouses.

The budget for the year ending February 28, 2007, was finalized in January of 2006 and based on the assumption that the 10 percent annual growth rate that WestWood had experienced since 2005 would continue.

Stove sales are seasonal, and the first quarter of WestWood's fiscal year is usually a slack period. As a consequence, inventory levels were down at the start of the current fiscal year on March 1, 2006.

WestWood's sales orders for the first quarter ended May 31, 2006, were up 54 percent over the same period last year and 40 percent above the first quarter budget. Unfortunately, not all of the sales orders could be filled due to the reduced inventory levels at the beginning of the quarter. WestWood's plant was able to increase production over budgeted levels, but not in sufficient quantity to compensate for the large increase in orders. Therefore, it has a large backlog of orders. Furthermore, preliminary orders for the busy fall season are 60 percent above the budget, even though the projections for the winter of 2006–2007 indicate no decrease in demand. WestWood's president attributes the increase to effective advertising, the products' good reputation, increased installations of woodstoves in new houses, and the bankruptcy of WestWood's principal competitor.

Required

1. WestWood's sales for the remainder of the 2006–2007 fiscal year will be much higher than predicted five months ago. Explain the effect this increase will have on the operations in the following functional areas of WestWood:

   a. Production   c. Marketing

   b. Finance and accounting d. Personnel

2. Some companies follow the practice of preparing a continuous budget.

   a. Explain what a continuous budget is.

   b. Explain how WestWood could benefit by preparing a continuous budget.

(CMA Adapted)

8–56 **Cash Budget**   Higgins Technologies manufactures plasma flat screen digital monitors. Use the following data to complete Higgins' quarterly cash budgets for the year ending December 31, 2007.

1. Higgins plans a major innovation over a six-month period starting at the beginning of the second quarter. The firm estimates the total cost to be $80 million with a 25 percent down payment at the end of the first quarter and equal installments at the end of each month for the remainder over the next six months. The firm expects to sell the replaced equipment at the end of the fourth quarter for $5 million.

2. Higgins sold $250 million 10-year 9 percent bonds three years earlier. Interest on these bonds is payable semiannually on May 31 and November 30. The bond covenant requires the firm to maintain a minimum cash balance of $30 million at all times and to deposit $20 million into a sinking fund on or before May 31 of each year.

3. Higgins has an open credit line with the U of A Bank for short-term loans at an interest rate of 12 percent per year. The firm can draw up to $100 million at the beginning of each quarter and repay outstanding balances at the end of each quarter. All borrowings and repayments are to be made in multiples of $1 million. Interest on the loans is payable at the end of each month. Higgins has yet to draw any funds on this account as of the end of the current year.

4. Debbie Hoskins, CFO, has determined that any excess cash on hand over $50 million should be applied to pay down short-term bank loans or invest in marketable securities at the end of the quarter. The firm is likely to earn a 5 percent annual return on marketable securities.

Required   Fill in the blanks:

	Quarters				
	I	II	III	IV	Year
Cash balance, beginning	$ 30,000	?	?	?	?
Add cash receipts:					
Collections from customers	425,000	?	?	460,000	?
Equipment disposal	?	?	?	?	?
Total cash available	?	$475,000	$510,000	?	?

(continued)

Subtract cash disbursements					
Raw materials purchases	$200,000	$220,000	?	$270,000	940,000
Payroll	?	120,000	115,000	?	474,000
S, G, & A expenses	60,000	62,000	58,000	64,000	?
Equipment purchase	?	?	?	?	?
Bond interest	?	?	?	?	?
Bond sinking fund	?	?	?	?	?
Income taxes	20,000	21,000	25,000	18,000	?
Total cash disbursement	?	?	?	?	?
Minimum cash balance required	?	?	?	?	?
Total cash needed	?	?	?	?	?
Short-term financing:					
Borrowing	0	?	?	?	?
Repayment	?	?	?	?	?
Interest	?	?	?	?	?
Total effects of financing	?	?	?	?	?
Cash balance, ending	$ 38,000	?	?	?	?

8–57 **Comprehensive Budget** Gold Sporting Equipment (GSE) is in the process of preparing its budget for the third quarter of 2007. The budgeting staff has gathered the following data:

1. Account balances as of June 30:

Cash	$ 25,000
Accounts receivable	15,000
Inventory	47,520
Building and equipment (net)	200,000
Liabilities	0

2. Recent and forecasted sales:

June (actual)	$75,000
July	80,000
August	82,000
September	90,000
October	100,000

3. Sales are 80 percent cash and 20 percent on credit. Credit accounts are all collected 30 days after sale.

4. At gross purchase prices of inventories, GSE's gross margin averages 40 percent of revenues. GSE records all inventory purchases at net prices.

5. Operating expenses: Salaries and wages, $8,000 per month plus 5 percent of revenue; rent and property tax, $1,000 per month; other operating expenses, excluding depreciations, 2 percent of revenues; depreciations $800 per month. All cash operating expenses are paid before the end of the month.

6. GSE has no minimum inventory requirement. The policy is to purchase each month on the 15th the expected sales for the following month. Terms on purchases are 1/10, n/30. Purchases usually arrive on or before the 20th. GSE's policy is to take all cash discounts offered.

7. GSE is negotiating the purchase of new equipment for $127,000 to be installed in September. Terms are 50 percent in the month before and 50 percent after the month of installation.

8. Minimum cash balance is $30,000. All borrowings are effective at the beginning of the month and all repayments are made at the end of the month of repayment. Loans are repaid when sufficient cash is available. The interest rate is 15% per year, payable at the end of each month. Both borrowings and repayments are in multiple of $10,000. Management does not want to borrow any more cash than is necessary and wants to repay whenever the cash on hand exceeds the minimum requirement.

9. GSE plans to pay no dividend to stockholders.

Required

1. Complete schedules A through E.

Schedule A: Budgeted Monthly Cash Receipts

Item	June	July	August	September
Cash sales				
Credit sales				
Total sales				
Receipts:				
Cash sales	N/A			
Collections on accounts	N/A			
Total cash collections				

Schedule B: Budgeted Monthly Cash Disbursements for Purchases

Item	July	August	September	3rd Quarter
Purchases				
Cash discount				
Total				

Schedule C: Budgeted Monthly Cash Disbursements for Operating Costs

Item	July	August	September	3rd Quarter
Salaries and wages				
Rent and Property Taxes				
Other cash operating costs				
Total				

Schedule D: Budgeted Total Monthly Cash Disbursements

Item	July	August	September	3rd Quarter
Purchases				
Cash operating costs				
Interest payment on short-term loan				
Equipment				
Total				

Schedule E: Cash Budget and Budgeted Financing

Item	July	August	September	3rd Quarter
Cash balance, beginning				
Total cash receipts				
Total cash available				
Total cash disbursements				
Cash balance before financing				
Borrowing required				
Borrowing repaid				
Cash balance, ending				

2. Prepare a budgeted income statement for the third quarter and a budgeted balance sheet as of September 30. GSE estimates its income tax rate at 25 percent, payable in the second quarter of the following year.

3. Gold Sporting Equipment has been using the loan described in Item 8 to meet its needs for funds. Alternatively, Gold can issue long-term bonds at no more than 12 percent annual interest rate to increase funds available for operations. What is the most sensible type of loan GSE should use to meet its needs? Explain your reasoning.

4. The underlying business situation has been greatly simplified. List at least three complicating factors that may exist in a real business setting.

Solutions to Self-Study Problems

1. Master Budget

A. HANSELL COMPANY
Sales Budget
For July 2007

Budgeted sales in units	6,000
Budgeted selling price per unit	× $ 80
Budgeted sales	$480,000

B. HANSELL COMPANY
Production Budget (in units)
For July 2007

Desired ending inventory (July 31)	
(The higher of 100 and 7,000 × 0.1)	700
Budgeted sales for July 2007	+ 6,000
Total units needed for July 2007	6,700
Beginning inventory (July 1)	
(The higher of 100 and 6,000 × 0.1)	− 600
Units to manufacture in July	6,100

C. HANSELL COMPANY
Production Budget (in units)
For August 2007

Desired ending inventory (8,000 × 0.1)	800
Budgeted sales	+ 7,000
Total units needed	7,800
Beginning inventory	− 700
Units to manufacture in August	7,100

D. HANSELL COMPANY
Direct Materials Purchases Budget (in pounds)
For July 2007

	Direct Materials	
	Dura-1000 **(4 lb. each)**	**Flexplas** **(2 lb. each)**
Materials required for budgeted production (6,100 units of duraflex)	24,400	12,200
Add: Target inventories (lower of 1,000 or 5 percent of August production needs	+ 1,000	+ 710
Total materials requirements	25,400	12,910
Less: Expected beginning inventories (lower of 1,000 or 5 percent)	− 1,000	− 610
Direct materials to be purchased	24,400	12,300

E. HANSELL COMPANY
Direct Materials Purchases Budget (in dollars)
For July 2007

	Budgeted Purchases Pounds	Expected Purchase Price per Unit	Total
Dura-1000	24,400	$1.25	$30,500
Flexplas	12,300	$5.00	61,500
Budgeted purchases			$92,000

F. HANSELL COMPANY
Direct Manufacturing Labor Budget
For July 2007

	Direct Labor Hours per Batch	Number of Batches	Total Hours	Rate per Hour	Total
K102 Hours	1	61	61	$50	$ 3,050
K175 Hours	10	61	610	$20	12,200
Total			671		$15,250

2. Cash Budget and Budgeted Income Statement

A. HANSELL COMPANY
Cash Budget
For July 2007

Cash Available		
Cash balance, beginning		$ 40,000
Add: Cash receipts from July cash sales	$480,000 × 20% = $ 96,000	
Collections of receivables from sales in June		
Collection within the discount period	5,500 × $80 × 80% × 60% × 98% = $206,976	
Collection after the discount period	5,500 × $80 × 80% × 25% = 88,000	
Collections of receivables from sales in May	5,400 × $80 × 80% × 10% = 34,560	425,536
Total cash available in July		$465,536
Cash Disbursement		
Materials purchases:		
June purchases	($25,000 + $22,000) × 20% × 98% = $ 9,212	
July purchases	$ 92,000 × 80% × 98% = 72,128	$ 81,340
Direct manufacturing labor		15,250
Variable factory overhead	($1,200 × 61 + $80 × 671) × 60% =	76,128
Fixed factory overhead	$50,000 − $20,000 =	30,000
Variable marketing, customer services, and administrative expenses	[($2,400,000 − $1,200,000) ÷ $4,000,000] × $480,000 =	144,000
Fixed marketing, customer services, and administrative expenses	($1,200,000 − $120,000) ÷ 12 =	90,000
Total cash disbursements		$436,718
Cash balance before financing		$ 28,818
Financing		
Amount to borrow		12,000
Cash balance, July 31, 2007		$ 40,818

B. HANSELL COMPANY
Budget Income Statement
For July 2007

Sales			$480,000
Cost of goods sold*	$38.30 × 6,000 =		229,800
Gross margin			$250,200
Selling and administrative expenses			
Variable		$144,000	
Fixed	$1,200,000 ÷ 12 =	100,000	244,000
Net income			$ 6,200

* Cost per unit:			
Direct materials			
Dura-1000	4 lb. × $1.25 =	$ 5.00	
Flexplas	2 lb. × $5.00 =	10.00	$ 15.00
Direct labor			
K102 labor	0.01 hour × $50 =	$ 0.50	
K175 labor	0.1 hour × $20 =	2.00	2.50
Factory overhead			
Applied based on batch	$1,200 ÷ 100 =	$ 12.00	
Applied based on direct labor-hour	$80 × 0.11 hour =	8.80	20.80
Cost per unit			$ 38.30

CHAPTER NINE

Decision Making with Relevant Costs and a Strategic Emphasis

After studying this chapter, you should be able to . . .

1. Define the decision-making process and identify the types of cost information relevant for decision making
2. Use relevant and strategic cost analysis to make special order decisions
3. Use relevant and strategic cost analysis in the make, lease, or buy decision
4. Use relevant and strategic cost analysis in the decision to sell before or after additional processing
5. Use relevant and strategic cost analysis in the decision to keep or drop products or services
6. Use relevant and strategic cost analysis to evaluate programs
7. Analyze decisions with multiple products and limited resources
8. Discuss the behavioral, implementation, and legal issues in decision making

The family sedan segment of the U.S. auto market—especially the Honda Accord, Ford Taurus, and Toyota Camry—experiences an intense level of competition. The Camry and the Taurus have traded places as the top-selling car in the United States.[1] The Camry is now on top, as it has been since 1997. The competition between these two cars illustrates an important cost management issue—striking a balance between product features and price. The two cars do not differ greatly in price, but most analysts argue that the cost and price reductions in the 1997 remake of the Camry brought it to the top of U.S. car sales. In contrast, the remake of the 1996 Taurus added features, cost—and price.

In the 2000 model year, Ford added further improvements to the Taurus, mainly safety features. It added seat belt pretensioners and other design features that improved the Taurus' performance in crash tests. Ford officials believe that safety could become the defining issue for the family sedan in the coming years. Toyota thinks differently; it believes that reliability is still the critical success factor. Honda thinks differently than Toyota and Ford, opting to focus on adding space and a smoother ride in the Accord's redesign.

Toyota, Ford, and Honda are saying that a number of strategic issues are involved in developing a competitive car, including safety features, low-cost manufacturing methods, and a competitive price. In this chapter we will discuss how to conduct relevant cost analysis and strategic analysis of decisions about product pricing, selecting cost-effective manufacturing methods, and deciding when to keep or drop a product, among others.

The decision maker has both short-term and long-term objectives for each type of decision. A decision with a short-term objective is one whose effects are expected to

---

[1] For further reading, see "Ford Bets on Safety, Not Style, for Comeback of Taurus," *The Wall Street Journal,* March 30, 1999, p. B1; "More Camry for Less Cash," *Business Week,* November 18, 1996, p. 186; "The Americanization of a Japanese Icon," *Business Week,* April 15, 2002; and "Machete Time," *Business Week,* April 7, 2001, pp. 42–43.

occur within about a year from the time of the decision. A decision with a long-term objective is expected to affect costs and revenues for a period longer than a year. Both types of decisions should reflect the firm's overall strategy, but it is often said that the decision maker has a long-term strategy if the focus is primarily on the decision's long-term objectives and a short-term strategy if the focus is on the short term.

Decision makers usually consider both short-term and long-term effects in making the best decision. Although the art and science of decision making has many elements, including leadership, vision, execution, and other characteristics, cost management provides two important resources to improve decisions: relevant cost analysis and strategic cost analysis. Relevant cost analysis has a short-term focus; strategic cost analysis has a long-term focus. Relevant cost analysis and strategic cost analysis are an important part of the financial manager's decision process.

The Decision-Making Process

In deciding among alternative choices for a given situation, managers employ the five step process outlined in Exhibit 9.1. The first step, and in many ways the most important, is to consider the strategic issues regarding the decision context. This helps focus the decision maker on answering the right question, in part by identifying a comprehensive list of decision options. Strategic thinking is important to avoid decisions that might be best only in the short term. For example, a plant manager might incorrectly view the choice as either to make or to buy a part for a manufactured product when the correct decision might be to determine whether the product should be redesigned so the part is not needed.

The manager's second step is to specify the criteria by which the decision is to be made. Most often the manager's principal objective is an easily quantified, short-term, achievable goal, such as to reduce cost, improve profit, or maximize return on investment. Other interested parties (e.g., owners or shareholders) have their own criteria for these decisions. Therefore, a manager most often is forced to think of multiple objectives, both the quantifiable short-term goals, and the more strategic, difficult-to-quantify goals.

In the third step, a manager performs an analysis in which the relevant information is developed and analyzed, using relevant cost analysis and strategic cost analysis. This step involves three sequential activities. The manager (1) identifies and collects relevant information about the decision, (2) makes predictions about the relevant information, and (3) considers the strategic issues involved in the decision.

EXHIBIT 9.1
The Decision-Making Process

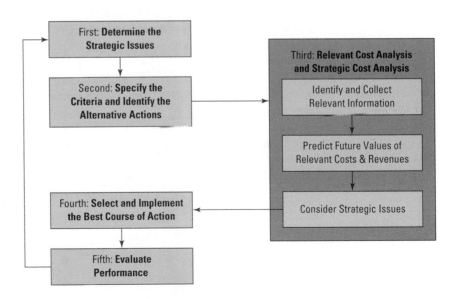

Fourth, based on the relevant cost analysis and strategic cost analysis, the manager selects the best alternative and implements it. In the fifth and final step, the manager evaluates the performance of the implemented decision as a basis for feedback to a possible reconsideration of this decision as it relates to future decisions. The decision process is thus a feedback-based system in which the manager continually evaluates the results of prior analyses and decisions to discover any opportunities for improvement in decision making.

Relevant Cost Analysis

Relevant Cost Information

Relevant costs

are costs that will be incurred at some future time; they differ for each option available to the decision maker.

Relevant costs are costs that will be incurred at some future time; they differ for each option available to the decision maker. A cost that does not differ for each of the decision maker's options is irrelevant because that choice has no effect on the cost. For example, in choosing which new car to buy, a consumer can ignore the cost of licenses and fees as long as these costs are the same for all cars. A cost that has already occurred or has been committed to is also irrelevant; the decision cannot influence these costs. Thus, the cost of the buyer's present car is irrelevant. The only relevant amount for the old car is the future amount—its potential trade-in value. The decision maker's rule is that *only future costs that differ among options are relevant for the decision.* (See Exhibit 9.2.)

LEARNING OBJECTIVE 1

Define the decision-making process and identify the types of cost information relevant for decision making.

A relevant cost can be either variable or fixed. Generally, variable costs are relevant for decision making because they differ for each option and have not been committed. In contrast, fixed costs often are irrelevant, since typically they do not differ for the options. Overall, variable costs often are relevant but fixed costs are not. So the use of the concept of relevant cost follows naturally from the development of the methods we used in cost estimation, cost-volume-profit analysis, and master budgeting.

Occasionally, some variable costs are not relevant. For example, assume that a manager is considering whether to replace or repair an old machine. If the electrical power requirements of the new and old machines are the same, the variable cost of power is not relevant. Some fixed costs can be relevant. For example, if the new machine requires significant modifications to the plant building, the cost of the modifications (which are fixed costs) are relevant because they are not yet committed.

To illustrate, assume a machine was purchased for \$4,200 a year ago, it is depreciated over two years at \$2,100 per year, and it has no trade-in or disposal value. At the end of the first year, the machine has a net book value of \$2,100 (\$4,200 − \$2,100) but the machine needs to be repaired or replaced. Assume that the purchase price of a new machine is \$7,000 and it is expected to last for one year with little or no expected trade-in or disposal value. The repair of the old machine would cost \$3,500 and would be sufficient for another year of productive use. The power for either machine is expected to

EXHIBIT 9.2
Relevant and Not Relevant Costs: The Car Purchase Decision

Cost Classification and Cost Relevance
(With examples for the car purchase decision)

	Committed, or "Sunk" (Generally, in the Past)	Not Committed, Discretionary (Generally, in the Future)
Costs That Differ Among Options	Not Relevant Example: Purchase of Buyer's Guide for the new car	Relevant Costs Example: Price of new car
Costs That Do Not Differ Among Options	Not Relevant Example: Price of old car	Not Relevant Example: American Auto Club membership

cost $2.50 per hour. The new machine is semiautomated, requiring a less-skilled operator and resulting in a reduction of average labor costs from $10.00 to $9.50 per hour for the new machine. If the firm is expected to operate at a 2,000-hour level of output for the next year, the total variable costs for power will be 2,000 × $2.50 = $5,000, and labor costs will be $19,000 ($9.50 × 2,000) and $20,000 ($10 × 2,000) for the new and old machines respectively.

Data for Machine Replacement Example

Old machine	
Current net book value	$2,100
Useful life (if repaired)	1 year
Operating cost (labor)	$10 per hour
New machine	
Purchase price	$7,000
Useful life	1 year
Operating cost (labor)	$9.50 per hour

The summary of relevant costs for this decision is in Exhibit 9.3, showing a $2,500 advantage for repairing the old machine. The $1,000 decrease in labor costs for the new machine is less than the $3,500 difference of replacement cost over repair cost ($7,000 − $3,500). Note that the power costs and the depreciation on the old machine are omitted because they are not relevant for the decision.

To show that the analysis based on total costs provides the same answer, Exhibit 9.4 shows the analysis for total costs that includes the power costs and the depreciation of the old machine; neither cost is relevant. The left portion of Exhibit 9.4 is the same as Exhibit 9.3. Note that both analyses lead to the same conclusion. The relevant cost approach in Exhibit 9.3 is always preferred, however, because it is simpler, less prone to error, and provides better focus for the decision maker.

EXHIBIT 9.3
Relevant Cost Analysis in Equipment Replacement

	Relevant Costs		Difference
	Repair	Replace	Replace Minus Repair
Variable costs			
Labor	$20,000	$19,000	$(1,000)
Fixed costs			
Old machine repair cost	3,500		(3,500)
New machine		7,000	7,000
Total costs	$23,500	$26,000	$ 2,500
Repair cost lower by: $2,500			

Variable Costs and Activity-Based Cost Drivers

Although most relevant costs for many decisions are variable, the concept of variable cost does not mean only a cost tied to changes in the output level. A variable cost varies directly with changes in a given cost driver, whether it is the number of products produced, the number of batches of product produced, or the number of design features for each product. For example, certain costs that are fixed at the output level (e.g., the cost of setting up machinery) are variable at the batch level because setup costs are incurred with each new batch of product. If we add features to a product, costs increase not only at the output level (additional direct materials and labor) but also at the batch level (increased setup costs) and the product level (increased engineering design costs, inspection and testing costs). In determining the costs that differ for options, managers must consider cost drivers in the broadest possible sense as those that might vary at any level of manufacture—units of output, batches, and products.

EXHIBIT 9.4 **Relevant Cost and Total Cost Analysis in Equipment Replacement**

	Relevant Costs		Total Costs		Difference
	Repair	Replace	Repair	Replace	Replace − Repair
Variable costs					
Labor	$20,000	$19,000	$20,000	$19,000	$(1,000)
Power			5,000	5,000	0
Fixed Costs					
Old machine					
Depreciation			2,100	2,100	0
Repair cost	3,500		3,500		(3,500)
New machine					
Depreciation		7,000		7,000	7,000
Total costs	$23,500	$26,000	$30,600	$33,100	$ 2,500
Repair cost lower by		$ 2,500		$ 2,500	

Consider again the decision in Exhibit 9.3 and assume that the cost of setting up the machines (a batch level cost) has been ignored because these costs are fixed (do not change with the number of units or labor hours). There will be the same number of setups (assume 120 setups) whether we repair or replace the machine. Because the new machine is semiautomated, the setup time is significantly less—1 hour per setup—while the old machine requires 4 hours per setup. Assume also that the lower wage rate of $9.50 applies both to setup labor as well as direct labor. The analysis of setup costs is as follows:

Setup Costs for New Machine	Setup Costs for Old Machine
$9.50 per hour for labor	$10 per hour for labor
× 120 setups per year	× 120 setups per year
× 1 hour per setup	× 4 hours per setup
= $1,140	= $4,800

The new machine saves $3,660 ($4,800 − $1,140) in setup labor as well as $1,000 in direct labor. The labor savings total is $4,660 ($3,660 + $1,000). This more than offsets the excess of the cost of the new machine over the cost of repair, $3,500 ($7,000 − $3,500), for a $1,160 = ($4,660 − $3,500) net benefit of replacing the machine. See the revised analysis in Exhibit 9.5.

Fixed Costs and Depreciation

A common misperception is that depreciation of facilities and equipment is a relevant cost. In fact, depreciation is a portion of a committed cost (the allocation of a purchase cost over the life of an asset); therefore, it is sunk and irrelevant. There is an exception to this rule: when tax effects are considered in decision making. In this context, depreciation has a positive value in that, as an expense, it reduces taxable income and tax expense. If taxes are considered, depreciation has a role to the extent that it reduces tax liability. The decision maker often must consider the impact of local, federal, and sometimes international tax differences on the decision situation.

Other Relevant Information: Opportunity Costs

Managers should include in their decision process information such as the capacity usage of the plant. Capacity usage information is a critical signal of the potential relevance of *opportunity costs,* the benefit lost when one chosen option precludes the

EXHIBIT 9.5   Relevant Costs in Equipment Replacement (including consideration of setup costs)

	Relevant Costs		Total Costs		Difference
	Repair	Replace	Repair	Replace	Replace − Repair
Variable costs					
Labor	$20,000	$19,000	$20,000	$19,000	$(1,000)
Power			5,000	5,000	0
Fixed Costs					
Setup costs	4,800	1,140	4,800	1,140	(3,660)
Old machine					
Depreciation			2,100	2,100	0
Repair cost	3,500		3,500		(3,500)
New machine					
Depreciation		7,000		7,000	7,000
Total costs:	$28,300	$27,140	$35,400	$34,240	$(1,160)

EXHIBIT 9.6
Determining Relevant Costs versus Strategic Cost Analysis

Determine Relevant Costs	**Strategic Cost Analysis**
Short-term focus	Long-term focus
Not linked to strategy	Linked to the firm's strategy
Product cost focus	Customer focus
Focused on individual product or decision situation	Integrative; considers all customer-related factors

benefits from an alternative option. When the plant is operating at full capacity, opportunity costs are an important consideration because the decision to produce a special order or add a new product line can cause the reduction, delay, or loss of sales of products and services currently offered. In contrast, a firm with excess capacity might be able to produce for current demand as well as handle a special order or new product; thus, no opportunity cost is present. When opportunity costs are relevant, the manager must consider the value of lost sales as well as the contribution from the new order or new product.

Another important factor is the *time value of money* that is relevant when deciding among alternatives with cash flows over two or more years. These decisions are best handled by the methods described in Chapter 20. Also, differences in quality, functionality, timeliness of delivery, reliability in shipping, and service after the sale could strongly influence a manager's final decision and should be considered in addition to the analysis of relevant costs. Although these factors often are considered in a qualitative manner, when any factor is strategically important, management can choose to quantify it and include it directly in the analysis.

Strategic Cost Analysis

Strategic information keeps the decision maker's attention focused on the firm's crucial strategic goal. Management decisions usually involve several strategic issues. For example, focusing on the short-term monthly and annual periods should not lead the manager to ignore the long-term strategic factors about markets and production processes. Failing to attend to the long-term, strategic factors could cause the firm

REAL-WORLD FOCUS Accounting Knowledge and the Use of Opportunity Costs

Research studies have consistently found that decision makers often ignore opportunity costs. For this reason, it is particularly important that the development of decision-making skills place particular emphasis on identifying and incorporating opportunity costs. Interestingly, a recent study found that decision makers with greater expertise in developing comparative income statements appeared to ignore fixed costs more than those with less experience. This was interpreted as resulting in part from the experienced decision makers' strong focus on computing and comparing net income. The problem is that the calculation of accounting net income does not include opportunity costs, thus, a focus on accounting net income could have caused the decision makers to ignore opportunity costs.

Source: Sandra C. Vera-Munoz, "The Effects of Accounting Knowledge and Context on the Omission of Opportunity Costs in Resource Allocation Decisions," *The Accounting Review,* January 1998, pp. 47–72.

to be less competitive in the future. Strategic factors include choices about the nature and amount of manufacturing capacity, product diversity, and product design for cost efficiency.

For example, a strategic decision to design the manufacturing process for high efficiency to produce large batches of product reduces overall production costs. At the same time, it might reduce the firm's flexibility to manufacture a variety of products and thus could increase the cost to produce small, specialized orders. The decision regarding cost efficiency cannot be separated from the determination of marketing strategy, that is, deciding what types and sizes of orders can be accepted.

By identifying *only* relevant costs, the decision maker might fail to link the decision to the firm's strategy. The decision maker also must consider strategic issues. For example, the decision to buy rather than to make a part for the firm's product might make sense on the basis of relevant cost but might be a poor strategic move if the firm's competitive position depends on product reliability that can be maintained only by manufacturing the part in-house. A good indication of a manager's failing to take a strategic approach is that the analysis will have a product cost focus, while a strategic relevant cost analysis also addresses broad and difficult-to-measure strategic issues. The strategic analysis directly focuses on adding value to the customer, going beyond only cost issues. (See Exhibit 9.6.)

We now consider the application of the relevant cost analysis and strategic cost analysis to four types of decisions that management accountants often face. For each decision, we develop the cost information that should be used. This cost information includes both relevant cost information and the strategic cost information discussed earlier. The four decisions are as follows: (1) the special order decision, (2) the make, lease, or buy decision, (3) the decision to sell before or after additional processing, and (4) profitability analysis.

Special Order Decision

Cost Analysis

LEARNING OBJECTIVE 2
Use relevant and strategic cost analysis to make special order decisions.

The so-called special order decision occurs when a firm has a one-time opportunity to sell a specified quantity of its product or service. It is called a *special order* because it is typically unexpected. The order frequently comes directly from the customer rather than through normal sales or distribution channels. Special orders are infrequent and commonly represent a small part of a firm's overall business. To make the special order decision, managers need critical information about relevant costs, revenues, and any opportunity costs. Consider, for example, the special order situation facing Tommy T-Shirt, Inc. (TTS). TTS is a small manufacturer of specialty clothing, primarily

EXHIBIT 9.7
Master Budget for TTS's Manufacturing Costs
Expected Output of 200,000
Units in 200 Batches

Cost Element	Costs Per Unit	Batch-Level Costs Per Batch	Batch-Level Costs Fixed Costs	Plant-Level Costs (all fixed)
Shirt	$3.25			
Ink	0.95			
Operating labor	0.85			
Subtotal	$5.05			
Setup		$130	$29,000	
Inspection		30	9,000	
Materials handling		40	7,000	
Subtotal		$200	$45,000	
Machine related				$315,000
Other				90,000
Total	$5.05	$200	$45,000	$405,000

T-shirts and sweatshirts with imprinted slogans and brand names. TTS has been offered a contract by a local college fraternity, Alpha Beta Gamma (ABG) for 1,000 T-shirts printed with artwork publicizing a fund-raising event. The fraternity offers to pay $6.50 for each shirt. TTS normally charges $9.00 for shirts of this type for this size order.

TTS's master budget of manufacturing costs for the current year is given in Exhibit 9.7. The budget is based on expected production of 200,000 T-shirts from an available capacity of 250,000. The 200,000 units are expected to be produced in 200 different batches of 1,000 units each. The three groups of cost elements are as follows:

1. **Unit-level costs** vary with each shirt printed and include the cost of the shirt ($3.25 each), ink ($0.95 each), and labor ($0.85), for a total of $5.05.

2. **Batch-level costs** vary, in part, with the number of batches produced. The batch-level costs include machine setup, inspection, and materials handling. These costs are partly variable (change with the number of batches) and partly fixed. For example, setup costs are $130 per setup ($26,000 for 200 setups) plus $29,000 fixed costs that do not change with the number of setups (e.g., setup tools or software). Setup costs for 200 batches total $55,000 ($26,000 + $29,000). Similarly, inspection costs are $30 per batch plus $9,000 fixed costs—$15,000 total ($30 × 200 + $9,000). Materials-handling costs are $40 per batch plus $7,000 fixed costs—$15,000 total ($40 × 200 + $7,000).

3. **Plant-level costs** are fixed and do not vary with the number of either units produced or batches. These costs include depreciation and insurance on machinery ($315,000) and other fixed costs ($90,000), for a total of $405,000. Total fixed cost is the sum of fixed batch-level costs ($45,000) and fixed facilities-level costs ($405,000), or $450,000. And the total cost estimation equation for TTS is

Total Cost = $5.05 per unit + $200 per batch + $450,000.

Exhibit 9.8 presents TTS's analysis of the relevant costs. The ABG order requires the same unprinted T-shirt, ink, and labor time as other shirts, for a total of $5.05 per unit. In addition, TTS uses $200 of batch-level costs for each order.

Analysis of Contribution from the Alpha Beta Gamma Order		
Sales	1,000 units @ $6.50	$6,500
Relevant costs (Exhibit 9.8)	1,000 units @ $5.25	5,250
Net contribution	1,000 units @ $1.25	$1,250

The correct analysis for this decision is to determine the relevant costs of $5.25, and then to compare the relevant costs to the special order price of $6.50. The not relevant

EXHIBIT 9.8
Special Order Decision
Analysis for TTS

Cost Type	Unit Costs	Total Cost for One Batch of 1,000 units
Relevant Costs		
Unit-level costs		
Unprinted shirt	$3.25	$3,250
Ink and other supplies	0.95	950
Machine time (operator labor)	0.85	850
Total unit-level costs	$5.05	$5,050
Batch-level costs (that vary with the number of batches)		
Setup		130
Inspection		30
Materials handling		40
Total ($200/batch; $0.20/unit)	0.20	$ 200
Total relevant costs	$5.25	$5,250

costs are not considered because they remain the same whether TTS accepts the ABG order. There is a $1.25 ($6.50 − 5.25) contribution to income for each shirt sold to Alpha Beta Gamma, or a total contribution of $1,250, so the order is profitable and should be accepted.

Strategic Analysis

The relevant cost analysis developed for TTS provides a useful decision regarding the order's profitability. However, for a full decision analysis, TTS also should consider the strategic factors of capacity utilization, short-term versus long-term pricing, the trend in variable costs, and the use of activity-based costing, as follows.

Is TTS Now Operating at Full Capacity?

TTS currently has 50,000 units of excess capacity, more than enough for the ABG order. But what if TTS is operating at or near full capacity; would accepting the order cause the loss of other possibly more profitable sales? If so, TTS should consider the opportunity cost arising from the lost sales. Assume that TTS is operating at 250,000 units and 250 batches of activity, and that accepting the ABG order would cause the loss of sales of other T-shirts that have a higher contribution of $3.75 ($9.00 − $5.25). The opportunity cost is $3.75 per shirt and the proper decision analysis is as follows:

Contribution from Alpha Beta Gamma order	$ 1,250
Less: Opportunity cost of lost sales (1,000 units × $3.75)	(3,750)
Net contribution (loss) for the order	$(2,500)

Exhibit 9.9 shows the effect of accepting the Alpha Beta Gamma order at full capacity; under full capacity, the Alpha Beta Gamma order would reduce total profits by $2,500 due to lost sales.

Excessive Relevant Cost Pricing

The relevant cost decision rule for special orders is intended only for those infrequent situations when a special order can increase income. Done on a regular basis, relevant cost pricing can erode normal pricing policies and lead to a loss in profitability for

Short-term pricing for special orders uses relevant cost information. For long-term pricing, the firm considers competitive issues as well as cost information. The two following examples illustrate this.

Some firms take a "value" approach to pricing. In what is commonly known as *value-based pricing,* many firms set prices based on the overall value the firm can deliver to the customer, including customer service, assistance with installation and training for the product or service, and finding ways for the product or service to save the customer money.

Some firms "pad" prices to increase margins. Kenneth Merchant and Michael Shields report examples of firms that pad, or overstate, product prices to compensate for the expected large discounts typically granted by the firm's salespersons. The net price received, even after large discounts, is sufficient to meet the firm's profit goals.

In another example, Dell Computer Corp. continues its dominance in the PC market by using a computer-based pricing system that allows the firm to adjust prices throughout the day for different customers in different industries with different order quantities and delivery dates. One key ingredient of the pricing system is accurate, up-to-date cost information, and precise forecasts of materials

costs and availability for the next six months. The system helps Dell maintain its position as the low-cost, low-price source for PCs.

In a somewhat similar instance, the Commerce Committee of the U.S. House of Representatives recently studied pharmaceutical firms' apparent practice of increasing prices when their products are subject to increased competition. Although this may seem counterintuitive, the price increase actually makes the drug more attractive to physicians who dispense it. This happens because doctors are reimbursed by Medicare on the basis of the "average wholesale price" (AWP) of the drug, which is typically far less than the price the doctors pay for it. In one example cited, the price to the doctor was less than one-half of the drug's AWP.

Sources: "The Power of Smart Pricing," *Business Week,* April 10, 2000, pp. 160–64; "Chemical Pricing Strategies in Competitive Markets," *Chemical Market Reporter,* New York, November 2, 1998; Kenneth Merchant and Michael D. Shields, "When and Why to Measure Costs Less Accurately to Improve Decision Making," *Accounting Horizons,* June 1993; "How Drug Makers Influence Medicare Reimbursements to Doctors," *The Wall Street Journal,* September 21, 2000, p. B1; and Gary McWilliams, "Dell Fine-Tunes Its PC Pricing to Gain an Edge in a Slow Market," *The Wall Street Journal,* June 8, 2001.

EXHIBIT 9.9
Special Order Decision for TTS under Full Capacity

	With ABG Order	Without ABG Order
Sales		
250,000 units at $9.00		$2,250,000
249,000 at $9.00; 1,000 at $6.50	$2,247,500	
Variable cost at $5.25	1,312,500	1,312,500
Contribution margin	$ 935,000	$ 937,500
Fixed cost	450,000	450,000
Operating income	$ 485,000	$ 487,500
Advantage in favor of rejecting the ABG order		$ 2,500

firms such as TTS. The failure of large companies in the airline, auto, and steel industries has been attributed to their excessive relevant cost pricing because a strategy of continually focusing on the short term can deny a company a successful long term. Special order pricing decisions should not become the centerpiece of a firm's strategy.[2]

Other Important Factors

In addition to capacity utilization and long-term pricing issues, TTS should consider Alpha Beta Gamma's credit history, any potential complexities in the design that might cause production problems, and other strategic issues such as whether the sale might lead to additional sales of other TTS products.

[2] See John K. Shank and Vijay Govindarajan, *Strategic Cost Management* (New York: Free Press, 1993); and Peter F. Drucker, *Managing for the Future* (New York: Truman Talley Books, 1993), pp. 251–55.

Make, Lease, or Buy Decision

Cost Analysis

LEARNING OBJECTIVE 3
Use relevant and strategic cost analysis in the make, lease, or buy decision.

Generally, a firm's products are manufactured according to specifications set forth in what is called the bill of materials, which is a detailed list of the components of the manufactured product. A bill of materials for the manufacture of furniture is illustrated in Chapter 4. An increasingly common decision for manufacturers is to choose which of these components to manufacture in the firm's plant and which to purchase from outside suppliers.

The relevant cost information for the make-or-buy decision is developed in a manner similar to that of the special order decision. The relevant cost information for making the component consists of the short-term costs to manufacture it, ordinarily the variable manufacturing costs, which would be saved if the part is purchased. These costs are compared to the purchase price for the part or component to determine the appropriate decision. Costs that will not change whether the firm makes the part or not are ignored. For example, consider Blue Tone Manufacturing, maker of clarinets and other reed-based musical instruments. Suppose that Blue Tone is currently manufacturing the mouthpiece for its clarinet but has the option to buy it from a supplier. The following cost information assumes that fixed overhead costs will not change whether Blue Tone chooses to make or buy the mouthpiece:

Cost to buy the mouthpiece, per unit		$24.00
Cost to manufacture, per unit		
Materials	$16.00	
Labor	4.50	
Variable overhead	1.00	
Total variable costs	$21.50	
Fixed overhead	6.00	
Total costs	$27.50	
Total relevant costs		$21.50
Savings from continuing to make		$ 2.50

In this example, the relevant cost to make is $21.50. Since the decision will not affect fixed overhead, the total $27.50 cost is irrelevant. The relevant cost to make is $2.50 less than the purchase cost, so Blue Tone should manufacture the mouthpiece. However, much like the TTS analysis, the make-or-buy analysis for Blue Tone is not complete without a strategic analysis that considers, for example, the quality of the part, the reliability of the supplier, and the potential alternative uses of Blue Tone's plant capacity.

A similar situation arises when a firm must choose between leasing or purchasing a piece of equipment. Such decisions are becoming ever more frequent as the cost and terms of leasing arrangements continue to become more favorable.[3]

To illustrate the lease or buy decision, we use the example of Quick Copy, Inc., a firm that provides printing and duplicating services and other related business services. Quick Copy uses one large copy machine to complete most big jobs. It leases the machine from the manufacturer on an annual basis that includes general servicing. The annual lease includes both a fixed fee of $40,000 and a per copy charge of $0.02.

The copier manufacturer has suggested that Quick Copy upgrade to the latest model copier that is not available for lease but must be purchased for $160,000. Quick Copy

[3] The attractiveness of leasing is especially apparent in the case of auto leasing. See "The Business Auto Decision," by Cherie O'Neil, Donald Samuelson, and Matthew Wills, *Journal of Accountancy*, February 2001, pp. 65–73. The lease-or-buy decision can also be aided by specialized computer software, such as Expert Lease Pro (www.autoleasing.com).

would use the purchased copier for one year, after which it could sell it back to the manufacturer for one-fourth the purchase price ($40,000). In addition, the new machine has a required annual service contract of $20,000. Quick Copy's options for the coming year are to renew the lease for the current copier or to purchase the new copier. The relevant information is outlined in Exhibit 9.10. The lease-or-buy decision will not affect the cost of paper, electrical power, and employee wages, so these costs are irrelevant and are excluded from the analysis. For simplicity, we also ignore potential tax effects of the decision.

The initial step in the analysis is to determine which machine produces a lower cost. The answer depends on the expected annual number of copies. Using cost-volume-profit analysis (Chapter 7 and Exhibit 9.11), Quick Copy's manager determines the indifference point, the number of copies at which both machines cost the same. The calculations are as follows, where Q is the number of copies:

$$\text{Lease cost} = \text{Purchase cost}$$

$$\text{Annual fee} = \text{Net purchase cost} + \text{Service contract}$$

$$\$40,000 + \$0.02 \times Q = (\$160,000 - \$40,000) + \$20,000$$

$$Q = \$100,000/\$0.02$$

$$= 5,000,000 \text{ copies per year}$$

The indifference point, 5,000,000 copies, is lower than the expected annual machine usage of 6,000,000 copies. This indicates that Quick Copy will have lower costs by purchasing the new machine. Costs will be lower by $20,000:

$$\text{Cost of Lease Minus Cost of Purchase}$$

$$(\$40,000 + \$0.02 \times 6,000,000) - (\$160,000 - \$40,000 + \$20,000)$$

$$= \$160,000 - \$140,000$$

$$= \$20,000$$

EXHIBIT 9.10
Quick Copy Lease or Buy Information

	Lease Option	Purchase Option
Annual lease	$40,000	N/A
Charge per copy	0.02	N/A
Purchase cost	N/A	$160,000
Annual service contract	N/A	$20,000
Value at end of period	N/A	$40,000
Expected number of copies a year	6,000,000	6,000,000

EXHIBIT 9.11
The Lease-or-Buy Example

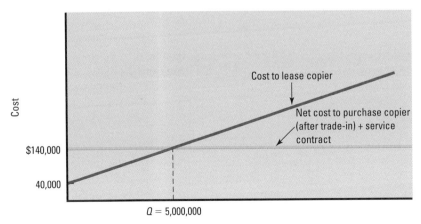

REAL-WORLD FOCUS   Make or Buy: Human Resources Management

Although the make-or-buy decision is commonly thought to affect parts and components of products, it can also apply to services, including human resource management, internal auditing, security, maintenance and repair, and other service activities performed within the firm. Many firms have chosen to outsource these functions, based in part on the concepts of relevant and strategic cost analysis. For example, to maintain a human resource (HR) function within a firm requires certain fixed and variable costs related to the number of employees. Alternatively, to outsource the function, the firm incurs a fixed fee or a fee that combines fixed and variable elements. The firm can determine the short-term cost of either approach as a basis for deciding between them. The firm also must consider the longer term strategic factors in the decision, as noted in the results of a recent study of the HR policies at 25 large companies. The survey showed that these human resource management functions should not be outsourced:

- Labor/union relations
- Employee relations
- Performance measurement

For example, one human resource manager participating in the study said that his company keeps the employee relations function within the firm but outsources other HR functions. When an employee relations problem arises, he explained, we need "someone from the company who can do something about the problem, and we can't outsource the mechanism that communicates to employees that we care about them."

Source: Charles R. Greer and Stuart A. Youngblood, "Human Resource Management Outsourcing: The Make or Buy Decision," *The Academy of Management Executive,* August 1999, pp. 85–96.

In addition to the relevant cost analysis, Quick Copy should consider strategic factors such as the quality of the copy, the reliability of the machine, the benefits and features of the service contracts, and any other factors associated with the use of the machine that might properly influence the decision.

Strategic Analysis

The make, lease, or buy decision often raises strategic issues. For example, a firm using value-chain analysis could find that certain of its activities in the value chain can be more profitably performed by other firms. The practice of choosing to have an outside firm provide a basic service function is called *outsourcing*. Make, lease, or buy analysis has a key role in the decision to outsource by providing an analysis of the relevant costs. Many firms recently have considered outsourcing manufacturing and data processing, janitorial, or security services to improve profitability. For example, Eastman-Kodak Corporation has outsourced its data processing requirements, and some airlines are outsourcing food preparation, baggage handling, and reservation systems.

Contract manufacturing describes the practice of having another firm (sometimes a direct competitor) manufacture a portion of the firm's products.

IBM, Texas Instruments, Cisco Systems, and other firms have taken the idea of outsourcing a step further, to what is called **contract manufacturing,** in which another firm manufactures a portion of the first firm's products. When one firm has excess capacity or expertise and the other lacks capacity or know-how, contract manufacturing can be a cost-effective strategy for both firms.[4]

Sell Before or After Additional Processing

Cost Analysis

LEARNING OBJECTIVE 4
Use relevant and strategic cost analysis in the decision to sell before or after additional processing.

Another common decision concerns the option to sell a product or service before an intermediate processing step or to add further processing and then selling the product or service for a higher price. The additional processing might add features or functionality to a product or add flexibility or quality to a service. For example, a travel agent

[4] See "The Airlines to Labor: Buy in—or Get Bashed," *Business Week,* November 1, 1993, p. 40; also "Farming Out Work—To IBM, DEC, NCR…," *Business Week,* May 17, 1993, pp. 92–94.

preparing a group tour faces many decisions related to optional features to be offered on the tour, such as side-trips, sleeping quarters, and entertainment. A manufacturer of consumer electronics faces a number of decisions regarding the nature and extent of features to offer in its products.

The analysis of features also is important for manufacturers in determining what to do with defective products. Generally, they can either be sold in the defective state to outlet stores and discount chains or be repaired for sale in the usual manner. The decision is whether the product should be sold with or without additional processing. Relevant cost analysis is again the appropriate model to follow in analyzing these situations.

To continue with the TTS example, assume that a piece of equipment used to print its T-shirts has malfunctioned, and 400 shirts are not of acceptable quality because some colors are missing or faded. TTS can sell the defective shirts to outlet stores at a greatly reduced price ($4.50) or can run them through the printing machine again. A second run will produce a salable shirt in most cases. The costs to run them through the printer a second time are for the ink, supplies, and labor, totaling $1.80 per shirt, plus the setup, inspection, and materials-handling costs for a batch of product. See the relevant cost analysis in Exhibit 9.12. Note that the cost of the unprinted T-shirt is the same for both options and is therefore irrelevant.

The analysis shows there is an $880 advantage to reprinting the shirts rather than selling the defective shirts to discount stores.

EXHIBIT 9.12
Analysis of Reprinting 400 Defective T-Shirts

	Reprint	Sell to Discount Store
Revenue (400 @ $9.00, $4.50)	$3,600	$1,800
Relevant Costs		
Supplies and ink ($.95)	380	
Labor ($.85)	340	
Setup	130	
Inspection	30	
Materials handling	40	
Total relevant costs	$ 920	
Contribution margin	$2,680	$1,800
Net advantage to reprint	**$2,680 − $1,800 = $880**	

Strategic Analysis

Strategic concerns arise when considering selling to discount stores. Will this affect the sale of T-shirts in retail stores? Will the cost of packing, delivery, and sales commissions differ for these two types of sales? TTS management must carefully consider these broader issues in addition to the key information provided in the relevant cost analysis in Exhibit 9.12.

Profitability Analysis

Profitability Analysis: Keep or Drop a Product Line

LEARNING OBJECTIVE 5
Use relevant and strategic cost analysis in the decision to keep or drop products or services.

An important aspect of management is the regular review of product profitability. This review should address issues such as these:

- Which products are most profitable?
- Are the products priced properly?
- Which products should be promoted and advertised most aggressively?
- Which product managers should be rewarded?

These and related issues can be addressed through relevant cost analysis. To illustrate, we use Windbreakers, Inc., a manufacturer of sport clothing. Windbreakers manufactures three jackets: Calm, Windy, and Gale. Management has requested an analysis of Gale due to its low sales and low profitability (see Exhibit 9.13).

The analysis of Gale should begin with the important observation that the $3.54 fixed cost per unit is irrelevant for the analysis of the current profitability of the three products. Because the $168,000 total fixed costs are unchangeable in the short run, they are irrelevant for this analysis. That is, no changes in product mix, including the deletion of Gale, will affect the total fixed costs to be expended in the coming year. The fact that the fixed costs are irrelevant is illustrated by comparing the contribution income statements in Exhibit 9.14, which assumes that Gale is dropped, and Exhibit 9.15, which assumes that Gale is kept. The only changes caused by dropping Gale are the loss of its revenues and the elimination of variable costs. Thus, dropping Gale causes a reduction in total contribution margin of $4 per unit times 3,750 units of Gale sold, or $15,000, and a corresponding loss in net income ($15,000 = $147,000 − $132,000).

Benefit: Saved variable costs of Gale	$135,000	$(36 × 3,750)
Cost: Opportunity cost of lost sales of Gale	(150,000)	$(40 × 3,750)
Decrease in profit from decision to drop Gale	$(15,000)	$ (4 × 3,750)

EXHIBIT 9.13
Sales and Cost Data for Windbreakers, Inc.

	Calm	Windy	Gale	Total
Units sold last year	25,000	18,750	3,750	47,500
Revenue	$750,000	$600,000	$150,000	
Price	$ 30.00	$ 32.00	$ 40.00	
Relevant costs				
Unit variable cost	24.00	24.00	36.00	
Unit contribution margin	$ 6.00	$ 8.00	$ 4.00	
Nonrelevant fixed costs	3.54	3.54	3.54	168,000
Income per unit	$ 2.46	$ 4.46	$ .46	

EXHIBIT 9.14
Contribution Income Statement Profitability Analysis: Gale Dropped

	Calm	Windy	Total
Sales	$750,000	$600,000	$1,350,000
Relevant costs			
Variable cost ($24 ea)	600,000	450,000	1,050,000
Contribution margin	$150,000	$150,000	$ 300,000
Nonrelevant costs			
Fixed cost			168,000
Net income without Gale			$ 132,000

EXHIBIT 9.15
Contribution Income Statement Profitability Analysis: Gale Kept

	Calm	Windy	Gale	Total
Sales	$750,000	$600,000	$150,000	$1,500,000
Relevant costs				
Variable cost ($24, 24, 36)	600,000	450,000	135,000	1,185,000
Contribution margin	$150,000	$150,000	$ 15,000	$ 315,000
Nonrelevant costs				
Fixed cost				168,000
Net income with Gale				$ 147,000

EXHIBIT 9.16
Profitability Analysis: Including Traceable Advertising Costs

	Calm	Windy	Gale	Total
Sales	$750,000	$600,000	$150,000	$1,500,000
Relevant costs				
Variable cost	600,000	450,000	135,000	1,185,000
Contribution margin	$150,000	$150,000	$ 15,000	$ 315,000
Other relevant costs (traceable)				
Advertising	25,000	15,000	20,000	60,000
Contribution after all relevant costs	$125,000	$135,000	$ (5,000)	$ 255,000
Nonrelevant costs (not traceable)				
Fixed cost				$ 108,000
Net income with Gale				$ 147,000

Assume that further analysis shows that $60,000 of the $168,000 fixed costs are advertising costs to be spent directly on each of the three products: $25,000 for Calm, $15,000 for Windy, and $20,000 for Gale. The remainder of the fixed costs, $108,000 ($168,000 − $60,000), are not traceable to any of the three products and are therefore allocated to each product as before. Because advertising costs are directly traceable to the individual products, and assuming that the advertising plans for Gale can be canceled without additional cost, the $5,000 of advertising costs for Gale should be considered a relevant cost in the decision to delete Gale. This cost will differ in the future.

Exhibit 9.16 shows that the total contribution margin after all relevant costs for Gale is now a net loss of $5,000, providing a potential $5,000 gain by dropping Gale because of the expected $20,000 savings in avoidable advertising costs. We can interpret the contribution figures for Calm and Windy in the same way. The loss in deleting Calm or Windy would be $125,000 and $135,000, respectively.

In addition to the relevant cost analysis, the decision to keep or drop a product line should include relevant strategic factors, such as the potential effect of the loss of one product line on the sales of another. For example, some florists price cards, vases, and other related items at or below cost to better serve and attract customers to the most profitable product, the flower arrangements.

Other important factors include the potential effect on overall employee morale and organizational effectiveness if a product line is dropped. Moreover, managers should consider the sales growth potential of each product. Will a product considered to be dropped place the firm in a strong competitive position sometime in the future? A particularly important consideration is the extent of available production capacity. If production capacity and production resources (such as labor and machine time) are limited, consider the relative profitability of the products and the extent to which they require different amounts of these production resources.

Profitability Analysis: Evaluating Programs

Managers use the concept of relevant cost analysis to measure the financial effectiveness of programs or projects. A good example of such an analysis is the evaluation of the Health and Weight Loss Program, a primary component of the Health Management

EXHIBIT 9.17
Health and Weight Loss Program Income Statement for Kimberly-Clark Corporation

Revenues and savings	
Health care cost savings	$ 9,416
Sick leave absenteeism savings	4,973
Program fees	2,168
Total revenues and savings	$16,557
Relevant costs	
Program materials	112
Consultant's salary	7,804
Total relevant costs	$ 7,916
Contribution after relevant costs	$ 8,641

LEARNING OBJECTIVE 6
Use relevant and strategic cost analysis to evaluate programs.

Program at Kimberly-Clark Corporation in Neenah, Wisconsin.[5] Kimberly-Clark has traced the costs of this program and measured its dollar benefits in three categories: (1) health care savings, (2) sick leave and absenteeism savings, and (3) program fees for the participating employees. Exhibit 9.17 shows the relevant cost analysis of the profitability of this program.

Profitability Analysis: Service and Not-for-Profit Organizations

Triangle Women's Center (TWC) uses relevant cost analysis to determine the desirability of new services. TWC provides several services to the communities in and around a large southeastern city. It has not offered child care services but has received a large number of requests to do so in recent years. Now TWC is planning to add this service. The relevant cost analysis follows. TWC expects to hire a director ($29,000) and two part-time assistants ($9,000 each) for the child care service. TWC estimates variable costs per child at $60 per month. No other costs are relevant because none of the other operating costs of TWC are expected to change. TWC expects to receive funding of $25,000 from the United Way plus $30,000 from the city council. The analysis for the child care service's first year of operation is shown in Exhibit 9.18, which assumes that 20 children, the maximum number, will use the service.

The TWC analysis shows that the child care service will have a deficit of approximately $6,400 in the first year. Now TWC can decide whether it can make up the deficit from current funds or by raising additional funds. Relevant cost analysis provides TWC a useful method to determine the resource needs for the new program.

EXHIBIT 9.18
Triangle Women's Center Analysis of Child Care Services

Relevant costs	
Salary of director	$29,000
Salary for two part-time assistants	18,000
Variable costs for 20 children at $60 per month each	14,400
Total relevant costs	$61,400
Total funding	
United Way	$25,000
City Council	30,000
	$55,000
Expected deficit in the first year	$ 6,400

[5] The application is described in Kenneth J. Smith, "Differential Cost Analysis Techniques in Occupational Health Promotion Evaluation," *Accounting Horizons*, June 1988, pp. 58–66.

REAL-WORLD FOCUS — Sales Commissions at IBM and Ford Motor Co.

The use of relevant cost analysis in determining product profitability is also important in motivating and rewarding the sales staff. Since the best measure of short-term profitability is *contribution after relevant costs,* this measure should be used for sales commissions to motivate the sales staff to sell the most profitable products, that is, those with the highest contribution margin. The common approach of using sales revenue as a basis for commissions is not consistent with the goal of improving profitability. IBM Corporation recognized the importance of this idea by tying 60 percent of its sales commissions to the **profit** generated by the products sold.

The IBM plan also attends to important strategic factors, such as customer satisfaction. To make sure that salespeople do not simply push for sales of high-margin products, IBM links the remaining 40 percent of their commissions to customer satisfaction. Thus, the compensation plan makes salespeople think like managers—their focus is on profits and customer satisfaction, as is the focus of top management.

Similarly, Ford Motor Co. recently changed the way its sales force is compensated from one based on units sold to one based on profit margins. Previously, salespeople had tended to push the low-price, low-margin vehicles to increase volume and save marketing costs. The change has motivated increased sales of the higher margin vehicles.

Source: "IBM Leans on Its Sales Force," *Business Week,* February 17, 1994, p. 110; and "The Power of Smart Pricing," *Business Week,* April 10, 2000, pp. 160–64.

Multiple Products and Limited Resources

LEARNING OBJECTIVE 7
Analyze decisions with multiple products and limited resources.

The preceding relevant cost analyses were simplified by using a single product and assuming sufficient resources to meet all demands. The analysis changes significantly with two or more products and limited resources. The revised analysis is considered in this section. We continue the example of Windbreakers, Inc., except that we assume that the Calm product is manufactured in a separate plant under contract with a major customer. Thus, the following analysis focuses only on the Windy and Gale products, which are manufactured in a single facility.

A key element of the relevant cost analysis is to determine the most profitable sales mix for Windy and Gale. If there are no production constraints, the answer is clear; we manufacture what is needed to meet demand for both Windy and Gale. However, when demand exceeds production capacity, management must make some trade-offs about the quantity of each product to manufacture, and therefore, what demand is unmet. The answer requires considering the production possibilities given by the production constraints. Consider two important cases: (1) one production constraint and (2) two or more production constraints.

Case 1: One Production Constraint

Assume that the production of Windy and Gale requires an automated sewing machine to stitch the jackets and that this production activity is a limited resource: sales demand for the two products exceeds the capacity on the plant's three automated sewing machines. Each machine can be run up to 20 hours per day five days per week, or 400 hours per month, which is its maximum capacity allowing for maintenance. This gives 1,200 (3 × 400) available hours for sewing each month. Assume further that the machine requires three minutes to assemble a Windy and two minutes to assemble a Gale.

Because only 1,200 hours of machine time are available per month and the Gale jacket requires less machine time, more Gale jackets can be made in a month than Windy jackets. The maximum number of Windy jackets is 24,000 jackets per month (1,200 hours times 20 jackets per hour, at 3 minutes per jacket). Similarly, if the sewing machine were devoted entirely to Gale jackets, then 36,000 jackets per month could be produced (1,200 times 30 jackets per hour). This information is summarized in Exhibit 9.19.

A continuous trade-off possibility exists for the extreme situations: zero output of Windy and 36,000 of Gale or 24,000 of Windy and zero of Gale. These production and

EXHIBIT 9.19
Windbreakers Data for the Windy and Gale Plant
One Constraint: The Sewing Machine

Find the most profitable product this way:		Windy	Gale
Since			
Contribution margin/unit		$8	$4
Sewing time per jacket		3 min	2 min
Then, because sewing time is limited to 1,200 hours per month, we determine the contribution margin per machine-hour			
Number of jackets per hour		20	30
(60 min/3 min = 20; 60/2 = 30)			
Contribution margin per hour		$160	$120
(20 × $8; 30 × $4)			
Also, the maximum production for each product, given the 1,200-hour constraint			
For Windy: 1,200 × 20		24,000	
For Gale: 1,200 × 30			36,000

EXHIBIT 9.20
Windbreakers Production and Sales Possibilities
One Production Constraint—The Sewing Machine

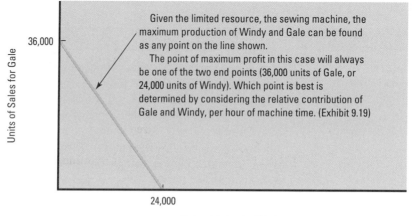

Given the limited resource, the sewing machine, the maximum production of Windy and Gale can be found as any point on the line shown.

The point of maximum profit in this case will always be one of the two end points (36,000 units of Gale, or 24,000 units of Windy). Which point is best is determined by considering the relative contribution of Gale and Windy, per hour of machine time. (Exhibit 9.19)

sales mix possibilities can be shown graphically; all sales mix possibilities are represented by all possible points on the line in Exhibit 9.20. The line in Exhibit 9.20 can be determined as follows:

$$\text{Slope} = -36,000/24,000 = -3/2$$

$$\text{Intercept} = 36,000$$

The line in Exhibit 9.20 is thus given by

$$\text{Units of Gale} = 36,000 - 3/2 \times \text{Units of Windy}$$

To illustrate, assume that Windbreakers is producing 12,000 units of Windy so that

$$\text{Units of Gale} = 36,000 - 3/2 \times 12,000 = 18,000$$

Now that we know the production possibilities, we can determine the best product mix. Note from Exhibit 9.19 that Windy has the higher overall contribution margin, $160 per hour (20 jackets per hour × $8 per jacket). Because 1,200 machine-hours are available per month, the maximum total contribution from the production possibilities is to produce only Windy and achieve the total contribution of 1,200 × $160 = $192,000 (or $8 per unit × 24,000 units = $192,000) per month. If Windbreakers were to produce and sell only Gale, the maximum total contribution margin would be $144,000 per month (1,200 hours × $120 per hour), a $48,000 reduction over the contribution from selling only Windy. *Thus, when there is only one production constraint and excess demand, it is generally best to focus production and sales on the product with the highest contribution per unit of scarce resource.* Of course, it is unlikely in a practical situation that a firm would be able to adopt the extreme position of deleting one product and focusing entirely on the other. However, the previous results show the value of considering a strong focus on the more profitable product based on the contribution per unit of a scarce resource.

Case 2: Two or More Production Constraints

When the production process requires two or more production constraints, the choice of sales mix involves a more complex analysis, and in contrast to one production constraint, the solution can include both products. To continue with the Windbreakers case, assume that in addition to the automated sewing machine, a second production activity is required. The second activity inspects the completed jackets, adds labels, and packages the completed product. This operation is done by 40 workers, who can complete the operation for the Windy jacket in 15 minutes and for the Gale jacket in 5 minutes (because of differences in material quality, less inspection time is required for the Gale jacket). This means that 4 (60/15) Windy jackets can be completed in an hour, or 12 Gale (60/5). Because of the limited size of the facility, no more than 40 workers can be employed effectively in the inspection and packaging process. These employees work a 40-hour week, which means 35 hours of actually performing the operation, given times for breaks, training, and other tasks. Thus, 5,600 hours (40 workers × 35 hours × 4 weeks) are available per month for inspecting and packing.

The maximum output per month for the Windy jacket is 22,400 (5,600 hours × 4 jackets per hour). Similarly, the maximum output for the Gale jacket is 67,200. All of this information is summarized in Exhibit 9.21.

The production possibilities for two constraints are illustrated in Exhibit 9.22. In addition to the production possibilities for machine time, we show the production possibilities for inspection and packing. The darker shaded area indicates the range of possible outputs for both Gale and Windy. Note that it is not possible to produce more than the 22,400 units of Windy because all 40 workers inspecting and packing full time would not be able to handle more than that number, even though the sewing machine is capable of producing 24,000 units. Similarly, although Windbreakers could pack and ship 67,200 units of Gale by having all 40 packers work full-time on that jacket, the firm could manufacture only 36,000 units of Gale because of limited capacity on the sewing machine.

The production planner can determine the best production mix by examining all of the possible production possibilities in the darker shaded area, from 36,000 on the Gale axis to point A where the constraints intersect, and then to the point 22,400 on the Windy axis. The sales mix with the highest contribution must be one of these three points: 36,000 of Gale, point A, or 22,400 units of Windy. The solution, called the *corner point analysis,* is obtained by finding the total contribution at each point and then

EXHIBIT 9.21
Windbreakers Data for the Windy and Gale Plant
The Second Constraint: Inspecting and Packing

	Windy	Gale
Since		
Contribution margin/unit	$8	$4
Inspection and packaging time per jacket	15 min	5 min
Then		
Number of jackets per hour	4	12
Contribution margin per hour (4 × $8; 12 × $4)	$32	$48
Also		
The maximum production for each product, given the 5,600-hour constraint		
For Windy: 5,600 × 4	22,400	
For Gale: 5,600 × 12		67,200

EXHIBIT 9.22
Windbreakers Production and
Sales Possibilities
Two Production Constraints—
Sewing Machine and Inspection

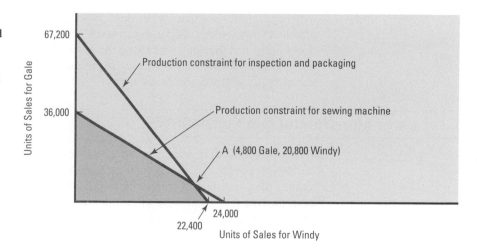

choosing the point with the higher contribution. The solution achieved in this manner is for production at point A, 20,800 units of Windy and 4,800 units of Gale.[6]

The analysis of sales mix and production constraints is a useful way for managers to understand both how a difference in sales mix affects income and how production limitations and capacities can significantly affect the proper determination of the most profitable sales mix.

Behavioral and Implementation Issues

Consideration of Strategic Objectives

LEARNING OBJECTIVE 8
Discuss the behavioral,
implementation, and legal issues
in decision making.

A well-known problem in business today is the tendency of managers to focus on short-term goals and neglect the long-term strategic goals because their compensation is based on short-term accounting measures such as net income. Many critics of relevant cost analysis have raised this issue. As noted throughout the chapter, it is critical that the relevant cost analysis be supplemented by a careful consideration of the firm's long-term, strategic concerns. Without strategic considerations, management could improperly use relevant cost analysis to achieve a short-term benefit and potentially suffer a significant long-term loss. For example, a firm might choose to accept a special order because of a positive relevant cost analysis without properly considering that the nature of the special order could have a significant negative impact on the firm's image in the marketplace and perhaps a negative effect on sales of the firm's other products. The important message for managers is to keep the strategic objectives in the forefront in any decision situation.

Predatory Pricing

The Robinson Patman Act, administered by the U.S. Federal Trade Commission, addresses pricing that could substantially damage the competition in an industry. This is called *predatory pricing*, which the U.S. Supreme Court defined in a 1993 decision,

---

[6] The point A, 20,800 for Windy and 4,800 for Gale, is obtained by solving the two equations:

$$15W + 5G = 35 \times 40 \times 4 \times 60 = 336,000 \text{ minutes}$$
$$3W + 2G = 400 \times 3 \times 60 = 72,000 \text{ minutes}$$

Linear programming, a mathematical method, permits the solution of much larger problems involving many products and production activities. A linear program technique to solve the Windy and Gale case is shown in Appendix A of this chapter. This technique uses the Solver function of Microsoft Excel.

Brooke Group Ltd. vs. Brown & Williamson Tobacco Corp. (B&W), as a situation in which a company has set prices below average variable cost and planned to raise prices later to recover the losses from lower prices. This law is relevant for short-term *and* long-term pricing since it could require a firm to justify significant price cuts. However, the Court in the *Brooke* decision concluded that on the basis of economic theory, predatory pricing does not work and concluded in favor of B&W, the defendant in the case. The Court's reasoning has stood the test of time, because all 37 predatory pricing cases since its 1993 decision have been found in favor of the defendant. In spite of this, some economists and lawyers in 1999–2000 believed that economic theories of competition had changed since 1993. On the basis of these new theories, they took issue with the aggressive pricing practices of American Airlines, especially at the Dallas–Fort Worth airport, where a number of competing carriers had been driven to financial distress. In 2001 their suit against American was thrown out by a federal judge, causing some to argue this is the end of suits regarding predatory pricing. The judge in the case noted that the law states predatory pricing exists when the firm sets price below average variable cost, which was not the case at American. Of course, at American as for any airline, variable costs are a small portion of total costs, so it was possible for American to drive prices very low and still be in compliance. The result could strengthen dominant firms in price-competitive industries such as the airlines and personal computers.[7]

A variation on the issue of predatory pricing is the recent increase in the number of countries levying fines against global firms for "dumping" their products at anticompetitive prices. A World Trade Organization report shows the number of cases per year has increased by 35 percent from 1995 to 2000. The U.S. antidumping laws were enacted more than 80 years ago to protect against predatory pricing by global firms exporting to the United States. The laws state that the import price cannot be lower than the cost of production or the price in the home market. Unfortunately the laws often have been used to protect uncompetitive industries in the home country. Facing increasing global pressure on the issue, U.S. congressional leaders are debating the need to reform the U.S. law.[8]

Replacement of Variable Costs with Fixed Costs

Another potential incentive associated with relevant cost analysis is for managers to replace variable costs with fixed costs. This might happen if mid-level and lower-level managers realize that because they rely on relevant cost analysis, upper management tends to overlook fixed costs. Lower-level managers might choose to replace their assets and other productive resources to reduce variable costs, although this increases fixed costs significantly. For example, a new machine might replace direct labor. The overall costs increase because of the cost of the machine, although variable costs under the manager's control decrease and the contribution margin increases. Management's proper goal is to maximize contribution margin and to minimize fixed operating costs at the same time. Managers should use relevant cost analysis as a tool to maximize contribution and must also develop methods to manage fixed costs.

Proper Identification of Relevant Factors

Another possible problem area of cost analysis is that managers can fail to properly identify relevant costs. In particular, untrained managers commonly include irrelevant,

---

[7] Based on information in "Caveat Predator," *Business Week,* May 22, 2000, pp. 116-18; "Legend Air, Unable to Get Financing, Suspends Flights," *The Wall Street Journal,* December 4, 2000; and Dan Carney, "Predatory Pricing: Cleared for Takeoff," *Business Week,* May 14, 2001, p. 50.

[8] Paul Magnusson, "A U.S. Trade Ploy That Is Starting to Boomerang," *Business Week,* July 29, 2002, pp 64–65; "The WTO Rules Against a Globally Unpopular U.S. Legislation," *Business Standard,* February 13, 2003; and "Steel Wire Imports May Have Violated Antidumping Laws," *The Wall Street Journal,* March 18, 2003, p. A12.

REAL-WORLD FOCUS   °Examples of Decision Biases:
Mutual Fund Investors Show "Loss Aversion"

A recent study indicates that mutual fund investors show an unfortunate decision bias when evaluating the returns of individual funds. The average investor is 2.5 times more likely to sell a fund with strong returns than a fund with weak returns (the good news is that they tend to buy strong funds). The researchers call this bias to sell strong funds "loss aversion," and explain it in terms of human emotions: You feel a lot better about selling a winner than you do about selling a loser. From a decision-making point of view, this emotional aspect is unfortunate because the investor simultaneously dumps a winning stock and incurs capital gains taxes on the gain made on the sale.

Source: Robert Barker, "Why Not Lose Those Mutual-Fund Losers," *Business Week,* October 23, 2000, p. 170.

sunk costs in their decision making.[9] Similarly, many managers fail to see that allocated fixed costs are irrelevant. When fixed costs are "unitized" in this manner, many managers tend to improperly find them relevant. It is easier for these managers to see the fixed cost as irrelevant when it is given in a single sum.

These are illustrations of the pervasive biases present in many managers' decision making. To repeat, effective use of relevant cost analysis requires careful identification of relevant costs, those future costs that differ among decision alternatives, and correctly recognizing sunk costs and unit fixed costs as irrelevant in the short term.

Summary

Relevant cost analysis uses future costs that differ for the decision maker's options. The principle of relevant cost analysis can be applied in a number of specific decisions involving manufacturing, service, and not-for-profit organizations. The decisions considered in the chapter include

- The special order decision for which the relevant costs are the direct manufacturing costs and any incremental fixed costs.
- The make, lease, or buy decision for which the relevant costs are the direct manufacturing costs and any avoidable fixed costs.
- The decision to sell a product before or after additional processing for which the relevant costs are the additional processing costs.
- The decision to keep or drop a product line or service for which the relevant costs are the direct costs and any fixed costs that change if the product or service is dropped.
- The evaluation of programs and projects.
- The decision of a not-for-profit organization to offer a service.

Strategic cost analysis complements relevant cost analysis by having the decision maker consider the strategic issues involved in the situation.

[9] For a comprehensive coverage of decision-making biases, see John S. Hammond, Ralph L. Keeney, and Howard Raiffa, "The Hidden Traps in Decision Making," *Harvard Business Review,* September–October 1998, pp. 47–58; also D. L. Heerema and R. L. Rogers, "Is Your Cost Accounting System Benching Your Team Players?" *Management Accounting,* September 1991, pp. 35–40, gives useful illustrations of the improper use of relevant cost analysis in the automobile industry, the military, and elsewhere. Prospect theory suggests that people underweigh alternatives that are uncertain in comparison to alternatives known to be certain. The theory has been offered as a potential explanation of the tendency people have to include sunk costs in decision making. See D. Kahneman and A. Tversky, "Prospect Theory: An Analysis of Decision under Risk," *Econometrica,* March 1979, pp. 263–92; and Glen Whyte, "Escalating Commitment to a Course of Action: A Reinterpretation," *Academy of Management Review,* 1986, pp. 311–21.

When two or more products or services are involved, another type of decision must be made: to determine the correct product mix. The solution depends on the number of production activities that are at full capacity. With one production constraint, the answer is to produce and sell as much as possible of the product that has the highest contribution margin per unit of time on the constrained activity. With two or more constrained activities, the analysis uses graphical and quantitative methods to determine the correct product mix.

A number of key behavioral, implementation, and legal issues must be considered in using relevant cost analysis. Many who use the approach fail to give sufficient attention to the firm's long-term, strategic objectives. Too strong a focus on relevant costs can cause the manager to overlook important opportunity costs and strategic considerations. Other issues include the tendency to replace variable costs with fixed costs when relevant cost analysis is used in performance evaluation, the pervasive tendency of people not to correctly view fixed costs as sunk but to view them as somehow controllable and relevant.

Appendix A

Linear Programming and the Product Mix Decision

This appendix explains how linear programming can be used to solve product mix decisions such as the Windbreakers case illustrated in the chapter. Linear programming is particularly useful when the product mix decision involves three or more constraints since these larger problems are difficult to solve graphically or with the simple corner point analysis explained in the chapter. A number of linear programming tools are available; we use the Solver function of Microsoft Excel because of its wide availability. To access this tool, you simply install it when installing Excel; Solver will appear as an option on Excel's Tool menu.

The first step in using Solver is to enter the data for the problem into an Excel spreadsheet, in the form shown in Exhibit 9.23:

Column A: Shows the product names.

Column B: Solver requires an initial guess at what might be an appropriate solution; for this purpose, we chose the point 10,000 units of Windy and 2,000 units of Gale; the point should be any of the possible points within the feasible region shown as the darker shaded area in Exhibit 9.22.

Columns C, D, and E: These contain data entered from the problem information.

Columns F, G, and H: These contain formulas based on the data in columns, C, D, and E; for example, cell F5 contains B5×C5; cell G5 contains B5×D5, and so on.

The second step in using Solver is to enter the parameters as shown in the dialog box in Exhibit 9.23. The dialog box appears by selecting **Solver** from the Tool menu. Note that the target cell is total contribution, located in cell F7, which currently shows the total contribution for sales of 10,000 units of Windy and 2,000 units of Gale. The "By Changing Cells" section includes those cells representing the total sales of Windy and Gale, now set at an initial value of 10,000 and 2,000 units, respectively. Then the constraints for sewing time and inspect and pack time are entered in the "Subject to the Constraints" section as shown. Finally, select Solve in the dialog box, and the solution appears, as shown in Exhibit 9.24. (See also footnote 6 on p. 354.)

Notice that cells B5 and B6 in Exhibit 9.24 now show the solution values for the two products, and the cells in columns F, G, and H show the total contribution and total use of the two constraints. At this time, it is possible to see any of three possible additional reports, the Answer, Sensitivity, and Limit reports as shown in the dialog box. We have selected only the Answer report for illustration at this time, which is shown in Exhibit 9.25. This report summarizes the initial and final values for the problem data.

EXHIBIT 9.23   Enter Data and Solver Parameters: Solution for the Windy and Gale Problem

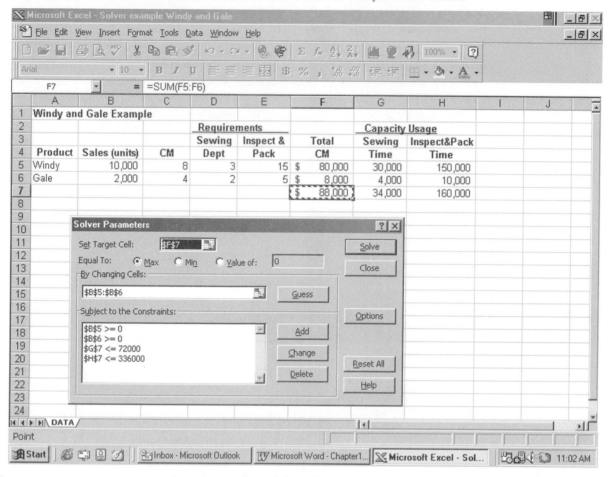

EXHIBIT 9.24   Solver Solution for the Windy and Gale Problem

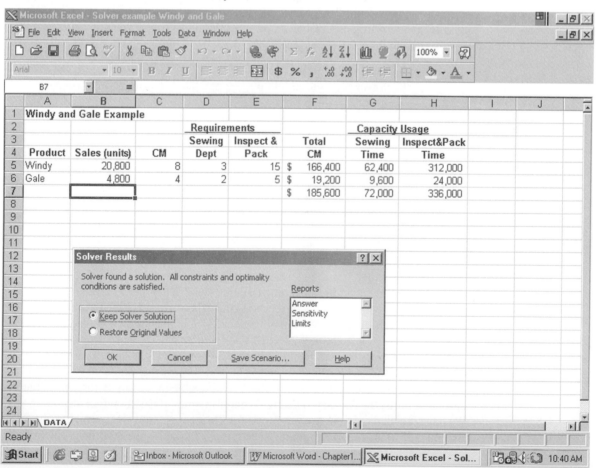

EXHIBIT 9.25 Solver Solution for the Windy and Gale Problem: Answer Report

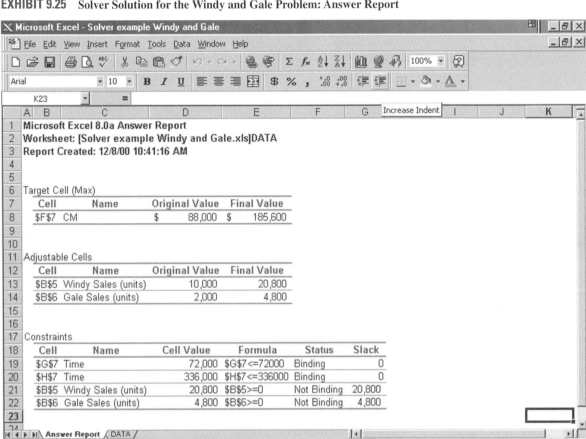

Key Terms

Comments on Cost Management in Action

Make-or-Buy Strategies: A Survey of U.S. Firms

Toyota Motor Company is able to maintain a small number of suppliers by using two key strategies. First, it develops a hierarchy of suppliers; Toyota deals directly with approximately 200, which are called the *top-tier suppliers*. These 200 suppliers in turn deal with second-tier suppliers who provide products and services to those at the top tier. These second-tier suppliers in turn deal with third-tier suppliers. In this way, Toyota delegates the responsibility for managing the supply function in a way that motivates suppliers at each tier to work effectively with those above and below it in the supply chain. Second, Toyota distinguishes two types of suppliers, general and specialty. Toyota has relatively simple relationships with those in the general category of suppliers but develops close financial and technological ties with the specialty suppliers. The objective is to recognize the strategic importance of the specialty suppliers and to develop strong relationships with them to ensure success.

A recent survey of 328 U.S. purchasing managers showed that they were taking steps to reduce both the number of suppliers and the frequency with which they change suppliers, in effect moving closer to the Toyota model.

Source: Hong Y. Park, C. Surender Reddy, and Sam Sarkar, "Make or Buy Strategy of Firms in the U.S.," *Multinational Business Review,* Fall 2000, pp. 89–97; "Machete Time," *Business Week,* April 9, 2001, pp. 42–43.

Self-Study Problems

(For solutions, please turn to the end of the chapter.)

1. Special Order Pricing

HighValu Inc. manufactures a moderate-price set of lawn furniture (a table and four chairs) that it sells for $225. It currently manufactures and sells 6,000 sets per year. The manufacturing costs include $85 for materials and $45 for labor per set. The overhead charge per set is $35, which consists entirely of fixed costs.

HighValu is considering a special purchase offer from a large retail firm, which has offered to buy 600 sets per year for three years at a price of $150 per set. HighValu has the available plant capacity to produce the order and expects no other orders or profitable alternative uses of the plant capacity.

Required   Should HighValu accept the offer?

2. The Make-or-Buy Decision

Assume that HighValu Inc., as described, currently purchases the chair cushions for its lawn set from an outside vendor for $15 per set. HighValu's chief operations officer wants an analysis of the comparative costs of manufacturing these cushions to determine whether bringing the manufacturing in-house would save the firm money. Additional information shows that if HighValu were to manufacture the cushions, the materials cost would be $6 and the labor cost would be $4 per set and that it would have to purchase cutting and sewing equipment, which would add $10,000 to annual fixed costs.

Required   Should HighValu make the cushions or continue to purchase them from the vendor?

3. Profitability Analysis

Consider again the Windbreakers firm described in the text. Suppose that it determines that dropping the Gale product line will release production capacity so that it can manufacture additional units of Windy. Assume that, as described in the text, the two production constraints are the automated sewing machine and the inspection and packing operation. The automated sewing machine can make 20 Windys or 30 Gales per hour. As before, the inspection operation requires 15 minutes for a Windy (4 per hour) and 5 minutes for a Gale (12 per hour). Currently, 3,750 Gales and 18,750 Windys are being manufactured and sold. Sales projections show that sales of Windy could be increased to 30,000 units if additional capacity were available.

Required

1. If Windbreakers deletes Gale entirely, how many units of Windy can it manufacture with the released capacity?
2. What is the dollar effect on net income if Windbreakers drops the production and sale of Gale and uses the released capacity for Windy?
3. What other factors should Windbreakers consider in its decision to drop Gale and use the released capacity to produce additional units of Windy?

Questions

9–1   What are relevant costs? Provide several examples for the decision to repair or replace a piece of equipment.

9–2   Define *outsourcing* and explain how the relevant cost analysis model is used in the outsourcing decision.

9–3   List at least four different decisions for which the relevant cost analysis model can be used effectively.

9–4   How does the relevant cost analysis model differ for manufacturing and service firms?

9–5   Define *contract manufacturing* and provide several examples.

9–6   List four to six strategic factors that are often important in the make-or-buy decision.

9–7   Explain what *not relevant* cost means and provide two examples of it.

9–8   Why are variable costs usually more relevant than fixed costs in short-term decision making?

9–9   Give an example of how a firm can decrease variable costs by increasing fixed costs.

9–10 Give an example of how a firm can decrease fixed costs by increasing variable costs.

9–11 How do short-term evaluations affect a manager's incentives and performance?

9–12 List four or five important limitations of relevant cost analysis.

9–13 How do strategic factors affect the proper use of relevant cost analysis?

9–14 List some of the behavioral, implementation, and legal problems to be anticipated in the use of relevant cost analysis.

9–15 How does the presence of one production constraint affect the relevant cost analysis model? Two or more production constraints?

9–16 What is the relationship, if any, between the relevant cost analysis method and cost-volume-profit analysis?

9–17 Explain why depreciation is a nonrelevant cost.

Exercises

9–18 **Special Order Analysis** Marshall Company recently approached Johnson Corporation regarding manufacturing a special order of 4,000 units of product CRB2B. Marshall would reimburse Johnson for all variable manufacturing costs plus 35 percent. The *per-unit* data follow:

Unit sales price	$28
Variable manufacturing costs	13
Variable marketing costs	5
Fixed manufacturing costs	4
Fixed marketing costs	2

Johnson would have a retooling cost of $12,000 but otherwise has sufficient plant capacity to manufacture the order. It would incur no marketing costs for this special order.

Required Should the special order be accepted?

9–19 **Special Order** Alton Inc. is working at full production capacity producing 20,000 units of a unique product. Manufacturing costs per unit for the product are

Direct materials	$ 9
Direct labor	8
Manufacturing overhead	10
Total manufacturing cost	$27

The unit manufacturing overhead cost is based on a $4 variable cost per unit and $120,000 fixed costs. The nonmanufacturing costs, all variable, are $8 per unit, and the sales price is $45 per unit.

Sports Headquarters Company (SHC) has asked Alton to produce 5,000 units of a modification of the new product. This modification would require the same manufacturing processes. SHC has offered to share the nonmanufacturing costs equally with Alton. Alton would sell the modified product to SHC for $35 per unit.

Required

1. Should Alton produce the special order for SHC? Why or why not?
2. Suppose that Alton Inc. had been working at less than full capacity to produce 16,000 units of the product when SHC made the offer. What is the minimum price that Alton should accept for the modified product under these conditions?

9–20 **Profitability Analysis, Dropping a Division** Rivera Financial Services is planning to drop one of its divisions that has a contribution margin of $20,000. In addition, $50,000 of Rivera's corporate overhead is allocated to the division. Of the $50,000, $30,000 can be eliminated if the division is discontinued.

Required What would be the increase or decrease in Rivera Industries' pretax income by dropping this division?

9–21 **Special Order** Grant Industries, a manufacturer of electronic parts, has recently received an invitation to bid on a special order for 20,000 units of one of its most popular products. Grant currently manufactures 40,000 units of this product in its Loveland, Ohio, plant. The plant is operating at 50 percent capacity. There will be no marketing costs on the special order. The sales manager of Grant wants to set the bid at $9 because she is sure that Grant will get the business at that price. Others on the executive committee of the firm object, saying that Grant would lose money on the special order at that price.

Units	40,000	60,000
Manufacturing costs		
Direct materials	$ 80,000	$120,000
Direct labor	120,000	180,000
Factory overhead	240,000	300,000
Total manufacturing costs	$440,000	$600,000
Unit cost	$ 11	$ 10

Required

1. Why does the unit cost decline from $11 to $10 when production level rises from 40,000 to 60,000 units?

2. Is the sales manager correct? What do you think the bid price should be?

3. List some additional factors Grant should consider in deciding how much to bid on this special order.

9–22 **Profitability Analysis**   Maitax Corporation, located in Buffalo, New York, is a retailer of high-tech products known for their excellent quality and innovation. Recently the firm conducted a relevant cost analysis of one of its product lines that has only two products, RAM and ROM. The sales for ROM are decreasing and the purchase costs are increasing. The firm might drop ROM and sell only RAM.

Maitax allocates fixed costs to products on the basis of sales revenue. When the president of Maitax saw the income statement, he agreed that ROM should be dropped. If this is done, sales of RAM are expected to increase by 10 percent next year; the firm's cost structure will remain the same.

	RAM	ROM
Sales	$180,000	$260,000
Variable cost of goods sold	70,000	130,000
Contribution margin	$110,000	$130,000
Expenses		
Fixed corporate costs	50,000	75,000
Variable selling and administration	18,000	50,000
Fixed selling and administration	12,000	21,000
Total expenses	$ 80,000	$146,000
Net income	$ 30,000	$(16,000)

Required

1. Find the expected change in annual net income by dropping ROM and selling only RAM.

2. What strategic factors should be considered?

9–23 **Relevant Cost Exercises**

a. **Make or Buy**   Murray Inc. manufactures machine parts for aircraft engines. CEO Bucky Walters is considering an offer from a subcontractor to provide 2,000 units of product OP89 for $124,000. If Murray does not purchase these parts from the subcontractor, it must continue to produce them in-house with these costs:

	Costs per Unit
Direct materials	$28
Direct labor	18
Variable overhead	6
Fixed overhead	4

In addition to these costs, Murray would also incur a retooling and design cost of $8,000 to produce part OP89.

Required   Should Murray Inc. accept the offer from the subcontractor? Why or why not?

b. **Disposal of Assets**   A company has an inventory of 2,000 different parts for a line of cars that has been discontinued. The net book value of inventory in the accounting records is $50,000. The parts can be either remachined at a total additional cost of $25,000 and then sold for $30,000 or sold as is for $2,500. What should it do?

c. **Replacement of Asset**   An uninsured boat costing $90,000 was wrecked the first day it was used. It can be either sold as is for $9,000 cash and replaced with a similar boat costing $92,000 or rebuilt for $75,000 and be brand new as far as operating characteristics and looks are concerned. What should be done?

d. **Profit from Processing Further**   Almond's Corporation manufactures products A, B, and C from a joint process. Joint costs are allocated on the basis of relative sales value at the end of the joint process. Additional information for Almond's Corporation follows:

	A	B	C	Total
Units produced	12,000	8,000	4,000	24,000
Joint costs	$144,000	$ 60,000	$36,000	$240,000
Sales value after joint processing	$240,000	$100,000	$60,000	$400,000
Additional costs for further processing	28,000	20,000	12,000	60,000
Sales value if processed further	280,000	120,000	80,000	480,000

Required   Should product A, B, or C be processed further and then sold?

e. **Make or Buy**   Strawn Company needs 20,000 units of a part to use in producing one of its products. If Strawn buys the part from McMillan Company for $85 instead of making it, Strawn could not use the released facilities in another manufacturing activity. Fifty percent of the fixed overhead will continue regardless of CEO Donald Mickey's decision. The cost data are

Cost to make the part	
Direct materials	$35
Direct labor	11
Variable overhead	19
Fixed overhead	20
	$85

Required   Determine which alternative is more attractive to Strawn and by what amount.

f. **Selection of the Most Profitable Product**   Video Company produces two basic types of video games, Bash and Gash. Pertinent data for Video Company follows:

	Bash	Gash
Sales price	$200	$140
Costs		
Direct materials	56	26
Direct labor	30	50
Variable factory overhead*	50	25
Fixed factory overhead*	20	10
Marketing costs (all variable)	28	20
Total costs	$184	$131
Operating income	$ 16	$ 9

*Based on labor hours.

The video craze is at its height so that either Bash or Gash alone can be sold to keep the plant operating at full capacity. However, labor capacity in the plant is insufficient to meet the combined demand for both games. Bash and Gash are processed through the same production departments.

Required   Which product should be produced? Briefly explain your answer.

g. **Special Order Pricing**   Barry's Bar-B-Que is a popular lunch-time spot. Barry is conscientious about the quality of his meals, and he has a regular crowd of 600 patrons for his $5 lunch. His variable cost for each meal is about $2, and he figures his fixed costs, on a daily basis, at about $1,200. From time to time, bus tour groups with 50 patrons stop by. He has welcomed them since he has capacity to seat about 700 diners in the average lunch period, and his cooking and wait staff can easily handle the additional load. The tour operator generally pays for the entire group on a single check to save the wait staff and cashier the additional time. Due to competitive conditions in the tour business, the operator is now asking Barry to lower the price to $3.50 per meal for each of the 50 bus tour members.

Required   Should Barry accept the $3.50 price? Why or why not? What if the tour company were willing to guarantee 200 patrons (or four bus loads) at least once a month for $3.00 per meal?

9–24 **Make or Buy**   Three Stars Inc. manufactures prefabricated houses. The firm's president, Michelle Brown, is interested in determining whether it would be better to manufacture the doors used in the houses or to buy them from a supplier. The following information, based on production of 500 doors, has been gathered to help determine the best option:

	Costs per Unit
Direct materials	$ 35
Direct labor	50
Variable overhead	10
Fixed overhead	
Administrative salaries	$ 7
Property taxes	2
Insurance	5
Utilities	5
Miscellaneous fixed overhead	6
Total costs	$120

Of the fixed overhead costs, Three Stars could save $5 per unit of miscellaneous fixed overhead if it purchases the doors from a supplier and allocates all other fixed costs elsewhere. The cost to purchase 500 doors would be $55,000.

Required   Should Three Stars make or purchase the doors? What is the savings per unit?

Problems

9–25 **Special Order**   Award Plus Co. manufactures medals for winners of athletic events and other contests. Its manufacturing plant has the capacity to produce 10,000 medals each month; current monthly production is 7,500 medals. The company normally charges $175 per medal. Variable costs and fixed costs for the current activity level of 75 percent follow:

	Current Product Costs
Variable costs	
Manufacturing	
Labor	$ 375,000
Material	262,500
Marketing	187,500
Total variable costs	$ 825,000
Fixed costs	
Manufacturing	$ 275,000
Marketing	175,000
Total fixed costs	$ 450,000
Total costs	$1,275,000

Award Plus has just received a special one-time order for 2,500 medals at $100 per medal. For this particular order, no variable marketing costs will be incurred. Cathy Senna, a management accountant with Award Plus, has been assigned the task of analyzing this order and recommending whether the company should accept or reject it. After examining the costs, Senna suggested to her supervisor, Gerard LePenn who is the controller, that they request competitive bids from vendors for the raw materials as the current quote seems high. LePenn insisted that the prices are in line with other vendors and told her that she was not to discuss her observations with anyone else. Senna later discovered that LePenn is a brother-in-law of the owner of the current raw materials supply vendor.

Required

1. Determine if Award Plus Co. should accept the special order. In explaining your answer, compute both the new average unit cost for Award Plus and the incremental unit cost for the special order.
2. Discuss at least three other considerations that Cathy Senna should include in her analysis of the special order.
3. Explain how Cathy Senna should try to resolve the ethical conflict arising out of the controller's insistence that the company avoid competitive bidding.

(CMA Adapted)

9–26 Special Order Analysis Jordan Industries produces high-quality automobile seat covers. Its success in the industry is due to its quality, although all of its customers, the automakers, are very cost conscious and negotiate for price cuts on all large orders. Noting that the auto supply business is becoming increasingly competitive, Jordan is looking for a way to meet the challenge. It is negotiating with JepCo, Inc., a large mail-order auto parts and accessories retailer, to purchase a large order of seat covers. Much of Jordan's business is seasonal and cyclical, fluctuating with the varying demands of the large automakers. Jordan would like to keep its plants busy throughout the year by reducing these seasonal and cyclical fluctuations. Keeping the flow of product moving through the plants at a steady level is helpful in keeping costs down; extra overtime and machine setup and repair costs are incurred when production levels fluctuate. JepCo has agreed to a large order but only at a price of $28 per set. The special order can be produced in one batch with available capacity. Jordan prepared these data:

Next month's operating information without the special order (per unit, for 10,000 units, made in 10 batches of 1,000 each)	
Sales price	$68
Per unit costs	
Variable manufacturing costs	21
Variable marketing costs	8
Fixed manufacturing costs	25
Fixed marketing costs	3
Special order information	
Sales	2,000 units
Sales price per unit	$28

No variable marketing costs are associated with this order, but Marc Jordan, the firm's president, has spent $2,000 during the past three months trying to get JepCo to purchase the special order.

Required

1. How much will the special order change Jordan Industries' total operating income?
2. How might the special order fit into Jordan's competitive situation?

9–27 Special Order: ABC Costing (Continuation of Problem 9–26) Assume the same information as for Problem 9–26, except that the $25 fixed manufacturing overhead consists of $10 per unit batch related costs and $15 per unit facilities level fixed costs. Also, assume that each new batch causes increased costs of $10,000 per batch; the remainder of the fixed costs do not vary with the number of units produced or the number of batches.

Required

1. Calculate the relevant unit and total cost of the special order, including the new information about batch related costs.
2. If accepted, how would the special order affect Jordan's operating income?
3. Suppose that JepCo notifies Jordan it must reduce its order to 1,000 units because of changes in orders it has received. How would this change affect your answer in Parts 1 and 2?

9–28 **Special Order**   BallCards Inc. manufactures baseball cards sold in packs of 15 in drugstores throughout the country. It is the third leading firm in an industry with four major firms. Ball-Cards has been approached by Pennock Cereal Inc., which would like to order a special edition of cards to use as a promotion with its cereal. BallCards would be solely responsible for designing and producing the cards. Pennock wants to order 25,000 sets and has offered $23,750 for the total order. Each set will consist of 33 cards. BallCards currently produces cards in sheets of 132.

Production, marketing, and other costs (per sheet)	
Direct materials	$1.20
Direct labor	0.20
Variable overhead	0.40
Fixed overhead	0.15
Variable marketing	0.10
Fixed marketing	0.35
Insurance, taxes, and administrative salaries	0.10
Costs for special order	
Design	2,000
Other setup costs	5,500

BallCards would incur no marketing costs for the special order. It has the capacity to accept this order without interrupting regular production.

Required

1. Should it accept the special order? Support your answer with appropriate computations.
2. What are the important strategic issues in the decision?

9–29 **Special Order**   Green Grow Inc. (GGI) manufactures lawn fertilizer and because of the quality often receives special orders from agricultural research groups. For each type of fertilizer sold, each bag is carefully filled to have the precise mix of components advertised for that type of fertilizer. GGI's operating capacity is 22,000 one-hundred-pound bags per month, and it currently is selling 20,000 bags manufactured in 20 batches of 1,000 bags each. The firm just received a request for a special order of 5,000 one-hundred-pound bags of fertilizer for $125,000 from APAC, a research company. The production costs would be the same, although delivery and other packaging and distribution services would cause a one-time $2,000 cost for GGI. The special order would be processed in two batches of 2,500 bags each. The following information is provided about GGI's current operations:

Sales and production cost data for 20,000 bags, per bag	
Sales price	$38
Variable manufacturing costs	15
Variable marketing costs	2
Fixed manufacturing costs	12
Fixed marketing costs	2

No marketing costs would be associated with the special order. Since the order would be used in research and consistency is critical, APAC requires that GGI fill the entire order of 5,000 bags.

Required

1. Should GGI accept the special order? Explain why or why not.
2. What would be the change in operating income if the special order is accepted?

3. Suppose that after GGI accepts the special order, it finds that unexpected production delays will not allow it to supply all 5,000 units from its own plants and meet the promised delivery date. It can provide the same materials by purchasing them in bulk from a competing firm. The materials would then be packaged in GGI bags to complete the order. GGI knows the competitor's materials are very good quality, but it cannot be sure that the quality meets its own exacting standards. There is not enough time to carefully test the competitor's product to determine its quality. What should GGI do?

9–30 **Special Order; ABC Costing (Continuation of Problem 9–29)**   Assume the same information as for Problem 9–29, except that the $12 fixed manufacturing overhead consists of $8 per unit batch related costs and $4 per unit facilities level fixed costs. Also, assume that each new batch causes increased costs of $5,000 per batch; the remainder of the batch level costs consists of tools and supervision labor that do not vary with the number of batches. The remainder of fixed costs do not vary with the number of units produced or the number of batches.

Required

1. Calculate the relevant unit and total cost of the special order, including the new information about batch related costs.
2. If accepted, how would the special order affect GGI's operating income?

9–31 **Make Or Buy; Special Order**   Lester-Smith Company manufactures three wood construction components: wood trusses, wood floor joists, and beams. The plant is operating at full capacity. It can produce 200 trusses, 1,000 joists, and 600 beams per month and sells everything it produces. The monthly revenues and expenses for the three products are

Sales revenues	
Trusses	$ 12,000
Joists	40,000
Beams	90,000
Total revenue	$142,000
Expenses	
Variable cost	
Trusses	$ 10,000
Joists	24,000
Beams	48,000
Total variable cost	$ 82,000
Fixed cost allocated	
Trusses	$ 4,000
Joists	12,000
Beams	24,000
Total fixed cost	$ 40,000
Total cost	$122,000
Total profit	$ 20,000

Required

1. The firm makes wood trusses mainly to satisfy certain customers by offering a full line of wood components. Lately, it has had a problem making a profit on the trusses and is considering buying them from another manufacturer at $55 a truss. Should the firm buy these trusses or continue to make its own?
2. Lester-Smith has an opportunity to produce an additional 400 beams for a customer at a price of $100 each. If it accepts this special order, the firm cannot produce trusses because the plant will be operating at full capacity. Should the firm accept this special order?

9–32 **Profitability Analysis, Scarce Resources**   Santana Company has met all production requirements for the current month and has an opportunity to produce additional units of product with its excess capacity. Unit selling prices and costs for three models of one of its product lines are as follows:

	No Frills	Standard Options	Super
Selling price	$30	$35	$50
Direct materials	9	11	11
Direct labor ($10/hour)	5	10	15
Variable overhead	3	6	9
Fixed overhead	3	6	6

Variable overhead is charged to products on the basis of direct labor dollars; fixed overhead is charged to products on the basis of machine-hours.

Required

1. If Santana Company has excess machine capacity and can add more labor as needed (neither machine capacity nor labor is a constraint), the excess production capacity should be devoted to producing which product or products?

2. If Santana Company has excess machine capacity but a limited amount of labor time, the production capacity should be devoted to producing which product or products?

9–33 **Special Order Analysis**   New Life, Inc., manufactures skin creams, soaps, and other products primarily for people with dry and sensitive skin. It has just introduced a new line of product that removes the spotting and wrinkling in skin associated with aging. It sells these products in pharmacies and department stores at prices somewhat higher than those of other brands because of New Life's excellent reputation for quality and effectiveness.

New Life currently has very low utilization of plant capacity. Two years ago, in anticipation of rapid growth, the company opened a large new manufacturing plant, which has yet to be utilized more than 50 percent. Partly for this reason, New Life has sought new partners and was able, with the help of financial analysts, to locate suitable business partners. The first potential partner identified in this search was a large supermarket chain, SuperValue, which is interested in the partnership because it wants New Life to manufacture an age cream to sell in its stores. The product would be essentially the same as the New Life product but packaged with the SuperValue brand name. The agreement would pay New Life $2.00 per unit and would allow SuperValue a limited right to advertise the product as manufactured for SuperValue by New Life. New Life's CFO has made some calculations and has determined that the direct materials, direct labor, and other variable costs needed for the SuperValue order would be about $1.00 per unit as compared to the full cost of $2.50 (materials, labor, and overhead) for the equivalent New Life product.

Required   Should New Life accept the proposal from SuperValue? Why or why not?

9–34 **Project-Analysis, Sales Promotions**   Clear Lake Furniture Company makes outdoor furniture from recycled products, including plastics and wood by-products. Its three furniture products are gliders, chairs with footstools, and tables. The products appeal primarily to cost-conscious consumers and those who value the recycling of materials. The company wholesales its products to retailers and various mass merchandisers. Because of the seasonal nature of the products, most orders are manufactured during the winter months for delivery in the early spring. Michael King, founder and owner, is dismayed that sales for two of the products are tracking below budget. The following chart shows pertinent year-to-date data regarding the company's products.

Certain that the shortfall was caused by a lack of effort by the sales force, Michael has suggested to Lisa Buck, financial analyst, that the company announce two contests to correct this situation before it deteriorates. The first contest is a trip to Hawaii awarded to the top salesperson if incremental glider sales are attained to close the budget shortfall. The second contest is a golf weekend, complete with a new set of golf clubs, awarded to the top salesperson if incremental sales of chairs with footstools are attained to close the budget shortfall. The Hawaiian vacation would cost $8,800 and the golf trip would cost $4,685.

	Glider		Chair with Footstool		Table	
	Actual	**Budget**	**Actual**	**Budget**	**Actual**	**Budget**
Number of units	2,750	4,000	7,100	8,000	3,500	3,300
Average sales price	$80.00	$85.00	$61.00	$65.00	$24.00	$25.00
Variable costs						
Direct labor						
Hours of labor	2.50	2.25	3.25	3.00	0.60	0.50
Cost per hour	$ 9.00	$10.00	$ 9.50	$ 9.25	$ 9.00	$ 9.00
Direct material	$16.00	$15.00	$11.00	$10.00	$ 6.00	$ 5.00
Sales commission	$15.00	$15.00	$10.00	$10.00	$ 5.00	$ 5.50

Required   Explain whether either contest is desirable or not.

(CMA Adapted)

9–35   **Make or Buy; Strategy**   GianAuto Corporation manufactures parts and components for manufacturers and suppliers of parts for automobiles, vans, and trucks. Sales have increased more
than 10 percent each year based in part on the company's excellent record of customer service
and reliability. The industry as a whole has also grown dramatically in recent years as auto
manufacturers continue to outsource more of their production, especially to cost-efficient manufacturers such as GianAuto. To take advantage of lower wage rates and favorable business
environments around the world, Gian has located its plants in six different countries around
the world.

   Among the various GianAuto plants around the world is the Denver Cover Plant, one of
GianAuto's earliest plants. The Denver Cover Plant prepares and sews coverings made primarily of leather and upholstery fabric and ships them to other GianAuto plants where they are
used to cover seats, headboards, door panels, and other GianAuto products.

   Ted Vosilo is the plant manager for the Denver Cover Plant, which was the first GianAuto
plant in the region. As other area plants were opened, Ted was given the responsibility for managing them in recognition of his management ability. He functions as a regional manager although the budget for him and his staff is charged to the Denver Cover Plant.

   Ted has just received a report indicating that GianAuto could purchase the entire annual
output of Denver Cover from outside suppliers for $60 million. He was astonished at the low
outside price because the budget for Denver Cover Plant's operating costs for the coming year
was set at $82 million. He believes that GianAuto will have to close operations at Denver
Cover to realize the $22 million in annual cost savings.

   Denver Cover's budget for operating costs for the coming year follows:

DENVER COVER PLANT
Budget for Operating Costs
For the Year Ending December 31, 2004
(000s omitted)

Materials		$32,000
Labor		
Direct	$23,000	
Supervision	3,000	
Indirect plant	4,000	30,000
Overhead		
Depreciation—equipment	$ 5,000	
Depreciation—building	3,000	
Pension expense	4,000	
Plant manager and staff	2,000	
Corporate allocation	6,000	20,000
Total budgeted costs		$82,000

Additional facts regarding the plant's operations are as follows:

- Due to Denver Cover's commitment to use high-quality fabrics in all its products, the purchasing department placed blanket purchase orders with major suppliers to ensure the receipt of sufficient materials for the coming year. If these orders are canceled as a result of the plant closing, termination charges would amount to 15 percent of the cost of direct materials.

- Approximately 400 plant employees will lose their jobs if the plant is closed. This includes all direct laborers and supervisors as well as the plumbers, electricians, and other skilled workers classified as indirect plant workers. Some would be able to find new jobs, but many would have difficulty doing so. All employees would have difficulty matching Denver Cover's base pay of $14.40 per hour, the highest in the area. A clause in Denver Cover's contract with the union could help some employees; the company must provide employment assistance to its former employees for 12 months after a plant closing. The estimated cost to administer this service is $1 million for the year.

- Some employees would probably elect early retirement because GianAuto has an excellent plan. In fact, $3 million of the 2004 pension expense would continue whether Denver Cover is open or not.

- Ted and his staff would not be affected by closing Denver Cover. They would still be responsible for managing three other area plants.

- Denver Cover considers equipment depreciation to be a variable cost and uses the units-of-production method to depreciate its equipment and the customary straight-line method to depreciate its building.

Required

1. Explain GianAuto's competitive strategy and how this strategy should be considered with regard to the Denver Plant decision. Identify the key strategic factors that should be considered in the decision.

2. GianAuto Corporation plans to prepare an analysis to use in deciding whether to close the Denver Cover Plant. Using the preceding information, identify the relevant and nonrelevant costs in this decision.

(CMA Adapted)

9–36 **Make or Buy** Raymond's Specialty Manufacturing (RSM) produces custom vehicles—limousines, buses, conversion vans, and small trucks—for special order customers. It customizes each vehicle to the customer's specifications. RSM has been growing at a steady rate in recent years in part because of the increased demand for specialty luxury vehicles. The increased demand has also caused new competitors to enter the market for these types of vehicles. RSM management considers its competitive advantage to be the high quality of its manufacturing. Much of the work is handmade, and the company uses only the best parts and materials. Many parts are made in-house to control for highest quality. Because of the increased competition, price competition is beginning to become a factor for the industry, and RSM is becoming more concerned about cost controls and cost reduction. It has controlled them by purchasing materials and parts in bulk, paying careful attention to efficiency in scheduling and working different jobs, and improving employee productivity.

The increased competition has also caused RSM to reconsider its strategy. Upon review with the help of a consultant, RSM management has decided that it competes most effectively as a differentiator based on quality of product and service. To reinforce the differentiation strategy, RSM has implemented a variety of quality inspection and reporting systems. Quality reports are viewed at all levels of management, including top management.

To decrease costs and improve quality, RSM has begun to look for new outside suppliers for certain parts. For example, RSM can purchase a critical suspension part, now manufactured in-house, from Performance Equipment Inc. for a price of $105. Buying the part would save RSM 10 percent of the labor and variable overhead costs and $68 of materials costs. The current manufacturing costs for the suspension assembly are as follows:

Materials	$192
Labor	75
Variable overhead	150
Fixed overhead	150
Total cost for suspension assembly	$567

Required

1. How would total costs be affected if RSM chose to purchase the part rather than to continue to manufacture it?
2. Should RSM purchase or manufacture the part? Include strategic considerations in your answer.

9–37 **Make or Buy, Review of Learning Curves** Henderson Equipment Company has produced a pilot run of 50 units of a recently developed cylinder used in its finished products. The cylinder has a one-year life, and the company expects to produce and sell 1,650 units annually. The pilot run required 14.25 direct labor-hours for the 50 cylinders, averaging 0.285 direct labor-hours per cylinder. Henderson has experienced an 80 percent learning curve on the direct labor-hours needed to produce new cylinders. Past experience indicates that learning tends to cease by the time 800 parts are produced.

Henderson's manufacturing costs for cylinders follows:

Direct labor	$12.00 per hour
Variable overhead	10.00 per hour
Fixed overhead	16.60 per hour
Materials	4.05 per unit

Henderson has received a quote of $7.50 per unit from Lytel Machine Company for the additional 1,600 cylinders needed. Henderson frequently subcontracts this type of work and has always been satisfied with the quality of the units produced by Lytel.

Required

1. If Henderson manufactures the cylinders, determine
   a. The average direct labor-hours per unit for the first 800 cylinders (including the pilot run) produced. Round calculations to three decimal places.
   b. The total direct labor-hours for the first 800 cylinders (including the pilot run) produced.
2. After completing the pilot run, Henderson must manufacture an additional 1,600 units to fulfill the annual requirement of 1,650 units. Without regard to your answer in requirement 1, assume that
   • The first 800 cylinders produced (including the pilot run) required 100 direct labor-hours.
   • The 800th unit produced (including the pilot run) required 0.079 hour.

   Calculate the total manufacturing costs for Henderson to produce the additional 1,600 cylinders required.
3. Determine whether Henderson should manufacture the additional 1,600 cylinders or purchase them from Lytel. Support your answer with appropriate calculations.

(CMA Adapted)

9–38 **Special Order; Strategy, International** Williams Company, located in southern Wisconsin, manufactures a variety of industrial valves and pipe fittings that are sold to customers in nearby states. Currently, the company is operating at about 70 percent capacity and is earning a satisfactory return on investment.

Glasgow Industries Ltd. of Scotland has approached management with an offer to buy 120,000 units of a pressure valve. Glasgow Industries manufactures a valve that is almost identical to Williams' pressure valve; however, a fire in Glasgow Industries' valve plant has shut down its manufacturing operations. Glasgow needs the 120,000 valves over the next four months to meet commitments to its regular customers; the company is prepared to pay $21 each for the valves.

Williams' product cost for the pressure valve, based on current attainable standards, is:

Direct materials	$ 6.00
Direct labor (0.5 hr per valve)	8.00
Manufacturing overhead (1/3 variable)	9.00
Total manufacturing cost	$23.00

Additional costs incurred in connection with sales of the pressure valve are sales commissions of 5 percent and freight expense of $1 per unit. However, the company does not pay sales commissions on special orders that come directly to management. Freight expense will be paid by Glasgow.

In determining selling prices, Williams adds a 40 percent markup to product cost. This provides a $32 suggested selling price for the pressure valve. The marketing department, however, has set the current selling price at $30 to maintain market share.

Product management believes that it can handle the Glasgow Industries order without disrupting its scheduled production. The order would, however, require additional fixed factory overhead of $12,000 per month in the form of supervision and clerical costs.

If management accepts the order, Williams will manufacture and ship 30,000 pressure valves to Glasgow Industries each month for the next four months. Shipments will be made in weekly consignments, FOB shipping point.

Required

1. Determine how many additional direct labor-hours will be required each month to fill the Glasgow order.
2. Prepare an analysis showing the impact of accepting the Glasgow order.
3. Calculate the minimum unit price that Williams' management could accept for the Glasgow order without reducing net income.
4. Identify the strategic factors that Williams should consider before accepting the Glasgow order.
5. Identify the factors related to international business that Williams should consider before accepting the Glasgow order.

(CMA Adapted)

9–39 **Profitability Analysis; Review of Master Budget, Strategy**   RayLok Incorporated has invented a secret process to improve light intensity and manufactures a variety of products related to this process. Each product is independent of the others and is treated as a separate profit/loss division. Product (division) managers have a great deal of freedom to manage their divisions as they think best. Failure to produce target division income is dealt with severely; however, rewards for exceeding one's profit objective are, as one division manager described them, lavish.

The DimLok Division sells an add-on automotive accessory that automatically dims a vehicle's headlights by sensing a certain intensity of light coming from a specific direction. DimLok has had a new manager in each of the three previous years because each manager failed to reach RayLok's target profit. Donna Barnes has just been promoted to manager and is studying ways to meet the current target profit for DimLok.

DimLok's two profit targets for the coming year are $800,000 (20 percent return on the investment in the annual fixed costs of the division) plus an additional profit of $20 for each DimLok unit sold. Other constraints on division operations are

- Production cannot exceed sales because RayLok's corporate advertising program stresses completely new product models each year, although the models might have only cosmetic changes.

- DimLok's selling price cannot vary above the current selling price of $200 per unit but may vary as much as 10 percent below $200.

- A division manager can elect to expand fixed production or selling facilities; however, the target objective related to fixed costs is increased by 20 percent of the cost of such expansion. Furthermore, a manager cannot expand fixed facilities by more than 30 percent of existing fixed cost levels without approval from the board of directors.

Donna is now examining data gathered by her staff to determine whether DimLok can achieve its target profits of $800,000 **and** $20 per unit. A summary of these reports shows the following:

- Last year's sales were 30,000 units at $200 per unit.

- DimLok's current manufacturing facility capacity is 40,000 units per year but can be increased to 80,000 units per year with an increase of $1,000,000 in annual fixed costs.

- Present variable costs amount to $80 per unit, but DimLok's vendors are willing to offer raw materials discounts amounting to $20 per unit, beginning with unit number 60,001.

- Sales can be increased up to 100,000 units per year by committing large blocks of product to institutional buyers at a discounted unit price of $180. However, this discount applies only to sales in excess of 40,000 units per year.

Donna believes that these projections are reliable and is now trying to determine what Dim-Lok must do to meet the profit objectives that RayLok's board of directors assigned to it.

Required

1. Determine the dollar amount of DimLok's present annual fixed costs.

2. Determine the number of units that DimLok must sell to achieve both profit objectives. Be sure to consider all constraints in determining your answer.

3. Without regard to your answer in requirement 2, assume that Donna decides to sell 40,000 units at $200 per unit and 24,000 units at $180 per unit. Prepare a master budget income statement for DimLok showing whether her decision will achieve DimLok's profit objectives.

4. Assess DimLok's competitive strategy.

5. Identify the strategic factors that DimLok should consider.

(CMA Adapted)

9–40   **Make or Buy; Strategy; Ethics**   The Midwest Division of the Paibec Corporation manufactures subassemblies used in Paibec's final products. Lynn Hardt of Midwest's profit planning department has been assigned the task of determining whether Midwest should continue to manufacture a subassembly component, MTR-2000, or purchase it from Marley Company, an outside supplier. Marley has submitted a bid to manufacture and supply the 32,000 units of MTR-2000 that Paibec will need for 2004 at a unit price of $17.30. Marley has assured Paibec that the units will be delivered according to Paibec's production specifications and needs. The contract price of $17.30 is applicable only in 2004, but Marley is interested in entering into a long-term arrangement beyond 2004.

Lynn has submitted the following information regarding Midwest's cost to manufacture 30,000 units of MTR-2000 in 2003.

Direct material	$195,000
Direct labor	120,000
Factory space rental	84,000
Equipment leasing costs	36,000
Other manufacturing costs	225,000
Total manufacturing costs	$660,000

Lynn has collected the following information related to manufacturing MTR-2000:

- Equipment leasing costs represent special equipment used to manufacture MTR-2000. Midwest can terminate this lease by paying the equivalent of one month's lease payment for each of the two years left on its lease agreement.

- Forty percent of the other manufacturing overhead is considered variable. Variable overhead changes with the number of units produced, and this rate per unit is not expected to change in 2004. The fixed manufacturing overhead costs are not expected to change whether Midwest manufactures or purchases MTR-2000. Midwest can use equipment other than the leased equipment in its other manufacturing operations.

- Direct materials cost used in the production of MTR-2000 is expected to increase 8 percent in 2004.

- Midwest's direct labor contract calls for a 5 percent wage increase in 2004.

- The facilities used to manufacture MTR-2000 are rented under a month-to-month rental agreement. Midwest would have no need for this space if it does not manufacture MTR-2000. Thus, Midwest can withdraw from the rental agreement without any penalty.

John Porter, Midwest divisional manager, stopped by Lynn's office to voice his opinion regarding the outsourcing of MTR-2000. He commented, "I am really concerned about outsourcing MTR-2000. I have a son-in-law and a nephew, not to mention a member of our bowling team, who work on MTR-2000. They could lose their jobs if we buy that component from Marley. I really would appreciate anything you can do to make sure the cost analysis shows that we should continue making MTR-2000. Corporate is not aware of materials cost increases and maybe you can leave out some of those fixed costs. I just think we should continue making MTR-2000."

Required

1. Prepare a relevant cost analysis that shows whether the Midwest Division should make MTR-2000 or purchase it from Marley Company for 2004.

2. Identify and briefly discuss the strategic factors that Midwest should consider in this decision.

3. By referring to the specific ethical standards for management accountants outlined in Chapter 1, assess the ethical issues in John Porter's request of Lynn Hardt.

(CMA Adapted)

9–41 **Profitability Analysis**   High Point Furniture Company (HPF) manufactures very high-quality furniture for sale directly to exclusive hotels, interior designers, and select retail outlets throughout the world. HPF's products include upholstered furniture, dining tables, bedroom furniture, and a variety of other products, including end tables. Through attention to quality and design innovation, and by careful attention to changing consumer tastes, HPF has become one of the most successful furniture manufacturers worldwide. Hal Blin, the chief operating officer of HPF, is reviewing the most recent sales and profits report for the three best selling end tables in HPFs product line—the Parker, Virginian, and Weldon end tables. Hal is concerned about the relatively poor performance of the Weldon line. He discusses the prospects for the line with HPF's marketing and sales vice-president, Joan Hunt. Joan notes that there has been no significant trend up or down in any of the end table lines, though the direction of consumer tastes would probably favor the Virginian and Parker lines. Hal and Joan agree that this may be the time for further analysis to determine whether the Weldon line should be discontinued.

HPF Sales and Profits Report: End Tables

| | Parker | | Virginian | | Weldon | | |
	Per Unit	Total	Per Unit	Total	Per Unit	Total	Total
Sales units		150,000		335,000		165,000	
Sales dollars	$459.00	$68,850,000	$365.00	$122,275,000	$248.00	$40,920,000	$232,045,000
Factory Costs							
Labor	125.00	18,750,000	118.00	39,530,000	62.00	10,230,000	68,510,000
Raw Materials	88.50	13,275,000	66.00	22,110,000	78.00	12,870,000	48,255,000
Power	23.50	3,525,000	15.60	5,226,000	13.80	2,277,000	11,028,000
Repairs	12.25	1,837,500	12.25	4,103,750	12.25	2,021,250	7,962,500
Factory Equipment	33.50	5,025,000	33.50	11,222,500	33.50	5,527,500	21,775,000
Other Costs	14.00	2,100,000	12.50	4,187,500	13.25	2,186,250	8,473,750
Total Factory Cost	296.75	44,512,500	257.85	86,379,750	212.80	35,112,000	166,004,250
Selling and Administrative Expenses							
Selling Expense	45.00	6,750,000	36.00	12,060,000	25.00	4,125,000	22,935,000
Office Expense	16.80	2,520,000	16.80	5,628,000	16.80	2,772,000	10,920,000
Administrative Expense	27.50	4,125,000	27.50	9,212,500	27.50	4,537,500	17,875,000
Interest	6.50	975,000	6.50	2,177,500	6.50	1,072,500	4,225,000
Total Cost	392.55	58,882,500	344.65	115,457,750	288.60	47,619,000	221,959,250
Operating Profit (Loss)	$ 66.45	$ 9,967,500	$ 20.35	$ 6,817,250	$ (40.60)	$ (6,699,000)	$ 10,085,750

Note: Selling expense consists of salaries for the sales staff, advertising, and the cost of marketing management and research. Power is for equipment used in manufacturing and varies with the number of units produced. Other factory costs are primarily fixed. Repairs are done when needed, sometimes by available manufacturing staff, and other times by outside vendors.

Required

1. Using Excel or an equivalent spreadsheet, develop an analysis that can help Hal decide about the future of the Weldon line. Should the Weldon line be dropped? Why or why not?

2. Using the spreadsheet you developed in Part 1, determine whether your answer would change if sales of Weldon are expected to fall by 80 percent.

3. Again using the spreadsheet in Part 1, determine whether the Weldon line should be discontinued if the resources devoted to Weldon could be used to increase sales by 10 percent in each of the other two lines.

4. Again using the spreadsheet in Part 1 and using Goal Seek in Excel or an equivalent, determine the sales increase (or decrease) in the sales of the Parker line that would be necessary if the Weldon line were discontinued to maintain the firm's overall profit in Part 1.

E
x

9–42 Profitability Analysis; Linear Programming (Appendix) Home Cooking Company offers monthly service plans to provide prepared meals that are delivered to customers' homes and need only be heated in a microwave or conventional oven. Home Cooking offers two monthly plans, premier cuisine and haute cuisine. The premier cuisine plan provides frozen meals that are delivered twice each month; the premier generates a contribution of $120 for each monthly service plan sold. The haute cuisine plan provides freshly prepared meals delivered on a daily basis and generates a contribution of $90 for each monthly plan sold. Home Cooking's strong reputation enables it to sell all meals that it can prepare.

Each meal goes through food preparation and cooking steps in the company's kitchens. After these steps, the premier cuisine meals are flash frozen. The time requirements per monthly meal plan and hours available per month follow:

	Preparation	Cooking	Freezing
Hours required			
Premier cuisine	2	2	1
Haute cuisine	1	3	0
Hours available	60	120	45

For planning purposes, Home Cooking uses linear programming to determine the most profitable number of premier and haute cuisine meals to produce.

Required

1. Using the Solver function of Microsoft Excel, determine the most profitable product mix for Home Cooking given the existing constraints and contribution margins.

2. Using the Solver function of Microsoft Excel, determine the most profitable product mix for Home Cooking given the existing contribution margins and all constraints except the preparation time constraint.

(CMA Adapted)

Solutions to Self-Study Problems

1. Special Order Pricing

The key to this exercise is to recognize that the variable manufacturing costs of $130 ($85 material and $45 labor) are the relevant ones and that the fixed overhead costs, since they will not change, are not relevant.

Thus, the correct decision is to accept the offer, since the price of $150 exceeds the variable manufacturing cost of $130. HighValu also should consider strategic factors. For example, will the three-year contract be desirable? Perhaps the market conditions will change so that HighValu will have more profitable uses of the capacity in the coming years. Will the special order enhance or diminish the firm's competitive position?

2. The Make-or-Buy Decision

The relevant costs for this analysis are the outside purchase cost of $15 per set versus the make costs of $10 per set ($6 material plus $4 labor), and $10,000 annual fixed costs.

First, determine the amount of annual savings from the reduction in variable costs for the make option:

6,000 annual sales × ($15 − $10) = $30,000 annual savings

Second, compare the savings in variable costs to the additional fixed costs of $10,000 per year. The net savings, an advantage to make rather than buy, is $20,000 ($30,000 − $10,000).

HighValu also should consider relevant strategic factors, such as the quality and reliability of the supply for the cushion. How will HighValu use the released capacity at its plant? Are any employees' jobs affected?

3. Profitability Analysis

1. To determine the number of Windys that can be manufactured if the 3,750 units of Gale are no longer produced, we consider the capacity released for each of the two constraints.

   For the automated sewing machine: The machine produces 20 Windys per hour or 30 Gales per hour, so that the number of Windys that could be produced from the released capacity of Gale is

   $$3,750 \times 20/30 = 2,500 \text{ Windys}$$

   For the inspection and packing operation: The operation requires 15 minutes for Windy (4 per hour) and 5 minutes for Gale (12 per hour), so the number of Windys that could be inspected and packed in the released time is

   $$3,750 \times 4/12 = 1,250 \text{ Windys}$$

   In this case, the inspection and packing is the effective limitation, so that if Gale is deleted, the firm can produce *1,250 Windys* with the released capacity.

2. If 3,750 units of Gale are replaced with 1,250 units of Windy, the proper relevant cost analysis should consider the contribution margin of each product:

	Windy	**Gale**
Unit contribution margin	$ 8	$ 4
Units sold (giving up 3,750 units Gale gives 1,250 of Windy, per part 1)	1,250	3,750
Total contribution margin	$10,000	$15,000

   Thus, the deletion of Gale and replacement with Windy would reduce the total contribution margin by $5,000 ($15,000 − $10,000).

3. Since the effect on total contribution is significant (as shown in part 2), Windbreakers should continue to make Gale. Other factors to consider follow:

   a. At existing sales levels of 18,750 of Windy and 3,750 of Gale, Windbreakers is operating at full capacity; if there are additional sales opportunities for Windy, the firm should consider adding to available capacity so that the current sales of Gale can be made plus the additional sales of Windy. The analysis of the cost benefit of additional capacity is best addressed through the techniques of capital budgeting as described in Chapter 20.

   b. The effect of the loss of Gale on the firm's image and therefore the potential long-term effects on the sales of Windy.

   c. The long-term sales potential for Gale. Will its sales likely exceed the current 3,750 level in future years?

Cost Planning for the Product Life Cycle: Target Costing, Theory of Constraints, and Long-Term Pricing

After studying this chapter, you should be able to . . .

1. Explain how to use target costing to facilitate strategic management
2. Apply the theory of constraints to strategic management
3. Describe how life-cycle costing facilitates strategic management
4. Outline the objectives and techniques of long-term pricing

Having two of the world's best selling cars, the Camry and the Corolla, as well as a number of other popular models, Toyota is among the world's most successful automakers. The reason for Toyota's success is that it is able to consistently produce high-quality cars with attractive features at competitive prices. Target costing, a method Toyota pioneered in the 1960s, is one method it uses to achieve high quality and desirable features at a competitive price.[1] Target costing is a design approach in which cost management plays a large part, as we will see in this chapter. Using target costing, a company designs a product to achieve a desired profit while satisfying the customer's expectations for quality and product features. The balancing of costs, features, and quality takes place throughout the design, manufacturing, sale, and service of the car but has the strongest influence in the first phase, design. When design alternatives are being examined and selected, Toyota has the maximum flexibility for choosing options that affect manufacturing and all other product costs such as customer service and warranty work.

Once the design is complete and manufacturing has begun, the cost consequences of the choice of features and manufacturing methods are set until the next model change. As a result, the development of a good, cost-effective design is critical. Target costing places a strong focus on using the design process to improve the product and reduce its cost. For example, in the redesign of the Camry, Toyota made the running lamps part of the headlamp assembly and made the grill part of the bumper, which saves time and materials in manufacturing and produces a more crash-resistant bumper—a win/win for Toyota and the car buyer.

---

[1] A. Taylor III, "How Toyota Defies Gravity," *Fortune*, December 1997, pp. 100–8; Takao Tanaka, "Target Costing at Toyota," *Journal of Cost Management*, Spring 1993, pp. 4–11; Durward K. Sobek II, Allen C. Ward, and Jeffry K. Liker, "Toyota's Principles of Set-Based Concurrent Engineering," *Sloan Management Review*, Winter 1999, pp. 67–83; "Toyota Motor Corporation: Target Costing System," Harvard Business School Case No. 9-197-031 (May 30, 1997); and "Machete Time," *Business Week*, April 9, 2001, pp. 42–43.

EXHIBIT 10.1
The Cost Life Cycle of a Product or Service

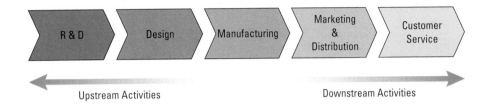

EXHIBIT 10.2
The Sales Life Cycle of a Product or Service

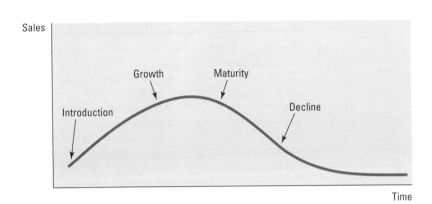

Target costing is the first of four costing methods we study in the chapter. The others are the theory of constraints, life-cycle costing, and long-term pricing. The common element of all four methods is that they are involved with the entire product life cycle. While once managers focused only on manufacturing costs, they now look at costs upstream (before manufacturing) and downstream (after manufacturing) in the product life cycle to get a comprehensive analysis of product cost and profitability (Exhibit 10.1). For example, in target costing we consider the role of product design (an upstream activity) in reducing costs in the manufacturing and downstream phases of the life cycle. Then, we see how the theory of constraints is used in the manufacturing phase to reduce manufacturing costs and to speed up delivery downstream. Then we look at life-cycle costing, which provides a comprehensive evaluation of the profitability of the different products, including costs throughout the product life cycle. Finally, long-term pricing uses life-cycle concepts in pricing decisions. Long-term pricing takes two important and very different views of the product life cycle.

The **cost life cycle** is the sequence of activities within the firm that begins with research and development followed by design, manufacturing (or providing the service), marketing/distribution, and customer service. It is the life cycle of the product or service from the viewpoint of costs incurred. The cost life cycle is illustrated in Exhibit 10.1.[2] The **sales life cycle** is the sequence of phases in the product's or service's life in the market from the introduction of the product or service to the market, the growth in sales, and finally maturity, decline, and withdrawal from the market. Sales are at first small, peak in the maturity phase, and decline thereafter, as illustrated in Exhibit 10.2. Both the sales and the cost views of the product life cycle are important in long-term pricing.

Three methods are commonly used by manufacturing firms, where new product development, manufacturing speed, and efficiency are important. The three methods are target costing, the theory of constraints, and life-cycle costing. Because a product with

The **cost life cycle**
is the sequence of activities within the firm that begins with research and development followed by design, manufacturing, marketing/distribution, and customer service.

The **sales life cycle**
is the sequence of phases in the product's or service's life in the market from the introduction of the product or service to the market, growth in sales, and finally maturity, decline, and withdrawal from the market.

---

[2] The *cost life cycle* also is called a *value chain* by many writers to emphasize that each activity must add value for the ultimate consumer [Michael Porter, *Competitive Advantage* (New York: Free Press, 1985)]. Note that this concept of the value chain differs from that introduced in Chapter 2. Chapter 2 describes the industry-level value chain; the cost life-cycle concept in this chapter describes the firm-level value chain. We use the broader concept of the industry-level value chain in Chapter 2 to facilitate the strategic focus in that chapter. For a discussion of the two types of value chains, see Joseph G. San Miguel, "Value Chain Analysis for Assessing Competitive Advantage," *Management Accounting Guideline Number 41* (The Society of Management Accountants of Canada, 1996); and Mike Partridge and Lew Perren, "Assessing and Enhancing Strategic Capability: A Value-Driven Approach," *Management Accounting* (UK), June 1994, pp. 28–29.

physical characteristics is involved, applications in manufacturing firms are more intuitive and easily understood. However, each method can also be used in service firms. For example, a local government could use the theory of constraints to speed the process of billing residents for water services (and to reduce the processing cost) or to speed the operations for processing and depositing the collections from these residents.

Target Costing

Our policy is to reduce the price, extend the operations, and improve the article. You will notice that the reduction of price comes first. We have never considered costs as fixed. Therefore we first reduce the price to the point where we believe more sales result. Then we go ahead and try to make the prices. We do not bother about the costs. The new price forces the costs down. The more usual way is to take the costs and then determine the price, and although that method may be scientific in the narrow sense; it is not scientific in the broad sense, because what earthly use is it to know the cost if it tells you that you cannot manufacture at a price at which the article can be sold? But more to the point is the fact that although one may calculate what a cost is, and of course all of our costs are carefully calculated, no one knows what a cost ought to be. One of the ways of discovering is to name a price so low as to force everybody in the place to the highest point of efficiency. The low price makes everybody dig for profits. We make more discoveries concerning manufacturing and selling under this forced method than by any method of leisurely investigation.

Henry Ford, *My Life and My Work*, 1923

LEARNING OBJECTIVE 1

Explain how to use target costing to facilitate strategic management.

Henry Ford's thinking would fit well in today's corporate boardrooms, where global competition, increased customer expectations, and competitive pricing in many industries have forced firms to look for ways to reduce costs year after year at the same time producing products with increased levels of quality and functionality. Ford is describing a technique called *target costing,* in which the firm determines the allowable (i.e., "target") cost for the product or service, given a competitive market price, so the firm can earn a desired profit:

$$\text{Target cost} = \text{Competitive price} - \text{Desired profit}$$

The firm has two options for reducing costs to a target cost level:

1. By integrating new manufacturing technology, using advanced cost management techniques such as activity-based costing, and seeking higher productivity.
2. By redesigning the product or service. This method is beneficial for many firms because it recognizes that design decisions account for much of total product life-cycle costs.[3] By careful attention to design, significant reductions in total cost are possible. This approach to target costing is associated primarily with Japanese manufacturers.[4]

Many firms employ both options: efforts to achieve increased productivity gains and target costing to determine low-cost design. Some managers argue that, unlike programs for productivity improvement, target costing provides a more distinct goal, a specific cost level. Because the goal is more definite, it appears more achievable and therefore more motivating.

---

[3] The Westinghouse Corporate Services Council estimates that 85 percent of a product's life-cycle cost is determined in the design phase (Karlos A. Artto, "Life Cycle Cost Concepts and Methodologies," *Journal of Cost Management,* Fall 1994, pp. 28–32); see also "Implementing Target Costing," *Management Accounting Guideline Number 28* (The Society of Management Accountants of Canada, 1994). The portion of life-cycle costs that is determined in the design stage is sometimes referred to as *locked-in* or *designed-in* cost to emphasize that, after the design is complete, it is difficult to reduce these costs.

[4] Robin Cooper and Regine Slagmulder, *Target Costing and Value Engineering* (Portland, OR: Productivity Press, 1997).

EXHIBIT 10.3
Target Costing in the Cost Life Cycle

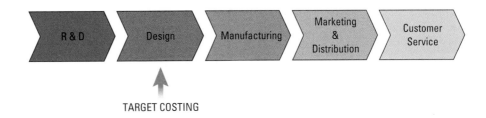

Many auto manufacturers, software developers, and other consumer product manufacturers must also determine in the design process the number and types of features to include in periodic updates of a product using cost and market considerations. Target costing, based on analysis of functionality/cost trade-offs, is an appropriate management tool for these firms. With its positioning in the early, upstream phases of the cost life cycle, target costing can clearly help a firm reduce total costs (see Exhibit 10.3).

Japanese industry and a growing number of firms worldwide are using target costing. The Cadillac division at General Motors Corporation; Toyota; Honda Motor Company; Compaq Computer Inc.; Intel, Inc.; and many others are using target costing. Many firms find it difficult to compete successfully on cost leadership or differentiation alone; they must compete on both price and functionality.[5] Target costing is a very useful way to manage the needed trade-off between functionality and cost.

Implementing a target costing approach involves five steps:

1. Determine the market price.
2. Determine the desired profit.
3. Calculate the target cost at market price less desired profit.
4. Use value engineering to identify ways to reduce product cost.
5. Use kaizen costing and operational control to further reduce costs.

The first three steps require no additional explanation. The following sections explain the fourth and fifth steps: the use of value engineering and of kaizen costing and operational control.

Value Engineering

Value engineering
is used in target costing to reduce product cost by analyzing the trade-offs between different types of product functionality and total product cost.

Value engineering is used in target costing to reduce product cost by analyzing the trade-offs between different types of product functionality (different types of product features) and total product cost. An important first step in value engineering is to perform a consumer analysis during the design stage of the new or revised product. The consumer analysis identifies critical consumer preferences that define the desired functionality for the new product.

The type of value engineering used depends on the product's functionality. For one group of products—including automobiles, computer software, and many consumer electronic products such as cameras and audio and video equipment—functionality can be added or deleted relatively easily. These products have frequent new models or updates, and customer preferences change frequently. The manufacturer in effect chooses the particular bundle of features to include with each new model of the product. For automobiles, this can mean new performance and new safety features; for computer software, it might mean the ability to perform certain new tasks or analyses.

In contrast, for another group of products, the functionality must be designed into the product rather than added on. These are best represented by specialized equipment and industrial products such as construction equipment, heavy trucks, and specialized medical equipment. In contrast to the first group, customer preferences here are rather stable.

---

[5] Robin Cooper, *When Lean Enterprises Collide* (Boston: Harvard Business School Press, 1995); see also the discussion of hypercompetition in the Appendix to Chapter 2.

Many global automakers use target costing and focus on design to speed the development of new products and to improve the features and quality of their products while keeping costs in check.

FORD MOTOR COMPANY

Ford has a new product design program, the Ford Product Development System, to speed the development of new vehicles and to improve the quality and cost-effectiveness of the designs. The system uses a Web-based tool allowing Ford engineers around the world to collaborate on design efforts; in a recent example, 4,500 engineers in the United States, the United Kingdom, and Germany used the tool. Ford also uses computer-aided design software developed by Structural Dynamics Research Corp. to speed its design process, improve the cost-effectiveness of the designs, and reduce the cost of developing product prototypes. Ford is hoping to use these new tools to reduce the average assembly time for a vehicle from two days to one day, and to reduce the overall lead time for order delivery by more than one-half.

GENERAL MOTORS

In an effort to improve profitability, GM has removed some features from the 2003 Buick Regal GS. The Monsoon speaker system, the Onstar telecommunications service, and the side airbags are now extra cost options. Similarly, the Pontiac Grand Am Sedan SE no longer has antilock brakes, a rear spoiler, or floor mats.

BMW

BMW has cut its development time for new cars in half through the use of computer-aided design software.

PORSCHE

The manufacturing time for the 911 Carrera was cut from 120 hours to 60 hours through the use of computer-aided design and computer-aided engineering.

DAIMLERCHRYSLER

The U.S. unit of DaimlerChrysler uses the rare metal palladium in catalytic converters to reduce auto emissions, as do many other automakers. The price of the metal, whose principal source is Russia, was stable until political and economic changes there disrupted the supply and caused the price of the metal to jump tenfold. Engineers at the U.S. unit are working to find new ways to meet pollution control standards that do not rely on this rare metal.

Source: Gregory L. White, "Russian Maneuvers Are Making Palladium Ever More Precious," *The Wall Street Journal,* March 6, 2000, p. 1; Gina Imperato, "SDRC Want You to Go Faster," *Fast Company,* October 1999, pp. 90–92; "Hot Wheels," *Business Week,* September 15, 1997, pp. 56–57; Steve Hamm and Marcia Stepanek, "From Reengineering to E-Engineering," *Business Week E-Biz,* March 22, 1999, p. EB15; and Karen Lundgaard and Sholnn Freeman, "Detroit's Latest Offer: Pay More, Get Less," *The Wall Street Journal,* July 24, 2002, p. D1.

Functional analysis
is a common type of value engineering in which the performance and cost of each major function or feature of the product is examined.

Target costing is more useful for products in the first group because the firm has some discretion about a larger number of features. A common type of value engineering employed in these firms is **functional analysis,** a process of examining the performance and cost of each major function or feature of the product. The objective of the analysis is to determine a desired balance of performance and cost. An overall desired level of performance achievement for each function is obtained while keeping the cost of all functions below the target cost.

Benchmarking is often used at this step to determine which features give the firm a competitive advantage. In a release of new software, for example, each desired feature of the updated version is reviewed against the cost and time required for its development. The objective is an overall bundle of features for the software that achieves the desired balance of meeting customer preferences while keeping costs below targeted levels. In another example, auto manufacturers must decide which performance and safety features to add to the new model. This decision is based on consumer analysis and a functional analysis of the feature's contribution to consumer preferences compared to its cost. For instance, improved safety air bags could be added, but target cost constraints could delay an improved sound system until a later model year.

Design analysis
is a common form of value engineering in which the design team prepares several possible designs of the product, each having similar features with different levels of performance and different costs.

Design analysis is the common form of value engineering for products in the second group, industrial and specialized products. The design team prepares several possible designs of the product, each having similar features with different levels of performance and different costs. Benchmarking and value chain analysis help guide the design team in preparing designs that are both low cost and competitive. The design team works with cost management personnel to select the one design that best meets customer preferences while not exceeding the target cost.

A useful comparison of different target costing and cost-reduction strategies in three Japanese firms, based on the field research of Robin Cooper, is illustrated in Exhibit 10.4. Note that the different market demands for functionality result in different

Cost Management in Action
Why Go Abroad (to Latin America)?
HP, Ericsson, IBM, Ford, Volkswagen

In competitive industries such as computers, consumer electronics, and autos, manufacturers continuously look for ways to reduce cost and increase value throughout the value chain. Because of intense pricing pressures and increased customer expectations, target costing methods can help identify and analyze the options for competitive advantage. Going abroad is the solution for many firms but for different reasons. We look at the practices in two industries: consumer electronics and computer products, and automakers.

CONSUMER ELECTRONICS AND COMPUTER PRODUCTS

Computer and electronics companies including HP, Ericsson, and IBM have outsourced manufacturing to plants operated by contract manufacturers in Mexico, such as Flextronics International, Ltd., Solectron Corp., and SCI Systems. IBM, for example, owns relatively few manufacturing plants, opting instead to contract out its manufacturing needs. Why is this an advantage to these three companies?

GLOBAL AUTOMAKERS

Ford, Volkswagen, DaimlerChrysler, General Motors, Renault, and Peugeot have invested in these new manufacturing plants in Mexico and Brazil. Why?

Automaker	Investment in Plants	Country
Ford	$1.9 billion	Brazil
Volkswagen	$1.5 billion	Mexico
Renault	$1.4 billion	Brazil
DaimlerChrysler	$815 million	Brazil
PSA Peugeot Citreon	$600 million	Brazil
General Motors	$600 million	Brazil

(Refer to Comments on Cost Management in Action at the end of the chapter.)

EXHIBIT 10.4 Target Costing in Three Japanese Firms

Firm/Industry	Functionality	Cost Reduction Approach	Strategy
Olympus/Cameras	Increasing rapidly; is designed in	Target costing using value engineering; the concept of distinctive functionality for the **price point**, plus supportive functionality	Heavy focus on managing functionality, like Nissan, but more so; importance of price points
Nissan/Auto	Rapidly increasing; easy to add or delete functionality	**Value engineering** by product and by each component of each product; then increase price or reduce functionality	Prices are set by desired customers' expectations about functionality; after functionality is set, target cost is used to find savings, especially from suppliers
Komatsu/Construction equipment	Static; must be designed in	**Design analysis** to determine alternative designs. **Functional analysis** to develop cost/functionality trade-offs. **Productivity programs** to reduce the remaining costs	Primary focus is on cost control rather than redesign or functionality analysis

cost-reduction approaches. Where customers' expectations for functionality are increasing, as for Nissan and Olympus, there is more significant use of target costing. In contrast, at Komatsu, the emphasis is on value engineering and productivity improvement. Note also that firms such as Nissan, which use both internal and external sourcing for parts and components, use target costing at both the product level and the component level. The overall product-level target cost is achieved when targeted costs for all components are achieved.[6]

Other cost-reduction approaches include cost tables and group technology. **Cost tables** are computer-based databases that include comprehensive information about the firm's cost drivers. Cost drivers include, for example, the size of the product, the materials used in its manufacture, and the number of features. Firms that manufacture parts of different size from the same design (pipe fittings, tools, and so on) use cost tables to show the difference in cost for parts of different sizes and different types of materials.

Cost tables

are computer-based databases that include comprehensive information about the firm's cost drivers.

[6] Ibid. Also see Robin Cooper and Regine Slagmulder, "Develop Profitable New Products with Target Costing," *Sloan Management Review,* Summer 1999, pp. 23–33; and Robin Cooper and Regine Slagmulder, "Target Costing for New Product Development; Component-Level Target Costing," *Journal of Cost Management,* September–October, 2001, pp. 36-43.

Group technology
is a method of identifying similarities in the parts of products a firm manufactures so the same part can be used in two or more products, thereby reducing costs.

Group technology is a method of identifying similarities in the parts of products a firm manufactures so the same parts can be used in two or more products, thereby reducing costs. Large manufacturers of diverse product lines, such as in the automobile industry, use group technology in this way. A point of concern in the use of group technology is that it reduces manufacturing costs but might increase service and warranty costs if a failed part is used in many different models. The combination of group technology and total quality management can, however, result in lower costs in both manufacturing and service/warranty.

Target Costing and Kaizen

The fifth step in target costing is to use Continuous Improvement (kaizen) and operational control to further reduce costs. Kaizen occurs at the manufacturing stage so that the effects of value engineering and improved design are already in place; the role for cost reduction at this phase is to develop new manufacturing methods (such as flexible manufacturing systems) and to use new management techniques such as operational control (Chapters 13, 14, and 15), total quality management (Chapter 16), and the theory of constraints (next section) to further reduce costs. *Kaizen* means *continual* improvement, that is, the ongoing search for new ways to reduce costs in the manufacturing process of a product with a given design and functionality.

Exhibit 10.5 shows the relationship between target costing and kaizen. Price is assumed to be stable or decreasing over time for firms for which target costing is appropriate because of intense competition on price, product quality and product functionality. These firms respond to the competitive pressure by periodically redesigning their products using target costing to simultaneously reduce the product price and improve their value. Consider the two points in Exhibit 10.5 labeled first and second target cost. The time period between product redesigns is approximately the product's *sales life cycle.* In the time between product redesigns, the firm uses kaizen to reduce product cost in the manufacturing process by streamlining the supply chain and improving both manufacturing methods and productivity programs. Thus, target costing and kaizen are complementary methods used to continually reduce cost and improve value.

The Use of Target Costing in Health Product Manufacturing

Health Products International, Inc. (HPI), is conducting a value engineering project by making a target costing analysis of a major product, a hearing aid. HPI sells a reliable second-generation hearing aid (HPI-2) for $750 (cost of $650) and has obtained 30 percent of this market worldwide at a profit of $100 per aid. However, a competitor recently introduced a new third-generation hearing aid that incorporates a computer chip that improves performance considerably and increases the price to $1,200. Through consumer analysis, HPI has determined that cost-conscious consumers will stay with

EXHIBIT 10.5
Price, Cost, Kaizen, and Target Costing

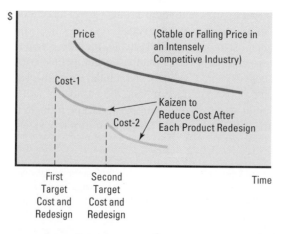

HPI, which will maintain its market share as long as its price does not exceed $600. HPI must meet the new lower price and maintain its current rate of profit ($100 per unit) by redesigning the hearing aid and/or the manufacturing process.

The target cost for the new aid is $600 − $100 = $500, a reduction in cost of $150 ($650 − $500) from the current model. Because the product has no add-on features, HPI decides to use design analysis with the following alternatives for changes and related savings per unit:

Alternative A. Reduce research and development expenditures ($50), replace the microphone unit with one of nearly equivalent sensitivity ($30), replace toggle power switch with a cheaper and almost as reliable slide switch ($30), replace the current inspection procedure with an integrated quality review process at each assembly station ($40). Total savings: $150.

Alternative B. Replace the amplifier unit with one having slightly less power, not expected to be a noticeable difference for most users ($50), replace the microphone unit with one of nearly equivalent sensitivity ($30), replace toggle power switch with a cheaper and almost as reliable slide switch ($30), replace the current inspection procedure with an integrated quality review process at each assembly station ($40). Total savings: $150.

Alternative C. Increase research and development activity to develop the new third-generation computer chip type of hearing aid (HPI-3, *increase* of $40). Replace the amplifier unit with one of slightly less power, not expected to be a noticeable difference for most users ($50), replace the microphone unit with one of nearly equivalent sensitivity ($30), replace toggle power switch with a cheaper and almost as reliable slide switch ($30), replace the current inspection procedure with an integrated quality review process at each assembly station ($40), renegotiate contract with supplier of plastic casing ($20), replace plastic earpiece material with material of slightly lower quality but well within the user's expectations for 6 to 10 years of use ($20). Net savings: $150.

After a review of its alternatives, HPI chose alternative C, primarily because it included an increase in research and development expenditures that would enable the firm at some future time to compete in the market for the new type of hearing aid. Manufacturing and marketing managers agreed that the design changes proposed in all the options would not significantly alter the market appeal of the current product. Key managers also determined that this alternative was strategically important because the new technology, while only a fraction of the market now, could be dominant in the next 10 to 15 years as prices come down on the new units and user awareness of the benefits of the computer chip become more well known.

The Theory of Constraints

> Remember that time is money.
>
> **Benjamin Franklin**

LEARNING OBJECTIVE 2
Apply the theory of constraints to facilitate strategic management.

Benjamin Franklin must be right. Most strategic initiatives undertaken by firms today focus on improving the speed of their operations throughout the cost life cycle. Why is speed so important? For many companies, it is a competitive edge. Customers expect quick response to inquiries and fast delivery of the product. Shorter sales life cycles in many industries mean that manufacturers are working to reduce product development time. Some of the most successful business models of recent years, such as those of Dell Computer and Amazon.com, are built on speed. Amazon's website states when the product will be shipped; many times this is within 24 hours.

In this part of the chapter, we present one of the key methods used to improve speed, the theory of constraints (TOC), a technique used to improve speed in the

EXHIBIT 10.6   **Measures of Speed and How to Improve It At Each Step of the Cost Life Cycle**

	R & D	Design	Manufacturing	Marketing & Distribution	Customer Service
Measures of Speed	Product development time (months)		Cycle time (hours or days), manufacturing cycle efficiency (a ratio)	Delivery time (days)	Customer response time for inquiries and service problems
How to Improve Speed	Design software, web-based engineering tools		**The Theory of Constraints (TOC)**	Reduce complexity, automate the shipping function	Customer service software, such as that provided by Siebel Systems, Inc.
Examples of Speed	BMW reduces new model development time by 100%, to 3 years		Porsche reduces cycle time on the 911 Carrera from 120 to 60 hours	Amazon.com— shipment of many items in less than 24 hours	Siebel customers include Otis Elevator, Bank of America, and American Cancer Society

Cycle time
is the amount of time between the receipt of a customer order and the shipment of the order.

Manufacturing cycle efficiency (MCE)
is the ratio of processing time to total cycle time.

Constraints
are those activities that slow the product's cycle time.

manufacturing process and thus speed. Before looking closely at TOC, we consider the issue of how speed is measured and improved throughout the cost life cycle, as illustrated in Exhibit 10.6. The measures are defined in different ways by different firms, depending on the nature of the firm's operations. For example, manufacturing **cycle time** (or manufacturing *lead time* or *throughput time*) is commonly defined as follows:

$$\text{Cycle time} = \text{Amount of time between the receipt of a customer order and the shipment of the order}$$

Depending on the firm's operations and objectives, the start of the cycle time can also be defined as the time a production batch is scheduled, the time the raw materials are ordered, or the time that production on the order is started. The finish time of the cycle can also be defined as the time that production is completed or the time the order is ready for shipping.

Another useful measure is **manufacturing cycle efficiency (MCE)**:

$$\text{MCE} = \frac{\text{Processing time}}{\text{Total cycle time}}$$

MCE separates total cycle time into the time required for each of the various activities: processing (value-adding work on the product), inspection, materials handling, waiting, and so on. Most firms would like to see their MCE close to 1, which reflects less time wasted on moving, waiting, inspecting, and other non-value-adding activities.[7]

The theory of constraints (TOC) was developed to help managers reduce cycle times and operating costs.[8] Prior to TOC, managers often devoted efforts to improve efficiency and speed *throughout* the manufacturing process instead of focusing attention on just those activities that were constraints (i.e., bottlenecks) in the process. **Constraints** are activities that slow a product's total cycle time. Goldratt and Cox use as

[7] While 100 percent is a theoretical maximum for MCE, many firms find their MCE ratios to be close to zero because of delays and wasted time in the manufacturing process. Also, note that the terms used here are *manufacturing* measurements, and that similar measures are used by firms to examine the firm's progress in *filling customer orders.* For example, customer lead time (or customer cycle time) is usually defined as the time from the receipt of an order to the delivery of the product.

[8] E. Goldratt and J. Cox, *The Goal* (New York: Free Press, 1986); and E. Goldratt, *The Theory of Constraints* (New York: North River Press, 1990). See also Thomas Corbett, *Throughput Accounting* (New York: North River Press, 1998); and "Measuring the Cost of Capacity," *Management Accounting Guideline Number 42* (The Society of Management Accountants of Canada, 1996).

an example a troop of boy scouts on a hike; the slowest hiker is the constraint and sets the overall pace for the troop. Manufacturers have learned that increased efficiency and speed with activities that are not constraints could be dysfunctional. Unnecessary efficiency is likely to result in the buildup of work-in-process inventory for activities prior to the constraint (just as the scouts would be "bunched up" behind the slowest scout) and to divert attention and resources from the actual slow-down cycle time. TOC has turned the attention to improving speed at the constraints, which causes a decrease in the overall cycle time.

The Use of the Theory of Constraints Analysis in Health Product Manufacturing

To illustrate the use of TOC and its five steps, we again consider Healthcare Products International, Inc. (HPI). Suppose that HPI is currently manufacturing both the second generation (HPI-2) and third generation (HPI-3) of hearing aids. The prices for the HPI-2 and HPI-3 are competitive at $600 and $1,200, respectively, and are not expected to change. Because of manufacturing delays and increasing cycle times, HPI has a backlog of orders for both the HPI-2 and the HPI-3. Its monthly number of orders for the HPI-2 is 3,000 units and for the HPI-3 is 1,800 units. New customers are told that they may have to wait three weeks or more for their orders. Management is concerned about the need to improve speed in the manufacturing process and is planning to use TOC. Here are the steps HPI would take to use TOC.

Steps in the Theory of Constraints Analysis

TOC analysis has five steps:

1. Identify the constraint.
2. Determine the most profitable product mix given the constraint.
3. Maximize the flow through the constraint.
4. Add capacity to the constraint.
5. Redesign the manufacturing process for flexibility and fast cycle time.

The theory of constraints (TOC) is a method for identifying and managing constraints in the manufacturing process to speed up the flow of product through the plant. Because of management concerns, the company decides to perform TOC analysis.

Step 1: Identify the Constraint

A **flow diagram** is a flowchart of the work done that shows the sequence of processes and the amount of time required for each.

The management accountant works with manufacturing managers and engineers to identify any constraint in the manufacturing process by developing a **flow diagram** of the work done. The flow diagram shows the sequence of processes and the amount of time each requires. The five processes for HPI follow, and their flow diagram is shown in Exhibit 10.7.

Process 1. Assemble earpiece.
Process 2. Test and program computer chip (product HPI-3 only).
Process 3. Install other electronics.
Process 4. Perform final assembly and test.
Process 5. Pack and ship.

The raw materials cost for each unit is $300 for the HPI-2 and $750 for the HPI-3 ($450 for the computer chip and $300 for other electronics).

The constraint is identified by using the flow diagram to analyze the total time required for each process given the current level of demand. Exhibit 10.8 shows a summary of the data for this analysis, including the number of employees available for each process and the total time available per month for all employees (assuming a 40-hour workweek in which 30 hours are available for work and 10 hours are used for breaks, training, etc.). HPI processes are very specialized, and employees are able to

EXHIBIT 10.7
Flow Diagram for HPI, Inc.

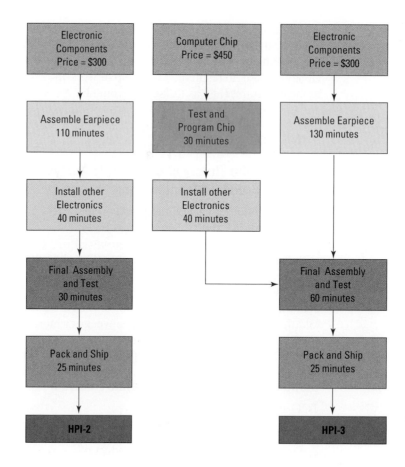

work only within their assigned process. Moreover, because of the specialized skills required, HPI has difficulty maintaining adequate staffing in all processes except process 5, pack and ship.

Step 1 in Exhibit 10.8 shows the total time required in each process given the current level of demand. Each of the five processes except process 4 has slack time. Therefore, the constraint occurs with process 4, perform final assembly and test. Because of inadequate time (900 hours too few) available in this process, HPI will not be able to meet the total demand for HPI-2 and HPI-3 and will delay some orders or perhaps not fill them at all. HPI must now determine which orders to fill and which not to fill. This takes us to the second step of TOC.

Step 2: Determine the Most Profitable Product Mix Given the Constraint

The most profitable product mix is the combination of products that maximizes total profits for both products. Should we produce all 3,000 units of HPI-2 and whatever we can of HPI-3, or should we produce all 1,800 units of HPI-3 and whatever we can of HPI-2? Or some other mix? The step 2 analysis in Exhibit 10.8 provides the answer.[9]

To determine the most profitable product mix, we first determine the most profitable product, given the constraint. TOC measures product profitability using the **throughput margin**, which is the product price less materials cost (includes the costs of all materials used, purchased components, and materials-handling costs). All other manufacturing costs are excluded in determining profitability because they are assumed to be fixed and will not change regardless of which product mix is chosen.[10] Step 2 in Exhibit 10.8

Throughput margin
is a TOC measure of product profitability; it equals price less materials cost, including all purchased components and materials handling costs.

---

[9] Note that the analysis in Step 2 and Step 3 of Exhibit 10.8 is identical to that explained in Chapter 9 under the heading of "Multiple Products and Scarce Resources," for one production constraint. The determination of the optimal product mix is arrived at in exactly the same manner.

[10] Note that TOC analysis assumes that factory labor is not a direct and variable cost but is a fixed cost. This assumption applies when labor is a small or an unchanging part of total cost.

EXHIBIT 10.8 **Summary of Key Data for HPI, Inc., TOC Analysis**

	HPI-2	HPI-3
Demand (Per Month)	3,000	1,800
Price	$600	$1,200
Materials Cost	$300	$ 750

Process	Minutes Required for Each Product Per Unit		Number of Employees	Total Hours Available Per Month
	HPI-2	HPI-3		
1: Assemble earpiece	110	130	80	9,600
2: Test and program computer chip	0	30	8	960
3: Install other electronics	40	40	30	3,600
4: Perform final assembly and test	30	60	20	2,400
5: Pack and ship	25	25	18	2,160

Step 1: Identify the Constraint (the process for which total hours required for the given demand exceeds available hours—Process 4)

	HPI-2	HPI-3	Total Hours	Hours Available	Slack Hours
Process 1: Assemble earpiece (HPI-2 3000 × 110/60)	5,500	3,900	9,400	9,600	200
Process 2: Test and program chip	0	900	900	960	60
Process 3: Install other electronics	2,000	1,200	3,200	3,600	400
Process 4: Perform final assembly and test	1,500	1,800	3,300	2,400	(900)
Process 5: Pack and ship	1,250	750	2,000	2,160	160

Step 2: Identify Most Profitable Product = HPI-2

	HPI-2	HPI-3
Price	$600.00	$1,200.00
Materials cost	300.00	750.00
Throughput margin	$300.00	$ 450.00
Constraint time (for Process 4)	30	60
Throughput per minute	$ 10.00	$ 7.50

Step 3: Identify the Most Profitable Product Mix

	HPI-2	HPI-3
Total demand in units	3,000	1,800
Units of product in optimal mix	3,000	900
Unmet demand	—	900

shows that throughput margins for the HPI-2 and HPI-3 are $300 and $450, respectively. Although HPI-3 has the higher margin, the profitability analysis is not complete without considering the time required by the constraint, final assembly, and test for each product. Since HPI-3 takes twice as much time in final assembly and test as HPI-2 (60 versus 30 minutes), we can produce twice as many HPI-2 models for each HPI-3 produced. In effect, the relevant measure of profitability is throughput margin *per minute of time in final assembly and test,* that is, a throughput per minute of $10 for HPI-2 and $7.50 for HPI-3. This means that each minute that final assembly and test is used to produce HPI-2 earns $10 while each minute used to produce HPI-3 earns only $7.50. HPI-2 is the most profitable product when final assembly and test is the constraint.

The best product mix is determined in Step 3 of Exhibit 10.8. HPI produces all 3,000 units or demand for HPI-2 since it is the most profitable product. Then HPI determines the remaining capacity in final assembly. Then HPI determines the number of units of HPI-3 it can produce with the remaining capacity on the constraint, Process 4. Despite the demand for 1,800 units of HPI-3, only 900 can be produced with the available capacity, determined as follows: First, the Process 4 capacity used in production of HPI-2 is calculated, 3,000 units × 30 minutes/unit equals 90,000 minutes or 1,500 hours. This leaves 900 (2,400 total Process 4 hours − 1,500) hours of time for HPI-3. Second, in 900 hours, HPI can produce 900 units of HPI-3, which requires one hour per unit processing time. Thus, the optimal product mix is 3,000 units of HPI-2 and 900 units of HPI-3, given the constraint on Process 4.

Step 3: Maximize the Flow through the Constraint

In this step, the management accountant looks for ways to speed the flow through the constraint by simplifying the process, improving the product design, reducing setup time, and reducing other delays due to unscheduled and non-value-added activities such as inspections or machine breakdowns, among others.

The **drum-buffer-rope system**
is a system for balancing the flow of production through a constraint, thereby reducing the amount of inventory at the constraint and improving overall productivity.

An important tool for managing product flow in step 3 is the **drum-buffer-rope (DBR) system,** which is a system for balancing the flow of production through a constraint, illustrated in Exhibit 10.9 for Health Products International, Inc. The DBR system works for HPI as follows. In the DBR system, all production flows are synchronized to the drum (the constraint), process 4. The rope is the sequence of processes prior to and including the constraint. The objective is to *balance the flow of production* through the rope by carefully timing and scheduling activity for processes 1 through 3. The buffer is a minimum amount of work-in-process input for process 4 that is maintained to ensure that process 4 is kept busy.

Takt time
is the speed at which units must be manufactured to meet customer demand.

Another commonly used method for identifying constraints and smoothing production flow is the use of Takt time. **Takt** is a German word meaning the conductor's baton, or rhythm. It is the ratio of the total time available given current capacity to the capacity required for the expected customer demand. For example, suppose a manufacturing plant operates for eight hours per day, and that after allowing for break time, 400 minutes of manufacturing time are available per day. Also, the average customer demand per day is 800 units, the Takt time is 30 seconds per unit:

$$\text{Takt time} = \frac{400 \text{ minutes}}{800 \text{ units}} = \text{½ minute or 30 seconds per unit}$$

This means that each unit must be manufactured in an average of 30 seconds to meet customer demand. Now suppose that two independent operations are needed to produce each unit, and that the first operation requires an average of 35 seconds and the second operation requires 25 seconds per unit. Because the two operations are independent the first operation is the constraint, and the firm will not be able to meet the expected demand of 800 units. The time for the first operation must be reduced to

EXHIBIT 10.9
**The Drum-Buffer-Rope
System for Production
Flow Management**

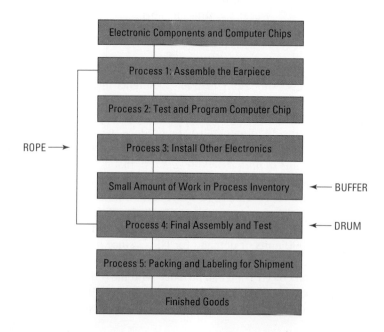

REAL-WORLD FOCUS   Focus on Cycle Time at Starbucks, Boozer Lumber Co., and England, Inc.

REDUCING CYCLE TIMES IN CUSTOMER PAYMENT

Starbucks has decided to deal with the long lines that scare off some customers by decreasing the time needed to pay from 20 seconds to 4 seconds. The swipeable card that allows customers to pay instantly also provides Starbucks with important marketing information. McDonald's is doing the same thing for fast food by using credit cards to reduce customer paying time to 5 seconds instead of the 10 seconds needed with cash. The U.S. Postal Service also has discovered that plastic is faster than cash.

CYCLE TIMES IN THE CONSTRUCTION INDUSTRY

Boozer Lumber Co. is a small lumber company in Columbia, South Carolina, which provides roof trusses and other products and services to the construction industry. Recently it adapted the production of trusses to accommodate the increased demand for more complex roof structures. The increased complexity of the product created constraints in the manufacturing process that were not immediately apparent to the company's managers. The machine operators were unfamiliar with the new designs, which were difficult to manufacture, resulting in a dramatic increase in machine setup time. The solution came when Bob Jones, owner of the company, read Goldratt and Cox's novel, *The Goal*. A quick investigation identified the setup for roof trusses as being a constraint in the business,

and the company employed experts to speed up the process using an automated system. Within two years, profits had improved enough that the company's 20 managers received a total of $800,000 in bonuses.

SPEEDING ORDER DELIVERY IN FURNITURE MANUFACTURING

England, Inc., a furniture manufacturer in Tazewell, Tennessee, has found a competitive advantage and increasing sales through speed in delivering customer orders. England, Inc. uses precision scheduling throughout the cost life cycle to achieve delivery times in as few as three weeks, much better than the industry average. This means tightly coordinated order taking, production scheduling, labor scheduling, purchasing, and the use of company-owned delivery trucks. As a result England's sales increased in 2001 while industry sales fell more than 9 percent.

Sources: John B. MacArthur, "Theory in Novel Spurs Turnaround for Lumber Firm," *Greensboro News and Observer,* August 24, 1999; Dan Morse, "Tennessee Producer Tries New Tactic in Sofas: Speed," *The Wall Street Journal,* November 19, 2002, p. 1; Shirley Leung and Ron Lieber, "The New Option at McDonald's: Plastic," *The Wall Street Journal,* November 26, 2002, p. D1; "Starbucks' Card Smarts," *Business Week,* March 18, 2002, p. 14; T. L. Carter, A. Segdhat, and T. Williams, "How ABC Changed the Post Office," *Strategic Finance,* February 1998.

30 seconds or less, the Takt time, in order for the production requirement to be met. A comparison of cycle time for each operation to overall Takt time for the plant quickly identifies constraints, and provides a basis for smoothing the flow of production through the different operations.

Step 4: Add Capacity to the Constraint

As a longer-term measure to relieve the constraint and improve cycle time, management should consider adding capacity to the constraints by adding new or improved machines and/or additional labor.

Step 5: Redesign the Manufacturing Process for Flexibility and Fast Cycle Time

The most complete strategic response to the constraint is to redesign the manufacturing process, including the introduction of new manufacturing technology, deletion of some hard-to-manufacture products, and redesign of some products for greater ease of manufacturing. Simply removing one or more minor features on a given product might speed up the production process significantly. The use of value engineering as described earlier might help at this point.

Theory of Constraints Reports

When a firm focuses on improving cycle time, eliminating constraints, and improving speed of delivery, the performance evaluation measures also focus on these critical success factors. A common approach is to report throughput margin as well as selected operating data in a *theory of constraints report.* An example of this report used by a manufacturer of automotive glass is shown in Exhibit 10.10. Note in the exhibit that window styles H and B are the most profitable because they have far higher throughput margin based on the binding constraint, hours of furnace time. The throughput

EXHIBIT 10.10
The TOC Report for an Auto Glass Manufacturer

Source: R. J. Campbell, "Pricing Strategy in the Automotive Glass Industry," *Management Accounting*, July 1989, pp. 26–34.

	March 2004			
	Style C	**Style A**	**Style H**	**Style B**
Window size	0.77	.073	7.05	4.95
Sales volume	High	Moderate	High	Moderate
Units in unfilled orders	1,113	234	882	23
Average lead time (days)	16	23	8	11
Market price	$2.82	$6.68	$38.12	$24.46
Direct production costs				
Materials	0.68	0.64	5.75	4.02
Scrap allowance	0.06	0.05	0.42	0.34
Material handling	0.12	0.12	1.88	1.61
Subtotal	.86	.81	8.05	5.97
Throughput margin	$1.96	$5.87	$30.07	$18.49
Furnace hours per unit	.0062	.0061	.0082	.0078
Throughput margin per hour	$316	$962	$3,667	$2,370

margin per hour is $3,667 and $2,370 for styles H and B, respectively; in contrast, the throughput margin per hour for styles C and A is less than $1,000. TOC reports are useful for identifying the most profitable product and for monitoring success in achieving the critical success factors.

ABC and the Theory of Constraints

Firms using such cost management methods as target costing and the theory of constraints commonly employ activity-based costing (ABC). ABC is used to assess the profitability of products, just as TOC was used in the previous illustration. The difference is that TOC takes a short-term approach to profitability analysis while ABC costing develops a long-term analysis. The TOC analysis has a short-term focus because of its emphasis on only materials-related costs, but ABC includes all product costs.

On the other hand, unlike TOC, ABC does not explicitly include the resource constraints and capacities of production activities. Thus, ABC cannot be used to determine the short-term best product mix, as for the auto window manufacturer in Exhibit 10.10. ABC and TOC are thus *complementary* methods; ABC provides a comprehensive analysis of cost drivers and accurate unit costs as a basis for strategic decisions about long-term pricing and product mix. In contrast, TOC provides a useful method for improving the short-term profitability of the manufacturing plant through short-term product mix adjustments and through attention to production constraints. The differences between ABC and TOC are outlined in Exhibit 10.11.[11]

Life-Cycle Costing

LEARNING OBJECTIVE 3
Describe how life-cycle costing facilitates strategic management.

Typically, product or service costs are measured and reported for relatively short periods, such as a month or a year. Life-cycle costing provides a long-term perspective because it considers the entire cost life cycle of the product or service (see Exhibit 10.12). It therefore provides a more complete perspective of product costs and product or service profitability. For example, a product that is designed quickly and carelessly, with little investment in design costs, could have significantly higher marketing and service

[11] For a comparison of TOC and ABC, see Robert Kee, "Integrating Activity-Based Costing with the Theory of Constraints to Enhance Production-Related Decision Making," *Accounting Horizons*, December 1995, pp. 48–61; Robin Cooper and Regine Slagmulder, "Integrating Activity-Based Costing and the Theory of Constraints," *Management Accounting*, February 1999, p. 2; and Robert Kee and Charles Schmidt, "A Comparative Analysis of Utilizing Activity-Based Costing and the Theory of Constraints for Making Product-Mix Decisions," *International Journal of Production Economics* 63 (2000), pp 1–17.

EXHIBIT 10.11
Comparison of the TOC and ABC Costing Methods

	TOC	ABC
Main objective	**Short-term focus;** throughput margin analysis based on materials and materials-related costs	**Long-term focus;** analysis of all product costs, including materials, labor, and overhead
Resource constraints and capacities	Included explicitly; a principal focus of TOC	Not included explicitly
Cost drivers	No direct utilization of cost drivers	Develop an understanding of cost drivers at the unit, batch, product, and facility levels
Major use	Optimization of production flow and short-term product mix	Strategic pricing and profit planning

EXHIBIT 10.12
Life-Cycle Costing in the Cost Life Cycle

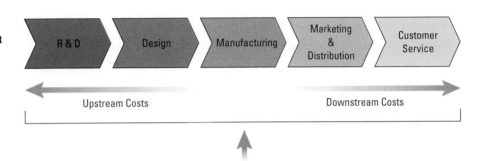

costs later in the life cycle. Managers are interested in the total cost, over the entire life cycle, not manufacturing costs only.

While cost management methods have tended to focus only on manufacturing costs, upstream and downstream costs can account for a significant portion of total life-cycle costs, especially in certain industries:

Industries with High Upstream Costs
Computer software
Specialized industrial and medical equipment

Industries with High Downstream Costs
Pharmaceuticals
Perfumes, cosmetics, and toiletries

Upstream and downstream costs are managed in a number of ways including improved relationships with suppliers and distributors; the most crucial way is the design of the product and the manufacturing process. Value-chain analysis, as explained in Chapter 2, can also provide a useful way to identify upstream and downstream linkages for a manufacturing or service firm (see Exhibit 10.13).

The Importance of Design

As managers consider upstream and downstream costs, decision making at the design stage is critical. Although the costs incurred at the design stage could account for only a very small percentage of the total costs over the entire product life cycle, design stage decisions commit a firm to a given production, marketing, and service plan. Therefore, they lock in most of the remaining life-cycle costs.

The critical success factors at the design stage include the following:

Reduced time to market. In a competitive environment where the speed of product development and the speed of delivery are critical, efforts to reduce time to market have the first priority.

EXHIBIT 10.13
Value Chain Showing Upstream and Downstream Linkages

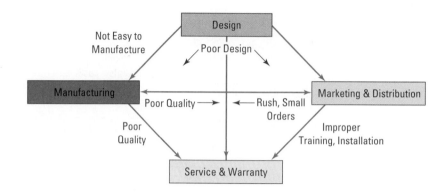

EXHIBIT 10.14 Characteristics of the Four Design Methods

Design Method	Design Speed	Design Cost	Downstream Costs
Basic engineering	Fast	Depends on desired complexity and functionality; should be relatively low	Can be very high because marketing and production are not integral to the design process
Prototyping	Slow	Significant; materials, labor, and time	Potentially can reflect a significant reduction
Templating	Fast	Modest	Unknown; can have costly unexpected results if the scaling does not work in the market or in production
Concurrent engineering	Continuous	Significant; design is an integral, ongoing process	Can result in greatest reduction

Reduced expected service costs. By careful, simple design and the use of modular, interchangeable components, the expected service costs can be greatly reduced.

Improved ease of manufacture. To reduce production costs and speed production, the design must be easy to manufacture.

Process planning and design. The plan for the manufacturing process should be flexible, allowing for fast setups and product changeovers, using agile manufacturing concepts, computer-integrated manufacturing, computer-assisted design, and concurrent engineering.

The four common design methods are basic engineering, prototyping, templating, and concurrent engineering. See Exhibit 10.14. **Basic engineering** is the method by which product designers work independently from marketing and manufacturing to develop a design from specific plans and specifications. An advantage of this approach is that it can be quick and less costly than the others. The disadvantage is that because basic engineering is independent from marketing and production, the product might be inappropriate for the market (hard to sell and/or service) or might be difficult and costly to manufacture. This method has high downstream costs as a result.

Prototyping is a method by which functional models of the product are developed and tested by engineers and trial customers. A good example of prototyping is the beta testing of software products by customers of the software vendor to provide a trial run of a new software system. The direct cost of prototyping can be high when significant materials and labor are needed to prepare the prototype products. On the other hand, it has great potential for reducing downstream costs since the feedback from the engineers and trial-run customers is used to improve the product and/or the production process.

Templating is a method in which an existing product is scaled up or down to fit the specifications of the desired new product. An example is the Big Mac, Biggie, Double, or Whopper hamburger sandwiches that are derived from simple sandwiches. Templating is a fast and low-cost design method; the impact on downstream costs depends on how well the scaling works and whether the production costs and market reaction are as expected.

Basic engineering
is the method in which product designers work independently from marketing and manufacturing to develop a design from specific plans and specifications.

Prototyping
is a method in which functional models of the product are developed and tested by engineers and trial customers.

Templating
is a method in which an existing product is scaled up or down to fit the specifications of the desired new product.

Concurrent engineering,
or *simultaneous engineering,* is
an important new method that
integrates product design with
manufacturing and marketing
throughout the product's life cycle.

Concurrent engineering, or *simultaneous engineering,* is an important new development in the design of products that is replacing the basic engineering approach in which product designers work in isolation on specialized components of the overall design project. In contrast, concurrent engineering relies on an integrated approach, in which the engineering/design process takes place *throughout the cost life cycle* using cross-functional teams. Information is solicited from and used at each phase of the value chain to improve the product design. For example, customer feedback in the service phase is used directly in the product design. Manufacturers such as Toyota Motor Corp. and Moen, Inc. are increasingly using product design in a very flexible manner; they incorporate improvements in the product continuously. Some experts argue that this approach has saved firms as much as 20 percent of total product cost.[12]

The Use of Life-Cycle Costing in a Software Firm

As an example of applying life-cycle costing, consider software developer Analytical Decisions, Inc. (ADI), that provides specialized software for banks and other financial institutions to use to analyze loan loss reserves and to plan loan portfolios. ADI has two products, ADI–1 for large banks and ADI–2 for small banks and savings and loans. Each product is updated annually, with an occasional special update during the year. Each update improves the product's functionality in some significant way.

Initially, ADI analyzed profitability by using the accounting software widely used in the industry, which provided the report shown in Exhibit 10.15. This analysis shows both products to be quite profitable, even in the presence of heavy R&D and selling costs; ADI–1 shows a somewhat higher gross margin (72%; $3,260,000/$4,500,000) than ADI–2 (60%; $1,495,000/$2,500,000). However, the analysis is incomplete since most of ADI's costs (R&D and selling) are not included in the product comparison. Because ADI's systems designers and programmers work in project teams, determining how the R&D costs should be assigned to the two products is relatively simple. Similarly, because ADI's sales and customer-service efforts are logged by product, these costs also can be traced, as shown in Exhibit 10.16.

The life-cycle cost analysis clearly identifies ADI–2 as the more profitable of the two products because ADI–1 incurs the bulk of the R&D and selling costs. Moreover,

[12] D. K. Sobek, A. C. Ward, and J. K. Liker, "Toyota's Principles of Set-Based Concurrent Engineering," *Sloan Management Review,* Winter 1999, pp. 67–83; F. Keenan, "Opening the Spigot," *Business Week,* June 4, 2001, p. EB17.

EXHIBIT 10.15
Product-Line Income Statement for Analytical Decisions, Inc.

	ADI–1	ADI–2	Total
Sales	$4,500,000	$2,500,000	$7,000,000
Cost of sales	1,240,000	1,005,000	2,245,000
Gross margin	$3,260,000	$1,495,000	$4,755,000
Research and development			2,150,000
Selling and service			1,850,000
Income before tax			$ 755,000

EXHIBIT 10.16
Life-Cycle Costing for Analytical Decisions, Inc.

	ADI–1	ADI–2	Total
Sales	$4,500,000	$2,500,000	$7,000,000
Cost of sales	1,240,000	1,005,000	2,245,000
Gross margin	$3,260,000	$1,495,000	$4,755,000
Research and development	1,550,000	600,000	2,150,000
Selling and service	1,450,000	400,000	1,850,000
Income before tax	$ 260,000	$ 495,000	$ 755,000

the revised analysis provides a basis for ADI management to seek possible cost reductions. For example, the ratio of research and development, selling and service costs to sales dollars is much higher for ADI–1 (67%; $3,000,000/$4,500,000) than for ADI–2 (40%; $1,000,000/$2,500,000). Management should investigate whether these higher costs are due to the nature of the different customers or quality problems in ADI–1. Management can use this breakdown of costs throughout the product's life cycle to identify opportunities for cost savings.

Pricing Products Using the Product Life Cycle

LEARNING OBJECTIVE 4
Outline the objectives and techniques of long-term pricing.

Management accountants are involved in three pricing situations: The first is the special order decision explained in Chapter 9 in which a nonrecurring sales opportunity arises; the proper price in this case is based on relevant cost analysis. The second context is target costing explained earlier in this chapter in which a firm faces a market price and determines how to achieve the level of costs necessary to make a profit, using product design and kaizen. The third type of pricing decision—not involving special orders or market-determined prices—is the focus in this section. These are the long-term, strategic pricing decisions facing most managers. They are complex decisions involving strategic issues and careful use of cost information. To assist in these pricing decisions, the management accountant prepares cost information from both the perspective of the cost life cycle and the sales life cycle.

Pricing Using the Cost Life Cycle

Pricing based on cost is a common approach for manufacturing firms and service firms. Firms that compete on cost leadership use cost information to improve operating efficiency to reduce costs and price. Prices are set by the most efficient producers, the ones that are best able to reduce costs. In contrast, firms that compete on differentiation have more discretion in setting prices. The differentiated firm's goal might be to increase profits by setting an initial high price for those willing to pay, followed by lower prices for the cost-conscious customers (called skimming). Alternatively, the firm's goal might be to increase market share by lowering the price (called penetration). A third approach would be to build longer-term customer relationships by utilizing "value pricing" in which pricing is based on meeting specific customer needs. A firm's pricing policy is also influenced by patterns in the industry. For example, firms with seasonal demand (clothing, appliances, furniture, among others) usually offer discounts and promotions during the slow periods of the year. Other industries are sensitive to interest rates, stock market returns, other factors in the economy (automobiles and construction, among others), and new products or pricing policies of competitors. To deal with the complexity of the pricing decision, firms like GE Lighting, DHL, and Hewlett-Packard use Web-based software systems to determine prices more quickly and accurately for different customers. The systems speed up the process of quoting prices and assist in determining the timing and location of discount programs. For example, the Stop & Shop supermarket chain is developing a new system, an electronic keypad on shopping carts, that will provide instant promotions to each shopper based on that shopper's buying pattern.[13] Thus, a number of seasonal, cyclical, economic, and other strategic factors influence the pricing policies of the firm, and cost information is only the starting point of the pricing decision. The cost information for pricing is commonly based on one of the four methods: (1) full manufacturing cost plus markup, (2) life cycle cost plus markup, (3) full cost and desired gross margin percent, and (4) full cost plus desired return.

[13] "The Price Is Right," *Business Week*, March 31, 2003, pp. 61–67.

Full Manufacturing Cost Plus Markup

In this method, a firm determines full manufacturing cost (the total of variable and fixed manufacturing costs) and applies a markup percentage to cover other operating costs plus profit. The markup percentage could be determined by industry practice, judgment, or a desired level of profit (equivalent to method 4). Suppose a firm has the following unit costs (using ABC costing), and a markup rate of 40 percent. Then, the price would be calculated as $210.

Manufacturing cost	
Materials	$ 40
Labor	50
Batch level costs	20
Other plant overhead	40
Total manufacturing cost	$150
Price based on full manufacturing cost: $150 × 140% = $210	

Life-Cycle Cost Plus Markup

The life-cycle approach to pricing uses the full life-cycle cost instead of manufacturing cost only. Suppose that in addition to manufacturing costs of $150 per unit, the previous firm has selling and administrative costs of $25 per unit, for a total of $175 life-cycle cost. The firm uses a markup rate of 25 percent based on life-cycle costs. The calculated price is now $218.75:

$$\text{Total life-cycle costs} \times \text{markup} = \text{price}$$

$$\$175 \times 125\% = \$218.75$$

The life-cycle approach has the advantage that all costs are included, so that the markup percentage can be directly tied to a desired level of profit. Both the full manufacturing cost and life-cycle cost approaches are commonly used according to a recent survey.[14]

Full Manufacturing Cost and Desired Gross Margin Percent

In this variation, the price is determined so that a desired gross margin percent is achieved. To continue with the previous example, suppose that the desired gross margin is 30 percent of sales. Then, the price would be $214.29:

$$\text{Price} = \frac{\text{Full manufacturing cost}}{(1 - \text{Desired gross margin percentage})}$$

$$= \frac{\$150}{(1 - .3)} = \$214.29$$

This price would produce a gross margin of $214.29 − $150 = $64.29, which is 30 percent of sales. Alternatively, a variation of this method could be used to achieve a desired percentage return on life-cycle costs. For example, if the desired percentage return on life-cycle costs is 15 percent, then the price would be $205.88:

$$\text{Price} = \frac{\text{Full life-cycle cost}}{(1 - \text{Desired life-cycle margin percentage})}$$

$$= \frac{\$175}{(1 - .15)} = \$205.88$$

Desired Return on Assets

Another common pricing approach is to set the price to achieve a desired return on assets. Assume again that the same information applies, that the firm has $3.5 million of assets committed to the production of the product, and desires a 10 percent before-tax

[14] E. Shim and E. F. Sudit, "How Manufacturers Price Products," *Management Accounting*, February 1995, pp 37–39.

return on assets. Sales are expected to be 10,000 units. Using a life-cycle cost approach (a full manufacturing-cost approach could be used in a similar manner), the markup percentage would be 20 percent.

$$\text{Markup rate} = \frac{\text{Desired before-tax return}}{\text{Life-cycle cost of expected sales}}$$

$$= \frac{\$3,500,000 \times 10\%}{10,000 \times \$175} = 20\%$$

And the price would then be $210:

$$\text{Price} = \text{Life-cycle cost} \times 120\% = \$175 \times 120\% = \$210$$

Each of these illustrations assumes that all sales are for the price determined. The desired price could be adjusted to reflect expected discounts or losses due to spoilage or theft.

Strategic Pricing for Phases of the Sales Life Cycle

Strategic pricing depends on the position of the product or service in the sales life cycle. As the sales life cycle becomes shorter (only months in some industries such as consumer electronics), the analysis of the sales life cycle becomes increasingly important.[15] In contrast to the cost life cycle just described, the sales life cycle refers to the phase of the product's or service's sales in the market, from introduction of the product or service to decline and withdrawal from the market. (Exhibit 10.2 illustrates the phases of the sales life cycle.)

Phase 1: Introduction. The first phase involves little competition, and sales rise slowly as customers become aware of the new product or service. Costs are relatively high because of high R&D expenditures and capital costs for setting up production facilities and marketing efforts. Prices are relatively high because of product differentiation and the high costs at this phase. Product variety is limited.

Phase 2: Growth. Sales begin to increase rapidly as does product variety. The product continues to enjoy the benefits of differentiation. Competition increases, and prices begin to fall.

Phase 3: Maturity. Sales continue to increase but at a decreasing rate. The number of competitors and of product variety decline. Prices fall further, and differentiation is no longer important. Competition is based on cost given competitive quality and functionality.

Phase 4: Decline. Sales and prices decline, as do the number of competitors. Control of costs and an effective distribution network are key to continued survival.

In the first phase, the focus of management is on design, differentiation, and marketing. The focus shifts to new product development and pricing strategy as competition develops in the second phase. In the third and fourth phases, management's attention turns to cost control, quality, and service as the market continues to become more competitive. Thus, the firm's strategy for the product or service changes over the sales life cycle from differentiation in the early phases to cost leadership in the final phases.

Similarly, the strategic pricing approach changes over the product or service life cycle. In the first phase, pricing is set relatively high to recover development costs and to take advantage of product differentiation and the new demand for the product. In the second phase, pricing is likely to stay relatively high as the firm attempts to build profitability in the growing market. In the latter phases, pricing becomes more competitive,

---

[15] Manash R. Ray, "Cost Management for Product Development," *Journal of Cost Management,* Spring 1995, pp. 52–64; "Product Life Cycle Management," *Management Accounting Guideline Number 29* (The Society of Management Accountants of Canada, 1994); and "Product Value Analysis: Strategic Analysis over the Entire Product Life Cycle," *Journal of Cost Management,* May/June 1999, pp. 22–29.

Chapter 10 *Cost Planning for the Product Life Cycle: Target Costing, Theory of Constraints, and Long-Term Pricing* 399

REAL-WORLD FOCUS — Strategic Pricing and New Product Development Using the Sales Life Cycle: Palm, Elcho, and Gateway

STRATEGIC PRICING AT PALM, INC.

Palm, Inc., provides innovative handheld computing devices used in organization, e-mail, sales data entry, wireless Internet access, and other applications. Palm introduces a number of new products each year, and each new model offers greater functionality than the ones before it. As the new handheld models are introduced at competitive prices, the prices on older models are reduced, and Palm has profitable markets in each of the different life-cycle phases for these products.

NEW PRODUCT DEVELOPMENT AT ELCHO PAINT COMPANY

Elcho Paint Co., which specializes in plastic coatings for automotive and other applications, is a $90 million business that relies heavily on new product development. Approximately one-third of Elcho's 540 employees work in research and technical service. Elcho uses sales life-cycle analysis to plan new product development by grouping its products into product families that represent different generations of a particular application. This helps Elcho to ensure that it

continues to offer its customers up-to-date products in each product family. This approach also assists in product costing by facilitating the tracing of research and development costs (using ABC costing) to the product families and to the individual products.

NEW PRODUCT DEVELOPMENT AT GATEWAY, INC.

Gateway, Inc., manufacturer of computer products, is aware of analysts' forecasts that computer sales and prices are expected to slow in the coming five years because of market saturation. Like other manufacturers, Gateway has begun to seek new sources of revenue by offering financing programs, developing software, providing training classes, and offering Internet and other computer services. Training courses, in particular, have been very profitable for Gateway, realizing 90 percent profit margins.

Sources: Mehmet C. Kocakulah, Dorn Fowler, and Brian L. McGuire, "Implementing an ABC System to Stay Competitive: A Case Study," *Journal of Cost Management,* March/April 2000, pp. 15–19; "Pocketful of Savings," *Business Week,* April 17, 2000, p. 10; and "How PC Makers Are Reprogramming Themselves," *Business Week,* October 30, 2000, p. 64.

EXHIBIT 10.17 Critical Success Factors, Strategic Pricing, and Research and Development at the Four Stages of the Sales Life Cycle for a Manufacturer of Computer Processors

Computer Processor	Sales Life-Cycle Phase	Critical Success Factors	Strategic Pricing	Research and Development
Z300	Introduction	Differentiation, innovation, performance	Price is set relatively high because of demand and differentiation	Expenditures are very high to develop differentiation, innovation, and performance
Y300	Growth	Development of financial resources and manufacturing capacity to sustain growth; development of distribution channels and marketing	As above	Expenditures are high to maintain differentiation, innovation, and performance
X300	Maturity	Effective cost control, quality, service; development of new product features	Target costing is used; price is set by a competitive market	Value engineering is used to determine value/cost relationships through target costing
W300	Decline	Control of costs and effective distribution; reduction of capacity; timing of divest/spin-off	Low price is set	None

and target costing and life-cycle costing methods are used as the firm becomes more a price taker than a price setter and makes efforts to reduce upstream (for product enhancements) and downstream costs.

The Use of the Sales Life Cycle in Computer Manufacturing

Exhibit 10.17 summarizes the relationship between life-cycle phases, critical success factors, and desired pricing for a manufacturer of computer processors. The firm makes four processors: the Z300, Y300, X300, and W300. The Z300 is a very fast processor; the Y300 and X300 are somewhat slower, and the W300 is the slowest.

Summary

The strategic cost management concepts introduced in the preceding chapters are extended here. First, we discuss four cost management methods used to analyze the product or service's life cycle: target costing, the theory of constraints, life-cycle costing, and strategic pricing. Target costing is a tool for analyzing the cost structure to help management identify the proper design features and manufacturing methods to allow the firm to meet a competitive price. The five steps in target costing are (1) determine the market price, (2) determine the desired profit, (3) calculate the target cost (market price less desired profit), (4) use value engineering to identify ways to reduce product cost, and (5) use kaizen costing and operational control to further reduce costs.

The theory of constraints (TOC) is a tool that assists managers in identifying bottlenecks (constraints) and scheduling production to maximize throughput and profits. TOC analysis has five steps: (1) identify the constraint, (2) determine the most efficient product mix given the constraint, (3) maximize the flow through the constraint, (4) add capacity to the constraint, and (5) redesign the manufacturing process for flexibility and fast throughput.

Life-cycle costing assists managers in minimizing total cost over the product's or service's entire life cycle. Life-cycle costing brings a focus to the upstream activities (research and development, engineering) and downstream activities (marketing, distribution, service), as well as the manufacturing and operating costs that cost systems focus on. Especially important is a careful consideration of the effects of design choices on downstream costs. The four common design methods: (1) basic engineering in which engineering is done separately from marketing and production, (2) prototyping in which a working model of the product is developed for testing, (3) templating in which a new product is developed from the design of a similar existing product, and (4) concurrent engineering, that integrates marketing, manufacturing, and design to continually improve a product's design.

Strategic pricing helps management determine the price of the product or service based on life-cycle costs or in its position in the different phases of its sales life cycle.

Appendix A

Using the Flow Diagram to Identify Constraints

This chapter has illustrated the use of the flow diagram to identify the constraint when there are two or more products being produced through a common set of processes, with no specific completion time. The flow diagram can also be used when there is a single product or project and a specific completion time. In the latter case, which is illustrated in this appendix, the flow diagram is used to identify the processes that must be finished on time for the product or project to be completed on time.

To illustrate, suppose that a small pharmaceutical firm, Skincare Products, Inc. (SPI), manufactures an insect repellent with sun screen. To produce a batch of product, the firm mixes the active and inert ingredients in a large vat. Because of Food and Drug Administration requirements, SPI provides three inspections: (1) the raw materials it receives, (2) the mix of raw materials during the mixing process, and (3) the final product. The first and second inspections check the materials for correct chemical content and potency; the third inspection focuses on correct weight or item count. The manufacturing process has six processes, which are illustrated in Exhibit 10.18:

Process 1: Receive and inspect raw materials
Process 2: Mix raw materials
Process 3: Perform second inspection
Process 4: Fill and package
Process 5: Perform third inspection
Process 6: Attach labels

EXHIBIT 10.18
Flow Diagram for Skincare Products, Inc.

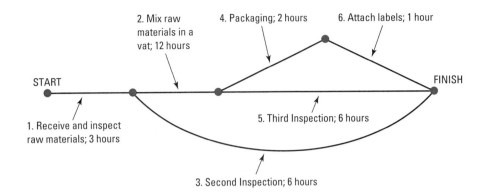

Exhibit 10.18 is a flow diagram of the work done that shows the sequence of processes and the amount of time required for each. The flow diagram is used to identify the constraints. Computer techniques do this for large networks, but the constraints for a smaller one such as Exhibit 10.18 can be identified by visual inspection. As defined earlier, a *constraint* is any process that delays the entire manufacturing process. The amount of the delay is often called *slack time*. Processes that can be delayed without delaying the finish time for the entire process are called *nonconstraints* or simply *slack* processes since the processes have some slack time in which to be completed. The constraints for SPI are as follows:

Process 1: Receive and inspect raw materials; required time, 3 hours

Process 2: Mix raw materials in vat; required time, 12 hours

Process 5: Perform third inspection; required time, 6 hours

The total time for the entire manufacturing process cannot be less than the total time of these three processes added together (3 + 12 + 6 = 21 hours) since these processes must follow in sequence and cannot overlap. The remaining processes—3, 4, and 6—are not constraints and can be delayed one or more hours without delaying the entire production process. The amount of the delay can be determined as follows. Process 3 requires 6 hours and must be finished while processes 2 and 5 are being completed, but because processes 2 and 5 require 18 hours (12 + 6) and process 3 requires only 6 hours, process 3 has 12 hours (18 − 6) of slack to be finished. Similarly, since processes 4 and 6 together require only 3 hours (2 hours plus 1 hour, respectively) and must be completed during process 5 (which requires 6 hours), in effect 3 hours of slack exist for processes 4 and 6 combined. Often the constraint processes (1, 2, and 5 in this case) are called critical processes since they cannot be delayed without delaying the entire batch of product. Also, the sequence of critical processes is often called the critical path.

Key Terms

Comments on Cost Management in Action

Why Go Abroad (to Latin America)? HP, Ericsson, IBM, Ford, and Volkswagen

In competitive industries such as computers, consumer electronics, and automobiles, manufacturers continuously look for ways to reduce cost and increase value throughout the value chain. These industries have chosen to locate extensive manufacturing operations and/or partners in Latin America to reduce cost and to benefit from innovative manufacturing methods and facilities. Wage costs are lower and, using target costing and value engineering, manufacturing processes are built around modular manufacturing methods that reduce the number of parts in the product, speeding the manufacturing process and reducing costs.

Consumer Electronics and Computer Products Why is outsourcing manufacturing to plants in Mexico an advantage to IBM, Ericsson, and HP? The contract manufacturers' manufacturing experience and technology give them a cost advantage. Flextronics and the other contract manufacturers also can focus on the manufacturing process rather than the entire product value chain. Moreover, they gain economies of scale by manufacturing similar products for different clients. The use of contract manufacturing is an important part of the strategy for HP and the others to achieve target costs while maintaining product leadership in design and customer service.

Global Automakers New manufacturing plants in Mexico and Brazil provide a number of global automakers innovative manufacturing processes as well as access to reduced costs for labor and other operations. The new plants utilize modular design/assembly approaches that significantly reduce the number of parts in the vehicle by combining parts into subassemblies provided by their suppliers. The plant becomes an automated assembler of these subassemblies, saving time and cost.

An additional benefit of the Latin American location for both electronics firms and automakers is that it substantially reduces transportation time and costs for shipments to major markets in North America relative to manufacturing plants located in Asia or other parts of the world.

Sources: Jonathan Friedland and Gary McWilliams, "How a Need for Speed Turned Guadalajara into a High-Tech Hub," *The Wall Street Journal,* March 2, 2000, p. 1; "Car Power: Special Report," *Business Week,* October 23, 2000, pp. 72–82; Peter Landers, "Why Some Sony Gear Is Made in Japan—By Another Company," *The Wall Street Journal,* June 14, 2001, p 1; Stephen H. Wildstrom, "Don't be Fooled by the Name on the Box," *Business Week,* June 17, 2002, p. 18; and "NAFTA's Scorecard: So Far, So Good," *Business Week,* July 9, 2001, pp. 54–56.

Self-Study Problem
(For solution, please turn to the end of the chapter.)

Best Brand Lighting, Inc.

Best Brand Lighting, Inc. (BBL) manufactures lighting fixtures. The two major markets for BBL products are major retailers, including Home Depot, Wal-Mart, and Kmart, and specialty lighting stores. The former sell primarily to homeowners, and the latter primarily to electrical contractors.

Although its standard sizes and models typically are sold to the large retailers, BBL sells its products with more specialized features and sizes only to the specialty stores. Thus, the design and manufacturing costs of the products going to the specialty stores are slightly higher. The products in both markets have similar sales life cycles of about two years.

Because of the difference in consumers, BBL has a larger marketing cost for the products sold to the large retailers—advertising in major media to attract homeowners. In contrast, the marketing for the specialty shops consists mainly of catalogs and advertisements in trade publications resulting in a lower overall marketing cost. The sales policies also differ somewhat for the two markets. Sales to specialty stores are priced higher but include significant discounts and attractive return policies. In contrast, sales to the major retailers have restrictive return policies and offer little, if any, discount.

BBL management is interested in an in-depth analysis of the profitability of its two markets. As a first step, it has asked for the average costs and other data for all BBL products:

	Major Retailers	Specialty Stores
Design costs	$ 0.80	$ 1.10
Manufacturing costs	5.20	5.90
Marketing costs	0.95	0.10
Returns	0.05	0.95
Discounts	0.10	0.95
Average price	10.55	12.50
Total market ($000) in BBL's sales region	188,000	32,000
Current unit sales	56,000	14,000

Required Using the methods discussed in this chapter, analyze BBL's two market segments. What questions would you want to ask management and which fact-finding studies would be appropriate to support this analysis?

Questions

10–1 Explain the two methods for reducing total product costs to achieve a desired target cost. Which is more common in the consumer electronics industries? In the specialized equipment manufacturing industries?

10–2   What does the term *sales life cycle* mean? What are the phases of the sales life cycle? How does it differ from the cost life cycle?

10–3   Do pricing strategies change over the different phases of the sales life cycle? Explain how.

10–4   Do cost management practices change over the product's sales life cycle? Explain how.

10–5   What is target costing? What types of firms use it?

10–6   What is life-cycle costing? Why is it used?

10–7   Name the five steps of the theory of constraints and explain the purpose of each. Which is the most important step and why?

10–8   What does the term *constraint* mean in the theory of constraint analysis?

10–9   What is the role of the flow diagram in the theory of constraints analysis?

10–10 What are the different methods of product engineering used in product design and life-cycle costing?

10–11 What does the concept of *value engineering* mean? How is it used in target costing?

10–12 What is the main difference between activity-based costing and the theory of constraints? When is it appropriate to use each one?

10–13 For what types of firms is the theory of constraints analysis most appropriate and why?

10–14 For what types of firms is target costing most appropriate and why?

10–15 For what types of firms is life-cycle costing most appropriate and why?

10–16 Explain the difference in intended application between strategic pricing and life-cycle costing.

Exercises

10–17 **Target Costing**   MaxiDrive manufactures a wide variety of parts for recreational boating, including a gear and driveshaft part for high-powered outboard boat engines. Original equipment manufacturers such as Mercury and Honda purchase the components for use in large, powerful outboards. The part sells for $610, and sales volume averages 25,000 units per year. Recently, MaxiDrive's major competitor reduced the price of its equivalent unit to $550. The market is very competitive, and MaxiDrive realizes it must meet the new price or lose significant market share. The controller has assembled these cost and usage data for the most recent year for MaxiDrive's production of 25,000 units:

	Standard Cost	Actual Quantity	Actual Cost
Materials	$6,500,000		$ 7,000,000
Direct labor	2,500,000		2,625,000
Indirect labor	2,500,000		2,400,000
Inspection (hours and cost)	—	1,000	350,000
Materials handling (number of purchases and cost)	—	3,450	485,000
Machine setups (number and cost)	—	1,500	725,000
Returns and rework (number of times and cost)	—	500	130,000
			$13,715,000

Required

1. Calculate the target cost for maintaining current market share and profitability.

2. Can the target cost be achieved? How?

10–18 **Target Costing**   Bowman Specialists Inc. (BSI) manufactures specialized equipment for polishing optical lenses. There are two models—one (A–25) principally used for fine eyewear and the other (A–10) for lenses used in binoculars, cameras, and similar equipment.

The manufacturing cost of each unit is calculated using activity-based costing, for these manufacturing cost pools:

Cost Pools	Allocation Base	Costing Rate
Materials handling	Number of parts	$2.25 per part
Manufacturing supervision	Hours of machine time	$23.50 per hour
Assembly	Number of parts	$2.55 per part
Machine setup	Each setup	$44.60 per setup
Inspection and testing	Logged hours	$35.00 per hour
Packaging	Logged hours	$15.00 per hour

BSI currently sells the A–10 model for $1,050 and the A–25 model for $725. Manufacturing costs and activity usage for the two products follow:

	A–10	A–25
Direct materials	$143.76	$66.44
Number of parts	121	92
Machine hours	6	4
Inspection time	1	0.6
Packing time	0.7	0.4
Setups	2	1

Required

1. Calculate the product cost and product margin for each product.

2. A new competitor has entered the market for lens-polishing equipment with a superior product at significantly lower prices, $825 for the A–10 model and $595 for the A–25 model. To try to compete, BSI has made some radical improvements in the design and manufacturing of its two products. The materials costs and activity usage rates have been decreased significantly:

	A–10	A–25
Direct materials	$78.65	$42.45
Number of parts	110	81
Machine hours	5	2
Inspection time	1	0.5
Packing time	0.7	0.2
Setups	1	1

Calculate the total product costs with the new activity usage data. Can BSI make a positive gross margin with the new costs, assuming that it must meet the price set by the new competitor?

3. Assume the information in requirement 2, but that BSI management is not satisfied with the gross margin on the A–10 after the cost improvements. BSI wants a $50 gross margin on A–10. Suppose you are able to change the number of parts to reduce costs further to achieve the desired $50 margin. How much would the number of parts have to change to provide the desired gross margin? [Hint: Use an Excel spreadsheet, and use the Goal Seek function.]

4. What cost management method might be useful to BSI at this time, and why?

10–19 **Determining the Impact of Evaluating Local Constraints**   Jim Gordon Nunes is a manufacturing manager at Perkins, Inc., with direct responsibility for the assembly department. Jim's department is the second of four manufacturing operations:

Receiving → Assembly → Heat Treatment → Shipping

He has just finished a class in the theory of constraints and is now doing his best to reduce the time and increase the flow through his department. He is the only Perkins manager trying to do this.

Required   Explain the likely outcome of Jim's actions and how you would have attempted to improve the throughput at Perkins, Inc.

10–20 **Pricing**   Johnson Inc. produces a single product, a part used in the manufacture of automobile transmissions. Known for its quality and performance, the part is sold to luxury auto manufacturers around the world. Because this is a quality product, Johnson has some flexibility in pricing the part. The firm calculates the price using a variety of pricing methods and then chooses the final price based on that information and other strategic information. A summary of the key cost information follows. Johnson expects to manufacture and sell 20,000 parts in the coming year. While the demand for Johnson's part has been growing in the past two years, management is not only aware of the cyclical nature of the automobile industry but also concerned about market share and profits during the industry's next downturn.

	Total Costs
Variable manufacturing	$1,800,000
Variable selling and administrative	240,000
Plant-level fixed overhead	350,000
Fixed selling and administrative	550,000
Batch-level fixed overhead	360,000
Total investment in product line	4,500,000
Expected sales (units)	20,000

Required

1. Determine the price for the part using a markup of 65 percent of full manufacturing cost.
2. Determine the price for the part using a markup of 35 percent of full life-cycle cost.
3. Determine the price for the part using a desired gross margin percentage to sales of 40 percent.
4. Determine the price for the part using a desired life-cycle cost percentage to sales of 25 percent.
5. Determine the price for the part using a desired before-tax return on investment of 18 percent.
6. Determine the contribution margin and operating profit for each of the methods in requirements 1 through 5. Which price would you choose, and why?

10–21 **Life-Cycle Costing**   Matt Simpson owns and operates Quality Craft Rentals, which offers canoe rentals and shuttle service on the Nantahala River. Customers can rent canoes at one station, enter the river there, and exit at one of two designated locations to catch a shuttle that returns them to their vehicles at the station they entered. Following are the costs involved in providing this service each year:

	Fixed Costs	Variable Costs
Canoe maintenance	$ 2,300	$2.50
Licenses and permits	3,000	0
Vehicle leases	5,400	0
Station lease	6,920	0
Advertising	6,000	0.50
Operating costs	21,000	0.50

Quality Craft Rentals began business three years ago with a $21,000 expenditure for a fleet of 30 canoes. These are expected to last seven more years, at which time a new fleet must be purchased.

Required Matt is happy with the steady rental average of 6,400 per year. For this number of rentals, what price should he charge per rental for the business to make a 20 percent life-cycle return on investment?

10–22 Matching Market Characteristics with Sales Life-Cycle Stages

Activities and Market Characteristics	Sales Life-Cycle Stage
Decline in sales	_____
Advertising	_____
Boost in production	_____
Stabilized profits	_____
Competitors' entrance into market	_____
Market research	_____
Market saturation	_____
Start production	_____
Product testing	_____
Termination of product	_____
Large increase in sales	_____

Required Insert the appropriate life-cycle stage in the space provided after each activity.

Problems

10–23 Target Costing in a Service Firm Alert Alarm Systems installs home security systems. Two of its systems, the ICU 100 and the ICU 900, have these characteristics:

Design Specifications	ICU 100	ICU 900	Cost Data
Video cameras	1	3	$150/ea.
Video monitors	1	1	$75/ea.
Motion detectors	5	8	$15/ea.
Floodlights	3	7	$8/ea.
Alarms	1	2	$15/ea.
Wiring	700 ft.	1,100 ft.	$0.10/ft.
Installation	16 hrs.	26 hrs.	$20/hr.

The ICU 100 sells for $810 installed, and the ICU 900 sells for $1,520 installed.

Required

1. What are the current profit margins on both systems?
2. Alert's management believes that it must drop the price on the ICU 100 to $750 and on the ICU 900 to $1,390 to remain competitive in the market. Recalculate profit margins for both products at these price levels.
3. Describe two ways that Alert could cut its costs to get the profit margins back to their original levels.

10–24 Target Costing, Strategy Benchmark Industries manufactures large workbenches for industrial use. Wayne Garrett, Benchmark's vice president for marketing, has concluded from his market analysis that sales are dwindling for the standard table because of aggressive pricing by competitors. This table sells for $875 whereas the competition sells a comparable table in the $800 range. Wayne has determined that dropping the price to $800 is necessary to regain the firm's annual market share of 10,000 tables. Cost data based on sales of 10,000 tables follow:

	Budgeted Amount	Actual Amount	Actual Cost
Direct materials	400,000 sq. ft.	425,000 sq. ft.	$2,700,000
Direct labor	85,000 hrs.	100,000 hrs.	1,000,000
Machine setups	30,000 hrs.	30,000 hrs.	300,000
Mechanical assembly	320,000 hrs.	320,000 hrs.	4,000,000

Required

1. Calculate the current cost and profit per unit.
2. How much of the current cost per unit is attributable to non-value-added activities?
3. Calculate the new target cost per unit for a sales price of $800 if the profit per unit is maintained.
4. What strategy do you suggest for Benchmark to attain the target cost calculated in requirement 3?

10–25 **Target Costing**   Morrow Company is a large manufacturer of auto parts for automakers and parts distributors. Although Morrow has plants throughout the world, most are in North America. Morrow is known for the quality of its parts and for the reliability of its operations. Customers receive their orders in a timely manner and there are no errors in the shipment or billing of these orders. For these reasons, Morrow has prospered in a business that is very competitive, with competitors such as Delphi, Visteon, and others.

Morrow just received an order for 100 auto parts from National Motors Corp., a major auto manufacturer. National proposed a $1,500 selling price per part. Morrow usually earned 20 per cent operating margin as a percent of sales. Morrow recently decided to use target costing in pricing its products. An examination of the production costs by the engineers and accountants showed that this part was assigned a standard full cost of $1,425 per part (this includes $1,000 production, $200 marketing, and $225 general and administration costs per part). Morrow's Value Assessment Group (VAG) undertook a cost reduction program for this part. Two production areas that were investigated were the defective unit rate and the tooling costs. The $1,000 production costs included a normal defective cost of $85 per part. Group leaders suggested that production changes could reduce defective cost to $25 per part.

Forty-five tools were used to make the auto part. The group discovered that the number of tools could be reduced to 30 and less expensive tools could be used on this part to meet National's product specifications. These changes saved an additional $105 of production cost per part. By studying other problem areas, the group found that general and administration costs could be reduced by $50 per unit through use of electronic data interchange with suppliers and just-in-time inventory management.

In addition, Morrow's sales manager told the group that National might be willing to pay a higher selling price because of Morrow's quality reputation and reliability. He believed National's proposed price was a starting point for negotiations. Of course, National had made the same offer to some of Morrow's competitors.

Required

1. What should be Morrow's target cost per auto part? Explain.
2. As a result of the Value Engineering Group's efforts, determine Morrow's estimated cost for the auto part. Will Morrow meet the target cost for the part? Do you recommend that Morrow take on the National offer? Explain your reasons.

(Adapted from a problem by Joseph San Miguel)

10–26 **Target Costing; Health Care**   MD Plus is a health maintenance organization (HMO) located in North Carolina. Unlike the traditional fee-for-service model that determines the payment according to the actual services used or costs incurred, MD Plus receives a fixed, prepaid amount from subscribers. The per member per month (PMPM) rate is determined by estimating the health care cost per enrollee within a geographic location. The average health care coverage in North Carolina sells for $115 per month. Because individuals are demanding quality care at reasonable rates, MD Plus must contain its costs to remain competitive. A major competitor, Doctors Nationwide, is entering the North Carolina market with a monthly premium of $109. MD Plus wants to maintain its current market penetration and hopes to increase its enrollees in 2005. The latest data on the number of enrollees and the associated costs follow:

Age	Number of Actual Enrollees in 2004	Number of Projected Enrollees in 2005	Average Monthly Cost in 2004
Less than 1 year	45,000	47,250	$ 3,825,000
1–4	80,500	84,525	6,842,500
5–14	95,000	99,750	8,075,000

(continued)

15–19	40,000	42,000	3,400,000
20–24	125,000	131,250	10,625,000
25–34	150,000	157,500	12,750,000
35–44	57,000	59,850	4,845,000
45–54	63,000	66,150	5,355,000
55–64	100,000	105,000	8,500,000
65–74	93,000	97,650	7,905,000
75–84	38,000	39,900	3,230,000
85 years and older	29,000	30,450	2,465,000
Total	915,500	961,275	$77,817,500

Required

1. Calculate the target cost required for MD Plus to maintain its current market share and profitability in 2004.
2. Because of rising inflation, MD Plus will charge $125 in 2005 while Doctors Nationwide will increase its premium by $15. Expenses for MD Plus are expected to increase by 6.8 percent in 2005. Based on the projected enrollees, calculate the target cost.
3. Identify the critical success factors for MD Plus. How can the HMO maintain its market share?

10–27 **Target Cost; Warehousing**   Johnson Supply, a wholesaler, has determined that its operations have three primary activities: purchasing, warehousing, and distributing. The firm reports the following pertinent operating data for the year just completed:

Activity	Cost Driver	Quantity of Cost Driver	Cost per Unit of Cost Driver
Purchasing	Number of purchasing orders	1,000	$100 per order
Warehousing	Number of moves	8,000	20 per move
Distributing	Number of shipments	500	80 per shipment

Johnson buys 100,000 units at an average unit cost of $5 and sells them at an average unit price of $10. The firm also has a fixed operating cost of $50,000 for the year.

Johnson's customers are demanding a 10 percent discount for the coming year. The company expects to sell the same amount if the demand for price reduction can be met. Johnson's suppliers, however, are willing to give only a 2 percent discount.

Required   Johnson has estimated that it can reduce the number of purchasing orders to 800 and can decrease the cost of each shipment $5 with minor changes in its operations. Any further cost saving must come from reengineering the warehousing processes. What is the maximum cost (i.e., target cost) for warehousing if the firm desires to earn the same amount of profit next year?

10–28 **Target Costing; International**   Harpers, Ltd., is a U.K. manufacturer of casual shoes for men and women. It has sustained strong growth in the U.K. market in recent years due to its close attention to fashion trends. Harpers' shoes also have a good reputation for quality and comfort. To expand the business, Harpers is considering introducing its shoes to the U.S. market, where comparable shoes sell for an average of $90 wholesale, more than $16 above what Harpers charges in the United Kingdom (average price, £46). Management has engaged a marketing consultant to obtain information about what features U.S. consumers seek in shoes if they desire different features. Harpers also has obtained information on the approximate cost of adding these features:

Features Desired in the United States	Cost to Add (in U.S. $)	Importance Rating (5 is most important)
Colorfast material	$4.50	3
Lighter weight	6.75	5
Extra-soft insole	3.00	4
Longer-wearing sole	3.00	2

The current average manufacturing cost of Harpers' shoes is £35 (approximately $56 U.S.), which provides an average profit of £11¼ ($18 U.S.) per pair sold. Harpers would like to maintain this profit margin; however, the firm recognizes that the U.S. market requires different features and that shipping and advertising costs would increase approximately $10 U.S. per pair of shoes.

Required

1. What is the target manufacturing cost for shoes to be sold in the United States?
2. Which features, if any, should Harpers add for shoes to be sold in the United States?
3. Critically evaluate Harpers' decision to begin selling shoes in the United States.

10–29 **Target Costing**   Westwind Yacht manufactures a line of family cruiser/racing sailboats. The boats are well-known for their quality, safety, and performance. Westwind hired Matthew Perry, a well-known sailboat designer and racer, to design a new sailboat, the M33. The M33 will have advanced materials in the hull and rigging to enhance the safety and performance of the boat, and also to improve its overnight comfort. Safety and comfort are the two most important boat-buying criteria of Westwind's customers, rated at 33 percent and 32 percent respectively, on a 100 point scale. The other two criteria are performance (20 percent) and styling (15 percent). The overall length of the boat is about 33 feet; its two sleeping areas have room for five or six people. Westwind projects a sale price of near $200,000 and estimates the costs of manufacturing the M33 as shown in Exhibit 10.19.

A team of engineers and sales managers studied the projected cost and were able to identify how each component of the planned boat contributed to satisfying the customers' criteria. The results of this study, based on careful estimates, is shown in Exhibit 10.20. For example, the estimates show that 30 percent of the customers' desire for safety is satisfied by the construction of the hull and keel, another 30 percent by the standing rigging.

EXHIBIT 10.19
Sailboat Components and Target Cost for the M33

Component	Target Cost	Percentage of Total
Hull and keel	$23,000	23%
Standing rig	15,000	15
Sails	22,000	22
Electrical	14,000	14
Other	26,000	26
		100%

EXHIBIT 10.20
Contribution of Each Component to Satisfying Customer Criteria for the M33

Component/Criteria	Safety	Styling	Performance	Comfort
Hull and keel	30%	20%	40%	20%
Standing rig	30	5	30	10
Sails	10	5	30	10
Electrical	20	10	—	—
Other	10	60	—	60
	100%	100%	100%	100%

Required

1. Using the component/criteria results in Exhibit 10.20 developed by the team of engineers and sales managers, together with the customer criteria, determine which components of the boat are most important to customers, and why.
2. Take your findings in requirement 1 and compare them against the target cost figures in Exhibit 10.19. What conclusions can you draw from this comparison?

10–30 **Theory of Constraints**   Precision Engineering Inc. (PEC) is a small manufacturer of precision tools used to construct research equipment for engineering departments at colleges and universities. It sells its two main products, PEC-1 and PEC-2, for $200 and $250, respectively. Due to increasing demand and shortage of specialized labor, PEC has found it increasingly difficult to meet the current weekly demand of 40 units of PEC-1 and 15 units of PEC-2. The following flow diagram shows the manufacturing requirements for the two products and the three types of materials required. Material A is used in PEC-1 only, Material C is used in PEC-2 only, and Material B is used in both PEC-1 and PEC-2.

The amount of weekly labor available for the four manufacturing operations follows:

Receiving and testing materials: 2,000 minutes
Machining (for Material A only): 3,500 minutes
Assembly: 2,000 minutes
Finishing: 3,500 minutes

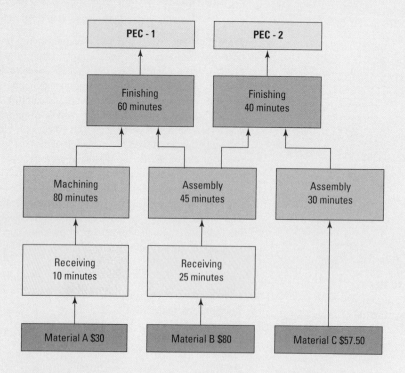

Assume that the labor for each operation is specialized and cannot be moved from one activity to another, that all operations except receiving and testing require a high level of skill, and that PEC cannot increase the capacity on these operations in the short run.

Required What is the best production plan for PEC? Why?

10–31 **Theory of Constraints; Strategy** Highpoint Furniture Co. is a small but fast-growing manufacturer of living room furniture. Its two principal products are end tables and sofas. The flow diagram for the manufacturing at Highpoint follows. Highpoint's manufacturing involves five processes: cutting the lumber, cutting the fabric, sanding, staining, and assembly. One employee cuts fabric and one does the staining. These are relatively skilled workers who could be replaced only with some difficulty. Two workers cut the lumber, and two others perform the sanding operation. There is some skill to these operations, but it is less critical than for staining and fabric cutting. Assembly requires the lowest skill level and is currently done by one full-time employee and a group of part timers who provide a total of 175 hours of working time per week. The other employees work a 40-hour week, with 5 hours off for breaks, training, and personal time. Assume a four-week month and that by prior agreement, none of the employees can be switched from one task to another. The current demand for Highpoint's products and sales prices are as follows, although Highpoint expects demand to increase significantly in the coming months if it is able to successfully negotiate an order from a motel chain.

	End Tables	Sofas
Price	$300	$550
Current demand (units per month)	300	180

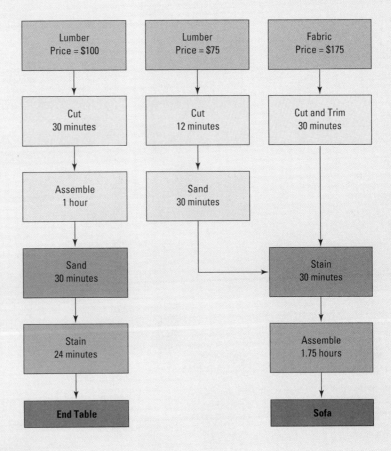

Required

1. What is the most profitable production plan for Highpoint? Explain your answer with supporting calculations.

2. How would you apply the five steps of the theory of constraints to Highpoint's manufacturing operations? What would you recommend for each step?

10–32 **Theory of Constraints**   Industrial Products Company (IPC) produces a variety of chemicals, primarily adhesives, lubricants, and polymers for industrial use by manufacturers to produce plastics and other compounds. Don Leo, the production vice president, has been informed of a disturbing trend of increasing customer complaints regarding late deliveries from the Canton, Kentucky, plant. The Canton plant is one of the firm's newest and most modern plants and is dedicated to the manufacture of two products, Polymer 1 and Polymer 2. Don has downloaded some incomplete recent information about the Canton plant onto his laptop; he plans to analyze the information in the hour or so he has before his next meeting of the IPC executive committee. He is concerned that some comments will be made about the problems at Canton, and he wants to have an idea of how to respond. Because IPC views Polymer 1 and Polymer 2 as very promising in terms of both sales and profit potential, the news of these problems is likely to spark some comment. The data downloaded by Don is as follows:

	Number of Hours Required for Each Product		Number of Hours Available per Week
Activity	**Polymer 1**	**Polymer 2**	
Filtering	?	?	320
Stripping	?	?	320
Reacting	3.0	5.0	320
Final filtering	2.0	1.0	160
Mixing	?	?	320
Other information			
Current sales demand (per week)	60	40	
Price	$105	$150	

Don has sketched the following flow diagram for the Canton plant. He believes it is relatively accurate because of his frequent contact with the plant.

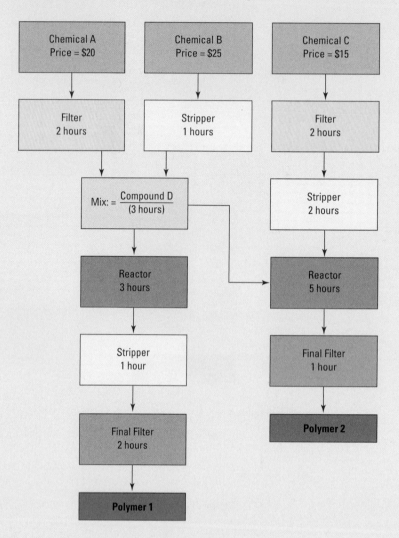

Required Prepare a short set of notes that Don can use in the executive meeting if questions come up about the problems at the Canton plant.

10–33 **Theory of Constraints** Bakker Industries sells three products (611, 613, and 615) that it manufactures in four departments. Both labor and machine time are applied to products in each of the four departments. The machine-processing and labor skills required in each department prohibit switching either machines or labor from one department to another. However, Bakker has a good supply of both full-time and part-time labor and does not expect hiring or retention of employees to be a problem. Because of the availability of part-time labor, Bakker considers labor a variable cost and includes it in the calculation of throughput margin.

Bakker's management is planning its production schedule for the next several months. Some machines will be out of service for extensive overhauling. Available machine times by department for each of the next six months are as follows:

	Department			
	1	**2**	**3**	**4**
Normal machine capacity in machine-hours	3,500	3,500	3,000	3,500
Capacity of machines being repaired, in machine-hours	500	400	300	200
Available capacity in machine-hours	3,000	3,100	2,700	3,300

Labor and machine specifications per unit of product follow:

Product	Labor and Machine Time	Department			
		1	2	3	4
611	Direct labor-hours	2	3	3	1
	Machine-hours	2	1	2	2
613	Direct labor-hours	1	2	0	2
	Machine-hours	1	1	0	2
615	Direct labor-hours	2	2	1	1
	Machine-hours	2	2	1	1

The Sales Department's forecast of product demand over the next six months is as follows:

Product	Monthly Sales
611	500 units
613	400 units
615	1,000 units

Bakker's inventory levels will not increase or decrease during the next six months. The unit price and cost data valid for the next six months follow:

	Product		
	611	613	615
Price	$196	$123	$167
Direct materials	7	13	17
Direct labor			
Department 1	12	6	12
Department 2	21	14	14
Department 3	24	—	16
Department 4	9	18	9
Variable overhead	27	20	25
Fixed overhead	15	10	32
Variable selling	3	2	4

Required

1. Determine whether Bakker can meet the monthly sales demand for the three products. What department is a constraint, if any?
2. What monthly production schedule would be best for Bakker Industries?

(CMA Adapted)

10-34 **Life-Cycle Costing** Tim Waters, the COO of BioDerm, has asked his cost management team for a product-line profitability analysis for his firm's two products, Xderm and Yderm. The two skin care products require a large amount of research and development and advertising. After receiving the following statement from BioDerm's auditor, Tim concludes that Xderm is the more profitable product and that perhaps cost-cutting measures should be applied to Yderm.

	Xderm	Yderm	Total
Sales	$3,000,000	$2,000,000	$5,000,000
Cost of goods sold	(1,900,000)	(1,600,000)	(3,500,000)
Gross profit	$1,100,000	$ 400,000	$1,500,000
Research and development			(900,000)
Selling expenses			(100,000)
Profit before taxes			$ 500,000

Required

1. Explain why Tim may be wrong in his assessment of the relative performances of the two products.

2. Suppose that 80 percent of the R&D and selling expenses are traceable to Xderm. Prepare life-cycle income statements for each product and calculate the return on sales. What does this tell you about the importance of accurate life-cycle costing?

3. Consider again your answers in requirements 1 and 2 with the following additional information. R&D and selling expenses are substantially higher for Xderm because it is a new product. Tim has strongly supported development of the new product, including the high selling and R&D expenses. He has assured senior managers that the Xderm investment will pay off in improved profits for the firm. What are the ethical issues, if any, facing Tim as he reports to top management on the profitability of the firm's two products?

10–35 Life-Cycle Costing   Starcom Communications Technologies, Inc., has introduced a new phone so small that it can be carried in a wallet. Starcom invested $400,000 in research and development for the technology and another $800,000 to design and test the prototypes. It predicts a four-year life cycle for this phone and has gathered this cost data for it:

	Monthly Fixed Costs	**Variable Costs**
Manufacturing costs	$25,000	$20
Marketing costs	20,000	5
Customer service costs	3,000	8
Distribution costs	5,000	15

Sales predictions:
For price of $150—average annual sales of 20,000 units.
For price of $180—average annual sales of 15,000 units.
For price of $225—average annual sales of 12,000 units.

If the price of a wallet phone is $225, Starcom must increase its research and development costs by $100,000 and the prototyping costs by $400,000 to improve the model for the higher price. Fixed customer service costs would also increase by $500 per month and variable distribution costs would increase by $5 per unit to improve the customer service and distribution at the $225 level. At the lowest price level of $150, fixed marketing costs would be reduced by $5,000 per month because the low price would be the principal selling feature.

Required

1. Determine the life-cycle costs for each pricing decision.

2. What price for the wallet phone's life cycle will produce the most profit for Starcom?

10–36 Life-Cycle Costing   The following revenue and cost data are for Turner Manufacturing's two radial saws. The L40 is for the commercial market and the L50 is for industrial customers. Both products are expected to have three-year life cycles.

L40 ($ in thousands)	2001	2002	2003
Revenues	$ 800	$2,300	$3,100
Costs			
Research and development	1,400	—	—
Prototypes	350	50	—
Marketing	60	600	475
Distribution	60	120	130
Manufacturing	20	770	1,350
Customer service	—	60	85
Total cost	$ 1,890	$1,600	$2,040
Operating margin	$(1,090)	$ 700	$1,060

L50 ($ in thousands)	2001	2002	2003
Revenues	$ 900	$1,900	$2,200
Costs			
Research and development	650	—	—
Prototypes	300	30	10
Marketing	124	200	260
Distribution	170	200	410
Manufacturing	85	700	770
Customer service	—	20	300
Total cost	$1,329	$1,150	$1,750
Operating margin	$ (429)	$ 750	$ 450

Required

1. How would a product life-cycle income statement differ from the above income statements?
2. Prepare a three-year life-cycle income statement for both products. Which product appears to be more profitable?
3. Prepare a schedule showing each cost category as a percentage of total annual costs. What do you think this indicates about the profitability of each product over the three-year life cycle?

10–37 **Life-Cycle Costing, Health Care, Present Value**   Cure-all, Inc., has developed a drug that will diminish the effects of aging. Cure-all has spent $1,000,000 on research and development and $2,108,000 for clinical trials. Once the drug is approved by the FDA, which is imminent, it will have a five-year sales life cycle. Laura Russell, Cure-all's chief financial officer, must determine the best alternative for the company among three options. The company can choose to manufacture, package, and distribute the drug; outsource only the manufacturing; or sell the drug's patent. Laura has compiled the following annual cost information for this drug if the company were to manufacture it:

Cost Category	Fixed Costs	Variable Cost per Unit
Manufacturing	$5,000,000	$68.00
Packaging	380,000	20.00
Distribution	1,125,000	6.50
Advertising	2,280,000	12.00

Management anticipates a high demand for the drug and has benchmarked $235 per unit as a reasonable price based on other drugs that promise similar results. Management expects sales volume of 3,000,000 units over five years and uses a discount rate of 10%.

If Cure-all chooses to outsource the manufacturing of the drug while continuing to package, distribute, and advertise it, the manufacturing costs would result in fixed costs of $1,500,000 and variable cost of $80. For the sale of the patent, Cure-all would receive $300,000,000 now and $25,000,000 at the end of every year for the next five years.

Required   Determine the best option for Cure-all. Support your answer.

10–38 **Manufacturing Cycle Efficiency**   Waymouth Manufacturing operates a contract manufacturing plant in Dublin, Ireland. The plant produces a variety of electronics products and components to manufacturers around the world. Cycle time is a critical success factor for Waymouth, which has developed a number of measures of manufacturing speed. The company has studied the matter and found that competitive contract manufacturers have manufacturing cycle efficiency (MCE) times of about 40 percent. When last measured, Waymouth's MCE was 35 percent.

Some key measures from the most recent month's production, averaged over all the jobs during that period, are as follows:

Activity	Average Number of Hours
New product development	30 hours
Materials handling	3
Order setup	6
Machine maintenance	3
Order scheduling	1
Inspection of completed order	5
Packaging and move to storage or ship	2
Manufacturing assembly	23
Order taking and verification	3
Raw materials receipt and stocking	6
Inspection of raw materials	2

Required   Determine the MCE time for the most recent month. What can you infer from the MCE time that you calculated?

10–39 **Constraint Analysis, Flow Diagrams (Appendix)**   Silver Aviation assembles small aircraft for commercial use. The majority of its business is with small freight airlines serving areas whose airports do not accommodate larger planes. The remainder of Silver's customers are commuter airlines and individuals who use planes in their businesses, such as the owners of larger ranches. Silver recently expanded its market into Central and South America, and the company expects to double its sales over the next three years.

To schedule work and track all projects, Silver uses a flow diagram. The diagram for the assembly of a single cargo plane is shown in Exhibit 10.21. The diagram shows four alternative paths with the critical path being *ABGEFJK*. Bob Peterson, president of Coastal Airlines, recently placed an order with Silver Aviation for five cargo planes. During contract negotiations, Bob agreed to a delivery time of 13 weeks (five work days per week) for the first plane with the balance of the planes being delivered at the rate of one every four weeks. Because of problems with some of the aircraft that Coastal is currently using, Bob contacted Grace Vander, sales manager for Silver Aviation, to ask about improving the delivery date of the first cargo plane. Grace replied that she believed the schedule could be shortened by as much as 10 work days or two weeks, but the cost of assembly would increase as a result. Bob said he would be willing to consider the increased costs, and they agreed to meet the following day to review a revised schedule that Grace would prepare.

Because Silver Aviation previously assembled aircraft on an accelerated basis, the company has a list of crash costs for this purpose. Grace used the data shown in Exhibit 10.22 to develop a plan to cut 10 working days from the schedule at a minimum increase in cost to Coastal Airlines. Upon completing her plan, she reported to Bob that Silver would be able to cut 10 working days from the schedule for an associated increase in cost of $6,000. Grace's Exhibit 10.23 shows accelerated assembly schedule for the cargo plane starting from the regularly scheduled days and cost.

Required

1. Explain why Grace's plan is unsatisfactory.
2. Revise the accelerated assembly schedule so that Coastal Airlines will take delivery of the first plane ahead of schedule at the least incremental cost to Coastal.

EXHIBIT 10.21   Flow Diagram for Plane Assembly

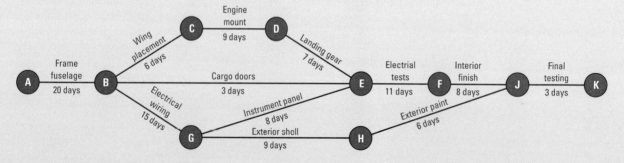

EXHIBIT 10.22
Crash Cost Listing

Activity		Expected Activity Times		Direct Cost		Added Crash Cost Per Reduced Day
		Regular	Crash	Regular	Crash	
AB	Frame fuselage	20 days	16 days	$12,000	$16,800	$1,200
BC	Wing placement	6	5	3,600	5,000	1,400
CD	Engine mount	9	7	6,600	8,000	700
DE	Landing gear	7	5	5,100	6,700	800
BE	Cargo doors	3	3	1,400	1,400	—
BG	Electrical wiring	15	13	9,000	11,000	1,000
GE	Instrument panel	8	6	5,700	8,300	1,300
EF	Electrical tests	11	10	6,800	7,600	800
GH	Exterior shell	9	7	4,200	5,200	500
FJ	Interior finish	8	7	3,600	4,000	400
HJ	Exterior paint	6	5	3,600	4,000	400
JK	Final testing	3	2	3,500	4,400	900
				$65,100	$82,400	

EXHIBIT 10.23
Accelerated Plane Assembly Schedule

Activity Crashed	Additional Cost per Day	Total Direct Cost
		$65,100
HJ by one day	$400	65,500
FJ by one day	400	65,900
GH by two days	500	66,900
CD by two days	700	68,300
EF by one day	800	69,100
DE by two days	800	70,700
BG by one day	1,000	71,700

3. Calculate the incremental costs that Bob will have to pay for this revised accelerated delivery.

(CMA Adapted)

10–40 **Production Planning and Control Strategy**   This is a story about manufacturing performance at one plant of a large company. It begins with Kristen Reynolds, a relatively new plant manager, coming to visit Bryan Simpkins, the plant's head of manufacturing. Kristen and Bryan work for ITR Incorporated, a manufacturer of lighting fixtures with plants located in six countries and worldwide sales. The plant that Kristen and Bryan manage is located in Canada near Hamilton, Ontario. It is the one plant in ITR's system that focuses on custom orders that require special materials, setup, and assembly. The other five plants supply ITR's high-volume, standardized products. Because of changes in the residential and commercial construction industries, the demand for custom orders at the Ontario plant has been increasing steadily. Unfortunately, it has not been filling these orders as quickly as Kristen would like. Many solid customers are waiting days or weeks longer for their orders than they did a year ago; moreover, some ITR sales people have begun to be evasive when customers ask how soon their orders can be filled. Kristen does not know how this is affecting sales or customer goodwill.

Kristen: Hi, Bryan. It's good to see you. I hope all is well with you and the family.

Bryan: Going great—though I just learned that Jimmy will have to have braces on his teeth. I don't even want to think of how much that will cost.

Kristen: Hey, I've been through that too. No fun. (pause) Bryan, I haven't visited the plant operations in some time. Would you take me for a quick tour?

Bryan: Let's go.

Bryan and Kristen first visit an operation where a skilled worker is operating a machine that molds a metal frame on which multiple light fixtures will later be installed. They watch as the worker (name badge says Ed) completes the last of a batch of 15 frames. Kristen asks how long this batch took him, and he says 82 minutes. "I know this exactly because I have productivity standards to meet, and I must record my time on all jobs. My standard is 6 minutes per item, so I beat my goal." Ed then examines each frame and finds that one has a bad twist and must be rejected; this takes about 10 minutes. He then pushes a button near the machine that calls another worker to remove the defective frame. Meanwhile, Ed loads the 14 good ones on a cart and moves them to the next manufacturing station. Bryan and Kristen note that many frames are already waiting at the next station.

The worker who was called to remove the defective frame tags it, writes up the potential cause(s) for the defect, and then moves the frame to the area of the plant designated for scrap and rework. Kristen and Bryan look at the defect report and note that it indicates two possibilities which will be studied further by another worker assigned to the scrap and rework area. The two possibilities are poor-quality materials, as determined by apparent weaknesses in portions of the framing material and poor work quality (Ed could have damaged the frame accidentally by banging it against one of the roof support beams located next to his work area). Kristen and Bryan note that Ed's workstation area is indeed pretty cramped.

They move to another workstation, which has no operator. By asking a worker at the adjacent station, they determine that the station is down because the machine needs repair. "Joe usually works that station, but he is helping out in the shipping department until his machine is repaired."

They move to another workstation that looks very busy. An order marked "urgent" is waiting at this station, while Dan, the operator, quickly finishes another order. Bryan asks Dan why he has not started the urgent order, and Dan explains that he cannot afford to stop the machine and set it up for another order. This would cost him some time that would lower his productivity on the current job. Dan explains that it is important that he get the items done in the current order quickly, within a standard level of productivity, or production supervisors will be coming to call. Dan says he sees the urgent sign and is working quickly to get to it. He says he might even delay lunch to start it.

To investigate some of the things they observed, Kristen and Bryan next visit the purchasing department. Here they find that the frame material Ed used was purchased from a relatively new vendor at an unbelievably low price. The purchasing department manager approved the purchase because other purchases in the month had gone over budget and this was a way to help meet the budget. The budget is a predetermined amount that the purchasing department is expected to spend each month. Plant policy requires an investigation of any large variances from the budget.

Next Kristen and Bryan inquire about Joe's machine. A check at the job scheduler's desk shows that the workstation had been in use constantly for the last few weeks. Joe said that he noticed a funny noise but had not reported it because he had some jobs to finish and his productivity is measured by how quickly he finished them. His time between jobs is not measured, but doing jobs quickly is important. Bryan asks the job scheduler why Ed's work area is so crowded since there appears to be plenty of room elsewhere in the plant. The job scheduler says that he is not sure, but that it probably has to do with the fact that each production department is charged a certain amount of plant overhead based on the amount of square feet of space that department occupies. Thus, the department manager for whom Ed works is likely to have reduced the space as much as possible to reduce these overhead charges.

As the story ends, Bryan and Kristen are looking for an answer to how urgent orders are scheduled and moved through the plant.

Required   Consider the manufacturing processes observed in ITR's Ontario plant. What recommendations do you think Bryan and Kristen should make?

Solution to Self-Study Problem

Best Brand Lighting, Inc.

A thorough analysis will require a good deal more inquiry of management and fact finding than is available from the limited information provided earlier, but a few useful observations can be made.

1. Encourage BBL to consider increasing the effort put into design to reduce manufacturing costs and to reduce the relatively high rate of product returns in the speciality segment. The cost of design appears low relative to manufacturing and downstream costs, especially in the specialty segment. Inquire about which types of design approaches are being used. Urge BBL to adopt concurrent engineering–based methods, especially because of the relatively short market life cycles in the industry.

2. Consider additional analysis of pricing. Because of BBL's strong acceptance in the specialty segment and because the differentiation strategy is likely to be important in that segment, a price increase might yield higher profits with little or no loss in market share.

Cost leadership appears to be the appropriate strategy in the major retail segment; inquire what methods the company is using to reduce overall product costs in this segment.

Also, investigate further the rate of customer returns for each product. Is this due to design problems or problems in sales management?

3. Consider a further analysis of marketing expenses. Would an increase in marketing effort in the major retailer segment improve sales in this segment?

4. Consider the need to perform a detailed analysis by product category within each market segment. A detailed analysis might uncover important information about opportunities to reduce cost and add value within the products' value chain.

5. Because of the relatively short sales life cycles, consider whether target costing could be used effectively at BBL. How intense is the level of competition in the industry, and to what extent are trade-offs made between functionality and price in the development and introduction of each new product? If the level of competition is very intense, and trade-offs between functionality and price are key strategic decisions, target costing should be a useful management tool.

6. Investigate the costing system. Is it activity-based? How accurate are the cost figures that it develops?

CHAPTER ELEVEN

Process Costing

After studying this chapter, you should be able to . . .

1. Identify the types of firms or operations for which a process costing system is most suitable
2. Explain and calculate equivalent units
3. Describe the five steps in process costing
4. Demonstrate the weighted-average method of process costing
5. Demonstrate the FIFO method of process costing
6. Analyze process costing with multiple departments
7. Prepare journal entries to record the flow of costs in a process costing system
8. Explain how process costing systems are implemented and enhanced in practice
9. Account for spoilage in process costing

The Coca-Cola Company is the world's leading manufacturer, marketer, and distributor of soft drink concentrates, syrups, and soft drinks. Coca-Cola's strategy focuses on both price and differentiation.[1]

Coca-Cola's differentiation strategy is apparent in its positioning: It positions itself as a unique and special product with a young, fresh image equal to none in the soft drink segment; it is a permanent reminder of classic values, of American culture inside and outside the country, and of all things American: entertainment, sports, and youth. Furthermore, its brand is recognized in practically every country in the world. Its exclusive formula makes it unique.

Coca-Cola uses process costing to track product and customer costs such as direct materials, direct labor, and overhead costs incurred in three major processes: (1) concentrate and syrup manufacturing, (2) blending, and (3) packaging. During the first process, mixing water with sugar, colorings, and other ingredients produces concentrates, and adding sweeteners and water to the concentrates produces syrups. In the second process, pure carbon dioxide is added to the blend of syrups and water to produce the beverage. In the third process, a filler injects a precise amount of the blended beverage into plastic bottles or cans, and a metal crown or plastic closure seals the package.

Process costing is a product costing system that accumulates costs according to processes or departments and assigns them to a large number of nearly identical products. The typical firm that uses process costing employs a standardized production process to manufacture homogeneous products. Process costing provides information for managers to analyze product and customer profitability and to make pricing, product-mix, and process improvement decisions.

In today's globally competitive environment, managers must know product costs to be able to make good decisions. Imagine a large corporation's top manager trying to decide whether to discontinue a product without knowing what it cost to produce. Managers need cost information for setting goals; forming strategy; developing long- and short-term planning; and for control, performance measurement, and decision-making purposes.

---

[1] For more about the Coca-Cola success story, see its website at www.coke.com; "Coca Cola Co.: Soft Drink Maker Opens $50 Million Plant in China," *The Wall Street Journal,* March 30, 1998; "Coca Cola CEO Speaks to Georgia CPAs," *Journal of Accountancy,* February 1999; and Keith Johnson, "Design Choice: Coke Bottle," *Marketing,* October 7, 1999, pp. 16–17.

Process costing also allows accountants to determine unit costs needed for valuing inventory and the cost of goods sold for external financial reports. For example, Milliken & Co. (www.milliken.com) uses an activity-based costing type of process costing to help managers focus on the actual costs in each process and to reduce non-value-added work in each process.[2]

Characteristics of Process Costing Systems

LEARNING OBJECTIVE 1
Identify the types of firms or operations for which a process costing system is most suitable.

Firms having homogeneous products that pass through a series of similar processes or departments use process costing. These firms usually engage in continuous mass production of a few similar products. Manufacturing costs are accumulated in each process. The departmental production cost report is a key document in tracking production quantity and cost information. Unit product cost is calculated by dividing process costs in each department by the number of equivalent units produced during the period.

The process cost system is used in many industries such as chemicals, oil refining, textiles, paints, flour, canneries, rubber, steel, glass, food processing, mining, automobile production lines, electronics, plastics, drugs, paper, lumber, leather goods, metal products, sporting goods, cement, and watches. Process costing can also be used by service organizations with homogeneous services and repetitive processes such as check processing in a bank or mail sorting by a courier. Companies using process costing include Coca-Cola (www.coca-cola.com), Royal Dutch Shell Group (www.shell.com), Bethlehem Steel (www.bethsteel.com), International Paper (www.internationalpaper.com), and Kimberly-Clark (www.kimberly-clark.com).

Equivalent Units

LEARNING OBJECTIVE 2
Explain and calculate equivalent units.

A manufacturing firm typically has partially completed units at the end of an accounting period. Under the job costing system, these partially completed units are not difficult to handle because job costs are available on job cost sheets.

In a process costing system, however, product costs for partially completed units are not readily available. Because the focus in cost accounting has shifted from jobs to processes or departments, the interest is in the unit cost of performing a certain *process* for a given period. The goal is to find the combined unit cost of all product units processed in that period, including those that are partially complete at either the beginning or the end of the accounting period. Note that by *partially complete,* we mean partially complete for that department; a unit could be complete for a given department but still be in the Work-in-Process Inventory account if this is not the final department.

The calculation of the product cost begins with determining the production cost per unit in each production department. These unit costs are incorrect if the amount of work done on partially complete units is not considered. Therefore, the cost calculations must be adjusted for partially complete units so that all units included in the computations reflect work actually done in the period.

With both complete and partially complete units, we need a way to measure the proper amount of production work performed during a period. An equivalent unit is one such measure. The problem of equivalent units arises because we take a continuous process and break it into separate, distinct time periods. The process is continuous, but the reporting is periodic, such as monthly or yearly.

Equivalent units
are the number of the same or similar complete units that could have been produced given the amount of work actually performed on both complete and partially complete units.

Equivalent units are the number of the same or similar complete units that could have been produced given the amount of work actually performed on both complete and partially complete units. Equivalent units are not the same as physical units. For example, suppose in a given month a chemical company had in process 30,000 gallons of a chemical, of which 20,000 gallons were complete at the end of the month but the remaining 10,000 gallons were only 50 percent complete. The equivalent units would be 25,000 gallons [20,000 + (10,000 × 50%)].

The equivalent units should be calculated separately for direct materials, direct labor, and factory overhead because the proportion of the total work performed on the product units in the work-in-process inventories is not always the same for each cost element. Partially complete units are often complete for direct materials but incomplete for direct labor and factory overhead. Examples include chemical or brewing processes that add direct materials in at the beginning but are not complete until the cooking process, which can extend over hours or days, is finished. Some firms divide costs into direct materials and conversion cost categories. *Conversion costs* are the sum of direct labor and factory overhead costs.

Conversion Costs

For many process industries, such as the oil refinery, aluminum, paper, chemical, and pharmaceutical industries, factory overhead and direct labor costs are often combined under conversion costs for the purpose of computing equivalent units of production. Linking these two cost elements is practical because the direct labor cost is not a significant cost element in most process industries.

Many manufacturing operations incur conversion costs uniformly throughout production. The equivalent units of conversion costs are therefore the result of multiplying the percentage of work that is complete during the period by the number of units on which work is partially complete. For example, for 1,000 units estimated to be 30 percent complete in the work-in-process ending inventory, the equivalent units of conversion in the period are 300 (30 percent × 1,000 units).

Firms using nonlabor-based cost drivers (such as machine-hours or the number of setups) for their factory overhead costs find that calculating separate equivalent units of production for factory overhead and direct labor costs is more appropriate.

Direct Materials

Direct materials can be added at discrete points of manufacturing or continuously over production. If the materials are added uniformly, the proportion used for computing equivalent units of direct materials is the same as the proportion for conversion costs. However, if the materials are added all at once, the proportion used in the computation depends on whether the point in the process where the materials are added has been reached.

Exhibit 11.1 illustrates the determination of equivalent units in direct materials for ending work-in-process (WIP) inventory. The example assumes that ending work-in-process (WIP) inventory has 1,500 product units that are 60 percent complete. Exhibit 11.1 has four materials-adding timing situations: (1) materials are added gradually throughout the process, (2) all materials are added at the beginning of the process, (3) all materials are added at the 40 percent point, and (4) all materials are added at the end of the process.

Flow of Costs in Process Costing

In process costing costs flow through different processes or departments. Exhibit 11.2 is a T-account model of direct materials, direct labor, and factory overhead cost flows in a two-department process costing system. Note four key points in this exhibit. First, a separate Work-in-Process Inventory account is used to record costs of each production department. Second, when Department A finishes its work, the costs of the goods completed are transferred to Department B's Work-in-Process Inventory account for further work. After this further work, the costs of goods completed are then transferred to the Finished Goods Inventory account. Third, direct materials, direct labor, and factory overhead costs can be entered directly into either production department's Work-in-Process Inventory account, not just that of the first department. Finally, starting with

EXHIBIT 11.1 Equivalent Units for Direct Materials under Ending Inventory

			Equivalent Units for Direct Materials This Period			
Type of Inventory	Physical Units Partially Complete	Percentage of Completion for Conversion	Materials Added Gradually	All Materials Added at the Beginning	All Materials Added at 40 Percent Point	All Materials Added at the End
Ending work-in-process inventory	1,500	60%	1,500 × 60% = 900	1,500 × 100% = 1,500	1,500 × 100% = 1,500	0

EXHIBIT 11.2 T-Account Model of Flow of Costs for Two Departments in Process Costing

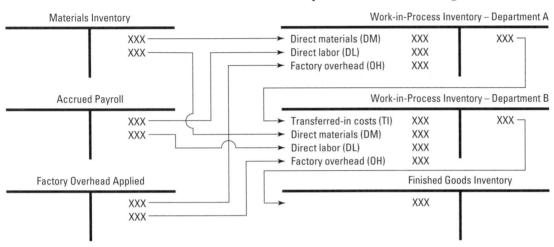

the second department (Department B), an additional cost element, *transferred-in-costs* (TI), appears. These are costs of the goods completed in the prior department and transferred into this department during the period.

Steps in Process Costing

The key document in a typical process costing system is the production cost report, prepared at the end of each period for each production process or department. The **production cost report** summarizes the number of physical units and equivalent units of a department, the costs incurred during the period, and the costs assigned to both units completed and transferred out and ending work-in-process inventories. The preparation of a production cost report includes the five steps in Exhibit 11.3.

Step 1: Analyze Flow of Physical Units

The first step determines which units were on hand at the beginning of the period, how many units were started (or received from the prior production department), which units were completed, and which units are in ending work-in-process inventory.

The analysis of physical units includes accounting for both input and output units. *Input units* include beginning work-in-process inventory and all units that enter a

EXHIBIT 11.3
Five Steps in Process Costs

1. Analyze the physical flow of production units.
2. Calculate equivalent units of production for all manufacturing cost elements.
3. Determine total cost for each manufacturing cost element.
4. Compute cost per equivalent unit for each manufacturing cost element.
5. Assign the total manufacturing costs to units completed and units of work in process at the end of the period.

production department during an accounting period. *Output units* include units that are complete and transferred out from a production department or are in the work-in-process inventory at the end of a period.

Step 2: Calculate Equivalent Units

The purpose of calculating equivalent units of production for direct materials, direct labor, and factory overhead is to measure the total work effort expended on production during an accounting period. The partially complete physical units are converted into the equivalent number of whole units.

Step 3: Determine Total Costs to Account For

The total manufacturing costs to account for include the current costs incurred and the costs of the units in the work-in-process beginning inventory. The amount of these costs is obtained from material requisitions, labor time cards, and factory overhead allocation sheets.

Step 4: Compute Unit Costs

The purpose of computing direct materials, direct labor, and factory overhead costs per equivalent unit of production is to have a proper product costing and income determination for an accounting period.

Step 5: Assign Total Manufacturing Costs

The objective of the production cost report is to assign total manufacturing costs incurred to the units completed and transferred out during the period and the units that are still in process at the end of the period. The total costs assigned in step 5 should equal the total costs to be accounted for in step 3.

Companies generally divide the five-step production cost report into three parts: production quantity information, unit cost determination, and cost assignment. The first part includes step 1, analyze flow of physical units, and step 2, calculate equivalent units. The second part includes step 3, determine total costs to account for, and step 4, compute equivalent unit cost. The third part includes step 5, assign total manufacturing costs (total costs accounted for).

Process Costing Methods

The two methods used to prepare the departmental production cost report when the firm uses process costing are the weighted-average method and the first-in, first-out (FIFO) method. The **weighted-average method** includes all costs in calculating the unit cost, including both those costs incurred during the current period and those costs incurred in the prior period that are shown as the beginning work-in-process inventory of this period. In this method, prior period costs and current period costs are averaged; hence, the name *weighted average*. The **FIFO method** includes in calculating the unit cost only costs incurred and work effort performed during the current period. FIFO considers the beginning inventory as a batch of goods separate from the goods started and completed within the same period. FIFO assumes that the first work done is to complete the beginning work-in-process inventory. Thus, all beginning work-in-process inventories are assumed to be completed before the end of the current period.

Under the weighted-average method, all units completed in the same period or in the ending inventory of that period are treated the same. When this method is used, the status of the product at the end of the period is the only element considered.

On the other hand, the status of the product at both the end and beginning of a period must be considered when the FIFO method is used to determine product costs. That is, the FIFO method looks at the input as well as the output of the production process, whereas the weighted-average method looks only at the output of the production process (completed and transferred out and ending work-in-process inventory).

The **weighted-average method** includes both current period and prior period costs in calculating unit cost.

FIFO method includes in calculating the unit cost only costs incurred and work effort performed during the current period.

In the early 1990s, the home appliance market, especially that for refrigerators, faced stiff competition. Whirlpool, Maytag, General Electric, and Electrolux tried to be the market leader. Whirlpool took specific steps to achieve this goal. The first step in Whirlpool's plan was to transform its largely domestic operation into a global powerhouse. The second step was to implement cost management techniques to reduce product and asset costs. How did Whirlpool reach its goal? (Refer to comments on Cost Management in Action at the end of the chapter.)

Illustration of Process Costing

To illustrate these two process costing methods, assume that Hsu Toy Company has two production departments, molding and finishing. The molding department places a direct material (plastic vinyl) into production at the beginning of the process. Direct labor and factory overhead costs are incurred gradually throughout the process with different proportions. The molding department uses machine-hours as the cost driver to apply factory overhead costs.

Exhibit 11.4 summarizes the molding department's units and costs during June.

Weighted-Average Method

LEARNING OBJECTIVE 4

Demonstrate the weighted-average method of process costing.

The weighted-average method makes no distinction between the cost incurred prior to the current period and the cost incurred during the current period. As long as a cost is on the current period's cost sheet for a production department, it is treated as any other cost regardless of when it was incurred. Consequently, the average cost per equivalent unit includes costs incurred both during the current period and in the prior period that carry over into this period through beginning work-in-process inventory. We use the five-step procedure to assign direct materials, direct labor, and factory overhead costs to the cost object, the molding department.

Step 1: Analyze Flow of Physical Units

The first step is to analyze the flow of all units through production. Exhibit 11.5 presents the procedures for this step.

EXHIBIT 11.4
Basic Data for Hsu Toy Company—Molding Department

Work-in-process inventory, June 1	10,000 units
Direct materials: 100 percent complete	$ 10,000
Direct labor: 30 percent complete	1,060
Factory overhead: 40 percent complete	1,620
Beginning work-in-process inventory	$ 12,680
Units started during June	40,000 units
Units completed during June and transferred out of the molding department	44,000 units
Work-in-process inventory, June 30	6,000 units
Direct materials: 100 percent complete	
Direct labor: 50 percent complete	
Factory overhead: 60 percent complete	
Costs incurred during June	
Direct materials	$ 44,000
Direct labor	22,440
Factory overhead	43,600
Total costs incurred	$110,040

EXHIBIT 11.5
Step 1: Analyze Flow of Physical Units—Molding Department

Input	Physical Units
Work-in-Process inventory, June 1	10,000
Units started during June	40,000
Total units to account for	50,000

Output	
Units completed and transferred out during June	44,000
Work-in-process inventory, June 30	6,000
Total units accounted for	50,000

Units to account for
are the sum of the beginning inventory units and the number of units started during the period.

Units accounted for
are the sum of the units transferred out and ending inventory units.

The two sections in Exhibit 11.5 show the two aspects of physical units flowing through production, *input units* and *output units*. This procedure ensures that all units in production are accounted for. Input units include all units that enter a production department during an accounting period or that entered during the prior period but were incomplete at the beginning of the period. These units come from two sources: (1) beginning work-in-process inventory started in a previous period that was partially complete at the end of the preceding period, which is 10,000 units in our example, and (2) work started or received in the current period, 40,000 units in our example. The sum of these two sources, 50,000 units here, is referred to as the number of **units to account for,** which is the sum of beginning inventory units and the number of units started during the period.

Output units include those that have been completed and transferred out and those not yet complete at the end of a period. These units can be in one of two categories: the 44,000 units completed or the 6,000 units in the ending work-in-process inventory. The sum of these two categories, 50,000 units, is referred to as the *number of units accounted for.* This number should match the number of units to account for. **Units accounted for** includes the sum of units completed and transferred out and the ending inventory units.

The primary purpose of this first step is to ensure that all units in production are accounted for before we compute the number of equivalent units of production for each production element.

Step 2: Calculate Equivalent Units

The second step in the process costing procedure is to calculate the number of equivalent units of production activity for direct materials, direct labor, and factory overhead. A table of equivalent units, presented in Exhibit 11.6, is based on the table of physical units prepared in step 1 (Exhibit 11.5).

The weighted-average method computes the total equivalent units produced to date. The number of units in production in the current period for each manufacturing

EXHIBIT 11.6
Step 2: Calculate Equivalent Units—Molding Department
Weighted-Average Method

	Physical Units	Completion Percentage	**Equivalent Units**		
			Direct Materials	Direct Labor	Factory Overhead
Work-in-process, June 1	10,000				
Direct materials		100%			
Direct labor		30			
Factory overhead		40			
Units started	40,000				
Units to account for	50,000				
Units completed	44,000	100%	44,000	44,000	44,000
Work-in-process, June 30	6,000				
Direct materials		100	6,000		
Direct labor		50		3,000	
Factory overhead		60			3,600
Units accounted for	50,000				
Total equivalent units			50,000	47,000	47,600

production element includes both (1) the units from previous periods that are still in production at the beginning of the current period and (2) the units placed into production in the current period.

In Exhibit 11.6, 44,000 physical units were complete and transferred out of the molding department. These units were 100 percent complete. Thus, they represent 44,000 equivalent units for direct materials, direct labor, and factory overhead. Note that the 44,000 units include 10,000 units placed into production prior to June and completed in June, and 34,000 units (44,000 units − 10,000 units) started and completed in June.

The 6,000 units in ending work-in-process inventory are complete with respect to direct materials because direct materials are added at the beginning of the process. Thus, they represent 6,000 equivalent units of direct materials. However, they are only 50 and 60 percent complete for direct labor and factory overhead, respectively. Therefore, the ending work-in-process inventories represent 3,000 equivalent units of direct labor (6,000 physical units × 50 percent complete) and 3,600 equivalent units of factory overhead (6,000 physical units × 60 percent complete).

From Exhibit 11.6, we calculate the total number of equivalent units as follows:

Completed and transferred out units

+ Ending work-in-process equivalent units

= Total equivalent units of production

Combining completed units and ending work-in-process equivalent units, the equivalent units of production for the molding department under the weighted-average method are 50,000 units of direct materials, 47,000 units of direct labor, and 47,600 units of factory overhead.

Step 3: Determine Total Costs to Account For

The third step determines how much money was spent both in the beginning work-in-process inventory and current production for direct materials, direct labor, and factory overhead.

Exhibit 11.7 summarizes the total manufacturing costs to account for. As given in our example data, total manufacturing costs ($122,720) consist of the beginning work-in-process inventory balance, $12,680, plus the current costs added during June, $110,040.

Step 4: Compute Unit Costs

For the fourth step in the process costing procedure, we compute the equivalent unit costs of production for direct materials, direct labor, and factory overhead; see Exhibit 11.8. The equivalent per-unit cost for direct materials ($1.08) is computed by dividing the total direct materials cost ($54,000), including the cost of the beginning work-in-process ($10,000) and the cost added during June ($44,000), by the total equivalent units (50,000). Similar procedures are used for direct labor and factory overhead costs. Notice that the total equivalent unit cost of $2.53 can be determined only by adding the unit direct materials cost of $1.08, the unit direct labor cost of $0.50, and the unit factory overhead cost of $0.95.

Step 5: Assign Total Manufacturing Costs

The final step of the process costing procedure is to assign total manufacturing costs to units completed and to units in the ending work-in-process inventory. Exhibit 11.9 summarizes the cost assignment schedule. Various unit numbers come directly from Exhibit 11.6; various unit costs come from Exhibit 11.8. Note that the total costs accounted for in this step ($122,720) should equal the total costs to account for in step 3 (Exhibit 11.7).

EXHIBIT 11.7
Step 3: Determine Total Costs to Account For—Molding Department

Beginning work-in-process inventory		
Direct materials	$10,000	
Direct labor	1,060	
Factory overhead	1,620	
Total		$ 12,680
Current costs added during June		
Direct materials	$44,000	
Direct labor	22,440	
Factory overhead	43,600	
Total costs added		110,040
Total costs to account for		$122,720

EXHIBIT 11.8
Step 4: Compute Unit Costs—Molding Department
Weighted-Average Method

	Direct Materials	Direct Labor	Factory Overhead	Total
Costs (from Exhibit 11.7)				
Work-in-process, June 1	$10,000	$ 1,060	$ 1,620	$ 12,680
Costs added during June	44,000	22,440	43,600	110,040
Total costs to account for	$54,000	$23,500	$45,220	$122,720
Divide by equivalent units from Exhibit 11.6	50,000	47,000	47,600	
Equivalent unit costs	$ 1.08 +	$ 0.50 +	$ 0.95 =	$2.53

EXHIBIT 11.9
Step 5: Assign Total Manufacturing Costs—Molding Department
Weighted-Average Method

	Completed and Transferred out	Ending Work-in-Process	Total
Goods completed and transferred out (44,000 × $2.53)	$111,320		$111,320
Ending work-in-process:			
Direct materials (6,000 × $1.08)		$ 6,480	6,480
Direct labor (3,000 × $0.50)		1,500	1,500
Factory overhead (3,600 × $0.95)		3,420	3,420
Total costs accounted for	$111,320	$11,400	$122,720

Cost Reconciliation

After finishing the five-step procedure, we need to determine whether the total manufacturing costs to account for in step 3 (i.e., total input costs) agree with the total costs accounted for in step 5 (i.e., total output costs). This checking procedure is called the *cost reconciliation*. For example, for Hsu Toy Company's modeling department, $122,720 total manufacturing costs accounted for in step 3 equal the total costs accounted for in step 5.

Production Cost Report

Steps 1 through 5 provide all information needed to prepare a production cost report for the molding department for June. This report is in Exhibit 11.10.

EXHIBIT 11.10
Production Cost Report—
Molding Department
Weighted-Average Method

Production Quantity Information

	Step 1: Analyze Flow of Physical Units		Step 2: Calculate Equivalent Units		
	Physical Units	Completion Percentage	Direct Materials	Direct Labor	Factory Overhead
Input					
Work-in-process, June 1	10,000				
Direct materials		100%			
Direct labor		30			
Factory overhead		40			
Units started	40,000				
Units to account for	50,000				
Output					
Units completed	44,000	100%	44,000	44,000	44,000
Work-in-process, June 30	6,000				
Direct materials		100	6,000		
Direct labor		50		3,000	
Factory overhead		60			3,600
Units accounted for	50,000				
Total equivalent units			50,000	47,000	47,600

Unit Cost Determination

Step 3: Determine Total Costs to Account For	Direct Materials	Direct Labor	Factory Overhead	Total
Work-in-process, June 1	$10,000	$ 1,060	$ 1,620	$ 12,680
Costs added during June	44,000	22,440	43,600	110,040
Total costs to account for	$54,000	$23,500	$45,220	$122,720
Step 4: Compute Unit Costs				
Divide by equivalent units	50,000	47,000	47,600	
Equivalent unit costs	$ 1.08	$ 0.50	$ 0.95	$ 2.53

Cost Assignment

Step 5: Assign Total Manufacturing Costs	Completed and Transferred out	Ending Work-in-Process	Total
Goods completed and transferred out (44,000 × $2.53)	$111,320		$111,320
Ending work-in-process			
Direct materials (6,000 × $1.08)		$ 6,480	6,480
Direct labor (3,000 × $0.50)		1,500	1,500
Factory overhead (3,600 × $0.95)		3,420	3,420
Total costs accounted for	$111,320	$11,400	$122,720

First-In, First-Out (FIFO) Method

Another way to handle inventory in a process costing application is the first-in, first-out (FIFO) method, which assumes that the first units to enter a production process are the first units to be completed and transferred out.

Our illustration of the FIFO method of process costing again uses Hsu Toy Company's molding department data (see Exhibit 11.4). Unlike the weighted-average method, the FIFO method does not combine beginning inventory costs with current costs when computing equivalent unit costs. The FIFO method considers the beginning inventory as a batch of goods separate from the goods started and completed within the same period. The costs from each period are treated separately. We follow the same five steps as in the weighted-average method, however, in determining product costs.

LEARNING OBJECTIVE 5

Demonstrate the FIFO method of process costing.

Step 1: Analyze Flow of Physical Units

The physical flow of product units is unaffected by the process costing method used. Therefore, step 1 for the FIFO method is the same as the weighted-average method in Exhibit 11.5.

Step 2: Calculate Equivalent Units

The FIFO method considers the beginning inventory as a batch of goods separate from the goods started and completed within the same period. The equivalent units in the beginning work-in-process—work done in the prior period—are not counted as part of the FIFO method equivalent units. Only that part of the equivalent units of the beginning work in process to be completed this period is counted.

Two equivalent, alternative procedures are used to calculate equivalent units of production under the FIFO method.

Step 2, Alternative A

One way to calculate FIFO equivalent units is to subtract the equivalent units in beginning work-in-process from the weighted-average equivalent units to obtain the FIFO method equivalent units, as shown in the last three rows of Exhibit 11.11. The 10,000 physical units in June 1 work-in-process have 100 percent of direct materials, so they have 10,000 equivalent units of direct materials prior to the current period. However, these units are only 30 percent and 40 percent complete for direct labor and factory overhead, respectively, so they contribute only 3,000 equivalent units of direct labor (10,000 × 30%) and 4,000 equivalent units of factory overhead (10,000 × 40%) prior to the current period. Notice that the $10,000 direct materials cost in the beginning work-in-process inventory is excluded from this calculation. Only current costs added in June are used to compute the equivalent unit cost under the FIFO method.

To calculate the total number of FIFO equivalent units, the following equations are given:

$$
\begin{array}{l}
\text{Completed and transferred out units} \\
\underline{+ \text{ Ending work-in-process equivalent units}} \\
= \text{Weighted-average equivalent units} \\
\underline{- \text{ Beginning work-in-process equivalent units}} \\
= \text{FIFO equivalent units of work done during this period}
\end{array}
$$

Exhibit 11.11 shows that Hsu Toy Company must account for a total of 50,000 units. Of these, 44,000 units are completed and 6,000 units are ending work-in-process inventory that is 100 percent complete for direct materials. The total equivalent units for the period for direct materials under the weighted-average method is 50,000. Of the 44,000 units completed during the period, 10,000 were in the beginning work-in-process inventory. These 10,000 units already had all direct materials added

EXHIBIT 11.11
Step 2: Calculate Equivalent Units—Molding Department
FIFO Method—Alternative A

			Equivalent Units		
	Physical Units	Completion Percentage	Direct Materials	Direct Labor	Factory Overhead
Input					
Work-in-process, June 1	10,000				
Direct materials		100%	10,000		
Direct labor		30		3,000	
Factory overhead		40			4,000
Units started	40,000				
Units to account for	50,000				
Output					
Units completed	44,000	100%	44,000	44,000	44,000
Work-in-process, June 30	6,000				
Direct materials		100	6,000		
Direct labor		50		3,000	
Factory overhead		60			3,600
Units accounted for	50,000				
Total equivalent units (weighted-average method)			50,000	47,000	47,600
Less: equivalent units in June 1 work-in-process			(10,000)	(3,000)	(4,000)
Equivalent units for work done in June only (FIFO method)			40,000	44,000	43,600

in the prior period. Subtracting 10,000 units from the 50,000 total equivalent units for the period, the FIFO equivalent units for work done only in June for direct materials is 40,000 units. Following the same procedure, equivalent units of production for the molding department using the FIFO method are 44,000 units of direct labor and 43,600 units of factory overhead.

The difference between the weighted-average method and the FIFO method is that under the weighted-average method, the equivalent units of production completed prior to the current period are not subtracted from the total completed units, so equivalent units under the weighted-average method are always as large as or larger than those under the FIFO method.

Step 2, Alternative B

An alternative way to determine the equivalent units using the FIFO method is to add equivalent units of work performed in the current period for each component constituting the output. These three components are (1) equivalent units added to complete the beginning work-in-process inventory, (2) units started and completed during the period, and (3) equivalent units of the ending work-in-process inventory. Exhibit 11.12 presents the FIFO equivalent units computation using the second procedure. Notice that under the FIFO method, the equivalent units in the beginning work-in-process inventory from last month's work effort are not added to equivalent units of work performed this month.

For example, the 10,000 units of beginning work-in-process inventory were 30 percent complete for direct labor. Hsu Toy Company completed the beginning work-in-process inventory by adding the remaining 70 percent of the direct labor during the current period to complete production. In addition, the firm started another 40,000 units in production during the period. Of these 40,000 units, the firm completed the production of 34,000, and the remaining 6,000 were still in the manufacturing process at the end of the period. The firm has completed only 50 percent of the total direct

EXHIBIT 11.12   **Step 2: Calculate Equivalent Units—Molding Department: FIFO Method—Alternative B**

	Physical Units	Completion Percentage	Equivalent Units		
			Direct Materials	Direct Labor	Factory Overhead
Input					
Work-in-process, June 1	10,000				
Direct materials		100%	10,000		
Direct labor		30		3,000	
Factory overhead		40			4,000
Units started	40,000				
Units to account for	50,000				
Output					
Completed and transferred out					
from work-in-process, June 1	10,000				
Direct materials 10,000 × (1 − 100%)			0		
Direct labor 10,000 × (1 − 30%)				7,000	
Factory overhead 10,000 × (1 − 40%)					6,000
Started and completed					
(44,000 − 10,000) =	34,000	100%	34,000	34,000	34,000
Work-in-process, June 30	6,000				
Direct materials		100	6,000		
Direct labor		50		3,000	
Factory overhead		60			3,600
Units accounted for	50,000				
Equivalent units for work for June only			40,000	44,000	43,600

labor to the ending work-in-process inventory, or an equivalent of 3,000 units. To summarize the direct labor spent during the period, the firm spent an equivalent of 7,000 units of direct labor to complete the beginning work-in-process inventory on hand, started and completed 34,000 units, and spent an equivalent of 3,000 units to complete 50 percent of the 6,000 units of ending work-in-process inventory. The total direct labor of the period is equivalent to a production of 44,000 FIFO units. Exhibit 11.13 graphically illustrates the difference between weighted average and FIFO equivalent units.

Step 3: Determine Total Costs to Account For

The total costs incurred to manufacture product units are unaffected by the process costing method used. Therefore, step 3 is the same as the weighted-average method in Exhibit 11.7. It shows that Hsu Toy Company's modeling department has $122,720 total manufacturing costs to account for.

Step 4: Compute Unit Costs

Under the FIFO method, equivalent unit costs are calculated by dividing the costs incurred during the current period by the equivalent units for work completed only during the current period. No cost in the work-in-process beginning inventory is included in determining equivalent unit costs for cost elements. Exhibit 11.14 presents such calculations. The equivalent unit cost for direct materials ($1.10) is computed by dividing the direct materials cost added during June ($44,000) by the equivalent units for work done in June only (40,000). Similar procedures are used for direct labor and factory overhead costs. Notice that the total equivalent unit cost of $2.61 can be determined only by adding the unit direct materials cost of $1.10, the unit direct labor cost of $0.51, and the unit factory overhead cost of $1.00.

EXHIBIT 11.13
Weighted-Average vs. FIFO
Equivalent Units

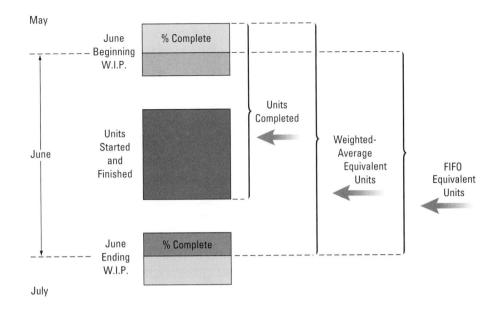

EXHIBIT 11.14
Step 4: Compute Unit Costs—
Molding Department
FIFO Method

	Direct Materials	Direct Labor	Factory Overhead	Total
Costs (from Exhibit 11.7)				
Work-in-process, June 1				$ 12,680
Costs added during June	$44,000	$22,440	$43,600	110,040
Total costs to account for				$122,720
Divide by equivalent units from Exhibit 11.11)	40,000	44,000	43,600	
Equivalent unit costs	$ 1.10 +	$ 0.51 +	$ 1.00 =	$ 2.61

Step 5: Assign Total Manufacturing Costs

The final step of the process costing procedure is to assign total manufacturing costs to units completed and to units in the ending work-in-process inventory. Like the weighted-average method, the FIFO method assigns the total costs of a period to the units completed, the units transferred out, and the units still in process at the end of the period. Unlike the weighted-average method, however, the FIFO method accounts for different batches of the completed units separately because work performed on different batches could be different.

The manufacturing process for units in the beginning work-in-process overlaps two periods. Thus, units completed from the beginning work-in-process inventory incurred costs prior to the current period as well as during the current period. This fact makes the assignment of total manufacturing costs to units completed during a period a two-part process. In the first part, the total manufacturing cost for units completed from beginning work-in-process is determined. In the second part, the total manufacturing costs for units started and completed during the manufacturing process in the current period are calculated.

Step 5, Part A: Total Cost of Units Completed from Beginning Work-in-Process Inventory

To determine the total manufacturing costs for the units completed from beginning work-in-process, the firm adds the manufacturing costs applied to the units during the current period to the costs from preceding periods already assigned to these units.

The total additional cost incurred in the current period to complete these units is the sum of the equivalent units of each cost element added to complete the element. These are applied to the units in beginning work-in-process and multiplied by the average unit cost for the cost element.

The costs assigned to the 10,000 units of the beginning work-in-process inventory that were completed and transferred out during the current period are calculated as follows:

Work-in-process inventory, June 1, 10,000 units	$12,680
Costs added during June to complete the beginning inventory	
Direct labor 7,000 equivalent units × $0.51	3,570
Factory overhead 6,000 equivalent units × $1.00	6,000
Total for beginning inventory	$22,250

Step 5, Part B: Total Cost for Units Started and Completed

The production cost of units started and completed in the current period can be computed by multiplying the number of units in this category by the cost per equivalent unit of the period.

The number of units started and completed in the period is the difference between the units completed and the number of units in beginning work-in-process. In the molding department example, we compute the units started and completed as follows:

$$\text{Units completed} - \text{Beginning work-in-process} = \text{Units started and completed}$$

$$44,000 \text{ units} - 10,000 \text{ units} = 34,000 \text{ units}$$

Then the cost assigned to units started and completed is

$$34,000 \text{ units} \times \$2.61 = \$88,740$$

The total costs transferred out are the sum of the total cost from the beginning inventory and the total cost for units started and completed; that is

$$\$22,250 + \$88,740 = \$110,990$$

Ending Work-in-Process Inventory The cost amount assigned to ending work-in-process units is derived by multiplying the average unit costs for the period of each manufacturing cost element by the equivalent units of the ending work-in-process inventory.

The cost of 6,000 units in ending work-in-process inventory of the molding department is computed as follows:

Direct materials, 6,000 equivalent units × $1.10	$ 6,600
Direct labor, 3,000 equivalent units × $0.51	1,530
Factory overhead, 3,600 equivalent units × $1.00	3,600
Total ending work-in-process inventory	$11,730

Exhibit 11.15 shows that the sum of the costs assigned to goods transferred out and in ending work-in-process inventory equals the total costs accounted for of $122,720.

Cost Reconciliation

Now we need to determine whether the total manufacturing costs to account for in step 3 agree with the total costs accounted for in step 5. Again, step 3 accounts for $122,720 total manufacturing costs; this equals the total costs of $122,720 accounted for in step 5.

EXHIBIT 11.15
Step 5: Assign Total
Manufacturing Costs—
Molding Department
FIFO Method

	Completed and Transferred out	Ending Work-in-Process	Total
Goods completed and transferred out			
Beginning work-in-process	$ 12,680		$ 12,680
Costs added during June			
Direct materials	0		0
Direct labor (7,000 × $0.51)	3,570		3,570
Factory overhead (6,000 × $1.00)	6,000		6,000
Total for beginning inventory	$ 22,250		$ 22,250
Started and completed			
(34,000 × $2.61)	88,740		88,740
Total costs completed and			
transferred out	$110,990		$110,990
Ending work-in-process			
Direct material (6,000 × $1.10)		$ 6,600	$ 6,600
Direct labor (3,000 × $0.51)		1,530	1,530
Factory overhead (3,600 × $1.00)		3,600	3,600
Total costs accounted for	$110,990	$11,730	$122,720

Production Cost Report

Steps 1 through 5 provide all information needed to prepare a production cost report for the molding department for June (Exhibit 11.16).

Comparison of Weighted-Average and FIFO Methods

The key difference between the weighted-average and FIFO methods is the handling of partially completed beginning work-in-process inventory units. The FIFO method separates the units in the beginning inventory from the units started and completed during the period. In contrast, the weighted-average method makes no separate treatment of the units in the beginning work-in-process inventory.

The FIFO method separates costs of the beginning work-in-process inventory from the current period costs, and it uses only the current period costs and work effort to calculate equivalent unit costs. As a result, the FIFO method separately calculates costs for units in the beginning inventory and units that were started during the period. In contrast, the weighted-average method uses the calculated average unit cost for all units completed during the period, including both the beginning work-in-process inventory and the units started and completed during the period.

The weighted-average method generally is easier to use because the calculations are simpler. This method is most appropriate when work-in-process is relatively small, or direct materials prices, conversion costs, and inventory levels are stable. The FIFO method is most appropriate when direct materials prices, conversion costs, or inventory levels fluctuate.

Many firms prefer the FIFO method over the weighted-average method for purposes of cost control and performance evaluation because the cost per equivalent unit under FIFO represents the cost for the current period's efforts only. Firms often evaluate department managers' performance on only current period costs without mixing in the effects of performance during different periods. Under the weighted-average method, the costs of the prior period and the current period are mixed, and deviations in performance in the current period could be concealed by interperiod variations in unit costs.

EXHIBIT 11.16
Production Cost Report—
Molding Department
FIFO Method

Production Quantity Information

| | Step 1: Analyze Flow of Physical Units | | Step 2: Calculate Equivalent Units | | |
	Physical Units	Completion Percentage	Direct Materials	Direct Labor	Factory Overhead
Input					
Work-in-process, June 1	10,000				
Direct materials		100%	10,000		
Direct labor		30		3,000	
Factory overhead		40			4,000
Units started	40,000				
Units to account for	50,000				
Output					
Units completed	44,000	100%	44,000	44,000	44,000
Work-in-process, June 30	6,000				
Direct materials		100	6,000		
Direct labor		50		3,000	
Factory overhead		60			3,600
Units accounted for	50,000				
Total equivalent units (weighted-average method)			50,000	47,000	47,600
Less: equivalent units in June 1 work-in-process			(10,000)	(3,000)	(4,000)
Equivalent units for work performed in June only (FIFO method)			40,000	44,000	43,600

Unit Cost Determination

Step 3: Determine Total Costs to Account For	Direct Materials	Direct Labor	Factory Overhead	Total
Work-in-process, June 1				$ 12,680
Costs added during June	44,000	22,440	43,600	110,040
Total costs to account for				$122,720

Step 4: Compute Unit Costs

	Direct Materials	Direct Labor	Factory Overhead	Total
Divide by equivalent units (from Step 2)	40,000	44,000	43,600	
Equivalent unit costs	$ 1.10	$ 0.51	$ 1.00	$ 2.61

Cost Assignment

Step 5: Assign Total Manufacturing Costs	Completed and Transferred out	Ending Work-in-Process	Total
Goods completed and transferred out			
Beginning work-in-process	$ 12,680		$ 12,680
Costs added during June			
Direct labor (7,000 × $0.51)	3,570		3,570
Factory overhead (6,000 × $1.00)	6,000		6,000
Total for beginning inventory	$ 22,250		$ 22,250
Started and completed (34,000 × $2.61)	88,740		88,740
Total costs completed and transferred out	$110,990		$110,990

EXHIBIT 11.16
(concluded)

Ending work-in-process			
Direct materials (6,000 × $1.10)		$ 6,600	$ 6,600
Direct labor (3,000 × $0.51)		1,530	1,530
Factory overhead (3,600 × $1.00)		3,600	3,600
Total costs accounted for	$110,990	$11,730	$122,720

Process Costing with Multiple Departments

Most manufacturing firms have multiple departments or use several processes that require a number of steps. As the product passes from one department to another, the cost passes from department to department. The costs from the prior department are called *transferred-in costs* or *prior department costs*. This section discusses the concept of transferred-in costs and describes the weighted-average methods of cost flow assumptions for firms with multiple departments. Appendix B to this chapter describes the use of the FIFO method of process costing for firms with multiple departments.

Transferred-In Costs

Transferred-in costs
are costs of work performed in the earlier department that are transferred into the present department.

Transferred-in costs (TI) are costs of work performed in the earlier department that are transferred into the present department. Including these costs is a necessary part of process costing because we treat each department as a separate entity, and each department's production cost report includes all costs added to the product up to that point. If transferred-in costs were not included, each completed unit transferred out of a department would include only the value of the work performed on it by that department. It might help you to think of transferred-in costs as similar to the direct materials introduced at the beginning of the production process. The equivalent units of production of transferred-in costs can be computed in the same manner as direct materials that are added at the beginning of a process. The difference between the direct materials cost and the transferred-in cost is that the former comes from the storeroom while the latter comes from another production department.

The equivalent units of the transferred-in cost for ending work-in-process inventory is always assumed to be the same as the number of units in ending work-in-process inventory. Because all units in process are complete for prior departments' costs, by definition the number of equivalent units transferred in is the same as the number of physical units transferred in.

Suppose that Hsu Toy Company's molding department transfers its production units to the finishing department. In the finishing department, direct materials are added at the end of the process. Conversion costs (direct labor and factory overhead) are applied evenly throughout the finishing department's process. The finishing department uses direct labor cost as the cost driver to apply factory overhead costs.

Data for the finishing department for June are shown in Exhibit 11.17.

Weighted-Average Method

LEARNING OBJECTIVE 6
Analyze process costing with multiple departments.

Follow the familiar five-step procedure as we illustrate the weighted-average method for process costing with multiple departments.

Steps 1 and 2: Analyze Flow of Physical Units and Calculate Equivalent Units

The first step is to analyze the physical units of production. The second step is to calculate equivalent units. Exhibit 11.18 summarizes the computation of physical units and equivalent units. Note that because overhead is charged to the product based on direct labor cost, direct labor and overhead are combined into a single element, conversion, to simplify the production cost report.

REAL-WORLD FOCUS Process Costing in Practice at the U.S. Department of Agriculture (USDA) and in the Pork Production Industry

The USDA's accounting standards manual urges the use of activity-based costing in conjunction with process costing. The USDA also suggests that process costing be used in situations involving a large volume of similar goods or services. An example is the use of process costing to cost the payment of entitlement benefits. The payment of entitlement benefits involves a series of processes: reviewing applications, computing the amount of benefits, and issuing checks. Process costing is well suited for this context.

A recent survey of financial managers in the pork production industry revealed a variety of cost systems used within the industry. Standard cost systems were the most common; job costing and process costing systems were also very common. Pork production can be described in terms of a value chain that includes breeding, nursing, and finishing, among other steps. Job and process cost systems are more often used in the later phases of the pork producer's value chain because the flow of production in lots or groups of swine makes tracking costs using job and/or process cost systems more convenient at this phase of the value chain.

Based on information in *U.S. Department of Agriculture Financial and Accounting Standards Manual,* Version 2.0, Chapter 5, Section 5.9 (U.S. Department of Agriculture, October 23, 1997). (http://www.usda.gov/ocfo/fasm/ch05/); and Steve Weiss, "Cost Accounting," presented at the 1998 Pork Financial Management Conference. (www.iowaselect.com/ind_cost.html).

EXHIBIT 11.17
Basic Data for Hsu Toy Company—Finishing Department

Work-in-process, June 1: 14,000 units	
Direct materials: 0 percent complete	
Transferred-in: 100 percent complete	$ 34,250
Conversion: 50 percent complete	7,000
Beginning work-in-process inventory	$ 41,250
Units transferred-in during June	44,000 units
Transferred-in costs during June	
Weighted-average method (From Exhibit 11.10)	$111,320
FIFO method(From Exhibit 11.15)	110,990
Units completed	50,000 units
Work-in-process, June 30	8,000 units
Transferred-in: 100 percent complete	
Direct materials: 0 percent complete	
Conversion: 50 percent complete	
Costs added during June	
Direct materials	$ 25,000
Conversion	47,000

The 8,000 units in ending work-in-process inventory are 100 percent complete with respect to transferred-in costs because they were 100 percent complete in the preceding department. There is no direct materials component because materials are added at the end of the finishing department. Because ending work-in-process inventory is only 50 percent complete with respect to conversion costs, ending work-in-process inventories represent 4,000 equivalent units of conversion costs (8,000 physical units × 50% complete).

As Exhibit 11.18 shows, the total number of equivalent units is calculated as follows:

Completed units
+ Ending work-in-process equivalent units
= Total equivalent units of production

That is, by using the weighted-average method, the equivalent units of production for the finishing department include 58,000 units transferred in, 50,000 units of direct materials, and 54,000 units of conversion.

EXHIBIT 11.18
Steps 1 and 2: Analyze Flow of Physical Units and Calculate Equivalent Units—Finishing Department
Weighted-Average Method

	Step 1		Step 2		
				Equivalent Units	
	Physical Units	Completion Percentage	Transferred-in Costs	Direct Materials	Conversion Costs
Input					
Work-in-process, June 1	14,000				
Transferred-in costs		100%			
Direct materials		0			
Conversion costs		50			
Transferred-in	44,000				
Units to account for	58,000				
Output					
Units completed	50,000	100%	50,000	50,000	50,000
Work-in-process, June 30	8,000				
Transferred-in costs		100	8,000		
Direct materials		0			
Conversion costs		50			4,000
Units accounted for	58,000				
Total equivalent units			58,000	50,000	54,000

EXHIBIT 11.19
Steps 3 and 4: Determine Total Costs to Account for and Compute Unit Costs—Finishing Department
Weighted-Average Method

Step 3	Transferred-in Costs	Direct Materials	Conversion Costs	Total
Work-in-process, June 1	$ 34,250	$ 0	$ 7,000	$ 41,250
Costs added during June	111,320	25,000	47,000	183,320
Total costs to account for	$145,570	$25,000	$54,000	$224,570

Step 4				
Divide by equivalent units (from Exhibit 11.18)	58,000	50,000	54,000	
Equivalent unit costs	$ 2.5098 +	$ 0.50 +	$ 1.00 =	$4.0098

Steps 3 and 4: Determine Total Costs to Account for and Compute Unit Costs

The third step is to determine the total manufacturing costs to account for, and the fourth step is to compute equivalent unit costs for transferred-in, direct materials, and conversion costs.

Exhibit 11.19 summarizes the total manufacturing costs to account for and unit costs for all cost components. Total manufacturing costs to account for ($224,570) consist of the beginning work-in-process inventory balance, $41,250, plus the current costs added during June, $183,320 ($25,000 + $47,000 + $111,320).

The equivalent unit cost for units transferred in ($2.5099) is computed by dividing the total transferred-in cost ($145,570), including the cost of beginning work-in-process ($34,250) and the cost added during June ($111,320), by the total equivalent units transferred in (58,000). Similar procedures are used for direct materials and conversion costs.

Step 5: Assign Total Manufacturing Costs

The final step of the process costing procedure is to assign total manufacturing costs to units completed and to units in ending work-in-process inventory. Exhibit 11.20 summarizes the cost assignment schedule with $224,574 total costs accounted for in this step 5.

REAL-WORLD FOCUS Process Industries Use Process Cost Information for Environmental Compliance

Many process industries such as paper manufacturing, chemical production, and steel processing among others, create environmentally sensitive waste products. A critical cost management goal for these firms is to find cost-effective means to manage these waste products. For example, a steel plating facility in the United States recently faced the need to redesign its plant to meet U.S. environmental standards. The firm sought bids from environmental engineering firms for the redesign work. The average bid was $800,000, each requiring a significant rebuilding of the plant and extensive downtime at the plant. To avoid the cost and disruption of such a plant redesign, the company used cost management methods based in part on process cost information to develop a plan to reduce cost within the plant's current facilities. The plan involved several changes in operations including new ways to handle raw materials, changes in product mix and scheduling, segregating wastewater flows, and treating some wastes within the plant rather than off-site. The redesign cost of the plan was less than 25 percent of the cost of the plant redesign and it also was projected to have lower operating costs. Moreover, the plan offered a better integration of day-to-day decision making with environmental compliance, in comparison to the redesign plan of the consulting environmental engineers.

Source: Jasbinder Singh, "Making Business Sense of Environmental Compliance," *Sloan Management Review,* Spring 2000, pp. 91–100.

EXHIBIT 11.20
Step 5: Assign Total Manufacturing Costs—Finishing Department
Weighted-Average Method

Step 5	Completed and Transferred out	Ending Work-in-Process	Total
Goods completed and transferred out (50,000 × $4.0098)	$200,490		$200,490
Ending work-in-process			
Transferred-in (8,000 × $2.5098)		$20,078	20,078
Conversion (4,000 × $1.00)		4,000	4,000
Total costs accounted for	$200,490	$24,078	$224,568

Cost Reconciliation

The small difference between the total cost accounted for in step 5 and the total cost in step 3 is due to a very small rounding error. To avoid unacceptable large rounding errors, at least three significant digits or more should be used in calculating the cost per equivalent unit in step 4.

Journal Entries For Process Costing

LEARNING OBJECTIVE 7
Prepare journal entries to record the flow of costs in a process costing system.

Process costing uses the same general ledger manufacturing accounts as job costing discussed in Chapter 4. However, instead of tracing product costs to specific jobs, we accumulate costs in production departments or other cost centers. Each department has a separate Work-in-Process Inventory account. These journal entries for Hsu Toy Company use weighted-average method data from Steps 3 and 5 of both Exhibit 11.10 (molding department) and Exhibit 11.20 (finishing department). Assume that 50 percent of the conversion costs in the finishing department are direct labor ($47,000 × 50% = $23,500).

The following direct materials were requisitioned and used:

(1)	Work-in-Process Inventory—Molding Department	44,000	
	Work-in-Process Inventory—Finishing Department	25,000	
	Materials Inventory		69,000
	To record direct materials costs added during June.		

The direct labor incurred follows:

(2)	Work-in-Process Inventory—Molding Department	22,440	
	Work-in-Process Inventory—Finishing Department	23,500	
	Accrued Payroll		45,940
	To record direct labor costs incurred during June.		

Factory overhead applied is as follows:

(3)	Work-in-Process Inventory—Molding Department	43,600	
	Work-in-Process Inventory—Finishing Department	23,500	
	Factory Overhead Applied		67,100
	To record the application of factory overhead to departments.		

Transferred-in costs from the molding department follows:

(4)	Work-in-Process Inventory—Finishing Department	111,320	
	Work-in-Process Inventory—Molding Department		111,320
	To record the weighted-average method of the cost of goods completed in the molding department and transferred out to the finishing department.		

Product units finished are as follows:

(5)	Finished Goods Inventory	200,490	
	Work-in-Process Inventory—Finishing Department		200,490
	To record the weighted-average method of the cost of goods completed in the finishing department.		

Implementation and Enhancement of Process Costing

Activity-Based Costing and the Theory of Constraints

LEARNING OBJECTIVE 8

Explain how process costing systems are implemented and enhanced in practice.

Process costing systems are uniquely appropriate where there are one or a few homogeneous products, as in many process industries such as chemical or paper manufacturing. The goal of the costing system is to account for production costs in the cost of work-in-process units and finished products in the production cost report. There is little need for cost information to identify the cost of *different products* or *different customer jobs,* because there are only one or a few products and they all go through the same processing and thus have the same unit cost. But sometimes the process-based manufacturer has very different products going through different processes, making the process costing system by itself inadequate. For example, Reichhold Inc. (www.reichhold.com), a manufacturer of industrial chemicals, adhesives, and other products, is a process company that uses processing costing, but has adapted the system to include activity-based costing, because of its product variety. While most of its products go through similar processing steps (cleaning, reacting, filtration, and blending) some products require much more time in some steps than other products. For example, one Reichhold product requires careful cleanup of the vat where it is processed, because even very small quantities of the chemical can contaminate other products that are later processed in the vat. So, activity-based costing is used to properly charge the extra cleanup costs to this product.[3] Activity-based costing is an important enhancement to process costing when product and process variety arises.

Similarly, process costing information is not intended to help the firm determine the most profitable product mix or to identify the most profitable use of the plant. These questions require analyses that utilize the products' contribution margins and the location of production constraints in the plant. To determine the most profitable product mix, the process firm would use the contribution methods explained in Chapter 9 and the theory of constraints method explained in Chapter 10. For example, Reichhold could use the theory of constraints to identify the bottlenecks in the manufacture of its products. After determining which processing step (such as cleaning or reacting) constrains throughput for the plant, Reichhold could adjust production schedules to most profitably use this constraint.

Just-in-Time Systems and Flexible Manufacturing Systems

Firms use the just-in-time (JIT) method to minimize inventory and improve quality by carefully coordinating the receipt of raw materials and the delivery of product with the manufacturing processes in the plant. The goal is to have little or no raw material, work-in-process, or finished goods inventory in the plant. This saves costs that arise from holding inventory, including the risk of damage, theft, loss, or failure to find a customer for the finished product. Since inventory is minimal in an effective JIT system, there is no need for a system such as process costing to determine equivalent units and to account for production costs in work-in-process and finished goods.[4] Simpler methods, such as **backflush costing** can be used instead. These methods charge current production costs (using standard unit costs) directly to finished goods inventory, without accounting for the flows in and out of the Work-in-Process account. Any difference between these standard unit costs and actual costs is typically very small and is charged to cost of goods sold at the end of the year. While not in compliance with generally accepted accounting principles (because the small amount of work-in-process inventory is not valued and placed on the balance sheet), the backflush method is reasonable and convenient for a JIT production environment.

Flexible manufacturing systems (FMS) are another means, like JIT, that help manufacturing firms reduce inventory levels. An FMS is an automated production system that produces one or more items using robots and computer-controlled materials-handling systems to reduce downtime and setup time. The result is a smooth flow of production with little or no work-in-process inventory. Again, the reduction of work-in-process inventory allows for simpler costing systems.

Backflush costing
is a simplified approach to determining product cost that is used when there is little or no work-in-process inventory.

Summary

Process costing is a product cost system that accumulates costs in processing departments and allocates them to all units processed during the period, including both completed and partially completed units. It is used by firms producing homogeneous products on a continuous basis to assign manufacturing costs to units in production during the period. Firms that use process costing include paint, chemical, oil-refining, and food-processing companies.

Process costing systems provide information so managers can make strategic decisions regarding products and customers, manufacturing methods, pricing options, overhead allocation methods, and other long-term issues.

Equivalent units are the number of the same or similar completed units that could have been produced given the amount of work actually performed on both complete and partially completed units.

[3] "Edward Blocher, Betty Wong, and Christopher T. McKittrick, "Making Bottom-Up ABC Work at Reichhold, Inc.," *Strategic Finance*, April 2002, pp. 51–55.

[4] A recent study of Canadian and British process firms shows that most of the firms surveyed had little work-in-process inventory and did not use equivalent units in the determination of unit cost. See John Parkinson, "Equivalent Units in Process Custing," presented at the American Accounting Association Annual Meeting, August 17, 2002.

The key document in a typical process costing system is the production cost report that summarizes the physical units and equivalent units of a production department, the costs incurred during the period, and the costs assigned to goods both completed and transferred out as well as to ending work-in-process inventories. The preparation of a production cost report includes five steps: (1) analyze physical units, (2) calculate equivalent units, (3) determine total costs to account for, (4) compute unit costs, and (5) assign total manufacturing costs.

The two methods of preparing the departmental production cost report in process costing are the weighted-average method and first-in, first-out (FIFO) method. The weighted-average method includes costs incurred in both current and prior periods that are shown as the beginning work-in-process inventory of this period. The FIFO method includes only costs incurred during the current period in calculating unit cost.

Most manufacturing firms have several departments or use processes that require several steps. As the product passes from one department to another, the costs from the prior department are transferred-in costs or prior department costs. Process costing with multiple departments should include the transferred-in cost as the fourth cost element in addition to direct materials, direct labor, and factory overhead costs.

Appendix A

Spoilage in Process Costing

LEARNING OBJECTIVE 9
Account for spoilage in process costing.

As discussed in Appendix A to Chapter 4, the two types of spoilage are normal and abnormal. *Normal spoilage* occurs under efficient operating conditions. It is uncontrollable in the short term and is considered a part of product cost. That is, the costs of lost units are absorbed by the good units produced. *Abnormal spoilage* exceeds expected losses under efficient operating conditions and is charged as a loss to operations in the period detected.

Two approaches are used to account for spoilage in process costing systems. The first approach is to count the number of spoiled units, prepare a separate equivalent unit computation with the cost per unit of the spoiled goods, and then allocate the cost to the good units produced. The second approach is to omit the spoiled units in computing the equivalent units of production; the spoilage cost is part of the total manufacturing costs. The first approach provides more accurate product costs because it computes the costs associated with normal spoilage and spreads them over the good units produced. The second approach is less accurate because it spread the costs of normal spoilage over all units—good completed units, units in ending work-in-process inventory, and abnormal spoiled units. This appendix discusses the first approach in detail.

Consider Diamond Company, which has the following data for the current period:

	Units	Cost
Beginning work-in-process inventory	2,000	
Direct materials (100 percent complete)		$100,000
Conversion costs (75 percent complete)		80,000
Units started in the period	8,000	
Costs incurred during the period		
Direct materials		300,000
Conversion costs		405,000
Ending work-in-process inventory	2,000	
Direct materials (100 percent complete)		
Conversion costs (80 percent complete)		
Completed and transferred out	7,000	
Normal spoilage is 10 percent of good production	700	

Diamond Company uses the weighted-average process costing method. The company inspects all products at the completion point. Using the five-step procedure described in the chapter, we need only add normal spoilage and abnormal spoilage components in calculations.

STEP 1. ANALYZE PHYSICAL UNITS

With 7,000 good production units completed in May, the normal spoiled units total 700 (7,000 × 10%). The calculation of abnormal spoiled units follows:

$$
\begin{aligned}
\text{Abnormal spoiled units} &= \text{Beginning work-in-process inventory} + \text{Units started} \\
&\quad - \text{Ending work-in-process inventory} - \text{Goods completed} \\
&\quad \text{and transferred-out units} - \text{Normal spoiled units} \\
&= 2{,}000 + 8{,}000 - 2{,}000 - 7{,}000 - 700 \\
&= 300 \text{ units}
\end{aligned}
$$

STEP 2. CALCULATE EQUIVALENT UNITS

Equivalent units for spoilage are calculated in the same way as good units. Following the first approach, all normal and abnormal spoiled units are included in the calculation of equivalent units. Since the company inspects all products at the completion point, the same amount of work is performed on each completed good unit and each completed spoiled unit.

STEP 3. DETERMINE TOTAL COSTS TO ACCOUNT FOR

These costs include all costs in the beginning work-in-process inventory and all costs added during the period. The detail of this step is similar to the process costing procedure without spoilage incurred.

STEP 4. COMPUTE UNIT COSTS

The detail of this step is similar to the process costing procedure without any spoilage.

STEP 5. ASSIGN TOTAL MANUFACTURING COSTS

This step now includes the costs of good units and spoiled units.

Exhibit 11.21 summarizes the five-step procedure for the weighted-average process costing method, including both normal and abnormal spoilage.

Exhibit 11.22 is the production cost report under the FIFO process costing method.

The journal entries for Diamond Company using the FIFO method follows:

Finished Goods Inventory	703,750	
Work-in-Process Inventory		703,750
To record the total cost of units completed, including the normal spoilage cost.		
Loss from Spoilage	26,250	
Work-in-Process Inventory		26,250
To record the abnormal spoilage cost.		

EXHIBIT 11.21
Diamond Company's
Production Cost Report
Weighted-Average Method

Production Quantity Information				
	Step 1: Flow of Costs		Step 2: Calculate Equivalent Units	
	Physical Units	Completion Percentage	Direct Materials	Conversion Costs
Input				
Work-in-process, May 1	2,000			
Direct materials		100%		
Conversion		75		
Number started	8,000			
Total to account for	10,000			
Output				
Number completed	7,000	100%	7,000	7,000
Normal spoilage (10%)	700		700	700
Abnormal spoilage	300		300	300
Work-in-process, May 31	2,000			
Direct materials		100	2,000	
Conversion		80		1,600
Total accounted for	10,000			
Total equivalent units			10,000	9,600

Unit Cost Determination			
Step 3: Determine Total Costs to Account for	**Direct Materials**	**Conversion Costs**	**Total**
Work-in-process, May 1	$100,000	$ 80,000	$180,000
Costs added during period	300,000	405,000	705,000
Total costs to account for	$400,000	$485,000	$885,000
Step 4: Compute Unit Costs			
Divide by number of equivalent units	10,000	9,600	
Equivalent unit costs	$ 40.00	$ 50.521	$ 90.521

Cost Assignment			
Step 5: Assign Total Manufacturing Costs	**Completed and Transferred out**	**Ending Work- in-Process**	**Total**
Goods completed and transferred out [(Goods units 7,000 + Normal spoilage 700) × $90.521]	$697,011		$697,011
Abnormal spoilage (300 × $90.521)			27,156
Work-in-process, May 31 Direct materials (2,000 × $40.00)		$ 80,000	80,000
Conversion (1,600 × $50.521)		80,833	80,833
Total costs accounted for	$697,011	$160,833	$885,000

EXHIBIT 11.22
Diamond Company's FIFO
Production Cost Report

Production Quantity Information

	Step 1: Analyze Flow of Physical Units	Step 2: Calculate Equivalent Units	
	Physical Units	Direct Materials	Conversion Costs
Input			
Work-in-process beginning inventory	2,000	(100%)	(75%)
Started this period	8,000		
Total to account for	10,000		
Output			
Completed	7,000	7,000	7,000
Normal spoilage (10 percent)	700	700	700
Abnormal spoilage	300	300	300
Work-in-process ending inventory	2,000 (80%)	2,000	1,600
Total accounted for	10,000		
Total work done to date		10,000	9,600
Work-in-process beginning inventory		(2,000)	(1,500)
Total work done this period (Total equivalent units)		8,000	8,100

Unit Cost Determination

Step 3: Determine Total Costs to Account For	Total	Direct Materials	Conversion Costs
Work-in-process beginning inventory	$180,000	$100,000	$ 80,000
Current cost	705,000	300,000	405,000
Total costs to account for	$885,000	$400,000	$485,000

Step 4: Compute Unit Costs			
		($300,000/ 8,000) =	($405,000/ 8,100) =
Cost per equivalent unit	$ 87.50	$ 37.50	$ 50.00

Cost Assignment

Step 5: Assign Total Manufacturing Costs	Total	Direct Materials	Conversion Costs
Units completed (7,000)			
From work-in-process, beginning inventory (2,000)	$180,000	$100,000	$ 80,000
Current costs incurred completing units (500)	25,000	0	25,000
Total cost from beginning inventory	$205,000	$100,000	$105,000
Normal spoilage (700)	61,250	26,250	35,000
Units started and completed this period (5,000)	437,500	187,500	250,000
Total cost of units completed	$703,750	$313,750	$390,000
Abnormal spoilage (300)	26,250	11,250	15,000
Work-in-process ending inventory		(2,000 × $37.5)	(1,600 × $50)
	155,000	= $75,000	= $80,000
Total costs accounted for	$885,000		

Appendix B

FIFO Method of Process Costing for Firms with Multiple Departments

Now we illustrate the FIFO method of process costing for multiple departments using data from the Hsu Toy Company's finishing department (see Exhibit 11.17).

STEPS 1 AND 2: ANALYZE FLOW OF PHYSICAL UNITS AND CALCULATE EQUIVALENT UNITS

Exhibit 11.23 summarizes the physical flow units and equivalent units of production for the finishing department.

The physical flow of product units is unaffected by the process costing method used. Therefore, step 1 is the same as with the weighted-average method.

The 14,000 physical units in the June 1 work-in-process inventory have 100 percent of transferred-in costs, so they represent 14,000 equivalent units of transferred-in work. Because the materials are added at the end of the process in the finishing department, zero equivalent units of direct materials for work-in-process inventory are on hand on June 1. The beginning work-in-process inventory is only 50 percent complete with respect to conversion activity, so this department has 7,000 equivalent units of conversion costs (14,000 × 50%).

As Exhibit 11.23 indicates, the total number of equivalent units is calculated as follows:

EXHIBIT 11.23
Steps 1 and 2: Analyze Flow of Physical Units and Calculate Equivalent Units—Finishing Department
FIFO Method

| | Step 1 | | Step 2 | | |
| | | | Equivalent Units | | |
	Physical Units	Completion Percentage	Transferred-in Costs	Direct Materials	Conversion Costs
Input					
Work-in-process, June 1	14,000				
Transferred-in		100%	14,000		
Direct materials		0		0	
Conversion		50			7,000
Transferred-in	44,000				
Units to account for	58,000				
Output					
Units completed	50,000	100%	50,000	50,000	50,000
Work-in-process, June 30	8,000				
Transferred-in		100	8,000		
Direct materials		0		0	
Conversion		50			4,000
Units accounted for	58,000				
Total equivalent units (weighted-average method)			58,000	50,000	54,000
Less: equivalent units in June 1 work-in-process			(14,000)	(0)	(7,000)
Equivalent units for work done in June only (FIFO method)			44,000	50,000	47,000

Completed units

+ Ending work-in-process equivalent units

− Beginning work-in-process equivalent units

= Equivalent units of work completed during this period

That is, equivalent units of production for the finishing department using the FIFO method are 44,000 transferred-in units, 50,000 direct material units, and 47,000 conversion activity units.

STEPS 3 AND 4: DETERMINE TOTAL COSTS TO ACCOUNT FOR AND COMPUTE UNIT COSTS

Exhibit 11.24 shows the computation of total costs to account for and equivalent unit costs for the finishing department.

The beginning work-in-process inventory has a cost of $41,250. The $182,990 total costs added during June include $110,990 transferred-in costs from the modeling department, $25,000 direct materials costs and $47,000 conversion costs incurred in the finishing department as shown in Exhibit 11.23.

The equivalent unit cost for transferred-in units ($2.5225) is computed by dividing the transferred-in cost during June ($110,990) by the equivalent units for work completed only in June (44,000). Similar procedures are used for direct materials and conversion costs. Notice that the costs of beginning inventory are excluded from this calculation. The calculations use only current costs added in June.

EXHIBIT 11.24

Steps 3 and 4: Determine Total Costs to Account For and Compute Unit Costs— Finishing Department
FIFO Method

Step 3	Transferred-in Costs	Direct Materials	Conversion Costs	Total
Work-in-process, June 1				$ 41,250
Costs added during June	$110,990	$25,000	$47,000	182,990
Total costs to account for				$224,240
Step 4				
Divide by equivalent units (from Exhibit 11.23):	44,000	50,000	47,000	
Equivalent unit costs	$ 2.5225 +	$ 0.50 +	$ 1.00 =	$4.0225

STEP 5: ASSIGN TOTAL MANUFACTURING COSTS

The final step of the process costing procedure is to assign total manufacturing costs to units completed and to units in the ending work-in-process inventory. Exhibit 11.25 summarizes the cost assignment schedule.

The costs assigned to the first batch of goods completed and from the 14,000 units of the beginning work-in-process are calculated as follows:

Work-in-process, June 1, 14,000 units	$41,250
Costs added during June to complete the beginning inventory:	
Direct material 14,000 equivalent units × $0.50	7,000
Conversion costs 7,000 equivalent units × $1.00	7,000
Total for beginning inventory	$55,250

The costs assigned to the 36,000 units started and completed during June are calculated:

$$50,000 \text{ units} - 14,000 \text{ units} = 36,000 \text{ units}$$

EXHIBIT 11.25
Step 5: Assign Total Costs—
Finishing Department
FIFO Method

	Completed and Transferred out	Ending Work-in-Process	Total
Goods completed and transferred out			
Beginning work-in-process	$ 41,250		$ 41,250
Costs added during June			
Direct materials (14,000 × $0.50)	7,000		7,000
Conversion (7,000 × $1.00)	7,000		7,000
Total from beginning inventory	$ 55,250		$ 55,250
Started and completed (36,000 × $4.0225)	144,810		144,810
Total costs completed and transferred out	$200,060		$200,060
Ending work-in-process:			
Transferred-in (8,000 × $2.5225)		$20,180	20,180
Conversion costs (4,000 × $1.00)		4,000	4,000
Total costs accounted for	$200,060	$24,180	$224,240

$$36,000 \text{ units} \times \$4.0225 = \$144,810$$

The total costs completed are the sum of the total costs from beginning inventory and the total costs for units started and completed, that is,

$$\$55,250 + \$144,810 = \$200,060$$

The cost of the finishing department's 8,000 units in ending work-in-process inventory is computed:

Transferred-in: 8,000 equivalent units × $2.5225	$20,180
Conversion: 4,000 equivalent units × $1.00	4,000
Total ending work-in-process inventory	$24,180

In Exhibit 11.25, the sum of the costs assigned to goods completed and ending work-in-process inventory is $224,240. Note that the amount of total costs accounted for in this step 5 should equal the total costs to account for in step 3 (as shown in Exhibit 11.24).

Key Terms

Comments on Cost Management in Action

Whirlpool Faces Competitive Pressure in Home Appliance Market

The Whirlpool Corporation acquired 47 percent of Philips Electronics' European appliance business unit in 1989 and the remainder in 1991. Whirlpool's European experience puts it far ahead of other U.S. firms such as Maytag, General Electric, and Electrolux in building an integrated global business. Operating income for the first three quarters of 1994 increased to 6.5 percent from 3.6 percent in 1990, and market share increased from 11.5 percent to 13 percent.

Whirlpool's most significant change is in the use of process cost information to improve processes and activities resulting in manufacturing cost reduction. Whirlpool also merged national designers and researchers into pan-European teams that work closely with the company's U.S. designers. This significantly reduced product costs for a series of new Whirlpool products using common "platforms" and processes that allow different models to be built on the same underlying chassis and process.

Whirlpool also reduced asset costs by streamlining Philips' scattered assets. By the end of 1994, it had slashed $400 million in annual costs. Whirlpool closed a surplus plant in Barcelona, trimmed 36 warehouses to 8, and centralized inventory control, chopping Philips' legion of 1,600 suppliers in half. Where Philips had purchased refrigerator power cords from 17 suppliers, Whirlpool buys from two. Together, these changes cut inventories by one-third.

Based on information in Patrick Oster and John Rossant, "Call It Worldpool," *Business Week*, November 28, 1994.

Self-Study Problems
(For solutions, please turn to the end of the chapter.)

1. Weighted-Average Method versus FIFO Method

Smith Electronic Company's chip-mounting production department had 300 units of unfinished product, each 40 percent complete on September 30. During October of the same year, this department put another 900 units into production and completed 1,000 units and transferred them to the next production department. At the end of October, 200 units of unfinished product, 70 percent completed, were recorded in the ending work-in-process inventory. Smith Company introduces all direct materials when the production process is 50 percent complete. Direct labor and factory overhead (i.e., conversion) costs are added uniformly throughout the process.

Following is a summary of production costs incurred during October:

	Direct Materials	**Conversion Costs**
Beginning work-in-process		$2,202
Current costs	$9,600	6,120
Total costs	$9,600	$8,322

Required

1. Calculate each of the following amounts using weighted-average process costing:
   a. Equivalent units of direct materials and conversion.
   b. Unit costs of direct materials and conversion.
   c. Cost of goods completed and transferred out during the period.
   d. Cost of work-in-process inventory at the end of the period.
2. Prepare a production cost report for October using the weighted-average method.
3. Repeat requirement 1 using the FIFO method.
4. Repeat requirement 2 using the FIFO method.

2. Weighted-Average Method versus FIFO Method with Transferred-In Cost

Reed Company has two departments, a machining department and a finishing department. The following information relates to the finishing department: work-in-process, November 1, was 10 units, 40 percent completed, consisting of $100 transferred-in costs, $80 direct materials, and $52 conversion costs. Production completed for November totaled 82 units; work-in-process, November 30, is 8 units, 50 percent completed. All finishing department direct materials are introduced at the start of the process; conversion costs are incurred uniformly throughout the process. Transferred-in costs from the machining department during November were $800; direct materials added were $720; conversion costs incurred were $861. Following is the summary data of Reed Company's finishing department:

Work-in-process, November 1, 10 units:	
Transferred-in: 100 percent complete	$ 100
Direct materials: 100 percent complete	80
Conversion: 40 percent complete	52
Balance in work-in-process, November 1	$ 232
Units transferred in from machining department	
during November	80 units
Units completed during November and	
transferred out to finished goods inventory	82 units
Work-in-process, November 30	8 units
Transferred-in: 100 percent complete	
Direct materials: 100 percent complete	
Conversion: 50 percent complete	
Costs incurred during November	
Transferred-in	$ 800
Direct materials	720
Conversion	861
Total current costs	$2,381

Required

1. Prepare a production cost report for November using the weighted-average method.
2. Prepare a production cost report for November using the FIFO method.

Questions

11–1 What are the typical characteristics of a company that should use a process costing system?

11–2 List three types of industries that would likely use process costing.

11–3 Explain the primary differences between job costing and process costing.

11–4 What does the term *equivalent units* mean?

11–5 How is the equivalent unit calculation affected when direct materials are added at the beginning of the process rather than uniformly throughout the process?

11–6 What is a production cost report? What are the five key steps in preparing a production cost report?

11–7 What is the distinction between equivalent units under the FIFO method and equivalent units under the weighted-average method?

11–8 Identify the conditions under which the weighted-average method of process costing is inappropriate.

11–9 Specify the advantages of the weighted-average method of process costing in contrast to the FIFO method.

11–10 From the standpoint of cost control, why is the FIFO method superior to the weighted-average method? Is it possible to monitor cost trends using the weighted-average method?

11–11 What are transferred-in costs?

11–12 Suppose that manufacturing is performed in sequential production departments. Prepare a journal entry to show a transfer of partially completed units from the first department to the second department.

11–13 Under the weighted-average method, all units transferred out are treated the same way. How does this differ from the FIFO method of handling units transferred out?

11–14 Under the FIFO method, only current period costs and work are included in unit costs and equivalent units computation. Under the weighted-average method, what assumptions are made when unit costs and equivalent units are computed?

11–15 What is the main difference between journal entries in process costing and in job costing?

11–16 What is the difference between process costing and operation costing?

11–17 Describe the effect of automation on the process costing system.

Exercises

11–18 **Physical Units**

Required In each case, fill in the missing amount.

1. Work-in-process inventory, February 1   80,000 units
   Work-in-process inventory, February 28   ?
   Units started during February   60,000
   Units completed during February   75,000

2. Work-in-process inventory, June 1   ?
   Work-in-process inventory, June 30   55,000 gallons
   Units started during June   75,000 gallons
   Units completed during June   83,000 gallons

3. Work-in-process inventory, September 1   5,500 tons
   Work-in-process inventory, September 30   3,400 tons
   Units started during September   ?
   Units completed during September   7,300 tons

4. Work-in-process inventory, November 1   45,000 units
   Work-in-process inventory, November 30   23,000 units
   Units started during November   57,000 units
   Units completed during November   ?

11–19 **Equivalent Units; Weighted-Average Method** Washington Fisheries, Inc., processes salmon for various distributors. Two departments, processing and packaging, are involved. Data relating to tons of salmon sent to the processing department during May follow:

		Percent Completed	
	Tons of Salmon	**Materials**	**Conversion**
Work-in-process inventory, May 1	1,500	80%	70%
Work-in-process inventory, May 31	2,300	50	30
Started processing during May	6,500		

Required

1. Calculate the number of tons completed and transferred out during the month.
2. Calculate the number of equivalent units for both materials and conversion for the month of May, assuming that the company uses the weighted-average method.

11–20 **Equivalent Units; Weighted-Average Method** Eastern Oregon Lumber Company grows, harvests, and processes timber for use as building lumber. The following data pertain to the company's sawmill:

Work-in-process inventory, January 1	
(materials: 60 percent; conversion: 40 percent)	30,000 units
Work-in-process inventory, December 31	
(materials: 70 percent; conversion: 60 percent)	15,000 units

During the year the company started 150,000 units in production.

Required Prepare a quantity schedule and compute the number of equivalent units of both direct materials and conversion for the year, using the weighted-average method.

11–21 **Equivalent Units; FIFO Method** Hardiston Chemical Company refines a variety of petrochemical products. These data are from the firm's Houston plant:

Work-in-process inventory, September 1	3,000,000 gallons
Direct materials	100 percent completed
Conversion	25 percent completed
Units started in process during September	4,850,000 gallons
Work-in-process inventory, September 30	2,400,000 gallons
Direct materials	100 percent completed
Conversion	80 percent completed

Required Compute the equivalent units of direct material and conversion for the month of September. Use the FIFO method.

11–22 **Equivalent Units; FIFO Method** Baker Company has the following information for December 1 to December 31. All direct materials are 100 percent complete; beginning materials cost $12,000.

Work-in-Process			
Beginning balance		Completed 800 units and	
December 1, 200 units,		transferred to finished	
9 percent complete	$14,000	goods inventory	$140,000
Direct materials	54,000		
Direct labor	34,000		*(continued)*

Factory overhead	
Property taxes	6,000
Depreciation	32,000
Utilities	18,000
Indirect labor	4,000
Ending balance December 31, 300 units, 12 percent complete	22,000

Required Calculate equivalent units using the FIFO method.

11–23 **Equivalent Units; FIFO Unit Cost** Young Company calculated the cost for an equivalent unit of production using the FIFO method.

Data for June	
Work-in-process inventory, June 1: 30,000 units	
Direct materials: 100 percent complete	$ 80,000
Conversion: 20 percent complete	24,000
Balance in work-in-process, June 1	$104,000
Units started during June	50,000
Units completed and transferred	60,000
Work-in-process inventory, June 30	
Direct materials: 100 percent complete	20,000
Conversion: 70 percent complete	
Cost incurred during June	
Direct materials	$150,000
Conversion costs	
Direct labor	120,000
Applied overhead	145,000
Total conversion costs	$265,000

Required Compute cost per equivalent unit.

11–24 **Journal Entries** NYI Corporation manufactures decorative window glass in two sequential departments. These data pertain to the month of August:

	Department 1	Department 2
Direct materials used for production	$ 55,000	$ 32,000
Direct labor	160,000	320,000
Applied factory overhead	340,000	250,000
Costs of goods completed and transferred	850,000	740,000

Required Prepare journal entries to record these events:

1. Incurrence of direct materials and direct labor. Application of factory overhead in department 1.
2. Transfer of products from department 1 to department 2.
3. Incurrence of direct materials and direct labor. Application of factory overhead in department 2.
4. Transfer of complete products from department 2 to finished goods inventory.

11–25 **FIFO Method** Phillips and Jones, an income tax preparation firm, uses the FIFO method of process costing for the monthly reports. The following shows its March 2004 information:

Returns in process, March 1 (30% complete)	100
Returns started in March	1,300
Returns in process, March 31 (90% complete)	200
Labor and overhead costs for returns in process, March 1	$ 330
Labor and overhead costs incurred in March	$148,500

Required   Calculate the following amounts using the FIFO method:

1. Equivalent units.
2. Cost per equivalent unit.
3. Cost of completed returns for the month of March.
4. Cost of returns in process as of March 31.

11–26 **Equivalent Units; Weighted-Average Method And FIFO Method**   Levittown Company employs a process costing system for its manufacturing operations. All direct materials are added at the beginning of the process, and conversion costs are added proportionately. Levittown's production schedule for November follows:

	Units
Work-in-process on November 1	
(conversion: 60 percent complete)	1,000
Started during November	5,000
Total to account for	6,000
Completed and transferred out from beginning inventory	1,000
Started and completed during November	3,000
Work-in-process on November 30	
(conversion: 20 percent complete)	2,000
Total accounted for	6,000

Required

1. Using the weighted-average method, compute the equivalent units for direct materials and conversion costs.
2. Using the FIFO method, compute the equivalent units for direct materials and conversion costs.

(CMA Adapted)

Problems

11–27 **Weighted-Average Method**   Hoffman, Inc. produces a single model of popular cell phones in large quantities. A single cell phone moves through two departments, assembly and testing. The manufacturing costs in the assembly department during March follow:

Direct materials added	$162,500
Conversion costs	133,100
	$295,600

The assembly department has no beginning work-in-process inventory. During the month, it started 25,000 cell phones, but only 23,000 were fully completed and transferred to the testing department. All parts had been made and placed in the remaining 2,000 watches, but only 60 percent of the labor had been completed. The company uses the weighted-average method of process costing to accumulate product costs.

Required

1. Compute the equivalent units and equivalent unit costs for March.
2. Compute the costs of units completed and transferred to the testing department.
3. Compute the costs of the ending work-in-process.

11–28 **Weighted-Average Method** Virginia Pulp Company processes wood pulp for manufacturing various paper products. The company employs a process costing system for its manufacturing operations. All direct materials are added at the beginning of the process, and conversion costs are incurred uniformly throughout the process. This is the company's production schedule for May:

| | Tons of Pulp | Percent Completed | |
		Materials	Conversion
Work-in-process inventory, May 1	3,000	100%	50%
Started during May	7,000		
Units to account for	10,000		
Units from beginning work-in-process, which were completed and transferred out during May	3,000		
Started and completed during May	5,500		
Work-in-process inventory, May 31	1,500	100%	50%
Total units accounted for	10,000		

The following cost data are available:

Work-in-process inventory, May 1	
Direct materials	$ 32,000
Conversion	44,000
Costs incurred during May	
Direct materials	240,000
Conversion	189,000

Required

1. Calculate equivalent units of direct materials and conversion during May. Use the weighted-average method.
2. Calculate the cost per equivalent unit for both direct materials and conversion during May. Use the weighted-average method.

11–29 **FIFO Method** Refer to the information in Problem 11–28.

Required Complete Problem 11–28 using the FIFO method.

11–30 **Weighted-Average Method** Yamamoto Company manufactures a single product that goes through two processes, mixing and cooking. These data pertain to the mixing department for August:

Work-in-process inventory, August 1	
Conversion: 80 percent complete	27,000 units
Work-in-process inventory, August 31	
Conversion: 40 percent complete	17,000 units
Units started into production	60,000
Units completed and transferred out	?
Costs	
Work-in-process inventory, August 1	
Material X	$ 64,800
Material Y	89,100
Conversion	119,880
Costs added during August	
Material X	152,700
Material Y	138,400
Conversion	302,520

Material X is added at the beginning of work in the mixing department. Material Y is also added in the mixing department, but not until product units are 60 percent complete with regard to conversion. Conversion costs are incurred uniformly during the process. The company uses the weighted-average cost method.

Required

1. Calculate equivalent units of material X, material Y, and conversion.
2. Calculate costs per equivalent unit for material X, material Y, and conversion.
3. Calculate the cost of units transferred out.
4. Calculate the cost of ending work-in-process inventory.

11–31 **FIFO Method**   Jenice Company uses FIFO process costing to account for the costs of its single product. Production begins in the fabrication department, where units of direct materials are molded into various connecting parts. After fabrication is complete, the units are transferred to the assembly department, which adds no material. After assembly is complete, the units are transferred to the packaging department, which packages units for shipment. After the units have been packaged, the final products are transferred to the shipping department. A partially completed production cost report for the month of May in the fabrication department follows:

JENICE COMPANY
Fabrication Department—Production Cost Report
For the Month Ended May 31, 2004

Quantity Schedule	Units		
Units to be accounted for			
Work-in-process inventory, May 1			
(materials: 100 percent; conversion: 40 percent)	3,000		
Started into production	?		
Total units to be accounted for	?		
Units accounted for as follows			
Transferred to department Y			
Units from the beginning inventory	?		
Units started and completed this month	?		
Work-in-process inventory, May 31	4,000		
(materials: 100 percent; conversion: 60 percent)			
Total units accounted for	?		

Equivalent Units and Unit Costs	Materials	Conversion	Total
Cost added during May	$172,500	?	?
Equivalent units	?	?	?
Unit Cost	?	?	?

Cost Reconciliation

Cost to be accounted for
    ?

Cost accounted for as follows:
    ?

The cost incurred in the fabrication department's work-in-process inventory at May 1 is $13,800. The assembly department's production cost report for the month of May shows that the number of transferred-in units is 68,000, costing $393,400.

Required

1. Fill in the missing amounts in the quantity schedule and complete the equivalent units and costs.
2. Complete the cost reconciliation part of the production cost report.

11–32 Weighted-Average Method   China Pacific Company manufactures a variety of natural fabrics for the clothing industry in a suburb of Shanghai. The following data in Chinese currency called *renminbi* pertain to the month of October.

Work-in-process inventory, October 1	25,000 units
Direct materials: 60 percent complete	57,000 renminbi
Conversion: 30 percent complete	45,000 renminbi
Cost incurred during October	
Direct materials	736,000 renminbi
Conversion	1,094,950 renminbi

During October, 175,000 units were completed and transferred out. At the end of the month, 30,000 units (direct materials 80 percent and conversion 40 percent complete) remain in work-in-process inventory.

Required   Calculate each of the following amounts using weighted-average process costing.

1. Equivalent units of direct materials and conversion.
2. Unit costs of direct materials and conversion.
3. Cost of goods completed and transferred out during October.
4. Cost of the work-in-process inventory at October 31.
5. Check the most recent issue of *The Wall Street Journal* or go to www.xe.com to learn the exchange rate between the U.S. dollar and the Chinese renminbi.

11–33 Weighted-Average Method; Transferred-in Costs   Hammond Toy Company has two departments, forming and finishing. Consider the finishing department, which processes the formed toys through hand shaping and the addition of metal. All other direct materials are added at the end of the process in the finishing department. The following summarizes the finishing department's July operations:

	Number of Units
Work-in-process, June 30, 50% complete for conversion costs	4,000
Transferred in during July	21,000
Completed during July	19,000
Work-in-process, July 31, 50% complete for conversion costs	6,000

	Costs
Work-in-process, June 30 (transferred-in costs: $25,000; conversion costs: $5,000)	$ 30,000
Transferred-in from forming department during July	100,000
Direct materials added during July	30,000
Conversion added during July	37,000
Total to account for	$197,000

Required   Calculate each of the following amounts using the weighted-average process costing method:

1. Equivalent units of transferred-in direct materials and conversion.
2. Unit costs of transferred-in direct materials and conversion.
3. Cost of goods completed and transferred out during July.
4. Cost of work-in-process inventory at July 31.

11–34 Weighted-Average Method   Lester-Smith Company has a department that manufactures wood trusses. The following information is for the production of these trusses for the month of February:

Work-in-process inventory, February 1	10,000 trusses
Direct materials cost: 100 percent complete	$100,000
Conversion: 20 percent complete	$115,000
Units started during February	15,000 trusses
Units completed during February and transferred out	20,000 trusses
Work-in-process inventory, February 29	5,000 trusses
Direct materials: 100 percent complete	
Conversion cost: 40 percent complete	
Costs incurred during February	
Direct materials	$50,000
Conversion	$95,000

Required   Using the weighted-average method, calculate the following:

1. Costs per equivalent unit.
2. Cost of goods completed and transferred out.
3. Cost remaining in the ending work-in-process inventory.
4. Assume that you are the company's controller. The production department's February unit cost is higher than standard cost. If the manager of the first department asks you to do him a favor by increasing the ending inventory completion percentage from 40 to 60 percent to lower the unit costs, what should you do?

11–35 **FIFO Method**   Refer to the information in problem 11–34.

Required   Repeat Problem 11–34 using the FIFO method.

11–36 **FIFO Method; Journal Entries**   You are engaged in the audit of the December 31, 2004, financial statements of Epworth Products Corporation. You are attempting to verify the costing of the work-in-process and finished goods ending inventories that were recorded on Epworth's books as follows:

	Units	Cost
Work-in-process (50 percent complete as to labor and overhead)	300,000	$660,960
Finished goods	100,000	504,900

Materials are added to production at the beginning of the manufacturing process, and overhead is applied to each product at the rate of 60 percent of direct labor costs. There was no finished goods inventory on January 1, 2004. Epworth uses the FIFO costing method. A review of Epworth's 2004 inventory cost records disclosed the following information:

		Costs	
	Units	Materials	Labor
Work-in-process inventory, January 1, 2004 (80 percent complete as to labor and overhead)	200,000	$ 200,000	$ 315,000
Started	1,000,000		
Completed	900,000		
Current period costs		1,300,000	1,995,000

Required   Prepare a production cost report to verify the inventory balances and prepare necessary journal entries to correctly state the inventory of finished goods and work-in-process, assuming that the books have not been closed.

11–37 **Weighted-Average Method; Transferred-in Costs**   Daewoo Corporation manufactures a popular model of business calculators in a suburb of Seoul, South Korea. The production process goes through two departments, assembly and testing. The following information (in thousands of South Korean currency, the *won*) pertains to the testing department for the month of July.

Work-in-process inventory, July 1		4,000 units
Transferred-in costs	57,800 won	(100 percent complete)
Costs added by the department		
Direct materials	23,400 won	(100 percent complete)
Conversion	23,360 won	(80 percent complete)

During the month of July, 15,000 units were transferred in from the assembly department at the cost of 141,700 won, and the mixing department added costs of 203,615 won.

Direct materials	93,475 won
Conversion	110,140 won

During the month, 16,000 units were completed and transferred to the warehouse. At July 31, the completion percentage of work-in-process was as follows:

Direct materials	90 percent
Conversion	60 percent

Required

1. Prepare the production report of the testing department for the month of July using the weighted-average process costing.

2. Check the most recent issue of *The Wall Street Journal* or www.xe.com to learn the exchange rate between the U.S. dollar and the South Korean won.

11–38 **FIFO Method; Transferred-in Costs (Appendix B)**   Wood Glow Manufacturing Company produces a single product, a wood refinishing kit that sells for $17.95. The final processing of the kits occurs in the packaging department. An internal quilted wrap is applied at the beginning of the packaging process. A compartmentalized outside box printed with instructions and the company's name and logo is added when units have 60 percent of the process. Conversion costs consisting of direct labor and applied overhead occur evenly throughout the packaging process. Conversion activities after the addition of the box involve package sealing, testing for leakage, and final inspection. Rejections in the packaging department are rare and can be ignored. The following data pertain to the packaging department's activities during the month of October.

- Beginning work-in-process inventory was 10,000 units, 40 percent complete as to conversion costs.

- In the month, 30,000 units were started and completed.

- Ending work-in-process had 10,000 units, 80 percent complete as to conversion costs.

The packaging department's October costs follow:

Quilted wrap	$80,000
Outside boxes	50,000
Direct labor	22,000
Applied overhead ($3 per direct labor dollar)	66,000

The costs transferred in from prior processing were $3 per unit. The cost of goods sold for the month was $240,000, and the ending finished-goods inventory was $84,000. Wood Glow uses the first-in, first-out (FIFO) method of inventory valuation.

Wood Glow's controller, Mark Brandon, has been asked to analyze the packaging department's activities for the month of October. Mark knows that to properly determine the department's unit cost of production, he must first calculate the equivalent units of production.

Required

1. Prepare an equivalent units of production schedule for the packaging department's October activity. Be sure to account for the beginning work-in-process inventory, the units started and completed during the month, and the ending work-in-process inventory.

2. Determine the October production's cost per equivalent unit.

3. Assuming that the actual overhead incurred during October was $5,000 more than the overhead applied, describe how to determine the value of the ending work-in-process inventory.

(CMA Adapted)

11–39 **FIFO Method** Superior Brands, Inc., manufactures a medium-quality rubber cement product in two departments. Cost and production data for the first department are given for June 2004:

Work-in-process inventory, June 1	
Conversion: 40 percent complete	15,000 units
Work-in-process inventory, June 30	
Conversion: 65 percent complete	25,000 units
Started into production	80,000 units
Completed and transferred out	?
Costs	
Work-in-process inventory, June 1	
Direct materials	$ 72,500
Conversion	12,937.50
Costs added during May	
Material A	260,000
Material B	403,750
Conversion	461,437.50

Material A is added at the beginning of work in the first department. Material B is also added in the first department but not until units of product are 50 percent complete with regard to conversion. Conversion costs are incurred uniformly during the process. The company uses the FIFO cost method.

Required

1. Calculate equivalent units of material A, material B, and conversion.

2. Calculate costs per equivalent unit for material A, material B, and conversion.

3. Calculate the cost of units transferred out.

4. Calculate the value of ending work-in-process inventory.

11–40 **Weighted-Average Method; Two Departments** Allgood, Inc., an automotive exhaust system manufacturer has two departments in muffler processing, the fabrication and the assembly departments. All materials for the fabrication department were added at the beginning of the process. Data recorded for January follow:

	Units	Percent Completed	Direct Materials	Conversion
Fabrication department				
Work-in-process inventory, January 1	6,000	20%	$ 15,000	$ 20,000
Transferred to assembly				
department in January	50,000			
Work-in-process inventory, January 31	4,000	40%		
Assembly department				
Work-in-process inventory, January 1	10,000	40		$200,000
(transferred-in cost: $92,000)				
Completed and				
transferred out in January	55,000			
Work-in-process inventory, January 31	5,000	40		

(continued)

Costs incurred in January		
Fabrication department	$117,500	$310,850
Assembly department		$723,400

Required Calculate the following using the weighted-average method:

1. Equivalent units of direct materials and conversion in the fabrication department.
2. Unit costs of direct materials and conversion in the fabrication department.
3. Cost of goods transferred to the assembly department from the fabrication department in the month of January.
4. Cost of the work-in-process ending inventory in the fabrication department.
5. Equivalent units of transferred-in and conversion in the assembly department.
6. Unit costs of transferred-in and conversion in the assembly department.
7. Cost of goods transferred to finished goods from the assembly department in January.
8. Cost of the work-in-process ending inventory in the assembly department.

11–41 **FIFO Method; Two Departments (Appendix B)** Graybill Company produces plastic photo frames. Two departments, molding and finishing, are involved in the manufacturing. The molding department fills the molds with hot liquid plastic that is left to cool and then opens them. The finishing department removes the plastic frame from the mold and strips the edges of the frames of extra plastic.

The following information is available for the month of January:

	January 1		January 31	
Work-in-Process Inventory	**Quantity (pounds)**	**Cost**	**Quantity (pounds)**	**Cost**
Molding department	None	—	None	—
Finishing department	5,000	$15,000	2,000	?

The work-in-process inventory in the finishing department is estimated to be 25 percent complete both at the beginning and end of January. Costs of production for January follow:

Costs of Production	**Materials Used**	**Conversion**
Molding department	$300,000	$50,000
Finishing department	—	40,000

The material used in the molding department weighed 50,000 pounds. The firm uses the FIFO method of process costing.

Required Prepare a report for both the molding and finishing departments for the month of January. The report should include equivalent units of production (in pounds), total manufacturing costs, cost per equivalent unit (pounds), cost of ending work-in-process inventory, and cost of goods completed and transferred out.

11–42 **Weighted-Average Method; FIFO Method; Two Departments** Porter Company manufactures its one product by a process that requires two departments. The production starts in department A and is completed in department B. Materials are added at the beginning of the process in department A. Additional materials are added when the process is 50 percent complete in department B. Conversion costs are incurred proportionally throughout the production processes in both departments.

On April 1, department A had 500 units in production estimated to be 30 percent complete; department B had 300 units in production estimated to be 40 percent complete. During April, department A started 1,500 units and completed 1,600 units; department B completed 1,400 units. The work-in-process ending inventory on April 30 in department A is estimated to be 20 percent complete, and the work-in-process ending inventory in department B is estimated to be 70 percent complete.

The cost sheet for department A shows that the units in the work-in-process beginning inventory had $3,000 in direct materials costs and $1,530 in conversion costs. The production costs incurred in April were $12,000 for direct materials and $10,710 for conversion. Department B's work-in-process beginning inventory on April 1 was $6,100; it incurred $38,000 in direct materials costs and $24,350 in conversion costs in April.

Department A's cost per unit in March is $14 regardless of which process costing method is used to determine costs. Porter Company uses the FIFO method for department A and the weighted-average method for department B.

Required

1. Prepare a production cost report for department A.
2. Prepare a production cost report for department B.

11–43 **Spoilage; Weighted-Average Method; Transferred-in Costs (Appendix A)** JC Company employs a process cost system. A unit of product passes through three departments—molding, assembly, and finishing—before it is completed. The following activity took place in the finishing department during May:

	Units
Work-in-process inventory—May 1	1,400
Transferred in from the assembly department	14,000
Spoiled	700
Transferred out to finished goods inventory	11,200

Direct materials are added at the beginning of the processing in the finishing department without changing the number of units being processed. The work-in-process inventory was 70 percent complete as to conversion on May 1 and 40 percent complete as to conversion on May 31. All spoilage was discovered at final inspection before the units were transferred to finished goods; 560 of the spoiled units were considered acceptable.

JC Company employs the weighted-average costing method. The equivalent units and the current costs per equivalent unit of production for each cost factor follow:

	Equivalent Units	Current Costs per Equivalent Unit
Cost of prior department	15,400	$5
Direct materials	15,400	1
Conversion cost	13,300	3
		$9

Required

1. What is the cost of production transferred to the finished goods inventory?
2. What is the cost assigned to the work-in-process inventory on May 31?
3. If the total costs of prior departments included in the finishing department's work-in-process inventory on May 1 amounted to $6,300, what is the total cost transferred in from the assembly department to the finishing department during May?
4. What is the cost associated with the abnormal spoilage?

(CMA Adapted)

11–44 **Spoilage, Weighted-Average Method; Transferred-in Costs (Appendix A)** Romano Foods Inc. manufactures 12-inch Roman Surprise Fresh Frozen Pizzas that retail for $4.69 to $5.99, depending upon the topping. The company employs a process costing system in which the product flows through several processes. Joe Corolla, vice president of production, has had a long-running disagreement with the controller, Sue Marshall, over the way to handle spoilage cost. Joe resists every attempt to charge production with variance responsibilities unless they are favorable. Spoilage costs have not been significant in the past, but, in November, the mixing department had a substantial amount of spoilage. Romano Foods has traditionally treated 10 percent of good output as normal spoilage. The mixing department input 120,000 units of ingredients; inspection rejected 13,000 dough units. Sue is concerned about the abnormal spoilage and wants Joe to take corrective steps. He maintains, however, that the mixing department is operating properly and has prepared the following report to support his contention:

ROMANO FOODS—MIXING DEPARTMENT
Production Cost Report
Month Ended November 30, 2004

Input Units	Total Cost	Good Output Units	Normal Spoilage (10 percent)	Abnormal Spoilage	Good Unit Cost
120,000	$45,360	107,000	12,000	1,000	$ 0.42
Budgeted unit cost					$ 0.435
Actual cost per good unit					0.420
Favorable variance					$ 0.015

Cost Reconciliation

Cost of 107,000 good units @ $0.42 each	$44,940
Abnormal spoilage (charge to purchasing for buying inferior materials):	
1,000 units @ $0.42 each	420
Total cost	$45,360

Sue read the report and found out that Joe miscalculated both normal and abnormal spoilage units, and he ignored the normal spoilage in calculating the unit cost.

Required

1. Revise Joe Corolla's production cost report for November 2004 by calculating the correct numbers or amounts for the following:

   a. The number of units of normal spoilage.

   b. The number of units of abnormal spoilage.

   c. The total and per-unit costs of the mixing department's production of good units in November.

   d. The total and per-unit costs of abnormal spoilage.

2. Prepare the journal entry to transfer costs for the mixing department for November to the assembly department.

3. Describe how Joe Corolla's production cost report has shown the performance of the mixing department to be less favorable than that shown in the revised report in requirement 1.

(CMA Adapted)

11–45 **Weighted-Average Process Costing; Spoilage** Cardona Paint Company, which manufactures quality paint to sell at premium prices, uses a single production department. Production begins by blending the various chemicals that are added at the beginning of the process and ends by filling the paint cans. The gallon cans are then transferred to the shipping department for crating and shipment. Labor and overhead are added continuously throughout the process. Factory overhead is applied on the basis of direct labor-hours at the rate of $3 per hour. The company combines labor and overhead in computing product cost.

Prior to May, when a change in the process was implemented, work-in-process inventories were insignificant. The change in the process allows increased production but results in considerable amounts of work-in-process for the first time. Also, the company had 1,000 spoiled gallons in May—one-half of which was normal spoilage and the rest abnormal spoilage.

These data relate to actual production during the month of May:

	Costs
Work-in-process inventory, May 1	
Direct materials—chemicals	$ 45,600
Direct labor ($10 per hour)	6,250
Factory overhead	1,875
May costs added:	
Direct materials—chemicals	228,400
Direct labor ($10 per hour)	35,000
Factory overhead	10,500

	Units
Work-in-process inventory, May 1 (25 percent complete)	4,000
Sent to shipping department	20,000
Started in May	21,000
Work-in-process inventory, May 31 (80 percent complete)	4,000

Required   Prepare a production cost report for May using the weighted-average method.

(CMA Adapted)

11–46 **Spoilage; Weighted-Average Method; Transferred-in Costs (Appendix A)**   APCO Company manufactures various lines of bicycles. Because of the high volume of each line, the company employs a process cost system using the weighted-average method to determine unit costs. Bicycle parts are manufactured in the molding department and then are consolidated into a single bike unit in the molding department and transferred to the assembly department where they are partially assembled. After assembly, the bicycle is sent to the packing department.

Cost per unit data for the 20-inch dirt bike has been completed through the molding department. Annual cost and production figures for the assembly department are presented in the schedules that follow.

Defective bicycles are identified at the inspection point when the assembly labor process is 70 percent complete; all assembly materials have been added at this point. The normal rejection for defective bicycles is 5 percent of the bicycles reaching the inspection point. Any defective bicycles above the 5 percent quota are considered to be abnormal. All defective bikes are removed from the production process and destroyed.

Required

1. Compute the number of defective, or spoiled, bikes that are considered to be
   a. Normal.
   b. Abnormal.
2. Compute the equivalent units of production for the year for
   a. Bicycles transferred in from the molding department.
   b. Bicycles produced with regard to assembly material.
   c. Bicycles produced with regard to assembly conversion.
3. Compute the cost per equivalent unit for the fully assembled dirt bike.
4. Compute the amount of the total production cost of $1,672,020 that will be associated with the following items:
   a. Normal spoiled units.
   b. Abnormal spoiled units.
   c. Good units completed in the assembly department.
   d. Ending work-in-process inventory in the assembly department.
5. Describe how to present the applicable dollar amounts for the following items in the financial statements:
   a. Normal spoiled units.
   b. Abnormal spoiled units.
   c. Completed units transferred in to the packing department.

Assembly Department Cost Data

	Transferred in from Molding Department	Assembly Materials	Assembly Conversion Cost	Total Cost of Dirt Bike through Assembly
Prior period costs	$ 82,200	$ 6,660	$ 11,930	$ 100,790
Current period costs	1,237,800	96,840	236,590	1,571,230
Total costs	$1,320,000	$103,500	$248,520	$1,672,020

Assembly Department Production Data

		Percentage Complete		
	Bicycles	Transferred in	Assembly Materials	Conversion
Beginning inventory	3,000	100%	100%	80%
Transferred in from molding during year	45,000	100	—	—
Transferred out to packing during year	40,000	100	100	100
Ending inventory	4,000	100	50	20

(CMA Adapted)

11–47 **Process Costing and Activity-Based Costing**   Hampton Chemical Specialties, Inc. (HCS) is a manufacturer of specialty chemicals sold to manufacturers, hospitals, and other users. HCS produces 10 to 15 million gallons of its main product HCS-22 each month. The data for July 2004 follows (in thousands of gallons). The chemical raw materials are added at the beginning of processing.

Beginning work-in-process inventory (60% complete for conversion; materials $55,000, conversion $7,250)	200 gallons
Units started	1,000 gallons
Good units finished (no spoilage)	800 gallons
Ending work-in-process inventory (30% complete for conversion)	400 gallons

Current manufacturing costs	
Materials	$176,000
Conversion	$66,900

Each month HCS averages 100 batches of product with approximately 12,000 gallons per batch, though some batches are as large as 50,000 gallons or more, and some are as small as a few hundred gallons. Also, the pattern of customer orders is that large orders come in at all times of the month, while small orders tend to cluster around the last few days of the month. The small orders are due to salespersons trying to meet monthly sales quotas and to the buying patterns of smaller customers who want their shipments early in the following month. As a result, in the average month three-fourths of the total orders are started in the last few days of the month, and most are not completed until early in the following month. For example, in July 2004, 100 batches were produced, and 75 were still in the ending work-in-process inventory at the end of the month. Ted Brown, plant controller for HCS, thinks that the current costing method, using weighted-average process costing, underestimates the costs of the ending work-in-process inventory as well as the smaller jobs.

Required

1. Calculate the production cost report using the weighted-average method.
2. Assume that $28,500 of the $66,900 current conversion costs could be traced to batch-related activities such as equipment setup. Further, assume that these batch-related costs are all incurred when the batch is started. Ted has asked you to recalculate the production

cost report to separate the batch-related costs from total conversion costs. How do the results differ from the method in requirement 1? Is Ted right about underestimating the cost of ending work-in-process inventory?

Solutions to Self–Study Problems

1. Weighted-Average Method versus FIFO Method

1. Weighted-average method
   a. Equivalent units

Direct materials: 1,000 + (200 × 100%)	1,200
Conversion: 1,000 + (200 × 70%)	1,140

   b. Cost per equivalent unit

Direct materials: ($9,600/1,200)	$8.00
Conversion: ($2,202 + $6,120)/1,140	$7.30
Total unit costs: $8.00 + $7.30	$15.30

   c. Cost of goods completed and transferred out: $15.30 × 1,000 $15,300

   d. Cost of work-in-process, 10/31

Direct materials: $8 × 200 × 100%	$1,600
Conversion: $7.30 × 200 × 70%	$1,022
Total: $1,600 + $1,022	$2,622

2. Weighted-average method production cost report

SMITH ELECTRONIC COMPANY
Chip-Mounting Production Department
Weighted-Average Production Cost Report

Production Quantity Information

	Step 1: Analyze Flow of Physical Units	Step 2: Calculate Equivalent Units	
	Physical Units	Direct Materials	Conversion Costs
Input			
Work-in-process beginning inventory	300		
Completion percentage			
Direct materials 0 percent			
Conversion 40 percent			
Started this period	900		
Total to account for	1,200		
Output			
Completed	1,000	1,000	1,000
Work-in-process ending inventory	200		
Completion percentage			
Direct materials 100 percent		200	
Conversion 70 percent			140
Total accounted for	1,200		
Total work done to date (Total equivalent units)		1,200	1,140

Unit Cost Determination

Step 3: Determine Costs to Account For	Total	Total Direct Materials	Conversion Costs
Work-in-process beginning inventory	$ 2,202		$2,202
Current cost	15,720	$9,600	$6,120
Total costs to account for	$17,922	$9,600	$8,322

Step 4: Compute Unit Costs			
Cost per equivalent unit		($9,600/1,200) =	($8,322/1,140) =
	$15.30	$8.00	$7.30

Cost Assignment

Step 5: Assign Total Manufacturing Costs	Total	Direct Materials	Conversion Costs
Units completed and transferred out	$15,300 ($15.30 × 1,000)		
Work-in-process ending inventory	2,622	(200 × $8) = $1,600	(140 × $7.30) = $1,022
Total manufacturing costs accounted for	$17,922		

3. FIFO method

   a. Equivalent units:

      Direct materials: (300 × 100%) + (1,000 − 300) + (200 × 100%)   1,200

      or 1,000 + (200 × 100%) − (300 × 0%)   1,200

      Conversion: [300 × (1 − 40%)] + (1,000 − 300) + (200 × 70%)   1,020

      or 1,000 + (200 × 70%) − (300 × 40%)   1,020

   b. Cost per equivalent unit

      Direct materials: $9,600/1,200 $ 8

      Conversion: $6,120/1,020 $ 6

      Total unit costs = $8 + $6 $14

   c. Cost of goods completed and transferred out

      From beginning work-in-process inventory:

         Direct materials: $0 + $8 × 300 × (1–0%) $ 2,400

         Conversion: $2,202 + $6 × 300 × (1–40%) $ 3,282

      Total: $2,400 + $3,282 $ 5,682

      Started and completed: $14 × (1,000 − 300) $ 9,800

      Total cost of goods completed: $5,682 + $9,800 $15,482

   d. Cost of work in process, 10/31

      Direct materials: $8 × 200 × 100% $1,600

      Conversion: $6 × 200 × 70% $ 840

      Total: $1,600 + $840 $2,440

4. FIFO method production cost report

SMITH ELECTRONIC COMPANY
Chip-Mounting Production Department
FIFO Production Cost Report

Production Quantity Information

	Step 1: Analyze Flow of Physical Units	Step 2: Calculate Equivalent Units	
	Physical Units	Direct Materials	Conversion Costs
Input			
Work-in-process beginning inventory	300		
Completion percentage			
Direct materials 0 percent		0	
Conversion 40 percent			120
Started this period	900		
Total units to account for	1,200		
Output			
Completed	1,000	1,000	1,000
Work-in-process ending inventory	200		
Completion percentage			
Direct materials 100 percent		200	
Conversion 70 percent			140
Total units accounted for	1,200	1,200	1,140
Total work performed to date			
Work-in-process beginning inventory	300	0	(120)
Total work performed this period		1,200	1,020
(FIFO equivalent units)			

Unit Cost Determination

Step 3: Determine Total Costs to Account For Flow	Total	Direct Materials	Conversion Costs
Work-in-process beginning inventory	$ 2,202		$2,202
Current cost	15,720	$9,600	6,120
Total costs to account for	$17,922	$9,600	$8,322

Step 4: Compute Unit Costs		($9,600/1,200) =	($6,120/1,020) =
Cost per equivalent unit	$14	$8	$6

Cost Assignment

Step 5: Assign Total Manufacturing Costs	Total	Direct Materials	Conversion Costs
Units completed (1,000):			
From work-in-process beginning inventory	$ 2,202		$2,202
Current costs incurred completing units	3,480	(300 × $8) = $2,400	(180 × $6) = $1,080
Total cost from beginning inventory	$ 5,682	$2,400	$3,282
Units started and completed this period	9,800 = [$8(1,000 − 300) + $6(1,000 − 300)]		
Total cost of units completed and transferred out	$15,482		
Work-in-process ending inventory	2,440	(200 × $8) = $1,600	(140 × $6) = $840
Total costs accounted for	$17,922		

2. Weighted-Average Method vs. FIFO Method with Transferred-In Cost

1. Weighted-average method

REED COMPANY
Finishing Department
Weighted-Average Production Cost Report

Production Quantity Information

	Step 1: Analyze Flow of Physical Units		Step 2: Calculate Equivalent Units	
	Physical Units	Transferred-in	Direct Materials	Conversion Costs
Input				
Work-in-process, November 1	10 (40%)			
Started this month	80			
Total units to account for	90			
Output				
Completed	82	82	82	82
Work-in-process, November 30	8 (50%)	8	8	4
Total accounted for	90			
Total work done to date		90	90	86
(Total equivalent units)				

Unit Cost Determination

Step 3: Determine Total Costs to Account For	Total	Transferred-in	Direct Materials	Conversion Costs
Work-in-process, November 1	$ 232	$100	$ 80	$ 52
Current costs	2,381	800	720	861
Total costs to account for	$2,613	$900	$800	$913

Step 4: Compute Unit Costs		Transferred-in	Direct Materials	Conversion Costs
		($900/90) =	($800/90) =	($913/86) =
Cost per unit	$29.51	$10.00	$8.89	$10.62

Cost Assignment

Step 5: Assign Total Manufacturing Costs	Total	Transferred-in	Direct Materials	Conversion Costs
Units completed (82):	$2,420 = 82 × $29.51			
Work-in-process, November 30 (8)	193	(8 × $10) = = $80	(8 × $8.89) = = $71	(4 × $10.62) = = $42
Total costs accounted for	$2,613			

2. FIFO method

REED COMPANY
Finishing Department
FIFO Production Cost Report

Production Quantity Information

	Step 1: Analyze Flow of Physical Units		Step 2: Calculate Equivalent Units	
	Physical Units	Transferred-in	Direct Materials	Conversion Costs
Input				
Work-in-process, November 1	10 (40%)			
Started this month	80			
Total units to account for	90			
Output				
Completed	82	82	82	82
Work-in-process, November 30	8 (50%)	8	8	4
Total accounted for	90			
Total work done to date		90	90	86
Work-in-process, November 1		(10)	(10)	(4)
Total work done this month— FIFO equivalent units		80	80	82

Unit Cost Determination

Step 3: Determine Total Costs to Account For	Total	Transferred-in	Direct Materials	Conversion Costs
Work-in-process, November 1	$ 232			
Current costs	2,381	$800	$720	$861
Total costs to account for	$2,613			

Step 4: Compute Unit Costs		Transferred-in	Direct Materials	Conversion Costs
		($800/80) =	($720/80) =	($861/82) =
Cost per unit	$29.50	$10.00	$9.00	$10.50

Cost Assignment

Step 5: Assign Total Manufacturing Costs	Total	Transferred-in	Direct Materials	Conversion Costs
Units completed (82):				
From work-in-process, November 1 (10)	$ 232	$100	$80	$52
Current costs added	63	—	—	(6 × $10.50)
Total from beginning inventory	$ 295	$100	$80	$115
Units started and completed (82 − 10 = 72)	2,124 = 72 × $29.50			
Total cost of units completed and transferred out	$2,419			
Work in process, November 30 (8)	194	(8 × $10) = $80	(8 × $9) = $72	(4 × $10.50) = $42
Total costs accounted for	$2,613			

CHAPTER TWELVE

Cost Allocation: Service Departments and Joint Product Costs

After studying the chapter, you should be able to . . .

1. Identify the strategic role of cost allocation
2. Explain the ethical issue of cost allocation
3. Use the three steps of departmental cost allocation
4. Explain the problems in implementing the different departmental cost allocation methods
5. Explain the use of cost allocation in service firms
6. Use the three joint product costing methods
7. Use the four by-product costing methods

In keeping with their firms' mission of continual improvement and superiority in their products and services, General Electric (GE) and many other firms such as Ford Motor Company, Johnson & Johnson, IBM, and Marriott have sought improved methods of providing administrative services within their firms. These administrative services are often called *shared services* because they are shared among the company's operating units. Shared services generally include such transaction-processing services as payroll processing, claims processing, human resources, and many accounting services, among others. The firms named have studied the cost to provide the services and have been alarmed at the relatively high costs, such as $10 or more to process a single vendor invoice. Some firms have chosen to outsource these services or to have the operating units provide the services locally, but, like GE, most firms are centralizing these services to reduce cost, provide a high and standardized level of service quality, and provide a single base of technology for easy use, communication, and future modification.[1]

With the growth of these centralized services, the need for effective methods to allocate the shared costs to the operating units has increased. Generally, the allocation issue arises when cost is shared because of a shared facility, program, production process, or service. The methods used to allocate these common costs to products are explained in this chapter.

This chapter explains methods for allocating common costs to products for two broad types of common costs: (1) the costs of production and service departments shared by two or more individual products and (2) the joint manufacturing costs for products that are not separately identifiable until later in the manufacturing process. An example of the latter is the cost of refining crude oil (the joint cost) into the individual products: gasoline, heating oil, and other products.

---

[1] For more information on company practices, see Ann Triplett and Jon Scheumann, "Managing Shared Services with ABM," *Strategic Finance*, February 2000, pp. 40–45; and "A Day of Reckoning for Bean Counters," *Business Week*, March 14, 1994, pp. 75–76.

We take a strategic perspective in developing these allocation methods and ask key strategic questions: How do the allocation methods we have chosen affect the motivations and behaviors of those in the operating units as well as the service units? Can we use ABC costing principles to develop more accurate methods of cost allocation? Does this service add value or should it be outsourced? The firm's answers to these questions can have a significant impact on its competitiveness and success.

The Strategic Role of Cost Allocation

The strategic role of cost allocation has four objectives:

1. Determine *accurate departmental and product costs* as a basis for evaluating the cost efficiency of departments and the profitability of different products.
2. *Motivate* managers to exert a high level of effort to achieve the goals of top management.
3. Provide the right *incentive* for managers to make decisions that are consistent with the goals of top management.
4. *Fairly determine the rewards* earned by the managers for their effort and skill and for the effectiveness of their decision making.

LEARNING OBJECTIVE 1

Identify the strategic role of cost allocation.

The first and most important objective requires the cost allocation method to be sufficiently accurate to support effective management decision making about products and departments.

The second objective, motivating managers, means that, to be effective, the cost allocation used must reward department managers for reducing costs as desired. A key motivation issue is whether the manager *controls* the allocated cost. For example, when a department's cost allocation for equipment maintenance is based on the number of the department's machine breakdowns, the manager has an incentive to reduce them and therefore reduce the maintenance costs. On the other hand, when the cost of maintenance is allocated on the basis of a department's square feet of floor space, the manager—who cannot affect the amount of floor space—is not motivated.

The third objective, providing the incentive for decision making, is achieved when cost allocation effectively provides the incentives for the individual manager to act autonomously in a manner that is consistent with top management's goals. For example, a major advantage of cost allocation methods is that they draw managers' attention to shared facilities. The cost allocation provides an incentive for individual and joint efforts to manage these costs and to encourage the managers to use these facilities to improve the performance of their units.

The fourth objective, fairness, is met when the cost allocation is clear, objective, and consistently applied. The most objective basis for cost allocation exists when a *cause-and-effect relationship* can be determined. For example, the allocation of maintenance costs on the basis of the number of equipment breakdowns is more objective and fair than an allocation based on square feet, the number of products produced, or labor costs in the department. The reason is that a cause-and-effect relationship exists between maintenance costs and the number of breakdowns; square feet or labor costs, however, do not have a clear relationship to maintenance costs.

In some situations, cause-and-effect bases are not available and alternative concepts of fairness are used. One such concept is *ability-to-bear,* which is commonly employed with bases related to size, such as total sales, total assets, or the profitability of the user departments. Other concepts of fairness are based on equity perceived in the circumstance, such as *benefit received,* which often is measured in a nonquantitative way. For example, the cost of a firm's computer services might be allocated largely or entirely to the research and development department because the computer is more critical to this department's functioning and this department uses it more than other departments do.

Recording artists Courtney Love, LeAnn Rimes, Beck, Clint Black, and others are suing the music industry for millions of dollars of unpaid royalties. The artists claim that the music industry unfairly cut into their royalties by improperly accounting for expenses. At issue lies the often complex recording contracts between the artists and the record companies that contain the details of how the expenses of producing and distributing the artist's work are to be calculated and charged to the artist's account. The artists think they are being cheated, while an industry spokesman says that the contracts reflect a "complex business relationship where both the artists and the label understandably angle to secure the best possible contract—in negotiations or renegotiations—while still preserving a mutually beneficial relationship." In other words, both sides should be well represented by management accountants who understand how the costs are to be calculated and allocated.

Source: Jennifer Ordonez, "Rockers vs. Bean Counters," *The Wall Street Journal*, September 24, 2002, p. B1.

The Ethical Issues of Cost Allocation

LEARNING OBJECTIVE 2
Explain the ethical role of cost allocation.

A number of ethical issues are important in cost allocation. First, ethical issues arise when costs are allocated to products or services that are produced for both a competitive market and a public agency or government department. Although government agencies very often purchase on a cost-plus basis, products sold competitively are subject to price competition. The incentive in these situations is for the manufacturer, using cost allocation methods, to shift manufacturing costs from the competitive products to the cost-plus products. Evidence of this was shown in a study reported by former Secretary of the Navy John F. Lehman. The study, performed for the Navy by a CPA firm, found that defense contractors' profits on military work were higher than profits on nonmilitary work.

A second ethical issue in implementing cost allocation methods is the equity or fair share issue that arises when a governmental unit reimburses the costs of a private institution or when it provides a service for a fee to the public. In both cases, cost allocation methods are used to determine the proper price or reimbursement amount. Although no single measure of equity exists in these cases, the objectives of cost allocation identified at the beginning of the chapter are a useful guide.

A third important ethical issue is the effect of the chosen allocation method on the costs of products sold to or from foreign subsidiaries. The cost allocation method usually affects the cost of products traded internationally and therefore the amount of taxes paid in the domestic and the foreign countries. Firms can reduce their worldwide tax liability by increasing the costs of products purchased in high-tax countries or in countries where the firm does not have favorable tax treatment. For this reason, international tax authorities closely watch the cost allocation methods used by multinational firms. The methods most acceptable to these authorities are based on sales and/or labor costs.[2]

Cost Allocation to Service and Production Departments

LEARNING OBJECTIVE 3
Use the three steps of departmental cost allocation.

The preceding chapters on activity-based costing (Chapter 5), job costing (Chapter 4), and process costing (Chapter 11) provide a useful context for introducing cost allocation. The processes discussed in those chapters allocated overhead costs either *directly* to products (job costing) or *indirectly* in an allocation first to production departments and then to the products (process costing) or by using production activities (activity-based costing), as illustrated in Exhibit 12.1. Direct allocation pools all overhead into a single amount and allocates overhead using a single rate. In contrast, the departmental approach pools overhead costs in departmental cost pools and allocates overhead

[2] Eric G. Tomsett, "Allocation of Central Costs in an International Group," *World Tax* (a publication of Deloitte & Touche International), January 1992.

REAL-WORLD FOCUS   Cost Allocation and Cost Shifting by Federal Reserve
                      Banks and Nonprofit Organizations

FEDERAL RESERVE BANKS REALLOCATE COMMON COSTS TO LESS COMPETITIVE SERVICES

The Monetary Control Act of 1980 required the Federal Reserve (FED) to charge explicitly for certain services, in effect placing Federal Reserve banks in direct competition with large commercial banks for these services. The act also required the FED to price these services based on full cost, including allocated indirect costs. Recent research indicates that the FED responded to the act by both improving the efficiency with which it provides these services and reallocating indirect costs to the less price-competitive services. In this manner, the FED was able to lower the full cost and, therefore, the price of its most price-competitive services.

COST ALLOCATION AND TAXATION OF UNRELATED BUSINESS INCOME AT NONPROFIT ORGANIZATIONS

Nonprofit organizations are exempt from federal income tax except for income from any activities that are unrelated to the nonprofit's exempt purpose. An example is the use of a laboratory for both tax-exempt basic medical research and testing a taxable product for commercial pharmaceutical firms. A concern in these cases is that the tax-exempt nonprofit organization will be able to compete un-

fairly with for-profit firms because of their tax-exempt status. The key argument is that common costs for the nonprofit's exempt and business activities will be used to "subsidize" the for-profit business (in this case, the taxable product testing). The nonprofit clearly has an incentive to allocate a relatively large portion of the common costs to the business activity to reduce taxes, but current Treasury regulations require that the cost allocation be reasonable. This has led some to argue that common costs should not be allocated in these cases. However, a recent analytical study (using economic models) of the economic productivity of for-profit and not-for-profit firms competing in the same business shows that failure to allocate common costs would lead to economic inefficiency by deterring the nonprofit manager from engaging in economically efficient unrelated businesses. The study supports the Treasury stance, which allows "reasonable" cost allocations.

Based on information in Ken S. Cavalluzzo, Christopher D. Ittner, and David F. Larcker, "Competition, Efficiency, and Cost Allocation in Government Agencies: Evidence on the Federal Reserve System," *Journal of Accounting Research,* Spring 1998, pp. 1–32; and Richard Sansing, "The Unrelated Business Income Tax, Cost Allocation, and Productive Efficiency," *National Tax Journal,* June 1998, pp. 291–302.

EXHIBIT 12.1
Three Types of Overhead Allocation

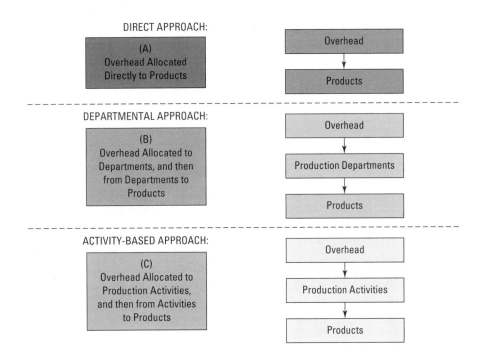

from each department to the products using a separate rate, one for each department. The departmental approach is preferred because it more accurately traces overhead costs to the products when different products require different amounts of resources in the various production departments.

The activity-based approach is the most accurate and the most preferred of the three approaches because it identifies cost behavior at the activity level, a much more detailed level of analysis than either the department level, as used in the departmental

EXHIBIT 12.2 The Three Phases in Departmental Cost Allocation

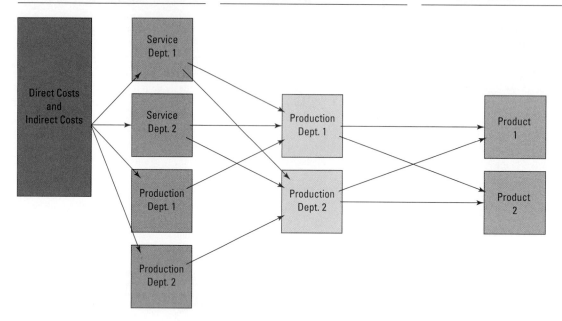

allocation approach, or plant level, as used in the direct approach.[3] Firms that have not been able to implement an activity-based costing system or cannot use the activity-based approach for cost-benefit or other reasons usually apply the departmental allocation approach. In the following section, we explain the application of the departmental approach.

Departmental Approach

The departmental approach recognizes that the typical manufacturing operation involves two types of manufacturing departments: production departments and service departments. Service departments provide human resources, maintenance, engineering, and other support to the production departments; production departments directly assemble and complete the product. The departmental approach has three phases: (1) trace all direct costs and allocate overhead costs to both the service departments and the production departments, (2) allocate the service department costs to the production departments, and finally (3) allocate the production department costs to the products. These phases are illustrated in Exhibit 12.2.

First Phase: Trace Direct Costs and Allocate Overhead Costs to Departments

The first phase in the departmental allocation approach traces the direct and indirect manufacturing costs in the plant to each service and production department that used them and identifies the overhead costs in the plant and allocates them to each of the service and production departments.

For the first-phase allocation, see the information for Beary Company in Exhibit 12.3. Beary manufactures two products and has two manufacturing departments and two service departments. A $36,000 direct cost can be traced to each department, and an indirect cost of $30,000 ($25,000 labor and $5,000 materials) is common to all departments but cannot be traced directly to the departments. Beary uses both labor-hours and machine-hours for allocating the indirect costs.

---

[3] For a recent survey of the use of activity-based costing in the allocation of shared facility costs, see Ann Triplett and Jon Scheumann, "Managing Shared Services with ABM," *Strategic Finance,* February 2000, pp. 40–45.

EXHIBIT 12.3
Data for Beary Company

	Service Department 1	Service Department 2	Production Department 1	Production Department 2	Total Hours	Total Amount
Labor-hours	1,800	1,200	3,600	5,400	12,000	
Machine-hours	320	160	1,120	1,600	3,200	
Direct costs	$1,600	$5,500	$15,500	$13,400		$36,000
Indirect labor		Not Traceable				25,000
Indirect materials		Not Traceable				5,000
						$66,000

EXHIBIT 12.4   **Departmental Allocation, First Phase: Beary Company**

Departmental Allocation Bases		Departments				
		Service 1	Service 2	Production 1	Production 2	Total
Direct labor-hours (DLH)		1,800	1,200	3,600	5,400	12,000
Percent		15%	10%	30%	45%	100%
Machine-hours (MH)		320	160	1,120	1,600	3,200
Percent		10%	5%	35%	50%	100%
First Phase: Trace Direct Costs and Allocate Overhead Costs to Departments						
Direct costs		$1,600	$5,500	$15,500	$13,400	$36,000
Overhead Costs to Departments						
Indirect Labor	DLH	3,750	2,500	7,500	11,250	$25,000
		= 15% × $25,000	= 10% × $25,000	= 30% × $25,000	= 45% × $25,000	
Indirect Materials	MH	500	250	1,750	2,500	$5,000
		= 10% × $5,000	= 5% × $5,000	= 35% × $5,000	= 50% × $5,000	
Totals for all departments		**$5,850**	**$8,250**	**$24,750**	**$27,150**	**$66,000**

The first-phase allocation for Beary Company is shown in Exhibit 12.4. Total direct costs of $36,000 are traced to the four departments, and the overhead costs are allocated using labor-hours (for indirect labor) and machine-hours (for indirect materials). The exhibit presents the allocation base information for labor-hour and machine-hour usage. The $25,000 of indirect labor is allocated to the four departments using the labor-hours allocation base. For example, the amount of indirect labor allocated to service department 1 is $3,750 (service department 1's share of total indirect labor, or 15% × $25,000). The allocations of indirect labor costs to the other departments are made in the same way. Similarly, the $5,000 of indirect materials cost is allocated to the four departments using machine-hours. The amount of indirect materials allocated to service department 1 is $500 (10% × $5,000). The totals for direct costs and allocated indirect costs are $66,000, the same as the total cost to allocate (from Exhibit 12.3).

Service department 1	$ 5,850
Service department 2	8,250
Production department 1	24,750
Production department 2	27,150
Total	$66,000

Second Phase: Allocate Service Department Costs to Production Departments

The second phase allocates service department costs to the producing departments. This is the most complex of the allocation phases because services flow back and forth between the service departments. These are often called **reciprocal flows**. For example, assume that 40 percent (720 hours) of service department 1's 1,800 labor-hours are

Reciprocal flows represent the movement of services back and forth between service departments.

EXHIBIT 12.5
Reciprocal Relationships in Beary Company

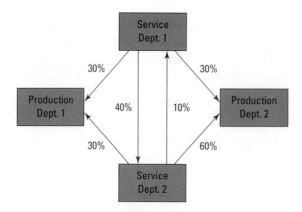

spent serving service department 2. Also assume that 10 percent of service department 2's time is spent serving service department 1. You can see these two reciprocal flows for Beary Company in Exhibit 12.5.

The percentage of service relationships is commonly determined by reference to labor-hours, units processed, or some other allocation base that best reflects the service provided in the departments. At Beary Company, the service flow percentages for each service department are determined according to the labor-hours used for services provided to the other service department and to the production departments. Beary's first service department spends 40 percent of its labor time serving the service department 2 and 30 percent serving each of the two production departments. Service department 2 serves the service department 1 approximately 10 percent of the time, the first production department 30 percent of the time, and the second production department 60 percent of the time.

Accountants use three common methods to allocate costs under the departmental approach: (1) the direct method, (2) the step method, and (3) the reciprocal method.

The Direct Method

The **direct method**
of cost allocation is accomplished by using the service flows *only to production departments* and determining each production department's share of that service.

The **direct method** is the simplest of the three methods because it ignores the reciprocal flows. The cost allocation is accomplished by using the service flows *only to production departments* and determining each production department's share of that service. For example, for service department 1, the share of time for each production department is 50 percent of the total production department service, determined as follows.

For service department 1:

> Net service to both production departments from service department 1:
> = 100% − Time of service to second service department
> = 100% − 40% = 60%
> Production department 1's share: 30 percent/60 percent = <u>50 percent</u>
>
> Production department 2's share: 30 percent/60 percent = <u>50 percent</u>

For service department 2:

> Net service to both production departments from service department 2:
> 100 percent − 10 percent = 90 percent
> Production department 1's share: 30 percent/90 percent = <u>33.33%</u>
>
> Production department 2's share: 60 percent/90 percent = <u>66.67%</u>

These percentage shares are used to allocate the costs from service departments to production departments, as shown in the second-phase section at the top of Exhibit 12.6. In that panel, for example, $5,850 of service department 1's costs are allocated

EXHIBIT 12.6   **Departmental Allocation Second and Third Phases, Using the Direct Method: Beary Company**

Second Phase: Allocate Service Department Costs to Production Departments

Direct Method		Production 1	Production 2	Total
Service 1	Service percent to producing departments	30%	30%	
	Allocation percent per direct method	50% = 30/(30 + 30)	50% = 30/(30 + 30)	
	Allocation amount	**$2,925**	**$2,925**	
		= 50% × $5,850	= 50% × $5,850	
Service 2	Service percent to producing departments	30%	60%	
	Allocation percent per direct method	33.33% = 30/(30 + 60)	66.67% = 60/(30 + 60)	
	Allocation amount	**2,750**	**5,500**	
		= 33.33% × $8,250	= 66.67% × $8,250	
Plus: First-phase allocation		24,750	27,150	
Totals for Production Departments		**$30,425**	**$35,575**	**$66,000**

Third Phase: Allocate Production Department Costs to Products

	Product 1	Product 2	
Base: labor-hours			
Amount	1,800	1,800	3,600
Percent	50%	50%	
Machine-hours			
Amount	400	1,200	1,600
Percent	25%	75%	
Production 1 (labor-hour basis)	$15,212.50	$15,212.50	
	= 50% × $30,425	= 50% × $30,425	
Production 2 (machine-hour basis)	$8,893.75	$26,681.25	
	= 25% × $35,575	= 75% × $35,575	
Totals for each product	**$24,106.25**	**$41,893.75**	**$66,000**

equally to the production departments; 50 percent each is $2,925. The $8,250 of service department 2's costs are allocated 33.33 percent or $2,750 to production department 1 and 66.67 percent or $5,500 to production department 2. Total costs in production departments 1 and 2 at the end of the first phase allocations are $30,425 and $35,575, respectively.

The third and final phase is much like the first phase. The allocation from production departments to products typically is based on the number of labor-hours or machine-hours used in the production departments that produce the products. For Beary Company, using the direct method, costs are allocated to production department 1 on the basis of labor-hours and to production department 2 on the basis of machine-hours; see the third-phase panel of Exhibit 12.6. Assume that the production of product 1 required 1,800 hours of production department 1's total labor time of 3,600 hours, and thus is allocated 50 percent (1,800/3,600) of the total cost in production department 1. Similarly, assume that product 1 required 400 of the 1,600 machine-hours used in production department 2, it is allocated 25 percent (400/1,600) of the costs of production department 2. Product 2's costs are determined in a similar manner, as shown in Exhibit 12.6. The total cost of $66,000 is allocated as $24,106.25 to product 1 and $41,893.75 to product 2.

The Step Method   The second method to allocate service department costs is the **step method,** so-called because it uses a sequence of steps in allocating service department costs to production departments. In the first step, one service department is selected to be allocated fully, that is, to the other service department as well as to each production department. The department to be allocated fully usually is chosen because it provides the most service to other service departments. At Beary Company, service department 1 provides more service (40%) and it goes first in the allocation. Service department 2 is

The **step method**
uses a sequence of steps in the allocating service department costs to production departments.

allocated only to the production departments, in the same manner as the direct method. Overall, this means that the step method provides more accurate allocations because one of the reciprocal flows between the two service departments (the one in the first step) is considered in the allocation, unlike the direct method that ignores all reciprocal flows.

The first phase of the step method (tracing direct costs and initial allocation of indirect costs) is the same as for the direct method as shown in Exhibit 12.4. However, in the second phase (Exhibit 12.7), service department 1, which is in the first step, is allocated to service department 2 and the two production departments. The allocation to service department 2 is $2,340 (40 percent × $5,850). The allocations for the two production departments are determined in a similar manner. Then, in the second step, service department 2 is allocated to the two production departments using the direct method in the same manner as in Exhibit 12.6. The only difference is that the total cost in service department 2 ($10,590) now includes the original cost in service department 2 ($8,250) plus the cost allocated from service department 1 in the first step ($2,340).

The third phase of the step method is completed as in Exhibit 12.6. Using the step method, the total cost allocated to product 1 is $24,008.75 and the total cost allocated to product 2 is $41,991.25, for a total of $66,000.

The **reciprocal method** considers *all* reciprocal flows between service departments through simultaneous equations.

The Reciprocal Method The **reciprocal method** is the most preferred of the three methods because, unlike the others, it considers *all* reciprocal flows between the service departments. This is accomplished by using simultaneous equations; the reciprocal flows are simultaneously determined in a system of equations.

An equation for each service department represents the cost to be allocated, consisting of the first-phase allocation costs plus the cost allocated from the other department. For Beary Company, the equation for service department 1 is as follows, using the symbol S1 to represent service department 1 costs and the symbol S2 to represent costs in service department 2.

Cost Management in Action

Health Care Providers Allocate Cost for Medicare Reimbursement

Since the advent of Medicare in 1966 to cover medical expenses of aged, blind, and disabled individuals, health care providers have been required to use cost allocation methods to receive reimbursement from the federal government for services covered by Medicare. The costs of health care service activities are allocated to the patient revenue-generating services. Some examples of service activities and patient revenue-generating services in a hospital follow.

How do hospitals respond to Medicare requirements and allocate the costs of service activities to the patient revenue-generating services? What methods are likely to be preferred?

(Refer to comments on Cost Management in Action at the end of the chapter.)

Patient Revenue-Generating Services

Intensive care unit	Laboratory
Psychiatric care	Radiology
Coronary care	Emergency Room
Surgery	Pharmacy
Anesthesia	

Service Activities

Dietary	Nursing administration
Laundry and linen	Operation of hospital buildings
Admissions	Administrative and general
Social services	Housekeeping

EXHIBIT 12.7   Departmental Allocation, Second and Third Phases Using the Step Method

Second Phase: Allocate Service Department Costs to Production Departments: Using the Step Method

	Service 2	Production 1	Production 2	Total
First Step				
Service 1				
Service percent	40%	30%	30%	
Amount	$ 2,340	$ 1,755	$ 1,755	
	= 40% × $5,850	= 30% × $5,850	= 30% × $5,850	
Second Step				
Service 2				
Service percent		30%	60%	
Allocation percent per direct method		33.33	66.67	
Amount	10,590	3,530	7,060	
	= $8,250 + $2,340	= 33.33% × $10,590	= 66.67% × $10,590	
Plus: First-phase allocation		24,750	27,150	
Totals for production departments		30,035	35,965	$66,000
Third Phase: Allocate Production Department Costs to Products				
Labor-hours				
Amount		1,800	1,800	3,600
Percentage		50%	50%	
Machine-hours				
Amount		400	1,200	1,600
Percentage		25%	75%	
Production 1 (labor-hour basis)		$15,017.50	$15,017.50	
		= 50% × $30,035	= 50% × $30,035	
Production 2 (machine-hour basis)		$8,991.25	$26,973.75	
		= 25% × $35,965	= 75% × $35,965	
Totals for each product		$24,008.75	$41,991.25	$66,000

Allocated S1 Costs = Initial allocation + Cost allocated from S2

$$S1 = \$5,850 + 10\% \times S2$$

Similarly, the equation for the second service department is as follows:

Allocated S2 Costs = Initial allocation + Cost allocated from S1

$$S2 = \$8,250 + 40\% \times S1$$

481

These two equations can be solved for S1 and S2 by substituting the second equation into the first as follows:

$$S1 = \$5,850 + 10\% \times (\$8,250 + 40\% \times S1)$$

$$S1 = \$6,953.13$$

And substituting S1 back into the second equation:

$$S2 = \$11,031.25$$

These values for S1 and S2 are allocated to the producing departments using the percentage service amounts for each department. We illustrate the process for Beary Company in Exhibit 12.8. Note that since the reciprocal method has considered all reciprocal service department activities, the allocation is based on the actual service percentages for each production department. For example, production department 1, which receives 30 percent of service department 1's work, is allocated 30 percent of service department 1's cost, $2,086 (30% × $6,953.13). The allocations are made in a similar manner to the allocation of service department 2's costs and to production department 2.

The third phase analysis in Exhibit 12.8 is done in the same manner as in Exhibits 12.6 and 12.7. The total cost allocated to product 1 is $24,036.25 and for product 2, $41,963.75.

Implementation Issues

The key implementation issue is the choice of the most accurate allocation method. Briefly review Exhibits 12.6, 12.7, and 12.8. Note that although total costs are the same ($66,000), the amounts allocated to the two products vary. Although these

EXHIBIT 12.8   **Departmental Allocation Second and Third Phases, Using the Reciprocal Method**

Second Phase: Allocate Service Department Costs to Production Departments Using the Reciprocal Method

First: Solve the simultaneous equations for Service 1 and Service 2 (see text):
  Amount allocated from service 1 $6,953.13
  Amount allocated from service 2 $11,031.25

	Production 1	Production 2	Total
Second: Allocate to producing departments			
Service 1			
Service %	30%	30%	
Allocated amount	$2,086	$2,086	
	= 30% × $6,953	= 30% × $6,953	
Service 2			
Service %	30%	60%	
Allocated amount	3,309	6,619	
	= 30% × $11,031	= 60% × $11,031	
Plus: Costs allocated in first phase	24,750	27,150	
Totals for Production Departments	$30,145	$35,855	$66,000
Third Phase: Allocate Production Department Costs to Products			
Base: Direct labor-hours			
Amount	1,800	1,800	3,600
Percent	50%	50%	
Machine-hours			
Amount	400	1,200	1,600
Percent	25%	75%	
Production 1 (direct labor-hour basis)	$15,072.50	$15,072.50	
	= 50% × $30,145	= 50% × $30,145	
Production 2 (machine-hour basis)	$8,963.75	$26,891.25	
	= 25% × $35,855	= 75% × $35,855	
Totals for each product	$24,036.25	$41,963.75	$66,000

amounts do not vary greatly for Beary Company, wide variations can occur in practice. When significant differences exist, a management accountant should consider the value of the reciprocal method, which is more complete and accurate than the others because it fully considers the reciprocal flows between service departments.

Excel can be used to solve the reciprocal allocation method using the tool, Solver. The solution technique is illustrated in Exhibit 12.9.

Four additional issues to consider when implementing the departmental allocation approach are (1) difficulty in determining an appropriate allocation base, (2) separation of variable and fixed costs (called *dual allocation*), (3) use of budgeted rather than actual amounts, and (4) allocated costs exceeding the outside purchase price.

Difficulty in Determining the Allocation Base Determining an appropriate allocation base and a percentage amount for service provided by the service departments is often difficult. For example, using labor hours could be inappropriate in an automated

LEARNING OBJECTIVE 4

Explain the problems in implementating the different departmental cost allocation methods.

EXHIBIT 12.9 **Solving for the Reciprocal Allocation Method Using the Solver Function in Microsoft Excel**

Solving reciprocal departmental allocation problems can become tedious if three or more departments are involved. In this case, we suggest the use of software programs such as the Solver function in Excel. The following screen capture illustrates how the Solver tool can be used to solve the Beary Company example in the text. The column for "Allocated Cost" in the spreadsheet contains the cost in each service department, while the columns for "Service Rates" contain the reciprocal service rates. The column for "Initial Allocation to" contains the product of the "Allocated Cost" and "Service Rates" columns,

using cell-based formulas. Cells E7 and F7 contain the formula-based sums of these columns. After selecting "Solver" from the Tools menu, the Dialog Box in Exhibit 12.9 appears and must be completed as shown. For example, the Target Cell (E7) must be set to a value of $5,850 (the cost of the first service department). When the dialog box is complete, select Solve, and the solution will appear in cells B5 and B6 (overwriting the amounts originally entered in the Allocated Cost column). The solution is $6,953.13 in cell B5 and $11,031.25 in cell B6. For more information on how to use Solver, see the Appendix for Chapter 9.

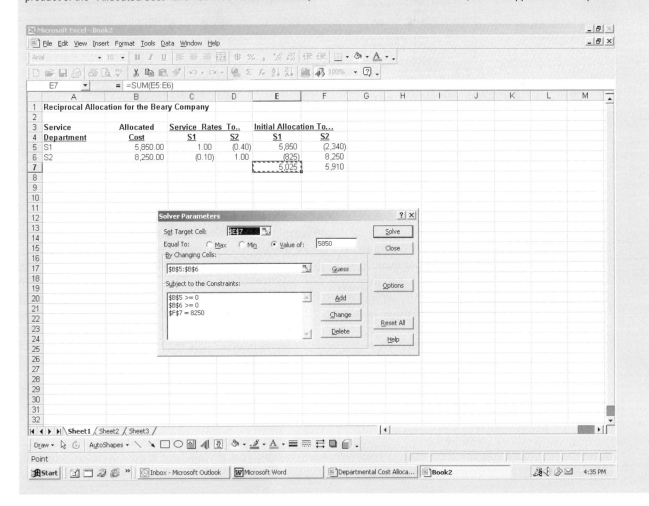

Organizations of all types incur insurance costs to minimize the potential effect of losses from their liability for injury to employees and customers. These costs are usually allocated to all of the organization's revenue-producing units. The allocation is often made in proportion to the total revenue in each unit, based on the fact that larger units should pay more than the smaller units and that more sales usually means more loss liability. Alternatively, the number of employees in the units can be used in the same way. In other cases, the insurance premium costs are not allocated to the units because unit managers have little control over the occurrence of the losses.

In contrast, a common argument currently used is that the insurance costs should be allocated on the basis of loss experience, usually determined over the two or three prior years, to provide a direct incentive for unit managers to reduce product and employee liability losses in their units. Unit managers can do this by consistently reminding employees of the importance of safety in the workplace and offering incentives to enhance workplace safety.

Based on information in: David M. Katz, "Cost Allocation Should Spur Safety," *National Underwriter,* November 9, 1998, pp. 27–30.

EXHIBIT 12.10
Disincentive Effects of Certain Allocation Methods

	Department A	Department B	Total Maintenance Cost
Panel 1: Basic information			
Square feet of floor space	5,000	5,000	
Average number of maintenance requests	50	50	
Total maintenance costs			$200,000
Panel 2: Maintenance cost allocation in an average month using square feet of floor space			
Allocated maintenance cost	$100,000	$100,000	$200,000

Panel 3: Maintenance cost allocation based on square feet for a month when department A increases usage of maintenance from 50 to 80 maintenance requests, while department B's usage remains the same at 50 requests. Here we assume that maintenance costs are variable with the number of maintenance requests, or $2,000 per request ($200,000/[50 + 50]), so that total maintenance costs increase to $260,000 ($2,000 × [50 + 80]).

| Allocated maintenance cost: | $130,000 | $130,000 | $260,000 |

plant where labor is a small part of total cost. Similarly, square feet of floor space could be inappropriate to allocate certain costs when a great deal of idle space exists. Furthermore, the use of square feet of floor space can have undesirable motivational consequences. For example, if we are allocating plantwide maintenance costs to production departments using floor space as a base, a department has inadequate incentive to limit its use of maintenance expense. Since the actual use of maintenance is unrelated to floor space, if a given department increases its use of maintenance, then the other departments pay for the increase as well, as illustrated in Exhibit 12.10. Here, department A increases its use of maintenance by $6,000 (from panel 2 to panel 3 in Exhibit 12.10), while department B's usage stays the same. The effect of department A's increased usage (when allocation is based on square feet) is that department B pays one-half of the increased cost. A preferred approach in this example would be to allocate on the basis of maintenance requests in order to achieve the desired objectives of motivation and fairness. Exhibit 12.11 provides some suggested allocation bases that can address some of these difficulties.

Distinguish Fixed and Variable Costs: Dual Allocation

A preferred departmental allocation approach is dual allocation, which separates variable and fixed costs and traces the variable costs directly to the departments that caused the cost. Tracing variable costs in this way satisfies the allocation objectives of motivation and fairness. However, firms sometimes find that separating the variable

EXHIBIT 12.11
Allocation Bases for Selected Types of Costs

Source: Institute of Management Accountants, "Allocation of Service and Administrative Costs," *Statement Number 4B* (Montvale, NJ, 1985).

Personnel-related costs—number of employees
Payroll-related costs (pensions, fringe benefits, payroll taxes)—labor cost
Materials-related costs—materials cost or quantity used
Space-related costs—square feet or cubic feet
Energy-related costs—motor capacity
Research and development costs—estimated time, sales, or assets employed
Public relations costs—sales
Executives' salaries costs—sales, assets employed
Property taxes costs—square feet, real estate or insurance valuation, market value of assets

EXHIBIT 12.12
Disincentive Effects of Actual Usage-Based Allocation Methods

	Department A	Department B	Total Maintenance Cost
Panel 1: Basic information			
Actual number of direct labor-hours	10,000	10,000	
Budgeted number of direct labor-hours	10,000	10,000	
Average number of maintenance requests	50	50	
Total maintenance costs			$200,000
Panel 2: Maintenance cost allocation in an average month using the number of direct labor-hours			
Allocated maintenance cost	$100,000	$100,000	$200,000

Panel 3: Maintenance cost allocation based on direct labor-hours for a month when department A decreases usage of direct labor-hours from 10,000 to 6,000 hours while department B's usage remains the same at 10,000 hours. Here we assume that maintenance costs have both a variable ($5 per direct labor-hour) and a fixed ($100,000) component. Total maintenance costs decrease to $180,000 (= $100,000 + $5 × (6,000 + 10,000)) and cost/hr is $180,000/16,000 = $11.25

| Allocated maintenance cost: | **$67,500**
 = 6,000 hrs
 × $11.25 | **$112,500**
 = 10,000 hrs
 × $11.25 | $180,000 |

and fixed costs of the departments is difficult or uneconomical. The firm then allocates the total costs (both variable and fixed) in the same manner. Because variable costs are not traced, the latter approach based on total cost does not meet the allocation objectives as well as dual allocation.

Budgeted versus Actual Amounts   When the allocation base is determined from actual amounts (for example, labor-hours incurred in the current period), each department's cost allocation affects the other departments' actual usage of the allocation base. The reason is that each department's actual usage affects total actual usage. Unfavorable incentives arise because one department's usage now affects the amount allocated to the other departments. Exhibit 12.12 continues the example of allocating maintenance costs used in Exhibit 12.10 except that maintenance is allocated on the basis of direct labor-hours. Also, we assume that maintenance costs are both variable and fixed relative to direct labor-hours; there are $100,000 in total fixed costs and a $5 per direct labor-hour variable cost. Exhibit 12.12 shows that department B's allocated costs increased from $100,000 (part 2) to $112,500 (part 3) even though department B did not increase its usage of direct labor-hours or of maintenance requests. The reason for this is that department A reduced its usage of direct labor from 10,000 hours to 6,000 hours. As a result, the $100,000 *total fixed costs in maintenance are allocated over a smaller number of total labor-hours,* thus increasing department B's total cost allocation. The direct labor-hours-based allocation is unfair and unmotivating for department B.

EXHIBIT 12.13 **Cost Allocation Using External Prices**

(A)	(B)	(C)	(D)	(E)	(F)	(G)
User Department	Direct Labor-Hours	Direct Labor-Hour Allocation Base	Cost Allocation Based on Labor-Hours	Outside Price	Allocation Base for Outside Price	Allocation Based on Outside Price
A	3,000	30% (3,000/10,000)	$ 300	$ 360	30% (360/1,200)	$300
B	4,000	40% (4,000/10,000)	400	600	50% (600/1,200)	500
C	1,000	10% (1,000/10,000)	100	120	10% (120/1,200)	100
D	2,000	20% (2,000/10,000)	200	120	10% (120/1,200)	100
Total	10,000	100%	$1,000	$1,200	100%	$1,000

For this reason, using budgeted or predetermined amounts rather than actual amounts for allocating fixed costs is preferable. When budgeted direct labor-hours are used, each department's fixed cost allocation is predictable and is not influenced by the usage in other departments. In contrast, allocating variable costs on the basis of actual usage is preferable, since variable costs can be directly traced to the different users. This is another reason that it is important to separate variable and fixed costs using dual allocation. An important limitation of the use of budgeted rates is that sometimes the budget information could be difficult to obtain. For example, budgeted rates would be difficult to implement when the allocation base varies significantly from period to period or is difficult to predict accurately.

Allocated Costs Exceed External Purchase Cost   Another limitation of the three departmental methods is that they can allocate to a department a higher cost than the cost of the service that the department could purchase from an outside supplier. Should the department pay more for a service internally than an outside vendor would charge? To motivate managers to be efficient and to make the right decisions, the allocation should be based on the cost as if each department had to obtain the service outside the firm. Consider the data in Exhibit 12.13 for a firm with four departments that share a common data processing service costing $1,000. Data processing costs are allocated using direct labor-hours in each department as shown in columns (B), (C), and (D) of Exhibit 12.13. The data processing service can also be obtained from an outside firm at the cost shown in column (E).

The direct labor-hours allocation base in this example penalizes department D, which can obtain the service outside the firm for $80 less than the inside cost ($200 − $120), perhaps because of the simplified nature of the requirements in department D. In contrast, department B can obtain the service outside only at a much higher price ($600 versus $400 inside), perhaps because of the specialized nature of the service. In this case, the allocation based on the *outside price* (column G in Exhibit 12.13) is fair to both departments B and D. It is a better reflection of the competitive cost of the service. The question of whether, and under what conditions, the department should be allowed to purchase outside the firm is a different issue, which is addressed in the coverage of management control in chapters 17 and 18.

Cost Allocation in Service Industries

LEARNING OBJECTIVE 5
Explain the use of cost allocation in service firms.

The concepts presented in this chapter apply equally well to manufacturing, service, or not-for-profit organizations that incur joint costs. For example, financial institutions such as commercial banks also use cost allocation. To illustrate, we use the Community General Bank (CGB), which provides a variety of banking services, including

EXHIBIT 12.14
**Cost Flows in Community
General Bank**

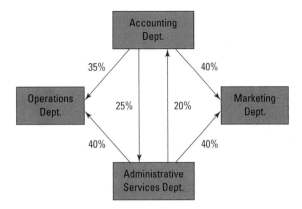

deposit accounts, mortgage loans, installment loans, investment services, and other services. Currently, CGB is analyzing the profitability of its mortgage loan department, which has two main businesses, commercial construction loans and residential construction loans. An important part of the analysis of these loan businesses is determining how to trace or allocate costs to the two businesses.

The cost allocation begins by identifying which departments directly support the two mortgage loan businesses, the loan operations department and the marketing department. The *operations department* handles the processing of loan applications, safekeeping of appropriate documents, billing, and maintaining accounts for both commercial and residential loans. The *marketing department* provides direct advertising, promotions, and customer service for both types of loans.

Other departments support the two loan businesses indirectly by supporting the operations and marketing departments. Two important support departments are the administrative services department and the accounting department. The *administrative services department* provides legal and technical support. The *accounting department* provides financial services, including regular financial reports and the maintenance of customer records. The administrative services and accounting departments provide services to each other as well as to the operations and marketing departments, as illustrated in Exhibit 12.14. Each of the four departments has labor and certain supplies costs that can be traced directly to it. In addition, CGB's human resources department and computer services department provide services to all four departments.

CGB uses the step method to allocate costs from support departments to the loan businesses. See the step method in Exhibit 12.15, which follows the same approach as for Beary Company in Exhibit 12.7. The top of Exhibit 12.15 shows the allocation bases that CGB uses to allocate human resources costs and computer services costs to each department. The allocation base for human resources costs is the number of employees, or the head count, in each department, and the allocation of computer services costs is based on the number of computers in each department. The number of employees and the number of computers in each department are given.

The first phase of the allocation in Exhibit 12.15 shows tracing the totals of $1,560,000 of direct labor and $33,000 for supplies costs to each department as well as the allocation of the human resources costs ($80,000) and computer services costs ($66,000), using the allocation bases head count and number of computers, respectively. The result is that the total cost of $1,739,000 is allocated as follows

Accounting department	$ 253,700
Administrative services department	381,500
Operations department	623,700
Marketing department	480,100
Total cost	$1,739,000

In the second phase, the accounting and administrative service department costs are allocated to the operations and marketing departments using the step method and the service percentages in Exhibit 12.14. The result is that the $1,739,000 of total cost is now allocated to the operations department ($934,957.50) and the marketing department ($804,042.50).

In the third and final phase, the costs from the operations and marketing departments are allocated to the two businesses, commercial and residential loans. The base that CGB uses to allocate operations department costs is the number of banking transactions handled within operations (15,000 for commercial loans and 10,000 for residential loans) and to allocate marketing costs is the number of loans of either type (900 commercial loans and 3,600 residential loans). The result of the final allocation is that the total cost of $1,739,000 is allocated to the commercial loans department ($721,783) and the residential loans department ($1,017,217), as illustrated for the third phase in Exhibit 12.15.

EXHIBIT 12.15   Use of the Step Method for Cost Allocation at Community General Bank

Departmental Allocation Bases	Accounting	Administrative Services	Operations	Marketing		Total
Human Resources						
Headcount	80	100	160	60		400
	20.0%	25.0%	40.0%	15.0%		100.0%
Computer Services						
Number of computers	60	60	150	30		300
	20.0%	20.0%	50.0%	10.0%		100.0%
First Phase: Trace Direct Costs and Allocate Overhead Costs to Departments						
Direct costs (given)						
Labor	$221,000	$339,500	$554,500	$445,000		$1,560,000
Supplies	3,500	8,800	4,200	16,500		33,000
Indirect costs						
Human Resources	16,000	20,000	32,000	12,000	(e.g., $12,000 = 15% × $80,000)	80,000
Computer Services	13,200	13,200	33,000	6,600	(e.g., $6,600 = 10% × $66,000)	66,000
Totals for all departments	$253,700	$381,500	$623,700	$480,100		$1,739,000
Second Phase: Allocate Service Department Costs to Operations and Marketing, Using the Step Method						
First step						
Accounting Department Service percent		25%	35%	40%		
Amount		$63,425	$88,795	$101,480	(e.g., $101,480 = 40% × $253,700)	
Second step						
Administrative services Service percent			40%	40%		
Allocation percent (per direct method)			50%	50%		
Amount			$222,462.50	$222,462.50	[e.g., $222,462.50 = 50% ×	
Totals for production departments			$934,957.50	$804,042.50	($381,500 + $63,425)]	$1,739,000

Third Phase: Allocate Operations and Marketing Costs to Commercial and Residential Loans	Commercial Loans	Residential Loans	
Base: Number of banking transactions	15,000	10,000	25,000
Percent	60%	40%	
Number of loans	900	3,600	4,500
Percent	20%	80%	
Operations (Number of transactions)	$560,974.50	$ 373,983	
Marketing (Number of loans)	$160,808.50	$ 643,234	
Totals for commercial and residential loans	$ 721,783	$1,017,217	$1,739,000

EXHIBIT 12.16
Profitability Analysis of Mortgage Loans Community General Bank

	Commercial Loans	Residential Loans
Revenues	$2,755,455	$2,998,465
Less expenses		
Cost of funds	1,200,736	1,387,432
Allocated operating costs	721,783	1,017,217
Contribution	$ 832,936	$ 593,816
Key ratios		
Contribution/revenue	30.23%	19.80%
Cost of funds/revenues	43.58%	46.27%

Cost allocation provides CGB a basis for evaluating the cost and profitability of its services. By taking the allocated operating costs just determined, the cost of funds provided, and the revenue produced by both commercial and residential loans, a profitability analysis of mortgage loans can be completed. Assume that the commercial loan departments have revenues of $2,755,455 and $2,998,465, respectively, and direct cost of funds of $1,200,736 and $1,387,432, respectively.

The profitability analysis in Exhibit 12.16 shows that the relatively high allocated operating costs of the residential loan department are an important factor in its overall poor performance (only 19.8 percent contribution per dollar of revenue in contrast to more than 30 percent for the commercial loan area). In contrast, the cost of funds appears to be comparable for both types of loans (43.58 percent of revenues for commercial loans and 46.27 percent of revenues for residential loans). The analysis indicates that the bank should investigate the profitability of residential loans and, in particular, the cost of operations and marketing for these loans.

Joint Product Costing

LEARNING OBJECTIVE 6
Use the three joint product costing methods.

Many manufacturing plants yield more than one product from a joint manufacturing process. For example, the petroleum industry processes crude oil into multiple products: gasoline, naphtha, kerosene, fuel oils, and residual heavy oils. Similarly, the semiconductor industry processes silicon wafers into a variety of computer memory chips with different speeds, temperature tolerances, and life expectancies. Beef and hides are products linked in the meatpacking process; neither of these items can be produced without producing the other. Other industries that yield joint products include lumber production, food processing, soap making, grain milling, dairy farming, and fishing.

Joint products and by-products are derived from processing a single input or a common set of inputs. **Joint products** are products from the same production process that have relatively substantial sales values. Products whose total sales values are minor in comparison to the sales value of the joint products are classified as **by-products**.

Joint products and by-products both start their manufacturing life as part of the same raw material. Until a certain point in the production process, no distinction can be made between the products. The point in a joint production process at which individual products can be identified for the first time is called the **split-off point**. Thereafter, separate production processes can be applied to the individual products. At the split-off point, joint products or by-products might be salable or require further processing to be salable, depending on their nature.

Joint costs include all manufacturing costs incurred prior to the split-off point (including direct materials, direct labor, and factory overhead). For financial reporting purposes, these costs are allocated among the joint products. Additional costs incurred after the split-off point that can be identified directly with individual products are called **additional processing costs** or **separable costs**.

Other outputs of joint production include scrap, waste, spoilage and defective units. Scrap is the residue from a production process that has little or no recovery value. Waste, such as chemical waste, is a residual material that has no recovery value and

Joint products
are products from the same production process that have relatively substantial sales value.

By-products
are products whose total sales values are minor in comparison with the sales value of the joint products.

The **split-off point**
is the first point in a joint production process at which individual products can be identified.

Additional processing costs
or **separable costs**
are those that occur after the split-off point and can be identified directly with individual products.

must be disposed of by the firm as required. In addition to waste and scrap, some products do not meet quality standards and can be reworked for resale. Spoiled units are not reworked for economic reasons. Defective units are reworked to become salable units.

Methods for Allocating Joint Costs to Joint Products

Joint costs are most frequently allocated to joint products using (1) the physical measure, (2) the sales value, and (3) the net realizable value methods.

The Physical Measure Method

The **physical measure method**
uses a physical measure such as pounds, gallons, or yards or units or volume produced at the split-off point to allocate the joint costs to joint products.

The **average cost method**
uses units of output to allocate joint costs to joint products.

The **physical measure method,** naturally enough, uses a physical measure such as pounds, gallons, or yards or units or volume produced at the split-off point to allocate the joint costs to joint products. The first step is to select the proper physical measure as the basis for allocation. We can use units of input or units of output. For example, if we are costing tuna products, the production of 100 pounds of tuna into quarter-pound cans would have an input measure of 100 pounds and an output measure of 400 cans. When units of output are used, this also is called the **average cost method.**

Assume that Johnson Seafood produces tuna filets and canned tuna for distribution to restaurants and supermarkets in the southeastern United States. The cost of 14,000 pounds of raw, unprocessed tuna plus the direct labor and overhead for cutting and processing the tuna into filets and canned tuna is the joint cost of the process. The flow of production is illustrated in Exhibit 12.17.

The production process starts at point 1. A total $16,000 joint cost ($7,000 direct materials, $5,000 direct labor, and $4,000 overhead) is incurred. Point 2 is the split-off point where two joint products are separated: 2,000 pounds of tuna filets and 8,000 pounds of canned tuna. The remaining 4,000 pounds of by-products, scrap, and waste are not accounted for. (The appendix to the chapter explains how to account for by-products.) If we use a physical measure method, the joint cost of $16,000 is allocated as shown in Exhibit 12.18.

Based on the physical measure method (pounds in this example), when the joint products reach the split-off point, we can compute the relationship of each of the joint products to the sum of the total units. The joint cost allocated to the products is the average cost per pound of the joint cost, which is $1.60 per pound.

The physical measure used to determine the relative weights for allocating the joint cost should be the measure of the products at the *split-off point,* not the measure when the production of the products is completed. Thus, the relevant measure in the example is the 2,000 pounds of filets and 8,000 pounds of canned tuna.

EXHIBIT 12.17
Diagram of Two Joint Product Cost Flows for Johnson Seafood

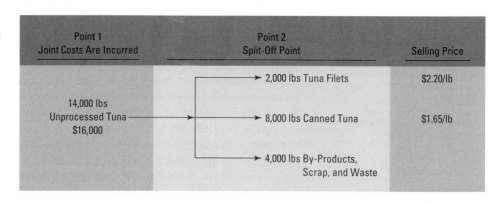

EXHIBIT 12.18
Physical Measure Method

Product	Physical Measure	Proportion	Allocation of Joint Cost	Cost per Pound
Tuna filets	2,000 lbs	0.20	$16,000 × 20% = $ 3,200	$1.60
Canned tuna	8,000 lbs	0.80	16,000 × 80% = 12,800	1.60
Total	10,000 lbs	1.00	$16,000	

The production costs per pound for both products follow:

Filets $1.60 per pound = $3,200/2,000 pounds

Canned tuna $1.60 per pound = $12,800/8,000 pounds

Advantages and Limitations   Among the advantages of the physical measure method are that (1) it is easy to use and (2) the criterion for the allocation of the joint costs is objective. This method, however, ignores the revenue-producing capability of individual products that can vary widely among the joint products and have no relationship at all to any physical measure. Each product can also have a unique physical measure (gallons for one, pounds for another) and, hence, the physical measure method might not be applicable. The following method addresses these limitations.

The Sales Value at Split-Off Method

The sales value at split-off method is an alternative and widely used method. The **sales value at split-off method** (or more simply, *sales value method*) allocates joint costs to joint products on the basis of their relative sales values at the split-off point. This method can be used only when joint products can be sold at the split-off point. If we assume that Johnson can sell a pound of filets for $2.20 and a pound of canned tuna for $1.65 and that Johnson has produced 2,000 pounds of filets and 8,000 pounds of canned tuna, the $16,000 joint cost should be allocated between the products as shown in Exhibit 12.19.

The first step in the sales value method (Exhibit 12.19) is to compute the total sales value of the joint products at the split-off point. Note that the sales value is the sales price multiplied by the number of production units, *not the actual number of sales units*. Determining the proportion of the sales value of each joint product to the total sales value is the second step. The final operation allocates the total joint cost among the joint products based on those proportions.

In the Johnson Seafood example, the sales value of filets is $4,400 and of canned tuna is $13,200, a total of $17,600. The proportion of the individual sales values of the products to the total sales value are 0.25 ($4,400/$17,600) for filets and 0.75 ($13,200/$17,600) for canned tuna. The allocated costs are $4,000 to filets and $12,000 to canned tuna.

The production costs per pound for both products are calculated as follows:

Filets $2.00 per pound = $4,000/2,000

Canned tuna $1.50 per pound = $12,000/8,000

Note that filets have a higher unit cost under the sales value method than under the physical measure method. The reason is that filets have a higher sales value. If the sales prices are estimated accurately and no additional processing costs are involved, the sales value at split-off method generates the same gross margin percentage for both filets and canned tuna as shown in Exhibit 12.20.

Advantages and Limitations   The advantages of the sales value method are that it (1) is easy to calculate and (2) is allocated according to the individual product's revenues. This method is superior to the physical measure method because it allocates the joint costs in proportion to the products' ability to absorb these costs. This is an application of the ability-to-bear concept of fairness included in the objectives of cost allocation at the beginning of the chapter.

EXHIBIT 12.19
Sales Value at Split-off Method

Product	Units	Price per unit	Sales Value	Proportion	Joint Cost Allocated	Cost per Pound
Filets	2,000 lbs	$2.20	$ 4,400	0.25	$16,000 × 25% = $ 4,000	$2.00
Canned tuna	8,000 lbs	1.65	13,200	0.75	16,000 × 75% = 12,000	1.50
Total			$17,600	1.00	$16,000	

The **sales value at split-off method** allocates joint costs to joint products on the basis of their relative sales values at the split-off point.

EXHIBIT 12.20
Product-Line Profitability
Analysis

	Tuna Filets	Canned Tuna
Sales	$2.20 × 2,000 = $4,400	$1.65 × 8,000 = $13,200
Cost of goods sold	$2.00 × 2,000 = 4,000	$1.50 × 8,000 = 12,000
Gross margin	$ 400	$ 1,200
Gross margin percent	9.09%	9.09%

One limitation of the sales value method is that market prices for some industries change constantly. Also, the sales price at split-off might not be available because additional processing is necessary before the product can be sold.

The Net Realizable Value Method

Not all joint products can be sold at the split-off point. Thus, there is no market price to attach to some products at the split-off point. In these cases, the concept of net realizable value is used. The **net realizable value (NRV)** of a product is the product's *estimated sales value* at the split-off point; it is determined by subtracting the additional processing and selling costs beyond the split-off point from the estimated ultimate sales value of the product.

The **net realizable value (NRV)** of a product is the estimated sales value of the product at the split-off point; it is determined by subtracting the additional processing and selling costs beyond the split-off point from the ultimate sales value of the product.

NRV = Ultimate sales value − Additional processing and selling cost

In the Johnson Seafood example, assume that in addition to filets and canned tuna, the firm processes cat food from raw, unprocessed tuna. Assume also that 14,000 pounds of tuna yield at the split-off point 2,000 pounds of filets and 8,000 pounds of canned tuna as before but now an additional 3,000 pounds of cat food. The remaining 1,000 pounds are scrap, waste, and by-products. For cat food the tuna must be processed further for sale to pet food distributors. The additional processing cost is $850 for minerals and other supplements that are important for cat nutrition but that add no weight to the product. The pet food distributors buy the prepared cat food from Johnson at $1.75 per pound and package it into 3-ounce cans for sale to pet stores and supermarkets. Exhibit 12.21 is a diagram of this situation.

Exhibit 12.22 shows the joint cost allocation calculation using the net realizable value method.

If Johnson Seafood sold all products it produced during the period, its gross margin amounts for the products would be as shown in Exhibit 12.23. Note that the gross margin percentage is lower for cat food than for filets because of the additional processing cost of $850.

EXHIBIT 12.21 **Diagram of Three Joint Product Cost Flows for Johnson Seafood**

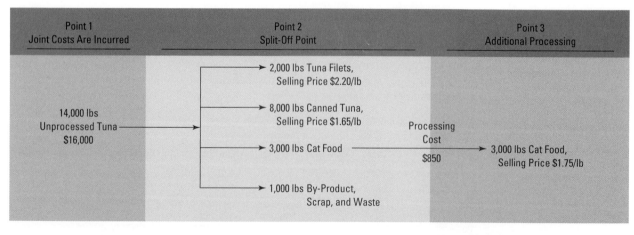

EXHIBIT 12.22   **Joint Cost Allocation Using the Net Realizable Value Method**

Product	Pounds	Price	Sales Value	Additional Processing	Net Realizable Value	Percent of NRV	Allocated Cost	Total Cost	Cost per Pound
Filets	2,000	$2.20	$ 4,400	—	$ 4,400	20%	$ 3,200	$ 3,200	$1.60
Canned tuna	8,000	1.65	13,200	—	13,200	60	9,600	9,600	1.20
Cat food	3,000	1.75	5,250	$850	4,400	20	3,200	4,050	1.35
Total	13,000		$22,850	$850	$22,000	100%	$16,000	$16,850	

EXHIBIT 12.23
Johnson Seafood's Product-Line Profitability Analysis

	Tuna Filets	Canned Tuna	Cat Food
Sales	$2.20 × 2,000 = $4,400	$1.65 × 8,000 = $13,200	$1.75 × 3,000 = $5,250
Cost of goods sold	$1.60 × 2,000 = 3,200	$1.20 × 8,000 = 9,600	$1.35 × 3,000 = 4,050
Gross margin	$1,200	$ 3,600	$1,200
Gross margin percent	27.27%	27.27%	22.86%

Advantages and Limitations   The NRV method is superior to the physical measure method because, like the sales value at split-off method, it produces an allocation that yields a predictable, comparable level of profitability among the products. The physical measure method might provide misleading guidance to top management regarding product profitability, which can be very frustrating to product-line managers.

Summary

This chapter introduces the objectives, concepts, and methods of cost allocation. There are two main cost allocation applications—departmental cost and joint product costing. Most important, the objectives and methods for cost allocation are determined based on the firm's strategy. Cost allocation is concerned with strategy in four key ways: (1) to determine accurate departmental and product costs as a basis for evaluating the departments' cost efficiency and profitability of different products, (2) to motivate managers to work hard, (3) to provide the proper incentive for managers to achieve the firm's goals, and (4) to provide a fair basis for rewarding managers for their effort.

Ethical issues often arise in cost allocation when managers must choose between alternative allocation methods. The manager must choose between methods that might decrease the cost of one product, customer, or business unit at the expense of increased costs for another product, customer, or unit.

Departmental cost allocation is performed in three phases: (1) trace all direct costs and allocate overhead to service and production departments, (2) allocate service department costs to production departments, and (3) allocate production department costs to products. The second phase is the most complex. Service department costs can be allocated to production departments using three methods—the direct method, the step method, and the reciprocal method. The three methods differ in the way they deal with service flows among service departments. The direct method ignores these flows, the step method includes some of them, and the reciprocal method includes all. For this reason, the reciprocal method is preferred.

A number of implementation issues arise when applying cost allocation methods including the strategic and ethical issues of the cost allocation. It is also important to allocate variable and fixed costs separately (in a process called *dual allocation*), to use budgeted rather than actual amounts in the allocation, and to consider alternative allocation methods when the result of an allocation to a department is a cost that is greater than the department could purchase the item from an outside entity.

The need for joint product costing arises when two or more products are made simultaneously in a given manufacturing process. The three methods for costing joint products are the (1) the physical measure method, (2) sales value at split-off method, and (3) net realizable value method. The physical measure method is the simplest to use but also has a significant disadvantage. Because the allocation ignores sales value, the gross margins of joint products determined using the physical measure method can differ in significant and unreasonable ways. In contrast, the sales value and net realizable value methods tend to result in similar gross margins among the joint products. The sales value at split-off method is used when sales value at split-off is known; otherwise the net realizable value is used.

APPENDIX A

LEARNING OBJECTIVE 7
Use the four by-product costing methods.

By-Product Costing

A by-product is a product of relatively small sales value that is produced simultaneously with one or more joint products. Two approaches are used for by-product costing: (1) the asset recognition approach and (2) the revenue approach. The main difference between these approaches lies in whether they assign an inventoriable value to by-products at the split-off point. The asset recognition approach records by-products as inventory at net realizable values; the value of the by-product is therefore recognized when the by-product is produced. In contrast, the revenue approach does not assign values to the by-products in the period of production but recognizes by-product revenue in the period sold.

Each of the two approaches contain two alternative methods, depending on the way in which by-products are reported in the income statement. The two asset recognition methods follow:

Net Realizable Value Method. This method shows the net realizable value of by-products on the balance sheet as inventory and on the income statement as a deduction from the total manufacturing cost of the joint products. This is done in the *period in which the by-product is produced.*
Other Income at Production Point Method. This method shows the net realizable value of by-products on the income statement as an other income or other sales revenue item. This is done in the *period in which the by-product is produced.*

The two revenue methods follow:

Other Income at Selling Point Method. This method shows the net sales revenue from a by-product sold *at time of sale* on the income statement as an other income or other sales revenue item.
Manufacturing Cost Reduction at Selling Point Method. This method shows the net sales revenue from a by-product sold *at time of sale* on the income statement as a reduction of the total manufacturing cost.

In Exhibit 12.24 we summarize the four major by-product costing methods.

ASSET RECOGNITION METHODS

To illustrate the asset recognition methods, assume that Johnson Seafood believes that it can make additional profit by taking a portion of the 1,000 pounds of scrap and waste in each batch of unprocessed tuna and reprocessing them to produce a high-quality garden fertilizer. However, the selling price of the fertilizer is expected to be relatively low, 50 cents per pound. Moreover, additional processing and selling costs of 30 cents per pound would be necessary for preparing, packaging, and distributing the product.

EXHIBIT 12.24
A Summary of By-Product Costing Methods

	Place in Income Statement	
Time to Recognize	**As Other Income**	**As a Deduction of Manufacturing Cost**
At time of production (asset recognition methods)	Other income at time of production	Net realizable value method; reduction in joint product cost at time of production
At time of sale (revenue methods)	Other income at time of sale	Reduction in cost of joint products at time of sale

EXHIBIT 12.25   Diagram of Three Joint Products and One By-Product Cost Flows for Johnson Seafood

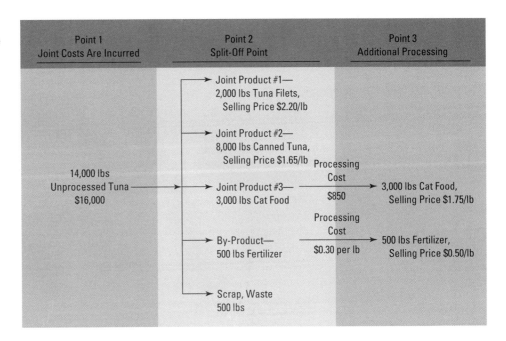

Since the sales value of fertilizer is relatively low, the firm decides to treat tuna filets, canned tuna, and cat food as joint products and fertilizer as a by-product. Suppose that Johnson sold all production of filets, canned tuna, and cat food, but sold only 400 of the 500 pounds of the fertilizer produced. Exhibit 12.25 shows the cost flows of the three joint products and one by-product.

From Exhibit 12.22, the total sales value of filets, canned tuna, and cat food is $22,850 ($4,400 + $13,200 + $5,250) and the total cost of the goods sold is $16,850 ($3,200 + $9,600 + $4,050). The net realizable value (NRV) of the 500 pounds of fertilizer produced is

$$NRV = \text{Sales value} - \text{Additional processing cost}$$
$$= \$0.50 \times 500 - \$0.30 \times 500$$
$$= \$100$$

Johnson's accounting for the by-product using the asset recognition methods (the net realizable value method and the other income at production point method) appears in Exhibit 12.26.

Asset recognition methods are based on the financial accounting concepts of asset recognition, matching, and materiality. By-products are *recognized* as assets with probable future economic benefits because a market exists for them. Asset recognition methods also have the preferred effect of *matching* the value of the by-product with its manufacturing cost; when the by-product is sold, its inventory cost is shown as the cost of sales. If the net realizable value of a by-product is *material* (that is, it will have a significant effect on inventory or profit), the asset recognition methods should be used because of the matching concept.

EXHIBIT 12.26
By-Product Costing—Asset Recognition Methods

	Net Realizable Value Method	Other Income at Production Method
Sale of joint products (Exhibit 12.22)	$22,850	$22,850
Cost of goods sold		
Cost of joint products sold (Exhibit 12.22)	$16,850	$16,850
Less net realizable value of by-product	(100)	—
Cost of goods sold	$16,750	$16,850
Gross margin	$ 6,100	$ 6,000
Other income at production	—	100
Income before tax	$ 6,100	$ 6,100

EXHIBIT 12.27
By-Product Costing—Revenue Recognition Methods

	Other Income at Selling Point Method	Manufacturing Cost Reduction Method
Sales of joint products	$22,850	$22,850
Cost of goods sold		
Cost of joint products sold	$16,850	$16,850
Less net sales revenue of by-product sold		
($0.50 − $0.30) × 400	—	(80)
Cost of goods sold	$16,850	$16,770
Gross margin	$ 6,000	$ 6,080
By-product revenue	80	—
Income before tax	$ 6,080	$ 6,080

REVENUE METHODS

Revenue methods recognize by-products at the time of sale. Exhibit 12.27 illustrates the two methods.

Revenue methods are justified on the financial accounting concepts of revenue realization, materiality, and cost benefit. These methods are consistent with the argument that by-product net revenue should be recorded at the time of sale because this is the *point revenue is realized.* Revenue methods are also appropriate when the value of the by-product is *not material,* that is, very small in relation to net income. For *cost-benefit* considerations, many firms use a revenue method because of its simplicity.

Key Terms

additional processing (separable) costs, *489*
average cost method, *490*
by-products, *489*
direct method, *478*

joint products, *489*
net realizable value (NRV), *492*
physical measure method, *490*
reciprocal flows, *477*
reciprocal method, *480*

sales value at split-off method, *491*
split-off point, *489*
step method, *479*

Comments on Cost Management in Action

Health Care Providers Allocate Cost for Medicare Reimbursement

The direct method of the departmental approach to cost allocation explained in this chapter has never been permitted for Medicare cost reports. The only permissible method is the step method, which must be performed under Medicare guidelines and audited by a private intermediary (e.g., Blue Cross). A hospital chooses the order in which the step method occurs and the allocation bases (e.g., square feet, pounds of laundry, time spent, number of meals served). The order of the step method and the choice of

Source: David T. Meeting and Robert O. Harvey, "Strategic Cost Accounting Helps Create a Competitive Edge," *Healthcare Financial Management,* December 1998, pp. 42–51; and Leslie Eldenburg and Sanjay Kallapur, "Changes in Hospital Service Mix and Cost Allocations in Response to Changes in Medicare Reimbursement Schemes," *Journal of Accounting and Economics,* May 1977, pp. 31–51.

EXHIBIT 12.28
Joint Cost Flows for
Northern Company

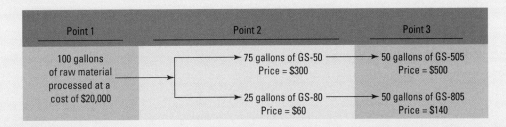

Point 1	Point 2	Point 3
100 gallons of raw material processed at a cost of $20,000	75 gallons of GS-50 Price = $300	50 gallons of GS-505 Price = $500
	25 gallons of GS-80 Price = $60	50 gallons of GS-805 Price = $140

allocation base are widely recognized to have a significant effect on allocated costs. Hospitals naturally choose methods that favor them in cost reimbursement. Many consultants, authors, and policy makers have called for improved guidance regarding the allocation of costs for Medicare reimbursement. Some have argued that since software tools are readily available to allocate costs using the reciprocal method, Medicare should require this more accurate method.

Self-Study Problem

(For solution, please turn to the end of the chapter.)

Joint Product Costing

Northern Company processes 100 gallons of raw materials into 75 gallons of product GS-50 and 25 gallons of GS-80. GS-50 is further processed into 50 gallons of product GS-505 at a cost of $5,000, and GS-80 is processed into 50 gallons of product GS-805 at a cost of $2,000. Exhibit 12.28 depicts this manufacturing flow.

The production process starts at point 1. A total of $20,000 in joint manufacturing costs are incurred in reaching point 2. Point 2 is the split-off point of the process that manufactures GS-50 and GS-80. At this point, GS-50 can be sold for $300 a gallon, and GS-80 can be sold for $60 a gallon. The process is completed at point 3—products GS-505 and GS-805 have a sales price of $500 a gallon and $140 a gallon, respectively.

Required   Allocate the joint product costs using each of the three methods: (1) physical measure, (2) sales value at split-off, and (3) net realizable value.

Questions

12–1   What are the objectives of cost allocation? Which are most important in a retail firm? In a manufacturing firm? In a service firm?

12–2   Explain the difference between joint products and by-products.

12–3   Explain the difference between spoilage, waste, rework, and scrap.

12–4   What are the three methods of departmental cost allocation? Explain how they differ, which is the most preferred, and why.

12–5   What are the three phases of the departmental allocation approach? What happens at each phase?

12–6   Give two or three examples of the use of cost allocation in service industries and not-for-profit organizations.

12–7   What are the four methods used in by-product costing, and how do they differ? Which is the preferred method and why?

12–8   What are the limitations of joint product cost allocation?

12–9   What are the limitations of departmental cost allocation?

12–10 What is the role of cost allocation from a strategic point of view?

Exercises

12–11 **Cost Allocation, General**   An organization's service and administrative costs can be substantial, and some or all of these costs usually are allocated to cost objects. Thus, the allocations of service and administrative costs can have a significant impact on product cost and pricing, asset valuation, and segment profitability.

Required

1. What are service and administrative costs?

2. When service and administrative costs are allocated, they are grouped into homogeneous pools and then allocated to cost objects according to some allocation base.

   a. Compare and contrast the benefit and cost criteria for selecting an allocation base.

   b. Explain what the ability-to-bear costs criterion means in selecting an allocation base. Discuss why this criterion has limited use.

(CMA Adapted)

12–12　By-Products and Decision-Making Strategy　Lowman Gourmet Products produces a wide variety of gourmet coffees (sold in pounds of roasted beans), jams, jellies, and condiments such as spicy mustard sauce. The firm has a reputation as a high-quality source of these products. Lowman sells the products through a mail-order catalog that is revised twice a year. Joe, the president, is interested in developing a new line of products to complement the coffees. The manufacture of the jams and jellies presently produces an excess of fruit liquid that is not used in these products. The firm is now selling excess liquid to other firms as flavoring for canned fruit products. Joe is planning to refine the liquid and add other ingredients to it to produce a coffee-flavoring product instead of selling the liquid. He figures that the cost of producing the jams and jellies, and therefore the fruit liquid, is irrelevant; the only relevant concern is the lost sales to the canneries and the cost of the additional ingredients, processing, and packaging.

Required　Does this plan make financial and strategic sense?

12–13　Joint Products　Bravo Company produces joint products J, K, and B from a process. This information concerns a batch produced in April at a joint cost of $60,000:

| | | After Split-Off | |
Product	Units Produced and Sold	Total Additional Costs	Total Sales Value
J	1,000	$10,000	$90,000
K	2,000	10,000	50,000
B	4,000	5,000	10,000

Required　How much of the joint cost should be allocated to each joint product using the net realizable value method?

12–14　Joint Products　Nebraska Corporation manufactures liquid chemicals A and B from a joint process. It allocates joint costs on the basis of sales value at split-off. Processing 500 gallons of product A and 1,000 gallons of product B to the split-off point costs $4,560. The sales value at split-off is $10 per gallon for product A and $14 for product B. Product B requires an additional process beyond split-off at a cost of $2.50 per gallon before it can be sold.

Required　What is Nebraska's cost to produce 1,000 gallons of product B?

12–15　Joint Product Costing; By-Products (Appendix)　Barnwell Company produces 15,000 units of A, 27,500 units of B, and 10,000 units of C from the same manufacturing process at a cost of $330,000. A and B are joint products; C is regarded as a by-product. The unit selling prices of the products are $30 for A, $20 for B, and $1 for C. None of the products require additional processing. Of the units produced, Barnwell Company sells 12,000 units of A, 26,000 units of B, and 10,000 units of C. The firm uses the net realizable value method to allocate joint costs and by-product costs. Assume no beginning inventory.

Required

1. What is the value of the ending inventory of Product A?
2. What is the value of the ending inventory of Product B?

12–16　Departmental Cost Allocation　HomeLife Life Insurance Company has two service departments (actuarial and premium rating) and two production departments (advertising and sales). The distribution of each service department's efforts (in percentages) to the other departments is

| From | | To | | |
	Actuarial	Premium Rating	Advertising	Sales
Actuarial	—	80%	10%	10%
Premium	20%	—	20%	60%

The direct operating costs of the departments (including both variable and fixed costs) are

Actuarial	$80,000
Premium rating	15,000
Advertising	60,000
Sales	40,000

Required

1. Determine the total cost allocated to the advertising and sales departments using the direct method.
2. Determine the total cost allocated to advertising and sales using the step method.
3. Determine the total cost allocated to advertising and sales using the reciprocal method.

12–17 **Departmental Cost Allocation**   Robinson Products Company has two service departments (S1 and S2) and two production departments (P1 and P2). The distribution of each service department's efforts (in percentages) to the other departments is

From	To			
	S1	**S2**	**P1**	**P2**
S1	—	10%	20%	?%
S2	10%	—	?%	30%

The direct operating costs of the departments (including both variable and fixed costs) are

S1	$180,000
S2	60,000
P1	50,000
P2	120,000

Required

1. Determine the total cost of P1 and P2 using the direct method.
2. Determine the total cost of P1 and P2 using the step method.
3. Determine the total cost of P1 and P2 using the reciprocal method.

Problems

12–18 **Departmental Cost Allocation; Outsourcing**   Williams Company produces two software products (NetA and NetB) in two separate departments (A and B). These products are highly regarded network maintenance programs. NetA is used for small networks and NetB is used for large networks. Williams is known for the quality of its products and its ability to meet dates promised for software upgrades.

Department A produces NetA, and department B produces NetB. The production departments are supported by two support departments, systems design and programming services. The source and use of the support department time are summarized as follows:

From	To				Total
	Design	Programming	Department A	Department B	Labor-Hours
Design	—	4,000	3,000	9,000	16,000
Programming	600	—	600	800	2,000

The costs in the two service departments are as follows:

	Design	Programming
Labor and materials (all variable)	$36,000	$25,000
Depreciation and other fixed costs	38,000	45,000
Total	$74,000	$70,000

Required

1. What are the costs allocated to the two production departments from the two service departments using (a) the direct method, (b) the step method (both possible sequences), and (c) the reciprocal method?

2. The company is considering outsourcing programming services to RJB Services, Inc., for $25 per hour. Should Williams do this?

12–19 **Departmental Cost Allocation; Outsourcing; Outside Price**   McKeoun Enterprises is a large machine tool company now experiencing alarming increases in maintenance expense in each of its four production departments. Maintenance costs are currently allocated to the production departments on the basis of labor-hours incurred in the production department. To provide pressure for the production departments to use less maintenance, and to provide an incentive for the maintenance department to become more efficient, McKeoun has decided to investigate new methods of allocating maintenance costs. One suggestion now being evaluated is a form of outsourcing: The producing departments could purchase maintenance service from an outside supplier. That is, they could choose either to use an outside supplier of maintenance or to be charged an amount based on their use of labor-hours. The following table shows the labor-hours in each department, the allocation of maintenance cost based on labor-hours, and the cost to purchase the equivalent level of maintenance service from an outside maintenance provider.

Production Department	Direct Labor-Hours Allocation Base (Percent)	Direct Labor-Hours Allocation Cost	Outside Price
A	20%	$ 90,000	$115,000
B	30	135,000	92,000
C	10	45,000	69,000
D	40	180,000	184,000
Total	100%	$450,000	$460,000

Required

1. As a first step in moving to the outsourcing approach, McKeoun is considering an allocation based on the price of the outside maintenance supplier for each department. Calculate the cost allocation on this basis and compare it to the current labor-hour basis.

2. If McKeoun follows the proposed plan, what is likely to happen to the overall use of maintenance? How will each department manager be motivated to increase or decrease the use of maintenance? What will be the overall effects of going to the new plan?

12–20 **Departmental Cost Allocation**   Synergies Corporation prepares business plans and marketing analyses for start-up companies in the Boston area. Synergies has been very successful in recent years in providing effective service to a growing number of clients. The company provides its service from a single office building in Boston, and is organized into two main client-service groups: one for market research and the other for financial analysis. The two groups are treated as cost centers with budgeted annual costs of $550,000 and $850,000, respectively. In addition, Synergies has a support staff that is organized into two main functions: one for clerical, facilities, and logistical support (called the CFL group) and another for computer-related support. The CFL group is also a cost center with budgeted annual costs of $350,000, while the annual cost of the computer group is $250,000.

Tom Miggs, CFO of Synergies, plans to prepare a departmental cost allocation for his four groups, and he assembles the following information:

Percentage of estimated dollars of work and time by CFI:

20%—service to the computer group
30%—service to market research
50%—service to financial analysis

Percentage of estimated dollars of work and time by the computer group:

10%—service to the CFL group
60%—service to market research
30%—service to financial analysis

Required Determine the total cost in the financial analysis and market research groups, after departmental allocation, using the direct method, the step method, and the reciprocal method.

12–21 **Departmental Cost Allocation** Dundee Corporation distributes its service department overhead costs to product departments. This information is for the month of June:

	Service Departments	
	Maintenance	**Utilities**
Overhead costs incurred	$30,000	$15,000
Service provided to departments		
Maintenance	—	10%
Utilities	20%	—
Producing—A	40	30
Producing—B	40	60
Totals	100%	100%

Required What is the amount of maintenance and utility department costs distributed to producing departments A and B for June using (1) the direct method, (2) the step method, and (3) the reciprocal method?

12–22 **Joint Product Costing** Choi Company manufactures two skin care lotions, Smooth Skin and Silken Skin, from a joint process. The joint costs incurred are $420,000 for a standard production run that generates 180,000 gallons of Smooth Skin and 120,000 gallons of Silken Skin. Smooth Skin sells for $2.40 per gallon, while Silken Skin sells for $3.90 per gallon.

Required

1. Assuming that both products are sold at the split-off point, how much of the joint cost of each production run is allocated to Smooth Skin on a net realizable value basis?
2. If no additional costs are incurred after the split-off point, how much of the joint cost of each production run is allocated to Silken Skin on the physical measure method basis?
3. If additional processing costs beyond the split-off point are $1.40 per gallon for Smooth Skin and $0.90 per gallon for Silken Skin, how much of the joint cost of each production run is allocated to Silken Skin on a net realizable value basis?
4. If additional processing costs beyond the split-off point are $1.40 per gallon for Smooth Skin and $0.90 per gallon for Silken Skin, how much of the joint cost of each production run is allocated to Smooth Skin on a physical measure method basis?

(CMA Adapted)

12–23 **Joint Product Costing** Sonimad Sawmill manufactures two lumber products from a joint milling process: mine support braces (MSB) and unseasoned commercial building lumber (CBL). A standard production run incurs joint costs of $300,000 and results in 60,000 units of MSB and 90,000 units of CBL. Each MSB sells for $2 per unit, and each CBL sells for $4 per unit.

Required

1. Assuming that no further processing occurs after the split-off point, how much of the joint costs are allocated to commercial building lumber (CBL) on a physical measure method basis?
2. If no further processing occurs after the split-off point, how much of the joint cost is allocated to the mine support braces (MSB) on a sales value basis?
3. Assume that the CBL is not marketable at split-off but must be planed and sized at a cost of $200,000 per production run. During this process, 10,000 units are unavoidably lost and

have no value. The remaining units of CBL are salable at $10 per unit. The MSB, although salable immediately at the split-off point, are coated with a tarlike preservative that costs $100,000 per production run. The braces are then sold for $5 each. Using the net realizable value basis, how much of the completed cost should be assigned to each unit of CBL?

4. Should Sonimad Sawmill choose to process the MSB beyond split-off? What would be the contribution if it did so?

(CMA Adapted)

12–24 Joint Products The Salinas Company produces three products, X, Y, and Z, from a joint process. Each product can be sold at the split-off point or processed further. Additional processing requires no special facilities, and the production costs of further processing are entirely variable and traceable to the products involved. Last year all three products were processed beyond split-off. Joint production costs for the year were $80,000. Sales values and costs needed to evaluate Salinas' production policy follow:

Product	Units Produced	Sales Value at Split-Off	If All Units Processed Further Sales Value	If All Units Processed Further Additional Costs
X	5,000	$25,000	$55,000	$9,000
Y	4,000	41,000	45,000	7,000
Z	1,000	24,000	30,000	8,000

Required

1. Determine the unit cost and gross profit for each product if Salinas allocates joint production costs in proportion to the relative physical volume of output.
2. Determine unit costs and gross profit for each product if Salinas allocates joint costs using the sales value method.
3. Should the firm sell any of its products after further processing?
4. Salinas has been selling all of its products at the split-off point. Selling any of the products after further processing will entail direct competition with some major customers. What strategic factors does the firm need to consider in deciding whether to process any of the products further?

12–25 Joint Products Hathaway Chemical makes three widely used industrial adhesives: SH–1, SH–2 and SH–3. See sales and production information for a gallon of each of the three adhesives in the following table. Most of Hathaway's customers ask for a special blend of the three products which improves heat-resistance. The additional processing requires additional time and materials, and the price is increased accordingly, as shown in the table. Assume that Hathaway produces only for specific customer orders, so there is no beginning or ending inventory. Assume also that all of Hathaway's customers requested the heat-resistant version of the product, so that all production required additional processing.

	SH–1	SH–2	SH–3
Units sold	144,000	125,000	88,000
Price (after addt'l processing)	$ 21	$ 14	$ 18
Separable processing cost	$433,000	$145,000	$589,000
Total joint cost $2,745,000			
Sales price at split-off	$ 10	$ 12	$ 8

Required

1. Calculate the product cost of each of the three product lines using the following methods: (a) physical unit method, (b) sales value at split off method, and (c) the net realizable value method.
2. Which of the three methods do you think would be preferred in this case? Why?

12–26 Joint Products; By-Products (Appendix) Multiproduct Corporation is a chemical manufacturer that produces two main products (Pepco–1 and Repke–3) and a by-product (SE–5) from a joint process. If Multiproduct had the proper facilities, it could process SE-5 further into a main product. The ratio of output quantities to input quantity of direct material used in the joint process remains consistent with the processing conditions and activity level.

Multiproduct currently uses the physical measure method of allocating joint costs to the main products. It uses the first-in, first-out (FIFO) inventory method to value the main products. The by-product is inventoried at its net realizable value, which is used to reduce the joint production costs before they are allocated to the main products.

Jim Simpson, Multiproduct's controller, wants to implement the sales value method of joint cost allocation. He believes that inventory costs should be based on each product's ability to contribute to the recovery of joint production costs. The net realizable value of the by-product would be treated in the same manner that the physical method would.

Data regarding Multiproduct's operations for November 2004 are presented in the following report. The joint cost of production totaled to $2,640,000 for November 2004.

	Main Products		By-Product
	Pepco–1	Repke–3	SE–5
Finished goods inventory in gallons on November 1, 2004	20,000	40,000	10,000
November sales in gallons	800,000	700,000	200,000
November production in gallons	900,000	720,000	240,000
Sales value per gallon at split-off point	$2.00	$1.50	$0.55*
Additional process costs after split-off	$1,800,000	$720,000	—
Final sales value per gallon	$5.00	$4.00	—

*Disposal and selling costs of 5 cents per gallon are incurred to sell the by-product.

Required

1. Describe the sales value method and explain how it would accomplish Jim's objective.

2. Assuming Multiproduct adopts the sales value method for internal reporting purposes, calculate the following:

   a. The allocation of the joint production cost for November 2004.

   b. The dollar values of the finished goods inventories for Pepco–1, Repke–3, and SE–5 as of November 30, 2004.

3. Multiproduct plans to expand its production facilities to further process SE–5 into a main product. Discuss how the allocation of the joint production costs under the sales value method would change when SE–5 becomes a main product.

(CMA Adapted)

12–27 Joint Products   Alderon Industries manufactures chemicals for various purposes. One process that Alderon uses produces SPL–3, a chemical used in swimming pools; PST–4, a chemical used in pesticides; and RJ–5, a by-product sold to fertilizer manufacturers. Alderon uses the net realizable value of its main products to allocate joint production costs and the first-in, first-out inventory method to value the main products. The by-product is inventoried at its net realizable value, which is used to reduce the joint production costs before they are allocated to the main products. The ratio of output to input of direct material used in the joint process remains consistent from month to month.

Data regarding Alderon's operations for the month of November 2004 follow. During this month, Alderon incurred joint production costs of $1,702,000 in the manufacture of SPL–3, PST–4, and RJ–5.

	SPL–3	PST–4	RJ–5
Finished goods inventory in gallons (November 1, 2004)	18,000	52,000	3,000
November sales in gallons	650,000	325,000	150,000
November production in gallons	700,000	350,000	170,000
Sales value per gallon at split-off	—	$3.80	$0.70*
Additional processing costs	$874,000	$816,000	—
Final sales value per gallon	$4.00	$6.00	—

*Disposal costs of 10 cents per gallon are incurred to sell the by-product.

Required

1. Determine Alderon Industries' allocation of joint production costs for the month of November 2004. Be sure to present appropriate supporting calculations.

2. Determine the dollar values of the finished goods inventories for SPL–3, PST–4, and RJ–5 as of November 30, 2004.

3. Alderon has an opportunity to sell PST–4 at the split-off point for $3.80 per gallon. Prepare an analysis showing whether Alderon should sell PST–4 at the split-off point or process further.

4. As a production supervisor for Alderon, you have learned that small quantities of the critical chemical compound in PST–4 might be present in SPL–3. What should you do?

(CMA Adapted)

12–28 **Joint Products; By-Products (Review of Chapters 7 and 9)**   Lond Company produces joint products Jana and Reta, and by-product Bynd. Jana is sold at split-off; Reta and Bynd undergo additional processing. Production data pertaining to these products for the year ended December 31, 2004, were as follows:

	Jana	Reta	Bynd	Total
Joint costs				
Variable				$ 88,000
Fixed				148,000
Separate costs				
Variable		$120,000	$3,000	$123,000
Fixed		90,000	2,000	92,000
Production in pounds	50,000	40,000	10,000	100,000
Sales price per pound	$4.00	$7.50	$1.10	

Lond had no beginning or ending inventories and no materials were spoiled in production. Bynd's net realizable value is deducted from joint costs. Joint costs are allocated to joint products to achieve the same gross margin percentage for each joint product.

Although 2004 performance could be repeated for 2005, Lond is considering operation of the plant at its full capacity of 120,000 pounds. The relative proportions of each product's output with respect to cost behavior and production increases would be unchanged. Market surveys indicate that prices of Jana and Bynd would have to be reduced to $3.40 and $0.90, respectively. Reta's expected price decline cannot be determined.

Required

1. Prepare the following information for Lond Company for the year ended December 31, 2004:

   a. Total gross margin.

   b. Allocation of joint costs to Jana and Reta.

   c. Separate gross margins for Jana and Reta.

2. Compute Lond's breakeven point in pounds for the year ended December 31, 2004.

3. Prepare the following information for Lond Company for the year ending December 31, 2005:

   a. Projected production in pounds for each product at full capacity.

   b. Differential revenues (excluding Reta).

   c. Differential costs.

   d. Sales price per pound of Reta required for Lond to achieve the same gross margin as that for 2004.

(CMA Adapted)

12–29 **Departmental Cost Allocation**   Marfrank Corporation is a manufacturing company with six functional departments: finance, marketing, personnel, production, research and development (R&D), and information systems, each administered by a vice president. The information systems department (ISD) was established in 2003 when Marfrank decided to acquire a mainframe computer and develop a new information system.

While systems development and implementation is an ongoing process at Marfrank, many basic systems needed by each functional department were operational at the end of 2004. Thus, calendar year 2005 is considered the first year for which the ISD costs can be estimated with a high degree of accuracy. Marfrank's president wants the other five functional departments to be aware of the magnitude of the ISD costs by allocating them in the reports and statements prepared at the end of the first quarter of 2005. The allocation to each department was based on its actual use of ISD services.

Jon Werner, vice president of ISD, suggested that the actual ISD costs be allocated on the basis of pages of actual computer output. He chose this basis because all departments use reports to evaluate their operations and make decisions. The use of this basis resulted in the following allocation:

Department	Percentage	Allocated Cost
Finance	50%	$112,500
Marketing	30	67,500
Personnel	9	20,250
Production	6	13,500
R&D	5	11,250

After the quarterly reports were distributed, the finance and marketing departments objected to this allocation method. Both departments recognized that they were responsible for most of the report output, but they believed that these output costs might be the smallest of ISD costs and requested that a more equitable allocation basis be developed.

After meeting with Jon, Elaine Jergens, Marfrank's controller, concluded that ISD provides three distinct services: systems development, computer processing represented by central processing unit (CPU) time, and report generation. She recommended that a predetermined rate be developed for each service based on budgeted annual activity and costs. The ISD costs would then be assigned to the other functional departments using the predetermined rate times the actual activity used. ISD would absorb any difference between actual costs incurred and costs allocated to the other departments.

Elaine and Jon concluded that systems development could be charged on the basis of hours devoted to systems development and programming, computer processing based on CPU time used for operations (exclusive of database development and maintenance), and report generation based on number of pages of output. The only cost they thought should not be included in any of the predetermined rates was for purchased software; these packages usually were acquired for a specific department's use. Thus, Elaine concluded that purchased software would be charged at cost to the department for which it was purchased. To revise the first-quarter allocation, she gathered this information on ISD costs and services:

	Estimated Annual Costs	Actual First-Quarter Costs	Percentage Devoted to		
				Computer Report	
			Systems Development	Processing	Generation
Wages/benefits					
Administration	$100,000	$25,000	60%	20%	20%
Computer operators	55,000	13,000		20	80
Analysts/programmers	165,000	43,500	100		
Maintenance					
Hardware	24,000	6,000	75	25	
Software	20,000	5,000	100		
Output supplies	50,000	11,500			100
Purchased software	45,000	16,000*	—	—	—
Utilities	28,000	6,250	100		
Depreciation					
Mainframe computer	325,000	81,250	100		
Printing equipment	60,000	15,000		100	
Building improvements	10,000	2,500	100		
Total department costs	$882,000	$225,000			

*All software purchased during the first quarter of 2005 was for the production department.

Information Systems Department Services			
	Systems Development	Computer Operations (CPU)	Report Generation
Annual capacity	4,500 hours	360 CPU hours	5,000,000 pages
Actual usage during first quarter, 2005			
Finance	100 hours	8 CPU hours	600,000 pages
Marketing	250	12	360,000
Personnel	200	12	108,000
Production	400	32	72,000
R&D	50	16	60,000
Total usage	1,000 hours	80 CPU hours	1,200,000 pages

Required

1. For ISD, determine the following:

   a. The predetermined rates for each service category: systems development, computer processing, and report generation.

   b. Using the predetermined rates developed in requirement 1a, the amount each of the other five functional departments would be charged for ISD's services provided during the first quarter of 2005.

2. With the method proposed by Elaine Jergens for charging the ISD costs to the other five functional departments, ISD's actual costs incurred and the costs assigned to the five user department might differ.

   a. Explain the nature of this difference.

   b. Discuss whether this proposal will improve cost control in ISD.

3. Explain whether Elaine's proposed method of charging user departments for ISD costs will improve planning and control in the user departments.

4. Assume that a finance manager has suggested outsourcing ISD. What factors should Marfrank consider in deciding whether to outsource ISD functions?

(CMA Adapted)

12–30 **Departmental Cost Allocation**   Computer Intelligence, a computer software consulting company, has three major functional areas: computer programming, information systems consulting, and software training. Carol Bingham, a pricing analyst in the accounting department, has been asked to develop total costs for the functional areas. These costs will be used as a guide in pricing a new contract. In computing these costs, Carol is considering three different methods of the departmental allocation approach to allocate overhead costs: the direct method, the step method, and the reciprocal method. She assembled the following data from the two service departments, information systems and facilities:

	Service Departments		Production Departments			
	Information Systems	Facilities	Computer Programming	Informations Systems Consulting	Software Training	Total
Budgeted overhead	$80,000	$45,000	$150,000	$190,000	$135,000	$600,000
Information systems* (hours)		200	1,200	600	1000	3,000
Facilities† (thousand square feet)	200		400	600	800	2,000

*Allocated on the basis of hours of computer usage.
†Allocated on the basis of floor space.

Required

1. Using as the application base computer usage time for the information systems department and square feet of floor space for the facilities department, apply overhead from these

service departments to the production departments, using these three methods. Use Excel and Solver to determine the allocations.

   a. Direct method.

   b. Step method.

   c. Reciprocal method.

2. Rather than allocate costs, how might Computer Intelligence better assign the information systems department's costs?

(CMA Adapted)

12–31 Joint Products and By-Products   Princess Corporation grows, processes, packages, and sells three apple products: slices that are used in frozen pies, applesauce, and apple juice. The outside skin of the apple, which is removed in the cutting department and processed as animal feed, is treated as a by-product. Princess uses the net realizable value method to assign costs of the joint process to its main products. The apple skin by-product is inventoried at its market value, and its net realizable value is used to reduce the joint production costs prior to allocation to the main products. Details of Princess' production process follow:

- The cutting department washes the apples and removes the outside skin. The department then cores and trims the apples for slicing. At this point, each of the three main products and the by-product are recognizable. Each product is then transferred to the next department for final processing.

- The slicing department receives the trimmed apples and slices and freezes them. Any juice generated during the slicing operation is frozen with the slices.

- The crushing department trims pieces of apple and processes them into applesauce. The juice generated during this operation is used in the applesauce.

- The juicing department pulverizes the core and any surplus apple from the cutting department into a liquid. This department experiences a loss equal to 8 percent of the weight of the good output produced.

- The feed department chops the outside skin into animal food and packages it. A total of 270,000 pounds of apples entered the cutting department during November. The following information shows the costs incurred in each department, the proportion by weight (based on pounds) transferred to the four final processing departments, and the selling price of each end product. Assume no beginning or ending inventory of apple slices, applesauce, or juice.

Department	Costs Incurred	Proportion of Product by Weight Transferred to Departments	Selling Price per Pound of Final Product
Cutting	$60,000	—	—
Slicing	11,280	33%	$.80
Crushing	8,550	30	.55
Juicing	3,000	27	.40
Feed	700	10	.10
Total	$83,530	100%	

Required

1. Princess Corporation uses the net realizable value method to determine inventory values for its main products and by-products. For the month of November, calculate each of the following:

   a. Output in pounds for apple slices, applesauce, apple juice, and animal feed.

   b. Net realizable value at the split-off point for each of the three main products.

   c. Cutting department cost assigned to each of the three main products and to the by-product in accordance with corporate policy.

   d. Gross margin in dollars for each of the three main products.

2. Comment on the significance to management of the gross margin dollar information by main product for planning and control purposes as opposed to inventory valuation.

3. List the important issues that Princess faces as a global company. What are its critical success factors? Which key issues arise because Princess operates in several countries? Should any of these issues affect the way Princess allocates costs, as determined in requirement 1?

(CMA Adapted)

12–32 Joint Products and By Products Goodson Pharmaceutical Company manufactures three main products from a joint process: Altox, Lorex, and Hycol. Data regarding these products for the fiscal year ended May 31, 2004, follow:

	Altox	Lorex	Hycol
Units produced	170,000	500,000	330,000
Sales value per unit at split-off	$3.50	—	$2.00
Allocation of joint costs*	$450,000	$846,000	$504,000
Separable costs	—	$1,400,000	—
Final sales value per unit	—	$5.00	—

*Joint costs are allocated on the basis of net realizable value, and the net realizable value of any by-product is deducted from the joint costs before allocation.

Altox is currently sold at the split-off point to a vitamin manufacturer. Lorex is processed further after the split-off point and sold as a cold remedy. Hycol, an oil produced from the joint process, is sold at the split-off point to a cosmetics manufacturer.

Arlene Franklin, president of Goodson, is reviewing opportunities to change the processing and sale of these three products. Altox can be refined for use as a high blood pressure medication, but this would result in a loss of 20,000 units. The costs to further process Altox are estimated to be $250,000 annually. The medication would sell for $5.50 per unit. The company has an offer from another pharmaceutical company to purchase Lorex, at the split-off point for $2.25 per unit. Goodson's research department has suggested that the company process Hycol further and sell it as an ointment to relieve muscle pain. The additional processing would cost $75,000 annually and would increase the units of product by 25 percent. The product would be sold for $1.80 per unit.

The joint process that Goodson currently uses also produces 50,000 units of Dorzine, a hazardous chemical waste product that costs the company $0.35 per unit for proper disposal. Dietriech Mills Inc. is interested in using the Dorzine as a solvent; however, Goodson must refine the Dorzine at an annual cost of $43,000. Dietrich would purchase all Dorzine Goodson can refine and is willing to pay $0.75 for each unit.

Required

1. Which of the three main products should Goodson Pharmaceutical Company sell at the split-off point? Which of them should the company process further to maximize profits? Support your answers with appropriate calculations, using a spreadsheet system.

2. Assume that Goodson has decided to refine the waste product Dorzine as a by-product of the joint process in the future and to sell it to Dietriech Mill.
   a. Did Goodson make the correct decision regarding Dorzine? Support your answer with appropriate calculations.
   b. Explain whether the decision to treat Dorzine as a by-product will affect your answer to requirement 1.

(CMA Adapted)

12–33 Cost Allocation; Equal Gross Margin Percentage; New Method Ted Brown is the chief financial officer of Haywood Inc., a large manufacturer of cosmetics and other personal care products. Ted is conducting a financial analysis of the firm's line of hand lotions which consists of three products: SkinSalve, SkinCream, and SkinBalm. Total sales for the three products in the recent year were $400,000, $250,000 and $500,000, respectively. Because there is a small amount of additional processing cost for each of the three products, which differs between the products ($20,000, $50,000 and $30,000, respectively), Ted has been using the net realizable value method for allocating the joint production cost of $500,000. However, he is not satisfied with the result of somewhat different gross margin percentage ratios (gross margin/sales) for the three products when using this approach. He knows only of the physical units method, the sales value at split-off method, and the net realizable value method for allocating joint cost.

Required Devise a new method of cost allocation for Ted so that after allocation of joint costs and separable costs, the gross margin percentage is the same for all three products.

Joint Product Costing

The Physical Measure Method If we use a physical measure method, the joint cost of $20,000 is allocated as shown in Exhibit 12.29.

The production costs per gallon for both products are the same:

Product GS–50: $15,000/75 = $200
Product GS–80: $ 5,000/25 = $200

The Sales Value at Split-Off Method Assume that Northern Company sold 60 gallons of GS–50 and 20 gallons of GS–80. Then the $20,000 joint cost should be allocated among the products as shown in Exhibit 12.30.

Note that the gallons sold do not figure in the analysis, which is based on *units produced* only. The production costs per gallon for both products are calculated:

Product GS–50 $18,750/75 = $250
Product GS–80 $ 1,250/25 = $ 50

The Net Realizable Value Method The net realizable values of GS–50 and GS–80 are $20,000 and $5,000, respectively, as shown in Exhibit 12.31. The allocated costs are $16,000 to GS–50 and $4,000 to GS–80.

The costs per gallon for products GS–505 and GS–805 are calculated:

Product GS–505 ($16,000 + $5,000)/50 = $420
Product GS–805 ($ 4,000 + $2,000)/50 = $120

EXHIBIT 12.29
Physical Measure Method

Product	Physical Measure	Proportion	Allocation of Joint Cost
GS–50	75 gallons	75%	$20,000 × 75% = $15,000
GS–80	25 gallons	25%	20,000 × 25% = 5,000

EXHIBIT 12.30
Sales Value at Split-Off Method

Product	Units	Price	Sales Value	Proportion	Joint Cost Allocated
GS–50	75	$300	$22,500	93.75%	$20,000 × 93.75% = $18,750
GS–80	25	60	1,500	6.25%	20,000 × 6.25% = 1,250
Total			$24,000	100%	$20,000

EXHIBIT 12.31 Net Realizable Value Method

Product	Production Units	Sales Price	Sales Value	Separable Cost	Net Realizable Value	Weight	Joint Cost Allocated
GS–50	50	$500	$25,000	$5,000	$20,000	80%	$20,000 × 80% = $16,000
GS–80	50	140	7,000	2,000	5,000	20%	20,000 × 20% = 4,000
Total	100		$32,000	$7,000	$25,000	100%	$20,000

Solution to
Self-Study Problem

The Flexible Budget and Standard Costing: Direct Materials and Direct Labor

After studying this chapter, you should be able to . . .

1. Evaluate the effectiveness and efficiency of an operation and calculate and interpret the operating income variance
2. Develop and use flexible budgets to analyze operating results
3. Set proper standard costs for planning, control, and performance evaluation
4. Identify factors contributing to variances and analyze and explain variances
5. Assess the effects of the contemporary manufacturing environment on operational control and standard costing
6. Recognize behavioral implications in implementing standard cost systems
7. Describe cost flows through general ledger accounts and prepare journal entries for the acquisition and use of direct materials and direct labor in a standard cost system

Founded in 1907 to provide private messenger and delivery services in Seattle, Washington, United Parcel Services (UPS) has become the world's largest package delivery company and a leading global provider of specialized transportation and logistics services.[1] Its primary business is the time-definite delivery of packages and documents that UPS guarantees will arrive at times customers specify. In addition to making deliveries throughout the United States, the firm delivers to more than 200 countries and territories. On average, UPS delivers more than 13 million packages and documents per day worldwide. It generated revenue of more than $31 billion in 2002 and earned a higher profit than its competitors. How does UPS do it?

An early adopter of standards in all phases of its operations, UPS has become known for its demand for strict adherence to these standards. Every day each driver of a UPS delivery truck knows the exact number of packages and documents he or she must deliver that day. Long-haul drivers who carry UPS packages are expected to travel a certain distance within a specific time. UPS customers can track packages on its website to find out the whereabouts of a package and the time that the package was or will be delivered. By maintaining strict work standards, UPS has been able to deliver as promised and has become one of the best-run companies in the United States and a global company with one of the most recognized brands in the world.

Budgets and standards are performance guidelines and goals. Organizations and businesses—be they service, merchandising, or manufacturing firms, for profit or not for profit—use budgets and standards to set performance expectations, evaluate and

---

[1] United Parcel Service *Annual Report, 2003.* Find out more about the company at its website: ups.com/.

control operations, motivate employees, and encourage efforts toward their goals. Manufacturing firms such as Ford, Caterpillar, Toshiba, Siemens, and Thomasville specify the amount of materials and the number of hours in manufacturing their products. Retail stores such as The Limited, Wal-Mart, and Target have specific standards for their employees and monitor their adherence to these standards closely. Farmers have standards for the amount of fertilizers to use per acre and the quantity of food to feed each pig. This chapter explores the uses of budgets and standard costing systems in operations.

He who controls the past controls the future.

George Orwell

You can't get caught up in things that you can't control. . . . We cannot control our selling price. We can control our cost of manufacturing. We can control our efficiencies.

Steven Appleton, CEO of Micro Technology

Budgets help firms plan and coordinate activities and serve as the bases for control operations and performance evaluations. Chapter 8 discussed preparation of budget. In this chapter, we turn our attention to how budgets can be used and the roles that standards play in controlling operations and evaluating operating results. Controlling operations assists managers in attaining the budgeted goals they set out to accomplish. Assessments of operating results provide feedbacks to managers and help them to gain insights into the causes that led to the operating results. By learning from the past, managers can, as George Orwell says, control the future.

Evaluating Operating Results

Evaluating operating results involves identification of variances. A variance is the amount that the actual operating result deviates from the expected amount for the operation. A variance is a surprise and is likely not a good characteristic of a well-managed operation. Managers need to anticipate and be aware of surprises, so that they can keep deviations at a minimum.

A good accounting system identifies variances and makes managers aware of significant variances at the earliest time so that managers can *manage by exception.* The production manager of an ice cream manufacturer needs not spend time in the mixing operation as long as this process operates as expected. However, the manager needs to pay attention to the operation if the mixing department requested or used 50 pounds of sugar to manufacture 50 gallons of ice cream, when the standard called for eight ounces of sugar for every gallon of ice cream. No manager has time to be everywhere at all times. Variances help managers to not spend time on operations that are under control and focus on the areas that need their attention. Variance identification helps managers to attain better operating results.

A favorable variance improves the operating result. A firm earns a higher operating income and a favorable variance if it

- Sold more units
- Received a higher selling price per unit
- Incurred lower costs

A firm that sells its product at $50 per unit when the budget selling price is $45 has a favorable variance in selling price. The firm has an unfavorable variance if it paid $36 per pound for direct materials when the budget specified the direct materials costing $32 per pound. A favorable variance is denoted by F and an unfavorable variance is denoted by U in this book.

Two aspects of operations are generally of interest to management in assessing operations: effectiveness in attaining goals and efficiency in carrying out operations.

Effectiveness

An **effective operation**
attains the goal set for
the operation.

LEARNING OBJECTIVE 1

*Evaluate the effectiveness and
efficiency of an operation and
calculate and interpret the
operating income variance.*

An **effective operation** is one that attains or exceeds the goal set for the operation. A firm that was budgeted to earn $50 million net operating income for the year but earned $51 million by the end of the year was effective. A student with a goal of maintaining her grade point average at 3.0 who had a 3.25 grade point average for the semester was effective. A social service organization that has a goal of serving 50,000 hot meals to homeless people and serves 55,000 hot meals has an effective operation.

The firm that had a goal to earn $50 million net operating income for the year and earns $49 million is ineffective. The student who wanted to maintain a 3.0 grade point average and earned a 2.75 average was not effective; even if the two part-time jobs the student had during the semester were not part of the plan when the 3.0 goal was chosen. The social service organization was not effective if it served only 48,000 hot meals when it budgeted to serve 50,000 hot meals, despite food price increases of more than 10 percent over the budgeted amount.

Effective operations are essential for a successful strategy. Ineffective operations render disappointing results, drain cash and other resources, and may lead an organization to its demise. Repeated ineffective operations often force a firm to either abandon or modify its strategy. Intel's effective operations enable the firm to be successful in carrying out its strategy of bringing new computer chips to the market before the competition. Intel has enjoyed high profitability and dominated the market since the mid-1980s. Its failure to be the company that introduced the fastest PC processor to the market in 2000 allowed one of its main competitors to gain 50 percent in market share and might have caused Intel to decide to expand into other markets. A series of setbacks in IBM's operations has forced it to retreat and redirect its strategies several times between the early 1980s and the mid-1990s. IBM is no longer the same company that it once was.

Most organizations have multiple strategic goals. A firm should assess its goals so that management has a clear grasp of the overall effectiveness of operations and the feasibility of attaining the strategic goals.

Some firms measure their effectiveness by analyzing one or a few of their critical success factors. A business firm may assess its effectiveness based on whether it has earned the desired operating income, gained the target market share, introduced new products by the deadlines, or attained the rate of return on net assets as specified in the master budget. School districts may use the average SAT score of their high school graduates or the number of students graduated as a measure of their effectiveness. Students may assess their effectiveness according to the number of credit hours completed or the grade point average earned.

A master budget delineates the desired operating results for the period and is a common starting point in assessing the effectiveness of operations. The difference between the actual result attained and the master budget measures the degree to which a firm was effective in meeting the goal or objective.

Efficiency

An **efficient operation**
wastes no resources in operations.

An **efficient operation** wastes no resources in carrying out the operation. An operation is inefficient if the firm spent more than the necessary amount of resources to complete the tasks. A firm that spent $40,000 to manufacture and sell 10,000 units is efficient if the standard is $4 per unit. The same firm would be inefficient if it cost $50,000 to manufacture and sell the same 10,000 units.

Assessments of efficiency are independent of assessments of effectiveness. A firm can be effective in attaining the goal set for its operation, but still be inefficient. Conversely, a firm can be efficient yet ineffective if it fails to attain the goal for the operations. Consider the manufacturing firm just mentioned. If it made and sold 9,000 units in a period when the plan is to manufacture and sell 10,000 units for the period, it was ineffective. It did not meet its sales goal of 10,000 units. The firm, however, was efficient if it spent $35,000, not the $36,000 ($4 per unit × 9,000 units) allowed, to manufacture and sell the 9,000 units. The firm was effective if it manufactured and sold 12,000 units and attained the goal of selling 10,000 units during the period. The firm was not efficient, however, if it spent $60,000 to manufacture and sell the 12,000 units.

Assessing Effectiveness

An important short-term goal for a company is to earn the budgeted operating income for the period. At the end of a period, management wants to know whether the operation has earned the desired operating income the firm set out to earn for the period. The desired operating income for a period usually is the budgeted operating income for the period. The difference between the actual operating income and the master budget operating income is the **operating income variance** and is a measure of the effectiveness of the period.

> The **operating income variance** of a period is the difference between the actual operating income of the period and the budgeted operating income in the master budget for the period.

Consider the analysis of operations for Schmidt Machinery Company in Exhibit 13.1. The bottom line of column (2) shows that the budgeted operating income for the period is $200,000, while column (1) reports that the firm earned an operating income of $128,000 for the period. The difference is the operating income variance for the period, $72,000 unfavorable [column (3)]. Schmidt Machinery Company was not effective in attaining its goal for the period; its operation fell 36 percent short of its budgeted operating income.

In addition to the operating income variance, Exhibit 13.1 reports the difference between the master budget and the actual operating result for each of reported items such as units sold, sales, and others. The results show that the actual units sold, 780 units, is 220 units less than the sales units in the master budget, a 22 percent decrease in units. As a result the total sales revenue is below that of budgeted sales by $160,400, or 20 percent.

Exhibit 13.1 reports that the variable expense incurred in October is $99,050 less than the budgeted amount—a favorable variance. This comparison probably would lead us to conclude that the primary reason for Schmidt's failure to be effective in earning its budgeted net income is the shortfall in sales. The shortfall is so large that even with a good control of expenses, as evidenced by the substantial favorable variance in variable expenses, the firm still suffers a substantial decrease in operating income and, as a result, failed to be effective in earning the budgeted $200,000 in operating income.

That conclusion is misleading. Direct comparisons, between the actual amounts incurred and the master or static budget amounts for variable expenses can be meaningless. In this instance, the variable expenses in the master or static budget are for operations at a higher level than that actually achieved. Variable expenses for 780 units should be less than the variable expenses for 1,000 units. Schmidt should not credit its

EXHIBIT 13.1
Comparison of Operating Results with Master Budget

	SCHMIDT MACHINERY COMPANY Analysis of Operations For October 2005		
	(1) **Actual** **Operating Result**	**(2)** **Master Budget**	**(3)** **Variance**
Units	780	1,000	220 U*
Sales	$639,600 100%	$800,000 100%	$160,400 U
Variable expenses	350,950 55	450,000 56	99,050 F†
Contribution margin	$288,650 45%	$350,000 44%	$ 61,350 U
Fixed expenses	160,650 25	150,000 19	10,650 U
Operating income	$128,000 20%	$200,000 25%	$ 72,000 U

*U denotes an *unfavorable effect* on the budgeted operating income
†F denotes a *favorable* effect.

management for having good control of its variable expenses based only on the fact that the variable costs incurred are below the budgeted amount for the period. Differences in the amount for variable expenses between the actual operation and the master budget figure have no implication on the effectiveness of the operation, nor are they measures of efficiency, as we discuss later.

The operating income variance reveals only whether the firm achieved the budgeted operating income for the period; it does not identify causes for the deviation or help the firm identify courses of action to reduce or eliminate similar deviations in the future. The firm needs to conduct additional analyses to learn the reason for missing the target. An analysis of the efficiency of the operation can shed insights on this question. Flexible budgets play important roles in such analyses.

The Flexible Budget

LEARNING OBJECTIVE 2
Develop and use flexible budgets to analyze operating results.

The budget prepared prior to the beginning of a period as discussed in Chapter 8 is a *master budget* for the period; it lays out expectations and provides blueprints of operations for the coming period. The budget is a *static budget* because the budget is developed for only a specific output level. For example, the budget Kerry Industrial Company prepares (Exhibits 8.4 through 8.15) is for sales of 20,000 units in April; 25,000 units in May; and 35,000 units in June. The budgeted amount of cost of goods sold in April, $371,750, is the expected cost of goods sold when Kerry sells 20,000 units.

The budget for a period (master or static budget) is useful for initial planning and coordination of activities of the period. It also serves as an important guideline or benchmark in monitoring and controlling operations and for performance evaluation. Operating conditions, however, seldom turn out exactly the way they were expected or forecasted when the budget was prepared. Whenever the output attained differs from the budgeted output, or the actual operating conditions deviate from those budgeted due to factors beyond the control of the firm, the organization needs to incorporate these changes and revises the master budget before assessing operating efficiency.

If Kerry sold 22,000 units in April, the budgeted cost of goods sold, $371,750, would no longer be appropriate for assessing operating efficiency during the period. We need to use the amount of cost that Kerry should have spent in operating at the 22,000 unit level.

Efficiency of an operation is determined by comparing the amount of resources used in the operation to the amount of the resource that should have been used for the actual output of the operation. A tool that can help in determining the amount of resources that should have been used for the operation of a period is the flexible budget for the output of the period.

The **flexible budget**
is a budget that adjusts revenues and costs to the output achieved.

A **flexible budget** is a budget that adjusts revenues and expenses to the actual output achieved. Changes in output (for example, units manufactured or sold for a manufacturing firm, number of patient-days for a hospital, or number of students for a school district) change the firm's revenues and expenses. A firm usually prepares a flexible budget at the end of a period when the total work done or actual output achieved during the period is known.

Flexible budgets can help management answer many important questions about an operation. The data for Schmidt Machinery Company in Exhibit 13.1 show that the period's operating income is $72,000 less than the budgeted amount. On receiving the report, management likely would want to know:

1. Why net income has gone down?
2. Why the expenses have gone from 75 to 80 percent of sales. Can management do something to prevent the same thing from happening next year?
3. Why selling and general expenses have increased $10,650?
4. What are the reasons for the deterioration in operating results? Is it because of changes in
   a. units sold?

b. sales price?

c. sales mix?

d. manufacturing or merchandising cost?

e. selling and general expenses?

Preparing a flexible budget allows management to adjust the budget to the output level achieved and answer these questions.

Flexible budgets differ from the master budget in the number of budgeted output units. Other factors, such as unit selling prices and unit variable costs, are the same in flexible budgets as the amounts in the master budget. The total fixed expenses usually remain the same in both the flexible and the master budgets unless the actual level of operation differs substantially from the planned operation level (outside the relevant range) and the firm had the time to adjust its operation level. Exhibit 13.2 illustrates the flexible budget for Schmidt for October 2005. Schmidt developed the flexible budget in three steps:

Step 1: Determine the output of the period. Schmidt manufactured and sold 780 units. The flexible budget, therefore, would be at the 780 units level of operation.

Step 2: Use the selling price and the variable cost per unit in the master budget to calculate the sales revenues and variable expenses, respectively, for the output quantity of the period and to compute the flexible budget contribution margin. The selling price per unit and variable cost per unit in the master budget are $800 and $450, respectively. Thus, at 780 units output level,

Flexible budget total sales = 780 units × $800 per unit $624,000

Flexible budget total variable expenses = 780 units × $450 per unit   351,000

Flexible budget contribution margin $273,000

Alternatively, the flexible budget contribution margin can be computed using the output unit and the budget contribution margin per unit.

Contribution margin per unit in the master budget:

$350,000 total contribution margin ÷ 1,000 units = $350 per unit

Total flexible budget contribution margin:

780 units × $350 per unit = $273,000

Step 3: Determine the budget amount of fixed cost and compute the flexible budget operating income. Schmidt Company has determined that the manufacturing and selling of 780 units is within the same operating range as the master budget operating level. The fixed cost for the flexible budget, therefore, is $150,000. Thus, the flexible budget operating income is

$273,000 − $150,000 = $123,000.

EXHIBIT 13.2

Flexible and Master Budgets for Schmidt Machinery Company

	(1) Flexible Budget		(2) Master Budget	
Units	780		1,000	
Sales ($800)	$624,000	100.00%	$800,000	100.00%
Variable expenses ($450)	351,000	56.25	450,000	56.25
Contribution margin ($350)	$273,000	43.75%	$350,000	43.75%
Fixed expenses	150,000	24.04	150,000	18.75
Operating income	$123,000	19.71%	$200,000	25.00%

EXHIBIT 13.3
Comparison of the Master
Budget and the Flexible
Budget

	Master Budget	**Flexible Budget**
Time prepared	Before the period	Before, during, or after the period
Activity levels	Single level	One or more levels
Level of detail	All aspects of operations	Selected aspects

The amount of fixed cost in a flexible budget may differ from the amount in the master budget if the actual operating level is substantially different from the operating level anticipated by the firm at the time when it prepared the master budget and the firm had sufficient time to adjust its level of operation.

Total sales and total expenses for a flexible budget are calculated using these formulas:

$$\text{Total sales} = \text{Number of units sold} \times \text{Budgeted selling price per unit}$$

$$\text{Total variable expenses} = \text{Number of units sold} \times \text{Budgeted variable cost per unit}$$

$$\text{Total fixed expenses} = \text{Amount of fixed expenses in the master budget}$$

A firm can prepare flexible budgets for different levels of output or activity. In addition, a firm usually prepares flexible budgets after the period is over while it always prepares the master budget before the beginning of the period. Flexible budgets also may differ in the level of detail. Flexible budgets typically contain fewer details than master budgets. Exhibit 13.3 highlights these differences.

Assessing Efficiency

With the help of a flexible budget, we can separate the difference between the operating result and the master budget into two components: the flexible budget variance and the sales volume variance.

Sales Volume Variance

Sales volume variance
is the difference between the flexible budget and the master or static budget of the period.

The **sales volume variance** of a period is the difference between the flexible budget amount and the amount in the master or static budget of the period for the corresponding item. A sales volume variance measures the effect of changes in units of sales on sales revenues, expenses, contribution margins, or operating income of the period. Column (4) of Exhibit 13.4 shows the sales volume variances for Schmidt's operations in October 2005.

The master budget [column (5)] shows that the firm planned to sell 1,000 units in October 2005. Schmidt Machinery Company, however, sold only 780 units in October. Column (3) shows the budget for 780 units (the flexible budget at the actual output level of the period). The difference between the flexible and the master budgets is the sales volume variance. Thus, the sales volume variance is 220 unfavorable in units and $77,000 unfavorable in operating income [column (4)].

Note that the operating income sales volume variance is the same as the contribution margin sales volume variance. This happens because fixed expenses in the master budget and the flexible budget usually are the same. Thus, an alternative way to compute the operating income sales volume variance is to multiply the difference between the units sold and the units in the master (static) budget by the master budget contribution margin per unit.

$$\text{Sales volume variance} = \text{Flexible budget amount} - \text{Master budget amount}$$

$$\text{Operating income sales volume variance} = \left[\begin{array}{c} \text{Units sold} \end{array} - \begin{array}{c} \text{Units budgeted to be sold} \end{array} \right] \times \begin{array}{c} \text{Master budget contribution margin per unit} \end{array}$$

$$= (780 - 1{,}000) \times \$350$$

$$= \$77{,}000 \text{ U}$$

EXHIBIT 13.4   Assessment of Operating Results with a Flexible Budget

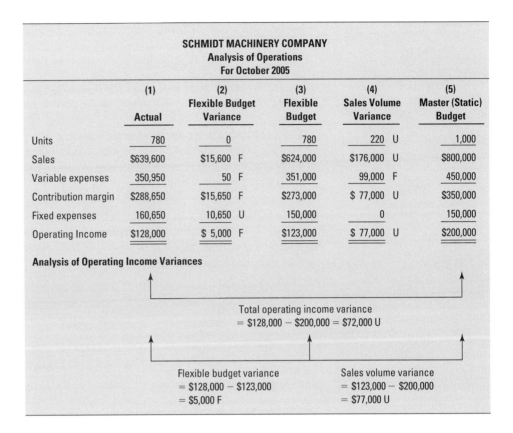

SCHMIDT MACHINERY COMPANY
Analysis of Operations
For October 2005

	(1) Actual	(2) Flexible Budget Variance	(3) Flexible Budget	(4) Sales Volume Variance	(5) Master (Static) Budget
Units	780	0	780	220 U	1,000
Sales	$639,600	$15,600 F	$624,000	$176,000 U	$800,000
Variable expenses	350,950	50 F	351,000	99,000 F	450,000
Contribution margin	$288,650	$15,650 F	$273,000	$ 77,000 U	$350,000
Fixed expenses	160,650	10,650 U	150,000	0	150,000
Operating Income	$128,000	$ 5,000 F	$123,000	$ 77,000 U	$200,000

Analysis of Operating Income Variances

Total operating income variance
= $128,000 − $200,000 = $72,000 U

Flexible budget variance
= $128,000 − $123,000
= $5,000 F

Sales volume variance
= $123,000 − $200,000
= $77,000 U

The operating income sales volume variance shows that a decrease of 220 units in units sold decreased the firm's operating income by $77,000. The sales volume variance may be a result of one or more of the following:

1. The market for the product has changed. The total demand for the product grows (declines) at a rate higher than expected.
2. The firm lost its market share to competitors.
3. The firm failed to set a proper goal for the period.

Each of these causes may be a result of one or more contributing factors. For example, a firm might have lost its market share because of quality problems that led to customers' dissatisfaction, shifts in customer preferences and tastes, ineffective advertising, reduction in the number of sales calls or salespeople, or products not available due to production problems, among others. The proper response for a sales volume variance depends on the cause of the variance. Chapter 15 discusses further analyses of sales volume variances to identify variances attributable to changes in market conditions and market shares.

Significant sales volume variances can have serious implications on the effectiveness of the chosen strategy of the firm. A significant unfavorable sales volume variance can indicate that the market is smaller than the level planned when the firm set its strategy and the goal for the period. The firm might need to modify or abandon its strategy. A small sales volume variance can indicate that the firm's strategy and operating plans are on track to attain its goals. A significant favorable sales volume variance can indicate that the firm needs to pursue a more aggressive strategy or operative goal.

Flexible Budget Variance

The **flexible budget variance** is the difference between the operating result and the flexible budget amount at the actual output level of the period. A flexible budget variance

Flexible budget variance
is the difference between the operating result and the flexible budget at the output level of the period.

measures efficiency in using input resources to attain the operating results of the period.

$$\text{Flexible budget variance} = \text{Actual results} - \text{Flexible budget}$$

The operating income flexible budget variance
of a period is the difference between the flexible budget operating income for a period and the operating income earned during the period.

Of all the flexible budget variances, the operating income flexible budget variance reflects the overall operating efficiency of the period and is likely to be of most interest to firms.

The **operating income flexible budget variance** of a period is the difference between the flexible budget operating income that would have been budgeted for the units sold, or the operating income that the firm would have earned if it carried out the operation according to the master budget except the output of the period, and the operating income earned during the period. In Exhibit 13.4, the operating income flexible budget variance is the difference in operating income between columns (1) and (3). Column (1) reports the operating income the firm earned from selling 780 units. Column (3) shows the budget for selling 780 units in a period. The bottom of column (3) is the operating income that the firm would have earned according to the budget to sell 780 units.

$$\begin{aligned}\text{Operating income flexible}\atop\text{budget variance} &= {\text{(Actual) operating}\atop\text{income earned}} - {\text{Flexible budget}\atop\text{operating income}} \\ &= \$128,000 \quad\quad - \$123,000 \\ &= \$5,000 \text{ F}\end{aligned}$$

Operating income flexible budget variances reflect efficiencies and inefficiencies in managing factors that are primarily internal to the firm. Factors contributing to operating income flexible budget variances include deviations in selling prices, variable costs, and fixed costs. For example, Schmidt's $5,000 favorable operating income flexible budget variance is the result of $15,600 favorable sales variance, $50 favorable variable expenses variance, and $10,650 unfavorable fixed expenses variance. Management is likely to have controls or influences on these factors.

Substantial or continuous unfavorable operating income flexible budget variances can diminish the feasibility of the strategy and may even jeopardize the continuation of the firm or organization.

The remainder of this chapter and the next one examine the operating income flexible budget variance in more detail. This further examination of the contributing factors to the operating income flexible budget variances requires a good understanding of standard costs, so we turn to that topic next.

Standard Cost

LEARNING OBJECTIVE 3
Set proper standard costs for planning, control, and performance evaluation.

How many strokes should a golfer take to play a course? What should Ford Motor Company's cost be to manufacture an Explorer? How much should Wal-Mart's cost be to sell a hair dryer? How much should a New York City mission's cost be to serve a hot meal to a homeless person?

A golfer uses the par for the course as a gauge for performance. *Par* is the number of strokes a golfer expects to take to cover a course competently—a *standard* that the golfer strives to attain. The costs that Ford Motor Company, Wal-Mart, and the New York City mission set for their operations are *standard costs*. A **standard cost** is a carefully determined cost a firm or organization sets for its operation—the cost the firm or organization should incur for the operation. A standard cost usually is expressed on a per unit basis.

A standard cost
is the cost a firm should incur for an operation.

Standard costs are bases in planning and control activities including preparing budgets, monitoring and control operations, and evaluating performances. A furniture manufacturer, for example, budgets the dollar amount of direct materials required to produce 5,000 entertainment centers based on the standard usage of direct materials per entertainment center and standard prices of the materials. If the standard calls for 3 square feet of Plexiglas for each entertainment center at $15 per square foot, the firm has a materials budget of 15,000 square feet of Plexiglas and $225,000 ($15 × 15,000) for producing the planned 5,000 entertainment centers. The firm also uses the $15 standard price per foot and the 3-foot standard per unit in monitoring manufacturing operations and assessing performance.

Components of a Standard Cost System

A standard cost prescribes expected performance. A complete standard cost for an operation includes carefully established standards for each operating cost element, including manufacturing, selling, and administrative expenses. Although the discussions in this and the next chapter focus on standard cost systems for manufacturing operations, these concepts and procedures also can be applied to other operations.

A manufacturing operation has three manufacturing cost elements: direct materials, direct labor, and factory overhead. This chapter focuses on standard costs for direct materials and direct labor. Chapter 14 discusses standard costs for factory overhead costs.

Types of Standards

Firms have different expectations for the proper levels at which to set their standards. Differences in expectations lead to two types of standards: ideal and currently attainable standards.

Ideal Standard

An **ideal standard** demands perfect implementation and maximum efficiency in every aspect of the operation. A firm can meet the ideal standard set for its operations when all relevant operating factors occur as expected and the firm carries out its operations as prescribed. An ideal standard is forward looking; rarely is it a historical standard.

Suppose that a firm manufactures 4-by-4-foot tabletops from cutting each 8-by-4-foot sheet of plywood in half so that each tabletop measures exactly 4-by-4 feet. An ideal standard sets the materials requirement for producing 1,000 tabletops at 500 sheets of plywood. A firm can meet such a standard if all equipment and instruments are in proper working condition, it has no defective plywood, employees cut all pieces perfectly, and all other relevant manufacturing factors are in proper condition and operate as expected.

An ideal standard is not easily attained. During an operation, accidents happen, unexpected events arise, and undesirable circumstances manifest themselves. Perfect performance, however, is not impossible. Today's highly competitive environment and demands for total quality management in all aspects of an operation have made many industry leaders realize the importance of attaining ever higher ideal standards in all operations. This is often referred to as a continuous improvement strategy.

At times an ideal standard can be met only if everybody involved, including those performing the task and those in support functions, exert extraordinary efforts throughout the operation. While possible, extraordinary efforts to achieve an ideal standard can lead to undue stress over a long period that decreases morale, increases apathetic attitudes among employees, and decreases the organization's long-term productivity. Such concerns have led some firms to adopt ideal standards for their operations only infrequently. Some firms set ideal standards for their operations because they are facing a crisis and need their employees to exert extraordinary efforts.

Firms that use ideal standards often modify performance evaluations and reward structures so that employees are not frustrated by frequent failures to attain the ideal standard. Firms can, for example, use progress toward the ideal standard rather than deviations from it as the primary benchmark in its performance evaluation and reward system.

Currently Attainable Standard

A **currently attainable standard** sets the performance criterion at a level that a person with proper training and experience can attain most of the time without having to exert extraordinary effort. A currently attainable standard emphasizes normality and allows for some deviations.

An **ideal standard** demands perfect implementation and maximum efficiency in every aspect of the operation.

A **currently attainable standard** sets the performance criterion at a level that a person with proper training and experience can attain most of the time without having to exert extraordinary effort.

Suppose that a firm sets the standard for the amount of plywood needed to produce 1,000 tabletops at 525 sheets of plywood, although two tabletops can be cut from one sheet. The additional 25 sheets allow for such things as less than ideal input quality, occasional maladjustment of the equipment used in production, and varying experience and skill levels of the personnel involved in the production. By using a standard that allows for normal fluctuations in relevant manufacturing factors, a firm usually can meet the currently attainable standard with reasonable effort.

Selection of Standards

Which standards—ideal or currently attainable—should a firm use in its standard cost system? There is no single answer for all situations. The most suitable standard for a firm is the one that helps it to attain its strategic goals.

Firms struggling for survival in intensely competitive industries may choose to set an ideal standard to motivate employees to put forth their best efforts. An ideal standard is not effective, however, if frequent failures in meeting the standard discourage employees or lead them to ignore the standards.

A currently attainable standard, however, may have built into it some degree of inefficiency. Allowing some inefficiencies is strategically unwise if the firm operates in an intensely competitive environment. A standard that allows 25 additional sheets of plywood conveys to production that it has attained an excellent performance as long as it does not make more than 25 mistakes for every 500 sheets of plywood it cuts.

Inefficiencies cost the firm, decrease its operating income, and weaken its competitive position. An ideal standard prescribes a high yet achievable performance. Any deviation from the ideal standard is an imperfection and undesirable to the firm. A world-class firm can ill afford any inefficiency and, most likely, would use ideal standards for its operations.

Today's dynamic and intensely competitive environment requires all organizations to reexamine their standards periodically and to cultivate continuous improvement. New technologies, equipment, and production processes often make existing standards obsolete. Without continuously updating standards, a firm can find survival difficult in a fiercely competitive global economy that demands total quality and high efficiency.

Nonfinancial Measures

Although most measures in standard cost systems eventually are expressed in dollar amounts as costs to the firm, nonfinancial measures often play important roles in standard cost systems. Managers do not manage costs; they manage activities. Losses and profits are the results of activities. Managers must control all activities that are strategically important in meeting the firm's goals. Some activities, such as friendly service, on-time delivery, and high quality, have no financial measures. Management at McDonald's, for example, considers quality, service, cleanliness, and value (QSCV) to be the foremost factors for its success, yet none of these four factors is reflected directly by a financial measure. Poor performances in QSCV activities often lead to decreased sales, lower operating income, diminishing firm values, as McDonalds found out in 2003.[2]

Sources of Standards

Firms often use several sources in determining appropriate standards for their operations. These sources include activity analysis, historical data, standards used in other firms for similar operations (a technique known as *benchmarking*), market expectations (target costing), and strategic decisions.

Activity Analysis

As discussed in Chapter 1, *activity analysis* is the process of identifying, delineating, and evaluating the activities required to complete a job, project, or operation. A thorough activity analysis includes all input factors and activities required to complete

---

[2] David Grainger, "Can McDonald's Cook Again?" *Fortune*, April 14, 2003, pp. 120–129.

At Westinghouse Air Brake Company in Chicago, workers are expected to "feed" a conveyor belt a finished part at fixed intervals. Having done this successfully, the workers in that work cell are rewarded with a $1.50 per hour bonus for that day's work. The bonus, a 12.5 percent increase in pay for the same hours, is a significant boost to the regular pay of $12 per hour and an effective incentive for most workers at the plant.

The speed of the conveyor changes from time to time to reflect changes in customer demand. When demand falls, the rate slows, and vice versa. The firm installed the bonus plan upon the recommendations of consultants and specialists in kaizen (continuous improvement). The bonus plan allowed Westinghouse to improve productivity in the plant by over 10 times the 1991 level. This seems to be a win-win situation for Westinghouse and Westinghouse workers. Do you see any problems?

the task efficiently. The analysis involves personnel from several functional areas including product engineers, industrial engineers, management accountants, and production workers.

Because each product is different, product engineers must specify product components in detail. Based on the firm's facilities and equipment and the product design, industrial engineers analyze the steps or procedures necessary to complete the task or product. Management accountants then work with engineers to complete the analyses.

For example, an activity analysis for preparing a hamburger at a fast-food restaurant starts with determining the ingredients and the tasks involved in preparing, cooking, and wrapping a hamburger. The analysis specifies the quantities and qualities of onion, lettuce, tomato, pickle, ground beef, buns, and other ingredients. It then determines the tools, steps, or procedures, and time needed to chop onions, cut lettuce, slice tomatoes and pickles, cook the meat, add buns, and wrap a hamburger. The analysis specifies the required skill level and experience of the employees, the equipment to be used, and other relevant factors affecting performance. The management accountant adds the cost of the ingredients, the employee wage rates for the required skill levels, the overhead and other relevant cost items to arrive at the total standard cost for a hamburger. The standard for the same operation is likely to vary for different firms because of differences in equipment, personnel skill levels and experience, operating policies, or other relevant factors. For example, the standard cost for making french fries at McDonald's is likely to differ from the standard cost for the same activity at a mom-and-pop burger shop. The mom-and-pop shop could be using 30-year-old equipment and cooking one order at a time. In contrast, the McDonald's across the street may be using state-of-the-art equipment that can cook 10 orders at a time.

Activity analysis, if properly executed, offers the most precise specifications for determining standards. It is time consuming and expensive, however, because determining standards via activity analyses require careful analyses of most, if not all, activities.

Historical Data

The cost to develop standards through activity analysis or other alternative methods can be prohibitively high. The high cost of developing standards through an alternative method leaves many firms, especially small businesses, with little choice but to rely on historical data if they want to take advantage of standard costing and flexible budget systems.[3] Historical data for making a similar product can be a good source for determining the standard cost of an operation when reliable and accurate data are available and no significant changes have occurred in operating conditions or technologies.

Through careful analyses of historical data for manufacturing a product or executing a task, management can determine appropriate standards for operations. A common practice is to use the average or the median of historical amounts of an operation as the standard for the operation. A firm determined to excel, however, would use the best performance in the past as its standard.

---

[3] William C. Lawler and John Leslie Livingstone, "Profit and Productivity Analysis for Small Businesses," *Journal of Accountancy,* December 1986, pp. 190–196.

Analysis of historical data is usually much less expensive than activity analysis. Historical data analysis also has the advantage of being inclusive of all manufacturing factors relevant to the way in which a firm operates in determining the standard for the firm. A standard based on the past can be biased, however, and leave out improvements or expected changes, and perpetuate past inefficiencies. Furthermore, although historical standards are likely to be more attainable than ideal standards, historical standards may not be consistent with continuous improvements required of many firms in today's worldwide competitive environment.

Benchmarking

Associations of manufacturers often collect industry information and have data available that managers can use to determine operation standards. Current practices of similar operations in other firms, not necessarily firms in the same industry, also can be good guidelines for setting the standard.

In recent years, many world-class firms were not satisfied with using the best operations of firms in the same industry; they have adopted as standards the best operations of any firm anywhere. Bath Iron Works, the fourth-largest shipyard in the United States, uses as its standard the benchmarks of the German firm Thyssen for pipe bending, Walt Disney World for preventive maintenance, and L.L. Bean for receipt inspection and paper reduction. IBM's plant in Austin, Texas, uses as benchmarks such plants as Tatung, Sampo, and DTK in Taiwan for its circuit board manufacturing. Allen-Bradley benchmarks a Hewlett-Packard Company plant in Colorado.

The advantage of benchmarking world-class firms is that standards based on the best performance anywhere help the firm to sustain its competitive edge. Data from trade associations or other firms, however, might not be completely applicable to the unique situation in which a firm operates. Furthermore, the best performance today may not be the best performance tomorrow.

Market Expectations and Strategic Decisions

Market expectations and strategic decisions often play important roles in standard setting, especially for firms using target costing (Chapter 10). With a set selling price for which the firm is able or desires to sell the product, the target cost is the cost that yields the desired profit margin for the product; it is the difference between the expected selling price and the desired profit margin of the product. A firm that has a target selling price of $200 and desires to earn $50 gross margin, for example, has a target cost and total standard cost of $150. Detailed standards then are determined for manufacturing the product at the target cost.

Strategic decisions also have effects on a product's standard cost. A strategic decision to strive for continuous improvement (known by the Japanese term *kaizen*) and zero defects require the firm to continuously set the standard for the product at the most challenging level. A strategic decision to replace a manual drilling machine with a high-precision automatic drilling machine would require the firm to alter the standard for its manufacturing process.

Standard-Setting Procedures

An **authoritative standard** is determined solely or primarily by management.

A **participative standard** calls for active participation throughout the standard-setting process by employees affected by the standard.

Using one or more of these sources of standards as the starting point, a firm can use either an authoritative or a participative procedure in setting standards.

An **authoritative standard** is determined solely or primarily by management. In contrast, a **participative standard** calls for active participation of employees affected by the standard throughout the standard-setting process. A firm uses an authoritative process to ensure proper consideration of all operating factors, to incorporate management's desires or expectations, or to expedite the standard-setting process. Firms using an authoritative process in standard setting, however, should keep in mind that a perfect or desirable standard is useless if employees ignore the standard.

Employees are more likely to accept standards they helped to determine. Participation also reduces the chance that employees will view the standard as unreasonable and increases the likelihood that they will buy into or adopt it as their own. Management, however, needs to be persuasive to ensure that the standards from participative processes will not prevent the firm from achieving its strategic goals or operating objectives.

Establishing Standard Cost

In organizations with successful standard cost systems, establishing a standard cost often is a joint effort of management, product design engineers, industrial engineers, management accountants, production supervisors, the purchasing department, the personnel department, and employees affected by the standard. Although not all of them are always involved, they participate at various points in establishing the standard cost. Even in an authoritative standard-setting process, the process is likely to involve some participation. After all, no management knows everything and better standards are often the result of incorporating input from subordinates.

Costs are the results of activities to create products or render services, and as we have said, managers manage activities, not costs. All standards, therefore, should be established for cost drivers underlying the costs associated with the product or service cost object.

Establishing Standard Cost for Direct Materials

A standard cost for direct materials of a product has three facets: quality, quantity, and price. The first step in establishing a standard cost is to specify clearly the quality of the direct materials. The quality of direct materials determines the quality of the product and affects many phases of the manufacturing process including quantity of direct materials needed or used in manufacturing, prices of direct materials, processing time, and the extent and frequency of supervision needed to complete manufacturing.

Trade-offs often are needed between uses of more expensive, higher-quality direct materials or less expensive, lower-quality direct materials in operations. The marketing department, engineering department, production department, and management accountants need to assess these trade-offs and determine the proper quality of the direct materials for products.

Once a firm determines the quality of the direct materials, management accountants need to work with the industrial engineering and production departments to set the standard for the quantity of direct materials for the manufacturing. Among factors considered in setting direct materials quantity standards are product design, cost drivers of manufacturing activities, quality of the direct materials, and the conditions of the production facility and equipment to be used for the manufacturing of the product.

Quality, quantity, and at times, the timing of purchases can affect price standards of materials. In a competitive environment, many companies emphasize long-term relationships with selected suppliers that are reliable in delivering quality materials on time. For a firm that emphasizes long-term benefits and reliability of its supply chain, the price standard needs to be revised only when a change occurs in the underlying long-term factors that affect material prices.

Establishing Standard Cost for Direct Labor

Direct labor costs vary with types of work, product complexity, employee skill level, nature of the manufacturing process, and the type and condition of the equipment to be used. After considering these factors, industrial engineering, production, personnel, labor union representatives, and management accountants determine jointly the quantity standard for direct labor.

The personnel department determines the standard wage rate for the type and skill level of employees needed for the manufacturing process. The standard labor rate for either direct or indirect labor includes not only the wage paid but also the fringe benefits provided to employees and the required payroll taxes associated with wages and salaries. Fringe benefits include health and life insurance, pension plan contributions, and paid vacations. Payroll taxes include unemployment taxes and the employer's share of an employee's Social Security assessment.

Standard Cost Sheet

A **standard cost sheet** specifies the standard costs (including both price and quantity) for all manufacturing cost elements required in the production of one unit of a product; it includes prices and quantities for each of the required direct materials, direct labor, and factory overhead.

Exhibit 13.5 shows a simplified standard cost sheet for selected manufacturing costs of Schmidt Machinery Company for manufacturing one unit of XV–1. The standard cost sheet specifies that the standard cost for one unit of XV–1 includes 4 pounds of aluminum at $25 per pound, 1 pound of PVC at $40 per pound, 5 hours of direct labor at $40 per hour, and factory overhead of $36 ($12 + $24) per direct labor-hour. One of the items not included in the standard cost sheet is the budgeted variable selling and administrative expense of $50 per unit. Exhibit 13.6 contains a more detailed standard cost sheet for Merrill-Continental Company, Inc.

A **standard cost sheet** specifies the standard price and quantity of each manufacturing cost element in the production of one unit of a product.

Operating Income Flexible Budget Variance

LEARNING OBJECTIVE 4
Identify factors contributing to variances and analyze and explain variances.

Factors that contribute to the operating income flexible budget variance include deviations in selling prices, variable expenses, and fixed expenses from their standard or budgeted amounts. Deviations of fixed expenses are discussed in Chapter 14.

Selling Price Variance

As the name implies, selling price variance reflects the effect of difference in selling prices. The **selling price variance** of an operation is often determined by finding the difference between the total sales revenues received and the total sales revenues in the flexible budget for the units sold during the period. The difference between these two sales revenues, if any, results from deviations of the actual selling prices from the budgeted selling price:

Selling price variance
is the difference between the total sales revenues received and the total sales revenues in the flexible budget for the units sold during the period.

EXHIBIT 13.5
Standard Cost Sheet

SCHMIDT MACHINERY COMPANY
Standard Cost Sheet
Product: XV–1

Descriptions	Quantity	Unit Cost	Subtotal	Total
Direct materials				
Aluminum	4 pounds	$25	$100	
PVC	1 pound	40	40	$140
Direct labor	5 hours	40		200
Factory overhead				
(based on direct labor-hours)				
Variable	5 hours	12	60	
Fixed	5 hours	24	120	180
Standard cost per unit				$520

EXHIBIT 13.6

A Standard Cost Sheet of Merrill-Continental Company, Inc.

Source: Thomas A. Faulhaber, Fred A. Coad, and Thomas J. Little, "Building a Process Cost Management System from the Bottom Up," *Management Accounting*, May 1988, p. 60.

Product		A	B	C
Color		Black	Black	White
Felt		Y	N	Y
Width	Inches	48	48	48
Thickness of rubber	Inches	0.060	0.080	0.060
Roll length	Feet	100	80	100
Package type		1	2	1
Production rate	Feet/Min	6	4	6
Trim loss	Percent	5.0%	5.0%	10.0%
Trim recovery	Percent	2.0%	3.0%	5.0%
Glue usage	Pounds/sf	0.05	0.05	0.10
Materials				
Compound 1	$/lb	0.41	1	1	0
Compound 1	S.G.	1.60			
Compound 2	$/lb	0.41	0	0	1
Compound 2	S.G.	1.58			
Felt 1	$/S.F.	0.06	1	0	0
Felt 2	$/S.F.	0.08	0	0	1
Glue 1	$/lb	0.60	1	0	0
Glue 2	$/lb	0.80	0	0	1
Package 1	$/Each	2.00	1	0	1
Package 2	$/Each	4.00	0	1	0
Labor	**$/Hour**			
Direct				
Extruder	$10.00	1.00	1.00	1.00
Operator	$ 6.00	3.00	2.00	3.00
Indirect				
Maintenance	$12.00	0.50	0.50	0.50
Forklift	$ 8.00	0.30	0.30	0.30
Changeover—Setup				
Line hours	Each	0.50	0.50	0.50
Scrap	S.F. Each	500	500	50

$$\text{Actual sales revenue} = \text{Units sold} \times \text{Actual selling price per unit}$$

$$\text{Flexible budget sales revenue} = \text{Units sold} \times \text{Budgeted selling price per unit}$$

Both sales revenues are for the same number of units—those sold during the period. The difference between these two sales revenues is in the selling price and, therefore, is the selling price variance of the period.

$$\begin{aligned} \frac{\text{Sales revenue flexible}}{\text{budget variance}} &= \frac{\text{Actual sales}}{\text{revenue}} - \frac{\text{Flexible budget}}{\text{sales revenue}} \\[2mm] &= \left[\begin{array}{c} \text{Units} \\ \text{sold} \end{array} \times \begin{array}{c} \text{Actual selling} \\ \text{price per unit} \end{array} \right] - \left[\begin{array}{c} \text{Units} \\ \text{sold} \end{array} \times \begin{array}{c} \text{Budgeted selling} \\ \text{price per unit} \end{array} \right] \\[2mm] &= \left[\begin{array}{c} \text{Actual selling} \\ \text{price per unit} \end{array} - \begin{array}{c} \text{Budgeted selling} \\ \text{price per unit} \end{array} \right] \times \begin{array}{c} \text{Units} \\ \text{sold} \end{array} \\[2mm] &= \text{Selling price variance} \end{aligned}$$

Since there is no difference in sales quantity between the sales revenue for the units sold and the sales revenue in the flexible budget for the units sold, the selling price variance of a period also is the sales revenue flexible budget variance of the period.

Exhibit 13.4 shows that Schmidt Machinery Company sold 780 units of XV–1 for $639,600, or $820 per unit. The budgeted selling price, however, is $800 per unit. Using the budgeted selling price of $800 per unit, the total sales revenue in the flexible budget for 780 units is $624,000. The difference, $15,600, is a result of the actual selling price per unit being $20 higher than that of the budgeted selling price per unit for the 780 units sold, as shown here:

$$\begin{aligned} \frac{\text{Selling price}}{\text{variance}} &= \left[\begin{array}{c} \text{Actual selling} \\ \text{price per unit} \end{array} - \begin{array}{c} \text{Flexible budget} \\ \text{selling price per unit} \end{array} \right] \times \begin{array}{c} \text{Units} \\ \text{sold} \end{array} \\[2mm] &= (\$820 - \$800) \times 780 \text{ units} \\[2mm] &= \$15,600 \text{ F} \end{aligned}$$

Variable Cost Flexible Budget Variance

The **variable cost flexible budget variance** is the difference between variable expenses incurred and the total variable expenses in the flexible budget for the period.

Variable cost flexible budget variance is the difference between the variable cost incurred during operation and the total variable cost in the flexible budget for the period, which is the total standard variable cost for the operation of the period. This variance reflects the deviation of the actual variable cost incurred during the period from the standard variable cost for the output of the period (units sold or manufactured).

Note in Exhibit 13.4 that Schmidt incurred $350,950 total variable expense in October 2005 to produce and sell 780 units of XV–1. On the standard cost sheet (Exhibit 13.5), the standard variable manufacturing expense is $400 per unit, including $140 for direct materials, $200 for direct labor, and $60 for variable manufacturing overheads. For 780 units, the total standard variable manufacturing expense is $312,000 ($400 per unit × 780 units). In addition, the standard variable selling and administrative expense is $50 per unit, or $39,000 in total ($50 per unit × 780 units). This brings the total variable expense for manufacturing and selling 780 units to $351,000 ($312,000 + $39,000). The difference between the actual variable expenses incurred during the period and the total variable expenses in the flexible budget for the units manufactured and sold during the period is the variable cost flexible budget variance, which is $50 favorable:

$$\begin{aligned} \frac{\text{Variable cost flexible}}{\text{budget variance}} &= \text{Variable cost incurred} - \text{flexible budget variable cost} \\[2mm] &= \$350,950 - (\$140 + \$200 + \$60 + \$50) \times 780 \text{ units} \\[2mm] &= \$350,950 - \$450 \times 780 \end{aligned}$$

$$= \$350,950 - \$351,000$$
$$= \$50 \text{ F}$$

The total actual variable expense incurred in October, $350,950, is $50 less than the total standard variable expense for manufacturing and selling 780 units of XV–1, $351,000. This suggests that the operation met the standards set in the standard cost sheet and that the operation appears to be under control.

Need for Further Analysis of the Variable Cost Flexible Budget Variance

A variable cost flexible budget variance is the sum of flexible budget variances of all variable costs and expenses, including flexible budget variances of direct materials, direct labor, variable overhead, and variable selling and administrative expense.

Variable cost flexible budget variance	=	Direct materials flexible budget variance	+	Direct labor flexible budget variance	+	Variable overhead flexible budget variance	+	Variable selling and administrative expenses flexible budget variance

Contributing factors to each of these variable expense flexible budget variances are likely to be different and may offset each other in the aggregate. An aggregated total amount, such as the total variable cost flexible budget variance, can mask poor performance in one or more of the cost components or operating divisions, as is true in the operating results of the Schmidt Machinery Company.

Schmidt's operating results for the period show a $50 favorable total variable cost flexible budget variance—a small variance that should not be of concern to the management. Further analyses of the costs shown in Exhibit 13.7, however, reveal that Schmidt spent $94,380 for 3,630 pounds of aluminum to manufacture 780 units of XV–1. The standard quantity of aluminum for 780 units of XV–1 is 3,900 pounds for

EXHIBIT 13.7
Comparison of Actual Variable Costs and Flexible Budget Variable Costs

SCHMIDT MACHINERY COMPANY October 2005			
Product XV–1 **Units Manufactured: 780**			
Operating Results			
Direct materials			
Aluminum	3,630 pounds at $26 per pound	$94,380	
PVC	720 pounds at $41 per pound	29,520	$123,900
Direct labor	3,510 hours at $42 per hour		147,420
Variable factory overhead			40,630
Total variable cost of goods manufactured			$311,950
Variable selling and administrative expenses			39,000
Total variable expenses incurred			$350,950
Flexible Budget			
Total standard variable cost of goods manufactured:			
Standard variable manufacturing cost per unit (from Exhibit 13.5)		$400	
Number of units manufactured		× 780	$312,000
Standard variable selling and administrative expenses		780 × $50	39,000
Total standard variable expense			$351,000
Flexible budget variable expense variance			$50 F*

*F denotes a *favorable* result.

$78,000. The amount spent on aluminum exceeds the standard cost allowed by $16,380, or 21 percent. In contrast, the labor and variable overhead variances are $8,580 favorable and $6,170 favorable, respectively. The variance for PVC is $1,680 favorable. By coincidence, the combined total of the variable cost flexible budget variances is a mere $50, a negligible amount.

As we demonstrate in Exhibit 13.7, conducting separate analyses of variances for different costs can prevent the offsetting of variances in opposite directions and reduce the likelihood that one or more inefficient operations is hiding behind efficient uses in one or more of the operating resources. Examining only the total costs can be misleading.

Direct Materials Variances

The direct materials flexible budget variance is the difference between the total direct materials cost incurred during an operation and the total standard direct materials cost for the output of the operation (units manufactured during the period). This variance reflects the efficiency in buying and using the direct materials. Attaining efficiency in buying and using materials requires good controls over both the price paid for the materials and the quantity of the materials used in the operation. Since price and usage can move in opposite directions, we must analyze a total direct materials variance further and identify direct material price variance (PV) and direct material quantity variance or usage variance (UV) so that the firm can gain a better understanding of the causes for variations in costs of materials.

Exhibits 13.8 and 13.9 illustrate analyses of direct materials costs using the October 2005 operating data of the Schmidt Company. Exhibit 13.8 shows that Schmidt used 3,630 pounds of aluminum at a total cost of $94,380 to manufacture 780 units of XV–1. The standard cost sheet reported in Exhibit 13.5 indicates that the standard cost for one unit of XV–1 is 4 pounds of aluminum at $25 per pound. Exhibit 13.9 shows computations for variances relating to the usage of aluminum to manufacture 780 units of XV–1 during the period.

Total Direct Materials Standard Cost for the Period

The total direct materials standard cost for a period is based on the output unit of the period. The following five steps describe the calculation of the total standard cost of direct materials:

Step 1: **Find the total number of output units of the period from the accounting records.** Schmidt Machinery Company manufactured 780 units of XV–1 in October.

Step 2: **Determine the standard quantity of direct materials for one unit of the product from the firm's standard cost sheet.** Schmidt's standard cost sheet specifies that the production of one unit of XV–1 should use 4 pounds of aluminum.

Step 3: **Calculate the total standard quantity of the direct materials for the period by multiplying the two amounts obtained in Steps 1 and 2.** Step 1 indicates that the firm manufactured 780 units of XV–1. Step 2 shows that the firm should use 4 pounds of aluminum for each unit of XV–1. The total standard amount of aluminum for the 780 units the company manufactured in October is, therefore, 3,120 pounds (4 pounds per unit × 780 units).

Step 4: **Find the standard unit cost of the direct materials from the firm's standard cost sheet.** Exhibit 13.5 specifies that the standard cost of aluminum is $25 per pound.

Step 5: **Calculate the total standard direct materials cost for the period by multiplying the amounts from Steps 3 and 4.** At $25 standard cost per pound (Step 4), the total standard cost for the 3,120 pounds of aluminum that Schmidt should have used in the production of 780 units of XV–1 (Step 3) is $78,000 ($25 per pound × 3,120 pounds). Therefore, the total direct materials cost for the output of the period is $78,000, the total variable cost in the flexible budget for the output of the period.

EXHIBIT 13.8
A Detailed Comparison of Actual Operating Results and Flexible Budget

---

SCHMIDT MACHINERY COMPANY
October 2005

Product XV–1
Units Manufactured: 780

Operating Results

Direct materials			
Aluminum	3,630 pounds at $26 per pound	$94,380	
PVC	720 pounds at $41 per pound	29,520	$123,900
Direct labor	3,510 hours at $42 per hour		147,420
Variable factory overhead			40,630
Total variable cost of goods manufactured			$311,950
Variable selling and administrative expenses			39,000
Total variable expenses incurred			$350,950

Flexible Budget

Direct materials			
Aluminum	780 units × 4 pounds × $25 =	$78,000	
PVC	780 units × 1 pound × $40 =	31,200	$109,200
Direct labor	780 units × 5 hours × $40 =		156,000
Variable factory overhead	780 units × 5 hours × $12 =		46,800
Total standard variable cost of goods manufactured			$312,000
Variable selling and administrative expenses			39,000
Total flexible budget variable expense			$351,000

Variances

Direct materials			
Aluminum	$94,380 − $78,000 = $16,380 U†		
PVC	29,520 − 31,200 = 1,680 F*		$14,700 U
Direct labor	147,420 − 156,000 =		8,580 F
Variable factory overhead	40,630 − 46,800 =		6,170 F
Variable manufacturing cost flexible budget variance			$50 F
Variable selling and administrative expense variance			0
Variable expense flexible budget variance			$50 F

---

*F denotes a *favorable* result.
†U denotes an *unfavorable* result.

EXHIBIT 13.9
Direct Materials Variance—Aluminum

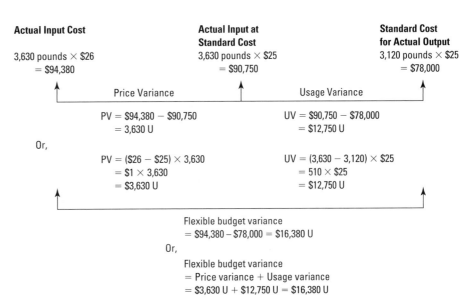

Direct Materials Flexible Budget Variance

Direct materials flexible budget variance
is the difference between total direct material costs incurred and total direct materials standard cost for the units manufactured during a period.

Direct materials flexible budget variance is the difference between total direct material costs incurred and total direct materials standard cost for the units manufactured during a period. Schmidt spent $94,380 for aluminum. The total standard aluminum cost for the 780 units manufactured during the period is $78,000, the flexible budget amount for direct materials. The direct materials—aluminum flexible budget variance, therefore, is $16,380 unfavorable ($94,380 − $78,000).

Further Analyses of the Direct Materials Flexible Budget Variance

Direct materials price variance
is the difference between the actual and the standard cost per unit of the direct material multiplied by the quantity of the direct materials purchased.

Price Variance The **direct materials price variance** is the difference between the actual and the standard cost per unit of the direct material multiplied by the quantity of the direct materials purchased during the period. It reflects the effect deviations of direct materials costs have on operating income. Schmidt Machinery Company paid $26 per pound for 3,630 pounds of aluminum. The standard cost sheet (Exhibit 13.5) specifies the standard price to be $25 per pound. The actual price paid is $1 per pound more than the price specified in the standard cost sheet for aluminum. For the 3,630 pounds purchased, the price variance for aluminum is $3,630 unfavorable (Exhibit 13.9).

$$\text{Direct material price variance} = \left[\begin{array}{l} \text{Actual price paid for one unit of direct material} \end{array} - \begin{array}{l} \text{Standard price for one unit of direct material} \end{array} \right] \times \begin{array}{l} \text{Total number of units of the direct material purchased} \end{array}$$

$$PV_{DM} = (AP_{DM} - SPDM) \times AQDM$$
$$PV_{Aluminum} = (AP_{Aluminum} - SP_{Aluminum}) \times AQ_{Aluminum}$$
$$= (\$26 - \$25) \times 3,630$$
$$= \$1 \times 3,630$$
$$= \$3,630 \text{ Unfavorable}$$

Interpreting the Direct Materials Price Variance

A direct materials price variance can result from failure to take purchase discounts, unexpected price change of materials, changes in freight costs, variation in grades of materials, or other causes. The purchasing department is often the office most likely to provide an explanation or have the responsibility for materials price variances.

Care must be taken in interpreting direct materials price variances. A favorable direct materials price variance could lead to high manufacturing costs if the low-cost materials are of poor quality. Downstream costs such as scrap, rework, schedule disruptions, or field services could exceed the price savings from lower materials prices. A firm with a differentiation strategy is likely to fail when it pursues favorable price variances through purchases of low-quality materials. A firm that competes on low cost also is likely to be doomed if the quality of its products is below the customers' expectations or increases downstream costs.

Carrying costs and additional materials-handling costs can cost the firm more than the savings from low purchase prices. A firm with a cost-effective purchasing department that has several warehouses full of materials and supplies purchased in bulk at low prices could have a higher total overall cost than a firm that buys in small quantities as needed, and maintains only a minimum amount of direct materials on hand, even though the firm paid higher purchase prices for materials.

Materials usage ratio
is the ratio of quantity used over quantity purchased.

In addition to price variances, many firms also use usage ratios in evaluating the performance of purchasing departments. A **materials usage ratio** is the ratio of quantity used over quantity purchased. A low materials usage ratio suggests that the purchasing department purchased for materials inventory, rather than the operational needs of the period. Such a move can be costly if the firm considers all costs. The benefit of any favorable price variance should be evaluated along with the cost of inventory storage of the surplus purchases.

Usage Variance

Direct materials usage variance
is the difference in the number of
units of the direct materials
between the actual units used
during the period and the standard
units of the direct materials that
should have been used for the
output of the period multiplied by
the standard cost per unit of the
direct materials.

Usage Variance

Direct materials usage variance is the difference in direct materials between the actual units used during the period and the standard units of the direct materials that should have been used for the output of the period multiplied by the standard cost per unit of the direct materials. The variance reports the effects on operating costs of deviations in direct materials usage from the standard. The total standard units of the direct materials that should have been used for the units of the product manufactured are also the flexible budget units for direct materials. This variance is also referred to as an *efficiency* or *quantity variance.*

Schmidt Machinery Company used 3,630 pounds to manufacture 780 units of XV–1. According to the standard cost sheet (Exhibit 13.5), each unit of XV–1 requires 4 pounds of aluminum. The total standard quantity of aluminum for the 780 units manufactured during the period, therefore, is 3,120 pounds (780 units × 4 pounds per unit). This says that the 3,630 pounds of aluminum used in production is 510 pounds more than the total standard quantity for the 780 units of XV–1 manufactured during the period. At the standard price of $25 per pound, the usage variance is $12,750 unfavorable (Exhibit 13.9):

$$\begin{matrix} \text{Direct} \\ \text{materials} \\ \text{usage variance} \end{matrix} = \begin{bmatrix} \text{Total quantity} & & \text{Total standard quantity of} \\ \text{of the direct} & - & \text{the direct materials for} \\ \text{materials used} & & \text{the units manufactured} \end{bmatrix} \times \begin{matrix} \text{Standard cost per} \\ \text{unit of the direct} \\ \text{usage materials} \end{matrix}$$

$$UV_{DM} = (AQ_{DM} - SQ_{DM}) \times SP_{DM}$$
$$UV_{Aluminum} = (AQ_{Aluminum} - SQ_{Aluminum}) \times SP_{Aluminum}$$
$$= (3,630 - 3,120) \times \$25$$
$$= 510 \times \$25$$
$$= \$12,750 \text{ Unfavorable}$$

Interpreting the Direct Materials Usage Variance

A significant direct materials usage variance suggests that the operation has used a significantly different amount of direct materials than the amount specified for the output of the operation. This variance measures efficiency in using direct materials. A direct materials usage variance can result from the efforts of production personnel, substitutions of materials or production factors, variation in the quality of direct materials, inadequate training or inexperienced employees, poor supervision, excess spoilage, or other factors.

Direct Labor Variances

A direct labor flexible budget variance is a result of the total direct labor cost of a period being different from the total standard direct labor cost for the output of the period. Like a direct materials flexible budget variance, a direct labor flexible budget variances also can be divided into two components: direct labor rate (price) and efficiency (quantity) variances. The procedure for further analyses of direct labor flexible variances is similar to those of further analyses of direct materials flexible budget variances. Exhibit 13.10 shows calculations of the direct labor rate variance and direct labor efficiency variance for Schmidt Machinery Company's operation in October 2005 when it manufactured 780 units of XV–1.

Direct Labor Rate Variance

Direct labor rate variance
is the difference in wage rates
between the actual rate paid and
the standard rate multiplied by the
actual direct labor-hours spent
in operation.

Direct labor rate variance is the difference in wage rates between the actual rate paid and the standard rate multiplied by the actual direct labor-hours spent in operation. It arises when all the wages paid are not at the standard wage rate. Schmidt Machinery Company paid an average wage rate of $42 per hour for 3,510 direct labor-hours in October. The standard cost sheet, however, calls for a wage rate of $40 per hour. The firm paid $2 per hour more than the standard hourly rate. With 3,510 total hours actually worked, the total direct labor rate variance is $7,020 unfavorable.

EXHIBIT 13.10
Direct Labor Variances—
Schmidt Machinery Company
October 2005

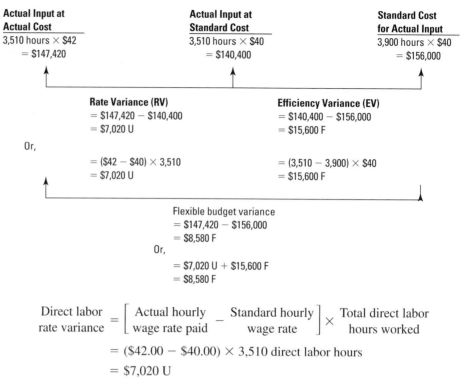

Actual Input at Actual Cost	Actual Input at Standard Cost	Standard Cost for Actual Input
3,510 hours × $42	3,510 hours × $40	3,900 hours × $40
= $147,420	= $140,400	= $156,000

Rate Variance (RV)
= $147,420 − $140,400
= $7,020 U

Efficiency Variance (EV)
= $140,400 − $156,000
= $15,600 F

Or,

= ($42 − $40) × 3,510
= $7,020 U

= (3,510 − 3,900) × $40
= $15,600 F

Flexible budget variance
= $147,420 − $156,000
= $8,580 F

Or,

= $7,020 U + $15,600 F
= $8,580 F

$$\frac{\text{Direct labor}}{\text{rate variance}} = \left[\begin{array}{c}\text{Actual hourly} \\ \text{wage rate paid}\end{array} - \begin{array}{c}\text{Standard hourly} \\ \text{wage rate}\end{array}\right] \times \begin{array}{c}\text{Total direct labor} \\ \text{hours worked}\end{array}$$

$$= (\$42.00 - \$40.00) \times 3,510 \text{ direct labor hours}$$

$$= \$7,020 \text{ U}$$

A direct labor rate variance reflects the effect on the operating income when the actual hourly wage rate paid deviates from the standard hourly wage rate. In addition, direct labor rate variances also could result from not using the skill-level workers specified in the standard cost sheet for the work.

The personnel department usually is responsible for direct labor rate variances. Production, however, could be responsible for the variance if it chooses to use employees with a different skill level than that specified in the standard cost sheet.

Direct Labor Efficiency Variance

The direct labor efficiency variance is the difference in direct labor hours between the hours worked and the total standard hours for the units manufactured multiplied by the standard direct labor hourly wage rate.

A **direct labor efficiency variance** occurs when the total direct labor-hours worked deviates from the total standard direct labor-hours for the output of the period. It is calculated by multiplying the difference in direct labor-hours between the hours worked and the total standard hours for the units manufactured and the standard direct labor hourly wage rate.

$$\frac{\text{Direct labor}}{\text{efficiency}}_{\text{variance}} = \left[\begin{array}{c}\text{Total direct} \\ \text{labor hours} \\ \text{worked}\end{array} - \begin{array}{c}\text{Total standard} \\ \text{direct labor hours} \\ \text{for the output}\end{array}\right] \times \begin{array}{c}\text{Standard} \\ \text{direct labor} \\ \text{hourly rate}\end{array}$$

Schmidt Machinery Company spent 3,510 direct labor-hours to manufacture 780 units of XV–1 in October 2005. The standard cost sheet allows five direct labor-hours for one unit of XV–1. The total standard hours allowed for 780 units of XV–1, therefore, is 3,900 hours (780 × 5). Thus, Schmidt used 390 fewer direct labor-hours than the total standard hours for 780 units. At a standard wage rate of $40 per hour, the total direct labor efficiency (quantity) variance is $15,600 favorable.

$$\frac{\text{Total standard direct}}{\text{labor hours for the output}} = \frac{780 \text{ units}}{\text{manufactured}} \times \frac{5 \text{ standard direct}}{\text{labor hours per unit}}$$

$$= 3,900 \text{ hours}$$

$$\frac{\text{Direct labor}}{\text{efficiency variance}} = \left[\begin{array}{c}3,510 \text{ actual} \\ \text{hours}\end{array} - \begin{array}{c}3,900 \text{ total} \\ \text{standard hours}\end{array}\right] \times \$40 \text{ per hour}$$

$$= \$15,600 \text{ F}$$

A direct labor efficiency variance reflects the effect on operating income when the total direct labor-hours spent to manufacture during the period deviates from the total standard direct labor-hours for the output of the period. Because this difference is a result of the difference in direct labor-hours, the resulting variance is called *direct labor efficiency variance.*

A direct labor efficiency variance usually is the responsibility of the production department. Besides the employees' efficiency or inefficiency in carrying out their tasks, however, several other factors—including these—can lead to a direct labor efficiency variance:

1. Employees or supervisors are new on the job or inadequately trained.
2. Employees' skill levels are different from those specified in the standard cost sheet.
3. Batch sizes are different from the standard size.
4. Materials are different from those specified.
5. Machines or equipment are not in proper working condition.
6. Supervision is inadequate.
7. Scheduling is poor.

Timing of Variance Recognition

Identification of variances helps managers to be aware of deviations from the expected performance. To realize the full benefit of determining and reporting variances, managers should recognize variances at the earliest feasible time.

A direct materials price variance can be identified either at the *time of purchase* or at the *time of issuing* the materials to production. The difference in the timing of recognizing direct materials price variances also affects the way in which direct materials are recorded in the materials control account. Early recognition of variances, such as identifying a price variance at the time of purchase, increases the likelihood that firms will be aware at an early time of any discrepancy between the price paid for the purchase and the standard price. Early recognitions of variances allow the firm to take proper actions preventing continuation of unfavorable price variances or attaining most benefit from favorable price variance.

Recognizing material price variances at the time of purchase lets the firm carry all units of the same materials at one price—the standard cost of the material, even if the firm did not purchase all units of the materials at the same price. Using one price for the same materials facilitates management control and simplifies accounting work.

If a direct materials price variance is not recorded until the materials are issued to production, the direct materials are carried on the books at their actual purchase prices. Deviations of actual purchase prices from the standard price may not be known until the direct materials are issued to production.

Regardless of when a direct materials price variance is recognized, the purchase price variance is computed based on the actual quantity purchased, not the actual quantity used in the production.[4] Consequently, the quantity purchased is used in the price variance computation, while the number of units actually consumed in production is used to compute the usage variance, as shown in Exhibit 13.11.

The analysis of variances for direct labor costs need not be conducted in two steps because direct labor has no inventory. The number of hours paid to employees is the same number of hours worked in production during the period.

The last couple of decades have seen increased bashing of the usefulness of direct labor variances in both research and practitioners' journals and books. Reasons cited include decreasing importance of direct labor as a manufacturing cost element, cost and increased complexity in variance reporting, and directing managers to mundane details rather than focusing managers' attention on matters of strategic importance to the firm.[5] Believing in these arguments, many companies have stopped reporting direct labor variances.

---

[4] Some writers refer to a price variance computed on the quantity used in production as *usage price variance.*

[5] Among them are H. Thomas Johnson and Robert S. Kaplan, *Relevance Lost: The Rise and Fall of Management Accounting* (Boston: Harvard Business School Press, 1987); D. R. Berlant, et al. *Harvard Business Review* (January–February 1990), pp. 178–85.

EXHIBIT 13.11
Analyzing Materials Variances When the Quantity Purchased and Quantity Used Are Different

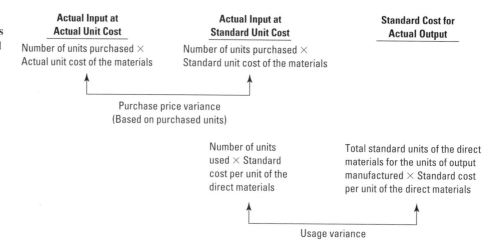

Several authors have argued that without direct labor cost variance information, however, managers will not be able to monitor workers as effectively and make appropriate resource allocation decisions, and worker productivity will decline.[6] A field study of 18 plants over a three-year period found plants that stopped direct labor variance reporting experienced a substantially greater decline in labor productivity than the plants that continued the reporting.[7]

Effect of the New Manufacturing Technology

LEARNING OBJECTIVE 5
Assess the effects of the contemporary manufacturing environment on operational control and standard costing.

Recent advances in manufacturing concepts and technologies have greatly impacted manufacturing processes, costing methods, and standard costing systems. With the introduction of just-in-time (JIT), automation, manufacturing cells, total quality management, throughput time, supply-chain management, and other modern manufacturing concepts and technologies, many firms have changed their focuses of cost control and management. No distinction between units purchased and units used is necessary in determining direct materials variances for firms that maintain a minimal inventory or that use a JIT system. For these firms, the quantity purchased in a period is almost the same as the amount used or needed during the period.

Furthermore, firms using JIT systems or supply-chain management often have less interest in materials purchase price variances. These firms often purchase materials from suppliers under long-term contracts to ensure deliveries of quality materials as scheduled or needed. These firms emphasize the total cost of their materials procurements, not just materials purchase costs. Factors such as quality, reliability, and availability often outweigh the purchase cost.

The arrival of new manufacturing technologies such as automation, flexible manufacturing systems, and cluster or cell manufacturing has deemphasized the importance of direct labor variances. Firms that use automated manufacturing systems use little or no direct labor and attach little importance to labor rate and efficiency variances.

More and more firms emphasize zero-defects and continuous improvement. The utmost concerns of these firms are satisfying customers and providing better products than the competition. A well-managed firm is not the one with the lowest unfavorable variances or the highest favorable variances but one with happy customers and consistently better products.

[6] A. H. Amershi, R. D. Banker, and S. M. Datar, "Economic Sufficiency and Statistical Sufficiency in the Aggregation of Accounting Signals," *The Accounting Review* 65 (1990), pp. 113–130.

[7] Rajiv D. Banker, et al. "Performance Impact of the Elimination of Direct Labor Variance Reporting: A Field Study," *Journal of Accounting Research,* September 2002, pp. 1013–1036. Plants that eliminated direct labor variance reporting experienced improvement in the quality of products delivered to customers.

The theory of constraints (Chapter 10) emphasizes that improving a firm's overall efficiency lies in decreasing throughput time from the beginning of the process through completion and delivery, not in individual efficiency variances. While decreasing unfavorable labor efficiency variances of nonbottleneck operations might give managers satisfaction, such efforts would not have any effect on overall efficiency.

Behavioral and Implementation Issues

LEARNING OBJECTIVE 6
Recognize behavioral implications in implementing standard cost systems.

A standard cost system provides guidelines for operations and criteria or benchmarks for performance evaluations. However, firms should use variances strictly as inputs to gain a better understanding of and to improve the operations; they should never use variances as means of finding scapegoats. Research in organizational behavior has shown that successful operations are often a result of proper rewards. The focus in using a standard cost system should be on influencing behavior through positive reinforcement and appropriate motivation. Seldom does long-term success result from penalties and punishments.

Standards perceived to be unreasonable exert excessive pressure, are inflexible, or viewed as part of an unfair or uneven performance evaluation and reward systems. Managers or employees with negative perceptions often are discouraged and adopt protective or defensive behavior. Some may even try to sabotage the system using tactics such as padding the budget, decreasing product and service quality, increasing absenteeism, having lackadaisical attitudes, and decreased initiative, among others. On the other hand, managers and other employees who have positive perceptions of a standard cost system show enthusiasm, creativity, and productivity.

The controller and supporting staff are responsible for reporting to management the results of operations, comparing the operating results with the budgeted goals, and identifying variances. The primary function of the controller and supporting staff is to help management to attain better results. They should not usurp line authority nor give the impression that they can do so. Staff personnel should not be directed to exercise authority over operating line personnel. Nor should the controller reprimand operating personnel for unfavorable results reflected on performance reports. Any action in responding to either favorable or unfavorable variances is strictly a line function. The controller is responsible for designing an effective cost control system. The line executives and supervisors have direct responsibility for implementing cost control.

Not all variances should be treated equally. A favorable efficiency variance of a *nonbottleneck* operation has little benefit to the firm, except the cost savings in the amount of the favorable efficiency variance. A favorable efficiency variance of a *bottleneck* operation, on the other hand, improves the overall operating efficiency of the firm, in addition to the cost savings of the favorable efficiency variance. Similarly, an unfavorable direct labor efficiency variance incurred by a *nonbottleneck* operation does not affect the firm other than in the increased level of manufacturing costs. An unfavorable direct labor efficiency variance in a *bottleneck* operation, on the other hand, can lead to sizable negative ripple effects on the firm's total manufacturing costs and operations. The unfavorable efficiency variance of an upstream operation that is a bottleneck, is likely to curtail the output of the downstream operations. A series of unfavorable efficiency variances in one or more bottleneck operations can severely cripple the firm's operation.

Cost Flows in General Ledgers Using a Standard Cost System

Standard cost systems use the same accounts for inventory control and for recording manufacturing cost accounts that other costing systems use. Similar to actual or normal cost systems, standard cost systems have accounts such as Materials Inventory, Accrued Payroll, Factory Overhead, Work-in-Process Inventory, Finished Goods

LEARNING OBJECTIVE 7
Describe cost flows through general ledger accounts and prepare journal entries for the acquisition and use of direct materials and direct labor in a standard cost system.

Inventory, and Cost of Goods Sold. Manufacturing costs flow through inventory and manufacturing cost accounts in ways that are similar to cost flows in an actual or normal cost system. One notable difference is that standard cost systems use standard costs instead of actual or normalized costs in inventory accounts.

Another difference is the use of variance accounts in standard cost systems. Most firms that use a standard cost system have a separate ledger account for each type of variance to identify source(s) of variances and to assist operational controls. Such firms record discrepancies between costs actually incurred and standard costs for the operation in variance accounts.

Direct Materials Cost

A firm that uses a standard cost system records purchases of direct materials as follows:

	Account	Amount
Debit:	Direct materials inventory	Total standard cost of the purchased materials
	Direct materials price variance *(if unfavorable)*	Amount of *unfavorable* variance
Credit:	Cash or Accounts Payable	The amount agreed to pay for the purchase
	Direct materials price variance *(if favorable)*	Amount of *favorable* variance

To illustrate, on October 7, Schmidt Machinery Company purchased 3,630 pounds of aluminum at $26 per pound. The term of the purchase is 1/EOM, n/180. The standard cost sheet (Exhibit 13.5) lists the cost to be $25 per pound. The firm records all cash discounts when earned. The journal entry for the purchase is as follows:

Date	Account	Amount	
Oct. 7	Materials Inventory (3,630 × $25)	90,750	
	Materials Purchase Price Variance—Aluminum (3,630 × $1)	3,630	
	Accounts Payable (3,630 × $26)		94,380
	Purchase of 3,630 pounds aluminum from Dura-Igor Corporation at $26 per pound. Terms 1/EOM, n/180; standard price $25 per pound.		

The purchase price Schmidt agreed to pay is $3,630 higher than the total standard cost for 3,630 pounds of aluminum—an unfavorable direct materials price variance. Schmidt records the unfavorable variance by *debiting* the variance account.

The journal entries at the time of issuing direct materials to manufacturing are as follows:

	Account	Amount
Debit:	Work-in-Process Inventory	Total standard quantity of materials for the output at standard cost
	Direct materials usage variance *(if unfavorable)*	Amount of *unfavorable* variance
Credit:	Direct materials inventory	Total materials used at standard cost
	Direct materials usage variance *(if favorable)*	Amount of *favorable* variance

On October 9, the production department requested 3,630 pounds of aluminum for the production of 780 units of XV–1.

Date	Account	Amount
Oct. 9	Work-in-Process Inventory (780 × 4 = 3,120; 3,120 × $25)	78,000
	Materials Usage Variance—Aluminum (3,630 − 3,120 = 510; 510 × $25)	12,750
	Materials Inventory (3,630 × $25)	90,750
	Issued 3,630 pounds of aluminum to production for the manufacture of 780 units of XV–1. Standard usage is 4 pounds per unit of XV–1.	

Direct Labor Cost

The cost of the units manufactured is increased by the wages incurred for the production. Thus, the Work-in-Process Inventory account is debited for the total standard direct labor wages for the units manufactured. The credit account is the Accrual Payroll for the total direct labor wages incurred for the operation.

	Account	Amount
Debit:	Work-in-Process Inventory	Total number of standard hours for the units manufactured at the standard hourly wage rate
	Direct labor rate or efficiency variance *(if unfavorable)*	Amount of variance
Credit:	Accrual Payroll	Total wage paid or accrued
	Direct labor rate or efficiency variance *(if favorable)*	Amount of variance

The difference between the amount debited (the amount that *should have been incurred* for the units of the product manufactured) and the amount credited (the total amount of direct labor wages paid) can result from difference in either the wage rate or the total number of direct labor-hours spent in production and the amounts according to the standard for the operation. Differences in actual wage rate and the standard wage rate are recorded in Direct Labor Rate Variance account. Differences in the number of total hours spent in production and the number of total standard hours that should have been spent for the output of the period are recorded in the Direct Labor Efficiency Variance account.

On October 15, Schmidt recognizes that the production department spent 3,510 direct labor-hours for $147,420 to complete the production of 780 units of XV–1, or $42 per hour. The standard (Exhibit 13.5) calls for 5 direct labor-hours per unit of XV–1 at $40 per hour.

Date	Account	Amount	
Oct. 15	Work-in-Process Inventory (780 × 5 = 3,900; 3,900 × $40)	156,000	
	Direct Labor Rate Variance (3,510 × [$42 − $40 = 2])	7,020	
	Direct Labor Efficiency Variance (390 × $40)		15,600
	Accrued Payroll (3,510 × $42)		147,420
	Spent 3,510 direct labor-hours to manufacture 780 units of XV–1.		
	Standard cost allows 5 hours per unit of XV–1 at $40 per hour		

Completion of Production

Upon completion of manufacturing, the standard cost of the units manufactured is transferred out of the Work-in-Process Inventory account and entered into the Finished Goods Inventory account at the standard total product cost. There is no entry to any variance account.

The standard cost sheet (Exhibit 13.5) specifies that the total standard cost per unit of XV–1 is $520. These journal entries record the completion of manufacturing and transfer of 780 units of XV–1 on October 15:

Date	Account	Amount	
Oct. 15	Finished Goods Inventory (780 × $520)	405,600	
	Work-in-Process Inventory		405,600
	Completed 780 units of XV–1 at standard cost per unit $520.		

Exhibit 13.12 summarizes cost flows through ledger accounts in a standard cost system.

Summary

Measures of effectiveness and efficiency help managers assess operations. Managers are interested in effectiveness to determine if they have attained the goals set for the operations and in efficiency to see if they have performed operations with the expected amounts of resources. A commonly used measure of effectiveness is the operating income variance, which is the difference in operating income between the master budget and the actual results.

An operation is efficient if it wastes no resources. A flexible budget plays an important role in assessing operating efficiency. Using the flexible budget for the output attained, management can separate the operating income variance between the actual amount earned and the budgeted amount into sales volume and flexible budget variances. A sales volume variance is the difference between a master budget amount and the flexible budget amount for the corresponding item. It measures the effects of changes in sales on the item. A flexible budget variance is the difference between the actual amount incurred or earned and the amount in the flexible budget for the corresponding item. It measures efficiency in carrying out the operation.

Establishing a standard requires careful analyses of the operation. A standard can be an ideal or a currently attainable standard. A manufacturing operation usually has a standard cost sheet that details the standard quantity and cost for all significant manufacturing elements of the operation. A firm uses activity analysis, historical data,

EXHIBIT 13.12
Cost Flows and Ledger Entries in Standard Cost System

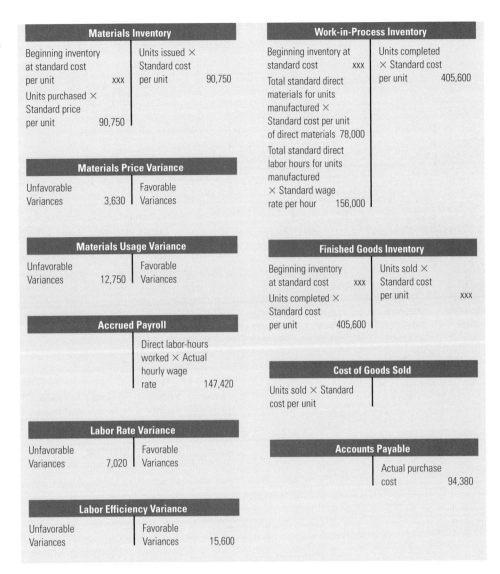

benchmarking, market expectation, or strategic considerations, among others, to set standards. Typical standards include standards for direct materials and direct labor. Comparing the actual amount of direct materials used and the number of direct labor-hours spent to the standard amounts, respectively, a firm identifies materials usage variance and labor efficiency variance. Exhibit 13.13 summarizes the relationships of these variances. Used properly, these variances can be a powerful tool for controlling operations and identifying factors that can help firms to improve their operations.

Recent advances in manufacturing technology such as JIT, flexible manufacturing systems, total quality management, and the theory of constraints have had a significant impact on manufacturing and standard costs, including decreased importance of materials purchase price variance, labor variances, and variances in nonbottleneck operations.

Use of a standard cost should focus on influencing behavior with positive reinforcements rather than imposing penalties and punishments.

EXHIBIT 13.13   **Hierarchy of Variances**

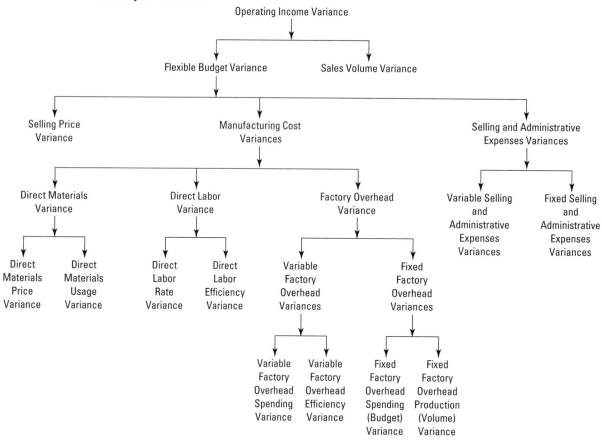

Comments on Cost Management in Action

The Kaizen Productivity Program Saves Jobs, Creates Stress

The improvement in plant productivity brought about by the bonus system and conveyor belt system at Westinghouse Air Brake Company was just what was needed to save the old Chicago plant. Without these improvements, the business would likely have gone overseas. However, the increased demand on workers' attention and effort caused stress. Workers found themselves operating two or more machines, each of which could operate at a different speed. Workers were usually in constant motion. To decrease stress, the machines were located close together in U-shaped cells when the plant was renovated. This allowed the workers to operate the machines more efficiently, and reduced the time required to move parts around the plant.

An unfortunate side effect of the system is that workers often would set aside a half-dozen or more finished parts to have some to feed the conveyor belt if there was a distraction or disruption of any kind. The few extra finished parts each worker set aside added up to a substantial amount for the plant. Plant managers frowned upon this hidden inventory practice and were constantly on the lookout for it.

Source: Timothy Aeppel, "Factory Lifts Productivity, But Staff Finds It's No Picnic," *The Wall Street Journal,* May 18, 1999, p. A10.

Self–Study Problems
(For solutions, please turn to the end of the chapter.)

1. Sales Volume and Flexible Budget Variances

Solid Box Fabrications manufactures boxes for workstations. The firm's standard cost sheet and the operating result of October 2006 follows:

	Standard Cost per Unit		Operating Result October 2006
Units			9,500
Sales	$ 50.00		$551,000
Variable costs			
Direct materials			
5 pounds at $2.4 per pound =	$ 12.00	48,000 pounds × $3 =	$144,000
Direct labor			
0.5 hour at $14 per hour =	7.00	4,800 hours × $16 =	76,800
Variable manufacturing overhead	2.00		19,000
Variable selling and administrative expenses	5.00		55,100
Total variable cost	$ 26.00		$294,900
Contribution margin	$ 24.00		$256,100
Fixed costs			
Manufacturing costs	$50,000		$ 55,000
Selling and administrative	20,000		24,000
Total fixed costs	$70,000		$ 79,000
Operating income			$177,100

In preparing the master budget for October 2006, the firm recognized that several costs on the standard cost sheet would change. For example, the selling price of the product would increase by 8 percent. Suppliers have notified the firm that starting October 1, materials prices would be 5 percent higher. The labor contract prescribes a 10 percent increase, starting October 1, on wages and benefits. Fixed manufacturing costs will increase $5,000 for insurance, property taxes, and salaries. Fixed selling and administrative expenses will increase as follows: $2,000 in managers' salaries, and $2,000 for advertising during October 2006. The unit sales for October 2006 are expected to be 10,000 units. Solid Box Fabrications uses JIT systems in all of its operations including materials acquisitions and product manufacturing.

Required

1. Prepare the master budget and flexible budgets for 9,500 units and 11,000 units for October 2006.
2. Compute the operating income sales volume variance, operating income flexible budget variance, selling price variance, and variable cost flexible budget variance for October 2006.
3. Determine the direct materials price variance, direct materials usage variance, direct labor rate variance, and direct labor efficiency variance.

2. Direct Materials Price and Usage Variances, Direct Labor Rate and Efficiency Variances, and Journal Entries

Chemical, Inc., has set the following standards for direct materials and direct labor for each 20-pound bag of Weed-Be-Doom:

	Per Bag
Direct materials: 25 pounds XF–2000 @ $0.08	$2.00
Direct labor: 0.05 hour @ $32	1.60

The firm manufactured 100,000 bags of Weed-Be-Doom in December, used 2,700,000 pounds of XF–2000 and spent 5,200 direct labor-hours. The firm purchased 3,000,000 lbs. of XF–2000 at $0.075 per pound and incurred a total payroll of $182,000 for direct labor during the month. The firm identifies all variances when it incurs the costs.

Required

1. Compute the price and usage variances for direct materials and the rate and efficiency variances for direct labor.

2. Prepare journal entries to record the company's data.

Questions

13–1 Tobias Company earned $5 million last year from selling 25,000 units of a special drill that makes no sound annoying dental patients. The master budget calls for sales of 30,000 units to earn $7.5 million in operating income. The operating income in the flexible budget for 25,000 units, however, is $4.5 million. A member of the operation review committee comments that the firm was neither efficient in its operations nor effective in attaining the operating goal. Do you agree with this assessment?

13–2 Can a standard cost system be used in job order costing? In process costing?

13–3 Can an organization be effective but not efficient in its operation? Efficient but not effective?

13–4 What is the difference between a standard and a budget?

13–5 What is the difference between a master budget and a flexible budget?

13–6 Can flexible budgets adapt to changes in both inflation rate and activity?

13–7 Verbatim Company's budget for last year included $80,000 for prime costs. The total actual prime costs for the period were $72,000. Can we say that the plant manager has done a good job in controlling the cost if actual production were 80 percent of the budgeted production?

13–8 Which of the following should a firm use as the standard in assessing production efficiencies: standards based on ideal performance, standards based on attainable performance, or standards based on the average of recent historical performance?

13–9 Why does management need to separate direct labor variances into rate variances and efficiency variances?

13–10 The manager of a firm is happy to receive a report that shows a favorable total materials variance of $75 and the manager decides that no more action is needed since the total variance is such an insignificant amount for an operation that has a total direct materials cost of over $100,000. Do you agree?

13–11 Which variances would be directly affected by a learning curve phenomenon?

13–12 Will overtime premiums affect direct labor variances? If so, which variances?

13–13 Should the performance of a division be deemed less than satisfactory if all of its variances are unfavorable?

13–14 At the end of its fiscal year, Graham Company had several substantial variances from standard variable manufacturing costs.

Required Which of the following scenarios is the most justifiable for the firm's allocation of the resulting variances to inventories and cost of sales?

1. Additional cost of raw materials acquired under a speculative purchase contract.
2. Equipment breakdown.
3. Overestimates of production volume for the period resulting from failure to predict an unusual decline in the market for the company's product.
4. Increased labor rates won by the union as a result of a strike.

(CMA Adapted)

13–15 Todco planned to produce 3,000 units of its single product, Teragram, during November. The standard specifications for one unit of Teragram include 6 pounds of material at $0.30 per pound. The firm uses JIT in all operations. Actual production in November was 3,100 units of Teragram. The accountant computed a $380 favorable materials purchase price variance and a $120 unfavorable materials usage variance.

Required Which of the following conclusions do these variances best support?

1. More materials were purchased than were used.
2. More materials were used than were purchased.
3. The actual cost of materials was less than the standard cost.

4. The actual usage of materials was less than the standard allowed.

5. The actual cost and usage of materials were both less than standard.

(CMA Adapted)

13–16 Why do firms using JIT systems often have little interest in materials price variances?

13–17 Identify the effects that new technologies such as JIT, flexible manufacturing systems, and TQM have on standard cost systems.

13–18 Discuss behavioral concerns in establishing and implementing a standard cost system.

13–19 At year-end, how should a firm handle immaterial variances for the year?

13–20 Portfolio management is a powerful concept in finance and marketing. The marketing application of the concept is to develop and manage a balanced portfolio of products. Market share and market growth can be used to classify products for portfolio purposes, and the product classifications often are extended to the organizational units that make the product. The market share/growth classifications can be depicted as follows:

	Market Share	
Market Growth Rate	**High**	**Low**
High	Rising star	?
Low	Cash cow	Dog

The question mark is the classification for products that show high-growth rates but have small market shares, such as new products that are similar to their competitors. A rising star is a high-growth, high-market-share product that tends to mature into a cash cow. A cash cow is a slow-growing established product that can be milked for cash to help the question mark and introduce new products. The dog is a low-growth, low-market-share item that is a candidate for elimination or segmentation. Understanding where a product falls within this market share/growth structure is important when applying a standard cost system.

Required

1. Discuss the major advantages of using a standard cost accounting system.

2. Describe the types of information that are useful in setting standards and the conditions that must be present to support the use of standard costing.

3. Discuss the applicability or nonapplicability of using standard costing for a product classified as a (a) cash cow and (b) question mark.

(CMA Adapted)

13–21 When should a firm enter journal entries recording variances?

13–22 A firm updates its standard costs once a year. Six months after the current standard costs are adopted, the firm is experiencing changes in cost due to better usage of material and efficiency in labor. Does a change in cost merit changing the standard cost?

Exercises

13–23 **Flexible Budget and Variances** Schmidt Machinery Company (Exhibit 13.1) manufactured and sold 900 units for $840 each in June. The firm incurred $414,000 total variable expenses and $180,000 total fixed expenses.

Required for the Month of June,

1. Prepare a flexible budget for the manufacturing and sales of 900 units

2. Compute for June

   a. The operating income sales volume variance.

   b. The contribution margin sales volume variance.

3. Calculate for June

   a. The operating income flexible budget variance.

   b. The contribution margin flexible budget variance.

   c. The selling price variance.

13–24 Flexible Budget and Variances   Kermit Company's master budget calls for production and sales of 12,000 units for $48,000; variable costs of $18,000; and fixed costs of $16,000. The firm incurred $24,000 variable cost to produce and sell 15,000 units for $64,000 and earned $25,000 operating income.

Required

1. Determine Kermit Company's
   a. Operating income in the flexible budget for the units sold.
   b. Contribution margin flexible budget variance.
   c. Operating income flexible budget variance.
   d. Contribution margin sales volume variance.
   e. Operating income sales volume variance.
2. Explain why the contribution margin sales volume variance and the operating income sales volume variance for the same period are likely to be identical.
3. Explain why the contribution margin flexible budget variance is likely to differ with the operating income flexible budget variance for the same period.

13–25 Sales Volume Variance   The following information is available for Mitchelville Products Company for the month of July:

	Master Budget	Actual
Units	4,000	3,800
Sales revenue	$60,000	$53,200
Variable manufacturing costs	16,000	19,000
Fixed manufacturing costs	15,000	16,000
Variable selling and administrative expense	8,000	7,700
Fixed selling and administrative expense	9,000	10,000

Required

1. Compute the July sales volume variance and flexible budget variance in contribution margin and operating income.
2. Discuss implications of the variances on strategic cost management.
3. Set up an electronic spreadsheet that will allow the firm to prepare flexible budgets for activities within its relevant range of operation and prepare flexible budgets when sales are
   a. 3,800 units.
   b. 4,100 units.

(CMA Adapted)

13–26 Direct Materials and Direct Labor Variances   Schmidt Machinery Company (Exhibit 13.7) used 3,375 pounds of aluminum in June to manufacture 900 units. The firm paid $30 per pound during the month to purchase aluminum. On June 1, the firm had 50 pounds of aluminum on hand. At the end of June, the firm only had 25 pounds of aluminum in its warehouse. The firm spent 4,200 direct labor hours in June and the average wage during the month is $42 per hour.

Required   Compute for June, Schmidt Machinery Company's

1. Purchase price and usage variances for aluminum.
2. Direct labor rate and efficiency variances.

13–27 Journal Entry   Use the data in Exhibit 13.5. On October 7, Schmidt Machinery Company purchased 720 pounds of PVC at $41 per pound. On October 9, Schmidt's production department requested 720 pounds of PVC for the 780 units of XV–1 to be manufactured.

Required   Make the necessary journal entries to record the purchase and the issuance of PVC to production.

13–28 Materials Purchase Price Joseph Company's direct materials costs are as follows:

Standard price per pound of direct materials	$5.00
Direct materials purchased (pounds)	2,000
Total standard direct materials for product manufactured (pounds)	1,600
Direct materials used in production (pounds)	1,800
Direct materials purchase price variance—favorable	$200

Required Compute the following:

1. The actual purchase price per pound of direct material (rounded to the nearest penny).
2. The direct materials usage variance.

13–29 Direct Materials Variances SMP Company has the following data from its operations for the month just completed:

Direct materials purchased	30,000 pounds
Direct materials used	28,000 pounds
Total direct materials purchased costs	$90,000
Standard price of direct materials	$3.25 per pound
Direct materials usage variance—unfavorable	$6,500

Required Compute for SMP Company the following:

1. Price per pound paid to purchase direct materials.
2. Direct materials price variance.
3. Total standard quantity of direct materials for the operation.

13–30 Materials Price Variance Rexon Company's direct materials costs for May follow:

Increase in direct materials inventories	2,000 pounds
Direct materials used	60,000 pounds
Cost of direct materials purchased	$220,000
Direct materials usage variance—unfavorable	$24,000
Standard quantity of direct materials allowed for May production	54,000 pounds

Required Compute for the month of May the following:

1. Standard cost per pound of the direct material.
2. Total purchases (in pounds) of direct materials during the period.
3. Direct materials price variance.

13–31 Direct Materials Variances Osbon Company uses a standard costing system. It had 700 gallons of direct material X in its inventory on June 1, which were purchased in May for $1.50 per gallon and carried at the standard cost of $1 per gallon. The following information pertains to direct material X for the month of June:

Gallons purchased	1,400
Standard gallons for productions in June	1,300
Standard cost per gallon	$1.00
Actual cost per gallon in June	$1.10
Direct materials inventory, June 30	600 gallons

Required Compute the materials purchase price and usage variances for direct material X for June.

13–32 Materials Price and Usage Variances Steinberg Company had the following direct materials costs for the manufacturing of product T in March:

Actual purchase price per pound	$7.50
Standard direct materials for Product T produced	2,100 pounds
Decrease in direct materials inventories	100 pounds
Direct materials used in production	2,300 pounds
Standard price per pound	$7.25

Required   What were Steinberg's direct materials price and usage variances for March?

13–33 Materials Price and Usage Variances   Bechtal Company uses a standard cost system to account for its only product. The direct materials standard per unit of the product is 4 pounds at $5.10 per pound. Operating data for April follow:

Total flexible budget variance for materials	$640 unfavorable
Materials purchase	8,300 pounds
Number of finished units produced	2,000
Increase in direct materials inventory	500 pounds

Required   Determine for Bechtal Company:

1. The materials price and usage variances for April.
2. The actual cost of direct materials per pound.

13–34 Standard Direct Materials Cost   Agrichem manufactures Insect-Be-Gone. Each bag of the product contains 60 pounds of direct materials. Twenty-five percent of the materials evaporate during manufacturing. The budget allows the direct materials to be purchased at $2.50 a pound under terms of 2/10, n/30. The company takes all cash discounts. Determine the standard direct materials cost for one bag of Insect-Be-Gone.

13–35 Standard Direct Materials Cost   Rusty Industries manufactures a sugar-substitute, SS–2, from a natural ingredient, natura. Each 10-pound package of SS–2 is manufactured using twelve pounds of natura. The firm has determined purchase price per pound of natura to be $5.00 with a purchase term of 3/15, n/45 and FOB, destination. The firm has a policy of taking all discounts offered. Determine the standard direct materials cost for one package of SS–2.

13–36 Materials Price and Usage Variances   Durable Company installs shingle roofs on houses. The standard materials cost for a type R house is $1,250, based on 1,000 shingles at $1.25 each. During April, Durable installed roofs on 20 type R houses, using 22,000 shingles at a total actual cost of $26,400. The firm maintains no inventory. What are Durable's materials price and usage variances for April?

13–37 Materials Usage Variance   Buckler Company manufactures desks with vinyl tops. The standard materials cost for vinyl per Model S desk is $27.00 per desk using 12 square feet of vinyl. A production run of 1,000 desks in March used 12,600 square feet of vinyl at a cost of $2 per square foot. What was the direct materials usage variance in March?

13–38 Labor Rate Variance   Skousen Company's direct labor costs for the month of January follow:

Total direct labor-hours worked	40,000
Total standard direct labor-hours for units manufactured	42,000
Average hourly wage rate paid for direct labor	$25
Direct labor efficiency variance	$48,000 favorable

Required   What is Skousen's

1. Standard hourly rate?
2. Direct labor rate variance?

13–39 Standard Labor Rate and Efficiency Variance   Elof's direct labor costs for the month of January follow:

Direct labor hourly rate paid	$30.00
Total standard direct labor-hours for productions	12,000
Direct labor-hours worked	11,000
Direct labor rate variance	$33,000 favorable

Required Compute these:

1. Standard direct labor wage per hour in January.
2. Direct labor efficiency variance.

13–40 **Standard Labor Rate and Total Hours** Propitt Company's records for April disclosed these data relating to direct labor:

Cost incurred	$1,000
Rate variance	100 F
Efficiency variance	165 U
Direct labor-hours worked	200

Required Compute these:

1. Standard direct labor-hour wage rate per hour.
2. Total standard direct labor-hours for the units manufactured in April.

13–41 **Labor Efficiency Variance** Nelof Company's direct labor costs for the month of January follow:

Direct labor-hours worked	20,000
Direct labor rate variance—unfavorable	$6,000
Total payroll for direct labor	$378,000
Budgeted units to manufacture	8,000
Budgeted total direct labor hours	24,000
Units manufactured	6,000

Required

1. What is Nelof's standard direct labor-hour wage rate?
2. What is Nelof's direct labor efficiency variance in January?

13–42 **Labor Rate and Efficiency Variances** The direct labor standards for one unit of Orego are 2 labor-hours at $20 per hour. Budgeted production for the period was 1,500 units of Orego. The firm manufactured 1,600 units and spent $69,000 for 3,000 direct labor-hours.

Required

1. What is the direct labor rate variance?
2. What is the direct labor efficiency variance?

13–43 **Labor Rate and Efficiency Variances** Keck Company's direct labor costs to manufacture its only product in October follow:

Standard direct-labor hours per unit of product	1.5
Number of finished units produced	10,000
Standard wage rate per direct labor-hour	$16
Total payroll for direct labor	$207,000
Wage paid per direct labor-hour	$18

Differences in hourly wage rates reflect skill levels of workers.

Required Determine these for October:

1. Direct labor rate variance.

2. Direct labor efficiency variance.

3. Production manager's performance in managing direct labor costs.

13–44 **Labor Rate and Efficiency Variances**   The following information pertaining to the operating data of Roy William Sports for September:

Standard direct labor cost per gallon of output at 20 gallons/hour	$1
Standard direct labor cost for 8,440 gallons manufactured	$8,440
Total payroll for direct labor (410 hours)	$8,610

Required   Compute for Roy William,

1. Direct labor rate variance.

2. Direct labor efficiency variance.

13–45 **Actual Labor Hours**   Cott Company's direct labor costs follow:

Standard direct labor-hours for the work done	10,000
Standard direct labor rate per hour	$25.00
Actual direct labor rate per hour	$22.00
Direct labor efficiency variance—unfavorable	$27,000

Required

1. How many total direct hours were worked, rounded to the nearest hour?

2. What is the direct labor rate variance?

13–46 **Actual Labor Hours**   Tubbard Company uses a standard cost system. The following information pertains to direct labor for product B for the month of October:

Standard hours for the output	2,000
Direct labor rate paid per hour	$22.50
Standard labor rate per hour	$20.00
Labor efficiency variance	4,000 U

Required

1. How many total direct hours were worked?

2. What is the direct labor rate variance?

3. What is the flexible budget variance for direct labor cost of the period?

13–47 **Total Payroll**   Tommy Company's direct labor costs for May follow:

Standard direct labor hourly wage rate	$50.00
Total standard direct labor-hours for work done	16,000
Total direct labor-hours worked	18,000
Total direct labor variance	$20,000 F

Required   Compute for Tommy,

1. Direct labor efficiency variance

2. Direct labor rate variance.

3. Total direct labor payroll in May.

13–48 **Total Payroll**   Susana Corporation's direct labor costs for the month of March follow:

Standard direct labor-hours	12,000
Direct labor-hours worked	10,500
Direct labor rate variance—favorable	$8,400
Standard direct labor rate per hour	$24.00

Required   What was Susana's total direct labor payroll for March?

13–49 **Standard Direct Labor Cost per Unit**   Saswana manufactures a product that requires three direct labor-hours per unit. Employee benefit costs are treated as direct labor costs. Data on direct labor follow:

Number of employees	25
Number of hours paid weekly per employee	40
Weekly productive hours per employee	35
Hourly wages	$30
Employee benefits	40%

Required   Determine the standard direct labor cost per unit of the product.

13–50 **Actual and Standard Labor Rates**   Data relating to Junior Company's direct labor costs follow:

Standard direct labor-hours for the units manufactured	30,000
Direct labor-hours worked	27,000
Direct labor rate variance—favorable	$16,200
Total payroll	$675,000

Required   Compute for Junior:

1. Actual direct labor rate.
2. Standard direct labor rate.
3. Direct labor efficiency variance.

13–51 **Direct Materials in Flexible Budget**   Koch Company uses flexible budgets for cost control. It produced 11,400 units of product during March, incurred $22,000 direct materials cost. Its master budget for the year has a direct materials cost of $273,600 for 144,000 units.

Required

1. Compute the direct materials cost in the flexible budget for March production.
2. Determine the direct materials flexible budget variance.

(CMA Adapted)

13–52 **Flexible Budget and Direct Labor Variances**   Duo Co. has the following processing standards for its clerical employees:

Number of hours per 1,000 papers processed	150
Normal number of papers processed per year	1,500,000
Wage rate per 1,000 papers	$600
Total standard variable cost of processing 1,500,000 papers	$2,700,000
Fixed costs per year	$150,000

The following information pertains to the 1,200,000 papers processed during the year:

Total cost	$1,995,000
Labor cost	$ 855,000
Labor-hours	190,000

Required   Compute for Duo Co. the following:

1. Expected total cost for the year to process 1,200,000 papers, assuming standard performance.
2. Labor rate variance for the year.
3. Labor efficiency variance for the year.

(CPA Adapted)

Problems

13–53 **Standard Cost System**   Mark-Wright Inc. (MWI) is a specialty frozen food processor located in the midwestern states. Since its founding in 1982, MWI has enjoyed a loyal local clientele willing to pay premium prices for the high-quality frozen foods prepared from special recipes. In the last two years, MWI has experienced rapid sales growth in its operating region and has had many inquiries about supplying its products on a national basis. To meet this growth, MWI expanded its processing capabilities, which resulted in increased production and distribution costs. Furthermore, MWI has been encountering pricing pressure from competitors outside its normal marketing region.

Because MWI desires to continue its expansion, Jim Condon, CEO, has engaged a consulting firm to assist the company in determining its best course of action. The consulting firm concluded that, although premium pricing is sustainable in some areas, MWI must make some price concessions if sales growth is to be achieved. Also, to maintain profit margins, the company must reduce and control its costs. The consulting firm recommended using a standard cost system that would facilitate a flexible budgeting system to better accommodate the changes in demand that can be expected when serving an expanding market area.

Jim met with his management team and explained the consulting firm's recommendations. He then assigned the team the task of establishing standard costs. After discussing the situation with their respective staffs, the management team met to review the matter.

Jane Morgan, purchasing manager, noted that meeting expanded production would necessitate obtaining basic food supplies from sources other than MWI's traditional ones. This would entail increased raw materials and shipping costs and could result in supplies of lower quality. Consequently, the processing department would have to make up these increased costs if current cost levels are to be maintained or reduced.

Stan Walters, processing manager, countered that the need to accelerate processing cycles to increase production, coupled with the possibility of receiving lower-grade supplies, can be expected to result in a slip in quality and a higher product rejection rate. Under these circumstances, per-unit labor utilization cannot be maintained or reduced, and forecasting future unit labor content becomes very difficult.

Tom Lopez, production engineer, advised that failure to properly maintain and thoroughly clean the equipment at prescribed daily intervals could affect the quality and unique taste of the frozen food products. Jack Reid, vice president of sales, stated that if quality could not be maintained, MWI could not expect to increase sales to the levels projected.

When the management team reported these problems to Jim, he said that if agreement could not be reached on appropriate standards, he would arrange to have the consulting firm set the standards, and everyone would have to live with the results.

Required

1. List for the use of a standard cost system:
   a. Its major advantages.
   b. Its disadvantages.
2. Identify those who should participate in setting standards and describe the benefits of their participation.
3. Explain the general features and characteristics associated with the introduction and operation of a standard cost system that make it an effective tool for cost control.
4. What could the consequences be if Jim Condon, CEO, has the outside consulting firm set Mark-Wright's standards?

(CMA Adapted)

13–54 **Standard Cost Sheet**   Singh Company is a small manufacturer of wooden household items. Al Rivkin, corporate controller, plans to implement a standard cost system. He has information from several co-workers that will help him develop standards for Singh's products.

One product is a wooden cutting board. Each cutting board requires 1.25 board feet of lumber and 12 minutes of direct labor time to prepare and cut the lumber. The cutting boards are inspected after they are cut. Because they are made of a natural material that has imperfections, one board is normally rejected for each five boards accepted. Four rubber pads are attached to the corners of each good cutting board. A total of 15 minutes of direct labor time is required to attach all four pads and finish each cutting board. The lumber for the cutting boards costs $3 per board foot, and each pad costs 5 cents. Direct labor is paid at the rate of $8 per hour.

Required

1. Develop the standard cost for the direct cost components of the cutting board. For each direct cost component, the standard cost should identify these:
   a. Standard quantity.
   b. Standard rate.

    c. Standard cost per unit.

2. Identify the advantages of implementing a standard costing system.

3. Explain the role of each of the following persons in developing standards:

    a. Purchasing manager.

    b. Industrial engineer.

    c. Cost accountant.

(CMA Adapted)

13–55 **Standard Cost Sheet** ColdKing Company is a small producer of fruit-flavored frozen desserts. For many years, its products have had strong regional sales because of brand recognition; however, other companies have begun marketing similar products in the area, and price competition has become increasingly important. Janice Wakefield, the company's controller, is planning to implement a standard cost system for ColdKing and has gathered considerable information from her co-workers about production and materials requirements for ColdKing's products. Janice believes that the use of standard cost will allow the company to improve cost control, make better pricing decisions, and enhance strategic management.

    ColdKing's most popular product is raspberry sherbet. The sherbet is produced in 10-gallon batches, each of which requires 6 quarts of good raspberries and 10 gallons of other ingredients. The fresh raspberries are sorted by hand before they enter the production process. Because of imperfections in the raspberries and normal spoilage, one quart of berries is discarded for every four accepted. The standard direct labor time for sorting to obtain one quart of acceptable raspberries is 3 minutes. The acceptable raspberries are then blended with the other ingredients; blending requires 12 minutes of direct labor time per batch. After blending, the sherbet is packaged in quart containers. Janice has gathered the following price information:

- ColdKing purchases raspberries for 80 cents per quart. All other ingredients cost 45 cents per gallon.

- Direct labor is paid at the rate of $9 per hour.

- The total cost of materials and labor required to package the sherbet is $0.38 per quart.

Required

1. Develop the standard cost for the direct cost components of a 10-gallon batch of raspberry sherbet. For each direct cost component, the standard cost should identify the following:

    a. Standard quantity.

    b. Standard rate.

    c. Standard cost per batch.

2. As part of the implementation of a standard cost system at ColdKing, Janice plans to train those responsible for maintaining the standards to use variance analysis. She is particularly concerned with the causes of unfavorable variances.

    a. Discuss the possible causes of unfavorable materials price variances, identify the individuals who should be held responsible for them, and comment on the implications of these variances on strategic cost management.

    b. Discuss the possible causes of unfavorable labor efficiency variances, identify the individuals who should be held responsible for them, and comment on the implications of these variances on strategic cost management.

(CMA Adapted)

13–56 **Fill In Missing Data** Valley Forge Company maintains no inventory and has these data for its fiscal year just ended:

	Operating Result	Flexible Budget Variance	Flexible Budget	Sales Volume Variance	Master Budget
Units	900	*a*	*b*	*c*	800
Sales revenue	$9,500	*e*	*d*	*f*	$8,800
Variable cost:					
Manufacturing	*i*	$600 F	*h*	$600 U	*g*
Selling and administrative	*j*	*l*	*k*	*m*	$1,600

Contribution margin	$2,400	n	p	r	q
Fixed cost	s	w	u	v	t
Operating income	$1,200	y	x	z	$1,400

Required   Find the amounts of the missing items *a* through *z* (there is no *o*).

13–57 Fill In Missing Data   V-Grip Company uses the JIT system in all its operations and has these data for its fiscal year just ended:

	Operating Result	Flexible Budget Variance	Flexible Budget	Sales Volume Variance	Master Budget
Units	b		a	100 F	1,500
Sales revenue	$ e	$1,600 U	$ d	$ c	$37,500
Variable cost:					
Manufacturing	h	$1,600 U	f	g	$24,000
Selling and administrative	4,000	i	3,200	k	j
Contribution margin	l	m	n	p	q
Fixed cost	r	u	s	v	t
Operating income	$1,000	w	$3,600	y	x

Required

1. Find the amounts of the missing items *a* through *y* (there is no *o*).
2. Compute the actual selling price per unit.

13–58 Fill In Missing Data   Paul, Inc., which manufactures dummy dolls, misplaced some of its data. Use the following information to replace the lost data:

	Actual	a	Flexible Budget	b	Static Budget
Units	900	c	d	e	825
Revenues	$52,600	$1,300 F	$f	$g	$ h
Variable costs	i	k	j	l	23,100
Fixed costs	10,350	n	m	p	11,425
Operating income	$22,175	q	r	s	$12,500

Required   Identify or find the missing items *a* through *s* (there is no *o*).

13–59 Fill In Missing Data   Pokeman Bunch, Inc., manufactures PokeMonster figures and has the following data from its operation for the year just completed:

	Actual Result	Flexible Budget Variance	Flexible Budget	Sales Volume Variance	Master Budget
Units	1,200	a	b	c	1,000
Revenues	$69,600	e	d	f	$60,000
Variable costs	j	i	g	h	40,000
Contribution margin	k	$11,200 U	l	m	n
Fixed costs	p	s	r	q	5,000
Operating income	$5,800	w	v	u	t

Required   Find the missing items *a* through *w* (there is no *o*).

13–60 **Basic Analysis of Direct Labor Variances**   Day-Mold was founded several years ago by two designers who developed several popular lines of living room, dining room, and bedroom furniture for other companies. The designers believed that their design for dinette sets could be standardized and would sell well. They formed their own company and soon had all the orders they could handle in their small plant in Dayton, Ohio.

The owners bought a microcomputer and software to produce financial statements. They thought all the information they needed was included in these statements.

Recently the employees have been requesting raises. The owners wonder how to evaluate these requests. At the suggestion of Day-Mold's CPA, who prepares the tax return, the owners have hired a CMA as a consultant to implement a standard cost system. The consultant believes that the calculation of variances will aid management in setting responsibility for labor performance.

The supervisors believe that under normal conditions, a dinette set can be assembled with 5 hours of direct labor at a cost of $20 per hour. The consultant has assembled labor cost information for the most recent month and would like your advice in calculating direct labor variances.

During the month, the firm paid $127,600 direct labor wages for 5,800 hours. The factory produced 1,200 dinette sets during the month.

Required

1. Compute direct labor variances for management's consideration.
2. Provide management with reasons for the variances.

(CMA Adapted)

13–61 **Working Backward**   Nelson Company uses a standard cost system. During the past month, the manufacturing operations had the following direct labor variances:

Direct labor rate variance	$11,600 F
Direct labor efficiency variance	24,000 U

The firm allows 2 standard direct labor-hours per unit; its standard direct labor-hour rate is $30. During the month, Nelson spent 16 percent more in direct labor-hours than the total standard hours for the units manufactured.

Required   Determine the following for Nelson Company:

1. The total standard hours for the units manufactured.
2. The total direct labor-hours worked.
3. The actual direct labor-hour wage rate.
4. The number of units manufactured.

13–62 **All Variances**   Funtime Inc. manufactures video game machines. Market saturation and technological innovations caused pricing pressures that resulted in declining profits. To stem the slide in profits until new products can be introduced, top management turned its attention to both manufacturing economics and increased production. To realize these objectives, management developed an incentive program to reward production managers who contribute to an increase in the number of units produced and a decrease in costs.

The production managers responded to the pressure of improving manufacturing in several ways that increased the number of completed units beyond normal production levels. The assembly group puts together video game machines that require parts from both the printed circuit boards (PCB) and the reading heads (RH) groups. To attain increased production levels, the PCB and RH groups began rejecting parts that previously would have been tested and modified to meet manufacturing standards. Preventive maintenance on machines used to produce these parts has been postponed; only emergency repair work is being performed to keep production lines moving. The maintenance department is concerned about serious breakdowns and unsafe operating conditions.

The more aggressive assembly group production supervisors pressured maintenance personnel to attend to their machines rather than those of other groups. This resulted in machine downtime in the PCB and RH groups that, when coupled with demands for accelerated parts delivery by the assembly group, led to more frequent rejection of parts and increased friction among departments.

Funtime operates under a standard cost system. The standard costs for video game machines are as follows:

Cost Item	Standard Cost per Unit		Total
	Quantity	Cost	
Direct materials			
Housing unit	1.0	$20	$20
Printed circuit boards	2.0	15	30
Reading heads	4.0	10	40
Direct labor			
Assembly group	2.0 hours	10	20
PCB group	1.0 hour	11	11
RH group	1.5 hours	12	18
Total standard cost per unit			$139

Funtime prepares monthly performance reports based on standard costs. The following is the contribution report for May 2005 when production and sales both reached 2,200 units.

FUNTIME INC.
Contribution Report
For the Month of May 2005

	Budget	Actual	Variance
Units	2,000	2,200	200 F
Revenue	$400,000	$396,000	$ 4,000 U
Variable costs			
Direct materials	$180,000	$220,400	$40,400 U
Direct labor	98,000	112,260	14,260 U
Total variable costs	278,000	332,660	54,660 U
Contribution margin	$122,000	$ 63,340	$58,660 U

Funtime's top management was surprised by the unfavorable contribution margin variance in spite of the increased sales in May. Jack Rath, the firm's cost accountant, was asked to identify and report on the reasons for the unfavorable contribution margin as well as the individuals or groups responsible for them. After his review, Jack prepared the following usage report:

FUNTIME INC.
Usage Report
For the Month of May 2005

Cost Item	Quantity	Actual Cost
Direct materials		
Housing units	2,200 units	$ 44,000
Printed circuit boards	4,700 units	75,200
Reading heads	9,200 units	101,200
Direct labor		
Assembly	3,900 hours	31,200
Printed circuit boards	2,400 hours	31,060
Reading heads	3,500 hours	50,000
Total variable cost		$332,660

Jack reported that the PCB and RH groups supported the increased production levels but experienced abnormal machine downtime, causing idle time that required the use of overtime to keep up with the accelerated demand for parts. This overtime was charged to direct labor. He also reported that the production managers of these two groups resorted to parts rejections, as opposed to testing and modifying them following former procedures. Jack determined that the assembly group met management's objectives by increasing production while utilizing fewer than standard hours.

Required

1. Calculate these six variances:
   a. Direct material price variance.
   b. Direct material usage variance.
   c. Direct labor efficiency variance.
   d. Direct labor rate variance.
   e. Selling price variance.
   f. Contribution margin sales volume variance.
2. Explain the $58,660 unfavorable variance between budgeted and actual contribution margin during May 2005.
3. Identify and briefly explain the behavioral factors that could promote friction among the production managers and between them and the maintenance manager.
4. Evaluate Jack Rath's analysis of the unfavorable contribution results in terms of its completeness and its effect on the behavior of the production groups.

(CMA Adapted)

13–63 **Changes of Standards** NuLathe Co. produces a turbo engine component for jet aircraft manufacturers. It has used a standard costing system for years with good results.

Unfortunately, NuLathe recently experienced production problems. The source for its direct materials went out of business. The new source produces similar but higher quality materials. The price per pound from the old source averaged $7.00; the price from the new source is $7.77. The use of the new materials results in a reduction in scrap that lowers the actual consumption of direct materials from 1.25 to 1.00 pounds per unit. In addition, the direct labor decreased from 24 to 22 minutes per unit because of less scrap labor and machine setup time.

The direct materials problem occurred when labor negotiations resulted in an increase of more than 14 percent in hourly direct labor costs. The average rate rose from $12.60 per hour to $14.40 per hour. Production of the main product requires a high level of skilled labor. Because of a continuing shortage in that skill area, NuLathe had to sign an interim wage agreement.

NuLathe began using the new direct materials on April 1 of this year, the same day the new labor agreement went into effect. The firm had been using standards set at the beginning of the calendar year. The direct materials and direct labor standards for the turbo engine are as follows:

Direct materials 1.2 lbs. @ $6.80/lb.	$ 8.16
Direct labor 20 min. @ $12.30 DLH	4.10
Standard prime cost per unit	$12.26

Howard Foster, cost accounting supervisor, had been examining the following performance report that he had prepared at the close of business on April 30. Jane Keene, assistant controller, came into Howard's office. He said, "Jane, look at this performance report. Direct materials price increased 11 percent and the labor rate increased over 14 percent during April. I expected larger variances, but prime costs decreased over 5 percent from the $13.79 we experienced during the first quarter of this year. The proper message just isn't coming through."

"This has been an unusual period," Jane said. "With the unforeseen changes, perhaps we should revise our standards based on current conditions and start over."

Howard replied, "I think we can retain the current standards but expand the variance analysis. We could calculate variances for the specific changes that have occurred to direct materials and direct labor before we calculate the normal price and quantity variances. What I really think would be useful to management right now is to determine the impact the changes in direct labor had in reducing our prime costs per unit from $13.79 in the first quarter to $13.05 in April—a reduction of $0.74."

NULATHE CO.
Analysis of Unit Prime Costs
Standard Cost Variance Analysis for April

	Standard	Price Variance	Quantity Variance	Actual
Direct materials	$6.8 × 1.2 = $8.16	($7.77 − $6.80) × 1.0 = $0.97 U	(1.0 − 1.2) × $6.8 = $1.36 F	$7.77 × 1.0 = $7.77
Direct labor	$12.3 × 0.33 = $4.10	($14.4 − $12.3) × 22/60 = $0.77 U	(22/60 − 20/60) × $12.30 = $0.41 U	$14.4 × 22/60 = $5.28
	$12.26			$13.05

Comparison of Actual Costs

	First Quarter	April	Percentage
Direct materials	$ 8.75	$ 7.77	(11.2)%
Direct labor	5.04	5.28	4.8
Total	$13.79	$13.05	(5.4)%

Required

1. Discuss the advantages of immediately revising the standards and retaining the current standards and expanding the analysis of variances.

2. Prepare an analysis that reflects the impact of the new direct materials supplier and the new labor contract on reducing NuLathe Co.'s costs per unit from $13.79 in the first quarter to $13.05 in April. This analysis should be in sufficient detail to identify the changes due to the direct materials price, the direct labor rate, the effect of direct materials quality on direct materials usage, and the effect of direct materials quality on direct labor usage. The analysis should show the changes in costs per unit due to the following.

   a. Use of the direct materials from new suppliers.

   b. The new labor contract.

(CMA Adapted)

13–64 **Standard Cost in Process Costing; All Variances and Journal Entries**   Dash Company adopted a standard costing system several years ago. The standard costs for the prime costs of its single product are

Material	(8 kilograms × $5.00/kg)	$40.00
Labor	(6 hours × $8.20/hr.)	$49.20

All materials are added at the beginning of processing. These operating data were taken from the records for November:

In-process beginning inventory	none
In-process ending inventory	800 Units, 75 percent complete as to labor
Units completed	5,600 Units
Budgeted output	6,000 Units
Purchases of materials	50,000 Kilograms
Total actual labor costs	$300,760
Actual hours of labor	36,500 Hours
Materials usage variance	$1,500 Unfavorable
Total materials variance	$750 Unfavorable

Required

1. Compute for November:
   a. The labor efficiency variance.
   b. The labor rate variance.

c. The actual number of kilograms of material used in the production process during the month.

d. The actual price paid per kilogram of material during the month.

e. The total amounts of material and labor cost transferred to the finished goods account.

f. The total amount of material and labor cost in the ending balance of work-in-process inventory at the end of November.

2. Prepare journal entries to record all transactions including the variances in requirement 1.

(CMA Adapted)

13–65 **Joint Direct Materials Variances** Benderboard produces corrugated board containers that the nearby wine industry uses to package wine in bulk. Benderboard buys kraft paper by the ton, converts it to heavy-duty paperboard on its corrugator, and then cuts and glues it into folding boxes. The boxes are opened and filled with a plastic liner and then with the wine.

Many other corrugated board converters are in the area and competition is strong. Benderboard is eager to keep its costs under control. The firm has used a standard cost system for several years. Responsibility for variances has been established. For example, the purchasing agent was responsible for the raw materials price variance, and the general supervisor answered for the raw materials usage variance.

Recently, the industrial engineer and the accountant participated in a workshop sponsored by the Institute of Management Accountants at which there was some discussion of variance analysis. They noted that the workshop proposed that the responsibility for some variances was properly dual. The accountant and engineer reviewed their system and were not sure how to adapt the new information to it.

The firm has the following standards for its raw materials:

Standard direct raw materials per gross of finished boxes at 4½ tons of Kraft paper at $10 per ton = $45.00

During May, the accountant assembled the following data about raw materials:

Finished product: 5,000 gross of boxes
Actual cost of raw materials during month: $300,000 for 25,000 tons
Direct raw materials put into production (used): 25,000 tons
Benderboard began and finished the month of May with no inventory

---

Required Determine the following for Benderboard:

1. Direct materials price variance.
2. Direct materials efficiency (usage) variance.
3. Direct materials joint variance.

(CMA Adapted)

13–66 **Flexible Budget and Variances** Phoenix Management helps rental property owners find renters and charges the owners one-half of the first month's rent for this service. For August 2006, Phoenix expects to find renters for 100 apartments with an average first month's rent of $700. Budgeted cost data per tenant application for 2006 follow:

- Professional labor: 1.5 hours at $20 per hour.
- Credit checks: $50.

Phoenix expects other costs, including a lease payment for the building, secretarial help, and utilities, to be $3,000 per month. On average, Phoenix is successful in placing one tenant for every three applicants.

Actual rental applications in August 2006 were 270. Phoenix paid $9,500 for 400 hours of professional labor. Credit checks went up to $55 per application. Other support costs in August 2006 were $3,600. The average first monthly rentals for August 2006 were $800 per apartment unit for 90 units.

Required

1. Compute the operating income flexible budget and sales volume variances for Phoenix's operations in August 2006.

2. Determine the professional labor rate and efficiency variances for August 2006.

3. What nonfinancial factors should Phoenix consider in evaluating the effectiveness and efficiency of professional labor?

13–67 **Acquisition Costs**   Amy Booker is the newly appointed manager of the consumer electronics division of Price Mart. Price Mart has several hundred retail stores in the United States, Canada, and Mexico. Amy has just come back from a tour of the division's suppliers in other countries including several potential suppliers in emerging countries.

Amy is pondering using companies in emerging countries as suppliers for some of Price Mart's most popular electronic products. Switching to these suppliers will greatly enhance the firm's competitive position. By changing, the firm can reduce the purchase cost of a popular MP3 player, for example, from $12 to $8. The firm's standard acquisition cost for this MP3 player is $11 per unit. Amy's predecessor tried and could never meet the standard.

Price Mart relies heavily on data from its standard cost system in performance evaluations. Amy knows that she could become CEO of the company in two years if she is successful in running the division.

Two companies, Free Enterprise and Continental Electronic, have agreed to sell up to 1 million MP3 players at $8, F.O.B. shipping point. Amy, however, is somewhat uncomfortable in doing business with both companies. In its recent annual report, Amnesty International described most of Free Enterprise's workers are prisoners. Continental Electronic is a state-owned company whose president demands as a sales term that an additional 1 percent be deposited in a "scholarship" fund account he has set up at a small bank in New York City.

Required

1. What variances might be reported if Amy purchases MP3 players from either of these two companies?

2. What ethical issues do Amy and Price Mart face in preparing variance reports?

13–68 **Price Variance**   Applied Materials Science (AMS) purchases its materials from several countries. As part of its cost control program, AMS uses a standard cost system for all aspects of its operations including materials purchases. The firm establishes standard costs for materials at the beginning of each fiscal year.

Pat Butch, the purchasing manager, is happy with the result of the year just ended. He believes that the purchase price variance for the year will be favorable and is very confident that his department has at least met the standard prices. The preliminary report from the controller's office confirms his jubilation. This is a portion of the preliminary report:

Total quantity purchased	36,000 kilograms
Average price per kilogram	$50
Standard price per kilogram	$60
Budgeted quantity per quarter	4,000 kilograms

In the fourth quarter, the purchasing department increased purchases from the budgeted normal volume of 4,000 to 24,000 kilograms to meet the increased demands, which was a result of the firm's unexpected success in a fiercely competitive bidding. The substantial increase in the volume to be purchased forced the purchasing department to search for alternative suppliers. After frantic searches, it found suppliers in several foreign countries that could meet the firm's needs and could provide materials with higher quality than that of AMS's regular supplier. The purchasing department, however, was very reluctant to make the purchase because the negotiated price was $76 per kilogram including shipping and import duty.

The actual cost of the purchases, however, was much lower because of currency devaluations before deliveries began, which was a result of the financial turmoil of several countries in the region.

Patricia Rice, the controller, does not share the purchasing department's euphoria. She is fully aware of the following quarterly purchases:

	First Quarter	Second Quarter	Third Quarter	Fourth Quarter
Quantity	4,000	4,000	4,000	24,000
Purchase price (per kilogram)	$68	$69	$73	?

Required

1. Calculate price variances for the fourth quarter and for the year. How much of the price variance is attributable to changes in foreign currency exchange rates?
2. Evaluate the purchasing department's performance.

13-69 **Direct Materials and Direct Labor Variances, Working Backwards** Cintani Industries makes laminated architectural panels, walkways, and canopies. The company's main products are the laminated panels for interior and exterior walls. A typical laminated panel consists of two layers of aluminum with one or more layers of other materials in between. The manufacturing process begins with mills grinding glass to a thin powder. Meanwhile, coils of thin aluminum are rolled over an open flame to remove impurities. The glass powder is then applied to the aluminum and fused in a 1,100-degree oven—hot enough to melt the glass and open the microscopic pores of the aluminum—to create a permanent finish that will never come off.

Cintani uses a standard cost system to account for manufacturing costs. The standard costs for a unit of PAP, a graffiti-resistant porcelain-on-aluminum panel popular with school districts, include the following:

Direct materials (6 lbs. at $5 per pound)	$30.00
Direct labor (2/3 hour at $30 per hour)	20.00
Manufacturing overhead (ABC-based)	10.00
	$60.00

At the end of May, the ledgers show the following data:

	Debit	Credit
Sales		$500,000
Accounts payable for purchases of direct materials		136,500
Direct materials price variance	$ 6,500	
Direct materials usage variance	5,000	
Direct labor rate variance	4,200	
Direct labor efficiency variance		6,000

The firm pays all its purchases in the month following the purchases. There is no beginning direct materials inventory on May 1. The firm manufactured and sold 4,500 units in May. All variances are identified and recorded at the earliest possible time.

Required Compute each of the following items for the firm for the month of May. Show all your computations.

1. Total standard direct labor cost.
2. Total direct labor hours worked.
3. Actual direct labor hourly wage rate.
4. Total standard quantity of direct materials for the panels manufactured.
5. Total direct materials used.
6. Total direct materials purchased.
7. Actual direct materials price per pound.

Solutions to Self-Study Problems

1. Sales Volumes and Flexible Budget Variances
   1. Master and flexible budgets

	Master Budget	Flexible Budget	
Units	10,000	9,500	11,000
Sales	$540,000	$513,000	$594,000

Variable costs			
Direct materials	$126,000	$119,700	$138,600
Direct labor	77,000	73,150	84,700
Variable manufacturing overheads	20,000	19,000	22,000
Variable selling and administrative expenses	50,000	47,500	55,000
Total variable cost	$273,000	$259,350	$300,300
Contribution margin	$267,000	$253,650	$293,700
Fixed costs			
Manufacturing costs	$ 55,000	$ 55,000	$ 55,000
Selling and administrative	24,000	24,000	24,000
Total fixed costs	$ 79,000	$ 79,000	$ 79,000
Operating income	$188,000	$174,650	$214,700

2. Operating income sales volume variance:

   $174,650 - $188,000 = $13,350$ Unfavorable

   Operating income flexible budget variance:

   $177,100 - $174,650 = $2,450$ Favorable

   Selling price variance $= $551,000 - $513,000 = $38,000$ Favorable

   Variable cost flexible budget variance:

   $294,900 - $259,350 = $35,550$ Unfavorable

3. Direct materials price variance, direct materials usage variance, direct rate variance, and direct labor efficiency variance

Direct Materials

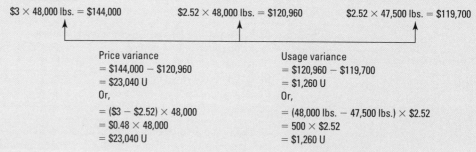

$3 \times 48,000$ lbs. $= $144,000$ $2.52 \times 48,000$ lbs. $= $120,960$ $2.52 \times 47,500$ lbs. $= $119,700$

Price variance
= $144,000 - $120,960
= $23,040 U
Or,
= ($3 - $2.52) × 48,000
= $0.48 × 48,000
= $23,040 U

Usage variance
= $120,960 - $119,700
= $1,260 U
Or,
= (48,000 lbs. - 47,500 lbs.) × $2.52
= 500 × $2.52
= $1,260 U

Direct Labor

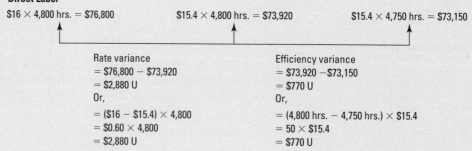

$16 \times 4,800$ hrs. $= $76,800$ $15.4 \times 4,800$ hrs. $= $73,920$ $15.4 \times 4,750$ hrs. $= $73,150$

Rate variance
= $76,800 - $73,920
= $2,880 U
Or,
= ($16 - $15.4) × 4,800
= $0.60 × 4,800
= $2,880 U

Efficiency variance
= $73,920 - $73,150
= $770 U
Or,
= (4,800 hrs. - 4,750 hrs.) × $15.4
= 50 × $15.4
= $770 U

2. Direct Materials Price and Usage Variances, Direct Labor Rate and Efficiency Variances, and Journal Entries

1.

Direct Materials—XF-2000

Total standard quantity of direct materials for the product manufactured (SQ)

= 100,000 bags × 25 pounds of XF-2000 per bag

= 2,500,000 pounds

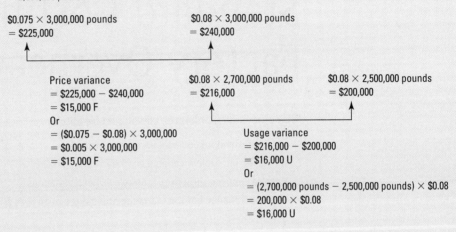

$0.075 × 3,000,000 pounds
= $225,000

$0.08 × 3,000,000 pounds
= $240,000

Price variance
= $225,000 − $240,000
= $15,000 F
Or
= ($0.075 − $0.08) × 3,000,000
= $0.005 × 3,000,000
= $15,000 F

$0.08 × 2,700,000 pounds
= $216,000

$0.08 × 2,500,000 pounds
= $200,000

Usage variance
= $216,000 − $200,000
= $16,000 U
Or
= (2,700,000 pounds − 2,500,000 pounds) × $0.08
= 200,000 × $0.08
= $16,000 U

Direct Labor

Actual wage rate per direct labor-hour (AR)

= $182,000 ÷ 5,200 hours

= $35 per hour

Total standard direct labor-hours for the product manufactured (SH)

= 100,000 bags × 0.05 hours per bag

= 5,000 hours

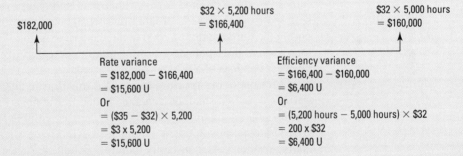

$182,000

$32 × 5,200 hours
= $166,400

$32 × 5,000 hours
= $160,000

Rate variance
= $182,000 − $166,400
= $15,600 U
Or
= ($35 − $32) × 5,200
= $3 x 5,200
= $15,600 U

Efficiency variance
= $166,400 − $160,000
= $6,400 U
Or
= (5,200 hours − 5,000 hours) × $32
= 200 x $32
= $6,400 U

2.

Materials inventory (3,000,000 × $0.08)	240,000	
Materials purchase price variance (3,000,000 × $0.005)		15,000
Accounts payable (3,000,000 × $0.075)		225,000
Purchased 3,000,000 pounds of XF–2000 at $0.075/per pound from Johnson Chemical Suppliers.		
Work-in-process inventory ($0.08 × 2,500,000)	200,000	
Materials usage variance (200,000 × $0.08)	16,000	
Materials inventory (2,700,000 × $0.08)		216,000
Issued 2,700,000 pounds of XF–2000 for the production of 100,000 bags of Weed-Be-Doom.		
Work-in-process inventory (5,000 × $32)	160,000	
Labor rate variance (5,200 × $3)	15,600	
Labor efficiency variance (200 × $32)	6,400	
Accrued payroll (5,200 × $35)		182,000
Direct labor wages for the manufacturing of 100,000 bags of Weed-Be-Doom for 5,200 hours at $35 per hour.		

CHAPTER FOURTEEN

Standard Costing: Factory Overhead

After studying this chapter, you should be able to . . .

1. Establish standard costs for variable overhead
2. Calculate and explain variable overhead variances
3. Compute and interpret fixed factory overhead variances
4. Use two-variance or three-variance procedures to analyze and interpret factory overhead variances
5. Dispose of variances in financial accounting systems
6. Apply standard costs to service organizations
7. Analyze and explain the variances in an activity-based standard cost system
8. Describe the effects of advances in new manufacturing technologies and changes in operating environments on standard cost systems
9. Determine whether to investigate variances

"The third quarter was a difficult period for United. Revenue performance suffered significantly from the operational disruptions we experienced throughout the quarter," James Goodwin, United Airlines chairman and chief executive, said.[1] United (UAL) suffered from thousands of labor and weather-related flight cancellations and delays during the third quarter of 2000 while the airline negotiated a labor contract with its pilots. The earnings per share for the quarter decreased from a profit of $2.89 the previous year to a loss of $1.29.

UAL's operating results experienced this drastic change although the decrease in traffic was only a small percentage of total traffic during the third quarter of 2000. As it is for other companies with high fixed costs, volume is a critical success factor for UAL. Fluctuations in traffic volume at UAL often explain the bulk of changes in operating results. UAL constantly monitors volume variance or passenger-miles variance, which measures the effect that deviations in actual volume (passenger miles) from the budget or planned level have on operation results. The goal to have minimum disruptions to planned operations and to achieve or exceed the expected operation level leads airlines to constantly seek to get that last passenger on board through price restructuring or other maneuvers.

Firms with high fixed costs experience wide variations in operating results when their levels of operation fluctuate. Management of these firms monitor business volumes closely and attempt the best they can to reduce fluctuations in business activities. This chapter examines production volume and other overhead-related variances that organizations use to monitor operations to gain better control and improve operating results.

A man should never be ashamed to own that he has been in the wrong, which is but saying in other words, that he is wiser today than yesterday.

Jonathan Swift

---

[1] "UAL to Post Loss to 3rd Period, Probably for 4th," *The Wall Street Journal*, October 2, 2000, p. A12.

Although reporting a variance in a standard cost system is not analogous to saying that something is wrong in the operation, it is true that one important function of a standard cost system is to help firms to attain better operating results. In Chapter 13, we discussed the basic concepts of a standard cost system, its applications to direct materials and direct labor, and the recording of standard costs. Building on that knowledge, we extend the application of the standard cost system to variable and fixed overheads. In addition, we examine further the effects that recent advances in manufacturing technologies and rapid changes in operating environments have had on the use of standard cost systems.

Standard Costs for Factory Overhead

LEARNING OBJECTIVE 1
Establish standard costs for variable overhead.

Variable factory overhead costs are costs of energy, lubricants, soaps in factory washrooms, glue used in products, maintenance labors, equipment repairs, and maintenance, among others. It is not unusual for a factory to have hundreds of variable factory overheads, all of them small amounts. As with direct materials or direct labor costs, the amount of variable factory overhead varies with the activity of the firm, and the procedure for analyzing variable factory overhead variances is similar to the procedures for analyzing direct materials or direct labor variances.

Fixed factory overhead costs include costs such as salaries for factory managers and plant security guards, depreciation expenses for equipment and factory buildings, and insurance and property taxes for factory buildings and equipment. Because fixed factory overheads have different cost behavior patterns than those of variable factory overhead, the procedure for analyzing each is different.

Standard Cost for Variable Factory Overhead

Adopting a standard cost system for variable factory overheads includes establishing standard variable factory overhead costs, using the standard to monitor and control variable factory overhead costs during operations, and assessing operations based on the standard.

Steps in Establishing the Standard Cost for Variable Factory Overhead

Establishing the standard variable factory overhead cost for an operation involves four steps:

1. Determining the behavioral patterns of variable factory overhead costs.
2. Selecting one or more appropriate activity measures for applying variable factory overhead to cost objects such as products, services, or divisions.
3. Choosing the levels of operation and estimating the total variable factory overhead and the total amount of the selected activity measure.
4. Computing the standard variable factory overhead rate.

Step 1: Determining the Behavioral Patterns of Variable Factory Overheads
A manufacturing process often has many variable factory overhead items. Most variable factory overheads are small in amount. Although the amount of variable factory overhead changes as the firm's activity changes, not all variable factory overhead items vary at the same rates or with the same activity. For example, as a furniture manufacturer produces more furniture, more sandpaper is used. The quantity of sandpaper used in a period is likely to vary in proportion to the number of pieces of furniture manufactured. Oil for machinery is also likely to increase as a factory operates more hours or manufactures more units. However, the amount of oil used can be a step function. If, say, a machine needs one quart of fresh oil for every 25 units processed, the increase in oil cost occurs in discrete steps rather than in direct proportion to the units produced, as it does for sandpaper. Exhibit 14.1 illustrates one such overhead pattern. Other variable factory overhead items can have widely divergent variation rates, patterns, or manufacturing activities.

EXHIBIT 14.1
Amount of Oil Needed for a
Lathe Machine

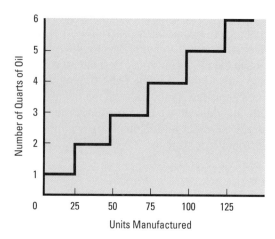

Changes in some variable factory overhead costs, however, are not due entirely to changes in manufacturing activity. Some overhead costs change as result of management decisions. Setup cost is an example of these costs. A manufacturer incurs a $5,000 setup cost to produce 10,000 units if it processes 10,000 units in one batch. The setup cost increases to, say, $9,800 if the firm manufactures the 10,000 units in two batches, and to $14,000 in three batches.

In general, the standard variable factory overhead for a manufacturing operation is a function of the number of units manufactured and other manufacturing activities. The first step in determining standard costs for variable factory overhead costs is to understand cost behavioral patterns of variable factory overhead costs. Because a number of different activities influence variable factory overhead costs, firms need to carefully select the most appropriate activity measure or measures as the base(s) for standard variable overhead rate(s). Selection of appropriate activity measures enhances the usefulness of the standard cost system as a management tool in planning and control of operations. These activity measures can be volume based or activity based.

Step 2: Selecting Activity Measures to Apply Variable Factory Overheads to Cost Objects An operation usually has a vast number of variable factory overheads involving many different usage patterns. Finding a single activity measure whose behavioral pattern conforms to all the variable factory overheads of an operation is an impossible task. One solution is to use a different activity measure for each variable overhead that has a different behavioral pattern. Such a solution is not likely to be justifiable in view of its complexity and implementation cost.

Many firms use a single activity measure, such as direct labor-hours or direct labor cost, as the activity measure for applying variable factory overhead. This practice is satisfactory so long as the total variable factory overhead is small or it relates to the selected activity measure. The increasing importance of factory overhead and the decreasing amount of direct labor-hours in many operations in recent years, however, have led many firms to reexamine this conventional practice. Their efforts to find more appropriate activity measures have led to increased uses of activity-related factory overhead measures.

An activity-based cost measure applies factory overheads to products or services based on activities involved in manufacturing operations. Using activity-based factory overhead cost measures requires identifying activities that cause factory overhead costs to change. Items that change with similar activities are grouped together.

Cooper identifies activities that change the amount of factory overhead as unit-based, batch-based, product-based, and facility-based factory overhead.[2] Unit-based

[2] Robin Cooper, "Cost Classification in Unit-Based and Activity-Based Manufacturing Cost Systems," *Journal of Cost Management for the Manufacturing Industry*, Fall 1990, pp. 4–14.

EXHIBIT 14.2
Standard Cost Sheet

SCHMIDT MACHINERY COMPANY
Standard Cost Sheet
Product Number: XV–1

Description	Quantity	Unit Cost	Subtotal	Total
Direct materials				
Aluminum	4 pounds	$25	$100	
PVC	1 pound	40	40	$140
Direct labor	5 hours	40		200
Factory overhead (based on 5,000 direct labor-hours)				
Variable	5 hours	12	60	
Fixed	5 hours	24	120	180
Standard cost per unit				$520

activity measures include machine-hours, direct labor-hours, and units of materials. Batch-based activity measures include the number of times materials and parts are moved during manufacturing, the number of setups, and the number of times that materials and parts are received and inspected. Product-based activity measures include the number of products, number of processes, and number of schedule changes. Facility-based activity measures primarily relate to the size of operations, not production activities.[3]

For simplicity of illustration, the early part of this chapter uses a single activity measure, direct labor-hour. A later example uses multiple activity measures for variable factory overhead. Exhibit 14.2 is the standard cost sheet of Schmidt Machinery Company originally presented as Exhibit 13.5. This standard cost sheet shows that the firm applies variable factory overhead at the rate of $12 per direct labor-hour.

Step 3: Choosing the Level of Operation and Estimating the Total Variable Factory Overhead and the Total Activity of the Selected Activity Measure   Activity measures for different variable factory overhead items can be diverse. Furthermore, a variable overhead and its activity measure do not always change at a constant rate at different operating levels. Before the standard variable factory overhead rate can be determined, firms must determine their expected level of operation and estimate the total variable factory overhead and the total amount for the selected activity for applying variable overhead at the expected level of operation.

Schmidt plans to manufacture 1,000 units. At 1,000 units, the accountant estimates the total variable factory overhead to be $60,000 and the total amount of the selected activity for applying variable overhead, direct labor-hours, to be 5,000 hours.

Step 4: Computing the Standard Variable Factory Overhead Rate   A standard variable factory overhead rate is determined by dividing the amount of the selected activity for applying variable factory overhead into the estimated total variable factory overhead.[4] Schmidt's accountant determines the standard variable factory overhead rate by dividing the estimated (budgeted) total variable factory overhead, $60,000, by the estimated (budgeted) direct labor-hours, 5,000, to arrive at the standard variable factory overhead rate of $12 per direct labor-hour.

---

[3] Robert D. McIlhattan, "How Cost Management Systems Can Support the JIT Philosophy," *Management Accounting,* September 1987, pp. 20–26.

[4] An alternative procedure is to use a multiple regression analysis discussed in Chapter 6 to determine the standard variable factory overhead rates. Uses of multiple regression analysis permit incorporations of multiple activity measures that affect the amount of variable factory overhead in determining the standard variable factory overhead rates. For example, a firm may include several measures of activity—machine-hours, labor-hours, number of setups, number of parts, and other relevant activity measures that drive variable factory overhead—in determining its standard variable factory overheads.

Exhibit 14.3 summarizes the steps for determining the standard variable factory overhead rate for an operation.

Analyzing Variable Factory Overhead

LEARNING OBJECTIVE 2
Calculate and explain variable overhead variances.

Firms use standard variable factory overhead rate(s) to monitor, control, evaluate, and analyze variable factory overheads in operations. This section examines uses of the standard variable factory overhead and determinations of variable factory overhead variances.

Determining the Total Variable Factory Overhead Variance

The difference between the total variable factory overhead incurred and the total standard variable factory overhead for the output (manufactured) of a period is the **total variable factory overhead variance** of the period. The total standard variable factory overhead for the output (manufactured) of a period also is the flexible budget variable factory overhead for the units manufactured during the period. Some companies refer to total variable factory overhead variance as *variable factory overhead flexible budget variance*.

The **total variable factory overhead variance** of a period is the difference between the total actual variable factory overhead incurred during operation and total standard variable factory overhead for the output of the period.

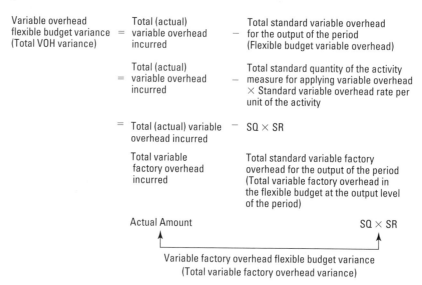

Schmidt Machinery Company incurred a total of $40,630 variable factory overhead cost and spent 3,510 direct labor-hours to manufacture 780 units of XV–1 in October

EXHIBIT 14.3
Steps in Determining the Standard Variable Factory Overhead Rate

Step	Example
1. Determine the behavioral patterns of variable factory overhead.	Management must understand cost behavior patterns.
2. Select the activity measure for applying total variable factory overhead to cost objects.	The firm chose to use direct labor-hours as the basis to apply variable factory overheads to cost objects and estimated that the total direct labor to manufacture 1,000 units requires 5,000 direct labor-hours.
3. Choose the level of operation and estimate the total variable factory overhead and the total amount of the selected activity.	The management accountant estimated that the total variable factory overhead to manufacture 1,000 units is $60,000.
4. Compute the standard variable factory overhead rate.	Divide the total variable factory overhead identified in step 3 ($60,000) by the number of direct labor-hours in step 2 (5,000) to obtain the standard variable factory overhead rate ($12 per direct labor-hour).

EXHIBIT 14.4
Variable Factory Overhead Flexible Budget Variance

SCHMIDT MACHINERY COMPANY	
Variable Factory Overhead Flexible Budget Variance	
For October 2005	
Total standard variable factory overhead:	
1. Units manufactured	780 units
2. Standard quantity of the activity measure for applying variable factory overhead for the units manufactured	
a. Activity measure for applying variable factory overhead	Direct labor-hours
b. Standard quantity of the activity measure per unit	× 5 Direct labor-hours
c. Total standard quantity of the activity measure for the units manufactured	3,900 Direct labor-hours
3. Standard variable overhead rate	× $12 per direct labor-hour
4. Total standard variable overhead	$46,800
Total variable factory overhead incurred	40,630
Variable factory overhead flexible budget variances	$ 6,170 F

2005. The amount of the total variable factory overhead incurred is determined by finding the sum of the amounts in the subsidiary ledgers for all items pertaining to variable factory overhead.

The total standard variable factory overhead for 780 units manufactured during the period is $46,800, as shown in Exhibit 14.4. You may notice that the procedure shown in Exhibit 14.4 to determine the total standard variable factory overhead is similar to those of determining the total standard costs for direct materials or direct labor costs. One notable exception is that the total standard variable factory overhead is determined based on a substitute activity measure for the variable factory overhead, instead of an activity measure of the variable factory overhead item itself.

Schmidt's accountant determines the total standard variable factory overhead for the period by first calculating the total standard direct labor-hours (the activity measure Schmidt Machinery Company uses to apply variable factory overheads) for the output of the period, 780 units of XV–1.

Schmidt manufactured 780 units of XV–1 in October 2005. At 5 direct labor-hours for each unit of XV–1 manufactured, the total standard direct labor-hours for the units manufactured in October is 3,900. Schmidt's accountant has determined the standard variable factory overhead rate to be $12 per direct labor-hour. The total standard variable factory overhead for its operations in October, therefore, is $46,800 (3,900 hours × $12 per hour).

The difference between the total variable factory overhead incurred and the total standard variable factory overhead for the units manufactured is the *variable factory overhead flexible budget variance*. Schmidt Machinery Company incurred a total variable factory overhead of $40,630 in its operations during October 2005. The total standard variable factory overhead for the output of the period as calculated based on the standard activity measure for applying standard variable factory overhead, 3,900 standard direct labor-hours for the 780 units manufactured, is $46,800, as shown in step 4 of Exhibit 14.4. The variable factory overhead flexible budget variance, therefore, is $6,170, favorable ($46,800 − $40,630).

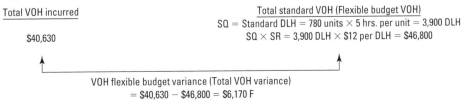

Managers commonly refer to variable factory overhead flexible budget variances as *overapplied* if they are favorable or *underapplied* if they are unfavorable. In October 2005, Schmidt Machinery Company has an overapplied (favorable) variable factory overhead of $6,170.

Further Analysis of the Variable Factory Overhead Flexible Budget Variance Some firms analyze the variable factory overhead flexible budget variance further into two components: spending and efficiency variances. **Variable factory overhead spending variance** is the difference between variable factory overhead incurred and the total standard variable factory overhead for the actual quantity of the activity measure for applying variable factory overhead.

> **Variable factory overhead spending variance**
>
> is the difference between variable factory overhead incurred and the total standard variable factory overhead for the actual quantity of the activity measure for applying the variable factory overhead.

$$\begin{array}{l} \text{Variable} \\ \text{overhead} \\ \text{spending} \\ \text{variance} \end{array} = \begin{array}{l} \text{Total} \\ \text{variable} \\ \text{overhead} \\ \text{incurred} \end{array} - \left[\begin{array}{l} \text{Actual quantity of} \\ \text{activity measure} \\ \text{for applying} \\ \text{variable overhead} \end{array} \times \begin{array}{l} \text{Standard variable overhead} \\ \text{rate per unit of the activity} \\ \text{measure for applying} \\ \text{variable overhead} \end{array} \right]$$

$$= \text{Actual VOH} - \text{AQ} \times \text{SR}$$

Variable factory overhead efficiency variance is the difference between the total standard variable factory overhead for the actual quantity of the activity measure for applying standard variable overhead and the standard variable factory overhead for the output of the period.

> **Variable factory overhead efficiency variance**
>
> is the difference between the total standard variable factory overhead for the actual quantity of the activity measure for applying variable factory overhead and the total standard variable factory overhead cost for the units manufactured during the period.

$$\begin{array}{l} \text{Variable} \\ \text{overhead} \\ \text{efficiency} \\ \text{variance} \end{array} = \left[\begin{array}{l} \text{Actual quantity of} \\ \text{activity measure} \\ \text{for applying} \\ \text{variable overhead} \end{array} - \begin{array}{l} \text{Total standard} \\ \text{quantity of activity} \\ \text{measure for the} \\ \text{output attained} \end{array} \right] \times \begin{array}{l} \text{Standard variable overhead} \\ \text{rate per unit of activity} \\ \text{measure for applying} \\ \text{variable overhead} \end{array}$$

$$= (\text{AQ} - \text{SQ}) \times \text{SR}$$

The sum of variable factory overhead spending variance and variable factory overhead efficiency variance is the variable factory overhead flexible budget variance, or simply total variable factory overhead variance.

$$\begin{array}{c} \text{Variable factory overhead} \\ \text{flexible budget variance} \\ \text{(Total variable factory} \\ \text{overhead variance)} \end{array} = \begin{array}{c} \text{Variable factory} \\ \text{overhead} \\ \text{spending} \\ \text{variance} \end{array} + \begin{array}{c} \text{Variable factory} \\ \text{overhead} \\ \text{efficiency} \\ \text{variance} \end{array}$$

Exhibit 14.5 illustrates this procedure using the October 2005 operating data of Schmidt Machinery Company. Schmidt uses direct labor-hours to apply variable factory overhead to cost objects. Further analyses of its variable factory overhead flexible budget variances are based on the number of direct labor-hours.

The procedures to further analyze variable factory overhead flexible budget variances are similar to those for analyzing direct materials or direct labor flexible budget variances. The procedures differ, however, in the activity measure of the cost item being analyzed. Further analyses of direct materials or direct labor flexible budget variance use a direct measure of the cost item. In contrast, there is no single direct measure for variable factory overheads because the total variable factory overhead is the sum of many overhead activities: inspection, setup, materials handling, and so forth. The amounts of these variable factory overheads are likely to vary with levels of different activities. For example, indirect materials cost may vary with the number of units manufactured; factory electricity may be a function of units manufactured, number of machines, number of hours operated, and/or number of square feet of the factory; indirect labor costs may change with the number of setups and/or the number of units.

Schmidt Machinery Company spent 3,510 direct labor-hours in October 2005. At the standard rate of $12 per hour, the standard variable factory overhead for the direct labor-hours spent is $42,120, as shown in point B of Exhibit 14.5. Using this amount, we can separate the variable factory overhead flexible budget variance into two components. The difference between the variable factory overhead incurred, point A, and the total standard variable factory overhead for the actual quantity of the activity

EXHIBIT 14.5
Analysis of Variable
Overhead Variances

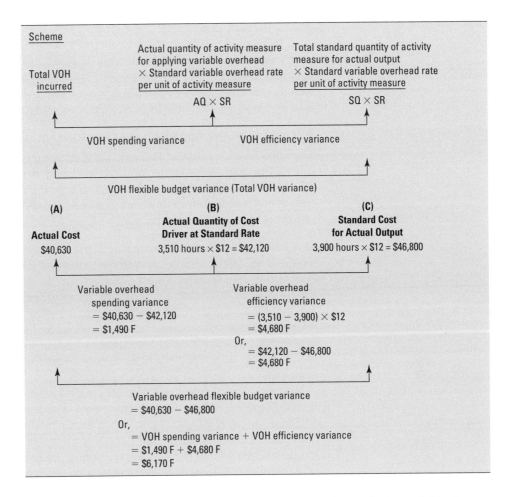

measure for applying the variable factory overhead, point B, is the variable factory overhead spending variance. This is $1,490, favorable. The difference between point B and the total standard variable factory overhead for the output of the period, point C, is the variable factory overhead efficiency variance, $4,680, favorable.

Differences between Variable Factory Overhead Variances and Direct Cost Variances

Although the procedures for analyzing variable factory overhead costs are similar to those for analyzing direct materials or direct labor variances described in Chapter 13, implications of variable factory overhead variances differ for two reasons. First, in addition to varying with volume, the total variable factory overhead cost may vary with activities that change categorically or at intervals such as number of production runs, number of batches, and type of products. In contrast, total direct materials or total direct labor costs vary in proportion to changes in production volume.[5]

Second, firms use a single activity measure (cost driver) such as pounds of materials or hours of direct labor to assign direct materials or direct labor costs to cost objects. In contrast, a firm can use two or more activity measures to assign factory overhead costs to cost objects because of the many different overhead activities involved. In fact, many firms find that assigning variable factory overhead with two more properly selected activity measures yields better cost assignments.

Some managers perceive the amount of work needed to maintain a multiple activity measures costing system exceeds the benefit derived from using the system. As a result, these firms assign factory overhead to cost objects by using a single activity measure such as direct labor-hours, machine-hours, direct material cost, or other easily identifiable factory activities. When a single activity measure is used for a number of overhead activities, however, the relationship between factory overhead and the

[5] Exceptions are firms with guaranteed wages or employment. The guaranteed portions of labor costs are fixed costs.

activity measure is not perfect. The amount of factory overhead incurred per machine-hour, for example, can vary from 1 cent to $5, depending on what transpires during the hour measured, although the firm applies, say, $2 of factory overhead per machine-hour to cost objects. The imperfect relationships can have significant effects on the results of variance analysis for factory overhead. As Chapter 5 points out, uses of activity-based costing yield more accurate cost assignments.

Interpretation and Implications of Variable Factory Overhead Variances

The imperfect relationships between variable factory overheads and the activity measures a firm uses to assign these variable factory overheads to cost objects mandate careful interpretations of variable factory overhead variances. The meaning and implications of variable factory overhead variances are not the same as those for direct materials or direct labor variances.

Variable Factory Overhead Spending Variance Determinations of variable factory overhead spending variances are similar to those of direct materials price variances or direct labor rate variances. Direct materials price or direct labor rate variances measure the effect on manufacturing cost of differences in prices between the actual price paid and the standard price for the cost element. All effects of differences in quantities are reflected by usage or efficiency variances for direct materials or direct labor costs. The same cannot be said for variable overhead spending variances. In addition to the effects of differences in prices a variable factory overhead spending variance can contain some or all the effects of differences in quantities.

Assume, for example, that a firm uses machine-hours to apply variable factory overheads. The standard calls for 1 machine-hour with 2 ounces of oil per machine-hour at $2.50 per ounce, or $5 per machine-hour, for the production of 10 units.[6] The firm used 6,000 machine-hours and 12,500 ounces of oil at a cost of $31,250 (12,500 × $2.50) to manufacture 55,000 units during the period just completed.

According to the standard, the manufacture of 55,000 units should have taken 5,500 machine-hours and 11,000 (2 × 5,500) ounces of oil. The accountant calculates variable factory overhead efficiency variances based on the difference in machine-hours because the firm uses machine-hours to apply variable factory overheads. The operation used 500 machine-hours more than the standard allowed for 55,000 units. At the standard application rate of $5 per machine-hour, the firm has an unfavorable efficiency variance of $2,500 (500 × $5), as shown in panel 1 of Exhibit 14.6. The efficiency variance represents the excess variable overhead costs that the firm would have incurred because of the excess number of machine-hours spent during the period.

The firm used 12,500 ounces of oil during the operation, an excess of 1,500 ounces over the standard for the units manufactured (given the standard of 2 ounces of oil for every 10 units, the total standard quantity of oil for 55,000 units manufactured during the period is 11,000 ounces). At the standard price of $2.50 per ounce, the efficiency variance would have been $3,750 unfavorable (1,500 ounces × $2.50 per ounce) using the procedure discussed in Chapter 13 for analyzing direct cost variances as shown in panel 2 of Exhibit 14.6.

Exhibit 14.6 shows that at least part of the variable factory overhead efficiency variance is included in the variable factory overhead spending variance. The difference between the actual quantity of oil used in the operation, 12,500 ounces, and the standard quantity of oil for the actual machine-hours operated, 12,000 ounces, is 500 ounces. At $2.50 standard price per ounce, the 500-ounce excess usage costs $1,250. Both the $1,250 and the $2,500 result from excess usage of oil. The $1,250, however, is included in the variable factory overhead spending variance when the variable factory overhead is analyzed based upon machine-hours as the activity measure for applying overheads. The inclusion of both the price variance and a portion of the efficiency

---

[6] The cost of oil is a direct cost if we know that the firm manufactures 10 units per machine-hour and uses 2 ounces of oil per machine-hour. The firm could treat the cost of oil as a direct cost if the cost is significant. However, the cost of oil needed to operate machinery is most likely insignificant and is, therefore, an overhead.

EXHIBIT 14.6

Inclusion of Variable Factory Overhead Efficiency Variance in Variable Factory Overhead Spending Variance

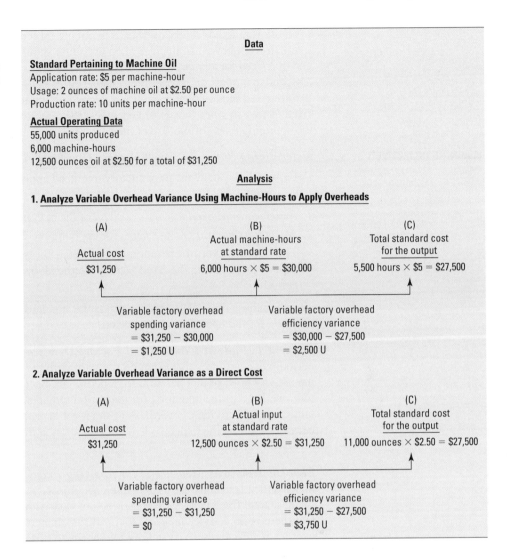

Data

Standard Pertaining to Machine Oil
Application rate: $5 per machine-hour
Usage: 2 ounces of machine oil at $2.50 per ounce
Production rate: 10 units per machine-hour

Actual Operating Data
55,000 units produced
6,000 machine-hours
12,500 ounces oil at $2.50 for a total of $31,250

Analysis

1. Analyze Variable Overhead Variance Using Machine-Hours to Apply Overheads

(A)	(B)	(C)
	Actual machine-hours at standard rate	Total standard cost for the output
Actual cost		
$31,250	6,000 hours × $5 = $30,000	5,500 hours × $5 = $27,500

Variable factory overhead
spending variance
= $31,250 − $30,000
= $1,250 U

Variable factory overhead
efficiency variance
= $30,000 − $27,500
= $2,500 U

2. Analyze Variable Overhead Variance as a Direct Cost

(A)	(B)	(C)
	Actual input at standard rate	Total standard cost for the output
Actual cost		
$31,250	12,500 ounces × $2.50 = $31,250	11,000 ounces × $2.50 = $27,500

Variable factory overhead
spending variance
= $31,250 − $31,250
= $0

Variable factory overhead
efficiency variance
= $31,250 − $27,500
= $3,750 U

variance in a variable factory overhead spending variance must be considered in interpreting the variance and determining its implications.

Variable Factory Overhead Efficiency Variance

Using a single activity measure to apply variable factory overhead also can render interpretations of variable factory overhead variances difficult because of the imperfect relationship between the chosen activity measure and variable factory overhead.

Each element of variable factory overhead (for example, lubricant, indirect labor, setup materials, or labor) often has a unique activity measure. The use of a single activity measure for all variable factory overheads imperfectly measures the usage (efficiency) variance for many of them. A firm can reduce or avoid the problem of imperfect measures of the chosen activity for usages of overheads by breaking the variable factory overhead into its elements, choosing an appropriate activity measure for each of the variable overhead cost elements, and calculating the spending and efficiency variances accordingly. Thus, if lubricant, indirect labor, and setup cost are significant variable factory overhead items, we would have a spending variance and an efficiency variance for each of these three elements rather than a single spending variance and a single efficiency variance for all variable factory overhead.

Standard Cost for Fixed Factory Overhead

Many firms include standard cost for fixed factory overhead in their standard cost system. One reason is that the GAAP requires full costing, including all variable and fixed costs, for financial reporting. Federal government procurements also mandate inclusion of all relevant fixed factory overheads in pricing for federal procurements. Furthermore, many firms believe that all costs of an operation should be included in the product cost and that fixed factory overhead costs are part of the cost of an operation and should be assigned to outputs of the operations. Other firms believe that using a standard cost system for fixed factory overhead allows them to determine whether their operations incur fixed factory overheads as expected, assess the effectiveness of their facilities, or weigh the appropriateness of the size of their facilities.

LEARNING OBJECTIVE 3
Compute and interpret fixed factory overhead variances.

Determining Standard Fixed Factory Overhead Application Rate

Determining the standard fixed factory overhead application rate involves three essential elements:

1. *Budgeted total fixed factory overhead* of the operation.
2. An *activity measure or* measures for applying the fixed factory overhead.
3. The normal level of operations as reflected by the quantity of the activity measure(s) for applying the fixed factory overhead, or the *denominator activity* for the period.

Together, these three elements determine the standard fixed factory overhead *application rate* for the operation of the period.

Element 1: Budgeted Total Fixed Factory Overhead   Fixed factory overheads are periodic expenditures that often do not vary with the activity level of a period. Once the activity level of an operation for a period has been determined, the total fixed factory overhead of the operation for the period remains relatively constant within a certain range of activities, regardless of the level at which the firm operated during the period. Based on the expected level of operation, a firm sets budgeted total fixed factory overheads.

Element 2: Activity Measure(s) for Applying Fixed Factory Overhead   Fixed factory overheads usually are assigned to cost objects via one or more activity measures. Because total fixed factory overheads do not vary with changes in activity levels, in effect there is no activity measure that reflects changes in the amount of fixed factory overheads.[7] To apply fixed factory overheads to products or processes, firms usually use the same activity measure that they use for applying variable factory overheads as the base for applying fixed factory overheads.

Denominator activity
is the desired or planned operating level that a firm uses to assign fixed overheads to cost objects or outputs.

Element 3: Denominator Activity   **Denominator activity** is the desired or planned operating level that a firm uses to assign fixed overheads to cost objects or outputs. A firm often expresses its denominator activity in quantity of the activity measure for applying fixed factory overhead. For example, the denominator activity for a firm will be 30,000 machine-hours if the firm plans to manufacture 10,000 units each period, has a standard of 3 machine-hours for each unit manufactured, and considers machine-hours to be an appropriate base for applying fixed factory overheads.

A **fixed factory overhead application rate**
is the rate at which a firm applies fixed overhead costs to cost objects.

Using these three elements, a firm determines its standard **fixed factory overhead application rate** by dividing the budgeted total fixed factory overhead for the period by the denominator activity. Firms then use the standard fixed factory overhead application rates to apply fixed overhead costs to cost objects.

$$\frac{\text{Fixed factory overhead}}{\text{(application) rate}} = \frac{\text{Budgeted total fixed factory overhead}}{\text{Denominator activity}}$$

Schmidt Machinery Company has a total budgeted fixed factory overhead of $120,000 per period and uses direct labor-hours as the activity measure to apply factory overhead. The planned manufacturing activity is 1,000 units of product XV–1 per period. With a labor standard of 5 direct labor-hours per unit of XV–1, the

---

[7] Recent studies on activity-based costing reveal that many so-called fixed factory overheads in the past do vary with some activities. For these cost items, firms need to find appropriate activity levels and bases for proper product cost determinations.

EXHIBIT 14.7
Steps in Determining Standard Fixed Factory Application Rate

Step	Example
1. Determine the *budgeted* total fixed factory overhead for the period.	Management decided to manufacture 1,000 units. The budgeted total fixed factory overhead to manufacture 1,000 units is $120,000 per month.
2. Select an activity measure or measures for applying fixed factory overhead.	The firm decided to use direct labor hours as the activity measure to apply fixed factory overhead.
3. Calculate the denominator activity quantity for the selected activity measure at the planned level of operation.	At 5 standard direct labor-hours per unit, the firm expected the total direct labor-hours of the period to be 5,000, the denominator activity for the period.
4. Compute the standard fixed factory overhead application rate by dividing the amount in Step 1 by the amount in Step 3.	Divide the amount in Step 1 ($120,000) by the amount in Step 3, identified as the denominator activity (5,000) of the period, to arrive at the standard fixed factory overhead rate of $24 per direct labor-hour.

denominator activity per period is 5,000 direct labor-hours. The fixed factory overhead application rate therefore is $24 per direct labor-hour.

Exhibit 14.7 summarizes the steps in determining a standard fixed factory overhead application rate for an operation.

Analyzing Fixed Factory Overhead Variances

Total fixed factory overhead variance is the difference in fixed factory overheads between the amounts incurred and the amount applied to the output or operation of the period.

The first step in analyzing fixed factory overhead variances is to determine the total fixed overhead variance. The **total fixed factory overhead variance** is the difference in fixed factory overheads between the amounts incurred and the amount applied to the output or operation of the period. Schmidt Company spent $130,650 on fixed factory overheads to manufacture 780 units of XV–1. Exhibit 14.8 shows an analysis of fixed overhead variances. The standard calls for 5 direct labor hours per unit. The total standard direct labor hours for the 780 units manufactured in October 2005, therefore, is 3,900 (5 hours per unit × 780 units). At the standard fixed factory overhead application rate of $24 per direct labor hour, the firm applied $93,600 (3,900 hours × $24 per hour) fixed factory overheads to the 780 units manufactured during the month. The total fixed factory overhead variance for October, is $37,050 unfavorable ($130,650 − $93,600).

Fixed factory overhead spending (budget) variance is the difference in fixed factory overheads between the amount incurred during the period and the budgeted amount for the period.

Fixed Factory Overhead Spending (Budget) Variance   Similar to further analyses of total variable factory overhead variances, a total fixed factory overhead variance can be further analyzed into two detailed variances: spending and product volume variances. **Fixed factory overhead spending (budget) variance** is the difference in fixed factory overheads between the amount incurred during the period and the budgeted amount for the period. Some firms refer to this variance as *fixed factory overhead (flexible) budget variance*. Schmidt Machinery Company incurred a total of $130,650 fixed factory overhead in October 2005 (Exhibit 14.8, point A). The budgeted fixed factory overhead was $120,000 for the month (Exhibit 14.8, point B). The difference between the total fixed factory overhead incurred (point A) and the budgeted fixed factory overhead for the period (point B), $10,650, unfavorable is fixed factory overhead spending (flexible budget) variance.

The **fixed factory overhead production volume variance** is the difference between the budgeted fixed factory overhead for the period and the fixed factory overhead applied to the output (units manufactured) of the period.

Fixed Factory Overhead Production Volume Variance   **Fixed factory overhead production volume variance** is the difference between the budgeted fixed factory overhead for the period and the fixed factory overhead applied to the output (units manufactured) of the period. As pointed out earlier, firms apply fixed factory overhead to outputs based on the standard fixed factory overhead application rate.

Fixed factory overhead production volume variances arise when a firm's actual operating level differs from the budgeted level for the period. Schmidt manufactured 780 units of XV–1 in October 2005, which requires 3,900 standard direct labor-hours (780 units × 5 hours) according to the standard cost sheet. At a standard fixed factory overhead application rate of $24 per direct labor-hour, the total standard fixed factory

EXHIBIT 14.8
Analysis of Fixed Factory
Overhead Variances

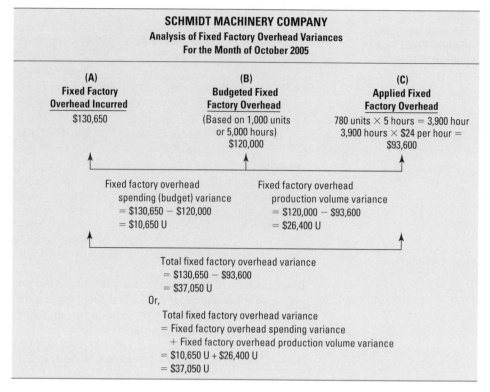

SCHMIDT MACHINERY COMPANY
Analysis of Fixed Factory Overhead Variances
For the Month of October 2005

| (A)
Fixed Factory
Overhead Incurred
$130,650 | (B)
Budgeted Fixed
Factory Overhead
(Based on 1,000 units
or 5,000 hours)
$120,000 | (C)
Applied Fixed
Factory Overhead
780 units × 5 hours = 3,900 hour
3,900 hours × $24 per hour =
$93,600 |

Fixed factory overhead
spending (budget) variance
= $130,650 − $120,000
= $10,650 U

Fixed factory overhead
production volume variance
= $120,000 − $93,600
= $26,400 U

Total fixed factory overhead variance
= $130,650 − $93,600
= $37,050 U

Or,

Total fixed factory overhead variance
= Fixed factory overhead spending variance
+ Fixed factory overhead production volume variance
= $10,650 U + $26,400 U
= $37,050 U

overhead applied to units manufactured in October 2005 was $93,600 (3,900 hours × $24 per hour; point C of Exhibit 14.8). The firm budgeted $120,000 for fixed factory overhead. The amount applied is $26,400 less than the budgeted amount. Schmidt has an unfavorable fixed factory overhead production volume variance of $26,400 in October.

The difference between the budgeted fixed factory overhead and the applied fixed factory overhead is the production volume variance. This variance is a result of the deviation of the number of units manufactured from the budgeted (denominator) units to be manufactured during the period. In the determination of the fixed factory overhead application rate the denominator is based on the budgeted level of operation. A variance arises when the units actually manufactured during the period is not the same as the budgeted units for the period. Therefore, the variance is a *production volume* or *denominator variance*.

Exhibit 14.9 provides alternative computations for the amounts at points B and C in Exhibit 14.8. This exhibit demonstrates that the production volume variance arises from the difference between the budgeted (denominator) and the actual units of output. The production volume variance is favorable when the firm manufactured more units during the period than the budgeted (denominator) units and is unfavorable when the actual production is less than the budgeted units. No production volume variance exists when the number of units manufactured during the period is the same as the denominator number of units that the firm budgeted (1,000 units).

Some firms view production volume variances as measures of facility or capacity utilization because they reflect differences in capacity utilization between the planned and the actual uses of the firm's facility or capacity as measured by the activity for applying factory overheads. Schmidt planned to operate 5,000 direct labor-hours to manufacture 1,000 units. The production of 780 units in October 2005 indicates that the firm operated only at the level of 3,900 direct labor-hours (780 units × 5 standard direct labor-hours per unit). The firm underused its facility by 220 units, or 1,100 direct labor-hours (5,000 − 3,900). At the standard fixed factory overhead application rate of $24 per hour, the production volume variance is $26,400 unfavorable (bottom panel of Exhibit 14.9). This unfavorable variance indicates that the lower operating level in October 2005 had an implicit cost of $26,400 to the firm.

Under- or Over-Applied Fixed Factory Overhead Variance The sum of the fixed factory overhead spending and production volume variances is the total fixed factory

EXHIBIT 14.9
An Alternative Computation of Production Volume Variance

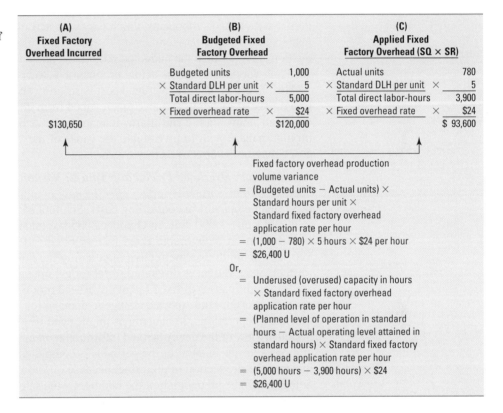

(A) Fixed Factory Overhead Incurred	(B) Budgeted Fixed Factory Overhead		(C) Applied Fixed Factory Overhead (SQ × SR)	
	Budgeted units	1,000	Actual units	780
	× Standard DLH per unit ×	5	× Standard DLH per unit ×	5
	Total direct labor-hours	5,000	Total direct labor-hours	3,900
	× Fixed overhead rate ×	$24	× Fixed overhead rate ×	$24
$130,650		$120,000		$ 93,600

Fixed factory overhead production volume variance
= (Budgeted units − Actual units) × Standard hours per unit × Standard fixed factory overhead application rate per hour
= (1,000 − 780) × 5 hours × $24 per hour
= $26,400 U
Or,
= Underused (overused) capacity in hours × Standard fixed factory overhead application rate per hour
= (Planned level of operation in standard hours − Actual operating level attained in standard hours) × Standard fixed factory overhead application rate per hour
= (5,000 hours − 3,900 hours) × $24
= $26,400 U

overhead variance of the period. This is also the difference between the fixed factory overhead incurred and the standard fixed factory applied to the output of the period. Some firms refer to this amount as *underapplied* (if unfavorable) *or overapplied* (if favorable) *fixed factory overhead.*

Schmidt Machinery Company incurred $130,650 fixed factory overhead during October 2005 to manufacture 780 units of XV–1. The firm applied $93,600 fixed factory overhead to the 780 units manufactured in October 2005. Schmidt Machinery Company, therefore, has an unfavorable total fixed factory overhead variance, or underapplied fixed factory overhead, of $37,050 for the period.

Interpretation of Fixed Factory Overhead Variances

Differences in activities underlying variable and fixed overheads and in behavioral patterns between fixed and variable factory overheads require that variable and fixed factory overhead variances be interpreted differently.

Fixed Factory Overhead Spending Variance A fixed factory overhead spending variance arises when the budget procedure failed to anticipate or incorporate changes in fixed factory overhead. For example, a budget that inadvertently neglected scheduled raises for factory managers, changes in property taxes on factory buildings and equipment, or purchases of new equipment creates unfavorable fixed overhead spending (budget) variances. Conversely, overestimates of fixed factory overheads lead to favorable fixed factory overhead spending (budget) variances. Significant fixed factory overhead spending variances that result from ineffective budget procedures suggest that the firm needs to improve its budgeting processes.

Unfavorable fixed factory overhead spending (budget) variances can be a result of excessive spending due to improper or inadequate control of operations. Events such as emergency repairs, impromptu replacement of equipment, or addition of managers for an unscheduled second shift increase fixed factory overheads and unfavorable fixed factory overhead spending (budget) variances of the period. Management should investigate the causes of such unfavorable fixed factory overhead spending variances and take proper actions to prevent similar events from recurring.

Fixed factory overhead spending (budget) variances can arise when a firm's cost classifications system fails to reflect its true cost behavior patterns. Classifying a cost item that includes components which vary with activity level as fixed overhead would lead to an unfavorable fixed factory overhead spending variance when the actual production is higher than the budgeted production and a favorable fixed factory overhead spending variance when the actual production is lower than the budgeted level.

Most likely no factory overhead cost is strictly variable or fixed. A small fixed factory overhead spending variance that resulted from imprecise classifications of factory overhead items should not alarm management. A large variance, however, should prompt management to investigate the cause of the variance, including reexamining cost behavior patterns of factory overheads.

Fixed Factory Overhead Production Volume Variance Fixed factory overhead production volume variances reflect *effectiveness* in attaining the goal set for the period rather than *efficiency* in controlling costs. Schmidt Machinery Company had a budget to manufacture 1,000 units in October 2005 but manufactured 780 units. As a result, the firm has an unfavorable fixed factory overhead production volume variance of $26,400. Schmidt was ineffective in attaining the goal set for October 2005. In contrast, all other variances discussed so far reflect operation efficiencies.

Among the causes of fixed factory overhead production volume variances are management decisions, unexpected change in demand for the product, or problems in manufacturing operations. Management might need to alter the production plan for the period in view of the newly arrived information on market outlook or strategic considerations after the budget for the period was completed. It could decide to phase out or increase the production of a product because of knowledge gained about a new technology since the preparation of the budget. Or the sales volume since the beginning of the year could suggest a larger or smaller market than expected in the budget. Management, therefore, could decide to step up or reduce production of the product. A fixed factory overhead production volume variance that results from one or more of these causes most likely is beyond the control of factory management.

Unexpected production problems can also be a source of fixed factory overhead production volume variance. Among the production problems a factory might encounter are equipment not functioning properly due to inadequate maintenance or unexpected breakdowns, a product not designed for easy production, or unexpected high labor turnovers. A production volume variance that results from manufacturing problems very likely is the responsibility, either partially or fully, of the factory management.

Alternative Analyses of Factory Overhead Variances

LEARNING OBJECTIVE 4
Use two-variance or three-variance procedures to analyze and interpret factory overhead variances.

Our discussion of analyzing factory overhead variances separated each of the total variable and the total fixed factory overhead variances into two variances. Such an analysis is referred to as a four-variance analysis of factory overhead variances. Not all firms, however, want or need to analyze factory overhead in such detail. Furthermore, a firm's chart of accounts may not separate variable and fixed factory overhead costs or management may not consider a detailed analysis of factory overhead variances cost effective. Alternative ways to analyze factory overhead that are less detailed include three-variance and two-variance analyses.

Three-Variance Analysis of Factory Overhead Variances

Three-variance analysis of factory overhead variances separates the difference between total factory overhead incurred and total standard factory overhead costs applied to the operations of the period for both variable and fixed factory overhead into three variances. These three factory overhead variances are *factory overhead spending, (variable) factory overhead efficiency,* and *production volume variances.*

Factory overhead spending variance is the difference between the total factory overheads incurred during operations and the expected total factory overheads at the operating level of the actual quantity of the activity for applying overheads. The expected total factory overheads for the operation at the actual quantity level of the activity for applying factory overheads includes both variable and fixed overheads. The expected variable factory overhead (for the operation at the actual quantity level of the activity for applying overheads) is the total standard variable factory overhead for the actual quantity of the activity for applying factory overheads during the period (point Q in panel 1 of Exhibit 14.10). This quantity is also the product of the actual hours spent during the period and the standard variable overhead rate per hour when the activity for applying overheads is either machine or direct labor hour. The expected fixed factory overhead for operations at the actual quantity level of the activity for applying overheads is the budgeted fixed factory overhead (point T).

In effect, three-variance analysis of factory overhead combines the variable factory overhead spending variance and the fixed factory overhead spending (budget) variance into one variance and refers to the variance as *(total) factory overhead spending variance* while the other two factory overhead variances remain unchanged.

The factory overhead efficiency variance arises only from variable factory overhead; it is the difference in standard variable factory overheads between the standard variable factory overhead for the actual activity for applying overheads and the standard variable factory overhead for the output of the period. The factory overhead efficiency variance is the variable factory overhead efficiency variance in the four-variance analysis discussed earlier. The factory overhead production volume variance is the same as the fixed factory overhead production volume variance analyzed earlier.

Schmidt Machinery Company spent 3,510 direct labor-hours in October 2005. At 3,510 direct labor-hours the total standard variable factory overhead is $42,120 ($12 standard variable factory overhead per direct labor-hour × 3,510 direct labor-hours the firm spent during the period). The standard (budget) total fixed factory overhead remains at $120,000. The total standard factory overhead for 3,510 direct labor-hours, therefore, is $162,120. The firm incurred $171,280 total factory overhead. The $9,160 difference ($162,120 − $171,280) is the factory overhead spending variance for the period, which is unfavorable as shown in panel 2 of Exhibit 14.10.

Alternatively, Schmidt Machinery Company can combine the $1,490 favorable variable factory overhead spending variance and the $10,650 unfavorable fixed factory overhead budget variance in the four-variance analysis of factory overhead to find the factory overhead spending variance, $9,160 unfavorable.

Finding three variances requires four points. Point A in Exhibit 14.10 is the total factory overhead incurred in operations of the period. Point B is the total standard factory overhead applied based on the actual quantity of the activity for applying factory overhead during the period. Point C is the total standard factory overhead in the flexible budget for the output of the period; it is the sum of the total standard variable factory overhead cost for the output of the period and the budgeted total fixed factory overhead. Point D is the total standard factory overhead cost applied to the standard quantity of the activity for applying factory overhead for the units manufactured (output) during the period.

The total fixed factory overhead in points B and C are always the same. Both points represent the budgeted total fixed factory overhead, $120,000. The only difference between these two points is the amount of the standard variable factory overhead. In point B the standard variable factory overhead is based on the *actual quantity of the activity* for applying factory overhead. Schmidt Machinery Company, which uses direct

EXHIBIT 14.10
Three-Variance Analysis of Factory Overhead Variances

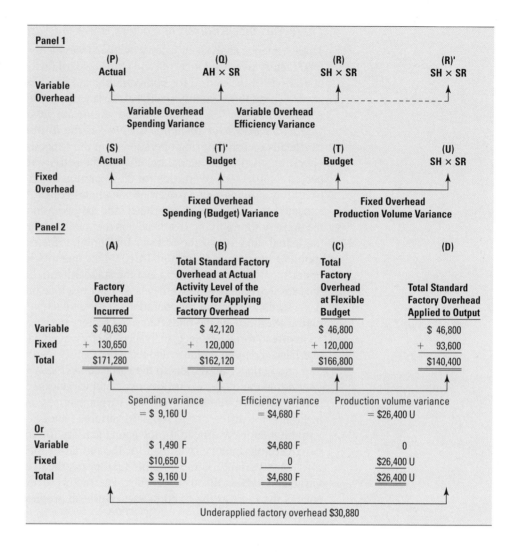

labor-hours as the activity measure for applying factory overhead, spent 3,510 direct labor-hours in October 2005. At a standard variable factory overhead rate of $12 per direct labor-hour, the total variable factory overhead at point B is $42,120 (= 3,510 × $12). Adding the budgeted fixed factory overhead of $120,000, the total factory overhead at point B is $162,120.

The difference between points A and B is the factory overhead spending variance. For the operation in October 2005 of Schmidt Machinery Company, point A is $171,280 and point B is $162,120. Thus, Schmidt's factory overhead spending variance in October 2005 is $9,160, unfavorable.

Point C is the total standard factory overhead for the operation of the period. The total standard variable factory overhead at point C is the product of the standard variable factory overhead application rate and the total standard quantity of the activity for applying variable factory overhead for the units manufactured during the period. Schmidt manufactured 780 units of XV–1 in October 2005. The standard allows 5 direct labor-hours for each unit of XV–1 manufactured. The total standard direct labor-hours for the 780 units of XV–1 manufactured in October 2005 is 3,900 (= 5 hours per unit × 780 units). The standard variable factory overhead rate is $12 per direct labor-hour. The total standard variable factory overhead for October 2005, therefore, is $46,800 (3,900 hours per unit × $12 variable overhead rate per hour). This amount also is the variable factory overhead flexible budget amount. As shown in Exhibit 14.10, both the variable and the fixed factory overhead at point C are the flexible budget amounts for the units manufactured during the period. The fixed factory overhead in the flexible budget is $120,000 and the total factory overhead at point C is $166,800.

The difference between points B ($162,120) and C ($166,800) is factory overhead efficiency variance ($4,680). Schmidt has a favorable factory overhead efficiency variance of $4,680 for its operations in October 2005.

Point D is the total standard factory overhead applied to the output (units manufactured) of the period. The total standard variable factory overhead applied to units manufactured during the period is the same as the flexible budget amount computed for point C. Schmidt applies $12 variable factory overhead for each direct labor-hour. For the 780 units manufactured in October 2005, which has a total standard direct labor-hours of 3,900, Schmidt applies $46,800 total variable factory overhead to the units manufactured.

Schmidt Machinery Company budgeted $120,000 fixed factory overhead for the month and applies fixed factory overhead at the rate of $24 per direct labor-hour. The firm applies $93,600 (780 units × 5 hours × $24) total fixed factory overhead to the 780 units of XV–1 manufactured during the period. The sum of the $46,800 applied variable factory overhead and the $93,600 applied fixed factory overhead, $140,400, is the total factory overhead applied to the units manufactured in October 2005, shown as point D in Exhibit 14.10. The difference between points C and D is factory overhead production volume variance. The factory overhead production volume variance for Schmidt's operations in October 2005 is $26,400, unfavorable.

Four-variance analyses can provide a more detailed analysis of the operation. If this additional analysis of variances provides little useful information to management, however, a three-variance or even a two-variance analysis may be sufficient.

Two-Variance Analysis of Factory Overhead Variances

Two-variance analyses of factory overhead separate the difference in total factory overhead between the amount incurred and the amount applied to the output of the period into two variances: *factory overhead flexible budget variance* and *factory overhead production volume variance*. The factory overhead flexible budget variance also is called a *factory overhead controllable variance*. Exhibit 14.11 shows two-variance analysis of factory overhead variances for Schmidt Machinery Company's operation in October 2005.

Note that the two-variance analysis in Exhibit 14.11 uses three of the four points employed in the three-variance analysis. Point A is the same in all analyses, the total factory overhead incurred during the period. Point C is the factory overhead in the flexible budget for the units manufactured during the period. Point D is the total standard factory overhead applied to the units manufactured during the period. Point B in Exhibit 14.10 for three-variance analysis is not used in two-variance analysis.

EXHIBIT 14.11
Two-Variance Analysis of Factory Overhead Variances

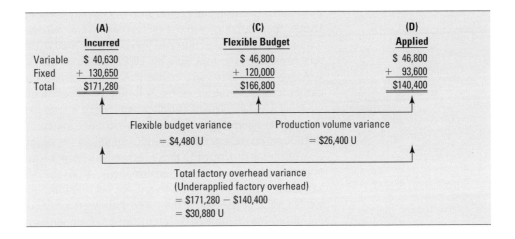

EXHIBIT 14.12
Analysis of Factory
Overhead Variance

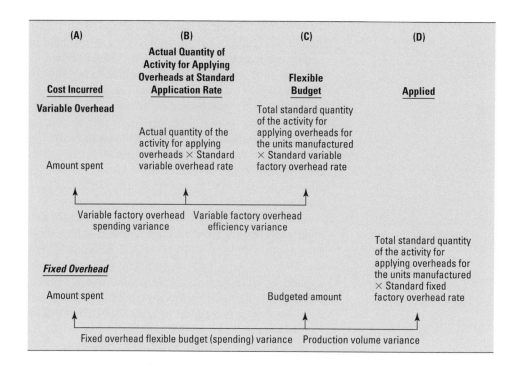

The difference between points A and C is the factory overhead flexible budget variance. This variance also can be determined by merging the spending and efficiency variances from the three-variance analysis. Schmidt Machinery Company incurred $171,280 for factory overheads to manufacture 780 units of XV–1 in October 2005. The total standard variable factory overhead to manufacture 780 units of XV–1 is $46,800. The total budgeted fixed factory overhead for the period is $120,000. The total amount at point C, therefore, is $166,800. Schmidt had an unfavorable factory overhead flexible budget variance of $4,480 for its operations during October 2005. Alternatively, we can determine the factory overhead flexible budget variance by combining two of the variances in the three-variance analysis of factory overhead variances, the unfavorable spending variance of $9,160 and the favorable efficiency variance of $4,680.

The production volume variance is the same as in four-variance or three-variance analysis.

Summary of Factory Overhead Variances

A firm can analyze factory overhead variances separately for variable and fixed factory overhead costs, or it can perform variance analyses without distinguishing the variances from either variable or fixed factory overhead. When both variable and fixed factory variances are separated into two variances, the analysis is a four-variance analysis of factory overhead variances. Exhibit 14.12 illustrates the determination of factory overhead variances using four-variance analysis. Exhibit 14.13 summarizes the analyses presented earlier for the operations of the Schmidt Machinery Company in October 2005.

A detailed analysis of variances can assist a firm to identify effects of different factors on the operating results. A four-variance analysis for example, shows separately the effects on the operating result of spending on variable overhead items and on fixed overhead items. Knowing these factors can help a firm gain effective control of operations and better assess its performances. Analyses performed at an aggregated level, say identifying only the total variance between the operating result and the budgeted total amount or the total standard cost allowed for the operation, might mask important variations attributable to different causes or in one or more of the individual overhead items that have opposite effects on costs.

EXHIBIT 14.13
Analysis of Factory Overhead Variance

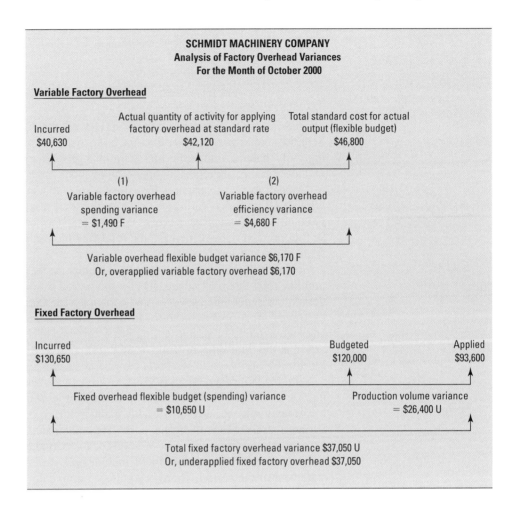

SCHMIDT MACHINERY COMPANY
Analysis of Factory Overhead Variances
For the Month of October 2000

Variable Factory Overhead

| Incurred $40,630 | Actual quantity of activity for applying factory overhead at standard rate $42,120 | Total standard cost for actual output (flexible budget) $46,800 |

(1) Variable factory overhead spending variance = $1,490 F

(2) Variable factory overhead efficiency variance = $4,680 F

Variable overhead flexible budget variance $6,170 F
Or, overapplied variable factory overhead $6,170

Fixed Factory Overhead

| Incurred $130,650 | Budgeted $120,000 | Applied $93,600 |

Fixed overhead flexible budget (spending) variance = $10,650 U

Production volume variance = $26,400 U

Total fixed factory overhead variance $37,050 U
Or, underapplied fixed factory overhead $37,050

Detailed analyses of variances add value, however, only if management understands the variances and is able to use them, if the personnel affected by the result can comprehend and accept the variances, and if the firm's cost system has data to support the analyses. A detailed analysis can be misleading, dysfunctional, or even detrimental if cost items are not properly identified as variable or fixed costs, if the behavioral patterns of the designated activity or activities for applying overheads do not represent the behavioral patterns of the underlying overhead costs, or if management or its subordinates do not understand the analysis.

Disposition of Variances

LEARNING OBJECTIVE 5
Dispose of variances in financial accounting systems.

How a firm reports and disposes of variances can affect the reported cost of goods sold, gross margin, operating income, and asset values. There are two alternative approaches in reporting and disposing of variances. A firm can dispose of the variance in the period in which the variance occurs. Alternatively, the firm can prorate cost variances among Work-in-Process Inventory, Finished Goods Inventory, and Cost of Goods Sold accounts.

Variance as a Current Period Savings or Expense

Firms using a standard cost system determine their cost of goods sold and operating expenses based on the standard costs. For example, at the budget selling price and the standard manufacturing cost Schmidt Machinery Company would have reported the following gross margin for its operations in October 2005:

Sales (780 units × $800 per unit, Exhibit 13.4)	$624,000
Cost of goods sold (780 units × $520 per unit)	405,600
Gross margin	$218,400

Such a report, however, fails to reflect all the operating results of the period. Schmidt sold at prices higher than the budgeted price and incurred higher manufacturing costs than the standard costs. Schmidt's gross margin is not $218,400. It needs to include variances in reporting operating results.

Unfavorable cost variances increase the total standard cost of goods sold and unfavorable selling price variances decrease the total flexible budget sales of the period. Favorable cost variances decrease the total standard cost of goods sold and favorable selling price variances increase the total flexible budget sales of the period. Exhibit 14.14 illustrates this procedure.

Schmidt Machinery Company sold 780 units. At the budgeted $800 selling price per unit, the total flexible budget sales for the period is $624,000. The firm sold the products for $820 per unit, however, and earned a $15,600 favorable selling price variance ($20 per unit × 780 units sold). In its income statement for October 2005, Schmidt adds the $15,600 favorable selling price variance to the total flexible budget sales to arrive at the total sales revenue of $639,000 received during the month, as shown in Exhibit 14.14.

The standard cost per unit is $520 (Exhibit 14.2). The total standard cost for the 780 units sold, therefore, is $405,600 ($520 per unit × 780 units). The firm, however, has a $50 favorable variance on variable manufacturing costs and a $37,050 unfavorable variance on fixed manufacturing costs. The total manufacturing cost variance, $37,000 unfavorable, increases the cost of goods of the period to $442,600.

The procedure in Exhibit 14.14 includes all variances of a period in the income statement of the period. There is no effect on inventory accounts reported in the balance sheet of the period or any subsequent periods. Many firms follow this procedure when the amounts of the variances are relatively small. Some firms, however, dispose of all variances at year-end even when the firm experienced significant amounts of variances. They do so on the ground that the variances of a period are the results of operations in that period and should therefore be disposed of in the statement that reports the operating results of the period.

EXHIBIT 14.14
Income Statement with Disposition of Variance in the Period Incurred

SCHMIDT MACHINERY COMPANY		
Income Statement		
For the Period Ended October 31, 2005		
Sales (Exhibit 13.4)	$624,000	
Add: Selling price variance (Exhibit 13.4)	15,600 F	
Net sales		$639,600
Cost of goods sold (at standard)	$405,600*	
Add: Manufacturing cost variances	+ 37,000† U	
Total cost of goods sold		442,600
Gross margin		$197,000
Selling and administrative expenses		69,000
Operating income		$128,000

*Standard manufacturing cost per unit (Exhibit 14.2)	$	520
Number of units manufactured and sold	×	780
Total standard cost of goods manufactured and sold		$405,600
† Total variable manufacturing cost variance (Exhibit 13.6)	$	50 F
Total fixed manufacturing cost variance (Exhibit 14.8)		37,050 U
Total manufacturing cost variance		$ 37,000 U

EXHIBIT 14.15
Proration of Manufacturing
Cost Variance

Accounts	Standard Cost	Percent	Proration of Variance	Adjusted Total Cost
Work in progress—Ending	$ 36,400	7%	$37,000 × 7% = $ 2,590	$ 38,990
Finished goods—Ending	78,000	15	$37,000 × 15% = 5,550	83,550
Cost of goods sold	405,600	78	$37,000 × 78% = 28,860	434,460
Total	$520,000	100%	$37,000	$557,000

Proration of Variance

Inventories are the result of operations. Costs of inventories increase (decrease) when the operations in which a firm created inventories experience unfavorable (favorable) variances on its manufacturing costs. Some firms believe that the costs of inventories should not be valued at their standard costs if the firm had significant variances on manufacturing costs of the period because the costs incurred to manufacture these inventories deviate significantly from their standard costs. Using standard costs for inventories failed to report the actual costs incurred for these inventories. These firms prorate manufacturing cost variances among the cost of goods sold and the ending inventories of the period.

Assume that in addition to the 780 units sold with $405,600 in standard costs, Schmidt Machinery Company had $36,400 of work-in-process inventory and $78,000 of finished goods inventory as of the end of October 2005. The firm desires to prorate manufacturing cost variances among ending inventories and the cost of goods sold of the period.[8] The total manufacturing cost variance in October 2005 was $37,000, unfavorable. Exhibit 14.15 shows the proration of the manufacturing cost variances.[9]

Prorations of manufacturing cost variances among ending inventories and the cost of goods sold carry the savings from efficient or the additional cost because of inefficient operations of a period into future periods. When Schmidt Machinery Company sells the finished goods ending inventory in a future period, say 2006, the unfavorable variance added to the finished goods ending inventory of October 2005 will increase the cost of goods sold of 2006 by $5,550. As a result, the operating income of 2006 will decrease by $5,550 because of the unfavorable variance the firm incurred in 2005. Inclusions of effects of efficient or inefficient operation in one period in the report of operating results of one or more future periods are likely to be misleading and inappropriate. Mixtures of operating results from more than one period render the analyses of operating results and the performance evaluations ambiguous and diminish their usefulness.

Prorations of manufacturing cost variances among ending inventories of work-in-process, finished goods, and cost of goods sold are appropriate, however, if the cost variance is a result of inappropriate standards or bookkeeping errors. In these circumstances, management must revise the standard or take action to prevent recurrences of the same bookkeeping error.[10]

Standard Cost in Service Organizations

LEARNING OBJECTIVE 6
Apply standard costs to service organizations.

Using standard cost systems facilitates budget preparation, eases monitoring and controlling operations, assists performance evaluation, and aids management in making decisions such as product pricing and resource management. These benefits are not limited to manufacturing firms. All organizations can benefit from standard cost systems.

---

[8] This example assumes that Schmidt carries no materials ending inventories. When materials purchased differ from materials used, however, the proration of the direct materials price variance should include direct materials ending inventory as well as the direct materials usage variance.

[9] When different activity measures are used for different cost elements, the proration should be done separately for each cost element based on its activity measure.

[10] Neither GAAP nor the Internal Revenue Code specifically addresses the issue on proration of variances. Because the total amount of variance is most likely an immaterial amount, firms can use either method to dispose of variances. Many firms, however, prorate variances in financial reports and for tax purposes.

In today's highly competitive environment, more and more service firms recognize the importance of standard cost in productivity monitoring, quality control, product-line planning, and other cost management concepts and techniques in their efforts to make their organizations or units efficient, competitive, and profitable. Using standard costs helps managers to grasp behavioral patterns of cost items, assess and monitor the efficiency and profitability of their organizations, identify deviations in operations, and target areas that need attention.

To best use a standard cost system, an organization must adapt the system to its operating characteristics and objectives. Objectives are likely to differ for different organizations. Some general characteristics, however, distinguish a service firm from a manufacturing or merchandising firm. Among them are the absence of output inventory, labor-intensive products, the predominance of fixed costs, and the lack of a uniform measure for outputs.

Service outputs cannot be stored for uses in a future period. Service bays in an automobile repair shop not used today do not increase the number of service bays available tomorrow. Empty airline seats on a flight do not increase the seats available on the next flight. Vacant hospital beds today do not increase the beds available tomorrow. Service outputs cannot be generated before they are needed; a service output exists only when a customer exists. In contrast, a manufacturer can make products for future deliveries. Consequently, a service firm has no favorable production volume variance. Furthermore, any unfavorable production volume variances are also the sales volume variances of the period.

People provide services and most service organizations are labor intensive. The bulk of expenses of service organizations are salary and wage-related expenditures and overheads. Material costs are incidental expenses. Consequently, labor-related measures such as labor rate and efficiency variances are much more important than materials variances to managers of service firms. In addition, labor-intensiveness leads service firms to monitor activities and gauge operating results using labor-based measures.

Equipment in service organizations enables staff members to perform better services. Service organizations acquire equipment to (1) replace labor, (2) reduce production costs, (3) improve process efficiency, or (4) improve the quality of services. Cost reductions often are not among service organizations' primary reasons for acquiring equipment or updating facilities.

New equipment added by a service organization often increases, rather than decreases, its total operating cost and the cost of providing services. A hospital that adds a piece of equipment, say, a state-of-the-art MRI scanner, improves the quality of treatment it provides; the equipment, however, adds costs to the hospital and ultimately to the patients. A multimedia classroom not only improves the quality of instruction but also increases the cost of instruction. A simple cost/output ratio often is not a good efficiency measure. Improper use of a cost/output ratio generated by standard cost systems can be detrimental to the ultimate objective of the service organization—providing better services to customers.

Most costs in service organizations are fixed costs. The bulk of labor costs are for professional personnel who usually are paid monthly salaries. Variations in salaries from one period to the next are few, if any. Other overhead costs often consist of expenses related to facilities and equipment and are fixed in amounts for each time period. The predominance of fixed costs in service organizations increases the importance of monitoring fixed cost variances.

Unlike a manufacturing firm that produces many identical products, each output unit of a service organization is likely to be unique. Two patients with similar conditions who check out of a hospital likely did not receive the same care. The likelihood of two students receiving degrees from the same institution at the same time having received the same education is almost nil.

Furthermore, service organizations often use measures other than units of output to measure their output. Exhibit 14.16 lists some measures of output often used by service organizations. As shown in Exhibit 14.17, hospitals use patient-days to measure

EXHIBIT 14.16
Output Measures of Service Organizations

Organization	Output Measure
Airline	Revenue-producing passenger-miles
Hospital	Patient-days
Hotel	Occupancy rate or number of guests
Accounting, legal, and consulting firms	Professional staff hours
Colleges and universities	Credit hours
Primary and secondary schools	Number of students

EXHIBIT 14.17
Standard Cost Sheet for a Hospital

Source: Based on Table 14 in *Managerial Cost Accounting for Hospitals* (Chicago: American Hospital Association, 1980), p. 97.

LANCASTER COUNTY HOSPITAL
Standard Cost Sheet for Pediatrics Floor

Direct Expenses	Rate/Price	Amount	Fixed
Salaries and wages			
Supervisors			$4,500
RNs	$15.00 per hour	1.3 hours per patient-day	
LPNs	10.00 per hour	1.7 hours per patient-day	
Nursing assistants	6.50 per hour	0.9 hour per patient-day	
Supplies—Inventory	0.20 per unit	10 units per patient-day	
Supplies—noninventory			300
Pediatrician fees	100 per hour	0.5 hour per patient-day	
Other direct expenses			250
Transferred Expenses			
Housekeeping	5.00 per hour	48 hours + 0.4 hour per patient day + 1.50 hours per patient discharge	
Laundry	0.25 per pound	500 pounds + 15 pounds per patient-day + 30 pounds per discharge + 50 pounds per surgery	
Allocated Expenses			
Personnel	0.08 per hour	242 hours + 3.9 hours per patient-day	
Other administrative and general	3.00 per hour	118 hours + 0.05 hour per patient-day + 1.5 hours per patient discharge	

their products. Colleges and universities use credit-hour production to show their outputs. These output measures seldom are perfect indicators of the outputs of service organizations. Patients or their families are likely to place different values on the same number of patient-days, depending on the results of treatments. A patient who is cured of an illness is likely to be more pleased with the care received than is the family of a patient who died of the same disease, although the numbers of patient-days were identical for both. In addition, the amount and type of work performed by a service organization to complete an output unit often varies from one client to the next or from one patient-day to another. The amounts and types of work performed for two patients with identical heart diseases during their 10-day stays can be vastly different although the number of patient-days is identical and their illnesses are the same.

Educational institutions seldom use their outputs—knowledge learned—as a measure of their output. Instead, these institutions frequently cite credit-hour production as the measure of their output. One hundred credit hours of mediocre instruction, however, do not have the same value as one hundred hours of excellent instruction. Intangible attributes, in addition to units of output, play dominant roles in determining the value of outputs from a service organization. These characteristics often lead service firms to rely on input-related measures such as patient-days and the number of credit hours produced to measure and monitor operations.

REAL-WORLD FOCUS   How a Hospital Unit Responds to a Performance Report

Date: November 5, 2005
To: Cynthia DeCamp, Hospital Director
From: Stan DeVine, Pediatric Unit Manager
Subject: Direct expenses, October 2005

Direct Labor Last month, my unit recruited three new RNs at the entry-level pay scale, replacing two retired RNs who had been with us for more than 20 years and were at the top of the pay scale. The average hourly salary for all RNs on the unit was reduced to $34 per hour, resulting in a favorable labor rate variance. The replacements, however, increased my RN nursing hours per patient-day to 1.5 hours, resulting in an unfavorable labor efficiency variance in last month's average daily staffing. To compensate for the increased RN staffing, one LPN was transferred to the Emergency Room, which needs his help. This resulted in both a favorable rate and efficiency variance for LPNs. We expect, however, that the favorable rate variance will be lost in approximately six months when the RNs reach the next pay level. Therefore, I recommend that plans be made to replace one RN with one LPN.

For a period of five consecutive days in the middle of the month, the unit had more than 20 patients and required the use of 48 overtime hours for the nurse assistants, causing an unfavorable rate and efficiency variance for this group.

Supplies—Inventory Uses of inventory supplies followed the standard level of 10 items per patient-day. However, two brands were changed. The purchasing department informs me that the new brands are less expensive and resulted in a $3,500 savings last month. Furthermore, the new items appear to be better than the previous brands, and we will continue to use them.

Supplies—Noninventory The unfavorable quantity variance resulted primarily from purchasing items that had been deferred the last several months. Year-to-date spending on these items, however, still remains favorable.

Pediatrician Fees The resident pediatrician, Dr. Kiddear, and other staff were required to provide some overtime night-shift services during the period that the patient census was more than 20 patients. Overtime night-shift work is paid at a rate higher than standard, thus causing an unfavorable price variance. The 48 additional hours for overtime night-shift work were responsible for the unfavorable usage variance.

Source: Adapted from *Managerial Cost Accounting for Hospitals* (Chicago: American Hospital Association, 1980), pp. 98–99.

The differences in operating characteristics between service organizations and typical manufacturing firms make it a necessity to modify standard cost systems before applying them to service organizations.

Standard Cost in the New Manufacturing Environment

The manufacturing environment evolved in the last few decades and many new management techniques developed during the same periods emphasize continual improvement, total quality control, and managing activity rather than cost. These emphases have changed product costing, strategic and operational decisions, and cost determination methods, as discussed in the preceding chapters. They also influence the ways in which many firms use standard cost systems and variance analyses as management tools, including the preparation of flexible budgets, the selection of evaluation criteria, and the implication of the variances.

Effect of the New Manufacturing Environment on Flexible Budgeting

LEARNING OBJECTIVE 7
Analyze and explain the variances in an activity-based standard cost system.

The traditional approach often uses a single-cost driver for all factory overheads in preparing flexible budgets. Exhibit 14.18 illustrates a typical traditional flexible budget for an output of 2,000 units (1,000 direct labor-hours) when the firm's master budget calls for output of 3,000 units (1,500 direct labor-hours) and the firm uses direct labor-hours to assign factory overhead to cost objects. The firm spent 1,200 direct labor-hours to manufacture 2,000 units. Exhibit 14.19 shows a typical traditional performance report for the operations.

Many firms in today's new manufacturing environments no longer use a single activity measure, such as direct labor-hours or machine-hours, to determine overhead rates and assign overhead to cost objects. Recent advances in activity-based costing have led many firms to measure and monitor different overheads based on the

EXHIBIT 14.18   **Master Budget and Traditional Flexible Budget**

Variable	Cost Function Fixed	Cost Function Cost Item	Flexible Budget 2,000 Units (1,000 direct labor-hours)	Master Budget 3,000 Units (1,500 direct labor-hours)
$20/unit		Direct materials	$ 40,000	$ 60,000
30/Direct labor-hours		Direct labor	30,000	45,000
2/Direct labor-hours		Indirect material	2,000	3,000
5/Direct labor-hours		Repair and maintenance	5,000	7,500
	$ 5,000	Receiving	5,000	5,000
	30,000	Engineering support	30,000	30,000
	75,000	Setup	75,000	75,000
		Total	$187,000	$225,500

EXHIBIT 14.19
Traditional Performance Report

	Actual Cost	Flexible Budget	Variance
Direct material	$ 50,000	$ 40,000	$10,000 U
Direct labor	36,000	30,000	6,000 U
Indirect material	3,000	2,000	1,000 U
Repair and maintenance	6,500	5,000	1,500 U
Receiving	3,000	5,000	2,000 F
Engineering support	30,000	30,000	—
Setup	50,000	75,000	25,000 F
Total	$178,500	$187,000	$ 8,500 F

EXHIBIT 14.20   **Cost Functions of Manufacturing Costs**

Cost Item	Activity Measure	Cost Function Variable	Fixed	Flexible Budget	Master (Static) Budget
Operating Data					
Output	Number of units			2,000 units	3,000 units
Direct labor-hours				1,000 hours	1,500 hours
Machine-hours				300,000 hours	450,000 hours
Number of setups				2 setups	3 setups
Cost Data					
Direct materials	Number of units	$20/unit	—	$ 40,000	$ 60,000
Direct labor	Direct labor	$30/hour, 0.5 hour/unit	—	30,000	45,000
Indirect materials	Direct labor-hours	$2/direct labor-hours	—	2,000	3,000
Repair and maintenance	Machine-hours	$0.01/machine-hours	$ 3,000	6,000	7,500
Receiving	Number of setups	$1,500/setup	500	3,500	5,000
Setup	Number of setups	$25,000/setup	—	50,000	75,000
Engineering support	Per period		$30,000	30,000	30,000
Total				$161,500	$225,500

activities that drive overheads. These firms also use several activity measures in preparing flexible budgets. The budgeted total factory overhead no longer varies with changes of a single activity; instead, it uses different activities for different factory overheads. Exhibit 14.20 illustrates the preparation of a flexible budget using an activity-based approach. Exhibit 14.21 is a performance report that uses the activity-based cost functions in determining the flexible budget for the product manufactured during the period.

EXHIBIT 14.21   **Performance Report Using Activity-Based Costing**

	Cost Incurred	Flexible Budget	Variance
Direct materials	$ 50,000	$ 40,000 (2,000 units × $20 per unit)	$10,000 U
Direct labor	36,000	30,000 (2,000 units × 0.5 hour per unit × $30 per hour)	6,000 U
Indirect materials	3,000	2,000 (1,000 hours × $2 per hour)	1,000 U
Repair and maintenance	6,500	6,000 (300,000 machine hours × $0.01 per machine hour + $3,000)	500 U
Receiving	3,000	3,500 (2 setups × $1,500 per setup + $500)	500 F
Engineering support	30,000	30,000 ($30,000 per period)	—
Setup	50,000	50,000 (2 setups × $25,000 per setup)	—
Total	$178,500	$161,500	$17,000 U

EXHIBIT 14.22
Comparison of Traditional and Activity-Based Costing

	Variance		
	Traditional	Activity-Based	Difference
Direct materials	$10,000 U	$10,000 U	—
Direct labor	6,000 U	6,000 U	—
Indirect materials	1,000 U	1,000 U	—
Repair and maintenance	1,500 U	500 U	$ 1,000
Receiving	2,000 F	500 F	1,500
Engineering support	—	—	
Setup	25,000 F	—	25,000
Total	$ 8,500 F	$17,000 U	$25,500

The total manufacturing cost variance for the period is $8,500, favorable, in a traditional performance report that uses a single activity for all factory overheads (Exhibit 14.19). In contrast, the operation has a $17,000 unfavorable variance when the firm uses an activity-based flexible budget to prepare the performance report for the same period (Exhibit 14.21). Exhibit 14.22 compares these performance reports.

Exhibit 14.22 demonstrates that variances identified using a traditional approach (single activity for applying factory overheads) can be misleading. Substantial differences are found in variances for repair and maintenance, receiving, and setups. The traditional approach considers repair and maintenance a variable cost that varies with direct labor hours. In contrast, the activity-based approach identifies repair and maintenance as a mixed cost with the variable portion of the cost varying with machine-hours. As a result, the variance of repair and maintenance decreases from $1,500 unfavorable to $500 unfavorable. The traditional approach considers both receiving and setups as fixed costs while the activity-based costing approach classifies these two costs as batch-related costs. The net result of these changes in cost variances has a $27,500 total difference.

Variance Determination in the New Manufacturing Environment

LEARNING OBJECTIVE 8
Describe the effects of advances in new manufacturing technologies and changes in operating environments on standard cost systems.

In today's new manufacturing environment, not all firms choose to calculate and report all variances that traditional standard cost systems usually report. Among variances that some firms no longer compute and report are materials price, materials usage, labor efficiency, variable overhead budget, and overhead production volume variances. Chapter 13 discussed materials and labor variances. The next sections examine overhead variances in a new manufacturing environment.

Overhead Flexible Budget Variance

Using an activity-based costing system allows firms to calculate overhead variances in more detail. These variances can reveal more precisely the underlying causes of variances that afford opportunities for firms to take appropriate responses.

Firms should not, however, overemphasize individual overhead variances. The focus should be on the total factory overhead variance, not variances of individual overhead items. Overemphasizing unfavorable setup variances, for example, could encourage large production runs that lead to increases in inventory costs and needs for working capital. Overconcern about unfavorable factory overhead variances might lead to decreased inspection of processes, products, or both; curtailed preventive maintenance; or taking other actions that might have long-term ill-effects on the firm.

Production Volume Variance

Production volume variances arise when units manufactured differ from the units budgeted to be manufactured. The units budgeted to be manufactured (master budget) in a period is the denominator activity for the period. The difference in units and the standard fixed factory overhead rate determine the magnitude of production volume variance. The standard fixed factory overhead rate is determined by dividing the total budgeted fixed factory overhead by the denominator activity. Thus, the denominator activity level a firm chooses determines the difference in units, the standard fixed overhead rate, and the magnitude of production volume variance.

Firms should use as the denominator the capacity of the equipment or division that is the constraint of their entire manufacturing process rather than the operating level of the division or firm itself. When more than one constraint exists, the denominator should be the smallest capacity among the constrained production processes. Using a nonconstrained activity or an activity other than the one for the process with the lowest constraint as the denominator of a division encourages the division to manufacture the denominator quantity to minimize their production volume variances. The excess units manufactured by a nonconstrained division or equipment over the production capacity of the constrained divisions or equipment increases work-in-process inventories and uses resources earlier than needed. Manufacturing for inventory does not increase productivity. Nor does it increase the firm's operating income. In fact, favorable production volume variances of nonconstrained equipment or divisions increase the cost of the firm.[11]

A division can achieve a favorable production volume variance by stepping up production activities to increase the number of units manufactured. This favorable production volume variance could be achieved, however, by manufacturing for inventory—a practice in which a JIT firm should never engage. The production volume variance should never be calculated and reported for performance evaluation purposes because it encourages the unwanted behavior of manufacturing for inventory. If calculated, the fixed factory overhead production volume variance should be reported only to top managers. It should never be used to evaluate the performances of lower operating units.

Furthermore, no production volume variance should be reported alone. The reporting of a production volume variance, either favorable or unfavorable, should be accompanied by the ratio of units used or shipped to the total units manufactured. So long as the ratio is 1 or close to 1, any production volume variance can have only long-term implications; it has no significance in short-term evaluation of operations.

Investigation of Variances

LEARNING OBJECTIVE 9
Determine whether to investigate variances.

Identifying and reporting variances are the first steps in reducing variances and improving operations. An effective standard cost system requires management to respond promptly and take proper actions to prevent the variances from recurring. Left uncorrected, variances are likely to repeat period after period. Abuse and waste of resources, falling morale, and declining performance are common among firms that pay no heed to variances.

[11] Eliyahu M. Goldratt, *The Goal* (Croton-on-Hudson, NY: North River Press, 1986).

REAL-WORLD FOCUS   What Effects Does Cell Manufacturing Have on Factory Overhead?

After almost a century of movement toward mass production, use of ever larger machinery, and the facility of Henry Ford's assembly line, the National Association of Manufacturers found in 1994 that the majority of factories are now using cell manufacturing. In cell manufacturing, a small team of workers group around manufacturing equipment and make entire products. A single cell makes, checks, and even packages an entire product or component. Each worker performs several tasks, and every cell is responsible for the quality of its products.

The benefits of manufacturing cells include speed, productivity, flexibility, and higher quality. After Gore-Tex adopted cell manufacturing at several of its 46 plants, it cut production time in half and delivered 97 percent, as compared to 75 percent, of the products on time. At both Harley-Davidson and Lexmark, productivity has increased by 25 percent. Harley-Davidson's cell-based plants have experienced substantial improvements in quality, despite the fact that the number of quality inspectors have been cut significantly. Mr. Kathuria, a factory manager at Harley-Davidson, attributed the success of cells to employee satisfaction. Working on an assembly line allows each worker to spend only a few seconds on each product.

Few workers would see the finished product. In cells employees see their product from start to finish." As Mr. Kathuria says, "they own the serial number."

However, does cell manufacturing have effect on factory overheads?

Firms adopting cell manufacturing have found their factory overheads decreased both in total and in unit cost. At Harley-Davidson, the floor space occupied by the factory was reduced by a third. Gore-Tex decreased the space taken up by the plant by one-quarter. Factors contributing to the need for less space are clustering of equipment and decrease or elimination of work-in-process and finished inventories.

Increased productivity further allows the reduced total factory overhead to be borne by higher volumes and, thus, decreases factory overhead per unit. In 1981, Harley-Davidson took a week to make a cylinder head and turned over its product only 4.5 times a year. In 1994, it took a two-man cell less than three hours to make a cylinder head and the firm turned over its stock 40 times a year.

Source: Based on "The Celling Out of America," *The Economist,* December 1994, pp. 63–64.

Not all variances call for investigation and corrective action, however. The proper response to a variance depends on the type of standard the firm uses, the firm's expectation, the magnitude and impact of the variances, and the causes and controllability of variances.

Type of Standard

A firm may set its standards based on a currently attainable standard or an ideal standard. Proper actions for variances from these two standards differ. A material variance from a currently attainable standard, either favorable or unfavorable, often requires management's immediate attention.

The same variance from an ideal standard, in contrast, can require no management action beyond noting improvements in operations as indicated by the magnitude and direction of the variance. So long as the organization is making good progress over time toward the ideal standard, management might not need to take any corrective action, even if the variance is rather substantial in amount.

Expectations of the Firm

Firms have different expectations on their operations. A firm experiencing a crisis needs and demands peak performance from all employees. A struggling firm might need to attain the established standards in all cases. To survive, the firm is likely allowing no exception to the standard, even if the firm adopts an ambitious ideal standard. In contrast, a highly profitable firm could be satisfied with making steady progress toward its established standard, especially when it uses an ideal standard to communicate its desired ultimate goal to members and divisions of the firm. The firm would not be overly alarmed by minor deviations from the standard. Companies with good management and caring workers, however, care about meeting the standards regardless of whether the firm is struggling or profitable.

Experience also can affect an organization's reaction to a variance. A firm in the early stages of using an ideal standard should not be alarmed by small deviations; a firm further along the path toward an ideal standard might see the same amount of deviation as a setback that requires immediate corrective action.

Magnitude, Pattern, and Impact of a Variance

The magnitude of variances and their impacts on future operations affect the firm's reaction to variances. Rarely do operating results meet the standards exactly. Small variances are expected, and most of them need no special attention from management unless a pattern develops. A persistent but small unfavorable variance might require management's attention because its cumulative effect on operating results can be quite substantial and reflect deteriorating operations.

Large variances usually catch the attention of management and receive immediate responses. The responses, however, might not be warranted. A large variance does not require action if it is not a result of aberrations of the underlying operations or if it is a one-time occurrence. A large unfavorable factory overhead efficiency variance identified with direct labor-hours as the base for applying factory overhead might not indicate runaway factory overhead costs if the bulk of factory overhead is driven by activities other than direct labor-hours. Similarly, a large unfavorable direct materials usage variance requires no further action if it is a result of, for example, a poorly adjusted machine that has since been properly calibrated.

Causes and Controllability

The causes of variances and the degree to which an organization can control them determine whether corrective actions are needed. No action is needed if management has no control over the variance even if the variance has a significant impact on the firm's operations.

The causes of variances and the controllability of variances fall into two categories: random and systematic. **Random variances** are beyond the control of management, either technically or financially, and are often considered as *uncontrollable variances*. Many standards are point estimates of a long-term average performance of operations. Small variances in either direction occur in operations, and firms usually cannot benefit from investigating or responding to them. For example, prices of goods or services acquired in open markets fluctuate with, among other factors, supply and demand at the time of acquisition and the amount of time allowed to acquire the goods or services. These variances are random and require no management action. A firm with a 10 percent excess material usage would most likely not investigate the variance if the firm chose to purchase the equipment that, on average, had a spoilage rate of 12 percent and the standard allowed no spoilage.

Systematic variances are persistent and are likely to recur until corrected. They usually are controllable by management or can be eliminated or reduced through actions of management. Systematic variances that are material in amount require management to take proper corrective action immediately.

Among causes for systematic variances are errors in prediction, modeling, measurement, and implementation. Each of these factors has its own implications on the needs for further investigation or proper managerial actions to correct the variance. Exhibit 14.23 classifies variances according to controllability, causes, and actions to be taken.

Prediction errors result from inaccurate estimation of the amounts of variables included in the standard-setting process. For example, a firm expected a 5 percent price increase for a direct material when the material price increased 10 percent, or it expected to have adequate $10-per-hour workers available when a shortage forced the firm to hire workers at $15 per hour.

Modeling errors result from failing to include all relevant variables or from including wrong or irrelevant ones in the standard-setting process. A modeling error occurs when a firm uses as standards the production rates of experienced workers although most of its workers were new hires and had little or no experience. The unfavorable direct labor efficiency variance that the firm experienced is a result of the modeling

Random variances
are variances beyond the control of management, either technically or financially, and often are considered as uncontrollable variances.

Systematic variances
are variances that are likely to recur until corrected.

A prediction error
is a deviation from the standard because of inaccurate estimation of the amounts of variables in the standard-setting process.

Modeling errors
are failures in not including all relevant variables or including wrong or irrelevant variables.

EXHIBIT 14.23   Cause of Variance and Corrective Action

Controllability	Cause	Corrective Action	Example
Uncontrollable (random)	Random error	None	Overtime wages paid to make up time lost by employees ill with flu
			Materials lost in a fire
Controllable (systematic)	Prediction error	Modify standard-setting processes	Increases in materials prices faster than expected
	Modeling error	Revise model or modeling process	Failed to consider learning curve effect in estimating product costs
			Not allowing for normal materials lost
	Measurement error	Adjust accounting procedure	Bonus attributed to the period paid, not the period earned
			Costs assigned to wrong jobs
	Implementation error	Take proper actions to correct the causes	Failure to provide proper training for the task

error, not of inefficient operations. The standard of making 100 gallons of output from every 100 gallons of input material is a modeling error when the manufacturing process has a 5 percent normal evaporation rate.

Corrective actions for both prediction and modeling errors require the firm to change its standard and the standard-setting process.

Measurement errors

are uses of incorrect numbers because of improper or inaccurate accounting systems or procedures.

Measurement errors are uses of incorrect numbers because of improper or inaccurate accounting systems or procedures. Including bonuses for extraordinary productivity as a cost of the period in which the bonuses were paid rather than the period in which they were earned is a measurement error. Charging overhead incurred for setups based on direct production labor-hours rather than the number of setups is a measurement error. Corrective actions for measurement errors include redesigning the firm's accounting systems or procedures and conducting training courses for cost accountants.

Failure to correct prediction, modeling, or measurement errors would, in the long term, frustrate employees and lead them to focus on showing the best reported results, even at the expense of improving the firm's performance. Employees of firms using standard cost systems that have uncorrected prediction, modeling, or measurement errors often lose confidence in accounting reports.

Implementation error

are deviations from the standard due to operators' errors.

Implementation errors are deviations from the standard due to operators' errors. Unfavorable materials usage variances from using materials of lesser quality than those specified by the standard are implementation errors. The direct labor rate or efficiency variance in an operation that assigned workers with a different skill level than the one called for in the standard is an implementation error. Setting a cutting machine to cut tubes in lengths of 2 feet 9.7 inches, instead of 2 feet 10 inches as required, is an implementation error.

Some implementation errors are temporary and disappear in subsequent periods in a normal course of operation. Other implementation errors could be persistent and reappear until the firm takes proper corrective actions. An incorrectly set cutting machine continues to manufacture products with wrong lengths until the problem is corrected. Use of wrong or excessive materials in production, on the other hand, might occur in one or only a few production runs.

Control Chart

A control chart plots measures of an activity or event over time; this widely used tool helps managers identify out-of-control variances. A control chart has a horizontal axis, a vertical axis, a horizontal line at the level of the desirable characteristic, and one or two additional horizontal lines for the allowable range of variation. The horizontal line represents time intervals, batch numbers, production runs, or other measures over time of interest to the firm. In Exhibit 14.24, the horizontal line denotes months, from January through December. The vertical line denotes scales for the characteristic of interest

EXHIBIT 14.24
**Direct Labor Efficiency
Variance—Finishing
Department**

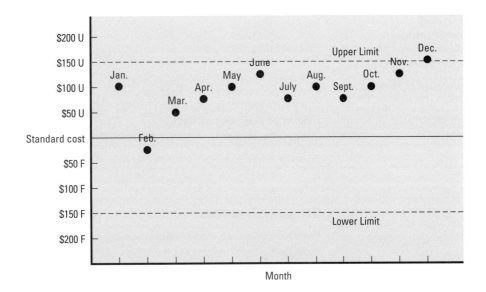

such as cost incurred. The scale of interest in Exhibit 14.24 is the amount of variance, ranging from $200 favorable to $200 unfavorable. The horizontal line at the level of the desirable characteristic in Exhibit 14.24 represents conformity with the standard ($0 variance). The two additional horizontal lines in Exhibit 14.24, are the upper and lower limits that indicate the allowable range of the variance. Management has decided that a variance less than $150 is acceptable. Variances within the limits are deemed random variances and no further action is needed unless a pattern emerges.

A control chart enables managers to grasp the size and the trend, if any, of variances over time. Exhibit 14.24 reflects an upward trend of unfavorable variances in March through June and repeated in September through December. An alert manager would very likely monitor the operations closely starting from, say, April or May. If corrective actions were taken in April or May, the upward pattern of unfavorable variances starting in September might not have occurred. The chart also suggests that the firm tends to have larger unfavorable variances at the beginning and end of a year. Management needs to examine this phenomenon and determine whether corrective actions are warranted.

Firms often set control limits in control charts. Typically, the two limits are upper and lower limits. Although the limits in Exhibit 14.24 are equal in distance from the standard cost, they are not necessarily so, especially when a variance in one direction is more costly to the firm than an equal amount of variance in the opposite direction. For example, if unfavorable variances are more costly than favorable variances, a firm might allow a narrower band for the upper limit than for the lower limit.

When the control limits are established using a statistical procedure, the chart is a **statistical control chart.** A common practice is to set the control limits at ± 3 standard deviations from the standard cost. Assume that the characteristics of interest have a normal distribution, a statistical control chart with ±3 standard deviations as the control limits suggest that the likelihood for an observation to be outside of the control limit is only 0.13 percent in either direction. For example, assume that the direct labor efficiency variance in Exhibit 14.24 has a normal distribution and $150 variance is three standard deviations away from the standard cost, then the chance for a variance such as the ones observed in December or February is only 0.13%—a rare occurrence that is not likely a result of random cause. Management may need to investigate the reason for the variance.

The control limits, however, vary with the type of standard the firm uses and management's expectations.

The chapter Appendix examines a cost-benefit approach in decisions to investigate variances under uncertainty.

Source: B. Gaumnitz and F Kollaritsch, "Manufacturing Variances: Current Practice and Trends," *Journal of Cost Management*, Spring 1991, pp. 58–64.

EXHIBIT 14.25
Company Practice for Investigating Direct Material and Direct Labor Variances

	Direct Materials	Direct Labor
All variances investigated	6.9%	5.3%
Variances above prescribed dollar limits investigated	34.8	31.0
Variances above prescribed percentage limits investigated	12.2	14.1
Statistical procedures used to select cases for investigation	0.9	0.9
Judgment used to decide whether investigation is needed	45.2	47.8
Variances never investigated	0.0	0.9
Total	100.0%	100.0%

Company Practices

Experienced managers usually have a good intuitive feeling about whether a variance requires further investigation. Others follow a magnitude rule of thumb, either in dollar amounts or in percentage of variation, to determine whether to further investigate variances. Often, the cause for a variance is corrected before the variance is reported. Visual inspections during operation might alert the operator of a cutting machine that the cuttings are not square as required. Most likely the operator would have adjusted the alignment that caused the improper cutting and corrected the problem before the manager received the variance report.

Note in Exhibit 14.25 that U.S. managers showed vastly different approaches to investigating direct materials and direct labor variances.

Summary

Establishing standard variable factory overheads require determination of cost behavior patterns of overhead cost items, selection of proper measure(s) of activity, and calculation of the overhead application rates.

The variable factory overhead flexible budget variance or the total variable factory overhead variance, shown as (A) in Exhibit 14.26, is the difference between the total variable factory overhead cost incurred and the total standard variable factory overhead for the number of units manufactured. Variable factory overhead spending and efficiency variances are detailed analyses of the total (flexible budget) variance. The variable factory overhead spending variance, (B), is the difference between the variable factory overhead incurred and the standard variable factory overhead for the actual quantity of the activity for applying variable factory overhead. The variable factory overhead efficiency variance, (C), is the difference between the standard variable factory overhead for the actual quantity of the activity for applying variable factory overhead and the standard variable factory overhead for the output of the period. Because of the imperfect association between the activity for applying overhead and the variable factory overhead costs, a variable factory overhead spending variance could include both price and usage variances. A variable factory overhead efficiency variance might not measure efficiency in the usage of variable factory overhead items; it might measure merely efficiency in use of the activity for applying overhead.

Uses of standard costs for fixed factory overhead include establishing the budgeted fixed factory overhead for the operation, selecting one or more activities for applying fixed factory overhead, and choosing the denominator activity level for the period as measured by the chosen activity measure. A fixed factory overhead application rate is determined by dividing the quantity of the activity for applying fixed factory overheads at the denominator activity level into the budgeted total fixed factory overhead. Fixed overhead variances include the fixed factory overhead spending (budget) variance and the production volume variance. In Exhibit 14.26, the fixed factory overhead spending variance, (E), is the difference between the actual and the budgeted fixed factory overhead for the period. Neither the actual units manufactured nor the actual level of the activity for applying fixed factory overheads incurred during the period has any

EXHIBIT 14.26   **Analysis of Overhead**

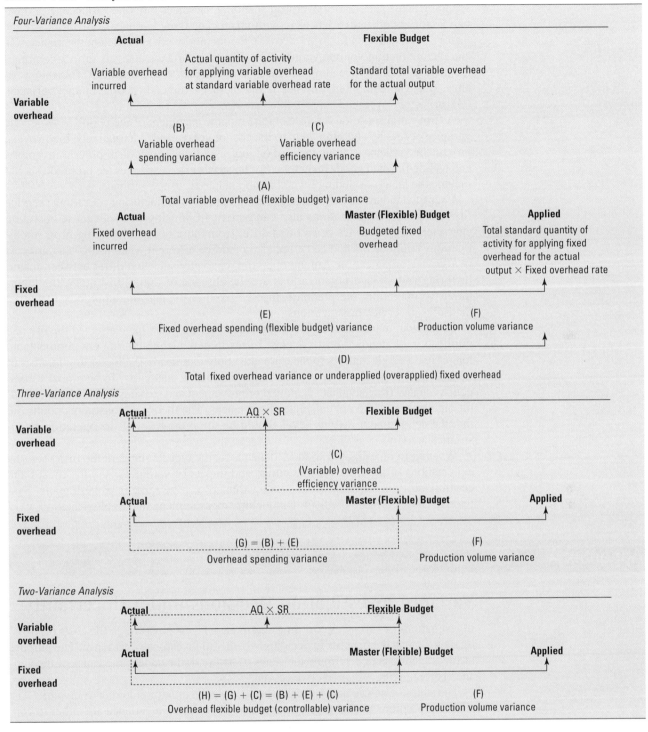

effect on the amount of the fixed factory overhead spending variance. The production volume variance, (F), is the difference between the total budgeted fixed factory overhead and the total fixed factory overhead applied to the units manufactured. The difference between the actual and the applied fixed factory overhead (or the sum of spending and production volume variances), (D), also is referred to as *underapplied* or *overapplied fixed factory overhead.*

The variances identified for variable factory overhead and fixed factory overhead can be combined into either three or two variances. The three-variance analysis creates a factory overhead spending variance, (G), by combining variable factory overhead spending and fixed factory overhead spending variances into one variance. The other two factory overhead variances remain intact. The three variances, therefore, are the factory overhead spending variance (G), the factory overhead efficiency variance (C), and the production volume variance (F). The two-variance analysis further combines the factory overhead spending variance, (G), with the factory overhead efficiency variance, (C). The combined variance is the factory overhead flexible budget variance, (H), or factory overhead controllable variance.

A firm can dispose of variances in the income statement of the period in which the variance occurs by charging them to the cost of goods sold. Alternatively, the firm can prorate the variances among the cost of goods sold, ending work-in-process inventory, and ending finished goods inventory. For materials price variances the proration should include the materials ending inventory and materials usage variance.

Uses of standard cost systems are not limited to manufacturing operations; service firms and other organizations also can benefit from using them. Because operating characteristics of service firms often differ from those of manufacturing firms, modifications might be needed and emphases could be different when using standard cost in a service organization. Among operating characteristics that differ between manufacturing and service organizations are the absence of output inventory, the labor-intensive operation, the predominance of fixed costs, and the ambiguity of output measures in service organizations.

Changes in manufacturing environments in recent years have affected the use and implication of standard cost systems. Firms in new manufacturing environments no longer use a single activity to measure and apply overheads. An increasing number of firms are using ideal, rather than currently attainable, standards. To be globally competitive, many firms mandate continual improvement and striving for perfection. In addition, these firms do not calculate all variances. The theory of constraints points out that the denominator activity level should be set at the level of the operation's constrained activity.

Whether to investigate variances depends on the type of standard the firm uses, the expectations of the firm, the magnitude and impact of variances, and the causes and controllability of variances. Causes of variances can be random or systematic. Systematic causes include prediction, modeling, measurement, and implementation.

Appendix A

Variance Investigation Decisions under Uncertainty

Investigations of variances cost time and money. Firms must weigh the costs of investigation against the benefits in deciding whether to investigate a variance. The purpose of investigation is to determine the states of nature or the underlying cause of the variance before taking any corrective action.

The states of nature underlying a variance can be either random or *systematic*. The alternative actions available to management when facing a variance are either to conduct an investigation or to take no action. With two possible states of nature and two courses of action, there are four combinations, each of which entails a different cost to the firm. These four combinations follow:

IR Investigate and find the reported variance to be a **r**andom fluctuation. No further action is needed.

IN Investigate and determine the reported variance is a result of systematic or **n**onrandom causes. Management may need to take corrective action.

NR Do **n**ot investigate and the reported variance is a result of **r**andom variations.

NN Do **n**ot investigate and the reported variance is a result of systematic or **n**onrandom causes.

PAYOFF TABLE

The cost to the firm for different courses of action and states of nature is likely to be different. Exhibit 14.27 shows the consequences of alternative management action under different states of nature. The cost of an investigation is **I.** When the variance is the result of a nonrandom factor, the cost to the firm to correct the variance is **C.** The cost of correction includes the cost to correct the nonrandom factor that led to the variance and the cost of the variance that the firm is likely to continue to experience until the variance is corrected. If management decides not to investigate the reported variance and the variance is systematic and persistent, the firm suffers a total cost, **L** (the present value of all losses the firm will suffer before the next decision time).

The decision not to investigate is correct when the variance is a random occurrence. The firm wastes no resources at all; it will, however, suffer a loss of L if the reported variance is the result of a nonrandom cause.

Management should also estimate the likelihood that the operation is in control or out of control, based on its understanding of the state of nature of the operation. Being in control implies that the reported variance is a random phenomenon. Being out of control suggests that the reported variance is the result of one or more systematic causes. The estimated probabilities of the states of nature enable management to compute the expected costs for each alternative action. The expected costs then serve as the input to the variance investigation decision.

Assuming that upon receiving the variance report, management estimates the probability to be 90 percent that the reported variance is a random fluctuation. The cost to conduct an investigation is approximately $1,000. Corrective actions, if needed, will likely cost the firm approximately $5,000, including the loss from the variance that it will continue to incur before the cause is corrected. The firm will suffer losses with a present value of $30,000 if it conducts no investigation but the variance stemmed from a nonrandom cause. Exhibit 14.28 summarizes this information.

Management has a 90 percent chance of finding that the variance is merely a random fluctuation and that an investigation, if conducted, is therefore a waste of time and resources. However, there is a 10 percent chance that the variance results from one or more nonrandom factors that should be corrected to avoid further losses. With the cost of investigation, $1,000, and the cost of corrective action, $5,000, the firm's total cost will be $6,000 if the investigation finds that the cause of the variance is nonrandom. The expected value of investigation is, therefore, $1,500, as shown in this computation:

$$E(\text{Investigate}) = (\$1,000 \times 90\%) + (\$6,000 \times 10\%) = \$1,500$$

The states of nature in Exhibit 14.28 suggest a 90 percent chance that the variance is random. The firm incurs no cost if it decides not to investigate. However, there is a 10 percent chance that the variance is a result of one or more nonrandom factors. The firm is likely to suffer a total loss of $30,000 if the variance is a result of one or more

EXHIBIT 14.27
Payoff Table for Variance Investigation

	States of Nature	
Management Action	**Random**	**Nonrandom**
Investigate	*I*	*I + C*
Do not investigate	none	*L*

EXHIBIT 14.28
Decision Based on a Payroll Table

	States of Nature		
Management Action	**Random (90%)**	**Nonrandom (10%)**	**Expected Value**
Investigate	$1,000	$6,000	$1,500
Do not investigate	0	30,000	3,000

EXHIBIT 14.29
Use Payoff Table to Determine
Indifference Probability

	States of Nature	
Management Action	**Random** $(1 - p)$	**Nonrandom** (p)
Investigate	I	I + C
Do not investigate	0	L

non-random factors and the firm allows the variance to continue by conducting no investigation. Thus, the expected cost of the decision not investigating the cause of the variance is $3,000, as shown here:

$$E(\text{Do not investigate}) = (\$0 \times 90\%) + (\$30,000 \times 10\%) = \$3,000$$

The $1,500 expected cost of investigation is lower than the $3,000 cost of not investigating and, according to the payoff table, the firm will incur a lower cost if it conducts an investigation to find the cause of the reported variance and takes appropriate action based on the finding of the investigation.

INDIFFERENCE PROBABILITY

A firm also can use a payoff table based on the cost of actions and inactions to determine the maximum probability level for a nonrandom variance to occur. As long as the probability for a nonrandom variance to occur is at or below the calculated probability, then according to the payoff table, the preferred action is not to investigate the cause of the reported variance.

Let p be the probability for a nonrandom variance to occur. Then the probability of a random variance is $1 - p$. Exhibit 14.29 shows the payoff table.

The expected costs of management actions can be represented as follows:

$$E(\text{Investigate}) = I \times (1 - p) + (I + C) \times p$$

and

$$E(\text{Do not investigate}) = L \times p$$

If the costs of the alternative actions are the same, it makes no difference to the firm which course of action it takes. That is, for management to be indifferent to either course of action (to investigate or not to investigate), the expected costs must be equal. Expressed in equation, at the indifference point,

$$I \times (1 - p) + (I + C) \times p = L \times p$$

Simplifying the equation, we get

$$I + C \times p = L \times p$$

Rewritten,

$$p = \frac{I}{L - C}$$

For data presented in Exhibit 14.28, the indifference probability is 4 percent:

$$p = \frac{\$1,000}{\$30,000 - \$5,000} = 4\%$$

This result suggests that if the probability is 4 percent for the cause of variance to be one or more nonrandom factors, it makes no difference which course of action management takes. The final cost of taking either course of action will be the same to the firm. The optimal action is to conduct an investigation when the probability for nonrandom factors exceeds 4 percent. If the probability for the cause to be nonrandom is below 4 percent, the optimal action is not to investigate. Our earlier calculation confirms this conclusion. The probability of a nonrandom variance was estimated to be 10 percent, which exceeds 4 percent calculated above, and the payoff table suggests that the recommended course of action is for the firm to investigate the cause of the variance.

Key Terms

denominator activity, *572*
fixed factory overhead
   application rate, *572*
fixed factory overhead
   production volume
   variance, *573*
fixed factory overhead
   spending (budget)
   variance, *573*

implementation error, *592*
measurement error, *592*
modeling error, *591*
prediction error, *591*
random variances, *591*
statistical control charts, *593*
systematic variances, *591*
total fixed factory overhead
   variance, *573*

total variable factory overhead
   variance, *566*
variable factory overhead
   efficiency variance, *568*
variable factory overhead
   spending variance, *568*

Self-Study Problems
(For solutions, please turn to the end of the chapter.)

1. Analysis of Overhead Variance

Simpson Manufacturing has the following standard cost sheet for one of its products:

		Total
Direct materials	5 pounds at $2 per pound	$ 10
Direct labor	2 hours at 25 per hour	50
Variable factory overhead	2 hours at 5 per hour	10
Fixed factory overhead	2 hours at 20 per hour	40
Cost per unit		$110

The firm applies factory overhead based on direct labor-hours and determines the factory overhead rate based on manufacturing 400 units of the product.

The firm has the following actual operating results for the year just completed:

Units manufactured	360	
Direct materials purchased and used	1,800 pounds	$19,800
Direct labor incurred	750 hours	20,250
Variable factory overhead incurred		4,800
Fixed factory overhead incurred		15,800

Before closing the periodic accounts, the balances in selected accounts follow:

Account	Debit (total)	Credit (total)
Work-in-process inventory	$153,000	$134,640
Finished goods inventory	134,640	111,690
Cost of goods sold	111,690	

Required

1. Determine for the period the following items:
   a. Total standard variable factory overhead for the period.
   b. Total variable factory overhead applied during the period.
   c. Total budgeted fixed factory overhead.
   d. Total fixed factory overhead applied.
2. Compute the following variances using four-variance analysis:
   a. Total variable factory overhead variance.
   b. Variable factory overhead spending variance
   c. Variable factory overhead efficiency variance.
   d. Total underapplied or overapplied variable factory overhead variance.
   e. Fixed factory overhead spending variance.
   f. Production volume variance.
   g. Total fixed factory overhead variance.
   h. Total underapplied or overapplied fixed factory overhead variance.
3. Compute the following variances using three-variance analysis:
   a. Factory overhead spending variance.

   b.   Factory overhead efficiency variance.

   c.   Production volume variance.

4.   Compute the factory overhead controllable flexible budget and production volume variances using two-variance analysis.

5.   Make proper journal entries for

   a.   Incurrence of factory overhead costs.

   b.   Application of factory overhead costs to production.

   c.   Identification of factory overhead variances assuming that the firm uses the four-variance analysis identified in requirement 2.

   d.   Close all factory overhead cost items and their variances of the period if

   (1)   The firm closes all variances to the Cost of Goods Sold account of the period.

   (2)   The firm prorates variances to the inventory accounts and the Cost of Goods Sold account of the period.

2. Variance Investigation (Appendix A)

David Smiley is the manager of Photobonics Manufacturing. He notices that the operation in the last four weeks has had an unfavorable materials usage variance of $25,000. He is trying to decide whether to investigate this variance. If he investigates and discovers that the process is out of control (not due to a random occurrence that is likely to correct itself), corrective actions will cost the firm $5,000. The cost of investigation is $2,500. The firm would suffer a total loss of $55,000 if it continues with the out of control operation. Smiley estimates the probability for the operation to be out of control at 60 percent.

Required

1.   What are the expected costs of investigating and of not investigating? Should the operation be investigated?

2.   What is the maximum level of probability that the operation can be out of control and Smiley would be indifferent as to the course of action to be taken?

Questions

14–1   Verbatim Company budgeted $80,000 factory overhead to manufacture 1,000 units in 2005. At the end of 2005, the firm found out that it manufactured only 850 units. The firm spent $80,000 on factory overhead in 2005. Did the plant manager do a good job in controlling factory overheads if (a) the firm had only fixed factory overhead or (b) the budgeted factory overhead included $60,000 variable factory overhead?

14–2   What are the relationships between the variable factory overhead efficiency variance and the direct labor efficiency variance for a firm that uses direct labor-hours to apply factory overhead?

14–3   What are the relationships among factory overhead spending variance, variable factory overhead spending variance, fixed factory overhead budget variance, and variable factory overhead efficiency variance?

14–4   What is a factory overhead flexible budget variance?

14–5   "The direction of a variance (favorable or unfavorable) is irrelevant in decisions on whether or not to investigate the variance." Do you agree?

14–6   "As long as the total actual factory overhead is not significantly different from the total standard factory overhead for the operation, there is no need to conduct further analyses of the factory overhead variance." Do you agree?

14–7   Why do some firms choose to use a two-variance instead of a three-variance or four-variance analysis in analyzing their manufacturing overheads?

14–8   What is the difference between the applied variable factory overhead and the total variable factory overhead in the flexible budget? Between the applied fixed factory overhead and the total flexible budget fixed factory overhead?

14–9   Would the choice of denominator level affect the amount of a fixed factory overhead (flexible) budget variance? Production volume variance?

14–10 Sipple Furniture's master budget for the year includes $360,000 for fixed supervisory salaries. The budgeted monthly volume is 500 units. Supervisory salaries are expected to incur uniformly throughout the year. During August, the firm produced 250 units, incurred production supervisory salaries of $29,000 and reported $14,000 underapplied fixed overhead for supervisory salaries. What is Sipple Furniture's supervisory salaries flexible budget variance for August?

14–11   Baxter Corporation's master budget calls for the production of 5,000 units per month and $144,000 indirect labor for the year. Baxter considers indirect labor cost a variable overhead. During April, the firm produced 4,500 units and incurred indirect labor costs of $10,100. What amount would be reported as flexible budget variance for indirect labor?

(CMA Adapted)

14–12   Can a factory overhead variance be separated into price and efficiency variances?

14–13   List causes that could lead to a variable factory overhead spending variance.

14–14   List causes that could lead to a variable factory overhead efficiency variance.

14–15   List causes that could lead to a fixed factory overhead spending variance.

14–16   List causes that could lead to a production volume variance.

14–17   How do the characteristics of service and manufacturing firms differ? Discuss the effects, if any, that these characteristics could have on the use of a standard cost system by service firms.

14–18   Why do many firms in today's new manufacturing environment no longer compute and report a direct materials price variance?

14–19   What factors should be considered in determining whether or not to investigate a variance?

Exercises

14–20   **Variable Factory Overhead Variance**   The Platter Valley factory of Bybee Industries manufactures field boots. The cost of each boot includes direct materials, direct labor, and factory overhead. The firm traces all direct costs to products. However, it assigns overhead based on direct labor hours.

The firm budgeted $15,000 variable factory overhead and 2,500 direct labor hours to manufacture 5,000 pairs of boots in March 2006.

The factory spent 2,700 direct labor hours in March 2006 to manufacture 4,800 pairs of boots and spent $15,600 on variable factory overhead during the month.

Required

1. Compute the flexible-budget variance, the spending variance, and the efficiency variance for variable factory overhead.

2. Comment on the factory's operation in March 2006 with regard to variable factory overhead.

14–21   **Fixed Factory Overhead Variance**   (Continuation of Exercise 14–20) For March 2006 the Platter Valley factory of Bybee Industries budgeted $90,000 fixed factory overhead and 2,500 direct labor hours to manufacture 5,000 pairs of boots.

The factory spent 2,700 direct labor hours in March 2006 to manufacture 4,800 pairs of boots. The actual fixed factory overhead incurred for the month was $92,000.

Required

1. Compute the spending variance and the production volume variance for fixed factory overhead.

2. Compute fixed factory overhead flexible budget variance.

3. Comment on the factory's operation in March 2006 with regard to fixed factory overhead.

14–22   **Three-Variance Analysis of Factory Overhead**   (Continuation of Exercises 14–20 and 14–21) The Platter Valley factory of Bybee Industries uses three-variance analysis to determine factory overhead variances.

Required

1. Use the data given in Exercises 14–20 and 14–21 to compute the spending variance, the efficiency variance, and the production volume variance for factory overhead.

2. Use your answers for Requirement 1 for Exercises 14–20 and 14–21 to determine the spending variance, the efficiency variance, and the production volume variance for factory overhead.

14–23   **Two-Variance Analysis of Factory Overhead**   (Continuation of Exercises 14–20 and 14–21) The Platter Valley factory of Bybee Industries uses two-variance analysis to determine factory overhead variances.

Required

1. Use the data given in Exercises 14–20 and 14–21 to compute the controllable (flexible budget) variance and production volume variance for factory overhead.
2. Use your answers for Requirement 1 for Exercises 14–20 and 14–21 and determine the controllable (flexible budget) variance and the production volume variance for factory overheads.
3. Comment on implications of overhead variances using a two-variance analysis.

14–24 **Factory Overhead Analysis—Two, Three, and Four Variances**   Walkenhorst Company's machining department prepared its 2005 budget based on the following data:

Maximum capacity	50,000 units
Machine-hours per unit	2
Variable factory overhead	$3.00 per hour
Fixed factory overhead	$360,000

At the time when the department prepared its budget, it expected to operate at 80 percent of the maximum capacity. The department uses machine-hours to apply factory overhead. In 2005, the firm spent 85,000 machine-hours and $625,000 in manufacturing overhead to manufacture 42,000 units.

Required   Determine for the year

1. The factory overhead application rate.
2. The total flexible budget factory overhead for the operation in 2005.
3. The production volume variance.
4. The factory overhead spending variance.
5. The factory overhead efficiency variance.
6. The variable and fixed factory overhead spending variances if the actual fixed factory overhead for the year was $375,000.

14–25 **Factory Overhead Flexible Budget and Variance Analyses**   Bush & Co. uses flexible budgets for cost control. During March, Bush spent 2,850 machine-hours to produce 10,800 units and incurred $13,000 in total factory overhead, of which $4,500 was for fixed factory overhead.

The master budget for the year called for production of 150,000 units using 37,500 machine-hours and a total factory overhead of $180,000. The total fixed factory overhead in the annual budget was $60,000.

Required   Compute the following for March production:

1. Total flexible budget overhead for the units manufactured.
2. Factory overhead flexible budget variance.
3. All variances, including
   a. Variable and fixed factory overhead spending variances.
   b. Variable factory overhead efficiency variance.
   c. Fixed factory overhead production volume variance.
4. Reconcile your answers in Requirements 2 and 3 above.

14–26 **Three-Variance and Two-Variance Analyses**   (Continuation of Exercise 14–25) Using data given in Exercise 14–25 for Bush & Co.

Required

1. Use three-variance analysis to determine the following variances:
   a. Factory overhead spending variance.
   b. Factory overhead efficiency variance.
   c. Factory overhead production volume variance.
2. Use two-variance analysis to determine the following variances:
   a. Factory overhead controllable variance.
   b. Factory overhead production volume variance.

14–27 Flexible Budget and Variances For Depreciation   Somson SuperKlean Service's master budget includes $258,000 for equipment depreciation. The master budget was prepared for an annual volume of 103,200 chargeable hours. This volume is expected to occur uniformly throughout the year. During September, Somson performed 8,170 chargeable hours, and the firm reported $20,500 for depreciation on equipment.

Required

1. Determine the flexible budget amount for equipment depreciation in September.
2. Compute spending variance for the depreciation expense on equipment.
3. Calculate the production volume variance for the depreciation expenses.
4. List possible reasons for the spending variance.

14–28 Four-Variance Analysis   The following information is available from Swinney Company for its operations in March:

Factory overhead incurred	$20,000
Fixed overhead expenses, incurred	$ 8,000
Fixed overhead expenses, budgeted	$ 9,000
Direct labor hours spent	4,200
Standard direct labor hours for the units manufactured	4,000
Total budgeted direct labor hours	4,500
Standard variable overhead rate per DLH	$ 2.50

Swinney uses direct-labor hours to apply factory overheads.

Required   Compute for Swinney Company:

1. Variable factory overhead spending variance.
2. Variable factory overhead efficiency variance.
3. Fixed factory overhead spending (budget) variance.
4. Fixed factory overhead production volume variance.

14–29 Three-Variance Analyses   (Continuation of Exercise 14–28) Using data given in Exercise 14–28 for Swinney Company, analyze factory overheads using three-variance analyses.

Required

1. Use the data given and compute these variances:
    a. Factory overhead spending variance.
    b. Factory overhead efficiency variance.
    c. Factory overhead production volume variance.
2. Use your answers in Exercise 14–28 and compute these variances:
    a. Factory overhead spending variance.
    b. Factory overhead efficiency variance.
    c. Factory overhead production volume variance.

14–30 Two-Variance Analyses   (Continuation of Exercise 14–28) Using data given in Exercise 14–28 for Swinney Company, analyze factory overheads using two-variance analyses.

Required

1. Use the data given and compute these variances:
    a. Factory overhead controllable variance.
    b. Factory overhead production volume variance.
2. Use your answers in Exercise 14–28 and compute these variances:
    a. Factory overhead controllable variance.
    b. Factory overhead production volume variance.
3. Use your answers in Exercise 14–29 and compute these variances:
    a. Factory overhead controllable variance.
    b. Factory overhead production volume variance.

14–31 **Fixed Overhead Rate, Denominator Level, and Two-Variance Analysis**   Overhead information for Danielson Company for October follows:

Total overhead incurred	$28,800
Fixed overhead budgeted	$7,200
Total standard overhead rate per direct labor-hour (DLH)	$4.50
Standard variable overhead rate per DLH	$3.00
Standard production hours for the units manufactured	3,500

Required

1. What is the standard fixed factory overhead rate per direct labor-hour?
2. What is the denominator level at direct labor-hour?
3. What is the total factory overhead flexible budget variance?
4. What is the factory overhead production volume variance?
5. What is the total underapplied or overapplied factory overhead?

14–32 **Variance Analysis, Applied Overhead, and Operating Level**   Conehead Company's overhead costs for May are

Total standard overhead applied	$60,000
Flexible budget overhead for the units produced	54,000
Budgeted total overhead in the master budget for the period	72,000
Overhead incurred	63,000

Conehead budgeted to manufacture 7,500 units in May.

Required

1. What is the total overhead flexible budget variance?
2. What is the factory overhead production volume variance?
3. What is the total underapplied or overapplied factory overhead?
4. How many units were manufactured in May?

14–33 **Overhead at Two Activity Levels and Four-Variance Analysis**   Greenhat Company applies factory overhead based on machine-hours. The firm had the following budget for its operation in 2005, which was at 80 percent level:

Standard direct machine-hours (MH)	20,000
Variable factory overhead	$72,000
Total factory overhead rate per MH	$12.60

Greenhat budgeted its operation for 2006 at 90 percent level. The standard called for 2 machine-hours per unit manufactured. During 2006 Greenhat operated 23,000 machine-hours to manufacture 11,300 units. The firm incurred $12,000 more factory overhead than the flexible budget amount for the units manufactured, of which $5,000 was due to fixed factory overhead.

Required

1. What is the budgeted total fixed factory overhead at an 80 percent level of operation? At a 100 percent level of operation?
2. What are the standard variable factory overhead rate and the standard fixed factory overhead rate in 2006?
3. What is the total factory overhead flexible budget amount for the operation in 2006?
4. Using four-variance analysis, compute these for Greenhat Company:
   a. Variable factory overhead spending variance.
   b. Variable factory overhead efficiency variance.
   c. Fixed factory overhead spending variance.
   d. Factory overhead production volume variance.

14-34 Three-Variance Analysis   Use the data for Greenhat Company in Exercise 14–33.

Required   Compute the following variances using three-variance analysis:

1. Factory overhead spending variance.
2. Variable factory overhead efficiency variance.
3. Factory overhead production volume variance.

14-35 Two-Variance Analysis   Use the data for Greenhat Company in Exercise 14–33.

Required   Compute the following variances using two-variance analysis:

1. Factory overhead flexible budget variance.
2. Factory overhead production volume variance.

14-36 Two-Variance Analysis and Direct Labor Variance   Marilyn, Inc., uses standard cost system and analyzes overhead using two-variance analysis. The following information relates to its operations for the month of April:

Actual total cost for direct labor	$43,400
Total direct labor-hours worked	14,000
Total standard hours for the output	15,000
Direct labor rate variance—unfavorable	$ 1,400
Actual total overhead	$32,000
Budgeted fixed costs	$ 9,000
Normal activity in hours	12,000
Total overhead application rate per standard direct labor-hour	$ 2.25

Required

1. What was Marilyn's direct labor efficiency variance for April?
2. What was Marilyn's factory overhead flexible budget (controllable) variance for April?
3. What was Marilyn's production volume variance for April?

(CMA Adapted)

14-37 Three-Variances Analysis   Use the data in Exercise 14–36 for Marilyn, Inc.

Required   Using three-variance analysis, compute the following:

1. Factory overhead spending variance.
2. Variable overhead efficiency variance.
3. Factory overhead production volume variance

(CMA Adapted)

14-38 Four-Variance Analyses   (Continuation of Exercise 14–36) Use the data given in Exercise 14–36 for Marilyn Inc. In addition, the firm has determined that its variable factory spending variance in April was $360 favorable.

Required   Compute the following items:

1. Variable factory overhead efficiency variance.
2. Actual variable factory overhead in April.
3. Actual fixed factory overhead in April.
4. Fixed factory overhead spending variance.

14-39 Working Backward—Total Factory Overhead   Shonburger Company applies factory overhead based on machine-hours (MH) and had a favorable total factory overhead variance of $120,000 for 2006. Additional data pertaining to 2006 follow:

Variable overhead	
Applied based on standard MH for the units manufactured	$600,000
Applied to the actual MH	500,000

Fixed overhead	
Applied based on standard MH for the units manufactured	$360,000
Budgeted	300,000

Required

1. What is the total overhead incurred in 2006 if the favorable total overhead variance includes the production volume variance?

2. What is the total overhead incurred in 2006 if the favorable total overhead variance is defined as the flexible budget overhead variance?

3. What are the production volume variances in Requirement 1 and 2?

14–40 **Factory Overhead Variances**   Shateau Job Shop had the following operating data for its operations in 2007:

Budgeted fixed overhead	$20,000
Standard variable overhead	$3 per MH
Fixed overhead incurred	$21,400
Variable overhead incurred	$32,500
Budgeted volume (5,000 units)	10,000 MH
Machine-hours spent	9,500
Units produced	4,500

Required   Compute these for Shateau Job Shop:

1. Variable factory overhead spending variance.

2. Variable factory overhead efficiency variance.

3. Fixed factory overhead spending variance.

4. Factory overhead production volume variance.

5. Factory overhead spending variance using three-variance analysis.

6. Factory overhead controllable variance using two-variance analysis.

14–41 **ABC Costing**   Alden Company uses two-variance analysis for overhead variances. Its master budget calls for 32 setups and 32,000 machine hours to manufacture 6,400 units for the year. Selected data for the 2006 production activity follow:

Budgeted fixed factory overhead:		
Setup	$ 64,000	
Other	200,000	$264,000
Total factory overhead incurred		$480,000
Variable factory overhead rate:		
Per setup		$600
Per machine-hour		$5
Total standard machine-hour for the units manufactured		30,000 hours
Machine-hours worked		35,000 hours
Actual total number of setups		28

Required

1. Compute the factory overhead spending, efficiency, and flexible budget variances for 2006.

2. Assume that the firm includes all setup costs as variable factory overhead. The budgeted total fixed factory overhead, therefore, is $200,000, and the standard variable factory overhead rate per setup is $2,600. What is the factory overhead spending, efficiency, and flexible budget variances for the year?

3. Assume that the firm uses only machine-hours as the activity measure to apply both variable and fixed factory overhead and includes all setup costs as variable factory overhead. What is the factory overhead spending, efficiency, and flexible budget variances for the year?

14–42 Variance Analysis   The following information is taken from Tyro Company's operating data for the year just ended:

Total factory overhead incurred	$15,000
Fixed factory overhead incurred	$ 7,200
Budgeted fixed overhead	$ 8,000
Total hours worked	3,600
Total standard direct labor-hours for the units manufactured	4,000
Overhead application rate based on direct labor-hour	
Standard variable factory overhead rate	$2.00
Standard fixed factory overhead rate	$2.50

Required   Determine the following:

1. Variable factory overhead spending variance.
2. Variable factory overhead efficiency variance.
3. Fixed factory overhead spending variance.
4. Production volume variance.
5. Denominator volume for the master budget.

14–43 Fixed Overhead Variance   The annual master budget for Selo Imports includes $324,000 for fixed production supervisory salaries and production volume of 180,000 units. Supervisory salaries are expected to incur uniformly throughout the year. The firm spent $28,000 in production supervisory salaries to manufacture 15,750 units in September.

Required   Determine the following variances regarding production supervisory salaries that will be included in the performance report for September.

1. Budget (spending) variance.
2. Efficiency variance.
3. Production volume variance.

14–44 Variance Analysis   Savanah Shipping Co. had the following operating results for its operation in August:

Total standard factory overhead applied	$80,000
Total standard factory overhead for the units manufactured	84,000
Total standard factory overhead for the hours worked	83,000
Total factory overhead incurred	86,000

Required   Compute the following factory overhead variances for Savanah Shipping Co.

1. Overhead spending variance.
2. Overhead efficiency variance.
3. Overhead production volume variance.
4. Total factory overhead variance.

14–45 Four-Variance Analysis   Dickey Company had total underapplied factory overhead of $15,000 and unfavorable variable factory overhead spending variance of $6,000 for the year just ended. Additional data follow:

Variable factory overhead	
Applied based on the total standard direct labor-hours (DLH)	
for the units manufactured	$42,000
Total standard amount for the actual DLH worked	38,000
Fixed factory overhead	
Applied to the units manufactured	$30,000
Budgeted for period	27,000

Required Compute the following for the year:

1. Total variable factory overhead incurred.
2. Variable factory overhead efficiency variance.
3. Total fixed factory overhead incurred.
4. Fixed factory overhead spending variance.
5. Factory overhead production volume variance.

Problems

14–46 **Four-Variance Analysis** Franklin Glass Works budgeted to manufacture 200,000 units for the year ended November 30, 2006. The standard cost sheet specifies two direct labor-hours for each unit manufactured. Total factory overhead was budgeted at $900,000 for the year with a fixed factory overhead rate of $3 per unit. Both fixed and variable factory overhead are assigned to products on the basis of direct labor-hours. The actual data for the year ended November 30, 2006, follow:

Units manufactured	198,000
Direct labor-hours spent	440,000
Variable factory overhead incurred	$352,000
Fixed factory overhead incurred	$575,000

Required Determine the following for the year just completed:

1. Total standard hours for the output.
2. Variable factory overhead efficiency variance.
3. Variable factory overhead spending variance.
4. Fixed factory overhead spending variance.
5. Total fixed factory overhead applied.
6. Fixed factory overhead production volume variance.

14–47 **All Manufacturing Variances** Eastern Company manufactures special electrical equipment and parts. The firm uses a standard cost system with separate standards established for each product.

The transformer department manufactures a special transformer. This department measures production volume in direct labor-hours and uses a flexible budget system to plan and control department overhead.

Standard costs for the special transformer are determined annually in September for the coming year. The standard cost of a transformer at its DeCatur plant for the year just completed is $67 per unit, as shown here:

Direct materials		
Iron	5 sheets × $2	$10
Copper	3 spools × $3	9
Direct labor	4 hours × $7	28
Variable overhead	4 hours × $3	12
Fixed overhead	4 hours × $2	8
Total		$67

Overhead rates were based on normal and expected monthly capacity for the year, both of which were 4,000 direct labor-hours. Practical capacity for this department is 5,000 direct labor-hours per month. Variable overhead costs are expected to vary with the number of direct labor-hours actually used.

During October, the plant produced 800 transformers. This number was below expectations because a work stoppage occurred during labor contract negotiations. When the contract was settled, the department scheduled overtime in an attempt to reach expected production levels.

The following costs were incurred in October:

Direct Material	
Iron	Purchased 5,000 sheets at $2.00/sheet and used 3,900 sheets
Copper	Purchased 2,200 spools at $3.10/spool and used 2,600 spools

Direct Labor	
Regular time:	2,000 hours at $7.00 and 1,400 hours at $7.20
Overtime:	600 of the 1,400 hours were subject to overtime premium. The total overtime premium of $2,160 is included in variable overhead in accordance with company accounting practices.

Factory Overhead	
Variable	$12,000
Fixed	$ 8,800

Required

1. What is the most appropriate time to record any variance of actual materials prices from standard?
2. What is the direct labor rate (price) variance?
3. What is the direct labor efficiency variance?
4. What is the total direct materials price variance?
5. What is the total direct materials usage variance?
6. What is the variable overhead spending variance?
7. What is the variable overhead efficiency variance?
8. What is the budget (spending) variance for fixed overhead?
9. What is the factory overhead production volume variance?

(CMA Adapted)

14–48 Four-Variance Analysis Derf Company applies overhead on the basis of direct labor-hours. Each product requires two direct labor-hours. Planned production for the period was set at 9,000 units. Manufacturing overhead is budgeted at $135,000 for the period, of which 20 percent is fixed. The 17,200 hours worked during the period resulted in production of 8,500 units. Variable manufacturing overhead cost incurred was $108,500, and fixed manufacturing overhead cost was $28,000. Derf Company uses four-variance analysis to analyze manufacturing overheads.

Required Compute the following for Derf Company:

1. The variable overhead spending variance for the period.
2. The variable overhead efficiency (quantity) variance for the period.
3. The fixed overhead budget (spending) variance for the period.
4. The factory overhead production volume variance for the period.

(CMA Adapted)

14–49 Four-Variance Analysis Able Control Company, which manufactures electrical switches, uses a standard cost system and carries all inventory at standard costs. The standard factory overhead costs per switch are based on direct labor-hours:

Variable overhead	(5 hours at $8/hour)	$ 40
Fixed overhead	(5 hours at $12*/hour)	60
Total overhead		$100

*Based on budget of 300,000 direct labor-hours per month.

The following information is for the month of October:

- The firm produced 56,000 switches, although 60,000 switches were scheduled to be produced.

- The firm spent 275,000 direct labor-hours at a total cost of $2,550,000.
- Variable overhead costs were $2,340,000.
- Fixed overhead costs were $3,750,000.

The production manager argued during the last review of the operation that it should use a more up-to-date base for charging factory overhead costs to operations. She commented that her factory had been highly automated in the last two years and has hardly any direct labor. The factory hires only highly skilled workers to set up productions and to do periodic adjustments of machinery whenever the need arises.

Required

1. Compute the following for Able Control Company:
   a. The fixed overhead spending variance for October.
   b. The factory overhead production volume variance for October.
   c. The variable overhead spending variance for October.
   d. The variable overhead efficiency variance for October.
2. Comment on the implications of the variances and suggest any action that the firm should take to improve its operations.

(CMA Adapted)

14–50   **Find the Unknowns, Four-Variance Analysis**   Consider each of the following independent cases (1), (2), and (3) and fill in the unknowns. For each case, assume a standard cost system with machine-hours as the base to apply factory overheads.

	Case 1	Case 2	Case 3
Actual Operation and Cost Incurred			
Actual machine-hours spent	A	K	U
Variable factory overhead incurred	$7,500	L	W
Fixed factory overhead incurred	$11,400	M	$11,500
Flexible budget data			
Budgeted variable factory overhead	B	N	X
Budgeted fixed factory overhead	$10,000	O	$16,500
Total budgeted factory overhead	C	$11,960	Y
Standard cost data			
Variable factory overhead rate per machine-hour	D	$6.60	$5
Fixed factory overhead rate per machine-hour	E	P	Z
Denominator level in machine-hours	800	Q	1,200
Total standard machine-hours for the output	F	600	AA
Total standard variable factory overhead applied	$8,800	R	BB
Total standard variable overhead for the actual MH	G	S	CC
Total standard fixed factory overhead applied	$10,000	T	DD
Variances			
Variable factory overhead spending variance	$900*	$0	$450*
Variable factory overhead efficiency variance	H	$0	$200*
Fixed factory overhead spending variance	I	$800#	EE
Fixed factory overhead production volume variance	J	$500*	$550#

*Unfavorable
#Favorable

14–51   **Comprehensive**   Organet Stamping Company manufactures a variety of products made of plastic and aluminum components. During the winter months, substantially all production capacity is devoted to lawn sprinklers for the following spring and summer seasons. Other products are manufactured during the remainder of the year. Because a variety of products are manufactured throughout the year, factory volume is measured using production labor-hours rather than units of production.

Production volume has grown steadily for the past several years, as the following schedule of production labor indicates:

This year	32,000 hours
1 year ago	30,000 hours
2 years ago	27,000 hours
3 years ago	28,000 hours
4 years ago	26,000 hours

The company has developed standard costs for its several products. It sets standard costs for each year in the preceding October. The standard cost of a sprinkler this year was $4.00, computed as follows:

Direct materials		
Aluminum	0.2 pound × $0.40 per pound	$0.08
Plastic	1.0 pound × $0.38 pound	0.38
Production labor	0.3 hour × $9.00 per hour	2.70
Overhead*		
Variable	0.3 hour × $1.60 per hour	0.48
Fixed	0.3 hour × $1.20 per hour	0.36
Total		$4.00

*Calculated using 30,000 production labor-hours as normal capacity.

During February of this year, 8,500 good sprinklers were manufactured. The following costs were incurred and charged to production:

Materials requisitioned for production		
Aluminum	(1,900 pounds × $0.40 per pound)	$ 760
Plastic: Regular	(6,000 pounds × $0.38 per pound)	2,280
Low grade†	(3,500 pounds × $0.38 per pound)	1,330
Production labor		
Straight time	(2,300 hours × $10.00 per hour)	23,000
Overtime	(400 hours × $15.00 per hour)	6,000
Overhead		
Variable	$5,200	
Fixed	3,100	8,300
Costs charged to production		$41,670

Materials price variations are not charged to production but to a materials price variation account at the time the invoice is entered. All materials are carried in inventory at standard prices. Materials purchases for February follow:

Aluminum	(1,800 pounds × $0.48 per pound)	$864
Plastic		
Regular grade	(3,000 pounds × $0.50)	1,500
Low grade†	(6,000 pounds × $0.29)	1,740

†Plastic shortages forced the company to purchase lower-grade plastic than called for in the standards, which increased the number of sprinklers rejected on inspection.

Required Compute the following for February:

1. The total variance from standard cost of the costs charged to production.
2. The spending or budget variance for the fixed portion of the overhead costs.
3. The labor efficiency variance.
4. The labor rate variance.

5. The total variable cost variance.

6. The variable overhead spending, efficiency, and flexible budget variances.

7. The factory overhead production volume variance.

8. The materials variances. Also comment on the effects of using materials of different grades.

(CMA Adapted)

14–52 **Standard Cost Per Unit**   Cain Company has an automated production process; consequently, it uses machine-hours to describe production activity. The company employs a full absorption cost system. The annual profit plan for the coming fiscal year is finalized each April. The profit plan for the fiscal year ending May 31 called for production of 6,000 units, requiring 30,000 machine-hours. The full absorption cost rate for the fiscal year was determined using 6,000 units of planned production. Cain develops flexible budgets for different levels of activity to use in evaluating performance. During the fiscal year, Cain produced 6,200 units requiring 32,000 machine-hours. The following schedule compares Cain Company's actual costs for the fiscal year with the profit plan and the budgeted costs at two different activity levels:

CAIN COMPANY
Manufacturing Cost Report
For the Fiscal Year Ended May 31
(in thousands of dollars)

		Flexible Budget		
Item	Profit Plan (6,000 units)	31,000 Machine-Hours	32,000 Machine-Hours	Actual Costs
Direct material				
G27 aluminum	$ 252.0	$ 260.4	$ 268.8	$ 270.0
M14 steel alloy	78.0	80.6	83.2	83.4
Direct labor				
Assembler	273.0	282.1	291.2	287.0
Grinder	234.0	241.8	249.6	250.0
Manufacturing overhead				
Maintenance	24.0	24.8	25.6	25.0
Supplies	129.0	133.3	137.6	130.0
Supervision	80.0	82.0	84.0	81.0
Inspector	144.0	147.0	150.0	147.0
Insurance	50.0	50.0	50.0	50.0
Depreciation	200.0	200.0	200.0	200.0
Total cost	$1,464.0	$1,502.0	$1,540.0	$1,523.4

Required   Compute these:

1. The actual cost of material used per one unit of product.

2. The cost of material that should be processed per machine-hour.

3. The budgeted direct labor cost for each unit produced.

4. The variable manufacturing overhead rate per machine-hour in a flexible budget formula.

5. The manufacturing overhead production volume variance for the current year.

6. The manufacturing overhead spending variance for the year using three-variance analysis.

7. The total budgeted manufacturing cost for an output of 6,050 units.

(CMA Adapted)

14–53 **Capacity and Fixed Overhead Rate**   Yuba Machine Company manufactures nut shellers at its Sutter City plant and sells to nut processors throughout the world. Since its inception, the family-owned business has used actual factory overhead costs in costing factory output. On December 1, 2006, Yuba began using a predetermined factory overhead application rate to determine manufacturing costs on a more timely basis. This information is from the 2006–2007 budget for the Sutter City plant:

Plant practical capacity	100,000 direct labor-hours
Variable factory overhead costs	$3.00 per direct labor-hour
Fixed factory overhead costs	
Salaries	$ 80,000
Depreciation and amortization	50,000
Other expenses	30,000
Total fixed factory overhead	$160,000

Based on these data, the predetermined factory overhead application rate was established at $4.60 per direct labor-hour.

A variance report for the Sutter City plant for the six months ended May 31, 2007, follows. The plant incurred 40,000 direct labor-hours that represent one-half of the company's expected activity in the master (static) budget.

	Variance Report		
	Actual Costs	**Budgeted Costs***	**Variance[†]**
Total variable factory overhead	$120,220	$120,000	$ (220)
Fixed factory overhead			
Salaries	$ 39,000	$ 32,000	$ (7,000)
Depreciation and	25,000	20,000	(5,000)
Other expenses	15,300	12,000	(3,300)
Total fixed factory overhead	$ 79,300	$ 64,000	$(15,300)

*Based on 40,000 direct labor-hours,
[†]Favorable (Unfavorable)

Yuba's controller, Sid Thorpe, knows from the inventory records that one-quarter of the applied fixed factory overhead costs remain in the work-in-process and finished goods inventories. Based on this information, he has included $48,000 of fixed factory overhead as part of the cost of goods sold in the following interim income statement:

YUBA MACHINE COMPANY
Interim Income Statement
For Six Months Ended May 31, 2007

Sales	$625,000
Cost of goods sold	380,000
Gross profit	$245,000
Selling expense	44,000
Depreciation expense	58,000
Administrative expense	53,000
Operating income	$ 90,000
Provision for income taxes (40%)	36,000
Net income	$ 54,000

Required

1. Define practical capacity and explain why it might not be a satisfactory basis for determining fixed factory overhead application rate.

2. Prepare a revised variance report for Yuba Machine Company using the expected activity in its master (static) budget as the basis for applying fixed factory overhead.

3. Determine the effect on Yuba's reported operating income of $90,000 at May 31, 2007, if the fixed factory overhead rate was based on the expected activity in the company's master (static) budget rather than on practical capacity.

4. What capacity should the firm use to determine its factory overhead application rate if the firm (a) considers the product a cash cow or (b) is striving to capture market share?

(CMA Adapted)

14–54 **Four-Variance Analysis**   Nolton Products developed its overhead application rate from its current annual budget. The budget is based on expected output of 720,000 units with 3,600,000 direct labor-hours. The company schedules production uniformly throughout the year. Nolton produced 66,000 units requiring 315,000 direct labor-hours during May, when its actual overhead costs amounted to $375,000. A comparison of the actual costs with the annual budget and with one-twelfth of the annual budget follows.

	Annual Budget				Actual
	Total Amount	Per Unit	Per Direct Labor-Hour	Monthly Budget	Costs for May 2007
Variable					
Indirect labor	$ 900,000	$1.25	$0.25	$ 75,000	$ 75,000
Supplies	1,224,000	1.70	0.34	102,000	111,000
Fixed					
Supervision	648,000	0.90	0.18	54,000	51,000
Utilities	540,000	0.75	0.15	45,000	54,000
Depreciation	1,008,000	1.40	0.28	84,000	84,000
	$4,320,000	$6.00	$1.20	$360,000	$375,000

Nolton uses a standard cost system and applies factory overhead on the basis of direct labor-hours.

Required   Calculate the following amounts for Nolton Products for May 2007. Be sure to identify each variance as favorable (F) or unfavorable (U).

1. Applied overhead costs.
2. Variable overhead spending variance.
3. Variable overhead efficiency variance.
4. Fixed overhead spending variance.
5. Production volume variance.

(CMA Adapted)

14–55 **Proration of Variances**   Butrico Manufacturing Corporation uses a standard cost system, records materials price variances when raw materials are purchased, and prorates all variances at year-end. Variances associated with direct materials are prorated based on the balances of direct materials in the appropriate accounts, and variances associated with direct labor and manufacturing overhead are prorated based on the balances of direct labor in the appropriate accounts.

The following Butrico information is for the year ended December 31:

Finished goods inventory at 12/31	
Direct materials	$ 87,000
Direct labor	130,500
Applied manufacturing overhead	104,400
Raw materials inventory at 12/31	$ 65,000
Cost of goods sold for the year ended 12/31	
Direct materials	$348,000
Direct labor	739,500
Applied manufacturing overhead	591,600
Direct materials price variance (unfavorable)	10,000
Direct materials usage variance (favorable)	15,000
Direct labor rate variance (unfavorable)	20,000
Direct labor efficiency variance (favorable)	5,000
Manufacturing overhead incurred	690,000

The firm had no beginning inventories and no ending work-in-process inventory. It applies manufacturing overhead at 80 percent of standard direct labor.

Required Compute these:

1. The amount of direct materials price variance to be prorated to finished goods inventory at December 31.
2. The total amount of direct materials in finished goods inventory at December 31, after all materials variances have been prorated.
3. The total amount of direct labor in finished goods inventory at December 31, after all variances have been prorated.
4. The total cost of goods sold for the year ended December 31, after all variances have been prorated.

(CMA Adapted)

14–56 **Working Backward—Two-Variance Analysis** Beth Company has budgeted fixed factory overhead costs of $50,000 per month and a variable factory overhead rate of $4 per direct labor-hour. The standard direct labor-hours for the output of October production were 18,000. An analysis of the factory overhead indicates that Beth had an unfavorable budget (controllable) variance of $1,000 and a favorable production volume variance of $7,600 in October. Beth uses two-variance analysis for overheads.

Required Compute these:

1. Actual factory overhead incurred in October.
2. Beth's applied factory overhead in October.
3. Budgeted total direct labor-hours.

(CMA Adapted)

14–57 **Four-Variance Analysis** Edney Company employs a standard cost system for product costing. The standard cost of its product is

Raw materials	$14.50
Direct labor (2 direct labor-hours × $8)	16.00
Manufacturing overhead (2 direct labor-hours × $11)	22.00
Total standard cost	$52.50

The manufacturing overhead rate is based on a normal annual activity level of 600,000 direct labor-hours. The firm has the following annual manufacturing overhead budget:

Variable	$3,600,000
Fixed	3,000,000
	$6,600,000

Edney spent $433,350 direct labor cost for 53,500 direct labor-hours to manufacture 26,000 units in November. Costs incurred in November include $260,000 for fixed manufacturing overhead and $315,000 for variable manufacturing overhead.

Required Determine these for November:

1. The variable manufacturing overhead spending variance.
2. The variable manufacturing overhead efficiency variance.
3. The fixed manufacturing overhead spending (budget) variance.
4. The manufacturing overhead production volume variance.
5. The amount of under- or overapplied manufacturing overhead.

(CMA Adapted)

14–58 **Compute All Variable Variances** Aunt Molly's Old Fashioned Cookies bakes cookies for retail stores. The company's best-selling cookie is chocolate nut supreme, which is marketed as a gourmet cookie and regularly sells for $8 per pound. The standard cost per pound of chocolate nut supremes, based on Aunt Molly's normal monthly production of 400,000 pounds is:

Cost Item	Quantity	Standard Unit Cost	Total Cost
Direct materials			
Cookie mix	10 ounces	$0.02/ounce	$0.20
Milk chocolate	5 ounces	0.15/ounce	0.75
Almonds	1 ounce	0.50/ounce	0.50
			$1.45
Direct labor*			
Mixing	1 minute	14.40/hour	0.24
Baking	2 minutes	18.00/hour	0.60
			0.84
Variable overhead†	3 minutes	32.40/hour	1.62
Total standard cost per pound			$3.91

*Direct labor rates include employee benefits.
†Applied on the basis of direct labor-hours.

Aunt Molly's management accountant, Karen Blair, prepares monthly budget reports based on these standard costs. April's contribution report compares budgeted and actual performance:

Contribution Report
April 2007

	Budget	Actual	Variance
Units (in pounds)	400,000	450,000	50,000 F
Revenue	$3,200,000	$3,555,000	$355,000 F
Direct material	580,000	865,000	$285,000 U
Direct labor	336,000	348,000	12,000 U
Variable overhead	648,000	750,000	102,000 U
Total variable costs	1,564,000	1,963,000	$399,000 U
Contribution margin	$1,636,000	$1,592,000	$ 44,000 U

Justine Molly, president of the company, is disappointed with the results. Despite a sizeable increase in cookies sold, the product's contribution to the overall profitability of the firm decreased. Justine has asked Karen to identify the reasons for the decreases in contribution margin. Karen has gathered this information to help in her analysis of the decrease:

Usage Report
April 2007

Cost Item	Quantity	Actual Cost
Direct materials		
Cookie mix	4,650,000 ounces	$ 93,000
Milk chocolate	2,660,000 ounces	532,000
Almonds	480,000 ounces	240,000
Direct labor		
Mixing	450,000 minutes	108,000
Baking	800,000 minutes	240,000
Variable overhead		750,000
Total variable costs		$1,963,000

Required

1. Explain the $44,000 unfavorable variance between the budgeted and actual contribution margin for the chocolate nut supreme cookie product line during April 2007 by calculating the following variances. Assume that all materials are used in the month of purchase.

   a. Sales price variance.

   b. Materials price variance.

   c. Materials usage variance.

   d. Labor efficiency variance.

   e. Variable overhead efficiency variance.

   f. Variable overhead spending variance.

   g. Contribution margin volume variance.

2. a. Explain the problems that might arise in using direct labor-hours as the basis for allocating overhead.

   b. How might activity-based costing (ABC) solve the problems described in Requirement 2a?

(CMA Adapted)

14–59 **Compare Actual with Budgeted Costs**   Talbot Company manufactures shirts sold to customers for embossing with various slogans and emblems. Bob Ricker, manufacturing supervisor, recently received the following November production report; the November budget is based on the manufacture of 80,000 shirts.

November 2007 Production Report

Cost Item	Standard	Actual	Variance
Direct materials	$160,000	$162,000	$ (2,000)
Direct labor	240,000	246,000	(6,000)
Factory overhead	200,000	241,900	(41,900)

Bob was extremely upset by the negative variances in the November report because he had worked very closely with his people for the past two months to improve productivity and to ensure that all workers are paid their standard wage rates. He immediately asked to meet with his boss, Chris Langdon. Also disturbed by the November results, Chris suggested that Bob meet with Sheryl Johnson, Talbot's controller, to see if he can gain further insight into the production problems. Sheryl was extremely helpful and provided Bob with the additional information on the annual budget and these actual amounts for November:

Variable Overhead Expenditures

	Annual	Per Unit	November
Indirect material	$ 450,000	$0.45	$36,000
Indirect labor	300,000	0.30	33,700
Equipment repair	200,000	0.20	16,400
Equipment power	50,000	0.05	12,300
Total	$1,000,000	$1.00	$98,400

Fixed Overhead Expenditures

	Annual	November
Supervisory salaries	$ 260,000	$ 22,000
Insurance	350,000	29,500
Property taxes	80,000	6,500
Depreciation	320,000	34,000
Heat, light, telephone	210,000	21,600
Quality inspection	220,000	29,900
Total	$1,440,000	$143,500

- Factory overhead at Talbot includes both variable and fixed components and is applied on the basis of direct labor-hours. The company's 2007 budget includes the manufacture of 1 million shirts and the expenditure of 250,000 direct labor-hours.
- The standard labor rate at Talbot is $12 per hour, and the standard materials cost per shirt is $2.
- Actual production for November was 82,000 shirts.

With these data, Sheryl and Bob analyzed the November variances, paying particular attention to the factory overhead variance because of its significance. Sheryl knows that part of the problem is that Talbot does not use flexible budgeting, and she will try to explain this to Bob as they analyze the data.

Required

1. By calculating the following four variances, explain the $41,900 unfavorable variance between budgeted and actual factory overhead during the month of November 2007:
   a. Variable factory overhead sales volume variance.
   b. Variable overhead efficiency variance.
   c. Variable overhead spending variance.
   d. Fixed overhead spending variance.
2. Describe the likely behavioral impact of the information provided by the calculations in Requirement 1 on Bob Ricker. Be sure to make specific reference to the variances calculated, indicating his responsibility in each case.

(CMA Adapted)

14–60 **Variance Investigation under Uncertainty (Appendix A)** The internal auditor of Transnational Company estimates the probability of its internal control procedure being in control to be 80 percent. She estimates the cost to conduct an investigation to find areas for improvement to be about $20,000 and the cost to revise and improve the internal control procedure to be approximately $50,000. The present value of savings from having the new procedure is expected to be $250,000.

Required

1. Construct a payoff table for the firm to use in determining its best course of action.
2. What is the expected cost to the firm if it conducts an investigation? If it does not investigate? Should the firm investigate?
3. What is the expected cost of perfect information?

14–61 **Variance Investigation under Uncertainty (Appendix A)** The manager of MMX Digital must decide whether to initiate an advertising campaign for the firm's newest multimedia computer chip. There has been some discussion among division managers about the chip's market condition. The marketing department assesses the probability of having a strong market to be 0.6.

The manager, with the help of the marketing staff, has estimated the profits she believes the firm could earn:

Profits with advertising	
Strong market	$10 million
Weak market	4 million
Profits without advertising	
Strong market	8 million
Weak market	5 million

Required

1. Should the firm undertake the advertising campaign?
2. What is the probability level regarding the state of the market that will render the manager indifferent as to the courses of action?

3. What is the maximum amount the firm should pay to obtain the perfect information regarding the state of the market if such information is available?

14–62 Variance Investigation under Uncertainty (Appendix A) A student organization is planning to raise funds by selling flower bouquets on Valentine's Day. The sales booth costs $100, which can be sold to another student organization for $30 after the project. The bouquets can be purchased at $7 each and will be sold for $12 each. The cost of having bouquets delivered to the booth is $20 per delivery. Once delivered, no bouquet can be returned.

Required

1. Assume that the organization predicts sales to be 60 bouquets. If actual sales are 48 bouquets, what is the cost of the prediction error?
2. Assume that the organization must place its order in 12-bouquet bundles. With good weather, the organization believes it can sell 100 bouquets, but it will most likely sell 36 bouquets if the weather is inclement. A member of the organization majoring in meteorology has predicted, after consulting with meteorologists at the National Weather Bureau and local TV stations, that the probability of having good weather on Valentine's Day is 60 percent.
   a. Construct a payoff table for the situation that the organization faces.
   b. What is the organization's best course of action?
   c. What is the expected value of perfect information?

14–63 Variance Investigation under Uncertainty (Appendix A) Ron Bagley is contemplating whether to investigate a labor efficiency variance the firm experienced in the assembly department. The investigation will cost $6,000. If it finds that the department is operating improperly, corrective action will cost another $18,000. If the department is operating improperly and Ron failed to make the investigation, additional operating costs because of inefficiencies are expected to be $33,000. At what level of probability for improper operations would Ron be indifferent about conducting an investigation to find the cause of the variance?

14–64 Two-Variance Analysis International Finance Incorporated issues letters of credit to importers for overseas purchases. The company charges a nonrefundable application fee of $3,000 and, on approval, an additional service fee of 2 percent of the amount of credit requested.

The firm's budget for the year just completed included fixed expenses for office salaries and wages of $500,000, leasing office space and equipment of $50,000, and utilities and other operating expenses of $10,000. In addition, the budget also included variable expenses for supplies and other variable overhead costs of $1,000,000. The firm estimated these variable overhead costs to be $2,000 for each letter of credit approved and issued. The firm approves, on average, 80 percent of the applications received.

During the year, the firm received 600 requests and approved 75 percent of them. The total variable overhead was 10 percent higher than the standard amount applied; the total fixed expenses were 5 percent lower than the amount allowed.

In addition to these expenses, the firm paid a $270,000 insurance premium for the letters of credit issued. The insurance premium is 1 percent of the amount of credits issued in U.S. dollars. The actual amount of credit issued often differs from the amount requested due to fluctuations in exchange rates and variations in the amount shipped from the amount ordered by importers. The strength of the dollar during the year decreased the insurance premium by 10 percent.

Required

1. Calculate the variable and fixed overhead rates for the year.
2. Prepare an analysis of the overhead variances for the year just completed.

14–65 Ethics and Overhead Variance New Millennium Technologies uses a standard cost system and budgeted 50,000 machine-hours to manufacture 100,000 units in 2006. The budgeted total fixed factory overhead was $9,000,000. The firm manufactured and sold 80,000 units in 2006 and would report a loss of $9,600,000 after disposing of all the production volume variance in the operating income of the period.

Bob Evans, VP–Finance, believes that the denominator activity level of 50,000 machine-hours is too low. The maximum capacity of the firm is between 5,000,000 and 6,000,000 machine-hours. Bob considers a denominator level at half the low-end capacity to be reasonable. Furthermore, he believes that the unfavorable production volume variance should be capitalized because the demand for the firm's products has been increasing rapidly. A conservative projection of the firm's sales places the total sales at a level that will require at least 5 million machine-hours in less than 5 years. Bob was able to show a substantial improvement in operating income after revising the cost data. He used the revised operating result in briefing financial analysts.

Required

1. Compute the effect of the changes on operating income.
2. Is it ethical for Bob to make the changes?

Solutions to Self–Study Problems

1. Analysis of Overhead Variance

1. a. | | |
        |---|---:|
        | Units manufactured during the period | 360 |
        | Standard direct labor-hours per unit | × 2 |
        | Total standard direct labor-hours for the units manufactured | 720 |
        | Standard variable factory overhead rate per direct labor-hour | × $5.00 |
        | Total standard variable factory overhead for the period | $3,600 |

    b. | | |
        |---|---:|
        | The total variable factory overhead applied (same as the total standard variable overhead for the period) | $3,600 |

    c. | | |
        |---|---:|
        | Budgeted units of production | 400 |
        | Standard direct labor-hours per unit | × 2 |
        | Total standard direct labor-hours for units budgeted for the period | 800 |
        | Standard fixed factory overhead rate per direct labor-hour | × $20 |
        | Total budgeted fixed factory overhead for the period | $16,000 |

    d. | | |
        |---|---:|
        | Total standard direct labor-hours for the units manufactured (from 1a) | 720 |
        | Standard fixed factory overhead rate per direct labor-hour | × $20 |
        | Total fixed factory overhead applied | $14,400 |

2. a, b, and c.

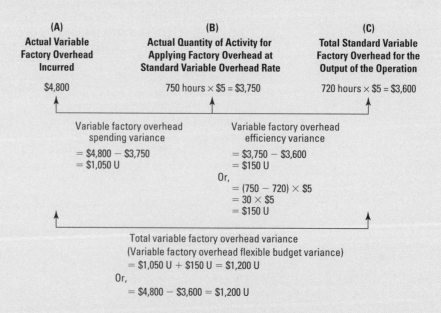

d. Total underapplied variable factory overhead variance = variable factory overhead flexible budget variance = $1,200.

e, f, and g.

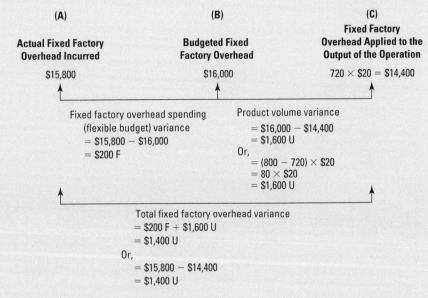

	(A) Actual Fixed Factory Overhead Incurred	(B) Budgeted Fixed Factory Overhead	(C) Fixed Factory Overhead Applied to the Output of the Operation
	$15,800	$16,000	720 × $20 = $14,400

Fixed factory overhead spending (flexible budget) variance
= $15,800 − $16,000
= $200 F

Product volume variance
= $16,000 − $14,400
= $1,600 U
Or,
= (800 − 720) × $20
= 80 × $20
= $1,600 U

Total fixed factory overhead variance
= $200 F + $1,600 U
= $1,400 U
Or,
= $15,800 − $14,400
= $1,400 U

h. Total underapplied fixed factory overhead variance = total fixed factory overhead variance = $1,400

3. a. Factory overhead spending variance = Variable factory overhead spending variance + Fixed factory overhead spending variance
= $1,050 U + $200 F
= $850 U

b. Factory overhead efficiency variance = Variable factory overhead efficiency variance = $150 U

c. Production volume variance = $1,600 U

4. Factory overhead controllable (flexible budget) variance = Factory overhead spending variance + Factory overhead efficiency variance
= $850 U + $150 U
= $1,000 U

Production volume variance is $1,600 U, the amount identified in both four-variance and three-variance analyses.

5.a.	Factory Overhead	20,600	
	Cash, Prepaid accounts, Accumulated Depreciations; or Sundry Payable accounts		20,600
b.	Work-in-Process Inventory	18,000	
	Factory Overhead Applied		18,000
c.	Factory Overhead Applied	18,000	
	Variable Factory Overhead Spending Variance	1,050	
	Variable Factory Overhead Efficiency Variance	150	
	Production Volume Variance	1,600	
	Factory Overhead		20,600
	Fixed Factory Overhead Spending Variance		200
d.	(1) Cost of Goods Sold	2,600	
	Fixed Factory Overhead Spending Variance	200	
	Variable Factory Overhead Spending Variance		1,050
	Variable Factory Overhead Efficiency Variance		150
	Production Volume Variance		1,600

(2) Ending balances at standard are

Work-in-process inventory ($153,000 − $134,640)	$ 18,360
Finished goods Inventory ($134,640 − $111,690)	22,950
Cost of goods sold	$111,690
Total	$153,000

Account	Standard Cost	Percent of Total	Proration of Variance	Adjusted Total Cost
Work-in-process, ending	$ 18,360	12%	$2,600 × 0.12 = $ 312	$ 18,672
Finished goods, ending	22,950	15	2,600 × 0.15 = 390	23,340
Cost of goods sold	111,690	73	2,600 × 0.73 = 1,898	113,588
Total	$153,000	100%	$2,600	$155,600

Cost of Goods Sold	1,898	
Work-in-process	312	
Finished Goods	390	
Fixed Factory Overhead Spending Variance	200	
Variable Factory Overhead Spending Variance		1,050
Variable Factory Overhead Efficiency Variance		150
Production Volume Variance		1,600

2. Variance Investigation (Appendix A)

Courses of Action

A_1: Investigate to determine the cause(s) of the efficiency variance.
A_2: Do not investigate.

States of Operation

S_1: The operation is in control (operates normally).
S_2: The operation is out of control.

Cost and Probability

I = Cost of investigation = $2,500
C = Cost of corrective action, if the process is found to be out-of-control = $5,000
L = Losses from being out of control with no correction taken = $55,000
P = Probability of the operation being in control = 40%

	Payoff Table	
	States of Operation	
Management Action	**In Control (random) (0.40)**	**Out of Control (systematic) (0.60)**
Investigate	$2,500	$2,500 + $5,000
Do not investigate	0	$55,000

1. E(investigate) = (40% × $2,500) + (60% × $7,500) = $5,500

   E(do not investigate) = 60% × $55,000 = $33,000

   The expected total cost to the firm will be lower if Smiley investigates the variance and takes proper actions to correct the cause of the variance, if the investigation finds the operation to be out of control.

2. Smiley is indifferent on the alternative courses of action if the probability of in control (P) is at a level that renders the expected costs of investigation and not investigating to be equal.

$$\$2,500P + \$7,500(1 - P) = \$55,000(1 - P)$$

$$50,000P = 47,500$$

$$P = 0.95$$

If the probability of the operation being in control is less than 95 percent, Smiley should investigate to find out the cause of variances.

Productivity, Marketing Effectiveness, and Strategic Profitability Analysis

After studying this chapter, you should be able to . . .

1. Describe productivity and identify effects of productivity changes on operating results
2. Compute and interpret partial operational and financial productivity
3. Separate change in financial productivity into productivity change, input price change, and output change
4. Calculate and interpret total productivity
5. Identify issues of productivity in the new manufacturing environment and the advantages and limitations of applying productivity measures to service firms and not-for-profit organizations
6. Disaggregate sales variance into selling price and sales volume variances
7. Separate sales volume variance into sales mix and sales quantity variances
8. Explain how market size and market share variances lead to sales quantity variances
9. Analyze factors leading to changes in profitability

Prior to the 1980s, almost no consumers owned a personal computer. Computers were for businesses firms and organizations and used by trained professionals. When Apple Computer introduced Apple II, it pretty much had the entire personal computers market to itself. Individual consumers—many of them were teenagers—snatched millions of affordable, user-friendly Apple computers.

Apple Computer chose to seek high profit margins, ignored the expanding market size, and overlooked the importance of market share. Apple Computer held fast to its operating systems and licensed no other computer manufacturer to use the operating systems.[1] Not willing to give up high profit margins, its prices often are higher than those of IBM PCs. As Apple's market share dwindled, so did the application software that made Apple computers useful. Decreased availability of application software deterred buyers. Apple's small market share further discouraged software developers from writing new applications, updating and improving existing applications, and adapting software for computers manufactured by Apple Computer. This vicious cycle caused Apple Computer's market share to dwindle from more than 95 percent to less than 3 percent today.

Sustaining profitability and maintaining or improving market share requires effective marketing activities. Effectiveness in marketing activities demands proper consideration of factors such as selling price, sales volume, market size, market share, and productivity. The first section examines measures of productivity and analyzes

---

[1] For a very brief period, Apple licensed its operating system to a couple of manufacturers.

productivity changes over the years. The second section discusses the impact of changes in selling prices, sales volume, market share, and market size on marketing effectiveness. The last section analyzes operating results over the years to assess the success of the firm's strategy.

Managing Productivity

Productivity isn't the villain—It's the hero.

BusinessWeek, **November 17, 2003, p. 37**

LEARNING OBJECTIVE 1

Describe productivity and identify effects of productivity changes on operating results.

The desire to produce more with less is the story behind progress. The last century has seen firms in the industrialized countries increase their productivity over 45-fold. As a result, the average number of working hours per year per person in the United States has decreased from more than 3,000 hours to around 1,800 hours while the output per worker increased several times. As Peter Drucker pointed out, the productivity explosion has paid for the 10-fold expansion in education and the expansion of health care. Productivity has become the wealth of nations.[2]

Improvements in productivity occur when fewer workers, materials, machines, or other resources are used to manufacture and sell the same or better products. Firms with higher productivity than their competitors enjoy competitive advantages, earn higher-than-average returns, and command long-term success. Producing more with less is a strategic critical success factor that all firms and organizations, regardless of their chosen competitive strategy, strive to attain.

Firms may choose to compete on cost leadership or product differentiation (Chapter 2). Those competing on cost leadership succeed by performing tasks with fewer resources than their competitors. Firms competing on product differentiation can strengthen their profit margins and competitive positions by using the same or fewer resources than their competitors in carrying out operations. Governments and not-for-profit organizations often require their employees to do more with fewer resources. Economists and financial analysts often use the amount of output produced per unit of input to measure a firm's or a country's competitiveness. Almost everywhere we look, the ability to do more with less is critically important.

What Is Productivity

Productivity
is the ratio of output to input.

Productivity is the ratio of output to input.

$$\text{Productivity} = \frac{\text{Output}}{\text{Input}}$$

A firm that spends five days to manufacture 100 units has a productivity of 20 units per day. A social service worker who processes 75 cases over a four-week period has a productivity of 3.75 cases per day. A firm that uses 24.5 pounds of material for each

---

[2] Peter F. Drucker, *Managing for the Future* (New York: Truman Talley Books, 1993), pp. 93–94.

REAL-WORLD FOCUS An Effective Stimulus to Improve Productivity

At the Murray, Kentucky, factory of Briggs & Stratton, the world's largest manufacturer of lawn mowers, pay starts at $9.64 an hour, plus productivity bonuses that add $1.72 an hour to the base wage. Because of that incentive, "our workers go to extremes to take even a half a cent of cost out of each engine," notes Paul M. Neylon, senior vice-president for engine products. Engines that took one hour to build at the old plant now require just 30 minutes.

Source: Michael Arndt, "How Briggs Is Revving the Engines," *Business Week,* May 5, 2003, p. 92.

unit manufactured is more productive than a firm that uses 25 pounds of the same materials to manufacture one unit of the same product. To improve productivity, firms need to know the productivity levels of their operations.

Measuring Productivity

Operational productivity is the ratio of output units to input units.

Financial productivity is the ratio of output to input with either the numerator or the denominator a dollar amount.

A measure of productivity can be either an operational or a financial productivity measure. **Operational productivity** is the ratio of output units to input units. Both the numerator and the denominator are physical measures (units). **Financial productivity** is also a ratio of output to input, except that either the numerator or the denominator is a dollar amount. For example, the number of tables made from a sheet of plywood involves operational productivity; the number of tables per dollar cost of plywood reflects financial productivity. The amount of sales per square foot of store space involves financial productivity. The amount of sales per dollar cost of plywood also reflects financial productivity.

A productivity measure may include all production factors or focus on a single factor or part of the production factors that the firm uses in manufacturing. A productivity measure that focuses on the relationship between one or part of the input factors and the output attained is a **partial productivity** measure. The following are examples of partial productivity:

Partial productivity focuses on the relationship between one or part of the input factors and the output.

- Direct materials yield (output/units of materials).
- Workforce productivity such as output per labor-hour or output per person employed.
- Process (or activity) productivity such as output per machine-hours or output per kilowatt-hour.

Total productivity includes all input resources in the computation of the ratio of output attained to input resources consumed.

A productivity measure that includes all input resources used in production is a **total productivity.** The number of tables manufactured per dollar of manufacturing costs is a total productivity measure because the denominator, manufacturing costs, includes all manufacturing costs incurred to make the tables. Exhibit 15.1 summarizes productivity measures.

Exhibit 15.2 presents selected production data of Erie Precision Tool Company in 2006 and 2007 for manufacturing DB2 drill bits. The manufacturing costs include total fixed factory overhead and other operating expenses of $300,000 per year and variable manufacturing costs consisting of metal alloy (direct materials) and direct labor-hours.

EXHIBIT 15.1
Productivity Measures

Productivity
- Partial productivity
    - Partial operational productivity
    - Partial financial productivity
- Total productivity (financial productivity)

EXHIBIT 15.2
Operating Data of Erie Precision Tool Company in 2006 and 2007

ERIE PRECISION TOOL COMPANY Operating Data for DB2 (Dollars in 000s)		
	2006	**2007**
Units of DB2 manufactured and sold	4,000	4,800
Total sales ($500 per unit)	$2,000	$2,400
Direct materials (25,000 pounds at $24/pound in 2006 and 32,000 pounds at $25/pound in 2007)	600	800
Direct labor (4,000 hours at $40 per hour in 2006 and 4,000 hours at $50/hour in 2007)	160	200
Fixed factory overhead and other operating expenses	300	300
Operating income	$ 940	$1,100

The firm earned $1,100,000 operating income in 2007, a 17 percent increase over the $940,000 earned in 2006. Without examining the operating data in detail, management would probably be happy with the improvement in operating result. The increase in operating income, however, compares unfavorably to the improvement in total sales. The total sales in 2007 are 120 percent of the total sales in 2006. With the fixed factory overhead and other operating expenses remaining unchanged at $300,000 each year even when the total sales increased in 2007, the increase in operating income should have been more than the 20 percent increase in total sales. The lower increase in operating income is a result of a higher-than-proportional increase in the firm's variable costs for direct materials and direct labor. The total variable costs increased 32 percent [($1,000−$760)/$760] while the total sales increased only 20 percent.

Several factors could have contributed to the increase in direct materials and direct labor costs, including increases in the units manufactured and sold, changes in the amounts and/or the proportions of the inputs used in production; and increases in the unit cost of resources. The firm should identify factors that caused the changes so that management can decrease manufacturing costs and increase operating income. (Chapters 13 and 14 discuss analyses based on the firm's standard costs for the period to determine the effect of changes in cost elements—such as wage rates, labor-hours, materials prices, and materials usage—on the firm's production cost.)

Productivity measurements discussed in this chapter examine the effect of a firm's productivity on its operating income. Increased productivity decreases costs and increases operating income. Changes in the productivity of different resources, however, do not always occur in the same direction or at an equal pace. A firm's productivity or use of direct materials can improve while its direct labor productivity may deteriorate. For instance, a furniture manufacturer increased materials productivity by reducing waste due to improper cutting. However, to reduce improper cutting of materials, workers spent more labor-hours to cut the boards carefully. The labor-hour productivity decreased. Management needs to know the changes in productivities of individual production resources, which partial productivities provide.

Partial Productivity

LEARNING OBJECTIVE 2
Compute and interpret operational and financial partial productivity.

A partial productivity measures the relationship between the output and one or part of the required input resources used in producing the output.

$$\text{Partial Productivity} = \frac{\text{Number of units or value of output manufactured}}{\text{Number of units or cost of a single or part of the input resources}}$$

The denominator is the number or cost of a manufacturing factor such as direct materials, direct labor-hours, or selected input resources; the numerator is the number of units or the value of the goods or services produced.

EXHIBIT 15.3
Partial Productivity of Erie Precision Tool Company in 2006 and 2007

ERIE PRECISION TOOL COMPANY		
Partial Productivity—Direct Materials and Direct Labor for DB2		
	Partial Operational Productivity	
	2006	**2007**
Direct materials	4,000 / 25,000 = 0.16	4,800 / 32,000 = 0.15
Direct labor	4,000 / 4,000 = 1.00	4,800 / 4,000 = 1.20
	Partial Financial Productivity	
	2006	**2007**
Direct materials	4,000 / $600,000 = 0.0067	4,800 / $800,000 = 0.006
Direct labor	4,000 / $160,000 = 0.025	4,800 / $200,000 = 0.024

For example, partial productivity of the direct materials for DB2 for the Erie Precision Tool Company in 2006 is 0.16 as computed here:

$$\text{Partial productivity of DM in 2006} = \frac{4,000}{25,000} = 0.16$$

Partial Operational Productivity

A partial operational productivity reflects the conversion ratio of an input or selected input resource to the output attained. The numerator, the output, is the number of units produced; the denominator is the number of units of input resources used. Exhibit 15.3 presents the partial operational productivity of Erie Precision Company in 2006 and 2007. The partial productivity of 0.16 for direct materials in 2006 indicates that the firm manufactured 0.16 unit of output for every pound of direct materials used in production.

Firms often use benchmarks or criteria in assessing productivity. Among benchmarks or criteria often used are past productivity measures of the firm, productivity of another firm in the same industry, the industry standard or average, or benchmarks established by the top management as the goal for the firm to attain. We'll use Erie Precision Tool Company productivity level in 2006 as the benchmark to assess productivity in 2007.

A comparison of partial productivity over time shows the change in the productivity of the input resource from the base year. Erie Company's operating results show that the partial productivity of the direct materials decreased over time. The firm manufactured 0.16 unit of DB2 in 2006 but only 0.15 unit of DB2 in 2007 from 1 pound of direct materials, a 6.25 percent decrease in productivity [(0.16 − 0.15) ÷ 0.16 = 0.0625]. Partial productivity of direct labor, however, improved in 2007. The firm manufactured one unit for each direct-labor hour in 2006 and 1.2 units in 2007, a 20 percent increase in productivity [(1.2 − 1) ÷ 1 = 0.20].

Changes in productivity also can be examined by computing the amount of input resources that the firm would have used in 2007 had it maintained the 2006 partial productivity, as shown in Exhibit 15.4. In this case, the 4,800 units of DB2 manufactured and sold in 2007 would have required only 30,000 pounds of direct materials (4,800 ÷ 0.16). The decreased partial productivity necessitated the use of an additional 2,000 pounds in 2007 (32,000 − 30,000). Similarly, the firm would have spent 4,800 direct labor-hours in 2007 had it had the same direct labor partial productivity in 2007 as in 2006. The firm saved the cost for 800 hours of direct labor (4,800 − 4,000) when its partial productivity in 2007 for direct labor increased from 1.0 to 1.2.

LEARNING OBJECTIVE 3
Separate change in financial productivity into productivity change, input price change, and output change.

Partial Financial Productivity

The bottom panel of Exhibit 15.3 reports the partial financial productivities of direct materials and direct labor. The partial financial productivity indicates the number of units of output manufactured for each dollar the firm spent on the input resource. The

EXHIBIT 15.4
Changes in Partial
Productivity of Erie Precision
Tool Company in 2007

	ERIE PRECISION TOOL COMPANY				
	Effects of Changes in Partial Productivity of Direct Materials and Direct Labor in the Production of DB2				
Input Resource	(1) 2007 Output	(2) 2006 Partial Operational Productivity	(3) = (1) ÷ (2) 2007 Output at 2006 Productivity	(4) Input Used in 2007	(5) = (3) − (4) Saving (Loss) in Units of Input
Direct materials	4,800	0.16	30,000	32,000	(2,000)
Direct labor	4,800	1.00	4,800	4,000	800

partial financial productivity for direct materials is determined by dividing the output (4,000 units in 2006 and 4,800 units in 2007) by the cost of the resource for the year (cost of direct materials: $600,000 in 2006 and $800,000 in 2007). The partial financial productivities are 0.0067 in 2006 and 0.006 in 2007. The partial financial productivity decreased from manufacturing 0.0067 units of DB2 in 2006 to 0.006 units in 2007 for every dollar spent on direct materials, a decrease in productivity from 2006 to 2007 of 10 percent [(0.0067 − 0.006) ÷ 0.0067).

The direct labor partial financial productivity is 0.025 for 2006 and 0.024 for 2007, a decrease of 4 percent [(0.025 − 0.024) ÷ 0.025]. This result contradicts the direct labor partial operational productivity reported earlier (20 percent improvement). These results suggest that although employee productivity per hour increased, the cost increase due to higher hourly wages more than offset the gain in productivity per hour.

Factors that may contribute to the difference in manufacturing costs between two operations are differences in output level, input cost, or productivity. Panel 1 of Exhibit 15.5 shows an analytical framework for determining the effects of each of these factors. Point A is the operating result of 2007. The amounts for all three factors at point A are the actual 2007 figures: units of output, productivity, and input cost. Point B is the cost to manufacture the 2007 output at the *2006 productivity level* and 2007 input cost. The only difference between points A and B is in productivity. Thus, any difference between points A and B is attributable to changes in productivity in 2007 and 2006.

Point C is the cost to manufacture the 2007 output at the 2006 productivity level and *2006 input cost*. Recall that point B is the cost to manufacture the 2007 output at the 2006 productivity level and *2007 input cost*. The only difference between points B and C is in the unit cost of the input resource in each of the years: point B uses the 2007 cost per unit for the input resource while point C uses the 2006 cost per unit for the input resource. The difference between the amounts in points B and C, if any, results from the difference in unit cost of the input resource.

Point D is the cost to manufacture the *2006 output* at 2006 productivity and 2006 unit cost of the input resource. Recall that point C is the cost to manufacture the *2007 output* at the 2006 productivity and the 2006 unit cost of the input resource. Any difference in the costs between points C and D is because of different output levels between these two points. The output is then divided by the total cost of the required resource to manufacture the output. Because the total cost of the required resource in each of the years is determined using the same productivity level (2006 productivity) and the same unit cost of the input resource (2006 cost per unit of the input resource), the total cost of the required resource in each of the years is in proportion to their respective output level. As a result, the ratios of output to input (costs) at points C and D are always identical.

The analysis shows that, of the 10 percent decrease in partial financial productivity of direct materials (from 0.0067 to 0.006, Exhibit 15.3), 6 percent (0.0004/0.0067, bottom of panel 4, Exhibit 15.5) is attributable to productivity change. The remaining 4 percent (0.000267/0.0067, bottom of panel 4, Exhibit 15.5) reflects the price change in the cost per pound of direct materials ($24 in 2006 to $25 in 2007).

EXHIBIT 15.5   Decomposition of Partial Financial Productivity

ERIE PRECISION TOOL COMPANY
Decomposition of Partial Financial Productivity

Panel 1: Framework

	A	B	C	D
Output	2007	2007	2007	2006
Productivity	2007	2006	2006	2006
Input Cost	2007	2007	2006	2006

Productivity Change   Input Price Change   Output Change

Panel 2: Operating Data for Decomposing Partial Financial Productivity

	Actual 2007 Operating Results	2007 Output at *2006 Productivity* and 2007 Input Cost	2007 Output at 2006 Productivity and *2006 Input Cost*	Actual 2006 Operating Results
Output units	4,800	4,800	4,800	4,000
Input units and costs				
Direct materials	$32,000 \times \$25 = \$ 800,000$	$30,000 \times \$25 = \$750,000$	$30,000 \times \$24 = \$720,000$	$25,000 \times \$24 = \$600,000$
Direct labor	$4,000 \times \$50 = 200,000$	$4,800 \times \$50 = 240,000$	$4,800 \times \$40 = 192,000$	$4,000 \times \$40 = 160,000$
Total	$\$1,000,000$	$\$990,000$	$\$912,000$	$\$760,000$

Part 3: Decompostion

	2007 Operation			2006 Operation
	2007 output/ (2007 input × 2007 input costs)	2007 output/(2006 input for 2007 output × 2007 input costs)	2007 output/(2006 input for 2007 output × 2006 input costs)	2006 output/ (2006 input × 2006 input costs)
Direct materials	$4,800/\$800,000 = 0.006$	$4,800/\$750,000 = 0.0064$	$4,800/\$720,000 = 0.006667$	$4,000/\$600,000 = 0.006667$
Direct labor	$4,800/\$200,000 = 0.024$	$4,800/\$240,000 = 0.0200$	$4,800/\$192,000 = 0.025000$	$4,000/\$160,000 = 0.025000$

Productivity Change   Input Price Change   Output Change

	Productivity Change	Input Price Change	Output Change
Direct materials	$0.0060 - 0.0064 = 0.0004$ U	$0.006400 - 0.006667 = 0.000267$ U	$0.006667 - 0.006667 = 0$
Direct labor	$0.0240 - 0.0200 = 0.0040$ F	$0.02000 - 0.025000 = 0.005000$ U	$0.025000 - 0.025000 = 0$

Part 4: Summary of Results

	Productivity Change from 2006						
	Productivity Change		Input Price Change		Output Change		Total Change
Direct materials	0.0004 U	+	0.000267 U	+	0	=	0.000667 U
Direct labor	0.0040 F	+	0.005000 U	+	0	=	0.001000 U

	Change as Percent of 2006 Productivity						
	Productivity Change		Input Price Change		Output Change		Total Change
Direct materials	6% U	+	4% U	+	0%	=	10% U
Direct labor	16% F	+	20% U	+	0%	=	4% U

The 2007 financial partial productivity of direct labor is 4 percent lower than that of 2006 (from 0.025 to 0.024, Exhibit 15.3). The lower partial financial productivity of direct labor in 2007 is not due to decreased productivity of direct labor in 2007, however. The partial productivity of direct labor increased by 16 percent (0.004/0.025, bottom of panel 4, Exhibit 15.5). The 25 percent increase in wages ($40 per hour in 2006 and $50 per hour in 2007) more than offsets the gain in labor productivity. As a result, total direct labor cost increased and the partial financial productivity decreased.

Partial Productivity: Operational versus Financial

Both the numerator and the denominator of a partial operational productivity measure are physical units. Using physical measures makes partial operational measures easy for operational personnel to understand and use in operations. The fact that an operational productivity measure is unaffected by price changes or other factors also makes it easier to benchmark.

A partial operational productivity focuses on the physical measure of one input resource at a time and allows management to know the effect of changes in productivity of the input resource on the operation. Executives in the auto industry often use partial operating productivity measures to compare labor productivity in the United States to that in Japan as a gauge of their competitive positions in the market. For example, in the early 1980s, auto executives demanded improvements in productivity on the grounds that Toyota produced one vehicle every 16 to 18 hours while some U.S. auto manufacturers produced one car every 40-plus hours.

A partial financial productivity has the advantage of considering the effects of both cost and quantity of an input resource on productivity. At a management level, the effect of cost, not merely the physical quantity, is a concern. In addition, partial financial productivity can be used in operations that use more than one production factor. Partial operational productivity, on the other hand, measures only one input resource at a time.

Limitations of Partial Productivity Analysis

A partial productivity measure has several limitations. First, it measures only the relationship between an input resource and the output; it ignores any effect that changes in other manufacturing factors have on the productivity. An improved partial productivity measure could have been obtained by decreasing the productivity of one or more other input resources. For example, Erie Precision Tool Company can improve its partial productivity of direct labor if wastes on direct materials are not a concern. Or, it can boost direct materials partial productivity through reduction in direct materials wasted by spending more labor hours to cut each piece of the materials carefully.

A second limitation is that partial productivity ignores any effect that changes in other production factors have on productivity. For example, increases in materials quality are likely to raise the partial productivity of direct materials as well as direct labor. Erie Precision Tool Company might have workers with more experience or higher skill in 2007 than those in 2006. As a result, the partial productivity of labor increased in 2007. The average hourly wage rate for workers with more experience or higher skill also earned higher hourly wage rates. Is it worthwhile for the firm to make the trade-off? Unfortunately, an analysis of operational partial productivity cannot provide an answer.

Third, partial productivity ignores effects that changes in the firm's operating characteristics have on the productivity of the input resource. Installation of high-efficiency equipment improves direct labor partial operational productivity. The improvement in labor partial operational productivity can hardly be attributed to increased labor productivity.

Fourth, an improved partial productivity does not imply that the firm or division operates efficiently. No efficiency standard is involved in the determinations of partial productivity measures.

Total Productivity

LEARNING OBJECTIVE 4
Calculate and interpret total productivity.

Total productivity is the ratio of output to the total cost of all input resources used to produce the output.

$$\text{Total productivity} = \frac{\text{Units or sales value of output}}{\text{Total cost of all input resources}}$$

Total productivity is a financial productivity measure. The numerator can be either the number of units or the sales value of the output attained. The denominator is the total amount of all resources used in the production of the output. The sum of units of

EXHIBIT 15.6
Total Productivity for DB2

ERIE PRECISION TOOL COMPANY 2006 and 2007		
Panel 1: Total Productivity in Units	**2006**	**2007**
(a) Total units manufactured	4,000	4,800
(b) Total variable manufacturing costs incurred	$760,000	$1,000,000
(c) Total productivity: (a) / (b)	0.005263	0.004800
(d) Decrease in productivity: 0.005263 − 0.004800 = 0.000463, or 8.8% (0.000463 ÷ 0.005263)		
Panel 2: Total Productivity in Sales Dollars	**2006**	**2007**
(a) Total sales	$2,000,000	$2,400,000
(b) Total variable manufacturing costs incurred	$760,000	$1,000,000
(c) Total productivity: (a) / (b)	$2.6316	$2.4000
(d) Decrease in productivity: $2.6316 − $2.4000 = $0.2316, or 8.8% ($0.2316 ÷ $2.6316)		

resources in their physical measures usually is not meaningful because the resources are likely to include resources measured differently. For example, materials, labor, and utilities are resources used in the manufacturing of a product. Materials are measured in pounds; labor is measured in hours; and utilities are measured in kilowatt-hours. The sum of these three measures is not meaningful. Costs of these resources serve as a common factor that allows measures for different resources such as materials, labor, and other production factors to be added together.

The first panel of Exhibit 15.6 shows the computation of Erie Precision Tool Company's total productivity of variable manufacturing costs for 2006 and 2007 in the manufacturing of DB2. The computation of total productivity involves three steps: First, determine the output of each period: 4,000 units in 2006 and 4,800 units in 2007. Second, calculate the total variable costs incurred to produce the output: $760,000 in 2006 and $1,000,000 in 2007 (Panel 2, Exhibit 15.5). Third, compute the total productivity by dividing the amount of output by the total cost of variable input resources: 0.005263 in 2006 and 0.004800 in 2007.

The total productivity indicates that for every dollar of variable cost incurred in 2006, the firm manufactured 0.005263 unit of the output. Or, for every thousand dollars of variable cost the firm manufactured 5.263 units of the output. The total productivity in 2007 is 0.0048, suggesting that the firm manufactures 0.0048 unit of DB2 for every dollar of resources (4.8 units for every thousand dollars). The total productivity decreased by 0.000463 units or 8.8 percent [(0.005263 − 0.004800) ÷ 0.005263].

Also, we can use the total sales revenue of the output units manufactured for the numerator to compute the total productivity, as shown in Panel 2 of Exhibit 15.6. For every dollar the firm spent on variable costs, it generated sales of $2.6316 in 2006 and $2.40 in 2007. The total productivity decreased by $0.2316, or 8.8 percent [(2.6316 − 2.4000) ÷ 2.6316].

The total productivity of all resources required to manufacture the output is often used in assessing production operations. Achieving higher productivity by making more units is an important first step for a successful firm. An investment that generates higher revenues than other investments for each dollar it spends on resources is a good investment.

Advantages and Limitations of Total Productivity

Total productivity measures the combined productivity of all operating factors. As such, use of a total productivity measure in performance evaluations decreases the possibility of manipulating some of the manufacturing factors to improve the productivity measure of other manufacturing factors. The same cannot be said for partial productivity measures. Managers of a firm that uses direct labor partial productivity as the primary basis in performance evaluations might not pay due care to minimizing materials wastes.

REAL-WORLD FOCUS   ALCOA Made Safety a Productivity Issue

When Paul O'Neill became CEO of Alcoa, Inc., in June 1987, the Pittsburgh-based firm earned $264 million on sales of $4.6 billion and had 35,000 employees. It was just another wheezing industrial giant with an unremarkable financial record and a workforce that was biding its time, according to *Business Week*.

O'Neill did not hold his troops to criteria that CEOs commonly use, such as profit margins, sales growth rates, or share price appreciation. His singular standard was time lost to employee injuries. In 1987, Alcoa had already outperformed most U.S. manufacturers in this area: Its rate of time lost because of employee injuries was one-third of the U.S. average. Nevertheless, O'Neill believed that "to be a world-class company, it first had to become the safest."

The emphasis on safety fundamentally altered Alcoa's culture. To meet the CEO's targets, managers and even bottom-rung employees began showing initiative instead of mutely waiting for orders. Productivity soon began rising, "Paul came in and got us to do things we never thought we could do," says L. Richard Milner, head of Alcoa's automotive unit.

When O'Neill retired at the end of 2000, Alcoa boasted the industry's safety record. Its rate of time lost for employee injuries is less than one-twentieth of U.S. average. For fiscal year 2000, the firm had profits of $1.5 billion on sales of $22.9 billion and a payroll of 140,000.

Source: Based on Michael Arndt, "How O'Neill Got Alcoa Shining," *Business Week*, February 5, 2001, p. 39.

By necessity, total productivity is a financial productivity measure. Personnel at the operational level may have difficulty linking financial productivity measures to their day-to-day operations. Furthermore, deterioration in total productivity can result from increased costs of resources that were beyond the manager's control, or decreased productivity of some of the input resources that were outside the realm of the manager. Ambiguity in the relationship between the controllability of operations and a performance measure based on total productivity could defeat the purpose of having a productivity measurement.

Another consideration in using a total productivity measure is that the basis for assessing changes in productivity could vary over time. For instance, Erie Precision Tool Company assesses the change in productivity in 2007 from 2006 using the productivity in 2006 as the criterion. The evaluation of the 2006 change in productivity from 2005 would have used 2005 productivity as the criterion. This procedure makes it impossible to compare changes in productivity from 2006 to 2007 to those of changes from 2005 to 2006 because the two measures use different years as the base. One solution to this problem is the use of a constant base year.

In addition, productivity measures can ignore the effects of changes in demand for the product, changes in selling prices of the goods or services, and special purchasing or selling arrangements on productivity.

Changes in demand alter the size of operations. The size of operations can affect total productivity as well as partial productivity for materials, labor, or processes. Economies of scale often imply improved productivity as the size of operation increases. The improved productivity per unit of input resource of a larger operation may not be a result of higher productivity of one or more of the input resources.

Increases or decreases in selling prices of the output goods or services change productivity in dollars of output for each unit of input either in part or in total. Management would be pleased to learn that the productivity as measured by the sales revenues per dollar spent on direct materials increased from $4.00 last year to $4.50 this year. The jubilation could not be justified, however, if the firm raised its selling price from an average of $20 per unit last year to an average of $25 per unit this year. The increased selling price alone would have increased the productivity per dollar of direct materials from $4.00 to $5.00. The partial productivity of direct materials decreased rather than increased.

Special arrangements in either sale of outputs or purchases of input resources also can disrupt the underlying relation between input and output measured by productivity. A special arrangement to sell products at a discount price decreases the productivity in dollars of output per input unit. Alternatively, a special purchase of materials increases financial productivity. Neither of these actions can be attributed to a loss or gain in productivity.

Productivity in the New Manufacturing Environment

LEARNING OBJECTIVE 5
*Identify issues of productivity
in the new manufacturing
environment and the advantages
and limitations of applying
productivity measures to service
firms and not-for-profit
organizations.*

Productivity and Total Quality Management

A common misconception is that firms attain improvements in quality at the expense of productivity. One reason for the misconception is that improvements in quality require additional resources or that a higher quality standard decreases units of good output. The experience of many firms, however, is the opposite—improvements in quality *increase* productivity.

Quality improvements often decrease wastes and the number of spoiled units of the manufacturing and downstream divisions. The total amounts of input resources needed for the division and the firm are likely to decrease. Improvements in quality at Kangall Manufacturing decreased the rejected units in the total units manufactured from 10 percent to 2 percent. The improvement in quality improved the firm's productivity from 1.60 to 1.74.[3]

Furthermore, quality improvements decrease the resources needed in production by decreasing or eliminating rework. Decrease or elimination of rework saves the consumption of materials, production hours, and processes (machine-hours, energy, space). Productivity improves because less input is required to produce the output.

Productivity and Business Process Reengineering

Productivity and business process reengineering go hand in hand; these two important approaches can help a firm attain a higher level of profitability and improve competitiveness.

Improving productivity requires determination of how a firm can manufacture a product or complete a task with fewer inputs, including materials, time, and facility. Productivity improvement need not be restricted to efforts to reduce the inputs needed for the same output or to increase the level of output from the same input. A thorough improvement in productivity goes deeper. In efforts to increase productivity, especially in service organizations, firms must identify the task, why it is being done, and whether it needs to be accomplished.[4] These are the same issues that business process reengineering considers. The easiest and perhaps the largest increases in productivity come from redefining the task to be done, especially from eliminating low-value-added activities and redesigning the processes to perform the task with fewer resources.

Productivity is often computed for all inputs and processes, including both high-value-added and low-value-added activities. Improving productivity for a low-value-added activity is not a productive use of resources. Low-value-added activities should be eliminated through reengineering. Productivity should be assessed only on high-value-added activities and efforts to improve productivity should focus only on high-value-added activities.

There is no such thing as a limit on productivity improvement. To be competitively productive requires continuous improvement. Only with continuous productivity improvements can a firm remain competitive in the long term.

Productivity improvement is not a synonym of employee layoff or capacity reduction. Although laying off workers and closing plants raises the level of productivity, these actions have only short-term effects and do not increase the growth rate of the firm. Furthermore, a reduced workforce may not be able to meet the increased demand when situations change. The cost of lost profit, yielding opportunities to competitors, and deteriorated competitive position can exceed the benefits of slimming down and restructuring. Boeing benefited from trimming fat in the early 1990s to increase productivity

[3] If the firm spent $3,937.50 to manufacture 7,000 units, of which 700 were rejected, its productivity is 6,300/$3,937.50 = 1.6. A decrease in the rejection rate to 2 percent of total units produced increases the output to 6,860 units with the same amount of the input resource. The productivity improves to 6,860/$3,937.50 = 1.74 unit per dollar spent.

[4] Drucker, *Managing for the Future*, p. 98.

and decrease cost. As the demand for aircraft rose, however, the firm struggled and failed to keep pace with demand. Production constraints forced Boeing to delay scheduled deliveries in October 1997 and opened opportunities for Airbus, its chief rival.

Productivity in Service Firms and Not-For-Profit Organizations

The basic concept for measuring productivity in service firms and not-for-profit organizations is similar to those for measuring productivity of manufacturing firms. To the extent that a service firm or not-for-profit organization can clearly define and identify its output and the required tasks or input resources, organizations can use the procedure discussed for manufacturing operations to examine service productivity. The productivity of a homeless shelter, for example, can be measured using the ratio of the number of persons housed to the total expenses incurred. An airline can gauge productivity by computing the ratio of paid-passenger-miles to total operating expenses.

Unfortunately, many outputs and required tasks of service firms and not-for-profit organizations cannot be measured precisely. Hospitals often use patient-days to measure their outputs and productivity. Although the number of patient-days can be measured unequivocally, not all patient-days require the same amount of work or generate the same revenue. The level of patient-day care needed for an open-heart surgery patient most likely is much higher than that of a normal appendectomy patient.

Indefinite relationships between the output and input resources required by service firms and not-for-profits often lead their management to measure only financial productivities that use dollar amounts for both the numerator and denominator of the ratio. An open-heart patient demands more input resources than does a person having an appendectomy. On the other hand, the open-heart patient's patient-day also generates higher revenue than does the patient-day of an appendectomy patient. Financial productivity can be a good measure for service firms if the relationship between the revenue generated and the cost of the input resources required to generate the revenue is relatively constant and if the dollar amount is a critical factor for the organization. Unfortunately, dollar amounts can seldom represent a not-for-profit organization's major objective, and revenues of service firms are more likely determined by the quality of the services rendered, not the cost of input resources.

One other difficulty in measuring productivity in a not-for-profit organization is the absence of revenue as the common measure for output. The output of a higher education institution includes the number of students graduated, the total number of credit hours taught, contributions to the advancement of knowledge, and services to the community. It is difficult to obtain a clear measure for some of these outputs; also, no revenue is attached to most, if not all, of these outputs. Consequently, identifying a revenue-based financial measure of the output of a higher education institution is impossible.

Managing Marketing Effectiveness

A firm's market is the place where it earns profits, fulfills its strategic goals, and attains long-term successes. No firm can gain long-term success without effective marketing activities that allow it to accomplish the following:

- Earn the budgeted operating income.
- Attain the budgeted market share.
- Adapt to market change.

Many factors affect marketing effectiveness. In the next section we analyze effects of changes in selling price, sales quantity, product mix, market size, and market share on operating results. Variances in any of these factors can prevent a firm from achieving its short-term performance objectives and strategic goals, including earning the desired income and sustaining long-term success. Exhibit 15.7 depicts the components of sales variances.

The difference between the actual sales revenues of a period and the sales revenues in the master budget is the sales variance of the period. Since sales revenue is the product of selling price per unit and the sales volume in units, a sales variance can result from deviation in either selling prices or sales volumes, as discussed in Chapter 13. Before examining further analyses of sales variances, we review selling price and sales volume variances.

Selling Price and Sales Volume Variances

LEARNING OBJECTIVE 6

Disaggregate sales variance into selling price and sales volume variances.

A *selling price variance* is the difference between the total sales revenue of the period and the amount that the firm would have received had it sold the same units at the budgeted selling price. It is computed by finding the difference between the actual and the budgeted selling price per unit and multiplying the difference by the number of units sold.

$$\text{Selling price variance} = \left[\begin{array}{c} \text{Actual selling} \\ \text{price per unit} \end{array} - \begin{array}{c} \text{Budgeted selling} \\ \text{price per unit} \end{array} \right] \times \begin{array}{c} \text{Number of} \\ \text{units sold} \end{array}$$

The selling price variance is also the *sales revenue flexible budget variance*—the difference between the actual total sales and the total sales in the flexible budget for the units sold. Selling price variance measures the impact that deviations of the actual selling prices from the budgeted selling prices have on operating results. The sum of the selling price variance and the total variable cost variance is the flexible budget contribution margin variance for the period.

A *sales volume variance* is the difference between an amount in the flexible budget for the number of units sold and the corresponding amount in the master budget for the period. This variance is a result of the difference in units between the actual units sold and the budgeted units to be sold in the master budget of the period. Thus, a sales volume variance measures the effect on operating results deviations in the number of units

EXHIBIT 15.7

Components of Sales Variances

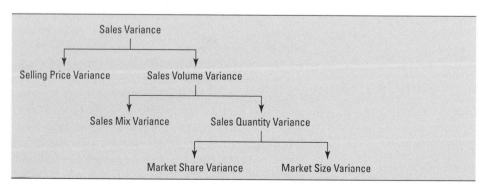

sold from the budgeted units in the master budget of the period. Depending on the purpose of an analysis, the effects can be in sales revenues, contribution margin, or operating income. The sales volume variance was introduced in Chapter 13 as part of the analysis of flexible budget variances. Exhibit 13–4 is reproduced here as Exhibit 15.8 as the starting point for further analyses of the sales volume variance.

Schmidt Machinery Company budgeted $200,000 operating income from sales of 1,000 units of XV–1 at $800 per unit ($800,000 ÷ 1,000 units), $450 variable expense per unit ($450,000 ÷ 1,000 units), and $150,000 total fixed expense for the month. At the end of the month, the actual operating results show that the firm sold 780 units for $639,600, or an average selling price of $820 per unit. The average actual selling price per unit exceeds the budgeted selling price per unit by $20. Thus, the firm has a favorable selling price variance of $15,600.

$$\text{Selling price variance} = (\$820 - \$800) \times 780 \text{ units sold}$$
$$= \$20 \text{ per unit} \times 780 \text{ units sold}$$
$$= \$15,600 \text{ F}$$

The total contribution margin flexible budget variance, $15,650 favorable, is the difference between the actual contribution margin of the period, $288,650, and the flexible budget contribution margin for the unit sold, $273,000. We also can compute the contribution margin flexible budget variance by summing up its components: sales revenue flexible budget variance (or selling price variance), $15,600 favorable, and variable cost flexible budget variance, $50 favorable.

$$\frac{\text{Contribution margin}}{\text{flexible budget variance}} = \frac{\text{Actual contribution}}{\text{margin earned}} - \frac{\text{Flexible budget}}{\text{contribution margin}}$$

$$= \quad \$288,650 \quad - \quad \$273,000 = \$15,650 \text{ F}$$

Or, $$\frac{\text{Contribution margin}}{\text{flexible budget variance}} = \frac{\text{Selling price}}{\text{variance}} + \frac{\text{Variable cost flexible}}{\text{budget variance}}$$

$$= \quad \$15,600 \text{ F} \quad + \quad \$50 \text{ F} \quad = \$15,650 \text{ F}$$

The master budget called for total sales of 1,000 units. Schmidt sold 780 units. The number of units sold is 220 units less than the budgeted sales units for the period. At a standard contribution margin of $350 per unit ($800 − $450, or $350,000 ÷ 1,000 units), the decrease in units sold reduces both the total contribution margin and the operating income by $77,000 ($350 × 220 units). This is the contribution margin or operating income *sales volume variance* of the period. It is the difference between the flexible budget contribution margin (operating income) for the units sold and the master (static) budget contribution margin (operating income) for the period. It is also the

EXHIBIT 15.8
Actual and Budget Operating Data

SCHMIDT MACHINERY COMPANY
Analysis of Operations
For the Month Ended October 31, 2006

	Actual	Flexible Budget Variances*	Flexible Budget	Sales Volume Variances	Master Budget
Units sold (XV–1)	780	0	780	220	1,000
Sales	$639,600	$15,600 F	$624,000	$176,000 U	$800,000
Variable expenses	350,950	50 F	351,000	99,000 F	450,000
Contribution margin	$288,650	$15,650 F	$273,000	$ 77,000 U	$350,000
Fixed expenses	160,650	10,650 U	150,000	—	150,000
Operating income	$128,000	$ 5,000 F	$123,000	$ 77,000 U	$200,000

*Including both price and efficiency variances.

product of the difference between the number of units sold and the budgeted number of sales units in the master budget multiplied by the budgeted (standard) contribution margin per unit.

$$
\begin{array}{c}
\text{Contribution} \\
\text{margin sales} \\
\text{volume variance}
\end{array}
=
\begin{array}{c}
\text{Flexible budget} \\
\text{contribution} \\
\text{margin}
\end{array}
-
\begin{array}{c}
\text{Master budget} \\
\text{contribution} \\
\text{margin}
\end{array}
$$

$$
= \quad \$273,000 \quad - \quad \$350,000 = \$77,000 \text{ U}
$$

Or,
$$
\begin{array}{c}
\text{Contribution} \\
\text{margin sales} \\
\text{volume variance}
\end{array}
=
\left[
\begin{array}{c}
\text{Actual} \\
\text{units} \\
\text{sold}
\end{array}
-
\begin{array}{c}
\text{Budgeted units} \\
\text{(master budget)} \\
\text{to be sold}
\end{array}
\right]
\times
\begin{array}{c}
\text{Budgeted} \\
\text{contribution} \\
\text{margin per unit}
\end{array}
$$

$$
= (\quad 780 \quad - \quad 1,000) \quad \times \quad \$350 = \$77,000 \text{ U}
$$

Several factors can contribute to a sales volume variance, including sales quantity and sales mix variances, which we examine next.

Sales Mix Variance

LEARNING OBJECTIVE 7
Separate sales volume variance into sales mix and sales quantity variances.

Most firms sell or manufacture more than one product, and not all of them are equally profitable. Even if a firm sold the same number of units as the budgeted total units for the period, the firm might still not have earned the budgeted operating income and have a significant sales volume variance. To illustrate, let's assume that, in addition to XV–1, Schmidt Machinery Company carries another product, FB–33. Exhibit 15.9 shows a condensed master budget for November 2006, and Exhibit 15.10 shows the operating results of the month.

During November 2006, Schmidt sold 780 units of XV–1 at an average price of $800 per unit ($624,000 ÷ 780 units = $800), the same as the budgeted selling price per unit. The firm also sold 3,220 units of FB–33 at $600 per unit ($1,932,000 ÷ 3,220 units = $600). Again, there is no difference between the budgeted selling price per unit and the actual selling price per unit. The firm had no selling price variance in November 2006.

The firm carried out its operation in November 2006 with the same operating expenses as specified in the budget of the period. The actual variable expenses per *unit* for both XV–1 and FB–33 (Exhibit 15.10) are the same as the budgeted variable expenses per *unit* (Exhibit 15.9). The actual fixed expenses also are the same as the budgeted amounts. There is no variance due to differences in the actual operating expenses from the standard or budgeted amounts.

EXHIBIT 15.9
Condensed Master Budget

	XV–1		FB–33		Both Products	
SCHMIDT MACHINERY COMPANY						
Condensed Master Budget						
For the Month Ended November 30, 2006						
	Total	Per Unit	Total	Per Unit	Total	Per Unit
Units	1,000		3,000		4,000	
Sales	$800,000	$800	$1,800,000	$600	$2,600,000	$650.00
Variable expenses	450,000	450	960,000	320	1,410,000	352.50
Contribution margin	$350,000	$350	$ 840,000	$280	$1,190,000	$297.50
Fixed expenses	150,000		450,000		600,000	
Operating income	$200,000		$ 390,000		$ 590,000	

EXHIBIT 15.10
Income Statement

SCHMIDT MACHINERY COMPANY
Income Statement
For the Month Ended November 30, 2006

	XV–1		FB–33		Both Products
	Total	Per Unit	Total	Per Unit	Total
Units	780		3,220		4,000
Sales	$624,000	$800	$1,932,000	$600	$2,556,000
Variable expenses	351,000	450	1,030,400	320	1,381,400
Contribution margin	$273,000	$350	$ 901,600	$280	$1,174,600
Fixed expenses	150,000		450,000		600,000
Operating income	$123,000		$ 451,600		$ 574,600

The total number of units sold, 4,000, is also the same as the budgeted total units to be sold. When the actual selling prices, variable expenses, fixed expenses, and total units sold are all the same as the amount budgeted, the firm can expect the actual operating income earned to be the same as the budgeted amount.

Nevertheless, the actual operating income of the period reported in Exhibit 15.10, $574,600, is $15,400 lower than the budgeted operating income shown in Exhibit 15.9, $590,000. When all operating factors—selling prices, variable expenses, fixed expenses, and total units sold—are the same as those in the master budget, why does the firm have an unfavorable operating income (and contribution margin) variance of $15,400?

The answer is that the operating income (and contribution margin) variance results from a change in the relative proportion of products. This variance is part of sales volume variance since there is no flexible budget variance (*why?*).[5] Contributing factors to sales volume variances of firms with multiple products include differences in (1) sales quantity—the actual units sold different from the budgeted units, and (2) sales mix—the actual relative proportion of one or more of the products differ from that of the budgeted proportion.

Sales mix is the relative proportion of each product. There are two sales mixes: budgeted and actual. For the operation of November 2006, the actual sales units for products XV–1 and FB–33 are not the same as the budgeted amounts, although the combined sales volume for the products is the same as that budgeted. The firm sold 220 fewer units of XV–1 than the number budgeted while it sold 220 more units of FB–33 than the budgeted units to be sold. The actual sales mixes differed with the budgeted sales mixes. Because the contribution margins per unit of XV–1 and FB–33 are not the same, changes in sales mixes lead to the deviation of the actual operating income (or total contribution margin) from the budgeted operating income (or total contribution margin). For a multiproduct firm with different contribution margins per unit for different products, selling the same total number of units as specified in the master budget does not imply that the flexible budget's operating income (or total contribution margin) will be the same as that in the master budget for the period.

A change in the sales mix can affect the firm's contribution margin and operating income. A product's **sales mix variance** is the effect that a change in the relative proportion of the product from the budgeted proportion has on the total contribution margin or operating income of the period. It is calculated by multiplying the difference in the sales mixes by the number of total units sold and the budget contribution margin per unit:

Sales mix
is the relative proportion of each product.

Sales mix variance
is the effect that changes in the relative proportions of products from the budgeted proportions have on the total contribution margin or operating income of the period.

[5] The firm has no flexible budget variance in November 2006 because there is no variance in any of the components of flexible budget variance—there is no selling price, variable cost, and fixed cost variance.

EXHIBIT 15.11
Sales Mix Ratio

Product	Budget Units	Budget Sales Mix	Actual Units Sold	Actual Sales Mix
XV–1	1,000	1,000 / 4,000 = 0.25	780	780 / 4,000 = 0.195
FB–33	3,000	3,000 / 4,000 = 0.75	3,220	3,220 / 4,000 = 0.805
Total	4,000	1.00	4,000	1.00

$$\begin{matrix} \text{Sales mix} \\ \text{variance of} \\ \text{a product} \end{matrix} = \left[\begin{matrix} \text{Actual sales} \\ \text{mix of the} \\ \text{product} \end{matrix} - \begin{matrix} \text{Budgeted sales} \\ \text{mix of the} \\ \text{product} \end{matrix}\right] \times \begin{matrix} \text{Total} \\ \text{units} \\ \text{sold} \end{matrix} \times \begin{matrix} \text{Budgeted contribution} \\ \text{margin per unit of} \\ \text{the product} \end{matrix}$$

Before computing a sales mix variance, we need to determine the actual sales mix ratio and the budgeted sales mix ratio for each product.

Exhibit 15.11 shows computations of budget and actual sales mixes for XV–1 and FB–33 for November 2006. The firm budgeted to sell 1,000 units of XV–1 and 3,000 units of FB–33. With total budgeted units of 4,000 units, the budgeted sales mix is 0.25 for XV–1 and 0.75 for FB–33.

Following the procedure to calculate sales mix variance, the sales mix variances for November 2006 are as follows:

$$\text{Sales mix variance of XV–1} = (0.195 - 0.25) \times 4{,}000 \text{ units} \times \$350 = \$77{,}000 \text{ U}$$

$$\text{Sales mix variance of FB–33} = (0.805 - 0.75) \times 4{,}000 \text{ units} \times \$280 = \$61{,}600 \text{ F}$$

$$\text{Total sales mix variance} = \$77{,}000 \text{ U} + \$61{,}600 \text{ F} = \$15{,}400 \text{ U}$$

The focus of the computation is on the deviation of the actual sales mix from the budgeted sales mix for each of the products. The number of units in the computations is the same for both products — the total units sold, or 4,000 units. The computation uses the *budgeted contribution margin* per unit of each of the products to arrive at the sales mix variances.

The 780 units of XV–1 that the firm sold in November is 19.5 percent of the total units the firm sold during the month. The budget calls for 25 percent of the total units sold to be XV–1. The actual sales mix is 5.5 percent less than the budgeted sales mix for XV–1—5.5 percent of the 4,000 units sold equals 220 units. Were the actual sales mix the same as the budgeted sales mix, the firm would have sold 220 more units of XV–1 in November. With budgeted contribution margin of $350 per unit of XV–1, the 5.5 percent in unfavorable sales mix (or 220 units) decreases the contribution margin (and operating income) by $77,000. The firm suffered an unfavorable sales mix variance of $77,000 in November on XV–1.

The actual sales mix for FB–33, 80.5 percent, is 5.5 percent more than the budgeted sales mix of 75 percent for the product. At a budgeted contribution margin of $280 per unit, the sales mix variance for FB–33 is $61,600 favorable.

The firm's total sales mix variance is the sum of the sales mix variances of all products, which is $15,400 unfavorable for Schmidt Machinery Company.

Sales Quantity Variance

Another contributing factor to the sales volume variances of firms with multiple products is the difference between the budgeted and the actual sales units—sales quantity variance. **Sales quantity variance** measures the effect of deviation in the number of units sold from the number of units budgeted to be sold on operating results, including total contribution margin and operating income.

Sales quantity variance focuses on the effects of deviation of the actual sales quantity from the budgeted sales quantity. Similar to the computation of sales mix variance, a product's sales quantity variance is the product of three elements:

1. The difference in *total units of all products* between the actual units sold and the units budgeted, which is the focus of this computation

Sales quantity variance measures the effect of deviation in the number of units sold from the number of units budgeted to be sold on operating results.

EXHIBIT 15.12
Income Statements for Two Products

SCHMIDT MACHINERY COMPANY
Income Statement
For the Month Ended December 31, 2006

	XV–1	FB–33	Total
Units	1,600	3,400	5,000
Sales	$1,280,000	$2,040,000	$3,320,000
Variable expenses	720,000	1,088,000	1,808,000
Contribution margin	$ 560,000	$ 952,000	$1,512,000
Fixed expenses	150,000	450,000	600,000
Operating income	$ 410,000	$ 502,000	$ 912,000

2. The budgeted sales mix ratio of the product
3. The budgeted contribution margin per unit of the product

With the focus of a sales quantity variance being the difference in total units between the actual units sold and the budgeted units, we use the budgeted amounts for the other two elements, sales mix and contribution margin per unit, to compute the sales quantity variance.

$$
\begin{array}{c}\text{Sales} \\ \text{quantity} \\ \text{variance of} \\ \text{a product}\end{array} = \left[\begin{array}{c}\text{Total units} \\ \text{of all} \\ \text{products} \\ \text{sold}\end{array} - \begin{array}{c}\text{Budgeted} \\ \text{total units} \\ \text{of all} \\ \text{products}\end{array}\right] \times \begin{array}{c}\text{Budgeted} \\ \text{sales mix} \\ \text{of the} \\ \text{product}\end{array} \times \begin{array}{c}\text{Budgeted} \\ \text{contribution} \\ \text{margin per unit} \\ \text{of the product}\end{array}
$$

Notice that the calculation of the sales quantity variance for a product uses the budgeted sales mix and the budgeted contribution margin per unit of the product. However, the difference in quantity is the difference between the total number of units sold and the total number of units budgeted to be sold for all of the firm's products.

The example used earlier, the November 2006 operation of Schmidt Machinery Company, had no sales quantity variances because the total number of units sold is the same as the total number budgeted. To illustrate the determination of a sales quantity variance, we examine operating data from another month.

In December 2006, Schmidt sold 1,600 units of XV–1 and 3,400 units of FB–33, all at the budgeted selling price, budgeted unit variable expense, and budgeted total fixed expense. The budget for December is the same as the budget for November. Exhibit 15.12 shows the actual operating result of December 2006. With total budgeted sales of 4,000 units, the 5,000 total units sold exceeds the number of budgeted units by 1,000.

With no difference between the actual and the budgeted selling prices for both products, there is no selling price variance for December. The selling price variance shown in the top panel of Exhibit 15.13 confirms this conclusion. The difference between the actual operating income ($912,000, Exhibit 15.12) and the budgeted operating income ($590,000, Exhibit 15.9), $322,000 favorable, can thus be attributed to the sales volume variance of the period. The bottom panel of Exhibit 15.13 confirms this result.

The sales volume variance can be separated further into sales mix and sales quantity variances. Following the procedure for calculating the sales quantity variance, we see that Schmidt has a total $297,500 favorable sales quantity variance in December 2006, as shown in Exhibit 15.14.

The total sales quantity variance can help managers in examining the effect of changes in the total number of units on the total contribution margin (or operating income). The previous example shows that the firm earned $297,500 more in total contribution margin (or operating income) from selling 1,000 units more than the 4,000 units budgeted.

In determining sales quantity variance, we hold all other factors constant at their budget amounts, including sales mix, contribution margin per unit, and fixed costs. The sales quantity variance is the difference between (1) the budgeted contribution

EXHIBIT 15.13
Selling Price and Sales
Volume Variance

SCHMIDT MACHINERY COMPANY
Selling Price and Sales Volume Variances
For December 2006

Selling Price Variance: (Actual price per unit − Budgeted price per unit) × Actual unit

XV–1	($800 − $800) × 1,600 = 0
FB–33	($600 − $600) × 3,400 = 0
Total	0

Sales Volume Variance: (Actual unit − Budgeted unit) × Budgeted CM per unit

XV–1	(1,600 − 1,000) × $350 = $210,000 F
FB–33	(3,400 − 3,000) × $280 = 112,000 F
Total	$322,000 F

EXHIBIT 15.14
Sales Quantity Variance

SCHMIDT MACHINERY COMPANY
Sales Quantity Variance
For December 2006

$$\text{Sales quantity variance of a product} = \left[\begin{array}{c} \text{Total units of} \\ \text{all products} \\ \text{sold} \end{array} - \begin{array}{c} \text{Budgeted total} \\ \text{units of all} \\ \text{products} \end{array} \right] \times \begin{array}{c} \text{Budgeted} \\ \text{sales mix of} \\ \text{the product} \end{array} \times \begin{array}{c} \text{Budgeted contribution} \\ \text{margin per unit of} \\ \text{the product} \end{array}$$

XV–1	(5,000 − 4,000) × 0.25 × $350 = $ 87,500 F
FB–33	(5,000 − 4,000) × 0.75 × $280 = 210,000 F
Total	$297,500 F

EXHIBIT 15.15
Further Analysis of Sales
Quantity Variance

SCHMIDT MACHINERY COMPANY
Further Analysis of Sales Quantity Variance
For December 2006

Product	Budgeted Sales Mix	Total Units at the Budgeted Mix	Contribution Margin per Unit	Total Contribution Margin
XV–1	0.25	5,000 × 0.25 = 1,250	$350	$350 × 1,250 = $ 437,500
FB–33	0.75	5,000 × 0.75 = 3,750	$280	$280 × 3,750 = 1,050,000
Total contribution margin of the total units sold at the budgeted mix				$1,487,500
Budgeted fixed expenses				600,000
Operating income from the sale of the total actual units at the budgeted mix				$ 887,500
Operating income of the master budget				590,000
Sales quantity variance				$ 297,500

margin based on the total units sold of all products at the budgeted sales mix and (2) the budgeted contribution margin based on the budgeted total units of all products at the budgeted sales mix. Exhibit 15.15 illustrates this analysis.

Had Schmidt sold the 5,000 units at the budgeted sales mix, it would have sold 1,250 units of XV–1 and 3,750 units of FB–33. With the budgeted contribution margin of $350 and $280 per unit of XV–1 and FB–33, respectively, the firm would have earned a total contribution margin of $1,487,500. After subtracting the budgeted fixed cost of $600,000, the operating income would be $887,500, which is $297,500 higher than the budgeted operating income of $590,000.

The company, however, did not sell its products at the budgeted sales mix in December 2006, as shown here:

Product	Units Sold	Actual Sales Mix	Budgeted Sales Mix
XV–1	1,600	32%	25%
FB–33	3,400	68%	75%
Total	5,000	100%	100%

The firm had sales mix variances for the period. Exhibit 15.16 computes the sales mix and sales quantity variances using a columnar form similar to the form used in Chapters 13 and 14.

Column A in Exhibit 15.16 is the flexible budget for the total number of units sold with the *actual sales mixes* of the period. Column B is the flexible budget for the total number of units sold with the *budgeted sales mixes*. Column C is the master (static) budget for the period.

Schmidt Machinery Company sold 1,600 units of XV–1 and 3,400 units of FB–33 in December. The actual sales mixes in column A are 32 percent and 68 percent for XV–1 and FB–33, respectively.

Column B in Exhibit 15.16 uses the number of units the firm would have sold had the firm sold all the products at the budgeted sales mixes. Schmidt sold 5,000 units in December. According to the budgeted sales mix, 25 percent of the units sold should be XV–1. Had the firm sold the 5,000 units at the budgeted sales mix, the number of units of XV–1 sold would have been

$$5,000 \text{ units} \times 25 \text{ percent} = 1,250 \text{ units}$$

All three points use the budgeted (standard) contribution margin per unit. Thus, the only difference between columns A and B is in the sales mixes. Column A uses the *actual* sales mix and column B uses the *budgeted* sales mix. The difference in total contribution margin between these two points is a result of the difference in sales mixes, or the sales mix variance.

The difference between points B and C is in the number of total units. The total units in point B is the number of units sold while the total units in point C is the budgeted unit for the period. The other two elements in these two points are the same. Both points B and C use the budgeted sales mix and the budgeted contribution margin per unit. The difference between points B and C, thus, stems from the difference in the total units: a sales quantity variance.

The sum of the sales quantity variance and the sales mix variance for each individual product and for the firm should be the same as the sales volume variance. The summary in panel 5 of Exhibit 15.16 confirms this result.

Market Size and Market Share Variances

LEARNING OBJECTIVE 8
Explain how market size and market share variances lead to sales quantity variances.

Two contributing factors of sales quantity variance are changes in the market size and the firm's share of the market. As the total market for its products expands, a firm is likely to sell more units. Conversely, the firm is likely to sell fewer units when the market for its products contracts. A *market size variance* measures the effect of changes in the market size of the firm's product on the operating results of the firm, including total contribution margin and the operating income of the firm.

When a firm's share of the market increases, the firm sells more units. *Market share variance* assesses the effect that changes in a firm's proportion of the total market have on the operating results of the firm, including total contribution margin and the operating income of the firm.

EXHIBIT 15.16
Sales Mix and Quantity
Variance

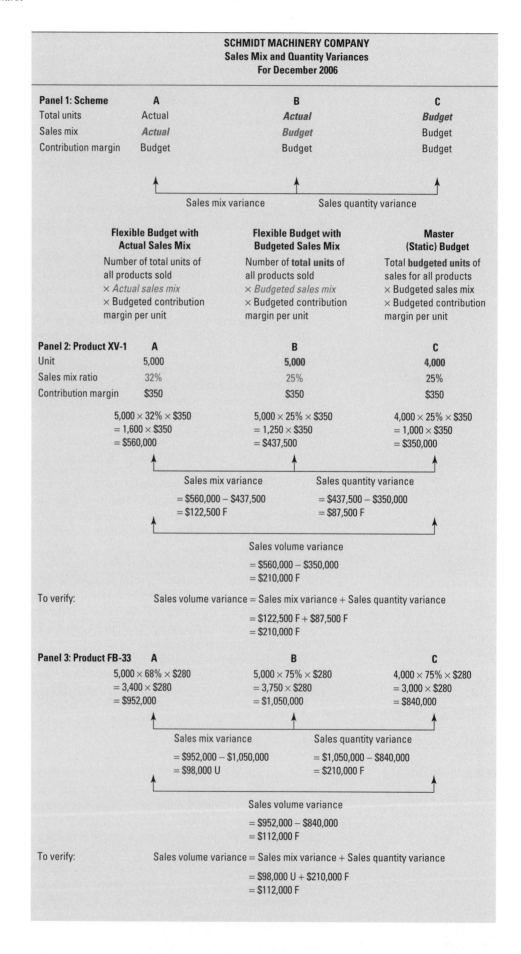

SCHMIDT MACHINERY COMPANY
Sales Mix and Quantity Variances
For December 2006

Panel 1: Scheme	A	B	C
Total units	Actual	*Actual*	*Budget*
Sales mix	*Actual*	*Budget*	Budget
Contribution margin	Budget	Budget	Budget

Sales mix variance   Sales quantity variance

Flexible Budget with Actual Sales Mix	**Flexible Budget with Budgeted Sales Mix**	**Master (Static) Budget**
Number of total units of all products sold × *Actual sales mix* × Budgeted contribution margin per unit	Number of **total units** of all products sold × *Budgeted sales mix* × Budgeted contribution margin per unit	Total **budgeted units** of sales for all products × Budgeted sales mix × Budgeted contribution margin per unit

Panel 2: Product XV-1	A	B	C
Unit	5,000	**5,000**	**4,000**
Sales mix ratio	32%	25%	25%
Contribution margin	$350	$350	$350

$5,000 \times 32\% \times \$350$	$5,000 \times 25\% \times \$350$	$4,000 \times 25\% \times \$350$
$= 1,600 \times \$350$	$= 1,250 \times \$350$	$= 1,000 \times \$350$
$= \$560,000$	$= \$437,500$	$= \$350,000$

Sales mix variance   Sales quantity variance
= $560,000 − $437,500   = $437,500 − $350,000
= $122,500 F   = $87,500 F

Sales volume variance
= $560,000 − $350,000
= $210,000 F

To verify: Sales volume variance = Sales mix variance + Sales quantity variance
= $122,500 F + $87,500 F
= $210,000 F

Panel 3: Product FB-33	A	B	C
	$5,000 \times 68\% \times \$280$	$5,000 \times 75\% \times \$280$	$4,000 \times 75\% \times \$280$
	$= 3,400 \times \$280$	$= 3,750 \times \$280$	$= 3,000 \times \$280$
	$= \$952,000$	$= \$1,050,000$	$= \$840,000$

Sales mix variance   Sales quantity variance
= $952,000 − $1,050,000   = $1,050,000 − $840,000
= $98,000 U   = $210,000 F

Sales volume variance
= $952,000 − $840,000
= $112,000 F

To verify: Sales volume variance = Sales mix variance + Sales quantity variance
= $98,000 U + $210,000 F
= $112,000 F

EXHIBIT 15.16
Concluded

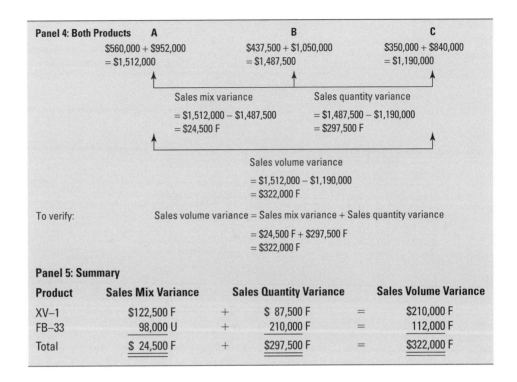

Panel 4: Both Products	A	B	C
	$560,000 + $952,000	$437,500 + $1,050,000	$350,000 + $840,000
	= $1,512,000	= $1,487,500	= $1,190,000

Sales mix variance
= $1,512,000 − $1,487,500
= $24,500 F

Sales quantity variance
= $1,487,500 − $1,190,000
= $297,500 F

Sales volume variance
= $1,512,000 − $1,190,000
= $322,000 F

To verify: Sales volume variance = Sales mix variance + Sales quantity variance
= $24,500 F + $297,500 F
= $322,000 F

Panel 5: Summary

Product	Sales Mix Variance		Sales Quantity Variance		Sales Volume Variance
XV–1	$122,500 F	+	$ 87,500 F	=	$210,000 F
FB–33	98,000 U	+	210,000 F	=	112,000 F
Total	$ 24,500 F	+	$297,500 F	=	$322,000 F

When Schmidt prepared the budget, the firm expected that the total worldwide market for its products, XV–1 and FB–33, would be 40,000 units per month and that Schmidt would have 10 percent of the total market. The master budget data for December were reported in Exhibit 15.9. Exhibit 15.12 showed the actual operations of the month. Exhibit 15.14 reported that the firm had a favorable total sales quantity variance of $297,500 in December.

Market Size Variance

Market size variance
is the effect of changes in market size on a firm's total contribution margin.

Market size is the total unit for the industry. **Market size variance** measures the effect of changes in market size on a firm's total contribution margin. As the market size expands, firms are likely to sell more units. Conversely, as the market size contracts, firms are likely to sell fewer units. In computing market size variance, the focus is on the change in market size: the difference between the actual and budgeted market sizes (units). When determining the market size variance of a firm, we assume that the firm maintains the budgeted market position (market share) and the budgeted average contribution margin per unit. The equation for computing a market size variance follows:

$$\begin{matrix} \text{Market} \\ \text{size} \\ \text{variance} \end{matrix} = \begin{bmatrix} \text{Actual} & & \text{Budgeted} \\ \text{market size} & - & \text{market size} \\ \text{(in units)} & & \text{(in units)} \end{bmatrix} \times \begin{matrix} \text{Budgeted} \\ \text{market} \\ \text{share} \end{matrix} \times \begin{matrix} \text{Weighted-average} \\ \text{budgeted contribution} \\ \text{margin per unit} \end{matrix}$$

The first term on the right side of the equation is the focus of the variance: the difference in market sizes (in units) between the actual and the planned or budgeted market size. The second term is the budgeted or desired market share. The product of the first two terms is the effect of the change in market sizes on the unit sales if the firm maintains the budgeted market share. To estimate the dollar effect of the change in sales units, we multiply the number of units by contribution margin per unit, the last term in the equation. Notice that the contribution margin per unit is the weighted-average budgeted contribution margin per (composite) unit of all of the firm's products in the same market, not the contribution margin per unit of an individual product. The weighted-average budgeted contribution margin per unit for a firm is determined by dividing the total units of the firm into the total contribution margin of the firm. Some managers

EXHIBIT 15.17
Market Size and Market
Share Variances

SCHMIDT MACHINERY COMPANY
Market Size and Share Variances
For December 2006

Panel 1: Market Size Variance

= **Difference in market size × Budgeted market share × Weighted-average budgeted
contribution margin per unit**

= (31,250 − 40,000) × 10% × $297.50 = $260,312.50 U

Panel 2: Market Share Variance

= **Difference in market share × Actual market size × Weighted-average budgeted
contribution margin per unit**

= (16% − 10%) × 31,250 × $297.50 = $557,812.50 F

Panel 3: Reconciliation

Market size variance	$260,312.50 U
Market share variance	557,812.50 F
Sales quantity variance	$297,500.00 F

refer to this contribution margin as the *composite contribution margin per unit*. Schmidt
Company budgeted to sell 4,000 units of XV–1 and FB–33 to earn a total contribution
margin of $1,190,000, as shown in Exhibit 15.9. Thus, the weighted-average budgeted
contribution per unit is $297.50 ($1,190,000 / 4,000 units).

The firm budgeted to sell 4,000 units and expected the total market to be 40,000
units. The budgeted market share is 10 percent of the total market. The total market for
December 2006 turned out to be 31,250 units, the total market size contracted. Panel 1
of Exhibit 15.17 shows the calculation of Schmidt's market size variance, which is
$260,312.50 unfavorable.

The actual market size of the industry (31,250 units) is a decrease of 8,750 units
from the budgeted market size of 40,000 units. If the firm maintained its budgeted market share of 10 percent, the 8,750 units decrease in market size would have decreased
Schmidt's total sales by 875 units. With a weighted-average contribution margin of
$297.50 per unit, the decrease in units (875) would have decreased Schmidt's total
contribution margin and operating income by $260,312.50.

Market Share Variance

Market share is a firm's proportion of a particular market. The market share of a firm
is a function of its core competitive competencies and competitive environment and reflects the firm's competitive position. A successful firm maintains or increases its market share. A firm experiencing continuous erosion in its market share would likely
experience financial difficulties and may suffer eventual demise.

Market share variance compares a firm's actual market share to its budgeted market
share and measures the effect of the difference in market shares on the firm's total contribution margin and operating income. Three items are involved in determining market share variance: the difference between the firm's actual and budgeted market share,
the total actual market size, and the weighted-average budgeted contribution margin
per unit. Notice that the computation uses the *actual,* not budgeted, total market size
and the *budgeted,* not actual, weighted-average contribution margin per unit. The product of these three factors—the difference in market shares, total actual market size, and
weighted-average budget contribution margin per unit—is the market share variance.
The equation is

Market share variance
measures the effect of changes in
market share on total contribution
margin and operating income.

$$\begin{matrix} \text{Market} \\ \text{share} \\ \text{variance} \end{matrix} = \begin{bmatrix} \text{Actual} & & \text{Budgeted} \\ \text{market} & - & \text{market} \\ \text{share} & & \text{share} \end{bmatrix} \times \begin{matrix} \text{Total actual} \\ \text{market size} \\ \text{(in units)} \end{matrix} \times \begin{matrix} \text{Weighted-average} \\ \text{budgeted contribution} \\ \text{margin per unit} \end{matrix}$$

Panel 2 of Exhibit 15.17 shows the calculation of the market share variance for Schmidt Machinery Company's December 2006 operations.

Although the total market for the industry decreased to 31,250, Schmidt's total units sold are higher than the budgeted sales for the period. Its market share increases from the budgeted 10 percent to 16 percent (5,000 units ÷ 31,250 units = 16 percent)—an increase of 6 percent. With the actual total market size being 31,250 units, the 6 percent increase in the market share would have increased Schmidt's total sales by 1,875 units. At a budgeted weighted-average contribution margin of $297.50 per unit, the increase of 1,875 units would have increased its total contribution margin and operating income by $557,812.50.

Reconciliation

Market size variance and market share variance are further analyses of sales quantity variance, as pointed out in Exhibit 15.7. Together, the market size variance and market share variance should equal the sales quantity variance of the period. Panel 3 of Exhibit 15.17 confirms this result. For December 2006, Schmidt has a favorable market share variance of $557,812.50 and an unfavorable market size variance of $260,312.50. The total of these two variances is $297,500 favorable, which is the sales quantity variance reported earlier.

Exhibit 15.18 calculates market size and market share variances using a columnar form. Remember that market share and market size variances explain the firm's sales quantity variance. The total variance in Exhibit 15.18, the difference between points A and C, is the total sales quantity variance for both products shown in Exhibit 15.16 as the difference between points B and C for both products. Point A of Exhibit 15.18 is the budgeted total contribution margin that the firm would have earned from the actual number of units sold. Point B of Exhibit 15.16 is the sum of the flexible budget for both products at the budgeted sales mix. Exhibit 15.18 calculates the same amount using market size. Starting from the industry's total market size, the total number of units sold by the firm is the product of the industry's total actual market size and the firm's actual market share:

$$31,250 \text{ units} \times 16 \text{ percent} = 5,000 \text{ units}$$

The weighted-average budgeted contribution margin per unit is $297.50. Therefore, the total contribution margin from 5,000 units is $1,487,500, as shown at point A of panel 2.

Point B is the budgeted total contribution margin the firm would have earned, given the actual market size, had it maintained the budgeted market share. With the actual market size of 31,250, the firm would have sold 3,125 total units if it had maintained its budgeted market share of 10 percent. At the weighted-average budgeted contribution margin of $297.50 per unit the total contribution margin would be $929,687.50. The only difference between point A and point B is in market share. The $557,812.50 difference ($1,487,500 − $929,687) between these two points, therefore, is a market share variance. This variance is favorable because the actual market share is 16 percent, as opposed to the budgeted 10 percent.

Point C is the master budget. The budgeted total units of sales in the master budget is the product of the budgeted market size and the budgeted market share:

$$40,000 \times 10 \text{ percent} = 4,000 \text{ units}$$

At the weighted-average budgeted contribution margin of $297.50 per unit the total contribution margin in the master budget is

$$4,000 \text{ units} \times \$297.50 \text{ per unit} = \$1,190,000$$

The only difference between point B and point C (the master budget) is in the total market size: actual market size at Point B and budgeted market size at point C. The difference, therefore, is a market size variance, which is $260,312.50 in our example. The variance is unfavorable because the actual market size is smaller than the budgeted market size anticipated at the time when the firm prepared the master budget for December 2006.

EXHIBIT 15.18
Analyzing Market Size and
Share Variances Using
Columnar Form

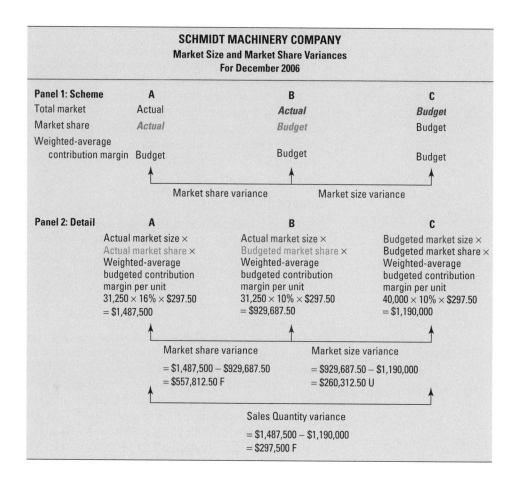

SCHMIDT MACHINERY COMPANY
Market Size and Market Share Variances
For December 2006

Panel 1: Scheme

	A	B	C
Total market	Actual	*Actual*	*Budget*
Market share	*Actual*	*Budget*	Budget
Weighted-average contribution margin	Budget	Budget	Budget

Market share variance   Market size variance

Panel 2: Detail

A	B	C
Actual market size × Actual market share × Weighted-average budgeted contribution margin per unit	Actual market size × Budgeted market share × Weighted-average budgeted contribution margin per unit	Budgeted market size × Budgeted market share × Weighted-average budgeted contribution margin per unit
31,250 × 16% × $297.50 = $1,487,500	31,250 × 10% × $297.50 = $929,687.50	40,000 × 10% × $297.50 = $1,190,000

Market share variance
= $1,487,500 − $929,687.50
= $557,812.50 F

Market size variance
= $929,687.50 − $1,190,000
= $260,312.50 U

Sales Quantity variance
= $1,487,500 − $1,190,000
= $297,500 F

Marketing Variances and Strategic Management

Sales variances such as selling price, sales volume, sales mix, sales quantity, market share, and market size variances help firms to understand factors leading to operating results and to assess the effectiveness of sales activities in attaining the strategic and budgeted goals. These variances also facilitate firms' planning for improvements in operations, modifying current strategy, and devising new strategy.

Strategic Implications of Selling Price Variance

Price change is a tool that firms often use as a competitive weapon. Firms decrease selling prices to expand market shares, drive out competition, establish market position, implement cost leadership competitive strategy, or attain other desired objectives. A fast-food chain decreases the price of a hamburger from 99¢ to 49¢ to drive out competition. An airline reduces the round-trip airfare between Chicago and Paris to $250 to maintain its market share. Firms set premium prices to implement differentiation strategy or take advantage of an expanding market, among other reasons. Sidney Frank, CEO of Frank Importing Co., decided to introduce Grey Goose vodka to the U.S. market as a "superpremium" liquor and set the price three times higher than other premium vodka liquors. The strategy is a success; total sales increased from 100,000 cases in 1999 to more than one million cases in 2002.[6]

A significant unfavorable selling price variance reduces profitability and can jeopardize the firm's financial condition. No firm can afford to allow significant unfavorable selling price variances to continue. Whether a firm has a cost leadership strategy

[6] Christopher Lawton, "A Liquor Maverick Shakes Up Industry with Pricey Brands," *The Wall Street Journal*, May 21, 2003, p. A1.

or a differentiation strategy, it needs to find the factors leading to the significant unfavorable selling price variance.

No single variance tells the whole story, however. Selling price variances need be assessed along with the directions and magnitudes of other sales-related variances. Decreases in selling prices to secure a higher sales volume or market share reduce profit if the unfavorable selling price variance exceeds the favorable sales volume variance. In the late 1970s 7-Up engaged in heavy discounting to gain growth. Increases in volumes were insufficient to make up for the decreases in profits due to the heavy discount. Decreases in selling prices reduced net income and cash flows. Financial difficulties eventually led the firm to be acquired by Cadbury Schweppes. Similarly, an increase in total sales quantity through lower prices might not be beneficial to the firm if a disproportionate amount of the increase in sales quantity comes from low-margin items (an unfavorable sales mix variance). When the combined unfavorable selling price and sales mix variances exceed the favorable sales quantity variance, net income, and cash flow from operations decrease.

A firm needs to consider its current position and the likely reactions of competitors before changing its selling prices. A price change taken by a market leader is likely to prompt competitors to follow the act immediately. For example, airlines usually reduce their fares within hours in response to competitors' fare cuts. Price wars often follow. More often than not, total sales dollars for the airline decrease. Price reductions that competitors will likely match immediately make sense only if the firm initiating them has a lower cost structure than its competitors. Unless accompanied by other actions, any gain in market share by the market leader through price reductions is likely to be temporary. A favorable selling price variance experienced by a market leader is a confirmation on the properness of actions taken by the management if the firm experiences no meaningful deterioration in its market share (unfavorable market share variance) and sales quantity (unfavorable sales quantity variance).

A non-market leader with a meaningful gain in market share and a significant unfavorable price variance should assess its ability to sustain continuous price reductions and competitors' reactions to the firm's gain in market share. A firm needs to assess the difference between favorable price variance and unfavorable market share variance if it has a favorable selling price variance with a significant loss of market share. An unfavorable selling price variance for a non-market leader without a significant gain in market share indicates that the price reduction decision is questionable.

Conversely, a firm needs to assess the difference between a favorable selling price variance and an unfavorable market share variance if the firm endures a significant loss of market share. Continuous deterioration of market share may reduce a firm to a relatively insignificant player in the industry, as experienced by the Apple Computer Inc.

A pricing policy is successful if it results in a favorable price variance with no decrease in either market share or sales quantity. The pricing policy is also a success if the unfavorable price variance is accompanied by an even greater combined total of favorable market share and sales quantity variances. Favorable variances in selling price, sales quantity, and market share variances signal unexplored potential.

Strategic Implications of Market Share Variance

A firm that intends to build market share expects to see favorable market share variances. In the short-run, however, the firm may experience unfavorable selling price variances. The unfavorable selling price variance needs not be a grave concern to the management because the primary strategy of the firm is to build market share. As long as the firm gains market share as the firm's strategy prescribes, unfavorable selling price, contribution margin, or operating income variances may not be of significance to the firm. Microsoft followed this strategy in marketing its word processing software, Microsoft Word. WordPerfect was the market leader in the 1980s and early 1990s. Microsoft gradually built Word's market share by offering Microsoft Word at low prices. As Word's market share grew, WordPerfect users were forced to switch to Word to be compatible with their colleagues, bosses, or friends.

REAL-WORLD FOCUS   The Myth of Market Share and Price

GM's market share has declined from more than 50 percent of the U.S. car market before the 1980s to below 30 percent by the early 2000s. To keep car sales humming, GM and other auto companies pile on ever more rebates, 0 percent loans, barely profitable lease rates, and other incentives to entice car buyers into showrooms. However, these sweet arrangements soured the carmakers' bottom lines. In 2002, GM's net vehicle prices fell 2 percent and its profit weakened.

Caught in the same vicious pull of incentives, Ford surprised the auto industry when it revealed that its net price per vehicle rose a small but promising 0.2 percent for the same quarter and its market share gained a half-point to 21.2 percent.

How did Ford do it? Smart pricing and careful spending of its marketing cash make the difference for Ford. "Ford collects sales data daily from dealerships and feeds them into computer models that predict which incentives will spark the best results. The output also shows marketers which cars need a boost and in which regional markets—and which cars don't. . . . In contrast, GM prefers the simplicity of promoting a single deal, say 0% financing, across the board."

Raising prices does not entail a lower market share. Lower prices make the bottom-line disappear.

Source: David Welch, "Ford Tames the Rebate Monster," *Business Week,* May 5, 2003, p. 38; and Richard Miniter, "Manager's Journal," *The Wall Street Journal,* June 15,1998.

Management should always be alert to declines in market share. A decrease in market share indicates erosion of its competitive position and encroachments of competitors. Ignoring declining market shares can lead to the firm's eventual demise. However, maintaining or increasing market share at the expense of current profit may not be a wise move either, especially when the firm competes in a mature market. Mature products are cash cows to most firms. Price reductions decrease cash inflows and defeat the strategy. Avoiding unfavorable market share variances at the expense of unfavorable selling price variances is questionable for a mature product.

The high profitability of a firm with a differentiation strategy requires the firm to monitor closely its sales quantity and market share variances. A small change in sales quantity and market share can impact significantly the firm's current and future operating income.

Strategic Implications of Market Size Variance

Misdirected expansion undertaken during periods of declining market size could cause overcapacity, decline in revenue, or financial distress. Shrinking market sizes, however, do not necessarily result in downsizing, as the experience of textile manufacturer Unifi demonstrates. Market size is never a static, well-defined figure. A mature market does not always mean that the total market is fixed or declining in size. Indeed, abundant evidence suggested that firms that took actions to redefine and expand the market size of their products often experience high profitability. McDonald redefined the total market size for its products when it expanded in the early 1980s into several foreign countries.

Defining *market* in *market size* is a challenge. Companies expend substantial resources to increase their *share* of a *market,* but they often have difficulty justifying a similar investment to expand market size, although the potential returns from a larger market can substantially exceed those from gaining a few percentages of market share. Success stories of pharmaceutical companies often result from market expansions. Introduction of a new drug for a previously untreatable ailment increases the number of potential customers, the market size, and the firm's earnings.

Strategic Profitability Analysis

LEARNING OBJECTIVE 9
Analyze factors leading to changes in profitability.

The purpose of strategic profitability analysis is to analyze the difference in operating income between two periods to assess successful implementation of the firm's strategy. To facilitate the analysis, changes in operating income are separated into effects of changes in sales volume (growth), selling price and cost of input resources (price-recovery), and productivity.

EXHIBIT 15.19
Operating Data—CSD Division

	2005	2006
Units produced and sold	9,360	9,600
Total market (units)	234,000	257,400
Selling price per unit	$ 900	$ 920
Total sales	$8,424,000	$8,832,000
Direct materials		
Cost per pound	$ 45	$ 48
Total direct materials used (pounds)	51,480	58,560
Total direct materials cost	$2,316,600	$2,810,880
Other variable costs		
Cost per hour	$ 60	$ 56
Total hours	33,696	36,480
Total other variable costs	$2,021,760	$2,042,880
Total variable operating cost	$4,338,360	$4,853,760
Manufacturing capacity (in units)	15,000	10,000
Fixed costs (excluding R&D)	$1,200,000	$ 960,000
R&D	$ 727,800	$ 570,000
R&D employees	12	10

EXHIBIT 15.20
Income Statement—CSD Division For 2005 and 2006

	2005		2006	
Sales	$8,424,000	100.00%	$8,832,000	100.00%
Total variable costs	4,338,360	51.50%	4,853,760	54.96%
Contribution margin	$4,085,640	48.50%	$3,978,240	45.04%
Fixed costs				
Manufacturing and operating	1,200,000	14.25%	960,000	10.87%
R&D	727,800	8.64%	570,000	6.45%
Operating income	$2,157,840	25.62%	$2,448,240	27.72%
Increase in operating income		$290,400 F		

Exhibit 15.19 presents the operating data pertaining to 2005 and 2006 of the Circuit-Switching Division (CSD) of the Schmidt Machinery Company. CSD manufactures an error-free circuit switch, EF10. Exhibit 15.20 shows the operating results.

Compared to the operating results in 2005 the division sold 240 units more in 2006, or 2.56 percent, and earned $290,400 more in operating income, or 13.46 percent. It appears that the division did a good job in 2006. Did the division move along the strategic direction set for the division? To find an answer to this question, we need to know factors contributing to the improved operating results. Changes in operating results can arise from changes in units sold (growth), selling price and cost of production factors (price recovery), and productivity in using production factors.

Growth Factor

The **growth factor** measures the change in operating income attributable to change in sales quantity. The analysis is similar to the analysis of quantity (efficiency) variance for a direct materials (direct labor) variance. As sales quantities change, both sales revenues and operating costs change and the change in operating income is a result of the changes in the sales revenue and operating costs. The net effect of growth on the operating income is the combined growth effects of sales revenue and operating costs.

Revenue Effect of Growth

Total sales revenues change as the units of sales fluctuate. To determine the effect of changes in sales units on total sales revenue we assume that the selling price per unit remains unchanged.

$$\begin{array}{c} \text{Revenue effect} \\ \text{of growth} \end{array} = \left[\begin{array}{c} \text{Units sold} \\ \text{in 2006} \end{array} - \begin{array}{c} \text{Units sold} \\ \text{in 2005} \end{array} \right] \times \begin{array}{c} \text{2005 selling} \\ \text{price per unit} \end{array}$$

$$= (9{,}600 - 9{,}360) \times \$900$$

$$= \$216{,}000 \text{ F}$$

The analysis uses 2005 operating data as the benchmark and calculates the change in total revenue when the unit of sales increased from 9,360 in 2005 to 9,600 in 2006 using the 2005 selling price per unit. Since the unit selling price remains unchanged, the result, $216,000 favorable, is attributable solely to the increase in units sold.

Cost Effect of Growth

Fluctuations in units of sale also affect operating costs of the firm. The cost effect of growth measures the change in operating costs because of the change in units of sales, assuming no changes in both the cost per unit of input resources and the productivity of these input resources.

$$\begin{array}{c} \text{Cost} \\ \text{effect of} \\ \text{growth} \end{array} = \left[\begin{array}{c} \text{Actual units of} \\ \text{input resources} \\ \text{used in 2005} \end{array} - \begin{array}{c} \text{Units of input resources that} \\ \text{would have been used to produce} \\ \text{2006 output at 2005 productivity} \end{array} \right] \times \begin{array}{c} \text{2005 cost per} \\ \text{unit of input} \\ \text{resources} \end{array}$$

The calculation assumes no change in either productivity or cost of input resources. The second term in the parentheses estimates the total units of input resources that the firm would have used to manufacture the 2006 unit of output if the firm maintains its 2005 productivity in using the input resources. The amount calculated in the parentheses on the right side, therefore, is the change in input resources needed to meet the changed output level if the input-output relationship (productivity) remains unchanged at the 2005 level. The effect in dollars is determined using the 2005 unit cost of input resource for the change in the required input resources for the output. A positive amount denotes favorable variance.

The cost effect of growth applies only to variable input resources. A fixed operating cost will have cost effect of growth only if the changed output quantity required the firm to operate at a different level such as the addition of a factory.

Direct Materials   CSD used 51,480 pounds of direct materials to produce 9,360 units of the product, or 5.5 pounds per unit in 2005. To produce the 9,600 units in 2006 at the 2005 productivity, CSD would require 52,800 pounds (9,600 × 5.5) of direct materials, or 1,320 pounds of additional direct materials for the additional 240 units. At the 2005 cost of $45 per pound, the cost of direct materials would have increased by $59,400.

$$\begin{array}{c} \text{Direct} \\ \text{materials} \\ \text{cost effect} \\ \text{of growth} \end{array} = \left[\begin{array}{c} \text{Actual units} \\ \text{of direct} \\ \text{materials} \\ \text{used in 2005} \end{array} - \begin{array}{c} \text{Units of direct materials} \\ \text{that would have been used} \\ \text{to produce 2006 output at} \\ \text{2005 productivity} \end{array} \right] \times \begin{array}{c} \text{Cost of direct} \\ \text{materials} \\ \text{per pound} \\ \text{in 2005} \end{array}$$

$$= (51{,}480 \text{ pounds} - 9{,}600 \times 5.5 \text{ pounds}) \times \$45$$

$$= (51{,}480 \text{ pounds} - 52{,}800 \text{ pounds}) \times \$45$$

$$= \$59{,}400 \text{ U}$$

Other Variable Costs   CSD spent 33,696 hours on other variable cost to manufacture 9,360 units in 2005, an average of 3.6 hour per unit. If CSD maintains the same productivity in 2006 as in 2005, the manufacturing of 9,600 would require 34,560 hours, or 864 additional hours. At the same hourly rate of $60, the additional hours would have increased the other variable costs by $51,840.

$$\text{Other variable cost effect of growth} = (33,696 - 9,600 \times 3.6) \times \$60$$

$$= \$51,840 \text{ U}$$

Fixed Costs and R&D   Both fixed and R&D costs would remain unchanged to manufacture the slightly higher units of output in 2006. Therefore, there is no cost effect of growth attributable to fixed and R&D costs.

In summary, the net effect in operating income resulting from the increase in units of sales (growth) is

Revenue effect of the growth		$216,000 F
Cost effect of the growth		
Direct materials	$59,400 U	
Other variable costs	51,840 U	
Fixed costs and R&D costs	0	111,240 U
Increase in operating income attributable to growth		$104,760 F

Further Analysis of Growth Effect

Variations in units sold can be a result of changes in either the total market size for the product, the firm's share of the market, or both. The total market for CSD's products increased 10 percent ($257,400 \div 234,000 = 110\%$) in 2006. CSD would have increased its total sales units by 10 percent, 936 units, if it maintained the same market share as in 2005.

$$9,360 \text{ units in } 2005 \times 10\% = 936 \text{ units}$$

The contribution margin per unit is $436.50 in 2005:

$$\$900 - (\$45 \times 5.5 \text{ pounds}) - (\$60 \times 3.6 \text{ hours}) = \$436.50 \text{ per unit}$$

The increase in operating income from selling 936 more in units, or the effect of the market size on growth effect of operating income, is

$$936 \times \$436.50 = \$408,564 \text{ F}$$

However, the firm's market share decreased in 2006. In 2005, CSD had 4 percent of the total market ($9,360 \div 234,000 = 4\%$). The firm managed to have only 3.73 percent of the total market in 2006 ($9,600 \div 257,400 = 3.7296\%$). The decrease in market share cost CSD a decrease of 696 units in units sold.

$$\begin{bmatrix} 2005 \\ \text{market} \\ \text{share} \end{bmatrix} - \begin{bmatrix} 2006 \\ \text{market} \\ \text{share} \end{bmatrix} \times \begin{matrix} 2006 \\ \text{market} \\ \text{size} \end{matrix}$$

$$= (4\% - 3.7296\%) \times 257,400 \text{ units}$$

$$= 696 \text{ units, unfavorable}$$

The effect of the market share on growth effect of operating income is[7]

$$696 \text{ U} \times \$436.50 = \$303,804 \text{ U}$$

---

[7] Using the procedures discussed earlier on determination of market share and market size variances, these variances are calculated as follows,

Contribution margin per unit in 2005: $900 − ($45 × 5.5 pounds) − ($60 × 3.6 hours) = $436.50 per unit

Market size variance:	(257,400 − 234,000) × 4% × $436.50 =	$408,564 F
Market share variance:	(4% − 3.7296%) × 257,400 × $436.50 =	303,804 U
Total growth effect on operating income		$104,760 F

Price-Recovery Factor

The **price-recovery factor** measures changes in operating income attributable to changes in the selling prices of products and the costs of input resources. This factor reflects the extent to which a firm was able to recover changes in the costs of input resources through changes in selling prices of the firm's products. Similar to the growth factor, the price-recovery factor is determined separately for revenues and costs. The calculations of price-recovery effects are similar to the computation of price variance for direct materials discussed in Chapter 13.

Revenue Effect of Price Recovery

$$\begin{array}{l} \text{Revenue effect} \\ \text{of price recovery} \end{array} = \left[\begin{array}{c} \text{Output selling price} \\ \text{per unit in 2006} \end{array} - \begin{array}{c} \text{Output selling price} \\ \text{per unit in 2005} \end{array} \right] \times \begin{array}{c} \text{Units of output} \\ \text{sold in 2006} \end{array}$$

$$= (\$920 - \$900) \times 9{,}600$$

$$= \$192{,}000 \text{ F}$$

CSD sold 9,600 units in 2006 at $920 per unit, which is $20 higher than the selling price in 2005. The increase in selling price brings in an additional $192,000 for CSD.

Cost Effect of Price Recovery

$$\begin{array}{l} \text{Cost} \\ \text{effect of} \\ \text{price} \\ \text{recovery} \end{array} = \left[\begin{array}{c} \text{Cost per} \\ \text{unit of input} \\ \text{resource} \\ \text{in 2005} \end{array} - \begin{array}{c} \text{Cost per unit} \\ \text{of input} \\ \text{resource} \\ \text{in 2006} \end{array} \right] \times \begin{array}{c} \text{Units of input resources} \\ \text{that would have been used} \\ \text{to produce 2006 output at} \\ \text{2005 productivity} \end{array}$$

The calculation focuses on changes in the cost of input resources. The last term in the equation, units of input resources that would have been used to produce the 2006 output units at 2005 productivity has been determined in the calculation for the cost effect of growth, except for fixed costs. The capacity level of fixed costs that would have been used to produce the 2006 output quantity remains the same at the 2005 level.

The cost effect of price recovery is also determined separately for each of the input resources or capacity.

Cost effect of price recovery		
Direct materials costs	($45 − $48) × 52,800 pounds =	$158,400 U
Other variable costs	($60 − $56) × 34,560 hours =	138,240 F
Fixed operating costs	($80 − $96) × 15,000 units =	240,000 U
R&D	($60,650 − $57,000) × 12 =	43,800 F
Total cost effect of price recovery on operating income		$216,360 U

The cost of direct materials increased from $45 to $48 per pound. At the 2005 productivity (5.5 pounds of direct materials per unit of the output), CSD needs 52,800 pounds to manufacture the 2006 output of 9,600 units (9,600 units × 5.5 pounds per unit). The higher direct materials price in 2006 decreased operating income by $158,400. However, CSD reduced the hourly rate for other variable costs from $60 in 2005 to $56 in 2006. The saving of $4 per hour for the 34,560 total hours that CSD would need to manufacture 9,600 units at the 2005 productivity for the other variable costs added $138,240 to 2006 operating income.

2005 other variable costs productivity: 33,696 hours ÷ 9,360 units = 3.6 hours per unit

Total hours of other variable costs needed to manufacture 2006 output of 9,600 units at the 2005 productivity other variable costs:

$$9{,}600 \text{ units} \times 3.6 \text{ hours per unit} = 34{,}560 \text{ hours}$$

CSD paid $1,200,000 fixed costs for 15,000 units of manufacturing capacity and $727,800 for 12 employees in R&D in 2005, or average costs of $80 per unit of the manufacturing capacity and $60,650 per R&D employee. The average costs for 2006 are $96 and $57,000 for fixed manufacturing capacity and R&D, respectively. Even though CSD lowered its manufacturing capacity in 2006 to save fixed costs, the fixed cost per unit of manufacturing capacity in 2006 was higher than that of 2005. As a result, the price-recovery effect of fixed manufacturing capacity costs is $240,000 unfavorable. However, the cost per R&D employee decreased and the price-recovery effect of R&D cost is $43,800 favorable.

The net price-recovery effect is the sum of revenue and cost effects, $24,360 unfavorable:

Revenue effect of price recovery	$192,000 F
Cost effect of price recovery	216,360 U
Price-recovery effect on operating income	$ 24,360 U

The result suggests that the cost increases in the firm's resource is higher than the increase in selling prices of the firm's products.

Productivity Factor

The **productivity factor** measures impacts of changes in the input-output relationship on the 2006 operating income based on the 2006 costs of input resources capacity.

$$\begin{array}{c} \text{Productivity} \\ \text{factor of} \\ \text{resources} \end{array} = \left[\begin{array}{c} \text{Input units or capacity that would} \\ \text{have been used to produce 2006} \\ \text{output at 2005 productivity} \end{array} - \begin{array}{c} \text{Input units} \\ \text{or capacity} \\ \text{used in 2006} \end{array} \right] \times \begin{array}{c} \text{Actual cost} \\ \text{per unit} \\ \text{in 2006} \end{array}$$

The input units or capacity that would have been used to manufacture the 2006 output units at the 2005 productivity have already been calculated in determining the cost effect of growth. For the CSD division, the productivity effect is

Direct materials	= (9,600 × 5.5 pounds per unit − 58,560) × $48 =	$276,480 U
Other variable costs	= (9,600 × 3.6 hours per unit − 36,480) × $56 =	107,520 U
Fixed operating costs	= (15,000 − 10,000) × $96 per hour =	480,000 F
R&D	= (12 − 10) × $57,000 per employee =	114,000 F
Total productivity effect on operating income		$210,000 F

Productivity effects of manufacturing factors are determined similar to the productivity measures discussed in the first section of this chapter. Notice that the calculation uses 2006 cost for the resources. At 2005 productivity, CSD should have used 52,800 pounds of direct materials to manufacture 9,600 units in 2006. Instead, CSD used 58,560 pounds, an excess of 5,760 pounds. At $48 per pound that CSD paid for the direct materials in 2006, the excess usage added $276,480 to the total cost. Similarly, CSD should have spent 34,560 hours on other variable costs in 2006 to manufacture 9,600 units. It used 36,480 hours and, at $56 per hour in 2006, increased costs by $107,520.

However, CSD reduced its manufacturing capacity from 15,000 units in 2005 to 10,000 units in 2006. At $96 average cost per unit (2006 cost), the reduction saved CSD $480,000 in cost. Similarly, the division saved $114,000 in R&D by reducing the number of employees from 12 to 10.

Summary of Strategic Profitability Analysis

Exhibit 15.21 summarizes variances for strategic profitability analysis. The top panel shows that the firm increased its operating income by $290,400 in 2006. The strategic profitability analysis in the middle panel shows that the increase in operating incomes is attributable to favorable growth and productivity. The firm was not successful in recovering increases in resources through higher selling prices of its products.

The bottom panel of Exhibit 15.21 is a further analysis of the effect of growth factor on operating income. The analysis points out that the $104,760 favorable growth

EXHIBIT 15.21
Summary of Strategic Profitability Analysis—CSD Division 2006

Change in operating income:

2005 operating income	$2,157,840
2006 operating income	2,448,240
Changes in operating income	$ 290,400 F

Strategic profitability analysis:

	Growth	Price Recovery	Productivity	Total
Total sales	$216,000 F	$192,000 F		
Direct materials	$ 59,400 U	$158,400 U	$276,480 U	
Other variable costs	$ 51,840 U	$138,240 F	$107,520 U	
Fixed costs of manufacturing capacity	$ 0	$240,000 U	$480,000 F	
R&D	$ 0	$ 43,800 F	$114,000 F	
Total cost variances	$111,240 U	$216,360 U	$210,000 F	
Total effect on operating income	$104,760 F	$ 24,360 U	$210,000 F	$290,400 F

Further analyses of growth factor effect:

Market size	$408,564 F
Market share	$303,804 U
Total	$104,760 F

factor effect the firm experienced is a result of the expansion in the market size of the firm's product. The firm is fortunate in a growing industry. However, the significant unfavorable market share variance (12.4 percent of the total operating income in 2006) raises the question of whether the firm is successful in executing its strategy. An unfavorable market share variance is always a warning signal management seldom can afford to ignore.

A firm with a differentiation strategy is not successful if it loses market share. It signals that the market did not recognize the value of the firm's products and the firm failed in differentiating the value of its products. The lower market share of a cost leadership firm indicates that the firm is not competitive against its competitors.

Increase in selling price can also decrease market share. As costs increase, firms are likely to raise selling prices to preserve profitability. Firms may also raise prices to earn a higher operating income. Costs of input resources for CSD increased during 2006 because of the increased direct materials prices and decreased productivity. Increases in selling prices contribute $192,000 to operating income. However, increases in direct materials costs and decreases in direct materials productivity add $434,880 ($158,400 + $276,480) to the cost of 2006. CSD benefited from the decreased hourly cost of other variables costs (from $60 to $56 per hour). The lower hourly cost contributed $138,240 to the operating income. However, the lower productivity on using other variable costs lessened the benefit by $107,520. Overall, the increase in selling prices that added $192,000 to the operating income failed to cover the increase in variable costs of $404,160 ($158,400 + $276,480 − $138,240 + $107,520).

Through reductions in fixed costs and R&D expenses, CSD added $397,800 (−$240,000 + $43,800 + $480,000 + $114,000) to 2006 operating income. Reductions in excess capacity increased operating income of the period. The reduction is a good decision if the firm will not need the reduced capacity in the foreseeable future or the savings from the reduced capacity is greater than the cost to restore the capacity in the event that the firm needs the capacity. The savings from R&D would be questionable, especially for a firm with a differentiation strategy. CSD reduced the number of employees in R&D and lowered the average salary from $60,650 to $57,000 per employee. Continuous improvements often are critical for a firm competing on a differentiation strategy. Decreases in R&D expenditures may diminish competitiveness of the firm. The decreases in manufacturing capacity and R&D are appropriate for a cost leadership firm if the firm will not need the reduced manufacturing capacity to meet market demands in the future and the reduced R&D is not needed to maintain competitiveness.

CSD's increases in selling price lagged behind faster increases in costs in 2006. This suggests that the firm was not effective if it competes on a cost leadership strategy. A cost leadership firm rarely can afford unfavorable variances on input resources, especially for variable manufacturing resources. Unfavorable cost variances take away the firm's competitiveness on cost leadership.

Summary

Productivity is the ratio of output to input. Improvements in productivity enable firms to do more with fewer resources. A productivity measure is often compared to the performance of a prior period, another firm, the industry standard, or a benchmark in assessing a firm's productivity.

Partial productivity is the ratio of output level attained to the amount of an input resource used in the operation. The higher the ratio is, the better. A partial operational productivity is the required physical amount of an input resource to produce one unit of output. The partial financial productivity of an input resource is the number of units or the value of output manufactured for each dollar spent on the input resource. A partial financial productivity measure can be separated into changes in productivity, input price, and output. The productivity change is the difference between the actual amount used and the expected amount of input resources to manufacture the output. The input price change accounts for the effects of the difference between the budgeted (or benchmark) and the actual prices for the input resource on the operating income of the period. The output change variance accounts for the change in cost due to changes in the number of output units.

A total productivity measures the relationship between the output achieved and the total input costs and is usually a financial productivity.

Measures of productivity are applicable to all organizations including service firms and not-for-profit organizations. However, imprecise measures for output, lack of definite relationships between output and input resources, or absence of revenue for not-for-profits may limit the usefulness of productivity measures for service or not-for-profit organizations.

Increasing global competition and rapid changes in technologies require management to be constantly alert to changes in resource productivity as well as opportunities and changes in marketing. Management must be aware of levels and changes in its productive factors, such as materials, labor, energy, and processes. To market effectively, management must be fully informed of the effects of changes in selling prices, sales volumes, sale mixes, market sizes, and market shares on operations and the firm's strategy. Management must monitor the effects of these changes on operating results to be able to take an appropriate action at the earliest time.

A sales volume variance reflects the difference in contribution margin or operating income between a flexible budget and the master (static) budget. The sales volume variance for a single product firm can be determined by multiplying the standard contribution margin per unit of the product and the difference in units between the number of units sold and the budgeted units to be sold. The sale volume variance of firms with multiple products can be separated into sales mix and sales quantity variances. Determination of sales mix variance includes three components:

1. The difference between the actual sales mix (defined as the ratio of the unit of the product to the total units of all products) and the budget sales mix
2. The total number of units of all products sold during the period
3. The product's standard contribution margin

The product of these three components is the sales mix variance of the product. The variance is favorable if the actual sales mix is greater than the budget sales mix [component (1)].

A product's sales quantity variance has three elements: (1) the difference between the firm's total actual units sold and the budgeted units, (2) the product's budget sales mix, and, (3) its standard contribution margin. The product of these three elements is the product's sales quantity variance. A sales quantity variance assesses the effect of the difference between the units sold and the number of units budgeted to be sold on total contribution margin and operating income.

A sales quantity variance can be separated further into market size and market share variances. A market size variance assesses the effect of changes in the industry's total market size on the firm's total contribution margin and operating income. A market size variance is the product of three factors: (1) the difference between the actual and the budgeted number of total market sizes (in number of units), (2) the firm's budgeted market share, and (3) the weighted-average budgeted contribution margin per unit. The market size variance is favorable if the actual total market size is larger than the market size expected when the master budget was prepared. A market share variance measures the effect of changes in the firm's market share on its operating income. A market share variance is the product of three elements: (1) the actual total number of units in the market (actual market size), (2) the difference between the firm's actual and budgeted market shares, and (3) the weighted average budgeted contribution margin per unit.

The change of a firm's operating income over periods can be separated into effects attributable to growth, price recovery, or productivity factors. The growth factor identifies the impacts on sales revenues and costs from selling a different number of units from the base year, assuming no change in selling prices, cost of input resources, operating capacity, and productivity. The price-recovery factor measures the changes in revenues and costs attributable to changes in selling prices of products and costs of input resources, assuming no change in productivity and at the changed operating level. The productivity factor determines the effect on operating costs from the changed input-output relationships based on the changed input costs.

Key Terms

financial productivity, *626*
growth factor, *652*
market share variance, *646*
market size variance, *645*
operational productivity, *626*

partial productivity, *626*
price-recovery factor, *654*
productivity, *625*
productivity factor, *655*
sales mix, *639*

sales mix variance, *639*
sales quantity variance, *640*
total productivity, *626*

Self-Study Problems

(For solutions, please turn to the end of the chapter.)

1. Productivity Variances

Carlson Automotive Company manufactures fuel-injection systems. It manufactured and sold 60,000 units in 2005 and 64,000 units in 2006 at $25 per unit. In 2005, the firm used 75,000 pounds of alloy TPX–45 at $7.20 per pound and spent 10,000 direct labor-hours at an hourly wage rate of $30. In 2006, the firm used 89,600 pounds of alloy TPX–45 at $6.80 per pound and spent 10,847 direct labor-hours at an hourly wage rate of $32. The total amount of all other expenses remains the same at $450,000 each year. Jerry Olson, CEO, was disappointed that although the total sales increased in 2006, the $195,616 operating income earned in 2006 is only 93 percent of the amount earned in 2005, which was $210,000.

Required Analyze the following:

1. Partial operational productivity of the direct material and direct labor for both 2005 and 2006.
2. Partial financial productivity of the direct material and direct labor for both 2005 and 2006.
3. Detailed composition of partial financial productivity.
4. Total productivity for 2005 and 2006 as measured in both units and sales dollars.

2. Sales Variances

Springwater Brewery has two main products: premium and regular ale. Its operating results and master budget for 2006 (000s omitted) follow:

	Operating Results of 2006			Master Budget for 2006		
	Premium	**Regular**	**Total**	**Premium**	**Regular**	**Total**
Barrels	180	540	720	240	360	600
Sales	$28,800	$62,100	$90,900	$36,000	$43,200	$79,200
Variable expenses	16,200	40,500	56,700	21,600	27,000	48,600
Contribution margin	$12,600	$21,600	$34,200	$14,400	$16,200	$30,600
Fixed expenses	10,000	5,000	15,000	10,000	5,000	15,000
Operating income	$ 2,600	$16,600	$19,200	$ 4,400	$11,200	$15,600

Pam Kuder, CEO, expected the total industry sales to be 1,500,000 barrels during the period. After the year, Mark Goldfeder, the controller, reported that the total sales for the industry were 1,600,000 barrels.

Required   Calculate the following:

1. Selling price variances for the period for each product and for the firm.
2. Sales volume variances for the period for each product and for the firm.
3. Sales quantity variances for each product and the firm.
4. Sales mix variances for the period for each product and for the firm.
5. The sum of the sales quantity variance and sales mix variance and verifying that this total equals the sales volume variance.
6. Market size variances.
7. Market share variances.
8. The sum of market size variance and market share variance and verifying that this total equals the sales quantity variance.

Questions

15–1   What is productivity? What does it measure?

15–2   Discuss why improving productivity is important for a firm that competes on a cost leadership strategy.

15–3   List benchmarks or criteria often used in assessing productivity, and discuss their advantages and disadvantages.

15–4   What is operational productivity? Financial productivity?

15–5   What is partial productivity? Total productivity?

15–6   "A financial productivity measure contains more information than an operational productivity measure does." Do you agree?

15–7   "A total productivity measure encompasses all partial productivity measures." Do you agree?

15–8   "Partial productivity measures should be calculated only for high-value-added activities." Do you agree?

15–9   Why do manufacturing personnel prefer operational productivity measures to financial productivity measures?

15–10   "An activity productivity measure such as machine-hour productivity is more important in a JIT environment than in a non-JIT environment." Do you agree?

15–11   Which of the following statements is true? (a) The lower the partial productivity ratio, the greater the productivity, (b) productivity improves when partial productivity increases, (c) prices of inputs are incorporated in the partial productivity ratio, (d) the partial productivity ratio measures the number of outputs produced per multiple input, and (e) more than one of the above is true.

15–12   List important measures in assessing marketing effectiveness.

15–13   What are the components of sales variance?

15–14   Distinguish between a selling *price variance* and a *sales volume variance.*

15–15   What is the difference between a *sales quantity variance* and a *sales volume variance?*

15–16   "As long as a firm sells more units than the units specified in the master budget, it will not have an unfavorable sales volume variance." Do you agree? Why?

15–17 What are the relationships among a selling price variance, a sales mix variance, a sales quantity variance, and a sales volume variance?

15–18 Distinguish between market size variance and market share variance.

15–19 "A favorable sales quantity variance indicates that the marketing manager has done a good job." Do you agree? Can you give an example in which a market size variance or market share variance is opposite to that of the sales quantity variance?

15–20 What are the relationships between market size variance, market share variance, sales quantity variance, and sales volume variance?

15–21 An improvement in earnings growth can be achieved at the expense of market share (an unfavorable market share variance). Do you agree?

15–22 What does growth factor explain in strategic profitability analysis?

15–23 What does price recovery factor explain in strategic profitability analysis?

15–24 What do market size and market share help to explain in strategic profitability analysis?

Exercises

15–25 **Partial Operational Productivity**   Darwin, Inc., provided the following information for a production factor:

Budgeted production	10,000 units
Actual production	9,500 units
Budgeted input	9,750 gallons
Actual input	8,950 gallons

Required   What is the partial operational productivity ratio of the production factor?

    a. 0.97 unit per gallon

    b. 1.02 units per gallon

    c. 1.06 units per gallon

    d. 1.12 units per gallon

    e. None of the above

15–26 **Partial Financial Productivity and Total Productivity**   RFD Corporation makes small parts from steel alloy sheets. Management has the flexibility to substitute direct materials for direct manufacturing labor. If workers cut the steel carefully, more parts can be manufactured from a metal sheet, but this requires additional direct manufacturing labor-hours. Alternatively, RFD can use fewer direct manufacturing labor-hours if it is willing to tolerate more waste of direct materials. RFD provides this information for the years 2005 and 2006:

	2005	2006
Output units	400,000	486,000
Direct manufacturing labor-hours	10,000	13,500
Wages per hour	$26	$25
Direct materials used	160 tons	180 tons
Direct materials cost per ton	$3,375	$3,125

Required   Carry all computations to four digits after the decimal point.

    1. Compute the partial financial productivity for both manufacturing factors for 2005 and 2006.

    2. Calculate RFD's total productivity in units per dollar in 2005 and 2006.

    3. Evaluate management's decision in 2006 to substitute one production factor for another.

15–27 **Partial Operational and Financial Productivity**   Software Solution (SOS) helps subscribers solve software problems. All transactions are made over the telephone. For the year 2006, 10 engineers, most of whom are recent graduates, handled 100,000 calls. The average yearly salary for software engineers was $45,000. Starting in 2007, the firm retained and hired only software engineers with at least two years of experience. SOS raised the engineers' salary to $60,000 per year. In 2007, eight engineers handled 108,000 calls.

Required

1. Calculate the partial operational productivity ratio for both years.
2. Calculate the partial financial productivity ratio for both years.
3. Did the firm make the right decision to hire only software engineers with at least two years' experience?
4. List other factors that should be considered in making the decision.

15–28 Sales Quantity, Sales Mix, and Sales Volume Variances CompuWorld sells two RISC chips, R66 and R100, to small machine tool manufacturers. Pertinent data for 2005 follow:

	Budgeted		Actual	
	R66	R100	R66	R100
Selling price per chip	$50	$160	$55	$155
Variable cost per chip	40	90	43	95
Contribution margin	$10	$ 70	$12	$ 60
Fixed cost per chip	6	30	5	25
Operating income	$ 4	$ 40	$ 7	$ 35
Sales in units	1,200	400	1,000	1,000

Required

1. What is the R66 sales quantity variance?
   a. $400 F   d. $3,000 F
   b. $1,000 F   e. $3,600 F
   c. $1,200 F

2. What is the R100 sales mix variance?
   a. $20,000 F   d. $40,000 F
   b. $30,000 F   e. $70,000 F
   c. $35,000 F

3. What is the total sales volume variance?
   a. $10,000 F   d. $22,000 F
   b. $12,400 F   e. $40,000 F
   c. $13,000 F

15–29 Basic Market Share, Market Size, and Sales Volume Variances C. W McCall sells a gold-plated souvenir mug; it expects to sell 1,600 units for $45 each to earn a $25 contribution margin per unit. Janice McCall, president, expects the year's total market to be 32,000 units. For the year just completed, the local college won the national hockey championship, and the total market was 100,000 units. C. W McCall sold 3,000 at $75 each. The variable cost to the firm is $40 per unit.

Required

1. What is the market share variance?
   a. $8,000 U   d. $50,000 U
   b. $11,200 U   e. $70,000 U
   c. $40,000 U

2. What is the market size variance?
   a. $51,000 F   d. $85,000 F
   b. $68,000 F   e. $119,000 F
   c. $71,400 F

3. What is the firm's sales volume variance?
   a. $35,000 F   d. $85,000 F
   b. $49,000 F   e. $135,000 F
   c. $51,000 F

15–30 **Sales Volume, Sales Quantity, and Sales Mix Variances**   The Varner Performing Arts Center has a total capacity of 7,500 seats: 2,000 center seats, 2,500 side seats, and 3,000 balcony seats. The budgeted and actual tickets sold for a Broadway musical show are as follows:

		Percentage	
	Ticket Price	Budgeted Seats	Actual Seats
Center	$60	80%	95%
Side	50	90	85
Balcony	40	85	75

The actual ticket prices are the same as those budgeted. Once a show has been booked, the total cost does not vary with the total number of attendance.

Required   Compute these for the show:

1. The budgeted and actual sales mix percentages for different types of seats.
2. The budgeted average contribution margin per seat.
3. The total sales quantity variance and the total sales mix variance.
4. The total sales volume variance.

15–31 **Growth in Operating Income**   The CSD division has the following operating result for the year 2007.

	2007
Units produced and sold	10,368
Total market (units)	270,270
Selling price per unit	$ 930
Direct materials	
Cost per pound	$ 50
Total direct materials used (pounds)	59,616
Other variable costs	
Cost per hour	$ 57
Total hours	41,472
Manufacturing capacity (in units)	10,000
Fixed costs (excluding R&D)	$930,000
R&D	$540,000
R&D employees	9

Required   Refer to the 2006 operating data of CSD division in the chapter (Exhibit 15.19, p. 651). Calculate the growth effect of the change in operating income from 2006 to 2007.

15–32 **Price-Recovery Effect**   Use the data in Exercise 15–31.

Required   Calculate the price-recovery effect of the change in operating income from 2006 to 2007.

15–33 **Productivity Effect**   Use the data in Exercise 15–31.

Required   Calculate the productivity effect of the change in operating income from 2006 to 2007.

15–34 **Market Size Variance, Market Share Variance, and Growth Effect**   Use the data in Exercise 15–31.

Required   Determine the effects of market size and market share on the growth effect of the change in operating income from 2006 to 2007.

15–35 **Strategy**   Use the results of your analyses for Exercises 15–31 through 15–34.

Required   Was CSD effective if it was competing on a differentiation strategy?

15–36 Strategy Use the results of your analyses for Exercises 15–31 through 15–34.

Required Was CSD effective if it was competing on a low-cost strategy?

15–37 Strategic Analysis of Operating Income JD Company manufactures a special alloy in its fully automated factories. Direct material cost is the only variable manufacturing cost. JD has the following operating data for 2005 and 2006.

	2005	2006
1. Units (50 pounds boxes) produced and sold	600	630
2. Selling price per box of 50 pounds	$2,400	$2,700
3. Direct materials used (pounds)	360,000	402,000
4. Direct material cost per pound	$2.00	$1.80
5. Manufacturing capacity (number of boxes)	1,000	1,000
6. Total conversion costs	$450,000	$480,000
7. Total R&D costs	$300,000	$220,000
8. Total number of R&D staff	5	4

Required

1. Calculate the operating income of JD Company in 2005 and 2006. What is the change in operating income from 2005 to 2006?
2. Calculate the effects of growth, price recovery, and productivity factors to explain the change in operating income from 2005 to 2006.
3. Comment on your answers in requirements 1 and 2 and explain their implications.

15–38 Strategic Analysis of Operating Income (continuation of Exercise 15–37) There are only two other companies that manufacture and sell the same product. JD Company estimated that these two firms sold approximately 400 units in 2005 and 630 units in 2006.

Required

1. Calculate how much of the change in operating income from 2005 to 2006 is attributable to the change in market size and market share.
2. Was JD Company successful in implementing product differentiation competitive strategy over the two-year period?

15–39 Strategic Analysis of Operating Income Lammer Cap Company purchases generic caps and imprints logos of local sports teams in Kansas, Missouri, and Oklahoma. On average 5 percent of the caps are lost during the process. The firm purchased 600,000 caps in 2005 at $4.18 per cap. Printing cost $0.38 per cap. The firm sold 570,000 in 2005 at $10 per cap and paid $1.00 commission for each cap sold. In addition, the firm incurred $300,000 administrative costs. The firm sold caps to 12,000 teams, although it could easily serve 15,000 teams. The firm estimated that it had 25 percent of the total market in the three-state area.

In an attempt to reduce cost, Lammer purchased generic caps from an emerging country at $1.98 per cap in 2006. Printing added $0.50 to the cost per cap. However, Lammer had to reject approximately 10 percent of the caps upon delivery due to quality problems. Another 10 percent were rejected after the printing process. The firm sold 646,380 caps in 2006 at $8.00 per cap. The sales commission remained at $1.00 per cap. However, Lammer had to increase administrative costs to $400,000 to handle additional work involved in buying the caps from the new supplier. The firm sold caps to 10,000 teams. However, the firm could still serve 15,000 teams. The firm calculated its market share was 30 percent of the total market in the three-state area.

Required

1. Calculate the operating income of Lammer Cap Company in 2005 and 2006 and determine the change in operating income from 2005 to 2006.
2. Calculate the effects of growth, price-recovery, and productivity factors to explain the change in operating income from 2005 to 2006.
3. Comment on your answers in requirements 1 and 2 and explain their implications.

15–40 Strategic Analysis of Operating Income (continuation of Exercise 15–39)   The total market has not changed in the three-state area.

Required

1. Calculate how much of the change in operating income from 2005 to 2006 is attributable to the change in market size.
2. Was Lammer Cap Company successful in implementing cost leadership strategy?

Problems

15–41 Partial Operational Productivity   Frisen Communication Inc. manufactures a scrambling device for cellular telephones. The device's main component is a delicate part, CSU10. CSU10 is easily damaged and requires careful handling. Once damaged, it must be discarded. The firm hires only skilled laborers to manufacture and install CSU10; however, some are still damaged. Robotic instruments process all other parts. Frisen's operating data for 2006 and 2005 follow:

	2006	2005
Units manufactured	500,000	600,000
Number of CSU10 used	800,000	825,000
Number of direct labor-hours spent	150,000	200,000
Cost of CSU10 per unit	$156	$135
Direct labor wage rate per hour	$56	$63

Required

1. Compute the partial operational productivity for 2005 and 2006.
2. On the basis of the partial operational productivity that you computed, what conclusions can you draw about the firm's productivity in 2006 relative to 2005?

15–42 Financial Partial Productivity   Use the data for Frisen Communication Inc. in problem 15–41 to complete the requirements.

Required

1. Compute the partial financial productivity ratios for 2005 and 2006.
2. On the basis of the partial financial productivity ratios you computed, what conclusions can you draw about the firm's productivity in 2006 relative to 2005?
3. Separate the change of the partial financial productivity ratio from 2005 to 2006 into productivity changes, input price changes, and output changes.
4. Does the detailed information provided by separating the change of the partial financial production ratio offer any additional insight into the relative productivity for 2005 and 2006?

15–43 Total Productivity   Use the data for Frisen Communication Inc. in problem 15–41 to do the following.

Required

1. Compute the total productivity ratios for 2005 and 2006.
2. On the basis of the total productivity that you computed, what conclusions can you draw about the firm's productivity in 2006 relative to 2005?

15–44 Partial Operational and Financial Productivity   In the fourth quarter of 2005 Simpson Company embarked on a major effort to improve productivity. It redesigned products, reengineered manufacturing processes, and offered productivity improvement courses. The effort was completed in the last quarter of 2005. The controller's office has gathered the following year-end data to assess the results of this effort.

	2005	2006
Units manufactured and sold	15,000	18,000
Selling price of the product	$40	$40
Materials used (pounds)	12,000	12,600
Cost per pound of materials	$8	$10
Labor-hours	6,000	5,000
Hourly wage rate	$20	$25
Power (kwh)	1,000	2,000
Cost of power per kwh	$2	$2

Required

1. Prepare a summary contribution approach income statement for each of the two years and calculate the change in operating income.
2. Compute the partial operational productivity ratios for each production factor in 2005 and 2006.
3. Compute the partial financial productivity ratios for each production factor in 2005 and 2006.
4. On the basis of the partial operational and financial productivity you computed, what conclusions can you make about the firm's productivity in 2005 relative to 2006?
5. Separate the changes in the partial financial productivity ratio from 2005 to 2006 into productivity changes, input price changes, and output changes.
6. Discuss additional insight on the relative productivity between 2005 and 2006 from the detailed information provided by separating the change in the financial partial productivity ratios.

15–45 **Partial Operational and Financial Productivity** Varceles Design has decided to experiment with two alternative manufacturing approaches, identified as MF and LI, for producing men's fashions. The firm expects the total demand to be 20,000 suits. The manufacturing factors required to produce these outputs differ. The management estimates the required input resources using different manufacturing approaches are:

	Materials (yds.)	Labor (hrs.)
MF	300,000	100,000
LI	200,000	120,000

The cost of materials is $8 per yard; the cost of labor is $25 per hour.

Required

1. Compute the partial operational productivity ratios for each of the production approaches. Which approach would you select based on the partial operational productivity ratios?
2. Calculate the partial financial productivity ratios for each of the production approaches. Which approach would you select based on the partial financial productivity ratios?
3. Compute the total productivity ratios for each of the production approaches. Which approach would you select based on the total productivity ratios?

15–46 **Direct Labor Rate and Efficiency Variances, Productivity Measures, and Standard Costs** Textron Manufacturing Inc. assembles industrial testing instruments in two departments, assembly and testing. Operating data for 2005 and 2006 follow:

	2005	2006
Assembly department		
Actual direct labor-hours per instrument	25	20
Actual wage rate per hour	$30	$36
Standard direct labor-hours per instrument	24	21
Standard wage rate per hour	$28	$35

Testing department

Actual direct labor-hours per instrument	12	10
Actual wage rate per hour	$20	$24
Standard direct labor-hours per instrument	14	11
Standard wage rate per hour	$21	$25

The firm assembled and tested 20,000 instruments in both 2005 and 2006.

Required

1. Calculate the direct labor rate and the efficiency variances for both departments in both years.
2. Compute the direct labor partial operational productivity ratio for both departments in both years.
3. Determine the partial financial productivity for both departments in both years.
4. Compare your answers for requirements 2 and 3. Comment on the results.
5. Do productivity measures offer different perspectives for the firm's strategic decisions from those of variance analysis?

15–47 **Productivity and Ethics**   Janice Interiors installs custom interiors for luxury mobile homes. In its most recent negotiation with the union, the firm proposed to share productivity gains in direct labor equally with the union. In return, the union agreed not to demand wage increases. Most union members, however, are skeptical about management's honesty in calculating productivity measures. Nevertheless, union members voted to try the program. Kim Tomas, the management accountant responsible for determining productivity measures, collected these data at the end of 2006:

	2006	2005
Number of installations	560	500
Direct labor-hours	112,000	99,000

Steve Janice, the CEO, is very anxious to demonstrate the firm's good intentions by showing the labor union a positive result. He suggests to Kim that some of the direct labor-hours are actually indirect. For example, the hours spent on details are indirect because these hours cannot be allocated to specific types of work. Following his suggestion, Kim reclassifies 12,000 hours as indirect labor.

Required

1. Evaluate whether Steve's suggestion to reclassify some of the direct labor-hours as indirect labor is ethical.
2. Would it be ethical for Kim to modify his calculations?

15–48 **Market Size, Market Share, Working Backward**   Triple Delight is a food stand located on a busy corner in the local business district. On average it sells three cheeseburgers and one fishwich for every four hamburgers sold. The following data were culled from its operation for 2006:

Total operating income variance	
Hamburger	$18,000 Unfavorable
Cheeseburger	50,000 Favorable
Fishwich	10,000 Unfavorable
Sales quantity variance	
Hamburger	14,000 Favorable
Cheeseburger	15,000 Favorable
Fishwich	?
Sales mix variance	
Hamburger	2,240 Unfavorable
Cheeseburger	4,800 Unfavorable
Fishwich	1,600 Favorable

Fixed costs variances		0
Market share variance		$96,000 Unfavorable
Market size variance		126,000 Favorable
Change in market share		4%
Fixed cost flexible budget variance		0

The estimated total volume for the food stands in the region was 2,500,000 units. Consistent good weather pushed the total volume for the year to 4,000,000.

Required   Determine the following:

1. Budget weighted-average contribution margin.
2. Budget and actual market shares.
3. Budget and actual total units of sales.
4. Sales quantity variances for fishwich.
5. Budget contribution margin of each product.
6. Actual sales mix of each product.
7. Budget and actual units for each product.

15–49 **Flexible Budget, Sales Volume, Sales Mix, and Sales Quantity Variances**   Melinda Company has two products, A and B. Melinda's budget for August 2006 follows:

	Product A	Product B	Total
Master budget			
Sales	$200,000	$300,000	$500,000
Variable costs	120,000	150,000	270,000
Contribution margin	$80,000	$150,000	$230,000
Fixed costs	100,000	90,000	190,000
Operating income	$ (20,000)	$ 60,000	$ 40,000
Selling price per unit	$ 100	$ 50	

On September 1, these operating results for August were reported:

	Product A	Product B	Total
Operating results			
Sale	$180,000	$320,000	$500,000
Variable costs	120,000	140,000	260,000
Contribution margin	$ 60,000	$180,000	$240,000
Fixed costs	100,000	90,000	190,000
Operating income	$ (40,000)	$ 90,000	$ 50,000
Units sold	1,900	5,000	

Required

1. For each product determine the following variances in the contribution margins:

	Product A	Product B
Flexible budget variance	_____	_____
Sales volume variance	_____	_____
Sales quantity variance	_____	_____
Sales mix variance	_____	_____

2. Explain the flexible budget variance using selling price and variable cost variances.

15–50 **Flexible Budget, Sales Volume, Sales Mix, and Sales Quantity Variances**   Jerry Tidwell, CEO, and a major stockholder of Tidwell Company, was unhappy with its operating results in 2005. The company manufactures two environmentally friendly industrial cleaning machines used primarily in automobile repair shops, gas stations, and auto dealerships. The master budget and operating results of the year (000s omitted except for the selling price per unit) follow:

	Master Budget			Actual Result		
	SK-100	SK-50	Total	SK-100	SK-50	Total
Sales	$100,000	$50,000	$150,000	$90,000	$60,000	$150,000
Variable costs	50,000	20,000	70,000	50,000	22,000	72,000
Contribution margin	$ 50,000	$30,000	$ 80,000	$40,000	$38,000	$ 78,000
Fixed costs	20,000	20,000	40,000	30,000	20,000	50,000
Operating income	$ 30,000	$10,000	$ 40,000	$10,000	$18,000	$ 28,000
Unit selling price	$ 100	$ 50				
Units sold				900	1,200	

Required

1. Compute the operating income flexible budget variance, operating income sales volume variance, contribution margin sales quantity variance, and contribution margin sales mix variance for each product and for the firm.

2. Write a memo to Jerry Tidwell about the implications of the variances that you just computed on planning and operational control.

15–51 **Market Size, Market Share, and Sales Quantity Variances, Single Product**   Prolite Company manufactures one product. Its budget and operating results for 2005 follows:

	Budgeted	Actual
Units sold	90,000	100,000
Unit contribution margin	$ 8.00	$10.00
Unit selling price	$20.00	$21.00

Industry volume was estimated to be 1,500,000 units when the budget was prepared. Actual total volume of the industry for the period was 2,000,000 units.

Required

1. What is the market size variance?
2. What is the market share variance?
3. What is the sales quantity variance?

15–52 **Market Size, Market Share Variances**   Lau & Lau, Ltd., of Hong Kong manufacture two products for the same market. Its budget and operating results for the year just completed follow:

	Budget	Actual
Unit of sales		
Product A	30,000	35,000
Product B	60,000	65,000
Contribution margin per unit		
Product A	$ 4.00	$ 3.00
Product B	10.00	12.00
Selling price per unit		
Product A	$10.00	$12.00
Product B	25.00	24.00

At the time of budget preparation, the budgeting department and sales department agreed that the industry volume for the year would likely be 1,500,000 units. Actual industry volume turned out to be 2,000,000 units.

Required

1. What is the average budgeted contribution margin per unit?
2. What is the sales volume contribution margin variance for each product?

3. What is the sale mix contribution margin variance for each product?

4. What is the sales quantity contribution margin variance for each product?

5. What is the market size contribution margin variance?

6. What is the market share contribution margin variance?

7. What is the total flexible budget contribution margin variance?

8. What is the total variable cost price variance if the total contribution margin price variance is $50,000 favorable?

9. What is the total variable cost efficiency variance if the total contribution margin price variance is $50,000 favorable?

15–53 Sales Volume, Sales Quantity, and Sales Mix Variances   I Can't Believe It's Gelatin operates several stores in a major metropolitan city and its suburbs. Its budget and operating data for 2006 follow:

Flavor	Budgeted Data for 2006			Actual Operating Results in 2006		
	Gallons	Selling Price per Gallon	Variable Costs per Gallon	Gallons	Selling Price per Gallon	Variable Costs per Gallon
Vanilla	250,000	$1.20	$0.50	180,000	$1.00	$0.45
Chocolate	300,000	1.50	0.60	270,000	1.35	0.50
Strawberry	200,000	1.80	0.70	330,000	2.00	0.75
Anchovy	50,000	2.50	1.00	180,000	3.00	1.20

Required

1. Compute these variances for the individual flavors and total sold:

   a. Sales volume.

   b. Sales mix.

   c. Sales quantity.

2. Assess the operation of 2006 based on your analyses.

15–54 Market Size and Market Share Variances   Use the data in problem 15–53 for I Can't Believe It's Gelatin. The total market for ice cream, yogurt, and gelatin was expected to be 10 million gallons. The industry group for the area reported that 9,600,000 gallons were sold for the year.

Required   Compute the market size and market share variances for I Can't Believe It's Gelatin.

15–55 Sales Volume, Sales Quantity, and Sales Mix Variances; Working Backward   DOA Alive is a group of aspiring musicians and actors who perform in theaters and dinner clubs. It has a matinee and evening show. These operating data pertain to the month of July:

Master budget data	
Total operating income	$10,000
Total monthly fixed cost	$39,200
Total number of shows	100
Contribution margin per show: Matinee	$240
Evening	$600
Actual operating results	
Total sales quantity variance	$4,920 U
The actual matinees were 150 percent of the evening shows	

Required

1. Calculate for each type of show and the total

   a. Sales mix variances.

   b. Sales quantity variances.

   c. Sales volume variances.

2. What strategic conclusions can you draw from the variances?

15–56 **Market Size and Share Variances** Transpacific Airlines (TPA) budgeted 80 million passenger-miles, or 5 percent of the total market for the year just completed at a contribution margin of 40 cents per mile. The budgeted variable cost is 12 cents per mile.

The operating data for the year show that TPA flew 69.12 million passenger-miles with an average price of 48 cents per passenger-mile. The SARS epidemic in the early part of the year in several countries in the region decreased the total miles flown by all airlines for the year by 10 percent. There is no flexible budget variance for all costs.

Required Assess the effects of the price, sales volume, market size, and market share on the firm's operating results for the year.

15–57 **Market Size and Market Share Variances for Small Business** Diane's Designs is a small business run out of its owner's house. For the past six months, the company has been selling two products, a welcome-sign and a birdhouse. The owner has been concerning about the company's marketing effectiveness. The master budget and actual results for March of this year follow:

	Master Budget		
	Welcome Sign	**Birdhouse**	**Total**
Units	50	25	75
Sales	$1,000	$250	$1,250
Variable costs	890	120	1,010
Contribution margin	$ 110	$130	$ 240
Fixed costs	75	75	150
Operating income	$ 35	$ 55	$ 90

	Actual Results		
	Welcome Signs	**Birdhouses**	**Total**
Units	45	35	80
Sales	$675	$420	$1,095
Variable costs	580	270	850
Contribution margin	$ 95	$150	$ 245
Fixed costs	75	75	150
Operating income	$ 20	$ 75	$ 95

The total market for welcome signs for the last six months are 3,000 budgeted and 3,000 actual. Diane expected the total market for birdhouses to be 200 units per month; the actual volume for the entire market, however, turned out to be only 175 units per month.

Required

1. Compare Diane's Designs' market share for welcome signs and birdhouses.
2. What is the market share variance?
3. What is the market size variance?
4. Explain possible reasons for these variances.
5. How might Diane's Designs improve in the future?

(Contributed by Stacy Armstrong)

15–58 **Strategic Profitability Analysis** Yesley Company sells high-tech lightweight portable refrigerator. Yesley offers excellent customer service and charges a premium price. The firm has the following operating results for 2005 and 2006.

	2005	2006
Units sold	40,000	42,000
Average selling price per unit	$600	$630
Average cost per unit	$360	$400
Units purchased	42,000	43,260
Total market size	100,000	120,000
Average selling and customer service cost per unit	$50	$45
Budget selling and customer service capacity	42,000 units	45,000 units
Total purchasing and administrative capacity	60,000 units	60,000 units
Average purchasing and administrative cost per unit	$10	$12

$20 of the selling and customer service cost per unit is fixed and is a function of the budget capacity. The remainder is variable cost incurred for each unit sold. The purchasing and administrative costs are fixed cost and do not vary with the actual number of units sold during the year. The firm follows a strict JIT operation and maintains no inventory. Discrepancies between units sold and units purchased are results of damages, lost, or otherwise unaccounted for.

Required

1. Calculate the change in operating income from 2005 to 2006.
2. Calculate the effects of the growth, price-recovery, and productivity factors on the difference in operating income between 2005 and 2006.
3. Determine the effect of market size and market share on the growth effect of change in operating income.
4. Based on your analyses above would you say that the firm followed its strategy of product differentiation successfully?

15–59 **Strategic Profitability Analysis—Working Backward**   Chesterfield Inc., a chain of 20 stores, specializes in one-of-a-kind fashions for 16- to 18-year-olds. The firm has operating income of $6,900,000 in 2005 and $9,000,000 in 2006. There has been no change in either the total number of stores or the total fixed expenses. The total units sold increased from 3 million in 2005 to 3.36 million in 2006 and the growth added $600,000 to operating income. Had the growth in Chesterfield's sales kept up with market growth, the operating income would have increased by $1,500,000. Improved productivity added $700,000 to operating income. However, the cost effect of price recovery is $800,000 unfavorable.

Required

1. Determine the revenue effect of price recovery and the net effect of price recovery factor on 2006 operating income.
2. Was Chesterfield's increase in 2006 operating income consistent with its differentiation competitive strategy?

Solutions to Self-Study Problems

1. Productivity Variances

1. Operational partial productivity

	2005				2006			
	Output		Input Resource Used	Partial Productivity	Output		Input Resource Used	Partial Productivity
TPX–45	60,000	÷	75,000 =	0.8	64,000	÷	89,600 =	0.7143
Direct labor	60,000	÷	10,000 =	6.0	64,000	÷	10,847 =	5.9002

2. Financial partial productivity

	2005			2006		
	Units of Output	Cost of Input Resource Used	Partial Productivity	Units of Output	Cost of Input Resource Used	Partial Productivity
TPX–45	60,000 ÷	$540,000 =	0.1111	64,000 ÷	$609,280 =	0.1050
Direct labor	60,000 ÷	$300,000 =	0.2000	64,000 ÷	$347,104 =	0.1844

3. Separation of financial partial productivity

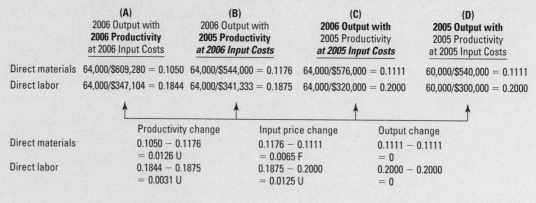

	(A) 2006 Output with **2006 Productivity** at 2006 Input Costs	**(B)** 2006 Output with **2005 Productivity** *at 2006 Input Costs*	**(C)** **2006 Output with** 2005 Productivity *at 2005 Input Costs*	**(D)** **2005 Output with** 2005 Productivity at 2005 Input Costs
Direct materials	64,000/$609,280 = 0.1050	64,000/$544,000 = 0.1176	64,000/$576,000 = 0.1111	60,000/$540,000 = 0.1111
Direct labor	64,000/$347,104 = 0.1844	64,000/$341,333 = 0.1875	64,000/$320,000 = 0.2000	60,000/$300,000 = 0.2000

	Productivity change	Input price change	Output change
Direct materials	0.1050 − 0.1176 = 0.0126 U	0.1176 − 0.1111 = 0.0065 F	0.1111 − 0.1111 = 0
Direct labor	0.1844 − 0.1875 = 0.0031 U	0.1875 − 0.2000 = 0.0125 U	0.2000 − 0.2000 = 0

Summary of result

				Change as Percent of 2005 Productivity*		
	Productivity Change	Input Price Change	Total Change	Productivity Change	Input Price Change	Total Change
Direct materials						
TPX–45	0.0126 U	0.0065 F	0.0061 U	11.34% U	5.85% F	5.49% U
Direct labor	0.0031 U	0.0125 U	0.0156 U	1.55% U	6.25% U	7.8% U

*2005 productivity: Direct materials − TPX–45   60,000 units ÷ (75,000 pounds × $7.20 per pound) = 0.111111
                     Direct labor   60,000 units ÷ (10,000 hours × $30 per hour) =   0.2

Change as percent of 2005 productivity:

	Productivity Change	Input Price Change	Total Change
DM − TPX–45	0.0126 ÷ 0.111111 = 11.34%	0.0065 ÷ 0.111111 = 5.85%	0.0061 ÷ 0.111111 = 5.49%
Direct labor	0.0031 ÷ 0.2 = 1.55%	0.0125 ÷ 0.2 = 6.25%	0.0156 ÷ 0.2 = 7.8%

4. Total productivity

Total productivity in units	2005	2006
(a) Total units manufactured	60,000	64,000
(b) Total variable manufacturing costs incurred	$840,000	$956,384
(c) Total productivity (a) / (b)	0.071429	0.066919
(d) Decrease in productivity	0.071429 − 0.0669191 = 0.00451	

Total productivity in sales dollars	2005	2006
(a) Total sales	$1,500,000	$1,600,000
(b) Total variable manufacturing costs incurred	$840,000	$956,384
(c) Total productivity (a) / (b)	$1.7857	$1.6730
(d) Decrease in productivity	$1.7857 − $1.6730 = 0.1127	

2. Sales Variances

1. Selling price variances (in 000)

Flexible budget sales:

	Master Budget for 2006 Total Sales	Units		Budgeted Selling Price per Unit		Total Units Sold in 2006		Flexible Budget Sales
Premium	$36,000	÷ 240	=	$150	×	180	=	$27,000
Regular	43,200	÷ 360	=	120	×	540	=	64,800

Selling price variances:

	Premium			Regular		
	Actual	Flexible Budget	Selling Price Variance	Actual	Flexible Budget	Selling Price Variance
Barrels	180	180		540	540	
Sales	$28,800	$27,000	$1,800 F	$62,100	$64,800	$2,700 U

Total selling price variance of the firm = $1,800 F + $2,700 U = $900 U

2. Sales volume variances for the period for each product and for the firm.

Flexible budget variable expenses:

	Master Budget for 2006 Total Variable Expenses	Number of Units		Budgeted Variable Expenses per Unit		Total Units Sold in 2006		Flexible Budget Variable Expenses
Premium	$ 21,600	÷ 240	=	$90	×	180	=	$16,200
Regular	27,000	÷ 360	=	75	×	540	=	40,500

Sales volume variances:

	Premium			Regular		
	Flexible Budget	Master Budget	Sales Volume Variance	Flexible Budget	Master Budget	Sales Volume Variance
Barrels	180	240	60 U	540	360	180 F
Sales	$27,000	$36,000	$9,000 U	$64,800	$43,200	$21,600 F
Variable expenses	16,200	21,600	5,400 F	40,500	27,000	13,500 U
Contribution margin	$10,800	$14,400	$3,600 U	$24,300	$16,200	$ 8,100 F
Fixed expenses	10,000	10,000	—	5,000	5,000	—
Operating income	$ 800	$ 4,400	$3,600 U	$19,300	$11,200	$ 8,100 F

3. Sales quantity variances for the firm and for each product. (See the solution for 4.)
4. Sales mix variances for the period for each product and for the firm (000 omitted).

Sales mixes:

	Budgeted		Actual	
	Total Sales in Units	**Sales Mix**	**Total Sales in Units**	**Sales Mix**
Premium	240	0.40	180	0.25
Regular	360	0.60	540	0.75
Total	600	1.00	720	1.00

Budgeted contribution margin per unit =
    Budget selling price per unit (item 1 above) − Budgets, variable
                cost per unit (item 2 above)

Premium = $150 − $90 = $60
Regular = $120 − $75 = $45

Sales mix and sales quantity variances:

Flexible Budget		Master Budget
Total units of all products sold × **Actual sales mix** × Budgeted (standard) contribution margin per unit	*Total units of all products sold* × **Budgeted sales mix** × Budgeted (standard) contribution margin per unit	*Total budgeted units of all products to be sold* × Budgeted sales mix × Budgeted (standard) contribution margin per unit

Premium

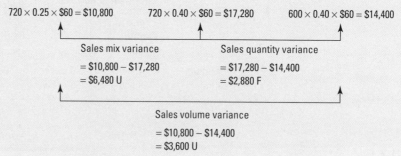

$720 \times 0.25 \times \$60 = \$10,800$ $720 \times 0.40 \times \$60 = \$17,280$ $600 \times 0.40 \times \$60 = \$14,400$

Sales mix variance
= $10,800 − $17,280
= $6,480 U

Sales quantity variance
= $17,280 − $14,400
= $2,880 F

Sales volume variance
= $10,800 − $14,400
= $3,600 U

To verify: Sales volume variance = Sales mix variance + Sales quantity variance
                = $6,480 U + $2,880 F
                = $3,600 U

Regular

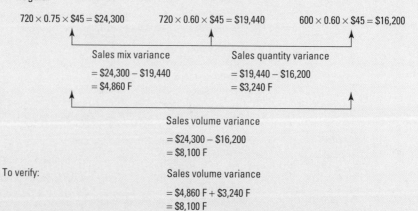

$720 \times 0.75 \times \$45 = \$24,300$ $720 \times 0.60 \times \$45 = \$19,440$ $600 \times 0.60 \times \$45 = \$16,200$

Sales mix variance
= $24,300 − $19,440
= $4,860 F

Sales quantity variance
= $19,440 − $16,200
= $3,240 F

Sales volume variance
= $24,300 − $16,200
= $8,100 F

To verify: Sales volume variance
                = $4,860 F + $3,240 F
                = $8,100 F

Total (both premium and regular)

$$\text{Sales mix variance} = \$6{,}480\ U + \$4{,}860\ F = \$1{,}620\ U$$

$$\text{Sales quantity variance} = \$2{,}880\ F + \$3{,}240\ F = \$6{,}120\ F$$

5. Verification

$$\text{Sales mix variance} + \text{Sales quantity variance} = \text{Sales volume variance}$$

Premium	$6,480 U	+	$2,880 F	=	$3,600 U
Regular	4,860 F	+	3,240 F	=	8,100 F
Total	$1,620 U	+	$6,120 F	=	$4,500 F

6. Market size variances. (See the solution for 7.)

7. Market share variances (000 omitted).

Weighted-Average Budgeted Contribution Margin Per Unit

Master budget total contribution margin	$30,600
Master budget total sales units	÷ 600
Total	$ 51

Market Shares:

Budgeted: Total sales in units 600 ÷ Total sales of the industry 1,500 = 0.40
Actual: Total sales in units 720 ÷ Total sales of the industry 1,600 = 0.45

Market Share and Size Variances:

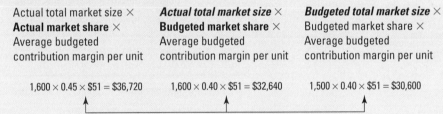

8. The sum of market size variance and market share variance follows. It verifies that this total equals the sales quantity variance.

Total market size variance + total market share variance = Total quantity variance
$2,040 F + $4,080 F = $6,120 F

CHAPTER SIXTEEN

Total Quality Management

After studying this chapter, you should be able to . . .

1. Define *quality* and *total quality management,* and devise guidelines for implementing total quality management

2. Distinguish between the two types of conformance and explain their effects on workers' behavior

3. Identify four major categories of quality costs

4. Prepare and interpret cost of quality reports

5. Describe methods commonly used to identify significant quality problems and their causes

6. Identify distinct characteristics of total quality management in service organizations

7. Explain the relationships between total quality management and productivity

8. Describe the role of management accountants in total quality management and the challenges they face

---

You can't turn quality on like a spigot. It's a culture, a lifestyle within a company.

A Ford Engineer

For decades, management experts in the United States, including W. Edwards Deming and J. M. Juran, urged manufacturers to "design in" quality at the beginning of the process, not to "inspect-in" quality at the end of the production line. The quality call to arms mainly fell on deaf ears in the United States, but not in Japan. More than 40 years ago, Juran predicted that a focus on quality would help turn Japan into an economic powerhouse.

Juran's prediction proved true.[1] In the late 1970s and the early 1980s, many U.S. firms had a rude awakening. Many U.S. executives realized, for the first time, that *Made in the U.S.A.* no longer stood for the best that was available. Once a term of mockery, *Made in Japan* became a term synonymous with quality. U.S. executives, especially those working for firms employing the traditional management techniques that had paid off so well a scant 20 years earlier, found themselves searching frantically for answers and desperately seeking to remain competitive.

U.S. auto manufacturers realized in the late 1970s that Japanese auto manufacturers were somehow able to sell automobiles that performed better, had far fewer defects, and cost less than those made in the United States and still earn high returns. Likewise, when Hewlett-Packard tested the quality of more than 300,000 new computer chips, it found those made by Japanese manufacturers had zero defects per thousand. Those made by U.S. manufacturers had 11 to 19 defects per thousand. After 1,000 hours of use, the failure rate of U.S. chips was 27 times higher than those of the Japanese chips.

---

[1] N. Gross, M. Stepanek, O. Port, and J. Carey, "Will Bugs Eat Up the U.S. Lead in Software?" *Business Week,* December 6, 1999.

Many industry and government leaders in the United States saw the handwriting on the wall: Get quality or lose the race.[2]

The world had changed. Global competition gave consumers abundant choices and they became more cost and value conscious, demanding high-quality products and services. Firms that failed to pay attention to quality often found eroding market shares and operating profits.

Many U.S. firms have made remarkable changes in the last two decades. Consumers have witnessed major efforts by U.S. manufacturers to improve quality. Many firms in the United States have engaged in relentless efforts to improve the quality of their products and services. Manufacturers in the United States and other countries have made tremendous progress in quality improvement in the last two decades, and continuous improvements have become a way of life for many firms and organizations. Facing massive discounting in the telecommunications sector and severe competitions, AT&T implemented "Concept of One," which means "do it once, do it right, and do it everywhere." In four years, AT&T saved about $2 billion in payroll alone.[3]

In 1987, Congress established the Malcolm Baldrige National Quality Award to enhance the competitiveness of U.S. businesses by promoting quality awareness, recognizing quality and performance achievements, and publicizing successful performance strategies of U.S. organizations in the areas of manufacturing, service, small business, and—added in 1999—education and health care. Seven broad categories make up the criteria: leadership, strategic planning, customer and market focus, information and analysis, human resource focus, process management, and business results. The fierce competition to win the award is evidence of the importance these firms place on being recognized for their quality operations. Simply applying for the award requires substantial investments in both time and money; the odds of winning are slim.[4] More than 800 organizations have applied and less than 5% had received the award.[5]

The Malcolm Baldrige National Quality Award program has helped applicants, award winners, and many other U.S. businesses and organizations to become more competitive. Studies by the National Institute of Standards and Technology, university researchers, and government and business organizations have found that incorporating the Baldrige quality performance concepts pays off in increased productivity, satisfied employees and customers, and improved profitability for both the companies and their investors. In each year since 1995, the hypothetical "Baldrige Stock Index," made up of publicly traded U.S. companies that have received the Malcolm Baldrige National Quality Award, has outperformed the Standard & Poor's 500 by almost three to one. In a recent study of 600 quality award-winning firms including the Baldrige, state, and other quality award programs and a control group, Singhal and Hendricks found that the award-winning companies significantly outperformed the control group in many aspects of their business, including the value of their common stock, operating income, sales, return on sales, and asset growth. Saccomano reported that companies with effective total quality management (TQM) programs had higher stock prices, sales, and income.[6] Agus and Hassan found that long-term TQM adopters had better financial performance than companies that had implemented TQM more recently.[7]

[2] James R. Evans and William M. Lindsay, *The Management and Control of Quality*, 3rd ed. (New York: West Publishing Co., 1996), p. 7.

[3] Stephanie N. Mehta, "How to Thrive When Prices Fall," *Fortune*, May 12, 2003, p. 132.

[4] Each applicant undergoes a rigorous examination process that takes 300 to 1,000 hours over six months after the applicant completes a detailed self-assessment. The examination process includes visits and reviews by an independent board of examiners primarily from business and quality experts in the private sector of achievements and improvements in every aspect of the organization's business, from strategic planning to human resources to customer satisfaction and performance and business results. Each applicant receives a detailed report on its strengths and opportunities for improvement.

[5] Some firms have won the award more than once. Winners include 3M, ADAC Laboratories, Ames Rubber Corporation, Armstrong, AT&T, BI, Cadillac, Corning, Custom Research, Dana, Eastman Chemical, Federal Express, Globe Metallurgical, Granite Rock Co., GTE, IBM, Marlow, Merrill Lynch, Milliken, Motorola, Solectron, STMicroelectronics, Sunny Fresh Foods, Texas Instruments, Ritz-Carlton, Trident, Wainwright, Wallace, Westinghouse, Xerox, and Zytec.

[6] Ann Saccomano, "TQM Works Over Time," *Traffic World*, 1998, p. 37.

[7] A. Agus and Z. Hassan, "Exploring the Relationship between the Length of Total Quality Management Adoption and Financial Performance: An Empirical Study in Malaysia," *International Journal of Management*, September 2000, pp. 323–33.

REAL-WORLD FOCUS   How Have U.S. Firms Done So Far?

In a survey of U.S. business, *The Economist* reports that U.S. firms have made tremendous progress in quality improvement. Many U.S. firms have introduced vigorous quality-raising initiatives and have discovered their own versions of the Japanese *kaizen*, or continuous quality improvement. Six Sigma programs that aim to reduce manufacturing defects to 3.4 per million have become part of quality lore. Many firms, including General Electric, Motorola, and Hewlett-Packard, have not only installed Six Sigma programs in their own factories and offices but also demanded that their suppliers implement similar programs. Some management consultants believe that for U.S. firms, quality is now old hat. They preach that it is time to take quality for granted and move on to the next new idea.

Source: "American Business Survey," *The Economist,* September 16, 1995, p. 5.

REAL-WORLD FOCUS   No Excuses at the Navy

When results are not as expected, many people blame bad luck. Some organizations, though, cannot afford to have bad luck. These organizations manage complex, high-risk technologies that must have everything occur as specified with no room for deviation. For them, a bit of bad luck threatens far more than a dip in the quarterly profits, and any role that luck might play must be removed completely.

Launching an airplane from an aircraft carrier requires flinging of the airplane into the air by one of the carrier's four steam-powered catapults. The airplane is held in place while its pilot applies full thrust, then the catapult is released, and the plane accelerates to 180 miles per hour in just over two seconds. Less than a minute later, the next catapult in line slingshots its own load off the deck, then the next, and the next, so that a group of 20 planes is airborne in less than 15 minutes. In readying each airplane for its launch, the catapult petty officer must calculate and set the steam pressure, taking into account the weight of the plane and the wind speed, while the crew must check for fuel leaks and other problems. A tiny bit of bad luck—a sudden wind shift, a last-minute mechanical breakdown, a miscommunication between pilot and catapult crew—could send an airplane—and perhaps its pilot, too—to the bottom of the ocean.

Launching a plane often takes place on a deck that is wet, slick with oil in places, and rocking back and forth to the rhythm of the waves. To further complicate matters, a number of other shipboard operations are being performed at the same time, including performing maintenance on the planes, fueling and arming them, moving them around a crowded deck, and parking them. Despite the many ways that things could go wrong, flight deck operations are generally smooth and accidents are quite rare.

Source: Robert Pool, "In the Zero Luck Zone," *Forbes ASAP,* November 27, 2000, pp. 85–91.

ISO 9000
is a set of guidelines for quality management and quality standards developed by the International Organization for Standardization in Geneva, Switzerland.

Worldwide, ISO 9000 has become a certification sought after by global companies to gain the stamp of approval on the quality of their products and services.

ISO 9000 is a set of guidelines for quality management and quality standards developed by the International Organization for Standardization in Geneva, Switzerland. More than 90 countries have adopted it. ISO 9000 certification has become a seal of quality since the revised standards became effective in 1987. Many firms and organizations require all their suppliers to be ISO 9000 certified.

To become ISO 9000 certified, a firm must prove that it is following ISO 9000 operating procedures; these include inspecting production processes, maintaining equipment, training workers, testing products, and dealing with customer complaints. An independent test company audits the firm's operations and makes recommendations concerning certification.

Recognizing the high cost of failing to meet quality standards and the benefit from being recognized as having high-quality products or services has also prompted firms to improve the quality of their products and services.

The cost of quality can be substantial; on average, it is 20 to 25 percent of sales for many U.S. firms.[8] One consultant estimates that 40 percent of the cost of doing business in the service sector can be attributed to poor quality.[9] On the other hand, firms

---

[8] Michael R. Ostrega, "Return on Investment through Cost of Quality," *Journal of Cost Management,* Summer 1991, pp. 37–77; Richard K. Youde, "Cost of Quality Reporting: How We See It," *Management Accounting,* January 1992, pp. 33–38.

[9] Ted Wolf, "Becoming a 'Total Quality' Controller," *The Small Business Controller,* Spring 1992, pp. 24–27.

with quality products or services gain sales and earn high profits. Attaining high quality and continuous improvement in the quality of products and services has become a way of life for most, if not all, organizations. Pursuing quality has become a global revolution affecting every facet of business. Quality reduces costs, increases customer satisfaction, and induces and maintains long-term success and profitability.

This chapter explains total quality management, defines quality and measurement of quality costs, illustrates the preparation of quality reports, examines approaches to detecting causes of deviations in quality, and explores decisions to investigate quality defects.

Quality And Strategic Cost Management

In the last two decades, the CEOs of many firms have come to realize that a strategy driven by quality improvements can lead to significant market advantages, improved profitability, and long-term prosperity. The line between planning for quality improvements and planning a business strategy has become increasingly blurred. Whether a firm competes through a strategy of cost leadership or product differentiation, quality issues permeate every aspect of its operations. A firm choosing to compete through low prices is not choosing to produce low-quality products. Its low-priced products must meet customers' expectations. Similarly, a differentiation strategy will not be successful if the firm fails to build quality into its products. The guiding principles underlying most quality-improvement programs are to satisfy customers' needs and to meet or exceed customers' expectations. Improved quality increases customer satisfaction. Increased customer satisfaction raises the firm's market share and revenues and enhances its competitive position. This is also the goal of a strategic plan to gain competitive advantage.

Quality is significant for other reasons, too. Quality costs can be substantial. In many organizations, few other factors have as much effect on costs and the bottom line. It is not surprising, therefore, that the current trend is to integrate planning for quality improvements with business strategic planning, recognizing that quality drives the success of the organization.

PIMS Associates, Inc., examined more than 1,200 companies to determine the impact of product quality on corporate performance and found that

- Product quality and profitability are closely related.
- Businesses that offer premium-quality products and services are more likely to have large market shares.
- Quality relates positively to a higher return on investment.[10]

Exhibit 16.1 shows that a firm with improved quality has several strategic competitive advantages and enjoys higher profitability and a higher return on investment. Firms can reap many benefits from improved quality. Improved quality decreases product returns. Lower returns decrease warranty costs and repair expenses. Improved quality lowers inventory levels for raw materials, components, and finished products because the firm has more reliable manufacturing processes and schedules. Improved product quality also lowers manufacturing costs as the firm reduces or eliminates rework and increases productivity. Customers are likely to perceive quality products as having higher values. Perceived high values allow the firm to command higher prices and enjoy a larger market share. Higher prices and greater market shares increase revenues and profits. Improved quality also decreases cycle time. Faster cycle times speed deliveries, and prompt delivery makes happy customers, creates new demand, and increases market shares. Higher revenues and lower costs boost net income and increase the firm's return on investment. Focus on quality also expands the firm's opportunity and decreases its competitive threats.

[10] Evans and Lindsay, *The Management and Control of Quality,* pp. 18–19.

EXHIBIT 16.1
Results of Improved Quality on Profitability and Return on Investment

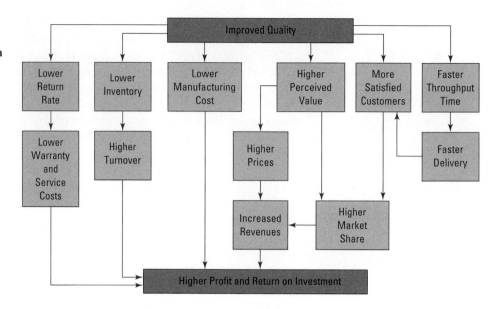

Cost, quality, and time are among the critical factors in successful strategies. Having quality products allows firms that compete on differentiation to be effective in sustaining their strategy. A firm with low costs and quality products provides its customers with products equal to or better in quality at lower prices. Only with quality products can the firm truly be a cost leader. Continuous improvements in the quality of products and services and in processes should be a fundamental strategic objective and a major item in the balanced scorecard of every firm and organization.

Total Quality Management

LEARNING OBJECTIVE 1
Define **quality** *and* **total quality management**, *and devise guidelines for implementing total quality management.*

To survive and be successful in today's global competitive environment, firms must manufacture quality products and provide quality services. A pollster of automotive products, J. D. Power observes that quality is becoming the price of entry for automotive marketers. Consumers everywhere have come to demand high-quality products. Firms must produce quality products and provide quality services to survive, maintain market shares, earn desired returns and sustain a competitive strategy. But what is quality?

The Meaning of Quality

There are many definitions of quality, and people often view it differently because of differences in their roles in the production-marketing-consumption chain and in their expectations for products or services. In simpler times, many CEOs perceived quality as a characteristic revealed by "I know it when I see it." Such an approach to quality provides no clear guideline for meeting it and makes quality management very difficult.

The ultimate test of a quality product or service is whether the product or service meets or exceeds customers' expectations. The requirements to meet or exceed customers' expectations then serve as specifications for operations throughout the organization. All individuals, departments, or subdivisions of an organization must strive for conformity to specifications that meet or surpass customer expectations.

Not all customers have the same expectations for a product or service. All 3/8-inch drill bits can drill 3/8-inch holes. Nevertheless, a firm can manufacture a 3/8-inch drill bit that costs $3 for home use and an industrial-strength drill bit that costs $15. The specifications and quality expectations for the less expensive drill bit are not the same as those for the more expensive one. The industrial strength drill bit is designed for heavy, continuous use and can be used for, say, 100 hours before it needs to be replaced. A drill bit for home use, on the other hand, is not designed for continuous use for long hours and has a shorter expected life of, say, 10 hours.

Each can be a quality product if it meets its respective specifications and customers' expectations. A product is a **quality** product if it conforms with the design or specification that meets or exceeds the expectations of customers at a competitive price they are willing to pay.

Expectations for services also differ. A tourist does not expect the same services from a Motel 6 as from a Ritz-Carlton Hotel, although both provide rooms for tourists. A mechanic performs quality service by changing a car's oil as specified: draining old oil, installing a new oil filter, lubricating the chassis, and adding clean new oil. The service is a quality service even if the mechanic used a regular oil, not a new synthesized oil that improves engine performance, if the customer asked for a regular, not a deluxe, oil change. The mechanic has failed to deliver a quality service, however, if the new oil filter falls off the next morning due to improper installation or if the refill is four or six quarts of oil instead of the five quarts specified by the manufacturer. Conformity to specifications determines the quality service of the job.

Characteristics of Total Quality Management

Total quality management (TQM) is the unyielding and continuous effort by everyone in the firm to understand, meet, and exceed the expectations of customers.[11] Although each organization is most likely to develop its own approach to total quality management to suit its particular culture and management style, certain characteristics are common to most TQM systems. These characteristics are as follows:

- Focusing on satisfying the customer.
- Striving for continuous improvement.
- Fully involving the entire work force.
- Actively supporting and involving top management.
- Using unambiguous and objective measures.
- Recognizing quality achievements in a timely manner.
- Continuously providing training on total quality management.

Exhibit 16.2 describes the critical factors for successful total quality management.

Focus on the Customer

TQM begins by identifying the firm's customers; determining their needs, requirements, and expectations; and then doing whatever it takes to satisfy them. Customers include both external and internal. External customers are the ultimate recipients of the firm's products or services. Internal customers are individuals or subunits within the firm involved in manufacturing the product or providing the services. At some stage, everyone in a process or organization is a customer or supplier to someone else, either inside or outside the organization.

Upon identifying the requirements and expectations of external customers, these requirements and expectations become the bases for specifications for internal customer/suppliers and external suppliers to the firm.

The identified expectations and requirements of external customers are translated into specifications for each successive internal customer/ supplier, including design requirements, part characteristics, and manufacturing operations, and requirements for external vendors. A firm can serve its ultimate, external customer better if the firm fully meets all requirements of each internal customer.[12]

A quality product or service conforms with the design or specification and meets or exceeds customers' expectations at a competitive price they are willing to pay.

Total quality management (TQM) is the unyielding and continuous effort by everyone in the firm to understand, meet, and exceed the expectations of customers.

[11] Ibid., p. 17.
[12] Ibid., p. 5.

EXHIBIT 16.2
Critical Total Quality Management Factors

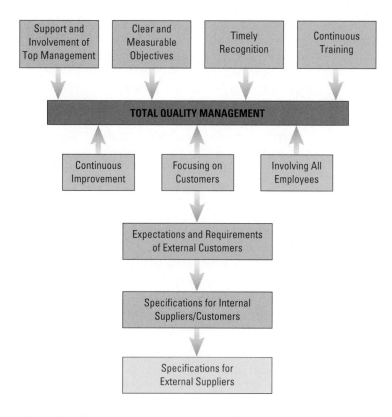

Strive for Continuous Improvement (Kaizen)

The Coca-Cola Company believes that quality is not a destination; it is a way of life. Coca-Cola Company states: "We know we will never arrive; there is no finish." Quality is a moving target. Without continuous improvement, quality disappears.

Taguchi and Wu believe that continuous quality improvement and cost reduction (kaizen) are necessary to remain competitive in today's global marketplace.[13] "With competitors forever trying to outperform us and customers exhibiting ever-changing expectations, a firm can never reach the ideal quality standard." The processes described in Exhibit 16.2 never end; firms need to continuously update specifications for both internal customers/suppliers and external suppliers to better serve external customers.

Full Involvement of the Entire Workforce

A firm can meet the requirements of its external customers only if each of the internal customers/suppliers in the process satisfies the requirements of the downstream process or customer. A breakdown in the process, no matter how insignificant, leads to a defective product or service and unsatisfied customers. Top management must encourage everyone in the firm, from the lowest level employees, office clerks, factory workers, accountants, and engineers to upper echelon professionals and managers, to be actively involved and participate in the firm's efforts to continuously improve quality. Employee involvement can range from simple information sharing, dialogue, or group problem solving, all the way to total self-direction. One proven effective approach for employee involvement is **quality (control) circles** or **quality circles** (QCs for short). A quality circle is a small group of employees from the same work area that meets regularly to identify and solve work-related problems and to implement and monitor solutions to the problems.

Quality circle
is a small group of employees from the same work area that meet regularly to identify and solve work-related problems and to implement and monitor solutions to the problems.

Active Support and Involvement of Top Management

Management personnel from the CEO to subdivision managers must participate actively in quality improvements for the program to be successful. They need to demonstrate their dedication to total quality to employees at every level, all vendors

---

[13] G. Taguchi and Y. Wu, *Introduction to Off-Line Quality Control* (Nagoya, Japan: Central Japan Quality Control Association, 1980).

and suppliers to the firm, all customers, and the community at every opportunity so that everyone is aware of the primary importance of total quality in every aspect of the firm's operations.

Unambiguous and Measurable Objectives

Clear objectives make progress visible. Measurable objectives forge efforts toward the common goal. To ensure success of total quality management, a firm must set unambiguous and measurable objectives. Effective measurement can help to ensure and facilitate quality improvements and supporting systems.

Timely Recognition of Quality Achievement

Timely recognition of the quality achievements of people and subunits is the best way to emphasize the firm's continuous striving for better quality and to ensure efforts toward total quality at every level.

Continuing Education

The race to total quality is never over. Mandatory continuing education and training of employees at all levels is necessary to achieve the culture change and continuous focus required in a total quality management environment.

TQM Implementation Guidelines

A firm cannot implement a successful TQM program overnight. Superficial copying techniques of successful TQM firms such as quality circles, teamwork, kaizen, does not make a TQM firm. It took Japanese companies more than 20 years to approach and surpass the quality level of many U.S. firms. It will take any organization serious about achieving TQM several years of concerted and dedicated efforts by all its members to become a world-class quality firm.

The implementation of TQM is not an easy task and is time consuming. The Institute of Management Accountants (IMA) believes that a typical organization takes three to five years to move from traditional management to TQM. Most likely, the firm will not see many tangible benefits in the early years of implementation, although some specific projects along the way can quickly yield high returns.

Drawing from the experiences of winners of the Malcolm Baldrige Award for effectively managing quality, IMA has devised an 11-phase process spanning three years to establish TQM.[14] Throughout the process, the full and genuine involvement of all employees is essential to a successful TQM implementation.

Year One—Preparation And Planning

• Create quality council and staff.
• Conduct executive-quality training programs.

[14] "Managing Quality Improvements," *Statement on Management Accounting No. 4-R* (Montvale, NJ: Institute of Management Accountants, 1993), pp. 10–11.

- Conduct quality audits.
- Prepare gap analysis.
- Develop strategy on quality improvements.

Year Two—Training And Implementation

- Conduct employee communication and training programs.
- Establish quality teams.
- Create a measurement system and set goals.

Year Three—Assessment, Review, And Revise

- Revise compensation/appraisal/recognition systems.
- Launch external initiatives with suppliers.
- Review and revise.

Create Quality Council and Staff

Most companies have found that successful implementation of TQM requires unwavering and active leadership from the CEO and senior managers. TQM is an undertaking that needs cooperation and the best efforts of all units of the organization. Without management support, a quality improvement program is likely to fail. As Shilliff and Motiska point out, "Every member of the [quality] team is important, but the most important member is the chief executive officer or top management. Without top management's wholehearted support, guidance, and direction, the quality program is doomed to mediocrity or eventual failure."[15]

However, the CEO or top management alone cannot bring forth all the desired benefits from TQM. Only with support from all managers in the top echelon can TQM attain the most desirable results. The necessary leadership often takes the form of an executive-level quality council. The quality council should include the top management team with the CEO chairing the council. The council's primary function is to develop quality mission and vision statements, companywide goals, and a long-term strategy.

Conduct Executive Quality Training Programs

To ensure senior management's unwavering and continuous support of TQM, the firm needs to conduct executive-quality training programs. The primary function of the program is to (1) raise senior management's awareness of the need for a systematic focus on and continuous support of quality improvement, (2) create a common knowledge base on total quality, and (3) establish reasonable expectations and goals. Conducting executive-quality training programs also helps avoid misunderstandings and miscommunication as the change effort progresses.[16]

Conduct Quality Audits

A quality audit assesses the firm's quality practices and analyzes the quality performance of the best practices, including those of other companies. Conducting a quality audit enables the firm to identify the company's strengths and weaknesses, develops a long-term strategic quality improvement plan, and identifies quality improvement opportunities that will yield the greatest return to the company in both the short and long term.

Gap analysis
is a benchmarking approach that determines the gap between the best in class and the firm's current practices.

Prepare Gap Analysis

A **gap analysis** is a benchmarking approach that determines the gap between the best in class and the firm's current practices. Following a quality audit that identifies the strengths and weaknesses of the firm's quality programs, a gap analysis identifies

[15] Karl A. Shilliff and Paul J. Motiska, *The Team Approach to Quality* (Milwaukee, WI: ASQC Quality Press, 1992), p. xi.
[16] Ibid., p. 11.

Total quality management (TQM) is a key strategic and operational issue for most firms, as their customers continue to have higher expectations for product and service quality. Because it involves most if not all the activities in the firm, the implementation of TQM is usually a complex and difficult process. The full implementation of TQM may take several years. The IMA has identified implementation guidelines that can assist managers in the process. Some firms such as General Electric (http://ge.com), Honeywell (http://honeywell.com/), and Weyerhaeuser (http://weyerhaeuser.com/) take additional steps to ensure the success of their quality initiatives. What do you think these additional steps might include?

target areas for quality improvements and provides a common objective database for the firm to develop its strategy on quality improvements.

Develop Strategy on Quality Improvement

The gap analysis results and the goal for quality improvement serve as bases for developing both short-term (one-year) and long-term (three-to-five-years) strategic plans for setting priorities in quality improvements. The initial plan should be limited and specific and have the potential of yielding high, measurable quality benefits.

Conduct Employee Communication and Training Programs

Employee training programs serve as a communication tool to convey management's commitment to total quality and provide employees with the necessary skills to achieve total quality; they play critical roles in successful quality improvement programs. To launch a $200 million quality improvement program to slash defects to no more than four per million, GE began by training 200 "master black belts" who became full-time quality teachers.[17]

Establish Quality Teams

A cross-functional quality team includes members from a variety of employee and management teams and functional units. The cross-functional quality team oversees the continuous improvement efforts and quality task forces throughout the organization and coordinates work to optimize the quality efforts, ensure adequate resources, and resolve issues.

Team members from throughout the organization should include individuals who can identify specific quality requirements and quality costs. Typical team members are product managers, engineers, production workers, customer service representatives, and management accountants.

Once established, quality teams become the main forces behind quality incentives, implementation and monitoring of quality programs, and continuous improvement. One major function of a quality team is to involve all employees in quality programs.

Create a Measurement System and Set Goals

A crucial factor for TQM success is having measures that truly reflect the needs and expectations of customers, both internal and external. A good measurement system that helps TQM often entails developing a new accounting system, because the current accounting system in use divides and spreads important quality data among myriad accounts. A good measurement system for TQM should also enable all employees to know at all times the progress being made toward total quality and the additional improvements needed.

Being an integral part of the firm's financial performance evaluation system, a traditional accounting system can impede quality improvement. All employees of the organization must understand that the measurements generated by a TQM system are tools for improvement, not punishment. A separate measurement system also facilitates TQM by reducing the concerns that the effect of expenditures for quality improvement will have on short-term operating results.

Revise Compensation/Appraisal/Recognition Systems

Reward and recognition are the best means to reinforce the emphasis on TQM. Moreover, a proper reward and recognition structure based on quality measures can be a powerful stimulus to promote TQM in a company. Efforts and progress will most likely be short lived if the firm makes no change to its compensation/appraisal/recognition system.

Launch External Initiatives with Suppliers

A supplier is as much a part of the company's operations as one of its divisions. Suppliers that fail to deliver quality materials and components doom the firm's effort to improve product quality before it starts. TQM includes the entire business system from suppliers of raw materials to services to the final customer. The following are among the practices successful TQM firms use to ensure having quality suppliers:

- Reducing the supplier base. A reduced supplier base reduces variations in quality, increases supplier commitment, and improves efficient use of resources.
- Selecting suppliers based not only on price and capability and willingness to improve quality, cost, delivery, and flexibility but also on dedication to continuous improvement.
- Forming long-term relationships with suppliers as working partners.
- Specifying precise supplier expectations and ensuring suppliers' consistent delivery.[18]

Review and Revise

All employees, led by the quality council and quality team need to conduct periodic reviews of quality progress and reassess quality improvement efforts. These reviews should be held monthly or, at a minimum, annually. All members of the firm, especially members of the review team, need to remember that, as many firms do, there is no finish line in quality improvement.

Types of Conformance

LEARNING OBJECTIVE 2
Distinguish between the two types of conformance and explain their effects on workers' behavior.

Quality involves conformance with specifications for products or services that meet or exceed customer requirements and expectations. Conformance, however, can differ among individuals or firms, as it did at Sony, as we describe in the next section.

Goalpost Conformance

Goalpost conformance (zero-defects conformance)
is conformance to a quality specification expressed as a specified range around the target.

Goalpost conformance is conformance to a quality specification expressed as a specified range around the target. The target is the ideal or desirable outcome of the operation.

For example, the target for a production process to manufacture 0.5-inch sheet metal is 0.5-inch thickness for all sheet metal manufactured. Recognizing that meeting the target every time in manufacturing is difficult, a firm often specifies a tolerance range. A firm that specifies a tolerance of ± 0.05 inch meets the quality standard when the thickness of its products is between 0.55 inch and 0.45 inch.

A goalpost conformance is a **zero-defects conformance.** With the specified range allowed for variations, management expects all outputs to be within the specified range of variations and achieves zero-defect conformance. Exhibit 16.3 depicts the goalpost conformance specifications for the sheet metal.

[18] Ibid., p. 17.

EXHIBIT 16.3
Goalpost Conformance

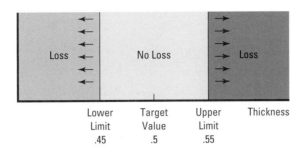

EXHIBIT 16.4
Absolute Conformance
(Robust Quality Approach)
and Taguchi Quality Loss
Function

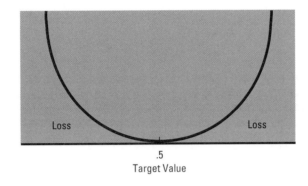

Absolute Quality Conformance

Absolute quality conformance
(robust quality approach)

requires all products or services to
meet the target value exactly with
no variation.

Absolute quality conformance or the **robust quality approach** requires all products or services to meet the target value *exactly* with no variation. An absolute conformance requires all sheet metal to have a thickness of 0.5 inch, not 0.5 inch ±0.05 inch or even 0.5 inch ±0.0005 inch. Exhibit 16.4 depicts the robust quality conformance approach.

Variations from the target value are less than ideal and have negative economic consequences. Robustness in quality comes with meeting the exact target consistently. Any deviation from the target is a quality failure and weakens the overall quality of the product or service. Whenever a product deviates from its target value it costs the firm.

Goalpost or Absolute Conformance?

Goalpost conformance assumes that a firm incurs no quality or failure cost or loss if all quality measures fall within the specified limits and the firm suffers quality costs or losses only when the measure is outside the limits. No such quality tolerance exists in absolute conformance, which views quality costs or losses as a continuously increasing function starting from the target value. Quality costs, hidden or out of pocket, occur whenever the quality measure deviates from its target value.

Which of these two approaches, goalpost or absolute conformance, is better? Perhaps we can find an answer in the experience Sony had in two of its plants that manufacture color televisions.[19]

The two Sony plants manufacture the same television sets and follow the same specification for color density. The two plants, however, adopt different types of quality conformance. The San Diego plant uses goalpost conformance, and the Tokyo plant adopts absolute conformance. On examining the operating data over the same period, Sony found that all the units produced at the San Diego plant fell within the specifications (zero defect), but some of those manufactured at the Japanese plant did not. The quality of the Japanese units, however, was more uniform around the target value, while the quality of the San Diego units was uniformly distributed between the lower and upper limits of the specification, the goalpost, as depicted in Exhibit 16.5.

[19] Evans and Lindsay, *The Management and Control of Quality*, p. 244.

EXHIBIT 16.5
Color Density of Sony TV Sets Manufactured in the San Diego Plant and a Japanese Plant

Source: James R. Evans and William M. Lindsay, *The Management and Control of Quality,* 3rd ed. (New York: West Publishing Co., 1996), p. 245.

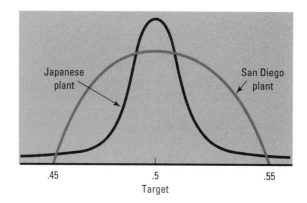

The average quality cost (loss) per unit of the San Diego plant, however, was \$0.89 higher than that of the Japanese plant. One reason for the higher quality cost for units produced at the San Diego plant was the need for more frequent field service. Customers are more likely to complain when the density is farther away from the target value. Although the plant in Tokyo had a higher rejection rate, it experienced lower warranty and repair costs for its products. For firms desiring to attain long-term profitability and customer satisfaction, absolute conformance is the better approach.

Taguchi Quality Loss Function

Genichi Taguchi and Y. Wu proposed the absolute quality conformance approach as an *off-line* quality control.[20] This approach pays more attention to upstream activities such as product design and planning of manufacturing or operation processes. Taguchi believes that these dimensions need to be perfected before embarking on manufacturing.

Taguchi and Wu recognize that any variation from the exact specifications entails a cost or loss to the firm. The cost or loss can be depicted by a quadratic function similar to the one shown in Exhibit 16.4.

Taguchi quality loss function
depicts the relationship between the total loss to a firm due to quality defects.

The **Taguchi quality loss function** depicts the relationship between the total loss to a firm due to quality defects. The loss grows larger as the variation increases (a quadratic function): the total loss increases as the magnitude of a quality characteristic of the product or service moves farther away from the target value. In a quadratic function the loss quadruples when the deviation from the target value doubles. For instance, if the loss is \$4 when the deviation is 0.1 from the target value the loss will be \$16 when the deviation doubles, or is 0.2 from the target value. The exact nature of the loss function for different quality characteristics can differ.

The total cost of deviations from the quality standard include direct costs in manufacturing and service, and hidden quality costs. Direct costs are costs such as rework, warranty repair or replacement, additional production costs, and loss on disposal. The hidden quality losses include customer dissatisfaction, loss of future business, loss of market share, additional engineering costs, additional management costs, and additional inventory.

Quality Loss Function

Taguchi and Wu show that a quadratic function provides a good approximation of quality losses. Losses increase at twice the rate of deviations from the target value; larger deviations from target cause increasingly larger losses. For a quality characteristic with the target value *T*, the loss from having a quality characteristic *x* can be estimated by this quadratic function:

$$L(x) = k(x - T)^2$$

---

[20] Taguchi and Wu, *Introduction to Off-Line Quality Control.* See also Evans and Lindsay, *The Management and Control of Quality,* pp. 243–48; and Thomas L. Albright and Harold P. Roth, "The Measurement of Quality Costs: An Alternative Paradigm," *Accounting Horizon,* June 1992, pp. 15–27.

where:

x = an observed value of the quality characteristic

T = the target value of the quality characteristic

k = the cost coefficient, determined by the firm's costs of failure

k is a constant estimated for the quality characteristic based on the total production and service costs and hidden costs to the firm due to deviation of the quality characteristic from the target value. The value of k for a quality characteristic can be determined using this relationship:

$$k = \frac{\text{Total quality cost}}{(\text{Tolerance allowed})^2}$$

Say, for example, that a firm has determined that no customer will accept sheet metal deviating more than 0.05 inch from the target value in thickness, that the target thickness is 0.5 inch, and that the cost to the firm is $5,000 for each rejection by a customer. The $5,000 cost to the firm includes repair or replacement, processing, service costs, and other costs due to customer dissatisfaction. Then

$$k = \frac{\$5,000}{0.05^2}$$

$$k = \$2,000,000$$

If the actual thickness of a unit is 0.47, then the estimated total loss for the unit is

$$L(0.47) = \$2,000,000(0.47 - 0.5)^2 = \$1,800$$

If, however, the thickness is 0.46, then the estimated total loss from the deviation increases to $3,200.

$$L(0.46) = \$2,000,000(0.46 - 0.5)^2 = \$3,200$$

Total Loss and Average Loss

The loss just calculated is the loss from having one unit with the observed quality characteristic. The total loss for all the units manufactured during a period is the sum of the losses from all units with their observed values of the quality characteristic deviated from the target value of the quality characteristic.

Alternatively, the total loss due to variations in the quality characteristic can be determined by multiplying the average loss per unit by the total number of units manufactured. The average loss per unit is the expected loss due to variations in the quality characteristic. Exhibit 16.6 shows the calculations of the expected total losses in two

EXHIBIT 16.6
Total Quality Loss

(1)	(2)	(3)	(4) = (2) × (3)	(5)	(6) = (2) × (5)
		Plant A		Plant B	
x Measured Thickness	L(x) Quality Loss	Probability	Weighted Loss	Probability	Weighted Loss
0.43	$9,800	0	$ 0	0.02	$196
0.46	3,200	0.20	640	0.03	96
0.48	800	0.20	160	0.15	120
0.50	0	0.20	0	0.60	0
0.52	800	0.20	160	0.15	120
0.54	3,200	0.20	640	0.03	96
0.57	9,800	0	0	0.02	196
Expected loss			$1,600		$824

plants identified as A and B. These two plants have different probability distributions of deviations from the target value, as noted in columns (3) and (5).

The output from plant A spreads evenly over the range from 0.46 to 0.54, with no unit falling outside the tolerance limits. In contrast, the output from plant B concentrates near the specified target value, but not all units lie within the tolerance limits.

Albright and Roth show that the expected, or average, loss per unit can be determined using variance and the square of the mean deviation from the target value as follows:[21]

$$EL(x) = k(\sigma^2 + D^2)$$

where:

$EL(x)$ = expected or average loss from having quality characteristic x

σ^2 = variance of the quality characteristic about the target value[22]

D = the deviation of the mean value of the quality characteristic from the target, or $D = \bar{x} -$ Target value

The variance is 0.0008 for plant A[23] and 0.000412 for plant B. The value of D is 0 for both plants.[24] Thus,

Plant A: $EL(x)$ = $2,000,000(0.0008 + 0) = $1,600

Plant B: $EL(x)$ = $2,000,000(0.000412 + 0) = $824

Notice the similarity in the quality characteristic between plant A and those observed in the Sony plant at San Diego: all units are within the specified tolerance limits and spread somewhat evenly between the specified tolerance limits. The quality characteristic of plant B is similar to those observed in the Sony plant in Japan: not all units lie within the tolerance limit, but most units cluster around the target value. Some units, however, fall outside the tolerance limits. Plant B, like the Sony plant in Japan, incurs a smaller average cost per unit. Even though all units of plant A fall within the tolerance limits while some units of plant B are outside the limits, plant B has a lower expected loss than that of plant A.

Using Quality Loss Function for Tolerance Determination

Taguchi quality loss function can also be used to set tolerances for an operation. A firm can repair rejected units that exceed the tolerance level. Even though repairs cost money, repairs that correct defects save downstream quality costs such as field repairs, warranty costs, and loss of goodwill. By contrasting the cost of repair with the quality cost of not detecting and repairing defects, firms can determine acceptable tolerance levels. Rewriting the equation for estimating the value of k:

$$\text{Total quality cost} = k \times (\text{Tolerance})^2$$

Assume that in the sheet metal example, the cost to the firm is $300 if the firm repairs the product that failed before shipping. The firm repairs all units that exceed

---

[21] Albright and Roth, "The Measurement of Quality Costs," p. 23.

[22] Variance, σ^2, is computed as follows:

$\sigma^2 = \Sigma(x - \bar{x})^2 f(x)$

where, x = quality characteristic, e.g. measured thickness in Exhibit 16.6.

$\bar{x}$ = mean value of quality characteristics, $\bar{x} = \Sigma x f(x)$

$f(x)$ = probability for observing quality characteristics, x, each value of $f(x)$ lies between 0 and 1, and all value of $f(x)$ sum to 1.

[23] For plant A,

$\bar{x}$ = column (1) $\times$ column (3) = $\Sigma x f(x)$ = 0.46 $\times$ 0.20 + 0.48 $\times$ 0.20 + 0.50 $\times$ 0.20 + 0.52 $\times$ 0.20 + 0.54 $\times$ 0.20 = 0.50

and, σ^2 = (0.46 − 0.50)^2 $\times$ 0.20 + (0.48 − 0.50)^2 $\times$ 0.20 + (0.50 − 0.50)^2 $\times$ 0.20 + (0.52 − 0.50)^2 $\times$ 0.20 + (0.54 − 0.50)^2 $\times$ 0.20 = 0.0008

[24] The mean value of the quality characteristic, 0, is 0.50 for plant A as calculated in footnote 23. The target value of the quality characteristic is also 0.50. Therefore D = 0.50 − 0.50 = 0. Verify that the value of D is also zero for plant B by carrying out the same procedure.

the tolerance level for thickness. Then, the firm can determine the tolerance as follows:

$$\$300 = \$2,000,000(\text{tolerance})^2$$

Solve the equation,

$$\text{Tolerance} = 0.0122$$

Alternatively, the tolerance can be determined as shown below.

$$\text{Tolerance} = T_0\sqrt{C_1/C_2}$$

where,

T_0 = current (or customer) tolerance

C_2 = manufacturer's cost of quality when the product failed to meet customer's specification

C_1 = manufacturer's cost to rework or scrap the unit before shipping

In the example above, the firm expects the external failure cost, C_2, to be \$5,000; the cost to the firm to be \$300 if the firm repairs, reworks, or scraps the defective unit before shipping (C_1); and the customer's tolerance to be 0.05. The firm would then set the tolerance at,

$$\text{Tolerance} = \$0.05\sqrt{\$300/\$5,000} = 0.0122$$

Costs Of Quality

Costs of quality
are costs of activities associated with the prevention, identification, repair, and rectification of poor quality and opportunity costs from lost production time and sales as a result of poor quality.

Costs of quality are costs of activities associated with prevention, identification, repair, and rectification of poor quality and opportunity costs from lost production time and lost sales as a result of poor quality. In the past, many firms considered quality costs to include only costs of inspections and costs of testing finished units. Other costs of poor quality were included as overhead and not identified as quality costs.

Many firms have realized that in addition to manufacturing costs, quality costs include costs associated with supporting functions such as product design, purchasing, public relations, and customer services. Recognizing the importance of identifying all costs of quality, Joseph Juran classifies costs of quality into four categories—prevention, appraisal, internal failure, and external failure—based on the time when firms incur quality costs. Exhibit 16.7 illustrates the components of quality costs.

LEARNING OBJECTIVE 3
Identify four major categories of quality costs.

Prevention Costs

Prevention costs
are costs incurred to keep quality defects from occurring.

Prevention costs are expenditures incurred to keep quality defects from occurring. Prevention costs include the following:

- **Quality training costs.** Expenditures incurred to conduct internal training programs for employees to participate in external programs to ensure proper manufacturing,

EXHIBIT 16.7
Components of Quality Costs

Prevention Cost

Training
  Instructor fees
  Testing equipment
  Tuition for external training
  Wages and salaries for time spent on train-
    ing and education
Planning and execution of quality program
  Salaries
  Cost of preventive equipment
  Cost of meetings
Promotion of quality
  Awards and recognition expenditure
  Printing and distribution of quality program
    pamphlets and posters
  Product redesign
  Process improvement
  Quality circles

Internal Failure Cost

Scrap
Rework
Loss due to downgrades
Reinspection costs
Loss due to work interruptions

Appraisal Cost

Raw materials inspection
Work-in-process inspection
Finished goods inspection
Test equipment
  Acquisition
  Salaries and wages
  Maintenance

External Failure Cost

Sales returns and allowance due to quality
  deficiency
Warranty cost
Contribution margin of cancelled sales
  orders due to quality deficiency
Contribution margin of lost sales orders
  due to perceived unsatisfactory quality

delivering, and servicing of products and services and to improve quality. These costs include salaries and wages for time spent in training, instruction costs, clerical staff expenses and miscellaneous supplies, and costs expended to prepare hand-books and instructional manuals.

- **Quality planning costs.** Wages and overheads for quality planning and quality circles, new procedure designs, new equipment designs to enhance quality, reliability studies, and supplier evaluations.
- **Equipment maintenance costs.** Costs incurred to install, calibrate, maintain, repair, and inspect production instruments, processes, and systems.
- **Supplier assurance costs.** Costs incurred to ensure that materials, components, and services received meet the firm's quality standards. These costs include costs of selection, evaluation, and training of suppliers to conform with the requirements of TQM.
- **Information systems costs.** Costs expended for developing data requirements and measuring, auditing, and reporting of data on quality.
- **Product redesign and process improvement.** Costs incurred to evaluate and improve product designs and operating processes to simplify manufacturing processes or to reduce or eliminate quality problems.
- **Quality circle.** Costs incurred to establish and operate quality control circles to identify quality problems and to offer solutions to improve the quality of products and services.

Firms have found that as prevention costs increase other costs of quality decrease much faster than the prevention costs increase. By far the best way a firm can spend its cost of quality money is to invest in preventive actions. Prevention costs eliminate or reduce quality problems and are likely the only value-added costs among costs of quality. Prevention costs are voluntary or discretionary. Nevertheless, prevention costs are the most cost-effective way to improve quality.

Appraisal Costs

Appraisal (detection) costs are expenditures spent in the measurement and analysis of data to determine conformity to specifications. These costs are incurred during production and prior to deliveries to customers. Through measurement, analysis, and monitoring of manufacturing processes and examination of products and services prior to delivery, firms identify defective items and ensure that all units meet or exceed customer requirements. Incurring these costs does not reduce the errors or keep defects from happening again; it detects defective units before they are delivered to customers. Appraisal costs include the following:

- **Test and inspection cost.** Costs incurred to test and inspect incoming materials, work in process, and finished goods or services.
- **Acquisition cost of test equipment and instrument.** Expenditures incurred to acquire, operate, or maintain facilities, software, machinery, and instruments for testing or appraising the quality of products, services, or processes.
- **Quality audits.** Salaries and wages of all personnel involved in appraising the quality of products and services and other expenditures incurred during quality appraising.
- **Laboratory acceptance testing.**
- **Field evaluation and testing.**
- **Information costs.** Costs to prepare and verify quality reports.

Internal Failure Costs

Internal failure costs are expenditures spent as a result of poor quality found through appraisal prior to delivery to customers. These costs are not value added and are never necessary. These are some internal failure costs:

- **Costs of corrective action.** Costs for time spent to find the cause of failure and to correct the problem.
- **Rework and scrap costs.** Materials, labor, and overhead costs for scrap, rework, and reinspection.
- **Process costs.** Costs expended to redesign the product or processes, unplanned machine downtime for adjustment, and lost production due to process interruption for repair or rework.
- **Expediting costs.** Costs incurred to expedite manufacturing operations due to time spent for repair or rework.
- **Reinspect and retest costs.** Salaries, wages, and expenses incurred during reinspection or retesting of reworked or repaired items.
- **Lost contributions due to increased demand on constraint resources.** Constraint resources spent on defective units increase cycle time and reduce total output. Contributions not earned from units not produced because of the unavailability of the constraint resources reduce the operating income of the firm.

External Failure Costs

External failure costs are costs incurred to rectify quality defects after unacceptable products or services reach the customer and costs of profits lost from missed opportunities as a result of the unacceptable products or services delivered. In addition to items listed as costs of internal failure, external failure costs include the following:

- **Repair or replacement costs.** Repair or replacement of returned failed products.
- **Costs to handle customer complaints and returns.** Salaries and administrative overheads of the customer service department; allowance or discount granted for poor quality and freight charges.

REAL-WORLD FOCUS   How Much Does External Failure Cost?

Ford Motor Company unveiled the 2001 model of its best-selling sport-utility vehicle, the Ford Explorer, in late 2000. The 2001 model added a host of new safety features that enhanced the most popular SUV on the market since its introduction a few years earlier. Ford expected the new model to increase the firm's market share and to add substantial amounts to its bottom line. Yet, three months after the redesigned Explorer began rolling off the assembly line not a single one of the 5,000 built was in dealer showrooms. Instead, they were parked outside factories in St. Louis and Louisville while Ford engineers pored over them looking for defects. Jacques Nasser, CEO of the Ford Motor Company, ordered factory managers to hold off on shipping the new Explorer until engineers had the opportunity to correct quality problems.

When asked by financial analysts to comment on the cost of delay and repairing defects, Nasser responded, "Pick a number. It is over $1 billion." The delay was expensive, but Ford executives say the cost of fixing warranty claims later would be far higher. One defect caught by engineers was an internal steering-column switch that might have led motorists to start the engine in the "drive" position. Left uncorrected, this problem had the potential of resulting in big-time safety recalls. What was the root cause of the problem? It was traced to a supplier who used too much solder on a $1 circuit board. "When you get to the bottom of it, they are that trivial," says a company official of such glitches. "But when you let them escape, they are just huge."

Source: N. Muller, "Putting the Explorer under the Microscope," *Business Week*, February 12, 2001. p. 40.

- **Product recall and product liability costs.** Administrative costs to handle product recalls, repairs, or replacements; legal costs; and settlements resulting from legal actions.
- **Lost sales due to unsatisfactory products and customer ill will.** Lost contribution margins on canceled orders, lost sales, and decreased market shares.
- **Costs to restore reputation.** Costs of marketing activities to minimize damages from a tarnished reputation and to restore the firm's image and reputation.

Among the costs of quality, external failure costs are likely the most expensive. External failure costs are non-value-added costs. In many instances, a firm's largest external failure costs are opportunity costs, such as contribution margins not earned from lost or decreased sales. Opportunity costs are neither reported by nor available through the firm's accounting system. As a result, the magnitude of external failure cost may go unnoticed. Management needs to exert conscientious special efforts to seek out information on opportunity costs due to external failures.

The goal of measuring and reporting cost of quality is to eliminate external failure costs, minimize appraisal and internal failure costs, and invest effectively in prevention costs.

Conformance and Nonconformance Costs

Costs of conformance
are prevention costs and appraisal costs.

Costs of nonconformance
are internal failure costs and external failure costs.

Quality expert Philip Crosby believes there are no quality problems, only product design, materials, labor, and manufacturing problems that lead to poor quality. Crosby proposes that quality costs have two components: the price of conformance and the price of nonconformance.[25] Prevention and appraisal costs are **costs of conformance** because they are incurred to ensure that products or services meet customers' expectations. Internal failure costs and external failure costs are **costs of nonconformance.** They are costs incurred and opportunity costs because of rejection of products or services. The cost of quality is the sum of conformance and nonconformance costs.

Prevention costs are usually the lowest and the easiest among the four costs of quality for management to control. Internal and external failure costs are among the most expensive costs of quality, especially external failure costs. In a typical scenario, the cost of prevention may be $0.10 per unit, the cost of testing and replacing poor quality parts or components during production may be $5, the cost of reworking or

[25] Philip B. Crosby, *Quality Without Tears* (New York: McGraw-Hill, 1984), p. 86.

reassembling may be $50, and the cost of field repair and other external costs may be $5,000 or higher.

External failure costs can be rather substantial. For instance, Firestone Tire Company was forced to recall and replace 6.5 million ATX tires in 2000. In the first two months of the recall, the firm spent more than $500 million of out-of-pocket cost and suffered sales decreases of more than 40 percent. The price of its stock fell to less than half of the value prior to the recall. With the damage to its reputation, lost prospective business, and the legal and liability costs in the years to come, the firm's future is, to say the least, not very bright. Although well-known for quality products for more than a century, some industry experts speculate that Firestone could not even survive this quality problem.

Better prevention of poor quality reduces all other costs of quality. With fewer problems in quality, less appraisal is needed because the products are made right the first time. Fewer defective units also reduce internal and external failure costs as repairs, rework, and recalls decrease. By spending more on prevention, companies spend less on internal or external failure costs. The savings alone can be substantial. Meanwhile, the firm enjoys higher perceived values of its products, increased sales and market share, and improved earnings and return on investment.

Theoretically, a firm's success in prevention efforts incurs neither appraisal costs nor internal or external failure costs. It is easier to *design* and *build* quality in rather than to *inspect* or *repair* quality in. Appraisal costs decreases as quality improves.[26] Nonconformance costs decrease at much faster rates than prevention costs increase.

Reporting Quality Costs

LEARNING OBJECTIVE 4
Prepare and interpret cost of quality reports.

The purpose of reporting quality costs is to make management aware of the magnitude of quality costs and to provide a baseline against which the impact of quality improvement activities could be measured. Tasks for reporting quality costs include data definitions, identification of data sources, data collection, and preparation and distribution of quality cost reports.

Data Definition, Sources, and Collection

The first step in generating a quality cost report is to define quality cost categories and identify quality costs within each category. The preceding discussion described common quality cost categories. However, definitions of cost categories can vary among firms. Considering its unique operating conditions and experience, each firm identifies appropriate cost categories and clearly states operational definitions of all quality costs. Every member of the team needs to have a clear understanding of the firm's quality cost categories.

Ideally, each quality cost should have its own account so that quality cost information is readily apparent, not buried in myriad accounts. These quality cost accounts are the source of quality cost information.

Cost of Quality Report

A report on cost of quality is useful only if its recipients understand, accept, and can use the content of the report. Reports can be prepared in many ways. Each firm should select and design a reporting system that (1) can be integrated into its information system and (2) promotes TQM. Among considerations in establishing a quality cost report system are proper stratifications of quality cost reports by product line, department, plant, or division, and the time periods of the reports so that the firm can identify clearly the origins of quality costs easily. To facilitate assessment of the magnitude of

---

[26] One reason is that once suppliers have been tested, screened, and certified, a firm spends much less time verifying compliance than it would otherwise.

REAL-WORLD FOCUS   Analyzing Quality Costs in Formosa Plastics Group

Formosa Plastics Group developed an analytical program to evaluate its quality costs. In its corporate manual, the firm specifies these quality costs based on the ratio of

• Total quality cost to sales revenue and cost of goods sold.
• External failure cost to sales revenue.
• Total failure cost to sales revenue.

• Voluntary cost (prevention and appraisal costs) to sales revenue.
• Total quality cost to direct labor hours.
• Total quality cost to plant assets.

Source: Thomas P. Edmonds, Bor-Yi Tsay, and Wen-Wei Lin, "Analyzing Quality Costs," *Management Accounting*, November 1989, p. 29.

EXHIBIT 16.8   Cost of Quality Matrix

Source: James R. Evans and William M. Lindsay, *The Management and Control of Quality*, 3rd ed. (New York: West Publishing Co., 1996), p. 303.

	Design Engineering	Purchasing	Production	Finance	Accounting	Other	Totals
Prevention costs							
Quality planning							
Training							
Other							
Appraisal costs							
Test and Inspect							
Instruments							
Other							
Internal failure costs							
Scrap							
Rework							
Other							
External failure costs							
Returns							
Recalls							
Other							
Totals							

quality costs and their impact, firms often express costs of quality in percentages of net total sales.

A cost of quality matrix, as illustrated in Exhibit 16.8, is a convenient and useful tool in reporting quality costs. With columns identifying functions or departments and rows delineating cost of quality categories, a cost of quality matrix enables each department, function, process, or product line to identify and recognize the effects of its actions on the cost of quality and to pinpoint areas of high-quality costs. The matrix can contain dollar amounts (actual or estimate) or relative percentages of the amounts in a base period. The base period can be the amount in the first year of implementing the TQM program, preselected benchmark amounts, or other appropriate amounts that management decides to use for monitoring progress.

Illustration of a Cost of Quality Report

Exhibit 16.9 illustrates a cost of quality report.[27] Bally Company is a small midwestern manufacturing company with annual sales of around $9 million. The firm operates

[27] Adapted from *IMA Statement No. 4R.*

EXHIBIT 16.9
Cost of Quality Report for
Bally Company

	Year 2		Year 0		Percent Change
Prevention Costs					
Training	$ 90,000		$ 20,000		350%
Quality planning	86,000		20,000		330
Other quality improvement	60,000		40,000		50
Supplier evaluation	40,000		30,000		33
Total	$ 276,000	3.07%	$ 110,000	1.38%	151
Appraisal Costs					
Testing	120,000		100,000		20
Quality performance measurement	100,000		80,000		25
Supplier monitoring	60,000		10,000		500
Customer surveys	30,000		10,000		200
Total	$ 310,000	3.44%	$ 200,000	2.5%	55
Internal Failure Costs					
Rework and reject	55,000		150,000		(63)
Reinspection and testing	35,000		30,000		16
Equipment failure	30,000		50,000		(40)
Downtime	20,000		50,000		(60)
Total	$ 140,000	1.56%	$ 280,000	3.5%	(50)
External Failure Costs					
Product liability insurance	70,000		250,000		(72)
Warranty repairs	100,000		120,000		(17)
Customer losses (estimated)	600,000		1,400,000		(57)
Total	$ 770,000	8.56%	$1,770,000	22.13%	(56)
Total quality costs	$1,496,000	16.62%	$2,360,000	29.50%	(37)
Total Sales	$9,000,000	100%	$8,000,000	100%	

in a highly competitive environment and has been experiencing increasing pressures to raise quality and lower cost from new and existing competitors. The report shows that the external failure costs for such items as warranty claims, customer dissatisfaction, and market share loss accounted for 75 percent of the total cost of quality in year 0 ($1,770,000 ÷ $2,360,000 or 22.13% ÷ 29.5%).

To be more competitive and to increase market shares, Bally began a corporatewide three-year TQM process. The firm started with substantial increases in prevention and appraisal expenditures. The investment started to pay off in year 2. The internal failure, external failure, and total quality costs have all decreased.

Exhibit 16.9 compares the current year's quality costs to those of a base year. Alternative bases for comparisons can be the budgeted amounts, flexible budget costs, or long-range goals. A cost of quality report also should include output measures whenever possible.

Problem Finding

LEARNING OBJECTIVE 5
Describe methods commonly used to identify significant quality problems and their causes.

To achieve total quality management, firms need to identify and understand truly significant quality problems. Many helpful tools to identify significant quality problems are available, including control charts, histograms, Pareto diagrams, brainstorming, and cause-and-effect diagrams. These tools are most effective if management accountants take a proactive role throughout the process.

EXHIBIT 16.10
Control Charts for 1/8-Inch Drill Bit

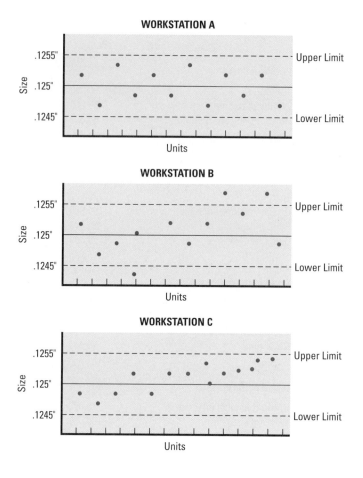

Control Charts

A **control chart**
plots successive observations of an operation taken at constant intervals.

A **control chart** plots successive observations of an operation, taken at constant intervals, to determine whether all observations fall within the specified range for the operation. The operation can be a machine, workstation, individual worker, work cell, part, process, or department. Intervals can be time periods, batches, production runs, or other demarcations of the operation.

A typical control chart has a horizontal axis representing time intervals, batch numbers, or production runs, and a vertical axis denoting a measure of conformance to the quality specification. The vertical measure also has a specified allowable range of variations, which are referred to as *upper* and *lower limits,* respectively. Exhibit 16.10 contains control charts for manufacturing 1/8-inch drill bits in three workstations.

Say that a firm has determined all drill bits must be within 0.0005 inch of the specified diameter. All units from workstation A are within the specified range ($\pm 0.0005''$), and no further investigation is necessary. Three units from workstation B are outside the specified range—an indication that not all operations in workstation B are in control. Management should investigate the cause of the aberration to prevent further quality failures. Although all units manufactured by workstation C are within the specified range acceptable to the firm, the control chart reveals that quality characteristics of workstation C are moving upward. Management may want to launch an investigation because the trend suggests that the operation will most likely produce drill bits outside the specified range in the near future.[28]

When the central line and the limits in a control chart are determined through a statistical process, the control chart is a *statistical quality control chart* (SQC) or *statistical process control chart* (SPC). The control charts showing in Exhibit 16.10 are SQC

---

[28] Using it in this manner, the control chart is often referred to as a *run chart.* A run chart shows the trend of observations over time.

or SPC charts if the line in the center, .125″, is determined by calculating the arithmetic mean (μ, read mu) of the observations and the limits, .1255″ and .1245″, are determined based on the standard deviation (Σ, read sigma) of the observations. For example, the standard deviation of the drill bits is, say, 0.00025″ and the firm has determined that variations within two standard deviations are acceptable. Thus the limits are $\mu \pm 2\Sigma$, or .125″ $\pm$ 2 $\times$ 0.00025″, which are .1255″ and .1245″ for upper and lower limits, respectively.

A firm sets the upper and lower limits based on experience, technology, customer expectation, and cost and benefit analysis that determine the extent of variations within which the firm is willing to accept or tolerate. The purpose of a control chart is to distinguish between random and nonrandom variations. A process is in *statistical control* if no sample observation is outside the established limits. Variations that fall within the established limits are deemed *random* variations and no further investigation is needed. Observations outside the limits signal quality failures.

However, for observations within the established limits to be considered random, the observations have to show no apparent patterns or runs, and an approximately equal number of observations are above and below the center line with most points nearing the center line. A process may be out of control if the observations show trends, cycles, clusters, or sudden shifts hugging the center line or the control limits. Many statistical techniques are available to help determine whether a process is in or out of control.[29]

Control charts are useful in establishing the state of control, monitoring processes, and identifying causes of quality variations. Posting control charts in a common area facilitates early detection of quality problems, promotes awareness of workers on the quality status of their products or services, and encourages active participation in efforts to raise quality. Ittner and Larcker find that firms in the computer industry that use quality control devices such as control charts have higher performance than firms not using them.[30]

Histogram

A histogram
is a graphical representation of the frequency of attributes or events in a given set of data.

A **histogram** is a graphical representation of the frequency of attributes or events in a given set of data. Patterns or variations that are often difficult to see in a set of numbers become clear in a histogram. Exhibit 16.11 contains a histogram of factors that contribute to the quality problems identified by a firm that makes chocolate mousse.

The firm has experienced uneven quality in one line of chocolate mousse. The firm identifies six contributing factors to the quality problem: substandard chocolate, improper liqueur mixture, uneven egg size, uneven blending speed, variant blending time, and improper refrigeration after production. It identified 210 batches as having poor quality. The histogram in exhibit 16.11 suggests that variations in egg size may be the largest contributor to the quality problem, followed by uneven speed in blending ingredients.

Pareto Diagram

A Pareto diagram
is a histogram of the frequency of factors contributing to the quality problem, ordered from the most to the least frequent.

A **Pareto diagram** is a histogram of factors contributing to the quality problem, ordered from the most to the least frequent. Joseph Juran observed in the 1950s that a few causes usually account for most of the quality problems, thus the name Pareto.[31] See the Pareto diagram of the chocolate mousse quality problem in Exhibit 16.12.

A Pareto diagram not only ranks the relative size of quality problems but also provides a useful visual aid. A Pareto diagram includes a cumulative curve that shows the cumulative effect of quality problems, as shown in Exhibit 16.12. Using a Pareto diagram, management can separate the few major causes of quality problems from the

---

[29] Evans and Lindsay, *The Management and Control of Quality,* pp. 697–98.

[30] Chris Ittner and David Larcker, "The Performance Effects of Process Management Techniques," *Management Science,* 1997, pp. 522–34.

[31] Vilfredo Pareto, a nineteenth-century Italian economist, observed that 80 percent of the wealth in Milan was owned by 20 percent of its residents.

EXHIBIT 16.11
Histogram of Quality
Problem: Contributing Factors

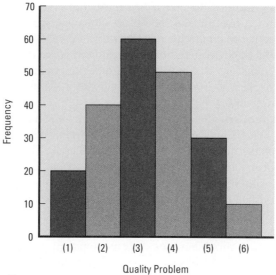

Key:

(1) Quality of chocolate   (4) Blending speed
(2) Liqueur   (5) Blending duration
(3) Egg size   (6) Improper refrigeration

EXHIBIT 16.12
Pareto Diagram of Quality
Problem: Ranking of
Contributing Factors

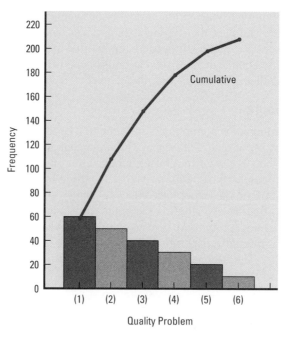

Key: (1) Egg size   (4) Blending duration
       (2) Blending speed   (5) Quality of chocolate
       (3) Liqueur   (6) Improper refrigeration

many trivial ones and identify areas that contribute most to poor quality. Thus management can focus its efforts on areas that are likely to have the greatest impacts on quality improvement. For example, the cumulative line in Exhibit 16.12 shows that improper egg size and erratic blending speed account for 110 quality problems in manufacturing the chocolate mousse. To improve quality, management would most likely demand that all suppliers deliver eggs uniform in size and regulate the speed of blenders. Pareto diagrams are especially useful in analyzing quality problems identified by a control chart as being outside the specified range.

EXHIBIT 16.13
Basic Cause-and-Effect Diagram

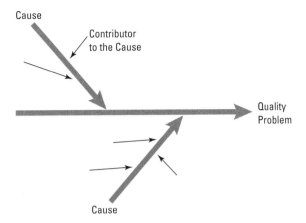

Brainstorming

Brainstorming is a way to elicit ideas from a group of people in a short time.[32] It is a way to identify problems, find causes of a problem, and develop a solution to a quality problem in a relaxed yet structured group session with members from a variety of backgrounds and responsibilities. Some basic rules for productive brainstorming follow:

1. No criticism of anyone's ideas by word or by gesture.
2. Once an idea has been put forth, there should be no further discussion of that idea during the session, except for clarification.
3. No idea is dumb or silly.
4. Each team member can introduce only one idea at a time.
5. Until most of the members have presented an idea, no member can introduce more than one idea.
6. No single individual should dominate the session.
7. No accusations of blame should occur during the session.[33]

Cause-and-Effect Diagram

The cause-and-effect, or Ishikawa, diagram organizes a chain of causes and effects to sort out root causes and identify relationships between causes and effects. Karou Ishikawa discovered that the number of factors that influenced a process or contributed to a quality problem were often overwhelming for situations with myriad factors. He developed cause-and-effect diagrams as an organizing aid.[34] Because of its shape, a fishbone diagram is another name for this diagram.

A cause-and-effect or fishbone diagram consists of a spine, ribs, and bones. At the right end of the horizontal spine is the quality problem at hand. The spine connects causes to the effect, the quality problem. Each branch or rib pointing into the spine describes a main cause of the problem. Bones pointing to each rib are contributing factors to the cause. In Exhibit 16.13 we illustrate the general structure of a cause-and-effect diagram.

Typical main causes for quality problems in manufacturing operations are

- Machines
- Materials

---

[32] Alex Osborn revived this ancient Greek technique in the 1940s. See A. F. Osborn, *Applied Imagination* (New York: Scribner's, 1963).

[33] Howard Gitlow, Alan Oppenheim, and Rosa Oppenheim, *Quality Management* (Burr Ridge, IL: Irwin, 1995), p. 309.

[34] Karou Ishikawa, *Guides to Quality Control*, 2nd ed. (Tokyo: Asian Productivity Organization, 1986). He first proposed the idea in 1943.

EXHIBIT 16.14
Cause-and-Effect Diagram for the Chocolate Mousse Quality Problem

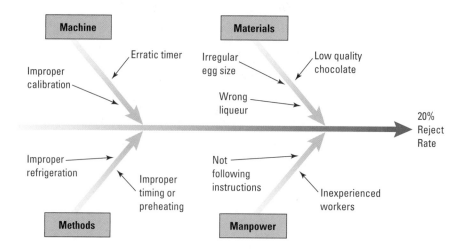

- Methods
- Manpower

Some users refer to the four main categories as *4M*.

In Exhibit 16.14 we show a cause-and-effect diagram for the quality problems in the manufacturing of chocolate mousse. The firm identified these main causes for the 20 percent rejection rate:

- Machines
  - Equipment not properly calibrated
  - Timer functions erratically
- Materials
  - Suppliers delivered wrong or irregular size eggs
  - Low-quality chocolate
  - Wrong liqueur used
- Methods
  - Improper refrigeration of ingredients
  - Ingredients not added at proper time or in prescribed sequence
  - Inappropriate preheating
- Manpower
  - Hiring of new workers without proper experience and not giving adequate training
  - Workers failed to follow instructions

Many firms have found brainstorming an effective technique in constructing cause-and-effect diagrams.

The two basic types of cause-and-effect diagrams are *dispersion analysis* and *process classification*. A dispersion analysis identifies and classifies causes for a specific quality problem (as previously illustrated for the chocolate mousse problem). A process classification diagram identifies key factors that may have contributed to the poor quality at each step of the process or flow. A process analysis is used when a series of events, steps, or processes creates a problem and it is not clear which one is the major cause of the problem.

Total Quality Management in Service Organizations

LEARNING OBJECTIVE 6
Identify distinct characteristics of total quality management in service organizations.

Service is an integral part of all corporations and organizations. Manufacturers like to add excellent service as another distinguishing characteristic of the firm. They know that retaining existing customers costs far less than recruiting new ones. Every service organization needs to deliver quality services to build businesses and maintain

REAL-WORLD FOCUS   Total Quality Management and Public Schools

The business world has known about total quality management (TQM) for years and has witnessed its successful implementation by Japanese companies. This popular business technique, designed to create and instill quality in companies' products and services, is now transcending the border from the business world into the educational arena. At Brooklyn's George Westinghouse Vocational & Technical High School, for example, students are participating in an educational experiment learning and using TQM. With help from corporate sponsors such as Ricoh, IBM, and Xerox, students use TQM principles in their electronics classes (finishing repairs before deadlines and with few mistakes) and receive feedback from the companies on their work. The school administration also uses TQM in its efforts to improve attendance and parental involvement.

Although there are differences between business and education, educators are applying TQM principles to their environment—and with initial success. Westinghouse is not alone in its use of TQM for reform. The number of U.S. public school districts using TQM has increased at a rapid pace in the last few years. The schools adopt a variety of TQM principles to create improvements specific to their particular needs. For example, in keeping with TQM's emphasis on gathering data to identify and help solve problems, Westinghouse teachers and administrators monitor attendance and test scores to pinpoint problems. They then use the information to brainstorm with students to resolve truancy and classroom failures. Other TQM principles at work at Westinghouse include using scatter diagrams to illustrate the relationship between two variables (e.g., how skipping homework leads to poor test grades), benchmarking (using a survey approach developed by Xerox to trace low attendance at parent-teacher events to scheduling conflicts); and cause-and-effect diagrams (using prompter students to make wake-up calls to classmates, thus decreasing tardiness).

School officials in Hillsborough County, Florida, implement a districtwide quality improvement mission. "Pinellas went 100 percent with a quality boot camp and invested an incredible amount of money," said Jodie Lamb, supervisor for staff development. "We wanted to just focus on the characteristics of a quality organization, focusing on building relationships, helping folks feel empowered, increasing their level of trust in the organization." Faculty and staff members established mission statements, values, and school rules. Principals and teachers serve as trainers.

TQM is not just practiced by teachers and administrators. Student-developed vision and mission statements, goals, and objectives are pinned to classroom bulletin boards and taped to walls. Even prekindergarten teachers trained at mandatory "quality boot camps" talk with children about why they are in school and what it means to be a high-performing student. "Businesses have been asking education to produce workers that are team players, problem solvers that can collaborate together," Sue Boyd, principal at Azalea Elementary School, the recipient of 2000 Governor's Sterling Award on quality education, said. "What this actually means is students are trained in that model. It's not just one child hitting the mark as a student. It extends beyond the classroom into the community, how we all get to the mark of excellence performance."

Sources: For further reading, see "Total Quality Management: Now, It's a Class Act," *Business Week,* October 31, 1994; and Pamela G. Leavy, "Total Quality Management Stressed in Public Schools," *The Tampa Bay Business Journal,* September 15, 2000, p. 22.

relationships with its customers. Providing quality service is especially important for service firms and organizations such as law firms, cleaning services, beauty shops, and hospitals. These firms earn revenues through services they provide.

Quality of service is also very important to merchandising or manufacturing corporations. Even though the cost of providing services is usually only a fraction of the total cost in a merchandising or manufacturing firm, quality of service can have significant effects on retaining customers and attracting new ones. A customer unhappy with the quality of service most likely will not come back. A customer rudely treated by a firm's receptionist may take her or his business elsewhere. A customer not satisfied with the help of a customer service representative is likely to look for alternative sources of supply next time. As Peter F. Drucker points out for service jobs in merchandising or manufacturing firms, "Quality is a condition and a restraint. It is external rather than in itself performance. It has to be built into the process."[35] Reichheld and Sasser report that companies can increase their profits by almost 100 percent if they retain just 5 percent more of their customers.[36] Retained customers are satisfied with the quality of products and services rendered by the firm.

Services are intangible outputs. A good service exists mostly in a customer's mind. While the goal in manufacturing is uniformity, the goal of service is customization. Medical doctors tailor their services to the need of each individual patient. Barbers

---

[35] Peter F. Drucker, *Managing for the Future* (New York: Truman Talley Books, 1993), p. 105.

[36] Frederick F. Reichheld and W. Earl Sasser, Jr., "Zero Defections: Quality Comes to Services," *Harvard Business Review,* September–October 1990, pp. 105–12.

provide quality service if they cut hair the way their customers want. Customization makes setting specifications difficult.

Furthermore, a service is not complete until the customer receives it. A manufacturing firm can recall a product of poor quality to repair or replace it. An automaker, for example, can recall cars to replace a defective brake system. A service firm that rendered poor-quality service often can offer only apologies or reparations. Rarely can a surgeon recall the patient to undo an operation wrongly executed.

These differences between service and manufacturing organizations make it necessary for service organizations to ensure that only qualified personnel can render services, that all personnel receive continuous education and training, and that quality is built into every step of the services provided to clients and customers.

Quality costs for services also include prevention and appraisal, as well as internal failure and external failure costs. However, the likely astronomical cost of service failures and the irreversibility of service outputs add the importance of prevention in total quality management of services.

Total Quality and Productivity

LEARNING OBJECTIVE 7
Explain the relationships between total quality management and productivity.

Improvement of quality requires additional resources and efforts with no increase in the output that the firm sets out to manufacture. A much too prevailing misconception is that efforts to improve quality decrease productivity because productivity measures the relationship between output and input resources, and an effort that requires additional input resources with no increase in output decreases productivity.

Studies have shown that improvements in quality lead to *increases* in productivity.[37] The belief that quality improvement and productivity have an inverse relationship could have grown out of the misperception that all units, once manufactured, are good outputs, whatever the quality of the output turned out to be or the required subsequent spending to rectify poor-quality products.

Many accounting systems do not include resources expended on rework or repair as direct costs in the manufacturing of the unit. Rather, repair or rework costs are treated as manufacturing overheads to be shared by all products and units. Facilities used and resources consumed for repairs, rework, retests, and other remedial work for poor-quality products are costs of a *hidden factory*. A hidden factory incurs manufacturing costs without increasing output and spreads its costs in accounts that are not easily traced. Were the costs of poor quality clearly identified and not considered as the cost of a hidden factory, the product cost of a firm with improved quality would likely be lower than the product costs of firms with no change in quality.

Furthermore, many actions or decisions taken to achieve total quality management improve productivity. For example, total quality management demands a simplified product design and a streamlined manufacturing process. A simple and easy-to-make product design decreases defects and, at the same time, increases productivity. A decision to streamline the manufacturing process to reduce the chance for errors to occur also can increase productivity because it eliminates unnecessary operations.

In their study, Leonard and Sasser found many examples of quality improvement leading to increased productivity, including these:

- Installation of a clean room to reduce contaminants on printed circuit boards increased output by almost 35 percent.

- Elimination of rework stations at one manufacturing factory for televisions forced workers to find and solve their own quality problems. As a result, the firm experienced an increase in production rates per direct labor-hour. The firm also saved money on rework and rework stations.

---

[37] Frank S. Leonard and W. Earl Sasser, "The Incline of Quality," *Harvard Business Review,* September–October 1982, pp. 163–71; and Y. K. Shetty, "Corporate Response to Productivity Challenges," *National Productivity Review,* Winter 1984–85, pp. 7–14.

REAL-WORLD FOCUS   Quality Gain Through Advanced Technology

Advanced technology is generating quality gains that help U.S. manufacturers distinguish themselves. For example, by digitizing the control of its factory, privately owned Latex Foam International (LFI) boosted its capacity, productivity, and quality. At a cost of $35 million, LFI built a state-of-the-art digital plant at Shelton, Connecticut. LFI's engineers can monitor all the factory's operations—from the mixing of latex and the distribution of liquid rubber into molding beds by mantis-like hanging robots to the heating, cooling, cleaning, and

drying of finished foam cores. The facility quickly achieved a 30 percent efficiency gain over its predecessor and boosted capacity by 50 percent, all in a smaller space with less than two-thirds of the workforce. The manufacturing system lets LFI track every mattress, right to when robots prod them to test for firmness with numerical precision.

Source: Adam Aston, "The Flexible Factory." *Business Week,* May 5, 2003, p. 91.

- Efforts to do it right the first time and every time by a firm increase not only its manufacturing productivity but also its sales productivity. Sales personnel no longer have to spend time processing returned defective products.[38]

Total Quality Management and Activity-Based Costing/Management

An activity-based costing system is ideally suited to total quality management. An ABC/M system facilitates implementation of TQM in two ways. First, it identifies cost with activities and thus increases the visibility of costs of quality. Costs of activities that are results of poor quality become clear to the organization. Traditional costing systems, in contrast, focus on organizational functions such as production, sales, and administrations. Management is likely not aware of the cost of quality without undertaking a special effort to gather data pertaining to cost of quality.

Second, organizations that use an ABC/M system most likely already have much of the cost information needed to implement TQM. A firm with a good ABC/M system in place needs only to identify costs and activities relating to costs of quality and quality improvement and classify these costs according to the cost of quality categories that the firm chooses to use. Firms with traditional costing systems require additional analyses to identify and measure cost of quality and to prepare cost of quality-reports. Additional tasks and costs of obtaining the necessary cost measures can discourage management from implementing TQM.

Just-in-Time Systems and Total Quality Management

A just-in-time system requires that all materials, components, and work meet quality specifications the first time and all the time. Defective materials, parts, or components bring production to grinding halts for JIT firms that operate with no inventory. These firms expect the required materials, parts, or components to be delivered when the processes expect them. If materials or components from upstream suppliers or departments are of low quality, the downstream departments must interrupt their work either to spend time to improve the materials or components so they meet the quality specification or to wait for new materials or components that meet the quality specifications to arrive. Delays or interruptions defeat JIT systems. To achieve a true JIT operation, a company strongly depends on its suppliers' ability to provide defect-free parts. A company must work closely with its suppliers so that all purchased materials and components meet its quality standard.

The Challenge of Total Quality Management to Management Accountants

The role of management accountants in total quality management includes gathering all relevant quality information, participating actively in all phases of the quality

[38] Leonard and Sasser, "*The Incline of Quality,*" pp. 163–71.

program, and reviewing and disseminating quality cost reports. A management system developed without active involvement of management accountants to improve quality is likely not to realize its full potential. Too often a firm includes quality costs in diverse and scattered accounts for products, marketing, engineering, and services. The impact of these costs and benefits disappears as the firm allocates account balances to several products or functions; some of them have at best remote relationships with the activities that cause the costs. As a result, the firm pays scant attention to quality costs and quality results on financial performance.

With their training and expertise in analyzing, measuring, and reporting information, management accountants can help design and conduct comprehensive quality information-gathering, measurement, and reporting systems. Management accountants can improve total quality management further by integrating the quality cost information into the existing management reporting and measurement systems. This integration facilitates the constant and continuous attention to improving quality by making measurement, reporting, and evaluation of quality a regular, routine activity rather than a special effort that will be dropped when the fad is over. A management accountant should be completely involved in all quality improvement activities of the enterprise. The IMA described these activities of an involved management accountant:

- Ensure full representation of management accountants on the main quality control committees and quality improvement teams.
- Make the company fully aware of the competitive benchmarks, competitive gaps, customers' retention rate, and cost of quality.
- Participate actively in identifying areas of greatest quality improvement opportunities and needs.
- Develop quality measures to monitor and assess ongoing progress toward quality goals.
- Be involved closely in vendor-rating decisions.
- Review and evaluate quality control effectiveness and the value of training courses for quality control personnel and human resources staff.
- Gather and continually review scrap and recovery costs.[39]

To meet the challenges of total quality management, management accountants must have a clear understanding of TQM methodology. They must be able to design, create, or modify information systems that measure and monitor quality and evaluate progress toward total quality as expected of each organizational unit and of the total enterprise. The following are some of the tasks:

- Determine which accounts contain significant TQM data.
- Reorganize and restructure the existing accounting system to provide accurate and complete quality cost data.
- Revise the chart of accounts to reflect each quality cost category.

A traditional accounting system often fails to associate costs with activities. As a result, quality teams do not have the necessary information readily available to focus on quality problems. A management accountant needs to relate quality costs to activities so that quality teams can focus their efforts appropriately to ensure the success of the TQM effort. One approach is to apply techniques from activity-based costing to TQM so that cost drivers for quality costs are identified clearly (see Chapter 5).

Content of cost of quality reports can vary widely, depending on the organization and its operating characteristics. Management accountants need to ensure that the measurement and reporting process meets the following criteria:

- Addresses the need of the internal customers.
- Includes all relevant cost of quality measures, including both financial and nonfinancial measures.

[39] *IMA Statement No. 4R*, p. 9.

- Adjusts measures to reflect quality and business challenges.
- Adapts measures as the need changes.
- Is simple and easy to use, execute, and monitor.
- Provides fast and timely feedback to users and managers.
- Fosters improvement rather than just monitoring.
- Motivates and challenges team members to strive for the highest quality gains.[40]

Summary

In today's global competition, with short product life cycles and rapidly changing technologies and consumer tastes, firms can sustain long-term survival and profitability only by manufacturing quality products and rendering quality services.

Providing quality is the best strategy for attaining long-term profitability. Businesses offering quality products and services gain market shares over the years; studies show that quality is positively and significantly related to higher returns on investment.

A quality product or service meets or exceeds customer's expectations at a price the customers are willing to pay. To achieve quality products or services, many firms adopt *total quality management,* which requires continuous efforts by everyone in an organization to understand, meet, and exceed the expectations of both internal and external customers.

Firms meet quality standards by conforming to goalpost or zero-defect conformance, which meets the quality standard within the specified range of the target, and absolute or robust quality conformance, which meets the specification exactly at the target value.

Four common categories for quality costs are prevention, appraisal, internal failure, and external failure. Prevention and appraisal costs are costs of conformance; and internal and external failure costs are costs of nonconformance.

Cost of quality reports should enable each department to identify and recognize the effects of its actions on the cost of quality and to pinpoint areas of high-quality costs. In generating a quality cost report, accountants define quality cost categories and identify all quality costs within each category. Ideally, each quality cost should have its own account so that its information is not buried in, or aggregated with, other accounts.

Tools that identify quality problems and are used to find solutions to those problems include control charts, histograms, Pareto diagrams, brainstorming, and cause-and-effect (fishbone or Ishikawa) diagrams. A control chart is a graph that depicts successive observations of an operation taken at constant intervals; it is often used to identify or discover quality problems. Both histograms and Pareto diagrams depict graphically the frequency of quality problems or observations. A Pareto diagram orders quality problems from the largest to the smallest. Brainstorming is a useful way to elicit ideas in identifying quality problems, finding causes of a quality problem, or developing solutions to a quality problem. The cause-and-effect diagram graphically represents a chain of causes and effects that lead to a quality problem. It is a useful way to sort out root causes and to identify relationships between causes or factors and the quality problem.

Organizations with quality services conform their performance standards with the needs and requirements of their customers. Although quality costs for a service organization or function include prevention, appraisal, internal failure, and external failure costs, service organizations pay the most attention to training and building quality into every step of service rendered because poor quality service usually cannot be recalled or replaced.

Improved quality increases productivity. Evidence has shown that the common misconception of inverse relationships between quality improvement and productivity is a result of including all units, regardless of quality, as good output.

[40] Ibid., p. 31.

Management accountants, with training and expertise in analyzing, measuring, and reporting information, can help design and implement comprehensive systems for quality information gathering, measurement, and reporting.

Key Terms

absolute quality conformance, *687*	gap analysis, *684*	quality, *681*
appraisal costs, *693*	goalpost conformance (zero-defects conformance), *686*	quality circle, *682*
control chart, *698*	histogram, *699*	Taguchi quality loss function, *688*
costs of conformance, *694*	internal failure costs, *693*	total quality management (TQM), *681*
costs of nonconformance, *694*	ISO 9000, *678*	
costs of quality, *691*	Pareto diagram, *699*	
external failure costs, *693*	prevention costs, *691*	

Comments on Cost Management in Action

To Implement TQM, Get a Black Belt

Companies such as General Electric, Weyerhauser, and Allied Signal are training their managers in quality management. The program is designed for business unit managers, quality managers, and engineers. First used by Motorola in 1986, these training programs provide an intense curriculum in measurement and statistical tools, cost management, team-building, and leadership. Successful candidates are awarded a green belt after months of training, which prepares them to lead their business units to Six Sigma goals in quality defects. Black belt and master black belt status is available for those who have more intensive training.

The key idea is to integrate Six Sigma thinking throughout the organization, and to provide the training so that local managers will be able to lead their units to success. Some firms have even extended the idea to include their business partners. For example, Cascade DieCasting in High Point, N.C., sent four of its managers off for Six Sigma training at the request of a major customer, Black and Decker.

Source: Hal Lancaster, "This Kind of Black Belt Can Help You Score Some Points at Work," *The Wall Street Journal,* September 14, 1999, p. B1.

Self-Study Problems
(For solutions, please turn to the end of the chapter.)

1. Cost of Quality Improvement

An automobile manufacturer plans to spend $1 billion to improve the quality of a new model. The manufacturer expects the quality improvement program to eliminate the need for recall and reduce the costs for warranty repairs. The firm's experience had been, on average, 1.5 recalls for each new model at the cost of $300 per vehicle per recall. The average cost per recall, if one is needed is expected to increase by 10 percent for the new model. Costs for other warranty repairs will decrease from $200 to $80 per unit. Sales of the new model were expected to be 500,000 units without the quality improvement program. The firm believes that the well-publicized quality improvement program will increase the total sales to 650,000 units. If there is a profit of $5,000 per unit, is the $1 billion expenditure justified?

2. Taguchi Quality Loss Function

Marlon Audio Company manufactures cassette tapes. The desired speed of its model SF2000 is 2 inches per second. Any deviation from this value distorts pitch and tempo resulting in poor sound quality. The firm sets the quality specification to 2 ±0.25 inches per second because an average customer is likely to complain and return the tape if the speed is off by more than 0.25 inch per second. The cost per return is $36. The repair cost before the tape is shipped, however, is only $3 per tape.

Required

1. Compute $L(x)$ if x is 2.12 inches per second.
2. Estimate the tolerance for the firm to minimize its cost.

3. Cost of Quality Report

Precision Electric Instruments manufacturers fans for mini and micro computers. As a first step to focus on quality improvements, the firm has compiled the following operating data for the year just completed (in thousands):

Line inspection	$ 55
Training	120
Returns	100
Warranty repairs	68
Preventive equipment maintenance	20
Recalls	157
Design engineering	67
Scrap	30
Downtime	40
Product-testing equipment	88
Product liability insurance	20
Supplier evaluation	15
Reworks	35
Inspection and testing of incoming materials	25
Litigation costs to defend allegation of defective products	240

Required Prepare a cost of quality report and classify the costs as prevention, appraisal, internal failure, and external failure.

Questions

16–1 Define *quality.*

16–2 What are the reasons that the cost of poor quality reached an epidemic level before U.S. companies were motivated to do something about the problem in the 1980s?

16–3 What is TQM? At what point can a firm consider its effort to achieve total quality management complete?

16–4 What is the Malcolm Baldrige National Quality Award and the ISO 9000 certificate? Why do many firms in the United States seek them?

16–5 What are the core principles of total quality management?

16–6 Why is continuous quality improvement essential to achieve TQM and critical to an organization's success and competitive position?

16–7 Describe the main elements for an effective implementation of TQM.

16–8 What are the purposes of conducting a quality audit?

16–9 What is a gap analysis?

16–10 Why is it often necessary to revise a firm's compensation and appraisal systems when implementing TQM?

16–11 Describe goalpost conformance.

16–12 Discuss the difference between goalpost conformance and absolute quality conformance.

16–13 Taguchi argues that being within specification limits is not enough to be competitive in today's global economy. Do you agree? Why?

16–14 What is the likely cost to a firm when its product or service does not conform to customers' expectations for features or performance?

16–15 Name three costs associated with each of the following cost categories:

  a. Prevention

  b. Appraisal

  c. Internal failure

  d. External failure

16–16 Which of the following cost categories tend to increase during the early years of TQM? Which of them tend to decrease over the years due to successful total quality management? Why?

  a. Prevention

  b. Appraisal

  c. Internal failure

  d. External failure

16–17 What is cost of conformance? Nonconformance?

16–18 Many organizations found that investments in prevention and appraisal usually resulted in major cost savings in other areas. Explain this phenomenon.

16–19 What functions does cost of quality reporting play in a quality improvement program?

16–20 Name and briefly describe three methods that companies use to identify quality problems.

16–21 What is a cause and effect diagram? What is its primary purpose?

16–22 What are the main causes of quality problems in a typical cause-and-effect diagram for manufacturing operations?

16–23 What is a Pareto chart? What is its function?

16–24 What are similarities and distinct characteristics in TQM for manufacturing and service firms?

16–25 What are the relationships between quality and productivity? Do efforts at productivity improvement help or hurt quality? Do quality improvement efforts help or hurt productivity? Why?

16–26 What roles do management accountants play in TQM?

16–27 How can management accountants meet the challenges of TQM?

Exercises

16–28 **Pareto Diagram**   The following causes of absenteeism for a fellow student are for the year just completed:

Cause of Absenteeism	Occurrences
Personal illness	12
Child's illness	26
Car broke down	8
Personal emergency	32
Overslept	9
Unexpected visitor	11

Required   Construct a Pareto diagram.

16–29 **Histogram Graph, Spreadsheet Application**   Genova Company classifies its costs of quality into four categories. The costs of quality as a percentage of cost of goods sold for the last three years are

	2007	2006	2005
Prevention costs	2.00%	4.00%	1.00%
Appraisal costs	1.50	2.50	3.00
Internal failure costs	14.00	23.00	27.00
External failure costs	12.00	18.00	31.00

Required

1. Use a spreadsheet to prepare a histogram that shows the costs of quality trends as a percentage of costs of goods sold.
2. Comment on the trends in cost of quality over the three-year period from 2005 to 2007.
3. What cost of quality can the firm expect as a percentage of its cost of goods sold in 2008?

16–30 **Quality Cost Classification**

Required   Classify each of the following costs into types of quality cost:

1. Materials, labor, and overhead costs of scrapped units.
2. Engineering time spent to determine the causes of failures to meet product specification.
3. Wages and salaries for the time spent by workers to gather quality measurements.
4. Information systems costs expended to develop data requirements.
5. Clerical staff expenses to coordinate training programs.
6. Salaries for members of problem-solving teams.
7. Payment to settle a product liability lawsuit.

16–31 Quality Cost Classification

Required   Identify the quality cost category for each of the following costs:

1. Materials, labor, and overhead costs spent on reworks for returned items.
2. Unplanned machine downtime to correct a mal-alignment.
3. Wages and salaries for the time spent by workers to analyze quality measurements.
4. Overtime premiums resulting from unplanned machine downtime.
5. Maintenance costs for measurement instruments.
6. Reengineering costs for operation processes.
7. Salaries and ancillary costs to conduct reliability studies.
8. Costs spent on implementing process control plans.
9. Costs spent to respond to complaints filed by federal regulation agencies.
10. Express freight premiums for returning products to customers.

16–32 Cost of Quality Improvement   PIM Industries, INC. manufactures electronics components. Each unit costs $30 before the final test. The final test rejects, on average, 5% of the 50,000 units manufactured per year. The average rejection rate of the industry is 3%. A consultant has determined that poor lighting is the most likely cause of this high rejection rate. It would cost $100,000 to install adequate lighting in the assembly department, which would be useful for 5 years. With adequate lighting that will cost an additional $5,000 in operating cost each year, the firm expects to reduce its rejection rate to no higher than the industry average.

Required   Should the firm install the lighting?

16–33 Cost of Quality Improvement   Office Pro sells office supplies to major corporations and institutions. Customers such as educational, religious, and not-for-profit institutions, and governmental agencies are exempt from sales tax. The firm estimates that it loses $600,000 each year by failing to collect sales tax from customers who are not entitled to be exempt from sales tax. The firm can hire three auditors to check the certification of each customer claiming sales-tax exemption and reduce the cost by 90 percent. The firm estimates that each auditor will cost $80,000, including salary, benefits, and expenses. In addition, the annual cost for necessary office space and equipment for the auditors is approximately $100,000.

Required   What is the cost to the firm to reduce the errors by 90 percent?

16–34 Taguchi Cost Coefficient   Solidtronic Inc., an OEM manufacturer, has a product specification of 75 ± 5. The cost for warranty services is estimated at $500 per unit.

Required   What is the value of k, the cost coefficient, in the Taguchi loss function?

16–35 Estimate Total Cost Using Taguchi Loss Function

Required   Use the data given in Exercise 16–34 to calculate the estimated total cost when the measured quality characteristic is 78.

16–36 Average Cost Per Unit Using Taguchi Loss Function   Use the data given in Exercise 16–34.

Required   What is the expected loss (cost) per unit if the manufacturing process is centered on the target specification with a standard deviation of 2?

16–37 Taguchi Cost Coefficient   Flextronchip, an OEM manufacturer, has a fifth generation chip for cell phones with a specification of 0.2 ± 0.0002 mm for the distance between two adjacent pins. The loss due to a defective chip is $20.

Required   Compute the value of k in the Taguchi loss function.

16–38 Expected Loss Using Taguchi Function   Use the data from Flextronchip given in Exercise 16–37.

The firm has taken a sample of 100 chips from the production process. The results are

Measurement	Frequency
0.1996	2
0.1997	5
0.1998	12
0.1999	11
0.2000	45
0.2001	10
0.2002	8
0.2003	5
0.2004	2

Required   Calculate the quality loss for each of the observed measurements and the expected loss for the production process.

16–39 **Expected Loss Using Taguchi Function**   Use the data from Flextronchip given in Exercises 16–37 and 16–38. Determine the variance and calculate the expected loss using the calculated variance.

16–40 **Using Taguchi Function To Determine Tolerance**   The desired distance for Flextronchip customers is 0.2 mm between two adjacent pins. Any deviation from this value causes interference. The process of handling complaints costs the firm at least $40 per chip. The engineers of the firm expect the average customer will be likely to complain when the distance is off the target by at least .0001. At the factory, the adjustment can be made at a cost of $1.60, which includes the labor to make the adjustment and additional testing.

Required   What should the tolerance be before an adjustment is made at the factory?

Problems

16–41 **Quality Cost Classification**   A partial list of Josephson Manufacturing Company's activities during the past year includes the following:
   a. Materials for repairs of goods under warranty.
   b. Inspection of goods repaired under warranty.
   c. Customer returns.
   d. Canceled sales orders due to unsatisfactory products previously delivered to its customers.
   e. Maintenance costs for testing equipment.
   f. Inspecting finished goods.
   g. Time spent to determine courses needed for quality training.
   h. Debugging software before production.
   i. Technical help to resolve a customer's production problems that could have been caused by bugs in the software shipped with the firm's equipment.
   j. Supervision of testing personnel.

Required

1. Classify each cost using one of the following categories: prevention cost, appraisal cost, internal failure cost, external failure cost, or not a quality cost.
2. Identify conformance and nonconformance costs in the list of activities.

16–42 **Quality Cost Classification**

Required   Classify these following items into types of cost of quality:

   a. Warranty repairs
   b. Scrap
   c. Allowance granted due to blemish
   d. Contribution margins of lost sales
   e. Tuition for quality courses
   f. Raw materials inspections
   g. Work-in-process inspection

h. Shipping cost for replacements

i. Recalls

j. Attorney's fee for unsuccessful defense of complaints about quality

k. Inspection of reworks

l. Overtime caused by reworking

m. Machine maintenance

n. Tuning of testing equipment

16–43 Cost of Quality Category The management of Brooks Company believes that its total costs of quality can be reduced if the firm increases expenditures in certain key costs of quality categories. Management has identified the following costs of quality:

Cost of Quality	Costs
Rework	$ 6,000
Recalls	15,000
Reengineering efforts	9,000
Repair	12,000
Replacements	12,000
Retesting	5,000
Supervision	18,000
Scrap	9,000
Training	15,000
Testing of incoming materials	7,000
Inspection of work in process	18,000
Downtime	10,000
Product liability insurance	9,000
Quality audits	5,000
Continuous improvement	1,000
Warranty repairs	15,000

Required

1. Classify these costs into cost of quality categories.

2. Determine the total dollars being spent on each category.

3. Based on the company's expenditures by cost of quality categories, on which cost category should the company concentrate its efforts to decrease its overall costs of quality?

16-44 Cost of Quality Analysis The Duncan Materials Company manufactures and sells synthetic coatings that can withstand high temperatures. Its primary customers are aviation manufacturers and maintenance companies. The following table contains financial information pertaining to cost of quality in 2005 and 2006 in thousands of dollars:

	2006	2005
Sales	$18,750	$15,000
Materials inspection	60	300
Production inspection	125	160
Finished product inspection	70	225
Preventive equipment maintenance	60	20
Scrap	300	500
Warranty repair	400	700
Product design engineering	270	150
Vendor certification	60	10
Direct costs of returned goods	80	250
Training of factory workers	140	40
Product testing equipment maintenance	60	60
Product testing labor	90	210
Customer support	30	70
Rework before shipment	180	240
Product liability settlement	60	360
Emergency repair and maintenance	60	190

Required

1. Classify the cost items in the table into cost of quality categories.

2. Calculate the ratio of each cost of quality category to revenues in each of the years.

3. Comment on the results.

4. In addition to the financial measures listed in the table, what other nonfinancial measures should Duncan Materials Company monitor in its effort to attain TQM?

16-45 **Spreadsheet Application**   Use the data in Problem 16-44 and a spreadsheet to complete this problem. Use the spreadsheet functions to carry out all calculations. Do not hard-code or carry out calculations elsewhere and type in the calculated amounts.

1. Determine the information you'll need to generate for a cost of quality report and set up a spreadsheet for the information. Among the items to be included in a cost of quality report are proper headings of the report, revenue and cost items (cost items should be in the cost of quality category), cost as a percentage of revenues for each of the years.

2. Input the data provided in 16-44 into the spreadsheet by the cost of quality category.

3. Enter functions or steps to calculate the total amount for each cost of quality category and the total cost of quality. Do not hard-code or type in the amounts.

4. Enter functions or steps to calculate the total cost of each cost of quality category as a percentage of revenues for each of the years. Use two digits after the decimal point for the percentages. Do the same for the total cost of quality. Do not hard-code or type in the amounts.

5. Move to another area of the spreadsheet or use a fresh sheet and title the area "Cost of Quality Trend Analysis." Enter functions or steps for the percentages; do not hard-code or type in the amounts.

6. Create a bar chart to compare the percentages of each of the cost of quality categories and the total cost of quality in 2005 and 2006.

7. Do a sensitivity analysis by making the following changes to the 2006 amounts:

   • Increase the total sales by 5 percent.

   • Increase total prevention cost by 6 percent.

   • Decrease total internal failure cost by 60 percent.

   • Decrease total external failure cost by 50 percent.

Required   What is the total cost of quality as a percentage of total sales?

16–46 **Cost of Quality Report**   Buster Company manufactures custom-designed milling machines and incurred the following cost of quality in 2005 and 2006:

	2006	2005
Rework	$200,000	$250,000
Quality manual	40,000	50,000
Product design	300,000	270,000
Testing	80,000	60,000
Retesting	50,000	90,000
Product recalls	360,000	500,000
Field service	230,000	350,000
Disposal of defective units	90,000	85,000

The sales in each of the two years totaled $6,000,000. The firm's cost of goods sold is typically one-third of net sales.

Required

1. Prepare a cost of quality report that classifies the firm's costs under the proper cost of quality category.

2. Calculate the ratio of each cost of quality category to sales in each of the two years. Comment on the trends in cost of quality between 2005 and 2006.

3. Give three examples of nonfinancial measures that Buster Company might want to monitor as part of a total quality management effort.

16–47 **Preparing a Cost of Quality Report**   Tarheel Company incurred these costs of quality:

	2005	2006
Calibration	$ 75,000	$100,000
Product design	150,000	175,000
Product liability	125,000	75,000
Product recalls	400,000	200,000
Retesting	250,000	200,000
Rework	325,000	100,000
Testing	50,000	150,000
Training	75,000	100,000
Warranty repairs	150,000	75,000

Required   Prepare a cost of quality report that classifies each of these costs under the proper cost of quality category. Indicate whether the costs are increasing or decreasing and by how much.

16–48 **Cost of Quality Report**   Scrabbling Enterprises (SE) is a pioneer in designing and producing scrabbling devices. SE's products were brilliantly designed, but management neglected the manufacturing process; as a consequence, quality problems have been chronic. When customers complained about defective units, SE simply sent a repairperson or replaced the defective unit. Recently, several competitors introduced similar products with much higher quality, causing SE's sales to decline. The firm's market share declined from 60 to 40 percent in 2006.

To rescue the situation, SE embarked on an intensive campaign to strengthen its quality control at the beginning of 2007. These efforts met with some success; the downward slide in sales was reversed, and the firm's market share increased from 40 percent in 2006 to 45 percent in 2007. To help monitor the company's progress, costs relating to quality and quality control were compiled for the previous year (2006) and for the first full year of the quality campaign (2007). The costs, which do not include the lost sales due to a reputation for poor quality, appear in thousands:

	2007	2006
Product recalls	$ 600	$3,500
Systems development	680	120
Inspection	2,770	1,700
Net cost of scrap	1,300	800
Supplies used in testing	40	30
Warranty repairs	2,800	3,300
Rework labor	1,600	1,400
Statistical process control	270	—
Customer returns of defective goods	200	3,200
Cost of testing equipment	390	270
Quality engineering	1,650	1,080
Downtime due to quality problems	1,100	600

Required

1. Prepare a quality cost report for both 2006 and 2007. Carry percentage computations to two decimal places.
2. Prepare a histogram showing the distribution of the various quality costs by category.
3. Write an analysis to accompany the reports you have prepared in requirements 1 and 2 on the effectiveness of the changes the firm made in the last year.
4. Suppose that the firm has just learned that its major competitor has reduced its price by 20 percent. SE can afford to lower its price only if it can cut costs. A sales manager suggests that the firm can reduce quality engineering and inspection work until the market stabilizes. The manager also points out that reduced inspections will decrease the net cost of scrap and losses of downtime due to quality problems. Do you agree?

16–49 **Cost of Quality Report**   Carrie Lee, the president of Lee Enterprises, was concerned about the result of her company's new quality control efforts. "Maybe the emphasis we've placed on upgrading our quality control system will pay off in the long run, but it doesn't seem to be helping us much right now. I thought improved quality would give a real boost to sales, but sales have remained flat at about $10,000,000 for the last two years."

Lee Enterprises has seen its market share decline in recent years because of increased foreign competition. An intensive effort to strengthen the quality control system was initiated a year ago (on January 1, 2007) in the hope that better quality would strengthen the company's competitive position and reduce warranty and servicing costs. These costs (in thousands) relate to quality and quality control over the last two years:

	2007	2006
Warranty repairs	$140	$420
Rework labor	200	140
Supplies used in testing	6	4
Depreciation of testing equipment	34	22
Warranty replacements	18	60
Field servicing	120	180
Inspection	120	76
Systems development	106	64
Disposal of defective products	76	54
Net cost of scrap	124	86
Product recalls	82	340
Product testing	160	98
Statistical process control	74	—
Quality engineering	80	56

Required

1. Prepare a cost of quality report that contains data for both 2006 and 2007. Carry percentage computations to two decimal places.

2. Prepare a histogram showing the distribution of the various quality costs by category.

3. Prepare a written evaluation to accompany the reports you have prepared in requirements 1 and 2. This evaluation should discuss the distribution of quality costs in the company, changes in this distribution that you detect have taken place over the last year, and any other information you believe would be useful to management.

4. A member of the management team believes that employees will be more conscientious in their work if they are held responsible for mistakes. He suggests that workers should do rework on their own time and that they also should pay for disposal of defective units and the cost of scraps. The proposal estimates that the firm can save another $400,000 in quality costs and the employees are less likely to make as many errors. Should the firm implement the proposal?

(CMA Adapted)

16–50 **Cost of Quality Program, Nonfinancial Information**   International Tractor (IT) manufactures tractor parts. A major customer has just warned IT that if it does not improve its quality, it will lose the firm's business. Duane Smith, IT's controller, must develop a cost of quality program. He seeks your advice on classifying each of the following items as (i) a prevention cost, (ii) an appraisal cost, (iii) an internal failure cost, or (iv) an external failure cost:

a. Cost of tractor parts returned to International Tractor.

b. Costs of having to rework defective parts detected by the engineering quality assurance team.

c. Cost of inspecting the products on the production line by the IT quality inspectors.

d. Labor cost of product designer at IT whose job is to design products that will not break under extreme pressure.

e. Payment for employees who visit customers with complaints.

Required

1. Classify the five individual items into one of the four categories.

2. Give two examples of nonfinancial performance measures that IT can use to monitor its total quality control effort.

3. Recommend an effective TQM implementation procedure to meet the customer's demand.

16–51 Relevant Costs and Quality Improvement   Lightening Bulk Company is a moving company specializing in transporting large items worldwide. The firm has an 85 percent on-time delivery rate. Twelve percent of the items are misplaced and the remaining 3 percent are lost in shipping. On average, the firm incurs an additional $60 per item to track down and deliver misplaced items. Lost items cost the firm about $300 per item. Last year the firm shipped 5,000 items with an average freight bill of $200 per item shipped.

The firm's manager is considering investing in a new scheduling and tracking system costing $150,000 per year. The new system is expected to reduce misplaced items to 1 percent and lost items to 0.5 percent. Furthermore, the firm expects the total sales to increase by 10 percent with the improved service. The average contribution margin is 40 percent.

Required

1. Should the firm install the new tracking system?
2. What other factors does the firm's manager need to consider in making the decision?
3. Upon further investigation, the manager discovered that 80 percent of the misplaced or lost items either originated in or were delivered to the same country. What is the maximum amount the firm should spend to reduce the problems in that country by 90 percent?

16–52 Quality Improvement, Relevant Cost Analysis   Worrix Corporation manufactures and sells 3,000 premium quality multimedia projectors at $12,000 per unit each year. At the current production level, the firm's manufacturing costs include variable costs of $2,500 per unit and annual fixed costs of $6,000,000. Additional selling, administrative, and other expenses, not including 15 percent sales commissions, are $10,000,000 per year.

The new model, introduced a year ago, has experienced a flickering problem. On average the firm reworks 40 percent of the completed units and still has to repair under warranty 15 percent of the units shipped. The additional work required for rework and repair causes the firm to add additional capacity with annual fixed costs of $1,800,000. The variable costs per unit are $2,000 for rework and $2,500, including transportation cost, for repair.

The chief engineer, Patti Mehandra, has proposed a modified manufacturing process that will almost entirely eliminate the flickering problem. The new process will require $12,000,000 for new equipment and installation and $3,000,000 for training. Patti believes that current appraisal costs of $600,000 per year and $50 per unit can be eliminated within one year after the installation of the new process. The firm currently inspects all units before shipment. Furthermore, warranty repair cost will be only $1,000 for no more than 5 percent of the units shipped.

Worrix believes that none of the fixed costs of rework or repair can be saved and that a new model will be introduced in three years. The new technology will most likely render the current equipment obsolete.

The accountant estimates that repairs cost the firm 20 percent of its business.

Required

1. What are the additional costs of choosing the new process?
2. What are the benefits of choosing the new process?
3. Should Worrix use the new process?
4. What factors should be considered before making the final decision?
5. A member of the board is very concerned about the substantial amount of additional funds needed for the new process. Because the current model will be replaced in about three years, the board member suggests that the firm should take no action and the problem will go away in three years. Do you agree?

16–53 Taguchi Loss Function   Duramold specializes in manufacturing molded plastic panels to be fitted on car doors. The blueprint specification for the thickness of a high-demand model calls for 0.1875 ±0.0025 inch. It costs $120 to manufacture and $150 to scrap a part that does not meet the specifications. The thickness measure for the unit just completed is 0.1893 inch.

Required   Use the Taguchi loss function to determine

1. The value of k.
2. The amount of loss for the unit.

16–54 **Taguchi Loss Function**   Use the data from problem 16–53 for Duramold. The firm can eliminate the uneven thickness by adding a production worker at the critical production point for $6 per unit.

Required   At what tolerance should the panel be manufactured?

16–55 **Taguchi Loss Function**   An electronic component has an output voltage specification of 125 ±5 millivolts. The loss to the firm for a component that does not meet the specification is $200. The output voltage for a sample unit is 122 millivolts.

Required   Use the Taguchi loss function to determine

1. The value of k.
2. The amount of loss.

16–56 **Taguchi Loss Function**   Use the data for problem 16–53. the firm can adjust the output voltage at the factory by changing a resistor at a cost of $12.

Required   At what voltage should the electronic component be manufactured?

16–57 **Taguchi Loss Function**   North Platt Machinery Company manufactures a shaft that must fit inside a sleeve. The firm has just received an order of 50,000 units from Southernstar Exploration Company for $80 per unit. North Platt can manufacture the shaft at $50 per unit. Southernstar desires the diameter of the shaft to be 1.275 cm. The diameter of the shaft must not be less than 1.25 cm, in order to fit properly inside the sleeve. To be able to insert the shaft into a sleeve without the use of force, the diameter cannot be larger than 1.30 cm. A defective shaft is discarded and a replacement has to be shipped via express freight to locations around the world. North Platt estimates that the average cost of handling and shipping a replacement shaft will be approximately $70. Shown below are the diameters from a sample of 80 shafts manufactured during a trial run.

Diameter	Number of Units	Diameter	Number of Units	Diameter	Number of Units
1.232	1	1.273	6	1.292	2
1.240	2	1.274	7	1.293	1
1.250	3	1.275	18	1.294	4
1.258	2	1.276	8	1.298	2
1.262	2	1.277	5	1.300	2
1.270	3	1.280	2	1.304	1
1.272	6	1.288	2	1.320	1

Required   Use the Taguchi loss function to determine

1. The expected loss
2. The tolerance in diameter that the amount should set for the shaft.

16–58 **Analyzing Cost of Quality Report**   Bergen Inc. produces telephone equipment at its Georgia plant. In recent years, the company's market share has been eroded by stiff competition from Asian and European competitors. Price and product quality are the two key areas in which companies compete in this market.

Jerry Holman, Bergen's president, decided to devote more resources to the improvement of product quality after learning that his company's products had been ranked fourth in product quality in a 2004 survey of telephone equipment users. He believed that Bergen could no longer afford to ignore the importance of product quality. Jerry set up a task force that he headed to implement a formal quality improvement program. Included on the task force were representatives from engineering, sales, customer service, production, and accounting because Jerry believed that this is a companywide program and all employees should share the responsibility for its success.

After the first task force meeting, Sheila Haynes, manager of sales, asked Tony Reese, production manager, what he thought of the proposed program. Tony replied, "I have reservations. Quality is too abstract to be attaching costs to it and then to be holding you and me responsible for cost improvements. I like to work with goals that I can see and count! I don't like my annual bonus to be based on a decrease in quality costs; there are too many variables that we have no control over!"

Bergen's quality improvement program has been in operation for 18 months, and the following cost report was recently issued.

As they were reviewing the report, Sheila asked Tony what he thought of the quality program now. "The work is really moving through the production department," replied Reese. "We used to spend time helping the customer service department solve their problems, but they are leaving us alone these days. I have no complaints so far. I'll be anxious to see how much the program increases our bonuses."

Cost of Quality Report by Quarter
(in thousands)

	June 30, 2006	September 30, 2006	December 31, 2006	March 31, 2007	June 30, 2007	September 30, 2007
Prevention costs						
Machine maintenance	$ 215	$ 215	$ 202	$ 190	$ 170	$ 160
Training suppliers	5	45	25	20	20	15
Design reviews	20	102	111	100	104	95
	$ 240	$ 362	$ 338	$ 310	$ 294	$ 270
Appraisal costs						
Incoming inspection	$ 45	$ 53	$ 57	$ 36	$ 34	$ 22
Final testing	160	160	154	140	115	94
	$ 205	$ 213	$ 211	$ 176	$ 149	$ 116
Internal failure costs						
Rework	$ 120	$ 106	$ 114	$ 88	$ 78	$ 62
Scrap	68	64	53	42	40	40
	$ 188	$ 170	$ 167	$ 130	$ 118	$ 102
External failure costs						
Warranty repairs	$ 69	$ 31	$ 24	$ 25	$ 23	$ 23
Customer returns	262	251	122	116	87	80
	$ 331	$ 282	$ 146	$ 141	$ 110	$ 103
Total quality cost	$ 964	$1,027	$ 862	$ 757	$ 671	$ 591
Total production cost	$4,120	$4,540	$4,380	$4,650	$4,580	$4,510

Required

1. Identify at least three factors that should be present for an organization to successfully implement a quality improvement program.

2. By analyzing the cost of quality report presented, determine whether Bergen's quality improvement program has been successful. List specific evidence to support your answer.

3. Discuss why Tony Reese's current reaction to the quality improvement program is more favorable than his initial reaction.

4. Jerry Holman believed that the quality improvement program was essential and that Bergen could no longer afford to ignore the importance of product quality. Discuss how Bergen could measure the opportunity cost of not implementing the quality improvement program.

(CMA Adapted)

16–59 **Expected Quality Cost, Confidence Interval, and Sample Size (Requires Chapter 6)** Paragon Manufacturing produces small motors for assembly in handheld tools such as chain saws and circular saws. The company recently began manufacturing a new motor, model EZ3, and forecasts an annual demand of 200,000 units for this model.

Each model EZ3 requires a housing manufactured to precise engineering specifications. Paragon purchases these housings, which are not subject to quality control inspection before entering the production process; however, paragon performance-tests the entire motor after final assembly. During pilot production runs of the new motor, several of the housings had wrong sizes and were rejected. If the housings were too shallow, they could not be assembled correctly; if they were too deep, the motor would not operate properly.

Ross Webster, Paragon's production manager, gathered the following information during the pilot production runs.

- When housings were rejected during assembly because they were too shallow, they were replaced with new housings. This change in housings required nine minutes of additional direct labor for each affected unit.

- The units that were rejected during performance testing because the housings were too deep had to be torn down and reassembled with new housings. This operation required 1 hour and 15 minutes of additional direct labor for each affected unit.

- The supplier of the housings is willing to take back the defective housings but will refund only one-half of the price. In the future, if Paragon inspects the housings before they enter the assembly process, the supplier will refund the full price of all rejected housings.

- The costs of model EZ3 follow:

Materials*	$ 44
Direct labor (3 hrs. @ $12/hr.)	36
Variable overhead ($18/hr.)	54
Total costs	$134

*Includes $7.00 for housing.

- The majority of the rejections experienced during the pilot runs were related to the housings. Ross's estimate of the probability of rejections for a lot of 800 housings follows:

Rejection during Assembly		Rejection during Performance Testing	
Quantity	Probability	Quantity	Probability
90	0.40	50	0.50
70	0.30	40	0.15
50	0.20	20	0.15
30	0.10	10	0.20

If Paragon decides to inspect the housings prior to assembly, Ross must select the appropriate sample size by using the following two formulas. The estimated sample size (formula 1) must be modified by the second formula (final sample size) because Ross will be sampling without replacement.

Formula 1	Formula 2

$$nc = C^2 pq/a^2 \qquad\qquad nf = \frac{nc}{1 + \dfrac{nc}{N}}$$

where:

nc = first estimate of sample size

nf = final sample size

c = confidence coefficient

p = maximum rejection rate

$q = 1 - p$

a = precision level

N = number of items in the population

Required

1. Determine the maximum amount that Paragon Manufacturing would be willing to spend annually to implement quality control inspection of the housings before assembly begins.

2. For the purpose of quality control inspection, determine the sample size that Ross should select from a lot of 800 housings if the desired level is 95.5 percent (confidence coefficient 2.00) with a precision of 1 percent and rejections not to exceed 1 percent.

3. Without prejudice to your answer in requirement 2, for quality control inspection purposes, assume that the sample size is 240 housings and the desired level is 95.5 percent (confidence coefficient 2.00) with a precision of 1 percent and rejections not to exceed 1 percent. Determine whether Ross should accept or reject a lot if there are

a. Two defective housings in the sample.

b. Three defective housings in the sample.

Explain your answer in each situation.

(CMA Adapted)

Solutions to Self-Study Problems

1. Cost of Quality Improvement

Cost of the quality improvement program		$1,000,000,000
Savings from eliminating recalls $300 × 110% × 1.5 × 500,000 =	$247,500,000	
Decreases in warranty repair cost ($200 − $80) × 500,000 =	60,000,000	
Profit from increased sales (650,000 − 500,000) × $5,000 =	750,000,000	1,057,500,000
Increase in Profit from the Quality Improvement Program		$ 57,500,000

Yes, the increase in profit from the additional sales and decrease in costs of warranty repairs and recalls exceed the $1 billion cost of quality improvement.

2. Taguchi Quality Loss Function

1. $36 = k (0.25)^2$

$k = \$576$

$L(x = 2.12) = \$576(2.12 - 2.0)^2 = \$8.2944$

2. $3 = \$576(\text{tolerance})^2$

Tolerance = 0.0722

Therefore, the specification should be set at 2 inches ±0.0722 inch.

3. Cost of Quality Report

Coolquietude Electric Instruments
Cost of Quality Report
For the Year 2006

Prevention costs		
Training	$ 120	
Design engineering	67	
Preventive equipment maintenance	20	
Supplier evaluation	15	
Total prevention costs	$ 222	
Appraisal costs		
Line inspection	$ 55	
Product-testing equipment	88	
Inspection and testing of incoming materials	25	
Total appraisal costs	$ 168	
Internal failure costs		
Scrap	$ 30	
Downtime	40	
Reworks	35	
Total internal failure costs	$ 105	
External failure costs		
Returns	$ 100	
Warranty repairs	68	
Recalls	157	
Product liability insurance	20	
Litigation costs	240	
Total external failure costs	$ 585	
Total cost of quality	$1,080	

CHAPTER SEVENTEEN

Management Control and Strategic Performance Measurement

After studying this chapter, you should be able to . . .

1. Identify the objectives of management control

2. Identify the types of management control systems

3. Define strategic performance measurement and show how centralized, decentralized, and team-oriented organizations can apply it

4. Explain the objectives and applications of strategic performance measurement in three common strategic business units: cost SBUs, revenue SBUs, and profit SBUs

5. Explain the role of the balanced scorecard in strategic performance measurement

6. Explain the role of strategic performance measurement in service firms and not-for-profit organizations

Talk about some of the most remarkable corporate turnarounds of the last decade! Mobil Oil North America was experiencing profits well below the industry average in the early 1990s, but soon after adopting a new performance measurement system, the firm became profitable. The performance measurement method is one of the most influential in many decades: the balanced scorecard. The same remarkable improvement occurred for CIGNA Property & Casualty Insurance and Chemical Bank when these two firms adopted the balanced scorecard.[1] In these instances, the success of the balanced scorecard is attributed to providing top management a way to effectively communicate strategic initiatives to the large number of managers throughout their firms and to enabling these managers to understand more clearly than perhaps ever before exactly how to implement that strategy. As Kaplan and Norton note (page 7):

The Balanced Scorecard made the difference. Each organization executed strategies using the same physical and human resources that had previously produced failing performance. The strategies were executed with the same products, the same facilities, the same employees, and the same customers. The difference was a new senior management team using the

---

[1] Robert S. Kaplan and David P. Norton, *The Strategy-Focused Organization: How Balanced Scorecard Companies Thrive in the New Business Environment* (Boston: Harvard Business School Press, 2001). For additional evidence, see William Fonvielle and Lawrence Carr, "Gaining Strategic Alignment: Making Scorecards Work," *Management Accounting Quarterly*, Fall 2001, pp. 5–14. For examples from the hospitality and financial services industries, see Rajiv D. Banker, Gordon Potter, and Dhinu Srinivasan, "An Empirical Investigation of an Incentive Plan that Includes Nonfinancial Performance Measures," *The Accounting Review*, January 2000, pp. 65–92; and, Christopher D. Ittner, David F. Larcker, and Taylor Randall, "An Examination of Strategic Performance Measurement Practices in Financial Service Firms," working paper, The Wharton School of the University of Pennsylvania, August 2001.

Balanced Scorecard to focus all organizational resources on a new strategy. The scorecard allowed these successful organizations to build a new kind of management system—one designed to manage strategy.

Moreover, the balanced scorecard is really a two-way device. Not only does it effectively communicate top management's strategy to the managers who will implement it, but also it provides a framework to consider, critique, and redevelop that strategy. That is, feedback from managers in the field regarding progress on scorecard measures can provide a useful way to continually reexamine the firm's strategy.

This chapter considers the systems used to measure and evaluate performance with a focus on the activities that most effectively help the firm achieve its strategy. We will study several performance systems, including the balanced scorecard. We begin by explaining the broad concepts underlying performance evaluation and control.

Performance Evaluation and Control

Performance evaluation
is the process by which managers at all levels gain information about the performance of tasks within the firm and judge that performance against preestablished criteria as set out in budgets, plans, and goals.

LEARNING OBJECTIVE 1
Identify the objectives of management control.

Management control
refers to the evaluation by upper-level managers of the performance of mid-level managers.

Operational control
means the evaluation of operating level employees by mid-level managers.

Performance evaluation is the process by which managers at all levels gain information about the performance of tasks within the firm and judge that performance against preestablished criteria as set out in budgets, plans, and goals.

Performance is evaluated at many different levels in the firm: top management, mid-management, and the operating level of individual production and sales employees. In operations, the performance of individual production supervisors at the *operating level* are evaluated by plant managers, who in turn are evaluated by executives at the *management level.* Similarly, individual salespersons are evaluated by sales managers who are evaluated in turn by upper-level sales management.

Management control refers to the evaluation by upper-level managers of the performance of mid-level managers. **Operational control** means the evaluation of operating-level employees by mid-level managers. Part IV covered operational control. Part V, which begins with this chapter, covers management control.

Operational Control versus Management Control

In contrast to operational control, which focuses on detailed short-term performance measures, management control focuses on higher-level managers and long-term, strategic issues. Operational control has a management-by-exception approach; that is, it identifies units or individuals whose performance does not comply with expectations so that the problem can be promptly corrected. In contrast, management control is more consistent with the management-by-objectives approach, in which long-term objectives such as growth and profitability are determined and performance is periodically measured against these goals.

Management control also has a broader and more strategic objective: to evaluate the unit's overall profitability as well as the performance of its manager, to decide whether the unit should be retained or closed, and to motivate the manager to achieve top management's goals. Because of this broader focus, various objectives for management control generally have multiple measures of performance rather than a single financial or operating measure, as is sometimes true in operational control. Exhibit 17.1 is an organization chart that illustrates the different roles of management control and operational control.

Objectives of Management Control

In a management-by-objectives approach, top management assigns a set of responsibilities to each mid-level manager. The nature of these responsibilities and, therefore, the precise nature of top management's objectives depends on the functional area involved (operations, marketing) and on the scope of authority of the mid-level manager (the extent of the resources under the manager's command).

EXHIBIT 17.1
Organization Charts:
Operational and Management
Control

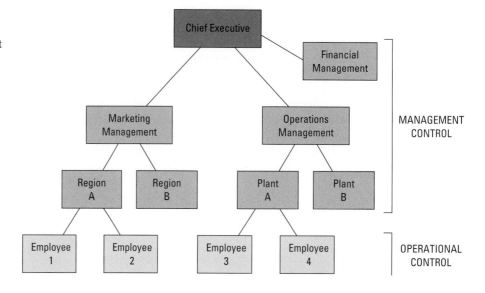

A **strategic business unit (SBU)** consists of a well-defined set of controllable operating activities over which an SBU manager is responsible.

An **employment contract** is an agreement between the manager and top management designed to provide incentives for the manager to act independently to achieve top management's objectives.

These areas of responsibility are often called *strategic business units* (SBUs). The concept of a strategic business unit is particularly useful for diversified firms that need performance measures to rationalize and manage the different business units. General Electric Company (GE) is widely cited as pioneering the concept.[2]

A **strategic business unit** consists of a well-defined set of controllable operating activities over which the SBU manager is responsible. Generally, managers have autonomy for making decisions and for managing the SBU's human and physical resources. The objectives of management control follow:

1. *Motivate* managers to exert a high level of effort to achieve the goals set by top management.
2. Provide the right *incentive* for managers to make decisions consistent with the goals set by top management.
3. *Determine fairly the rewards* earned by managers for their effort and skill and the effectiveness of their decision making.

A concise summary of top management's objectives is to provide fair compensation to the manager for working hard and making the right decisions, all within the context of autonomous action by the SBU manager. A common mechanism for achieving these multiple objectives is to develop an **employment contract** between the manager and top management that covers each of these points. Assuming that managers act in autonomous self-interest, the contract is designed to provide incentives for them to act independently while achieving top management's objectives and earning the desired compensation. This is called goal congruence. The contract specifies the manager's desired behaviors and the compensation to be awarded for achieving specific outcomes by using these behaviors. The contract can be written or unwritten, explicit or implied; some contracts are legal and enforceable by the courts.[3] For clarity and effectiveness, organizations often use explicit written contracts.

[2] The General Electric Company story is told in two Harvard Business School Cases (Cases Number 385–315 and 381–174). *Strategic Management: Concepts and Cases*, 12th ed. by Arthur Thompson Jr. and A. J. Strickland III (New York: McGraw-Hill/Irwin, 2001) provides a useful discussion of SBUs. An overall discussion of strategic performance measurement is provided by Robert Simons in *Performance Measurement and Control Systems for Implementing Strategy* (Upper Saddle River, NJ: Prentice Hall, 2000). In practice, some firms use the concept of SBU to refer to a business unit that is at a relatively high level in the organization, so that a firm will have only a dozen or fewer SBUs. In these cases, lower level units might be referred to as business units, centers, divisions, or simply units. To simplify the presentation in this chapter we use the single term *SBU* rather than the variety of terms used in practice for these units, at various levels of aggregation.

[3] For a good overview of the use of contracts in management control, see Kenneth A. Merchant, *Rewarding Results* (Boston: Harvard Business School Press, 1989), especially Chapters 1 and 2.

Employment Contracts

The **principal-agent model** is a conceptual model that contains the key elements that contracts must have to achieve the desired objectives.

An economic model called the **principal-agent model** is a prototype that contains the key elements that contracts must have to achieve the desired objectives. The model sets out two important aspects of management performance that affect the contracting relationship, uncertainty and lack of observability.

> **Uncertainty.** Each manager operates in an environment that is influenced by factors beyond the manager's control—operating factors such as unexpected and unpreventable machine breakdowns and external factors such as fluctuations in market prices and demands. The manager's lack of control means that there is some degree of *uncertainty* about the effectiveness of the manager's actions, independent of the efforts and abilities the manager brings to the job.

> **Lack of observability.** The efforts and decisions made by the manager are *not observable to top management.* The manager generally possesses information not accessible to top management. Because of the manager's independent and unobservable actions, top management is able to observe only the concrete outcomes of those actions, not the efforts that led to these outcomes.

The presence of uncertainty in the job environment and the lack of observability and the existence of private information for the manager complicate the contracting relationship. Ideally, with no uncertainty and perfect observability, the manager and top management would base their contract on the amount of effort the manager is to supply. An observable effort would assure both parties of the desired outcome. However, the presence of uncertainty and the lack of observability mean that the contract between the manager and top management must specifically incorporate both uncertainty and the lack of observability. This can be accomplished by understanding and applying the three principles of employment contracts:

1. Because of uncertainty in the manager's environment, the contract should recognize that other factors inside and outside the firm also influence the outcomes of the manager's efforts and abilities. Therefore, the contract should separate the outcome of the manager's actions from the effort and decision-making skills employed by the manager; that is, separate the performance of the manager from the performance of the SBU.
2. The contract must include only factors that the manager controls. This concept is similar to the first principle, which separates the manager from the SBU; this second principle excludes *known* uncontrollable factors from the contract.
3. Because of uncertainty and lack of observability, a *risk-averse manager is improperly biased* to avoid decisions with uncertain outcomes. In contrast, top management would prefer to see some of these relatively risky decisions implemented because of top management's greater tolerance for risk.

In effect, the contract between top management and the manager should recognize the manager's risk aversion and the role of uncertainty: the need to understand and to apply the three principles of contracting.

In the principal-agent model illustrated in Exhibit 17.2, top management supplies compensation to the manager who operates in an environment of uncertainty. The manager supplies effort and decision-making skills as well as a degree of risk aversion. The effect of the effort and decision-making skills on the factors in the environment produces the outcomes. The outcomes are multifaceted, including financial and nonfinancial results: earnings, customer satisfaction, operating efficiency, and so on. The accountant prepares a performance report consisting of financial and nonfinancial measures of the outcomes of the manager's decisions and efforts; the performance report goes to top management, which uses it to determine the manager's pay. In this way, the principal-agent model shows the relationships among the key factors that affect the manager's performance and compensation.

EXHIBIT 17.2
The Principal-Agent Model

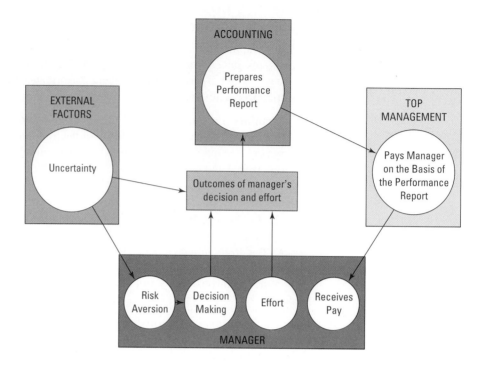

Design of Management Control Systems for Evaluation

LEARNING OBJECTIVE 2
Identify the types of management control systems.

Developing a management control system involves clearly identifying the *who, what,* and *when* for the evaluation. We start with the *who,* that is, who is interested in evaluating the organization's performance? The four recipients of performance reports are: (1) the firm's owners, directors, or shareholders, (2) its creditors, (3) the community or governmental units affected by its operations, and (4) its employees. Each has a different view about what performance is desired.[4]

The second aspect of management control is *what* is being evaluated. Commonly the evaluation is of the individual manager, to assess the effectiveness and efficiency of the manager's performance. Alternatively, the focus of the evaluation might be the SBU under the manager's control for the purpose of determining whether or not to expand or to divest the SBU. Rather than focusing on the individual manager, the evaluation might be directed to a team of managers. A manager's performance can be compared either with that of other managers or with the manager's own previous performance. Comparison to other managers is common, but comparison to the manager's previous performance is preferable when comparison to others is inappropriate or unfair in some way.

The third aspect of management control is *when* the performance evaluation is conducted. There are two considerations. First, the evaluation can be done on the basis of either *resources input* to the manager or *outputs* of the manager's efforts. The first approach uses the master budget (Chapter 8), while the second uses the flexible budget (Chapter 13). The focus is on inputs when measuring the outputs of the manager's efforts is difficult or the nature and extent of the manager's control over the outputs is not clear. Then the manager's evaluation is performed *ex ante,* that is, before the manager's efforts and decisions have been made. In effect, the manager negotiates with top management for the amount of resources needed. This approach is common in service and not-for-profit organizations for which the outputs are often difficult to measure. In

---

[4] For a useful discussion of strategic performance measurement in the context of diverse stakeholders, see Anthony A. Atkinson, John H. Waterhouse, and Robert B. Wells, "A Stakeholder Approach to Strategic Performance Measurement," *Sloan Management Review,* Spring 1997, pp. 25–37.

contrast, in manufacturing, where the inputs and outputs are often relatively easy to measure, the *ex post* approach based on actual outputs is more commonly used.

Another timing option is to tie the evaluation to the product life cycle. The life cycle of a product or service is the time from its introduction to its removal from the market. In the early stages of a product's sales life cycle, management focuses primarily on nonfinancial factors such as market penetration and success in developing certain customers. The appropriate performance measures at this time include revenue according to customer class and area, the number of back orders, the number of new customers, and customer satisfaction. As the product achieves market acceptance, profitability and asset management become more important, and the performance measures change. Finally, when the product is in its mature phase—when the nature of the competition is established and the future of the market is clear—the focus on profitability continues with the addition of interest in strategic issues such as customer satisfaction, information regarding product modifications, and potential new markets. Top management must choose the types of performance measures that are appropriate for the sales life cycle stage of the product or service, as illustrated in Exhibit 17.3.

EXHIBIT 17.3
Sales Life Cycle of Management Control

Stage of Product's Sales Life Cycle	Appropriate Performance Evaluation Measures
Early	Revenue, market penetration
Growth	Profitability, asset management
Mature	Profitability, strategy

The management accountant first determines the who, what, and when of management control and then designs a system to evaluate it. The systems for management control are of two types, formal and informal. Formal systems are developed with explicit management guidance while informal systems arise from the unmanaged, and sometimes unintended, behavior of managers and employees. Informal systems reflect the managers' and employees' reactions and feelings that result from the positive and negative aspects of the work environment. An example is the positive feelings of security and acceptance held by an employee in a company that has a successful product and offers generous employee benefits.

Informal Control Systems

Informal systems are used in firms at both the individual and the team levels. At the individual level, employees' performance is influenced by the individual drives and aspirations they bring to the workplace; these are separate from any incentives and guidance provided by management. Such individual motivators explain performance differences between employees.

When informal systems exist at the work group or team level, shared team norms, such as a positive attitude to help the firm achieve quality goals or to improve sales, influence the performance of team members. At a broader level, organization-level norms can influence the behavior of teams and of individual employees. For example, some firms have a culture of commitment to customer service (IBM and Wal-Mart); others have a culture devoted to quality (Toyota, FedEx) or innovation (Rubbermaid, Hewlett-Packard). Management accountants must consider these informal systems to properly develop control systems that have the desired impact on employees' performance.

Formal Control Systems

The three important formal management control systems at the individual employee level are (1) hiring practices, (2) promotion policies, and (3) strategic performance measurement systems. In each system, management sets expectations for desired employee performance. Hiring and promotion policies are critical in all companies and supplement strategic performance measurement systems. Strategic performance measurement systems are the most common method for evaluating managers.

EXHIBIT 17.4
Systems for Management Control

Little is known about formal systems for management control at the team or group level, although the increased emphasis on teamwork in recent years is likely to produce demand for such systems. Some U.S. companies have adopted the *keiretsu* system of shared responsibility prevalent in Japanese companies, and it is a likely starting place for such a development.[5] The four management control systems are summarized in Exhibit 17.4.

Strategic Performance Measurement

LEARNING OBJECTIVE 3
Define strategic performance measurement and show how centralized, decentralized, and team-oriented organizations can apply it.

Strategic performance measurement
is an accounting system used by top management for the evaluation of SBU managers.

Strategic performance measurement is a system used by top management to evaluate SBU managers. It is used when responsibility can be effectively delegated to SBU managers and adequate measures for evaluating the performance of the managers exist. Before designing strategic performance measurement systems, top managers determine when delegation of responsibility (called *decentralization*) is desirable.

Decentralization

A firm is decentralized if it has chosen to delegate a significant amount of responsibility to SBU managers. In contrast, a centralized firm reserves much of the decision making at the top management level. For example, in a centralized multi-store retail firm, all pricing decisions, product purchasing, and advertising decisions are made at the top management level, typically by top-level marketing and operations executives. In contrast, a decentralized retail firm allows local store managers to decide which products to purchase and the type and amount of advertising to use.

The strategic benefit of the centralized approach is that top management retains control over key business functions, ensuring a desired level of performance. Additionally, with top management involvement in most decisions, the expertise of top management can be effectively utilized, and the activities of the different units within the firm can be effectively coordinated. For many firms, however, a decentralized approach is preferable. The main reason is that top management cannot effectively manage the operations at a very detailed level; it lacks the necessary local knowledge. Decisions at lower levels in the firm must be made on a timely basis using the information at hand to make the firm more responsive to the customer. For example, the retail store manager must often make quick changes in inventory, pricing, and advertising to respond to local competition and changing customer buying habits and tastes.

Although the main reason for decentralization is the use of local or specialized knowledge by SBU managers, other important incentives exist. First, many managers would say that decentralized strategic performance measurement is more motivating because it provides them the opportunity to demonstrate their skill and their desire to

[5] For a recent description of one bank's approach to using team-based performance measures, see Dan Hill, "Cooperation or Competition?" *Strategic Finance*, February 2000, pp. 53–57.

achieve as well as to receive recognition and compensation for doing so. Second, because of the direct responsibility assumed by SBU managers, the decentralized approach provides a type of training for future top-level managers. Finally, most managers would agree that the decentralized approach is a better basis for performance evaluation. It is perceived to be more objective and to provide more opportunity for the advancement of hard-working, effective managers.

As shown in Exhibit 17.5, decentralization has a downside as well. It can hinder coordination within the firm. The increased focus on competition also could cause increased conflict among managers, which can lead to counterproductive actions and reduced overall performance.

EXHIBIT 17.5
Benefits and Drawbacks of Decentralization

Benefits of Decentralization	Drawbacks of Decentralization
• Uses local knowledge • Allows timely and effective response to customers • Trains managers • Motivates managers • Offers objective method of performance evaluation	• Can hinder coordination among SBUs • Can cause potential conflict among SBUs

Types of Strategic Business Units

The four types of strategic business units (SBUs) are cost SBUs, revenue SBUs, profit SBUs, and investment SBUs.

Cost SBUs are a firm's production or support SBUs that provide the best quality product or service at the lowest cost. Examples include a plant's assembly department, data processing department, and shipping and receiving department. When the focus is on the selling function, SBUs are called **revenue SBUs** and are defined either by product line or by geographical area. When an SBU both generates revenues and incurs the major portion of the cost for producing these revenues, it is a **profit SBU.** Profit SBU managers are responsible for both revenues and costs and therefore seek to achieve a desired operating profit. The use of profit SBUs is an improvement over cost and revenue SBUs in many firms because they align the manager's goals more directly with top management's goal to make the firm profitable.

The choice of a profit, cost, or revenue SBU depends on the nature of the production and selling environment in the firm. Products that have little need for coordination between the manufacturing and selling functions are good candidates for cost SBUs. These include many commodity products such as food and paper products. For such products, the production manager rarely needs to adjust the functionality of the product or the production schedule to suit a particular customer. For this reason, production managers should focus on reducing cost while sales managers focus on sales; this is what cost and revenue SBUs accomplish.

Cost SBUs
are production or support SBUs within the firm that have the goal of providing the best quality product or service at the lowest cost.

A revenue SBU
is defined either by product line or by geographical area.

A profit SBU
both generates revenues and incurs the major portion of the cost for producing these revenues.

In contrast, sometimes close coordination is needed between the production and selling functions. For example, high-fashion and consumer products require close coordination so that consumer information coming into the selling function promptly reaches the design and manufacturing functions. Cost and revenue SBUs could fail to provide the incentive for coordination; in this case, production managers would be focusing on cost and not listening to the ever-changing demands coming from the selling function. A preferred option is to use the profit center for both the revenue and production managers so that both coordinate efforts to achieve the highest overall profit for the firm.

When a firm has many different profit SBUs because it has many different product lines, comparing their performance could be difficult because they vary greatly in size and in the nature of their products and services. A preferred approach is to use **investment SBUs,** which include assets employed by the SBU as well as profits in the performance evaluation. Investment SBUs are covered in Chapter 18.

An **investment SBU** includes assets employed by the SBU as well as profits in performance evaluation.

The Balanced Scorecard

Each of the four types of SBUs described above focuses on a critical financial measure of performance. Rather than to focus on financial performance only, some firms use multiple measures of performance to evaluate SBUs, usually in the form of a balanced scorecard. The balanced scorecard provides a more comprehensive performance evaluation, and therefore an evaluation that can be more effective in meeting the evaluation objectives of motivation and fairness. Most often these methods will be used to evaluate the performance of the manager of the SBU. For example, managers of cost SBUs are expected to meet or exceed targets for cost reduction. Managers of SBUs using the balanced scorecard are evaluated on multiple measures. Sometimes investment SBU performance measures are used in two ways: to evaluate the manager of the SBU and to evaluate the SBU as a business investment. We examine each of these five methods in this and the following chapter.

Cost Strategic Business Units

LEARNING OBJECTIVE 4
Explain the objectives and applications of strategic performance measurement in three common strategic business units: cost SBUs, revenue SBUs, and profit SBUs.

Cost SBUs include direct manufacturing departments such as assembly and finishing and manufacturing support departments such as materials handling, maintenance, and engineering. The direct manufacturing and manufacturing support departments are often evaluated as cost SBUs since these managers have significant direct control over costs but little control over revenues or decision making for investment in facilities.

Strategic Issues Related to Implementing Cost SBUs

Three strategic issues arise when implementing cost SBUs. One is cost shifting, the second is excessively focusing on short-term objectives, and the third is the tendency of managers and top management to miscommunicate because of the pervasive problem of budget slack.

Cost Shifting

Cost shifting occurs when a department replaces its controllable costs with noncontrollable costs. For example, the manager of a production cost SBU that is evaluated on controllable costs has the incentive to replace variable costs with fixed costs. The reason for this is that the manager generally is not held responsible for increases in noncontrollable fixed costs. The net effect might be higher overall costs for the firm, although controllable costs in the manager's department might decrease. Fixed costs go up while variable costs go down. The effective use of cost SBUs requires top management to anticipate and prevent cost shifting by requiring an analysis and justification of equipment upgrades and any changes in work patterns that affect other departments. Top management's attention to cost shifting is particularly important because the foundation of strategic performance measurement systems is an SBU manager who is responsible only for controllable costs. The focus on controllable costs is necessary to achieve the objectives of motivation and fairness. However, as explained earlier, excessive focus on controllable costs can result in dysfunctional cost shifting.

Cost-shifting issues also arise in not-for-profit organizations. For example, many governmental units do not distinguish between direct and indirect costs in their performance reporting. This can lead to poor decision making, as illustrated by the U.S. Forest Service:

> Inappropriate accounting measures allegedly caused the United States Forest Service to cut down trees that an ordinary business would have left standing . . . the Forest Service is not charged for the cost of constructing roads into remote areas to reach the lumber. The Forest Service's response to these measures of its performance is to cut down a great deal of lumber and to construct costly, intricate roads to reach it. The Service already has 342,000 miles of logging roads and plans to build yet another 262,000 by 2040. Critics contend that these roads are constructed to reach increasingly poor quality timber and that they inflict considerable environmental damage. They recommend new measures of its performance that account for the full cost of logging, including the cost of raising the timber, building the roads to reach it, and replacing it.[6]

The Forest Service's failure to identify the full cost of the logging, including the costs of the roads as well as the logging of the trees, can cause poor decision making.

Another incentive for cost shifting in not-for-profit entities is that certain services are reimbursed on a cost-plus basis while others are charged as fixed fees. Cost shifting in this context means allocating joint costs (see Chapter 12) from the fixed-charge to the cost-plus services. The cost shifting can be done in a variety of ways. A number of hospitals, for example, have shifted the costs of Medicare and Medicaid (fixed-fee) patients to private (cost-plus) patients.[7] Cost shifting undermines the motivation and fairness of the performance evaluation systems within these hospitals.

In a related example, cost shifting can occur *within* the hospital:

> Kevin Schulman, a medical economist at Georgetown Medical School, tells of a hospital where the radiology department decided to save money by sending out only one copy of a report, instead of separate copies to each care provider. It won a hospital efficiency award, while the medical clinic in the same hospital had to hire someone to reproduce that lone report for all the doctors who needed a copy.[8]

The cost shifting was from one department in the hospital to another rather than from one type of patient to another.

Excessive Short-Term Focus

Another strategic issue is the broad concern that many performance measurement systems focus excessively on annual cost figures; this motivates managers to attend only to short-term costs and to neglect long-term strategic issues. This concern is an important reason why cost SBUs should use nonfinancial strategic considerations as well as financial information on costs.[9]

---

[6] Regina E. Herzlinger and Denise Nitterhouse, *Financial Accounting and Managerial Control for Nonprofit Organizations* (Cincinnati: South Western Publishing, 1994), p. 419; also, Cox et al., "Responsibility Accounting and Operational Control for Governmental Units," *Accounting Horizons,* June 1989, pp. 38–48, show the results of a survey of 830 governmental units in the United States and Canada with a principal finding that the strategic performance measurement systems in three-fourths of these units did not distinguish between controllable and uncontrollable costs.

[7] See Leslie Eldenburg and Sanjay Kallapur, "Changes in Hospital Service Mix and Cost Allocations in Response to Changes in Medicare Reimbursement Schemes," *Journal of Accounting and Economics,* May 1997, pp. 31–51.

[8] "Hospitals Attack a Crippler: Paper," *Business Week,* February 21, 1994, pp. 104–6.

[9] The problems caused by an excessive focus on short-term costs and profits are illustrated in "Corporate Liposuction Can Have Nasty Side Effects," *Business Week,* July 17, 2000, pp. 74–75.

Role of Budget Slack

A third strategic issue in implementing cost-based SBUs is to recognize both the negative and the positive roles of budget slack. **Budget slack** is the difference between budgeted and expected performance. The majority of SBUs have some amount of slack, evidenced by a budgeted cost target that is somewhat easier to attain than is reasonably expected. Managers often plan for a certain amount of slack in their performance budgets to allow for unexpected unfavorable events. However, a significant amount of slack might result from SBU managers' attempts to make their performance goals easier and therefore indicate an overall lower level of performance than should have been achieved.

The positive view of slack is that it effectively addresses the decision-making and fairness objectives of performance evaluation. By limiting managers' exposure to environmental uncertainty, it reduces their relative risk aversion. The resulting evaluation therefore satisfies fairness, and the reduced risk helps the managers make decisions that are more nearly congruent with the goals of top management.

Implementing Cost SBUs in Departments

Production and Support Departments

The two methods for implementing cost SBUs for production and support departments are the discretionary-cost method and the engineered-cost method. These two methods have different underlying cost behavior and a different focus: inputs or outputs, respectively. When costs are predominantly fixed, an input-oriented planning focus is appropriate because fixed costs are not controllable in the short term. The planning approach is taken so that top management can effectively budget for expected costs in each discretionary-cost SBU; the focus is on beginning-of-period planning for expected costs rather than end-of-period evaluation of the amount of costs expended. In contrast, if costs are primarily variable and therefore controllable, an output-oriented approach, based on end-of-period evaluation of controllable costs, is appropriate. The input-oriented approach is called the **discretionary-cost method** because costs are considered to be largely uncontrollable and discretion is applied at the planning stage. The output-oriented approach is called the **engineered-cost method** since costs are variable and therefore "engineered," or controllable.

Another factor in choosing between discretionary-cost and engineered-cost SBUs is the complexity of the work environment. SBUs that have relatively ill-defined outputs (for instance, research and development) have less well-defined goals and are therefore more likely to be evaluated as discretionary-cost SBUs; SBUs for which the operations are well defined and the output goals are more clearly determined will have engineered-cost SBUs. See Exhibit 17.6.

Cost behavior in a production SBU is therefore important in choosing the cost SBU method. As explained in Chapter 3, the behavior of an activity measure depends on the level of analysis: the facility, the product, the batch of production, or the unit of production. Similarly, when studying a cost SBU, we must know on which level of analysis it operates. For example, costs in the engineering department are driven primarily by product-level activity measures: the number of new products or product changes. Also, costs in the inspection department are caused primarily by batch-level activity measures: the number of production runs or setups.

Relatively few cost drivers exist at the facility level because most of its costs are fixed and do not fluctuate with changes in production level, production mix, or product. Costs at the facility level have few cost drivers; therefore, most departments at this level are evaluated as discretionary-cost SBUs.

For cost SBUs at the unit, batch, and product levels, managers commonly implement the engineered-cost method based on the appropriate cost driver for that production activity. For example, for the engineering department where the cost driver is at the product level, the engineered-cost method uses the number of engineering changes to new and existing products as the cost driver and evaluates the performance of the engineering

EXHIBIT 17.6
SBUs for Production and
Support Departments

Discretionary-Cost Approach	Engineered-Cost Approach
Costs are mainly fixed, uncontrollable	Costs are mainly variable, controllable
Firms use an input-oriented planning focus	Firms use an output-oriented evaluation focus
Operations are ill-defined	Operations are well-defined
The focus is on planning	The focus is on evaluation

department on its costs for each engineering change completed. Similarly, for the inspection department where the cost driver is at the batch level (inspection is done for each batch), the appropriate cost SBU method is again the engineered-cost method, in which management reviews the cost incurred versus the number of batches inspected.

Some production departments are more difficult to classify as batch, product, or facility level. For example, the maintenance department can be viewed as a facility-level activity because much of the demand for maintenance is for plant and equipment that is not influenced by production level (units or batches). However, because the wear on equipment is greater at a higher level of production or for a larger number of batches, batch and unit cost drivers also can be appropriate. The choice of method depends in part on management's objectives. If management wants to motivate a reduction in maintenance use (because of rising maintenance costs or of overall budget constraints), the engineered-cost method is appropriate since it rewards cost reduction.[10] In contrast, if management is concerned about the low overall serviceability of plant and equipment (due perhaps to a prior lack of maintenance), the discretionary-cost method provides the proper incentive by reducing the maintenance manager's risk aversion and thereby motivating proper additional expenditures on maintenance.

Another option for management control of the engineering department or maintenance department is to treat each of them as profit SBUs and to charge users a price for their services. The effects of using a profit SBU method are added emphasis on cost control and an incentive for the SBU to provide quality service and perhaps seek markets outside the firm.[11]

General and Administrative Departments

Administrative support departments such as human resources, research and development, information technology services, and printing and duplicating are also commonly evaluated as cost SBUs. They seldom have a source of revenue, but the department managers control most of the costs, so the cost SBU method is appropriate. The choice of a discretionary-cost or engineered-cost method for these departments depends on the cost behavior in the department and on management's philosophy and objectives, as explained earlier. The proper choice of method might change over time. For example, when cost reduction is a key objective, the human resources department might be treated as an engineered-cost SBU for a time. Later it might be changed to a discretionary-cost SBU to motivate managers to focus on long-term goals such as the design of new employee bonus systems.

Cost behavior in administrative support SBUs is often a step-fixed cost, as illustrated in Exhibit 17.7. As clerical and/or service support personnel are added, labor costs increase in a step-fixed pattern. Suppose that one clerk is required to process 100 new employee applications per month and that each clerk is paid $1,200 per month. If the firm processes 250 applications per month, it needs three clerks at a total cost of $3,600 per month. If the discretionary-cost method is used, the supervisor of personnel management

---

[10] Note, however, that Robin Cooper and Robert S. Kaplan, in "Activity-Based Systems: Measuring the Costs of Resource Usage," *Accounting Horizons,* September 1992, explain that methods such as the engineered-cost method do not necessarily achieve a reduction in costs unless the supply of resources is reduced following a reduction in the usage of resources.

[11] For example, some hospital departments such as radiology that are commonly viewed as cost SBUs can also be viewed as profit SBUs when management sees their revenue-producing potential. See Ed Egger, "Market Memo: Hospitals Should Look at Radiology as a Profit Center," *Health Care Strategic Management,* February 2000.

REAL-WORLD FOCUS   Outsourcing Allows Firms to Focus on Core Competencies

BP Amoco recently announced a $1.1 billion agreement with Price-waterhouseCoopers (PWC) in which PWC will provide much of the U.S.–based accounting and transaction-processing activities for BP Amoco. The change is expected to reduce BP's accounting costs by 10 to 20 percent. Moreover, it will allow BP to focus on its strategic business plans and core competencies. Similarly, GMAC Mortgage Corp. uses outsourcing to manage the firm's travel arrangements and to manage inventory.

Owens Corning, manufacturer of glass fiber, have outsourced the employee time and expense-reporting systems to reduce cost and allow employees to concentrate on core competencies. Many firms choose to outsource some part of the human resources function; the trends in outsourcing are noted in the publication, *Human Resources Outsourcing Today* (hrotoday.com/).

Sometimes outsourcing is to seek outside expertise. For example, many firms are now outsourcing security services, especially after

the tragedy of 9/11. Firms now look to security experts such as Krull, Inc., or Visionics Corp. to provide effective security measures. Cost pressures are the reason for hiring other firms. For example, Nokia, Motorola, and Ericsson are using outsourcing of manufacturing to save costs as the cell phone business becomes increasingly a commodity business driven by cost cutting. In sum, according to a recent survey of The Outsourcing Institute (outsourcing_institute.com), the top two reasons that firms go to outsourcing is to save on operating costs and to focus the company's operations on core activities.

Based on information in Charles E. Davis, Elizabeth B. Davis, and Lee Ann Moore, "Outsourcing the Procurement through Payable Process," *Management Accounting*, July 1998, pp. 38–44; "BP Amoco Is Set to Outsource Accounting in $1.1 Billion Deal," *The Wall Street Journal*, November 10, 1999; Tim Kearney, "Why Outsourcing Is In," *Strategic Finance*, January 2000, pp. 34–38; Louis Lavelle, "Professional Services," *Business Week*, January 14, 2002, p. 122; Stephen Baker, "Outsourcing Alone Won't Save Nokia's Rivals," *Business Week*, February 12, 2001, p. 38.

EXHIBIT 17.7
Step-Fixed Administrative Support Costs: Discretionary Cost versus Engineered Cost

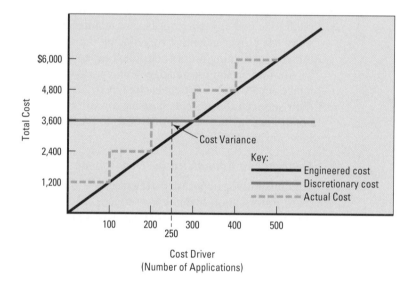

is likely to have negotiated for three clerks *at the beginning of the year*, and therefore the budget is $3,600 and there is no meaningful *ex post* evaluation. The discretionary-cost method is represented by the horizontal line in Exhibit 17.7.

Recognizing that processing each application in effect costs $12 ($1,200/100), management might choose to use an engineered-cost method that evaluates the personnel department manager by comparing the budget of $3,000 (250 applications times $12 per application) to the actual expenditure of $3,600. Because slack or overcapacity can exist due to the nature of the step-fixed cost, an unfavorable cost variance is likely; only when the operation is exactly at one of the full-capacity points (100, 200, 300 . . .) will there be no variance. Therefore, the interpretation of the cost variances must include both the productivity of labor and the underutilization of labor due to excess capacity.

Outsourcing Cost SBUs

Outsourcing is the term used to describe a firm's decision to have a service or product currently provided by a support department supplied by an outside firm in the future. For example, H. J. Heinz, Eastman-Kodak, and the Vatican in Rome are among the

A number of large firms, including Eastman Kodak, Xerox, and governmental units such as the U.S. Marine Corps and the State of Connecticut are outsourcing significant parts of their information technology (IT) operations. Approximately 20 percent of the largest U.S. firms have already outsourced this operation, according to current estimates, and the trend is for that percentage to increase. Some of the outsourcing is to application service providers (ASPs), which provide a wide range of

IT services (e-mail, transaction processing, and more), often over the Internet. In other cases, the IT tasks have been taken over by large consulting firms such as Accenture, IBM, Electronic Data Systems, and Computer Science Corp. Why are these firms outsourcing their IT function? How does outsourcing IT make the firm more competitive? (Refer to Comments on Cost Management in Action at the end of the chapter.)

organizations that have chosen to outsource information technology (IT) needs. These firms have found that the use of an outside source is an effective way to obtain reliable service at a reasonable cost without the risk of obsolescence and other potential management problems. It can also enable a firm to gain access to new technologies. The cost of outsourcing is that the firm loses control over a potentially strategic resource and must rely on the outside firm's competence and continued performance. For this reason, firms analyze this decision thoroughly, select the vendors carefully, and develop precisely worded contracts. Outsourcing is an option increasingly used by many firms for their IT, printing and duplicating, engineering, and other service needs.

Cost Allocation

A pervasive issue when using cost SBUs is how to allocate the jointly incurred costs of service departments, such as IT, engineering, human resources, or maintenance, to the departments using the service. The various cost allocation methods are explained in Chapter 12. The choice of method affects the amount of cost allocated to each cost SBU and therefore is critical in effective cost SBU evaluation. For example, if the cost of maintenance is allocated based on the square feet of space in each production department, the departments with more space have higher costs. The incentives of such an allocation method are not clear because the production departments likely cannot control the amount of space they occupy. Alternatively, if maintenance costs are allocated on the basis of the number of maintenance jobs requested, the production departments can control their allocated maintenance costs by controlling usage.

The criteria for choosing the cost allocation method, as explained in Chapter 12, are the same as the objectives for management control: to (1) motivate managers to exert a high level of effort, (2) provide an incentive for managers to make decisions consistent with top management's goals, and (3) provide a basis for a fair evaluation of managers' performance. For example, when management wants to encourage production departments to reduce the amount of maintenance, allocation based on usage provides the desired incentive. In contrast, if management wants the departments to increase the use of maintenance to improve the serviceability of the equipment, the most effective incentive might be not to allocate the maintenance cost or perhaps to subsidize it in some way.

Dual allocation

is a cost allocation method that separates fixed and variable costs. Variable costs are directly traced to user departments, and fixed costs are allocated on some logical basis.

A useful guide in choosing the cost allocation method, in addition to the three criteria just explained, is to use dual allocation. **Dual allocation** is a cost allocation method that separates fixed and variable costs. Variable costs are directly traced to user departments, and fixed costs are allocated on some logical basis. For example, the variable costs of maintenance, such as supplies, labor, and parts, can be traced to each maintenance job and charged directly to the user department. This approach is both fair and positively motivating. In contrast, the fixed costs of the maintenance department (training, manuals, equipment, etc.) that cannot be traced to each maintenance job should be allocated to the user departments using a basis that fairly reflects each department's use of the service. For example, those departments whose maintenance jobs require more expensive equipment might be allocated a higher proportion of the maintenance department's fixed costs.

To improve dual allocation, indirect costs could be traced to cost SBUs using activity-based costing (Chapter 4). This approach tends to produce the most accurate cost assignment and therefore would be the most motivating and fairest to the SBU managers.[12]

Revenue Strategic Business Units

Revenue drivers
are the factors that affect sales volume, such as price changes, promotions, discounts, customer service, changes in product features, delivery dates, and other value-added factors.

Management commonly uses revenue drivers in evaluating the performance of revenue SBUs. **Revenue drivers** in manufacturing firms are the factors that affect sales volume, such as price changes, promotions, discounts, customer service, changes in product features, delivery dates, and other value-added factors. In service firms, the revenue drivers focus on many of the same factors, with a special emphasis on the quality of the service—is it courteous, helpful, and timely?

The marketing department can be viewed as both a revenue SBU and a cost SBU. The revenue SBU responsibility stems from the fact that the marketing department manages the revenue-generating process. The marketing manager must therefore report revenues, typically by product line, and sometimes by sales area and salesperson. Top management uses the revenue reports to assess the performance of the marketing manager in achieving desired sales goals. Often this analysis is performed at a detailed level to determine the separate effects of changes in price, quantity, and sales mix on the overall sales dollars.[13]

Order-getting costs
are expenditures to advertise and promote the product.

The marketing department also can be a cost SBU. In the pharmaceuticals, cosmetics, software, games and toys, and specialized electrical equipment industries, the cost of advertising and promotion is a significant portion of the total cost of producing and selling the product. The marketing department incurs two types of costs: order-getting and order-filling costs. **Order-getting costs** are expenditures to advertise and promote the product. They include samples, demonstrations, advertising and promotion, travel and entertainment expenses, commissions, and marketing research. Because showing how these costs have directly affected sales is often difficult, managers frequently view order-getting costs as a discretionary-cost SBU and focus on planning these expenditures rather than evaluating their effectiveness. In contrast, other firms have developed extensive analyses of order-getting costs to identify the most effective activities for improving sales. Such additional analyses might consist of statistical analyses of general economic data and the firm's sales and operating data, with operational analyses consisting of ratios of sales per salesperson, sales per number of follow-ups on inquiries, and returns and allowances per product and salesperson.

Order-filling costs
include freight, warehousing, packing and shipping, and collections.

A second category of marketing costs is **order-filling costs**, which include freight, warehousing, packing and shipping, and collections. These costs have a relatively clear relationship to sales volume and as a result, they can often be effectively managed as an engineered-cost SBU. The engineered-cost method could be implemented by developing appropriate operating ratios—average shipping cost per item, average freight cost per sales dollar, and so on.

Profit Strategic Business Units

The profit SBU manager's goal is to earn profits. A key advantage of the profit SBU is that it brings the manager's incentives into congruence with those of top management: to improve the firm's profitability. Moreover, the profit SBU should also motivate in-

---

[12] For an example of how activity-based costing is used to allocate costs for the cost and profit units of an auto retailer, see Jonathan M. Booth and Bala V. Balachandran, "Using ABM to Identify Value: An Automotive Retailer Case Study," *Journal of Cost Management*, September–October 1999, pp. 4–10.

[13] This is explained in Chapter 15. Also, some marketing managers have a relatively broad view of the responsibility of the marketing function, which includes responsibility for sales and cost of sales. This is suggested, for example, by the Institute of Marketing's definition: "Marketing is the management process for identifying, anticipating, and satisfying customer requirements profitably."

dividual managers because by earning profits, the managers are contributing directly to the firm's success. For these reasons, the profit SBU meets the management control objectives of motivation and decision making explained earlier.

Strategic Role of Profit SBUs

Three strategic issues cause firms to choose profit SBUs rather than cost or revenue SBUs. First, profit SBUs provide the incentive for the desired coordination among the marketing, production, and support functions. The handling of rush orders is a good example. A cost SBU would view a rush order unfavorably because of the potential added cost associated with the disruption of the production process, but a revenue SBU would view it favorably. If they are in separate cost and revenue SBUs, the production manager has little incentive to meet with the marketing manager to coordinate the rush order. In contrast, if the production SBU is a profit SBU, its manager accepts the order if it improves the SBU's profit, a decision consistent with the goals of both the production SBU and top management.

A second reason that firms use profit SBUs rather than cost SBUs is to motivate managers to consider their product as marketable to outside customers. Production departments that provide products and services primarily for other internal departments might find that they can market their products or services profitably outside the firm, or that the firm might be able to purchase the product or service at a lower price outside the firm.

The third reason for choosing profit SBUs is to motivate managers to develop new ways to make profit from their products and services. For example, an increasing number of companies find that service contracts (for home entertainment equipment, business equipment, appliances, and so on) provide a significant source of profit in addition to the sale of the product. In the software industry, revenues from providing service and upgrades can be as important as the software's original sales price. Coordination between marketing, production, and design is critical for the success of these efforts, and since many of these contracts are for three years or more, the expected future costs of the service must be carefully analyzed. In a profit SBU, managers have the incentive to develop creative new products and services because the profit SBU evaluation rewards the incremental profits.

The Contribution Income Statement

The **contribution income statement** is based on the contribution margin developed for each profit SBU and for each relevant group of profit SBUs.

A common form of profit SBU evaluation is the **contribution income statement,** which is based on the contribution margin developed for each profit SBU and for each relevant group of profit SBUs. The contribution income statement is illustrated in Exhibit 17.8 for Machine Tools, Inc. (MTI). MTI has two operating divisions, A and B, each of which is considered a profit SBU. The level of detail at which the contribution income statement is developed varies depending on management's needs. For a firm with a limited number of products, the level of detail in Exhibit 17.8 is common. For a firm with several products, a more extensive contribution income statement would be required to provide sufficient detail for management analysis.

This contribution income statement is an extension of the income statement illustrated in Exhibits 9.14 and 9.15 of Chapter 9. Chapter 9 introduces the idea of traceable fixed costs; that is, fixed costs can be traced directly to a product line or production unit. Exhibit 9.15 shows both contribution margin and contribution margin less traceable fixed costs, **contribution by SBU (CSBU)**. The concept of CSBU is important because it measures *all* costs traceable to the individual profit SBUs. CSBU is a more complete and fair measure of performance than either the contribution margin or profit.

The **contribution by SBU (CSBU)** measures *all* costs traceable to, and therefore controllable by, the individual profit SBUs.

This chapter expands the contribution income statement by distinguishing controllable and noncontrollable fixed costs. **Controllable fixed costs** are fixed costs that the profit SBU manager can influence in approximately a year or less. That is, the manager typically budgets these costs in the annual budget; some of them involve contractual relationships for a year or less. Examples include advertising; sales promotion; certain

Controllable fixed costs are those fixed costs that the profit SBU manager can influence in approximately a year or less.

EXHIBIT 17.8 Machine Tools, Inc. Contribution Income Statement (000s omitted)

	Company as a Whole	Company Breakdown into Two Divisions		Breakdown of Division B by Product			
		Division A	Division B	Not Traceable	Product 1	Product 2	Product 3
Net revenues	$2,000	$600	$1,400		$400	$700	$300
Variable costs	900	200	700		100	350	250
Contribution margin	$1,100	$400	$ 700		$300	$350	$ 50
Controllable fixed costs	250	100	150	$ 25	25	100	0
Controllable margin	$ 850	$300	$ 550	(25)	$275	$250	$ 50
Noncontrollable fixed costs	400	120	280	20	10	130	120
Contribution by SBU	$ 450	$180	$ 270	$(45)	$265	$120	$ (70)
Untraceable costs	200						
Operating income	$ 250						

Noncontrollable fixed costs
are those that are not controllable
within a year's time, usually
including facilities-related costs
such as depreciation, taxes, and
insurance.

Controllable margin
is determined by subtracting short-
term controllable fixed costs from
the contribution margin.

engineering, data processing, and research projects; and management consulting. In contrast, **noncontrollable fixed costs** are those that are not controllable within a year's time; usually they include facilities-related costs such as depreciation, taxes, and insurance.

As illustrated in Exhibit 17.8, the firm develops a useful measure of the profit SBU manager's short-term performance by subtracting controllable fixed costs from the contribution margin to determine the **controllable margin.** In contrast, to measure the manager's performance in managing both short- and long-term costs, the CSBU measure is most appropriate since it includes both short-term and long-term fixed costs.

One complication in completing the contribution income statement is that some costs that are not traceable at a detailed level are traceable at a higher level of aggregation. The untraceable costs column in the income statement represents costs traceable to division B but not traceable to any of the product lines. For example, the $25,000 controllable fixed costs might consist of the cost of advertising that was arranged at the division level to benefit all three products, so it is not traceable to any one product.

In addition to providing useful measures of the manager's performance in managing costs, the contribution income statement can be used to determine whether a profit SBU should be dropped or retained, much like our contribution margin analysis in Exhibit 9.15. The analysis is now enhanced because of our ability to distinguish controllable and noncontrollable fixed costs. For example, using the analysis in Exhibit 17.8, MTI can determine that if it drops product 3, the short-term effect will be to reduce profit by $50,000, the amount of the controllable margin. All costs involved in the determination of the controllable margin are avoidable within a period of one year. Taking the longer-term view, suppose that MTI could ultimately save an additional $120,000 of noncontrollable fixed costs by dropping product 3. Then, in the long term, MTI can save a net of $70,000 by dropping product 3, the amount of the contribution by SBU (CSBU) for product 3.

Variable Costing versus Full Costing

The use of the contribution income statement often is called *variable costing* because it separates variable and fixed costs. Only variable costs are included in determining the cost of sales and the contribution margin. In contrast, full costing is a cost system that includes fixed cost in product cost and cost of sales. Full costing is the conventional costing system because it is required by financial reporting standards and by the Internal Revenue Service for determining taxable income.

The advantage of variable costing is that it meets the three objectives of management control systems by showing separately those costs that can be traced to, and controlled

EXHIBIT 17.9A
Comparison of Absorption and
Variable Costing

Panel 1 Data Summary	Period 1	Period 2	
Units			
Beginning inventory	0	40	
Price	$100	$100	
Sold	60	140	
Produced	100	100	
Unit variable costs			
Manufacturing	$30	$30	
Selling and administrative costs	$5	$5	
Fixed costs			Per unit
Manufacturing	$4,000	$4,000	$40
Selling and administrative costs	$1,200	$1,200	

Panel 2

Period 1 Income Statement	Full Costing		Variable Costing	
Sales (60 × $100)		$6,000		$6,000
Cost of goods sold				
Beginning inventory	$0		$0	
+ Cost of goods produced	7,000		3,000	
	(= 100 × $70)		(= 100 × $30)	
= Cost of goods available for sale	7,000		3,000	
− Ending inventory*	2,800		1,200	
	(= 40 × $70)		(= 40 × $30)	
= Cost of goods sold		4,200		1,800
Less: Variable selling and administrative costs		N/A		300
Gross margin		**$1,800**		
Contribution margin				**$3,900**
Less other costs				
Less: Fixed manufacturing costs	N/A		$4,000	
Less: Selling and administrative costs				
Variable	300		N/A	
Fixed	1,200		1,200	
Total other costs		1,500		5,200
Net income*		$ 300		$(1,300)

Recap
Difference in net income = $300 − $(1,300) = $1,600
Difference in ending inventory = $2,800 − $1,200 = $1,600 (or 40 units × $40/unit = $1,600)

*Notice that the difference in net income between full and variable costing is the same as the difference in ending inventory.

by, each SBU. In this section, we see an additional reason for using variable costing: Although net income determined using full costing is affected by changes in inventory levels, net income using variable costing is not affected. Exhibit 17.9A and B shows how using full costing affects net income.

Panel 1 in Exhibit 17.9A shows the data used in the illustration, including units produced and sold and costs for two periods. Panel 2 shows both the full and variable cost income statements for the first of two periods. Two periods are used to show the differences for both possible cases, increasing or decreasing inventory. In the first period, inventory increases; in the second period, it decreases. Exhibit 17.9B shows the comparison of the two income statements for period 2.

In period 1, inventory increases by 40 units because production of 100 units exceeds sales of 60 units. Inventory decreases by the same amount in period 2. Using full costing, the unit product cost is $30 variable plus $40 fixed, or $70 per unit in both periods. The $70 unit cost is used to calculate the cost of goods sold on the income

EXHIBIT 17.9B
Comparison of Full and Variable Costing

Period 2 Income Statement				
Sales (140 × $100)		$14,000		$14,000
Cost of goods sold				
Beginning inventory (from period one)	2,800		1,200	
+ Cost of goods produced (for 100 units, same as period 1)	7,000		3,000	
= Cost of goods available for sale	9,800		4,200	
− Ending inventory	0		0	
= Cost of goods sold		9,800		4,200
Less: Variable selling and administrative		N/A		700
Gross margin		**$ 4,200**		
Contribution margin				**$ 9,100**
Less: Other costs				
Less: Fixed manufacturing costs	N/A		4,000	
Less: Selling and administrative costs				
Variable	700		N/A	
Fixed	1,200		1,200	
Total other costs		1,900		5,200
Net income		**$ 2,300**		**$ 3,900**

Recap
Difference in net income = $3,900 − $2,300 = $1,600
Difference in beginning inventory = $2,800 − $1,200 = $1,600

statements in periods 1 and 2 for absorption costing. The selling and administrative costs ($5 variable and $1,200 fixed) are deducted after gross margin to determine the net income of $300 in period 1 and $2,300 in period 2.

The variable costing income statement uses only variable cost to determine product cost. The cost of sales and inventory figures are determined using a variable manufacturing cost of $30 per unit. To calculate the total contribution margin, the variable selling and administrative costs of $5 per unit sold are deducted along with the $30 variable cost of sales per unit. The result is a total contribution margin of $3,900 in period 1 and $9,100 in period 2. In variable costing, all fixed costs (both manufacturing fixed cost of $4,000 and selling and administration fixed costs of $1,200) are deducted from the contribution margin, to get a $1,300 loss in period 1 and $3,900 profit in period 2.

The difference in net income in period 1 for full and variable costing is $1,600 ($300 profit compared to a $1,300 loss), which is exactly the amount of fixed cost put into the increase in inventory under full costing ($1,600 = 40 units × $40 per unit fixed cost). Note that the amount of ending inventory in period 1 differs by $1,600 ($2,800 for absorption cost versus $1,200 for variable costing). This amount is also the difference in net income for variable and full costing for both periods 1 and 2, when inventory decreases by 40 units. The useful guide then is that *full costing net income exceeds variable costing net income (by the amount of fixed cost in the inventory change) when inventory increases, and variable costing net income is higher than full costing net income when inventory decreases.*

The important point is that variable costing is not affected by the change in inventory because all fixed costs are deducted from income in the period in which they occur; fixed costs are not included in inventory so that inventory changes do not affect net income. For this reason, variable costing net income can be considered a more reliable measure and is preferable for use in strategic performance measurement. When full costing is used (as is required for financial reporting), the management accountant must use special caution in interpreting the amount of net income and attempt to determine what portion of profit, if any, might be due to inventory changes. This is especially important if net income is used as a basis for performance evaluation, as it is in profit SBUs.

Strategic Performance Measurement and the Balanced Scorecard

The sacred obligation of senior leadership:
  Vision: What will it be?
  Goals: What four or five things must we do to get there?
  Alignment: Translate the work of each person into an alignment with the goals.
  Soichiro Honda, Founder of Honda Motor Company

LEARNING OBJECTIVE 5

Explain the role of the balanced scorecard in strategic performance measurement.

Cost, revenue, and profit SBUs are widely used methods to achieve strategic performance measurement. A common characteristic of these SBUs in practice is that they use little or no nonfinancial information. However, a complete strategic performance evaluation necessarily attends to all critical success factors of the business, including many nonfinancial factors. A useful approach for a complete strategic performance evaluation is to include both financial and nonfinancial factors for the SBU using the balanced scorecard. The balanced scorecard measures the SBU's performance in four key perspectives: (1) customer satisfaction, (2) financial performance, (3) internal business processes, and (4) learning and innovation. Cost, revenue, and profit SBUs focus on the financial dimension. The main concept of the balanced scorecard is that no single measure can properly evaluate the SBU's progress to strategic success. Rather, multiple measures typically grouped in the four key perspectives provide the desired comprehensive evaluation of the SBU's performance. Moreover, by attending directly to the firm's critical success factors, the balanced scorecard effectively aligns the performance measurement/evaluation process to the firm's strategy.

A recent survey of 203 firms indicated that customer perspective measures of the balanced scorecard are highly valued by 85 percent of the executives of these firms; 82 percent see the financial measures as highly valuable. Operations perspective measures are highly valued by 79 percent, and employee satisfaction/learning and innovation perspective measures are highly valued by more than 50 percent.[14] These results are strong support for the importance of the strategic approach of the balanced scorecard.

Unfortunately, not all balanced scorecards used by firms are utilized in evaluating and rewarding managers. A recent survey of 60 firms that use the balanced scorecard shows that about 50 percent of them employed the scorecard in evaluating managers, and of those, about 33 percent used it in determining compensation.[15] The reason that scorecards are utilized less often in performance evaluation might be that they are more difficult to compare *across* SBUs. Each SBU has its own scorecard; thus, the scorecard evaluation is more likely based on progress relative to the prior year or to a budget than on the more common, compare-across-all-managers approach. Other implementation issues related to the balanced scorecard for performance evaluation include these:

- Many large firms have installed extensive computer systems called *enterprise resource planning* systems (ERPs). They provide an information system base that stores the detailed information for the balanced scorecard. Firms without an ERP might have difficulty developing and maintaining the data needed for the scorecard.
- In contrast to financial data that are subject to financial audit and control systems, much of the nonfinancial information used in the scorecard is not subject to control or audit. Thus, the reliability and accuracy of some of the nonfinancial data could be questionable.

---

[14] Christopher D. Ittner and David F. Larcker, "Innovations in Performance Measurement: Trends and Research Implications," *Journal of Management Accounting Research,* 1998, p. 207, citing study by J. H. Lingle and W. A. Schiemann, "From Balanced Scorecard to Strategic Gauges: Is Measurement Worth It?" *Management Review,* March 1996, pp. 56–61.

[15] Ittner and Larcker, "Innovation in Performance Measurement," p. 222. Note, however, that a recent survey reported that of 214 firms surveyed, 88 percent are considering linking the balanced scorecard to compensation. See Kaplan and Norton, *The Strategy-Focused Organization,* p. 253.

EXHIBIT 17.10
Strategy Map Links Balanced Scorecard Perspectives

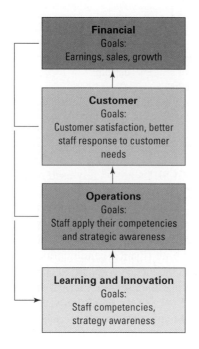

- The performance reviews of managers occur at regular intervals—usually every quarter or every year—which fits well with the typical firm's preparation of financial information quarterly and annually. In contrast, the nonfinancial information is often prepared on a weekly or daily basis for effective use in operations and decision making. This variance in preparation cycles can complicate the nature and timing of reviews.

- Typically, all financial data used by the cost or profit SBUs are developed internally, using well-developed information systems. In contrast, some of the most valuable nonfinancial information, such as customer surveys, are developed external to the firm, which creates additional issues regarding the timeliness and the reliability of this nonfinancial information.

A **strategy map** uses the balanced scorecard to describe the firm's strategy in detail by using cause-and-effect diagrams.

Whether or not the balanced scorecard is used for performance evaluation, it is a powerful method to guide managers in achieving the firm's strategic goals and in evaluating its progress to these goals. To contribute to these objectives, Kaplan and Norton have developed the concept of the **strategy map**, which uses the balanced scorecard to describe the firm's strategy in detail by using cause-and-effect diagrams. A simple strategy map is illustrated in Exhibit 17.10. The strategy map links the four scorecard perspectives, showing how measurable goals within each perspective contribute to performance at the next perspective. The map begins with the learning and innovation perspective, which includes the goals—staff competencies, strategy awareness, and technology infrastructure—that are necessary for learning and innovation to take place. The goals contribute directly to the internal business process (operations) perspective, in which the staff apply their competencies and strategic awareness and utilize the technology infrastructure. In a similar way, the goals in the operations perspective support the goals of the customer perspective. The goals within the customer perspective support the financial perspective. As each firm has a different balanced scorecard, so too it has a different strategy map. The strategy map is a detailed view of how the firm achieves its strategic goals, showing the interactions between the scorecard's perspectives.[16]

The strategy map also reinforces the idea that financial performance and shareholder value are the ultimate goals for most applications of the balanced scorecard. The other perspectives contribute directly to the ultimate financial goals. Recent research shows

---

[16] Kaplan and Norton illustrate the strategy maps for several firms, including Mobil and the city of Charlotte, NC. Kaplan and Norton, *The Strategy-Focused Organization*, pp. 42–43, 139.

REAL-WORLD FOCUS   Research and Development: Strategically Critical but Difficult to Evaluate

Effective use of research and development (R&D) is an important part of any firm's competitive strategy. Some firms take an "incrementalist" approach to R&D, continually striving to add value to their products and services. Other firms take the opposite approach by looking specifically for "breakthrough" results from R&D. The breakthrough results are those that fundamentally change the nature of the products, the services, and the competition in the industry. An example of a breakthrough result is General Electric's digital X-ray technology, first sold in 1996, which uses digital imaging to replace the conventional film-based technology. An example of a breakthrough approach is Xerox, whose famed Palo Alto Research Facility has been recognized for its significant research accomplishments.

Many firms employ both approaches. Some argue that a firm needs to use both R&D strategies: the incrementalist approach that focuses on continually improving existing products and the breakthrough approach that develops fundamental changes. The incrementalist R&D projects help to keep the current product lines competitive while the breakthrough projects hold the promise of a successful future.

Management of any R&D project is difficult, but breakthrough projects are especially difficult to evaluate because of the extensive uncertainty surrounding them. It is clear, however, that breakthrough projects must be evaluated differently than the incrementalist projects. They require more patience, and the pressure of short-term

cost reports is inappropriate. Nor can these projects be evaluated by comparing the amount spent on research (say, relative to total sales) to that of other firms in the industry. Emphasis must be on the researchers' skills, the funding levels, and other factors that can aid the progress of the research. For example, academic research at Rensselaer Polytechnic Institute shows that the most successful R&D researchers have wide-ranging networks in the research community. The skills of the researchers, the funding level, and the other factors can be evaluated in a balanced scorecard approach.

Recent research involving 75 industrial design managers reported that the firms surveyed use various financial and nonfinancial measures to evaluate new product development, although managers in these firms reported that relatively few of these measures reflect the key aspects of their firms' strategies. Clearly, R&D activities are difficult to evaluate, although they are critical to the strategies of many firms.

Sources: Based on Chris Sandlund, "Paradise Lost?" *Business2.com,* April 3, 2001, pp. 50–53; Julie Hertenstein and Marjorie B. Platt, "Performance Measures and Management Control in New Product Development," *Accounting Horizons,* September 2000, pp. 303–23; Peter Coy, "Research Labs Get Real: It's about Time," *Business Week,* November 6, 2000, p. 51; "R&D by the Numbers," *Business Week,* December 6, 1999, p. 86; and "Getting to Eureka!" *Business Week,* November 10, 1997.

that the nonfinancial measures in the other perspectives are in fact good predictors of financial performance.[17] The strategy map also emphasizes the important point that, by describing the firm's strategy in some detail, the balanced scorecard can also be used as a *means for developing strategy* and evaluating progress to achieving strategy.

The use of the balanced scorecard for developing strategy and evaluating progress in achieving it is illustrated by information regarding a food ingredients company taken from a recent study. The firm was actively involved in implementing the balanced scorecard at the time of the study, and management agreed to discuss its strategic goals, the relative importance of these goals (ranked by scorecard perspective), and the key performance measures for evaluating progress toward these goals (see Exhibit 17.11). The firm's perspectives are shown in order of importance from top to bottom in the exhibit.

We can infer the firm's strategy from reviewing Exhibit 17.11. The firm puts the financial perspective first and emphasizes market growth. This makes sense for a company in a commodity-type industry (food ingredients) where profit margins are small and sales volume is important. Cost control is also important for profitability, as noted in the strategic goals within both the customer and internal perspectives. In effect, the exhibit shows the outline from which a strategy map can be developed. Goals in the learning and growth perspective support the goals in the internal perspective, which in turn support the goals in the customer and financial perspective, as shown by the arrows in Exhibit 17.11.

[17] See for example, Rajiv D. Banker, Gordon Potter, and Dhinu Srinivasan, "An Empirical Investigation of an Incentive Plan that Includes Nonfinancial Measures," *The Accounting Review,* January 2000, pp. 65–92; and Christopher D. Ittner and David F. Larcker, "Are Nonfinancial Measures Leading Indicators of Financial Performance?" *Journal of Accounting Research,* 1998, pp. 1–35.

EXHIBIT 17.11 Strategic Goals and Scorecard Measures for a Food Ingredients Company

Goals	Measures
Financial Perspective	
Capture an increasing share of market growth.	Company growth versus industry growth
Secure the base business while remaining the preferred supplier to our customers.	Volume trend by line of business; revenue trend line of business; gross margin
Expand aggressively in global markets.	Ratio of North American sales to international sales
Commercialize a continuous stream of profitable new ingredients and services.	Percent of sales from products launched within five years; gross profit from new products
Customer Perspective	
Become the lowest-cost supplier.	Total cost of using our products and services relative to the total cost of using competitive products and services
Tailor products and services to meet local needs.	Cross-sell ratio
Expand those products and services that meet customers needs better than competitors do.	Percentage of products in R&D pipeline being test-marketed by our customers (percentage of pipeline value)
Increase customer satisfaction.	Customer surveys
Internal Perspective	
Maintain the lowest cost base in the industry.	Our total costs relative to number one competitor; inventory turns; plant utilization
Maintain consistently predictable production processes.	First-pass success rate
Continue to improve distribution efficiency.	Percentage of perfect orders
Build capability to screen and identify profitable products and services.	Change in pipeline economic value
Integrate acquisitions and alliances efficiently.	Revenues per salary dollar
Learning and Growth Perspective	
Link the overall strategy to the reward and recognition system.	Net income per dollar of variable pay
Foster a culture that supports innovation and growth.	Annual preparedness assessment; quarterly reports

Adapted from Chee W. Chow, Kamal M. Haddad, and James E. Williamson, "Applying the Balanced Scorecard to Small Companies," *Management Accounting*, August 1997.

Management Control in Service Firms and Not-for-Profit Organizations

LEARNING OBJECTIVE 6
Explain the role of strategic performance measurement in service firms and not-for-profit organizations.

Management control in service firms and not-for-profit organizations is commonly implemented in the form of a cost SBU or a profit SBU. As do manufacturing and retail firms, these organizations choose a cost SBU when the manager's critical mission is to control costs; a profit SBU is preferred when the department manager must manage both costs and revenues or, alternatively (in a not-for-profit), manage costs without exceeding budgeted revenues.

The most common type of SBU in service firms and not-for-profit organizations is the cost SBU. For example, the performance of a bank's consumer loan department often is monitored as a cost SBU, as illustrated in Exhibit 17.12. Note that the structure of the performance report is much like that of the profit SBU analysis in Exhibit 17.8. The difference is that the focus in Exhibit 17.12 is on costs, which are separated into variable costs such as labor and supplies, controllable fixed costs such as supervision salaries, and noncontrollable fixed costs such as data processing and facilities management. In addition, Exhibit 17.12 includes information regarding certain operating

REAL-WORLD FOCUS

Use of the Balanced Scorecard by The Mayo Clinic, the IRS, and the City of Charlotte, NC

The **Mayo Clinic** in Rochester, Minnesota, one of the most prestigious health care providers in the world, recently needed to measure performance in areas beyond the traditional financial and clinical productivity indicators. Various Mayo administrative and operating groups developed a balanced scorecard with six perspectives:

1. Customer satisfaction: internal and external customers.
2. Internal business processes: efficiency of operations.
3. Quality of service.
4. Continuous improvement efforts.
5. Public responsibility and social commitment.
6. Financial performance.

In developing the scorecard, the group learned a number of important lessons. First, its information systems infrastructure had to be improved to deal with the increased expectations developed from the balanced scorecard. Second, the balanced scorecard is really a process rather than a product. It requires continual commitment, critical thought, and an ongoing process of renewal.

The Internal Revenue Service (IRS) has adopted the balanced scorecard for performance management. The three perspectives of the scorecard are customer satisfaction, employee satisfaction, and operating results. The scorecard was developed to shift the focus of individual IRS managers from achieving specific targets to the overall mission, that is, to align the IRS performance measurement system with its strategic goals. The mission of the IRS is "to provide America's taxpayers top quality service by helping them understand and meet their tax responsibilities and by applying the tax law with integrity and fairness to all." The specific strategic goals of the IRS are developed by each organizational unit to support this broad mission. The details of the balanced scorecard are contained in the IRS *Internal Revenue Manual,* Part 1, Chapter 5 (http://irs.gov/irm/page/0,,id%3D26957,00.html).

In adopting the balanced scorecard, the **Charlotte, North Carolina,** City Council chose five key perspectives: community safety, transportation, economic development, neighborhoods, and restructuring government.

Sources: Jonathan W. Curtright, Steven C. Stolp-Smith, and Eric S. Edell, "Strategic Performance Management: Development of a Performance Measurement System at the Mayo Clinic," *Journal of Healthcare Management,* January–February 2000, pp. 58–68; See also, Dale A. Henderson, Bruce W. Chase, and Benjamin M. Woodson, "Performance Measures for NPOs," *Journal of Accountancy*, January 2002, pp. 63–68. Nancy Elliott and Lisa Schumacher, "Charlotte Adopts the Balanced Scorecard," *The American City & County,* October 1998, p. 32; Robert S. Kaplan and David P. Norton, *The Strategy-Focused Organization* (Boston: Harvard Business School Press, 2001).

EXHIBIT 17.12
Performance Report for the Consumer Loan Department August 31, 2004

Variable costs	
Direct labor	$23,446
Supplies	3,836
Controllable fixed costs	
Supervision salaries	15,339
Advertising	6,500
Fees and services	4,226
Other	766
Noncontrollable fixed costs	
Facilities	650
Data processing	2,200
Other	899
Total costs	$57,862
Operating performance	
Number of accounts at end of month	1,334
Number of new accounts	54
Number of closed accounts	22
Number of transactions processed	1,994
Number of inquiries processed	334

measures critical to the department's success: the number of new accounts, number of closed accounts, number of transactions processed, and number of inquiries handled. This information is used to evaluate department's performance over time and perhaps to compare its performance to that of related departments such as the mortgage loan department. Note that the report does not include the cost of funds provided for the loans since it is assumed that the department manager cannot control either the supply or the cost of those funds.

Summary

The principal focus of management control systems is strategic performance measurement. The goal of top management in using strategic performance measurement is to *motivate the managers* to provide a high level of effort, to *guide them to make decisions that are congruent with the goals of top management,* and to provide a basis for determining *fair compensation* for the managers.

A large number of management control systems are used in practice, including both formal and informal systems and individual or team-based systems. The chapter focuses on one type of formal control system at the individual level, the strategic performance measurement system.

Strategic performance measurement systems are implemented in four different forms, depending on the nature of the manager's responsibilities: the revenue SBU, cost SBU, profit SBU, and investment SBU.

The four types of SBUs are employed in manufacturing firms as well as service firms, not-for-profit and governmental organizations. Common cost SBUs in manufacturing firms are production and production-support departments. Cost SBUs often are evaluated as either engineered-cost SBUs or discretionary-cost SBUs. Discretionary-cost SBUs focus on planning desired cost levels; the engineered-cost SBUs focus on evaluation of achieved cost levels.

The marketing department can be either a cost SBU or a revenue SBU, or both. As a revenue SBU, the marketing department has goals for sales growth, as a cost SBU, there are goals for managing order-getting and order-filling costs.

The profit SBU is used when coordination between the marketing and production areas is needed, for example, in handling special orders or rush orders. Evaluation on profit provides the incentive for the departments to work together. Profit SBUs are also used to set a desirable competitive tone. All departments have the profit incentive to compete with other providers of the product or service, inside or outside the firm. The contribution margin income statement is an effective method for evaluating profit SBUs because it identifies each profit SBU's direct costs.

The contribution income statement is used for profit SBUs. It has the benefit of not being affected by changes in finished goods inventory. In contrast, the conventional income statement based on full costing is affected by inventory changes.

A key issue in the effective use of strategic performance measurement systems is the integration of strategic considerations into the evaluation. This requires an identification of the firm's critical success factors, and use of appropriate measurement and reporting of these factors, commonly in the form of a balanced scorecard. In many cases, a substantial portion of these factors is nonfinancial, including operating and economic data from sources external to the firm.

The different types of strategic performance measurement are used in service firms, not-for-profit organizations, and governmental units.

Key Terms

budget slack, *732*
contribution by SBU (CSBU), *737*
contribution income statement, *737*
controllable fixed costs, *737*
controllable margin, *738*
cost SBU, *729*
discretionary-cost method, *732*
dual allocation, *735*

employment contract, *724*
engineered-cost method, *732*
investment SBU, *730*
management control, *723*
noncontrollable fixed costs, *738*
operational control, *723*
order-filling costs, *736*
order-getting costs, *736*
performance evaluation, *723*

principal-agent model, *725*
profit SBU, *729*
revenue drivers, *736*
revenue SBU, *729*
strategic business unit (SBU), *724*
strategic performance measurement, *728*
strategy map, *742*

Comments on Cost Management in Action

Outsourcing Information Technology

In a recent survey of CFOs, 57 percent reported that their firms were outsourcing a portion or all of their information technology (IT) needs. The motivation for outsourcing IT is twofold. First, it can help to dramatically reduce the firm's overall cost of IT. Second, and perhaps most important, it helps the firm to keep up with advancing technology by partnering with an application service provider or consulting firm with a high level of expertise.

How does it make the firm more competitive? Consultants and analysts disagree on this point. Some argue that IT is a strategic resource in most industries and should be supported within the firm to achieve the desired integration of IT and business strategy. They point to firms such as Wal-Mart that have used IT to improve its strategic goal of low cost and low price. Similarly, ADP, Inc., and Levi Strauss have used IT to improve their competitive position through enhancements in customer service.

Others argue that the question is not *whether* to outsource but *which* of the IT activities to choose to outsource and *where* to outsource. For example, Xerox has an outsourcing arrangement with Electronic Data Systems (EDS) to handle its operational IT tasks while it maintains a partnership with the software developer Oracle to develop Xerox's strategic goals for IT. Also, IT outsourcing has gone global. Software engineers and database managers in India and the Philippines are getting the work for one-fifth to one-half the pay.

N. Venkatraman, a leading author on IT outsourcing, argues that IT should be viewed as a strategic SBU in either a cost, profit, investment, or service form (for Venkatraman, a "service" SBU puts customer service as top priority). Venkatraman proposes a simple formula for choosing the type of SBU based on two factors: (1) the degree to which the firm needs either operational efficiency or business capability from IT and (2) the degree of risk the firm is willing to bear. A low-risk firm that requires operational efficiency should choose the cost SBU form; a low-risk firm that requires business capability should use a service SBU. In contrast, a firm willing to accept risk and requiring business capability should choose an investment SBU because it will provide the desired long-term perspective for IT.

Self-Study Problem

(For solution, please turn to the end of the chapter.)

Discretionary-Cost and Engineered-Cost Methods

C. B. (Chuck) Davis is the manager of the claims processing department for Liberty Life Insurance Co. He has 12 clerks working for him to process approximately 900 claims per month. Each clerk earns a monthly salary of $2,400, including benefits. The number of claims varies somewhat, and, in recent years, it has been as low as 810 and as high as 1,020 per month. Chuck has argued with Liberty officials that his 12 clerks are not enough to handle 1,000 or more claims; he knows from a recent study of his department that it takes a well-trained clerk an average of 121 minutes to process a claim (processing time also varies widely, from as little as a few minutes to as much as several hours, depending on the claim's complexity). While Liberty management agrees that 12 clerks are not sufficient for a month with 1,020 claims, it notes that they are far too many when only 810 claims need to be processed. Management concludes, therefore, that 12 clerks are about right. Assume that each clerk works an eight-hour day except for 40 minutes of break time and that each month has an average of 22 working days. In the most recent month, January, the department processed 915 claims.

Required

1. What type of SBU does Liberty management appear to consider the claims processing department?
2. Assuming that Liberty uses the discretionary-cost method to implement cost SBUs, what is the budgeted cost in the claims department for January?
3. Assuming that Liberty uses the engineered-cost method to implement cost SBUs, what is the budgeted cost in the claims department for January?
4. If you were Chuck Davis, what would you use as a more effective argument to top management in requesting additional clerks?

Sources: Based on David J. Castellani, "ASPs: Changing Information Technology Delivery," *Strategic Finance,* March 2000, pp. 34–37; "The Promised Land for Outsourcing," *Business Week,* July 6, 1998, p. 39; N. Venkatraman, "Beyond Outsourcing: Managing IT Resources as a Value Center," *Sloan Management Review,* Spring 1997, pp. 51–64; and Tom Groenfeldt, "Who's in the Driver's Seat?" *The Journal of Business Strategy,* January–February 1997, pp. 36–41. "Out from the Source," *Business Week,* July 8, 2002, p 12; Pete Engardio, Aaron Bernstein, and Manjeet Kripalani, "Is Your Job Next," *Business Week,* February 3, 2003, pp. 48–60. For further information view the Outsourcing Institute's website at http://outsourcing.com/content.asp?page=01i/articles/itoutsourcing/index.html.

Questions

17–1   What is the difference between management control, performance evaluation, and operational control?

17–2   What is strategic performance measurement, and why is it important for effective management?

17–3   Does an effective performance evaluation focus on individual or team performance?

17–4   Explain the difference between informal and formal control systems. What type of control system is strategic performance measurement?

17–5   Name three types of organizational design and explain how they differ.

17–6   What are four types of SBUs, and what are the goals of each?

17–7   Since full costing is accepted for financial reporting purposes and variable costing is not, why should we be concerned about the difference between them? What is the difference, and why is it important?

17–8   What are some important behavioral and implementation issues in strategic performance measurement? How does the management accountant deal with these issues?

17–9   What is the role of cost allocation in strategic performance measurement?

17–10 Can strategic performance measurement be used for service firms and not-for-profit organizations? How?

17–11 In what situations is a cost SBU most appropriate? A profit SBU? A revenue SBU?

17–12 How do centralized and decentralized firms differ? What are the advantages of each?

17–13 Can the marketing department be both a revenue SBU and a cost SBU? Explain.

Exercises

17–14 **Departmental Cost Allocation in Profit SBUs**   Elvis Wilbur owns two restaurants, the Beef Barn and the Fish Bowl. Each restaurant is treated as a profit SBU for performance evaluation. Although the restaurants have separate kitchens, they share a central baking facility. The principal costs of the baking area include depreciation and maintenance on the equipment, materials, supplies, and labor.

Required

1. Elvis allocates the monthly costs of the baking facility to the two restaurants based on the number of tables served in each restaurant during the month. In April the costs were $24,000, of which $12,000 is fixed cost. The Beef Barn and the Fish Bowl each served 3,000 tables. How much of the joint cost should be allocated to each restaurant?

2. In May fixed and unit variable costs remained the same, but the Beef Barn served 2,000 tables and the Fish Bowl served 3,000. How much should be allocated to each restaurant? Explain your reasoning.

17–15 **Allocation of Marketing and Administrative Costs; Profit SBUs**   Hamilton Academy allocates marketing and administrative costs to its three schools based on total annual tuition revenue for the schools. In 2004 the allocations (000s omitted) were as follows:

	Lower School	Middle School	Upper School	Total
Tuition revenue	$1,500	$500	$2,000	$4,000
Marketing and administration	375	125	500	$1,000

In 2005, the middle and upper schools experienced no change in revenues, but the lower school's tuition revenue increased to $1.8 million. Marketing and administrative costs rose to $1,200,000.

Required

1. Using revenue as an allocation base, how should the costs be allocated for 2005?

2. What are the shortcomings of this allocation formula?

17–16 **Allocation of Administrative Costs**   Kuldigs Rental Management Services manages four local apartment complexes of varying sizes and degrees of luxury. Kuldigs' president has observed that the luxurious apartments tend to require more of her staff's time than the simpler units. Kuldigs incurs monthly operating expenses of $15,000, and its president desires a profit of 7 percent, for a total monthly billing of $16,050.

	Units	Average Rent per Unit
Pinnacle Point	100	$720
Whispering Woods	355	540
Hollow Rock	300	425
College Villa	550	340

Required How should the $16,050 be allocated to the four apartment complexes? Explain your answer.

17–17 Responsibility for Inefficiency; Ethics General Hospital leases its diagnostic equipment from Normed Leasing, which is also responsible for maintaining the equipment. Recently the hospital's MRI machine needed repair and physicians were required to order expensive nonemergency laboratory tests for their patients to diagnose conditions that could have been diagnosed more easily (and less expensively) using the MRI machine. Rather than bill its patients for the entire costs of these tests, the hospital billed the patients for the cost of an MRI and billed the difference to Normed. Normed disputes the charge, claiming that the physicians should have postponed diagnosis of the patients' conditions until the MRI machine could be repaired.

Required What issues should be addressed to determine how the charge should be handled properly? How can this situation be prevented? If appropriate, include ethical issues in your response.

17–18 Assigning Responsibility Kristen Langdon, the sales manager at a large bicycle manufacturer, has secured an order from a major department store that is due to ship on November 1. She is eager to please the department store in the hope of getting more future business. She asks Bryan Collins, the company's purchasing agent, to procure all necessary parts in time for production to begin on October 10. Bryan orders the parts from reputable suppliers, and most of them arrive by October 7. George Watkins, the production manager, begins production as scheduled on October 10, although the gears that Bryan ordered were delayed because of quality control problems at the manufacturer. Bryan assures George that the gear shipment will arrive before October 16 when those parts are scheduled to be attached to the bicycles. The shipment finally arrives on October 18 after production has been delayed for two days.

Required Which department should bear the responsibility for the two days' downtime? How can similar problems be avoided in the future?

17–19 Profit SBUs: Full and Variable Costing Fitzpatrick Inc. planned and manufactured 500,000 units of its single product in 2004, its first year of operations. Variable manufacturing costs were $40 per unit of production. Planned fixed manufacturing costs were $1,200,000. Marketing and administrative costs (all fixed) were $500,000 in 2004. Fitzpatrick sold 450,000 units of products in 2004 at $50 per unit.

Required

1. Determine Fitzpatrick Inc.'s operating income using full costing.

2. Determine Fitzpatrick Inc.'s operating income using variable costing.

3. Explain the difference between the operating incomes in requirements 1 and 2.

17–20 Centralization versus Decentralization; Health Care Doctors Health Care System has integrated health networks in three different regions: northern California, southern Florida, and Oklahoma. These three markets have vast regional differences. Because of the increasing penetration of the U.S. health care market by managed care companies, Doctors Health Care System must create a system that offers continuity of care across the continuum for a set price in order to remain competitive. Its board of directors set the system's goal as being a leader in developing and maintaining integrated health networks that improve the health status of their communities.

Required To meet this goal in the three regions, should the health system's management structure be decentralized or centralized? What are the advantages and disadvantages of each option?

Problems

17–21 Allocation of Central Costs; Profit SBUs Whispering Glen Resorts, Inc., operates four resort hotels in the heavily wooded areas of eastern Texas. The resorts are named after the predominant trees at the resort: Oak Glen, Pine Glen, Magnolia, and Pecan Arbor. Whispering Glen allocates its central office costs to each of its four hotels according to the annual revenue it generated. For the current year, these costs (000s omitted) were as follows:

Front office personnel	$ 6,000
Administrative and executive salaries	4,000
Interest on resort purchase	2,000
Advertising	300
Housekeeping	100
Depreciation on reservations computer	80
Room maintenance	80
Carpet-cleaning contract	50
Contract to repaint rooms	40
	$12,650

These are pertinent data relating to the four hotels:

	Pine Glen	Pecan Arbor	Oak Glen	Magnolia	Total
Revenue (000s)	$3,000	$7,000	$9,000	$5,000	$24,000
Square feet	52,500	75,000	32,500	75,000	235,000
Rooms	150	200	100	250	700
Assets (000s)	$65,000	$110,000	$88,000	$45,000	$308,000

Required

1. Based on annual revenue, how many of the central office costs are allocated to each hotel? What are the shortcomings of this allocation method?

2. Suppose that the current method were replaced with a system of four separate cost pools with costs collected in the four pools allocated on the basis of revenues, assets invested in each hotel, square footage, and number of rooms, respectively. Which costs should be collected in each of the four pools?

3. Using the cost pool system, how much of the central office costs would be allocated to each hotel? Is this system preferable to the single-allocation base system used in requirement 1? Why or why not?

17–22 Profit SBUs: Comparison of Variable and Full Costing   Harvard Company manufactures hair brushes that sell at wholesale for $2 per unit. The company had no beginning inventory in 2004. These data summarize the 2004 and 2005 operations:

	2004	2005
Sales	1,800 units	2,200 units
Production:	2,000 units	2,000 units
Production cost		
Factory—variable (per unit)	$0.60	$0.60
—fixed	$1,000	$1,000
Marketing—variable	$.40	$.40
Administrative—fixed	$500	$500

Required   Prepare the following, using a spreadsheet system.

1. An income statement for each year based on full costing.
2. An income statement for each year based on variable costing.
3. A reconciliation and explanation of the differences in the operating income resulting from using the full costing method and variable costing method.

17–23 Full versus Variable Costing   Jackson Jones Corp. (JJC) is a manufacturer of an electronic control system used in the manufacture of certain special-duty auto transmissions used primarily for police and military applications. The part sells for $45 per unit and had sales of 3,600 units in the current year, 2004. JJC has 400 units available for sale at the end of 2004 and is projecting sales of 4,400 units in 2005. JJC is planning the same production level for 2005 as in 2004, 4,000 units. The variable manufacturing costs for JJC are $16 and the variable selling costs are only $.50 per unit. The fixed manufacturing costs are $100,000 per year and the fixed selling costs are only $500 per year.

Required Prepare the following, using a spreadsheet:

1. An income statement for 2004 and 2005 using full costing.

2. An income statement for 2004 and 2005 using variable costing.

3. A reconciliation and explanation of the difference in the operating income resulting from the full and variable costing methods.

17–24 **Profit SBUs: Comparison of Variable and Full Costing (Under- And Overapplied Overhead)** Jason Reynolds, Inc. manufactures a specialized surgical instrument called the TDR–11. The firm has grown rapidly in recent years because of the product's low price and high quality. However, sales have declined this year due primarily to increased competition and a decrease in the surgical procedures for which the TDR–11 is used. The firm is concerned about the decline in sales, especially the decline in operating income over the past year. The firm has hired a consultant to analyze the firm's profitability. The consultant provided the following information:

	2004	2005
Sales (units)	2,300	1,900
Production	2,200	1,700
Budgeted production and sales	2,000	2,000
Beginning inventory	850	750
Data per unit (all variable)		
Price	$1,995	$1,885
Direct materials	440	440
Direct labor	255	255
Selling costs	125	125
Period cost (all fixed)		
Manufacturing overhead	$480,000	$480,000
Selling and administrative	160,000	160,000

Required

1. Using the full cost method, which Reynold's accountant used to prepare the annual financial statements, prepare the income statements for 2004 and 2005.

2. Using variable costing, prepare an income statement for each period, and explain the difference in net income from that obtained in requirement 1.

3. Write a brief memo to the firm to explain the difference in income between variable costing and absorption costing.

17–25 **Full versus Variable Costing** Conner Manufacturing has the following information for the years ended December 31, 2004, and December 31, 2005:

	2004	2005
Units		
Beginning inventory (units)	200	
Price	$80	$80
Units sold	1,000	1,900
Actual production (units)	1,200	1,700
Budgeted production (units)	1,500	1,500
Unit variable costs		
Manufacturing	$30	$30
Selling and administrative	$5	$5
Fixed costs		
Manufacturing	$24,000	$24,000
Selling and administrative	$5,000	$5,000

Required

    1. Prepare the variable cost and full cost income statements for 2004 and 2005.

    2. Prepare a reconciliation and explanation for the differences between full cost and variable cost income for both years.

17–26 Balanced Scorecard

Required   Complete problem 2–22.

17–27 Balanced Scorecard

Required   Complete problem 2–26.

17–28 Balanced Scorecard

Required   Complete problem 2–30.

17–29 Contribution Income Statement for Profit SBUs   Glamour, Inc., is an upscale clothing store in New York City and London. Each store has two main departments, Men's Apparel and Women's Apparel. Marie Phelps, Glamour's CFO, wants to use strategic performance measurement to better understand the company's financial results. She has decided to use the profit SBU method to measure performance and has gathered the following information about the two stores and the two departments of the New York City store:

Total net sales	$2,250,000
Fixed costs	
Partly traceable and controllable	200,000
Partly traceable but noncontrollable	160,000
Nontraceable costs	55,000
Total net sales (percent)	
London Store	40%
New York—Men's Apparel	30
New York—Women's Apparel	70
Cost of goods sold—variable (percent of sales)	
London	55%
New York—Men's Apparel	60
New York—Women's Apparel	40
Variable operating costs (percent of sales)	
London	34%
New York—Men's Apparel	24
New York—Women's Apparel	30
Fixed controllable costs—partly traceable (percent of total)	
London	40%
New York total	40
Men's Apparel	45
Women's Apparel	40
Could not be traced	15
Could not be traced to New York or London	20
Fixed noncontrollable costs—partly traceable (percent of total)	
London	50%
New York total	40
Men's Apparel	30
Women's Apparel	10
Could not be traced to either department	60
Could not be traced to London or New York	10

Required   Using this information and a spreadsheet system, prepare a contribution income statement for Glamour, showing contribution for both stores and for both departments of the New York store.

17–30 Contribution Income Statement for Profit SBUs; Strategy   Music Teachers, Inc., is an educational association for music teachers that had 20,000 members during 2004. The association operates from a central headquarters but has local membership chapters throughout the United States. The local chapters hold monthly meetings to discuss recent developments on topics of interest to members. The association's monthly journal, *Teachers' Forum,* has features about recent developments in the field. The association publishes books and reports and sponsors professional courses that qualify participants for continuing professional education credits. The association's statement of revenue and expense (000s omitted) for 2004 follows:

Revenue	$3,275
Expense	
Salaries	$ 920
Personnel costs	230
Occupancy costs	280
Reimbursement to local chapters	600
Other membership services	500
Printing and paper	320
Postage and shipping	176
Instructors' fees	80
General and administrative	38
Total expenses	$3,144
Excess of revenues over expenses	$131

The organization's board of directors has requested that a statement of operations be prepared showing the contribution of each profit SBU (i.e., membership, magazine subscriptions, books and reports, continuing education). Mike Doyle was assigned this responsibility and had gathered these data prior to statement preparation:

- Annual membership dues are $100, of which $20 covers a one-year subscription to the association's journal. Other benefits include membership in the association and chapter affiliation. The portion of the dues covering the magazine subscription ($20) should be assigned to the magazine subscriptions profit SBU.

- One-year subscriptions to *Teachers' Forum* are sold to nonmembers and libraries at $30 each. A total of 2,500 of these subscriptions were sold this year. In addition to subscriptions, the magazine generated $100,000 in advertising revenue. The costs for printing and paper and for postage and shipping per magazine subscription were $7 and $4, respectively.

- The books and reports department sold a total of 28,000 technical reports and professional texts at an average unit selling price of $25. Average costs per publication were as follows:

Printing and paper	$4
Postage and shipping	2

- The association offers a variety of continuing education courses to both members and nonmembers. The one-day courses cost $75 each and were attended by 2,400 students in 2004. A total of 1,760 students took two-day courses at a cost of $125 for each course. Outside instructors were paid to teach some courses.

- Salary and occupancy data are

	Salaries	Square Footage
Membership	$210,000	2,000
Magazine subscriptions	150,000	2,000
Books and reports	300,000	3,000
Continuing education	180,000	2,000
Corporate staff	80,000	1,000
	$920,000	10,000

Included in the $280,000 occupancy cost is rent for the books and reports department for an annual cost of $50,000. Personnel costs are an additional 25 percent of salaries.

- Printing and paper costs other than for magazine subscriptions and books and reports relate to the continuing education department.
- General and administrative expenses include all other costs incurred by the corporate staff to operate the association.

Mike has decided to assign all revenue and expense to the profit SBUs on the following basis:

1. Can be traced directly to a profit SBU.
2. Can be allocated on a reasonable and logical basis to a profit SBU.

The expenses that can be traced or assigned to corporate staff as well as any other expenses that cannot be assigned to profit SBUs will be grouped with the general and administrative expenses and not allocated to the profit SBUs. Mike believes that allocations often tend to be arbitrary and are not useful for management reporting and analysis. He believes that additional allocation of the general and administrative expenses associated with the operation and administration of the association would be arbitrary.

Required

1. Prepare a contribution income statement for Music Teachers, Inc.
2. What is the strategic role of the contribution income statement for Music Teachers, Inc.?
3. Mike Doyle is considering the possibility of not allocating indirect or nontraceable expenses to profit SBUs.
   a. What reasons are often presented for not allocating indirect or nontraceable expenses to profit SBUs?
   b. Under what circumstances might the allocation of indirect or nontraceable expenses to profit SBUs be acceptable?

(CMA Adapted)

17–31 **Contribution Income Statement for Profit SBUs; Strategy, International**   Stratford Corporation is a diversified company whose products are marketed both domestically and internationally. Its major product lines are pharmaceutical products, sports equipment, and household appliances. At a recent meeting, Stratford's board of directors had a lengthy discussion on ways to improve overall corporate profitability without new acquisitions. New acquisitions are problematic because the company already is heavily leveraged. The board members decided that they needed additional financial information about individual corporate operations to target areas for improvement. Dave Murphy, Stratford's controller, has been asked to provide additional data to assist the board in its investigation. Stratford is not a public company and, therefore, has not prepared complete income statements by product line. Dave has regularly prepared an income statement by product line through contribution margin. However, he now believes that income statements prepared through operating income along both product lines and geographic areas would provide the directors with the required insight into corporate operations. Dave has the following data available:

| | Product Lines | | | |
	Pharmaceutical	Sports	Appliances	Total
Production/Sales in units	160,000	180,000	160,000	500,000
Average selling price per unit	$8.00	$20.00	$15.00	
Average variable manufacturing cost per unit	4.00	9.50	8.25	
Average variable selling expense per unit	2.00	2.50	2.25	
Fixed factory overhead excluding depreciation				$500,000
Depreciation of plant and equipment				400,000
Administrative and selling expense				1,160,000

Dave had several discussions with the division managers from each product line and compiled this information:

- The division managers concluded that Dave should allocate fixed factory overhead on the basis of the ratio of the variable costs per product line or per geographic area to total variable costs.
- Each division manager agreed that a reasonable basis for the allocation of depreciation on plant and equipment would be the ratio of units produced per product line or per geographical area to the total number of units produced.
- There was little agreement on the allocation of administrative and selling expenses, so Dave decided to allocate only those expenses that were directly traceable to the SBU being delineated; that is, manufacturing staff salaries to product lines and sales staff salaries to geographic areas. He used these data for this allocation:

Manufacturing Staff		Sales Staff	
Pharmaceutical	$120,000	United States	$60,000
Sports	140,000	Canada	100,000
Appliances	80,000	Europe	250,000

- The division managers provided reliable sales percentages for their product lines by geographical area:

	Percentage of Unit Sales		
	United States	Canada	Europe
Pharmaceutical	40%	10%	50%
Sports	40	40	20
Appliances	20	20	60

Dave prepared this product-line income statement:

STRATFORD CORPORATION
Statement of Income by Product Lines
For the Fiscal Year Ended April 30, 2004

	Product Lines				
	Pharmaceutical	Sports	Appliances	Unallocated	Total
Sales in units	160,000	180,000	160,000		500,000
Sales	$1,280,000	$3,600,000	$2,400,000	—	$7,280,000
Variable manufacturing and selling costs	960,000	2,160,000	1,680,000	—	4,800,000
Contribution margin	$ 320,000	$1,440,000	$ 720,000	—	$2,480,000
Fixed costs					
Fixed factory overhead	$ 100,000	$ 225,000	$ 175,000	—	$500,000
Depreciation	128,000	144,000	128,000	—	400,000
Administrative and selling expense	120,000	140,000	80,000	$ 820,000	1,160,000
Total fixed costs	$ 348,000	$ 509,000	$ 383,000	$ 820,000	$2,060,000
Operating income (loss)	$ (28,000)	$ 931,000	$ 337,000	$(820,000)	$ 420,000

Required

1. Prepare a contribution income statement for Stratford Corporation based on the company's geographic areas of sales.

2. As a result of the information disclosed by both income statements (by product line and by geographic area), recommend areas on which Stratford Corporation should focus its attention to improve corporate profitability.

3. What changes would you make to Stratford's strategic performance measurement system? Include the role, if any, of the firm's international business operations in your response.

(CMA Adapted)

17–32 **Profit SBUs; Annual Financial Reports**   Greg Peterson was recently appointed vice president of operations for Webster Corporation. He has a manufacturing background and previously served as operations manager of Webster's tractor division. The business units of Webster Corporation include divisions that manufacture heavy equipment, process food, and provide financial services.

In a recent conversation with Carol Andrews, Webster's chief financial officer, Greg suggested evaluating unit managers on the basis of the business unit data in Webster's annual financial report. This report presents revenues, earnings, identifiable assets, and depreciation for each business unit for a five-year period. He believes that evaluating business unit managers by criteria similar to that used to evaluate the company's top management is appropriate. Carol has reservations about using information from the annual financial report for this purpose and suggested that Greg consider other criteria to use in the evaluation.

Required

1. Explain why the business unit information prepared for public reporting purposes might not be appropriate for the evaluation of unit managers' performance.

2. Describe the possible motivational impact on Webster Corporation's unit managers if Greg's proposal for their evaluation is accepted.

3. Identify and describe several types of information that would be appropriate for Greg Peterson to use when evaluating the performance of unit managers.

(CMA Adapted)

17–33 **Performance Measurement**   Divisional managers of SIU Incorporated have been expressing growing dissatisfaction with the current methods used to measure divisional performance. Divisional operations are evaluated every quarter by comparison with the static budget prepared during the prior year. Divisional managers claim that many factors are completely out of their control but are included in this comparison. This results in an unfair and misleading performance evaluation.

The managers have been particularly critical of the process used to establish standards and budgets. The annual budget, stated by quarters, is prepared six months prior to the beginning of the operating year. Pressure by top management to reflect increased earnings has often caused divisional managers to overstate revenues and/or understate expenses. In addition, once the budget had been established, divisions were required to live with the budget. Frequently, external factors such as the state of the economy, changes in consumer preferences, and actions of competitors have not been adequately recognized in the budget parameters that top management supplied to the divisions. The credibility of the performance review is curtailed when the budget cannot be adjusted to incorporate these changes.

Top management, recognizing the current problems, has agreed to establish a committee to review the situation and to make recommendations for a new performance evaluation system. The committee consists of each division manager, the corporate controller, and the executive vice president who serves as the chairman. At the first meetings, one division manager outlined an Achievement of Objectives System (AOS). In this performance evaluation system, divisional managers would be evaluated according to three criteria:

- Doing better than last year—Various measures would be compared to the same measures of the prior year.

- Planning realistically—Actual performance for the current year would be compared to realistic plans and/or goals.

- Managing current assets—Various measures would be used to evaluate the divisional management's achievements and reactions to changing business and economic conditions.

A division manager believed this system would overcome many of the inconsistencies of the current system because divisions could be evaluated from three viewpoints. In addition, managers would have the opportunity to show how they would react and account for changes in uncontrollable external factors.

A second division manager was also in favor of the proposed AOS. However, he cautioned that the success of a new performance evaluation system would be limited unless it had the complete support of top management. Further, this support should be visible within all divisions. He believed that the committee should recommend some procedures that would enhance the motivational and competitive spirit of the divisions.

Required

1. Explain whether the proposed AOS would be an improvement over the measure of divisional performance now used by SIU Incorporated.

2. Develop specific performance measures for each of the three criteria in the proposed AOS which could be used to evaluate divisional managers.

3. Discuss the motivational and behavioral aspects of the proposed performance system. Also, recommend specific programs which could be instituted to promote morale and give incentives to divisional management.

(CMA Adapted)

17–34 **Centralization vs. Decentralization: Banking** RNB is a bank holding company for a statewide group of retail consumer-oriented banks. RNB was formed in the early 1960s by a group of young investors who believed in a high level of consumer services. The number of banks owned by the holding company expanded rapidly. These banks gained visibility because of their experimentation with innovations such as free-standing 24-hour automated teller machines, automated funds transfer systems, and other advances in banking services.

RNB's earnings performance has been better than that of most other banks in the state. The founders organized RNB and continue to operate it on a highly decentralized basis. As the number of banks owned has increased, RNB's executive management has delegated more responsibility and authority to individual bank presidents, who are considered to be representatives of executive management. Although certain aspects of each bank's operations are standardized (such as procedures for account and loan applications and salary rates), bank presidents have significant autonomy in determining how each bank will operate.

The decentralization has led each bank to develop individual marketing campaigns. Several of them have introduced unique "packaged" accounts that include a combination of banking services; however, they sometimes fail to notify the other banks in the group as well as the executive office of these campaigns. One result has been interbank competition for customers where the market overlaps. The corporate marketing officer had also recently begun a statewide advertising campaign that conflicted with some of the individual banks' advertising. Consequently, customers and tellers have occasionally experienced both confusion and frustration, particularly when the customers attempt to receive services at a bank other than their "home" bank.

RNB's executive management is concerned that earnings will decline for the first time in its history. The decline appears to be attributable to reduced customer satisfaction and higher operating costs. The competition among the banks in the state is keen. Bank location and consistent high-quality customer service are important. RNB's 18 banks are well located, and the three new bank acquisitions planned for next year are considered to be in prime locations. The increase in operating costs appears to be directly related to the individual banks' aggressive marketing efforts and new programs. Specifically, expenditures increased for advertising and for the special materials and added personnel related to the "packaged" accounts.

For the past three months RNB's executive management has been meeting with the individual bank presidents to review RNB's recent performance and seek ways to improve it. One recommendation that appeals to executive management is to make the organization's structure more centralized. The specific proposal calls for reducing individual bank autonomy and creating a centralized individual bank management committee of all bank presidents to be chaired by a newly created position, vice president of individual bank operations. The individual banks' policies would be set by consensus of the committee to conform to overall RNB plans.

Required

1. Discuss the advantages of a decentralized organizational structure.

2. Identify disadvantages of a decentralized structure. Support each disadvantage with an example from RNB's situation.

3. Do you think the proposed more centralized structure is in the strategic best interests of RNB? Why or why not?

(CMA Adapted)

17–35 **Performance Measurement; Cost Accounting Standards; Ethics**   Callum Corporation is a diversified manufacturing company with corporate headquarters in St. Louis. The three operating divisions are the aerospace division, the ceramic products division, and the glass products division.

Much of the manufacturing activity of the aerospace division is related to work performed for the National Aeronautics and Space Administration (NASA) under negotiated contracts. The contracts provide that cost shall be allocated to the contracts in accordance with the federal government's Cost Accounting Standards (as promulgated by the Cost Accounting Standards Board and administered by the General Accounting Office).

Callum Corporation headquarters provide general administrative support and computer services to each of the three operating divisions. The Cost Accounting Standards provide that the cost of general administration may be allocated to negotiated defense contracts. Further, the standards provide that in institutions where computer services are provided by corporate headquarters, the actual costs (fixed and variable) of operating the computer department may be allocated to the defense division based on a reasonable measure of computer usage.

Another provision of the Cost Accounting Standards deals with the situation in which a defense division acquires noncommercial components from a sister division. The standards provide that when there is no established market price for the component, the component must be transferred to the defense division at cost without a markup for profit. This provision of the standards applies to Callum Corporation because the aerospace division purchases custom designed ceramic components from the ceramic products division. There is no established market price for these custom components.

The general managers of the three divisions are evaluated as profit center managers based on the before-tax profit of the division. The November 2004 performance evaluation reports for each of the divisions (in millions of dollars) are shown in the following table:

	Aerospace Division	Ceramic Products Division	Glass Products Division
Sales	$23.0	$15.0*	$55.0
Cost of goods sold	13.0	7.0	38.0
Gross profit	$10.0	$8.0	$17.0
Selling and administration:			
Division selling and administration	$5.0	$5.0	$8.0
Corporate—general administration	1.0	—	—
Corporate—computing	1.0	—	—
Total selling and administration	$ 7.0	$ 5.0	$ 8.0
Profit before taxes	$ 3.0	$ 3.0	$ 9.0

*Includes $3,000,000 of custom ceramic products sold to aerospace division at cost and the remainder ($12,000,000) sold to the glass products division and outside customers at established market prices.

Required

1. Review the November performance evaluation reports for the three operating divisions of Callum Corporation.

   a. Identify specific instances where the federal government's Cost Accounting Standards have influenced Callum's divisional performance reporting.

   b. For each specific instance identified, discuss whether the use of accounting practices based on Cost Accounting Standards is desirable for internal reporting and performance evaluation.

2. Considering the accounting practices and reporting methods currently employed by Callum Corporation, describe the improper decision making that could result for the company as a whole if the demand for commercial (nondefense related) ceramic products is equal to or greater than the productive capacity of the ceramic products division.

3. Without a charge for computing services, the operating divisions may not make the most cost-effective use of the resources of the computer systems department of Callum Corporation. Outline and discuss methods for charging the operating divisions for the use of computer services that would promote cost consciousness by the operating divisions and operating efficiency by the computer systems department.

 17–36 Balanced Scorecard; Strategic Business Units; Ethics Pittsburgh-Walsh Company, Inc. (PWC), manufactures lighting fixtures and electronic timing devices. The lighting fixtures division assembles units for the upscale and mid-range markets. The trend in recent years as the economy has been expanding is for sales in the upscale market to increase while those in the mid-range market have been relatively flat. Over the years, PWC has tried to maintain strong positions in both markets, believing it is best to offer customers a broad range of products to protect the company against a sharp decline in either market. PWC has never been the first to introduce new products but watches its competitors closely and quickly follows their lead with comparable products. PWC is proud of its customers service functions, which have been able to maintain profitable relationships with several large customers over the years.

The electronic timing devices division manufactures instrument panels that allow electronic systems to be activated and deactivated at scheduled times for both efficiency and safety purposes. Both divisions operate in the same manufacturing facilities and share production equipment.

PWC's budget for the year ending December 31, 2004, follows; it was prepared on a business unit basis under the following guidelines.

- Variable expenses are directly assigned to the division that incurs them.
- Fixed overhead expenses are directly assigned to the division that incurs them.
- Common fixed expenses are allocated to the divisions on the basis of units produced, which bears a close relationship to direct labor. Included in common fixed expenses are costs of the corporate staff, legal expenses, taxes, staff marketing, and advertising.
- The company plans to manufacture 8,000 upscale fixtures, 22,000 mid-range fixtures, and 20,000 electronic timing devices during 2004.

PITTSBURGH-WALSH COMPANY
Budget
For the Year Ending December 31, 2004
(amounts in thousands)

	Lighting Fixtures Upscale	Lighting Fixtures Mid-Range	Electronic Timing Devices	Totals
Sales	$1,440	$770	$800	$3,010
Variable expenses				
Cost of goods sold	720	439	320	1,479
Selling and admin.	170	60	60	290
Contribution margin	$ 550	$271	$420	$1,241
Fixed overhead	140	80	80	300
Divisional contribution	$ 410	$191	$340	$ 941
Common fixed expenses				
Overhead	48	132	120	300
Selling and admin.	11	31	28	70
Net income	$ 351	$ 28	$192	$ 571

PWC established a bonus plan for division management if the division exceeds the planned product line net income by 10 percent or more.

Shortly before the year began, Jack Parkow, the CEO, suffered a heart attack and retired. After reviewing the 2004 budget, Joe Kelly, the new CEO, decided to close the lighting fixtures mid-range product line by the end of the first quarter and use the available production capacity to grow the remaining two product lines. The marketing staff advised that electronic timing devices could grow by 40 percent with increased direct sales support. Increasing sales above that level and of upscale lighting fixtures would require expanded advertising expenditures to increase consumer awareness of PWC as an electronics and upscale lighting fixture company. Joe approved the increased sales support and advertising expenditures to achieve the revised plan. He advised the divisions that for bonus purposes, the original product-line net income objectives must be met and that the lighting fixtures division could combine the net income objectives for both product lines for bonus purposes.

Prior to the close of the fiscal year, the division controllers were given the following preliminary actual information to review and adjust as appropriate. These preliminary year-end data reflect the revised units of production amounting to 12,000 upscale fixtures, 4,000 mid-range fixtures, and 30,000 electronic timing devices.

PITTSBURGH-WALSH COMPANY, INC.
Preliminary Actual Information
For the Year Ending December 2004
(amounts in thousands)

	Lighting Fixtures Upscale	Lighting Fixtures Mid-Range	Electronic Timing Devices	Totals
Sales	$2,160	$140	$1,200	$3,500
Variable expenses				
Cost of goods sold	1,080	80	480	1,640
Selling and admin.	260	11	96	367
Contribution margin	$ 820	$ 49	$ 624	$1,493
Fixed overhead	140	14	80	234
Divisional contribution	$ 680	$ 35	$ 544	$1,259
Common fixed expenses				
Overhead	78	27	195	300
Selling and admin.	60	20	150	230
Net income (loss)	$ 542	$(12)	$ 199	$ 729

The controller of the lighting fixtures division, anticipating a similar bonus plan for 2005, is contemplating deferring some revenue into the next year on the pretext that the sales are not yet final and accruing in the current year expenditures that will be applicable to the first quarter of 2005. The corporation would meet its annual plan, and the division would exceed the 10 percent incremental bonus plateau in 2004 despite the deferred revenues and accrued expenses contemplated.

Required

1. Did the new CEO make the correct decision? Why or why not?
2. Outline the benefits that an organization realizes from SBU reporting, and evaluate profit SBU reporting on a variable cost basis versus an absorption cost basis.
3. Why would the management of the electronics timing devices division be unhappy with the current reporting? Should the current performance measurement system be revised?
4. Explain why the adjustments contemplated by the controller of the lighting fixtures division are unethical by citing specific standards in the Institute of Management Accountants' Standards of Ethical Conduct.
5. Develop a balanced scorecard for PWC, providing three to five perspectives and four to six measures of each perspective. Make sure your measures are quantifiable.

17–37 **Profit SBUs**   Charleston Manufacturing Company, a maker of building products for commercial and industrial construction, has four divisions: bathroom fixtures; roofing products; adhesives, paints, and other chemicals; and flooring. Each division is evaluated on its profit as determined by the annual financial report, and the profit figure is used to determine the division managers' compensation. The firm has continued to grow in both sales and profits over the recent years, but top management has observed that it is not growing as fast as other firms in the industry. Moreover, the building products business is experiencing strong overall growth due in part to the rapid increase in construction in the southeastern states where Charleston competes. The firm's CEO is concerned that it is losing ground in the industry at a time of improving opportunities. The CEO believes that the problem might be in the firm's performance measurement system and sets up a task force to determine how the firm should proceed.

Required You are assigned to lead the task force. What are your suggestions for the CEO regarding Charleston's performance measurement?

17–38 Design of Strategic Business Unit Hamilton-Jones, a large consulting firm in Los Angeles, has experienced rapid growth over the last five years. To better serve its clients and to better manage its practice, the firm decided two years ago to organize into five strategic business units, each of which serves a significant base of clients: accounting systems, executive recruitment and compensation, client-server office information systems, manufacturing information systems, and real-estate consulting. Each client SBU is served by a variety of administrative services within the firm, including payroll and accounting, printing and duplicating, report preparation, and secretarial support. Hamilton-Jones management closely watches the trend in the total costs for each administrative support area on a month-to-month basis. Management has noted that the costs in the printing and duplicating area have risen 40 percent over the last two years, a rate that is twice that of any other support area.

Required Should Hamilton-Jones evaluate the five strategic business units as cost or profit SBUs? Why? How should the administrative support areas be evaluated?

17–39 Design of Strategic Business Unit Martinsville Manufacturing Company develops parts for the automobile industry. The main product line is interior systems, especially seats and carpets. Martinsville operates in a single large plant that has 30 manufacturing processes: carpet dyeing, seat frame fabrication, fabric cutting, and so on. In addition to the 30 manufacturing units, there are six manufacturing support departments: maintenance, engineering, janitorial, scheduling, materials receiving and handling, and information systems. The costs of the support departments are allocated to the 30 manufacturing units on the basis of direct labor cost, materials costs, or the square feet of floor space in the plant occupied by the unit. In the case of the maintenance department, the cost is allocated on the basis of square feet. Maintenance costs have been relatively stable in recent years, but the firm's accountant advises that the amount of maintenance cost is a little high relative to the industry average.

Required What are the incentive effects on the manufacturing units of the current basis for allocating maintenance costs? What would be a more desirable way, if any, for allocating these costs? Explain your answer.

17–40 Design of Strategic Business Unit MetroBank is a fast-growing bank that serves the region around Jacksonville, Florida. The bank provides commercial and individual banking services, including investment and mortgage banking services. The firm's strategy is to continue to grow by acquiring smaller banks in the area to broaden the base and variety of services it can offer. The bank now has 87 strategic business units, which represent different areas of service in different locations. To support its growth, MetroBank has invested several million dollars in upgrading its information services function. The number of networked computers and of support personnel has more than doubled in the last four years and now accounts for 13 percent of total operating expenses. Two years ago, MetroBank decided to charge information services to the SBUs based on the head count (number of employees) in each SBU. Recently, some of the larger SBUs have complained that this method overcharges them and that some of the smaller SBUs are actually using a larger share of the total information services resources. MetroBank's controller has decided to investigate these complaints. His inquiry of the director of the information services department revealed that the larger departments generally use more services, but some small departments in fact kept him pretty busy. Based on this response, the controller is considering changing the charges for information services to the basis of actual service calls in each SBU rather than the head count.

Required Is the information services department at MetroBank a profit SBU or a cost SBU? Which type of unit should it be, and why? Evaluate the controller's decision regarding the basis for charging information services costs to the SBUs.

17–41 **Design of Strategic Business Unit**   Advanced Electronic Devices (AED) is a large manufacturer of electronic parts used in the manufacture of computers, automobiles, and a variety of consumer products. The firm manufactures approximately 3,500 different products each year. Approximately 10 percent of these are new products, and another 10 percent are dropped each year. AED is organized into 16 profit SBUs that cover the main areas of its business and 14 manufacturing support departments, each of whose cost is charged to the profit SBUs on the basis of product cost. The head of engineering, one of the largest support departments, has argued that the current system is dysfunctional. It does not encourage the longer-term type of engineering projects that she thinks are critical to the firm's success. She argues that the longer-term engineering projects will develop the key improvements in the products and production processes that will maintain the firm's "competitive edge."

Required   Assess the argument by the head of the engineering department. Is the engineering department currently evaluated as a cost SBU or profit SBU? How do you think the support departments, including engineering, should be evaluated, and how should their costs be charged to the manufacturing departments?

17–42 **Profit SBUs: Hospitals**   Suburban General Hospital owns and operates several community hospitals in North Carolina. One of its hospitals, Cordona Community Hospital, is a not-for-profit institution that has not met its financial targets in the past several years because of decreasing volume. It has been losing market share largely because of the entrance of a new competitor, Jefferson Memorial Hospital. Jefferson has successfully promoted itself as the premier provider of quality care; its slogan is "Patients Come First." To compete with Jefferson, Cordona has developed a new department, guest services, to improve patient relations and overall customer service. Guest services personnel will be positioned throughout the hospital and at major entrances to help patients and their families get where they are going. Guest services will also be visible in the waiting rooms of high-volume areas such as cardiovascular services and women's services to help guide the patients throughout their visit. Cordona's management is wrestling with how to charge guest services to the various profit SBUs in the hospital.

Required   What are some different ways to allocate the guest service costs, and what would be the effect of each on the behavior of the managers of the different profit SBUs?

17–43 **Strategy: Balanced Scorecard**   WaveCrest Boats, Inc., located in Kinston, North Carolina, is a large manufacturer of sailboats. The company was founded by brothers Tom and Bill Green, who started it to combine their work and hobby, sailing. The Greens's boats are intended primarily for the first-time boat buyer and accordingly include a number of design features for ease of use. Some of WaveCrest's innovative designs have received the attention of other manufacturers in the industry and of sailing magazine editors. The intended market for the boats is the recreational boating enthusiast and sailing camps and clubs that are looking for a durable and easy-to-use boat.

   The sailboat industry can be described as a very cyclical business and depends a great deal on overall economic conditions. Because most customers view sailing as a rather expensive recreational hobby, sales increase when the economy is at its best. The adoption of a boat for racing in a given area and the requirement that competitors use that particular boat to compete have dramatically affected sales.

   WaveCrest's plant occupies a single large building plus three smaller buildings for supplies, administration, and other manufacturing uses. The plant has two key manufacturing departments, each with a supervisor. The molding department develops the molds for the boats and produces the fiberglass hull for each boat. The assembly department installs the fittings, rub-rail and other hardware, and packs the mast, sails, lines, and other items for shipment.

   WaveCrest is currently manufacturing two boat designs, a 14-foot cat-rigged boat and a 16-foot sloop-rigged boat. The wholesale price of these boats is $2,500 and $4,500, respectively. The plant manufactures an average of 100 of the 14-foot boats and 50 of the 16-foot boats per month. The plant is staffed by six highly skilled workers in the molding department, and five additional employees in the assembly department. Tom and Bill work on marketing and customer relations in addition to boat design and testing. Tom is principally responsible for design and production and has been able to create two promising new designs that the firm is market testing and considering for production, as well as some new ideas for streamlining the production process. Bill is primarily responsible for marketing and customer relations and is on the road much of the time attending boat shows and visiting sailing camps and clubs.

Required

1. Develop what you think is or should be WaveCrest's competitive strategy.

2. The Green brothers are interested in evaluating their performance other than using the financial report. In particular, they want to be able to evaluate their progress toward specific goals in each business area. Because they do not see much of each other as a result of Bill's travel, they also want a way to be more aware of what the other is doing and accomplishing. Someone has suggested the use of a balanced scorecard for this purpose. Based on the firm's strategy, develop three to five perspectives of a potential balanced scorecard and four to six measures for each perspective. Do you think the balanced scorecard will provide the information the brothers are seeking?

17–44 **Performance Measurement; Balanced Scorecard; Hospital** Bridgeport Hospital and Health Care Services (BHHS) in Bridgeport, Connecticut, is a part of the Yale University Health System. BHHS is a 450-bed community-teaching hospital with the following mission: "In 2003, Bridgeport Hospital and Health Care Services, as an integral part of the Yale New Haven Health System, will be the system patients choose, the system to which physicians and payers refer, and the employer of choice for health care personnel."

To transform this mission to reality, BHHS recently adopted the balanced scorecard for performance measurement, and a plan to implement it by the end of 2003. In the first year of the scorecard, 2001, BHHS identified 12 scorecard perspectives and 56 critical success factors across these 12 perspectives. The following year, BHHS refined the scorecard to include the following five perspectives and 35 measurable critical success factors:

1. **Organizational health** (teamwork, leadership development, communications, facilities . . .)
2. **Process improvement** (reducing delays, streamlining processes, and maximizing the effective use of technology . . .)
3. **Quality improvement** (patient satisfaction, improving patient outcomes, external recognition for patient care . . .)
4. **Volume and market share growth** (expanded clinical services . . .)
5. **Financial health** (revenues, costs, system efficiencies . . .)

The scorecard is now in development and is expected to be fully implemented by 2003.

Required

1. Why did BHHS reduce the number of scorecard perspectives and measurable critical success factors in 2002? The number of perspectives was further reduced to four in 2003; state which are the remaining four perspectives and explain why.

2. For the five perspectives in the 2002 plan, develop two to five possible measurable critical success factors that the hospital might use to measure performance toward the goals of each perspective.

3. Will the scorecard as described be effective in helping BHHS achieve its mission?

4. Develop a strategy map for BHHS, incorporating each of its four perspectives. Explain why you have developed the map in this way.

Solution to Self-Study Problem

Discretionary-Cost and Engineered-Cost Methods

1. Liberty management is apparently using a cost SBU for its claims department because it generates no revenues. Since management has chosen not to adjust the number of clerks for the changing number of claims each month, it appears to be using a discretionary-cost method to budget these costs. That is, management has determined it is more effective to provide a reasonable resource (12 clerks) for the claims processing area and not to be concerned directly with the clerks' efficiency, the slack during slow times, or the hectic pace at peak load times. Management's view is that the work averages out over time.

2. If Liberty uses the discretionary-cost method, the budget would be the same each month and would not depend on the level of claims to be processed. The budget would include the costs to provide the number of clerks that management judges to be adequate for the job (12 clerks × $2,400 per month), or $28,800 per month.

3. If Liberty uses the engineered-cost method, each claim that is processed has a budgeted cost based on the average time used as determined by a work flow study. Assume that each clerk works an eight-hour day except for 40 minutes of break time; the number of claims a clerk can process each month (assuming 22 working days) is

$$\frac{[(8 \text{ hours} \times 60 \text{ minutes} - 40] \times 22 \text{ days}}{121 \text{ minutes}} = 80 \text{ claims per month}$$

The cost per claim is thus

$$\$2,400/80 = \$30 \text{ per claim}$$

The engineered-cost budget for January is

$$915 \text{ claims} \times \$30 \text{ per claim} = \$27,450$$

The unfavorable variance for January using the engineered-cost method is $1,350 ($28,800 actual expenditure less $27,450 budgeted expenditure). This unfavorable variance is best interpreted as the cost of unused capacity for processing claims. Since the capacity for processing claims is 80 × 12 = 960 claims, the department has unused capacity of 45 claims (960 − 915 = 45 claims), or approximately one-half of one clerk.

4. Chuck could make the strategic argument that the claims processing department should be staffed for peak capacity rather than for average capacity to ensure promptness and accuracy during the busy months and to provide a better basis for employee morale, which is an important factor in performance during the low-volume months as well.

CHAPTER EIGHTEEN

Strategic Investment Units and Transfer Pricing

After studying this chapter, you should be able to . . .

1. Identify the objectives of strategic investment units

2. Explain the use of return on investment (ROI) and identify its advantages and limitations

3. Explain the use of residual income and identify its advantages and limitations

4. Explain the use of economic value added (EVA) in evaluating strategic investment units

5. Explain the objectives of transfer pricing, the different transfer pricing methods, and when each method should be used

6. Discuss the important international tax issues in transfer pricing

The increasing intensity of competition and the growing importance of global trading requirements such as those of the World Trade Organization (WTO) and tax rules in each country are creating new challenges for global businesses. These elements have particularly affected the manner in which global firms evaluate their business units located throughout the world. In this chapter, we consider how firms evaluate their subsidiaries as strategic business units and how they develop transfer prices for sales between the firm's various units. Differences in accounting practices, tax rates, and foreign exchange rates for different countries seriously affect the evaluation and the transfer prices. According to Bill Gates:

Microsoft's international business grew really fast once we got rolling overseas. We made a point of moving into international markets as early as possible, and our subsidiaries had a lot of entrepreneurial energy. Giving them the freedom to conduct their businesses according to what made sense in each country was good for customers and profitable for us. Our international business shot up from 41 percent of revenues in 1986 to 55 percent in 1989.

The independence of our subsidiaries extended to their financial reporting, which came to us in a number of different formats driven by a number of different business arrangements and taxation rules. Some subsidiaries accounted for products from our manufacturing corporation in Ireland based on their cost; others used a percentage of customer price as the cost. They'd reconcile the actual sales and profits in different ways. Some of our subsidiaries got a commission on direct sales . . . other subs facilitated direct sales from the parent company, and we reimbursed them on a cost-plus basis. The half dozen or so different financial models gave us a lot of headaches. . . .

"Not knowing any better," as Mike Brown (Chief Financial Officer) likes to say, he and our controller, Jon Anderson, decided to take advantage of the fact that everyone already used PC spreadsheets for other kinds of analysis. They designed a cost-basis profit and loss financial that didn't show any of the inter-company markups or commissions. Mike and Jon showed the new P&L around via e-mail and got quick buy-off on it. When we looked at our subsidiary financials after that, we had a much easier time seeing how we were actually doing, especially when we could pivot the data to see it from angles. . . .One critical aspect is being able to easily control exchange rate assumptions in any view so you can see results either with or without the effects of exchange rates.[1]

Similarly, the changes in the local currencies of the countries in which they operate can seriously affect global firms such as Goodyear, Caterpillar, Coca-Cola, and McDonald's. For example, the decline in euro currency in European Union countries during 1999–2000 caused the operating income of these firms to fall by as much as 30 percent. In contrast, the euro has made strong advances against the dollar since 2002. The result is that some U.S. firms have gained from the weakening dollar. For example, the rise of the euro relative to the dollar in 2002 produced $16 million in foreign-exchange related profits for Amazon.com for the quarter ended December 31, 2002, enough to change what would have been a net loss into net income.[2] The complexities of evaluating SBUs of these global firms is covered in this chapter.

Part One: Strategic Investment Units

Most firms use profit SBUs and investment SBUs to evaluate managers. Profit SBUs are commonly used because of their strong effect on the motivation and goal congruence objectives of SBUs; managers are rewarded for their units' contribution to the firm's total profit. However, firms cannot use profit alone to compare one business unit to other business units or to alternative investments because the other business units and alternative investments are likely to be of different sizes or have different operating characteristics. The desired level of profit for a unit depends on its size and operating characteristics. Thus, although profit alone can be used effectively to evaluate a unit's performance over time, it should not be used to evaluate performance relative to other units or to alternative investments. A method to compare a unit to other units and to alternative investment is needed. The profit per dollar invested for each unit, usually called **return on investment (ROI),** can be used to compare a unit to others or to the profitability of alternative investments. Investment SBUs are based on the concept of return on investment.

Return on investment (ROI)

is profit divided by investment in the business unit.

The Strategic Role of Investment Units

The strategic role of investment SBUs is the same as those of the other SBUs:

1. To motivate managers to exert a high level of effort to achieve the goals set by top management.
2. To provide the incentive for managers to make decisions consistent with the goals set by top management.
3. To determine fairly the rewards earned by the managers for their effort and skill and the effectiveness of their decision making.

LEARNING OBJECTIVE 1

Identify the objectives of strategic investment units

How do investment SBUs achieve these three objectives? The first objective, motivation, can be achieved because the goal to increase return on investment is clear and intuitive and is generally within the manager's control. The second objective, goal congruence, is achieved since return on investment (ROI) is a critical financial performance measure for the firm as a whole. Each successful investment SBU contributes directly to the firm's success. The third objective, fairness of rewards, is achieved

---

[1] Bill Gates, *Business @ the Speed of Thought* (New York: Warner Books, 1999, p. 9).

[2] Debra Sparks, "Business Won't Hedge the Euro Away," *Business Week,* December 4, 2000, p. 157; and "The Euro: A Dismal Failure, a Ringing Success," *The Wall Street Journal,* November 2, 2000, p. A29; Michael M. Phillips, "Ship Those Boxes; Check the Euro," *The Wall Street Journal,* February 7, 2003, p. C1; Liliana Hickman-Riggs and William A. Riggs, "Accounting for the Euro," *Management Accounting Quarterly,* Spring 2001, pp. 34-40.

because the use of investment SBUs provides a sound basis for comparing the performance of units of different size; profits are measured relative to the amount of investment. Moreover, ROI contributes to achieving fairness because it is a clear, quantitative measure that managers understand well, and over which they typically have a great deal of control.

The principal measure of investment SBU performance is ROI. In addition, two related measures—residual income (RI) and economic value added (EVA)—are used. We consider each in the following sections.

Return on Investment

LEARNING OBJECTIVE 2
Explain the use of return on investment (ROI) and identify its advantages and limitations.

The most commonly used investment SBU measure is ROI, which is a percentage, and the larger the percentage, the better the ROI. The amount of ROI for a successful company depends on many factors, including general economic conditions and in particular, the current economic conditions of the company's industry. For example, cyclical industries such as airlines and home construction have ROIs that vary significantly under differing economic conditions. In calculating ROI, profit is typically determined from generally accepted accounting principles.[3] However, for internal purposes, the firm can choose to use alternative definitions of profit, for example, the variable costing approach explained in Chapter 17.

The amount of investment is often determined by the assets of the business unit based also on generally accepted accounting principles. Alternatively, investment can be measured by the value of the ownership interest, which can be determined from the shareholders' equity on the financial statements of a publicly owned firm. For a nonpublic firm, it can be determined from the amount of total assets less liabilities. When the value of the ownership interest is used for investment, return on investment often is called **return on equity (ROE)**. ROE is of special interest to shareholders and business owners because it is a direct measure of the firm's returns to owners. Because our focus in this chapter is on the performance of managers in meeting top management's goals, we hereafter focus on only ROI. The evaluation of the firm from the viewpoint of the shareholder is considered again in Chapter 19.

Return on equity (ROE),
is the return determined when investment is measured as shareholder's equity.

ROI Equals Return on Sales Times Asset Turnover

We can enhance the ROI measure's usefulness by showing it as the product of two components, return on sales and asset turnover. Since sales and profits relate to a period of time, for consistency the amount of assets used to calculate ROI usually is determined from the simple average of the value of assets at the start of the period and the value of assets at the end of the period.

$$\text{ROI} = \text{Return on sales} \times \text{Asset turnover}$$

$$\text{ROI} = \frac{\text{Profit}}{\text{Sales}} \times \frac{\text{Sales}}{\text{Assets}}$$

Return on sales (ROS),
a firm's profit per sales dollar, measures the manager's ability to control expenses and increase revenues to improve profitability.

Asset turnover,
the amount of dollar sales achieved per dollar of investment, measures the manager's ability to increase sales from a given level of investment.

Return on sales (ROS), a firm's profit per sales dollar, measures the manager's ability to control expenses and increase revenues to improve profitability. **Asset turnover,** the amount of dollar sales achieved per dollar of investment, measures the manager's ability to increase sales from a given level of investment. Together, the two components of ROI tell a more complete story of the manager's performance and enhance top management's ability to evaluate and compare the different units. For example, research has shown that firms with different operating strategies tend also to have a different mix of return on sales versus asset turnover. Firms with high operating leverage

---

[3] Generally accepted accounting principles are the body of accounting rules, methods, and procedures that are set forth as acceptable by the accounting profession for use in preparing financial statements.

(see Chapter 7) tend to have low asset turnover and high return on sales; those with low operating leverage and commoditylike products tend to have the highest asset turnover and the lowest return on sales.[4]

Illustration of Evaluation Using Return on Investment

Assume that CompuCity is a retailer with three product lines, computers, software, and computer help books. It has stores in three regions, the Boston area, South Florida, and the Midwest. Each store sells only books, computers, and software. CompuCity's profits for the Midwest declined last year, due in part to increased price competition in the computer unit.

Because of this decline in profits, top management uses ROI to study the performance of the Midwest region. Each product line is considered an investment SBU. CompuCity knows that the markups are highest in software and lowest for computers because of price competition. Investment in each unit consists of the inventory for sale and the value of the real estate and improvements of the retail stores. Inventory is relatively low in the computer unit since merchandise is restocked quickly from the manufacturers. Inventory is also low in the book unit because about 40 percent of CompuCity's books are on consignment from publishers.

The value of the real estate and store improvements is allocated to each of the three units on the basis of square feet of floor space used. The software unit occupies the largest amount of floor space, followed by computers and books. Panel 1 of Exhibit 18.1 shows the income, sales, and investment information for CompuCity in 2003 and 2004. Panel 2 shows the calculation of ROI, including ROS and asset turnover, for the Midwest region for both 2003 and 2004.

The data in Exhibit 18.1 indicate that CompuCity's ROI has fallen (from 14.4 percent in 2003 to 13.5 percent in 2004) due mainly to a decline in overall return on sales (from 6.1 percent in 2003 to 5.1 percent in 2004). Further analysis shows that the drop in return on sales is due to the sharp decline in ROS for the computer unit (from 4 percent in 2003 to 2 percent in 2004). The computer unit's decline in ROS is likely the result of the increased price competition.

The analysis also shows that software is the most profitable business unit (the highest ROI of 20 percent in 2004); this is so primarily because of the relatively high ROS (highest at 10 percent since the markup on software products is relatively high). In contrast, the computer and book units have higher asset turnovers due to the lower required levels of inventory and floor space than the computer unit and the large percentage of consignment inventory for the book unit. ROI has also improved significantly for the software unit because of the decline in investment, due either to a reduction in inventory or a decrease in floor space for software (recall that investment is allocated to the units on the basis of floor space).

Strategic Analysis Using ROI

Use of ROI enables CompuCity to evaluate the managers of the three units and to complete a strategic analysis of the entire firm. CompuCity can set performance goals for managers in terms of both return on sales and asset turnover. The unit managers then have very clear goals to increase sales and reduce costs, reduce inventory, and use floor space effectively. To be effective, the goals should recognize differences in the competitive factors among the units. For example, lower ROS should be expected of the computer unit because of competitive pricing that affects that unit.

---

[4] ROI based on asset turnover, and return on sales is often referred to as the *DuPont approach* since it was originated by Donaldson Brown, chief financial officer of DuPont Corporation early in the 1900s. See also Thomas I. Selling and Clyde P. Stickney, "The Effects of Business Environment and Strategy on a Firm's Rate of Return on Assets," *Financial Analysts Journal,* January–February 1989; Patricia M. Fairfield and Teri L. Yohn, "Using Asset Turnover and Profit Margin to Forecast Changes in Profitability," presented at the American Accounting Association Annual Meeting, Philadelphia, August 2000.

EXHIBIT 18.1 ROI, Return on Sales, and Asset Turnover for CompuCity *(Midwest Region)*

Panel 1: Income Investment, and Sales for CompuCity

	Income		Investment		Sales	
	2003	**2004**	**2003**	**2004**	**2003**	**2004**
Computers	$ 8,000	$ 5,000	$ 50,000	$ 62,500	$200,000	$250,000
Software	15,000	16,000	100,000	80,000	150,000	160,000
Books	3,200	5,000	32,000	50,000	80,000	100,000
Total	$26,200	$26,000	$182,000	$192,500	$430,000	$510,000

Panel 2: Return on Sales, Asset Turnover, and ROI for CompuCity

	Return on Sales		Asset Turnover		ROI	
	2003	**2004**	**2003**	**2004**	**2003**	**2004**
Computers	4% = 8,000/200,000	2% = 5,000/250,000	4.00 = 200,000/50,000	4.00 = 250,000/62,500	16% = 8,000/50,000	8% = 5,000/62,500
Software	10% = 15,000/150,000	10% = 16,000/160,000	1.50 = 150,000/100,000	2.00 = 160,000/80,000	15% = 15,000/100,000	20% = 16,000/80,000
Books	4% = 3,200/80,000	5% = 5,000/100,000	2.50 = 80,000/32,000	2.00 = 100,000/50,000	10% = 3,200/32,000	10% = 5,000/50,000
Total	6.10% = 26,200/430,000	5.10% = 26,000/510,000	2.36 = 430,000/182,000	2.65 = 510,000/192,500	14.40% = 26,200/182,000	13.50% = 26,000/192,500

Exhibit 18.1 data also reflect the way that competitive factors in the computer unit and business relationships regarding inventory in the computer and book units affect the firm's profitability. This provides a useful basis for an improved analysis: for determining how the firm should position itself strategically. How should CompuCity's competitive approach be changed in view of recent and expected changes in the competitive environment? Perhaps the computer unit should be reduced and the software unit expanded. Which stores in the Midwest are successful, and why? A value-chain analysis might provide insight into strategic competitive advantage and opportunity. For example, CompuCity might find it more profitable to reduce its computer unit and replace it with products that are potentially more profitable, such as printers, pagers, cell phones, fax machines, supplies, and computer accessories.

Overall, ROI provides a useful basis for evaluating not only the unit manager's performance, but also the entire firm's performance.

Use of Return on Investment

For ROI to be useful, income and investment must be determined consistently and fairly:

1. Income and investment must be measured in the same way for each unit. For example, all units must use the same inventory cost flow assumption (FIFO or LIFO) and the same depreciation method.
2. The measurement method must be reasonable and fair for all units. For example, if some units have much older assets than other units have, the use of historical cost-based net book value for assets can significantly bias the ROI measures in favor of the older units.

In the following sections, we consider the measurement issues affecting the determination of both income and investment.

Measuring Income and Investment: Effect of Accounting Policies

Accounting policies regarding the measurement of investments and the determination of income have a direct affect on ROI. The two main types of accounting policies that affect ROI are (1) revenue and expense recognition policies and (2) asset measurement methods. Revenue and expense recognition policies affect ROI by determining when a sale is recognized as revenue and when an expenditure is recognized as an expense. These policies affect the timing of sales and expenses. The firm's policy for revenue and expense recognition should be considered carefully since any differences between units might significantly influence the proper interpretation of ROI.

Similarly, the firm has accounting policies for measuring inventory and long-lived assets that affect income and investment:

For Long-Lived Assets

1. **Depreciation policy.** The determination of the useful life of the asset and the depreciation method used affect both income and investment. Larger depreciation charges reduce ROI.
2. **Capitalization policy.** The firm's capitalization policy identifies when an item is expensed or capitalized as an asset. If an item is expensed, the effect reduces ROI.

For Inventory

3. **Inventory measurement methods.** The choice of inventory cost flow assumption (FIFO, LIFO) affects income and the measurement of inventory. Methods that increase cost of goods sold and decrease inventory, as is often the effect with LIFO in times of rising prices, reduce ROI.
4. **Absorption costing** (explained in Chapter 17). The effect of absorption costing creates an upward bias on net income and therefore on ROI when inventory levels are rising and the reverse when inventory levels are falling.
5. **Disposition of variances** (explained in Chapter 14). Standard cost variances can be closed to the cost of goods sold accounts or prorated to the inventory accounts; the choice has a direct effect on income and the inventory balances.

These five measurement issues affect the proper interpretation of net income and investment and, therefore, of ROI.[5] To ensure comparability, all business units must use the same policies. Moreover, when interpreting ROI, top management should consider whether the existing accounting policies have a bias to overstate (or understate) income and investment.[6]

---

[5] Each of the policies also has the effect of either simultaneously increasing income and increasing investment or simultaneously decreasing income and decreasing investment. Since ROI is a ratio that normally is between zero and 1, an increase in income increases ROI although investment also has increased by the same amount, and vice versa.

[6] Frances L. Ayres summarizes the accounting policies that can affect income in "Perceptions of Earnings Quality: What Managers Need to Know," *Management Accounting,* March 1994, pp. 27–29. See also Alfred Rappaport, "Shortcomings of Accounting Numbers," *Creating Shareholder Value* (New York: Free Press, 1986), Chap. 2; Anne Tergesen, "Which Number Is the Real McCoy?" *Business Week,* October 11, 1999, p. 177; Susan Sherreik, "What Earnings Reports Don't Tell You," *Business Week,* October 16, 2000, pp. 201–4.

EXHIBIT 18.2
**Effect of Capitalizing Certain
Costs on ROI for CompuCity**
(Midwest Region)

Panel 1: ROI Prior to Capitalizing Display Materials (same as Exhibit 18.1)		
	Computer Unit	**Book Unit**
Assets	$62,500	$50,000
Income	$ 5,000	$ 5,000
ROI	8%	10%

Panel 2: Book Unit Expenses Display Costs While the Computer Unit Capitalizes These Costs		
Assets	$64,000 = $62,500 + $1,500	$50,000
Income	$ 6,500 = $ 5,000 + $1,500	$ 5,000
ROI	10.16% = $6,500/$64,000	10%

To illustrate the effect of an accounting policy, assume that all units of CompuCity expense all furniture and other items used to display products; these items cost $1,500 per year. Suppose the computer unit decides to capitalize these expenses. What is the effect on ROI? Exhibit 18.2 compares the computer unit to the books unit before the change (in panel 1) and after (in panel 2).

The illustration shows that the decision to capitalize the display costs increased the computer unit's assets, income, and ROI. Although the book unit has the higher ROI when both units expense display costs, the computer unit's decision to capitalize these costs while the book unit does not has caused the computer unit to have the higher ROI.

Other Measurement Issues for Income

In addition to the firm's accounting policies, other effects on income should be considered when using ROI:

1. **Nonrecurring items.** Income can be affected by nonrecurring charges or revenues and then would not be comparable to income of prior periods or of other business units. For example, the high promotion costs for introducing a new product might significantly distort net income in the period involved.

2. **Income taxes.** Income taxes can differentially affect the various units, with the result that after-tax net income may not be comparable. This could be true, for example, if the business units operate in different countries with different tax rates and tax treaties.

3. **Foreign exchange.** Business units that operate in foreign countries are subject to foreign exchange rate fluctuations that can affect the income and the value of investments of these units.

4. **Joint cost sharing.** When the business units share a common facility or cost, such as the personnel department or data processing cost, that cost is often allocated to the units on some fair-share basis. For example, the amount of square feet of floor space is used to allocate plant-level costs. (See Chapter 12 for a discussion of allocation objectives and methods.) Different allocation methods result in different costs for each unit, and therefore they affect the units' income.

Each of these effects on income can influence the proper interpretation of ROI and should be considered when using ROI to evaluate investment SBUs.

Measuring Investment: Which Assets to Include?

A common method for calculating ROI is to define investment as the net cost of long-lived assets plus working capital.[7] A key criterion for including an asset in ROI is the degree to which the unit controls it. For example, if the unit's cash balance is controlled at the firmwide level, only a portion (or perhaps none) of the cash balance should be included in the investment amount for calculating ROI. Similarly, receivables and inventory should include only those controllable at the unit level.

---

[7] *Working capital* is defined as current assets less current liabilities. For a discussion of the determination of assets for ROI, see R. N. Anthony and V. Govindarajan, *Management Control Systems,* 11th ed. (New York: McGraw-Hill/Irwin, 2004).

Coke and Its Bottlers: Two Units and Two ROIs

Coca-Cola is made up of two separate companies, the Coke company and the bottling company, Coca-Cola Enterprises (CCE). The Coke company produces and sells the highly profitable proprietary concentrate to the bottlers that compete in a price-sensitive market. Once a part of a combined company, CCE was spun off as a separate entity in 1986. A favorable result of the spin-off for the Coke company is that the bottling company carries most of the assets of the two entities, the bottling plants and equipment. This means that the Coke company has consistently high ROIs (averaging nearly 20 percent in recent years) while the CCE company has consistently low ROIs (averaging about 2 percent in recent years). The spin-off

clearly has had the effect of improving the reported ROIs for the Coke company that has a high return on sales because of the high margins on the concentrate and also a high asset turnover because the bottling facilities are carried by the CCE. Because CCE is 38 percent controlled by Coke, the Securities and Exchange Commission is considering whether the two entities should be combined for financial reporting, which would result in ROIs under 10 percent for the combined entity.

Source: "Has Coke Been Playing Accounting Games?" *Business Week,* May 13, 2002, pp. 98–99.

Long-lived assets commonly are included in investment if they are traceable to the unit (for shared assets, see the next section). Management problems arise, however, if the long-lived assets are leased or if some significant portion of them is idle. Leasing requires a clear firmwide policy regarding how to treat leases in determining ROI so that unit managers are properly motivated to lease or not to lease, as is the firm's policy. In general, the leased assets should be included as investments since they represent assets used to generate income, and the failure to include them can cause a significant overstatement of ROI.

For idle assets, the main issue is again controllability. If the idle assets have an alternative use or are readily saleable, they should be included in the investment amount for ROI. Also, if top management wants to encourage the divestment of idle assets, including idle assets in ROI would motivate the desired action since divestment would reduce investment and increase ROI. Alternatively, if top management sees a potential strategic advantage to holding the idle assets, excluding idle assets from ROI would provide the most effective motivation since holding idle assets would not reduce ROI.

Measuring Investment: Allocating Shared Assets

When shared facilities, such as a common maintenance facilities are involved, management must determine a fair sharing arrangement. As in joint cost allocation (Chapter 12), top management should trace the assets to the business units that used them and allocate the assets that cannot be traced on a basis which is as close to actual usage as possible. For example, the investment in a vehicle maintenance facility might be allocated on the basis of the number of vehicles used in each unit or on their total value in each unit.

Alternatively, the required capacity and therefore the investment in the joint facility are sometimes large because the user units require high levels of service at periods of high demand. The assets should be allocated according to the *peak demand* by each individual unit; units with higher peak-load requirements that cause the need for capacity then receive a relatively larger portion of the investment. For example, a computer services department might require a high level of computer capacity because certain users require a large amount of service at certain times.

Measuring Investment: Current Values

Historical cost
is the book value of current assets plus the net book value of the long-lived assets.

Net book value
is the asset's historical cost less accumulated depreciation.

The amount of investment is typically the historical cost of the assets. The **historical cost** amount is the book value of current assets plus the net book value of the long-lived assets. **Net book value** is the asset's historical cost less accumulated depreciation. A problem arises when the long-lived assets are a significant portion of total investment because most long-lived assets are stated at historical cost, and price changes since their purchase can make the historical cost figures irrelevant and misleading.

If the relatively small historical cost value is used for investment in ROI, the result is that *ROI can be significantly overstated* relative to ROI determined with the current value of the assets. The consequence is that the use of historical cost ROI can mislead strategic decision makers, since the inflated ROI figures can create an illusion of profitability. The illusion is removed when the assets are replaced later at their current value, and the amount of income might not have been sufficient to support the replacement of the asset at the current higher value.

For example, a firm that enjoys a relatively high ROI of 20 percent based on net book value (e.g., income of $200,000 and net book value of $1,000,000) would find that *if* replacement cost of the assets were four times book value ($4 \times \$1,000,000 = \$4,000,000$), the ROI after replacement would become a relatively low 5 percent ($200,000/$4,000,000). Strategically, the firm should have identified the low profitability in a timely manner, but use of historical cost ROI can delay this recognition. A proper strategic approach is to use an investment value in ROI that considers replacing the assets at their current market value so that decisions are made on the basis of the current and future profitability of the firm's products and services, not on the basis of their past profitability alone.

In addition to its strategic value, the use of current value helps to reduce the unfairness of historical cost net book value when comparing among business units with *different aged assets*. Units with older assets under the net book value method have significantly higher ROIs than units with newer assets because of the effect of price changes and of accumulating depreciation over the life of the assets. If the old and new assets are contributing equivalent service, the bias in favor of the unit with older assets is unfair to the manager of a unit with newer assets. The difference is also misleading for strategic decision makers. The use of current values helps to reduce this bias since current values are not affected as strongly by age of assets as are historical cost–based net book values. Note that the use of current values improves the use of ROI both as a measure of the performance of the manager and of the economic performance of the unit itself; current values make the ROI calculation both more relevant and comparable.

Measures of Current Values   The three methods for developing or estimating the current values of assets are (1) gross book value, (2) replacement cost, and (3) liquidation value. **Gross book value (GBV)** is the historical cost without the reduction for depreciation. It is an estimate of the current value of the assets. GBV improves on net book value because it removes the bias due to differences in the age of assets among business units. However, it does not address potential price changes in the assets.

The other two approaches, replacement cost and liquidation value, effectively handle both the issues of age of assets and current cost. **Replacement cost** represents the current cost to replace the assets at the current level of service and functionality. In contrast, **liquidation value** is the price that could be received from their sale. In effect, replacement cost is a purchase price and liquidation value is a sales price. Generally, replacement cost is higher than liquidation value.

GBV is preferred by those who value the objectivity of a historical cost number; purchase cost is a reliable, verifiable number. In contrast, replacement cost is preferred when ROI is used to evaluate the manager or the unit as a continuing enterprise because the use of replacement cost is consistent with the idea that the assets will be replaced at the current cost and the business will continue. On the other hand, the liquidation value is most useful when top management is using ROI to evaluate the business unit for potential disposal, and the relevant current cost is the sales value of the assets, or liquidation value.

To illustrate, consider CompuCity's three marketing regions. CompuCity has 15 stores in the Midwest, 18 in the Boston area, and 13 in South Florida. CompuCity owns and manages each store. Exhibit 18.3 shows the net book value, gross book value, replacement cost, and liquidation value for 2004 for the stores in each region.[8]

Gross book value (GBV)
is the historical cost without the reduction for depreciation.

Replacement cost
represents the current cost to replace the assets at the current level of service and functionality.

Liquidation value
is the price that could be received for the sale of the assets.

---

[8] The values for net book value and gross book value in Exhibit 18.3 represent the simple average of beginning-of-year and end-of-year values (beginning and ending values are not shown). Replacement cost and liquidation value are determined as of the point when ROI is calculated.

EXHIBIT 18.3
Investment Data and ROI for CompuCity in Its Three Marketing Regions (000s omitted)

Region	Income	Net Book Value	Gross Book Value	Replacement Cost	Liquidation Value
Financial data					
Midwest	$26,000	$192,500	$250,500	$388,000	$ 332,000
Boston area	38,500	212,000	445,000	650,000	1,254,600
South Florida	16,850	133,000	155,450	225,500	195,000
Return on investment					
Midwest		13.51%	10.38%	6.70%	7.83%
Boston area		18.16	8.65	5.92	3.07
South Florida		12.67	10.84	7.47	8.64

The stores in the Boston area, where CompuCity began, are among the oldest and are located in areas where real estate values have risen considerably. The newer stores in the Midwest and Florida are also experiencing significant appreciation in real estate values. ROI based on net book value shows the Boston area to be the most profitable. Additional analysis based on GBV, however, shows that when considering that the Boston area stores are somewhat older, the ROI figures for all three regions are comparable, illustrating the potentially misleading information from ROI based on net book value.

Replacement cost is useful in evaluating managers' performance because it best measures the investment in the continuing business. The ROI figures show that all three regions are somewhat comparable, with South Florida slightly in the lead.

Liquidation value provides a somewhat different answer. The ROI based on liquidation value for the Boston area is very low relative to the other two areas. Because of the significant appreciation in real estate values at the Boston area stores, the liquidation value for the Boston region is quite high. The replacement cost figure is lower than liquidation cost because of the assumption that if CompuCity replaces its stores in the Boston area, they would be located where the real estate values are somewhat lower. The analysis of liquidation-based ROIs is useful for showing CompuCity management that the real estate value of these stores could now exceed their value as CompuCity retail locations. Perhaps the company should sell these stores and relocate elsewhere in areas whose values are near that of the suggested replacement cost figure.

Strategic Issues in Using Return on Investment

In addition to the measurement issues described earlier, two key issues must be considered in using ROI for evaluating investment SBUs: First, use the balanced scorecard to avoid an excessive focus on short-term results. Second, ROI has a disincentive for new investment by the most profitable units.

The Balanced Scorecard: Avoiding Excessive Short-Term Focus

ROI evaluation, much like profit SBUs and cost SBUs, focuses the manager's attention on the current period's costs and revenues, perhaps discouraging new investment that would increase long-term profitability, unless a quick and significant improvement in current income occurs. The result, often called *investment myopia,* is that managers tend to avoid new investment because the returns could be uncertain and might not be realized for some time. If the manager is evaluated using current ROI performance, the urgency of meeting the current period's ROI target tends to eclipse efforts to improve long-term profits.[9] The ROI-based incentive is for the manager to reduce research and

[9] Investment myopia is discussed widely. See, for example, Judith H. Dobrzynski, "A Sweeping Prescription for Corporate Myopia," *Business Week,* July 6, 1992; Kenneth A. Merchant, *Rewarding Results: Motivating Profit Center Managers* (Boston: Harvard Business School Press, 1989), Chap. 4; and John Dearden, "The Case against ROI Control," *Harvard Business Review,* May–June 1969.

development spending, advertising, employee training, and productivity improvements in order to improve the current ROI; strategically, however, these decisions might have disastrous long-term effects.

The effects of an excessive focus on short-term results can be addressed by using ROI as *only one part* of an overall evaluation of a strategic investment unit. A good approach is to use a balanced scorecard in which ROI plays an important role in the financial dimension of critical success factors (CSFs). In addition, the balanced scorecard evaluation considers CSFs in the other three dimensions: (1) customer satisfaction, (2) internal business processes, and (3) learning and innovation. The main concept of the balanced scorecard is that no one measure properly evaluates the SBU's progress to strategic success. Moreover, by attending directly to the firm's CSFs, the balanced scorecard effectively links the performance measurement/evaluation process to the firm's strategy. Chapter 17 discusses a food ingredients company's use of the balanced scorecard in strategic performance measurement.

ROI: Disincentive for New Investment by the Most Profitable Units

Business units evaluated on ROI have an important disincentive that conflicts with their achieving the objectives of investment SBUs. ROI encourages units to only invest in projects that earn *higher than the unit's current ROI* so that the addition of the investment improves the unit's overall ROI right away. Thus, the most profitable units have a corresponding disincentive to invest in any project that does not exceed their current ROI, although the project would have a good return. A "good" return can be defined as an ROI in excess of some minimum threshold, usually based on the firm's cost of capital.[10]

The disincentive for new investment hurts the firm strategically in two ways. First, it rejects investment projects that would be beneficial. Second, to take advantage of a unit's apparent management skill, ROI evaluation provides a disincentive for the best units to grow. In contrast, the units with the lowest ROI have an incentive to invest in new projects to improve their ROI. Management skills could be lacking in the low-ROI units, however.

The disincentive can be illustrated if we assume that CompuCity's Boston region has an option to purchase for $22,500 a telephone switch that can increase the capacity of its 800 service number and reduce operating costs by $10,000 per year. The switch is expected to last for three years and have no salvage value. Exhibit 18.4 shows

---

[10] The cost of capital is a composite of the firm's cost for funds from different sources, including both debt and equity. It is explained and illustrated in Chapter 20.

EXHIBIT 18.4 **ROI for CompuCity Purchase of Switch**

	First Year	Second Year	Third Year
Depreciation expense (straight-line method)	$ 7,500 = $22,500/3	$ 7,500	$7,500
Net book value at year-end	$15,000 = $22,500 − $ 7,500	$ 7,500 = $15,000 − $7,500	$ 0 = $ 7,500 − $7,500
Average net book value for the year	$18,750 = ($22,500 + $15,000)/2	$11,250 = ($15,000 + $7,500)/2	$3,750 = ($ 7,500 + $0)/2
ROI	13.33% = $10,000 − $ 7,500	22.22% = $10,000 − $7,500	66.67% = $10,000 − $7,500
	$18,750	$11,250	$3,750

the determination of ROI for the purchase of the switch using the straight-line method of depreciation. The ROI for its purchase is 13.33 percent in the first year and 22.22 percent and 66.67 percent in the second and third years, respectively.[11]

Using net book value, the Boston region's ROI is currently 18.16 percent (Exhibit 18.3). It might not purchase the switch because the first year's return of 13.33 percent is less than the current ROI. Buying the switch would reduce Boston's ROI from 18.16 percent to 17.77 percent [($38,500 + $10,000 − $7,500)/($212,000 + $18,750)] in the first year. In later years, the ROI from the switch would substantially exceed Boston's current ROI, but the manager might not be able to wait for that improvement if strong pressure for current profits exists.

LEARNING OBJECTIVE 3

Explain the use of residual income and identify its advantages and limitations.

Moreover, from a firmwide perspective, since the return on the switch in each year exceeds the firm's threshold return of 12 percent, the Boston region should purchase it. Thus, a significant limitation of ROI is that it can cause SBU managers to decline some investments, in conflict with firmwide interests. A useful way to address this limitation is to use an alternative measure of investment SBU profitability, called *residual income.*

Residual Income

Residual income (RI)

is a dollar amount equal to the income of a business unit less a charge for the investment in the unit.

In contrast to ROI, which is a percentage, **residual income (RI)** is a dollar amount equal to the income of a business unit less a charge for the investment in the unit. The charge is determined by multiplying the firm's desired minimum rate of return by the investment amount. Residual income can be interpreted as the income earned after the unit has paid a charge for the funds it needs to invest in the unit.

The RI calculation for CompuCity is illustrated in Exhibit 18.5 using a minimum rate of return of 12 percent. Note that since all three units have an ROI higher than 12 percent, all also have a positive RI. Note too that the unit's ranking on ROI is the same as its ranking based on RI: the Boston area unit has the highest ROI and residual income.

The issues regarding the measurement of investment and income for RI are the same as those discussed for ROI. Because of the effect of different accounting policies and the tendency of net book value to understate investment, the residual income measure must be interpreted carefully. It has the advantage of enabling a unit to pursue an investment opportunity as long as the investment's return exceeds the minimum return set by the firm. For example, using RI, the Boston region would accept the opportunity to purchase the telephone switch described in Exhibit 18.4 because it would contribute to the unit's residual income. The RI in the first year after the investment in the switch would be

$$\$13,310 = (\$38,500 + \$10,000 - \$7,500) - 0.12 \times (\$212,000 + \$18,750)$$

a $250 improvement over the unit's RI without it ($13,060, from Exhibit 18.5).

---

[11] Using the discounted cash flow methods explained in Chapter 20, the purchase of the switch has an internal rate of return of approximately 16 percent ($22,500/$10,000 = 2.250; the PV factor for 16 percent and three years is 2.246). As noted in Chapter 20, the discounted internal rate of return provides a summary return for the entire life of a multiyear project in contrast to ROI for which the return increases each year over the life of the project under most depreciation methods.

REAL-WORLD FOCUS Use of Residual Income in Evaluating Federal Programs

A recent project report of the Federal Accounting Standards Advisory Board (FASAB) provides background and perspective for the federal government to consider including the cost of capital in program evaluation. Specifically, the report notes that the inclusion of the cost of capital is consistent with *Federal Financial Accounting Standards Number 4* (managerial cost accounting standards for the federal government), which states that full cost information is desirable in financial reporting by federal programs and projects. The report also explains the calculation of residual income (RI) and its benefits in evaluating federal programs and projects. Particular attention is given to the fact that certain federal regulatory and policy-making activities require small amounts of capital and should thus

have a smaller capital charge. In contrast, agencies with large amounts of assets (for example, with $10 billion or more in assets: The Army Corps of Engineers, General Services Administration, Veterans Affairs; the U.S. Air Force, Army, and Navy; the Departments of the Interior, Agriculture, Energy, and Transportation; and NASA) should have a higher capital charge. The report also notes that the current guidance regarding financial reporting of governmental agencies in Canada and the United Kingdom includes the cost of capital in a manner very much like that of the RI measure.

Source: Based on Federal Accounting Standards, "Accounting for the Cost of Capital by Federal Entities," July 1996.

EXHIBIT 18.5
Illustration of Residual Income for CompuCity

	Income	Net Book Value
Financial data		
Midwest	$26,000	$192,500
Boston area	38,500	212,000
South Florida	16,850	133,000
Return on investment		
Midwest	13.51%	
Boston area	18.16	
South Florida	12.67	
Residual income	(minimum rate of return = 12 percent)	
Midwest	$ 2,900 = $26,000 − 0.12 × $192,500	
Boston area	$13,060 = $38,500 − 0.12 × $212,000	
South Florida	$ 890 = $16,850 − 0.12 × $133,000	

An additional advantage of RI is that a firm can adjust the required rates of return for differences in risk. For example, units with higher business risk can be evaluated at a higher minimum rate of return. The increased risk might be due to obsolete products, increased competition in the industry, or other economic factors affecting the business unit.

Another advantage is that it is possible to calculate a different investment charge for different types of assets. For example, a higher minimum rate of return could be used for long-lived assets that are more likely to be specialized in use and thus not so readily salable.

Limitations of Residual Income

Although the residual income measure deals effectively with the disincentive problem of ROI, it has limitations. A key one is that because RI is not a percentage, it suffers the same problem of profit SBUs in not being useful for comparing units of significantly different sizes. Residual income favors larger units that would be expected to have larger residual incomes, even with relatively poor performance. Moreover, relatively small changes in the minimum rate of return can dramatically affect the RI for units of different size, as illustrated in Exhibit 18.6. Although both units A and B have the same ROI of 15 percent, the RI amount differs significantly: $300,000 for unit A but only $22,500 for unit B. The difference would be greater for a smaller minimum return.

ROI and RI can complement each other in the evaluation of investment SBUs. The advantages and limitations of each measure are summarized in Exhibit 18.7.

EXHIBIT 18.6   The Effect of Unit Size and Minimum Desired Rate of Return on Residual Income

	Business Unit A	Business Unit B
Investment	$10,000,000	$750,000
Income	$1,500,000	$112,500
ROI	15% = $1,500,000/$10,000,000	15% = $112,500/$750,000
Residual income, at a minimum desired return of 12 percent	$300,000 = $1,500,000 − 0.12 × $10,000,000	$22,500 = $112,500 − 0.12 × $750,000

EXHIBIT 18.7   Advantages and Limitations of ROI and Residual Income

	Advantages	Limitations
ROI	• Easily understood • Comparable to interest rates and to rates of returns on alternative investments • Widely used	• Disincentive for high ROI units to invest in projects with ROI higher than the minimum rate of return but lower than the unit's current ROI
Residual income	• Supports incentive to accept all projects with ROI above the minimum rate of return • Can use the minimum rate of return to adjust for differences in risk • Can use a different minimum rate of return for different types of assets	• Favors large units when the minimum rate of return is low • Not as intuitive as ROI • Can be difficult to obtain a minimum rate of return
Both ROI and residual income	• *Congruent* with top management goals for return on assets • *Comprehensive financial measure;* includes all elements important to top management: revenues, costs, and investment • *Comparability;* expands top management's span of control by allowing comparison of business units	• *Can mislead strategic decision making;* not as comprehensive as the balanced scorecard, which includes customer satisfaction, internal processes, and learning as well as financial measures; the balanced scorecard is linked directly to strategy • *Measurement issues;* variations in the measurement of inventory and long-lived assets and in the treatment of nonrecurring items, income taxes, foreign exchange effects, and the use/cost of shared assets • *Short-term focus;* investments with long-term benefits might be neglected

Economic Value Added

LEARNING OBJECTIVE 4

Explain the use of economic value added (EVA) in evaluating strategic investment units.

Economic value added (EVA) is a business unit's income after taxes and after deducting the cost of capital.

Economic value added (EVA)[12] is a business unit's income after taxes and after deducting the cost of capital.[13] The idea is very similar to what we have explained as residual income. The objectives of the measures are the same: to effectively motivate investment SBU managers and to properly measure their performance. In contrast to RI, EVA uses the firm's cost of capital instead of a minimum rate of return. The *cost of capital* is usually obtained by calculating a weighted average of the cost of the firm's two sources of funds: borrowing and selling stock (the cost of capital is defined and explained in Chapter 20). For many firms, the minimum desired rate of return and the cost of capital are very nearly the same, with small differences due to adjustments for risk and for strategic goals such as the firm's desired growth rate. Although RI is

---

[12] EVA is a registered trademark of Stern Stewart & Co.

[13] G. Bennett Stewart III, "EVA Works—But Not If You make These Common Mistakes," *Fortune,* May 1, 1995, pp. 117–18. See also Marc J. Epstein and S. David Young, "Greening with EVA," *Management Accounting,* January 1999, pp. 45–49; Paul Dierks and Ajay Patel, "What Is EVA and How Can It Help Your Company?" *Management Accounting,* November 1997, pp. 52–58.

A number of studies have investigated the association of EVA with measures of shareholder value, principally stock price and stock returns. In a 1993 report, Shawn Tully showed that the stock prices of an EVA adopter, the Coca-Cola Company, followed EVA better than either earnings per share or return on equity.

More recently, researchers have found less promising results. A study of 17 Canadian agribusiness firms found little association between EVA and shareholder value for these firms. An econometric study of stock returns for 773 firms from the Business Week 1,000 (for 1988) also found that EVA added only marginally to the information content of accounting earnings. A study of 325 firms from Standard & Poor's 500 and the Business Week 1,000 found that their stock returns have a higher association to residual income and return on investment than to EVA. S. David Young, arguing from accounting concepts, states in a recent article that the adjustments to earnings proposed by EVA advocates may not improve EVA over residual income.

Regardless of the controversy, numerous firms in addition to Coca-Cola are enthusiastic about using EVA. For example, Centura

Bank of Rocky Mount, North Carolina, also uses EVA in evaluating performance and determining executive bonuses. The bank explains that EVA has had a significant positive influence on managers' decision making: it offers a stronger focus on tax planning and a more careful analysis of new business plans, among others.

Based on information in Robert McGough, "EVA Pay Plans Aren't a Big Hit in New Study," *The Wall Street Journal,* May 3, 2000, p. C1. Calum G. Turvey, Linda Lake, Erna van Duren, and David Sparling, "The Relationship between Economic Value Added and the Stock Market Performance of Agribusiness Firms," *Agribusiness,* Autumn 2000, pp. 399–416: Gary C. Biddle, Robert M. Bowen, and James S. Wallace, "Does EVA Beat Earnings? Evidence on Associations with Stock Returns and Firm Values," *Journal of Accounting and Economics,* 1997, pp. 301–36; S. David Young, "Some Reflections on Accounting Adjustments and Economic Value Added," *Journal of Financial Statement Analysis,* Winter 1999, pp. 7–19; and "Centura Banks Promote Sales Culture, Measure Performance by Economic Value Added," *Journal of Retail Banking Services,* Winter 1997, pp. 33–36.

intended to deal with the undesirable effects of ROI, EVA is also used to focus managers' attention on creating value for shareholders by earning profits higher than the firm's cost of capital. The calculation of EVA is illustrated on p. 820.

Another difference is that EVA users do not follow conventional, conservative accounting policies. For example, these users usually capitalize expenses that contribute to the company's long-term value. These expenses include research and development, certain types of advertising, and training and employee development which usually are expensed according to generally accepted accounting principles. In addition, EVA users often adjust earnings for certain aspects of accrual accounting to make EVA earnings more useful in projecting the firm's cash flows and long-term earnings potential. One adjustment is to use current cost to value inventory for both the balance sheet and its cost of goods sold so that both total assets and earnings are stated in terms of current costs. A second adjustment is that deferred taxes are not considered in determining earnings or liabilities; this provides a more nearly cash-flow–based valuation of earnings.

A number of firms, such as CSX, Coca-Cola, and Briggs & Stratton have adopted EVA in recent years and attribute improvements in profitability to the change. These developments indicate a renewed interest in residual income, with modifications, and some evidence of its usefulness for evaluating investment SBUs.

Using Average Total Assets

For simplicity, the CompuCity example above has used the year-end value of total assets in the calculation of ROI, residual income and EVA. In practice, accountants use the average of the beginning and ending balances of the year for total assets in calculating ROI, residual income and EVA. The reason is that since net income is applicable to the entire year, then using a simple average of the amount of total assets for the year is more consistent with income, than simply using the year-end amount. For example, CompuCity's ROI for 2004 (using information from Exhibit 18.1 and assuming the investment amounts shown in the exhibit are for the year-end) would be calculated as 13.89%:

$$\text{ROI} = \frac{\$26,000}{(\$182,000 + \$192,500)/2} = 13.89\%$$

Part Two: Transfer Pricing

Transfer pricing
is the determination of an exchange price for a product or service when different business units within a firm exchange it.

Transfer pricing is the determination of an exchange price for a product or service when different business units within a firm exchange it. The products can be final products sold to outside customers or intermediate products.

Transfer pricing is one of the most strategic activities in SBU management. It not only directly affects the strategic objectives of the firm (such as the decision of which parts of the value chain the firm should occupy) but also requires coordination among the marketing, production, and financial functions. It affects materials and parts sourcing decisions, tax planning, and, potentially, the marketing of the final and intermediate products. Because significant decision-making autonomy is desirable to enhance the motivation of the business units, setting the transfer price using an arm's-length approach between the units is also desirable. That is, the units should behave as if they were independent businesses. This determination of the transfer price is desirable from both a management perspective and tax purposes, as explained in the next section. The arm's-length approach is not always possible, however, such as when no alternative suppliers exist. The transfer pricing methods explained here include techniques for handling a variety of circumstances.

When Is Transfer Pricing Important?

Transfers of products and services between business units is most common in firms with a high degree of vertical integration. Vertically integrated firms engage in a number of different value-creating activities in the value chain. Wood product, food product, and consumer product firms are examples. For instance, a computer manufacturer must determine transfer prices if it prepares the chips, boards, and other components and assembles the computer itself. (See Exhibit 2–4 in Chapter 2: Value Chain for the Computer-Manufacturing Industry.) A useful way to visualize the transfer pricing context is to create a graphic such as the one in Exhibit 18.8 that illustrates the business units involved in the transfer of products and services and identifies them as inside or outside the firm, international or domestic. Exhibit 18.8 shows the transfers for a hypothetical computer manufacturer, High Value Computer (HVC), that purchases a key component, the x-chip, from both internal and external suppliers and purchases other components from international sources. The internal unit that manufactures x-chips sells them both

EXHIBIT 18.8
Transfer Pricing Context for High Value Computer

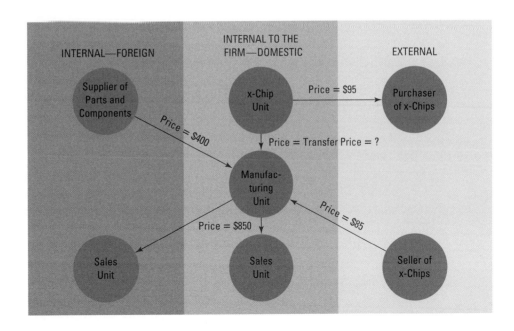

internally and externally. The manufactured units are transferred to both internal and external sales units. Where it is known, the transfer price is shown in Exhibit 18.8.

The management accountant's role is to determine the proper transfer price for the internal sales of the x-chip. We begin by considering the objectives of transfer pricing.

Objectives of Transfer Pricing

LEARNING OBJECTIVE 5
Explain the objectives of transfer pricing, the different transfer pricing methods, and when each method should be used.

The objectives for transfer pricing are the same as for SBUs: (1) to motivate managers, (2) to provide an appropriate incentive for managers to make decisions consistent with the firm's goals, and (3) to provide a basis for fairly rewarding the managers.

In satisfying these objectives, the transfer price determination also must recognize firmwide strategic goals. For example, an important strategic objective for transfer pricing is to minimize taxes locally and internationally. By setting a high transfer price for goods shipped to a relatively high tax country, the firm can reduce its firm-level tax liability. This would increase the cost and thus reduce the income of the purchasing unit in the high tax country, thereby minimizing taxes there. At the same time, the higher profits shown by the selling unit (as a result of the high transfer price) would be taxed at lower rates in the seller's home country.

Another strategic objective of transfer pricing is to develop strategic partnerships. A relatively high transfer price might also be used to encourage internal units to purchase from an external supplier, to encourage an external business relationship the firm wants to develop because of the supplier's quality, or to gain entrance to a market in a new country. It might also assist a newer or weaker unit to grow or build up a unit for spin-off or sale to outside investors.

International Transfer Pricing Objectives

Expropriation
occurs when the government in which a foreign company's investment assets are located takes ownership and control of those assets.

With the globalization of business, the international aspect of transfer pricing is becoming a critical concern, particularly with tax issues. Other international objectives include minimizing customs charges, dealing with currency restrictions of foreign governments, and dealing with the risk of expropriation by foreign governments. **Expropriation** occurs when a government takes ownership and control of assets a foreign investor has invested in that country. In managing the relationship with any one country, the management accountant attempts to find a strategic balance among these sometimes conflicting objectives.

Minimization of Customs Charges

The transfer price amount can affect the overall cost, including the customs charges, of goods imported from a foreign unit. For example, if customs charges are significant on the parts and components imported by the domestic manufacturing unit, High Value Computer's relatively low transfer price on these imports would be beneficial to reduce the amount of customs charges.

Currency Restrictions

As a foreign unit accumulates profits, a problem arises in some countries that limit the amount and/or timing of repatriation of these profits to the parent firm. One way to deal with these restrictions is to set the transfer price so that profits accumulate at a relatively low rate. This objective must be considered with other transfer pricing objectives.

Risk of Expropriation

When a significant risk of expropriation exists, the firm can take appropriate actions such as limiting new investment, developing improved relationships with the foreign government, and setting the transfer price so that funds are removed from the foreign country as quickly as possible.

Transfer Pricing Methods

The **variable cost method** sets the transfer price equal to the variable cost of the selling unit.

The **full cost method** sets the transfer price equal to the variable cost plus allocated fixed cost for the selling unit.

The **market price method** sets the transfer price as the current price for the selling unit's product in the market.

The **negotiated price method** involves a negotiation process and sometimes arbitration between units to determine the transfer price.

The four methods for determining the transfer price are variable cost, full cost, market price, and negotiated price. Each has advantages and limitations, and the choice of method depends on a careful consideration of the circumstances.

The **variable cost method** sets the transfer price equal to the selling unit's variable cost plus markup. This method is desirable when the selling unit has excess capacity and the transfer price's chief objective is to satisfy the internal demand for the goods. The relatively low transfer price encourages buying internally. This method is not suitable when the selling unit is a profit or investment SBU, because it adversely affects the seller's profit.

The **full cost method** sets the transfer price equal to variable costs plus selling unit's allocated fixed cost and markup. Advantages of this approach are that it is well understood and that the information is readily available in the accounting records. A key disadvantage is that it includes fixed costs, which can cause improper decision making (Chapter 9). To improve on the full cost method, firms can use the dual allocation method explained in Chapter 17 or, better yet, the activity-based method described in Chapter 5.[14]

The **market price method** sets the transfer price as the current price of the selling unit's product in the market. Its key advantage is objectivity; it best satisfies the arm's-length criterion desired for both management and tax purposes. A key disadvantage is that the market price, especially for intermediate products, is often not available.

The **negotiated price method** involves a negotiation process and sometimes arbitration between units to determine the transfer price. This method is desirable when the units have a history of significant conflict and negotiation can result in an agreed-upon price. The limitation is that the method can reduce the desired autonomy of the units.

Firms commonly use two or more methods, called *dual pricing*. For example, when numerous conflicts exist between two units, standard full cost might be used as the buyer's transfer price, while the seller might use market price.[15]

The advantages and limitations of the four methods are outlined in Exhibit 18.9.

Choosing the Right Transfer Pricing Method

The three key factors to consider in deciding whether to make internal transfers, and, if so, in setting the transfer price follow:

1. Is there an outside supplier?
2. Is the seller's variable cost less than the market price?
3. Is the selling unit operating at full capacity?

Exhibit 18.10 shows the influence of these three factors on the choice of a transfer price and on the decision to purchase inside or out.

First: Is there an outside supplier? If not, there is no market price, and the best transfer price is based on cost or negotiated price. If there is an outside supplier, we must consider the relationship of the inside seller's variable cost to the market price of the outside supplier by answering the second question.

Second: Is the seller's variable cost less than the market price? If not, the seller's costs are likely far too high, and the buyer should buy outside. On the other hand, if the seller's variable costs are less than the market price, we must consider the capacity in the selling unit by answering the third question. (Note: We

---

[14] For an illustration of dual allocation in transfer pricing, see David W. Young, "Two-Part Transfer Pricing Improves IDS Financial Control," *Healthcare Financial Management*, August 1998, pp. 56–65. For an explanation of the use of activity-based costing in transfer pricing, see Robert S. Kaplan, Dan Weiss, and Eyal Desheh, "Transfer Pricing with ABC," *Management Accounting*, May 1997, pp. 20–28, and Gary J. Colbert and Barry H. Spicer, "Linking Activity-Based Costing and Transfer Pricing for Improved Decisions and Behavior," *Journal of Cost Management*, May–June 1998, pp. 20–26.

[15] See a discussion of this issue in *The Wall Street Journal*, April 18, 1997, p. B1, regarding Koch Industries.

EXHIBIT 18.9   Advantages and Limitations of the Four Transfer Pricing Methods

Method	Advantages	Limitations
Variable cost	• Provides the proper motivation for the manager to make the correct *short-term decision*, in which the seller's fixed costs are not expected to change. When the seller's variable cost is less than the buyer's outside price, the variable cost transfer price will cause internal sourcing, the correct decision	• Inappropriate for long-term decision making in which fixed costs are relevant, and prices must cover fixed as well as variable costs • Unfair to seller if seller is profit or investment SBU
Full cost	• Easy to implement • Intuitive and easily understood • Preferred by tax authorities over variable cost • Appropriate for long-term decision making in which fixed costs are relevant, and prices must cover fixed as well as variable costs	• Irrelevance of fixed cost in short-term decision making; fixed costs should be ignored in the buyer's choice of whether to buy inside or outside the firm • If used, should be standard rather than actual cost (allows buyer to know cost in advance and prevents seller from passing along inefficiencies)
Market price	• Helps to preserve unit autonomy • Provides incentive for the selling unit to be competitive with outside suppliers • Has arm's-length standard desired by taxing authorities	• Intermediate products often have no market price • Should be adjusted for cost savings such as reduced selling costs, no commissions, and so on
Negotiated price	• Can be the most practical approach when significant conflict exists	• Need negotiation rule and/or arbitration procedure, which can reduce autonomy • Potential tax problems; might not be considered arm's length

EXHIBIT 18.10   Choosing the Right Transfer Price

	Decision to Transfer	Transfer Price
First: Is there an outside supplier? If there is *no* outside supply:	Buy inside	Cost or negotiated price
If there is an outside supply, answer the second question: **Second:** Is the seller's variable cost less than the outside price? *If it is greater than the outside price,* the seller must look for ways to reduce cost	Buy outside	No transfer price
If seller's variable costs are less than the outside price, answer the third question: **Third:** Is the selling unit operating at full capacity? *If seller has excess capacity,* then	Buy inside	**Low:** variable cost **High:** market price
If the seller is at full capacity → And if the contribution of the outside purchase to the entire firm is *greater than* the contribution of the inside purchase	Buy outside	No transfer price
And if the contribution of the outside purchase to the entire firm is *less than* the contribution of the inside purchase	Buy inside	Market price

focus on variable costs in this second step because commonly the transfer pricing decision is made in the context of a short-term decision in which fixed costs are not expected to differ whether the internal transfer is made or is not made. In this case, the analysis is very much like the make-or-buy decision explained in Chapter 9—the fixed costs of the seller are irrelevant since they will not change.)

Third: Is the selling unit operating at full capacity? That is, will the order from the internal buyer cause the selling unit to deny other sales opportunities? If not, the selling division should provide the order to the internal buyer at a transfer price somewhere between variable cost and market price. In contrast, if the selling unit is at full capacity, we must determine and compare the cost savings of internal sales versus the selling division's opportunity cost of lost sales. If the cost savings to the inside buyer are higher than the cost of lost sales to the seller, the buying unit should buy inside, and the proper transfer price should be the market price.

This three-question analysis is from top management's perspective and is thus the desired outcome of the units making these decisions autonomously. A good approach that preserves much of the units' autonomy is to set clear guidelines regarding top management's objectives in transfer pricing. Unit managers should know that their autonomous action to favor their unit over the interests of the firm as a whole will be viewed negatively in their annual performance evaluation.

Determining the correct transfer price and correct transfer decision can be illustrated using the High Value Computer case (Exhibit 18.8). High Value has the option to purchase the x-chip outside the firm for $85 or to manufacture it. Note that if the manufacturing unit purchases the x-chip from the outside suppler, it must add a component to the x-chip at a variable cost of $5 to make the x-chip function as desired; this additional step would not be necessary if the x-chip is purchased internally. Also, note that the x-chip unit can sell its chip outside for $95 but there is a variable selling cost of $2 per unit; there is no variable selling cost for internal transfer. The relevant information is presented in the top portion of Exhibit 18.11. The lower portion of Exhibit 18.11 shows the calculation of the relevant costs for each option.

A comparison of options 1 and 2 in Exhibit 18.11 shows that the firm as a whole benefits under option one when the manufacturing unit purchases the x-chip outside, and the x-chip unit also sells outside. The reason is that the computer manufacturing unit's savings of $30 from internal transfer ($30 = $85 outside price plus $5 for additional variable cost to add a component to the x-chip less $60 variable cost of the internal x-chip unit) is less than the x-chip unit's opportunity cost of lost sales, $33 ($95 less $60 manufacturing cost less $2 selling cost). The opportunity cost of the x-chip unit is important since the unit is at full capacity. The $450,000 difference between the two options is due to the net difference identified above, ($33−$30) × 150,000 = $450,000. In summary, we can answer the same three questions for High Value company in the following way:

> **First: Is there an outside supplier?** High Value has an outside supplier, so we must compare the inside seller's variable costs to the outside seller's price.
>
> **Second: Is the seller's variable cost less than the market price?** For High Value, it is, so we must consider the utilization of capacity in the inside selling unit.
>
> **Third: Is the selling unit operating at full capacity?** For High Value, it is, so we must consider the contribution of the selling unit's outside sales relative to the savings from selling inside. Again, for High Value, the contribution of the selling unit's outside sales is $33 per unit, which is higher than the savings from selling inside ($30), so High Value's selling unit should choose outside sales and make no internal transfers.

International Tax Issues in Transfer Pricing

LEARNING OBJECTIVE 6

Discuss the important international tax issues in transfer pricing.

Two recent surveys have found that more than 80 percent of multinational firms (MNCs) see transfer pricing as a major international tax issue, and more than half these firms said it was the most important issue.[16] Most countries now accept the Organization of Economic Cooperation and Development's model treaty, which calls for transfer prices to be adjusted using the arm's-length standard, that is, to a price that unrelated

[16] Based on information from two surveys: (1) the Ernst & Young Transfer Pricing Global Survey of 400 MNCs, as reported in the *Ernst & Young Business UpShot*, October 1997; and (2) a survey of 210 companies in the United States, United Kingdom, Japan, Australia, the Netherlands, France, and Germany, as reported in *Accounting Today*, August 21–September 10, 1995.

The recent fall in the value of Southeast Asian currencies (the Indonesian rupiah, Thai baht, Malaysian ringgit, and Sri Lanka rupee) relative to the U.S. dollar appeared to be an opportunity for some Southeast Asia manufacturers to increase their exports to U.S. retailers and manufacturers. The idea is that the falling currency prices will make the Asian goods less expensive in U.S. dollars, which will increase their appeal in the United States relative to other products and thus increase demand. Nike, which has a number of manufacturing plants in Southeast Asia, says, however, that these currency changes will not have much effect on U.S. prices. Is Nike likely to miss the potential to lower prices and increase U.S. sales? (Refer to Comments on Cost Management in Action at the end of the chapter.)

EXHIBIT 18.11

**Transfer Pricing Example
The High Value Computer
Company**

Key assumptions
  The manufacturing unit can buy the x-chip inside or outside the firm.
  The x-chip unit can sell inside or outside the firm.
  The x-chip unit is at full capacity (150,000 units).
  One x-chip is needed for each computer manufactured by High Value.
Other information

Sales price of computer for HVC's computer unit	$850
Variable manufacturing cost of the computer unit (excluding x-chip) ($400 parts and $250 labor)	650
Variable x-chip manufacturing cost for HVC's x-chip unit	60
Price of x-chip from outside supplier, to HVC computer unit	85
Variable cost to computer unit to add needed component to outside supplier's x-chip	5
Price of x-chip from HVC's x-chip unit to outside buyer	95
Variable selling cost to the x-chip unit for outside sales	2

Option 1: X-Chip Unit Sells Outside
High Value manufactures 150,000 computers, using x-chips purchased for $85 from outside supplier; High Value's x-chip unit sells 150,000 units for $95 each to outside buyer.

Contribution Income Statement*
(000s omitted)

	Computer Manufacturing Unit	X-Chip Unit	Total
Sales (price = $850, $95)	$127,500	$14,250	$141,750
Less: Variable costs			
X-chip ($85 + $5)	13,500		13,500
Other costs ($650, $60 + $2)	97,500	9,300	106,800
Contribution margin	$ 16,500	$ 4,950	$ 21,450

Option 2: X-Chip Unit Sells Inside
High Value manufactures 150,000 computers, using x-chips purchased for $60 (variable cost) from the inside supplier.

	Computer Manufacturing Unit	X-Chip Unit	Total
Sales (price = $850, $60)	$127,500	$9,000	$136,500
Less: Variable costs			
X-chip ($60)	9,000		9,000
Other costs ($650, $60)	97,500	9,000	106,500
Contribution margin	$ 21,000	—	$ 21,000

*It is assumed that in the short-term fixed costs will not differ for the two options and are excluded from the analysis.

parties would have set. The model treaty is widely accepted, but the way countries apply it can differ. However, worldwide support is strong for an approach to limit attempts by MNCs to reduce tax liability by setting transfer prices that differ from the arm's-length standard.[17]

The Arm's-Length Standard

The **arm's-length standard** calls for setting transfer prices to reflect the price that unrelated parties acting independently would have set. The arm's-length standard is applied in many ways, but the three most widely used methods are (1) the comparable price method, (2) the resale price method, and (3) the cost-plus method. The **comparable price method** is the most commonly used and the most preferred by tax authorities. It establishes an arm's-length price by using the sales prices of similar products made by unrelated firms.[18] A limitation is that it depends on the availability of comparable and unrelated prices.

The **resale price method** is used for distributors and marketing units when little value is added and no significant manufacturing operations exist. In this method, the transfer price is based on an appropriate markup using gross profits of unrelated firms selling similar products.

The **cost-plus method** determines the transfer price based on the seller's costs plus a gross profit percentage determined by comparing the seller's sales to those of unrelated parties or to unrelated parties' sales to those of other unrelated parties.

Advance Pricing Agreements

Advance pricing agreements (APAs) are agreements between the Internal Revenue Service (IRS) and the firm using transfer prices that establishes the agreed-upon transfer price. The APA usually is obtained before the firm engages in the transfer. The APA program's goal is to resolve transfer pricing disputes in a timely manner and to avoid costly litigation. The program supplements the dispute resolution methods already in place: administrative (IRS), judicial, and treaty mechanisms. Two-thirds of the MNCs in a recent survey indicated that they expected to use APAs in determining their transfer prices.[19]

The **arm's-length standard** says that transfer prices should be set so they reflect the price that unrelated parties acting independently would have set.

The **comparable price method** establishes an arm's-length price by using the sales prices of similar products made by unrelated firms.

The **resale price method** is based on determining an appropriate markup based on gross profits of unrelated firms selling similar products.

The **cost-plus method** determines the transfer price based on the seller's cost plus a gross profit percentage determined by comparing the seller's sales to those of unrelated parties.

Advance pricing agreements (APAs) are agreements between the Internal Revenue Service and the firm using transfer prices that establish the agreed-on transfer price.

[17] For further information on international taxation and transfer pricing, see B. J. Arnold and M. J. McIntyre, *International Tax Primer* (Boston: Kluwer Law International, 1995); also S. Crow and E. Sauls, "Setting the Right Transfer Price," *Management Accounting,* December 1994, pp. 41–47.

[18] In this context, *unrelated* indicates that the firm has no common ownership interest.

[19] *Accounting Today,* August–September 1995, p. 10. Also, for a recent survey of advance pricing agreements in 27 different countries, see Susan C. Borkowski, "Transfer Pricing Advance Pricing Agreements: Current Status by Country," *The International Tax Journal,* Spring 2000, pp. 1–16; for U.S. APA procedures, see Steven C. Wrappe, Ken Milani, and Julie Joy, "The Transfer Price Is Right," *Strategic Finance,* July 1999, pp. 39–43.

Survey of Transfer Pricing Practices for Tax Purposes

A recent survey of transfer pricing practices noted some interesting differences in the way firms in different countries determine transfer pricing for international taxation purposes. The survey included 23 firms in the United Kingdom, 14 in the United States, and 8 in Europe. Note the popularity of the cost-plus method in all three areas.

Based on information in: Jamie Elliott, "International Transfer Pricing: A Suvey of U.K. and non–U.K. Firms," *Management Accounting (UK)*, November 1998, pp. 48–50.

Method	United Kingdom	United States	Europe
Comparable price method	8	2	0
Resale price method	3	4	1
Cost-plus method	9	5	3
Other	3	3	4
Total	23	14	8

Summary

Return on investment (ROI) and residual income (RI) are two of the most commonly used and well-understood financial measures used in business today. Because of the advantage of investment SBUs in motivating managers and in providing a useful basis for top management to compare business units, most firms now commonly use these measures.

ROI, which has the advantages just mentioned has several disadvantages: a short-term focus, the difficulty in determining a unique measure for earnings and investment, and the disincentive for high ROI units to invest in projects with good but not very high returns.

RI is computed as the SBU's earnings less a capital charge based on a minimum desired rate of return. RI solves some, but not all, of the ROI's problems. For example, both have a short-term focus.

The increased interest in the balanced scorecard and in economic value added (EVA) suggest that firms are adapting investment SBUs to include a long-term strategic focus.

The management accountant can serve an important role by overseeing many objectives of transfer pricing: performance evaluation (of management and business units), tax minimization, management of foreign currencies and risks, and other strategic objectives. The common transfer pricing methods include variable costing, full costing, market value, and negotiated price. In setting the transfer price, management considers the availability and quality of outside supply, the internal selling unit's capacity utilization, and the firm's strategic objectives in determining the proper transfer price.

Perhaps the most important aspect in determining a transfer price for international transfers is minimizing international taxes. With the efforts of various international groups each country monitors transfer prices used in international trade. The most common transfer pricing methods used for international trade include the comparable price method, the resale price method, and the cost-plus method. A firm can determine the acceptability (to various countries) of its transfer pricing method by requesting what is called an *advance pricing agreement*.

Key Terms

advance pricing agreements (APAs), 787
arm's-length standard, 787
asset turnover, 768
comparable price method, 787
cost-plus method, 787
economic value added, (EVA) 779
expropriation, 782

full cost method, 783
gross book value (GBV), 774
historical cost, 773
liquidation value, 774
market price method, 783
negotiated price method, 783
net book value, 773
replacement cost, 774
resale price method, 787

residual income (RI), 777
return on equity (ROE), 768
return on investment (ROI), 767
return on sales (ROS), 768
transfer pricing, 781
variable cost method, 783

Comments on Cost Management in Action

Foreign Currency Translation, Transfer Pricing, and Profits

Nike is probably correct that U.S. prices for its products and those of its competitors will not change much. The reason is that the cost elements of its products from Southeast Asia affected by the falling local currencies, primarily labor costs, represent only a modest portion of the total product cost. Most of the cost of these manufactured products is for materials, which are imported from the United States and elsewhere outside Southeast Asia. Thus, the effect of the falling Southeast Asian currencies on *total* product cost is likely to be small; Nike estimates it to be 10 percent or less although some currencies have fallen to less than half of their previous value to the dollar.

Moreover, Southeast Asian manufacturers find that they have increased financing costs and sometimes reduced financing availability when the local currency falls and the raw materials from the United States and elsewhere become more expensive. For some of these manufacturers, the total operating and financing cost (in U.S. dollars) might even increase.

From a transfer pricing perspective, the dramatic change in currency value presents real problems in performance evaluation. Should the local manufacturing unit be responsible for costs in U.S. currency or in terms of the local currency? Are the currency fluctuations controllable by the local managers? The answers to these questions are difficult and complex, but many companies expect their local managers to take steps to mitigate the negative effects of currency fluctuations by buying or selling options or other financial instruments, for example.

Source: Based on Jonathan Moore and Moon Ihlwan, "Cheaper Exports? Not So Fast," *Business Week,* February 2, 1998, pp. 48–49.

Self-Study Problems
(For solutions, please turn to the end of the chapter.)

1. Return on Investment and Residual Income

Selected data from Irol Inc.'s accounting ledger follow:

Sales	$8,000,000
Net book value, beginning	2,500,000
Net book value, end	2,600,000
Net income	640,000
Minimum rate of return	12%

Required

1. Calculate return on investment, return on sales, and asset turnover.
2. Calculate residual income.

2. Proper Transfer Price

Johnston Chemical Company manufactures a wide variety of industrial chemicals and adhesives. It purchases much of its raw material in bulk from other chemical companies. One chemical, T-Bar, is prepared in one of Johnston's own plants. T-Bar is shipped to other Johnston plants at a specified internal price.

The Johnston adhesive plant requires 10,000 barrels of T-Bar per month and can purchase it outside the firm for $150 per barrel. Johnston's T-bar unit has a capacity of 20,000 barrels per month and is presently selling that amount to outside buyers at $165 per barrel. The difference between the T-Bar unit's price of $165 and the outside firm's T-bar price of $150 is due to short-term pricing strategy only; the materials are equivalent in quality and functionality. The T-Bar unit's selling cost is $5 per barrel, and its variable cost of manufacturing is $90 per barrel.

Required

1. Should the adhesive unit purchase T-Bar inside or outside the firm?
2. Based on your answer in requirement 1, what is T-Bar's proper transfer price?
3. How would your answer to requirements 1 and 2 change if the T-Bar unit had a capacity of 30,000 barrels per month?

Questions

18–1   Explain the advantages of investment SBUs. Why would a firm choose investment SBU evaluation rather than profit SBU or cost SBU evaluation?

18–2   What are the three investment SBU evaluation measures?

18–3 What is return on investment, and how is it calculated?

18–4 What are the measurement issues to consider when using return on investment?

18–5 What are the advantages and limitations of return on investment?

18–6 What is meant by the *arm's-length standard,* and for what is it used?

18–7 What are the components of return on investment, and how is each interpreted and used?

18–8 What are the advantages and limitations of residual income?

18–9 What are the objectives of investment SBU evaluation?

18–10 What is return on equity, how is it calculated, and how is it interpreted?

18–11 What are the three methods most commonly used in international taxation to determine a transfer price acceptable to tax authorities? Explain each method briefly.

18–12 What does *expropriation* mean, and what is the role of transfer pricing in this regard?

18–13 How does the concept of economic value added compare to return on investment and residual income?

Exercises

18–14 **Investment SBUs; The Sales Life Cycle (Review of Chapter 17)**   The sales life cycle is used to describe the phases a product goes through from introduction to withdrawal from the market. The four phases are (a) introduction, (b) growth, (c) maturity, and (d) decline and withdrawal.

In the introduction phase, the firm relies on product differentiation to attract new customers to the product. In the growth phase, the product attracts competition, although differentiation is still an advantage for the firm. In the maturity phase, competition is keen, and cost control and quality considerations become important. In the final decline phase, differentiation again becomes important as do cost control and quality (see Chapter 10 and Chapter 17 for more detail).

Required   At which phases of the sales life cycle, if any, should investment SBU evaluation methods be used, and why?

18–15 **Investment SBUs; The Cost Life Cycle**   As explained in Chapter 10, the cost life cycle consists of the phases the product goes through within a firm to prepare it for distribution and service. The five phases of the cost life cycle are (a) research and development, (b) design, (c) production, (d) marketing and distribution, and (e) customer service.

The early phases of the cost life cycle are particularly important in that a relatively high percentage (some say as high as 80 percent or more) of the product's life cycle costs are determined at these phases. That is, the downstream costs of manufacturing, service, and repair are a direct consequence of the quality of the design.

Required   At which phases of the cost life cycle, if any, should investment SBU evaluation methods be used, and why?

18–16 **Return on Investment and Residual Income**   Consider the following data from Midwest Financial, Inc. It uses investment SBU evaluation to analyze its two main divisions, mortgage loans and consumer loans (in millions):

	Mortgage Loans	**Consumer Loans**
Total assets	$2,000	$20,000
Operating income	$400	$2,500
Return on investment	20%	12.5%

Required

1. Based on ROI, which division is more successful? Why?
2. Midwest uses residual income as a measure of management success. What is the residual income for each division if the minimum desired rate of return is (a) 10 percent, (b) 15 percent, (c) 20 percent? Which division is more successful under each of these rates?

18–17 **Return On Investment; Comparisons of Three Companies**

Required   Fill in the blanks:

	Companies in the Same Industry		
	A	B	C
Sales	$1,500,000	$750,000	$_____
Income	200,000	75,000	_____
Investment (assets)	500,000	_____	2,500,000
Return on sales	_____	_____	0.5%
Asset turnover	_____	_____	1.5
Return on investment	_____	1%	_____

18–18 **Transfer Pricing; Decision Making**   Daniels Inc., which manufactures sports equipment, consists of several divisions, each operating as a profit SBU. Division A has decided to go outside the company to buy materials since division B informed it that the division's selling price for the same materials would increase to $200. Information for division A and division B follows:

Outside price for materials	$150
Division A's annual purchases	10,000 units
Division B's variable costs per unit	$140
Division B's fixed costs	$1,250,000
Division B's capacity utilization	100%

Required

1. Will the company benefit if division A purchases outside the company? Assume that division B cannot sell its materials to outside buyers.

2. Assume that division B can save $200,000 in fixed costs if it does not manufacture the material for division A. Should division A purchase from the outside market?

3. Assume the situation in requirement 1. If the outside market value for the materials drops $20, should A buy from the outside?

18–19 **Transfer Pricing; Decision Making**   Using the information from requirement 1 of problem 18–18, assume that division B could sell 10,000 units outside for $210 per unit with variable marketing costs of $8. Should division B sell outside or to division A?

18–20 **Target Sales Price; Return On Investment (ROI)**   Preferred Products, a bicycle manufacturer, uses normal volume as the basis for setting prices. That is, it sets prices on the basis of long-term volume predictions and then adjusts them only for large changes in pay rates or material prices. You are given the following information:

Materials, wages, and other variable costs	$300 per unit
Fixed costs	$200,000 per year
Target return on investment	20%
Normal volume	1,500
Investment (total assets)	$800,000

Required

1. What sales price is needed to attain the 20 percent target ROI?

2. What ROI rate will be earned at sales volumes of 2,000 and 1,000 units, respectively, given the sales price determined in requirement 1?

18–21 **ROI, Return On Sales, and Asset Turnover**   Eikelberry, Inc., has the following financial results for the years 2002 through 2004 for its three regional divisions:

	2002	2003	2004
Revenue			
Southwest	$12,000	$13,500	$16,000
Midwest	6,600	5,800	7,200
Southeast	9,300	11,100	12,000
Total	$27,900	$30,400	$35,200
Net Income			
Southwest	$ 1,200	$ 1,600	$ 1,450
Midwest	880	670	920
Southeast	1,200	1,500	1,600
Total	$ 3,280	$ 3,770	$ 3,970
Total Assets			
Southwest	$14,000	$14,000	$16,500
Midwest	4,200	4,200	4,200
Southeast	5,300	5,600	5,600
Total	$23,500	$23,800	$26,300

Required   Calculate return on investment, asset turnover, and return on sales for each division for each of the three years 2002, 2003, and 2004.

18–22   **ROI; Different Measures For Total Assets**   Michelle Jordan, Inc., has the following financial data for 2004 for its three regional divisions:

				Current Cost	
Region	Income	Net Book Value	Gross Book Value	Replacement Cost	Liquidation Value
North Atlantic	$45,000	$225,000	$450,000	$990,000	$350,000
Mid Atlantic	33,000	289,000	310,000	380,000	445,000
South Atlantic	22,000	115,000	166,000	650,000	980,000

Required   Calculate return on investment, investment turnover, and return on sales for each division for 2004. The sales in the North, Mid, and South Atlantic regions are $2,350,000, $1,450,000, and $500,000, respectively. Calculate ROI and investment turnover for each of the four measures of investment.

18–23   **ROI; Different Measures For Assets**   Ready Products, Inc., operates two divisions, each with its own manufacturing facility. The historical cost accounting system reports the following data for 2004:

HEALTH CARE PRODUCTS DIVISION
Income Statement for the Period Ended December 31, 2004
(000s)

Revenues	$600
Operating costs	470
Operating income	$130

COSMETICS DIVISION
Income Statement for the Period Ended December 31, 2004
(000s)

Revenues	$600
Operating costs	400
Operating income	$200

Ready estimates the useful life of each manufacturing facility to be 15 years. As of the end of 2004, the plant for the health care division is four years old, while the manufacturing plant for the cosmetics division is six years old. The purchase cost of the plant was the same at the time of purchase, and both have useful lives of 15 years with no salvage value. The company uses straight line depreciation and the depreciation charge is $70,000 per year for each division. The manufacturing facility is the only long-lived asset of either division. Current assets are $300,000 in each division.

An index of construction costs, replacement cost, and liquidation values for manufacturing facilities for the six-year period that Ready has been operating is as follows:

			Liquidation Value	
Year	Cost Index	Replacement Cost	Healthcare	Cosmetics
1998	80	$1,000,000	$800,000	$ 800,000
1999	82	1,000,000	800,000	800,000
2000	84	1,100,000	700,000	700,000
2001	89	1,150,000	600,000	700,000
2002	94	1,200,000	600,000	800,000
2003	96	1,250,000	600,000	900,000
2004	100	1,300,000	500,000	1,000,000

Required

1. Compute return on investment for each division using historical cost. Interpret the results.

2. Compute return on investment for each division, incorporating current-cost estimates as follows, using:

   a. Gross book values under historical costs.

   b. Gross book value at historical cost restated to current cost using the index of construction costs.

   c. Net book value of long-lived assets restated at current cost using the index of construction costs.

   d. Current replacement cost.

   e. Current liquidation value.

3. Which of the measures calculated in requirement 2 would you choose to (a) evaluate the performance of each division manager, (b) decide which division is most profitable for the overall firm. What are the strategic advantages and disadvantages to the firm of each measure for both (a) and (b)?

Problems

18–24 **Calculating ROI & RI And Comparing Results** Morgan Industries manufactures die machinery. To meet its expansion needs, it recently (2002) acquired one of its suppliers, Vienna Steel. To maintain Vienna's separate identity, Morgan reports Vienna's operations as an investment SBU. Morgan monitors all of its investment SBUs on the basis of return on investment. Management bonuses are based on ROI, and all investment SBUs are expected to earn a 12 percent minimum before income taxes.

Vienna's ROI has ranged from 14 percent to 18 percent since 2002. The company recently had the opportunity for a new investment that would have yielded 13 percent ROI. However, division management decided against the investment because it believed that the investment would decrease the division's overall ROI.

The 2004 operating statement for Vienna follows. The division's operating assets were $13,000,000 at the end of 2004, a 6 percent increase over the 2003 year-end balance.

VIENNA DIVISION
Operating Statement For Year Ended December 31, 2004
(000s omitted)

Sales	$25,000
Cost of goods sold	16,600
Gross profit	8,400

Operating expense		
Administration	$2,340	
Selling	3,810	6,150
Income before income taxes		$ 2,250

Required

1. Calculate the following performance measures for 2004 for the Vienna division:
   a. Return on average investment in operating assets employed.
   b. RI calculated on the basis of average operating assets employed.
2. Which performance measure (ROI or RI) should Morgan Industries use to provide the proper incentive for each division to act autonomously in the firm's best interests? Would Vienna's management have been more likely to accept the capital investment opportunity if RI had been used as a performance measure instead of ROI? Explain.
3. What type of strategic performance measurement do you recommend for Vienna Division? Explain.

18–25 **Transfer Pricing; Decision Making**   Phoenix Inc., a cellular communication company, has multiple divisions. Each division's management is compensated based on the division's operating income. Division A currently purchases cellular equipment from outside markets and uses it to produce communication systems. Division B produces similar cellular equipment that it sells to outside customers but not to division A at this time. Division A's manager approaches division B's manager with a proposal to buy the equipment from division B. If it produces the cellular equipment that division A desires, division B would incur variable manufacturing costs of $60 per unit.

Relevant Information about Division B

Sells 50,000 units of equipment to outside customers at $130 per unit.
Operating capacity is currently 80 percent; the division can perform at 100 percent.
Variable manufacturing costs are $70 per unit.
Variable marketing costs are $8 per unit.
Fixed manufacturing costs are $580,000.

Income per Unit for Division A (assuming parts purchased outside, not from division B)

Sales revenue		$320
Manufacturing costs		
Cellular equipment	80	
Other materials	10	
Fixed costs	40	
Total manufacturing costs		130
		190
Gross margin		
Marketing costs		
Variable	35	
Fixed	15	
Total marketing costs		50
Operating income		$140

Required

1. Division A wants to buy 25,000 units from division B at $75 per unit. Should division B accept or reject the proposal? How would your answer differ if (a) Division A requires all 25,000 units in the order to be shipped by the same supplier, or (b) Division A would accept partial shipment from Division B?
2. What range will the managers of divisions A and B agree is the best price for each division?

18–26 **Return on Investment; Residual Income**   Raddington Industries is a diversified manufacturer with several divisions, including the Reigis Division. Raddington monitors its divisions on the basis of both unit contribution and return on investment (ROI), with investment defined as average operating assets employed. All investments in operating assets are expected to earn a minimum return of 9 percent before income taxes.

Reigis's cost of goods sold is considered to be entirely variable; its administrative expenses do not depend on volume. Selling expenses are a mixed cost with 40 percent attributed to sales volume. The 2004 operating statement for Reigis follows. The division's operating assets employed were $80,750,000 at November 30, 2004, unchanged from the year before.

REIGIS STEEL DIVISION
Operating Statement
For the Year Ended November 30, 2004
(000s omitted)

Sales revenue		$35,000
Less expenses		
Cost of goods sold	$18,500	
Administrative expenses	3,955	
Selling expenses	2,700	25,155
Income from operations before tax		$ 9,845

Required

1. Calculate Reigis Steel Division's unit contribution if it produced and sold 1,484,000 units during the year ended November 30, 2004.
2. Calculate the following performance measures for 2004 for Reigis:
   a. Pretax ROI from average operating assets employed.
   b. Residual income calculated on the basis of average operating assets employed.
3. Reigis management is presented the opportunity to invest in a project that would earn an ROI of 10 percent. Is Reigis likely to accept the project? Why or why not?
4. Identify several items that Reigis should control if it is to be fairly evaluated as a separate investment SBU within Raddington Industries using either ROI or RI performance measures.

(CMA Adapted)

18–27 **Performance Evaluation**   Darmen Corporation is one of the major producers of prefabricated homes in the home building industry. The corporation consists of two divisions. (1) Bell Division, which acquires the raw materials to manufacture the basic house components and assembles them into kits, and (2) Cornish Division, which takes the kits and constructs the homes for final home buyers. The corporation is decentralized and the management of each division is measured by its income and return on investment.

Bell Division assembles seven separate home kits using raw materials purchased at the prevailing market prices. The seven kits are sold to Cornish for prices ranging from $45,000 to $98,000. The prices are set by corporate management of Darmen using prices paid by Cornish when it buys comparable units from outside sources. The smaller kits with the lower prices have become a large portion of the units sold because the final home buyer is faced with prices which are increasing more rapidly than personal income. The kits are manufactured and assembled in a new plant just purchased by Bell this year. The division had been located in a leased plant for the past four years.

All kits are assembled upon receipt of an order from Cornish Division. When the kit is completely assembled, it is loaded immediately on a Cornish truck. Thus, Bell Division has no finished goods inventory.

The Bell Division's accounts and reports are prepared on an actual cost basis. There is no budget and no product standards have been developed. A factory overhead rate is calculated at the beginning of each year. The rate is designed to charge all overhead to the product each year. Any under- or over-applied overhead is allocated to the cost of goods sold account and work in process inventories.

Bell Division's performance report follows. This report forms the basis of the evaluation of the division and its management by the corporate CFO. Additional information regarding corporate and division practices is as follows:

- The corporate office does all the personnel and accounting work for each division.
- The corporate personnel costs are allocated on the basis of number of employees in the division.
- The corporate accounting costs are allocated to the division on the basis of total costs excluding corporate charges.
- The division administration costs are included in factory overhead.
- The financing charges include a corporate imputed interest charge on division assets and any divisional lease payments.
- The division investment for the return on investment calculation includes division inventory and plant and equipment at gross book value.

BELL DIVISION
Performance Report
For the Year Ended December 31, 2004

	2004	2003	Increase or (Decrease) from 2003 Amount	Percent Change
Summary data				
Net income ($000 omitted)	$ 34,222	$ 31,573	$ 2,649	8.4%
Return on investment	37%	43%		
Production data (in units)				
Kits started	2,400	1,600	800	50.0
Kits shipped	2,000	2,100	(100)	4.8
Kits in process at year-end	700	300	400	133.3
Financial data ($000 omitted)				
Sales	$138,000	$162,800	($24,800)	(15.2)
Production costs of units sold				
Raw material	$ 32,000	$ 40,000	$ (8,000)	(20.0)
Labor	41,700	53,000	(11,300)	(21.3)
Factory overhead	29,000	37,000	(8,000)	(21.6)
Cost of units sold	$102,700	$130,000	$(27,300)	(21.0)
Other costs				
Corporate charges for				
Personnel services	$ 228	$ 210	$ 18	8.6
Accounting services	425	440	(15)	(3.4)
Financing costs	300	525	(225)	(42.9)
Total other costs	$ 953	$ 1,175	$ (222)	(18.9)
Adjustments to income				
Unreimbursed fire loss	—	$ 52	$ (52)	(100.00)
Raw material losses due to				
improper storage	$ 125	—	$ 125	—
Total adjustments	$ 125	$ 52	$ 73	140.4
Total deductions	$103,778	$131,227	$(27,449)	(20.9)
Division income	$ 34,222	$ 31,573	$ 2,649	8.4
Division Investment	$ 92,000	$ 73,000	$ 19,000	26.0
Return on Investment	37%	43%		

Required

1. What performance evaluation system does Darmen Corporation use? Discuss the value of the system in evaluating the Bell Division and its management.

2. Present specific recommendations to the management of Darmen Corporation to improve its performance evaluation system.

(CMA adapted)

18–28 **Performance Evaluation; Strategy Map; Review of Chapter 17; Correlation Analysis** Maydew Manufacturing Inc. is a large manufacturer of lawn and garden equipment including mowers, edgers, tillers, related equipment, and accessories. The firm has been very successful in recent years, and sales have grown more than 10 percent in each of the last five years. The firm is organized into 15 investment SBUs based on product line groups. Return on investment and residual income calculations have been made for each of the last four years and used in management compensation for the last two years. Recently Maydew top management has contracted with MM&PC, a large consulting firm to review the performance measurement process at the firm. One of MM&PC's key recommendations has been to consider the implementation of the balanced scorecard both for performance measurement and for strategic management. As a step in this direction, MM&PC has asked Maydew for some data on ROI and other measures being considered for the balanced scorecard to analyze the relationships among these data. It is hoped that the analysis will help MM&PC develop a strategy map for the firm. The following data show the last year's ROI for each SBU and the average for the last three years for training hours per employee in the SBU, customer retention rate in the SBU (customers are primarily large department store chains and other distributors of lawn and garden equipment), the QSV score, and the defect rate (per thousand products). The QSV score is a measure of the Quality-Service-Value of the SBU made by an analysis of a variety of operating data including the results of on-site inspection of each unit by key operating executives and other measures of operating performance (the highest score is 10, and the lowest is 0).

Manager	ROI	Training Hours per Employee	Customer Retention	QSV Score	Defect Rate
1	21.3	98	99.3	7	3.3
2	15.4	122	98.2	8	4.7
3	9.6	67	86.7	6	11.2
4	12.4	88	84.5	9	13.7
5	18.6	92	91.4	8	2.1
6	4.5	33	90.7	4	28.9
7	8.8	49	88.9	6	1.2
8	22.6	77	93.5	10	12.4
9	11.8	102	95.5	9	8.0
10	14.6	95	91.1	6	7.4
11	16.5	87	92.7	6	2.8
12	12.1	80	86.4	8	4.9
13	6.2	66	80.2	4	15.3
14	1.3	50	78.0	4	22.8
15	9.7	78	85.5	7	30.5

Required

1. Using the concept of the strategy map, consider how the nonfinancial factors (training hours, customer retention, QSV, and defect rate) affect ROI. Which of these variables has the greatest influence on ROI? Use regression and correlation analysis to perform your analysis.

2. Explain which two managers you would rate as the best overall and which you would rate as the worst overall, and give reasons why.

18–29 **Transfer Pricing Methods** Lynsar Corporation started as a single plant to produce its major components and then assembled its main product into electric motors. Lynsar later expanded by developing outside markets for some components used in its motors. Eventually, the company reorganized into four manufacturing divisions: bearing, casing, switch, and motor. Each manufacturing division operates as an autonomous unit, and divisional performance is the basis for year-end bonuses.

Lynsar's transfer pricing policy permits the manufacturing divisions to sell either externally or internally. The price for goods transferred between divisions is negotiated between the buying and selling divisions without any interference from top management.

Lynsar's profits for the current year have dropped although sales have increased, and the decreased profits can be traced almost entirely to the motor division. Jere Feldon, Lynsar's chief financial officer, has learned that the motor division purchased switches for its motors from an outside supplier during the current year rather than buying them from the switch division, which is at capacity and has refused to sell to the motor division. It can sell them to outside customers at a price higher than the actual full (absorption) manufacturing cost that has always been negotiated in the past with the motor division. When the motor division refused to meet the price that the switch division was receiving from its outside buyer, the motor division had to purchase the switches from an outside supplier at an even higher price.

Jere is reviewing Lynsar's transfer pricing policy because he believes that suboptimization has occurred. Although the switch division made the correct decision to maximize its division profit by not transferring the switches at actual full manufacturing cost, this was not necessarily in Lynsar's best interest because of the price the motor division paid for them. The motor division has always been Lynsar's largest division and has tended to dominate the smaller divisions. Jere has learned that the casing and bearing divisions are also resisting the motor division's expectation to use the actual full manufacturing cost as the negotiated price.

Jere has requested that the corporate accounting department study alternative transfer pricing methods to promote overall goal congruence, motivate divisional management performance, and optimize overall company performance. Three transfer pricing methods being considered follow. The one selected will be applied uniformly across all divisions.

- Standard full manufacturing costs plus markup.
- Market selling price of the products being transferred.
- Outlay (out-of-pocket) costs incurred to the point of transfer plus opportunity cost to the seller, per unit.

Required

1. Discuss the following:
   a. The positive and negative motivational implications of employing a negotiated transfer price system for goods exchange between divisions.
   b. The motivational problems that can result from using actual full (absorption) manufacturing costs as a transfer price.
2. Discuss the motivational issues that could arise if Lynsar Corporation decides to change from its current policy of covering the transfer of goods between divisions to a revised transfer pricing policy that would apply uniformly to all divisions.
3. Discuss the likely behavior of both buying and selling divisional managers for each transfer pricing method listed earlier, if it were adopted by Lynsar.

(CMA Adapted)

18–30 **Transfer Pricing Issues**   Often when transfer prices are based on cost, a supplying division has no incentive to reduce cost. For example, a design change that would reduce the supplying division's manufacturing cost would benefit only downstream divisions if the transfer price is based on a markup of cost.

Required   What can or should be done to provide the supplying division an incentive to reduce manufacturing costs when the transfer price is cost-based?

18–31 **Transfer Pricing; International Taxation**   Hirsch Company has a manufacturing subsidiary in Singapore that produces high-end exercise equipment for U.S. consumers. The manufacturing subsidiary has total manufacturing costs of $1,500,000 plus general and administrative expenses of $350,000. The manufacturing unit sells the equipment for $2,500,000 to the U.S. marketing subsidiary, which sells it to the final consumer for an aggregate of $3,500,000. The sales subsidiary has total marketing, general, and administrative costs of $300,000. Assume that Singapore has a corporate tax rate of 33 percent and that the U.S. tax rate is 46 percent. Assume that no tax treaties or other special tax treatments apply.

Required   What is the effect on Hirsch Company's total corporate level taxes if the manufacturing subsidiary raises its price by 10 percent to the sales subsidiary?

18–32   **Transfer Pricing; Decision Making**   Advanced Manufacturing Inc. (AMI) produces electronic components in three divisions: industrial, commercial, and consumer products. The commercial products division annually purchases 10,000 units of part 23–6711, which the industrial division produces for use in manufacturing one of its own products. The commercial division is growing rapidly due to rapid growth in its markets. The commercial division is expanding its production and now wants to increase its purchases of part 23–6711 to 15,000 units per year. The problem is that the industrial division is at full capacity. No new investment in the industrial division has been made for some years because top management sees little future growth in its products, so its capacity is unlikely to increase soon.

The commercial division can buy part 23–6711 from HighTech Inc. or from Britton Electric, a customer of the industrial division, now purchasing 650 units of part 88–461. The industrial division's sales to Britton would not be affected by the commercial division's decision about part 23–6711.

Industrial division	
Data on part 23–6711	
Price to commercial division	$185
Variable manufacturing costs	155
Price to outside buyers	205
Data on part 88–461	
Variable manufacturing costs	65
Sales price	95
Other suppliers of part 23–6711	
HighTech Inc., price	200
Britton Electric, price	210

Required

1. What is the proper decision regarding where the commercial division should purchase the additional 5,000 parts and what is the correct transfer price?

2. Assume that the industrial division's sales to Britton would be cancelled if the commercial division does not buy from Britton. What would be the unit cost to AMI in this case, and would the desired transfer price change?

3. What are the strategic implications of your answer to requirement 1? How can AMI become more competitive in one or more of its divisions?

18–33   **Return on Investment; Residual Income**   Jump-Start Co. (JSC), a subsidiary of Mason Industries, manufactures go-carts and other recreational vehicles. Family recreational centers that feature go-cart tracks as well as miniature golf courses, batting cages, and arcade games have increased in popularity. As a result, Mason management has been pressuring JSC to diversify into some of these other recreational areas. Recreational Leasing Inc. (RLI), one of the largest firms that leases arcade games to these family recreational centers, is looking for a buyer. Mason's top management believes that RLI's assets could be acquired for an investment of $3.2 million and has strongly urged Bill Grieco, JSC's division manager, to consider the acquisition.

Bill has reviewed RLI's financial statements with his controller, Marie Donnelly; they believe that the acquisition may not be in JSC's best interest. "If we decide not to do this, the Mason people are not going to be happy," Bill said. "If we could convince them to base our bonuses on something other than ROI, maybe this acquisition would look more attractive. How would we do if the bonuses were based on RI using the company's 15 percent cost of capital?"

Mason has traditionally evaluated all divisions on the basis of ROI, which is the ratio of operating income to total assets. The desired rate of return for each division is 20 percent. The management team of any division reporting an annual increase in the ROI is automatically eligible for a bonus. The management of divisions reporting a decline in ROI must provide convincing explanations for the decline to be eligible for a bonus. The bonus for divisions with declining ROI is limited to 50 percent of the amount of the bonus paid to divisions reporting an increase.

The following are the condensed financial statements of JSC and RLI for the fiscal year ended May 31, 2004.

	JSC	RLI
Sales revenue	$10,500,000	—
Leasing revenue	—	$2,800,000
Variable expenses	7,000,000	1,000,000
Fixed expenses	1,500,000	1,200,000
Operating income	$ 2,000,000	$ 600,000
Current assets	$ 2,300,000	$1,900,000
Long-term assets	5,700,000	1,100,000
Total assets	$ 8,000,000	$3,000,000
Current liabilities	$ 1,400,000	$ 850,000
Long-term liabilities	3,800,000	1,200,000
Shareholders' equity	2,800,000	950,000
Total liabilities and shareholders' equity	$ 8,000,000	$3,000,000

Required

1. If Mason Industries continues to use ROI as the sole measure of division performance, explain why JSC is reluctant to acquire RLI. Support your answer with appropriate calculations.
2. If Mason Industries could be persuaded to use RI to measure JSC's performance, explain why JSC would be more willing to acquire RLI. Support your answer with appropriate calculations.
3. Discuss how the behavior of division managers is likely to be affected by the use of
   a. ROI as a performance measure.
   b. RI as a performance measure.

(CMA Adapted)

18–34 **Return on Investment**   Videonet Company manufactures highly specialized products for networking video-conferencing equipment. Production of specialized units are, to a large extent, performed under contract, with standard units manufactured according to marketing projections. Maintenance of customer equipment is an important area of customer satisfaction. With the recent downturn in the computer industry, the video-conferencing equipment segment has suffered, causing a slide in Videonet's financial performance. Its income statement for the fiscal year ended October 31, 2004, follows.

VIDEONET COMPANY
Income Statement
For the Year Ended October 31, 2004
(000s omitted)

Net sales	
Equipment	$6,500
Maintenance contracts	1,800
Total net sales	$8,300
Expenses	
Cost of goods sold	4,600
Customer maintenance	1,000
Selling expense	600
Administrative expense	900
Interest expense	150
Total expense	$7,250
Income before taxes	1,050
Income taxes	420
Net income	$ 630

Videonet's return on sales before interest and taxes was 14.5 percent in fiscal 2004 when the industry average was 18 percent. Its total asset turnover was two times, and its return on average assets before interest and taxes was 29 percent, both well below the industry average. To improve performance and raise these ratios closer to, or above, industry averages, Bill Hunt, Videonet's president, established the following goals for fiscal 2005:

Return on sales before interest and taxes	15%
Total asset turnover	3 times
Return on average assets before interest and taxes	35%

To achieve Hunt's goals, Videonet's management team considered the growth in the international video-conferencing market and proposed the following actions for fiscal 2005:

- Increase equipment sales prices by 10 percent.
- Increase the cost of each unit sold by 3 percent for needed technology, and quality improvements and for increased variable costs.
- Increase maintenance inventory by $250,000 at the beginning of the year and add two maintenance technicians at total cost of $130,000 to cover wages and related travel expenses. These revisions are intended to improve customer service and response time. The increased inventory will be financed at an annual interest rate of 12 percent; no other borrowings or loan reductions are contemplated during fiscal 2005. All other assets will be held to fiscal 2004 levels.
- Increase selling expenses by $250,000 but hold administrative expenses at 2004 levels.
- The effective rate for 2005 federal and state taxes is expected to be 40 percent, the same as 2004.

These actions were taken to increase equipment unit sales by 8 percent, with a corresponding 8 percent growth in maintenance contracts.

Required

1. Prepare a budgeted income statement for Videonet for the fiscal year ending October 31, 2005, on the assumption that the proposed actions are implemented as planned and that the increased sales objectives will be met.
2. Calculate the following ratios for Videonet for fiscal year 2005 and determine whether Bill Hunt's goals will be achieved.
   a. Return on sales before interest and taxes.
   b. Total asset turnover.
   c. Return on average assets before interest and taxes.
3. Discuss the limitations and difficulties that can be encountered in using the ratios in requirement 3, particularly when making comparisons to industry averages.

(CMA Adapted)

18–35 **Strategy; Strategic Performance Measurement; Transfer Pricing** Ajax Consolidated has several divisions; however, only two transfer products to other divisions. The mining division refines toldine, which it transfers to the metals division where toldine is processed into an alloy and is sold to customers for $150 per unit. Ajax currently requires the mining division to transfer its total annual output of 400,000 units of toldine to the metals division at total manufacturing cost plus 10 percent. Unlimited quantities of toldine can be purchased and sold on the open market at $90 per unit. The mining division could sell all the toldine it produces at $90 per unit on the open market, but it would incur a variable selling cost of $5 per unit.

Brian Jones, the mining division's manager, is unhappy transferring the entire output of toldine to the metals division at 110 percent of cost. In a meeting with Ajax management, he said, "Why should my division be required to sell toldine to the metals division at less than market price? For the year just ended in May, metals' contribution margin was more than $19 million on sales of 400,000 units while mining's contribution was just over $5 million on the transfer of the same number of units. My division is subsidizing the profitability of the metals division. We should be allowed to charge the market price for toldine when we transfer it to the metals division."

The following is the detailed unit cost structure for both the mining and metals divisions for the fiscal year ended May 31, 2004:

	Cost per Unit	
	Mining Division	**Metals Division**
Transfer price from mining division	—	$66
Direct material	$12	6
Direct labor	16	20
Manufacturing overhead	32*	25†
Total cost per unit	$60	$117

*Manufacturing overhead in the mining division is 25 percent fixed and 75 percent variable.
†Manufacturing overhead in the metals division is 60 percent fixed and 40 percent variable.

Required

1. Explain whether transfer prices based on cost are appropriate as a divisional performance measure and why.

2. Using the market price as the transfer price, determine the contribution margin for both divisions for the year ended May 31, 2004.

3. If Ajax were to institute the use of negotiated transfer prices and allow divisions to buy and sell on the open market, determine the price range for toldine that both divisions would accept. Explain your answer.

4. Identify which of the three types of transfer prices—cost based, market based, or negotiated—is most likely to elicit desirable management behavior at Ajax and thus benefit overall operations. Explain your answer.

(CMA Adapted)

18–36 **Transfer Pricing; International**   Better Life Products (BLP), Inc., is a large U.S.–based manufacturer of health care products; it specializes in cushions, braces, and other remedies for a variety of health problems experienced by elderly and disabled persons. BLP knows that its industry is price competitive and hopes to compete through rapid growth, primarily within the United States, where it has a well-established brand image. Because of the competitive industry conditions, BLF is focusing on cost and price reductions as a principal way to attract customers. Because of rising domestic production costs, lower production costs in other countries, and a modest increase in global demand for its products, BLP manufactures some of these products outside the United States. Much of the materials for use by foreign manufacturers is shipped from the United States to the foreign manufacturer, which assembles the final product. In this way, BLP takes advantage of the foreign country's lower labor costs. For this purpose, BLP has formed three divisions, one in the United States to purchase and perform limited assembly of the raw materials; one a foreign division to complete the manufacturing, especially of the labor-intensive components of manufacturing; and one a marketing and sales division in the United States. Sales of BLP's products are approximately 80 percent in the United States, 10 percent in Canada, and 10 percent worldwide. The foreign divisions tend to focus only on manufacturing because of the specialized nature of the products and because of BLP's desire to have the U.S. sales division coordinate all sales activities. BLP now has 18 U.S. divisions and 23 foreign divisions operating in this manner.

Foreign divisions' shipments to the United States are subject to customs duties according to the U.S. Tariff Code, which adds to BLP's cost of the foreign-based manufacturing. However, the code requires U.S. companies to pay duty on only the value added in foreign countries. For example, a product imported from an Argentine company to BLP pays customs on only the amount of the product's cost resulting from labor incurred in Argentina. To illustrate, a product with $10 of materials shipped from the United States to Argentina that incurs $10 of labor costs in Argentina is charged a tariff based on the $10 of labor costs, not the $20 of total product cost. Thus, for tariff purposes, having as small a portion of total product cost from the foreign country as possible is advantageous to BLP.

BLP division managers, including those of the foreign manufacturing facilities, are evaluated on the basis of profit. Jorge Martinez is the manager of the manufacturing plant in Argentina; his compensation from BLP is based on meeting profit targets.

BLP uses a transfer pricing approach common in the industry to allow each of the company's divisions to determine the transfer pricing autonomously through interdivision negotiations. In recent years, however, top management has played an increased role in such negotiations. In particular, when the divisions determine a transfer price that can lead to increased taxes, foreign exchange exposure, or tariffs, the corporate financial function becomes involved. This has meant that the transfer prices charged by foreign divisions to U.S. sales divisions have fallen to reduce the value added by the foreign country and thereby reduce the tariffs. To avoid problems with U.S. and Argentine government agencies, the transfer prices have been reduced slowly over time.

One effect of this transfer pricing strategy has been the continued decline of the foreign divisions' profitability. Jorge and others have difficulty meeting their profit targets and personal compensation goals because of the continually declining transfer prices.

Required

1. Assess BLP's manufacturing and marketing strategies. Are they consistent with each other and with what you consider to be the firm's overall business strategy?

2. Assess BLP's performance measurement system. What changes would you suggest and why?

18–37 Transfer Pricing; International Taxes; Ethics Target Manufacturing, Inc., is a multinational firm with sales and manufacturing units in 15 countries. One of its manufacturing units, in country X, sells its product to a retail unit in country Y for $200,000. Country X unit has manufacturing costs of $100,000 for these products. The retail unit in country Y sells the product to final customers for $300,000. Target is considering adjusting its transfer prices to reduce overall corporate tax liability.

Required

1. Assume that both country X and country Y have corporate income tax rates of 40 percent and that no special tax treaties or benefits apply to Target. What would be the effect on Target's total tax burden if the manufacturing unit raises its price from $200,000 to $240,000?

2. What would be the effect on Target's total taxes if the manufacturing unit raised its price from $200,000 to $240,000 and the tax rate in country X is 20 percent and in country Y is 40 percent?

3. Comment on the ethical issues, if any, you observe in this case.

18–38 Strategic Performance Measurement: International; Strategy; Service Industry With the multinational company becoming a significant business structure throughout the world, a growing problem is developing in the analysis of the MNC's financial results. When the incidents in this problem occurred, the U.S. dollar was strengthening considerably relative to other currencies. Besides causing economic problems in many developing countries, it also created a problem in the proper evaluation of a multinational's subsidiaries and their contribution to its total results.

Security System Corporation provides financial services for dealers and consumers in a variety of construction and consumer product areas. The firm is searching for the proper method to evaluate its subsidiaries. Of concern is the subsidiaries' contribution to the company's overall earnings and how to evaluate whether the specific goals developed by the subsidiaries' management have been met.

In search of answers, the company is concerned with the following concepts:

- Analysis of results: In local currency or U.S. dollars?
- Management's explanation of variances: In local currency or U.S. dollars?
- What should the time frames be for comparative data: Plan or forecast?

The firm has six distinctive business segments in the new-residential-housing market: consumer appliance market, commercial nonresidential construction, consumer aftermarket, home furnishings market, automotive market, and capital goods markets. Last year the company achieved 30 percent of its revenues and 35 percent of its earnings from its international subsidiaries. However, years ago when one British pound sterling equaled $2.33 U.S. (whereas now it's one pound = $1.45 U.S.), the firm achieved 35 percent of its revenue—but more significantly, 47 percent of its earnings—from its international subsidiaries. During the past five years, although the U.S. dollar equivalent of earnings from the international subsidiaries has declined from 47 percent of the total to 35 percent, most operations have reported significant, steady gains from year to year in the local currency.

All operations report their monthly financial data to the firm's world headquarters in U.S. dollars. They use the existing exchange rate at the close of business on the last day of the month. The firm reports the exchange based on accounting guidelines (except for one or two special situations). The comparisons of the monthly financial data are made against a financial plan that uses a predetermined exchange rate for the various months of the year.

Over the past five years, as the U.S. dollar has fluctuated against foreign currencies, the firm has analyzed the financial results of its operations totally in U.S. dollars and then compares its results to a fixed-plan exchange rate.

The firm establishes exchange rates to be used each year, many times optimistically, and then sets an earnings per share target on that basis. If the dollar strengthens even more, the firm misses its targets and prepares statements showing that a particular group missed its planned targets when, in fact, all of the group's operations could have exceeded their local currency plans but are losing on the comparison because of unfavorable exchange rate effects.

Required   How should the firm measure its results to enhance its competitiveness? How can it safeguard its overall EPS target if it uses local currencies in the reporting system? Where does the responsibility for the U.S. dollar attainment of goals lie?

(CMA Adapted)

18–39   **Uses of Return on Investment: Dell Corporation**   One of the many factors that has been attributed to the success of the computer maker Dell is its extensive use of return on investment evaluation. Facing steep price cutting in the computer industry in 1993, and write-offs of $65 million in inventory, Michael Dell decided to recruit operations and finance top managers to the firm. One of the changes was to introduce the concept of return on investment throughout the firm. The importance of financial measures was emphasized to all 10,350 employees

Required   Return on investment is typically used to evaluate SBU managers. List several examples of how Dell might use ROI in addition to SBU evaluation.

Solutions to Self–Study Problems

1. Return on Investment and Residual Income

1. ROS = Net income/Sales

    = $640,000/$8,000,000

    = 0.08

    Asset turnover = Sales/Average investment

    = $8,000,000/($2,500,000 + $2,600,000)/2

    = 3.137 times

    ROI = ROS × Asset turnover

    = 0.08 × 3.137

    = 25.1%

2. Residual income = Net income − (Average investment × Minimum rate of return)

    = $640,000 − [($2,500,000 + $2,600,000)/2] × 0.12

    = $334,000

2. Determining the Proper Transfer Price

1. Since the T-Bar unit is at full capacity and the contribution on outside sales of $70 (= $165 − $5 − $90) is higher than the $60 cost saving of inside production (= $150 − $90), the T-Bar unit should sell outside and the adhesive unit should purchase T-Bar for $150 outside the firm.

2. Since the T-bar unit is at full capacity and there is an outside market, the best transfer price is market price for T-bar. The relevant market price is the price that the T-Bar unit can charge (assuming it is a reliable, long-term price), $165. This transfer price will cause the adhesive unit to do the correct thing, that is, to buy outside since the outside price is lower.

3. If the T-bar unit has excess capacity, it can sell T-Bar both internally and externally. The correct transfer price is then the price that will cause the adhesive unit to purchase internally; that is, any price between variable cost of the seller ($90) and the outside market price to the adhesive unit ($150). The units might agree on a price by considering what is a fair return to each unit and in effect split the profit on the sale between them. The actual outcome of the negotiations for the transfer price depends on a number of factors, including the negotiation skills of the two managers.

CHAPTER NINETEEN

Management Compensation and Business Valuation

After studying this chapter, you should be able to . . .

1. Identify and explain the types of management compensation
2. Identify the strategic role of management compensation and the different types of compensation used in practice
3. Explain the three characteristics of a bonus plan: the base for determining performance, the compensation pool from which the bonus is funded, and the bonus payment options
4. Describe the role of tax planning and financial reporting in management compensation planning
5. Explain how management compensation plans are used in service firms and not-for-profit organizations
6. Apply the different methods for business evaluation and business valuation.

There's no praise to beat the sort you can put in your pocket.

Moliére

The main issue in this chapter is how to determine management compensation and value the entire company. How do we fairly compensate managers for this success? We have emphasized strategy throughout the book. How do we quantitatively assess the firm's success in achieving its strategy?

Looking at large, publicly held firms, we focus first on a measure of success that many would use: the value of the firm as measured by its market capitalization, that is, the value of its outstanding shares. Fundamentally, all measures of the firm's value are predictions of future performance—an assessment of the future value of the current ownership in the firm. Choosing a method for predicting future value is a difficult task, as Bill Barker, a writer for the Motley Fool says: "I don't think there is any method that anyone will think is the perfect one. If you ask 10 investors what the Holy Grail method would be, you'd get 10 different answers." In this spirit, we consider a number of different valuation methods in this chapter.[1]

Part One: Management Compensation

LEARNING OBJECTIVE 1
Identify and explain the types of management compensation.

Recruiting, motivating, rewarding, and retaining effective managers are critical to the success of all firms. Effective management compensation plans are an important and integral part of the determination of a strategic competitive advantage and are important concerns of the management accountant.

---

[1] The Motley Fool (*www.fool.com*) is an organization that provides education and information for investors.

CEO Pay Up and Down

The years 2001 and 2002 were tough for U.S. corporations, with earnings falling sharply in most industries. CEO pay fell as well, with cash compensation falling an average of 33 percent in the 2003 *Business Week* survey. Moreover, benefits such as club memberships, company cars, and first-class air travel fell even more sharply, to approximately 10 percent of their 1988 levels. However, many CEOs continued to show steady or improved compensation because their companies adjusted bonus targets or bonus systems so that executive pay improved despite falling earnings. The rationale: we will do what is necessary to retain key executives.

While cash compensation fell on the average, there was no slowdown in granting stock options. Thus, total CEO compensation (cash plus deferred stock and stock options) remained relatively stable. Again, the rationale is to retain the best executive capability.

Stock options are a common part of executive pay in the United States, with approximately 90 percent of large corporations including them in executive compensation. Other countries differ significantly; for example, the percentage in Germany is less than 40 percent, and in Japan less than 20 percent.

Source: "Executive Pay," *Business Week,* April 21, 2003, pp. 86–90; "Disappearing Perks," *Business Week,* March 31, 2003, p. 10; Jesse Drucker, "Performance Out of Reach? Move the Target," *The Wall Street Journal,* April 29, 2003, p. B1; Louis Lavelle, "The Artificial Sweetener in CEO Pay," *Business Week,* March 26, 2001, pp.1, 3, 4; Patrick McGeehan, "A Remix in the Grants of Options and Stock," *The New York Times,* April 6, 2003, p. 4; "Love Those Options," *Business Week,* August 11, 2001, p. 10.

Types of Management Compensation

Management compensation plans are policies and procedures for compensating managers.

A salary is a fixed payment.

A bonus is based on the achievement of performance goals for the period.

Benefits include special travel, membership in a fitness club, tickets to entertainment events, and other extras paid for by the firm.

Management compensation plans are policies and procedures for compensating managers. Compensation includes one or more of the following: salary, bonus, and benefits. **Salary** is a fixed payment; a **bonus** is based on the achievement of performance goals for the period. **Benefits** include travel, membership in a fitness club, life insurance, medical benefits, tickets to entertainment events, and other extras paid for by the firm.

Compensation can be paid currently (usually an annual amount paid monthly, twice a month, or weekly) or deferred to future years. Salary and benefits are typically awarded currently; bonuses are either paid currently or deferred, though a wide variety of plans is found in practice.

The compensation plans for high-level managers are generally explained in the firm's proxy statements and must be approved by the shareholders. Base salary usually is an annual amount paid throughout the year, although it can also include predetermined future cash payments and/or stock awards. Perks are commonly awarded on an annual basis, although they can include future payments or benefits. Base salary and perks are negotiated when the manager is hired and when compensation contracts are reviewed and renewed. They are not commonly influenced by the manager's current performance, as is bonus pay. A recent study of top executives showed that bonus pay is the fastest growing part of total compensation: firms are moving to linking executive pay to performance. The median bonus was more than salary for the sampled firms. Moreover, bonus systems seem to be effective. Another recent study showed that relatively high-performing firms have on the average 60 percent compensation in bonuses and 40 percent in salary, while low-performing firms have 60 percent in salary and 40 percent in incentive pay.[2]

Strategic Role and Objectives of Management Compensation

The strategic role of management compensation has three aspects: (1) the strategic conditions facing the firm, (2) the effect of risk aversion on managers' decision making, and (3) certain ethical issues.

[2] In the study, company performance was measured by changes in the firm's stock price. See Nancy Thorley Hill and Kevin T. Stevens, "Structuring Compensation to Achieve Better Financial Results," *Strategic Finance,* March 2001, pp. 48–51. See also, "A Little Less in the Envelope This Week," *Business Week,* February 18, 2002, pp. 64–66.

Design the Compensation Plan for Existing Strategic Conditions

The compensation plan should be grounded in the strategic analysis of the firm: its competitive strengths and weaknesses and critical success factors. As the strategic conditions facing the firm change over time, the compensation plan should also change. For example, the firm's strategy changes as its products move through the different phases of the sales life cycle: product introduction, growth, maturity, and decline (Chapter 10). As a firm's product moves from the growth phase to the mature phase, the firm's strategy also moves from product differentiation to cost leadership. When this happens, the compensation plan should change in response to the new strategy. Exhibit 19.1 illustrates how the mix of salary, bonus, and perks might change as the firm and its products move through different phases of the sales life cycle.

Note in Exhibit 19.1 that the mix of the three parts of total compensation changes as strategic conditions change. For example, in the mature phase of the products' life cycle, when competition is likely to be the highest and the firm is interested in maintaining an established market and controlling costs, a balanced compensation plan of competitive salary, bonus, and benefits is needed to attract, motivate, and retain the best managers. In contrast, during the growth phase when the need for innovation and leadership is the greatest, the emphasis is on relatively large bonuses to effectively motivate managers. In effect, top management considers the specific strategic conditions facing the firm as a basic consideration in developing the compensation plan and making changes as strategic conditions change.

Risk Aversion and Management Compensation

The manager's relative risk aversion can have an important effect on decision making (see Chapter 17, "Employment Contracts"). Risk aversion is the tendency to prefer decisions with predictable outcomes over those that are uncertain. It is a relatively common decision-making characteristic of managers. A risk-averse manager is biased against decisions that have an uncertain outcome, even if the expected outcome is favorable.

For example, a risk-averse manager might cancel a planned investment in new equipment that would reduce operating costs if there is a chance that nonoperating costs from installation problems, employee training needs, or other reasons might increase. In contrast, the firm's top management and shareholders might not see the risk of additional nonoperating costs as significant relative to the potential for reduced operating costs. The difference in perspective comes about because the outcome of the decision, while likely to have a relatively small impact on the firm and therefore on top management and shareholders, is likely to directly and significantly impact the manager's bonus.

Compensation plans can manage risk aversion effectively by carefully choosing the mix of salary and bonus in total compensation. The higher the proportion of bonus in total compensation, the higher the incentive for the manager to avoid risky outcomes. To reduce the effect of risk aversion, a relatively large proportion of salary should be in total compensation, with a smaller portion in bonus. Determining the proper balance between salary and bonus must consider all three compensation objectives.

Ethical Issues

Two ethical issues must be addressed when designing and implementing compensation plans: (1) the overall level of compensation and (2) unethical actions that managers might perform to meet goals, such as misrepresenting actual results.

EXHIBIT 19.1
Compensation Plans Tailored for Different Strategic Conditions

Product Sales Life Cycle Phase	Salary	Bonus	Benefits
Product introduction	High	Low	Low
Growth	Low	High	Competitive
Maturity	Competitive	Competitive	Competitive
Decline	High	Low	Competitive

When Is Executive Pay Too High?

There is a common concern that executive pay is too high and that lower-level employees are not properly compensated relative to the very high salaries and bonuses of top executives, particularly during periods of corporate downsizing and falling earnings. High executive pay has caused some employee unions to seek proxy fights at corporate annual meetings with the goal of reducing executive pay.[3] High executive compensation is unjust, some argue, and compensation plans are unethical. Others point out that most executives are worth their high compensation because they bring far greater value to the firm than the cost of their compensation. Shareholders and bondholders who see their investments appreciate and attribute this to the executive are likely to see the compensation plans as just and ethical. For example, when a key manager left Wal-Mart, the firm's stock price fell 4 percent on the day of the announcement, indicating the very high importance investors placed on this executive.[4]

The Internal Revenue Service can deny a firm's right to deduct compensation that it determines to be unreasonable. The U.S. Tax Court analyzes 14 compensation factors to determine whether the compensation is reasonable, including the manager's qualifications, the nature of the work, the size and complexity of the firm, and the prevailing economic conditions.[5]

Unethical Actions

Sometimes the management compensation plan provides an incentive for unethical action. Recent examples include Kenneth Lay, CEO of Enron; Andrew Fastow, CFO of Enron; Scott Sullivan, CFO of Worldcom; Dennis Kozlowski, CEO of Tyco International; and Gary Winnick, CEO of Global Crossing. Each of these executives has been charged with illegal activities that have harmed their companies and the companies' shareholders. In all these cases, the incentive to increase cash or stock option-based compensation was present. The U.S. House of Representatives considered legislation that would seize the assets of executives under federal charges and hold these assets in escrow until their guilt or innocence is proven.[6]

Objectives of Management Compensation

The firm's key objective is to develop management compensation plans that support its strategic objectives, as set forth by management and the owners. The objectives of management compensation are therefore consistent with the three objectives of management control as defined in Chapter 17:

1. To motivate managers to exert a high level of effort to achieve the goals set by top management.
2. To provide the incentive for managers, acting autonomously, to make decisions consistent with the goals set by top management.
3. To determine fairly the rewards earned by managers for their effort and skill and the effectiveness of their decision making.

In Chapter 17 and Chapter 18, these objectives were used to develop performance measurement systems (e.g., cost, profit, and investment SBUs). In this chapter, the objectives are used to develop effective management compensation plans.

[3] Joann Lublin, "Executive Pay," *The Wall Street Journal,*" April 14, 2003, p. R1; "The Battle Royal Against Regal Paychecks," *Business Week,* February 24, 2003, p. 127; "Executive Pay: Labor Strikes Back," *Business Week,* May 26, 2003, p. 46.

[4] *The Wall Street Journal,* March 29, 1996. Bill Fields, a 25-year veteran of Wal-Mart, left his position as chief of the main discount store business department to accept a similar position at Viacom, Inc. A similar case is reported for Black & Decker, whose stock fell by 8 percent the day Joseph Galli, its chief executive, departed; see "Power Drain," *Business Week,* May 17, 1999, p. 50.

[5] The 14 factors are set out in the Tax Court ruling in *Pulsar Components International, Inc., v. Commissioner,* T.C. Memo 1996-129 (3/14/96).

[6] "Making Them Give Back the Cash," *Business Week,* August 26, 2002, p. 36.

The first objective is to motivate managers to exert a high level of effort to achieve the firm's goals. A performance-based compensation plan is best for this purpose. For example, a bonus plan that rewards the manager for achieving particular goals is appropriate. The goals could be financial or nonfinancial, current or long term.

The second objective is to provide the appropriate incentive for managers to make decisions that are consistent with the firm's objectives. The firm's objectives are identified in the strategic competitive analysis from which its critical success factors (CSFs) are derived. CSFs include customer satisfaction, quality, service, product development, and innovation in production and distribution. Firms attend to CSFs by making them part of the manager's compensation.

For example, McDonald's rewards managers who develop its CSFs—quality, service, cleanliness, and value—in addition to the conventional financial performance measures (earnings, growth in sales). International Paper Company includes nonfinancial factors such as quality, safety, and minority employee development as factors in management compensation plans. Research has shown that similar firms with clear strategic goals specified in CSFs include these factors in their compensation plans.[7]

In developing compensation plans, the management accountant works to achieve fairness by making the plan simple, clear, and consistent. Fairness also means that the plan focuses only on the controllable aspects of the manager's performance. For example, compensation should not be affected by expenses that cannot be tied directly to the manager's unit. Similarly, the manager's performance evaluation should be separate from that of the unit because economic factors beyond the manager's control are likely to affect the unit's performance. Fairness in this sense is often achieved by basing the manager's compensation on performance relative to prior years or to agreed-on goals rather than on comparison to the performance of other managers.

Bonus Plans

> As a general view, remuneration by fixed salaries does not in any class of functionaries produce the maximum amount of zeal.
>
> **John Stewart Mill, English philosopher and economist, 1806–1873**

As stated earlier, bonus compensation is the fastest growing element of total compensation and often the largest part. A wide variety of bonus pay plans can be categorized according to three key aspects:

- The **base of the compensation,** that is, how the bonus pay is determined. The three most common bases are (1) stock price, (2) cost, revenue, profit, or investment SBU–based performance, and (3) the balanced scorecard.
- **Compensation pools,** that is, the source from which the bonus pay is funded. The two most common compensation pools are earnings in the manager's own SBU and a firmwide pool based on the firm's total earnings.
- **Payment options,** that is, how the bonus is to be awarded. The two common options are cash and stock (typically common shares). The cash or stock can either be awarded currently or deferred to future years. Stock can either be awarded directly or granted in the form of stock options.

Bases for Bonus Compensation

Bonus compensation can be determined on the basis of stock price, strategic performance measures (cost, revenue, profit, or investment SBU), or the balanced scorecard (critical success factors). For example, when the manager's unit is publicly held, its

[7] C. Ittner and D. Larcker, "Total Quality Management and the Choice of Information and Reward Systems," *Journal of Accounting Research* (1995 Supplement), pp. 1–34; and R. Bushman, R. Indjejikian, and A. Smith, "CEO Compensation: The Role of Individual Performance Evaluation," *Journal of Accounting and Economics,* April 1996.

LEARNING OBJECTIVE 3

Explain the three characteristics of a bonus plan: the base for determining performance, the compensation pool from which the bonus is funded, and the bonus payment options.

stock price is a relevant base. When stock price is used, the amount of the bonus could depend on the amount of the increase in stock price or on whether the stock price reaches a certain predetermined goal. When an accounting measure or CSF is used, the amount of the bonus can be determined in any one of three ways: (1) by comparison of current performance to that of prior years, (2) comparison of performance to a predetermined budget, or (3) comparison of the manager's performance to that of other managers. A limitation of the first two methods, comparison to prior years or to budget, is that the economic situation of the manager's unit may have changed significantly from the prior year or from the time the budget target was set, thereby making the budget or prior year amount an unfair basis for evaluation and compensation. A problem with the third method is that it does not take into account the different economic circumstances of the different managers, some of whom may be in units that are in favorable economic times while others are not. The firm chooses its compensation plan to achieve the best balance of motivation and fairness from these options.

The choice of a base comes from a consideration of the compensation objectives, as outlined in Exhibit 19.2. A common choice is to use cost, revenue, profit, or investment

EXHIBIT 19.2 **Advantages and Disadvantages of Different Bonus Compensation Bases Relative to Compensation Objectives**

	Motivation	Right Decision	Fairness
Stock price	(+/−) Depends on whether stock and stock options are included in base pay and bonus (+) aligns management compensation with shareholder interests	(+) Consistent with shareholder's interests.	(−) Lack of controllability
Strategic performance measures (cost, revenue, profit, and investment SBUs)	(+) Strongly motivating if noncontrollable factors are excluded	(+) Generally a good measure of economic performance (−) Typically has only a short-term focus (−) If bonus is very high, creates an incentive for inaccurate reporting	(+) Intuitive, clear, and easily understood (−) Measurement issues: differences in accounting conventions, cost allocation methods, financing methods, and so on
Balanced scorecard (critical success factors)	(+) Strongly motivating if noncontrollable factors are excluded (+) aligns management compensation with shareholder interests	(+) Consistent with management's strategy (−) Can be subject to inaccurate reporting of nonfinancial factors	(+) If carefully defined and measured, CSFs are likely to be perceived as fair (−) Potential measurement issues, as above

Key: (+) means the base has a positive effect on the objective.
    (−) means the base has a negative effect on the objective.

SBUs because they are often a good measure of economic performance; therefore, they are motivating and perceived to be fair. As many firms move to a more strategic approach to cost management, however, the use of CSFs and stock-price-based measures in compensation is likely to increase. Ford Motor Company and International Paper Company, among others, are using CSFs in this way.

Once the base is chosen the firm also must choose a method for calculating the amount of the bonus based on the actual level of performance relative to the target. The most common approach is a simple linear calculation, that is, the greater the amount that performance exceeds the target (prior year, budget, or that of other managers) the greater the amount of the bonus. For example, if the bonus formula is 10 percent of profit over budget, and actual and budgeted profit are $200,000 and $100,000 respectively, then the amount of the bonus would be 10 percent × ($200,000 − $100,000) = $10,000. Sometimes firms will have a maximum amount for the bonus. Also, various nonlinear formulas can be used, as Daimler-Chrysler has used for dealer bonuses.[8]

Bonus Compensation Pools

A manager's bonus can be determined by the so-called **unit-based pool** that is based on the performance of the manager's unit. For example, the bonus pool might be determined as the amount of the unit's earnings that are more than 5 percent of the investment in the unit. The appeal of the unit-based pool is the strong motivation for effective managers to perform and to receive rewards for their effort; the upside potential to the individual manager is very motivating.

Alternatively, the amount of bonus available to all managers is often a **firmwide pool** set aside for this purpose. A firmwide pool, for example, might be the amount of firmwide earnings that are more than 5 percent of firmwide investment. Each unit manager's bonus is then drawn from this common pool. General Electric Corporation's bonus compensation plan includes the following in its 1995 Proxy Statement regarding the firm's pool:

the maximum amount in any year is 10% of the amount by which consolidated net earnings exceed 5% of average consolidated capital investment.

When the bonus pool is unit based, the amount of the bonus for any one manager is independent of the performance of the other managers. In contrast, when a firmwide pool is used, each manager's bonus depends in some predetermined way on the firm's performance as a whole. The sharing arrangements vary widely, although a common arrangement is for all managers to share equally in the firmwide bonus pool. Generally, the firmwide pool provides an important incentive for coordination and cooperation among units within the firm since all managers share in the higher overall firm profits that result from cross-unit efforts. Moreover, those who think executive pay is too high often argue that pay linked to overall firm performance is preferable since all managers share in this success. We summarize the advantages and disadvantages of each approach to bonus pools in Exhibit 19.3.

Bonus Payment Options

In recent years, the use of different payment options for bonus compensation plans has greatly increased. In the competition for top executives, firms are developing innovative ways to attract and retain the best.[9]

A unit-based pool is a basis for determining a bonus according to the performance of the manager's unit.

A firmwide pool is a basis for determining the bonus available to all managers through an amount set aside for this purpose.

[8] Michael C. Jensen, "Corporate Budgeting Is Broken—Let's Fix It," *Harvard Business Review,* November 2001, pp. 95–101.

[9] "Executive Pay," *Business Week,* April 21, 2003, pp. 86–90. Compensation practices also change as market conditions change. For example, after the decline in the share values of technology firms in March 2000, these firms shifted to cash-based executive pay; "New Dot-Com Mantra: Just Pay Me in Cash Please," *The Wall Street Journal,* November 28, 2000, p. C1.

REAL-WORLD FOCUS   The Hidden Cost of Stock Options

Many firms use stock options to provide an effective means of manager compensation. The stock options align managers' interests with those of shareholders. The stock option method also has another important benefit: its cost *does not affect net income.* Under current accounting rules, the effect of stock options on net income, determined by the Black-Scholes fair value option pricing model, *need be disclosed only in footnotes* to the financial statements.

For example, the reported net incomes of Merrill Lynch, Siebel Systems, and Hewlett-Packard would have been losses instead of profits, if options had been expensed. Both IBM and Microsoft would have shown 30 percent less profit, and Intel's profit would have fallen by 80 percent! Most accountants argue that options have a real value and a real cost (the expansion of ownership in the firm and dilution of current shareholders' interests), and should be accounted for as expense. Those opposed argue that expensing options will negatively affect some firms (particularly start-ups and tech firms that rely on options for employee and executive compensation) and limit their ability to attract employees and funding. Meg Whitman of ebay says:

Every single employee at ebay has stock options. If we're required to expense stock options, which I think may be coming, it will change the amount of stock options that we hand out. We might have to eliminate it altogether. I just think it's the wrong thing for new companies.

The Financial Accounting Standards Board, which sets financial reporting standards, announced in March 2003 that it will develop a new standard for expensing stock options to make U.S. standards more consistent with those of other countries, where options are typically expensed. Some firms, such as Coca-Cola, General Motors, General Electric, Dow Chemical, Home Depot, and Wal-Mart are already expensing options for financial reporting purposes.

Due in part to the likelihood that new accounting standards will require options to be expensed, a number of technology companies including Microsoft and Dell have changed compensation plans to rely less on stock options. Microsoft has moved to grants of restricted stock, while Dell is relying on cash bonuses.

Source: "Special Report: The Angry Market," *Business Week,* July 29, 2002, p. 36; "Piloting JetBlue and eBay," *Business Week,* March 17, 2003, p. 16; "Beyond Options," *Business Week,* July 28, 2003, pp. 34–38.

EXHIBIT 19.3 **Advantages and Disadvantages of Different Bonus Pools Relative to Compensation Objectives**

	Motivation	**Right Decision**	**Fairness**
Unit based	(+) Strong motivation for an effective manager—the upside potential (−) Unmotivating for manager of economically weaker units	(−) Provides the incentive for individual managers **not** to cooperate with and support other units when needed for the good of the firm.	(−) Does not separate the performance of the unit from the manager's performance
Firmwide	(+) Helps to attract and retain good managers throughout the firm, even in economically weaker units (−) Not as strongly motivating as the unit-based pool	(+) Effort for the good of the overall firm is rewarded—motivates teamwork and sharing of assets among units	(+) Separates the performance of the manager from that of the unit (+) Can appear to be fairer to shareholders and others who are concerned that executive pay is too high

Key: (+) means the pool has a positive effect on the objective.
     (−) means the pool has a negative effect on the objective.

We look at the four most common payment options:

Current bonus (cash and/or stock) based on current (usually annual) performance, the most common bonus form.

Deferred bonus (cash and/or stock) earned currently but not paid for two or more years. Deferred plans are used to avoid or delay taxes or to affect the manager's future total income stream in some desired way. This type of plan can also be used to retain key managers because the deferred compensation is paid only if the manager stays with the firm.

Stock options confer the right to purchase stock at some future date at a predetermined price. They are used to motivate managers to increase stock price for the benefit of the shareholders. When exercised, stock options also have the

EXHIBIT 19.4 **Advantages and Disadvantages of Bonus Payment Options Relative to Compensation Objectives**

	Motivation	Right Decision	Fairness
Current bonus	(+) Strong motivation for current performance; stronger motivation than for deferred plans	(−) Short-term focus (−) Risk-averse manager avoids risky but potentially beneficial projects	(+/−) Depends on the clarity of the bonus arrangement and the consistency with which it is applied
Deferred bonus	(+) Strong motivation for current performance, but not as strong as for the current bonus plan since the reward is delayed	Same as for current bonus	Same as for current bonus
Stock options	(+) Unlimited upside potential is highly motivating (−) Delay and uncertainty in reward reduces motivation	(+) Incentive to consider longer-term issues (+) Provides better risk incentives than for current or deferred bonus plans (+) Consistent with shareholder interests	(−) Uncontrollable factors affect stock price Also, same as for current bonus
Performance shares	Same as for stock options	(+) Incentive to consider long-term factors that affect stock price (+) Consistent with the firm's strategy, when critical success factors are used (+) Consistent with shareholder interests when earnings per share is used	(+/−) Depends on the clarity of the bonus arrangements and the consistency with which it is applied

Key: (+) means the payment option has a positive effect.
  (−) means the payment option has a negative effect.

positive effect of increasing the executive's ownership in the firm, thereby further increasing the executive's alignment with shareholder interests. For this reason, many firms require executives to own a significant amount of stock in the company.[10]

Performance shares grant stock for achieving certain performance goals over two years or more.

The current and deferred bonus plans generally focus the manager's attention on short-term performance measures, most commonly on accounting earnings. In contrast, stock options and performance shares focus attention directly on shareholder value. See the advantages and disadvantages of the four plans in Exhibit 19.4.

Tax Planning and Financial Reporting

LEARNING OBJECTIVE 4

Describe the role of tax planning and financial reporting in management compensation planning.

In addition to achieving the three main objectives of compensation plans, firms attempt to choose plans that reduce or avoid taxes for both the firm and the manager. By combining salary, bonus, and perks, accountants can maximize potential tax savings for the firm, and delay or avoid taxes for the manager. For example, many perks (club memberships, company car, entertainment) are deductible to reduce the firm's tax liability but are not considered income to the manager (and therefore not taxed).

In contrast, although salary is a deductible business expense for the firm, it is taxable income for the manager. Bonus plans have a variety of tax effects as outlined in

---

[10] "Three CEOs Who Need to Take Stock," *Business Week,* May 20, 2002, p. 14; "New Boss, New Plan," *Business Week,* February 2, 1998, pp. 122–32.

REAL-WORLD FOCUS   Indexed Options: Improving the Link of Performance to Pay

Many shareholders and analysts as well as Federal Reserve Chairman Alan Greenspan have argued that allowing the improvement in stock prices to result in a large financial reward for executives with stock options is not fair. In many cases, the executive might have had little to do with the improvement in stock price; for example, a general improvement in economic conditions increases all stock values. To link stock options more clearly to executive performance, firms can adopt "indexed options" that link the value of the stock option to whether the stock price meets a predetermined index. The index can be based on the performance of competitors in the firm's industry or on a broad index measure, such as the Standard & Poor's 500 index.

Indexed options can mean more or less total pay for the executive. For example, the data of a study of executive compensation in 1998 indicate that although Jack Welch at General Electric would have benefited from indexed options, Nolan Archibald at Black & Decker would have received much less pay.

Disadvantages of indexed options include the fact that an accounting rule requires companies to charge indexed options against earnings, which is not required for standard options. Some argue that indexed options will hinder firms' ability to attract the best executives.

Source: "Exploring Options," *Business Week*, February 3, 2003, pp. 78–79; Alfred Rappaport, "New Thinking on How to Link Executive Pay to Performance," *Harvard Business Review*, March–April 1999, pp. 91–101; and Jennifer Reingold, "An Options Plan Your CEO Hates," *Business Week*, February 28, 2000, pp. 82–84.

EXHIBIT 19.5   **Tax and Financial Report Effects of Compensation Plans**

Source: For more on taxation and compensation, see Russ Banham, "Sunk by Options," *Journal of Accountancy*, October 2001, pp. 43-46; also John C. Boma and Michael D. Rosenbaum, "Keep Executives Happy," *Journal of Accountancy*, February 1998, pp. 47–50.

			Tax Effect	
		Financial Statement Effect	**On the Firm**	**On the Manager**
Salary		Current expense	Current deduction	Currently taxed
Bonus	Current	Current expense	Current deduction	Currently taxed
	Deferred	Deferred expense	Deferred deduction	Deferred tax
	Stock options—nonqualified plans	Current (2003) accounting rules encourage but do not require recognition as expense for most stock grants; only footnote disclosure is required	Deduction when exercised	Taxed as ordinary income when exercised
	Stock options—qualified plans	As above	No deduction	Taxed as capital gains when stock is sold if held 18 months from exercise date
	Performance shares	As above	Deferred deduction	Deferred tax
Perks	Certain retirement plans	Current expense	Current deduction	Deferred tax
	Other perks	Current expense	Current deduction	Never taxed

Exhibit 19.5. Tax planning is complex and dynamic, an integral part of compensation planning. Exhibit 19.5 suggests general relationships; a thorough coverage of tax planning is beyond the scope of this text.

Firms also attempt to design compensation plans that have a favorable effect on the firm's financial report. For example, present accounting rules do not require current recognition of the expense for grants of stock or stock options in many compensation cases. This means that the financial report effects of stock-based compensation can be delayed, and earnings can be shown as currently higher than it would be under other types of compensation. A thorough coverage of financial reporting rules regarding management compensation is not attempted here. Exhibit 19.5 provides an overview of the issues.

Management Compensation in Service Firms and Not-For-Profit Organizations

LEARNING OBJECTIVE 5
Explain how management compensation plans are used in service firms and not-for-profit organizations.

Example of a Service Firm

Although most compensation plans are used by manufacturing or merchandising firms, an increasing number of service firms, especially financial and professional service firms, are using these plans. A good example is the compensation plan for the architectural and engineering design firm, Short-Elliott-Hendrickson, Inc. (SEH).[11] SEH provides professional services in a variety of markets, each of which is organized as a profit SBU: airport planning, water resources, waste management, municipal services, structural engineering, architecture, and others. SEH has developed a compensation plan for managers of each profit SBU. The plan uses a balanced scorecard approach that focuses on three areas: (1) financial results, (2) client satisfaction, and (3) improvement in the process of developing and providing the services. Management considers the financial results area to be the most important and has developed the following three criteria for evaluating managers and each profit SBU: profitability, efficiency, and collections of accounts receivable.

1. **Profitability** is measured by the *profit multiplier,* the ratio of net revenues to direct labor dollars.
2. **Efficiency** is measured by *staff utilization,* which is determined from the ratio of direct labor-hours chargeable (to clients) to total hours worked less vacation and holiday time.
3. **Collection of accounts** as measured by two ratios:
   a. The percentage of accounts receivable over 90 days, a measure of the ability to collect customer accounts.
   b. Average days of unbilled work outstanding, a measure of the ability to complete assignments and bill promptly for them.

As shown in Exhibit 19.6, SEH's compensation plan is based on three criteria and four measures (two measures for collection of accounts). Note that the water resources group fell short of its target in each of the three areas with scores of 79 percent for the profit multiplier, 88 percent for staff utilization, and 92 percent and 89 percent, respectively, for each of the two measures of collections of accounts. The advantage of this compensation plan is that it clearly places responsibility for financial results on the three criteria that are important to SEH's strategy and is therefore consistent with the objectives of management compensation. The objectives of motivation and correct decision making are achieved since the managers of SEH's profit SBUs have clear, attainable goals consistent with the firm's strategy. The objective of fairness is achieved by focusing on ratios rather than total profits, which increases comparability among managers.

Example of a Not-For-Profit Organization

A good example of compensation-based responsibility accounting in not-for-profit organizations is the bonus arrangement for the manager of the Greensboro, North Carolina, Coliseum. It is a large indoor arena used for sporting events such as basketball (the Atlantic Coast Conference Basketball Tournament) and a variety of musical and other performances. The city owns and manages the Coliseum; it has been running deficits of more than a million dollars per year in recent years.

To address the need to increase revenues, the Greensboro City Council decided to outsource the Coliseum management to a management company for a fee plus a bonus

[11] Mark Pederson and Gary A. Lidgerding, "Pay-for-Performance in a Service Firm," *Management Accounting,* November 1995, pp. 40–43. A similar balanced scorecard-based system, designed for public accounting firms, is described by Michael Hayes in "Pay for Performance," *Journal of Accountancy,* June 2002, pp. 24–28.

What does a company do when its stock price falls and its executive stock options are no longer attractive? If the firm does not move quickly, it can lose key executives to other employers that offer a more attractive compensation package. With the inevitable ups and downs of the stock market, firms are likely to face this problem at one point or another; most recently it has affected those in the technology sector. (Refer to Comments on Cost Management in Action at the end of the chapter.)

EXHIBIT 19.6   Management Compensation Plan for the Water Resources Group of SEH Inc.

1. Profit Multiplier (ratio: net revenues to direct labor dollars)		2. Staff Utilization (ratio: chargeable time to total time)		3. Collection of Accounts			
				Percentage of Accounts Receivable > 90 Days		Days Revenue Unbilled	
Actual	88%	Actual	79%	Actual	14%	Actual	50 days
Goal	95%	Goal	83%	Goal	10%	Goal	45 days
Variance	7%	Variance	4%	Variance	4%	Variance	5 days
Multiply by weight of	3	Multiply by weight of	3	Multiply by weight of	2	Divide by goal	45 days
Weighted variance	21%	Weighted variance	12%	Weighted variance	8%	Percent variance	11%
Less	100%	Less	100%	Less	100%	Less	100%
Score	**79%**		**88%**		**92%**		**89%**

incentive for reducing the deficit. The current Coliseum director proposed forming a management company with himself as director. The proposal included a $175,000 fee to the management company, a $125,000 salary for himself as director, and a bonus that would be available if he were able to generate revenues higher than 80 percent of expenses (i.e., reduce the deficit to less than 20 percent). The current ratio of revenues to expenses is 75 percent.

The city council approved the idea, although the city manager wanted the bonus threshold to be higher (88 percent), and one council member wanted the bonus arrangement to include both a percentage and a specified amount, "If the amount of the deficit is $3 million, I don't want to pay any incentive. If it is $1 million I will."[12]

The management contract is a useful means for Greensboro to achieve its goals for the Coliseum. The director and management company have strong motivation to increase revenues and thereby reduce the city's deficit. As in any type of performance measurement system, however, attention must be given to the measurement issues: How are revenue and expense to be determined?

Part Two: Business Evaluation and Business Valuation

LEARNING OBJECTIVE 6

Apply the different methods for business evaluation and business valuation.

In this second part of the chapter, we examine the evaluation of the firm as a whole. The goal of strategic cost management is the success of the firm in maintaining competitive advantage, so we evaluate the firm's overall performance as well as the performance of individual managers.

We take a broad approach that includes both the process of evaluating a firm's overall performance and the process of determining an overall value for the firm; ultimately, the objective of the firm's managers is to improve the overall value of the firm.

Business evaluation uses the balanced scorecard, financial ratio analysis, and economic value added as benchmarks to evaluate the firm's overall performance. In

[12] *Greensboro News & Record,* May 29, 1996.

contrast, business *valuation* values the firm by estimating its total market value, which can then be compared to the market value for prior periods or for comparable firms.[13]

Business Evaluation

To illustrate business evaluation—using the balanced scorecard, financial ratio analysis, and economic value added—we use EasyKleen Company, a manufacturer of paper products. For relevant information about EasyKleen, see Exhibit 19.7.

The Balanced Scorecard

The use of the balanced scorecard to evaluate the firm is similar to the use of critical success factors in evaluating and compensating the individual manager. When evaluating the firm using CSFs, the management accountant uses benchmarks from industry information and considers how the CSFs have changed from prior years. A favorable evaluation results when the CSFs are superior to the benchmarks and to prior years' performance. For example, assume that EasyKleen has three CSFs, one each from the three key performance categories:

1. Return on total assets (financial performance).
2. Number of quality defects (business processes).
3. Number of training hours for plant workers (human resources).

A target level of performance is set for each CSF based on a study of the performance of the best firms in the industry. The benchmark is set at 90 percent of the best performance in the industry, and EasyKleen is evaluated on its overall performance, as illustrated in Exhibit 19.8.

EasyKleen management sees from the balanced scorecard that the firm met its goal in the financial area but fell short in both the operations and human resources areas. The scorecard is a guide for directing attention to achieving desired goals.

Financial Ratio Analysis

Financial ratio analysis uses financial statement ratios to evaluate the firm's performance. Two common measures of performance are liquidity and profitability. *Liquidity* refers to the firm's ability to pay its current operating expenses (usually for a year or less) and maturing debt. The six key measures of liquidity are the accounts receivable turnover, the inventory turnover, the current ratio, the quick ratio, and two cash flow ratios. The higher these ratios the better and the higher the evaluation of the firm's liquidity. The four key profitability ratios are the gross margin percent, the return on assets, the return on equity, and the earnings per share. The six liquidity ratios and four profitability ratios are explained in other finance and accounting texts and are not covered here. Instead, we show how each of the ratios is calculated for EasyKleen Company in Exhibit 19.9. The information is taken from Exhibit 19.7 and assumes that the benchmark level of performance is 90 percent of the best in the industry.

As Exhibit 19.9 indicates, EasyKleen had a very good year financially. It met six of its ten goals. Profitability is the strongest area; it exceeded three of four ratios substantially; only the earnings per share target was unmet by a small margin. The liquidity goals were largely met, although receivables turnover and cash flow fell short. This points to the need to improve the collection of receivables, which would improve all three of these ratios. Overall, the financial ratio analysis shows that EasyKleen performed quite well.

[13] Some useful references on business valuation are Elizabeth Danziger, "Is Business Appraising for You?" *Journal of Accountancy,* March 2000, pp. 28–33; Frank C. Evans, "Tips for the Valuator," *Journal of Accountancy,* March 2000, pp. 35–41; Stephen Penman, *Financial Statement Analysis and Security Valuation;* (New York: McGraw–Hill, 2004); Krishna G. Palepu and Paul M. Healy, *Business Analysis and Valuation* (Cincinnati, OH: South-Western, 2004). Other resources for business valuation include the American Society of Appraisers (appraisers.org), the Institute of Business Appraisers (instbusapp.org), and the American Institute of CPAs (aicpa.org).

EXHIBIT 19.7
Selected Financial Information

EASYKLEEN COMPANY
Summary of Selected Financial Information
For the Year Ended December 31,

Financial Statements	2004	2003
Current assets		
Cash	$ 50,000	$ 70,000
Accounts receivable	100,000	80,000
Inventory	50,000	60,000
Total current assets	$ 200,000	$210,000
Long-lived assets	200,000	180,000
Total assets	$ 400,000	$390,000
Current liabilities	50,000	$ 60,000
Long-term debt	200,000	200,000
Total liabilities	$ 250,000	$260,000
Shareholders' equity	150,000	130,000
Total liabilities and equity	$ 400,000	$390,000
Sales	$1,000,000 (50% are credit sales)	
Cost of sales	500,000	
Gross margin	$ 500,000	
Operating expense	300,000	
Operating profit	$ 200,000	
Income taxes	100,000	
Net income	$ 100,000	

Asset Valuation, Total Assets

Net book value	$ 400,000
Gross book value	550,000
Replacement cost	600,000
Economic value of intangibles	100,000
Liquidation value	450,000

Other Information

Depreciation expense	$ 30,000
Capital expenditures	$ 50,000
Dividends	$ 80,000
Year-end share price	$ 16.25
Number of outstanding shares	50,000
Training expenses	$ 30,000 (26 hours per worker)
Quality defects	350 ppm (parts per million)
Cost of capital	12%

Cash Flow from Operations

Net income	$ 100,000
Depreciation expense	30,000
Decrease (increase) in accounts receivable	(20,000)
Decrease (increase) in inventory	10,000
Increase (decrease) in current liabilities	(10,000)
Total cash flow from operations	$ 110,000

Free Cash Flow

Cash flow from operations	$ 110,000
Capital expenditures	(50,000)
Dividends	(80,000)
Free cash flow	$ (20,000)

EXHIBIT 19.8 Balanced Scorecard

		EASYKLEEN COMPANY Balanced Scorecard For the Year Ended December 31, 2004		
Category	**CSF**	**Target Performance**	**Actual Performance***	**Variance**
Financial Operations	Return on total assets	22%	25.3%	3.3% (exceeded)
Operations	Quality defects	300 ppm	350 ppm	50 ppm (unmet)
Human Resources	Training hours	32 hours per employee	26 hours per employee	6 hours (unmet)

*See Exhibit 19.9 for return on assets and Exhibit 19.7 for quality defects and training hours.

EXHIBIT 19.9 Financial Analysis

	EASYKLEEN COMPANY Financial Analysis For the Year Ended December 31, 2004		
Ratio (how calculated)	**Benchmark**	**Actual**	**Percent Achievement**
Liquidity Ratios			
Accounts receivable turnover (Credit sales/Average receivables)	7	5.56 = $500,000/(100,000 + 80,000)/2	79% (unmet)
Inventory turnover (Cost of sales/Average inventory)	8	9.09 = $500,000/($50,000 + 60,000)/2	114% (met)
Current ratio (Current assets/Current liabilities)	2	4 = $200,000/$50,000	200% (met)
Quick ratio (Cash and receivables/Current liabilities)	1	3 = ($50,000 + $100,000)/$50,000	300% (met)
Cash flow ratio (Cash flow from operations/Current liabilities)	2.5	2.2 = $110,000/$50,000	88% (unmet)
Free cash flow ratio (Free cash flow/Current liabilities)	1.5	−.4 = −$20,000/$50,000	% (unmet)
Profitability Ratios			
Gross margin percent (Gross profit/Net sales)	35%	50% = $500,000/$1,000,000	143% (met)
Return on assets (Net income/Average total assets)	22%	25.3 = $100,000/($400,000 + 390,000)/2	115% (met)
Return on equity (Net income/Shareholders' equity)	44%	66.67% = $100,000/$150,000	152% (met)
Earnings per share (Net income/Weighted—average number of shares outstanding)	$2.15	$2.00 = $100,000/50,000	93% (unmet)

Economic Value Added

As discussed in Chapter 18, economic value added (EVA) is a business unit's income after taxes and after deducting the cost of capital. The cost of capital is usually obtained by calculating a weighted average of the cost of the firm's two sources of funds, borrowing and selling stock. EVA focuses managers' attention on creating value for shareholders. By earning higher profits than the firm's cost of capital, the firm increases its internal resources available for dividends and/or to finance its continued growth. Dividends and growth boost stock price and add shareholder value.

EVA for EasyKleen is determined as follows; *invested capital* is defined for EVA as total assets less current liabilities. Training expenses of $30,000 are added to total assets and back to net income for EVA calculations since training expenses are considered an investment for EVA purposes:

$$\text{EVA} = \text{EVA net income} - (\text{Cost of capital} \times \text{Invested capital})$$

$$= \text{Net income} + \text{Training expenses}$$

$$- 0.12 \times (\text{Average Total assets} + \text{Training expenses} - \text{Current liabilities})$$

$$= \$100,000 + \$30,000 - 0.12 \times [(\$400,000 + \$390,000)/2 + \$30,000 - \$50,000]$$

$$= \$85,000$$

The EVA of $85,000 for EasyKleen is a very positive value relative to net income and invested capital. It indicates of the firm's strong profitability and, in particular, its significant contribution to shareholder value.

Business Valuation

An intuitively appealing performance measure for the firm is its market value. Market value is an objective measure that clearly shows what investors think the firm is worth. It also has the advantage of being consistent with the objective of top management to add shareholder value:

> The essence of corporate strategy is to figure out how the corporation, as intermediary, can add value to the business it oversees. . . . The point here is not that businesses should not be trying to compete effectively in product and service markets; of course they should. But that effort has to be measured not only in terms of its impact on competition in a product or service market, but also in terms of its effect in the market for corporate control (*i.e., in the equity market; stock price*). A company that emphasizes the former at the expense of the latter can find itself in trouble very quickly. . . . To sum up, companies need strategies for competing in two kinds of markets: the familiar product and service markets, and the market for corporate control. Winning in the latter market depends on creating for shareholders superior value that derives from cash flow returns. (emphasis added)[14]

As this statement predicts, a public firm that advances its competitive position but fails to achieve acceptance in the market through improved stock price will find itself vulnerable in the market for corporate control. That is, the company might be purchased by investors who see that the market undervalues the firm. Success in the market is achieved by taking a value-oriented approach within the firm—orienting the firm's strategy to shareholder value. This can mean the spin-off of certain business units, financial restructuring, and outsourcing of certain activities.

The concept of adding shareholder value requires a new interpretation of management strategy and the value chain. The role of strategy goes beyond the policies and procedures to achieve competitive advantage. It must also include the overarching objective of adding shareholder value. Similarly, the firm's value chain goes beyond adding value for its customer to adding value also for the shareholders.

The Market Value Method

The four methods for valuing a firm are (1) market value, (2) asset valuation, (3) the discounted cash flow method, and (4) earnings-based valuation. The first method is the most simple and direct. The firm's value is determined by multiplying the number of outstanding shares by the current market price of the shares. For the EasyKleen Company, the value determined is:

$$\text{Number of shares} \times \text{Share price}$$
$$= 50,000 \times \$16.25 = \$812,500$$

The performance of the firm and of its top management can be evaluated by changes either in the firm's share price or its market value. The market value method is the most direct and objective measure of the shareholders' assessment of the firm's performance and its success in creating value for the shareholders.

For nonpublic firms a relevant stock price is not available, and one of the three other methods is needed to evaluate the firm.

---

[14] T. Copeland, T. Koller, and J. Murrin, *Valuation: Measuring and Managing the Value of Companies* (New York: John Wiley, 1992), pp. 3–26.

DELL USES ECONOMIC VALUE ADDED TO IMPROVE COMPETITIVENESS

Economic value added (EVA) has enabled a number of firms to significantly improve their competitiveness. Dell Computer was suffering from intense price competition with Compaq Corporation and other competitors in early 1993. It introduced EVA to focus managers and operating employees on their role in improving profitability. For example, the marketing department began to calculate the return on investment for each mailing, and the purchasing department computed the cost of unsold inventory.

EVA HELPS CSX UNIT BECOME MORE PROFITABLE

CSX Corporation's Intermodel unit uses trains to carry freight to trucks or cargo ships. In 1988, the unit was unprofitable, as shown by a negative EVA of $70 million. The unit managers were told to bring the EVA up to breakeven before 1993 or the unit would be sold.

By 1992, the unit had achieved a positive EVA of $10 million. This was accomplished by careful attention to the use of assets. A focus on idle assets led unit managers to reschedule certain routes. For example, on the route from New Orleans to Jacksonville, Florida, four locomotives pulled a freight train at 28 mph, arriving four to five hours prior to the time needed to load the trucks or freighters in Jacksonville. By removing one of the four locomotives and using a speed of 25 mph, the train arrived in time for the unloading with an hour to spare. The slow-down and removal of one locomotive was a significant saving to the unit in both capital costs (the locomotive) and operating costs (less fuel required). Looking at all the routes in a similar manner, the Intermodal group was able to achieve significant savings in capital usage and operating costs.

Sources: Based on information from Gary McWilliams, "Whirlwind on the WEB," *Business Week,* April 7, 1997, pp. 132–36; and Shawn Tully, "The Real Key to Creating Wealth," *Fortune,* September 20, 1993, pp. 38–50.

The Asset Valuation Method

Accountants have four options when using the asset valuation method: net book value, gross book value, replacement cost, and liquidation value (see Chapter 18). An important limitation of the net book value and gross book value methods is that they are affected by the firm's accounting policies, and they can be greatly distorted by the age of the assets and by the exclusion of intangible assets. Intangible assets include internally developed patents, trademarks, and trade secrets, and other competitive assets that are not included on the balance sheet under generally accepted accounting principles (GAAP). By excluding these assets, the economic value of the firm can be significantly understated by conventional GAAP-based financial statement, especially for technology companies. Intangibles usually would be less important for other types of firms such as savings and loan institutions or firms in regulated industries. Suppose that EasyKleen has developed a cleaning solvent that gives it a competitive advantage, and that a conservative estimate of the value of the solvent is $100,000. The liquidation value of the firm would normally include this value directly, and the replacement cost can be adjusted to include it to provide a more comprehensive measure of the value of the firm's assets.[15]

The replacement cost and liquidation value methods have weaknesses, however. Most important, an objective measure for replacement cost or liquidation value rarely exists, since the firm is not likely to be involved in either liquidation or replacement when the valuation is made. The asset values in Exhibit 19.10 show quite a range. EasyKleen is not considering liquidation, so the replacement cost (including intangibles) of $700,000 is likely to be the more useful of the two measures.

The Discounted Cash Flow Method

The discounted cash flow (DCF) method measures the firm's value as the discounted present value of its net cash flows. The DCF is based on the same concepts used in Chapter 20 for capital budgeting decisions. Cash flows a year or more into the future are discounted to consider the time value of money; cash flows in recent periods are more valuable than cash flows in distant periods. Since it is based on cash flows, the

[15] "Brainpower on the Balance Sheet," *Business Week,* August 26, 2002, pp. 110–111.

EXHIBIT 19.10
EasyKleen Company: Asset
Valuation Methods and Values

EASYKLEEN COMPANY
Asset Valuation Methods and Values

Method	Value
Net book value	$400,000 (from the financial statements)
Gross book value	550,000 (from the financial statements)
Replacement cost	600,000 (estimated, usually by appraisals of experts in commercial real estate)
Replacement cost plus economic value of intangibles	$700,000
Liquidation value	450,000 (estimated, usually by appraisals of experts in commercial real estate)

EXHIBIT 19.11
DCF Valuation of the
EasyKleen Company

Years	Cash Flow	Present Value Factor	Present Value of Cash Flows
1	$110,000	0.893	$ 98,230
2	120,000	0.797	95,640
3	130,000	0.712	92,560
4	140,000	0.636	89,040
5	150,000	0.567	85,050

Total present value of cash flows in the planning period ⟶ $ 460,520 (A)

| 6+ | $150,000 | 8.3333 | $1,249,995 (B) |

Total present value of 6+ years' cash flows ⟶ 0.567   708,747 (C) = (B) × .567

Plus: Marketable securities and investments   0 (D)

Less: Market value of debt   200,000 (E)

Value of the firm, shareholder value $ 969,267 = (A) + (C) + (D) − (E)

DCF method has the additional advantage of not being subject to the bias of different accounting policies for determining total assets and net income, as are the asset valuation and the financial analysis methods. The DCF method is commonly used when the share price is not available or is unreliable.

The DCF method distinguishes two types of value in determining a firm's value. The first is the value of the cash flows for the planning period (usually a three- to five-year period), and the second is the value of the cash flows beyond three to five years. Exhibit 19.11 shows how the method is used for the EasyKleen Company, assuming that the discount rate (the cost of capital) is 12 percent, the planning period is five years, and the net cash flows increase by $10,000 each year and then remain at $150,000 per year for the sixth year and thereafter. Exhibit 19.11 shows that the total discounted value of net cash flows for the first five years is $460,520.

The present values of the cash flows from the sixth year on are determined using the discount factor for an annuity with a continuing life, which is the inverse of the discount rate $(1/0.12 = 8.3333)$.[16] This gives a discounted value for these six-year-plus cash flows of $1,249,995. To discount this amount back from the beginning of the sixth year to the present, we discount $1,249,995 by the fifth year discount factor (0.567) to arrive at the discounted value of the continuing (six-year-plus) cash flows, $708,747.

To determine the firm's *net valuation*, we now add the discounted value of the planning period cash flows and the discounted value of six-year-plus cash flows to the

[16] Typically, the firm's cash flows are assumed to continue indefinitely, and thus the discount factor for an annuity is used in perpetuity (continuing life). This assumption is consistent with the idea that the firm is an ongoing entity with little or no likelihood of bankruptcy. If a shorter period is desired, the appropriate discount factor from the annuity table can be used for the desired number of years. For example, if the desired period, after the planning period, is from the 6th year to the 20th year, the discount factor is found in the annuity table for 15 years (6 through 20), or 6.811. The factor 6.811 is then used in place of the factor 8.3333 in the analysis in Exhibit 19.11.

REAL-WORLD FOCUS   Spin-offs of Business Units: Effect on Market Value and Compensation

WHY THE SPIN-OFF?

Many firms find that spin-offs of business units result in an increase in the market value of these units. The spin-off makes it easier for the market to assess the value of the spun off business since it is difficult for analysts and investors to assess the aggregate value of firms with multiple businesses. Research shows that spun off subsidiaries show better than average growth in sales, income, and capital expenditures. Research shows that business units that are not given much attention by top management tend to suffer and are therefore better spun off.

SPIN-OFFS AND CEO COMPENSATION AT ITT

We see also that management compensation follows the benefits of spin-offs. The total compensation of Rand V. Araskog, CEO of ITT Corporation, more than doubled in the year that ITT spun off two

business units, ITT Industries and ITT Hartford Group. ITT's stock price almost tripled from three years prior. Charles Peck, a senior associate of the Conference Board, a nonprofit business research center in New York, said, "You can make an argument that if a business, through splitting or downsizing, is increasing the earning performance of the company, then the compensation is legitimate. These days, we're going more toward measures of financial performance, rather than the sheer size of the company."

Sources: Hemang Desai and Prem Jain, "Firm Performance and Focus: Long-Run Stock Market Performance Following Spinoffs," *Journal of Financial Economics*, October 1999; Jeff D. Opdyke, "A New Way to Profit from a Company's Problems," *The Wall Street Journal*, March 4, 2003, p. D1; and "Araskog's Piece of ITT Empire Shrinks but Compensation More Than Doubles," *The Wall Street Journal*, April 1, 1996.

---

value of current nonoperating investments such as marketable securities, and we subtract the market value of long-term debt. The net valuation for the firm is then $969,267. This value is somewhat higher than the market value method amount ($812,500) or the replacement cost asset value of $700,000. If the cash flow estimates are reliable, the DCF method provides a useful measure in determining the firm's value.

Multiples-Based Valuation

A common approach to valuing a business is to use a multiple of some financial measure—usually sales, earnings, or cash flow. For example, the earnings-based multiple computes value as the product of expected annual accounting earnings and a multiplier. The multiplier is often estimated from the price-to-earnings ratios of the stocks of comparable publicly held firms. The earnings multiplier has important limitations. The accounting treatment of inventory, depreciation, and other important components of earnings might not be comparable to that of other firms in the industry. When earnings are not comparable for these reasons, determining a relevant and useful multiplier is difficult.

The price-to-earnings ratio measures the amount the investor is willing to pay for a dollar of the firm's earnings per share. If the price-to-earnings ratio is not available for a given firm, an average or representative value is taken from the price-to-earnings ratios of other firms in the industry. This ratio can then be adjusted upward to recognize a firm with future profit potential not recognized in current earnings or vice versa. Assume that the relevant price-to-earnings multiple for EasyKleen is 8.5. Then the value of EasyKleen using this method is determined as follows:

$$\text{Earnings multiplier} \times \text{Earnings}$$
$$= 8.5 \times \$100,000 = \$850,000$$

The earnings multiplier is easy to apply and can provide a useful evaluation of the firm, subject to the limitations noted. The sales-based multiple and the cash flow based multiples are applied in a similar fashion.

In practice, the management accountant commonly uses two or more of the valuation techniques and evaluates the assumptions in each to arrive at an overall valuation assessment. If the management accountant is confident of the forecasts of net cash flow, a valuation of approximately $900,000 is appropriate and reasonable.

Summary

In this chapter we discussed management compensation and the evaluation of a business. The first part introduces the objectives and methods for compensating managers. The three principal objectives for management compensation, which follow directly from the objectives for management control, are the *motivation* of the manager, the *incentive* for proper decision making, and *fairness* to the manager.

The three main types of compensation are *salary, bonus* and *benefits*. The bonus is the fastest growing part of total compensation and often the largest part. The three important factors in the development of a bonus plan are the base for computing the bonus (strategic performance measures, stock price, and critical success factors), the source of funding for the bonus (the business unit or the entire firm), and the payment options (current and deferred bonus, stock options, and performance shares). The development of an executive compensation plan is a complex process involving these three factors and the three types of compensation, as well as the objectives of management control.

Tax planning and financial reporting concerns are important in compensation planning because of management's desire to reduce taxes and report financial results favorably. Thus, accountants must consider taxes and financial reporting issues when they develop a compensation plan for managers.

Management compensation plans are used in service and not-for-profit organizations as well. The chapter illustrates actual examples for a professional services firm and the Greensboro, North Carolina, Coliseum (see also the self-study problem at the end of the chapter).

The second part of the chapter considers the evaluation of the entire firm in contrast to the previous two chapters and the first part of this chapter that focused on the individual manager. The evaluation of the firm is important for investors and as one part of an overall assessment of the performance of top management. The common evaluation methods include the balanced scorecard, financial ratio analysis, and economic value added. Methods used to directly value a business include the market value of stock, the asset valuation method, the discounted cash flow method, and the multiples-based methods.

Key Terms

benefits, *807*

bonus, *807*

firmwide pool, *812*

management compensation plans, *807*

salary, *807*

unit-based pool, *812*

Comments on Cost Management in Action

When Good Options Go Bad

When a company's stock price falls and its executive stock options no longer look attractive, it has a number of choices. One is to simply reprice the options to a lower price that is more in keeping with the lower market price of the firm's stock. Another choice is to grant new options that have a lower exercise price to replace the old.

Another approach is for the executive to hedge his or her own stockholding or stock options by buying "put" (right-to-sell) options on the firm's stock in the open market. If the stock price falls dramatically, the executive can still sell the stock or exercise the options at the relatively favorable ("put") price. This practice is very much like that engaged in by global firms to hedge their exposure to foreign exchange fluctuations.

The problem with executives hedging their stock holdings and options is that it undermines the principle of pay for performance. Through hedging, the executive can effectively protect against a fall in the stock. Hedging reduces the risk of stock ownership and therefore reduces the incentive for executives to take steps to sustain stock price.

Source: Pallavi Gogoi, "When Good Options Go Bad," *Business Week*, December 11, 2000, pp. EB96–98; Louis Lavelle, "Undermining Pay for Performance," *Business Week*, January 15, 2001, p. 70; and Michael Schroeder and Ruth Simon, "Tech Firms Object as SEC Gets Tougher on their Practice of Repricing Options," *The Wall Street Journal*, February 7, 2001, p. C10.

Self-Study Problem

(For solution, please turn to the end of the chapter.)

Management Compensation Plan

Davis-Thompson-Howard & Associates (DTH) is a large consulting firm that specializes in the evaluation of governmental programs. The lawyers, accountants, engineers, and other specialists at DTH evaluate both the performance of existing programs and the success of potential new government programs. DTH obtains most of its consulting engagements by completing proposals in open bidding for the services desired by governmental agencies. The competition for these proposals has increased in recent years, and as a result DTH's yield (the number of new engagements divided by proposals) has fallen from 49 percent a few years ago to only 26 percent in the most recent year. The firm's profitability has fallen as well. DTH has decided to study its management compensation plan as one step among the many it will take in attempting to return the firm to its previous level of profitability.

DTH has six regional offices, two located near Washington, D.C., and the others near large metropolitan areas where most of their clients are located. Each office is headed by an office manager who is one of the firm's professional associates. The firm's services in these offices are classified into financial and operational audit services, educational evaluation, engineering consulting, and financial systems. The Washington offices tend to provide most of the financial and audit services, and the other offices offer their own mix of professional services. No two offices are alike since each has adapted to the needs of its regional client base. DTH's objective is to be among the three most competitive firms in its areas of service and to increase its revenues by at least 10 percent per year.

DTH's compensation plan awards each office a bonus based on (1) the increase in billings over the prior year and (2) the number of net new clients acquired in the current year. The office manager has the authority to divide the office bonus as appropriate, although these same two criteria are generally used to allocate it to the office professionals. Top management is not aware of any problems with the compensation plan; there have been no significant complaints.

One observation by the CEO might suggest a reason for the firm's decline in yield of proposals. It has been losing out particularly on large new contract proposals that require a large number of staff and a significant professional travel commitment. These are jobs for which it would be necessary to coordinate two or more DTH offices. The CEO notes that DTH has as many regional offices as most of its competitors, which now seem to be winning a larger share of these contracts.

Required

Discuss the pros and cons of DTH's compensation plan. Is it consistent with the company's objectives and competitive environment?

Business Valuation

WebSmart is a relatively new Internet company that sells educational products on the Web. The firm focuses on students preparing for college entrance exams. The key competitive advantage at WebSmart is their highly regarded publication, *Guide to Competitive Colleges,* which is sold widely in bookstores and on Amazon.com. The firm has grown rapidly and now is seeking additional venture capital investment to allow it to improve its operations and provide additional advertising and promotion. One of the venture capital firms that WebSmart approached has asked WebSmart to provide an estimate of the firm's value. Relevant financial information about WebSmart from the most recent financial statement follows. WebSmart owns no significant fixed assets, but operates out of leased space. WebSmart management knows that the median stock price-to-sales multiple in the industry is approximately 7.

Total assets per most recent financial statement	$1,450,000
Estimated market value of *Guide to Competitive Colleges*	350,000
Net income	(85,000)
Cash flow from operations	(165,000)
Total revenues	$600,000

Required

Develop an estimate of the value of WebSmart and explain your reasoning.

Questions

19–1   Identify and explain the three objectives of management compensation.

19–2   Explain the three types of management compensation.

19–3   Explain how a manager's risk aversion can affect decision making and how compensation plans should be designed to deal with risk aversion.

19–4   Explain how management compensation can provide an incentive to unethical behavior. What methods can be used to reduce the chance of unethical activities resulting from compensation plans?

19–5   From a financial reporting standpoint, what form of compensation is most desirable for the firm?

19–6   From a tax-planning standpoint, what form of compensation is least desirable for the manager? For the firm?

19–7   List the three bases for bonus incentive plans; explain how they differ and how each achieves or does not achieve the three objectives of management compensation.

19–8   Identify and explain the five financial ratios used to evaluate liquidity as part of the firm's valuation.

19–9   What are the two types of bonus pools for bonus incentive plans? How do they differ, and how does each achieve or not achieve the three objectives of management compensation?

19–10 List the four types of bonus payment options and explain how they differ. How does each achieve or not achieve the three objectives of management compensation?

19–11 Develop arguments to support your view as to whether executive pay in the United States is too high.

19–12 What are the four valuation methods? Which do you think is superior and why?

19–13 What type of management compensation is the fastest growing part of total compensation? Why do you think this is the case?

19–14 Why do you think it is important for a management accountant to be able to complete an evaluation of the firm separate from an evaluation of individual managers?

19–15 How does the firm's management compensation plan change over the life cycle of the firm's products?

Exercises

19–16 **Compensation, Strategy, and Market Value**   Jackson Supply Company is a publicly owned firm that serves the medical supply needs of hospitals and large medical practices in six southeastern states. The firm has grown significantly in recent years, as the areas it serves have grown. Jackson has focused on customer service and has developed an excellent reputation for speed of delivery and overall quality of service. The company ensures that customer service is each manager's main focus by making it count for 50 percent of the management bonus. The firm measures specific indicators of customer service monthly; progress toward these measures as well as others is used to determine each manager's bonus. In the past several months, top management has noticed that although most managers are meeting or exceeding their customer service goals and receiving bonuses accordingly, the firm's stock price has been lagging while competitive firms' stock prices have been rising steadily.

Required   What modification, if any, should Jackson Supply Company make to its management compensation plan?

19–17 **Performance Evaluation and Risk Aversion**   Jill Lewis is the office manager of PureBreds, Inc. Her office has 30 employees whose collective job is to process applications by dog owners who want to register their pets with the firm. There is never a shortage of applications waiting to be processed, but random events beyond Lewis's control cause fluctuations in the number of applications that her office can process.

Alex Zale, the district manager to whom Jill reports, has no way to observe her effort other than to monitor the number of applications that are processed.

Required

1. If Jill is risk adverse, how should Alex compensate her? Why?

For requirements 2 and 3, assume that the correctness of the information is entered into the computers at Jill's office is as important as the volume of processed applications.

2. What are the disadvantages of a compensation package that is influenced by the number of processed applications but not by the correctness of the data input?

3. List at least two ways that Alex could measure how accurately Jill's office is processing the applications.

19–18 **Performance Evaluation and Risk Aversion**   Heartwood Furniture Corporation has a line of sofas marketed under the name NightTime Sleepers. Heartwood management is considering several compensation packages for Amy Johnson, NightTime's general manager. Amy's duties include making all investing and operating decisions for NightTime.

Required

1. Amy is risk neutral and prefers to receive the maximum reward for her hard work. Do you recommend compensation based on flat salary, an ROI-based bonus, or a combination of both? Why?

2. If Amy does not make investing decisions for NightTime, is ROI still a good performance measure? If so, then explain why. If not, suggest an alternative.

3. Heartwood Furniture wants to evaluate Amy by comparing NightTime's ROI to the ROI of Stiles Furniture, which operates in a business environment similar to that of NightTime. Both companies have the same capabilities, but Stiles uses a significantly different manufacturing strategy than NightTime does.

   a. Would evaluating Amy with this benchmark be fair?

   b. Would using residual income instead of ROI offer any advantages?

   c. What are the drawbacks to evaluating Amy using total sales instead of ROI?

19–19 **Evaluating An Incentive Pay Plan; Strategy**   Anne-Marie Fox is the manager of a new and used boat dealership. She has decided to reevaluate the compensation plan offered to her sales representatives to determine whether it encourages the dealership's success. The representatives are paid no salary, but they receive 20 percent of the sales price of every boat sold, and they have the authority to negotiate the boats' prices as far down as their wholesale cost if necessary.

Required   Is this plan in the dealership's strategic best interest? Why or why not?

19–20 **Alternative Compensation Plans**   ADM, Inc., an electronics manufacturer, uses growth in earnings per share (EPS) as a guideline for evaluating executive performance. ADM executives receive a bonus of $5,000 for every penny increase in EPS for the year. This bonus is paid in addition to fixed salaries ranging from $500,000 to $900,000 annually.

Cygnus Corporation, a computer components manufacturer, also uses EPS as an evaluation tool. Its executives receive a bonus equal to 40 percent of their salary for the year if the firm's EPS is in the top third of a list ranking the EPS ratios for Cygnus and its 12 competitors.

Required

1. Why are companies such as ADM, Inc., and Cygnus Corporation switching from stock option incentives to programs more like the ones described? What does the use of these plans by the two firms say about each firm's competitive strategy?

2. What are the weaknesses of incentive plans based on EPS?

19–21 **Business Evaluation**   Bakersfield Company is a manufacturer of auto parts having the following financial results for 2003-2004.

	2004	2003	2004 Industry Average
Cash	$ 385,000	$ 125,000	
Accounts receivable	300,000	275,000	
Inventory	200,000	175,000	
Long-lived assets	1,440,000	1,500,000	
Current liabilities	200,000	250,000	
Long-term debt	800,000	800,000	
Economic value of intangibles	—	—	
Capital expenditures	—	—	
Sales	3,500,000	3,600,000	
Cost of sales	2,500,000	2,600,000	
Operating expense*	500,000	450,000	
Training expense	40,000	20,000	
Income tax rate	40%	40%	40%
Depreciation expense	60,000	50,000	
Dividends	—	—	

(continued)

	2004	2003	2004 Industry Average
Year-End Stock Price	$ 2.55	$ 2.75	
Number of outstanding shares	1,800,000	1,800,000	
Sales multiplier			2
Free cash flow multiplier			18
Earnings multiplier			9
Cost of capital	6.0%	6.0%	
Accounts receivable turnover			9.2
Inventory turnover			11.3
Current ratio			2.8
Quick ratio			2.0
Cash flow from operations ratio			1.2
Free cash flow ratio			1.1
Gross margin percentage			30.0%
Return on assets (Net book value)			20.0%
Return on equity			30.0%

*Operating expense includes training expense and depreciation expense.

Required

1. Calculate and interpret the financial ratios (per Exhibit 19.9) for Bakersfield for 2003 and 2004. Since the calculation of many ratios requires the average balance in an account (e.g., average receivables is required in calculating receivables turnover) you may assume that the balances in 2002 are the same as 2003.

2. Calculate and interpret Economic Value Added (EVA) for Bakersfield for 2003 and 2004. Assume that capital is defined as average total assets plus training expenses.

19–22 **Business Valuation**   Refer to the information in Exercise 19–21.

Required   Develop a business valuation for Bakersfield Company for 2004 using (a) the market value method, (b) the asset valuation method, and (c) the multiples-based method. Which of the methods would you use and why?

Problems

19–23 **Compensation; Machine Replacement**   Choco-Lots Candy Co. makes chewy chocolate candies at a plant in Winston-Salem, North Carolina. Brian Main, the production manager at this facility, installed a packaging machine last year at a cost of $400,000. This machine is expected to last for 10 more years with no residual value. Operating costs for the projected levels of production are $80,000 annually.

Brian has just learned of a new packaging machine that would work much more efficiently in Choco-Lots' production line. This machine would cost $420,000 installed, but the annual operating costs would be only $30,000. This machine would be depreciated over 10 years with no residual value. He could sell the current packaging machine this year for $150,000.

Brian has worked for Choco-Lots for seven years. He plans to remain with the firm for about two more years, when he expects to become a vice president of operations at his father-in-law's company. Choco-Lots pays Brian a fixed salary with an annual bonus of 1 percent of net income for the year.

Assume that Choco-Lots uses straight-line depreciation and has a 10 percent required rate of return. Ignore income tax effects.

Required

1. As the owner of Choco-Lots, would you want Brian to keep the current machine or purchase the new one?

2. Why might Brian not prefer to make the decision that the owner of Choco-Lots desires?

19–24 **Compensation; Benefits; Ethics**   DuMelon Publishing Inc. is a nationwide company headquartered in Boston, Massachusetts. The firm's benefits are a significant element of employee compensation. All professional employees at DuMelon receive company-paid benefits including medical insurance, term life insurance, and paid vacations and holidays. They also receive a set reimbursement amount of $100 a day maximum for travel expenses when they conduct business for DuMelon. DuMelon offers a 25 percent match for money the professionals deposit in the company-sponsored 401(k) plan.

These benefits vary, depending on the employee's salary and level in the company. For example, the amount of vacation days increases as a professional is promoted to higher levels. The maximum amount that can be contributed to the 401(k) plan also increases as the employee's salary increases.

When a DuMelon employee attains the position of vice president of a function, such as operations or sales, that person qualifies for a special class of additional benefits: a company car, a larger office with decoration allowances, and access to the executive suite at the Boston office. (The executive suite features a dining room and lounge for the executives' use.) The perks also include total reimbursement for all business travel expenses.

Required

1. Explain the implications for employee behavior and performance of DuMelon's two levels of benefits for professional employees.

2. Suppose that the policy for benefits is not applied strictly at DuMelon. As a result, the following instances have occurred:

   a. The company has occasionally paid the travel expenses of VP's spouses. Company policy is unclear as to whether this is allowed.

   b. Some VPs have special-ordered their company-provided vehicles, which on average costs the company an additional $3,300 for each car.

   c. Passes to the executive suite have been lent to other DuMelon professionals.

   d. Some of the vice presidents have offices that are much larger than those of other vice presidents. No apparent factors determine who gets the larger offices.

   How might this situation affect the behavior of vice presidents and other professionals at DuMelon? What are the underlying implications for cost control of benefits? Use specific examples when applicable.

19–25   **Incentive Pay in The Hotel Industry**   Jorge Martinez is the general manager of Classic Inn, a local mid-priced hotel with 100 rooms. His job objectives include providing resourceful and friendly service to the hotel's guests, maintaining an 80 percent occupancy rate, improving the average rate received per room to $58 from the current $55, and achieving a savings of 5 percent on all hotel costs. The hotel's owner, a partnership of seven people who own several hotels in the region, want to structure Jorge's future compensation to objectively reward him for achieving these goals. In the past, he has been paid an annual salary of $42,000 with no incentive pay. The incentive plan the partners developed has each of the goals weighted as follows:

Measure	Percent of Total Responsibility
Occupancy rate (also reflects guest service quality)	40%
Operating within 95 percent of expense budget	25
Average room rate	35
	100%

If Jorge achieves all of these goals, the partners determined that his performance should merit total pay of $46,000. They agreed that for the incentive plan to be effective, it should comprise 50 percent of his total pay, $23,000.

The goal measures used to compensate Jorge are as follows:

Occupancy goal:	29,200 room-nights = 80 percent occupancy rate × 100 rooms × 365 days
Compensation:	40 percent weight × $23,000 target reward = $9,200 $9,200/29,200 = $0.315 per room-night
Expense goal:	5 percent savings
Compensation:	25 percent weight × $23,000 target reward = $5,750 $5,750/5 = $1,150 for each percentage point saved
Room rate goal:	$3 rate increase
Compensation:	35 percent weight × $23,000 target reward = $8,050 $8,050/300 = $26.83 per each cent increase

Jorge's new compensation plan will thus pay him a $23,000 salary plus 31.5 cents per room-night sold plus $1,150 for each percentage point saved in the expense budget plus $26.83 per each cent increase in average room rate.

Required

1. Based on this plan, what will Jorge's total compensation be if his performance results are
   a. 29,200 room-nights, 5 percent saved, $3.00 rate increase?
   b. 25,000 room-nights, 3 percent saved, $1.15 rate increase?
   c. 28,000 room-nights, 0 saved, $1.03 rate increase?
2. Comment on the expected effectiveness of this plan.

19–26 **Incentive Pay Formula Development** Use the concepts in problem 19–23 to complete the following requirements.

Required

1. Design an incentive pay plan for a restaurant manager whose goals are to serve 300 customers per day at an average price per customer of $6.88. The restaurant is open 365 days per year. These two goals are equally important. The incentive pay should comprise 40 percent of the manager's $32,000 target total compensation.
2. Calculate the manager's total compensation if the restaurant serves 280 customers per day at an average price of $6.75.

19–27 **Compensation Pools; Residual Income; Review of Chapter 18** Household Products Inc. (HPI) manufactures household goods in the United States. The company made two acquisitions in previous years to diversify its product lines. In 2002, Household Products Inc. acquired glass and plastic producing companies. HPI now (2004) has three divisions: glass, plastic, and paper. The following information (in millions) presents operating revenue, operating income, and invested assets of the company over the last three years.

Operating Revenue	2002	2003	2004
Paper	$12,000	$13,000	$14,000
Plastic	5,000	4,500	4,200
Glass	7,000	7,200	7,400
Operating Income			
Paper	$ 3,000	$ 3,200	$ 3,500
Plastic	500	300	120
Glass	1,100	900	700
Invested assets			
Paper	$ 7,000	$ 7,400	$ 7,900
Plastic	2,000	1,500	1,200
Glass	4,000	4,200	4,800

The number of executives covered by HPI's current compensation package follows:

	2002	2003	2004
Paper	300	350	375
Plastic	40	40	37
Glass	120	140	175

The current compensation package is an annual bonus award. Senior executives share in the bonus pool, which is calculated as 12 percent of the company's annual residual income. *Residual income* is defined as operating income minus an interest charge of 15 percent of invested assets.

Required

1. Use asset turnover, return on sales, and ROI to explain the differences in profitability of the three divisions.

2. Compute the bonus amount to be paid during each year; also compute individual executive bonus amounts.

3. If the bonuses were calculated by divisional residual income, what would the bonus amounts be?

4. Discuss the advantages and disadvantages of basing the bonus on HPI's residual income compared to divisional residual income.

19–28 Compensation; Strategic Issues   Mobile Business Incorporated (MBI) is a worldwide manufacturing company that specializes in high technology products for the aerospace, automotive, and plastics industries. State-of-the-art technology and business innovation have been key to the firm's success over the last several years. MBI has 10 manufacturing plants in six foreign countries. Its products are sold worldwide through sales representatives and sales offices in 23 countries. Performance information from these plants and offices is received weekly and is summarized monthly at the Toronto headquarters.

The company's current bonus compensation package focuses on giving rewards based on the utilization of capital within the company (i.e., management of inventory, collection of receivables, and use of physical assets). The board of directors is concerned, however, with the short-term focus of this plan.

Some employees believe that the company's current compensation plan does not reflect its stated goals of maintaining and enhancing its global position through innovative products.

Required   Develop a bonus package that considers MBI's strategic goals and the global environment in which it operates.

19–29 Executive Compensation; Teams; Ethics   Universal Air Inc. supplies instrumentation components to airplane manufacturers. Although only a few competitors are in this market, the competition is fierce.

Universal uses a traditional performance incentive plan to award middle-management bonuses on the basis of divisional profit. Recently, Charles Gross, chief executive officer, concluded that these objectives might be better served with new performance measures. On January 1, 2004, he assigned his executive team of top-level managers to develop these new measures.

The executive team conducted a customer survey. Although Universal has always prided itself on being on the technological forefront, the survey results indicated technology to be a low priority for customers, who were more concerned with product quality and customer service. As a result, the executive team developed 30 new criteria to measure middle-management performance and directed the controller to develop the necessary monthly reports and graphs to report on these new measures. Then the executive team announced to middle managers that these new indicators would be used to evaluate their performance. The managers were not enthusiastic and complained that some measures were influenced by the performance of other departments that they could not control. Over the next few months, customer complaints increased, and a major customer chose a competitor over Universal.

Upon seeing these results, Charles decided to review the new process. In a meeting with executive and middle managers, he emphasized that the new measures should help balance the company's performance between increased customer value and improved operating process efficiency. He set up two cross-functional teams of executive and middle managers to develop a second set of new measures: one to evaluate new product development and the other to evaluate the customer order and fulfillment process. Both teams are to focus on cost, quality, and scheduling time.

Richard Strong, quality inspection manager, is the brother-in-law of John Brogan, cost accumulation manager. On June 1, John telephoned Sara Wiley, the purchasing manager at Magic Aircraft Manufacturing Inc., one of Universal's major customers. Brogan said, "Listen Sara, we're jumping through all these hoops over here to measure performance, and management seems to be changing the measures every day. It was so easy before, getting a bonus based on the bottom line; now we have to worry about things out of our control based on how the customer perceives our performance. Would you do me a favor? If you have any complaints, please have your people call me directly so I can forward the complaint to the right person. All that really matters is for all of us to make money." In actuality, Richard was the only person to whom John reported the customer complaints that Sara offered.

Required

1. For Universal Air Inc. to remain competitive, it must implement the second set of new performance measures. Identify for the company

   a. At least three customer value-added measures.

   b. At least three process-efficiency measures.

2. Identify at least three types of employee behaviors that Universal can expect by having middle management participate in the development of the second set of new performance measures.

3. Describe what executive management at Universal needs to do to ensure the effectiveness of the cross-functional teams.

4. Referring to the specific standards for ethical conduct by a management accountant (Chapter 1), discuss whether John Brogan's behavior is unethical.

(CMA Adapted)

19–30 **Executive Compensation**   Jensen Corporation is a holding company with several diversified divisions operating throughout the United States. Jensen's management allows the divisions to operate on an autonomous basis in most areas; however, the corporate office becomes involved in determining some division strategies related to capital budgeting, development of marketing campaigns, and implementation of incentive plans. The area of incentive plans has often been a problem to Jensen because many of the companies it has acquired already had such plans in place. These plans are not easily changed without causing discontent among the managers. Jensen has striven for consistency among its divisions with regard to bonus and incentive plans, but this has not always been achievable.

The restaurant division operates a chain of vegetarian restaurants, Hobbit Hole, in the eastern United States. Jensen acquired it approximately three years ago and has made very few changes to it. The restaurant's reputation was well established and, aside from nominal changes in marketing strategy, the chain has been allowed to operate in much the same manner as it did before its acquisition. In addition to a base salary, Hobbit Hole unit managers participate in the restaurant's profits. This incentive plan was in place when Jensen acquired the chain; although the profit percentage might vary among restaurant units, the overall plans are basically the same. The unit managers are satisfied with this incentive strategy, and Jensen's management does not believe that changes are necessary.

Jensen's motel division was formed 15 years ago when Jensen purchased a small group of motels in the Midwest. Since that time, the division has grown significantly as the company has acquired motels throughout the country using the name Cruise and Snooze Inns. Since its initial motel purchase, Jensen has implemented its own incentive program for unit managers in the individual motels. The incentive program provides annual bonuses based on the achievement of specific goals that are not necessarily finance oriented but pertain to areas such as improved quality control and customer service. This program requires administrative time, but Jensen believes that the results have been satisfactory.

Required

1. Hobbit Hole's restaurant unit managers are covered by a profit participation incentive plan. Discuss the following for this incentive plan:

   a. Its benefits to Jensen Corporation.

   b. The negative behavioral problems that it could cause, if any.

2. The Cruise and Snooze Inns' motel unit managers participate in an incentive program based on goal attainment. Discuss the following for this type of incentive plan:

   a. Advantages to Jensen Corporation.

   b. Disadvantages to Jensen Corporation.

3. Having two different types of incentive plans for two operating divisions of the same company can create problems.

   a. Discuss the behavioral problems that having different types of incentive plans for Hobbit Hole and Snooze Inns could cause Jensen Corporation.

b. Present the rationale that Jensen Corporation can give to the unit managers of Hobbit Hole and Cruise and Snooze Inns to justify having different incentive plans for two operating divisions of the same company.

(CMA Adapted)

19–31 **Business Evaluation** Blue Water Sailboats is owned by a partnership of two businesspeople who are friends and avid sailors. At present, they are interested in expanding the business and have asked you to review its financial statements.

Blue Water Sailboats sells approximately 100 to 150 sailboats each year, ranging from 14-foot dinghies to 20-foot sailboats. Their sales prices range from $2,000 to more than $10,000. The company has a limited inventory of boats consisting primarily of one or two boats from each of the four manufacturers that supply Blue Water. The company also sells a variety of supplies and parts and performs different types of service. Most sales are on credit.

The company operates from a large building that has offices, storage, and sales for some of the smaller sailboats. The larger sailboats are kept in a fenced area adjacent to the main building, and an ample parking area is nearby. This year Blue Water purchased a boat lift to haul boats. The lift has brought in revenues for boat repairs, hull painting, and related services, as well as the boat hauls.

The balance sheet and income statement for Blue Water Sailboats for 1999 through 2003 and for the first eleven months of 2004 follow. The increase in net fixed assets in the recent two years is due to improvements in the building, paving of the parking area, and the purchase of the lift.

The company obtains its debt financing from two sources: a small savings and loan for its short-term funds, and a larger commercial bank, also for short-term loans, but principally for long-term financing. The terms of the loan agreement with the bank include a restriction that its current ratio must remain higher than 1.5.

Required Evaluate the liquidity and profitability of Blue Water Sailboats using selected financial ratios. Assess the company's overall profitability, liquidity, and desirability as an investment. Use a spreadsheet system to improve the speed and accuracy of your analysis.

BLUE WATER SAILBOATS COMPANY
Comparative Balance Sheet
For the Years Ended December 31,

	1999	2000	2001	2002	2003	2004 (11 months)
Cash	$23,260	$21,966	$18,735	$28,426	$43,692	$31,264
Accounts receivable	99,465	102,834	112,903	125,663	104,388	142,009
Allowance for bad debts	(9,304)	(8,786)	(8,824)	(11,266)	(7,282)	(12,506)
Inventory	35,009	56,784	61,792	67,884	58,994	95,774
Other current assets	11,894	12,894	9,024	11,006	18,923	22,903
Total current assets	$160,324	$185,692	$193,630	$221,713	$218,715	$279,444
Property and equipment	262,195	282,008	299,380	368,565	405,269	498,626
Accumulated depreciation	(65,984)	(93,442)	(122,892)	(158,099)	(187,227)	(226,307)
Total assets	$356,535	$374,258	$370,118	$432,179	$436,757	$551,763
Accounts payable	82,635	78,127	63,346	56,256	40,189	49,544
Taxes payable	11,630	10,983	11,780	14,083	3,738	15,632
Short-term loans	59,876	56,980	37,583	41,093	49,594	76,962
Accrued payroll payable	5,227	4,598	3,649	4,224	4,774	4,779
Total current liabilities	$159,368	$150,688	$116,358	$115,656	$98,295	$146,917
Long-term debt	158,173	172,388	179,490	214,997	229,471	262,258
Partners' equity	38,994	51,182	74,270	101,526	108,991	142,588
	$356,535	$374,258	$370,118	$432,179	$436,757	$551,763

BLUE WATER SAILBOATS COMPANY
Comparative Statement of Income and Cash Flow
For the Years Ended December 31,

	1999	2000	2001	2002	2003	2004 (11 months)
Sales	$767,580	$724,878	$777,480	$929,478	$764,610	$938,857
Returns and allowances	38,379	35,645	40,334	45,998	32,887	46,380
Cost of sales	473,908	441,298	458,015	545,778	453,669	530,597
Gross margin	$255,293	$247,935	$279,131	$337,702	$278,054	$361,880
Depreciation expense	$29,075	$27,458	$29,450	$35,208	$29,128	$35,563
Interest expense	18,597	19,557	20,998	21,475	24,889	28,993
Salaries and wages	81,923	73,664	77,846	95,764	92,903	99,447
Accounting and legal	9,304	8,786	9,323	11,834	13,108	11,380
Administration expense	79,666	75,234	80,693	96,469	87,995	97,441
Other expense	12,630	18,927	15,763	22,903	18,934	22,662
Total expense	$231,195	$223,626	$234,073	$283,653	$266,957	$295,486
Net income	$24,098	$24,309	$45,058	$54,049	$11,097	$66,394
Cash flow from operations						
Depreciation		$27,458	$29,450	$35,208	$29,128	$35,563
Decrease (increase) in receivables		(3,887)	(10,031)	(10,318)	17,291	(22,397)
Decrease (increase) in inventory		(21,775)	(5,008)	(6,092)	8,890	(36,780)
Decrease (increase) in other current assets		(1,000)	3,870	(1,982)	(7,917)	(3,980)
Increase (decrease) in current liabilities		(8,680)	(34,330)	(702)	(17,361)	48,622
Total		$16,425	$29,009	$70,163	$41,128	$77,422

19–32 Business Valuation Refer to the information in 19–31 for the Blue Water Sailboats Company.

Required Develop a business valuation for Blue Water Sailboats Company for 2004 using the asset valuation method and the multiples-based methods. Assume that the industry average earnings multiple is 8 and the industry average multiple on operating cash flow is 12. Which of the methods would you use and why?

19–33 Business Evaluation Georgia Home Products, Inc. (GHP) manufactures plumbing fixtures and other home improvement products that are sold in Home Depot and Wal-Mart as well as hardware stores. GHP has a solid reputation for providing value products, good quality, and a good price. The company has been approached by an investment banking firm representing a third company, Garden Specialties Inc. (GSI) that is interested in acquiring GHP. The acquiring firm (GSI) is a retailer of garden supplies; it sees the potential synergies of the combined firm and is willing to pay GHP shareholders $75 cash per share for their stock which is greater than the current stock price; the stock has traded at about $65 in recent months. Summary financial information about GHP follows.

Required

1. Evaluate GHP as a company using financial ratio analysis. Since the calculation of some ratios requires the averaging of balances, you may assume that the balances in 2002 are the same as 2003.
2. Evaluate GHP as a company using economic value added. Assume that capital is defined as average total assets plus training expenses.

SELECTED FINANCIAL INFORMATION
GEORGIA HOME PRODUCTS, INC.

	2004	2003	2004 Industry Average
Cash	$ 10,517,200	$ 2,546,000	
Accounts receivable	68,946,000	56,930,000	
Inventory	41,784,000	34,885,000	
Long-lived assets			
Gross book value	116,755,000	114,650,000	
Net book value	69,709,000	74,388,000	
Replacement cost	175,483,000	175,483,000	
Liquidation value	67,430,000	78,366,000	
Current liabilities	25,872,000	28,922,000	
Long-term debt	55,830,000	55,830,000	
Economic value of intangibles	11,236,000		
Capital expenditures	2,105,000		
Sales	345,074,000	322,087,000	
Cost of sales	218,648,000	189,374,000	
Operating expense*	82,664,000	69,374,000	
Training expense	11,947,000	45,389,000	
Income tax rate	40%	40%	40.0%
Depreciation expense	6,784,000	6,354,000	
Dividends	1,000,000	1,000,000	
Year end stock price	66.37	59.45	$12.00
Number of outstanding shares	3,285,774	3,285,774	
Sales multiplier			1.20
Free cash flow multiplier			16.00
Earnings multiplier			7.00
Cost of capital	5.5%	5.5%	
Accounts receivable turnover			6.50
Inventory turnover			7.00
Current ratio			2.20
Quick ratio			2.00
Cash flow form operations ratio			1.50
Free cash flow ratio			1.10
Gross margin percentage			30.0%
Return on assets (net book value)			18.0%
Return on equity			32.0%

*Operating expense includes training expense and depreciation expense

19–34 Business Valuation Refer to the information in Problem 19–33.

Required

1. Develop a business valuation for 2004 using the market value method, the asset valuation method, and the multiples-based methods.

2. Determine an estimated value for GHP using the discounted free cash flow method, assuming that the 2004 amount of free cash flow continues indefinitely.

3. Which of the methods would you use and why?

4. Is the GSI offer a good one? Why or why not?

Solution to Self-Study Problem

Management Compensation Plan

DTH's goal is to increase its business by at least 10 percent a year in a very competitive environment. The compensation plan is consistent with this goal because it rewards increases in revenues and new clients. It is likely, however, that under the current plan, each office is focusing only on the client base in its own region.

A problem occurs when DTH must make proposals that require joint cooperation and participation among two or more offices. The compensation plan does not have an incentive for cooperation. In fact, it could be a distraction and reduce the potential for a substantial bonus for any given office to develop a proposal for a large contract in which other offices might benefit. The cost of the proposal would be borne by the office, and the benefits would accrue to other offices as well as the originating office. The cost of the proposal for large contracts must therefore be shared among the offices in some way, or any one office will not have the incentive to spend the time and money necessary to develop a large proposal.

In addition to sharing the cost of the proposal, DTH should consider having a firmwide proposal development group for these large projects. The individual offices would then be charged for the cost of this group, perhaps in proportion to the fees received from large contracts in that office. Clearly, the firm is losing the larger contracts, and the compensation and proposal development plans must provide the needed incentive for each office to go after them aggressively.

Another alternative is to go to a firmwide compensation pool that would provide a direct and strong incentive for each office to cooperate in developing new business. A disadvantage of this approach is that it would reduce the motivation for each office to seek business in its own region because the revenues from these individual efforts would be shared firmwide.

Another issue concerning the current compensation plan is the office manager's discretion to divide the office bonus among the professionals in the office. Although no one has complained, a lower-level professional is unlikely to complain about the office manager's bonus decisions. The equity of this system should be reviewed to ensure that each office manager is using this discretion in a fair and appropriate way.

Business Valuation

Since WebSmart is a relatively new company currently showing losses and negative cash flows, the earnings-multiple and discounted cash flow approaches are not suitable. Moreover, since the company is not public, there is no current stock price. This leaves two possibilities: the asset valuation method and the revenues-multiple methods. In this case the most relevant asset figure is likely to be the total assets figure (which is largely a current replacement cost number since it includes few fixed assets) plus the economic value of WebSmart's key asset, the college guide, for a total of $1,800,000 ($1,450,000 plus $350,000). In contrast, the revenue multiple would estimate value at $4,200,000 = 7 × $600,000. Alternatively, WebSmart could use projected revenues in the multiple calculation. Moreover, it could use projected cash flows in a cash flow multiple or discounted cash flow calculation, since cash flow would presumably be positive in the coming year or two. The range of value, $1,800,000 to $4,200,000 is pretty wide, but not unexpected given a new company like this. Given that the value of the firm probably depends more on its prospects than its current asset values, a measure closer to the $4,200,000 is probably better.

Capital Budgeting

After studying this chapter, you should be able to . . .

1. Identify the major steps in capital budgeting
2. Use appropriate data in analyzing capital investments
3. Apply capital investment evaluation techniques to assess capital investments and identify advantages and limitations of these techniques
4. Identify the underlying assumptions of the two discounted cash flow methods
5. Explain the relationships between strategic cost management and capital budgeting
6. Identify behavioral factors in capital budgeting decisions

Over the last 40 years, nimble, low-cost Asian electronic manufacturers have gradually taken over markets from U.S. companies. Taiwan has the world's two largest chip foundries. Singapore had the third largest foundry until the summer of 2002 when IBM's new $3 billion chip-fabrication factory in East Fishkill, New York, started production. The new factory helped IBM to become the manufacturer of the smallest and most technologically advanced microprocessors.

After careful analyses and evaluations using capital budgeting techniques and considering technology, cash flows, and return on investment, IBM commissioned the construction of its new factory. The investment paid off. In 2002, when sales in the semiconductor business grew by 1.5 percent, the foundry's portion grew 15 percent. The foundry expects to grow another 25 percent in 2003. The fab factory is helping IBM steal prime customers from the Asian foundries. Nvidia Corp., a maker of advanced video chips and the showcase account for the industry leader Taiwan Semiconductor Manufacturer Co., switched to IBM for its next generation chips. The joint development deal the foundry signed with Advanced Micro Devices Inc. effectively scuttled plans for a state-of-the art fab factory that AMD and the second largest foundry in the world, Taiwan's United Microelectronics Corp., were planning to build. The No. 3 foundry, Singapore's Chartered Semiconductor Manufacturing Co. signed a deal to send its customers needing the most advanced manufacturing technology to IBM.[1]

Caterpillar Inc. the world's largest manufacturer of construction and mining equipment, diesel and natural gas engines, and industrial gas turbines, suffered three years of consecutive operating losses in the early 1980s that totaled more than $1.1 billion because of the increasing competitive pressures from Kamatsu of Japan and manufacturers in the United States and other countries.[2] The firm began a plant modernization in the early 1980s aiming to acquire modern manufacturing systems, termed plant with a future, to enable it to respond and adjust quickly to changes in demand and in product designs. Caterpillar management analyzed and evaluated the proposals using capital budgeting techniques including net present value, payback period, and internal rate of return. The investments paid off starting in the late 1980s and continued into the next decade. Caterpillar was able to restore profitability and regain its market share.

Through well-planned capital investments, IBM and Caterpillar respond to changing business climates, reduce costs, improve quality, and strengthen business processes

---

[1] "IBM Grabs Business from Asian Foundries," *The Wall Street Journal,* May 8, 2003, pp. B4 and B6. For more information about IBM, check the website: ibm.com/

[2] Find out more about the company at its website: cat.com/.

REAL-WORLD FOCUS   Can Olympic Hosts and Sponsors Grab the Gold?

When it comes to being a host city or corporate sponsor of the Olympics, the long-term result can be a boon—or a bust. Host cities not only face possible destruction of their image (e.g., Munich, 1972; Atlanta, 1996), but also they can suffer economic setbacks (e.g., Montreal, 1976). Of course, this is the negative side. Some host cities have benefited enormously from this large investment, enhancing their image and infrastructure and increasing the recognition of corporate sponsors (e.g., Los Angeles, 1984; Seoul, 1988; Barcelona, 1992). How large is the investment made by host cities? For the 1996 games, Atlanta raised an estimated $1.57 billion.

What's the risk of the particular investment? How can hosts and sponsors ensure a gold-medal return? When you go for the gold, you must be prepared for a few risks. Like the athletes who invest years of their lives training to reach the Olympics and encounter risks and returns along the way, host cities and corporate sponsors must invest large amounts and overcome obstacles. These financial sponsors understand these risks, but they also recognize the potential long-term gain, whether to their city's image or its bottom line.

"It's hard to allocate the costs and returns, but thanks to the Olympics we got a new bullet train to Tokyo, new expressway, and more sewers," says Shigekazu Nakamura of the 1998 Winter Olympics in Nagano, Japan. He is deputy managing editor of *Shinano Mainichi Shimbun,* the city's largest newspaper. Although these improvements total approximately $12.1 billion, Nagano and Olympic corporate sponsors believe that the long-term return was definitely worth the initial investment. For example, Eastman Kodak Company, a long-time sponsor of the Olympics, believes that its investment in the 1998 Winter Olympics (a minimum of $40 million) is money well spent. "We've always seen an uptick in revenues, in brand awareness [after the Olympics]," says Carl E. Gustin Jr., a senior vice president at Kodak. So, like the Olympic athletes, financial sponsors must be ready for a potential stellar performance or a less-than-fulfilling experience.

Sources: "Sponsorship: The Risks and Rewards of Going for the Gold," *Business Week,* February 9, 1998; "Atlanta's Big Leap," *Business Week,* July 29, 1996; and "A High Hurdle in Atlanta," *Business Week,* May 3, 1993.

throughout their value chains. This chapter presents these and other methods that IBM, Caterpillar, and many firms, organizations, and individuals use to analyze and evaluate capital investment projects.

My interest is in the future because I am going to spend the rest of my life there.

Charles Franklin Kettering

The Indian who sold Manhattan for $24 was a sharp salesman. If he had put his $24 away at 6% compounded semiannually, it would now be $9.5 billion and he could buy most of the now-improved land back.

S. Branch Walker

Businesses and organizations often need to commit large sums to projects with expenditures and benefits expected to stretch well into the future. Such projects are known as **capital investments.** Examples include purchase of new equipment, construction of new facilities, development and introduction of new products, installation of computer-based patient records, expansion into new sales territories, and, as the above feature discusses, hosting an Olympic game.[3]

A **capital investment** is a large sum of funds committed to a project with expected future benefits.

A good capital investment generates cash, decreases cash outlays, or both, over its projected lifetime to earn back the capital committed to the project and a desirable profit. No firm or organization can survive long without capital investments. A poorly executed capital investment can lead to financial hardship, tie up resources for extended periods of time, curtail opportunities available to the firm, demoralize employees, and disappoint suppliers and customers. Eventually, the failure to make good capital investments can

[3] Leslie A. Kian and Michael W. Stewart, "Justifying the Cost of a Computer-Based Patient Record," *Healthcare Financial Management* 49, no. 7, pp. 58–63.

doom a firm or organization. Poor capital investments in the late 1990s led to the continuous and considerable drops in the market capitalization of AT&T and forced it to cut its dividends by 80 percent in 2000—the first time in the firm's history of more than 100 years.

Successful capital investments often are results of projects undertaken by visionary entrepreneurs. Ford Motor Company grew by leaps and bounds in the early twentieth century as a result of Henry Ford's visionary investment in new manufacturing techniques at the time. History shows us that many venture capitalists have profited handsomely by making capital investments in new ideas.

The soundness of capital investment decisions is critical to organizations, whether for profit or not for profit. **Capital budgeting** is the process of identifying, evaluating, and selecting projects that require commitments of large sums of funds and generate benefits stretching well into the future. Sound capital investments are often a result of a careful capital budgeting.

Capital budgeting
is the process of identifying, evaluating, and selecting projects that require commitments of large sums of funds and generate benefits stretching well into the future.

Types of Capital Investment

Firms make capital investments to acquire assets for various reasons and purposes. In general, there are three categories of capital investments.[4]

1. **Assets to meet regulatory, safety, health, and environmental requirements.** Acquisition of these assets most likely cannot be deferred or rejected without potential huge penalties in the future. Costs to acquire these assets are unavoidable costs of doing business.

2. **Assets to enhance operating efficiency and/or increase revenue.** These assets improve or maintain efficient productive capacity or increase revenues. Acquisition of these assets can often be deferred in the short term at the manager's discretion.

3. **Assets to enhance competitive effectiveness.** These assets increase a firm's capacity, allow it to enter new markets, or alter or improve its fundamental operations.

Evaluation criteria and decision procedures for acquiring assets are most likely to differ according to the acquisition's reason or purpose. The extent to which a firm's strategy is applied to asset acquisition decisions also differs according to different needs. Acquisitions of assets to meet regulatory, safety, health, or environmental requirements are likely mandatory and not to be delayed. Too often, urgency underlies the need to acquire these assets. The focus of the decision in acquiring these assets is the selection of the most cost-effective way to satisfy the legal or regulatory requirements. The firm's strategy plays no role in the decision (other than to continue as a going concern).

A firm's strategy plays limited roles in capital investment decisions to acquire assets that enhance operating efficiency and/or increase revenue. Firms acquire these assets to maintain competitiveness or operating efficiency. Rarely do acquisitions of these assets have major impacts on a firm's product lines or market share. Critical factors in this type of investment decision are likely to be cost-benefit comparisons and availability of funds.

Acquisitions of assets that enhance competitive effectiveness are likely to have a significant impact on operating cash flows and profits in the short term and competitiveness in the long term. These assets should be acquired following the firm's strategy. Before acquiring these assets, the proposal should be reviewed in view of the firm's strategic goals and the importance of the proposed capital investment in meeting these goals. Because of the strategic impacts and substantial costs that such acquisitions often entail, these assets must be subject to a series of tests to ensure that they meet the firm's strategic and financial goals.

[4] Robert Simons, *Performance Measurement and Control Systems for Implementing Strategy* (Upper Saddle River, NJ: Prentice Hall, 1999).

Capital Budgeting Process

LEARNING OBJECTIVE 1
Identify the major steps in capital budgeting.

A capital budgeting process consists of three successive steps: project identification and definition, evaluation and selection, and monitoring and review.

Project Identification and Definition

A capital budgeting process begins with project identification and definition. This step is the most critical and the most difficult for a successful capital investment, as concurred by a majority of the firms responding to a survey of capital budgeting practices.[5]

Initial proposals for capital investments can come from all levels of management, from the top management, or managers of subunits, to conscientious and visionary employees at all levels. Initiatives for capital investments for equipment replacement or acquisition of assets to improve efficiency, increase revenue, or improve safety that require only marginal changes from current operations are likely to originate with a lower-level manager or employee. In contrast, higher management often initiates major changes such as construction of new plants, adoption of just-in-time or flexible manufacturing systems, development of new products, expansion into new territory, and additions to meet regulatory, safety, health, and environmental requirements.

Before undertaking a capital investment, firms must define clearly the objectives of the capital investment project and set unambiguous boundaries for the project. The management must know not only what the project will do but also what it will not do. Lack of a clear definition of a proposed investment project increases the difficulty in estimating revenues, costs, and cash flows. Too often a project without clear boundaries grows into a huge undertaking that exceeds the firm's available resources.

Evaluation and Selection

Evaluating a capital investment requires projection of revenues or benefits, costs, and cash flows over the project's entire life cycle. Knowing a project's benefits and costs helps management grasp its impact on the firm's resources and gauge whether the firm can absorb the cost. The benefits and costs of a capital investment include both financial and nonfinancial elements.

Uncertainty about future events often makes estimating the revenues or benefits, costs, and cash flows of a capital investment project a difficult task, especially for those with long lives. Changes in technology; shifts in market demand; actions of other firms in the same or a related industry; and the effects of international, national, regional, and local economies are among the general factors that firms need to consider in capital investment decisions. In addition, specific factors relating to the project must be identified. Many techniques are available to help make projections. (Chapter 6 discusses techniques on projecting cost behavior patterns and estimating costs. Chapter 9 examines issues relating to short-term decision making.)

Financial effects are not the only consideration in evaluating and selecting capital investments. A firm undertakes capital investment projects for both financial benefits and non-financial considerations. Among nonfinancial reasons for committing major capital expenditures are the safety of employees or the public; convenience or comfort of the employees; social concerns; pollution control; legal requirements; contractual commitments; and protection of existing programs, product lines, or market shares.[6]

---

[5] Of the three stages of the capital budgeting process, 51 percent of the firms participating in a survey consider the project identification and definition stage to be the most critical to the success of a capital investment. Forty-four percent of them also consider this step to be the most difficult. James M. Fremgen, "Capital Budgeting Practices: A Survey," *Management Accounting,* May 1973, pp. 19–25.

[6] Nonfinancial reasons often lead to uses of urgency as a criterion in capital investment projects. Such a concern is especially prevalent in government projects. For example, a new bridge was rebuilt because the existing one was deemed hazardous. A highway was built because the legislator from the district convinced the Department of Transportation that having a new highway through the area was urgent. For more examples, see "Report to the Congress of the United States by the Comptroller General," *Federal Capital Budgeting: A Collection of Haphazard Practices* (Washington, DC: General Accounting Office, 1981).

Budgeting on Faith or Strategic Investment Analysis

When it comes to investing in new technology, many corporations are known to make the investment decision on faith. The decision of a kitchen unit manufacturer with an established reputation for innovative design to invest heavily in computer-assisted design equipment was based on management's belief that its customers would ascribe high value to the use of sophisticated automatic technology in manufacturing.

Investing in new technology without a formal analysis using a capital budgeting technique is akin to theologians explaining the mysteries of the universe. Faith (capital) budgeting involves the basic assumption that the investment, especially when it is in new technology, differs fundamentally from other capital investments. The investment can so alter a business that its intangible benefits cannot be quantified or fully anticipated. Returns not anticipated or quantifiable cannot be incorporated into capital budgeting models. Traditional capital budgeting techniques such as the payback period, book rate of return, or discounted cash flows are of no use and, if used, most likely will lead to underinvestment in new technologies. Not investing in new technology can lead to an inexorable erosion of competitive capability, compounded by market perception that

the firm is behind in time and technology—an unacceptable stigma to many managers and CEOs.

Investing in new technology does not have to rely on faith budgeting. All investments involve future events. An investment, whether in a new technology or the addition of a newer and more efficient equipment, should be evaluated on its strategic fit and benefits as well as a formal quantitative analysis. Considerations of strategic fit and benefits can be informal. For example, a medium-size manufacturer and distributor of specialized leisure products adopted MRP, CAD/CAM, and robotized production, although these investments failed the company's three-year payback criterion. The firm approved these investments after a long and careful consideration of their informal strategic benefits. Included in its consideration were improvements on product quality, reductions in quality variations, increased manufacturing flexibility, more precise responses to fluctuating demands, increased skill base, and better control and planning.

Sources: Michael Bromwich and Al Bhimani, "Strategic Investment Appraisal," *Management Accounting,* March 1991, pp. 45–48; and John R. Brandt, "Budgeting on Faith," *Industry Week,* 247 (23).

The critical importance of one or more nonfinancial factors for undertaking a capital investment does not imply that it is unnecessary to conduct financial evaluation on the project. Although a firm needs to add pollution abatement equipment to satisfy a legal requirement, it must still perform a financial analysis to identify the equipment's costs and benefits. Even if management is fully aware that the firm's benefit from the capital expenditure is likely to be less than the costs entailed, a complete financial evaluation apprises management of the cost to comply with legal requirements and prepares management for the requisite cash outlays.

Monitoring and Review

A successful capital investment requires continual monitoring and review. A careful evaluation before selecting an investment is only the first step. As the investment project progresses, situations change, new variables surface, and fresh opportunities arise. The organization needs to be able to modify its original plan, incorporate new developments, and alter the course of action, if necessary, to attain the best results.[7]

Data for Capital Budgeting

LEARNING OBJECTIVE 2
Use appropriate data in analyzing capital investments.

Data used for capital investment decisions differ from those generated for routine accounting records and reports in two respects: their characteristics and the factors relevant to decisions.

Characteristics of Capital Budgeting Data

The characteristics of capital budgeting data differ from financial reporting data in three aspects: data period, measurement object, and time horizon. Exhibit 20.1 contrasts data characteristics for capital budgeting and those for routine financial reporting.

[7] Twenty-three percent of the firms participating in the capital budgeting survey conducted by Fremgen consider this stage to be the most critical to the success of an investment.

EXHIBIT 20.1
Selected Characteristics of
Capital Budgeting and
Financial Reporting Data

Characteristic	Capital Budgeting	Financial Reporting
Data period	Life of the project	Annually, quarterly, or monthly
Measurement object	Cash flows	Accrual revenues and expenses
Time horizon	Future events and transactions	Historical events and transactions

Data Period

Two underlying concepts of financial reporting data are periodicity and accrual basis accounting. *Periodicity* requires firms to record and report accounting data at specified regular intervals: monthly, quarterly, or annually. Only transactions or data pertaining to the period being reported are included in financial reports.

A capital budgeting process, however, evaluates the investment over its entire life cycle, not just one accounting period. A decision to introduce a new product, for example, must consider not only the investment required to develop and market the product initially but also the expected revenues and costs in all the years the product is to be on the market. In contrast, an accrual basis accounting system typically separates the life cycle of the new product into several time periods and focuses on only one period at a time.

Measurement Object

Accrual basis accounting requires firms to include in the period's accounting data and financial statements all figures pertaining to revenues earned and expenses incurred in that period. Receipt or disbursement of cash is not a factor in determining the period in which to include and report the amount.

A capital investment budget focuses on cash flows, not on accrual-based revenues and expenses. Thus, a noncash sale in a period is not included in the capital budget for that period if the firm receives no cash in that period from the sale. Similarly, an expense is not included in a capital budget as an expense of the period if the firm pays no cash for that expense during that period. In contrast, an accrual-based accounting procedure includes both the noncash sale and the unpaid expense in the period if the firm deems the transaction belongs to that period.

Time Horizon

Another difference between capital budgeting data and financial reporting data is in the time horizon. Capital budgeting data focus on future transactions and events, while financial reporting data are based on historical transactions and events. A proper financial report records and reports all transactions and events that have occurred during the period and the consequences of past actions. In contrast, historical data are seldom included in capital budgeting and are included only to the extent of their effects on current and future cash flows.

Relevant Factors in Capital Budgeting

The ultimate concern of a firm and its investors is its cash position. The relevant factor in capital budgeting, therefore, is the cash outflows for and inflows from a capital investment.

A business firm makes capital investments to improve profits. This interest in profit leads many firms to focus their attention on periodic net income when considering capital investments. Although net income is a measure of profit, overemphasizing its importance can lead to erroneous capital investment decisions because net income calculated based on accounting numbers for financial reporting is not a good measure of return on a capital investment.

Both the periodicity reporting requirement and the arbitrary process involved in determining net income lessen the usefulness of net income as an objective criterion. Net

844 Part Six Advanced Topics in Cost Management

income is the result of applying selected accounting rules and methods to transactions. A period's net income can differ substantially when the firm chooses to follow an alternative accounting rule and use different, yet equally acceptable, accounting methods.

Capital budgeting considers only cash flows. It includes all items affecting cash flows whether or not they are accounting revenues or expenses of the period.

Conversely, capital budgeting considers no noncash items. A noncash item, such as depreciation expense, is included in capital budgeting calculations only to the extent that it affects tax obligation cash flows. Depreciation expenses are not cash payments and are by themselves irrelevant in capital budgeting. This is true although they are expenses for income determination purposes. A depreciation expense is relevant to a capital budget only because it has an effect on the amount of income taxes the firm must pay for the period. In the same vein, the entire amount of cash paid in a period to purchase an asset is relevant for capital budgeting purposes, although the entire amount might not be an expense in computing the net income for the period.

Cash Flows

A capital investment often starts with a cash outflow that is a payment or commitment of funds, followed by decreases in cash expenditures, increases in cash inflows, or both in subsequent periods. Additional funds also could be needed for additional capital investments during the life of the project.

Cash inflows or *out*flows occur at three stages of a capital investment project:

1. **Project initiation.** Cash flows at this point include
   - Cash outflows to acquire the investment and to begin operations.
   - Cash commitments for working capital needed for the operations.
   - Cash inflow or outflow to dispose of the asset being replaced.
2. **Project operation.** Cash flows during the operation of a capital investment include
   - *Outflows for* operating expenditures and additional capital investment after the initial investment.
   - *Commitments for* additional working capital needed in operations.
   - *Inflows of cash* generated by the investment (revenues and cash savings) and cash released from working capital no longer needed in operations.
3. **Final project disposal.** Cash flows at final disposal include
   - Cash inflows or outflows related to the investment's disposal.
   - Cash inflows from the release of working capital no longer committed to the investment.

Determining Cash Flows in Capital Budgeting

Cash received increases and cash paid or committed decreases, cash available to an organization. The immediate effect that a cash receipt or cash payment or commitment has on cash flows often is referred to as the *direct effect.*

Paying $1,000 for repairs, for example, decreases the amount of cash available for other uses by $1,000 immediately and is a direct effect. An event or transaction often changes a tax-paying organization's tax obligations. The effect that an event or transaction has on the amount of an organization's tax payment for the period is the *tax effect or indirect effect.* If a firm that paid $1,000 for repairs is in the 25 percent tax bracket, for example, the payment decreases the firm's tax liability by $250. Thus, the payment has a tax or indirect effect of $250 cash inflow or cash saving.

Both direct and indirect effects affect cash flows of the period. The total of the direct effect and the tax effect is the *net effect* on cash flow. The net effect of the $1,000 payment for repairs is a cash outflow of $750 ($1,000 outflow − $250 cash inflow). Exhibit 20.2 summarizes these effects.

A $10,000 cash revenue for a *for-profit firm* in the 30 percent tax bracket has a net cash inflow of $7,000, not $10,000, because the additional $10,000 revenues increase

EXHIBIT 20.2
Effects of Cash Flow

Direct Effect:	Cash receipt, cash payment, or cash commitment
Tax Effect:	Changes in tax payments
Net Effect:	Direct effect + Tax effect

its taxes by $3,000. The amount of net cash outflow for a $6,000 payment by the same firm for expenses is $4,200 because the $6,000 expense decreases the firm's tax expenses by $1,800.

Noncash revenues or expenses that have tax effects also affect cash flows. Because tax liability is determined on an accrual-based income, a noncash revenue such as a credit sale does not increase the cash available to the firm but does increase the firm's taxable income for the period, which increases the amount of cash needed to pay for taxes. Thus, a noncash revenue *decreases,* not increases, cash available to the firm. The amount of the decrease is the increase in taxes resulting from the noncash revenue.

For example, a $10,000 noncash revenue, such as a credit sale, for a firm in the 30 percent tax bracket reduces, not increases, cash available to the firm by $3,000. Although the firm receives no cash from a noncash revenue, it nevertheless increases its tax liability by $3,000. Therefore, for a taxpaying organization, *a noncash revenue is a cash outflow,* not a cash inflow.

An increase in expenses, on the other hand, decreases taxable income, which reduces the taxes for the period. A noncash expense, therefore, increases, not decreases, cash inflow. Depreciation is a noncash expense that does not require a cash payment in the period in which the expense is recognized. The expense, however, reduces the firm's tax payment for the period. This increases cash available for other uses and results in a cash inflow to the firm.

Activities at various stages of a capital investment differ and have various effects on cash flows. As indicated, cash flows for capital investments occur at the project initiation, during project operation, and at the final disposal. In the next sections we examine in detail the effects on cash flows of activities at each of these three stages.

Project Initiation

Activities at the inception of a capital investment are likely to include

1. Acquisition of assets.
2. Commitment of additional working capital.
3. Disposal of assets replaced.

Effects of Initial Investment Acquisition on Cash Flow

Activities at the initial investment stage that entail cash outflow include constructing or buying a new facility; purchasing, installing, and testing new equipment; and training personnel. The bulk of the direct cash outflow for an investment usually occurs at its beginning. In capital budgeting, the time when initial cash outflows occur for the acquisition is referred to as *time 0* (or *year 0*).

Most of these cash outflows also have tax effects. For example, costs to hire or train personnel can be treated as expenses in the period they are incurred. Increases in expenses reduce income taxes, and decreases in tax payments reduce cash outflows or increase cash inflows.

Another effect that asset acquisition costs have on cash flows is the depreciation expenses to be taken on the acquired asset. Depreciation expenses themselves have no immediate cash effect. As a noncash expense that decreases operating (and taxable) income in subsequent periods, the depreciation expense reduces the firm's tax obligation in subsequent years. A reduction in the tax obligation is a cash inflow for a tax-paying organization. Exhibit 20.3 summarizes cash flow effects at the initiation stage.

Smith Company manufactures high-pressure pipe for deep-sea oil drilling. The firm is considering purchasing a milling machine for $500,000. The installation cost will be

EXHIBIT 20.3
Effects of Investment Acquisition on Cash Flow

Direct Effect (Outflow)

- Cost to purchase, construct, or manufacture buildings and equipment.
- Cost to install and test equipment.
- Cost to hire and train personnel.

Tax Effect (Inflow)

- Decrease in income taxes for acquisition costs treated as expenses.
- Decrease in income taxes due to depreciation on the investment.

approximately $5,000. Testing and adjusting before placing the machine in production will cost $10,000. After its expected useful life of four years, disposal costs related to the equipment follow: sale of the equipment, $100,000 (inflow); machine removal and site cleaning expenses, $20,000 (outflow). The firm uses straight-line depreciation with an estimated salvage value of $75,000 for the investment. The controller expects the firm to be in the 34 percent federal income tax bracket and the state and local governments to levy 6 percent income taxes.

The first segment (year 0) of Exhibit 20.4 shows that the initial cash outflow for the investment will be $515,000. The firm uses straight-line depreciation for the equipment.[8] With $75,000 expected salvage value after four years, the total depreciable cost is $440,000 and the depreciation expense for the equipment is $110,000 per year for the next four years, as Exhibit 20.4 shows. The depreciation expense itself has no direct effect on cash flow because the expense requires no cash payment. The depreciation expense, however, does have a tax effect by acting as a tax shield. The depreciation expense decreases the firm's taxable income and reduces its tax liability. For a for-profit firm in the 40 percent tax bracket (34 percent federal, 6 percent state and local income taxes), a $110,000 decrease in net income reduces tax liability by $44,000. The firm enjoys this reduced tax liability each year of the project's life. The reduced tax payment is a cash inflow to the firm.

Effects of Working Capital Commitment on Cash Flow

Working capital is the additional funds needed to meet the requirements of the operations.[9] An investment in plant and equipment often calls for additional working capital to pay for new payroll and other expenditures, materials, work-in-process, and finished goods inventories, supplies and accounts receivables, among others, required for operations of the investment.

---

[8] Most spreadsheet programs can calculate depreciation expense. For example, Microsoft Excel, Lotus, and Quattro Pro calculate depreciation expense using the straight-line depreciation method if you enter (preceded with = for EXCEL and @ for Lotus 1-2-3 or Quattro Pro)

SLN (cost, salvage value, number of years)

The function for depreciation expense using sum-of-the-years'-digits method is

SYD (cost, salvage value, number of years, period)

where *period* is the year for which depreciation expense is desired. Enter **1,** for example, if you want to know the depreciation expense for the first year.

The function for depreciation expense using the double-declining balance method is

DDB (cost, salvage value, number of years, period, factor)

where *factor* is the rate at which the balance declines. If factor is omitted, it is assumed to be 2 (the double-declining balance method). In addition, these programs have two other functions, DB and VDB, for calculating depreciation. DB computes an asset's depreciation for a specified period of time using a fixed rate declining balance method. VDB determines an asset's depreciation for any period the user specifies, including a partial period, using the double-declining balance method or another method the user specifies. The keystroke sequences for all depreciation functions are **Insert → Function → Financial.**

To calculate depreciation expenses using other methods such as the ACRS (Accelerated Cost Recovery System) or MACRS (Modified Accelerated Cost Recovery System), refer to the depreciation schedule described for each method in the Internal Revenue Code (see the appendix to this chapter).

[9] In accounting terms, working capital is the excess of current assets over current liabilities. The working capital needed for an investment is the excess of *additional* current assets over *additional* current liabilities, because of the investment.

EXHIBIT 20.4
Effects of Asset Acquisition on Smith Company's Cash Flow

Year 0

Cost of equipment	$ 500,000
Installation cost	5,000
Testing and adjusting	10,000
Total cash *outflow* in year 0	$(515,000)

Year 1 through Year 4

Total cost of acquisition	$ 515,000
Expected salvage value at the end of useful life	75,000
Total to be depreciated	$ 440,000
Years of useful life for depreciation purposes	4
Depreciation expense per year, straight-line basis	$ 110,000
Income tax rate (34% + 6%)	0.40
Total cash *inflow* (tax deduction) each period due to depreciation expense	$ 44,000

Alternative Schematic Form

Description	Year 0	Year 1	Year 2	Year 3	Year 4
Cost of equipment	$(500,000)				
Installation cost	(5,000)				
Testing and adjusting	(10,000)				
Tax saving on depreciation expense		$44,000	$44,000	$44,000	$44,000
Total	$(515,000)	$44,000	$44,000	$44,000	$44,000

Funds committed as working capital, though not spent, are not available for other uses. Funds restricted for working capital is a cash outflow in the year the firm commits the funds. The commitment, however, affects only direct cash flow. No tax implications exist because the working capital commitment has no effect on either revenue or expense and, therefore, on taxes.

Not all investments require additional working capital, however. Some investments may reduce the needs for working capital. The amount needed for some operations can even decrease as the result of an investment. The decreased need for working capital is a cash inflow in the period in which the firm reduces the amount of working capital. Firms that adopt supply-chain management, just-in-time, and computer-integrated manufacturing systems often experienced decreased needs for working capital. These firms enjoy cash inflows from the reduced working capital because the investment in new manufacturing technologies increases their operating efficiency through reduced inventory levels and other reductions in operating costs.

Smith Company estimates that once the proposed milling machine is in operation, its inventory and accounts receivable will increase. Although the firm expects the increases in current assets to be offset by increases in accounts payable and other current liabilities, the expected increases in current liabilities cover only part of the increases in inventories and accounts receivables. The firm needs to increase its working capital by $200,000 to cover inventories needed for operations and accounts receivable arising from the investment. This $200,000 tied up in inventories and accounts receivable will not be available for other uses. Earmarking these funds has the direct effect of increasing the cash *outflow* for the investment in year 0 from $515,000 to $715,000 (see Exhibit 20.5).

Effect of Assets Disposal on Cash Flow

Disposing of assets has both direct and tax effects on a firm's cash flows, as Exhibit 20.6 shows. A firm gains if the net proceeds from disposing an asset exceed its *net book value* (the difference between its original cost and the total amount of

EXHIBIT 20.5

Direct Effects on Smith Company's Cash Outflow in Year 0

Cost of equipment, installation, and testing	$(515,000)
Working capital needed for operations	(200,000)
Tax effect	0
Net investment (total cash outflow in year 0)	$(715,000)

EXHIBIT 20.6

Effect of Asset Disposal on Smith Company's Cash Flow

Direct Effect

- **Inflow:** Proceeds from disposal
- **Outflow:** Expenditures for equipment removal and site restoration

Tax Effect

- **Inflow:** Tax effect on loss of the disposal
- **Outflow:** Tax effect on gain of the disposal

EXHIBIT 20.7

Net Effect of Asset Disposal on Smith Company's Cash Flow

Terminology

Net book value	Original cost − Accumulated depreciation
Net proceeds	Proceeds from disposal − Expenditures for removal and restoration
Gain on disposal	Net proceeds > Net book value
Loss on disposal	Net proceeds < Net book value

Net Cash Effect (Inflow)

For Gain Net proceeds − (Gain on disposal × Tax rate)
For Loss Net proceeds + (Loss on disposal × Tax rate)

depreciation taken on it, or accumulated depreciation on the asset). A gain on the disposal of an asset is taxable, however, and the gain's tax liability decreases the firm's net cash inflow from the disposal.

A firm suffers a loss if the net proceeds from disposing an asset are less than its net book value. A loss reduces the firm's tax obligation. The effect of the disposal on cash inflow for an asset sold at a loss is the sum of (1) the net cash proceeds from the disposal and (2) the savings in taxes due to the loss from the disposal. Exhibit 20.7 summarizes the determination of the net effect of asset disposal on cash flow.

Acquisition of the new milling machine makes the milling machine that Smith Company is currently using redundant. Smith Company purchased the milling machine seven years ago for $320,000. The accumulated depreciation on the machine currently in use is $200,000 as of the replacement date. A used equipment broker who charges a commission of 10 percent of the selling price has found a buyer willing to pay $80,000 for the old machine. Smith Company, however, must pay all removal expenses, which Smith estimates to be $2,000.

Subtracted from the $80,000 selling price for the equipment are the $8,000 commission for the broker and $2,000 equipment removal expenses. The net proceeds to Smith Company from the disposal are $70,000, before considering tax effects.

Smith Company suffers a loss on the machine's disposal. The firm bought it for $320,000 and has taken $200,000 depreciation on it. This leaves a net cost, or book value, of $120,000 as of the date of disposal. The firm, however, sold the equipment for only $70,000—a $50,000 loss. This loss decreases taxable income for the period and reduces the firm's income tax liability. At the 40 percent tax rate, the $50,000 loss from the disposal of the old milling machine reduces Smith Company's tax bill by $20,000 (see Exhibit 20.8). The cash inflow from the tax saving, however, occurs at the end of the tax year.

EXHIBIT 20.8

Cash Flows from Smith Company's Disposal of Equipment

Immediate Cash Effect		
Selling price		$ 80,000
Expenses related to the disposal of the equipment		
Brokers' commission (10 percent of $80,000)	$8,000	
Equipment removal expenses	2,000	10,000
Net proceeds from the disposal of the equipment		$ 70,000
Cash Effect at End of Year (tax saving from the disposal)		
Acquisition cost of the equipment		$320,000
Accumulated depreciation		200,000
Net book value as of disposal date		$120,000
Net proceeds from the disposal		70,000
Loss from the disposal		$ 50,000
Income tax rate		0.40
Income tax saving from the loss on disposal		$ 20,000
Total Cash Effect from Disposal		
Immediate cash effect		$ 70,000
Cash effect at end of year		20,000
Total cash inflow from disposal		$ 90,000

Project Operation

A firm invests to increase revenues, decrease expenses, or both. Changes in revenues or expenses have both direct and tax effects on cash flows. Unlike other types of cash flows that occur perhaps once or twice during the life of the investment, cash flows from operations occur every year or several times during the investment's life.

Increases in sales revenue have direct effects on cash inflows. Smith Company expects its investment to bring in $1,000,000 in cash revenue from increases in production volume in each of the next four years. This investment will have a direct effect of $1,000,000 cash inflow in each of the next four years.

Increases in revenues are likely to increase activities and expenditures of the firm. Even without any effect on the firm's revenues, an investment may still have effects on the firm's activity, expenses, and cash expenditures. Increases in cash expenditures offset the increases in cash from revenues. The $1,000,000 increase in revenues that Smith Company expects from the new milling machine requires $750,000 annual cash expenditures for operating expenses such as direct materials, direct labor, manufacturing overhead, and selling and administrative expenses. The net cash inflow from the investment, therefore, is $250,000 per year. At a 40 percent tax rate, the additional $250,000 increases the firm's tax obligation by $100,000. This leaves a net after-tax cash inflow of $150,000 per year, before considering the depreciation tax shield for each of the four years of the investment and an additional one-time expenditure in the investment's first year.

In addition, an investment can entail changes in amortized costs and allocated expenses. An investment in plant and equipment also increases the firm's depreciation expenses, thus raising its amortized costs, which are tax deductible. Although depreciation expenses do not take the form of cash payments, they reduce tax liabilities and, therefore, decrease cash *outflows*. You can see this tax effect in Exhibit 20.4, where the savings in taxes from the depreciation expenses of Smith's milling machine investment decrease cash outflows by $44,000 each year for four years. The decreases in cash outflows due to the depreciation expenses increase the cash inflow from the investment from $150,000 to $194,000 in each of the four useful years of the machine as shown in panels A and B of Exhibit 20.9.

Smith Company expects other additional costs in the first year of operating the new milling machine, including expenditures for employee training, work adjustments, and learning effects. The firm expects the total additional costs in year 1 to be $50,000 before taxes. At a 40 percent tax rate the net after-tax effect on cash flow of the first year of the investment is a cash outflow of $30,000, which reduces the net cash inflow in year 1 from $194,000 to $164,000, as shown in the Year 1 column of Panel C of Exhibit 20.9.

An investment can increase the allocation base of a division and, thus, increase the indirect expenses allocated to it. Suppose that the headquarters allocates its expenses to divisions at a rate of $0.025 per dollar of sales. The investment brings in $1,000,000 additional sales per year and results in an additional charge of $25,000 in headquarters

EXHIBIT 20.9
Effects on Cash Flow

Panel A: Effect of Operations on Cash Flows	
Effect of cash revenue or expense	
Revenues	$1,000,000
Cash operating expenditures	750,000
Increase in cash inflows before taxes	$ 250,000
Income taxes (at 40 percent)	100,000
Increase in cash inflows from operations	$ 150,000
Effect of noncash expense	
Depreciation expenses	$ 110,000
Income tax rate	40%
Decrease in cash outflows due to taxes	$ 44,000
Summary of effect on cash flow	
From cash revenue or expense	$ 150,000
From noncash expense	44,000
Total cash *inflows* in each period	$ 194,000

Panel B: Alternative Financial Approach to Determine Periodic Cash Flow Effects		
Revenues		$1,000,000
Operating expenses		
Cash expenditures	$ 750,000	
Noncash expenditures: Depreciation	110,000	860,000
Operating income before taxes		$ 140,000
Income taxes (at 40 percent)		56,000
Operating income		$ 84,000
Noncash expenditures: Depreciation		110,000
Increase in cash inflow from operations		$ 194,000

Panel C: Total Effect on Cash Flow in Each of the Years

	Time Period				
Description	Year 0	Year 1	Year 2	Year 3	Year 4
Cost of equipment	$(500,000)				
Installation cost	(5,000)				
Testing and adjusting	(10,000)				
Working capital	(200,000)				$200,000
Disposal of displaced machine	90,000				
Cash inflow from operations (Panel A or B)		$194,000	$194,000	$194,000	194,000
One-time expenditure (net of taxes)		(30,000)			
Total cash inflow (outflow) effect	$(625,000)	$164,000	$194,000	$194,000	$394,000

EXHIBIT 20.10
Cash Flow Effects of Periodic Operation

Transaction	Effects on Cash Flow
Cash receipts	Amount received × (1 − Tax rate)
Cash expenditures	Amount paid × (1 − Tax rate)
Depreciated initial cost	Tax shield: Depreciation expense × Tax rate
Allocated cost	No effect

EXHIBIT 20.11
Determination of the Net Effect on Cash Flow of Final Disposal

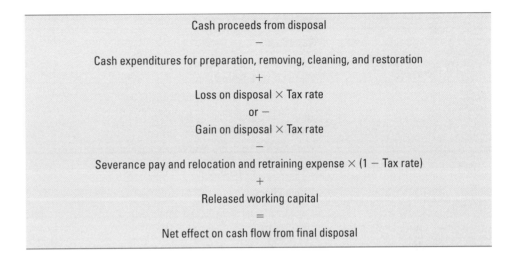

Cash proceeds from disposal

−

Cash expenditures for preparation, removing, cleaning, and restoration

+

Loss on disposal × Tax rate

or −

Gain on disposal × Tax rate

−

Severance pay and relocation and retraining expense × (1 − Tax rate)

+

Released working capital

=

Net effect on cash flow from final disposal

expenses to the division each year. The total expenses of the division thus will increase by $25,000 in each of the four years of the investment. The increase in a division's sales, however, does not increase the total overall costs of the company. Looking at the capital investment from the corporate viewpoint, the $25,000 additional charge to the division is not a cash outflow of the firm and, therefore, is not considered in capital budgeting.[10] Also, the tax effect results in no saving because the firm's total expenses remain unchanged.

Panel A of Exhibit 20.9 summarizes the effects of periodic operations on cash flow. Panel B shows an alternative financial approach determining the same effect. Panel C reports the total effects of initial acquisition activities and periodic operations on the cash flows of each period. Exhibit 20.10 summarizes the determination of the cash flow effects of various operating items.

Final Project Disposal

Direct Cash Effects   The disposal of an investment at the end of its useful life also can affect cash flows. A sale of the investment increases cash inflows. The disposal, however, often requires expenditures either to prepare assets for sale or to clean up and restore the site after the disposal.

Disposal also can decrease the need for personnel. A firm is likely obligated to pay severance or relocation and retraining expenses for employees associated with the operations to be discontinued. These payments or expenses are cash outflows. Anticipating decreasing needs for employees, many firms start to phase out employees a few years before the final year of an investment by encouraging early retirement, leaving vacated positions unfilled, transferring the employees to other divisions, or using other management techniques to ease effects of the impending change. Thus, some severance pay, relocation expenses, and retraining costs could occur a few years before the final disposal.

Tax Effects   A gain or loss from disposal of an asset has tax implications for a tax-paying firm. The firm pays taxes on any gain and receives tax credit benefits for any loss by way of decreased tax liability because of the loss.

[10] Unless, of course, the investment entails an increase in operating expenses at the headquarters.

EXHIBIT 20.12
Effects of Final Disposal on Smith Company's Cash Flow

	Cash Flows	Gain	Net Cash Flow
Panel A: Disposal of Machine			
Direct Effect			
Proceeds from sale of machine	$ 100,000		
Machine removal and site cleanup expenses	(20,000)		
Net proceeds from sale of machine		$80,000	$ 80,000
Tax Effect			
Cost of the milling machine	$ 515,000		
Accumulated depreciation	440,000		
Book value of the milling machine		75,000	
Gain on sale of the milling machine		$ 5,000	
Income taxes (at 40 percent)		× 0.40	2,000
Net after-tax cash proceeds from disposal of machine			$ 78,000
Panel B: Other Expenditures			
Direct Effect			
Relocation cost of displaced employees	$(150,000)		
Tax Effect			
Income taxes (at 40 percent)	60,000		
Net after-tax cash outflow for relocation of employees			$ (90,000)
Panel C: Released Working Capital			
Direct Effect			
Working capital no longer needed			200,000
Total effect of the final disposal on cash *inflow*			$188,000

Released Working Capital   Working capital committed to an investment is no longer needed after the firm terminates it. The funds tied up as working capital will now be available for other uses, and the released working capital is a cash inflow without any tax consequence when the funds are released. Exhibit 20.11 summarizes the procedure to determine the effects of final disposal on cash flows.

Effect of Final Disposal on Smith Company's Cash Flow

Smith Company expects to sell the new milling machine and related equipment at the end of year 4 for $100,000. The estimated salvage value for depreciation purposes, however, is $75,000. The cost of equipment removal and site cleanup is expected to be $20,000.

The disposal thus has a direct cash inflow of $80,000 ($100,000 − $20,000). The estimated salvage value for depreciation purposes is irrelevant in determining the direct cash effect of the disposal.

After disposing of the investment, Smith Company can reassign all but 10 employees to other divisions without incurring significant expenses. The firm expects to spend $150,000 for relocation, retraining, and work adjustment for these 10 employees in the investment's last year. This $150,000 is a cash outflow and has a direct effect on cash flow in the year that Smith discontinues the investment.

The net proceeds that Smith Company receives from disposing of the milling machine provide a $5,000 gain for tax purposes ($80,000 net proceeds − $75,000 book value). At a 40 percent tax rate, Smith Company must pay $2,000 in taxes on this gain. After taxes, Smith has a $78,000 cash inflow from the disposal as Panel A of Exhibit 20.12 shows.

EXHIBIT 20.13
Effects of Investment in Project B on Smith Company's Cash Flows (in thousands)

				Years		
		0	**1**	**2**	**3**	**4**
Initial Investment						
Cost of equipment		$(500)				
Installation cost		(5)				
Testing and adjusting		(10)				
Working capital		(200)				
Disposal of the displaced machine		90				
Net initial cash outflow		$(625)				
Operations						
Revenues			$1,000	$1,000	$1,000	$1,000
Operating expenses						
Cash items			$ 800	$ 750	$ 750	$ 750
Noncash item: Depreciation			110	110	110	110
Total operating expenses			$ 910	$ 860	$ 860	$ 860
Operating income before taxes			$ 90	$ 140	$ 140	$ 140
Income taxes (40 percent)			36	56	56	56
Operating income			$ 54	$ 84	$ 84	$ 84
Noncash expense: Depreciation			110	110	110	110
Net cash inflow from operations			$ 164	$ 194	$ 194	$ 194
Final Disinvestment (net of taxes)						
Working capital released						$ 200
Disposal of investment						78
Employee relocation, retraining, or						
severance pay						(90)
Net cash inflow from final disinvestment						$ 188
Net effect on cash flow		$(625)	$ 164	$ 194	$ 194	$ 382

Other cash expenditures also have tax implications. At 40 percent tax rate, the $150,000 relocation cost decreases the firm's tax liability by $60,000. The relocation expense's net after-tax effect on cash flow is therefore a $90,000 cash outflow, as shown in Panel B of Exhibit 20.12.

Smith Company committed $200,000 in working capital at the onset of the investment, which is no longer needed once the firm terminated the investment. The release of working capital adds a $200,000 *cash inflow* at the end of year 4, which has no tax effect because a decrease in working capital is not a gain. The addition of the $200,000 cash inflow released from the working capital no longer needed brings the total cash inflow from termination of the investment to $188,000 as shown in Panel C of Exhibit 20.12.

In Exhibit 20.12 you can see the effects of the final disposal of the investment on Smith Company's cash flows. Exhibit 20.13 summarizes the cash flow effects on Smith Company's milling machine investment in each year of its life.

Capital Investment Evaluation Techniques

LEARNING OBJECTIVE 3

Apply capital investment evaluation techniques to assess capital investments and identify advantages and limitations of these techniques.

The three most widely used techniques for evaluating capital investments are:

1. Payback period.
2. Book rate of return.
3. Discounted cash flow.

Each technique has its merits and shortcomings. None is definitely superior to the others in all aspects. Over the years surveys have found firms use several different

EXHIBIT 20.14
Data for Projects A and B

Project A

Required initial investment	$ 555,000
Estimated salvage value	$ 60,000
Annual operating data	
Revenues	$ 900,000 per year for four years
Cash operating expense	$ 660,000 per year for four years
Final disposal	
Cash proceeds from disposal	$ 200,000
Employee relocation, retraining, and severance pay	$ 240,000

Project B

Required initial investment	$ 625,000 (Exhibits 20.5 and 20.8)
Estimated salvage value	$ 75,000
Annual operating data	
Revenues	$1,000,000 per year for four years
Cash operating expense	$ 750,000 per year for four years
Other operating data	
Additional cash expenditure	$ 50,000 year 1 only
Final disposal	
Cash proceeds from disposal	$ 100,000
Machine removal and site cleanup	$ 20,000
Employee relocation, retraining, and severance pay	$ 150,000

Company

Depreciation method	Straight-line
Income tax rate	40 percent for combined federal, state, and local taxes

capital investment evaluation techniques.[11] Furthermore, firms use different methods for different types of projects or use more than one method to evaluate a capital investment. Many of the firms responding to the surveys use at least one secondary technique to supplement the primary analytical method in evaluating capital projects.

Data for Evaluating Investment Capital

We again use data for Smith Company to illustrate techniques for evaluating capital investment. In addition to the previous investment project, identified as Project B, Jennifer O'Clock, the manager, received another investment proposal, identified as Project A. Project A also has a four-year expected useful life and requires $555,000 total initial investments in year 0. O'Clock expects Project A to generate $900,000 revenue each year for four years. Its cash operating expense will be $660,000 each year, in addition to depreciation expenses and other allocated headquarters' expenses.

Project A does not require additional working capital and has a salvage value of $60,000 for depreciation purposes. O'Clock expects to sell the investment for $200,000 at the end of year 4. The total expenses for relocation, retraining, and severance pay for the displaced employees and for all other expenses relating to the disposal are expected to be $240,000. Exhibit 20.14 summarizes pertinent data for both projects.

Payback Period

Investors often ask how long it takes to get their money back when considering investments. The payback period answers this question.

The **payback period** of an investment is the length of time required for the cumulative total net cash inflows from the investment to equal the total initial cash outlays. At that point in time, the investor has recovered the amount of money invested in the project, hence, the payback period.

The **payback period** of an investment is the length of time required for its cumulative total net cash inflows to equal its total initial cash outlays.

[11] Thomas Klammer, Bruce Koch, and Neil Wilner, "Capital Budgeting Practices—A Survey of Corporate Use," *Journal of Management Accounting Research,* Fall 1991, pp. 113–30.

EXHIBIT 20.15 Payback Period for Project A with Uniform Net Cash Inflows: Total Initial Investment of $555,000

(1)	(2)	(3)	(4)	(5)	(6)	(7)	(8)	(9)	(10)
Period	Revenue	Operating Expenses	Cash Inflows Before Taxes	Depreciation Expense*	Operating Income Before Taxes	Income Taxes (40 percent)	After-Tax Operating Income	Net After-Tax Cash Inflows (4) − (7)	Cumulative Net After-Tax Cash Inflow from Operation
1	$900,000	$660,000	$240,000	$123,750	$116,250	$46,500	$69,750	$193,500	$193,500
2	900,000	660,000	240,000	123,750	116,250	46,500	69,750	193,500	387,000
3	900,000	660,000	240,000	123,750	116,250	46,500	69,750	193,500	580,500
4	900,000	660,000	240,000	123,750	116,250	46,500	69,750	193,500	—
Disposal	200,000†	240,000‡	<40,000>	60,000§	<100,000>	<40,000>	<60,000>	0	—

*Depreciation expense is $123,750 per year [($555,000 − $60,000)/4].

†The selling price of the investment at the end of the fourth year.

‡Employee relocation, retraining, and severance pay, $240,000.

§Salvage value, $60,000.

EXHIBIT 20.16
Payback Period for Project B with Uneven Cash Inflows: Total Initial Investment of ($625,000)

(1)	(2)	(3)
Years	Net After-Tax Cash Inflow (Exhibit 20.13)	Cumulative Net After-Tax Cash Inflow
1	$164,000	$164,000
2	194,000	358,000
3	194,000	552,000
4	382,000	

Determining the Payback Period

After determining the total required initial investment, the first step in computing a payback period is determining the after-tax cash flows from the investment for each year of the project's life. Exhibits 20.15 and 20.16 present the cash flows for Projects A and B, respectively, over their useful lives. The after-tax net cash inflows (column 9, Exhibit 20.15) for Project A are uniform over the years; the cash inflows for Project B (column 2, Exhibit 20.16) are uneven. Although the principle for calculating payback periods is the same, the details in determining payback periods differ when cash flow patterns of investments are not similar.

Determining the Payback Period with Uniform Annual Cash Flows

Project A generates $900,000 revenue each year for four years (column 2, Exhibit 20.15). The cash operating expenses are $660,000 per year, as reported in column 3, in addition to $123,750 depreciation expense (column 5) per year. The difference between the $900,000 revenue and the sum of the $660,000 cash operation expense and the $123,750 depreciation expense is the operating income before taxes, $116,250 (column 6 of Exhibit 20.15). This amount is taxable. At a 40 percent total income tax rate, the total income tax on the operating income generated by Project A is $46,500 per year (column 7), and the after-tax operating income is $69,750 in each of the four years (column 8).

The firm expects to terminate Project A after four years. The last row of Exhibit 20.15 shows the effects of transactions relating to the termination. The firm expects to sell Project A's equipment and related assets for $200,000 at the end of its useful life. However, the firm must spend $240,000 for employee relocation, retraining, and severance pay. Thus, the final disposal of Project A will have a $40,000 net cash outflow before taxes. With $60,000 book value for the project at the time of the disposal, the firm expects to have a total loss of $100,000. A loss of $100,000 for a firm in the 40 percent income tax bracket decreases taxes by $40,000 and the net after-tax operating income from the disposal is a net loss of $60,000 (column 8, Exhibit 20.15).

Project A's cash inflow from operations before taxes is $240,000 each year (column 4), the difference between revenues (column 2) and cash operating expenses (column 3). After paying income taxes (column 7), Project A generates a net after-tax cash inflow of $193,500 (column 9 = column 4 − column 7) from the operations each year. The net after-tax cash inflow (column 9) can also be computed by adding the noncash expense, depreciation expenses (column 5), to the after-tax operating income (column 8). Column 10 of Exhibit 20.15 shows the cumulative net cash proceeds starting from the project's first period of operation.

Project A's payback period is the number of periods for the cumulative total cash flow (column 10) equals the project's initial investment. Project A generates $193,500 net after-tax cash inflows each year in the first three years and will have cumulative net proceeds of $387,000 by the end of year 2, which is $168,000 short of the initial $555,000 investment. In the absence of detailed data on cash flow patterns during the year, we assume that both revenues and operating expenses flow evenly throughout the year. With the expected net after-tax cash inflows of $193,500 in year 3, the firm needs 0.87 ($168,000 ÷ $193,500) of a year in the third year to generate $168,000 net cash inflows. The payback period of Project A, therefore, is 2.87 years, or 2 years, 10 months, and 13 days.

Alternatively, the payback period for an investment with equal cash inflows every year like Project A can be determined by dividing the total initial investment by the expected annual net cash inflows:

$$\text{Payback period} = \frac{\text{Total initial capital investment}}{\text{Annual expected after-tax net cash inflow}}$$

For Project A, the payback period is

$$\text{Payback period} = \frac{\$555,000}{\$193,500} = 2.87 \text{ years}$$

Determining Payback Period with Uneven Annual Cash Flows Column 2 of Exhibit 20.16 reproduces the information in the last row of Exhibit 20.13 and provides the data for finding the payback period of Project B. With uneven net cash inflows, the payback period is the length of time before the cumulative net cash inflows equal the initial cash outlay.

Project B's cumulative net cash inflows is $552,000 by the end of year 3. This amount is $73,000 short of the initial cash investment of $625,000. With the estimated net cash inflow in year 4 of $382,000, it takes 0.19 of a year in year 4 to earn $73,000. The payback period for Project B therefore is 3.19 years:

$$3 \text{ years} + \frac{\$73,000}{\$382,000} = 3.19 \text{ years}$$

Evaluation of the Payback Period Technique

Advantages A major advantage of the payback period technique is that it is easy to compute and to comprehend. A payback period provides a quick estimate of the time needed for the firm to recoup the cash invested.

The length of payback period can serve as a measure of the investment's risk. The longer an investment's payback period, the riskier it is. This is true for two reasons. First, the farther into the future a payback period is, the more likely the projected revenues and expenses will not be as predicted. Second, the longer it takes to recover the investment, the more likely the product or service will become obsolete or attract competition, making it more difficult to earn cash flows as projected.

A payback period also indicates liquidity of funds generated from the investment. Cash inflows from a project are available for uses in other projects. A project with a four-year payback period is likely not as liquid as one with a payback period of three years or less.

The payback period technique emphasizes quick payoffs, an important consideration in some instances. Firms in industries with a high obsolescence risk often require short payback periods, as we have witnessed in recent years with investments in high-technology industries such as the computer chip and the personal computer. Short payback periods often become the determining factor for investments in these industries.

Limitations   Among limitations of the payback period technique are its failure to consider an investment's total profitability and the time value of money. The payback period technique considers cash flows from the initiation of the project until its payback period and ignores cash flows after the payback period.

The second limitation is that the payback period technique disregards the time value of money. It considers only the length of time required to recover the investment regardless of differences in the timing or pattern of cash flows. As long as the payback periods for two projects are the same, the payback period technique considers them equal to the firm as investments, even if one project generates most of its net cash inflows in the early years of the project while the other project generates most of its net cash inflows in the latter years of the payback period. The payback period method considers a $5,000 cash inflow in year 5, for example, to be the same as a $5,000 cash inflow in year 1.

To illustrate the effects of these two limitations of the payback period method, assume that a firm must select one of two investments: P and Q. The expected cash flows for these two projects follow:

Project	Year 0	Year 1	Year 2	Year 3	Year 4	Payback Period
P	$(100,000)	$90,000	$5,000	$5,000	$80,000	3 years
Q	(100,000)	5,000	95,000	10,000	10,000	2 years

Both projects require the same amount of initial investment. Of the two projects, Project Q has a shorter payback period. According to the payback period method, Project Q is the preferred investment of the two.

Project Q is the preferred investment, however, only if we can ignore both the amount of the total net cash inflows and their patterns. The payback period technique ignores the fact that Project P brings in $180,000 total cash inflows and Project Q brings in only $120,000 total cash inflows over the four-year period.

Furthermore, the cash flow patterns show that Project P brings in substantially more net cash inflows than Project Q in the first year of operations. If the firm invests all cash inflows from investments and earns a 10 percent return, Project P has a shorter payback period than Project Q (1.71 years versus 1.99 years) [12] If the time value of money is not ignored, at a 10 percent interest rate Project P has a shorter payback period.

---

[12] We assume that operating cash flows occur uniformly throughout the year. The estimated payback periods are as follows:

	Project P	Project Q
Initial investment	$100,000	$100,000
Cash inflow in year 1	90,000	5,000
Additional cash inflow needed to pay back the initial investment	$ 10,000	$ 95,000
Cash inflow in year 2		
From operations	5,000	95,000
From interest earned (10%) on the net cash inflow of year 1	9,000	500
Total cash inflow in year 2	$ 14,000	$ 95,500

Therefore, payback periods are

$$\text{Project P: } 1 \text{ year} + \frac{\$10,000}{\$14,000} \text{ year} = 1.71 \text{ years}$$

$$\text{Project Q: } 1 \text{ year} + \frac{\$95,000}{\$95,500} \text{ year} = 1.99 \text{ years}$$

One common error in using the payback period method is to demand too short a payback period. Companies require short payback periods to maintain a liquid financial position, fulfill the need to finance other investments, manage risk and uncertainty, or to avoid extended projections. Demanding too short a payback period, however, often hampers good investing by causing firms not to invest in long-term improvements. After all, an investment in hand tools takes a very short time to pay back the initial outlay, while an investment in a new technology—such as a computer-integrated-manufacturing (CIM) system—usually takes years to earn back the investment. A firm that stresses short payback periods in investments and avoids those projects that require long payback periods most likely do not fare very well in today's competitive global market.

Book Rate of Return

Determining Book Rate of Return

The book rate of return technique is another common method used widely in evaluating capital investments. The **book rate of return** of an investment is the net income from the investment as a percentage of its book value.

> The **book rate of return**
> is the average net income from an
> investment as a percentage of its
> book value.

$$\text{Book rate of return} = \frac{\text{Average annual net income}}{\text{Investment (book value)}}$$

Both numerator and denominator are numbers that normally appear in financial statements; thus, the rate of return is referred to as the *book rate of return*. It is an unadjusted rate of return because the procedure does not adjust for the difference in time value of money (returns) received in different periods.

The numerator is the average annual net income from the investment over its useful life. The denominator is either the initial total investment or the average investment (book value) over the useful life of the project. Some companies prefer the original investment because it is objectively determined and is not influenced by either the choice of the depreciation method or the estimation of the salvage value. Either amount is used in practice. It is important that the same method is used to determine the amount of investment for all investment projects under evaluation.

Recall the situation that Jennifer O'Clock faces, as described in Exhibit 20.14. She expects Project A to earn a net income of $69,750 per year:

$$\text{Net income} = \text{Revenues} - \underset{\text{expenses}}{\text{Cash operating}} - \underset{\text{expenses}}{\text{Noncash operating}} - \underset{\text{taxes}}{\text{Income}}$$

$$= \$900,000 - \$660,000 - \frac{\$555,000 - \$60,000}{4} - \$46,500$$

$$= \$69,750$$

The only noncash expense for Project A is the depreciation expense on the equipment.

The average investment is the average book value for the investment in its accounting records during the investment's life. (See Exhibit 20.17 for Project A.)

Project A requires an initial investment of $555,000, and the firm estimates the salvage value after four years to be $60,000. An investment's average book value for the year is the average of the book value at the beginning of the year and its balance at the

EXHIBIT 20.17
Smith Company's Average Investment for Project A

Year	Investment at the Beginning of the Year	Investment at the End of the Year	Average Investment for the Year
1	$555,000	$431,250	$ 493,125
2	431,250	307,500	369,375
3	307,500	183,750	245,625
4	183,750	60,000	121,875
Total			$1,230,000

Average book value = $1,230,000/4 years = $307,500

end of the year. According to the accounting records, the amount of investment is $555,000 at the beginning of year 1 and $431,250 at the end of the same year. The average investment for year 1, therefore, is $493,125 (last column, Exhibit 20.17). The average investment for the life of the investment is the sum of the average investments for each year divided by the number of years. With a total average investment of $1,230,000 over a 4-year period, the average investment over the entire four-year period is $307,500 ($1,230,000/4).

Dividing the average net income of the project, $69,750, by the average investment in the project, $307,500, we obtain 22.68 percent for the book rate of return for Project A.

$$\frac{\$69,750}{\$307,500} = 22.68 \text{ percent}$$

A firm that uses the straight-line depreciation method can compute the average investment by taking the simple average of the initial investment and its salvage value at the end of its useful life:

$$\text{Average investment} = \frac{\text{Original cost} + \text{Salvage value}}{2}$$

$$= \frac{\$555,000 + \$60,000}{2} = \$307,500$$

This shortcut computation for average investment is not applicable when the depreciation method is not the straight-line method based on years because the decrease in the book value of the investment is not constant over the years. Exhibit 20.18 shows the determination of the average investment for Project A if Smith Company uses the double-declining-balance depreciation method.

Some firms choose to calculate book rates of return on the original total investment. The book rate of return for Project A is 12.57 percent if the firm chooses to use the original investment as the denominator.

$$\frac{\$69,750}{\$555,000} = 12.57 \text{ percent}$$

Project A's expected annual net income remains stable throughout its useful life. The average net income thus is the same as its expected annual income. In contrast, the expected net income for Project B varies from year to year. The firm, therefore, needs to calculate the average expected net income of Project B before computing its book rate of return.

Exhibit 20.13 shows that Project B's net incomes over its four-year useful life are $54,000, $84,000, $84,000, and $84,000 for years 1 through 4, respectively. The average net income per year is $76,500:

$$\frac{\$54,000 + \$84,000 + \$84,000 + \$84,000}{4} = \$76,500$$

Project B has a book value of $515,000 at its onset and a salvage value of $75,000. The average investment is $295,000:

EXHIBIT 20.18
Smith Company's Average Investment When the Firm Uses the Double-Declining-Balance Depreciation Method

Year	Investment at the Beginning of the Year	Depreciation Expense for the Year	Investment at the End of the Year	Average Book Value (investment) for the Year
1	$555,000	$277,500	$277,500	$416,250
2	277,500	138,750	138,750	208,125
3	138,750	69,375	69,375	104,063
4	69,375	9,375	60,000	64,687
Total				$793,125

Average book value (investment) = $793,125/4 years = $198,281

$$\frac{\$515,000 + \$75,000}{2} = \$295,000$$

The book rate of return is 25.93 percent using the average investment or 14.85 percent using the total initial investment:

$$\frac{\$76,500}{\$295,000} = 25.93 \text{ percent} \qquad \frac{\$76,500}{\$515,000} = 14.85 \text{ percent}$$

Evaluation of the Book Rate of Return Technique

Advantages   The book rate of return technique uses the same kind of data routinely generated for financial reports. No special procedures are required to generate data to compute the book rate of return, which makes it easier to use than other capital investment evaluation techniques. Another advantage is that the book rate of return method is likely to be consistent with the method for performance evaluations on the operating results of the investment. Managers often are evaluated using a procedure similar to that of the book rate of return. Using the same procedure in both the decision-making and the periodic performance evaluation ensures consistency. The fact that financial reporting data will be audited for their conformance with the generally accepted accounting principles can add reliability.

In addition, the book rate of return enables decision makers to gauge the impacts that the capital investment has on the financial performance of the division or the firm. Using the book rate of return method, the firm can easily assess the impact that the capital investment has on the required returns specified by the firm's debt covenants or other contractual agreements with a third party.

The book rate of return has an additional advantage over the payback period method in that it includes the entire period of an investment in its capital investment analyses. Unlike the payback period method, which uses the data only to the point of recouping (payback) the original investment, the book rate of return method considers all net incomes over the entire life of the project and provides a measure of the investment's profitability.

Limitations   Like the payback period method, the book rate of return technique ignores the time value of money. Another limitation is its use of accounting numbers in both the denominator and the numerator in determining the book rate of return. Accounting numbers depend on the choice of accounting procedures. Different accounting procedures can lead to substantially different amounts for an investment's net income and book values. For example, Exhibit 20.18 shows that the average book value of Project A is $198,281 when the firm uses the double-declining-balance depreciation method—a $109,219 decrease from the amount shown in Exhibit 20.17.

Net income based on a straight-line depreciation method differs from the net income for the same period using, say, a declining-balance depreciation method. As a result, the book rates of return calculated based on the net incomes using different depreciation methods are different, although nothing has changed except in the choice of the accounting procedures. This is undesirable because the result for a capital investment should differ only if its underlying factors vary; the result should not vary because of a change in the accounting procedures.

Also, whereas net income can be a useful measure of the firm's profitability as a whole, the net cash flow is a better measure of an investment's performance for reasons cited earlier. Furthermore, inclusion of only the book value of the invested asset as the total investment ignores the fact that a project can require commitments of working capital and other outlays that are not included in the book value of the project.

Neither the payback period nor the book rate of return technique considers the time value of money in evaluating capital investment projects.

We next examine two discounted cash flow techniques that explicitly consider the time value of money.

Discounted Cash Flow

The **discounted cash flow (DCF) techniques** evaluate a capital investment using equivalent present values of future net cash inflows and the initial investment.

The **discounted cash flow (DCF) techniques** evaluate a capital investment using equivalent present values of future net cash inflows and the initial investment.

An investment has cash flows throughout its useful life. A dollar of cash flow in the early years of an investment is worth more than a dollar of cash flow in a later year. A simple addition or subtraction of money received or paid at different points in time to arrive at the total effect of an investment ignores the time value of money, an important consideration in all investments. Neither the payback period nor the book rate of return discussed earlier considers time value of money. The DCF techniques explicitly consider the time value of money in evaluating capital investments.

Two DCF approaches are in general use: the net present value method and the internal rate of return method. The *net present value (NPV) method* uses a specified discount rate to bring all subsequent net cash inflows after the initial investment to their present values (the time of the initial investment, or year 0). The NPV method focuses on the *dollar amount* at the time of the investment.

In contrast, the *internal rate of return (IRR) method* estimates the discount rate that makes the present value of all the subsequent net cash inflows after the initial investment equal the initial cash outlays of the investment. The IRR method's focus is on the *rate of return.*

Although the focus of these two approaches differ, they are variations of the same concept and use the same factors in evaluating capital investments:

1. The total initial investment.
2. The expected future cash receipts and disbursements.
3. The investor's desired rate of return.

We have already discussed the first two factors. The following section examines issues regarding the third factor, the desired rate of return before examining the two alternative discounted cash flow methods.

Desired Rate of Return

The **desired rate of return,** or the hurdle rate, is the minimum rate of return the investing firm requires from an investment.

The **desired rate of return,** or hurdle rate, is the minimum rate of return the investing firm requires from an investment. In seeking the best investment, a firm should not invest unless the investment will earn for the firm at least the same return as other investments available to the firm. Thus, the desired rate of return on an investment is the rate of return the firm would have earned by investing the same funds in the best available alternative investment that bears the same risk.

Determining the desired rate of return based on the best alternative opportunity available is often difficult in practical terms. It is difficult or impossible for management to know all investment opportunities available to the firm. Conducting an exhausting search and examining all opportunities can be very costly or time consuming, or both.

Rather than using the true opportunity cost, or the best return available anywhere, firms often use an alternative measure for the desired rate of return. Among the alternative measures of the desired rate of return are

1. Minimum rate of return.
2. Cost of capital.

A firm frequently has a minimum return requirement for all of its investments and considers only capital project proposals that meet it. Among factors a firm considers in determining the required minimum rate of return are its strategic plan, the industry average rate of return, and other investment opportunities.

Cost of capital is the cost that a firm incurred or expects to incur in raising the funds needed for an investment or operation. Uses of the firm's cost of capital can help the

The **cost of capital**

is a composite of the cost of various sources of funds comprising a firm's capital structure.

firm to ensure that the capital investment project will at least recover the firm's cost in obtaining the necessary funds for the investment.

Statement on Management Accounting No. 4A by the Institute of Management Accountants defines **cost of capital** as "a composite of the cost of various sources of funds comprising a firm's capital structure."[13] A firm obtains funds by issuing preferred or common stock; borrowing money using various forms of debt such as notes, loans, or bonds; or retaining earnings. The costs to the firm are the returns demanded by debt and equity investors through which the firm raises the funds for the investment.

The cost of the debt is the after-tax interest rate of the debt. If a firm pays 10 percent interest, for example, to secure a $5,000 loan from its bank, the cost of the debt is 7 percent or $350 if the firm is in the 30 percent tax bracket.[14]

The cost of equity securities is the return demanded by shareholders. Equities include preferred stocks, common stocks, and retained earnings. The cost of a preferred stock is the percentage of the dividend to be paid on it divided by the security's market value. To illustrate, George's Sports, Inc., has an income tax rate of 30 percent and issues 100 shares of $2.40, par $20 preferred stock for $25 per share. The cost of the preferred stock to George's Sports is 9.6 percent, computed as follows:

$$\frac{\text{Dividend per share}}{\text{Market price per share}} = \frac{\$2.40}{\$25.00} = 9.6\%$$

Notice that the dividend rate on the preferred stock is 12% ($2.40/$20). The cost of preferred equity is determined based on the value that investors are willing to pay—$25 for shareholders of preferred stocks issued by George's Sports. The firm's income tax is irrelevant in determining the cost of equities because the returns to shareholders are not tax deductible.

The cost of common stock and retained earnings is the ratio of the return demanded by shareholders of common stocks to the market value of the stock. If, for example, George's Sports, Inc., has 100 shares of $10 par common stock outstanding, the market price for this common stock is $200 per share and the investors demand a return of $25 per share on the stock. The cost of the common stock to George's Sports is 12.5 percent:

$$\frac{\text{Return demanded by investors}}{\text{Market price per share}} = \frac{\$25}{\$200} = 12.5\%$$

The cost of capital to a firm is a weighted average of the returns demanded by debt and equity investors. The weighted average cost of capital of a firm is the expected rate of return investors would demand on a portfolio of all the firm's outstanding securities.[15]

As an example, consider a firm in 40 percent tax bracket for federal and state taxes combined. This firm has a $100,000 bank loan with 12 percent interest; $500,000, 10 percent, 20-year mortgage bond selling at 90 with semi-annual interest payment; $200,000, 15 percent, $20 noncumulative, noncallable preferred stock with a total market value of $300,000; and 10,000 shares of $1 par common stock that the firm sold for $5 per share. The common stock's current market price is $75 per share. The market demands a return of $15 per share. The weighted cost of capital of the firm is 13.6016 percent, as computed:

[13] Institute of Management Accountants, *Statement Number 4A: Cost of Capital* (Montvale, NJ, 1984), p. 1.

[14] Cost of debt is the effective, not the nominal, interest rate of the debt. For example, the effective interest rate on a 10-year, 8 percent, $100,000 bond with semiannual interest payments that was sold for $88,448 is 10 percent, not 8 percent, since the effective interest rate on the bond is 10 percent. If the firm is at the 40 percent tax bracket, the cost of bond to the firm is 6 percent.

[15] Richard A. Brealey, Stewart C. Myers, and Alan J. Marcus, *Fundamentals of Corporate Finance* (New York: McGraw-Hill/Irwin, 2001).

	(1)	(2)	(3)	(4)	(5)	(6) = (3) × (5)
	Book Value	**Interest or Dividend Rate**	**After-Tax Rate or Expected Return**	**Total Market Value**	**Weight (Based on Market Value)**	**Weighted Average Cost of Capital**
Bank loan	$100,000	12%	7.20%	$100,000	0.06250	0.4500%
Bond	500,000	10	6.76#	450,000	0.28125	1.9013
Preferred stock	200,000	15	10.00*	300,000	0.18750	1.8750
Common stock	50,000		20.00†	750,000	0.46875	9.3750
Total	$850,000			$1,600,000	1.00	13.6013%

#Estimated effective interest rate using IRR function in Excel. Other spreadsheet programs also offer the same function.

*Total number of shares preferred stock: $200,000 ÷ 20 = 10,000 shares

Market value of per share of preferred stock: $300,000 ÷ 10,000 shares = $30 per share

Dividends per share: $20 × 15% = $3

Expected return on preferred stock: $3 ÷ $30 = 10%

†$15 ÷ $75 = 20%

Net Present Value

The **net present value (NPV)** of an investment is the difference between the sum of the present values of future net cash inflows from the investment and the initial investment.

The **present value** of a future net cash inflow is its current equivalent dollar value, given the desired rate of return.

Determining the Net Present Value   The **net present value (NPV)** of an investment is the difference between the sum of the present values of future net cash inflows from the investment and the initial investment. The **present value** of a future net cash inflow is its current equivalent dollar value at year 0 at the desired rate of return. The present value of $5,000 to be received a year from now by an investor with a 10 percent desired rate of return is $4,545:

$$\$5{,}000 \times 0.909 = \$4{,}545$$

where 0.909 is the discount factor for 10 percent in one period. The discount factor can be found in the present value table on page 900. With a 10 percent desired rate of return, receiving $4,545 now or $5,000 a year from now is the same to the investor.[16]

The NPV is the balance of the present value of the expected future net cash inflows after paying for the initial investment.

Present Value of Net Cash Flow

$$\text{Net present value} = \overbrace{\text{Present value of cash receipts} - \text{Present value of cash expenditure}} - \text{Total net initial investment}$$

The net present value is the amount, in current dollars, the investment earns after yielding the desired return in each period.

The first step in determining an investment's net present value is to determine the net cash inflow in each year of the investment. The net cash inflows then are converted, based on the desired rate of return, into their present equivalent dollar amounts. The net present value is the remainder after subtracting the total initial cash outlays for the investment from the sum of the present values of all future net cash inflows. These steps summarize the calculation of a project's NPV:

1. Determine the net cash inflow in each year of the investment.
2. Select the desired rate of return.

---

[16] To verify, calculate the total amount the investor has on hand one year after receiving $4,545:

Cash received now	$4,545
Interest for one year: $4,545 × 10 % =	455
Total cash on hand one year from now	$5,000

Thus, $4,545 is the present value equivalent of the $5,000 to be received one year from now.

3. Find the discount factor for each year based on the desired rate of return selected in step 2.
4. Multiply steps 1 and 3 to determine the present values of the net cash inflows.
5. Total the amounts in step 4 for all the years.
6. Subtract the initial investment from the amount obtained in step 5.

A capital project is desirable if it has a positive NPV and undesirable if it has a negative NPV.

Determining NPV with Uniform Net Cash Inflows   Jennifer O'Clock desires to earn a 10 percent after-tax rate of return on investments. These calculations show the determination of the present value of net cash inflows from Project A:

$$\text{Present value of net cash inflows} = \$193{,}500 \times 3.17$$
$$= \$613{,}395$$

The 3.17 is the discount factor for an annuity of four years at 10 percent. An *annuity* is a constant sum received or paid each year for a number of years. The discount factor varies according to the number of years and the rate of the desired return. The present value tables on page 900 show the discount factors for computing present values of annuities.

Project A generates an after-tax net cash inflow of $193,500 each year for four years. The preceding calculation shows that at 10 percent, the desired rate, these yearly net cash inflows have a present value (year 0) of $613,395.

Project A requires an initial investment (year 0) of $555,000. Subtracting the $555,000 initial investment from the present value of net cash inflows yields $58,395, the NPV of this investment:

$$\text{NPV of Project A} = \$613{,}395 - \$555{,}000 = \$58{,}395$$

The NPV indicates that a $555,000 investment in Project A will earn $58,395 in current dollars for the investor, in addition to earning a 10 percent return each year for four years on the $555,000 investment.

Using a Spreadsheet Program to Determine NPV   Most spreadsheet programs offer functions that allow users to calculate present values of cash flows.[17] These functions are:

For both Lotus 1-2-3 and Quattro Pro: @NPV (Rate, Range)
For Microsoft Excel: =NPV (Rate, Range)

where *rate* is the interest rate and *range* refers to the consecutive rows or columns in the spreadsheet that comprise net cash flows of the investment in each of the consecutive years. The first amount specified in *range* is either the amount or the cell of the net cash inflow at the end of the first year. The second amount is either the amount or the cell of the net cash inflow at the end of the second year, and so on. The program returns the present value of the future net cash inflows specified in the *range*. The user then calculates the net present value by finding the difference between the amount returned from the spreadsheet and the initial investment.

The NETPV function in Quattro Pro allows users to enter all cash flows, including the initial cash outflow. The program then returns the net present value:

NETPV (Rate, Range, Initial investment)

Interpretation of NPV   An investment that earns the same rate of return as the desired rate of return has an NPV of zero. It will be greater than zero (as in this case) when an investment earns a rate of return higher than the desired rate of return, and a

---

[17] Keystroke sequences are as follows:

For Microsoft Excel: Insert → Function → Financial → NPV

For Quattro Pro: Insert → Function → Financial-Cash Flow → NPV

negative amount when the investment earns a return less than the desired rate of return. Project A has an NPV of $58,395. This suggests that Project A earns a higher rate of return than the required 10 percent return and is a desirable investment. The investment will earn a 10 percent return on the funds invested plus $58,395 (in current dollars).

Alternative investments exist. The positive NPV of Project A simply shows that the return from investing in this project is higher than the discount rate used in the computation. Project A might or might not be the best investment available. Other investment opportunities could yield even higher returns. O'Clock must check alternative investments, such as Project B in our example, before making the final decision.

Determining NPV with Uneven Cash Inflows   Project B has uneven net cash inflows over four years. As a result, the computation of its NPV requires more detailed calculations than those for the NPV of Project A. Exhibit 20.19 shows the calculations of Project B's NPV. The procedure starts with the after-tax net cash inflows generated each year by the investment during its useful life. These cash flows are then discounted using the present value discount factors on page 900, as shown in the last column of Exhibit 20.19.

The total present value shown in the last column of Exhibit 20.19 tells us that the equivalent total present value of the cash inflows from Project B over the years is $715,920. After subtracting the initial investment, the NPV of Project B is $90,920. The positive NPV suggests that Project B is also a desirable investment.

Present Value (or Discounted) Payback Period   The payback period technique is often criticized for ignoring the time value of money. To avoid this criticism, users of the payback period method can use the present values of net cash inflows from an investment to determine its payback period. This payback period is the **present value payback period** that some users refer to as **breakeven time (BET).**

The **present value payback period** or **breakeven time (BET) method** is the span of time required for the cumulative present value of cash inflows to equal the initial investment of the project.

The present value payback period method uses the *present values* of net cash inflows rather than the undiscounted dollar amounts of net cash inflows to determine the payback period. As in the NPV method, the present value of net cash inflows from the investment is estimated using the firm's desired rate of return. The span of time required for the cumulative present value of net cash inflows to equal the initial investment of the project is the present value payback period. The present value payback period of Project A is 3.56 years, as calculated in Exhibit 20.20, in contrast to 2.87 years for the simple payback period.

The present value or discounted payback period method has an advantage over the simple payback period method because it considers one dollar today to be more valuable than one dollar in the future. Nevertheless, it suffers the same weakness as the payback period in other aspects. Both methods emphasize quick payoffs and ignore profitability and cash inflows after the payback period.

Internal Rate of Return Method

The **internal rate of return (IRR) method** is a discounted cash flow method that estimates the discount rate which makes the present value of subsequent net cash inflows to equal the initial investment.

The **internal rate of return (IRR) method** estimates the discount rate that makes the present value of subsequent net cash inflows to equal the initial investment. The NPV of the investment will be zero if we use this estimated rate as the desired rate of return to compute the NPV.

EXHIBIT 20.19
NPV of Project B: An Uneven Cash Flow Example

Years	Net After-Tax Cash Inflow	Discount Factor	Present Value
1	$164,000	0.909	$149,076
2	194,000	0.826	160,244
3	194,000	0.751	145,694
4	382,000	0.683	260,906
Total present value of net cash inflows			$715,920
Less: Initial investment			625,000
Net present value			$ 90,920

EXHIBIT 20.20
Present Value Payback Period for Project A

Year	Net After-Tax Cash Inflow	Discount Factor at 10 Percent	Present Value of Net Cash Inflow	Cumulative Present Value of Net Cash Inflow
1	$193,500	0.909	$175,892	$175,892
2	193,500	0.826	159,831	335,723
3	193,500	0.751	145,318	481,041
4	193,500	0.683	132,161	

Amount needed in year 4 to reach the payback period:

$$\$555,000 - \$481,041 = \$73,959$$

$$\text{Present value payback period} = 3 \text{ years} + \frac{73,959}{132,161} = 3.56 \text{ years}$$

The IRR method evaluates capital investments by comparing the estimated internal rate of return to the criterion rate of return. The criterion can be the firm's desired rate of return, the rate of return from the best alternative investment, or another rate the firm chooses to use for evaluating capital investments.

Determining the Internal Rate of Return

Like the NPV method, the IRR method considers the time value of money, initial cash investment, and all cash flows from the investment. Unlike the NPV method, the computation procedure of the IRR method does not use the desired rate of return to compute the present values of net cash inflows. The IRR method determines an investment's rate of return that makes the present value of net cash inflows after its initiation equal the investment's initial amount and then compares the estimated rate of return with the required rate in assessing the investment's desirability. In using this method, the investor computes the investment's rate of return and compares the computed rate of return to the firm's desired return.[18]

The computation procedures for IRR vary somewhat with the pattern of net cash inflows over an investment's useful life.

Uniform Cash Flows The IRR method estimates the discount rate that makes the present value of net cash inflows equal the initial total cash disbursements and commitments. The first step in using the IRR method, therefore, is to determine the investment's total net initial cash disbursements and commitments and its net cash inflows in each year of the investment.

The discount rate that causes the total initial investment and the investment's present value of subsequent net cash inflows to be equal is the IRR of the investment. For an investment with uniform net cash inflows over its life, the IRR is the discount rate that satisfies the following equation:

> Total initial investment = Present value of net cash inflows computed using the discount rate
>
> = Annual net cash inflow × Annuity discount factor of the discount rate for the number of periods of the investment's useful life

Using $A_{r,n}$ to denote the last term in this equation, the equation can be restated as follows:

---

[18] The book rate of return method discussed earlier appears to address the same issue; it provides a rate of return on investment. The IRR method, however, considers the time value of money; the book rate of return method does not. In estimating the rate of return, the IRR method uses cash flows while the book rate of return method uses the net income computed following the accounting rules and procedures the firm chooses to use.

$$A_{r,n} = \frac{\text{Total initial cash disbursements and commitments for the investment}}{\text{Annual (equal) net cash inflows from the investment}}$$

where $A_{r,n}$ is the annuity discount factor that makes the present value of the net cash inflows over the investment's life equal the initial investment, n is the number of periods for the project, and r is the discount rate.

The discount rate, r, for the calculated discount factor, $A_{r,n}$, is the interest rate that has the same discount factor as $A_{r,n}$ in the annuity table along the row for n periods, or the one closest to it. This discount rate is the IRR of the investment. To illustrate, the IRR for Project A is determined as follows:

$$\$555,000 = \$193,500 \times A_{r,4}$$

$$\text{Rearrange, } A_{r,4} = \frac{\$555,000}{\$193,500} = 2.868$$

Using the annuity factor in the present value tables (pp. 900–901) on the four-year (useful life of the investment) row,

$$r \approx 15 \text{ percent}$$

The computed IRR is compared to the firm's required rate of return or some other chosen criterion to assess the investment's desirability. An investment is desirable if the computed IRR exceeds the required rate of return. The computed 15 percent IRR for Project A is higher than the 10 percent rate of return that the firm set for this investment. Project A is, therefore, a desirable investment.

When the available annuity table does not have a discount factor reasonably close to the computed discount factor for the project, the IRR method requires an interpolation procedure to estimate the IRR.[19]

Uneven Cash Flows The procedure for estimating the IRR of a project with uneven net cash inflows over the years can involve trial and error and interpolation. The determination of the IRR for Project B, as shown in Exhibit 20.21, illustrates this procedure.

The present value of net cash inflows is $650,108 at an interest rate of 14 percent and $620,728 at 16 percent. The required investment on the project being evaluated, $625,000, is between these two present values. Therefore the rate of return of the

---

[19] To illustrate the interpolation procedure, let's assume that this is the only annuity table available:

n/r	12%	14%	16%
1	3.037	2.914	2.798

The $A_{r,4}$ for Project A is 2.868. The annuity table, however, does not have a discount factor of 2.868 in the row for 4 periods. The discount factor is 2.914 at 14 percent and 2.798 at 16 percent. The IRR, which has a discount factor of 2.868, is between these two discount rates. The following interpolation procedure estimates the IRR:

	Interest Rate		Discount Factor	
At lower rate	14%	14%	2.914	2.914
Target rate		?		2.868
At higher rate	16	—	2.798	—
Difference	2%	?	0.116	0.046

The difference in discount factors between the interest rates on either side of the target discount factor (2.868), discount factors for 14 and 16 percent, is 0.116. This suggests that an increase of 2 percent in interest rates from 14 percent to 16 percent decreases the discount factor by 0.116.

The interest rate we are looking for has a discount factor of 2.868, a decrease of 0.046 from the discount factor for interest rate of 14 percent. The interest rate, therefore, needs to be increased from 14 percent to make the discount factor to decrease from 2.914 to 2.868. The needed decrease in the discount factor, 0.046, is 40 percent (0.046/0.116) of the difference in the discount factors between 14 percent and 16 percent. With an increase of 2 percent in interest rates from 14 percent to 16 percent, the discount factor decreases by 0.116. The needed increase in interest rate to decrease the discount factor by 0.046, therefore, is 40 percent of the 2 percent, or 80 percent as shown here:

$$14\% + \left(\frac{0.046}{0.116} \times 2\%\right) = 14\% + (0.4 \times 2\%) = 14\% + 0.8\% = 14.80\%$$

EXHIBIT 20.21
Present Values of Project B with Interest Rates of 14 and 16 Percent

Year	Net After-Tax Cash Flow	Discount Factor at 16 Percent	Present Value at 16 Percent	Discount Factor at 14 Percent	Present Value at 14 Percent
1	$164,000	0.862	$141,368	0.877	$143,828
2	194,000	0.743	144,142	0.769	149,186
3	194,000	0.641	124,354	0.675	130,950
4	382,000	0.552	210,864	0.592	226,144
Total			$620,728		$650,108

	Interest Rate		Total Cash Flows	
	14%	14%	$650,108	$650,108
		?		625,000
	16		620,728	
Difference	2%	?	$ 29,380	$ 25,108
Internal rate of return				

$$14\% + 2\% \times \frac{\$25,108}{\$29,380} = 15.71\%$$

project must be between 14 percent and 16 percent. A 2 percent increase in interest rates from 14 percent to 16 percent decreases the present value of net cash inflows by $29,380. With $625,000 initial investment in the project, the IRR procedure calls for an increase in the interest rate from 14 percent so that the present value of net cash inflows will decrease from $650,108 to $625,000, a decrease of $25,108, which is 85.5 percent of $29,380. The interest rate needs to increase from 14 percent by 1.71 percent (0.855 of the 2 percent difference between 14 percent and 16 percent). The rate of return that makes the present value of the net cash inflows over the project's life to equal the initial investment ($625,000), therefore, is 15.71 percent (= 14 percent + 1.71 percent), which is the estimated internal rate of return.

Using a Spreadsheet Program to Determine IRR Many spreadsheet programs offer easy-to-use functions for estimating internal rate of return. For example, Lotus 1-2-3, Quattro Pro, and Microsoft Excel have an IRR function for estimating internal rate of return. The required inputs for the programs are as follows:

Lotus 1-2-3 and Quattro Pro: @IRR(Estimated rate of return in decimal, Range)
Microsoft Excel: =IRR(Range, Estimated rate of return in decimal)

The user provides a rough starting point for estimating the rate of return.[20] The *range* is the location of the data in the spreadsheet. The first cell of the range is the initial cash outlay expressed as a negative amount, followed, in sequence, the net cash inflows each period over the years.[21]

Using Financial Calculators to Determine NPV and IRR Many financial calculators have built-in functions for calculating NPV and IRR. Most financial calculators follow similar keystrokes. We use Project B as an example and illustrate keystrokes for three financial calculators. Remember to enter the initial cash outflow as a negative number.

---

[20] Microsoft Excel assumes that the estimated rate of return is 0.1 if none is provided.

[21] Both Microsoft Excel and Quattro Pro offer two additional programs, MIRR and XIRR, for estimating the internal rate of return. MIRR is for situations in which a firm finances the needed cash outflows at a different rate than the expected rate for cash inflows:

=MIRR (Range, Finance rate, Reinvest rate)

XIRR is used when cash flows are not necessarily periodic:

=XIRR (Range, Dates, Estimated rate)

The dates should correspond with the values specified in the range.

1. Net present value

Hewlett-Packard HP-10B		Sharp EL-733A		Texas Instrument BA II Plus	
−625,000	CF$_j$	−625,000	CF$_j$	CF	
164,000	CF$_j$	164,000	CF$_j$	2nd	{CLR Work}
				−625,000	ENTER ↓
194,000	CF$_j$	194,000	CF$_j$		
				164,000	ENTER ↓
194,000	CF$_j$	194,000	CF$_j$		
				194,000	ENTER ↓
382,000	CF$_j$	382,000	CF$_j$		
				194,000	ENTER ↓
10	I/YR	10	i		
				382,000	ENTER ↓
	{NPV}		NPV	NPV	
					ENTER
				10	
				↓	CPT

2. Internal Rate of Return

Hewlett-Packard HP-10B		Sharp EL-733A		Texas Instrument BA II Plus	
−625,000	CF$_j$	−625,000	CF$_j$	CF	
164,000	CF$_j$	164,000	CF$_j$	2nd	{CLR Work}
				−625,000	ENTER ↓
194,000	CF$_j$	194,000	CF$_j$		
				164,000	ENTER ↓
194,000	CF$_j$	194,000	CF$_j$		
				194,000	ENTER ↓
382,000	CF$_j$	382,000	CF$_j$		
				194,000	ENTER ↓
				382,000	ENTER ↓
	{IRR/YR}		IRR	IRR	
				CPT	

Comparison of the Net Present Value and the Internal Rate of Return Methods

LEARNING OBJECTIVE 4
Identify the underlying assumptions of the two discounted cash flow methods.

Among methods for analyzing capital investments, the discounted cash flow (DCF) methods are the most theoretically sound. The two DCF methods suggest the same answers in most instances. Sometimes, however, different DCF methods yield significantly different results. To use capital budgeting techniques properly, you must recognize situations in which the two DCF methods can reach different conclusions and the reasons for the differences.

Exhibit 20.22 summarizes factors that may lead the results from analyses using the NPV method and the IRR method to differ. The results may vary significantly when capital investment projects differ in (1) amount of initial investments, (2) net cash flow

EXHIBIT 20.22
Factors Affecting Results of NVP vs. IRR Analyses

Results from NPV and IRR can differ if projects differ as to

1. Amount of initial investment
2. Net cash flow pattern
3. Length of useful life
4. Fluctuating cost of capital over the project life
5. Results of multiple projects

patterns, or (3) length of useful lives. In addition, these two methods can yield different conclusions in situations with (4) varying costs of capital over the life of a project and (5) multiple investments.

Amount of Initial Investment

Although both the NPV and the IRR methods use net cash inflows in evaluating capital investments, they do so differently. The NPV method examines the excess amount of the present value of future net cash inflows generated by an investment over the project's initial investment. The project that has the highest NPV among the investments under consideration is the choice of the NPV method.

The net present value of a project with a large initial investment is more likely to have a higher net present value than one with a small initial investment. Consider two investment projects with these initial investments, years of useful life, and annual net cash inflows:

Project	Initial Investment	Annual Net Cash Inflows	Years of Useful Life	NPV at 10 percent	IRR
P	$5,000	$1,000	10	$1,145	15.13%
Q	1,000	300	10	843	27.38%

Project P has a higher NPV than Project Q does. The NPV suggests that Project P is the better investment of the two.

However, Project Q has an IRR of 27.38 percent while Project P has an IRR of only 15.13 percent. The IRR method favors Project Q. Project P has a higher NPV than Project Q because Project P has a much larger initial investment than that of Project Q. The NPV method does not consider the difference in initial investments. The NPV method focuses on the dollar amount of the difference between the present value of the net cash inflows from an investment and the amount initially invested. Once an investment has generated sufficient net cash inflows to pay for itself (earned the firm's desired rate of return), a project that requires a large investment is likely to generate a higher amount of NPV than a project that requires a small investment. A $500,000 investment in a project that earns 11 percent return has an NPV of $5,000 if the firm's required rate of return is 10 percent. In contrast, the NPV will be only $500 if the same firm invests $5,000 in another project that earns 20 percent. Notice that the initial investment for Project P is five times the amount for Project Q. The net cash inflows of Project P, however, are not five times of those of Project Q. Nevertheless, the NPV method suggests that Project P is the better investment of the two.

A comparison of the net present values of investments that require substantially different initial investments yields no meaningful results. The method should be used only to evaluate investments that are approximately equal in initial investment requirements.

The IRR method uses percentages to evaluate the relative profitability of the investments. Differences in the amount of initial investments have no effect on the relative profitability of investments. The IRR method, therefore, is more appropriate for assessing investments requiring significantly different initial investments.

Net Cash Flow Pattern

Firms invest to earn net cash inflows. Not all net cash inflows are the same, however. Variations in patterns of net cash inflows such as the timing, amount, or direction of net cash inflows can affect the overall returns on projects and alter capital investment decisions.

Timing and Amount of Net Cash Flow

Not all investment projects generate cash flows similarly at different points in time. Some projects generate the bulk of their net cash inflows early in the investment. Others might not have significant net cash inflows until the last years of the project. Some projects have relatively constant net cash inflows throughout their useful lives. Other projects have rather irregular net cash inflows. Differences in timing and amount of net cash inflows affect a project's internal rate of return.

Paton Implement Manufacturing Company considers two capital investments in September 2006; Projects A and B. Both projects require $100,000 initial investments and have 10 years of useful life. Project A will generate most of its net cash inflows in its early years, while Project B will earn the bulk of its net cash inflows toward its completion. Columns 2 and 3 of Exhibit 20.23 contain the expected after-tax net cash inflows for Projects A and B, respectively. The cost of capital for both projects is 10 percent.

Project B generates small net cash inflows in its early years. The amount increases, however, over the years. The net cash inflows of Project A follow a different pattern—higher net cash inflows in the early years. At 10 percent cost of capital, Project B has a higher net present value than Project A. The IRR method suggests the opposite. The internal rates of return are 19.34 percent for Project B and 26.18 percent for Project A.

Which project is a better investment? The preceding section suggests possible conflicting results from the two DCF methods when projects require different initial investments. However, the two projects, A and B, require the same amount of initial investment.

The two DCF methods involve different assumptions on earnings of net cash inflows from investment. The NPV method assumes that all net cash inflows from an investment earn the desired rate of return or the discount rate employed in calculating its NPV (10 percent in the previous example). In contrast, the IRR method assumes that all net cash inflows from a project earn the same rate of return as the project's internal rate of return.

EXHIBIT 20.23
Effects of Patterns of Net Cash Inflows on the Evaluation of Capital Investment Using DCF Methods

(1) Period	(2) Net After-Tax Cash Inflow of A	(3) Net After-Tax Cash Inflow of B	(4) 10 Percent Factor	(5) Present Value of A	(6) Present Value of B
0	$(100,000)	$(100,000)	1.000	$(100,000)	$(100,000)
1	$ 45,000	$ 13,000	0.909	$ 40,905	$ 11,817
2	39,000	14,800	0.826	32,214	12,225
3	25,000	16,600	0.751	18,775	12,467
4	17,000	20,200	0.683	11,611	13,797
5	23,000	23,800	0.621	14,283	14,780
6	20,000	27,400	0.564	11,280	15,454
7	17,000	35,500	0.513	8,721	18,212
8	15,000	49,000	0.467	7,005	22,883
9	13,000	49,000	0.424	5,512	20,776
10	13,000	43,000	0.386	5,018	16,598
Total	$ 227,000	$ 292,300		$ 155,324	$ 159,009
NPV				$ 55,324	$ 59,009
IRR				26.18%	19.34%

Project A has an internal rate of return of 26.18 percent. In arriving at this rate, the IRR method assumes that all of Project A's net cash inflows will earn 26.18 percent in each of the subsequent years until the end of its useful life. The $45,000 net cash inflows of Project A in year 1, for example, earns the firm $11,781 ($45,000 × 0.2618) in year 2 and $14,865 [($45,000 + $11,781) × 0.2618] in year 3, and so on until the end of Project A's useful life.

The internal rate of return of Project B is 19.34 percent. Thus, the IRR method assumes that all net cash inflows of Project B will earn 19.34 percent in each of the subsequent years.

Having earlier net cash inflows and a higher IRR than those of Project B, Project A raises its IRR in two ways. First, the firm earns returns on the early net cash inflows over a longer period of time than those from the late net cash inflows. For example, Project A has a net cash inflow of $45,000 in Year 1. This $45,000 earns interest in each of the subsequent nine years. In contrast, Project B has a net cash inflow of $13,000 in Year 1 and the firm earns interest on $13,000 in each of the subsequent nine years. Assuming 10 percent interest rate, the early higher net cash inflow of Project A adds $3,200 more to the project's return than that Project B does. Second, all net cash inflows, including the earnings from the net cash inflows of the early years, earn a higher rate of return, because Project A has a higher internal rate of return than Project B.

Which rate of return, the internal rate of return of the project or the discount rate employed in the NPV method, is more realistic for the net cash inflows that an investment generates? Earning a certain rate of return on a project does not imply that all net cash inflows of the project also will earn the same rate of return. Yet the IRR method assumes that *all* of a project's net cash inflows earn the *same* rate of return as the project's internal rate of return.

A desirable investment with a high rate of return is likely a unique, one time, investment opportunity. The likelihood for the high return of the project to repeat is likely to be slim. To expect the net cash inflows generated by an investment with a high rate of return to earn the same high return is an overly optimistic and most likely an unrealistic assumption.

The IRR method assumes that Project B's net cash inflows will earn a lower rate of return in subsequent years than those generated by Project A because the internal rate of return of Project B is lower, 19.34 percent. For example, the $13,000 net cash inflow that Project B generates in year 1 is assumed to earn 19.34 percent in each of the subsequent years while the $45,000 generated by Project A is assumed to earn 26.18 percent each year until the end of this project. Surely cash available for investment in a given year will not earn a different rate of return because the cash is from a different project.

In contrast, the NPV method assumes that all net cash inflows earn the same rate as the discount rate employed in calculating the project's net present value. The discount rate used by the NPV method usually is the firm's weighted-average cost of capital—a more conservative and more realistic expectation in most instances.

However, the discount rate used to compute NPV might not be the real rate of return that the net cash inflows in subsequent years will earn. To avoid misguided capital investment decisions, management should carefully estimate the rates of return that an investment can be expected to generate.[22]

Shift in Cash Flow Direction

A typical capital investment has net cash outflows in the project's early stage and generates net cash inflows thereafter. However, not every capital investment project follows such a neat and uneventful cash flow pattern. After the initial investment, some projects require additional investments that exceed the projects' cash inflows for that period. These projects then would have a net cash outflow, or negative net cash inflow, for the period. In a survey on capital budgeting practices, Fremgen found that 32 percent

---

[22] The IRR function in Microsoft Excel and Quattro Pro allows different discount rates to be used for different periods.

EXHIBIT 20.24
Investment with Multiple Rates of Return

(1) Period	(2) After-Tax Net Cash Flow	(3) Discount Factor at 10 Percent	(4) Present Value with 10 Percent Discount Rate	(5) Discount Factor at 16 Percent	(6) Present Value with 16 Percent Discount Rate
0	$(1,323)	1.000	$(1,323)	1.000	$(1,323)
1	3,000	0.909	2,727	0.862	2,586
2	(1,700)	0.826	(1,404)	0.743	(1,263)
NPV			0		0

of the respondents frequently experienced one or more mixed directions in cash flows.[23] A mixed cash flow pattern can cause projects to have more than one internal rate of return, as the next example demonstrates.

A firm invests $1,323 in a project that will bring in $3,000 in cash proceeds after one year. The project's required cost for equipment disposal and site restoration makes the net effect on cash flow at the end of year 2 an outflow of $1,700.

Exhibit 20.24 shows that the project has two internal rates of return because the cash flow changes from a net cash outflow in year 0 to a net cash inflow in year 1 and then to a net cash outflow again in year 2. The net present value is zero at 10 percent discount rate and also at 16 percent. Theoretically, an investment project can have as many internal rates of return as changes in the direction of net cash flows. The Fremgen survey found that 15 percent of the respondents who used the IRR method had experienced multiple internal rates of return.

Having multiple internal rates of return makes an investment's real rate of return a puzzle. Users should be cautious in applying the IRR method to projects with mixed cash flow directions.

Length of Useful Life

The IRR method considers each additional useful year of a project another year that its cumulative net cash inflow will earn a return equal to the project's internal rate of return. As a result, IRR is likely to favor projects with long useful lives.

Assume that Paton Implement Manufacturing Company also considers Project C. The investment requirement and expected net cash inflow returns for the first 10 years of Project C are the same as those of Project A. Project C has a useful life of 15 years. The net cash inflows of the last five years are a mere $1,000 per year, a 1 percent return for a $100,000 investment. Exhibit 20.25 shows that Project C's IRR is 26.29 percent. Recall that Project A's IRR is 26.18 percent. Project C earns a higher return than Project A, although Project C earns a mere 1 percent return in each of the last five years of its useful life.

This result is not unique to the IRR method. The NPV method also favors projects with long useful lives as long as the project earns a positive net cash inflow during the extended years. Exhibit 20.25 shows that, although Project C earns only a small net cash inflow in each of the last five years, its NPV increases from $55,344 to $56,805. As long as the net cash inflow in a year is positive, no matter how small it is, the net present value increases, and the project's desirability improves.

Maintaining an investment ties up resources that the firm could use elsewhere. Even if the project requires no additional out-of-pocket financial outlays in its last years, the firm is paying to continue the project in the form of lost opportunities. The firm could, for example, use the space occupied by the project for other projects, or managers can guide other projects better if they do not have to spend time on this project. Furthermore, with the proceeds from the project's termination, the firm might be able to earn a higher return on the proceeds elsewhere than the return from the continuation of the project.

[23]James M. Fremgen, "Capital Budgeting Practices: A Survey," *Management Accounting,* May 1973, pp. 19–25.

EXHIBIT 20.25
Effect of the Length of Useful Life on the Evaluation of Capital Investment Using DCF Methods
Net After-Tax Cash Inflow

Period	Net Cash Inflow A	Net Cash Inflow C	10 Percent Discount Factor	Present Value of A	Present Value of C
0	$(100,000)	$(100,000)	1.000	$(100,000)	$(100,000)
1	$ 45,000	$ 45,000	0.909	$ 40,905	$ 40,905
2	39,000	39,000	0.826	32,214	32,214
3	25,000	25,000	0.751	18,775	18,775
4	17,000	17,000	0.683	11,611	11,611
5	23,000	23,000	0.621	14,283	14,283
6	20,000	20,000	0.565	11,300	11,300
7	17,000	17,000	0.513	8,721	8,721
8	15,000	15,000	0.467	7,005	7,005
9	13,000	13,000	0.424	5,512	5,512
10	13,000	13,000	0.386	5,018	5,018
11		1,000	0.350		350
12		1,000	0.319		319
13		1,000	0.290		290
14		1,000	0.263		263
15		1,000	0.239		239
Total	$ 227,000	$ 232,000		$ 155,344	$ 156,805
NPV				$ 55,344	$ 56,805
IRR				26.18%	26.29%

EXHIBIT 20.26
Net Present Values of Project B with Different Desired Rates of Return over the Years

Year	Net After-Tax Cash Inflow	Desired Rate of Return	Discount Factor	Present Value
1	$164,000	0.10	0.909	$149,076
2	194,000	0.12	0.797	154,618
3	194,000	0.13	0.694	134,636
4	382,000	0.15	0.572	218,504
Total PV				$656,834
Initial Investment				625,000
NPV				$ 31,834

Fluctuating Cost of Capital over Project Life

A firm's cost of capital often fluctuates as situations change over the years. A firm might enjoy a low cost of capital when it has access to low-cost funds or the capital market has abundant funds. A firm could face a high cost of capital when it experiences adverse operating results or tight economic conditions. As the firm's financial condition or operating environment changes, its cost of capital could also change. A proper capital budgeting procedure should incorporate changes in the firm's cost of capital or desired rate of return in evaluating capital investments.

The NPV method can accommodate different rates of return over the years. As an example, Jennifer O'Clock realizes that the desired rates of return for Project B should be different in different years because of several factors relevant to the investment including fluctuations in foreign exchange rates, advances in technology, shifts in market tastes, and changes in the economy. Column 3 of Exhibit 20.26 depicts her desired rate of return at different years. She can still determine Project B's NPV by following the same procedure for determining the net present values when there is only one discount rate over the entire period. By using appropriate discount rates for the net cash inflow of different periods, she can determine the net present value of Project B as shown in the last column of Exhibit 20.26.

EXHIBIT 20.27
Comparison of NPV and IRR Methods

NPV	IRR
Not meaningful for comparing projects with different amounts of initial investments	Easy to compare projects with different amounts of initial investments
NPVs of multiple projects are additive	IRRs of multiple projects are not additive
Assumes that cash proceeds can be reinvested to earn the same rate of return used in the computation of the NPV	Assumes that cash proceeds can be reinvested to earn the same rate as the IRR on that particular project
Allows for multiple discount rates over the years	Allows for only one discount rate for the entire period

EXHIBIT 20.28
Summary of Factors Affecting Results of Analyses Using the DCF Methods

Factor	NPV Method	IRR Method
Amount of initial investment	Favors projects with large initial investment	Has no effect
Net cash flow pattern		
• Timing and amount	Has moderate effect	Effects in proportion to the internal rate of return
• Cash flow direction	Has no effect	Can have multiple rates of return for projects with multiple cash flow directions
Length of useful life	Moderately favors projects with long, useful lives	Favors projects with long, useful lives and in proportion to the internal rate of return
Fluctuating cost of capital	Incorporates easily	Incorporates with difficulty
Results of multiple projects	Is the sum of the results of individual projects	Requires recomputation

The IRR procedure determines a single rate that reflects the return of the project under consideration. The firm then compares its cost of capital or desired rate of return with the project's single rate of return in assessing the project's desirability. The IRR method cannot easily handle situations with varying desired rates of return.

Multiple Projects

The NPV method evaluates investment projects in dollar amounts while the IRR method evaluates investment projects in percentages or rates. The net present values from multiple projects can be added to arrive at a single total net present value for all investments that a firm will invest as a package while percentages or rates of return on multiple projects cannot be added. The total NPV of independent projects is the simple sum of these projects' net present values. If the NPV of a $120,000 investment is $35,000, and the NPV of a $50,000 investment in another independent project is $20,000, the total net present value of investing $170,000 in these two projects is $55,000, the sum of the two net present values. The additivity of net present values makes evaluating multiple investments easy.

Internal rates of return of different investments cannot be added to determine the overall internal rate of return of the multiple projects. Investments of $120,000 in one project that earns a 10 percent rate of return and $50,000 in another project that earns a 15 percent rate of return do not make 25 percent the rate of return from the entire $170,000 investment. A change in the composition of projects being considered requires a complete recalculation of the overall IRR.

Exhibit 20.27 compares the two DCF methods. Exhibit 20.28 summarizes factors that could lead the NPV method and the IRR method to reach different conclusions in evaluating the same investment project.

REAL-WORLD FOCUS

How a Hospital Justified a Computer-Based Patient Record System

The University of Texas M.D. Anderson Cancer Center in Houston, Texas, has a staff of about 8,000 located in several buildings that include a 518-bed hospital, a 10-story outpatient clinic, and several remote patient care sites. Although it kept some patient information on computer, many records were paper based. Files for repeat patients became unwieldy, requiring regular compiling and thinning. A computer-based patient record (CPR) that integrates financial and clinical information can be an important tool for improving the quality of care and lowering its cost. However, purchasing, implementing, and maintaining a CPR requires a significant investment that management must justify.

The CPR project was the responsibility of an executive team consisting of the vice president for patient care, the vice president for hospital and clinic operations, and the executive vice president for administration and finance. A project steering committee directed the cost-benefit analysis and other aspects of evaluation. A stakeholders group consisting of managers from departments that would be affected by CPR implementation provided much of the

data for the cost-benefit analysis. The chief information officer and the associate vice president of medical information served on all teams and were involved at all levels.

The cost-benefit analysis followed these steps:

- Identified goals for a CPR.
- Determined quantifiable and nonquantifiable benefits.
- Estimated costs.
- Projected costs and benefits over 10 years and calculated the net present value.
- Monitored the results.

The cost-benefit analysis enabled executives to make informed strategic and tactical decisions regarding acquisition and implementation of a CPR.

Based on Leslie A. Kian and Miceael W. Stewart, "Justifying the Cost of a Computer-Based Patient Record," *Healthcare Financial Management* 49, no. 7, pp. 58–63.

Strategic Cost Management and Capital Budgeting

LEARNING OBJECTIVE 5

Explain the relationships between strategic cost management and capital budgeting.

Capital investment is a critical factor in an organization's continued success and needs to be tailored to its strategy. A capital investment also can change or reshape an organization's strategy. A capital investment analysis that includes only immediate high-value-added activities and costs to the firm can be too narrowly focused and fail to capture the full impact of the investment on the firm. A proper analysis of capital investments should include consideration of the firm's competitive advantage, value chain, and strategic cost drivers.

Competitive Strategy and Capital Budgeting

As discussed in Chapter 2, competitive strategy is the way a firm chooses to compete to achieve its goals or mission. A firm can choose to build, hold, or harvest. Exhibit 20.29 shows the effect of differences in strategic missions on capital budgeting.

An organization that chooses to build often faces many uncertainties, uses evolving technologies, and traverses in environments that change rapidly. Capital budgeting processes in these firms are often less formal, use more nonfinancial or nonquantifiable data, and apply subjective criteria in evaluating investment projects. In contrast, a firm that chooses to harvest is likely a mature organization or competes on a mature market. Its capital budgeting processes are more likely to be formal, and most of the data for its capital budgeting are likely to be quantifiable and financial in nature.

Uncertainties often faced by an organization that chooses to build can require the firm to adopt a long-term perspective and allow for long payback periods or low hurdle rates. The long payback periods or low hurdle rates are justified because a firm chooses to build and enjoy a long payoff period if it is successful. However, these projects likely require approval at a relatively high level of management because of the high risk involved.

A mature market is likely ripe for change. By necessity, a capital investment's payback period in such a market needs to be short, and the hurdle rate must be at least the firm's average rate of return. A firm that decided to harvest most likely would not undertake major capital investments. Capital investments requiring small amounts of funds can be approved by managers at relatively low levels.

EXHIBIT 20.29
Strategic Missions and Capital Budgeting

Factor in Capital Budgeting	Strategic Mission		
	Build	**Hold**	**Harvest**
Formalization of capital expenditure decisions	Less formal DCF analysis	→	More formalized DCF analysis
Capital expenditure evaluation criteria	More emphasis on nonfinancial data (market share, efficient use of R&D dollars, etc.)	→	More emphasis on financial data (cost efficiency; straight cash-on-cash incremental return)
	Longer payback	→	Shorter payback
Hurdle rate	Relatively low	→	Relatively high
Capital investment analysis	More subjective and qualitative	→	More quantitative and financial
Project approval limit at business unit level	Relatively high	→	Relatively low
Frequency of postaudit	Frequent	→	Less frequent

Based on: Vijay Govindarajan and John K. Shank, "Strategic Cost Management: Tailoring Controls to Strategies," *Journal of Cost Management,* Fall 1992, pp. 14–25.

A firm, however, should never consider its strategic direction as given in its capital investment analysis. Assuming a continuing stable operating environment can be a fatal mistake. Moreover, a capital investment can help managers redefine strategy, establish new goals, and plan new tactics to reach its goals at a higher level. As a tool for analyzing long-term investment opportunities, capital budgeting is guided by strategy and goals, but it is also instrumental in redefining or enhancing the way a firm has chosen to compete. A new manufacturing technology acquired by a harvesting firm with a low-cost competitive strategy can transform the firm into a different competitive position, such as product differentiation with an increased emphasis to build. For instance, the adoption of a host of new technologies enabled Levi-Strauss to make individually tailored designer jeans embroidered with the owner's name. Moving into a custom-made market, the firm's most critical factor for its success was no longer cost. Levi-Strauss transformed its market from a commodity market (low-cost) to a custom-made market differ because of the investment in new information technology.[24]

Value Chain and Capital Budgeting

Critics often charge that conventional capital budgeting techniques render incomplete analyses in today's competitive environment with rapid changes in both technology and the markets. A common criticism is that the conventional capital budgeting techniques are project oriented; they start from the inception of a project, followed by the delivery of goods and services to market, and finish with the disposal of the project at the end of its useful life. Such an analysis, critics argue, fails to capture the full impact of a capital investment at different stages.

Through its activities, a firm adds or creates value and occupies a node in the linked set of value-creating activities from basic raw materials to the ultimate end-use product delivered to the consumer and the final disposals by the end-user. (This process has been defined as a *value chain* in Chapter 2.) Even though a firm can participate in only a segment of the entire value chain, the firm should analyze the impact of its capital investments over the entire value chain.

Shank and Govindarajan conducted a field study and demonstrated the importance of value-chain analysis in capital budgeting.[25] They examined a firm that undertook a conventional capital budgeting analysis, which included only the benefits to the operation

[24] Lawrence P. Carr, William C. Lawler, and John K. Shank, "Cost Analysis for Value Chain Reconfiguration: Adding the Strategic Dimension," Paper presented at 2000 Annual Meeting, Management Accounting Section, American Accounting Association.

[25] John K. Shank and Vijay Govindarajan, "Strategic Cost Analysis of Technological Investments," *Sloan Management Review,* Fall 1992, pp. 39–51.

Cost Management in Action — Is That Advanced Manufacturing Technology Worth It?

A manufacturer of telecommunications devices is about to review proposals for investment to increase its manufacturing capacity for manufacturing one of its key components. In the past, the proposals vary in the level of technology and the degree of computer integration required for manufacturing process. So far, the firm has minimal experience with advanced manufacturing technology and is using semiautomated machines in key parts of its manufacturing process of the components. Over the last several years, company executives have been conscious of the growing competitive pressures that may eventually require investment in advanced manufacturing technology. As a result the firm has been actively seeking out such investment proposals. Many proposals had been reviewed in the last few years. However, no proposals have ever passed the review stage. "The numbers just don't support it," according to one member of the review committee, who has been a staunch advocate of advanced manufacturing technologies.

The firm evaluates all major investment proposals using the net present value method with the estimated long-term (five years) cost of capital as the discount rate. In addition, the firm also uses the payback method in analysis. However, a short payback period is not necessary to justify investment in a project if the project is considered to be among the best in terms of investment proposals. A review of the proposals submitted over the last few years revealed that these proposals ranked consistently higher based upon the net present value method.

You believe that it is critically important for the long-term profitability of the firm to acquire new advanced manufacturing technology. You are of the opinion that the firm will lose its competitive edge, or may not even survive, if it fails to respond to this demand. As the manager of the manufacturing process, who has submitted several unsuccessful proposals for investment in advanced manufacturing technologies, how would you modify your proposal?

where the investment was to be made. The analysis showed no financial gain to the firm and indicated that it should not make the proposed capital investment. However, a value-chain analysis that included impacts to both upstream and downstream operations showed that the investment could save an estimated $33.6 million per year in just one of the firm's locations. The value-chain analysis demonstrated unequivocally the investment's benefit, and the firm changed its decision.

Cost Driver Analysis

Volume frequently is the only cost driver identified in many capital budgeting analyses. For many capital investments, however, structural and executional cost drivers can be as critical as, if not more than, volume in determining the investment's success and should be considered.

Structural cost drivers are factors that relate to the firm's strategic decisions on the fundamental structure of the investment such as its technology, scale, product-line complexity, scope of vertical integration, or experience. These structural cost drivers are likely to be found at levels in which the firm chooses to compete (Chapter 2).

A decision not to invest in a new technology leaves the firm with no choice but to continue operating with the same set of cost drivers. The cost drivers or their levels can differ entirely should the firm decide to invest in a new technology. The cost of a business unit with a complex product line is not the same as another one with a product line that is easy to make, service, and sell. McDonnell Douglas Corporation's decision in 1996 not to make the estimated $15 billion investment necessary to compete directly with larger rivals reduced the firm to a minor player in the commercial jet business.[26] A capital budgeting decision can change the firm's structural cost drivers, and the results of structural cost drivers often are the very ones that a capital investment seeks to obtain. A complete capital investment analysis should always include the effects of structural cost drivers.

Executional cost drivers affect a firm's cost position and its ability to work successfully within the economic structure it chooses. Executional cost drivers that are likely to be important include these:

- Workforce involvement (participative management).
- Workforce commitment to continuous improvement.

[26] *The Wall Street Journal,* October 29, 1996, p. A3. The firm eventually was acquired by Boeing, its main rival in the United States.

Overcapacity of the global shipping industry and decreased-demand forecasts made costcutting a priority at American President Lines (APL), a global shipping company founded in 1848. At the same time, the shipping industry was becoming more IT-intensive. Cost cutting and the emerging business model required increasing reliance on conducting transactions online. Investment in information technology has been a recurring issue throughout the firm.

Projects with a strong ROI get priority while those characterized by soft-dollar benefits get a harder look through a balanced-scorecard approach. APL's scorecard is heavily weighted toward ROI, payback, and net present value, while also considering a range of soft benefits. The scorecard requires weighted averages of scores on a long list of items, including strategic alignment, costs, benefits to the company and its customers, and risks, among others. All hard-dollar returns require identification of the cost center and account to which benefits will accrue. For example, to justify a project that claims a savings of $1 million in labor or 10 full-time employees, the scorecard has to specify which cost center will eliminate those jobs and which of the company's accounts will turn red ink into black.

A project that looks promising on paper must meet other requirements to win approval. These requirements include whether a detailed plan is in place for accomplishing the project's goals, whether the project has strong business ownership and commit-

ment, and whether the IT department can meet all the specific details required by the project.

Once approved, the project's progress is reviewed every month. The review committee assigns a red, yellow, or green light to the project. According to Chuck Lenatti, "A yellow light indicates that the project has a problem but can get back on track with some modifications." A red light means that there are significant issues. "The biggest challenge is saying, Stop the project. Once a project has gotten wheels and is moving along, it is very difficult to stop."

After a project is completed, the committee conducts two post-mortem reviews. Upon completion, the committee examines whether the project was completed on time and on budget, and if it delivered the benefits promised. The second review is conducted six months after completion.

APL's management believes that the balanced-scorecard approach strengths IT innovation because it aligns the company with the business strategy and ensures that the business unit is ready to make the most of a project. At APL, some projects were put on hold not because the ROI wasn't there, but because the business side wasn't ready to commit.

Source: Chuck Lenatti, "Grinding Away on ROI," *CFO*, Summer 2003, pp. 23–29.

- Adherence to total quality management concepts.
- Utilization of effective capacity.
- Efficiency of production flow layout.
- Effectiveness of product design or formulation.
- Exploitation of linkages with suppliers and customers throughout the value chain.[27]

In the early 1990s, Motorola derived one of its cost advantages from its ability to reduce defect rates to no more than three units per million in manufacturing integrated circuits achieved through years of continual capital investments in quality training and process improvements. This example shows the impact of an executional cost driver. The cost advantage led Motorola to enter the business of making billets for fluorescent lamps. Motorola management believed that its quality skills provided a strategic advantage for a successful entry into this new business that uses old technologies.

Behavioral Issues in Capital Budgeting

LEARNING OBJECTIVE 6
Identify behavioral factors in capital budgeting decisions.

Successful capital budgeting results from efforts of individuals and teams. Although it is often a product of careful corporate decision making, a proper and carefully executed capital investment decision does not necessarily lead to a successful capital investment because human behavior often plays an important role in the success of an investment.

A successful manager is often viewed as one who is responsible for a large or growing unit. Large or growing enterprises require capital investments. Furthermore, a new capital asset is visible and is often viewed as "progress" or an "accomplishment." This

---

[27] Shank and Govindarajan, "Strategic Cost Analysis," p. 47.

fact leads too many managers to be overly eager to promote capital investments. Firms must carefully contain aggressive managers who overestimate projections in attempting to earn approval for capital investments in their divisions.

Studies have found that escalating commitment is too commonly a phenomenon in capital investments. In an attempt to recoup past losses, a decision maker often considers past costs or losses as relevant in making capital investment decisions and includes elimination or reduction of losses from past investments as savings to benefit the new investment. Escalating commitments are more likely to occur when these managers are also responsible for the negative results of past actions.[28]

Although sunk costs should have no effect on decisions, research in prospect theory has found that sunk costs often play important roles in influencing the way decisions are framed. Sunk costs should not enter into consideration for either benefits or costs of capital investments. The existence of a negative operating result from investments or actions taken in the past could cause subsequent decisions to be framed as a choice between losses, and a positive operating result leads subsequent decisions to be framed as a choice between gains. Several studies show that decisions made on choices between losses differ from those between gains.[29]

Much-needed capital investments are often not pursued because of the amount of work and time required to secure their approval. Projects that cost less than those that must be approved as a capital investment are undertaken instead. As a result, managers may choose to invest in multiple small additions that require no approval from the supervisor or committee, rather than investing in a major capital project such as computer-integrated manufacturing or flexible manufacturing systems that would vastly improve the firm's competitive advantage. Failure to make necessary capital investments can reduce the firm's competitiveness, erode its market share, and jeopardize its long-term profitability and even survival.

Intolerance of uncertainty often leads managers to require short payback periods for capital investments. Once a project pays for itself, the amount of risk is reduced and the decision is home free. This makes projects with short payback periods the preferred choice to some decision makers. However, not all critical capital investments can have a short payback period. Many important projects require a lengthy time to install, test, adjust, train personnel, and gain market acceptance; examples include investments in new manufacturing technologies, new product development, and expanding into new territories. Requiring too short a payback period makes the acceptance of such projects unlikely, even if the firm will enjoy long-term benefits from the capital investments.

Summary

Capital investment decisions are among the most important decisions that a firm or organization makes. No business firm can survive for long without making sound capital investments. No governmental organization can provide good services to its constituents without intelligent capital investments.

Capital budgeting processes include project identification and definition, project evaluation, and monitoring and review. Initial proposals for capital investment often are made at the local or business subunit level. Investments that involve major technology change are more likely initiated at top management level, however.

Capital investment analyses focus on future events and operating environment. In analyzing capital investments, the primary focus is cash flow. An investment is not a financially sound decision if a firm receives less cash from it than the amount of funds it invests in the project.

Cash outflows in investments occur at three stages: (1) *project initiation:* to acquire the investment and begin operations, to provide its working capital, and to dispose of the replaced or discarded assets; (2) *project operation:* to cover operating expenditures

[28] Glen Whyte, "Escalating Commitment to a Course of Action: A Reinterpretation," *Academy of Management Review,* 1986, pp. 311–21.
[29] D. Kanamen and D. Tversky, "Prospect Theory: An Analysis of Decisions under Risk," *Econometrica,* 1979, pp. 263–90.

EXHIBIT 20.30   **Capital Investment Evaluation Techniques**

Technique	Definition	Computation Procedure	Advantages	Weaknesses
Payback period	Number of years to recover the initial investment	*Uniform flow:* $$\frac{\text{Investment}}{\text{Net cash inflow}}$$ *Uneven flow:* Number of years for the cumulative cash flow equal to the investment	1. Simple to use and understand 2. Measures liquidity 3. Appraises risk	1. Ignores timing and time value of money 2. Ignores cash flows beyond payback period
Book rate of return	Ratio of average annual net income to the initial investment or average investment (book value)	$$\frac{\text{Average net income}}{\text{Investment book value}}$$	1. Data readily available 2. Consistent with other financial measures	1. Ignores timing and time value of money 2. Uses accounting numbers rather than cash flows
Net present value	Difference between the initial investment and the present value of subsequent net cash inflows discounted at a given interest rate	Present value of net cash inflows—initial investment	1. Considers time value of money 2. Uses realistic discount rate for reinvestment 3. Additive for combined projects	1. Not meaningful for comparing projects requiring different amounts of investments 2. Favors large investments
Internal rate of return	Discount rate that makes the initial investment equal the present value of subsequent net cash inflows	Solving the following equation for discount rate i: Present value factor of $i \times$ Net cash inflows = Initial investment	1. Considers time value of money 2. Easy for comparing projects requiring different amounts of investment	1. Assumption on reinvestment rate of return could be unrealistic 2. Complex to compute if done manually

and any additional investments and to provide additional working capital; and (3) *final project disposal:* to dispose of the investment, to restore facilities, and to provide training or relocation for personnel whose positions have been terminated. An investment generates net cash inflows during its existence through increases in revenues or decreases in expenses. All cash flows for a business firm should be net of tax effects.

Many techniques for analyzing capital investments are available, including undiscounted techniques such as payback period and book rate of return and the discounted cash flow techniques such as net present value and internal rate of return. Exhibit 20.30 summarizes the definitions, computation procedures, advantages, and weaknesses of these techniques.

A capital investment analysis should consider the firm's competitive advantage, the effects of the investment on both upstream and downstream activities in the firm's value chain, and its impact of strategic structural and executional cost drivers.

Appendix A

Modified Accelerated Cost Recovery System (MACRS)

Firms often use different depreciation methods for various depreciable assets. To bring more uniformity into depreciation computations and to encourage businesses to invest in new plant and equipment by allowing them to recover the investment quickly through depreciation, Congress introduced the Accelerated Cost Recovery System (ACRS) in 1981. It was replaced in 1986 by the Modified Accelerated Cost Recovery System (MACRS). As a result, several systems are currently in uses for determineing depreciation expenses of depreciable assets.

EXHIBIT 20.31
Asset Classes (Recovery Periods) under MACRS

Class	Depreciation Method	Example
3-year property	200% declining balance	Light tools and handling equipment
5-year property	200% declining balance	Computers and peripheral equipment, office machinery, automobiles, light trucks
7-year property	200% declining balance	Office furniture, appliances, carpet, and furniture in residential rental property and any asset that does not have an assigned class
10-year property	200% declining balance	Manufacturing assets for food products, petroleum refining, tobacco
15-year property	150% declining balance	Road and shrubbery, telephone distribution plant
20-year property	150% declining balance	Multipurpose farm structures
27.5 year property	Straight line	Residential rental property
31.5 year property	Straight line	Nonresidential real property, office building, warehouse

EXHIBIT 20.32
MACRS Depreciation Rate

Year	3-year	5-year	7-year	10-year	15-year	20-year
1	33.33	20.00	14.29	10.00	5.00	3.75
2	44.45	32.00	24.49	18.00	9.50	7.22
3	14.81	19.20	17.49	14.40	8.55	6.68
4	7.41	11.52*	12.49	11.52	7.70	6.18
5		11.52	8.93*	9.22	6.93	5.71
6		5.76	8.92	7.37	6.23	5.28
7			8.92	6.55*	5.90*	4.89
8			4.47	6.55	5.90	4.52
9				6.56	5.91	4.46*

*First year of switching to the straight-line method.

Two of the factors that affect the amount of depreciation for an asset are (1) the year it was placed in service and (2) type of asset. All assets placed in service after 1986 use MACRS. ACRS is used for assets placed in service after 1980 but before 1987. Assets placed in service before 1981 can use either the straight-line or an accelerated depreciation method. This appendix discusses MACRS only. Publication 534 "Depreciation" from the Internal Revenue Service (IRS) provides detailed information on different depreciation methods.

MACRS assigns all depreciable assets to one of eight classes, referred to as *recovery periods* in the tax law. Exhibit 20.31 describes these classes and their depreciation methods with examples of assets in each class.

MACRS does not use disposable value; MACRS depreciation is calculated based on the entire original cost. With the exception of residential and nonresidential real properties in the last two classes, a half-year convention is used to determine the depreciation for the first year the asset is placed in service, and, if the firm owns the depreciable asset for the entire recovery period, for the year following the end of the recovery period.

A half-year convention allows one-half year of depreciation for the first year the firm places the property in service regardless of when during the year it was actually placed in service. To illustrate, the first-year depreciation for a five-year property would have been 40 percent (200 percent of the straight-line rate) of the original cost without the half-year convention. Because of the half-year convention, the allowable depreciation for the first year is 20 percent whether the asset is placed in service on January 3 or December 3. The depreciation for each remaining year of the recovery period is determined by using the 200 percent declining-balance method. The depreciation for the second year of a five-year property, for example, is 40 percent of the remaining 80 percent, which is 32 percent of the original cost. Exhibit 20.32 shows the depreciation rates for properties other than residential or nonresidential real properties.

Under a special rule, a mid-quarter convention instead of a half-year convention might be required. Residential and nonresidential rental properties use a mid-month convention in all situations. You should consult IRS publications or tax professionals for details.

Tax planning is a complex matter. The discussion in this appendix barely scratches the surface. Many issues such as loss carrybacks and carryforwards, qualification for capital assets, state income taxes, and foreign tax credits are not discussed. Always consult a tax professional to ensure that all tax considerations have been included.

Key Terms

book rate of return, *858*
breakeven time (BET) method, *865*
capital budgeting, *840*
capital investment, *839*
cost of capital, *862*

desired rate of return, *861*
discounted cash flow (DCF) techniques, *861*
internal rate of return (IRR) method, *865*
net present value (NPV), *863*

payback period, 854
present value, *863*
present value payback period, *865*

Comments on Cost Management in Action

Many benefits of advanced manufacturing technology are often difficult to quantify in dollar amounts or even in numbers. To make matters worse, these benefits, more often than not, are long-term in nature, and the firm will see no immediate tangible results. A large confectionery firm rejected an automated storage and distribution facility because it did not include the benefits that better customer services would bring. Better customer services often lead to higher sales volume and market share and, eventually, higher profits. Realizing these difficulties, middle managers of a kitchen unit manufacturer, with an established reputation for innovative design, forced an investment in computer-assisted design equipment by exaggerating financial benefits—a practice that should be discouraged and disallowed!

Appraisals of investments in advanced manufacturing technology need to be evaluated in terms of quantitative analysis and strategic consideration. Advanced manufacturing technology can expand the firm's product portfolio, enhance corporate image, and increase manufacturing flexibility, in addition to potentially decreasing production time and costs. Firms need to assess both the quantifiable short-term incremental cash inflows and the long-run strategic benefits in judging an investment's merits. In addition to cash flow analysis, an investment proposal can go a long way if it also includes the investment's strategic benefits. A firm manufacturing high-pressure casings decided to convert its manufacturing operations to cell manufacturing. The firm enjoyed such unplanned benefits as a 50 percent reduction in inventory, a 75 percent improvement in quality, substantial reduction in lead times, and flexible machining with overall labor reduction. An electrical switch gear products manufacturer with a sales of $32 million and a total staff of 550 invested in CAD to increase its design capacity in anticipation of a 25 percent growth. The firm's original expectations included reduced lead time in the drawing office and reduced number of employees and WIP inventory. The additional benefits offered more accurate and timely transfer of data that greatly improved the firm's competitive edge and propelled the firm into a new marketing position.

Based on Michael Bromwich and Al Bhimani, "Strategic Investment Appraisal," *Management Accounting*, March 1991, pp. 45–8.

Self-Study Problem
(For solution, please turn to the end of the chapter.)

Capital Budgeting for Expanding Productive Capacity

Ray Summers Company operates at full capacity of 10,000 units per year. The firm, however, is still unable to meet the demand for one of its products, estimated at 15,000 units annually. This level of demand is expected to continue for at least another four years.

To meet the demand, the firm is considering the purchase of a new equipment for $580,000. This equipment has a useful life of four years and can be sold for $50,000 at the end of the fourth year. The engineering division estimates that installing, testing, and adjusting the machine will cost $12,000 before it can be put in operation.

An adjacent vacant warehouse can be leased for the duration of the project for $10,000 per year. The warehouse needs $58,000 of renovations to make it suitable for manufacturing. The lease terms call for restoring the warehouse to its original condition at the end of the lease. The restoration is estimated to cost $20,000. Analysis of current operating data provides this information:

			Per Unit
Sales price			$200
Variable costs			
Manufacturing	$60		
Marketing	20	$80	
Fixed costs			
Manufacturing	$25		
Marketing and administrative	15	40	120
Net income			$ 80

The new equipment has no effect on the variable costs per unit. All current fixed costs are expected to continue with the same total amount. The per-unit cost includes depreciation expenses of $5 for manufacturing and $4 for marketing and administration.

Additional fixed manufacturing costs of $140,000 (excluding depreciation) will be incurred each year if the equipment is purchased. The firm must hire an additional marketing manager to serve new customers. The annual cost for the new marketing manager, support staff, and office expense is estimated at approximately $100,000. The accountant expects the firm to be in the 40 percent tax bracket for combined federal and state income taxes in the next four years. No investment credit is currently in effect. The firm requires a minimum rate of return of 12 percent on investments and uses straight-line depreciation.

Required

1. What is the total initial investment requirement (year 0)?
2. What effect will the acquisition of the new equipment have on net income in each of the four years?
3. What effect will the acquisition of the new equipment have on cash flows in each of the four years?
4. Compute the payback period of the investment.
5. Compute the book rate of return based on the average investment.
6. Compute the net present value.
7. Compute the internal rate of return.
8. Use a spreadsheet to verify your answers for 6 and 7.
9. The firm expects the variable manufacturing cost per unit to increase once the new equipment is in place. What is the most that the unit variable manufacturing cost can increase and allow the firm to still earn the required rate of return on the investment?

Questions

20–1   What are the major steps in capital budgeting decisions?

20–2   "If I have to name the one most important concern in capital budgeting, I'll say it is the effect on the bottom line." Do you agree? What factor might have led this company executive with more than 20 years of experience to come to this conclusion?

20–3   List cash flows that a hospital is likely to incur after it installs a CAT scanner.

20–4   Identify costs that a chemical plant may incur after 20 years in operation.

20–5   What is a direct cash effect? Give three examples of direct cash effects in acquiring a new factory.

20–6   What is tax effect? Give three examples of tax effect pertaining to acquisition of a new factory.

20–7   "Book value is nothing but a bookkeeper's figure and is irrelevant in capital budgeting." Do you agree?

20–8   What are limitations of the payback period technique? Does the present value payback period technique overcome these limitations?

20–9   Does the book rate of return method provide a true measure of return on investment? How about the internal rate of return?

20–10   What should be the decision criterion when using the NPV method to evaluate capital investments? Does the IRR method use the same criterion?

20–11 "Let's be more practical. DCF is not the only gospel. Many managers have become too absorbed with DCF." Can such a statement be justified? Why?

20–12 "Because business executives don't know how to run the numbers, companies are not acting decisively to put these technologies to work. . . . Urgently needed are new cost-benefit formulas and measurements . . . that go beyond the usual return on investment (ROI) evaluations." Do you agree? Why? If you agree, what cost-benefits do ROI evaluations leave out?

20–13 What criterion should be used to choose investment projects for a firm with unlimited funds available to the firm at a cost of 10 percent? Can the firm use the same criterion if it has only a limited amount of funds, say, $100 million, available for investments?

20–14 List at least three important behavioral factors in capital budgeting.

20–15 When analyzing a capital investment what conditions or factors may lead the results to differ between the two DCF (NPV and IRR) methods?

20–16 How does the size of the initial investment affect the IRR method and the NPV method?

20–17 "The net present value method weighs early receipts of cash much more heavily than late receipts of cash." Do you agree?

20–18 Depreciation expenses have no effect on cash flows and, therefore, is not relevant in capital investment decisions. Do you agree?

20–19 A firm alters its desired rate of return from year to year or from project to project. What underlying factors may have prompted a firm to change its desired rate of return for a capital investment under consideration?

20–20 Should the firm accept the independent projects described here? Why?

   a. A firm's cost of capital is 10 percent and the project's internal rate of return is 11 percent.

   b. A capital project requires $150,000 initial investment. The firm's cost of capital is 10 percent, and the present value of the expected net cash inflows from the project is $148,000.

20–21 How would a firm that chooses to build use capital budgeting differently than a firm that chooses to harvest? Why might they differ?

20–22 C.W. Yale, president of Hotchikiss, Inc., your client, recently attended a seminar at which a speaker discussed planning and control of capital expenditures, which he referred to as *capital budgeting*. Yale tells you that he is not quite sure he understands that concept.

Required

   1. Explain the nature of capital budgeting and identify several of its uses.

   2. What are the basic differences between the payback period technique and the net present value method of capital budgeting? Explain.

   3. Define *cost of capital.*

   4. Financial accounting data are not entirely suitable for use in capital budgeting. Explain.

(CPA Adapted)

Exercises

20–23 **Cash Flows Effects**

   a. A hospital incurred $500,000 out-of-pocket expenses in its billing and receivable department. The department also had $80,000 depreciation expense for office equipment. The hospital is a not-for-profit organization that pays no income taxes. What effects do these expenses have on the hospital's cash flow?

   b. Warren Elway Sports Shop paid $50,000 for advertising. It also had $30,000 depreciation expenses on shop equipment and fixtures. On average, the store pays about 20 percent of its income on income taxes. What effects do these expenses have on the store's cash flow?

20–24 **Basic Capital Budgeting Techniques**

   a. Project A costs $5,000 and will generate annual after-tax net cash inflows of $1,800 for five years. What is the payback period?

   b. Project B costs $5,000 and will generate after-tax net cash inflows of $500 in year one, $1,200 in year two, $2,000 in year three, $2,500 in year four, and $2,000 in year five. What is the payback period?

   c. Project C costs $5,000 and will generate net cash inflows of $2,500 before taxes for five years. The firm uses straight-line depreciation with no salvage value and has 25 percent tax rate. What is the payback period?

d. Project D costs $5,000 and will generate sales of $4,000 each year for five years. The cash expenditures will be $1,500 per year. The firm uses straight-line depreciation with an estimated salvage value of $500 and has a tax rate of 25 percent.

   (a) What is the book rate of return based on the original investment?

   (b) What is the book rate of return based on the average book value?

e. What are the NPV for each of the projects A through D? Assuming that the firm requires a minimum of 8 percent return on all investments.

20–25 Cost of Capital

a. Micro Advantage, Inc., issued a $5,000,000, 20-year bond a year ago at 98 with a coupon rate of 9 percent. Today, the debt is selling at 110. If the firm's tax bracket is 30 percent, what is its after-tax cost of bond?

b. Micro Advantage, Inc., has $5,000,000 preferred stock outstanding that it sold for $24 per share. The preferred stock has a per share par value of $25 and pays $3 dividend per year. The current market price is $30 per share. The firm's tax bracket is 30 percent. What is its cost of the preferred stock?

c. In addition bonds and preferred stocks described in A and B above, Micro Advantage has outstanding 50,000 shares of common stock that has a par value of $10 per share and a current market price of $170 per share. The expected market return on the firm's common equity is 20 percent. What is Micro Advantage's weighted average cost of capital?

20–26 Future and Present Values, Spreadsheet Application

a. Assume that the Indian referred to in the chapter opener put away the $24 he received from selling Manhattan on January 1, 1701.

Required

1. Use a spreadsheet to determine the balance (in billions) as of December 31, 2000, assuming a 6 percent interest rate compounded semiannually.

2. Carry out the same calculation using an 8 percent interest rate compounded semiannually.

3. What would be the balances for requirements 1 and 2 if the interests are compounded quarterly?

4. Assume that the account had a balance of $9.5 billion as of December 31, 2000. How much would the total amount be on December 31, 2006 if the rate is 8 percent compounded semiannually?

b. In 2000, Alex Rodriguez signed a 10-year $252 million contract with the Texas Rangers. Assuming equal payments each year and the owner's cost of capital was 12 percent, at the time the contract was signed. What is the cost of the contract to the owner as of January 1, 2000, the date the contract was signed, in each of the following independent situations?

Required

1. Alex will receive the first payment on December 31, 2000.

2. Alex will receive the first payment on January 1, 2000, the date the contract was signed.

3. Assuming the owner is in a 45 percent combined federal, state, and local income tax bracket, calculate your answer for requirement 1.

20–27 After-Tax Net Present Value and IRR

a. eEgg is considering the purchase of a new distributed network computer system to help handle its warehouse inventories. The system costs $60,000 to purchase and install and $30,000 to operate each year. The system is estimated to be useful for four years. Management expects the new system to reduce the cost of managing inventories by $62,000 a year. The firm's cost of capital is 10 percent.

Required   What is the net present value under these conditions?

1. The firm is not yet profitable and pays no taxes.

2. The firm is in the 30 percent income tax bracket and uses straight-line depreciation with no salvage value.

3. The firm is in the 30 percent income tax bracket and uses double-declining-balance depreciation with no salvage value.

b. Use the data for eEgg and answer the first two questions and compute the internal rate of return in each case.

20–28 **Basic Capital Budgeting Techniques, Uniform Net Cash Inflows, Spreadsheet Application**
Irv Nelson, Inc., purchased a $500,000 machine to manufacture specialty taps for electrical equipment. Nelson expects to sell all it can manufacture in the next 10 years. The government has exempted taxes on profits from new investments to encourage capital investments. This legislation is to be in effect in the foreseeable future. The machine is expected to have 10 years' useful life with no salvage value. Nelson uses straight-line depreciation. The net cash inflow is expected to be $120,000 each year for 10 years. Nelson uses 12 percent in evaluating capital investments.

Required

1. Compute for the capital investment the
   a. Payback period.
   b. Book rate of return based on (a) initial investment and (b) average investment.
   c. Net present value.
   d. Present value payback period.
   e. Internal rate of return.
2. Use a spreadsheet program to verify your answers for requirements c and e above.

20–29 **Basic Capital Budgeting Techniques, Uneven Net Cash Inflows With Taxes, Spreadsheet Application** Use the same information for this problem as you did for exercise 20–28, except that the investment is subject to taxes and that the net operating cash inflow is as follows:

Year	Cash Inflow	Year	Cash Inflow
1	$ 50,000	6	$300,000
2	80,000	7	270,000
3	120,000	8	240,000
4	200,000	9	120,000
5	240,000	10	40,000

Irv Nelson has been paying 30 percent for combined federal, state, and local income taxes, a rate that is not expected to change during the period of this investment. The firm uses straight-line depreciation.

Required

1. Compute for the project
   a. Payback period.
   b. Book rate of return based on (a) initial investment and (b) average investment.
   c. Net present value.
   d. Internal rate of return.
2. Use a spreadsheet program to find the answers for requirements c and d.

20–30 **Basic Capital Budgeting Techniques, Uneven Net Cash Inflows and Macrs** Use the data in exercise 20–29 for Irv Nelson, Inc., and MACRS. The asset qualifies as a 5-year property.

Required Compute for the investment

1. Payback period.
2. Book rate of return based on (a) the initial investment and (b) an average investment.
3. Net present value.
4. Internal rate of return.

20–31 **Straightforward Capital Budgeting with Taxes** Dorothy & George Company is planning to acquire a new machine at a total cost of $30,600. The machine's estimated life is six years and its estimated salvage value is $600. Dorothy & George Company estimates that annual cash savings from using this machine will be $8,000. The company's cost of capital is 8 percent and its income tax rate is 40 percent. The company uses straight-line depreciation.

Required

1. What is this investment's net after-tax annual cash inflow?
2. Assume that the net after-tax annual cash inflow of this investment is $5,000, what is the payback period?
3. Assume that the net after-tax annual cash inflow of this investment is $5,000, what is the net present value of this investment?

(CPA Adapted)

20–32 **Capital Budgeting with Tax and Sensitivity Analysis**   Gravina Company is planning to spend $6,000 for a machine that it will depreciate on a straight-line basis over 10 years with no salvage value. The machine will generate additional cash revenues of $1,200 a year. Gravina will incur no additional costs except for depreciation. Its income tax rate is 35 percent.

Required

1. What is the payback period?
2. What is the book rate of return on the initial increase in required investment?
3. What is the maximum amount that Gravina Company should invest if it desires to earn a minimum of 15 percent rate of return?
4. What is the minimum annual cash revenue required for the project to earn a 15 percent rate of return?

(CPA Adapted)

20–33 **Basic Capital Budgeting**   Rockyford Company must replace some machinery that has zero book value but a current market value of $1,800. One possibility is to invest in new machinery costing $40,000. This new machinery would produce estimated annual pretax operating cash savings of $12,500. Assume the new machine will have a useful life of four years and depreciation of $10,000 each year for book and tax purposes. It will have no salvage value at the end of four years. The investment in this new machinery would require an additional $3,000 investment of working capital.

If Rockyford accepts this investment proposal, the disposal of the old machinery and the investment in the new one will occur on December 31 of this year. The cash flows from the investment will occur during the next four calendar years.

Rockyford is subject to a 40 percent income tax rate for all ordinary income and capital gains and has a 10 percent after-tax cost of capital. All operating and tax cash flows are assumed to occur at year-end.

Required   Determine

1. The present value of the after-tax cash flow arising from disposing of the old machinery.
2. The present value of the after-tax cash flows for the next four years attributable to the operating cash savings.
3. The present value of the tax shield effect of depreciation at the end of year 1.
4. Which one of the following is the proper treatment for the $3,000 working capital required in the current year?
   a. It should be ignored in capital budgeting because it is not a capital investment.
   b. It is a sunk cost that needs no consideration in capital budgeting.
   c. It should be treated as part of the initial investment when determining the net present value.
   d. It should be spread over the machinery's four-year life as a cash outflow in each of the years.
   e. It should be included as part of the cost of the new machine and depreciated.

(CMA Adapted)

Problems

20–34 Equipment Replacement The management of Devine Instrument Company is considering the purchase of a new drilling machine, model RoboDril 1010K. According to the specifications and testing results, RoboDril will substantially increase productivity over AccuDril X10, the machine Devine is currently using.

The AccuDril was acquired 8 years ago for $120,000 and is being depreciated over 10 years expected useful life with an estimated salvage value of $20,000. The engineering department expects the AccuDril to keep going for another three years after a major overhaul at the end of its expected useful life. The estimated cost for the overhaul is $100,000. The overhauled machine will be depreciated using straight-line depreciation with no salvage value. The overhaul will improve the machine's operating efficiency approximately 20 percent. No other operating conditions will be affected by the overhaul.

RoboDril 1010K is selling for $250,000. Installing, testing, rearranging, and training will cost another $30,000. The manufacturer is willing to take the AccuDril as a trade-in for $40,000. The RoboDril will be depreciated using the straight-line method with no salvage value. New technology most likely will make RoboDril obsolete to the firm in five years.

Variable operating cost for either machine is the same: $10 per hour. Other pertinent data follow:

	AccuDril X10	RoboDril 1010K
Units of output (per year)	10,000	10,000
Machine-hours	8,000	4,000
Selling price per unit	$ 100	$ 100
Variable manufacturing cost (not including machine-hours)	$ 40	$ 40
Other annual expenses (tooling and supervising)	$95,000	$55,000
Disposable value—today	$25,000	
Disposable value—in five years	0	$50,000

Devine Instrument Company's cost of funds is 12 percent, and it is in the 40 percent tax bracket.

Required

1. Determine the effect on cash flow for items that differ for the two alternatives.
2. Compute the payback period for purchasing RoboDril 1010K rather than having AccuDril X10 overhauled in two years.
3. What is the present value of each alternative?
4. What other factors, including strategic issues, should the firm consider before making the final decision?

20–35 Sensitivity Analysis Use the information in problem 20–34 to answer the following questions:

Required

1. What is the maximum machine operating cost of the overhauled AccuDril for the replacement decision to be an incorrect financial decision?
2. New technologies developed since the purchase of AccuDril X10 make it possible to overhaul this machine now for $80,000. Both the overhaul cost and the salvage value are to be depreciated over two years. The overhaul will improve its productivity by 20 percent and reduce the cost of a major overhaul two years from now to $30,000. All overhaul costs will be depreciated using the straight-line method. With either overhaul, the machine will have no salvage value. Either overhaul can be scheduled during regular maintenance and will not affect production. Despite the old saying, "If it ain't broke, don't fix it," should you overhaul it now or wait for two years to do the overhaul as planned originally, assuming that no funds are currently available to purchase RoboDril 1010K?
3. Performing the overhaul now also improves product quality. Management believes that the quality improvement is rather subtle and very difficult to quantify. Should the firm overhaul now?

20–36 Comparison of Capital Budgeting Techniques, Sensitivity, Strategy Nil Hill Corporation has been using its present facilities at their annual full capacity of 10,000 units for the last three years. Still, the company is unable to keep pace with continuing demand for the product that is estimated to be 25,000 units annually. This demand level is expected to continue for at least another four years. To expand manufacturing capacity and take advantage of the demand, Nil Hill must acquire equipment costing $995,000. The equipment will double the current production quantity. This equipment has a useful life of 10 years and can be sold for $195,000 at the end of year 4 or $35,000 at the end of year 10. Analysis of current operating data provides the following information:

			Per Unit
Sales price			$195
Variable costs			
Manufacturing	$90		
Marketing	10	$100	
Fixed costs			
Manufacturing	$45		
Other	25	70	170
Net income			$ 25

The fixed costs include depreciation expense of the current equipment. The new equipment will not change variable costs, but the firm will incur additional fixed manufacturing costs (excluding depreciation) of $250,000 annually. The firm needs to spend an additional $200,000 in fixed marketing costs per year for additional sales. Nil Hill is in the 30 percent tax bracket. Management has set a minimum rate of return of 14 percent for all capital investments.

Required

1. What effects will the new equipment have on net income in each of the four years?
2. What effect will the new equipment have on cash flows in each of the four years?
3. Compute the investment's payback period.
4. Compute the book rate of return based on the average investment.
5. Compute the net present value.
6. Compute the internal rate of return.
7. Management is unsure of the reliability of the estimated unit variable cost. What is the maximum deviation allowed for the original decision to remain unchanged for each of the following independent situations if
   a. The change will affect only the variable cost of the additional units to be manufactured by the new machine?
   b. The firm anticipates increases in competition. Management believes it will have to reduce the selling price of the product. How much can the firm decrease the selling price per unit and still afford to increase production capacity so that making this product remains a sound financial decision?

20–37 **Replacing a Small Machine: Capital Budgeting Techniques and Sensitivity Analysis** Hightec Corporation has a seven-year contract with Magichip Company to supply 10,000 units of XT-12 at $5 per unit. Increases in materials and other costs since signing the contract two years ago make this product a cash drain to Hightec. As the manager of the subsidiary that manufactures and sells XT-12, you have discovered that a new machine, SP1000, has a higher productivity. The following is a summary of pertinent information:

	Machine in Use	**SP1000**
Capacity	10,000 units/year	18,000 units/year
Materials	$4.00 per unit	$3.00 per unit
Labor and other variable costs	$1.00 per unit	$0.20 per unit
Maintenance costs	$1.00 per unit	$0.10 per unit

(For simplicity, assume that all revenues and expenses are received and paid at year-end.)

The current machine can be sold for $3,000 today. Its salvage value will be $1,000 if the firm continues to use the machine for another five years. The new machine costs $100,000, will be depreciated over a five-year life, and will have a net disposal value of $5,000 in five years. The company's cost of capital is 6 percent. If the company decides to keep the old machine, which is fully depreciated, production can continue with it for at least another five years. All machines are depreciated on a straight-line basis with no salvage value. The firm expects to continue to pay approximately 20 percent for both federal and state income taxes in the foreseeable future. At present the Magichip Company is the only user of XT-12.

Required   Compute

1. The effects on the cash flow each year if the new machine is purchased.
2. The net present value of the new machine.
3. The payback period of the new machine.
4. The internal rate of return on the new machine, assuming that the new machine's annual cash inflows were $25,000 and the new machine will have no salvage value at the end of its useful life.
5. The internal rate of return assuming that the after-tax cash flow returns for each of the years are

Year 1	$20,000
Year 2	$22,000
Year 3	$25,000
Year 4	$30,000
Year 5	$40,000

6. By how much can the variable costs of the new machine increase (or decrease) and the company be indifferent on the replacement, assuming all the other costs will be as estimated?

20–38   Capital Budgeting with Sum-of-Years'-Digits Depreciation   Bernie Company purchased a new machine with an estimated useful life of five years and no salvage value for $45,000. The machine is expected to produce net cash inflows from operations, before income taxes, as follows:

1st year	$ 9,000
2nd year	12,000
3rd year	15,000
4th year	9,000
5th year	8,000

Bernie will use the sum-of-the-years'-digits method to depreciate the new machine in its accounting records. Bernie uses 10 percent for evaluating capital investments and is currently in a 24 percent income tax bracket.

Required   Compute the

1. Payback period.
2. Net present value.
3. Internal rate of return.

(CPA Adapted)

20–39   Working Backward: Determine Initial Investment Based on Book Rate of Return   Bread Company is planning to purchase a new machine that it will depreciate on a straight-line basis over 10 years. A full year's depreciation will be taken in the year of acquisition. The machine is expected to produce a net before taxes cash inflow of $6,750 from operations in each of the 10 years. The book rate of return is expected to be 10 percent on the initial increase in required investment. The firm's tax rate is 20 percent.

Required   What is the cost of the new machine?

(CPA Adapted)

20–40 **Working Backward: Determine Initial Investment Based on Internal Rate of Return**   Gene, Inc., invested in a machine with a useful life of six years and no salvage value. It depreciated the machine using the straight-line method; the machine was expected to produce a $20,000 annual cash inflow from operations, after cash expenses but before taxes. Gene has determined that the time-adjusted rate of return on the investment is 10 percent. The firm is in the 20 percent tax bracket.

Required   What was the cost of the machine?

(CPA Adapted)

20–41 **Working Backward: Determine Periodic Cash Flow Based on Book Rate of Return**   Dillon, Inc., purchased a new machine for $60,000 on January 1, 2006. The machine is being depreciated on a straight-line basis over five years with no salvage value. The book rate of return is expected to be 15 percent on the initial investment. The machine will generate a uniform cash flow. The firm's tax rate is approximately 25 percent.

Required   What is the expected annual before taxes cash flow from operations from this investment?

(CPA Adapted)

20–42 **Machine Replacement and Sensitivity Analysis Without Considering Taxes**   Ann & Andy Machine Company bought a cutting machine, Model KC12, on March 5, 2007, for $5,000 cash. The estimated salvage value and estimated life were $600 and 11 years, respectively. On March 5, 2008, Ann, the company CEO, learned that she could purchase a different cutting machine, Model AC1, for $8,000 cash. The new machine would save the company an estimated $750 per year in operating costs compared to KC12. AC1 has an estimated salvage value of $400 and an estimated life of 10 years. The company could get $3,000 for KC12 on March 5, 2008. The company uses the straight-line method for depreciations and 12 percent rate of return.

Required

1. Compute, for AC1, the
   a. Payback period.
   b. Book rate of return using the average investment.
   c. Net present value.
   d. Internal rate of return.
2. Should the firm purchase AC1? Why?
3. What is the minimum (or maximum) savings that AC1 must have without altering your decision in requirement 2?

20–43 **Value of Accelerated Depreciation**   Freedom Corporation acquired a fixed asset for $100,000. Its estimated life was four years, and it had no estimated salvage value. Assume a relevant interest rate of 8 percent and an income tax rate of 40 percent.

Required

1. What is the present value of the tax benefits resulting from calculating depreciation using the sum-of-the-years'-digits method as opposed to the straight-line method on this asset?
2. What is the present value of the tax benefits resulting from calculating depreciation using the double-declining-balance method as opposed to straight-line method on this asset?
3. What is the present value of the tax benefits resulting from using MACRS as opposed to straight-line depreciation? The asset qualifies as a three-year asset.

(CPA Adapted)

20–44 **Capital Budgeting with Sensitivity Analysis**   Meidi Johnson has owned a medical professional building for the last 20 years. She leased the land from an adjacent medical school 22 years ago for 30 years and had the building constructed. At the end of the lease period, the medical school becomes the sole owner of the land, its improvements, and any structures on the land. The construction took two years. The building is in excellent condition and fully occupied at favorable rental rates. The value of the property has appreciated considerably. Because depreciation is based on the original construction cost, Meidi's taxable income is unusually large.

George Kardell, a commercial real estate broker, has approached Meidi with a proposal from a group of investors. He believes that Meidi can sell the building and the balance of the leasehold at a price that will be profitable to all parties. The sale, if made, would be a cash sale that will provide her with the cash she needs for another project. She is currently negotiating with a bank for financing of this other project she is considering. The bank is asking for 12 percent interest. Meidi, however, would use 10 percent as her cost of capital if she can sell the building for cash. The potential investor group's cost of capital is 12 percent.

The buyer is in the 30 percent tax bracket. Meidi believes that she has been paying a marginal income tax rate of 40 percent in the last five years, and she expects no change in the next eight years. Unfortunately for her, the tax law in effect since last year eliminates any special tax rate for capital gains earned. This condensed income statement is taken from Meidi's latest tax return.

Income Statement for 2006

Rental revenue		$2,000,000
Expenses		
Operations	$950,000	
Administration	70,000	
Property taxes	280,000	
Depreciation (straight line)	100,000	1,400,000
Net income before taxes		$ 600,000
Income taxes at 40 percent		240,000
Net income after taxes		$ 360,000

The buyer will use the straight-line depreciation method. No change in either rental revenue or expenses is expected.

Required

1. What is the maximum the buyer should pay?
2. What is the minimum selling price Meidi can accept if she has to pay George a 5 percent commission?
3. What is the maximum the buyer would be willing to pay if the purchase is for a MACRS five-year property?

20–45 **Cash Flow Analysis and NPV**   Lou Lewis, the president of the Lewisville Company, has asked you to give him an analysis of the best use of a warehouse the company owns.

a. Lewisville Company is currently leasing the warehouse to another company for $5,000 per month on a year-to-year basis.

b. The warehouse's estimated sales value is $200,000. A commercial Realtor believes that the price is likely to remain unchanged in the near future. The building originally cost $60,000 and is being depreciated at $1,500 annually. Its current net book value is $7,500.

c. Lewisville Company is seriously considering converting the warehouse into a factory outlet for furniture. The remodeling will cost $100,000 and will be modest because the major attraction will be rock-bottom prices. The remodeling will be depreciated over the next five years using the double-declining-balance method.

d. The inventory, cash, and receivables needed to open and sustain the factory outlet would be $600,000. This total is fully recoverable whenever operations terminate.

e. Lou is fairly certain that the warehouse will be condemned in 10 years to make room for a new highway. The firm most likely would receive $200,000 from the condemnation.

f. Estimated annual operating data, exclusive of depreciation, are

Sales	$900,000
Operation expenses	$500,000

g. Nonrecurring sales promotion costs at the beginning of year 1 are expected to be $100,000.

h. Nonrecurring termination costs at the end of year 5 are $50,000.

    i. The minimum annual rate of return desired is 14 percent. The company is in the 40 percent tax bracket.

Required

1. Show how you would handle the individual items in determining whether the company should continue to lease the space or convert it to a factory outlet. Use the company's analysis form, which is set up as follows:

			Cash Flows in Year					
Item	Description	Net Present Value	0	1	2	3	4	5
a.								
b.								
.								
.								
.								
i.								

Identify any item that is irrelevant.

2. After analyzing all relevant data, compute the net present value. Indicate which course of action, based only on these data, should be taken.

20–46 Machine Replacement with Tax Considerations A computer chip manufacturer spent $2,500,000 to develop a special-purpose molding machine. The machine has been used for one year and will be obsolete after four years. The firm uses straight-line depreciation for this machine.

    At the beginning of the second year, a machine salesperson offers a new, vastly more efficient machine. It will cost $2,000,000, will reduce annual cash manufacturing costs from $1,800,000 to $1,000,000, and will have zero disposal value at the end of three years. Management has decided to use the double-declining-balance depreciation method for tax purposes for this machine if purchased.

    The old machine's salvage value is $300,000 now and will be $50,000 three years from now; however, no salvage value is provided in calculating straight-line depreciation for tax purposes. The firm's income tax rate is 45 percent. The firm desires to earn a minimum after-tax rate of return of 8 percent.

Required Using the net present value technique, show whether the firm should purchase the new machine.

20–47 Equipment Replacement Oilers Company makes a computer desk that it sells for $30 under a contract to a large computer retailer. The company operates one shift in its Ohio plant. The annual normal capacity is 100,000 units.

    Oilers pays direct labor at $8.00 per hour. An employee can produce a desk in 2 hours. Each desk requires 8 board feet of hard board costing $0.25 per board foot. Indirect manufacturing costs (manufacturing overhead) at normal capacity of 100,000 units are described by the following budget line:

Total costs = Fixed costs + Variable cost per unit × units manufactured
Total costs = $25,000 + $0.30/unit × units manufactured

    Some years ago, Oilers installed a saw that now has a carrying (book) value of $20,000, which is being depreciated at $2,000 a year. At the time of installation, the saw was expected to have no salvage value at the end of its useful life because that value would equal its dismantling costs.

    A sales agent from Whalers Company is encouraging Oilers Company to replace the saw with a numerical saw. In addition to being able to perform precision cutting, the new saw also will reduce the time to make a desk by half and reduce the direct labor-hours required to produce one desk from 2 hours to 1 hour. Because the new saw is more powerful than the present one, utility costs are expected to increase by $0.10 per unit.

The new saw will cost $100,000, including installation, testing, and transportation charges. Its estimated useful life is 10 years and will be depreciated using the straight-line method with $10,000 estimated salvage value.

Whalers Company agrees that, if Oilers buys the saw, Whalers will buy the old one for $4,000 and charge Oilers no dismantling costs. The income tax rate is 40 percent. Oilers management expects a 15 percent return on investment. The loss on the trade-in of the current saw is allowable as an income tax deduction.

Required

1. As a financial analyst for Oilers, you are charged with analyzing the purchase of the new saw. In preparing a report for the president, you must determine the following for management's consideration:

   a. The contribution margin per unit under current operating conditions.

   b. The standard overhead rate (application rate) per unit under current operating conditions.

   c. The budget line for indirect manufacturing costs (manufactured overhead), assuming the purchase and installation of the new saw.

   d. The new saw's manufacturing overhead standard rate (application rate) is expected to remain the same if normal capacity is 100,000 units.

   e. The contribution margin per unit, assuming the sales price remains unchanged, if the new saw is purchased and installed.

   f. The net additional investment for the new saw, assuming that Oilers decides to purchase and install it.

   g. The expected net additional cash flow per year if the new saw is purchased and installed. Assume that the company sells all that it produces.

2. The firm will be able to reduce approximately half of the hourly production workers currently on its payroll if the new saw is purchased. The plant has been in its current location for more than 50 years. Over 40 percent of the households in this small southeast Ohio town have at least one member who works for the firm. Should the firm purchase the state-of-the-art equipment?

(IMA Adapted)

20–48 Equipment Replacement, MACRS   VacuTech is a high-technology company that manufactures sophisticated instruments for testing microcircuits. Each instrument sells for $3,500 and costs $2,450 to manufacture. An essential component of the company's manufacturing process is a sealed vacuum chamber where the interior approaches a pure vacuum. The technology of the vacuum pumps that the firm uses to prepare its chamber for sealing has been changing rapidly. On June 1, 2004, VacuTech bought the latest in electronic high-speed vacuum pumps that can evacuate a chamber for sealing in only six hours. The company paid $400,000 for the pump. Recently, the pump's manufacturer approached VacuTech with a new pump that would reduce the evacuation time to two hours.

VacuTech's management is considering the purchase of this new pump and has asked Doreen Harris, the company controller, to evaluate the financial impact of replacing it with the new model. Doreen has gathered the following information prior to preparing her analysis:

- The new pump could be installed on May 31, 2007, and placed in service on June 1, 2007. The pump's cost is $608,000; installing, testing, and debugging it will cost $12,000. The pump would be assigned to the three-year class for depreciation under the Modified Accelerated Cost Recovery System (MACRS) and is expected to have an $80,000 salvage value when it is sold at the end of four years. Depreciation on the equipment would be recognized starting in 2007, and MACRS rates would be as follows:

Year 1	33%
Year 2	45
Year 3	15
Year 4	7

- The current pump is being depreciated under MACRS and will be fully depreciated by the time the new pump is placed in service. If the firm purchases the new pump, it will sell the current pump for $50,000, its estimated salvage value at the time of purchase.

- At the current rate of production, the new pump's greater efficiency will result in annual cash savings of $125,000.
- VacuTech is able to sell all testing instruments that it can produce. Because of the new pump's increased speed, output is expected to increase by 30 units in 2007, 50 units in both 2008 and 2009, and 70 units in 2010. Manufacturing costs for all additional units would be reduced by $150 per unit.
- VacuTech is subject to a 40 percent tax rate. For evaluating capital investment proposals, management assumes that annual cash flows occur at the end of the year and uses a 16 percent after-tax discount rate.

Required

1. Determine whether VacuTech should purchase the new pump by calculating the net present value at January 1, 2007, of the estimated after-tax cash flows that would result from its acquisition.
2. Describe the factors, other than the net present value, that VacuTech should consider before making the pump replacement decision.

(CMA Adapted)

20–49 **Joint Venture**   Perez Group has the opportunity to enter into a joint venture giving it a 49 percent ownership with local investors in an emerging country. The firm would be required to invest the entire $3,000,000 initial outlay needed for the venture and would receive 80 percent of the expected $900,000 yearly profit for 10 years. At the end of 10 years, ownership will be turned over to the local investors. Cost of capital is 10 percent. Perez will accept projects only if its return on investment is more than 20 percent.

Required   Should Perez invest in the project?

20–50 **Risk and NPV**   J. Morgan of SparkPlug Inc. has been approached to take over a production facility from B.R. Machine Company. The acquisition will cost $1,500,000, and the after-tax net cash inflow will be $275,000 per year for 12 years.

SparkPlug currently uses 12 percent for its cost of capital. Tom Morgan, production manager, is very much in favor of the investment. He argues that the total after-tax net cash inflow is more than the cost of the investment, even if the demand for the product is somewhat uncertain. "The project will pay for itself even if the demand is only half the projected level." Cindy Morgan believes, however, that the cost of capital should be 16 percent because of the declining demand for SparkPlug products.

Required

1. Should Morgan accept the project if its cost of capital is 12 percent?
2. If Morgan is correct and uses 16 percent, does that change the investment decision?
3. Is adjusting the discount rate or the desired rate of return an effective way to deal with risk or uncertainty?

20–51 **Sensitivity Analysis**   Griffey & Son operate a plant in Cincinnati and are considering opening a new facility in Seattle. The initial outlay will be $3,500,000 and should produce after-tax net cash inflows of $600,000 per year for 15 years. Due to the effects of the ocean air in Seattle, however, the plant's useful life may be only 12 years. Cost of capital is 14 percent.

Required

1. Will the project be accepted if 15 years' useful life is assumed? What if 12 years of useful life is used?
2. How many years will be needed for the Seattle facility to earn at least a 14 percent return?

20–52 **Uneven Cash Flows**   MaxiCare Corporation, a not-for-profit organization, specializes in health care for senior citizens. Management is considering whether to expand operations by opening a new chain of care centers in the inner city of large metropolises. For a new facility initial cash outlays for lease, renovations, working capital, training, and other costs are expected to be about $15 million in year 0. The firm expects the cash inflows of each new facility in its first year of operation to equal the total cash outlays for the year. Net cash inflows are expected to increase to $1 million in each of years 2 and 3, $2.5 million in year 4, and $3 million in each of years 5 through 10. The lease agreement for the facility will expire at the end of year 10, and the firm expects the cost to close a facility will pretty much exhaust all cash proceeds from the disposal. Cost of capital for the firm is 12 percent.

Required   Compute the net present value for this venture.

20–53   **Environment Cost Management**   Myers Manufacturing, Inc., wants to build a booth for painting the boxes it makes for small transformers to be used to power neon signs. The company can choose either a solvent-based or a powder paint process. The following table summarizes the costs and investment required by each approach:

	Solvent Paint System	Powder Paint System
Initial investment	$400,000	$1,200,000
Unit paint cost	0.19	0.20
Estimated life in years	10	10
Annual units	2,000,000	2,000,000

The firm will incur additional environmental costs with the solvent paint system but not with the powder paint system. The firm estimates annual environmental costs for the solvent paint system as follows:

	Units	Unit Cost
Monthly pit cleaning	12	$1,000
Hazardous waste disposal	183	3,000
Superfund fee	18,690	0.17
Worker training	2	1,500
Insurance	1	10,000
Amortization of air-emission permit	0.2	1,000
Air-emission fee	44.6	25
Record keeping	0.25	45,000
Wastewater treatment	1	50,000

The firm estimates its cost of capital to be 12 percent. Either system is a 10-year property under MACRS. The firm pays a total of 40 percent in income taxes.

Required

1. Without considering environmental costs, what is the difference in cost in today's dollar for the two systems?
2. What is the most the firm is willing to pay for the powder-based system?

   (Adapted from German Boer, Margaret Curtin, and Louis Hoyt, "Environmental Cost Management," *Management Accounting* [September 1998], pp. 28–38.)

Solution to Self-Study Problem

Capital Budgeting for Expanding Production Capacity

1. | Cost of the new equipment | $580,000 |
   |---|---|
   | Installation, testing, and training | 12,000 |
   | Renovation cost for the leased warehouse | 58,000 |
   | Total cash outflow in year 0 | $650,000 |

The total cash outflow for the initial investment is $650,000.

2.

Sales		$200 \times 5,000 =$		$1,000,000
Cost of goods sold				
Variable manufacturing costs per unit		$ 60		
Fixed manufacturing costs				
Additional fixed manufacturing overhead:				
($140,000 + 10,000)/5,000 units =		30		
Depreciation on new equipment				
(650,000 − $50,000)/4 = $150,000 per year				
$150,000/5,000 units per year =		30		
Manufacturing cost per unit		$ 120		
Number of units		$\times$ 5,000		600,000
Gross margin				$ 400,000
Marketing and administrative expenses				
Variable marketing expenses per unit	$20			
Number of units	$\times$ 5,000	$100,000		
Additional fixed marketing expenses		100,000		200,000
Net income before taxes				$ 200,000
Income taxes				80,000
Net income				$ 120,000

The firm can expect its net income to increase by $120,000 each year in years 1, 2, and 3; net income in year 4 will be $108,000 as computed here:

Net income before restoration expenses		$120,000
Restoration expenses	$20,000	
Decrease in income taxes	8,000	12,000
Increase in net income in year 4		$108,000

3.

	Each of Years 1 to 3	Year 4
Net income after taxes	$120,000	$108,000
Add: Expenses not requiring cash disbursement:		
Depreciation included in fixed costs $30 $\times$ 5,000 =	150,000	150,000
Cash inflow from disposal of equipment		50,000
Total cash flow return	$270,000	$308,000

Thus, the net cash inflow will be $270,000 each year for the first three years and will be $308,000 in year four.

4. Payback period $= \dfrac{\$650,000}{\$270,000} = 2.407$ years

Or 2 years and 5 months.

5. Average investment = ($650,000 + $50,000)/2 = $350,000
   Average net income = ($120,000 $\times$ 3 + $108,000)/4 = $117,000
   Book rate of return = $117,000/$350,000 = 33.43 percent

6. PV of net cash inflows in year 1 to year 3 at 12%:

$270,000 $\times$ 2.402 =	$648,540
PV of net cash inflows in year 4 at 12%:	
$308,000 $\times$ 0.636 =	195,888
Total PV of net cash inflows	$844,428
Initial investment	650,000
NPV	194,428

7.

PV of net cash inflows at 25 percent	$653,320	$653,320
Initial investment		$650,000
PV of net cash inflows at 30 percent	598,120	
Difference in PV of net cash inflows	$ 55,200	$ 3,320

Therefore, the internal rate of return is

$$25\% + \frac{\$3{,}320}{\$55{,}200} \times 5\% = 25.3\%$$

8. _____

	A	B	C
			Keystroke
1	**Cash Flow**		
2	Year 0	$(650,000)	
3	Year 1	$ 270,000	
4	Year 2	$ 270,000	
5	Year 3	$ 270,000	
6	Year 4	$ 308,000	
7	Present Value	$ 844,234	= NPV(0.12,B3:B6)
8	NPV	$ 194,234	= B7 + B2
9	IRR	25.27%	= IRR(B2:B6)

9. The most that the after-tax net cash inflows per year can be

decreased is $194,428/3.037 =	$ 64,020
Add income taxes	42,680
The most that variable cost per year can increase	$106,700

Therefore, the variable cost per unit can increase by $106,700/5,000, or $21.34 per unit, and the firm still will earn 12 percent on the investment.

PRESENT VALUE TABLES

Table 1 Present Value of $1

Periods	4%	5%	6%	7%	8%	9%	10%	11%	12%	13%	14%	15%	20%	25%	30%
1	0.962	0.952	0.943	0.935	0.926	0.917	0.909	0.901	0.893	0.885	0.877	0.870	0.833	0.800	0.769
2	0.925	0.907	0.890	0.873	0.857	0.842	0.826	0.812	0.797	0.783	0.769	0.756	0.694	0.640	0.592
3	0.889	0.864	0.840	0.816	0.794	0.772	0.751	0.731	0.712	0.693	0.675	0.658	0.579	0.512	0.455
4	0.855	0.823	0.792	0.763	0.735	0.708	0.683	0.659	0.636	0.613	0.592	0.572	0.482	0.410	0.350
5	0.822	0.784	0.747	0.713	0.681	0.650	0.621	0.593	0.567	0.543	0.519	0.497	0.402	0.328	0.269
6	0.790	0.746	0.705	0.666	0.630	0.596	0.564	0.535	0.507	0.480	0.456	0.432	0.335	0.262	0.207
7	0.760	0.711	0.665	0.623	0.583	0.547	0.513	0.482	0.452	0.425	0.400	0.376	0.279	0.210	0.159
8	0.731	0.677	0.627	0.582	0.540	0.502	0.467	0.434	0.404	0.376	0.351	0.327	0.233	0.168	0.123
9	0.703	0.645	0.592	0.544	0.500	0.460	0.424	0.391	0.361	0.333	0.308	0.284	0.194	0.134	0.094
10	0.676	0.614	0.558	0.508	0.463	0.422	0.386	0.352	0.322	0.295	0.270	0.247	0.162	0.107	0.073
11	0.650	0.585	0.527	0.475	0.429	0.388	0.350	0.317	0.287	0.261	0.237	0.215	0.135	0.086	0.056
12	0.625	0.557	0.497	0.444	0.397	0.356	0.319	0.286	0.257	0.231	0.208	0.187	0.112	0.069	0.043
13	0.601	0.530	0.469	0.415	0.368	0.326	0.290	0.258	0.229	0.204	0.182	0.163	0.093	0.055	0.033
14	0.577	0.505	0.442	0.388	0.340	0.299	0.263	0.232	0.205	0.181	0.160	0.141	0.078	0.044	0.025
15	0.555	0.481	0.417	0.362	0.315	0.275	0.239	0.209	0.183	0.160	0.140	0.123	0.065	0.035	0.020
16	0.534	0.458	0.394	0.339	0.292	0.252	0.218	0.188	0.163	0.141	0.123	0.107	0.054	0.028	0.015
17	0.513	0.436	0.371	0.317	0.270	0.231	0.198	0.170	0.146	0.125	0.108	0.093	0.045	0.023	0.012
18	0.494	0.416	0.350	0.296	0.250	0.212	0.180	0.153	0.130	0.111	0.095	0.081	0.038	0.018	0.009
19	0.475	0.396	0.331	0.277	0.232	0.194	0.164	0.138	0.116	0.098	0.083	0.070	0.031	0.014	0.007
20	0.456	0.377	0.312	0.258	0.215	0.178	0.149	0.124	0.104	0.087	0.073	0.061	0.026	0.012	0.005
22	0.422	0.342	0.278	0.226	0.184	0.150	0.123	0.101	0.083	0.068	0.056	0.046	0.018	0.007	0.003
24	0.390	0.310	0.247	0.197	0.158	0.126	0.102	0.082	0.066	0.053	0.043	0.035	0.013	0.005	0.002
25	0.375	0.295	0.233	0.184	0.146	0.116	0.092	0.074	0.059	0.047	0.038	0.030	0.010	0.004	0.001
30	0.308	0.231	0.174	0.131	0.099	0.075	0.057	0.044	0.033	0.026	0.020	0.015	0.004	0.001	0.000
35	0.253	0.181	0.130	0.094	0.068	0.049	0.036	0.026	0.019	0.014	0.010	0.008	0.002	0.000	0.000
40	0.208	0.142	0.097	0.067	0.046	0.032	0.022	0.015	0.011	0.008	0.005	0.004	0.001	0.000	0.000

Table 2 Present Value of Annuity of $1

Periods	4%	5%	6%	7%	8%	9%	10%	11%	12%	13%	14%	15%	20%	25%	30%
1	0.962	0.952	0.943	0.935	0.926	0.917	0.909	0.901	0.893	0.885	0.877	0.870	0.833	0.800	0.769
2	1.886	1.859	1.833	1.808	1.783	1.759	1.736	1.713	1.690	1.668	1.647	1.626	1.528	1.440	1.361
3	2.775	2.723	2.673	2.624	2.577	2.531	2.487	2.444	2.402	2.361	2.322	2.283	2.106	1.952	1.816
4	3.630	3.546	3.465	3.387	3.312	3.240	3.170	3.102	3.037	2.974	2.914	2.855	2.589	2.362	2.166
5	4.452	4.329	4.212	4.100	3.993	3.890	3.791	3.696	3.605	3.517	3.433	3.352	2.991	2.689	2.436
6	5.242	5.076	4.917	4.767	4.623	4.486	4.355	4.231	4.111	3.998	3.889	3.784	3.326	2.951	2.643
7	6.002	5.786	5.582	5.389	5.206	5.033	4.868	4.712	4.564	4.423	4.288	4.160	3.605	3.161	2.802
8	6.733	6.463	6.210	5.971	5.747	5.535	5.335	5.146	4.968	4.799	4.639	4.487	3.837	3.329	2.925
9	7.435	7.108	6.802	6.515	6.247	5.995	5.759	5.537	5.328	5.132	4.946	4.772	4.031	3.463	3.019
10	8.111	7.722	7.360	7.024	6.710	6.418	6.145	5.889	5.650	5.426	5.216	5.019	4.192	3.571	3.092
11	8.760	8.306	7.887	7.499	7.139	6.805	6.495	6.207	5.938	5.687	5.453	5.234	4.327	3.656	3.147
12	9.385	8.863	8.384	7.943	7.536	7.161	6.814	6.492	6.194	5.918	5.660	5.421	4.439	3.725	3.190
13	9.986	9.394	8.853	8.358	7.904	7.487	7.103	6.750	6.424	6.122	5.842	5.583	4.533	3.780	3.223
14	10.563	9.899	9.295	8.745	8.244	7.786	7.367	6.982	6.628	6.302	6.002	5.724	4.611	3.824	3.249
15	11.118	10.380	9.712	9.108	8.559	8.061	7.606	7.191	6.811	6.462	6.142	5.847	4.675	3.859	3.268
16	11.652	10.838	10.106	9.447	8.851	8.313	7.824	7.379	6.974	6.604	6.265	5.954	4.730	3.887	3.283
17	12.166	11.274	10.477	9.763	9.122	8.544	8.022	7.549	7.120	6.729	6.373	6.047	4.775	3.910	3.295
18	12.659	11.690	10.828	10.059	9.372	8.756	8.201	7.702	7.250	6.840	6.467	6.128	4.812	3.928	3.304
19	13.134	12.085	11.158	10.336	9.604	8.950	8.365	7.839	7.366	6.938	6.550	6.198	4.843	3.942	3.311
20	13.590	12.462	11.470	10.594	9.818	9.129	8.514	7.963	7.469	7.025	6.623	6.259	4.870	3.954	3.316
22	14.451	13.163	12.042	11.061	10.201	9.442	8.772	8.176	7.645	7.170	6.743	6.359	4.909	3.970	3.323
24	15.247	13.799	12.550	11.469	10.529	9.707	8.985	8.348	7.784	7.283	6.835	6.434	4.937	3.981	3.327
25	15.622	14.094	12.783	11.654	10.675	9.823	9.077	8.422	7.843	7.330	6.873	6.464	4.948	3.985	3.329
30	17.292	15.372	13.765	12.409	11.258	10.274	9.427	8.694	8.055	7.496	7.003	6.566	4.979	3.995	3.332
35	18.665	16.374	14.498	12.948	11.655	10.567	9.644	8.855	8.176	7.586	7.070	6.617	4.992	3.998	3.333
40	19.793	17.159	15.046	13.332	11.925	10.757	9.779	8.951	8.244	7.634	7.105	6.642	4.997	3.999	3.333

A

abnormal spoilage   An unacceptable unit that should not arise under efficient operating conditions

absolute quality conformance (robust quality approach)   Conformance that requires all products or services to meet the target value exactly with no variation

activity   Composed of actions, movements, or work sequences, it is work performed within an organization

activity analysis   The development of a detailed description of the specific activities performed in the firm's operations

activity-based budgeting (ABB)   A budgeting process that focuses on costs of activities or cost drivers necessary for production and sales

activity-based costing (ABC)   An analysis used to improve the accuracy of cost analysis by improving the tracing of costs to products or individual customers

activity-based management (ABM)   An activity analysis used to improve operational control and management control

activity cost driver   Measures how much of an activity a cost object uses

actual costing system   A costing process that uses actual costs incurred for direct materials and direct labor and assigns or applies actual factory overhead to various jobs

actual factory overhead   Costs incurred in an accounting period for indirect materials, indirect labor, and other indirect factory costs, including factory rent, insurance, property tax, depreciation, repairs and maintenance, power, light, heat, and employer payroll taxes for factory personnel

additional processing costs or **separable costs**   Costs that occur after the split-off point and can be identified directly with individual products

advance pricing agreement (APA)   An agreement between the Internal Revenue Service (IRS) and the firm using transfer prices, that establishes the agreed-upon transfer price

analysis of variance table   A table that separates the total variance of the dependent variable into both error and explained variance components

appraisal costs   Costs incurred in the measurement and analysis of data to ascertain if products and services conform to specifications

arm's-length standard   A transfer price set to reflect the price that unrelated parties acting independently would have set

asset turnover   The amount of sales dollar achieved per dollar of investment; measures the manager's ability to increase sales from a given level of investment

authoritative standard   A standard determined solely or primarily by management

average cost   The total of manufacturing cost (materials, labor, and overhead) divided by units of output

average cost method   A method that uses units of output to allocate joint costs to joint products

B

balanced scorecard   An accounting report that includes the firm's critical success factors in four areas: (1) financial performance, (2) customer satisfaction, (3) internal business processes, and (4) innovation and learning

basic engineering   The method in which product designers work independently from marketing and manufacturing to develop a design from specific plans and specifications

batch-level activity   An activity performed for each batch of products rather than for each unit of production

benchmarking   A process by which a firm identifies its critical success factors, studies the best practices of other firms (or other units within a firm) for achieving these critical success factors, and then implements improvements in the firm's processes to match or beat the performance of those competitors

benefits   Special benefits for the employee, such as travel, membership in a fitness club, tickets to entertainment events, and other extras paid for by the firm

bill of materials   A detailed list of the components of the manufactured product

bonus   Compensation based on the achievement of performance goals for the period

book rate of return   The average net income from an investment as a percentage of its book value

breakeven point   The point at which revenues equal total cost and profit is zero

budget   A quantitative plan of operations for an organization; it identifies the resources and commitments required to fulfill the organization's goals for the budgeted period

budgeting   The process of preparing a budget

budget slack   The difference between budgeted performance and expected performance

by-products   Products whose total sales values are minor in comparison with the sales value of the joint products

C

capital budgeting   A process for evaluating an organization's proposed long-range major projects

capital investment   An investment that requires committing a large sum of funds to projects with expenditures and benefits expected to stretch well into the future

cash budget   A budget that brings together the anticipated effects of all budgeted activities on cash

cause-and-effect diagram   A diagram that maps out a list of causes that affect an activity, process, stated problem, or a desired outcome

comparable price method   Establishes an arm's-length price by using the sales prices of similar products made by unrelated firms

computer-aided design (CAD)   The use of computers in product development, analysis, and design modification to improve the quality and performance of the product

computer-aided manufacturing (CAM)   The use of computers to plan, implement, and control production

computer-integrated manufacturing (CIM)   A manufacturing system that totally integrates all office and factory functions within a company via a computer-based information network, to allow hour-by-hour manufacturing management

concurrent engineering   An engineering method that integrates product design with manufacturing and marketing throughout the product's life cycle; also called simultaneous engineering

confidence interval   A range around the regression line within which the management accountant can be confident the actual value of the predicted cost will fall

constraints   Those activities that slow the product's total cycle time

continuous budget   A budgeting system that has in effect a budget for a set number of months, quarters, or years at all times

continuous improvement (The Japanese word is *kaizen.*)   A management technique in which managers and workers commit to a program of continuous improvement in quality and other critical success factors

contract manufacturing   The practice of having another manufacturer (sometimes a direct competitor) manufacture a portion of the firm's products

contribution by SBU (CSBU)   A measurement of *all* the costs traceable to, and therefore controllable by, the individual profit SBUs

contribution income statement   Focuses on variable costs and fixed costs, in contrast to the conventional income statement which focuses on product costs and nonproduct costs

contribution margin income statement   An income statement based on contribution margin that is developed for each profit SBU and for each relevant group of profit SBUs

contribution margin ratio   The ratio of the unit contribution margin to unit sales price $(p - v)/p$

control chart   A graph that depicts successive observations of an operation taken at constant intervals

controllable cost   A cost that a manager or employee has discretion in choosing to incur or can significantly influence the amount of within a given, usually short, period of time

controllable fixed costs   Fixed costs that the profit SBU manager can influence in approximately a year or less

controllable margin   A margin determined by subtracting short-term controllable fixed costs from the contribution margin

conversion cost   Direct labor and overhead combined into a single amount

core competencies   Skills or competencies that the firm employs especially well

correlation   A given variable tends to change predictably in the same or opposite direction for a given change in the other, correlated variable

cost allocation   The process of assigning indirect costs to cost pools and cost objects

cost assignment   The assignment of indirect costs to cost pools and cost objects

cost driver   Any factor that causes a change in the cost of an activity

cost driver analysis   The examination, quantification, and explanation of the effects of cost drivers

cost element   An amount paid for a resource consumed by an activity and included in a cost pool

cost estimation   The development of a well-defined relationship between a cost object and its cost drivers for the purpose of predicting the cost

cost leadership   A competitive strategy in which a firm succeeds in producing products or services at the lowest cost in the industry

cost life cycle   The sequence of activities within the firm that begins with research and development, followed by design, manufacturing, marketing/distribution, and customer service

cost management information   The information the manager needs to effectively manage the firm or not-for-profit organization

cost object   Any product, service, customer, activity, or organizational unit to which costs are accumulated for some management purpose

cost of capital   A composite of the cost of various sources of funds comprising a firm's capital structure

cost of goods manufactured   The cost of goods that were finished and transferred out of Work-in-Process Inventory account this period

cost of goods sold   The cost of the product transferred to the income statement when inventory is sold

cost of quality report   A report that shows the costs of prevention, appraisal, internal, and external failures. An important type of cost of quality report is the quality matrix, which shows the different quality costs for each operating and support function

cost-plus method   A method that determines the transfer price based on the seller's costs plus a gross profit percentage determined by comparing the seller's sales to that of unrelated parties

cost pools   Costs that are collected into meaningful groups

cost SBU   Production or support SBUs within the firm that have the goal of providing the best quality product or service at the lowest cost

costs of conformance   Costs of prevention and appraisal

costs of nonconformance   Costs of internal failure and external failure

costs of quality   Costs associated with the prevention, identification, repair, and rectification of poor quality and opportunity costs from lost production time and sales as a result of poor quality

cost tables   Computer-based databases that include comprehensive information about the firm's cost drivers

cost-volume-profit (CVP) analysis   A method for analyzing how various operating decisions and marketing decisions will affect net income

critical success factors (CSFs)   Measures of those aspects of the firm's performance that are essential to its competitive advantage and, therefore to its success

currently attainable standard   A level of performance that workers with proper training and experience can attain most of the time without extraordinary effort

customer cost analysis   Identifies cost activities and cost drivers related to customers

customer profitability analysis   Process that traces and reports customer revenues and customer costs

customer revenue analysis   Traces selling price, sales discounts, and cash discounts to customers and identifies financing costs associated with customer revenues

CVP graph   Illustrates how the levels of revenues and total costs change over different levels of output

cycle time   The amount of time between receipt of a customer order and shipment of the order

D

degrees of freedom   Represents the number of independent choices that can be made for each component of variance

denominator activity   The desired operating level at the expected operating efficiency for the period, expressed in the quantity of the activity measure for applying fixed factory overhead

departmental overhead rate   An overhead rate calculated for a single production department

dependent variable   The cost to be estimated

design analysis   A common form of value engineering in which the design team prepares several possible designs of the product, each having similar features with different levels of performance and different costs

desired rate of return   The minimum rate of return the investing firm requires for the investment

differential cost   A cost that differs for each decision option and is therefore relevant

differentiation   A competitive strategy in which a firm succeeds by developing and maintaining a unique value for the product as perceived by consumers

direct cost   A cost conveniently and economically traced directly to a cost pool or a cost object

direct labor cost   The labor used to manufacture the product or to provide the service

direct labor efficiency variance   The difference in the number of hours worked and the number of standard direct labor-hours allowed for the units manufactured multiplied by the standard hourly rate

direct labor rate variance   The difference between the actual and standard hourly wage rate multiplied by the actual direct hours used in production

direct materials cost   The cost of the materials in the product and a reasonable allowance for scrap and defective units

direct materials flexible budget variance   The difference between direct material costs incurred and the total standard cost for the direct materials in the flexible budget for the units manufactured during the period

direct materials price variance   The difference between the actual and standard unit price of the direct materials multiplied by the actual quantity of the direct materials purchased

direct materials usage budget   A plan that shows the direct materials required for production and their budgeted cost

direct materials usage variance   The product of the difference between the number of units of direct materials used during the period and the number of standard units of direct materials that should have been used for the number of units of the product manufactured during the period and the standard unit price of the direct materials

direct method   Cost allocation accomplished by using the service flows *only to production departments* and determining each production department's share of that service

discounted-cash flow (DCF techniques)   A technique that evaluates a capital investment by considering equivalent present values of all future cash flows from the initial investment

discretionary-cost method   Used when costs are considered largely uncontrollable; apply discretion at the planning stage; an input-oriented approach

drum-buffer-rope system   A system for balancing the flow of production through a constraint, thereby reducing the amount of inventory at the constraint and improving overall productivity

dual allocation   A cost allocation method that separates fixed and variable costs. Variable costs are directly traced to user departments, and fixed costs are allocated on some logical basis

Durbin-Watson statistic   A measure of the extent of nonlinearity in the regression

E

economic value added (EVA)   A business unit's income after taxes and after deducting the cost of capital

effective operation   The attainment of the goal set for the operation

efficient operation   An operation that wastes no resources

employment contract   An agreement between the manager and top management, designed to provide incentives for the manager to act independently to achieve top management's objectives

engineered-cost method   An output-oriented method that considers costs to be variable and therefore controllable

equivalent units   The number of the same or similar completed units that could have been produced given the amount of work actually performed on both completed and partially completed units

executional cost drivers   Factors that the firm can manage in the short term to reduce costs such as workforce involvement, design of the production process, and supplier relationships

expropriation   A foreign government takes ownership and control of assets a domestic investor has invested in that country

external failure costs   Costs incurred to rectify quality defects after unacceptable products or services reach the customer and lost profit opportunities caused by the unacceptable products or services delivered

F

facility-sustaining activity   An activity performed to support the production of products in general

factory overhead   All the indirect costs commonly combined into a single cost pool in a manufacturing firm

factory overhead applied   The amount of overhead assigned to a specific job using a predetermined factory overhead rate

FIFO method   A process costing method for calculating the unit cost that includes only costs incurred and work effort during the current period

financial budget   A plan that identifies sources and uses of funds for budgeted operations to achieve the expected operating results for the period

financial productivity   The ratio of output to the dollar amount of one or more input factors

finished goods inventory   The cost of goods that are ready for sale

firmwide pool   A basis for determining the bonus available to all managers through an amount set aside for this purpose

first difference   For each variable, the difference between each value and the succeeding value in the time series

fixed cost   The portion of the total cost that does not change with a change in the quantity of the cost driver, within the relevant range

fixed factory overhead application rate   The rate at which the firm applies fixed overhead costs to cost objects

fixed factory overhead production volume variance   The difference between the budgeted allowance for fixed factory overhead for the period and the applied fixed factory overhead

fixed factory overhead spending (budget) variance   The difference between the actual amount incurred and the budgeted amount for the fixed factory overhead

flexible budget   A budget that adjusts revenues and costs for changes in output achieved

flexible budget variance   The difference between the actual operating result and the flexible budget at the actual operating level of the period

flexible manufacturing system (FMS)   A computerized network of automated equipment that produces one or more groups of parts or variations of a product in a flexible manner

flow diagram   A flow chart of the work done that shows the sequence of processes and the amount of time required for each

F-statistic   A useful measure of the statistical reliability of the regression

full-cost method   The transfer price set equal to the variable cost plus allocated fixed cost for the selling unit

functional analysis   A common type of value engineering in which the performance and cost of each major function or feature of the product is examined

G

goal congruence   The consistency between the goals of the firm and the goals of its employees. It is achieved when the manager acts independently in such a way as to simultaneously achieve top management's objectives

goalpost conformance (zero-defects conformance)   Conformance to a quality specification expressed as a specified range around a target

gross book value (GBV)   The historical cost without the reduction for depreciation

group technology   A method of identifying similarities in the parts of products a firm manufactures, so the same part can be used in two or more products, thereby reducing costs

H

high-low method   A method using algebra to determine a *unique* estimation line between representative low and high points in the data

histogram   A graphical representation of the frequency of attributes or events in a given set of data

historical cost   The book value of current assets plus the net book value of the long-lived assets

I

ideal standard   A standard that demands perfect implementation and maximum efficiency in every aspect of the operation

implementation error   A deviation from the standard that occurs during operations as a result of operators' errors

independent variable   The cost driver used to estimate the value of the dependent variable

indirect cost   A cost that is not conveniently or economically traceable from the cost or cost pool to the cost pool or cost object

indirect labor cost   Supervision, quality control, inspection, purchasing and receiving, and other manufacturing support costs

indirect materials cost   The cost of materials used in manufacturing that are not physically part of the finished product

internal accounting controls   A set of policies and procedures that restrict and guide activities in the processing of financial data with the objective to prevent or detect errors and fraudulent acts

internal failure costs   Costs incurred as a result of poor quality found through appraisal prior to delivery to customers

internal rate of return (IRR) method   A discounted cash flow method that estimates the discount rate that causes the present value of subsequent net cash inflows to equal the initial investment

investment SBU   An SBU that includes assets employed by the SBU as well as profits in performance evaluation

ISO 9000   A set of guidelines for quality management and quality standards developed by the International Organization for Standardization in Geneva, Switzerland

J

job costing   A product costing system that accumulates and assigns costs to a specific job

job cost sheet   A cost sheet that records and summarizes the costs of direct materials, direct labor, and factory overhead for a particular job

joint products   Products from the same production process that have relatively substantial sales values

just-in-time (JIT) system   A comprehesive production and inventory system that purchases or produces materials and parts only as needed and just in time to be used at each stage of the production process

K

kaizen budgeting   A budgeting approach that explicitly demands continuous improvement and incorporates all the expected improvements in the resultant budget

kanban   A set of control cards used to signal the need for materials and products to move from one operation to the next in an assembly line

L

learning curve analysis   A systematic method for estimating costs when learning is present

learning rate   The percentage by which average time (or total time) falls from previous levels, as output doubles

least squares regression   One of the most effective methods for estimating costs, found by minimizing the sum of the squares of the estimation errors

life-cycle costing   A management technique used to identify and monitor the costs of a product throughout its life cycle

liquidation value   The price that could be received for the sale of the assets

long-range plan   A plan that identifies which actions are required during the 5- to 10-year period covered by the plan to attain the firm's strategic goal

M

management compensation plans   Policies and procedures for compensating managers

management control   The evaluation of mid-level managers by upper-level managers

manufacturing cycle efficiency (MCE)   The ratio of processing time to total cycle time

marginal cost   The additional cost incurred as the cost driver increases by one unit

margin of safety   A measure of the potential effect of a change in sales on profit

margin of safety ratio   A useful measure for comparing the risk of two alternative products, or for assessing the riskiness in any given product

market price method   The transfer price set as the current price for the selling unit's product in the market

market share variance   A comparison of the firm's actual market share to its budgeted market share and measurement of the effect of changes in the firm's market share on its total contribution margin and operating income

market size variance   A measure of the effect of changes in the total market size on the firm's total contribution margin and operating income

mass customization   A management technique in which marketing and production processes are designed to handle the increased variety that results from delivering customized products and services to customers

master budget   A plan of operations for a business unit during a specific period

materials inventory   The cost of the supply of materials used in the manufacturing process or to provide the service

materials requisition form   A source document that the production department supervisor uses to request materials for production

materials usage ratio   The ratio of quantity used over quantity purchased

mean squared variance   The ratio of the amount of variance of a component to the number of degrees of freedom for that component

measurement errors Incorrect numbers resulting from improper or inaccurate accounting systems or procedures

merchandise purchase budget A plan that shows the amount of merchandise the firm needs to purchase during the period

mixed cost The total cost when it includes both variable and fixed cost components

modeling error A deviation from the standard because of the failure to include all relevant variables or because of the inclusion of wrong or irrelevant variables in the standard-setting process

multicollinearity The condition when two or more independent variables are highly correlated with each other

N

negotiated price method The determination of a transfer price through a negotiation process and sometimes arbitration between units

net book value The asset's historical cost less accumulated depreciation

net present value (NPV) The excess of the present value of future cash flow returns over the initial investment

net realizable value (NRV) The estimated sales value of the product at the split-off point is determined by subtracting the additional processing and selling costs beyond the split-off point from the ultimate sales value of the product

network diagram A flowchart of the work done that shows the sequence of processes and the amount of time required for each

nonconstant variance The condition when the variance of the errors is not constant over the range of the independent variable

noncontrollable fixed costs Costs that are not controllable within a year's time, usually including facilities-related costs such as depreciation, taxes, and insurance

non-value-added activity An activity that does not contribute to customer value or to the organization's needs

normal costing system A costing process that uses actual costs for direct materials and direct labor and applies factory overhead to various jobs using a predetermined basis

normal spoilage An unacceptable unit that occurs under efficient operating conditions

O

operating budgets Plans that identify resources needed in operating activities and the acquisition of these resources

operating income flexible budget variance The difference between the flexible budget operating income for the units sold during the period and the actual operating income earned

operating income variance The difference between the actual operating income of the period and the master budget operating income projected for the period

operating leverage The ratio of the contribution margin to profit

operational control The evaluation of operating-level employees by mid-level managers

operational productivity The ratio of output to the number of units of an input factor

operation costing A hybrid costing system that uses job costing to assign direct materials costs and process costing to assign conversion costs to products or services

opportunity cost The benefit lost when choosing one option precludes receiving the benefits from an alternative option

order-filling costs Expenditures for freight, warehousing, packing and shipping, and collections

order-getting costs Expenditures to advertise and promote the product

outliers Unusual data points that strongly influence a regression analysis

overapplied overhead The amount of factory overhead applied that exceeds the actual factory overhead cost

overhead All the indirect costs commonly combined into a single cost pool

overhead application or allocation A process of assigning overhead costs to the appropriate jobs

P

Pareto analysis A management tool that shows 20 percent of a set of important cost drivers are responsible for 80 percent of the total cost incurred

Pareto diagram A histogram of the frequency of factors contributing to the quality problem, ordered from the most to the least frequent

partial productivity A productivity measure that focuses only on the relationship between one of the inputs and the output attained

participative standard Active participation throughout the standard-setting process by employees affected by the standard

payback period The length of time required for the cumulative total net cash inflows from an investment to equal the total initial cash outlays of the investment

performance evaluation The process by which managers at all levels gain information about the performance of tasks within the firm and judge that performance against preestablished criteria as set out in budgets, plans, and goals

performance measurement A measurement that identifies items that indicate the work performed and the results achieved by an activity, process, or organizational unit

period costs All nonproduct expenditures for managing the firm and selling the product

physical measure method A method that uses a physical measure such as pounds, gallons or yards or units or volume produced at the split-off point to allocate the joint costs to joint products

planning and decision making   Budgeting and profit planning, cash flow management, and other decisions related to operations

plantwide overhead rate   A single overhead rate used throughout the entire production facility

predetermined factory overhead rate   An estimated factory overhead rate used to apply factory overhead cost to a specific job

prediction error   A deviation from the standard because of an inaccurate estimation of the amounts for variables used in the standard-setting process

preparation of financial statements   Requires management to comply with the financial reporting requirements of regulatory agencies

present value   The current equivalent dollar value of a cash flow return, given the desired rate of return

present value payback method or breakeven time (BET)   A method using the span of time required for the cumulative present value of cash inflows to equal the initial investment of the project

prevention costs   Costs incurred to keep quality defects from occurring

prime costs   Direct materials and direct labor that are sometimes considered together

principal-agent model   A conceptual model that contains the key elements that contracts must have to achieve the desired objectives

process costing   A costing system that accumulates product or service costs by process or department and then assigns them to a large number of nearly identical products

product and service costing   In preparing financial statements, management complies with the financial reporting requirements of the industry and of regulatory agencies

product costing   The process of accumulating, classifying, and assigning direct materials, direct labor, and factory overhead costs to products or services

product costs   Only the costs necessary to complete the product (direct materials, direct labor, and factory overhead)

production budget   A plan for acquiring and combining the resources needed to carry out the manufacturing operations that allow the firm to satisfy its sales goals and have the desired amount of inventory at the end of the budget period

production cost report   A report that summarizes the physical units and equivalent units of a department, the costs incurred during the period, and the costs assigned to both units completed and transferred out and ending work-in-process inventories

productivity   The ratio of output to input

product-sustaining activity   An activity performed to support the production of a specific product

profit SBU   An SBU that generates revenues and incurs the major portion of the cost for producing these revenues

profit-volume graph   Illustrates how the level of profits changes over different levels of output

proration   The process of allocating underapplied or overapplied overhead to Work-in-Process Inventory, Finished Goods Inventory, and Cost of Goods Sold accounts

prototyping   A method in which functional models of the product are developed and tested by engineers and trial customers

Q

quality   A product or service that meets or exceeds customers' expectations at a competitive price they are willing to pay

quality circle   A small group of employees from the same work area that meet regularly to identify and solve work-related problems, and to implement and monitor solutions to the problems

R

random variances   The variances beyond the control of management, either technically or financially, that often are considered as uncontrollable variances

rank-order correlation   A statistic that measures the degree to which two sets of numbers tend to have the same order or rank

reciprocal flows   The movement of services back and forth between service departments

reciprocal method   A cost allocation method that considers all reciprocal flows between service departments through simultaneous equations

reengineering   A process for creating competitive advantage in which a firm reorganizes its operating and management functions, often with the result that jobs are modified, combined, or eliminated

regression analysis   A statistical method for obtaining the unique cost estimating equation that best fits a set of data points

relevant cost   A cost with two properties: it differs for each decision option and it will be incurred in the future

relevant range   The range of the cost driver in which the actual value of the cost driver is expected to fall, and for which the relationship is assumed to be approximately linear

replacement cost   The current cost to replace the assets at the current level of service and functionality

resale price method   A transfer pricing method based on determining an appropriate markup based on gross profits of unrelated firms selling similar products

residual income (RI)   A dollar amount equal to the income of a business unit less a charge for the investment in the unit

resource   An economic element applied or used to perform activities

resource driver   A measure of the amount of resources consumed by an activity

return on equity (ROE)   The return determined when investment is measured as shareholders' equity

return on investment (ROI) Profit divided by investment in the business unit

return on sales (ROS) A firm's profit per sales dollar measures the manager's ability to control expenses and increase revenues to improve profitability

revenue drivers The factors that affect sales volume, such as price changes, promotions, discounts, customer service, changes in product features, delivery dates, and other value-added factors

revenue SBU An SBU with responsibility for sales, defined either by product line or by geographical area

rework A produced unit that must be reworked into a good unit that can be sold in regular channels

risk preferences The way individuals differentially view decision options, because they place a weight on *certain* outcomes that differs from the weight they place on *uncertain* outcomes

robot A computer-programmed and controlled machine that performs repetitive activities

R-squared A number between zero and one. Often it is described as a measure of the explanatory power of the regression; that is, the degree to which changes in the dependent variable can be predicted by changes in the independent variable

S

salary A fixed payment

sales budget A schedule showing expected sales in units at their expected selling prices

sales life cycle The sequence of phases in the product's or service's life in the market—from the introduction of the product or service to the market, to growth in sales, and finally maturity, decline, and withdrawal from the market

sales mix The proportion of units of each product or service to the total of all unit products or services

sales mix variance The product of the difference between the actual and budgeted sales mix by the actual total number of units of all products sold and by the budgeted contribution margin per unit of the product

sales quantity variance The product of three elements: (1) the difference between the budgeted and actual total sales quantity, (2) the budgeted sales mix of the product, and (3) the budgeted contribution margin per unit of the product. It measures the effect of the change in the number of units sold from the number of units budgeted to be sold

sales value at split-off method A method that allocates joint costs to joint products on the basis of their relative sales values at the split-off point

sales volume or activity variance The difference between the flexible budget and the master or static budget. A measurement of the effect on sales, expenses, contribution margin, or operating income of changes in units of sales

schedule of cost of goods manufactured and sold A schedule that shows the manufacturing costs incurred, the change in the

work-in-process inventory, the cost of goods sold, and the change in finished goods inventory during the period

scrap Part of the product that has little or no value

selling price variance The difference between the total actual sales revenue and the total flexible budget sales revenue for the units sold during a period

sensitivity analysis The name for a variety of methods used to examine how an amount will change if factors involved in predicting that amount change

split-off point The first point in a joint production process at which individual products can be identified

spoilage An unaccepted unit that is discarded or sold for disposal value

standard cost The cost a firm ought to incur for an operation

standard cost sheet A listing of the standard price and quantity of each manufacturing cost element for the production of one product

standard error of the estimate (SE) A measure of the accuracy of the regression's estimates

statistical control charts Charts that set control limits using a statistical procedure

step cost A cost that varies with the cost driver, but in discrete steps

step method A cost allocation method that uses a sequence of steps in allocating of service department costs to production departments

strategic business unit (SBU) A well-defined set of controllable operating activities over which an SBU manager is responsible

strategic cost management The development of cost management information to facilitate the principal management function, strategic management

strategic management The development of a sustainable competitive position

strategic performance measurement An accounting system used by top management for the evaluation of SBU managers

strategy A set of policies, procedures, and approaches to business that produce long-term success

strategy map A device that uses the balanced scorecard to describe the firm's strategy in detail by using cause-and-effect diagrams

structural cost drivers Strategic plans and decisions that have a long-term effect with regard to issues such as scale, experience, technology, and complexity

sunk costs Costs that have been incurred or committed in the past, and are therefore irrelevant

sustainability The balancing of short- and long-term goals in all three dimensions of the company's performance—economic, social, and environmental

SWOT analysis   A systematic procedure for identifying a firm's critical success factors: its internal strengths and weaknesses, and its external opportunities and threats

systematic (controllable) variances   Variances that are likely to recur unless they are corrected

T

Taguchi quality loss function   Depicts the relationship between the total loss to a firm due to quality defects and the extent of quality defects

Takt time   The speed at which units must be manufactured to meet customer demand

target costing   The desired cost for a product is determined on the basis of a given competitive price, so the product will earn a desired profit

templating   A method in which an existing product is scaled up or down to fit the specifications of the desired new product

throughput margin   A TOC measure of product profitability; it equals price less materials cost, including all purchased components and materials handling costs

time ticket   A sheet showing the time an employee worked on each job, the pay rate, and the total cost chargeable to each job

total contribution margin   The unit contribution margin multiplied by the number of units sold

total productivity   A measure including all input resources in computing the ratio of the output attained and the input used to attain the output

total quality management (TQM)   A technique in which management develops policies and practices to ensure that the firm's products and services exceed customers' expectations

total variable factory overhead variance   The difference between total actual variable factory overhead incurred and total standard variable factory overhead for the output of the period

transfer pricing   The determination of an exchange price for a product or service when different business units within a firm exchange it

transferred-in costs   The costs of work performed in the earlier department that are transferred into the present department

trend variable   A variable that takes on values of 1, 2, 3, . . . for each period in sequence

t-value   A measure of the reliability of each of the independent variables; that is, the degree to which an independent variable has a valid, stable, long-term relationship with the dependent variable

two-stage allocation   A procedure that assigns a firm's resource costs, namely factory overhead costs, to cost pools and then to cost objects

U

underapplied overhead   The amount that actual factory overhead exceeds the factory overhead applied

unit-based pool   A basis for determining a bonus according to the performance of the manager's unit

unit contribution margin   The difference between unit sales price and unit variable cost; it is a measure of the increase in profit for a unit increase in sales

unit cost   The total manufacturing cost (materials, labor, and overhead) divided by units of output

unit-level activity   An activity performed for each unit of production

units accounted for   The sum of the units transferred out and ending inventory units

units to account for   The sum of the beginning inventory units and the number of units started during the period

V

value activities   Firms in an industry perform activities to convert raw material into the final product; includes customer service

value-added activity   An activity that contributes to customer value and satisfaction or satisfies an organizational need

value-chain analysis   A strategic analysis tool used to identify where value to customers can be increased or costs reduced, and to better understand the firm's linkages with suppliers, customers, and other firms in the industry

value engineering   Used in target costing to reduce product cost by analyzing the trade-offs between different types of product functionality and total product cost

variable cost   The change in total cost associated with each change in the quantity of the cost driver

variable cost method   The transfer price equals the variable cost of the selling unit

variable expense flexible budget variance   The difference between the actual variable expenses incurred and the total standard variable expenses in the flexible budget for the units sold during the period

variable factory overhead efficiency variance   The difference between the total standard variable factory overhead for the actual quantity of the substitute activity measure for applying variable factory overhead and the total standard variable factory overhead cost for the units manufactured during the period

variable factory overhead spending variance   The difference between variable factory overhead incurred and total standard variable factory overhead based on the actual quantity of the substitute activity measure to apply the overhead

W

weighted average after-tax cost of capital   The after-tax cost to the firm of securing funds with a given capital structure

weighted-average method   A method for calculating the unit cost that includes all costs, both those incurred during the current period and those incurred in the prior period that are shown as the beginning work-in-process inventory of this period

what-if analysis   The calculation of an amount given different levels for a factor that influences that amount

work cells   Small groups of related manufacturing processes organized in clusters to assemble parts of finished products

work-in-process inventory   Contains all costs put into manufacture of products that are started but not complete at the financial statement date

work measurement   A cost estimation method that makes a detailed study of some production or service activity to measure the time or input required per unit of output

work sampling   A statistical method that makes a series of measurements about the activity under study

Z

zero-base budgeting   A budgeting process that requires managers to prepare budgets from ground zero

INDEX